T

—

HILL'S MANUAL

OF

SOCIAL AND BUSINESS FORMS:

A

GUIDE TO CORRECT WRITING

Showing How to Express Written Thought Plainly, Rapidly, Elegantly and Correctly.

EMBRACING INSTRUCTION AND EXAMPLES IN

PENMANSHIP, SPELLING, USE OF CAPITAL LETTERS, PUNCTUATION, COMPOSITION, WRITING FOR THE PRESS, PROOF-READING,
EPISTOLARY CORRESPONDENCE, NOTES OF INVITATION, CARDS, COMMERCIAL FORMS, LEGAL BUSINESS FORMS,
FAMILY RECORDS, SYNONYMS, SHORT-HAND WRITING, DUTIES OF SECRETARIES, PARLIA-
MENTARY RULES, SIGN-WRITING, EPITAPHS, THE LAWS OF ETIQUETTE,
BOOK-KEEPING, VALUABLE TABLES OF REFERENCE,
WRITING POETRY, ETC., ETC.

BY THOS. E. HILL,
AUTHOR OF "HILL'S ALBUM OF BIOGRAPHY AND ART."

CHICAGO:
HILL STANDARD BOOK CO., PUBLISHERS.
1884.

1884, Dec. 15,
Fine money.

TWO HUNDRED AND SIXTIETH THOUSAND.

To

THE MILLIONS

WHO WOULD, AND MAY,

Easily and Gracefully Express the Right Thought,

THIS WORK IS

RESPECTFULLY DEDICATED.

PREFACE.

 O enable the individual to write with ease, and to do the right thing in the right place in many of the important positions in life, is the object of this book.

There have been many excellent works heretofore given to the world treating on Penmanship, that admirably served their purpose in their specialty; but the student when done with their study, though proficient in chirography, was yet ignorant of how to use the same in the transaction of business.

Good books in abundance have been published on Grammar, Letter-writing, Composition, and various Business Forms, but, though proficient in a knowledge of their contents, the student, often left with a miserable Penmanship, shrinks from making use of this knowledge, because of the disagreeable labor attendant upon a cramped and detestable handwriting.

The result sought to be accomplished in this book is to combine both a knowledge of penmanship and its application in the written forms which are in most general use. Added to these are the chapters on collection of debts, parliamentary rules, etiquette and other departments of action, which are calculated to teach how to do in many of the important social and business relations of life.

The Teacher of Penmanship will find its pages replete with information pertaining to the art of writing. As a treatise on Penmanship, it is more profusely illustrated than any work of the kind now before the public; and though condensed, it is yet sufficiently explicit in detail, and in the consideration of principles, to make the analysis of letters thoroughly understood by the student. The programme of exercises for a course of writing lessons, together with suggestions relating to the organization and management of the writing class, will be welcomed by young teachers, whose penmanship is sufficiently good to enable them to teach the art, but who fail of success through lack of knowledge of the course to be pursued in order to interest and entertain the class after it has assembled.

The Teacher of the public or private school will find abundant use for a manual of this kind in the school-room. The subject of letter-writing—an art almost universally neglected—should be a matter of daily exercise in the recitation-room. The correct form of writing the superscription, the complimentary address, the division into paragraphs, the complimentary closing, the signature, and folding of the

letter; the letters of introduction, of recommendation, excuse, sympathy, and business
—all these practical epistolary forms, such as enter into the every-day transactions
of life, should be thoroughly taught in our schools.

The gathering of news for the press, the rules and typographical marks for proof-
reading, the illustrations of printing types, visiting and business cards, notes of invitation, etc.—all these exercises and more, can be introduced with great benefit to
pupils. In short, nearly every chapter of this Manual, much of which has never been
published before in any form, can be used to supply practical lessons in the school-
room.

In the business walks of life, a work of this kind has long been required. In
penmanship, use of capital letters, punctuation, letter-writing; the forms of notes,
bills, orders, receipts, checks, drafts, bills of exchange, articles of agreement, bonds,
mortgages, deeds, leases, and wills; in selecting the kind of type in which to print
the hand-bill or card; the marking letters; the law of the different States concerning
the limitation of actions, rates of interest, usury, and amount of property exempt from
forced sale and execution,—all this and much more contained herein, will be of
especial service for reference in the transaction of business.

By the lady, much will be found in a Manual of this kind that will particularly
serve her in the writing of her social forms. As a text-book and self-instructor in
writing, it admirably serves to give her that delicate and beautiful penmanship which
pleases the eye as does fine music the ear. The rules of composition, writing for the
press, the letter-writing, the marriage anniversaries, the notes of invitation to the
cotton, paper, leather, wooden, tin, silk and other weddings; the fancy alphabets for
needle-work; the selections for the album, lists of common Christian names, and
synonyms, abbreviations, foreign words and phrases, the rules for writing poetry
and the laws of etiquette—all these will meet her especial favor.

The mistress of the household will find here the form of the testimonial suitable
to be given the servant upon his or her departure to seek a situation elsewhere. The
mother will find the written excuse to the teacher for the non-attendance of her
child at school; the servant, the form of letter when applying for a situation; and
the bashful, blushing maiden, the cautious, carefully worded letter, that will aid her
in giving expression to the hitherto closely guarded secrets of the heart.

The sign-painter has daily use for a reference book of this kind, arranged and
adapted, as it is, to the comprehension and wants of the knights of the pencil and
brush, with the rules of punctuation, prepared for his especial use, and abundant
examples of signs, so as to enable him not only to paint the letters and words
beautifully, but to punctuate the same correctly. In this department is given a
large number of plain and fancy alphabets, while the book throughout contains beautiful emblems and different kinds of lettering. The fine specimens of penmanship and
pen-flourishing, including round-hand writing, old English, German-text, and orna-

mental script letters, will particularly please, presenting, as they do, much that is entirely new, calculated to aid the young sign-painter in doing his work elegantly and correctly.

The artist in lettering on marble finds in this work a chapter presenting tombstone inscriptions and epitaphs, giving the modern and best forms of wording by which to perpetuate the memory of the departed. More especially will this be valued by the marble-worker as giving him the grammatical wording of the inscription, the abbreviation of words, and their correct punctuation. The grand and costly monument, designed to stand for a thousand years, to be gazed upon by multitudes, and the record that it bears to be read by millions! How important that, in this conspicuous place, in such enduring form, the inscription, in grammar, capitalization, and punctuation, should be given absolutely correct. The ornamental scripts, with the plain and fancy alphabets, will also admirably serve the wants of marble-workers. This chapter will likewise assist the mourner who is desirous of selecting an appropriate inscription to mark the last resting place of the departed.

The reader will appreciate the forms herein relating to inscriptions suitable for use by the engraver, when marking the spoon, the ring, the cane, the watch, the modest birth-day gift, or the costly wedding present. The engraver will more especially value these examples, from the fact that they enable the customer to select at once the words desired, and the style of lettering in which they shall be executed; while the forms of punctuation and arrangement of wording will teach the youngest apprentice at the bench how to execute the same correctly.

The secretary of the public meeting, the presiding officer, every member of the assemblage; in fact, every American citizen that aspires to discharge the duties of a freeman, will be aided by the chapter on parliamentary rules, the forms of resolutions appropriate for various occasions, petitions to public bodies, etc.

The individual who would appear at ease in general society, who would do the right thing at the right time, be self-possessed and free from embarrassment, will appreciate the chapter on etiquette. More especially will this be valued because of its beautiful and instructive illustrations.

The chapter assigned to the writing of poetry, and the dictionary of rhymes, will instruct and aid a certain class; while the poetic selections will be valued by all lovers of poetry, as presenting some of the most beautiful and charming poems in existence

In short, the varied character of this work appeals alike to the wants of the old and young of all classes. Realizing this, the book is launched on the sea of literature with the confident belief that it is demanded, and that it will accomplish its mission of usefulness.

8

✦Alphabetical Summary of Contents✦

PREFACE.

O enable the individual to write with ease, and to do the right thing in the right place in many of the important positions in life, is the object of this book.

There have been many excellent works heretofore given to the world treating on Penmanship, that admirably served their purpose in their specialty; but the student when done with their study, though proficient in chirography, was yet ignorant of how to use the same in the transaction of business.

Good books in abundance have been published on Grammar, Letter-writing, Composition, and various Business Forms, but, though proficient in a knowledge of their contents, the student, often left with a miserable Penmanship, shrinks from making use of this knowledge, because of the disagreeable labor attendant upon a cramped and detestable handwriting.

The result sought to be accomplished in this book is to combine both a knowledge of penmanship and its application in the written forms which are in most general use. Added to these are the chapters on collection of debts, parliamentary rules, etiquette and other departments of action, which are calculated to teach how to do in many of the important social and business relations of life.

The Teacher of Penmanship will find its pages replete with information pertaining to the art of writing. As a treatise on Penmanship, it is more profusely illustrated than any work of the kind now before the public; and though condensed, it is yet sufficiently explicit in detail, and in the consideration of principles, to make the analysis of letters thoroughly understood by the student. The programme of exercises for a course of writing lessons, together with suggestions relating to the organization and management of the writing class, will be welcomed by young teachers, whose penmanship is sufficiently good to enable them to teach the art, but who fail of success through lack of knowledge of the course to be pursued in order to interest and entertain the class after it has assembled.

The Teacher of the public or private school will find abundant use for a manual of this kind in the school-room. The subject of letter-writing—an art almost universally neglected—should be a matter of daily exercise in the recitation-room. The correct form of writing the superscription, the complimentary address, the division into paragraphs, the complimentary closing, the signature, and folding of the

LIST OF ILLUSTRATIONS.

FULL-PAGE PLATES.

STEEL PLATE PORTRAIT OF THE AUTHOR---FRONTISPIECE.

WRITING.

RITING is the art of placing thought, by means of written characters, upon any object capable of receiving the same. The origin of this art is completely veiled in obscurity, no history giving authentic account of its first introduction and use. Its first recorded mention is in the Bible, wherein it is said, referring to the preparation of the Ten Commandments by Moses on Mount Sinai, that "The Tables were *written* on both their sides."

Fifteen hundred years before Christ, Cadmus, the Phœnician, had introduced letters into Greece, being sixteen in number, to which several were afterwards added. It is certain that the Greeks were among the very earliest of the nations of the earth to invent and make use of written characters for the record of ideas, which could be clearly interpreted by succeeding generations; though the invention of the art came from the advancing civilization of mankind, and had its origin with various nations: at first in the form of hieroglyphics, or picture writing, which characters have, as mankind progressed, been simplified, systematized, and arranged in alphabets, giving us the various alphabetical characters now in use.

Writing and penmanship, though nearly synonymous terms, are quite different in meaning. Writing is the expression of thought by certain characters, and embraces penmanship, spelling, grammar and composition.

ENMANSHIP is the combination of peculiar characters used to represent the record of thought; and having, since its first invention, continued to change its form down to the present time, so it is probable the style of penmanship will continue to change in the future. The great defect existing in the present system of penmanship is the superabundance of surplus marks, that really mean nothing. This fault, along with our defective alphabet, consumes in writing, at present, a great amount of unnecessary time and labor. Thus, in writing the word *Though*, we make twenty-seven motions, whereas, being but two sounds in the word, we actually require but two simple marks.

That style of writing whereby we use a character to represent each sound, is known as phonography, which system of penmanship enables the penman to write with the rapidity of speech. The phonetic or phonographic system of spelling, wherein each sound is represented by a character, gives us the nearest approach to a perfect alphabet in existence, and is the method of spelling and the style of writing to which we will, beyond question, ultimately attain.

It has been found extremely difficult, however, to suddenly change a style of alphabet in general use in a living language: and the mass of the American and English people will, without doubt, use the present style of penmanship, with various modifications, many decades in the future. To the perfection of that system in general use, in the English and American method of writing, which the present generation will be most likely to have occasion to use throughout their lifetime, this work is directed, as having thus the most practical value; though Short-hand is illustrated elsewhere.

System of Penmanship.

Two styles of penmanship have been in use, and each in turn has been popular with Americans in the past fifty years; one known as the round hand, the other as the angular writing. The objection attaching to each is, that the round hand, while having the merit of legibility, requires too much time in its execution; and the angular, though rapidly written, is wanting in legibility. The best teachers of penmanship, of late, have obviated the objections attaching to these different styles, by combining the virtues of both in one, producing a semi-angular penmanship, possessing the legibility of the round hand along with the rapid execution of the angular.

To the Duntons, of Boston, and the late P. R. Spencer, as the founders of the semi-angular penmanship, are the people indebted for the beautiful system of writing now in general use in the schools throughout the country.

Copies.

The copies, accompanied by directions in this book, will be found ample in number and sufficiently explicit in detail to give the student a knowledge of writing and flourishing. In acquiring a correct penmanship it is not the practice of many different copies that makes the proficient penman, but rather a proper understanding of a few select ones, for a few copies embrace the whole art.

As will be seen by an examination of the copy plates, each letter of the alphabet is made in a variety of styles, both large and small, succeeded by words alphabetically arranged in fine

and coarse penmanship, which are excellently adapted to the wants of both ladies and gentlemen, according to the dictates of fancy in the selection of coarse and fine hand.

As a rule, however, the bold penmanship, indicating force of character, will be naturally adopted by gentlemen, while the finer hand, exhibiting delicacy and refinement, will be chosen by the ladies.

Principles.

The principles of penmanship, also represented, give the complete analysis of each letter, while the proper and improperly made letters, representing good and bad placed side by side, will have a tendency to involuntarily improve the penmanship, even of the person who makes a casual examination of the letters of the alphabet thus made in contrast.

The illustrations of curves, proportions and shades that accompany these directions should also be carefully studied, as a knowledge of these scientific principles in penmanship will be found of great service to the student in giving a correct understanding of the formation of letters.

Importance of Practice.

It is not sufficient, however, that the student merely study the *theory* of writing. To be proficient there must be actual *practice*. To conduct this exercise to advantage it is necessary to have the facilities for writing well. Essential to a successful practice are good tools with which to write. These comprise the following writing materials:

Pens.

Metallic pens have generally superseded the quill. They are of all styles and quality of metal, gold and steel, however, being the best. In consequence of its flexibility and great durability, many prefer the gold pen; though in point of fine execution, the best penmen prefer the steel pen, a much sharper and finer hair line being cut with it than with the gold pen.

Paper.

For practice in penmanship, obtain of the stationer five sheets of good foolscap paper. Midway from top to bottom of the sheet, cut the paper in two, placing one half inside the other. Use a strong paper for the cover, and sew the whole together, making a writing-book. Use a piece of blotting paper to rest the hand on. The oily perspiration constantly passing from the hand unfits the surface of the paper for receiving good penmanship. The hand should never touch the paper upon which it is designed, afterwards, to write.

Ink.

Black ink is best. That which flows freely, and is nearest black when first used, gives the most satisfaction. The inkstand should be heavy and flat, with a large opening, from which to take ink, and not liable to tip over. The best inkstand is made of thick cut glass, enabling the writer to see the amount of ink in the same, and shows always how deep to set the pen when taking ink from the stand. Care should be observed not to take too much ink on the pen ; and the surplus ink should be thrown back into the bottle, and never upon the carpet or floor. Close the bottle when done using it, thus preventing rapid evaporation of the ink, causing it soon to become too thick.

Other Writing Materials.

An important requisite that should accompany the other writing materials is the pen wiper, used always to clean the pen when the writing exercise is finished, when the ink does not flow readily to the point of the pen, or when lint has caught upon the point. A small piece of buckskin or chamois skin, obtained at the drug store, makes much the best wiper. The student should be provided with various sizes of paper, for different exercises to be written, such as commercial forms, letters, notes of invitation, etc., with envelopes to correspond in size ; together with lead-pencil, rubber, ruler,

and mucilage. Thus provided with all the materials necessary, the writing exercise, which otherwise would be an unpleasant task, becomes a pleasure.

How to Practice.

Having the necessary materials in readiness for writing, the student should set apart a certain hour or two each day for practice in penmanship, for at least one month, carefully observing the following directions:

See Plate 1. Carefully examine each copy on this plate. Devote one page in the writing book to the practice of each copy. Commence with copy No. 1. The practice of this copy is an important exercise for two reasons, being : first, to give sufficient angularity for rapidity in writing; and second, to give freedom of movement.

The student who carries a heavy, cramped hand, will find great benefit result from practicing this copy always at the commencement of the writing exercise. Rest the hand on the two lower fingers — never on the wrist, and rest the body and arm lightly upon the forearm. Assume thus a position whereby the pen can take in the entire sweep of the page, writing this exercise, in copy No. 1, from the left to the right side of the page, without removing the pen from the paper while making the same. The student may write both with pen and lead-pencil, and should continue the practice of this exercise until perfect command is obtained of the fingers, hand and arm ; and all evidence of a stiff, cramped penmanship disappears.

Copy No. 2 is a contraction of copy No. 1, making the letter *m*. Great care should be used in writing this letter to make the several parts of the same, uniform in height, size, and slope ; the downward slope of all the letters being at an angle of 52 degrees. See diagram illustrating slope of letters.

Position while Writing.

N object early to be attained, is to acquire an easy, graceful and healthful position of body while sitting or standing, when writing. To obtain this, the writer should sit with the right side to the desk, using a table so high as to compel the body to sit erect.

Rest the arm lightly upon the elbow and forearm, and the hand upon the two lower fingers, the wrist being free from the desk. Allow the body and head to incline sufficiently to see the writing, but no more.

Maintain a position such as will give a free expansion of the lungs, as such posture is absolutely indispensable to the preservation of health.

A desk or table, with a perfectly level surface, is best for writing. Where a decided preference is manifested for sitting with the left side, or square, to the desk, such position may be taken. If the desk slopes considerably, the left side is preferable.

Avoid dropping the body down into an awkward, tiresome position. If wearied with continued sitting, cease writing. Lay down the pen, step forth into the **fresh air, throw back the arms, expand the chest, inflate the lungs, and take exercise. When work is again resumed, maintain the same erect position, until the habit becomes thoroughly fixed of sitting gracefully and easily, while engaged in this exercise.**

Position for Sitting and Holding the Pen.

TO secure the correct slope of a plain, rapid penmanship, when writing, keep the paper at right angles with the arm, holding the same in position with the left hand, the edge of the paper being parallel with edge of the desk.

Hold the pen between the thumb and second finger, resting against the corner of the nail, with the fore-finger on the back of the pen, for the purpose of steady-ing it; having the thumb sufficiently bent to come opposite the forefinger joint, the two last fingers being bent under, resting lightly on the nails.

Avoid dropping or rolling the hand and pen too much to one side, thereby causing one point of the pen to drag more heavily than the other, thus producing a rough mark in writing. A smooth stroke indicates that the pen is held correctly; a rough one tells us when the position is wrong.

Sit sufficiently close to the desk to avoid the necessity of leaning for-ward or sidewise in order to reach the same, and occupy a chair that gives support to the back, using a table large enough to comfortably hold all the writing materials that are necessary when writing.

Copy No. 3 shows (see Plate I) the *m,* in words, and illustrates the distinction that should be made between the several letters, to make writing plain. See " Description of the Plates."

Legibility.

Legibility is of the greatest importance in penmanship ; and care should be observed to make each letter very distinctly what it is designed to be. While practicing with a view to improvement, the student should beware of writing too fast. The copies are very simple, and are easily imitated by the student who may give the subject earnest attention and care.

Proportion of Small Letters.

The following diagrams represent the relative proportion of the capital and small letters. As will be seen in the diagram for the finer hand, there are eight lines, containing seven spaces. In the middle space are made the contracted letters which occupy one space, excepting *i* and *a,* which are a little higher. The *t, d* and *p* are each of the same height ; *p* and *q* extend the same distance below the line. The loop letters are all of the same length above and below the line, the loop being two thirds the length of the letter. Capitals are of the same height as the loop letters above the line.

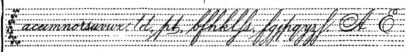

RELATIVE PROPORTION OF LETTERS IN LARGE, ROUND HAND.

Elements of Small Letters.

By examination of the small letters of the alphabet, it is seen that they can be resolved into a few fundamental elements (or principles, as they are called by many teachers), being five in number, as follows :

The 1st principle, *i,* is found in the following letters, viz : last of *a, d,* completely in the *i,* in the *p,* with the lower part omitted ; last of the *g,* first of the *i* and *s,* completely in the *t,* completely in the *u* and last of *w.*

The 2nd principle, *i,* forms the first of *m, n* and upper part of *y.*

The 3rd principle, *i,* forms the lower part of *h,* the lower part of *k,* last of *m, n* and *p* and first of *u, w, x* and *y.*

The 4th principle, *o,* forms the first part of *a,* left of *c,* lower part of *d,* left of *e,* lower part of *f,* upper part of *g,* the whole of *o,* upper part of *q* and right of *s.*

The 5th principle, *ℓ,* forms the upper part of *f, b, h, k* and *l.* Inverted, it forms the lower part of *q, j, y* and *z.*

General Hints for Small Letters.

Be careful to close the *a* at the top, else it will resemble a *u.* Observe the distinction between the *n* and the *u.* The *t* and *d* are shaded at the top, and made square. The *t* is crossed one third the distance from the top. The loop is of uniform length in all loop letters. Avoid a loop in the upper part of *t* and *d.* The dot of the *i* should be at a point twice the height of the letter. Beware of making the extended letters crooked. The left hand mark of the loop letters should be straight, from the center of the loop to the line, sloping at an angle of 52 degrees. See diagram of slope. Figures are twice the height of the *m.*

Principles of Capital Letters.

No. 1.

No. 2.

No. 3.

The capital stem (see No. 1) can be terminated at the bottom, as shown in the first character. Observe in Nos. 2 and 3 the disposition of shades, curves and parallel lines. Their application in capitals will be seen in the next column.

CAPITAL LETTERS.

THREE standard principles are used in the formation of Capital Letters, viz:

The 1st principle, called the capital stem, is found in A, B, D, F, G, H, I, J, K, L, M, N, P, R, S, T, W, X and Z.

The 2nd principle, occurs in C, D, E, K, M, O, R, U and X.

The 3rd principle, is found in the upper part of B, F, H, M, N, P and T, and forms the first of Q, U, V, W, X, and Y.

Capital letters, in a bold penmanship, are three times the height of the small letter *m.*

VIEWS OF THE CORRECT POSITION FOR HOLDING HAND AND PEN WHILE WRITING.

No. 1.

No. 1 Represents the first position to be taken, when placing the hand in correct position for writing. As will be seen, the hand is squarely on the palm, and not rolled to one side. The wrist is free from the desk, and the two lower fingers are bent under, resting upon the nails.

No. 2.

No. 2 Exhibits the hand elevated upon the two lower fingers, with the pen placed in correct position. The end of the large finger drops slightly beneath the penholder, giving a much greater command of the fingers than when it rests at the side or slightly on top of the holder.

No. 3.

No. 3 Shows another view of correct position. It will be seen that no space is shown between the pen and finger, the holder crossing the forefinger in front of the knuckle-joint. The thumb is sufficiently bent to come opposite the forefinger-joint, supporting the holder on the end of the thumb. The end of the large finger should be about three-quarters of an inch from the point of the pen.

No. 4.

No. 4 Represents the correct position when the pen is at the bottom of an extended letter below the line, the pen being, as shown, nearly perpendicular. With the holder held snugly beneath the forefinger and supported on the end of the thumb, the greatest command is thus given to the fingers.

No. 5.

No. 5 Exhibits the front view of the hand showing the position of the forefinger, which should rest squarely on the top of the holder. The large finger drops beneath the holder, which crosses the corner of the nail. The hand is held, as shown, squarely on the palm and not dropped to one side.

VIEWS REPRESENTING INCORRECT POSITIONS FOR HAND AND PEN WHILE WRITING.

No. 6 Represents the evil effect of rolling the hand too much to one side, and holding all of the fingers so straight as to completely lose command of them. The result is a stiff, heavy, cramped penmanship, and rough marks, resulting from one point of the pen dragging more heavily than the other.

No. 6.

No. 7 Exhibits the pen " held so tightly that the hand is wearied and the letters look frightfully." The large finger should be straightened, and the end caused to drop lightly beneath the holder. The forefinger should be brought down snugly upon the holder, and the end of the thumb brought back opposite the forefinger joint. Loosen the fingers, grasping the holder therein just firm enough to guide the pen and no more.

No. 7.

No. 8 Shows the result of dropping the hand too heavily upon the wrist and allowing it to roll to one side. The writer has thus lost command of the hand and arm, and the pen scratches, resulting from one point dragging more heavily than the other. The large finger should drop beneath the holder, and the hand should be brought up squarely upon the palm.

No. 8.

No. 9 Represents another bad position, with pen held too tightly. The writer loses a command of the fingers, in this case, by allowing the holder to fall below the knuckle-joint between the forefinger and thumb. All the fingers are likewise out of position.

No. 9.

The student should institute a rigid comparison between the correct and incorrect positions herewith shown, with an earnest resolve to reject the wrong and to hold fast that which is good.

As is exhibited in the above, those letters composed of curved lines present a grace and beauty not shown in those having straight lines and angles. As a rule, never make a straight line in a capital letter when it can be avoided.

Proportion.

Another important principle is that of proportion. Any object, to present a pleasing appearance to the eye, should have a base of sufficient size and breadth to support the same. Nature is full of examples. The mountain is broadest at the base; and the trunk of every tree and shrub that grows upon its sides, is largest near the earth, the roots spreading broader than the branches.

The good mechanic builds accordingly. The monument is broadest at the base. The house has a foundation large enough for its support, and the smallest article of household use or ornament, constructed to stand upright, is made with reference to this principle of proportion, with base broader than the top. This principle, applied in capital letters, is shown by contrast of various letters made in good and bad proportion, as follows:

Letters should be constructed self supporting in appearance, with a foundation sufficiently broad to support that which is above.

NATURE'S RULES.

HERE are a few general principles in Nature that are applicable to penmanship. These principles are eternal, and will never change.

Curved Lines.

The first is that of curved lines. Those objects in Nature that we most admire possess a grace and fullness of curve which elicit our admiration. The edge of the flower curves. The trunk of the tree, the leaf, the bud, the dewdrop, the rainbow, —all that is beautiful in Nature, in fact, is made up of curved lines. The human countenance, rounded and flushed with the rosy hue of health, is beautiful. Wasted by disease and full of angles, it is less attractive. The winding pathway in the park, the graceful bending of the willow, the rounded form of every object that we admire, are among the many illustrations of this principle. This is finely shown in the engraving of birds and flowers at the head of this chapter.

The same applied to the making of capital letters is shown in the following, representing in contrast letters made of curves and straight lines:

Contrast.

A very important principle, also, is that of contrast. Nature is again the teacher, and affords an endless variety of lessons. Scenery is beautiful that is most greatly diversified by contrast. That is more beautiful which is broken by mountain, hill, valley, stream, and woodland, than the level prairie, where nothing meets the eye but brown grass. The bouquet of flowers is beautiful in proportion to the many colors that adorn it, and the strong contrast of those colors. Oratory is pleasing when accompanied by changes in the tone of voice. Music is beautiful from the variety of tone. The city is attractive from contrast in the style of buildings; and the architecture of the edifice that is broken by striking projections, tall columns, bold cornice, etc., is beautiful from that contrast. Thus in penmanship. Made with graceful curves, and in good proportion, the letter is still more beautiful by the contrast of light and shaded lines, the heavy line giving life to the appearance of the penmanship. If desirous of observing this principle, care should be taken not to bring two shades together, as the principle of contrast is thus destroyed. The effect of shade is shown by the following letters in contrast.

In capitals, where one line comes inside another, it is important for beauty that the lines should run parallel to each other. The equi-distant lines of the rainbow, and the circles around the planets, are among Nature's illustrations. A uniformity of slope and height, in all letters should also carefully be observed.

Again, as the well-trimmed lawn and the cleanly kept park, with no unsightly weeds or piles of rubbish to meet the gaze, are objects of admiration, so the neatly-kept page of writing, marred by no blots or stains, is beautiful to the eye.

Position of the Hand in Flourishing.

In executing broad sweeps with the pen, and assuming a position that will give greatest command of the hand in flourishing, the position of the pen in the hand should be reversed; the end of the penholder pointing *from* the left shoulder, the pen pointing towards the body, the holder being held between the thumb and two first fingers, as shown above.

Plain Penmanship and Flourishing.

The chief merit of business penmanship is legibility and rapidity of execution. Without sacrificing these qualities, the student may add as much beauty as possible. The business penman should beware, however, of giving much attention to flourishing, its practice, aside from giving freedom with the pen, being rather to distract the mind from the completion of a good style of business writing. Especially in plain penmanship should all flourishing be avoided. Nothing is in worse taste, in a business letter, than various attempts at extra ornamentation.

To the professional penman, however, in the preparation of different kinds of pen work, a knowledge of scientific flourishing is essential to the highest development of the art.

The principles of curves, shades and proportion that govern the making of capital letters apply as well also in flourishing.

CORRECT POSITION

FOR STANDING

WHILE WRITING;

Showing Hands, Paper, and
Position of the Feet.

HE desk at which the individual stands when writing, should slightly incline from the front upward. It should so project as to give ample room for the feet beneath, which should be so placed as to be at nearly right angles with each other, the right foot forward, the principal weight of the body resting upon the left. Incline the left side to the desk, resting the body upon the left elbow, as shown in the above engraving, thus leaving the right arm free to use the muscular or whole arm movement, as may be desired.

The desk should be so high as to cause the writer to stand erect, upon which the paper should be placed with the edge parallel with the desk.

Rest the body lightly on the forearm, and the hand upon the two lower fingers, the end of the penholder pointing towards the right shoulder. Practice in the position herewith shown, either with lead pencil or pen, upon waste paper, entirely regardless of the form of letters, until the pen can be held easily and correctly, and writing can be executed rapidly. Strike off-hand exercises, and the whole arm capitals, making each letter as perfectly as may be, the practice, however, being with special reference to acquiring the correct position, and freedom of movement.

Steady the paper firmly with the left hand, holding it near the top of the sheet, as shown in the illustration. Beware of soiling the paper with perspiration from the left hand.

CORRECT & INCORRECT

POSITION

SITTING and HOLDING

THE PEN.

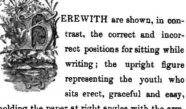

EREWITH are shown, in contrast, the correct and incorrect positions for sitting while writing; the upright figure representing the youth who sits erect, graceful and easy, holding the paper at right angles with the arm, steadying the same with the left hand.

As will be perceived, the correct position, here represented is at once conducive to health and comfort, being free from labored effort and weariness.

On the opposite side of the table sits a youth whose legs are tired, whose hands are wearied, and whose head and back ache from his struggles at writing. This boy will be liable to become, ere long, near-sighted, from keeping his eyes so close to his work. He will be round-shouldered, will have weak lungs, and will probably early die of consumption, caused from sitting in a cramped, contracted and unhealthy posture.

The bad positions liable to be assumed in writing, are, first, the one here shown; second, lying down and sprawling both elbows on the table; third, rolling the body upon one side, turning the eyes, and swinging the head, at the same time protruding and twisting the tongue every time a letter is made.

An earnest, determined effort should be made, when writing, to bring the body into an easy, graceful attitude, until the habit becomes thoroughly established.

This illustration should be carefully studied by youth when learning to write; and *all* writers should give the matter attention.

SMALL LETTERS CONTRASTED, SHOWING PROBABLE FAULTS.   RIGHT AND WRONG.

Wrong.	Right.	Wrong.	Right.	Wrong.	Right.
1st *a* is not closed at the top. It resembles a *u*. 2nd *a* contains a loop and resembles an *o*.		1st *j* is crooked and contains too much loop at the bottom. 2nd *j*, loop too short.		1st *s* is too short. 2nd *s* contains a loop, top and bottom.	
1st *b* is crooked. 2nd *b* has a loop too long.		1st *k* resembles an *h* and is crooked. 2nd *k*, loop too long; lower part spreads too much.		1st *t*, not crossed, is too round at the bottom, with bad connecting line. 2nd *t* slopes too much.	
1st *c* has the connecting line too high. 2nd *c* has a loop too large, causing it to resemble the *e*.		1st *l* is crooked. 2nd *l*, loop too broad and too long.		1st *u* resembles an *n*. 2nd *u* is irregular in height.	
1st *d* contains a loop at the bottom. 2nd *d* slopes too much.		1st *m* lacks uniformity of slope and appearance. 2nd *m* lacks uniformity of height, and too angular.		1st *v* is too angular at the top and bottom. 2nd *v* spreads too much.	
1st *e*, loop too small. 2nd *e*, loop too large.		1st *n* lacks uniformity of slope. 2nd *n* resembles a *u* with first part too high.		1st *w* is too angular. 2nd *w* is irregular in height.	
1st *f* is crooked. 2nd *f* has a loop too long, top and bottom.		1st *o* is left open at the top and resembles a *v*. 2nd *o* contains a loop.		1st *x* is spread too much. 2nd *x* is too angular.	
1st *g* is left open at the top. It resembles a *y*. 2nd *g* contains a loop at the top.		1st *p* is crooked. 2nd *p* has been patched and is badly shaded.		1st *y* is too high in the first part. 2nd *y* slopes too much.	
1st *h* is crooked. 2nd *h* has a loop too long.		1st *q* is left open at the top. 2nd *q* contains a loop in the top.		1st *z* has a loop at the top. 2nd *z* slopes too much.	
1st *i* has no dot, and the lines unite too low. 2nd *i* has the dot too near the letter; the lines are not sufficiently united.		1st *r* contains a loop. 2nd *r* is too flat.		The dollar mark should have parallel lines being crossed by a character similar to the letter *S*.	

CAPITALS CONTRASTED, SHOWING PROBABLE FAULTS. RIGHT AND WRONG.

Wrong.   **Right.**
1st *A* is too broad at the top.   2nd too much resembles the small *a*.

Wrong.   **Right.**
1st *J* is crooked. 2nd *J* is too broad at the top, and contains a bad loop at the bottom.

Wrong.   **Right.**
1st *S* has the loop too small at the top. 2nd *S* has the loop too large at the top.

Wrong.   **Right.**
1st *B* has a bad capital stem. 2nd *B*, like the first, is too large at the top.

Wrong.   **Right.**
1st *K* has a bad capital stem. 2nd *K* has an angular capital stem, and spreads too much.

Wrong.   **Right.**
1st *T* has a bad capital stem. 2nd *T* has a bad top.

Wrong.   **Right.**
1st *C* has the loop too large, with base too small. 2nd *C* contains an angle.

Wrong.   **Right.**
1st *L* loop too large in upper part. 2nd *L* has the loop in the top too small.

Wrong.   **Right.**
1st *U* contains angles in the upper part. 2nd *U* spreads too much at the top.

Wrong.   **Right.**
1st *D* contains several angles. 2nd *D* is out of proportion.

Wrong.   **Right.**
1st *M* spreads too much at the top and has a bad capital stem. 2nd *M* is too close at the top, has a bad capital stem, the last *O* part spreading too much.

Wrong.   **Right.**
1st *V* contains angles. 2nd *V* spreads too much at the top.

Wrong.   **Right.**
1st *E* contains angles. 2nd *E*, out of proportion by being too large at the top.

Wrong.   **Right.**
1st *N* has a bad capital stem, being too long and angular. 2nd *N* is out of proportion by spreading too much at the top.

Wrong.   **Right.**
1st *W* contains angles in the upper portion of the first of the letter. 2nd *W* is out of proportion by having too much slope.

Wrong.   **Right.**
1st *F* has the top too far to the left. 2nd *F* contains both a bad top and capital stem.

Wrong.   **Right.**
1st *O* is too slim. 2nd *O* contains an angle at both top and bottom.

Wrong.   **Right.**
1st *X* contains several angles where there should be none. 2nd *X* is spread too much.

Wrong.   **Right.**
1st *G* is too small at the top. 2nd *G* is too large at the top.

Wrong.   **Right.**
1st *P* is too small at the top. 2nd *P* has the top too large.

Wrong.   **Right.**
1st *Y* has the top too long. 2nd *Y* is too small at the top.

Wrong.   **Right.**
1st *H* has a bad capital stem. 2nd *H* resembles an *X*.

Wrong.   **Right.**
1st *Q* contains angles. 2nd *Q* is too large at the top.

Wrong.   **Right.**
1st *Z* resembles a small letter *y*. 2nd *Z* is also illegible.

Wrong.   **Right.**
1st *I* is too broad, and has the loop too large. 2nd *I* has a bad capital stem.

Wrong.   **Right.**
1st *R* is too large at the top. 2nd *R* contains angles.

Wrong.   **Right.**
1st character *&* is too slim. 2nd character spreads too much. Both slope badly.

DESCRIPTION OF THE PLATES.

VERY Copy on Plates Nos. 1, 2, 3 and 4 should be written with care by all students desirous of improving their penmanship. Ladies can, if they wish, terminate with the finer hand, while gentlemen will end with the bolder penmanship.

Plate I.

Copy 1 is a free, off-hand exercise, calculated to give freedom and ease in writing. Observe to make an angle, top and bottom. A sufficient amount of practice on this copy, with pen or pencil, will break up all stiffness in the writing.

Copy 2 is the contraction of copy No. 1 into the letter *m*, giving a free, open, bold, business hand.

Copy 3 is composed of words of greater length, which should be written, if possible, by the student, from the beginning to the end of the word, without removing the pen from the paper until the word is finished. The words are composed principally of the letter *m*, which should be written with much care.

Copies 4 and 5 are the small letters of the alphabet. Carefully observe the shades, and the uniformity in slope of letters.

Copy 6 exhibits the figures, which are twice the height of small letters. The **7** and **9**, in script, extend one-half their length below the line.

Copies 7 and 8 are the capital letters of the alphabet, which are of the same height as the small letter *l*. There is usually but one shade in a letter. Observe the directions, given elsewhere, for the making of capitals, and guard against the probable faults, as there expressed. Study also, carefully, the principles of curves, proportion and shades, as applied in the making of capital letters.

The remainder of copies on Plates 1 and 2 should be written with the greatest care, "Perseverance" being the motto. Do not leave these copies until they are thoroughly mastered.

Plate III.

This plate is composed of copies similar to the others, the same principles being applicable in the making of the letters. As will be seen, this is a much more delicate hand, and is especially adapted to fine epistolary writing.

Plate IV.

Plate IV illustrates the form of writing a letter of introduction, and may be copied by the student as a specimen business letter.

Plate V.

This plate exhibits the off-hand capitals, which should be made purely with the arm movement, the hand resting lightly on the two lower fingers. Practice, at first, in making them with a lead-pencil on waste paper, will be found quite beneficial.

Plate VI.

The copies of Round Hand on this plate should be written with especial care, being the style suitable for headings, etc. Observe in the small letters that each is round, and every down mark shaded. The alphabet of German Text on this page will be found useful for ornamental work.

Plate VII.

Plate VII exhibits a variety of pen work, containing both fine and bold penmanship, and will be found a superior copy in which the student can display a knowledge of penmanship and flourishing.

Plate VIII.

Plate VIII is an original off-hand specimen of flourishing, the curves, proportion and shades in which should be carefully observed. (*See view of holding pen in flourishing*, page 27.)

PLATE I

1 —————————————————————————

2 *mu. mumu. men. ment.*

3 *mammon. mammoth. m. n.*

4 *a b c d e f g h i j k l m n o p*

5 *q r s t u v w x y z & &c &c*

6 *1 2 3 4 5 6 7 8 9 0. 1st 2nd 3rd 4th 1881.*

7 *A B C D E F G H I K L M N*

8 *O P Q R S T U V W X Y Z*

9 *Albany Boston. Chicago. Detroit.*

10 *Edinburgh. Florence. Gettysburg.*

PLATE II

PLATE I

PLATE II

11 Hartford. Indianapolis. Jackson.

12 K London. Montreal. New York. C.

13 Pittsburg. Quincy. Rutland. S.

14 T U V W X Y Z & &c. ?!

15 A man's manners shape his fortune.

16 Samples of my business writing.

17 My success to day, due to good writing.

18   A beautiful hand writing is of
itself an ornament and does honor to
the executor. It is of that nature which
cannot be bought or sold, but is obtained
only by talents and application.

Blackboard Flourishing.

The plates, representing flourishing in white lines on dark groundwork, though designed to represent off-hand work upon the blackboard, will be found equally useful for practice with the pen. The figure of the Swan from Packard and Williams' "Gems of Penmanship" is a beautiful piece of flourishing, which finely illustrates how true to nature an object may be made with but very few strokes of the pen. As will be seen, the figures on these plates are composed wholly of curved lines.

TEACHING PENMANSHIP.

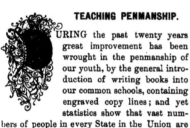

URING the past twenty years great improvement has been wrought in the penmanship of our youth, by the general introduction of writing books into our common schools, containing engraved copy lines; and yet statistics show that vast numbers of people in every State in the Union are unable to write; and some of these are to be found in nearly every locality. A majority of these persons have passed their school days, but the necessity is none the less urgent with them for improvement in penmanship; and they would gladly avail themselves of the opportunity for receiving instruction, if a competent teacher were to open a Writing School in their vicinity.

There exists a general demand for good instructors in Writing throughout the country, and teachers who will properly prepare themselves for the profession, can have excellent remuneration for their services. It is true that many persons attempt to teach writing as a profession, who, through bad management and want of moral principle, deservedly fail; but the earnest, faithful, competent teacher is wanted, and will be well rewarded for his labor.

The "12 Lesson" System.

There are but twenty-six letters in the alphabet to write; fifty-two in all, capital and small letters. The principles from which these letters are formed are, in reality, very few; and to obtain a mastery of these principles is the object of giving instruction. Therefore, to acquire a knowledge of *how* to write, a large number of lessons is not absolutely necessary. The course of instruction may be so arranged as to very completely include all the principles pertaining to penmanship in twelve lessons; and the class may have such practice, each lesson being two hours in length, as will, with many pupils, completely change their penmanship in that time. It is not pretended that any one can *perfect* their writing in twelve lessons. Real ease and grace in penmanship is the result of months and years of practice; but a knowledge of *how* to practice, to impart which is the mission of the teacher, may be learned in a short time. In fact, most people are surprised to see how much may be accomplished in few lessons when the class is properly instructed.

Should, however, the teacher wish to give a more extended term of instruction, it is only necessary to drill longer upon each principle, with elaborate blackboard illustration to correspond. If the time and means of the student prevent the taking of the longer course, the shorter term may be made proportionately beneficial. Should the Twelve-lesson term be adopted by the traveling teacher, the following suggestions may be of service in the organization and management of a Writing class.

Having acquired proficiency in penmanship, and having good specimens of writing to exhibit, let the young teacher, desirous of establishing a Writing school, visit any locality where live a civilized people. While it is true that the more ignorant most greatly need the advantage of such instruction, it is nevertheless a fact that the more intelligent and educated the people of a community, the better will be the teacher's patronage.

How to Organize the Class.

Secure, if possible, a school-room provided with desks and a blackboard. It is no more than justice to present the directors and the teacher of the school, upon whom the responsibility of management of the school building rests, each with a scholarship in the writing class. Having obtained a school-room, the next thing to be done to secure success, is to thoroughly advertise the nature and character of the school, and the time of commencement. The teacher may do this in the following ways :

First, By having editorial mention made in all newspapers published in the vicinity.

Second, By posters, announcing the school, liberally distributed about the town.

Third, By circulars, giving full description of the school, sent to each house.

Fourth, By visiting each school-room, supposing the day schools to be in session, in the vicinity, and, having obtained permission to do so, addressing the pupils of the school, accompanied by blackboard illustrations, showing method of teaching, announcing terms, time of commencing school, etc., and

Fifth, By personally calling at every public business place, and as many private houses as possible, in the neighborhood, exhibiting specimens and executing samples of writing when practicable.

A lady or gentleman well qualified as a teacher, pursuing this plan will seldom fail of obtaining a large class. Having secured an established reputation as a good teacher, personal canvass afterwards is not so necessary. Personal acquaintance with the patrons of the school, however, is always one of the surest elements of success with any teacher.

If the school is held in a rural district, newspaper and printed advertising can be dispensed with. In the village or city it is indispensable.

It is unwise to circulate a subscription paper, the establishment of the school being made contingent upon the number of subscribers to the class. A better way is to announce the school *positively* to commence at a certain time and *certainly* to continue through the course, which announcement inspires confidence and secures a much larger class.

Ask no one to sign a subscription paper, or to pay tuition in advance. The fact of doing so argues that the teacher lacks confidence in the people, who, in turn, suspect the stranger that seeks advanced pay, and thus withhold their patronage. The better way is to announce that no subscription is required to any paper, and no tuition is expected in advance ; that all are invited to attend the school, and payment of tuition may be made when students are satisfied of the worth of the school. The fairness of these terms will secure a larger attendance than could otherwise be obtained, and will induce the teacher to put forth the very best efforts to please the patrons of the school.

Commencing about the middle of the term to make collection, by good management on the part of the teacher, if the school has been really meritorious, all the tuition will be paid by the time the last lesson is reached.

How to Maintain Interest.

To secure the best attendance, and the most interest on the part of pupils, the school should be in session every evening or every day, Sundays excepted, until the close of the term. It is a mistaken idea that students do best receiving but one or two lessons per week. During the intervening time between lessons pupils lose their interest, and the probability is that the class will grow smaller from the beginning to the close, if the mind of the student is allowed to become pre-occupied, as it will be, with other matters that occur between lessons so far apart. On the contrary, a writing class that meets every day or evening, under the management of an enthusiastic, skillful master, will grow from the beginning in size and interest, and the student, like the daily attendant at the public school, will exhibit a good improvement, resulting from undivided

PLATE IV

Letter of Introduction

New York, June 1st 1873

Hill Standard Book Co.
Chicago, Ill

Dear Sirs

This will introduce
to your honorable house Mr Winfield Success
of this city who visits Chicago for the purpose
of procuring a situation as canvassing agent
for Hill's Manual.

From a knowledge of his honesty, industry
and steadiness of purpose I think him such
a person as you will be pleased to employ if
you need more canvassers. I therefore take
great pleasure in recommending him to your
favorable acquaintance.

Yours Very Respectfully

Daniel Cunningham

attention to the study, from the time of commencement to the close.

Each pupil in the class should be provided with pen, ink, and a writing book. Practicing in the evening, each should be provided with a lamp, covered with a shade, throwing as strong light as possible on the writing.

For the writing book, use five sheets of best foolscap paper. Cut in two, midway from top to bottom of the sheet; put one half inside the other; cover with strong paper, and sew the whole together, the cover extending one inch above the writing paper.

How to Arrange Copies.

Slips are best for copies, as they slide down the paper and can be kept directly above the writing of the pupil while practicing. Twenty-four copies will be generally sufficient to occupy the time of most pupils during the term, and should be arranged to embrace all the principles and exercises it is necessary for the student to understand in writing plain penmanship.

The copies may be written or printed. Written, if well executed; printed, if the teacher can obtain them, suitably arranged for the twelve-lesson term, as they are thus more perfect than written copies are likely to be, and save the teacher the drudgery of writing copies. If printed, the copy should be a fine, elegant lithographic *fac simile* of perfect penmanship; —perfect, because it takes the pupil no longer to learn to make a correct than an incorrect letter. Numbered in the order of their succession, from one to twenty-four, these slips should be wrapped together in a package, which should be pasted on the inside, at the top of the cover, whence they can be drawn as required by the student. When the copy is finished, the slip should be placed at the bottom of the package.

The wrapper, holding the copies, should be sufficiently firm and tight to prevent the copies falling from their places when the book is handled. If the copies are kept by the pupil free from wrinkles and blots, an advantage of this arrangement is, that when the book is written through the copies are yet carefully preserved in their place, when new writing paper may be added to the book and the copies used again by the same pupil or by others.

Another plan is, for the teacher to keep the copies and distribute the same at the commencement of the lesson among the members of the class, and collect them at the close. When the teacher is short of copies, this plan may be pursued, though the other is the most systematic, and is attended with the least labor.

The most advanced and rapid penmen of the class, who write out their copies before the close of the term, may be furnished with copies of various commercial forms, for practice, in the last of the term.

Should a *second term* of lessons be given, those students who attend it should review the copies of the first term for about six lessons, after which they may be drilled in the writing of commercial forms, business letters, compositions, etc., according to the capacity and advancement of the pupil.

The copy should always be ready before the class assembles. The teacher should never be compelled to write a copy while the school is in session, especially if the class be large.

Commencement of the School.

The teacher having arranged to give a course of lessons in writing, should open the school at the hour appointed, even if there be no more than one pupil in attendance at the time of commencement, and should *conduct the term through*, unless insurmountable obstacles prevent. If the school possesses real merit the class will steadily increase in size, until a hundred pupils may be in attendance, even though but a half dozen were in the class at the opening lesson.

PROGRAMME OF EXERCISES FOR EACH LESSON.

First Lesson.

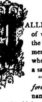

ALLING audience to order. Brief statement of what it is proposed to accomplish during the course of instruction. Assembling of the members of the class in front of the teacher, when each pupil, able to do so, should write a sample of penmanship, worded as follows: "*This is a sample of my penmanship before taking lessons in writing,*" each signing name to the same.

Pupils should be urged to present the best specimen it is possible for them to write, in order that the improvement made may be clearly shown when the student writes a similar exercise at the close of the term.

Specimens written, assume position for sitting and holding pen, full explanation being given by the teacher concerning correct and incorrect positions. Commence writing on the second page, the first page being left blank on which to write the name of the owner of the book. Let the first be a copy composed of quite a number of extended letters, containing such words as, "*My first effort at writing in this book.*" Writing these words in the first of the term enables the pupils to turn back from the after pages and contrast their writing with their first efforts in the book, on an ordinarily difficult copy, thus plainly showing their improvement as they could not perceive it by commencing with the simplest exercise. Students are encouraged to much greater exertion when they can plainly see their improvement. Having covered the first page with their ordinary penmanship, let the class commence with Copy No. 2, shown on page 41, in the set of writing-school copies, while the teacher fully explains, from the blackboard, the object of the copy. Give half an hour's practice on position and freedom of movement, making frequent use of the blackboard in illustrating the principles for making letters. The blackboard is, in fact, indispensable to the teacher of penmanship.

Intermission of fifteen minutes. Criticism of position, explanation on blackboard of letter *m*, and practice on the letter by the class. Remarks by the teacher on the importance of a good handwriting, with brief outline of what the next lesson is to be.

Second Lesson.

Drill on position; criticism. Use a separate slip of paper for ten minutes' practice on freedom of movement for hand and arm. See that every pupil has the requisite materials. Explanation again of letter *m* as made in words mum, man, mim, etc. Thorough drill, and examination by teacher of each pupil's writing. *Intermission.* Writing of short words, with special reference to perfecting the letter *m*. Blackboard explanation of slope of letters, with illustrations showing importance of uniformity of slope, etc. Hints in reference to neatness, order and punctuality, and encouragement, if the improvement of the class warrants the same. Love of appro-

bation is one of the ruling organs of the mind. Nothing is more gratifying, when the student has done well, than to be appreciated; and the pupil is stimulated to much greater exertion, when receiving judicious praise from the teacher for work well performed. Prompt and early attendance of the class at the next lesson should be urged, and close by giving outline of next lesson. The teacher should gather and keep the books. Students may each care for their pens, ink, and light.

Third Lesson.

Drill in movement. Explanation of letter *o* on the blackboard, and letters in which it is made, such as *a, d, g, q, e,* etc., showing, also, faults liable to be made. Careful examination and criticism of the writing of every student in the class individually. Explanation of *t, d,* and *p,* on the board, showing probable faults, with other exercises at the discretion of the teacher. *Intermission.* Explanation of length, size, and form of loop letters, the class being supposed to be practicing similar exercises to those illustrated on the board. Explanation and illustration concerning the writing of all the small letters, representing on the board the principles upon which they are made. During the lesson, two hours in length, the students should always be engaged in writing, except at intermission, and while the attention of the class is engaged with the blackboard illustrations.

Fourth Lesson.

A few minutes' drill on freedom of movement. Explanation of position for sitting and holding the pen, showing faults. Illustrations on the blackboard of the fundamental principles for making capital letters, representing curves, proportion, shades, parallel lines, etc.; students practicing the principles on a loose piece of paper. Careful drill on the capital stem. Caution by the teacher that students do not write too fast. General practice on copies including the capital letters. Individual examination by the teacher of all the writing books. *Intermission.* Blackboard illustration, showing faults in the making of the principles; careful drill on position for sitting, holding pen, and freedom of movement. Representation by teacher of evil effects of cramped penmanship, and weariness resulting from sitting improperly. Earnest effort to induce every pupil to practice as much as possible between lessons, a premium being given to the member of the class who shows greatest improvement at the close of the lessons, and a premium to the best penman.

Fifth Lesson.

Five minutes' drill on off-hand movement, special attention being paid by the class to the position for sitting and holding the pen. Illustration by the teacher, on the blackboard, of capital letters from *A* to *M*, making each capital correctly, beside which should be made the same letter as the pupil is liable to make it, showing probable faults. Examination by the teacher of the writing in each book. *Intermission.* Urgent appeal by the teacher to students to secure the greatest possible excellence in writing, by practice both in and out of the school; showing not only the reputation acquired by receiving the premium in the class, but the lasting advantage resulting

PLATE V

OFF HAND CAPITALS

Edw Mandel, Chicago

PLATE VI

Specimens of Round Hand,

for Day Book Headings and Ledger

and all Forms where Legibility is Required.

German Text.

𝕬 𝕭 𝕮 𝕯 𝕰 𝕱 𝕲 𝕳 𝕴 𝕵 𝕶 𝕷 𝕸 𝕹 𝕺 𝕻 𝕼 𝕽 𝕾 𝕿 𝖀 𝖁 𝖂 𝖃 𝖄 𝖅

a b c d e f g h i j k l m n o p q r s t u v w x y z.

PLATE VI

Specimens of Round Hand,

for Day Book and Ledger Headings

and all Forms where Legibility is Required.

German Text.

𝔄𝔅𝔈𝔇𝔈𝔉𝔊𝔥𝔍𝔍𝔎𝔏𝔐𝔑𝔒𝔓𝔔
𝔕𝔖𝔗𝔘𝔙𝔚𝔛𝔜𝔜

a b c d e f g h i j k l m n o p q r s t u v w x y z.

PLATE III

1. a b c d e f g h i j k l m n o p q r s t

2. u v w x y z 1 2 3 4 5 6 7 8 9 0 . & &c &c.

3. A B C D E F G H I J K L M N

4. O P Q R S T U V W X Y Z

5. Sunday Monday Tuesday Wednesday Thursday

6. Friday Saturday Jan Feb. March Apr May

7. June July Aug. Sept. Oct. Nov Dec   1st 2nd 3rd

8. A fine penmanship suitable for epistolary writing.

9. Copies of running hand penmanship for ladies

10. Samples of penmanship adapted to rapid writing

PLATE IV

Letter of Introduction.

New York, June 1st 1872

Hill Standard Book Co.
    Chicago, Ill.

        Dear Sirs.

            This will introduce
to your honorable house Mr Kinfield Success
of this city, who visits Chicago for the purpose
of procuring a situation as canvassing agent
for Hills Manual.

    From a knowledge of his honesty, industry,
and steadiness of purpose I think him such
a person as you will be pleased to employ if
you need more canvassers. I therefore take
great pleasure in recommending him to your
favorable acquaintance.

            Yours Very Respectfully,

                Daniel Cunningham

SUGGESTIONS TO TEACHERS.

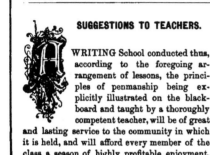

A WRITING School conducted thus, according to the foregoing arrangement of lessons, the principles of penmanship being explicitly illustrated on the blackboard and taught by a thoroughly competent teacher, will be of great and lasting service to the community in which it is held, and will afford every member of the class a season of highly profitable enjoyment. Of course the success of the school mainly depends upon the teacher. The instructor is, in fact, the life and soul of the class. If he possess love of order, tact, versatility, knowledge of human nature, self-possession, with ability to illustrate, explain and entertain his class with story and anecdote pertaining to writing, he will find his classes large and the profession of teaching writing as profitable to himself and as beneficial to the public as any upon which he can enter.

Should teaching writing be chosen as a profession for a series of years, it is well for the teacher to select a dozen or twenty villages in which to teach, and give instruction in each of these localities, once or twice a twelvemonth for years in succession rather than teach over a very wide range of country. The teacher's reputation thus becomes established, the profession is dignified and ennobled; people knowing the worth of the school are free to patronize, and thus the avocation is made much more pleasant and profitable to the teacher.

The outline of instruction given for the foregoing series of lessons is but a brief epitome of what each lesson ought to be. The enumeration of subjects may guide the young teacher somewhat, but the whole should be greatly elaborated, and will be, by the ingenious teacher, as circumstances demand.

The usual charge for a course of instruction of 12 lessons is from $2 to $5 per pupil.

Teachers should furnish paper for students, and care for the books when not in use by the pupils. Students may take charge of the other materials required.

The strictest order should be maintained. No whispering ought to be allowed. Such stillness should reign in the school that every scratching pen may be distinctly heard.

To secure order the teacher will notice when the first evidence of restlessness begins to manifest itself in the class; certain students becoming tired of writing. If this uneasiness is allowed to continue twenty minutes, the school will be oftentimes a scene of confusion, but upon the first appearance of weariness, the attention of the class should be directed for a short time to the blackboard, or the time may be occupied for a little while by some story, humorous or otherwise, having a bearing upon writing; listening to which the students become rested, and proceed with their practice afterwards with pleasure.

Having invited the leading citizens of the town to visit the school, call upon them frequently for remarks to the class on the subject of writing. From the business and professional men who may thus address the class, the teacher and pupils may oftentimes gain many valuable ideas, the class will be encouraged, and better discipline will be secured. The great secret of preserving good order in school is to keep the mind of the students constantly employed with the work in hand.

The subjects pertaining to writing are abundant, and it becomes the teacher to study and present them to the class in familiar lectures as occasion demands. Many of the succeeding chapters of this book afford subject matter, from which the teacher of penmanship can obtain topics to discuss, that will entertain and instruct the class, while the instructor should, at the same time, be on the alert for practical subjects to illustrate his work, from whatever source they may be obtained. For example, how character can be told from penmanship; what faculties of mind are employed in the execution of writing; why some pupils are naturally handsome penmen and others not; why Edward Everett should write elegantly and Horace Greeley with a scrawl; why gentlemen naturally write a large hand, and ladies fine, etc.

The effect of temperament on penmanship, and the result of using stimulants, should be thoroughly considered, and presented to the class. Students should be urged to avoid the use of tobacco as a noxious habit that lays the foundation for intemperance, and the use of strong drink as the destroyer of the soul; both tobacco and stimulants being also destructive to that steadiness of nerve essential to the execution of beautiful penmanship.

Many a boy may be deterred from an evil habit by the good example and advice of the teacher, admonishing him that superiority in penmanship and great excellence in life will come from being strictly temperate.

CONCLUDING SUGGESTIONS ON PENMANSHIP TO LEARNERS.

HIS book, as is designed, will fall into the hands of many who will never have an opportunity of receiving instruction from a professional teacher.

To practice penmanship to advantage, unaided by the teacher, students should provide themselves with necessary materials, as detailed elsewhere.

For the purpose of making steady progress in the acquisition of an elegant,plain penmanship, the student will be assisted by copying choice gems of poetry or prose, first writing each exercise on a separate slip of paper and afterwards transcribing the same in a book kept for the purpose. In the writing of original compositions and letters, each exercise should be copied as long as the student is desirous of improving in penmanship; the copy being always a great improvement upon the original, not only in penmanship,but in spelling, grammar, use of capital letters, and composition.

Writers should not rest satisfied until they have absolutely mastered a plain, rapid, and elegant penmanship. The art, being almost purely mechanical, is more easily acquired by some than others; but every person from eight years of age upwards, until the body becomes tremulous with age, having ordinary command of the hand, who will persevere in the attempt, can write a legible, easy penmanship.

Among the benefits arising from a good handwriting, some are shown in the following

Reasons why we should write well.

Because, 1st. Good penmanship of itself adds greatly to our *happiness*. The consciousness to the lady or gentleman of being able to write a letter that shall win the admiration and praise of the friend to whom it is written is a source of unspeakable pleasure to the writer, and to possess this ability throughout our lifetime is to be proficient in an accomplishment which adds to our happiness, as does excellence in oratory, painting or music. Good writing is a fine art, and is to the eye what good language is to the ear.

2nd. Good writing is of great benefit to us *pecuniarily*. The person who may apply for a situation as teacher, clerk, or any position where intellectual ability is required, finds a beautifully written letter the best recommendation that can be sent when applying for that position. Hundreds of instances are on record, many doubtless within the knowledge of the reader, where lucrative situations have been obtained through good penmanship, that could never have been secured had the applicant not had a good handwriting.

And, 3rd. A mastery of the art of writing is of great service to us *intellectually*. Persons who can write well, taking pleasure in the practice, will write more than they otherwise would. Every time they write a word

Blackboard Flourishing

Chalk and pencil Drawing.

they spell it, and thus improve in spelling. Every time a sentence is written, an application is made of grammar; and thus knowledge is obtained of how to speak correctly. The subject they write about, they become familiar with; and thus, in the act of writing, they are intellectually improved. The most intelligent and influential in any community are those who can express thought most easily and correctly on paper.

COPIES FOR WRITING-SCHOOL.

STANDARD copies for the twelve lessons may consist of the following script lines, though it is important that they be as perfectly prepared as the copies shown on Plates I, II, III and IV.

The extra practice, beyond the two copies assigned at each lesson, may be on a separate slip of paper, and should comprise the writing of the elements of letters, commercial forms, offhand capitals, letter writing, etc.

Students may join the class at any time, up to the last half of the term. Whatever may be the time of commencement, however, each pupil should begin with the first copies, and write as many of them as time will permit. The occasional review of the principles, by the teacher, will enable the students that join last to understand them; though it is desirable, for the sake of practice, that each pupil commence, if possible, with the first lesson.

As will be seen by examination, the style of penmanship, for ladies and gentlemen, is equally large up to the 17th copy. Beyond that, the size for ladies is decidedly finer. Though important that ladies should be able to write a bold penmanship for business and other writing, the lady involuntarily chooses a more delicate handwriting, by which she thus expresses her natural delicacy and refinement of character.

First Lesson.

1. My first effort at writing in this book.
2.

Second Lesson.

3. n n m m u u m n n m m u u n
4. mum min mam mem mind ment

Third Lesson.

5. o a d g g e d t p b f l o a d g g e
6. a b c d e f g h i j k l m n

42

COPIES FOR THE WRITING SCHOOL.

Fourth Lesson.

7. o p q r s t u v w x y z. &. &c. &c

8. A B C D E F G H I J K L M

Fifth Lesson.

9. N O P Q R S T U V W X Y Z

10. America Bavaria Canada Denmark

Sixth Lesson.

11. England France Germany Holland

12. India Japan Kentucky. Lapland

Seventh Lesson.

13. Mexico Norway Oregon Pennsylvania

14. Quito Russia Switzerland Turkey

Eighth Lesson.

15. Uruguay Vermont Wyoming X. Y. Z.

16. A sample of my business penmanship

Ninth Lesson.

17. By commendable deportment we gain esteem

18. Commendations generally animate men.

Tenth Lesson.

19. Improvement should be the object of all.

20. Honor and shame from no condition rise

---- Eleventh Lesson. ----

21. Learning is the ornament of youth

22. Prosperity gains friends; adversity tries them

---- Twelfth Lesson. ----

23. Running hand penmanship for business.

24. Samples of my off-hand, business writing

LADIES EPISTOLARY.

---- Ninth Lesson. ----

17. Emulation in acquiring knowledge is commendable. For value received

18. In time of prosperity prepare for adversity. Sunshine and Storm

---- Tenth Lesson. ----

19. Humiliation and repentance are ornaments of the Christian. Humiliation

20. Learn all that is possible to-day; you may require it to-morrow. Learn.

---- Eleventh Lesson. ----

21. Merit shall not go unrewarded. Trust to time and persevere. Persevere.

22. Nature unfolds a volume ever profitable for our study. Look and learn.

---- Twelfth Lesson. ----

23. This is a specimen of my hand-writing. Specimens of Penmanship

24. Running-hand penmanship for Ladies Epistolary Writing. Writing

Short-Hand Writing.

Short-Hand for Business Purposes.

VERY year adds proof, by the constantly increasing demand for it, how indispensable in a modern education is a knowledge of rapid writing. The young, by all means, should acquire it.

It may be used by the author in his study, the editor in his "sanctum," the clergyman in his library, the lawyer in his office — in fact, everywhere that writing is needed, the simplicity and dispatch of Short-hand make its value apparent.

The beginner should determine, at the outset, whether or not he will, for a time at least, do verbatim writing. If he wishes to do this, he must expect to give much time and close attention to it. The man or system that promises to give verbatim speed in a few weeks' time, is unworthy of confidence. It is useless to expect to be a good reporter and follow some other business at the same time. Reporting is a profession of itself, and requires the undivided attention of the person following it. If, however, the beginner, simply wishing relief from longhand in his daily writing, is content with a rate of speed that gives a fully written and absolutely legible manuscript, a style that is easy to learn, write, read, and remember, let him take up the simplest style, master it thoroughly, and depend for speed upon perfect familiarity with

the word-forms used, and the greatest facility in their execution, as in long-hand, and he will gain his object more easily and quickly than if he seeks it through shorter word-forms, which must necessarily be more difficult to learn and read. Very few people need to become verbatim reporters; every one, however, having much writing to do, can use a simple style of short-hand to advantage.

The grand principle upon which a system of short-hand should be built is that of phonetics. Every sound in the language should be represented by its individual sign, used for that sound and no other. As a simple sound is uttered by one impulse of the voice, so should the sign representing it be made by one movement of the hand; resulting in a single, simple sound being represented by a single, simple line. These lines should be of such a form that they may be easily joined, one to another, so that a word may be completely written without raising the pen. The most frequently occurring sounds should be represented by the most easily written signs; and all the sounds should be represented by such signs as will give a free, flowing, forward direction to the writing, without running either too far above or below the line upon which it is written. There should be a distinct line drawn between the simplest style for general use — which should contain no contracted, irregular, or exceptional word-forms — and the more brief and complicated styles for the reporter's use.

Of the various systems of Short-hand, that called Tachygraphy (*Ta-kíg-ra-fe*), a system invented and elaborated by D. P. Lindsley, of Andover, Mass., probably more nearly meets the requirements of the public than any now in use; the advantage of this system of Short-hand being, that it combines rapidity with completeness of detail in a very large degree. By permission of Mr. Lindsley we are enabled to present the following synopsis and illustrations from his work, "Elements of Tachygraphy," published by Otis Clapp, No. 3 Beacon St., Boston.

THE ALPHABET OF TACHYGRAPHY.

CONSONANTAL SIGNS.

SIGN.	NAME.	SOUND.	SIGN.	NAME.	SOUND.
	Be, b	in bay.		The, th	in they.
	Pe, p	in pay.		Ith, th	in oath.
	Ga, g	in go.		Em, m	in may.
	Ka, k	in key.		En, n	in nay.
	De, d	in do.		Ing, ng	in sing.
	Te, t	in to.		El, l	in lay.
	Ve, v	in eve.		Ra, r	in ray.
	Ef, f	in if.		Wa, w	in we.
	Zhe, z	in azure.		Ya, y	in ye.
	Ish, sh	in show.		Ha, h	in high.
	Ze, z	in ooze.		Ja, j	in jail.
	Es, s	in so.		Cha, ch	in each.

VOCAL SIGNS.

SIGN.	NAME.	SOUND.	SIGN.	NAME.	SOUND.
	E, e	in eve.		I, i	in it; y in duty.
	A, a	in ace.		ĕ, e	in ebb.
	Ai, ai	in air.		ă, a	in ask, at.
	Ah, ä	in are.		ŏŏ, oo	in foot; u in full.
	Oo, o	in do.		ŭ, û	in us, fun, but.
	O, o	in ode.		ŏ, o	in on, or.
	Au, au	in aught.		I, ĭ	in ice.
	Oi, oy	in boy.		Ew, ew	in dew.
	Ow, ow	in now.			

In writing Tachygraphy the pen should be held between the first and second fingers, and steadied by the thumb — as shown in the cut at the beginning of this chapter — so that such signs as may be easily made, without changing the position of the pen.

The alphabet should be thoroughly mastered by taking up the signs in pairs, and writing them many times, repeating the sound represented as the sign is made, so as to get the sound allied with the sign, and both well fixed in the mind. It will be noticed that all heavy signs represent vocal sounds, while nearly all the light signs represent whispered sounds.

The signs, are always written downward; from left to right; either upward or downward, and always upward.

In joining consonant signs with each other, acute angles should be made where possible, as they are more easily and rapidly made than obtuse angles. The joining of a vowel sign with a consonant, at its beginning, should always form an angle, thus:

Abe, eke, it, of, owes, on, oil, are.

At the end of a consonant, the semi-circular vowels are written, either in their alphabetic form or as hooks on the consonant, whichever is most convenient and adds most to facility in writing. The vowels (distinguished mainly by size), are determined by their being written in the direction the hands of a clock move — turning far enough to the right to form a proper angle with the following sign; and (also distinguished mainly by size), are determined by their being written in the opposite direction. Examples:

Be, kid, keen, deep, tick, fish, leap, hid, bad, car, tan, narrow, last.

The dash vowels should always form angles with consonant signs; ' ˙ are varied in their direction to facilitate this. Examples:

◟ ◠ goat, knowing, | ◥ up, cut.

Either the first or second, or both strokes of the vowel diphthongs may be made straight or curved to facilitate joining, thus:

◠ ◠ ◠ ◠ ◠

Nine,   size,   noise,   now,   hew.

The other vowel signs do not vary from the alphabetic position, and must be disjoined when they will not form a proper angle.

Disjoined vowels should be written to the left of upright and inclined, and above horizontal consonants, when the vowel sound precedes the consonant sound, and to the right of upright and inclined, and below horizontal consonants, when the vowel sound follows the consonantal.

CONSONANTAL DIPHTHONGS.

Br, as in brow.	Dl, as in meddle.
Pr, as in prow.	Tl, as in settle.
Gr, as in grow.	Vl, as in evil.
Cr, as in crow.	Fl, as in fly.
Dr, as in draw.	Zhl, as in ambrosial.
Tr, as in try.	Shl, as in special.
Vr, as in over.	Nl, as in kennel.
Fr, as in free.	
Zhr, as in measure.	Sp, as in spy.
Shr, as in shred.	Sk, as in sky.
Thr, as in other.	St, as in stay.
Thr, as in three.	Sf, as in sphere.
Nr, as in owner.	Sm, as in smith.
Bl, as in blow.	Sn, as in snow.
Pl, as in plow.	Sl, as in slat.
Gl, as in glow.	Sw, as in sweet.
Cl, as in clay.	

Bz, as in hubs.	Mz, as in hems.
Ps, as in hopes. also Gz, Ks, Ds, Ts, etc.	Nz, Ns, as in hens, hence.
Vz, as in loaves.	Ngz, as in brings.
Fs, as in roofs.	Lz, Ls, as in owls, else.
Zz, as in mazes.	Rz, Rs, as in wars, horse.
Sz, as in masses. also Thz, Ths, etc.	Wh, as in when.

These signs, it will be observed, are not new ones, but modifications of those already learned. They should be used only where no vowel sound occurs between the consonant sounds. A few examples will explain their use quite fully.

◠ ◠

Blow, glow, meddle, evil, brow, upper, gray, meeker, draw, utter, over, free, measure, shred, other, owner, spy, stay, sphere, smith, snow, sleep, sweet, when, special, kennel.

Where the final consonant of a word is either s or z, preceded by a consonant, a circle is used for the s or z, thus:

◠ ◠ ◠ ◠ ◠ ◠ ◠ ◠

Hope, hopes, lad, lads, owl, owls, war, wars. When preceded by a vowel, use the alphabetic form for s and z.

The circle is also used between two consonants, and is then written on the outside of the angle formed by the consonants — when both are straight lines, as ◡ ◠ ; on the inside of the curve, where one is a curve and the other a straight line, as ◠ ◠ ; and on the inside of both curves, when possible, as in

◠ ◠ ◠

It is sometimes necessary to write the circle on the inside of one curve and outside of the other, as in ◠

Two or more words, closely allied in sense, may be joined into a phrase, where the signs composing the words unite readily, thus adding to both the speed and legibility of the writing. Example;

Of the, with it, it is, in such a way, I will be, I have.

The first inclined or perpendicular consonant sign should rest upon the line — the other signs following in their proper direction. Example:

Seek always to form a free, flowing, graceful outline. The most easily written forms are the most beautiful, and *vice versa*.

We have given, of this system, only a synopsis of the fully written Common Style, but sufficient, however, to explain the merits and principles of Tachygraphy. Those who wish to fit themselves for verbatim writing are referred to the work entitled, " The Note Taker. A Treatise on the Second Style of Lindsley's Brief Writing, for the use of Lawyers, Editors, Reporters, Students, and all persons desirous of taking full notes in Courts of Record, Professional Schools, Seminaries, and Public Assemblies." Published by the firm to which we have before alluded.

The following Extracts are from Pope's Essay on Man.

Vice is a monster of so frightful mien,

As, to be hated, needs but to be seen;

Yet seen too oft, familiar with her face,

We first endure, then pity, then embrace.

Pope's Essay on Man.—Second Epistle.

SPELLING.

EAUTIFUL penmanship should be accompanied by correct spelling. If the person can possess but one accomplishment, it is, in fact, better to spell correctly than to write well. Nothing so mars the effect of beautiful chirography as bad spelling, which is the more conspicuous when set off by good penmanship. True, there are over a hundred thousand words in the English language, and we cannot reasonably be expected to remember the correct orthography of them all; and not until the phonetic system is received, by which every word is represented by a recognized sign, can we spell all words correctly without reference to the dictionary; but the few hundred words in general use are not so difficult to master. At any rate, the writer should have at hand a reliable dictionary, and no word should go from his hand without being correctly spelled.

The following will aid students somewhat in their knowledge of spelling:

Names of Elementary Sounds.

An elementary sound is the simplest sound of the English language, as a, e, b, k.

The English language contains about forty elementary sounds.

These sounds are divided into three *classes*— *vocals*, *sub-vocals*, and *aspirates*.

The *vocals* consist of a pure tone only, as a, e, i, o, u.

The *sub-vocals* consist of tone united with breath; as b, d, l, m, n, r.

The *aspirates* consist of pure breath only; as p, t, k, f.

The following words contain the different elementary sounds of the language:

VOCALS.— N-a-me, b-a-ll, a-t, m-e, m-e-t, f-i-ne, p-i-n, s-o-ld, m-o-ve, n-o-t, m-u-te, p-u-ll, c-u-p, f-ou-nd.

SUB-VOCALS.— B-at, d-og, g-o, j-oy, l-ife, m-an, n-o, so-ng, ba-r, th-ose, v-oice, w-ise, y-es, z-one, a-z-ure.

ASPIRATES.— F-aith, h-at, ar-k, p-ine, s-un, t-ake, th-ink, sh-one, ch-ur-ch, wh-cu.

Letters.

A letter is a *character* used to represent an elementary sound.

The English Alphabet contains twenty-six letters: A, a; B, b; C, c; D, d; E, e; F, f; G, g; H, h; I, i; J, j; K, k; L, l; M, m; N, n; O, o; P, p; Q, q; R, r S, s; T, t; U, u; V, v; W, w; X, x; Y, y; Z, z.

As will be seen, there are more elementary sounds than letters. It therefore follows that some letters must represent more than one sound each.

Those letters which represent vocals are called *vowels*. They are a, e, i, o, u, and sometimes w and y.

Those letters which represent sub-vocals and aspirates are called *consonants*.

The sub-vocals and consonants are b, d, g, l, m, n, r, v, z.

The aspirates and consonants are f, h, k, c, q, p, t, s.

Rules for Spelling.

1. Words of one syllable ending in F, L, or S, preceded by a single vowel, double th final consonant; as STAFF, MILL, PASS; except IF, OF, AS, GAS, HAS, JAS, YES, IS, HIS, THIS, US, THUS.

2. Words ending in any other consonant except F, L, and S, do not double the final letter; except ADD, ODD, EGG, EBB, INN, EBB, PURR, BUTT, BUZZ, and some proper names.

3. Words of one syllable, and words accented on the last syllable, when they end with a single consonant, preceded by a single vowel, double the final consonant before an additional syllable beginning with a vowel; as ROB, ROBBER; PERMIT, PERMITTING; but X final, being equivalent to KS, is an exception, and is never doubled.

4. A final consonant, when not preceded by a single vowel, or when the accent is not on the last syllable, should remain single before an additional syllable; as TOIL, TOILING; VISIT, VISITED. L and s are often doubled, in violation of this rule, when the accent is not on the last llabl ; as TRAVEL, TRAVELLER; BIAS, BIASSED. It is better to write TRAVELER and BIASED.

5. Primitive words ending in LL reject one L before LESS and LY; as SKILL, SKILLESS; FULL, FULLY; but words ending in any other double letter, preserve it double before these terminations; as FREE, FREELY; ODD, ODDLY.

6. The final E of a primitive word is generally omitted before an additional termination beginning with a vowel; as RATE, RATABLE; FORCE, FORCIBLE; but words ending in CE and GE retain the E before ABLE and OUS; as PEACE, PEACEABLE; OUTRAGE, OUTRAGEOUS.

7. The final E of a primitive word is generally retained before an additional termination beginning with a consonant; as PALE, PALENESS; but when the E is preceded by a vowel it is sometimes omitted; as TRUE, TRULY; and sometimes retained; as SHOE, SHOELESS.

Chalk and pencil Drawing.

Referrible.	Resistible.	Sensible.
Redexible.	Responsible.	Tangible.
Refrangible	Reversible.	Terrible.
Regible.	Revertible.	Transmissible.
Remissible.	Risible.	Visible.
Reprehensible.	Seducible.	

The following words end in **able**:

Approvable,	Manifestable,	Solvable,
Blamable,	Movable,	Tamable,
Conversable,	Provable,	Tenable,
Dilatable,	Ratable,	Transferable,
Dissolvable,	Referable,	Unsalable,
Incondensable,	Reprovable,	Untamable,
Inferable,	Salable,	Untenable.

The following words in spelling begin with **Im**. Other words of similar pronunciation begin with **Em**.

Imbibe,	Immingle,	Implant,
Imboil,	Immit,	Implead,
Imbound,	Immix,	Impart.
Imbrue,	Immure,	Impose,
Imbrute,	Impact,	Impound,
Imbue,	Impale,	Impregnate,
Imburse,	Impassioned,	Impress.
Immanuel,	Impawn.	Imprint,
Immaculate,	Impeach.	Impromptu.
Immense,	Impearl,	Impugn,
Imminent,	Impel,	Impulse.
Immigrant,	Impen.	Impunity,
Immerge,	Imperil,	Imputable.
Immerse,	Impinge.	Impute.
Immigrate.		

Ise and Ize.

The following words terminate with **ise**. Other words of like pronunciation terminate with **ise**.

Advertise,	Criticise,	Exercise,
Advise,	Demise,	Exorcise.
Affranchise,	Despise,	Merchandise,
Apprise,	Devise,	Misprise.
Catechise,	Disfranchise,	Recognise,
Chastise,	Disguise,	Reprise.
Circumcise,	Divertise,	Supervise,
Comprise,	Emprise,	Surmise,
Compromise,	Enfranchise,	Surprise.

Words ending in **d, de, ge, mit, rt, se,** or **ss,** take **sion** in derivatives. Other words of similar pronunciation in their ending are usually spelled with **tion.**

Abscission,	Confession,	Divulsion,
Abersion,	Confusion,	Emersion,
Adhesion,	Conversion,	Evasion,
Admission,	Declension,	Evulsion,
Cohesion,	Decursion,	Exesion,
Compulsion,	Depulsion,	Expulsion,
Condescension,	Dissension.	Impression.

Impulsion,	Recension.	Revulsion,
Incursion,	Recursion.	Tension.
Intrusion,	Remission.	Transcursion,
Propulsion,	Revision.	Version.

Exceptional words. Coercion, Suspicion, Crucifixion.

Words in En.

Encage.	Enfranchise,	Ensure,
Enchant,	Engender,	Entail,
Enchase,	Engorge,	Entangle.
Encircle,	Entrance,	Enthrone,
Enclose,	Enhance,	Entice,
Encroach,	Enjoin,	Entire,
Encumber.	Enlard,	Entitle,
Endamage,	Enlarge,	Entomb,
Endear,	Enlighten,	Entrap,
Endow.	Enlist,	Entreat,
Enfeeble.	Enroll,	Enure.

Words in In.

Inclasp,	Ingrain.	Intrust,
Incrust,	Ingulf,	Intwine,
Indict,	Inquire,	Inure,
Indite,	Insnare,	Inveigle.
Indorse.	Insure,	Inwheel.
Indue,	Interlace,	Inwrap,
Infold,	Interplead,	Inwreathe.
Ingraft,	Inthrall,	

Words ending in eive.

Conceive,	Deceive,	Perceive,
Receive,		

Words ending in ieve.

Achieve,	Relieve.	Sieve,
Aggrieve,	Reprieve.	Thieve.
Believe,	Retrieve.	

Nouns which change **f** or **fe** into **ves** in the plural.

Beeves,	Leaves,	Shelves,
Calves,	Lives,	Thieves.
Elves,	Loaves,	Wharves,
Halves,	Selves,	Wives,
Knives,	Sheaves,	Wolves.

Nouns ending in **f** or **fe** in which **s** is only used in the plural.

Briefs,	Turfs,	Woofs,
Chiefs,	Kerfs,	Hoofs,
Fiefs,	Surfs,	Roofs,
Griefs,	Fifes,	Proofs,
Mischiefs,	Strifes,	Beliefs,
Kerchiefs,	Safes,	Reliefs,
	Scarfs,	Gulfs.
Dwarfs.		

Nouns ending in **eau, ieu,** and **ou,** terminate the plural in **x.**

Beaux,	Flambeaux,	Morceaux,
Bureaux,	Rondeaux,	Rouleaux,
Chapeaux,	Plateaux,	Tableaux.
Chateaux,	Bijoux.	

SPELLING BY SOUND.

 SYSTEM OF ORTHOGRAPHY, whereby superfluous letters could be dispensed with, educational reformers have long sought to introduce. Of these, the following method of Spelling by Sound was published some time since by the Hon. Joseph Medill, editor of the Chicago Tribune, its advantage over the strictly phonetic system being that the same alphabet is employed as that in general use, which makes it much easier to introduce. It is at the same time more agreeable to the eye. By this system the student can spell any word after learning the sounds, and the reader can readily pronounce any word when reading. The great advantages gained are less space used in writing, less time, correct pronunciation, and correct spelling.

The application of this system of spelling is shown as follows:

A Specimen of His System.

The extreme iregûlarities ov our orthografy hav long ben a sours ov inconvéniens and anoians. Men eminent az scolars and státsmen hav often pointed out these absurdities ov speling. Yet the évil remanes. It encumbers our primary edûcásion and robs our yuth ov yeres ov time that shûd be dévóted tu the acquizision ov nolej. It imposes a burden upon the literary man thru life in thℇ ûse ov sûperflûus leters, and compels meny persons tu study speling from the crädle tu the grave or fale tu spel corectly. It is a fereful barier tu foriners hu wish tu lern our langwaje ; and wors than aul, it hinders thousands ov persons from lerning tu rede and rite, and thus largely augments the ranks ov ignórans and depravity.

Theze évils ar so énormus in the agrégate that we fele compeled tu endors the words ov the distinguished President ov the American Filólojical Asósiásion, Prof. F. A. March, ûzed in hiz opening adres at the last anûal méting ov the Sósiety :

" It iz no ûse tu try tu caracterize with fiting epithets the monstrous speling ov the English langwaje. The time lost by it is a larj part ov the hole skule time ov the most ov men. Count the ours which éch person wâsts at skule in lerning tu rede and spel, the ours spent thru life in képing up and perfecting hiz nolej ov speling, in consulting dicshunáries —a work that never ends—the ours that we spend in riting silent leters ; and multiplying this time by the number ov persons hu speak English, and we hav a tótal ov milyuns ov yeres wâsted by éch jenerásion. The cost ov printing the silent leters ov the English langwaje iz tu be counted by milyuns ov dolors for éch jenerásion."

" Sûner or láter English orthografy must be simplified and réformed."
—Benjamin Franklin.

" I fele very hopeful that a begining wil be made before long in réforming, not indede everything but at lést sumthing in the unhistorical. unsistematic, uninteljible, untéchable, but by no menes unamendable speling now curent in England."—Prof. Max Muller.

In spéking ov the disgráful state ov English orthografy and the best mode ov réforming it, the grate American lexicografer, Dr. Nóah Webster, in the introdúcsion tu hiz Quarto Dicshunary, says :

" Nothing can be more disrepûtable tu the literáry caracter ov a násion than the history ov English orthografy, unles it iz that ov our orthóepy." * * *

. " Dr. Franklin compíled a dicshunary on hiz skeme ov réform, and prócûred tîpes tu be cast, which he ofered tu me with a vû tu engaje me tu prosecute hiz dezine. This ofer I declîned tu accept ; for I wos then, and am stil, convinsed that the skeme ov introdûcing nu caracters intu the langwaje is néther practicable nor expedient. Eny atempt ov this kind must sertenly fale of sucses."

" The mode ov asertáning the prónunsiasion ov words by marks, points or trifling oltérásion. ov the present caracters, semes tu be the ónly won which can be rédûsed tu practis."

" Delitful task ! to rere the tender thaut,
Tu téch the yung fdéa hou tu shute,
Tu pore fresh instrucsion ó'er the mind,
Tu brethe the enlivening spirit, and tu fix
The jenerus purpos in the gióing brest."

"O, thautles mortals ! ever blind tu fate,
Tu sune dejected and tu sune élate."

" Worth makes the man and want ov it the felo ·
The rest is aul but lether or prúneis."

Where there is a wil there is a wa ; and while the evil continûes the nesesity for orthógrafic réform wil never cese. If there ar eny among us hu hav tu litle regard for there óne children tu smuthe for them the path on which there infant fete must stumble, we conjure them in the name ov God and hûmanity tu beware ov the gráter sin ov crushing by opósing inflûens the rising hopes ov milyuns les fortunate, hu hav néther mooy nor time tu squonder, but hu nede aul the ades posible tu enáble them tu take a posision among the intelijent, vertûus and hapy sitizens ov our grate and glórius cuntry.

The foregoing will suffice to represent Mr. Medill's idea of simplified orthography. It is almost phonetic and yet preserves most of the analogies and peculiarities of the English language. He retains the general rule that *e* ending a word and preceding a consonant indicates that the vowel is "long." Thus he spells such words as

belíeve,	beleve,	guide,	gide,	prove,	pruve,
receíve,	reseve,	course,	corse,	proof,	prufe,
release,	relese,	pique,	peke,	through,	thru,
fierce,	fêrse,	chaise,	shaze,	school,	skule,
repeal,	repele,	paid,	pade,	door,	dore,
feel,	fele,	repair,	repare,	four,	fore,
sleeve,	sleve,	gauge,	gage,	boar,	bore,
league,	lege,	pear,	pare,	blow,	blo.

Where the *e* sound does not indicate the long vowel sound, he proposes to use accented vowels, viz. : á, é, í, ó, û, and for the sound of *u* in full, should, etc , he uses û : thus, fûl, shûd. For the broad sound of *a* heard in ought, *caught*, *awful, all, brood,* he employs *au* and spells them out ; caut, auful, aul, braud, etc. For the terminals tion, sion, cian, scion, etc., he uses *sion.* He retains *ed* as the sign of the past tense, and *s* as that of the plural of nouns and singular of verbs. *Ble* as a terminal is also retained. *K* is written for *ch* in all words in which *ch* has the sound of *k*. Ex.. arkitect, monark, skule. etc. All double con-onants are reduced to single ones, as only one of them is heard in pronunciation. In all words now spelled with *ck*, as back, beck, lick, rock, luck, he drops the *c* as being wholly superfluous. In words ending in ous, he omits the *o*, as in curius, spurius, and when *ou* has the sound *u* he also drops the *o*, as in duble, jurny. He retains *y* at the end of nouns in the singular, as copy, foly. He writes *f* for *ph* in alfabet, fonetics, filosofy, etc. He omits all silent vowels in digraphs, and writes

head,	hed	said,	sed,	tongue,	tung,
earth,	erth	heifer,	hefer,	sieve,	siv,
though,	tho,	leopard,	lepard,	built,	bilt,
phthisic,	tizic,	cleanse,	clens,	inyrrh,	mer.

The proposed system is very easily written. After an hour's practice the pen runs naturally into it. The plan is one which would cost adults scarcely an effort to learn to write, and no effort at all to learn to read it. He thinks it is the simplest and most rational compromise with existing usage, prejudice, and etymologies, which can probably be devised with any hope of acceptance, and if accepted and adopted it would secure to the Anglo-American race throughout the world one of the simplest and best orthographies in existence. ·

CAPITAL LETTERS.

ANY people greatly disfigure their writing, and stamp themselves as illiterate, by the omission or improper use of capital letters.

What do we think of the man who, wishing to place his son in the care of a teacher, wrote a letter, introducing his boy, thus?

"deer sur yeW Bein a man of noleg i Wish tu Put Mi son in yure skull."

Or, of the mother who sends a line by her child to the boot and shoe merchant as follows?

"mister Grean Wunt you let mi Boay hev a Pare ov Esy toad shuz."

Fortunately the rules for using capitals are few, and once acquired, are easily remembered.

Rules for the Use of Capitals.

Begin every paragraph with a capital letter.

Begin every sentence following a period with a capital letter.

Begin each proper name with a capital letter.

Begin the names of places, as Boston, Newport, Niagara, with capital letters.

Begin the words, North, South, East, West, and their compounds and abbreviations, as North-east, S. W., with capital letters, when geographically applied.

Begin the names of the Deity and Heaven, or the pronoun used for the former, as, in His mercy — Thou, Father, etc., with capital letters.

Begin all adjectives formed from the names of places or points of the compass as English, Northern, each with a capital letter.

Begin each line of poetry with a capital letter.

Begin all quotations with a capital letter.

Begin all titles of books, and usually each important word of the title, as Hume's History of England, with capital letters.

Begin the name of any historical event, as the French Revolution, with capital letters.

The pronoun I and the interjection O must invariably be capital letters.

Begin names of the month, as June, April, with capital letters. Also the days of the week, as Monday, Tuesday, etc.

Begin all addresses, as Dear Sir — Dear Madam, with capital letters.

Capital letters must never be placed in the middle of a word.

PUNCTUATION.

HILE the omission of punctuation may not mar the appearance of writing, as do bad spelling and improper use of capitals, its correct use is, nevertheless, essential to the proper construction of a sentence.

Very ludicrous, and sometimes serious mistakes result from improper punctuation. In the following sentence, the meaning is entirely changed by the location of the semicolon.

"He is an old and experienced hand ; in vice and wickedness he is never found ; opposing the works of iniquity he takes delight."

"He is an old and experienced hand in vice and wickedness ; he is never found opposing the works of iniquity ; he takes delight."

Punctuation Marks.

The following are the principal characters or points used in punctuation :

Comma	,	Exclamation	!	Hyphen	-
Semicolon,	;	Interrogation	?	Apostrophe	'
Colon	:	Dash	—	Quotation Marks	" "
Period	.	Ellipsis	. . . .	Brackets	[ ]
Parenthesis	( )	The Caret	∧		

Rules for Punctuation.

The Comma (,). Wherever occurs a distinct natural division of a sentence; or where two or more words are connected, without the connecting word being expressed, the comma is used ; as

"Dealer in hats, caps, boots, shoes, etc." "Hedges, trees, groves, houses, and people, all went rushing by." "Towering far above us stood the pines, silent, majestic, and grand." "Verily, verily, I say unto you."

The Semicolon (;) is used where a sentence consists of several members each constituting a distinct proposition, and yet having dependence upon each other; as

"Some men are born great ; some acquire greatness ; some have greatness thrust upon them." "Contributors : Will. M. Carleton ; Wm. C. Bryant ; B. F. Taylor ; John G. Saxe." "Contents : Riches ; Poverty ; Religion."

The Colon (:) is used to divide a sentence into two or more parts, which, although the sense is complete in each, are not wholly independent ; as

"Temperance begets virtue : virtue begets happiness." "Two questions grow out of the subject : 1st : What is the necessity of a classical education ? 2d : How far can a classical education be made applicable to the ordinary business affairs of life ?"

The Period (.) is placed at the end of every complete and independent sentence ; before decimals ; between pounds and shillings ; after initial letters, and for abbreviations ; as

"Man, know thyself." "Chas. Williams, M.D." "J. Q. Adams." "Genl. Supt. of C., B., and Q. R. R." "£25. 8s. 4d." "4.24 miles."

The Exclamation Point (!) denotes sudden or violent emotion : as

"O blissful days! Ah me! How soon ye passed!" "Charge, Chester, charge! On, Stanley, on!" "Great bargains! Clothing sold at forty per cent. below cost!" "Rejoice! Rejoice! the summer months are coming."

The Note of Interrogation (?) is used after every sentence in which a question is asked ; as

"What season of the year do you enjoy most ?"

It is also used to denote sneeringly the unbelief of the speaker ; as

"His wise counsels (?) failed to accomplish their end."

Brackets [ ] *and Parentheses* ( ) are employed to enclose words thrown into a sentence by way of explanation, which could be omitted without injury to its construction ; as

"I have met (and who has not) with many disappointments." "Eight (8) miles and one hundred (100) yards." "In conclusion, gentlemen, I am for the constitution, the whole constitution, and nothing but the constitution." [Great applause.]

The Dash (—) is used when the subject breaks off suddenly, and to show the omission of words, letters and figures ; thus :

"I would — but ah! I fear it is impossible — I would — I *will* reform." "The pulse fluttered — stopped — went on — stopped again — moved — stopped."
"This agreement entered into this —— day of ——, 18—, between —————— of the first part, and —————— of the second part, witnesseth, etc."

The Hyphen (-) is employed as a character between two words to show that they are connected together as a compound word ; thus :

Thirty-fold, super-heated, four-leaved, etc.

It is also used at the end of a syllable when the remainder of the word follows on the next line. Also in dividing a word to show its pronunciation ; as

Pro-cras-ti-nate ; val-e-tud-i-na-ri-an ; co-op-e-rate.

The Ellipsis (. . . .) is used to represent the omission of words, syllables, and letters, and is sometimes represented by a dash ; thus, k —— g for king : occasionally by stars ; thus, * * * * : and sometimes by periods ; like these . . . . . The following examples illustrate its use.

"Mrs. W—— ——, of C——, is said to be the fortunate individual." "This was in 1850. * * * * Twenty years later, in 1870, we gather up, again, the thread of our discourse." "If he had married . . . . Ah, well! it was not so to be."

The Apostrophe (') is employed to distinguish the possessive case ; thus :

"John's Book." "Superintendent's Office." "Wells' Grammar : "

And the omission of letters in the beginning or middle of a word , thus ,

"I'll," for "I will." "Thou'lt," for "Thou wilt." "Prop'r," for "Proprietor." "In'st," for "Interest," etc.

See rules for punctuation, in the chapter relating to "Sign Painting."

The Caret (∧) is employed, in writing, to show where a word, or several words have been omitted in the sentence, and have been placed above the line ; as

handmaid of   e
"Temperance is the virtue." "Improvment."
∧   ∧

Quotation Marks (" ") are used by the writer to designate a word or sentence quoted or copied from another author ; as

"Three things bear mighty sway with men,
The Sword, the Sceptre, and the *Pen*."

The Marks of Reference (* † ‡ § ‖ ¶) are used to call attention to notes of explanation at the bottom of the page. If many notes are used and these are all exhausted, they can be

doubled.   Some writers use letters, and some
figures, for reference.

Marks of Pronunciation.

For the purpose of giving inflection to certain words, or to designate the prolongation of
occasional syllables in a word, the author
frequently finds it convenient to use certain
characters to denote such accents. To illustrate:

The Acute (á) gives the rising inflection ; as
" Will you ride ?"

The Grave (à) the falling ; as
" Will you wálk or ride."

The Circumflex (â) indicates the rising and
falling inflection in the same syllable ; as,
" Machine," Montreâl," etc.

The Macron (¯) placed above a letter designates a full, long vowel sound ; as
" Fāte." " Hōme." " Nōte." " Ēve," etc.

A Breve (˘) denotes a short sound, when
placed above a vowel ; as
" Ă-dore." " Glŏ-ri-ŏus."

The Diæresis (ä) is used for the purpose of
dividing a diphthong, or syllable into two distinct syllables ; as
" Avengëd." " Belovëd."

Also when two vowels come together, this
character is sometimes used to show that they
are not contracted into a diphthong ; as
" Coöperate." " Reïterate." " Reäppear."

The Cedilla (ç) is a mark placed under the
c to denote that its sound is the same as the
letter *s ;* as
" Çhaise." " Façade."

The Tilde (ñ) placed over an n gives it the
sound of *ny ;* as
" Miñon." " Señor."

Marks Directing Attention.

The Index (☞) is used to call special
attention to an important line or clause in the
writing or printing , as :
" ☞ Five per cent discount for cash."

The Asterism or Stars (⁂) is used to designate a general reference ; as

" ⁂ The teacher should make frequent use of the blackboard."

The Brace } is employed to unite two or
more parts of speech or names that are brought
into juxtaposition as

Gender { Masculine. Feminine. Neuter.   Committee { Wm. Smith. John Brown.

A Paragraph (¶) is used by the author frequently to designate, in the middle of a sentence, when he re-reads his manuscript, those
words that he wishes to have commence a paragraph. It shows where something new begins.

A Section (§) usually designates the smaller
distinct parts of a book.

As references they are frequently used with
numbers ; thus :

" ¶ 87.   Wedding Ceremonies in Different Countries."
" § 172.   The Law of Usury in Different States."

Leaders (----) are employed to lead the eye
from one portion of the page to another across
blank space ; as

London............................. 123
Paris.. 84
New York..304

Underscoring.

Words and sentences that the writer desires
should be emphatic, are designated by lines
drawn beneath the words that are to be empha-
sized.   Thus one line indicates *italics ;* two
lines, SMALL CAPITALS ; three lines, LARGE
CAPITALS ; four lines, *ITALIC CAPITALS.*
The words
" To arms ! to arms !! to arms !!! they cry,"

Underscored will appear in print thus —
" *To arms !* TO ARMS!! TO ARMS!!! they cry."

" Upward and upward we went! gradually the scene grew
more and more entrancing! until at length, *faster,* RICHER,
WILDER, *GRANDER* the weird objects came and went,
fading away at last in the long dim distance."

The Parts of Speech.

IMPROPER USE OF WORDS.

GRAMMAR is the art of writing or speaking a language correctly. There are eight distinct parts of speech, named as follows: *Noun, Pronoun, Adjective, Verb, Adverb, Preposition, Conjunction,* and *Interjection.*

The NOUN is the name of an object or some quality of the same; as, *knife, horse, house, sharpness, speed, beauty.* Nouns are of two classes, proper and common. A proper noun is the name of an individual object; as, *England, William, Washington;* and should always be capitalized. Names given to whole classes are common nouns; as, *sea, land, army, tree, etc.*

A PRONOUN is a word that takes the place of a noun; as, "*He* reads," "*She* studies," "*It* falls."

An ADJECTIVE is a word used to describe a noun; as, "*sweet* cider," "*educated* people," "*fast* horse."

The VERB is a word that expresses action; as, "He *runs,*" "She *sleeps,*" "It *falls.*"

The ADVERB tells how the action is performed, and modifies the meaning of verbs, adjectives, and other adverbs; as, "He walks *rapidly,*" "*Very* soon," "*More* pleasing," "*Directly* under," etc.

A PREPOSITION is a word that connects other words, and shows the relation between them; as, "The snow lies *on* the ground," "He went *to* Europe."

A CONJUNCTION is a part of speech used to connect words and sentences together; as, "Houses *and* lands;" "I walked in the meadows *and* in the groves, *but* I saw no birds *nor* animals of any kind, *because* of the darkness."

An INTERJECTION is a word used to express sudden or strong emotion; as, *O! Alas! Ah!*

As a full consideration of the subject of grammar requires a volume of itself, it is not, therefore, the purpose of this book to enter into a detailed explanation of the use of the various parts of speech, along with the rules for applying the same. Fuller instruction relating to the proper construction of language may be obtained in any of the various text-books on grammar, which may be procured at the bookstores.

Mistakes Corrected.

The object in introducing the subject of grammar here is to call attention to the faults liable to be made by the writer and speaker unacquainted with a knowledge of the correct use of language. To illustrate: special care should be taken to use the plural verb when the plural nominative is used; as, "Trees *grows*" should be "Trees *grow;*" "Birds *flies*" should be "Birds *fly;*" "Some flowers *is* more fragrant than others" should be "Some flowers *are* more fragrant than others."

Care should be exercised in the use of the adjective pronoun; as, "*Them* men" should be "*Those* men."

The past tense of the word *do* is frequently improperly used; as, "I *done* the example" should be "I *did* the example."

Care should be taken with words terminating with *ly;* as, "Birds fly swift" should be "Birds fly *swiftly;*" "She sang beautiful" should be "She sang *beautifully;*" "He walks rapid" should be "*rapidly;*" "He talks eloquent" should be "*eloquently.*"

The word *got* is frequently unnecessarily used; as, "I have got the book" should be "I have the book."

The word *learn* is often wrongly used in place of teach; as, "Will you *learn* me to write?" should be "Will you *teach* me to write?"

The verbs *lay* and *lie* are frequently misused.

The following examples illustrate the distinctions to be observed in their use: Thus, "I *lie* down; you *lie* down; he *lies* down." But, "I *lay* down the book; you *lay* down the carpet; he *lays* down the rules."

The verbs *sit* and *set* are often used improperly. The following sentences illustrate the difference between them: Thus, "I *sit* down; you *sit* down; he *sits* down." "I *set* the table; you *set* the trap; and he *sets* the saw."

Care should be used not to have two negatives in a sentence when affirmation is meant; thus, "Don't never tell a lie" should be "Never tell a lie;" "I can't see nothing" should be "I can see nothing," or, "I cannot see anything."

Slang Phrases, and Profanity.

A man is known by the company he keeps. He is also known by his language. No amount of good clothes or outside polish can prevent a man from being regarded as vulgar and low-bred who is addicted to the use of profane words. The use of profanity plainly indicates that the person employing it has such a limited knowledge of words suitable to express ideas, that he is compelled to use vulgar language in order to convey his thought. And the same measurably is true of slang phrases. Such terms as "*Level Best,*" "*Right Smart,*" "*Played out,*" "*You Bet,*" "*Bottom dollar,*" etc., while sometimes allowed among familiar acquaintances, are vulgarisms, and in all graver speaking and writing should be avoided.

The uniform use of a chaste, refined and beautiful language is not only an index to a pure, clear and cultivated intellect, but is always, to the lady or gentleman, one of the surest elements of success in any business where language is required.

ERRORS THAT ARE FREQUENT —IN— CONVERSATION.

Common Faults IN Writing and Speaking.

MISTAKES —IN— GRAMMAR WHICH ARE OFTEN HEARD.

Superfluous Words, Improper Phrases, and Errors of Grammar.

MANY of the following expressions may be heard in the ordinary conversation of every day life. They indicate a lack of knowledge or want of care in the use of words which those who have been trained to the use of correct language immediately observe.

In this connection it may be said that one of the most important studies is that of Grammar, which should be vigorously pursued until the student can properly construct sentences. On that qualification, in many positions of life, hangs success. Without this training the individual is liable at any time to use those expressions which indicate deficiency in this branch of a primary education.

These phrases are especially common in the language of those who are unskilled in knowledge of grammar. The corrections will aid the student somewhat in the acquisition of a better method of expression, but while they do this it is not pretended that they teach this art. They simply direct attention to the importance of this subject as a branch of education, and point out by example those phrases which are often used incorrectly.

"It is *me*," should be "It is *I*."	"Better than *me*," should be "Better than *I*."	"*Who* do you wish?" should be "*Whom* do you wish?"	"He was *to* Henry's," should be "He was *at* Henry's."	"Between you and *I*," should be "Between you and *me*."
"I *done* that," should be "I *did* that."	"How *far* is it," should be "How *far* is it."	"I *had* rather do it," should be "I *would* rather do it."	"He travels *rapid*." should be "He travels *rapidly*."	"It is three *foot* long," should be "It is three *feet* long."
"I *seen* him," should be "I *saw* him."	"I love beefsteak," should be "I *like* beefsteak."	"He had *laid* down," should be "He had *lain* down."	"As soon as *ever* I can," should be "As soon as I can."	"She sings *beautiful*," should be "She sings *beautifully*."
"We enter *in*," should be "We enter."	"*Was* you there?" should be "*Were* you there?"	"What *are* the news?" should be "What *is* the news?"	"The crops look *finely*," should be "The crops look *fine*."	"He won't *never* do it," should be "He *will* never do it."
"This *'ere* one," should be "This one."	"Who *done* that?" should be "Who *did* that?"	"*Set* down and rest," should be "*Sit* down and rest."	"*Don't* never do that," should be "*Never* do that."	"He made a *dicker*," should be "He made a *bargain*."
"Is that *him*?" should be "Is that *he*?"	"I don't think so," should be "I think not."	"See that *'ere* bird," should be "See that bird."	"Can you *learn* me?" should be "Can you *teach* me?"	"He fell on the floor," should be "He fell *to* the floor."
"Call *upon* him," should be "Call on him."	"How do you *do*?" should be "How are you?"	"I *had* ought to go," should be "I ought to go."	"I *have* got the book," should be "I *have* the book."	"Cover over the well," should be "Cover the well."
"Do *like* I do," should be "Do *as* I do."	"Give me *me* hat," should be "Give me my hat."	"They *was* talking," should be "They *were* talking."	"I enjoy *good* health," should be "I have good health."	"If I am *not mistaken*," should be "If I *mistake* not."
"*Once'* or *twice*," should be "*Once* or *twice*."	"A *summer's* day," should be "A *summer* day."	"*Me* and John saw it," should be "John and *I* saw it."	"I'll *bet* you'll go," should be "I *think* you will go."	"He is *up* on the house," should be "He is on the house."
"If I *was* him," should be "If I *were he*."	"I have *got back*," should be "I have *returned*."	"*Who* did you say?" should be "*Whom* did you say?"	"Let me dress *me*," should be "Let me dress *myself*."	"I cannot by *no* means," should be "I cannot by any means."
"In case I win," should be "*If* I win."	"Not as I know *of*," should be "Not that I know."	"I *swapped* horses," should be "I *traded* horses."	"The man was *beat*," should be "The man was *beaten*."	"The stone *sinks down*," should be "The stone *sinks*."
"Let you and *I*," should be "Let you and *me*."	"I am very *dry*," should be "I am very *thirsty*."	"Are you *was* going?" should be "Are you going?"	"He is as good as *him*," should be "He is as good as *he*."	"It was *her* who called," should be "It was *she* who called."
"That *there* one," should be "That one."	"I have *saw* him," should be "I have *seen* him."	"*Such another* error," should be "*Another such* error."	"They returned *back*," should be "They returned."	"There *was* some men," should be "There *were* some men."
"*Be* you cold?" should be "*Are* you cold?"	"Both *of* these men," should be "Both these men."	"I can't *stand* it," should be "I cannot *endure* it."	"The cloth was *wore*," should be "The cloth was *worn*."	"He must stay *to* home," should be "He must stay *at* home."

"First *of all* let me say,"
should be
"First, let me say."

"*New* furnished rooms,"
should be
"*Newly* furnished rooms."

"Do you see *them* men?"
should be
"Do you see *those* men?"

"*Is* your hands cold?"
should be
"*Are* your hands cold?"

"*Above* a year since,"
should be
"*More than* a year since."

"These *kind* of apples,"
should be
"These *kinds* of apples,"
or
"*This* kind of apples."

"He is *in under* the wall,"
should be
"He is *under* the wall."

"I *toted* him across,"
should be
"I *carried* him across."

"I came from *over yer*,"
should be
"I came from *yonder*."

"*Lay* down or *set* down,"
should be
"*Lie* down or *sit* down."

"Two *spoonsful* of tea,"
should be
"Two *spoonfuls* of tea."

"I'll give you *fits*,"
should be
"I will *attend* to you."

"A *new* pair of boots,"
should be
"A *pair* of new boots."

"The *best* of the two,"
should be
"The *better* of the two."

"I have *lit* the fire,"
should be
"I have *lighted* the fire."

"I *belong* to the church,"
should be
"I am a *churchmember*."

"He *climbed up* the hill,"
should be
"He *climbed* the hill."

"What *beautiful* sauce,"
should be
"What *excellent* sauce."

"I *had* rather ride,"
should be
"I *would* rather ride."

"Very *warmish* weather,"
should be
"Very *warm* weather"

"*There is* a great many,"
should be
"*There are* a great many."

"I *only* want five dollars,"
should be
"I *want only* five dollars."

"You *hadn't ought* to go,"
should be
"You *ought not* to go."

"*There's lots* of them,"
should be
"*There are many* of them."

"I have *rode* with him,"
should be
"I have *ridden* with him."

"I saw the *Miss Browns*,"
should be
"I saw the *Misses Brown*."

"Peaches were *plenty*,"
should be
"Peaches were *plentiful*."

"Continue *on* in this way,"
should be
"Continue in this way."

"*Don't* give him no more,"
should be
"Give him no more."

"Walter and *me* went down,"
should be
"Walter and *I* went down."

"*Who* does this belong to,"
should be
"*Whom* does this belong to."

"*As* far as I am concerned,"
should be
"*So* far as I am concerned."

"He had *near* ten dollars,"
should be
"He had *nearly* ten dollars."

"We had an *awful nice* time,"
should be
"We had a *delightful* time."

"He rose up from his seat,"
should be
"He rose from his seat."

"He came *ladened* with honor,"
should be
"He came *laden* with honor."

"I expected *to have seen* him,"
should be
"I expected *to see* him."

"Give me a *little bit of* piece,"
should be
"Give me a *small* piece."

"They despised *one another*,"
should be
"They despised *each other*."

"I was *tickled* to see him"
should be
"I was *pleased* to see him."

"He is heavier than I *be*,"
should be
"He is heavier than I *am*."

"When we *was* living here,"
should be
"When we *were* living here."

"He is better than you *be*,"
should be
"He is better than you *are*."

"Similarity *with* each other,"
should be
"Similarity *to* each other."

"When I get *off from* a car,"
should be
"When I get *off* a car"

"Do you *mean to do that*?"
should be
"Do you *intend to do that*?"

"*Either of them are* rich,"
should be
"*Each of them is* rich."

"I have a *couple of dollars*,"
should be
"I have *two* dollars."

"It spread *all over* the town,"
should be
"It spread *over all* the town."

"If I *sees* him I would do it,"
should be
"If I *were he* I would do it."

"I'll be blamed if I can tell,"
should be
"I *cannot* tell."

"Who is there?" "It is *me*,"
should be
"Who is there?" "It is *I*."

"I *took* you for another,"
should be
"I *mistook* you for another."

"His faith has been *shook*,"
should be
"His faith has been *shaken*."

"He died *with consumption*,"
should be
"He died *of consumption*."

"You are stronger than *me*,"
should be
"You are stronger than *I*."

"I reckon I'll go to-morrow,"
should be
"I *intend* to go to-morrow."

"I *guess* I'll go to-morrow,"
should be
"I *think of going* to-morrow."

"He has a *tarnal* lot of potatoes,"
should be
"He has a *large quantity* of potatoes."

"Make haste and dress *you*,"
should be
"Make haste and dress *yourself*."

"The two *first* men are the strongest,"
should be
"The *first two* men are the strongest."

"She sang *to* the Baptist church,"
should be
"She sang *at* the Baptist church."

"*Them is* large enough for you,"
should be
"*Those are* large enough for you."

"We *won't* say one *single* word,"
should be
"We *will not* say one word."

"He is *down in* the basement,"
should be
"He is *in* the basement."

"His manner admits of no *excuse*,"
should be
"His manner admits no excuse."

"Received *of* John Brown five dollars,"
should be
"Received *from* John Brown five dollars."

"No other means *but* this was left,"
should be
"No other means *than* this was left."

"They will go *from* thence next week,"
should be
"They will go thence next week."

"From *now* till Christmas,"
should be
"From *this time* till Christmas."

"He has *got over* his trouble,"
should be
"He has *recovered from* his trouble."

"I know better; that ain't so,"
should be
"Pardon me, I *understand* differently."

"I know little or nothing of it,"
should be
"I know little, *if anything*, of it."

"He has four *brother-in-laws*,"
should be
"He has four *brothers-in-law*."

"I know *Mr. and Mrs. Dr. Brown*,"
should be
"I know *Dr. and Mrs. Brown*."

"It's *funny* how long she *stays* sick,"
should be
"It is *singular* that she should *remain* sick so long."

"You *lie*; he got *tight*,"
should be
"You are *mistaken*; he was *drunk*."

"I'll be goll darned *if* I know where it is,"
should be
"I do not know where it is."

"*Somehow or another* I'm a failure,"
should be
"*For some reason* I am always a failure."

"Henry and John *is* coming,"
should be
"Henry and John *are* coming."

"He dropped *down* into the water,"
should be
"He dropped into the water."

"They differ *among* one another,"
should be
"They differ *among themselves*"

"Take *the* three-fourths, give me *the the balance*,"
should be
"Take *three-fourths*; give me the remainder."

"I *see* him *every now and then*,"
should be
"I see him *occasionally*."

"I never play if I can *help it*,"
should be
"I never play if I can *avoid it*."

"*Look out* or you'll get hurt,"
should be
"*Be careful* or you'll get hurt."

"Should have gloves like *Henry has*,"
should be
"Should have gloves like Henry's."

"I'd like *for you* to go,"
should be
"I would be *pleased to have* you go."

"May be I *mought* or I *moughtn't*,"
should be
"I *may* or I *may not*."

"I never *see* such a *slew* of people before,"
should be
"I never *saw* such a *large number* of people before."

"His works are approved *of* by many,"
should be
"His works are approved *by* many."

"I *don't* know nothing about it,"
should be
"I know nothing about it."

"He has a *heap* of cattle,"
should be
"He has a *large number* of cattle."

"He had a *right smart* crop of corn last year,"
should be
"He had a *large* crop of corn last year."

"He has a good *bit* of money,"
should be
"He has a good *deal* of money."

"I went to New York, *you know*, and when I *came back*, *you see*, I commenced attending school,"
should be
"I went to New York, and when I *returned* I commenced attending school."

Composition and Declamation.

IMPORTANCE OF ORIGINALITY.

HAVING acquired ideas and education, it is of the utmost importance that the facility of imparting knowledge to others be cultivated. The man or woman in any community who can express ideas correctly, plainly and readily, with good voice and self-possession, in the presence of others, wields always a commanding influence—provided this accomplishment is guided by good judgment, which teaches *when* to speak, *where* to speak, *what* to speak, and *how* to speak.

The correct and fluent expression of thought is largely a matter of practice. Our youth should be early taught to write their thoughts, and to declaim in public.

The writing of compositions in school is one of the most important of the studies pursued, and, with every student, in some form, should be among the daily exercises of the schoolroom; as in the writing of the composition are learned spelling, penmanship, punctuation, use of capital letters, grammar, and correct expression. Frequently, also, during the week, the student should declaim: the declamation being generally the student's own composition. Thus youths become accustomed to the speaking of their own thoughts correctly, and oftentimes eloquently.

This art, acquired under the guidance of an experienced teacher, will be of infinite service to the man in after life; and, with the rapidly widening sphere of woman's work, the ability to speak well in public is equally desirable for her.

True, many people who have an ambition for public speaking do not awake to the necessity and importance of this subject until the period of their school days has long passed, when the conviction is likely to force itself upon their minds that they are too late. Such, however, need not be discouraged in their efforts towards the acquisition of a pleasing style of oratory. Let a debating club be established, of half a dozen or more persons, to meet regularly during the week, at stated times, for the discussion of current topics of the day, either at a private residence, some hall chosen for the purpose, or at a schoolroom; the exercises of the occasion being interspersed with essays by members of the club, the whole to be criticised by critics appointed. A few weeks thus spent will oftentimes develop in the club several fluent essayists and speakers.

If desirous of distinction, it is not enough that the speakers utter their own thoughts. There should be especial effort made to present the idea in an original, attractive and efficient form. To be effective, the speaker must exhibit variety in gesture, tone of voice, and method of illustration. Gestures and sentences should be gracefully rounded; the illustrations, in strong and telling words, should be so proportioned,

THE READING OF THE ESSAY.

It is a public occasion. Coming to the front, upon the stage, confident, easy and natural, with manuscript held in the left hand, that the right may be free for gesture if required, the lady reads her essay; the exercise being effective by originality of composition, fitting words, new and important thoughts, appropriateness, ease, and clearness of enunciation.

and the arguments so arranged, as to grow stronger from the beginning to the end; while the thoughts should be so presented as to be appropriate, and in harmony with the occasion.

The speakers and essayists whom we know as wielding the greatest influence in the world's history, added to these graces of oratory depth of investigation, liberty of thought, and freedom of expression. They scorned to traverse the beaten paths, simply because of custom and popularity. They chose to be independent. Rather than follow, they preferred to lead the thoughts of others.

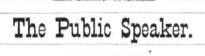

The Public Speaker.

MEANS BY WHICH TO WIN SUCCESS.

KNOWLEDGE is well; it is of great importance; but a person may be very wise, and yet lack influence because wanting in readiness of speech.

The ability to make an off-hand speech, without the aid of manuscript, at once entertaining and instructive, is an accomplishment very much to be desired; and it is one that can in most cases be acquired by the man or woman of average talent, who has the requisite amount of training for this purpose, accompanied by the necessary opportunities for intellectual culture. Such being the fact, the following suggestions may be opportune, as giving an outline of the requisites necessary for the production of a ready speaker.

First. The foundation of the discourse should be thoroughly fixed in the mind, and the order of succession in which the arguments are to follow.

Second. These should be so arranged that one thought should be the natural outgrowth of the other, and each idea should be so distinctly marked out as to be in readiness the moment it is wanted.

Third. The speaker should vividly feel all that he may design to speak, in order that clear ideas may be expressed. The mind should not, however, be so absorbed with the subject in hand as to prevent its acting readily in the development of the topic under consideration. It is possible for the feelings to become so vehement in their expression as to paralyze utterance from their very fullness.

BASHFULNESS.   SELF-POSSESSION.

The above illustrations represent the effect of practice and culture. While speaker No. 1, by his unpolished manner and diffidence is an object of pity or ridicule, and without influence as a public speaker, No. 2, representing John B. Gough, as he apostrophizes a glass of water, entrances his audience by his self-possession, his earnestness, and his naturalness.

Fourth. The feelings, in speaking, must be resolved into ideas, thoughts into images, to express which there must be suitable language. While the main idea should be firmly grasped, in its elucidation it should be separated into its principal members, and these again divided into subordinate parts, each under perfect command of the speaker, to be called upon and used at will, until the subject is exhausted.

Fifth. The full, complete and ready use of the imagination is of the greatest importance to the extemporaneous speaker, which power may be greatly cultivated by reading the works of Walter Scott, Dickens, and other standard writers who excel in imaginative description. To hold up before the audience a clear, distinct outline of the subject in hand, and paint the picture in fitting language so vividly that the auditors will delightedly follow its progress, step by step, is the distinguishing excellence of the off-hand speaker. With many persons of real talent, the powers of imagination work too slowly to hold the attention of the audience. This hindrance, however, can be largely overcome by practice.

Sixth. The difficulty of embarrassment, which afflicts some people upon public appearance, is overcome by practice, and by having a perfectly distinct understanding of what is to be said, which consciousness tends to give confidence and self-possession. To obtain the ability to present this clear conception of the subject, the speaker should study logic, geometry, and kindred subjects that arrive at conclusions through a process of analytical reasoning. The speaker should be able to think methodically, being able to decompose his thoughts into parts, to analyze these into their elements, to recompose, regather and concentrate these again in a manner such as will clearly illustrate the idea sought to be conveyed.

Seventh. One of the most efficient aids to public speaking is the ability to write. The public speaker will do well to commence by writing in full what he is desirous of saying. He should, at the same time, make a study of the various masters of oratory. Writing gives great clearness to the expression of thought, and, having plenty of time in its composition, the mind is able to look at the subject in every phase. With the main idea clearly defined and kept constantly in view, let the speaker examine the subject in every light, the different faculties of the mind concentrating upon a single point. Thus, step by step, the subject is considered in all its bearings, the various details of the idea being completely studied, and the whole matter thoroughly developed, until the subject has reached its perfect form.

Eighth. The daily study of synonymous words and their meanings will give greater facility of expression. The mind should also be stored with a great variety of information on subjects pertaining to the arts and sciences, from which one can constantly draw in cases of emergency. It is impossible for the speaker to extemporize what is not in the mind. And further, all reading and study should be done with such care that every idea thus acquired will be so thoroughly wrought out as to be available when we wish to communicate our ideas to others.

Ninth. In public speaking, one of the great secrets of success is a knowledge of human nature. To acquire this, the speaker should carefully study men — the passions and impulses that influence mankind — their phrenological characteristics, and know them as they are. To do this, he should freely mingle in society, interchanging ideas, and seeking every opportunity for the practice of extempore speaking.

Tenth. An important element necessary to success in the off-hand speaker is courage. While it is essential that he use choice and fitting language in the expression of ideas, let him not hesitate, when he has commenced a sentence, because be cannot readily call to mind the exact language necessary to beautifully clothe the thought. Push vigorously through to the end. even though at a sacrifice, for a time, of the most perfect forms of speech. This courage that dare stand up and speak a sentence ungrammatically, even, is necessary to make the good speaker of the future.

Finally, while all cannot become equally proficient in oratory, the industrious student of average talent, who earnestly resolves to win success as an extempore speaker, will find himself, in the majority of cases, in time, self-possessed in the presence of others. With ideas clear and distinct, vivified and quickened by imagination, clothed in fitting words and beautiful language, he will be enabled to instruct and entertain an audience in a manner vastly better than most people would suppose who may have listened to his maiden efforts in the commencement of his public speaking.

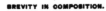

IDEAS EXPRESSED IN FEW WORDS.

BREVITY IN COMPOSITION.

O be able to talk correctly, the student should first be able to write properly. Not only should penmanship be plain and easy, words rightly spelled, capitals correctly used, and sentences grammatically constructed and punctuated, but much depends, also, beyond that, upon the style of composition, mode of expression, and language used, whether it be acceptable to readers and hearers or not.

As a rule, with the great sea of literature about us, the writer of to-day who is original and condenses ideas into the smallest space, whether in the sermon, book, business letter, or newspaper article, is much the most likely to have readers or hearers. The aim of the writer should therefore be, first, to say something new, presenting a subject fraught with original ideas; and second, to give those ideas in the fewest possible words consistent with agreeable expression.

"Why did you not make that article more brief?" said an editor to his correspondent.

"Because," said the writer, "I did not have time."

The idea sought to be conveyed, concerning brevity, is clearly shown in that answer of the correspondent. It is an easy matter to dress ideas in many words. It requires much more care, however, to clearly state the same idea in fewer words.

The chief merit of Shakespeare is the thought conveyed in few words; the meaning that we catch beyond the words expressed.

Those poets that will live in immortality have

written thus. The reader cannot fail to recognize the truth and thought conveyed in this stanza of Cowper's, beyond the words themselves:

"Judge not the Lord by feeble sense,
But trust Him for His grace;
Behind a frowning providence,
He hides a smiling face."

The idea expressed in these few lines brings up in long review the trials of a past life, and the recollection of sorrows and afflictions which we afterwards, not unfrequently, discovered to be blessings in disguise, and in reality seemingly designed for our best good.

There is much food for reflection in the following stanza from Gray's "Elegy":

"Full many a gem, of purest ray serene,
The dark, unfathomed caves of ocean bear;
Full many a flower is born to blush unseen,
And waste its sweetness on the desert air."

With this reading comes up the thought of those of our fellow men whom *we* know to be good, noble, and worthy, but whose names will go down to the grave unhonored and unknown.

Very plainly we see the meaning beyond the words in the following, also from Gray:

"Perhaps, in this neglected spot, is laid
Some heart, once pregnant with celestial fire—
Hand, that the rod of empire might have swayed,
Or waked to ecstasy the living lyre."

A similar idea is expressed by Whittier, though in fewer words:

"Of all sad words of tongue or pen,
The saddest are these, ' It might have been.' "

Both stanzas are deeply freighted with thought beyond what is expressed

Those extracts, whether in prose or poetry, that are destined to go down to coming generations, are so laden with ideas and suggestions that in listening or reading, the scenes they suggest seem to move before us, and we forget words in contemplating that which the words describe

Prose writings often contain gems of thought told very briefly, especially in the works of our best authors. In the following, from Irving's description of the grave, the reader becomes so absorbed in the picture portrayed that the words themselves are lost in the emotions they enkindle:

"O, the grave! the grave! It buries every error, covers every defect, extinguishes every resentment. From its peaceful bosom spring none but fond regrets and tender recollections. Who can look down upon the grave even of an enemy, and not feel a compunctious throb, that he should ever have warred with the poor handful of earth that lies mouldering before him.

"But the grave of those we loved—what a place for meditation! There it is that we call up in long review the whole history of virtue and gentleness, and the thousand endearments lavished upon us, almost unheeded, in the daily intercourse of intimacy; there it is that we dwell upon the tenderness, the solemn, awful tenderness of the parting scene—the bed of death, with all its stifled griefs, its noiseless attendants, its mute, watchful assiduities—the last testimonies of expiring love—the feeble, fluttering, thrilling—O how thrilling!—pressure of the hand—the last fond look of the glazing eye, turned upon us even from the threshold of existence—the faint, faltering accents struggling in death to give one more assurance of affection.

"Ay, go to the grave of buried love, and meditate! There settle the account with thy conscience for every past benefit unrequited, every past endearment unregarded, of that departed being who can never—never—never return to be soothed by thy contrition."

The Bible abounds in beautiful and expressive sayings, that reveal much in few words, as shown in the following:

"The wicked flee when no man pursueth." "Boast not thyself of to-morrow. Thou knowest not what a day may bring forth." "A soft answer turneth away wrath." "Better is a dinner of herbs where love is, than a stalled ox and hatred therewith." "Hope deferred maketh the heart sick." "Cast thy bread upon the waters, for thou shalt find it after many days."

Care should be taken to prune out the unnecessary words with an unsparing hand. Thus, in the sentence, "I have got back, having returned yesterday," it is better to say, "I returned yesterday."

Two young men, upon going into the army during the late civil war, were requested by their friends to telegraph at the close of any battle they might take part in, concerning their condition. At the close of the battle of Perryville, one telegraphed the following:

"PERRYVILLE, KY., Oct. 9, 1862.

"DEAR FRIENDS:

"As requested, I take the first opportunity after the late severe battle, fought at this place, to inform you that I came from the engagement uninjured.

"HENRY MOSELEY."

The other telegraphed as follows:

"PERRYVILLE, KY., Oct. 9, 1862.

"Uninjured.

"HIRAM MAYNARD."

Hiram well knew that his friends would hear immediately of the battle from the newspapers, and would learn from the same source that his regiment participated in the engagement. Their

next question would then be " How is Hiram ? "
To answer that, he had simply to telegraph one
word. In a letter afterwards, he gave the particulars.

The following rules should be observed in
writing :

First. Never use a word that does not add
some new thought, or modify some idea already
expressed.

Second. Beware of introducing so many subjects into one sentence as to confuse the sense.

Third. Long and short sentences should be
properly intermixed, in order to give a pleasing
sound in reading. There is generally a rounded
harmony in the long sentence, not found in the
short, though as a rule, in order to express
meaning plainly, it is better to use short sentences.

Fourth. Make choice of such words and
phrases as people will readily understand.

Rhetorical Figures.

HE beauty, force, clearness, and
brevity of language are frequently
greatly enhanced by the judicious
use of rhetorical figures, which are
named and explained as follows :

A **Simile** is an expressed comparison.

EXAMPLE — " Charity, *like the sun*, brightens every object on which
it shines."

The **Metaphor** is an implied comparison, indicating the resemblance of two objects by applying the name, quality or conduct of one directly
to the other.

EXAMPLE — " Thy word is a *lamp* to my feet." " Life is an *isthmus*
between two eternities." " The morning of life." " The storms of
life."

An **Allegory** is the recital of a story under
which is a meaning different from what is expressed in words, the analogy and comparison
being so plainly made that the designed conclusions are correctly drawn.

EXAMPLE — Thou hast brought a vine (the Jewish nation) out of
Egypt; thou hast cast out the heathen and planted it. Thou prepar-
edst room before it and didst cause it to take deep root, and it filled the
land. The hills were covered with the shadow of it, and the boughs
thereof were like the goodly cedars.— BIBLE.

In **Hyperbole**, through the effect of imagina-

tion or passion, we greatly exaggerate what is
founded in truth, by magnifying the good qualities of objects we love, and diminish and
degrade the objects that we dislike or envy.

EXAMPLES —" That fellow is so tall that he does not know when his
feet are cold." " Brougham is a *thunderbolt*."

Personification consists in attributing life to
things inanimate.

EXAMPLE — " *Hatred* stirreth up strife; but *love* covereth all sins."

A **Metonymy** (*Me-ton-y-my*) substitutes the
name of one object for that of another that
sustains some relation to it, either by some degree of mutual dependence or otherwise so
connected as to be capable of suggesting it ;
thus cause is used for effect or the effect for the
cause, the attribute for the subject and the subject for the attribute.

EXAMPLES — 1. Cause and effect; as " Extravagance is the *ruin* of
many,"— that is, the *cause of ruin.*
2. Attribute and that to which it belongs; as " *Pride* shall be
brought low"— that is, *the proud.*

A **Synecdoche** (*sin-ek-do-ke*) is a form of speech
wherein something more or something less is
substituted for the precise object meant, as
when the whole is put for a part, or a part for
the whole ; the singular for the plural or the
plural for the singular.

EXAMPLES — " His *head* is grey,"— that is, his *hair.* " The *world*
considers him a man of talent,"— that is, the *people.*

Antithesis is the contrasting of opposites.

EXAMPLES — " *Sink* or *swim, live* or *die, survive* or *perish,* I give
my hand and heart to this vote." " Though *deep* yet *clear.*"

Irony is a form of speech in which the writer
or speaker sneeringly means the reverse of what
is literally said, the words being usually mockery uttered for the sake of ridicule or sarcasm.
Irony is a very effective weapon of attack, the
form of language being such as scarcely to
admit of a reply.

EXAMPLE — " Have not the Indians been kindly and justly treated?
Have not the temporal things, the vain baubles and filthy lucre of
this world, which are too apt to engage their worldly and selfish
thoughts, been benevolently taken from them; and have they not
instead thereof, been taught to set their affections on things above?"

Paralipsis pretends to conceal what is really
expressed.

EXAMPLE — " *I will not call him villain*, because it would be unpar-
liamentary. *I will not call him fool*, because he happens to be chancellor of the exchequer."

Climax is the gradual ascending in the expression of thought, from things lower to a higher
and better. Reversed, it is called *anticlimax.*

EXAMPLES — "A Scotch mist becomes a shower; and a shower, a storm; and a storm, a tempest; and a tempest, thunder and lightning; and thunder and lightning, heavenquake and earthquake." "Then virtue became silent, heartsick, pined away, and died."

Allusion is that use of language whereby in a word or words we recall some interesting incident or condition by resemblance or contrast.

EXAMPLES — "Give them the Amazon in South America and we'll give them the Mississippi in the United States."

After the signing of the Declaration of Independence, Hancock remarked to his fellow signers that they must all *hang* together. "Yes," said Franklin "or we shall all *hang separately.*"

The allusion in this case turns to a *pun*, which is a play upon words.

EXAMPLE — "And the Doctor told the Sexton
And the Sexton *tolled* the bell."

A continued allusion and resemblance in style becomes a *parody.*

EXAMPLE — " 'Tis the last rose of summer, left blooming alone;
All her lovely companions are faded and gone;
No flower of her kindred, no rosebud is nigh,
To reflect back her blushes, or give sigh for sigh.
I'll not leave thee, thou lone one, to pine on thy stem;
Since the lovely are sleeping, go, sleep thou with them.
Thus kindly I scatter thy leaves o'er the bed
Where thy mates of the garden lie scentless and dead."

PARODY — " 'Tis the last golden dollar, left shining alone;
All its brilliant companions are squandered and gone;
No coin of its mintage reflects back its hue,
They went in mint juleps, and this will go too!
I'll not keep thee, thou lone one, too long in suspense;
Thy brothers were melted, and melt thou, to pence!
I'll ask for no quarter, I'll spend and not spare,
Till my old tattered pocket hangs centless and bare."

PUN — "Ancient maiden lady anxiously remarks,
That there must be peril 'mong so many *sparks;*
Roguish-looking fellow, turning to the stranger.
Says it's his opinion she is out of danger." — *Saxe.*

Exclamation is a figure of speech used to express more strongly the emotions of the speaker.

EXAMPLES — "Oh! the depth of the riches both of the wisdom and the knowledge of God!'"

" How poor, how rich, how abject, how august
How complicate, how wonderful is man
Distinguished link in being's endless chain!
Midway from nothing to the Deity!
A beam ethereal, sullied and absorbed!
Though sullied and dishonored, still divine!
An heir of glory! a frail child of dust!
A worm! a god! I tremble at myself,
And in myself am lost."

Interrogation is a rhetorical figure by which the speaker puts opinions in the form of questions for the purpose of expressing thought more positively and vehemently without expectation of the questions being answered.

EXAMPLES — "He that planned the ear shall he not hear? He that formed the eye, shall he not see?" "O Death, where is thy sting? O Grave, where is thy victory?"

"But when shall we be stronger? Will it be the next week or the next year? Will it be when we are totally disarmed, and when a British guard shall be stationed in every house? * * * Is life so dear, or peace so sweet, as to be purchased at the price of chains and slavery?"

" Can storied urn or animated bust
Back to its mansions call the fleeting breath?
Can Honor's voice provoke the silent dust,
Or Flattery soothe the dull, cold ear of death?"

Euphemism (*u-fe-miz-em*) is a word or sentence so chosen and expressed as to make a disagreeable fact sound more pleasantly than if told in plain language.

EXAMPLES — " Deceased " for " dead;" "stopping payment," instead of " becoming bankrupt;" " falling asleep," instead of " dying," "you labor under a mistake," for " you lie;" " he does not keep very correct accounts," instead of " he cheats when he can;" " she certainly displays as little vanity in her personal appearance as any young lady I ever saw;" for "she is an intolerable slattern."

" I see Anacreon laugh and sing;
His silver tresses breathe perfume;
*His cheeks display a second spring
Of roses taught by wine to bloom.*"

Apostrophe like the exclamation is the sudden turning away, in the fullness of emotion, to address some other person or object. In this we address the absent or dead as if present or alive, and the inanimate as if living.

This figure of speech usually indicates a high degree of excitement.

EXAMPLES — " O gentle sleep,
Nature's soft nurse, how have I frighted thee,
That thou no more wilt weigh my eyelids down,
And steep my senses in forgetfulness?"

Thus King David, on hearing of the death of Absalom, exclaims, "O, my son Absalom, my son, my son!"

Ossian's Address to the Moon, is one of the most beautiful illustrations of the apostrophe.

" Daughter of heaven, fair art thou! The silence of thy face is pleasant. Thou comest forth in loveliness. The stars attend thy blue steps in the East. The clouds rejoice in thy presence, O Moon! and brighten their dark-brown sides. Who is like thee in heaven, daughter of the night? The stars are ashamed in thy presence, and turn aside their sparkling eyes. Whither dost thou retire from thy course, when the darkness of thy countenance grows? Hast thou thy hall like Ossian? Dwellest thou in the shadow of grief? Have thy sisters fallen from heaven? and are they who rejoiced with thee at night no more? Yes, they have fallen, fair light ' and often dost thou retire to mourn. But thou thyself shall one night fail, and leave thy blue path in heaven. The stars will then lift their heads; they who in thy presence were astonished will rejoice."

"Thou lingering star with less'ning ray,
That lov'st to greet the early morn,
Again thou usher'st in the day
My Mary from my soul was torn.
O Mary! dear departed shade!'"

Vision is a figure of rhetoric by which the speaker represents the objects of his imagination as actually before his eyes and present to his senses.

EXAMPLES — "Soldiers! from the tops of yonder pyramids, forty centuries look down upon you!"

" We behold houses and public edifices wrapt in flames; we hear the crash of roofs falling in, and one general uproar proceeding from a thousand different voices; we see some flying they know not whither, others hanging over the last embraces of their wives and friends; we see the mother tearing from the ruffian's grasp her helpless babe, and the victors cutting each others' throats wherever the plunder is most inviting."

Onomatopœia is the use of such word or words as by their sound will suggest the sense, as *crash, buzz, roar, etc.* Motion is thus easily imitated, as is also sound, and even the reflections and emotions.

EXAMPLES:—"Away they went pell mell, hurry skurry, wild buffalo, wild horse, wild huntsmen, with clang and clatter, and whoop and halloo that made the forests ring." "The ball went *whizzing* past."

"While I nodded nearly napping, suddenly there came a tapping
As of some one gently rapping, rapping at my chamber door."

General Summary.

Dr. Blair's system of rhetoric sums up the most important qualities of style in the six following terms, being thus condensed by Kerl:

"*Purity, propriety,* and *precision* chiefly in regard to words and phrases; and *perspicuity, unity,* and *strength,* in regard to sentences. He who writes with *purity,* avoids all phraseology that is foreign, uncouth, or ill-derived; he who writes with *propriety,* selects the most appropriate, the very best expressions, and generally displays sound judgment and good taste; he who writes with *precision,* is careful to state exactly what he means—all that he means, or that is necessary, and nothing more; he who writes with *perspicuity,* aims to present his meaning so clearly and obviously, that no one can fail to understand him at once; he who observes *unity,* follows carefully the most agreeable order of nature, and does not jumble together incongruous things, nor throw out his thoughts in a confused or chaotic mass; and he who writes with *strength,* so disposes or marshals all the parts of each sentence, and all the parts of the discourse, as to make the strongest impression. A person's style, according as it is influenced by taste and imagination, may be *dry, plain, neat, elegant, ornamental, florid* or *turgid.* The most common faulty style is that which may be described as being stiff, cramped, labored, heavy and tiresome; its opposite is the easy, flowing, graceful, sprightly, and interesting style. One of the greatest beauties of style, one too little regarded, is simplicity or naturalness; that easy, unaffected, earnest, and highly impressive language which indicates a total ignorance, or rather innocence, of all the trickery of art. It seems to consist of the pure promptings of nature; though, in most instances, it is not so much a natural gift as it *is the perfection of art.*"

Laws of Language.

The following rules by Dr. Campbell, in reference to the construction of sentences and choice of words, will be found of service.

1. When the usage is divided as to any particular words or phrases, and when one of the expressions is susceptible of different meanings, while the other admits of only one signification, the expression which is strictly of one meaning should be preferred.
2. In doubtful cases, analogy should be regarded.
3. When expressions are in other respects equal, that should be preferred which is most agreeable to the ear.
4. When none of the preceding rules takes place, regard should be had to simplicity.
5. All words and phrases, particularly harsh and not absolutely necessary, should be dismissed.
6. When the etymology plainly points to a different signification from what the word bears, propriety and simplicity require its dismission.

7. When words become obsolete, or are never used but in particular phrases, they should be repudiated, as they give the style an air of vulgarity and cant, when this general clause renders them obscure.
8. All words and phrases which analyzed grammatically, include an imperfection of speech, should be dismissed.
9. All expressions which, according to the established rules of language, either have no meaning, or involve a contradiction, or according to the fair construction of the words, convey a meaning different from the intention of the speaker, should be dismissed.

Specific Directions.

PARAGRAPHS.—One or more sentences form a paragraph. When a deviation or change is made in the subject a new paragraph is commenced. The first line of each paragraph in writing should commence about one inch from the left side of the sheet. Preserve a space half an inch in width between the left of the writing and the edge of the sheet. Write as close to the right edge of the sheet as possible. When lack of space prevents the completion of a word on the line, place the hyphen (-) at the end of the line and follow with the remaining syllables on the next line. Words may be divided, but never divide syllables.

Rules of Construction.

1. The principal words in a sentence should be placed where they will make the most striking impression.
2. A weaker assertion or argument should not follow a stronger one.
3. The separation of the preposition from the noun which it governs, should be avoided
4. Concluding the sentence with an adverb, preposition, or other insignificant word, lessens the strength of the sentence.

ORDER OF ARRANGEMENT.—Young writers will find it well to prepare a memorandum of the subjects they wish to treat on a separate slip of paper, and the points they wish to make relating to each subject. Having the subjects clearly fixed in the mind, they should commence with the least important and follow through to the end, considering the most important at the close.

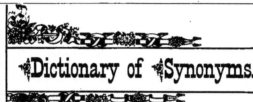

Dictionary of Synonyms.

SEVERAL THOUSAND SYNONYMOUS WORDS.
For the use of Writers and Speakers.

UITE a common fault is that of using, when writing, the same word several times in a sentence. To avoid this inelegant repetition, the writer should give careful attention to the selection of different words having a similar meaning. Observe the following:

Example.

He is *accurate* in figures, *accurate* in grammar, *accurate* in spelling, *accurate* in writing.

IMPROVED.

He is *accurate* in figures, *correct* in grammar, *exact* in spelling, *precise* in writing.

See the word *accurate* in the dictionary, accompanied by synonymous words.

Example.

He made an excellent *address* in the morning, and his colleague made an excellent *address* in the evening.

IMPROVED.

He made an excellent *address* in the morning, and his colleague entertained the assemblage with an eloquent *speech* in the evening.

Example.

The patient *suffered* untold *agony* for years; during which time he *suffered* not only *agony* of body, but *agony* of mind.

IMPROVED.

The patient *suffered* untold *agony* for years; during which time he *endured* not only *torture* of body, but *anguish* of mind.

A.

Abase — humble, lower, degrade, depress, disgrace.

Abate—lessen, reduce, subside, decrease, diminish.

Abbreviate — abridge, curtail, condense, compress, epitomise, lessen, reduce, shorten.

Abhor—abominate, detest, hate, loathe.

Ability—capacity, power, skill, means, talent.

Able—capable, competent.

Abode—dwelling, habitation, residence.

Abominate—abhor, detest, hate, loathe.

Abridge—contract, diminish, lessen, shorten.

Absent — abstracted, inattentive, heedless.

Absorb—engross, engulf, imbibe, swallow.

Abstain—forbear, refrain, withhold.

Abstruse—hidden, obscure, difficult.

Absurd — foolish, unreasonable, preposterous, ridiculous, silly.

Abundant—ample, copious, plentiful.

Abusive—insolent, offensive, scurrilous, disgraceful.

Accede — acquiesce, agree, consent, assent, comply, yield.

Accept—admit, receive, take.

Acceptable—agreeable, grateful, welcome.

Accession — addition, augmentation, increase.

Accommodate — adjust, adapt, serve, suit, fit.

Accomplice—abettor, ally, assistant, accessory, associate.

Accomplish — complete, effect, achieve, fulfil, execute, realise, finish.

Account—explanation, narration, description, recital.

Accumulate—heap, collect, gather, amass.

Accurate—precise, exact, correct.

Accuse—asperse, arraign, censure, impeach, defame, calumniate, detract, vilify.

Achieve—execute, complete, fulfil, realise, accomplish, effect.

Acknowledgment — confession, concession.

Acknowledge — confess, own, avow, grant.

Acquaint—inform, communicate, disclose, make known.

Acquiesce —comply, yield, consent, agree, assent.

Acquire — gain, attain, procure, win, obtain.

Acquirement—attainment, gain.

Acquit — free, pardon, forgive, discharge, clear.

Active — quick, nimble, agile, alert, prompt, industrious, busy, brisk, vigorous.

Actual—real, certain, positive.

Actuate—impel, induce, move.

Acute—sharp, keen, subtle, piercing, shrewd, pointed, penetrating.

Adapt—suit, fit, adjust, accommodate.

Add—join to, put to, increase.

Address—speech, utterance, ability, courtship, skill, direction.

Addition — augmentation, accession, increase.

Adhere — stick, cleave, hold, attach.

Adept—apt, quick, skilful, expert.

Adherent—disciple, follower, partisan.

Adhesion—sticking, attachment, adherence.

Adjacent—close, near, adjoining, contiguous.

Adjourn—postpone, defer, delay.

Adjust—settle, fix, suit, adapt, accommodate.

Administer—give, execute, dispense, manage, supply, serve.

Admiration — regard, esteem, wonder, surprise, amazement.

Admission—entrance, access, admittance.

Admit — allow, permit, tolerate, concede, grant.

Admonition — warning, advice, counsel, reproof.

Adorn—deck, embellish, beautify.

Adroit—agile, dexterous, clever, skilful.

Adulterate—corrupt, pollute, debase, defile.

Advancement—progression, improvement.

Advantage—profit, benefit, use, good.

Adventure — chance, casualty, contingency, incident, occurrence.

Adversary — opponent, antagonist, enemy.

Adverse — unfortunate, hostile, contrary, repugnant, opposed.

Advert—notice, turn, regard, allude.

Advise — consult, consider, deliberate, admonish.

Advocate—plead, argue, defend, support.

Affability — civility, courteousness, urbanity.

Affable—civil, courteous, urbane, pleasing.

Affair — business, concern, matter, transaction.

Abet—aim, assume, move, pretend, arrogate.

Affecting—feeling, touching, pathetic.

Affection—love, fondness, attachment, kindness, tenderness.

Affiliate—adopt, receive, initiate, associate.

Affinity — relationship, kindred, alliance, conformity, attraction.

Affirm — assure, assert, aver, declare, protest.

Affliction—pain, trouble, distress, grief, sadness, sorrow, tribulation, bereavement, calamity.

Affluence — plenty, abundance, riches, opulence, wealth, concourse, influx.

Afford—yield, grant, give, impart, spare.

Affright—alarm, dismay, shock, terrify, appall, frighten, dishearten, intimidate.

Affront—provoke, outrage, insult, offend.

Afraid — fearful, terrified, timid, timorous.

Aged — elderly, old, senile, advanced in years.

Agent—representative, deputy.

Aggregate — mass, collect, accumulate.

Agile—alert, active, lively, quick, sprightly, nimble, brisk.

Agitate — shake, disturb, move, discuss.

Agitation—disturbance, trepidation, tremor.

Agony — pain, distress, torture, anguish, suffering.

Agree—accede, acquiesce, assent, consent, concur, comply.

Agreeable—suitable, acceptable, pleasing, grateful.

Agreement — harmony, accordance, covenant, concurrence, contract, bargain.

Aid—assist, help, succor, relieve.

Aim — aspire, endeavor, level, point.

Air—aspect, manner, appearance, look, mien.

Alarm—fear, consternation, dread, apprehension, fright, terror, summons, surprise.

Alienate — transfer, withdraw, estrange.

Allege—adduce, affirm, advance, assert.

Alleviate — ease, abate, lessen, mitigate, relieve, diminish, soothe, lighten.

Alliance — coalition, union, combination, league, confederacy.

Allot — distribute, apportion, assign, appoint.

Allowance—wages, pay, stipend, salary, permission, concession, grant.

Allude—refer, suggest, hint, intimate.

Allure—tempt, entice, seduce, decoy, attract.

Alter—change, vary, modify, rearrange.

Always — ever, perpetually, constantly, continually, incessantly.

Amass—gather, heap, collect, accumulate.

Amazement—astonishment, surprise, wonder, admiration.

Ambiguous — obscure, doubtful, equivocal, uncertain.

Amenable — answerable, responsible, accountable.

Amend—correct, improve, better, rectify, reform, mend.

Amends—recompense, restoration, reparation, restitution.

Amiable—lovely, kind, charming, delightful, obliging.

Ample—large, extended, spacious, copious, abundant, plenteous.

Amusement—entertainment, diversion, sport, pastime, recreation.

Angry—passionate, hot, irascible, hasty.

Anguish—pain, distress, suffering, agony.

Animate—cheer, enliven, exhilarate, impel, incite, inspire, urge, encourage.

Animation — life, spirits, liveliness, buoyancy, gayety, vivacity.

Animosity—hatred, enmity, malignity, hostility.

Annex — attach, affix, add, subjoin.

Announce—proclaim, declare, advertise, publish.

Annul—destroy, revoke, abolish, cancel, repeal, annihilate.

Answer—reply, response, rejoinder.

Answerable—amenable, accountable, responsible.

Antagonist — enemy, foe, opponent, adversary.

Antecedent — previous, former, anterior, preceding, prior, foregoing.

Antipathy — aversion, abhorrence, dislike, detestation, hatred.

Anxiety—caution, care, perplexity, solicitude, uneasiness, disquietude.

Apathy—unfeelingness, indifference, insensibility, unconcern.

Aperture—cavity, opening.

Apology—defense, plea, excuse.

Apparent—evident, clear, plain, visible, distinct.

Appeal—invoke, refer, call upon.

Appearance—aspect, look, air, manner, mien, semblance.

Appease — calm, soothe, pacify, allay, assuage, tranquilize.

Applaud—praise, approve, extol, commend.

Applause — acclamation, shouting, approval.

Appoint—allot, fix, provide, order, prescribe, ordain, depute, constitute.

Appraise—value, estimate.

Appreciate—value, esteem, estimate, prize.

Apprehension — terror, alarm, fear, seizure, dread, suspicion, fright.

Apprise — inform, acquaint, disclose.

Approach — admittance, access, avenue, passage.

Approbation—approval, concurrence, consent, sanction, confirmation.

Appropriate — assume, usurp, set apart.

Appropriate — peculiar, exclusive, adapted.

Approve—allow, like, applaud, esteem, commend.

Arbitrator — judge, umpire, arbiter.

Archives—annals, records.

Ardent—hot, eager, passionate, fervent, fiery, vehement.

Arduous—hard, difficult, laborious.

Argument — proof, reason, dispute.

Arise—mount, ascend, rise, stand up.

Arraign — charge, accuse, impeach.

Arrange — place, dispose, class, range.

Arrogance — assumption, pride, self-conceit, haughtiness, presumption.

Artful—crafty, artificial, deceitful, cunning, dexterous.

Articulate — speak, pronounce, utter.

Artifice — deception, imposition, stratagem, cheat, deceit, finesse.

Attitude—posture, gesture.

Attract—charm, captivate, win, allure, draw, entice.

Attractiveness — charms, allurements, enticements.

Audacity — impudence, boldness, hardihood, effrontery.

Auspicious — favorable, propitious, prosperous, lucky, fortunate.

Authentic—genuine, authorized, true.

Authority — power, dominion, force, sway, influence, ascendency.

Avarice—greed, covetousness, cupidity.

Averse—loth, unwilling, reluctant, repugnant, unfortunate, unfavorable.

Aversion — dislike, repugnance, antipathy, abhorrence, detestation.

Avidity—eagerness, greediness.

Avocation—calling, trade, profession, office, business, employment, occupation.

Avoid—shun, elude, eschew.

Avow—own, confess, recognize, acknowledge.

Awake—rouse, provoke, excite.

Awe—fear, dread, reverence.

B

Babbling — idle talk, loquacity, chattering, prattling.

Backward—loth, unwilling, reluctant, averse.

Baffle—confound, defeat, disconcert, elude, confuse.

Balance—settle, adjust, regulate, equalize.

Banter—taunt, ridicule, deride, rally, joke, jest.

Bare—stripped, naked, destitute, uncovered, unadorned.

Bargain — purchase, cheapen, contract, buy.

Base—mean, low, vile.

Bashful—shy, modest, diffident, timid.

Basis—foundation, pedestal, base, ground.

Bastard—spurious, illegitimate.

Battle — combat, fight, engagement.

Bear—carry, bring forth, support, suffer, endure, sustain, undergo.

Beat — hit, strike, defeat, overthrow.

Beau—sweetheart, gallant, dandy, fop.

Beautiful—handsome, fine.

Beautify — embellish, decorate, adorn, deck, ornament.

Becoming — suitable, graceful, comely, decent, befitting, meet, fit.

Beg—crave, beseech, entreat, ask, request, implore, solicit, supplicate.

Begin—originate, enter upon, commence.

Beguile—delude, mislead, amuse, deceive, impose upon.

Behavior—conduct, carriage, deportment, manner, demeanor, address.

Behold—see, look, observe, view.

Beholder—spectator, looker on, observer.

Belief—credit, faith, trust, certainty, confidence, reliance, conviction, opinion, assent.

Below—under, beneath.

Bend—lean, incline, distort, bow, subdue.

Beneath—under, below.

Bequeath—devise, give by will.

Beseech—solicit, crave, implore, beg, entreat, request, urge, supplicate.

Bestow—grant, confer, give, present.

Better—improve, mend, reform, ameliorate.

Blame — reprove, reproach, condemn, censure, reprehend, inculpate, upbraid.

Blameless — unblemished, faultless, innocent, guiltless, spotless, irreproachable.

Blast—desolate, destroy, wither up, split.

Blemish—flaw, spot, defect, fault, speck.

Blunt—dull, uncouth, insentient, abrupt.

Blunder—error, mistake.

Boaster — braggard, braggart, braggadocio, vaunter, blusterer.

Boasting — parade, ostentation, vaunting.

Boisterous—violent, furious, impetuous.

Bold — courageous, daring, fearless, impudent, insolent, audacious.

Bondage—servitude, slavery, confinement, imprisonment.

Border—edge, verge, rim, brim, margin, brink, side.

Bore — pierce, penetrate, perforate.

Bound — define, confine, restrict, terminate, limit, circumscribe.

Bounty—liberality, benevolence, generosity, beneficence.

Brave—bold, daring, heroic, undaunted, courageous, intrepid, fearless.

Breach—gap, chasm, break, opening.

Break—destroy, batter, dissolve, rend, tame, demolish, shatter.

Breaker — surge, billow, wave, sand-bank, covered rock.

Brief — short, concise, succinct, compendious, summary, epitomized.

Bright—clear, shining, sparkling, brilliant, glistening, glittering, lucid, resplendent.

Brilliancy—brightness, radiance, splendor, luster.

Broad—far-reaching, ample, extensive, large, wide.

Brawl—fight, quarrel, altercation, affray.

Bruise — break, crush, squeeze, pound, compress.

Build—erect, establish, construct, found.

Bulk—greatness, largeness, size, extent, magnitude, dimensions.

Burden — load, freight, weight, cargo.

Burning — ardent, fiery, scorching, hot.

Burst—break, rend, crack, split.

Business—trade, occupation, calling, work, avocation, profession, employment.

Bustle — disorder, hurry, tumult, confusion.

But—except, still, however, save, nevertheless, yet, notwithstanding.

Butchery—havoc, slaughter, carnage, massacre.

Buy — procure, bargain, obtain, purchase.

C

Cabal—coalition, league, combination, conspiracy, intrigue, plot.

Calamity—mishap, disaster, misfortune.

Calculate—count, number, compute, reckon, estimate.

Call—exclaim, cry, invite, name, summon, subpœna.

"First of all let me say,"
should be
"First, let me say."

"New furnished rooms,"
should be
"Newly furnished rooms."

"Do you see them men!"
should be
"Do you see those men!"

"Is your hands cold!"
should be
"Are your hands cold!"

"Above a year since,"
should be
"More than a year since."

"These kind of apples,"
should be
"These kinds of apples,"
or
"This kind of apples."

"He is in under the wall,"
should be
"He is under the wall."

"I toted him across,"
should be
"I carried him across."

"I came from over yer,"
should be
"I came from yonder."

"Lay down or set down,"
should be
"Lie down or sit down."

"Two spoonsful of tea,"
should be
"Two spoonfuls of tea."

"I'll give you fits,"
should be
"I will attend to you."

"A new pair of boots,"
should be
"A pair of new boots."

"The best of the two,"
should be
"The better of the two."

"I have lit the fire,"
should be
"I have lighted the fire."

"I belong to the church,"
should be
"I am a churchmember."

"He climbed up the hill,"
should be
"He climbed the hill"

"What beautiful sauce,"
should be
"What excellent sauce."

"I had rather ride."
should be
"I would rather ride."

"Very scarmish weather,"
should be
"Very warm weather."

"There is a great many,"
should be
"There are a great many."

"I only want five dollars,"
should be
"I want only five dollars."

"You hadn't ought to go."
should be
"You ought not to go."

"There's lots of them,"
should be
"There are many of them."

"I have rode with him,"
should be
"I have ridden with him."

"I saw the Miss Browns,"
should be
"I saw the Misses Brown."

"Peaches were plenty,"
should be
"Peaches were plentiful."

"Continue on in this way,"
should be
"Continue in this way."

"Don't give him no more,"
should be
"Give him no more."

"Walter and me went down,"
should be
"Walter and I went down."

"Who does this belong to,"
should be
"Whom does this belong to."

"As far as I am concerned,"
should be
"So far as I am concerned."

"He had near ten dollars,"
should be
"He had nearly ten dollars."

"We had an awful nice time,"
should be
"We had a delightful time."

"He rose up from his seat,"
should be
"He rose from his seat."

"He came ladened with honor,"
should be
"He came laden with honor."

"I expected to have seen him,"
should be
"I expected to see him."

"Give me a little bit of piece,"
should be
"Give me a small piece."

"They despised one another,"
should be
"They despised each other."

"I was tickled to see him"
should be
"I was pleased to see him."

"He is heavier than I be,"
should be
"He is heavier than I am."

"When we was living here,"
should be
"When we were living here."

"He is better than you be,"
should be
"He is better than you are."

"Similarity with each other,"
should be
"Similarity to each other."

"When I get off from a car,"
should be
"When I get off a car."

"Do you mean to do that!"
should be
"Do you intend to do that!"

"Either of them are rich,"
should be
"Each of them is rich."

"I have a couple of dollars,"
should be
"I have two dollars."

"It spread all over the town,"
should be
"It spread over all the town."

"If I was him I would do it,"
should be
"If I were he I would do it."

"I'll be blamed if I can tell,"
should be
"I cannot tell."

"Who is there!" "It is me,"
should be
"Who is there!" "It is I."

"I took you for another,"
should be
"I mistook you for another."

"His faith has been shook,"
should be
"His faith has been shaken."

"He died with consumption,"
should be
"He died of consumption."

"You are stronger than me,"
should be
"You are stronger than I."

"I reckon I'll go to-morrow,"
should be
"I intend to go to-morrow."

"I guess I'll go to-morrow,"
should be
"I think of going to-morrow."

"He has a tarnal lot of potatoes,"
should be
"He has a large quantity of potatoes."

"Make haste and dress you,"
should be
"Make haste and dress yourself."

"The two first men are the strongest,"
should be
"The first two men are the strongest."

"She sang to the Baptist church,"
should be
"She sang at the Baptist church."

"Them is large enough for you,"
should be
"Those are large enough for you."

"We won't say one single word,"
should be
"We will not say any one word."

"He is down in the basement,"
should be
"He is in the basement."

"His manner admits of no excuse,"
should be
"His manner admits no excuse."

"Received of John Brown five dollars,"
should be
"Received from John Brown five dollars."

"No other means but this was left,"
should be
"No other means than this was left."

"They will go from thence next week,"
should be
"They will go thence next week."

"From now till Christmas,"
should be
"From this time till Christmas."

"He has got over his trouble,"
should be
"He has recovered from his trouble."

"I know better; that ain't so,"
should be
"Pardon me, I understand differently."

"I know little or nothing of it,"
should be
"I know little, if anything, of it."

"He has four brother-in-laws,"
should be
"He has four brothers-in-law"

"I know Mr. and Mrs. Dr. Brown,"
should be
"I know Dr. and Mrs. Brown."

"It's funny how long she stays sick,"
should be
"It is singular that she should remain sick so long."

"You lie; he got tight,"
should be
"You are mistaken; he was drunk."

"I'll be poll darned if I know where it is,"
should be
"I do not know where it is."

"Somehow or another I'm a failure,"
should be
"For some reason I am always a failure."

"Henry and John is coming,"
should be
"Henry and John are coming"

"He dropped down into the water,"
should be
"He dropped into the water."

"They differ among one another,"
should be
"They differ among themselves."

"Take three-fourths, give me the remainder,"
should be
"Take three-fourths; give me the remainder."

"I see him every now and then,"
should be
"I see him occasionally."

"I never play if I can help it,"
should be
"I never play if I can avoid it."

"Look out or you'll get hurt,"
should be
"Be careful or you'll get hurt."

"Should have gloves like Henry has,"
should be
"Should have gloves like Henry's."

"I'd like for you to go,"
should be
"I would be pleased to have you go."

"May be I mought or I moughtn't,"
should be
"I may or I may not."

"I never see such a slew of people before,"
should be
"I never saw such a large number of people before."

"His works are approved of by many,"
should be
"His works are approved by many."

"I don't know nothing about it,"
should be
"I know nothing about it."

"He has a heap of cattle,"
should be
"He has a large number of cattle."

"He had a right smart crop of corn last year,"
should be
"He had a large crop of corn last year."

"He has a good bit of money,"
should be
"He has a good deal of money."

"I went to New York, you know, and when I came back, you see, I commenced attending school,"
should be
"I went to New York, and when I returned I commenced attending school."

Consummation—perfection, completion.

Contagious—epidemic, infectious.

Contain—hold, include, embrace, comprehend.

Contaminate—pollute, taint, defile, corrupt, poison.

Contemn—scorn, despise, disdain.

Contemplate—consider, meditate, muse.

Contemptible—paltry, vile, disdainful, mean, despicable, disreputable, low.

Contend—quarrel, debate, contest, argue, vie, strive.

Contention—strife, conflict, contest, combat, dispute, dissension.

Contentment—acquiescence, happiness, satisfaction, gratification.

Contiguous—near, approximating, adjacent.

Continual—perpetual, constant, incessant, unceasing, continuous.

Continuation—continuance, duration.

Contract—arrangement, bargain, agreement, compact, covenant.

Contract—curtail, abridge, condense, abbreviate, reduce, shorten.

Contradict—gainsay, deny, oppose.

Contrary—opposite, adverse, inimical.

Contribute—assist, administer, aid, share.

Contrition—remorse, penitence, repentance, compunction, regret.

Contrivance—device, means, invention, plan, scheme.

Control—subdue, restrain, check, govern, curb.

Controversy—argument, debate, disputation, contest.

Convene—call together, assemble, convoke.

Convenient—handy, adapted, suitable.

Conversation—dialogue, discussion, conference, colloquy.

Converse—commune, speak, talk, discourse.

Convey—take, carry, bear, transport.

Conviction—persuasion, detection, satisfaction.

Convivial—agreeable, festal, social, sociable.

Convoke—gather, assemble, convene, call together.

Copious—ample, full, abundant, exuberant, plenteous, bountiful.

Cordial—hearty, warm, sincere.

Correct—mend, amend, reform, better, improve, rectify.

Corroborate—establish, confirm, strengthen.

Corruption—depravity, pollution, defilement, adulteration, contamination, infection, putridity.

Costly—expensive, precious, valuable.

Counsel—advice, instruction, exhortation.

Counteract—change, defeat, oppose, hinder, frustrate, prevent.

Countenance—uphold, favor, encourage, support, sanction.

Counterfeit—forged, feigned, false, spurious, imposture, imitation.

Couple—brace, pair, two, join, connect.

Courage—heroism, valor, bravery, firmness, intrepidity, fearlessness.

Course—mode, way, track, line, career, progress, method, passage, road, route, series, succession.

Courteous—kind, civil, affable, polished, respectful, polite, well-bred.

Covenant—arrangement, agreement, contract, pledge, stipulation.

Covering—concealing, screening, sheltering, hiding, overspreading.

Covetousness—greed, avarice, cupidity, inordinate desire.

Coward—mean, dastard, poltroon.

Cowardice—fear, timidity, cowardliness.

Crafty—underhanded, cunning, artful, wily, deceitful, sly, subtle.

Crave—beg, pray, beseech, entreat, implore, request, solicit, supplicate.

Create—build, form, make, cause, invent, originate, shape, produce.

Crime—evil, guilt, wickedness, sin, vice.

Crisis—juncture, critical point.

Criticism—stricture, censure, review, remark, judgment.

Crooked—bowed, turned, curved, awry, bent, disfigured, deformed.

Cross—ill-tempered, fretful, peevish, spleeny, petulant, splenetic.

Cruel—barbarous, brutal, pitiless, inhuman, inexorable, unmerciful, harsh.

Cultivation—advancement, civilization, improvement, refinement, tillage.

Cure—heal, restore, remedy.

Curious—prying, inquisitive.

Curse—imprecation, malediction, anathema, execration.

Cursory—hasty, careless, slight, desultory, superficial.

Curtail—shorten, contract, abbreviate, abridge.

Custom—habit, usage, practice, prescription, practice.

D

Damage—injury, hurt, loss, detriment.

Dampness—wet, moisture, humidity.

Danger—hazard, peril, risk, venture.

Daring—bold, fearless, valorous, courageous, intrepid, brave.

Dark—dismal, obscure, gloomy, dim.

Date—time, period, epoch, era, age.

Dead—still, lifeless, inanimate, deceased.

Deadly—fatal, mortal, destructive.

Dealing—trade, practice, traffic, commerce.

Dearth—famine, need, scarcity, want.

Debar—deter, hinder, prevent, exclude, preclude.

Debase—lower, degrade, humble, disgrace.

Debate—argue, wrangle, dispute, controvert, contest.

Debilitate—impair, weaken, enervate, enfeeble.

Debility—infirmity, weakness, incapacity, imbecility, feebleness.

Decay—decline, consumption.

Decease—demise, death, departure of life.

Deceit—fraud, duplicity, deception, cunning, artifice, trickery, guile.

Decent—comely, fit, seemly, becoming.

Decide—settle, resolve, fix, determine.

Decision—sentence, determination, judgment, resolution, conclusion.

Decisive—conclusive, convincing, ending.

Declare—announce, pronounce, testify, proclaim, assert, assert, affirm.

Decline—droop, decay, shun, reject, repel, sink, refuse.

Decorate—embellish, ornament, beautify, adorn.

Decoy—allure, tempt, seduce, entice, inveigle.

Decrease—lessen, diminish, subside, lower, abate.

Dedicate—devote, consecrate, set apart.

Deduction—abatement, inference, conclusion.

Deed—action, exploit, achievement, feat.

Deface—mar, disfigure, destroy, mutilate.

Defame—slander, vilify, scandalize, calumniate.

Defeat—beat, baffle, conquer, overcome, overthrow, vanquish, frustrate.

Defect—want, flaw, blemish, imperfection.

Defective—wanting, imperfect, deficient.

Defender—protector, advocate, pleader, vindicator.

Defense—apology, excuse, justification, protection, vindication.

Defer—delay, hinder, prolong, retard, postpone, protract, procrastinate.

Deference—respect, regard, condescension, submission, veneration.

Deficient—lacking, wanting, imperfect.

Defile—taint, poison, vitiate, corrupt, contaminate, pollute.

Definite—exact, precise, positive, certain, bounded, limited.

Defraud—swindle, cheat, rob, deceive, trick.

Degrade—lower, disgrace, lessen, reduce, decry, depreciate, disparage.

Degree—rank, position, station, class, order.

Dejection—depression, lowliness, melancholy.

Delay—hinder, defer, detain, prolong, protract, postpone.

Deliberate—slow, hesitating, considering, thoughtful, cautious.

Delicate—frail, fine, nice, weak, tender, beautiful, elegant, dainty.

Delighted—pleased, glad, grateful, joyful.

Delineate—describe, draw, paint, sketch, depict, represent.

Delinquent—criminal, offender.

Deliver—give up, save, yield, utter, surrender, concede, rescue, transmit.

Delusion—cheat, illusion, deception, fallacy.

Demand—claim, require, ask.

Demolish—overthrow, destroy.

Demonstrate—illustrate, show, prove, manifest.

Denominate—name, title, style, designate.

Denote—imply, signify, mark, betoken.

Deny—refuse, disown, contradict, oppose.

Departure—leaving, forsaking, going away, abandoning, exit.

Dependence—trust, reliance, confidence, connection.

Deplore—bemoan, bewail, mourn, lament.

Deportment—behavior, conduct, character, carriage, demeanor.

Depraved—degraded, corrupt, abandoned, profligate, wicked, vicious.

Deprecate—underrate, disparage, detract undervalue, degrade, traduce, lower.

Deprive—prevent, hinder, depose, divest, strip, abridge.

Depute—authorize, appoint, constitute.

Deputy—agent, substitute, representative, delegate.

Derange—disarrange, discompose, disorder, confuse, disconcert.

Deride—mock, ridicule, make fun of, banter, laugh at.

Describe—illustrate, narrate, delineate, recount, relate, represent.

Description—account, illustration, narration, explanation, recital, relation, detail.

Design—intend, plan, scheme, purpose, project, sketch.

Designate—name, show, point out, indicate, choose, distinguish, style.

Desist—stop, leave off, cease, discontinue.

Desperate—desponding, hopeless, mad, careless, furious, regardless.

Despicable—mean, vile, pitiful, worthless, outrageous, contemptible.

Despise—hate, scorn, loathe.

Despotic—arbitrary, self-willed, absolute.

Destination—point, location, lot, design, fate, purpose, appointment.

Destitute—bare, forlorn, poor, scanty, forsaken, needy.

Destroy—ruin, waste, demolish, consume, annihilate, dismantle.

Desultory—grow, unravel, clear, roving.

Detach—sever, separate, disjoin, divide.

Detail—account, tale, description, narration, recital.

Detain—keep, restrain, confine, hold.

Detect—find, discover, convict.

Determine—fix, decide, bound, limit, settle, resolve, adjust.

Determined—firm, resolute, decided, fixed, concluded, ended, immovable.

Detest—hate, loathe, abominate, abhor.

Detestable—hateful, loathsome, abominable, execrable.

Detract—defame, degrade, vilify, slander, calumniate, scandalize, derogate.

Detriment—inconvenience, loss, injury, disadvantage, damage, hurt, prejudice.

Develop—grow, unravel, clear, unfold, disclose, exhibit.

Deviate—stray, wander, err, digress, swerve.

Device—design, scheme, show, plan, contrivance, stratagem, invention.

Devote—give, apply, consecrate, set apart, dedicate.

Devout—pious, holy, religious, prayerful.

Dexterity—adroitness, ability, expertness, aptness, skillfulness, skill, tact.

Dialect—language, speech, tongue.

Dictate—propose, direct, order, prescribe, instruct, suggest.

Die—expire, depart, perish, languish, wither.

Differ—dispute, dissent, contend, vary, disagree.

Different—unlike, various, diverse.

Difficult—trying, arduous, hard, troublesome.

Difficulty—obstacle, obstruction, embarrassment, trouble, perplexity, trial, impediment.

Diffident—retiring, fearful, bashful, distrustful, modest, hesitating.

Dignified—exalted, elevated, honored, stately.

Diligent—industrious, assiduous, laborious, active, persevering, attentive.

Diminish—shorten, curtail, abate, decrease, lessen, subside.

Direct — show, guide, conduct, manage, regulate, sway.

Direction — command, order, address, superscription.

Directly — at once, quickly, immediately, instantly, promptly, instantaneously.

Disagree—dispute, dissent, differ, quarrel, vary.

Disappoint—foil, defeat.

Disaster — misfortune, calamity, mischance, mishap.

Disavow—disown, deny, disclaim, repudiate.

Discard — cast off, dismiss, discharge.

Discern — distinguish, discriminate, penetrate, behold, discover.

Discernible—plain, evident, perceptible, manifest, apparent.

Disclose — reveal, discover, divulge.

Disconcert — disorder, confuse, defeat, ruffle, fret, vex, unsettle, interrupt, derange.

Discord — contention, dissension, inharmony.

Discover — make known, detect, communicate, reveal, impart, tell, disclose.

Discredit—dishonor, scandal, disgrace, disrepute, ignominy, reproach.

Discretion—prudence, judgment.

Disdain—scorn, contempt, pride, arrogance, haughtiness.

Disease—sickness, distemper, malady, disorder.

Disgrace—degrade, debase, dishonor, abase.

Disguise — cover, disfigure, conceal, dissemble.

Disgust—loathing, nausea, dislike, aversion.

Dishonor—shame, disgrace.

Dislike—antipathy, aversion, repugnance, hatred, contempt, abhorrence.

Dismiss — discharge, divest, discard.

Disorder — confusion, bustle, disease, tumult, malady, distemper, irregularity.

Disparage — lower, undervalue, degrade, detract, decry, depreciate.

Disperse—scatter, dissipate, deal out, spread, distribute.

Display — parade, exhibit, show, ostentation.

Displease—offend, anger, vex.

Dispose—regulate, place, arrange, order, adapt.

Dispute—contest, debate, quarrel, altercation, difference, controversy.

Disseminate—spread, circulate, scatter, propagate.

Dissertation — discourse, essay, treatise, disquisition.

Dissipate — disperse, squander, waste, expend, consume, dispel.

Distaste—aversion, disgust, contempt, dislike, dissatisfaction, loathing.

Distinct—clear, obvious, different, separate, unlike, dissimilar.

Distinguish—discriminate, know, see, perceive, discern.

Distinguished—noted, eminent, conspicuous, celebrated, illustrious.

Distress—grief, sorrow, sadness, suffering, affliction, agony, pain, anguish, misery.

Distribute—deal out, scatter, assign, allot, apportion, divide.

District—locality, section, tract, region, territory, province, circuit, county.

Diversion—enjoyment, pastime, recreation, amusement, deviation, sport.

Divide—separate, part, share, distribute.

Divine—suppose, conjecture, foretell, guess.

Divulge—disclose, impart, reveal, communicate, publish.

Docile—gentle, tractable, pliant, teachable, yielding, quiet.

Doctrine—belief, wisdom, dogma, principle, precept.

Dogmatical—positive, authoritative, arrogant, magisterial, confident.

Doleful—awful, dismal, sorrowful, woeful, piteous, rueful.

Doubt—suspense, hesitation, perplexity, scruple, uncertainty.

Doubtful — unstable, uncertain, dubious, precarious, equivocal.

Drag—pull, bring, haul, draw.

Dread—fear, apprehension.

Dreadful—fearful, frightful, terrible, awful, horrible.

Dress—array, apparel, vestments, garments, attire.

Droop—pine, sink, fade, decline, languish.

Dumb—mute, still, silent, inarticulate.

Durable—lasting, constant, permanent, continuing.

Dutiful — submissive, obedient, respectful.

Dwelling — home, house, abode, habitation, residence, domicile.

E

Eager—earnest, excited, ardent, impetuous, quick, vehement.

Earn—acquire, win, make, gain, obtain.

Earth—globe, world, planet.

Ease—rest, quiet, repose, facility, lightness.

Economical—careful, close, saving, frugal, thrifty, sparing.

Ecstasy—happiness, joy, rapture, transport, delight, enthusiasm, elevation.

Edifice — building, fabric, structure.

Education — culture, cultivation, breeding, refinement, instruction, nurture, tuition.

Efface—destroy, obliterate, erase, expunge, annihilate.

Effect — consequence, result, purpose, event, issue, reality, meaning.

Effects — things, goods, chattels, furniture, movables, property.

Efficient — competent, capable, able, effectual, effective.

Effort—endeavor, essay, attempt, exertion, trial.

Elegant—graceful, lovely, beautiful, handsome.

Eligible — suitable, fit, worthy, capable.

Embarrass — trouble, entangle, puzzle, perplex, distress.

Embellish — ornament, decorate, adorn, illustrate, deck, beautify.

Emblem—symbol, figure, type.

Embrace—hold, clasp, hug, comprehend, comprise.

Emergency—necessity, exigency, casualty.

Emotion—feeling, tremor, excitement, agitation.

Employment—occupation, trade, profession, business, avocation.

Empower—enable, delegate, commission, authorize.

Empty—untenanted, vacant, void, evacuated, unfurnished, unfilled.

Enchant—beguile, charm, captivate, bewitch, fascinate, enrapture.

Encomium—eulogy, praise.

Encounter—quarrel, assault, attack, combat, engagement, meeting.

Encourage — cheer, stimulate, animate, incite, sanction, support, countenance, instigate.

Encroach—intrude, trespass, infringe.

End—finish, close, stop, extremity, termination, sequel, consequence, cessation, death, purpose.

Endeavor—aim, exertion, effort, attempt.

Endless — unending, everlasting, perpetual, interminable, infinite, incessant, eternal.

Endurance — submission, fortitude, patience, resignation.

Enemy—adversary, opponent, foe, antagonist.

Energy — determination, efficacy, force, vigor, strength, potency, power.

Enervate—weaken, enfeeble, unnerve, debilitate, deteriorate.

Engage — employ, enlist, fight, induce, pledge, promise, attract, win.

Enjoyment—happiness, pleasure, joy, gratification.

Enlarge — extend, widen, lengthen, increase.

Enmity—spite, hatred, hostility, malignity, animosity.

Enough—ample, sufficient, plenty, abundance.

Enrage—excite, irritate, inflame, incense, aggravate, exasperate.

Enrapture—charm, attract, captivate, fascinate, enchant.

Enterprise—business, adventure, attempt, undertaking.

Entertainment—pastime, sport, amusement, recreation, diversion, performance, banquet, feast.

Entice—tempt, decoy, seduce, attract, allure.

Entire—full, whole, perfect, complete, total, integral.

Entirely—perfectly, completely, wholly.

Entitle—style, designate, name, characterize, denominate.

Entreat—ask, solicit, crave, beg, beseech, implore, petition, supplicate.

Envy—suspicion, jealousy, grudging.

Epitomize—lessen, abridge, curtail, reduce, condense.

Equal—commensurate, adequate, uniform.

Equitable — just, right, honest, satisfactory, impartial, reasonable, fair.

Eradicate—exterminate, root out, extirpate.

Erase — expunge, efface, cancel, obliterate.

Erect—build, raise, found, set up, construct, elevate, establish, institute.

Error—blunder, mistake, fault.

Escape—elope, evade, elude, fly, avoid, pass.

Essential—important, necessary, requisite, indispensable.

Esteem — respect, regard, value, appreciate, prize, love.

Estimate—rate, compute, value, calculate, appraise, appreciate, esteem.

Eternal—perpetual, forever, endless, infinite, immortal, continual, everlasting.

Evade—escape, elude, avoid, prevaricate, shun.

Even—smooth, level, plain, equal, uniform.

Event—incident, adventure, issue, occurrence, result, consequence.

Ever—always, constantly, forever, unceasingly, continually, incessantly.

Evidence—proof, deposition, witness, testimony.

Evil—sinful, wicked, bad.

Exact—enjoin, demand, extract, extort.

Exact—sure, strict, punctual, precise, accurate.

Exalted—high, elevated, refined, dignified, raised, sublime, magnificent.

Examination—search, scrutiny, investigation, inquiry, research.

Example — copy, precedent, pattern.

Exasperate—excite, irritate, enrage, vex, provoke, aggravate.

Exceed — improve, outdo, excel, surpass, transcend.

Excellence — goodness, purity, superiority, perfection, eminence.

Except—but, besides, unless, object.

Exchange—barter, trade, traffic.

Excite—provoke, arouse, incite, stimulate, awaken, irritate.

Exculpate — forgive, exonerate, acquit, absolve, justify.

Excuse—pretense, pretext, plea, subterfuge, apology, evasion.

Execrable—hateful, detestable, contemptible, abominable.

Exemption—freedom, privilege, immunity.

Exercise—practice, exert, carry on.

Exhaust—empty, drain, spend.

Exigency—necessity, emergency.

Exonerate—clear, relieve, exculpate, justify, acquit, absolve, forgive.

Expectation—belief, trust, hope, confidence, anticipation.

Expedient — fit, suitable, necessary, requisite.

Expedite — hurry, hasten, accelerate, quicken.

Expeditious — speedy, diligent, quick, prompt.

Expel—exile, banish, cast out.

Expensive — dear, costly, valuable.

Experience — knowledge, trial, experiment, proof, test.

Expert — handy, ready, skillful, adroit, dexterous.

Explain—show, elucidate, unfold.

Explanation — detail, account, description, relation, explication, recital.

Explicit—clear, definite, express, plain.

Exploit — feat, accomplishment, achievement, deed, performance.

Explore—search, examine.

Extend—spread out, stretch out, enlarge, increase, distend, diffuse.

Extensive—wide, comprehensive, large.

Extenuate — palliate, diminish, lessen, excuse.

Exterior — outward, outside, external.

Exterminate — eradicate, extirpate, destroy.

External—outward, exterior.

Extol—commend, praise, admire, laud, eulogize, applaud.

F

Facetious — amusing, jocular, comic, jocose.

Fact—incident, circumstance.

Faculty—ability, gift, talent, power.

Failing—weakness, imperfection, frailty, misfortune, miscarriage, foible, fault.

Fair—clear, conspicuous, right, impartial, straight, honest, just, equitable.

Faith—trust, belief, credit, fidelity.

Fallacious — illusive, visionary, deceitful, delusive, fraudulent.

Falsehood — falsity, falsification, fabrication, fiction, lie, untruth.

Familiar — free, intimate, unceremonious.

Famous — celebrated, eminent, renowned, distinguished, illustrious.

Fanciful — ideal, imaginative, capricious, fantastical, whimsical, hypochondriac.

Fancy — imagination, taste, whim, caprice, inclination, liking, conceit, notion, conception, humor, ideality.

Fascinate — charm, attract, captivate, bewitch, enchant, enrapture.

Fashion — style, mode, custom, manner, way, practice, form, sort.

Fasten — fix, hold, stick, annex, attach, affix.

Fastidious — particular, disdainful, squeamish.

Fate — destiny, chance, fortune, lot, doom, lot.

Favor — civility, support, benefit, grace.

Favorable — auspicious, suitable, propitious.

Fault — failing, error, shortcoming, blemish, imperfection, offense.

Faultless — guiltless, blameless, spotless, innocent.

Fear — alarm, dread, timidity, terror, fright, trepidation, apprehension.

Fearful — dreadful, horrible, terrible, awful, afraid, timorous, timid.

Fearless — daring, brave, intrepid, undaunted, courageous.

Feasible — reasonable, plausible, practicable.

Feat — exploit, trick, achievement, act, deed.

Feeble — frail, infirm, weak.

Feeling — sensation, sympathy, generosity, sensibility.

Felicity — joy, delight, happiness, prosperity, bliss, blessedness.

Fertile — fruitful, prolific, abundant, productive.

Fervor — warmth, heat, ardor, vehemence, zeal.

Festivity — joyfulness, happiness, gayety, festival.

Fickle — unstable, changeable, inconstant, variable, capricious, impulsive.

Fiction — invention, lie, untruth, falsehood, fabrication.

Fidelity — faith, honesty, loyalty.

Fiery — hot, fervent, impulsive, ardent, passionate, vehement.

Figure — shape, semblance, form, representation, statue.

Fine — delicate, nice, pretty, lovely, showy, beautiful, elegant.

Finish — conclude, end, terminate, close, complete, perfect.

Firm — ready, strong, immovable, solid, steady, sturdy, partnership, resolute.

First — highest, chief, earliest, primary, primitive, pristine, commencement, original.

Fitted — suited, competent, qualified, adapted.

Flag — droop, languish, decline, pine, faint.

Flagitious — wicked, atrocious, flagrant, heinous.

Flavor — taste, odor, fragrance.

Flaw — spot, stain, speck, crack, blemish, defect.

Fleeting — transient, transitory, swift, temporary.

Fleetness — swiftness, rapidity, quickness, velocity, celerity.

Fluctuate — vary, waver, change, hesitate, vacillate.

Follower — adherent, successor, believer, disciple, partisan, pursuer.

Fondness — affection, love, attachment, tenderness.

Foolish — simple, stupid, silly, absurd, preposterous, irrational.

Forbear — refrain, spare, abstain, pause.

Forbid — deny, prohibit, interdict, oppose.

Force — oblige, compel, restrain.

Forcible — powerful, strong, irresistible, mighty, potent, cogent.

Forebode — foretell, presage, betoken, prognosticate, augur.

Forego — quit, give up, resign.

Foregoing — before, former, previous, prior, preceding, anterior, antecedent.

Forethought — expectation, foresight, anticipation, premeditation.

Forfeiture — penalty, fine.

Forge — counterfeit, frame, invent, fabricate.

Forgive — absolve, pardon, remit, acquit, excuse.

Forlorn — forsaken, lost, lonely, destitute, deserted.

Form — ceremony, observance, rite.

Formal — ceremonious, particular, methodical, exact, stiff, precise.

Forsake — desert, abandon, leave, abdicate, relinquish, quit.

Fortunate — successful, lucky, prosperous.

Fortune — estate, portion, success, fate.

Forward — confident, eager, bold, ardent, immodest, presumptuous, ready, progressive.

Foster — keep, harbor, nourish, cherish, nurse.

Fragile — brittle, weak, tender, frail.

Frailty — weakness, unsteadiness, instability, failing, foible.

Frame — fabricate, compose, plan, contrive, invent, form, adjust.

Fraternity — society, brotherhood.

Fraud — cheat, imposition, deceit, deception, guile.

Freak — whim, caprice, humor, fancy.

Free — generous, liberal, candid, open, frank, familiar, unconfined, unconstrained, unreserved, munificent, bounteous.

Free — deliver, liberate, rescue, clear, affranchise, enfranchise.

Freedom — liberty, independence, exemption, privilege, familiarity, unrestraint.

Freely — spontaneously, frankly, unreservedly, cheerfully, unhesitatingly, liberally.

Frequently — often, repeatedly, commonly, generally, usually.

Fresh — new, recent, cool, modern, novel.

Fret — chafe, anger, gall, corrode, agitate, vex.

Fretful — captious, peevish, angry, petulant.

Friendly — pleasant, kind, agreeable, sociable, amicable.

Fright — panic, consternation, terror, alarm.

Frighten — terrify, scare, alarm, intimidate, affright, daunt.

Frightful — horrid, horrible, terrible, terrific, dreadful, fearful.

Frugal — careful, saving, prudent, economical.

Fruitful — abundant, plentiful, fertile, productive, prolific.

Frustrate — defeat, hinder, foil, nullify, disappoint.

Fully — largely, amply, completely, copiously, abundantly.

Futile — useless, frivolous, trifling.

G

Gain — obtain, get, win, acquire, attain, profit.

Gait — bearing, mien, walk, carriage.

Gale — breeze, storm, hurricane, tempest.

Gather — collect, muster, infer, assemble, compress, fold.

Gay — dashing, showy, merry, fine, cheerful.

Generally — usually, commonly, frequently.

Generous — liberal, bounteous, beneficent, munificent, noble.

Genius — talent, intellect, wisdom, ingenuity, capacity, ability, taste.

Genteel — polished, refined, mannerly, cultured, polite.

Gentle — tame, meek, mild, quiet, peaceable.

Genuine — real, actual, authentic, unalloyed, unadulterated, true, natural.

Germinate — sprout, shoot, grow, bud, vegetate.

Gesture — action, motion, posture, attitude.

Get — gain, attain, obtain, procure, realize, acquire, possess.

Gift — donation, present, gratuity, benefaction, endowment, ability, talent.

Give — impart, confer, grant, bestow, consign, yield.

Glad — happy, gay, cheerful, joyful, joyous, delighted, gratified.

Glance — sight, look, glimpse.

Glitter — glisten, sparkle, shine, glare, radiate.

Glittering — glistening, sparkling, shining, bright, brilliant.

Gloom — dark, sad, dim, cloudy, dull, sullen, morose, melancholy.

Glory — fame, renown, splendor, praise, honor, reputation, brightness.

Graceful — comely, genteel, becoming, elegant, neat.

Grand — dignified, lofty, exalted, great, elevated, magnificent, sublime, majestic, glorious, superb, splendid.

Grant — give, bestow, cede, confer, concede, sell, yield.

Grasp — grip, seize, catch.

Grateful — thankful, agreeable, delicious, pleasing.

Gratification — indulgence, happiness, enjoyment, fruition, pleasure.

Grave — slow, solemn, thoughtful, serious, important, sedate.

Greatness — size, bulk, grandeur, magnitude, immensity, dignity, power.

Greediness — ravenous, rapacity, voracity, covetousness, eagerness.

Grief — sadness, sorrow, distress, regret, melancholy, affliction, anguish.

Grieve — bemoan, bewail, afflict, lament, hurt, mourn, sorrow.

Group — cluster, collection, assemblage.

Grow — sprout, vegetate, proceed, increase.

Guarantee — warrant, vouch for, secure.

Guard — protect, defend, shield, watch.

Guess — suppose, conjecture, think, surmise, divine.

Guest — stranger, visitor, visitant.

Guide — lead, direct, conduct, control, instruct, regulate.

Guilty — depraved, wicked, sinful, criminal, debauched.

H

Hale — strong, sound, hearty, robust.

Handsome — fine, fair, beautiful, pretty, graceful, lovely, elegant, noble.

Happiness — contentment, luck, felicity, bliss.

Harass — tire, molest, weary, disturb, perplex, vex, torment.

Harbinger — messenger, forerunner, precursor.

Hard — near, close, unfeeling, inexorable, arduous, difficult, firm, hardy, solid.

Hardened — unfeeling, obdurate, insensible, callous.

Hardihood — boldness, presumption, audacity, effrontery, daring, bravery.

Hardly — barely, scarcely, with difficulty.

Hardship — affliction, oppression, grievance, injury.

Harm — evil, injury, damage, misfortune, hurt, ill, mishap.

Harmless — gentle, unoffending, inoffensive, innocent.

Harmony — unison, concord, accordance, melody, agreement.

Harsh — rough, stern, severe, rigorous, austere, morose.

Hasten — hurry, expedite, accelerate, quicken.

Hastiness — dispatch, speed, precipitancy, hurry, rashness.

Hasty — rash, angry, quick, passionate, cursory.

Hate — dislike, abjure, detest, abhor, loathe, abominate.

Hateful — odious, contemptible, execrable, detestable, abominable, loathsome.

Haughtiness — vanity, self-conceit, arrogance, pride, disdain.

Hazard — trial, venture, chance, risk, danger, peril.

Headstrong — self-willed, stubborn, forward, violent, obstinate, venturesome.

Heal — restore, cure, remedy.

Healthy — well, sound, wholesome, salutary, salubrious.

Hear — harken, listen, watch, attend, overhear.

Hearty — sincere, zealous, warm, strong, cordial, ardent, healthy.

Heaviness — sorrow, gloom, dejection, weight, gravity.

Heedless — dilatory, thoughtless, negligent, remiss, careless, inattentive.

Heighten — raise, advance, improve, aggravate.

Heinous — wicked, sinful, flagrant, atrocious.

Help — provide, serve, assist, aid, relieve, support, succor.

Hence — from, thence, so, accordingly, therefore, wherefore, consequently.

Heroic — bold, noble, brave, fearless, valiant, courageous, intrepid.

Heroism — valor, boldness, courage, bravery, gallantry, fortitude.

Hesitate — pause, falter, wait, delay, doubt, demur, stammer.

Hidden — obscure, mysterious, secret, covert, concealed.

Hideous — awful, frightful, horrible, ghastly, grim, grisly.

Hilarity — jollity, joviality, mirth, merriment, cheerfulness, gayety.

Hinder — interfere, impede, embarrass, retard, prevent, oppose, stop, thwart, obstruct.

Hold — keep, occupy, maintain, retain, detain, grasp, possess.

Honesty — honor, fidelity, frankness, integrity, probity, purity, justice, sincerity, rectitude, uprightness, truthfulness.

Honor — exalt, dignify, respect, adorn, revere, esteem, venerate, reverence.

Hope — desire, belief, trust, confidence, expectation, anticipation.

Hopeless—desponding, dejected, despairing.

Horrible—dreadful, terrible, terrific, fearful, frightful, awful.

Hostile—unfriendly, contrary, opposite, repugnant.

Hostility — enmity, opposition, animosity, ill-will, unfriendliness.

House--domicile, dwelling, home, habitation, family, race, quorum.

However—notwithstanding, but, nevertheless, yet, still.

Humble—meek, lowly, subdued, submissive, modest, unpretending, unassuming.

Hurry--hasten, expedite, precipitate.

Hurtful — annoying, injurious, detrimental, mischievous, pernicious, prejudicial.

Hypocrisy — dissimulation, pretence, deceit.

I

Idea—notion, thought, conception, imagination, perception.

Idle—unoccupied, unemployed, inactive, indolent, still, lazy, slothful.

Ignorant — untaught, unskilled, uninformed, unlettered, illiterate, unlearned.

Illness — sickness, disorder, disease, malady.

Illusion—falsity, mockery, deception.

Imagine—think, suppose, fancy, conceive, deem, contrive, apprehend.

Imbecility — weakness, languor, feebleness, infirmity, debility, impotence.

Imitate—follow, copy, mimic.

Immaterial—unimportant, insignificant, inconsiderable, inconsequential, unimportant, spiritual, unsubstantial, unconditioned.

Immediately—instantly,directly.

Immense—vast, huge, enormous, prodigious, unlimited.

Immodest—impudent, bold, indelicate, shameless, indecent, unchaste.

Impair—lessen, weaken, injure, decrease.

Impart—gr..nt, bestow, disclose, communicate, reveal, divulge.

Impatient — uneasy, eager, restless, hasty.

Impeach—censure, reproach, arraign, accuse.

Impede—hinder, delay, obstruct, retard.

Impediment — obstruction, obstacle, hinderance.

Impel—urge, force, incite, induce, instigate, animate, encourage.

Impending—imminent, threatening.

Imperative — commanding, imperious. authoritative, despotic.

Imperfection—wanting, blemish, fault, defect, failing, frailty, foible, weakness.

Imperious — commanding, domineering, haughty, imperative, proud, lordly, overbearing, tyrannical.

Impertinent—rude, quarrelsome, intrusive, insolent, meddling, irrelevant, troublesome.

Impetuous—hasty, rough, vehement, violent, forcible, boisterous.

Implicate — involve, embarrass, entangle.

Implore — beg, beseech, ask, entreat, supplicate, solicit, request.

Imply—mean, signify, denote, infer, involve.

Importance — weight, moment, signification, consequence.

Imposture—deceit, cheat, fraud, deception, imposition, counterfeit, artifice.

Imprecation—execration, curse, malediction, anathema.

Improve—cultivate, correct, reform, rectify, amend, advance.

Impudent—insolent, bold, rude, saucy, impertinent, uncouth, immodest, shameless.

Impute—charge, ascribe, attribute.

Inability — disability, weakness, impotence.

Inactive — sluggish, lazy, idle, slothful, inert, drowsy.

Inadequate—insufficient, incompetent, unable, incapable.

Inattentive—negligent, heedless, careless, inadvertent, thoughtless, dilatory, remiss.

Incessantly—constantly, continually, unremittingly, unceasingly.

Incident — contingency, circumstance, event.

Incite—provoke, excite, stimulate, arouse, encourage, animate, aggravate.

Include—contain, enclose, comprise, embrace, comprehend.

Incommode—molest, disturb, inconvenience, trouble, annoy.

Incompetent—inapt, insufficient, incapable, inadequate, unsuitable.

Inconsistent—incongruous, contrary, ridiculous, absurd.

Inconstant—unstable, uncertain, fickle, variable, changeable, versatile.

Indecent—unbecoming, impudent, immodest, indelicate.

Indicate—show, mark, point out, reveal.

Indifferent—passive, neutral, regardless, unconcerned, impartial.

Indigence—poverty, need, want, penury.

Indigenous—native.

Indignation—temper, anger, displeasure, contempt, resentment, wrath.

Indiscretion—imprudence, folly, injudiciousness.

Indispensable — important, necessary, essential.

Indisputable — undeniable, indubitable, unquestionable, incontrovertible, conclusive, settled.

Indistinct—confused, ambiguous, doubtful, dark.

Induce—persuade, lead, influence, urge, instigate, actuate.

Industrious — diligent, persevering, laborious, assiduous, active.

Inevitable—unavoidable, certain.

Inexorable — immovable, relentless, unyielding, implacable.

Inexpedient — unsuitable, unfit, inconvenient.

Infect—taint, corrupt, defile, contaminate, pollute.

Inference—deduction, conclusion.

Inferior—less, lower, secondary, subservient, subordinate.

Infested—disturbed, troubled, annoyed, plagued.

Infinite — boundless, unbounded, illimitable, unlimited, immense, eternal.

Infirm — weak, sickly, decrepit, feeble, debilitated, imbecile.

Influence—authority, power, persuasion, credit, favor, sway.

Information — notice, counsel, intelligence, advice, instruction.

Ingenious — inventive, talented, skillful.

Ingenuity — capacity, invention, genius, skill, talent.

Inhabit — dwell, occupy, reside, stay, abide, sojourn.

Inherent—innate, inborn, inbred.

Inhuman—cruel, savage, barbarous, brutal.

Iniquitous—unjust, evil, wicked, nefarious.

Injunction—order, mandate, precept, command.

Injure—harm, hurt, impair, damage, deteriorate.

Innate—natural, inherent, inbred, inborn.

Innocent—pure, blameless, guiltless, faultless, inoffensive, harmless, spotless.

Inordinate — immoderate, intemperate, irregular, excessive.

Inquisitive — curious, inquiring, anxious, prying.

Insanity—derangement, madness, craziness, lunacy, mania.

Insensibility — dullness, apathy, indifference, stupidity, torpor, imperceptibility.

Insidious—deceitful, sly, crafty, cunning, subtle, treacherous.

Insignificant — worthless, meaningless, inconsiderable, trivial, unimportant.

Insinuate — hint, suggest, intimate.

Insolent—insulting, abusive, rude, haughty, saucy, offensive, impertinent.

Inspire—animate, invigorate, enliven, cheer, exhilarate, suggest.

Instigate — tempt, incite, urge, encourage, impel, move, stimulate.

Instill—infuse, implant, sow.

Instruction—education, precept, teaching, suggestion, counsel, advice.

Insufficient — inadequate, incapable, incompetent, unfit, unable, unsuitable.

Insult — abuse, affront, outrage, contempt, insolence, indignity.

Integrity—purity, probity, truthfulness, uprightness, honesty.

Intellect—understanding, genius, ability, capacity, talent.

Intelligence—intimation, understanding, information, notice, knowledge, intellect.

Intemperate—excessive, immoderate, inordinate.

Intend—purpose, mean, design.

Intercede — mediate, interpose, interfere.

Interline—insert, alter, correct, add.

Intermission — cessation, stop, rest, vacation, interruption.

Intermit — abate, suspend, subside, forbear.

Interpose — mediate, interfere, intermeddle.

Interpret—explain, demonstrate, elucidate, expound, decipher.

Interrogate—examine, question, inquire.

Interval—space, interstice, time.

Intervening — coming between, interposing, intermediate.

Intimidate — frighten, alarm, daunt, scare.

Intoxication — infatuation, inebriety, drunkenness.

Intractable—perverse, obstinate, stubborn, ungovernable, uncontrollable, unmanageable.

Intrepid — fearless, undaunted, bold, daring, valiant, courageous, brave.

Intrinsic—real, true, inherent, inward, essential, genuine.

Introductory—preliminary, previous, prefatory.

Intrude— invade, infringe, encroach, obtrude, entrench.

Intrust—confide, commit.

Invade — enter, attack, intrude, encroach, infringe.

Invalid—weak, sick, infirm, null, feeble, void.

Invalidate—weaken, injure, destroy, overthrow.

Invective—censure, abuse, railing, reproach, satire.

Invent—feign, fabricate, frame, conceive, discover, devise.

Invest—enclose, surround, confer, adorn, array, endow, endue.

Investigation—search, inquiry, examination, scrutiny, research.

Inveterate—obstinate, confirmed, constant, fixed.

Invigorate—restore, strengthen, fortify.

Invincible — unyielding, unconquerable.

Involve — envelop, enwrap, entangle, implicate.

Irascible—irritable, hasty, fiery, hot, angry.

Ire — anger, temper, wrath, passion, resentment.

Irony—ridicule, sarcasm, satire, burlesque.

Irrational — unreasonable, foolish, absurd, silly.

Irrefragable—undeniable, indisputable, incontrovertible, unquestionable.

Irritate — plague, anger, tease, excite, provoke, aggravate, exasperate.

Irruption—opening, invasion, inroad, bursting forth.

Issue—offspring, progeny, result, end, sequel, egress, evacuation, effect, consequence.

J

Jade — harass, weary, tire, dispirit.

Jealousy—suspicion, envy.

Jest—fun, joke, sport.

Jocose—funny, witty, merry, jocular, pleasant, facetious, waggish.

Jocund — joyful, lively, merry, gay, sprightly, sportive, light-hearted, vivacious, mirthful.

Join—unite, add, combine, close, adhere, confederate league.

Joke—rally, sport.

Jollity—hilarity, mirth, gayety, merriment, festivity, joviality.

Journey — travel, trip, voyage, tour.

Joy—happiness, delight, gladness, charm, rapture, ecstasy, felicity, exultation, pleasure, transport.

Judgment — sentence, decision, doom, opinion, discernment, discrimination, penetration, intelligence, sagacity.

Just — exact, accurate, correct, honest, barely, upright, righteous, equitable, incorrupt.

Justify — defend, excuse, clear, absolve, maintain.

Justness—exactness, correctness, accuracy, equity, propriety.

K

Keen—sharp, penetrating, acute, cutting, piercing, shrewd.

Keep—hold, detain, support, retain, maintain, guard, reserve, sustain.

Kind—indulgent, compassionate, tender, lenient, gentle, affable, courteous, benignant, bland.

Kind—sort, manner, class, race, species, way, genus.

Knowledge—understanding, perception, learning, erudition, skill, acquaintance.

L

Labor—toil, work, strive, exert, drudge.

Lament—sorrow, mourn, deplore, complain, bewail, grieve, regret.

Language—tongue, speech, dialect, idiom.

Languid — weary, weak, faint, exhausted, dull, drooping.

Large—comprehensive, capacious, extensive, big, great, huge.

Lassitude—prostration, languor, weariness, enervation, fatigue.

Last—latest, hindmost, ultimate, final, end.

Lasting—durable, continuous, forever, continual, permanent, perpetual, eternal.

Latent—unseen, hidden, secret.

Laudable — praiseworthy, commendable.

Laughable — droll, ridiculous, comical, mirthful.

Lavish—profuse, wasteful, extravagant.

Lazy—indolent, idle, slothful, inactive.

Lean—bend, incline, totter, waver

Learning — intelligence, knowledge, erudition, science, literature, information.

Leave—abandon, desert, resign, relinquish, bequeath.

Legitimate—real, legal, lawful, genuine.

Lengthen—protract, extend, continue, draw out.

Lessen—diminish, decrease, abate, reduce, subside, shrink, degrade.

Let—allow, permit, suffer, leave, hire.

Lethargic—dull, tired, weary, heavy, drowsy, sleepy.

Level—even, smooth, plain, flat.

Levity—giddiness, gayety, fickleness, vanity, lightness.

Liable—exposed, responsible, subject.

Liberal—benevolent, generous, munificent, charitable.

Liberate—free, set free, deliver, release

Liberty — freedom, permission, license, leave, exemption, privilege.

Lie — deception, untruth, fiction, fabrication, falsehood.

Life—being, energy, vitality, vivacity, briskness

Lifeless — deceased, dead, inanimate, inactive, stale, flat, dull.

Lift—raise, elevate, exalt, hoist.

Light—illuminate, enlighten, nimble, kindle.

Like—probable, similar, uniform, resembling.

Likeness — resemblance, picture, portrait.

Liking—inclination, attachment, fondness, affection.

Linger—wait, delay, loiter, hesitate, saunter, tarry, lag.

Liquid—fluid, liquor.

Listen — hearken, attend, hear, overhear.

Little — small, diminutive.

Live—exist, subsist, dwell, abide, reside

Lively—active, energetic, brisk, nimble, jocund, merry, sprightly, vigorous.

Lodge — accommodate, entertain, shelter, harbor.

Loftiness — height, haughtiness, stateliness, elevation, dignity, pride.

Loiter—lag, saunter, linger.

Lonely—dreary, lonesome, retired, solitary.

Look—see, behold, view, inspect, appearance.

Loose — unconnected, open, unrestrained, dissolute, licentious, unjointed.

Loss—injury, damage, detriment, waste.

Lot—share, portion, fate, fortune, destiny.

Loud—noisy, vociferous, clamorous, turbulent, vehement.

Love—liking, affection, fondness, kindness, attachment, adoration, esteem.

Lovely—attractive, amiable, elegant, charming, handsome, fine, delightful, beautiful.

Lover—beau, wooer, suitor.

Loving—kind, affectionate, attentive, tender, amorous.

Low—humble, mean, base, abject, debased, dejected, despicable.

Lower — humble, humiliate, debase, degrade.

Lucky — successful, fortunate, prosperous.

Ludicrous — amusing, comical, droll, laughable.

Lunacy—mania, derangement, insanity, madness.

Luxuriant — excessive, voluptuous, abundant, exuberant.

Luxury — profusion, abundance, excess.

M

Magnificent—noble, grand, sublime, glorious, splendid, superb.

Magnitude—size, greatness, bulk.

Maintain—sustain, keep, support, help, continue, assert, defend, vindicate.

Malady—evil, disease, affliction, disorder, distemper

Manage—control, direct, conduct.

Mandate—command, charge, injunction, order.

Mangle—cut, lacerate, mutilate, tear, maim.

Manifest—evident, clear, open, apparent, obvious, plain.

Margin—edge, verge, rim, brim, brink, border.

Mark—stamp, impress, imprint, brand, show, observe.

Marriage—matrimony, wedlock, nuptials.

Marvel—wonder, prodigy, miracle.

Massive—large, heavy, bulky, ponderous

Master—achieve, overcome, surmount, conquer.

Mature—perfect, complete, ripe.

Maxim—saying, adage, proverb.

Mean — abject, low, despicable, miserly, sordid, penurious, niggardly.

Meaning—sense, import, signification, intention, purpose, design.

Meanwhile—meantime, interim, intervening.

Mechanic—artisan, artificer.

Meddle—interpose, interfere, interrupt.

Mediate—intercede, interpose.

Meek—mild, soft, gentle, humble.

Meet—assemble, join, fit, becoming.

Meeting — assembly, company, auditory, congregation.

Melancholy — sadness, distress, depression, gloom, grief, dejection.

Melody—harmony, unison, happiness, concord.

Melt—dissolve, soften, liquefy.

Memory—remembrance, reminiscence, recollection.

Mend — improve, repair, rectify, correct.

Merciful—mild, tender, gracious, benignant, compassionate, forgiving.

Merciless—hard-hearted, pitiless, cruel, unmerciful.

Mercy — pity, clemency, compassion, lenity.

Merry—happy, joyous, cheerful, gay, lively, mirthful, sportive, sprightly, vivacious.

Messenger—bearer, carrier, harbinger, forerunner, precursor.

Metaphor—similitude, trope, emblem, allegory, symbol.

Method—order, manner, system, mode, rule, plan, regularity.

Mighty—strong, powerful, great, potent.

Mild — meek, gentle, kind, easy, sweet, tender, mellow.

Mindful—heedful, observant, attentive.

Minister—contribute, supply, administer.

Mirth—merriment, joy, hilarity, cheerfulness, vivacity, jollity.

Mischief—damage, harm, hurt, misfortune, injury.

Misery—stingy, covetous, niggardly, penurious, avaricious.

Misfortune—calamity, harm, disaster, mishap, ill-luck.

Mistake—error, blunder, misconception.

Misuse—ill-treat, pervert, abuse, misapply.

Mitigate — lessen, alleviate, appease, ameliorate, abate, assuage, soothe, mollify.

Model — pattern, copy, sample, mould, specimen.

Moderation—temperance, sobriety, frugality, forbearance, modesty.

Modern—recent, late, new, novel.

Modest—quiet, retiring, reserved, diffident, bashful, unassuming.

Modify — re-arrange, change, extenuate, alter, moderate.

Molest—annoy, vex, tease, incommode, trouble, disturb.

Mollify—ease, appease, moderate, mitigate, assuage, soften.

Morose — sour, sullen, gloomy, peevish, forbidding.

Motive—incentive, reason, cause, principle.

Mourn — grieve, lament, sorrow, bewail, bemoan.

Move—change, pass, stir, incite, influence, persuade, actuate, instigate, impel.

Munificent — bounteous, bountiful, generous, beneficent, liberal, plentiful.

Muse—study, ponder, wonder, reflect, think, meditate, contemplate.

Mutable—changeable, unsteady, inconstant, fickle, wavering, unstable, variable, alterable, irresolute.

Mutilate—deface, injure, destroy, deprive, mangle, maim.

Mutinous — turbulent, seditious, insubordinate.

Mysterious—hidden, dim, dark, obscure, mystic, latent.

N

Naked—exposed, nude, unclothed, uncovered, simple, plain.

Name — cognomen, appellation, title, reputation, credit, denomination.

Narrow — contracted, confined, limited, curtailed, close.

Native—indigenous, genuine, intrinsic.

Near—adjoining, adjacent, close, contiguous.

Necessary — needful, expedient, indispensable, essential, important, requisite.

Need—poverty, want, penury, indigence.

Nefarious—evil, wicked, unjust, wrong, iniquitous.

Negligent—careless, heedless, remiss, neglectful, inattentive.

New—fresh, late, modern, novel.

Nigh—close, adjoining, contiguous, near, adjacent.

Noble — distinguished, elevated, exalted, illustrious, great, grand.

Noisy—boisterous, turbulent, high, clamorous, loud sounding.

Noted — renowned, distinguished, conspicuous, celebrated, eminent, notorious, illustrious.

Notice—warning, information, intelligence, advice.

Notion — thought, opinion, sentiment, whim, idea, conception, perception.

Notorious—celebrated, renowned, distinguished, noted, public, conspicuous.

Notwithstanding—nevertheless, however, in spite of, yet.

Nourish—feed, uphold, maintain, cherish, nurture, support.

O

Obdurate — inflexible, unfeeling, callous, impenitent, hardened, insensible, obstinate.

Obedient—submissive, compliant, yielding, dutiful, obsequious, respectful.

Object—end, subject, aim.

Object — oppose, against, except to.

Oblige—compel, coerce, bind, engage, force, favor, please, gratify.

Obnoxious—offensive, liable, disagreeable, unpleasant, exposed

Obscure—hidden, concealed, indistinct, difficult, dark, abstruse.

Observance—ceremony, rite, attention, form, respect.

Observant—watchful, attentive, mindful, regardful.

Observe—see, notice, watch, follow, remark, keep

Obsolete—disused, old, worn-out, antiquated, ancient, old-fashioned.

Obstacle — impediment, obstruction, difficulty, hinderance.

Obstinate — stubborn, resolute, headstrong.

Obstruct—impede, hinder, stop, prevent

Obtain—gain, secure, get, win, acquire, procure, earn.

Obvious—plain, apparent, open, clear, evident, visible, manifest.

Occupation — work, profession, calling, trade, business, avocation, employment.

Occupy—keep, hold, use, possess.

Occurrence—event, contingency, adventure, incident.

Odor—smell, fragrance, perfume, scent.

Offense — trespass, crime, injury, sin, outrage, insult, misdeed, wrong, transgression.

Offensive—mean, abusive, insulting, impertinent, insolent, rude, scurrilous, obnoxious, opprobrious.

Officious—busy, active, forward, obtrusive, intrusive.

Only—solely, singly, alone, simply, merely.

Open — unravel, reveal, disclose, unlock.

Opening—fissure, aperture, hole, cavity.

Operation—performance, action, agency.

Opinion—belief, idea, sentiment, notion.

Opinionated — obstinate, stubborn, stiff, egotistical, conceited, self-willed.

Opponent — opposer, adversary, foe, enemy, antagonist.

Opposite — contrary, repugnant, adverse.

Opprobrious—reproachful, insolent, abusive, offensive, insulting, scandalous, scurrilous.

Opprobrium — shame, disgrace, reproach, infamy, ignominy.

Oration—speech, sermon, lecture, discourse, address, harangue.

Ordain — appoint, invest, order, prescribe.

Order — brotherhood, fraternity, rank, method, succession, series, degree, genus.

Order — mandate, injunction, precept, command.

Orderly — precise, regular, systematic, methodical.

Ordinary — usual, common.

Origin — rise, cause, source, foundation, beginning, descent, fountain.

Original — primitive, first, pristine, primary.

Ornament — decorate, beautify, adorn, deck, embellish.

Ornate — decorated, adorned, embellished, bedecked, garnished.

Ostentation — parade, show, display, boast.

Outrage — insult, injure, affront, violence.

Outward — extraneous, apparent, intrinsic.

Overbearing — repressive, impertinent, haughty, lordly.

Overcome — vanquish, conquer, surmount, subdue.

Overflow — fill, inundate, deluge, abound.

Oversight — mistake, error, misapprehension, inattention.

Overwhelm — overpower, crush, upturn, overthrow, subdue.

Owner — holder, proprietor, master, possessor.

P

Pacify — calm, still, quiet, soothe, conciliate.

Pain — distress, afflict, torture, torment, suffer, hurt.

Paint — portray, represent, depict, sketch, color, describe, delineate.

Pair — join, two, couple, brace.

Pale — fade, wan, white, pallid, fair.

Palpable — gross, plain, apparent, discernible, perceptible.

Palpitate — tremble, throb, beat, flutter, gasp, pant.

Pang — torture, torment, distress, agony, anguish, sorrow.

Pardon — acquit, forgive, clear, free, discharge, release, remit.

Parsimonious — mean, frugal, miserly, avaricious, penurious, niggardly.

Part — share, portion, division, piece, section.

Particular — individual, specific, exact, appropriate, circumstantial, peculiar, exclusive, punctual, distinct.

Particularly — chiefly, mainly, principally, especially, distinctly, specifically.

Partisan — disciple, adherent, follower.

Partner — associate, accomplice, colleague, coadjutor.

Passion — desire, feeling, love, anger, excitement.

Passionate — hot, angry, irascible, hasty, excitable.

Passive — submissive, unresisting, patient, resigned.

Pathetic — affecting, touching, moving.

Patience — endurance, fortitude, resignation.

Patient — resigned, composed, enduring, calm, passive, an invalid.

Peaceable — quiet, calm, serene, tranquil, mild, gentle.

Peevish — fretful, disagreeable, petulant, cross, captious, irritable.

Penalty — punishment, pain, fine, forfeiture, chastisement.

Penitence — contrition, remorse, compunction, repentance.

Penurious — parsimonious, sparing, miserly, niggardly, beggarly.

Penury — want, poverty, distress, indigence, need.

Perceive — observe, discern, distinguish.

Perception — belief, conception, sentiment, idea, sensation, notion.

Peremptory — positive, despotic, arbitrary, dogmatical, absolute.

Perfect — done, complete, finished.

Perfidious — false, treacherous, faithless.

Perforate — pierce, bore, penetrate.

Perform — execute, accomplish, effect, produce, achieve, fulfill.

Perfume — odor, smell, scent, exhalation, fragrance.

Period — circuit, date, age, epoch, era.

Permit — allow, suffer, consent, admit, tolerate, yield.

Pernicious — noisome, ruinous, destructive, mischievous, hurtful, noxious.

Perpetual — uninterrupted, incessant, unceasing, constant, continual.

Perplex — bewilder, annoy, confuse, involve, molest, puzzle, embarrass, harass, entangle.

Persevere — endure, continue, persist, insist, pursue, prosecute.

Perspicuity — clearness, transparency, brilliancy.

Persuade — urge, induce, exhort, influence, entice, prevail upon.

Perverse — stubborn, untractable, unmanageable, crooked, cross.

Pestilential — destructive, mischievous, epidemical, infectious, contagious.

Petition — prayer, supplication, request, suit, entreaty.

Picture — likeness, image, effigy, representation.

Pious — spiritual, devout, godly, religious.

Pique — offense, grudge, dislike, malice, spite, rancor.

Pity — sympathy, commiseration, compassion, condolence, mercy.

Place — site, ground, post, position.

Placid — still, calm, gentle, quiet, tranquil, serene.

Plague — perplex, embarrass, tantalize, annoy, importune, vex, torment.

Plain — perceptible, discernible, manifest, obvious, clear, apparent, evident, distinct.

Plan — design, contrivance, device, scheme, arrangement, project, stratagem.

Pleasant — cheerful, jocular, gay, vivacious, agreeable, facetious, witty.

Please — gratify, satisfy, humor, delight.

Pleasure — satisfaction, delight, happiness, enjoyment, joy.

Pledge — pawn, deposit, security, hostage, earnest.

Plentiful — bounteous, abundant, copious, exuberant, ample, plenteous.

Pliant — lithe, limber, yielding, bending, supple, flexible, pliable.

Plight — predicament, state, case, situation, condition, conjuncture.

Plot — plan, arrangement, project, conspiracy, combination, scheme, intrigue.

Polite — courteous, well-bred, civil, polished, refined, genteel, affable.

Politeness — good manners, civility, courtesy, suavity, good breeding.

Politic — wise, careful, artful, cunning, civil, prudent.

Pollute — corrupt, taint, defile, infect, contaminate.

Pompous — lofty, stately, ostentatious, showy, dignified, magnificent.

Ponder — study, reflect, think, muse, consider.

Portion — piece, part, quantity, share, division, dower, fortune.

Positive — confident, certain, real, dogmatic, sure, absolute.

Possess — keep, hold, have, enjoy, occupy.

Postpone — retard, delay, prolong, protract, defer, procrastinate.

Posture — figure, gesture, action, position, attitude.

Potent — powerful, strong, vigorous, mighty, forcible.

Poverty — want, need, indigence, penury, suffering.

Practicable — possible, feasible, available.

Practice — custom, style, manner, form, use, habit.

Praise — eulogize, applaud, laud, admire, commend.

Prayer — application, petition, request, suit, entreaty, supplication.

Precarious — uncertain, dubious, doubtful, equivocal, unreliable.

Precedence — priority, superiority, preference.

Preceding — anterior, previous, prior, antecedent, former, foregoing.

Precept — maxim, rule, principle, injunction, law, doctrine, mandate, command.

Precious — choice, costly, valuable, expensive, uncommon, rare.

Precise — careful, particular, exact, accurate, correct, nice.

Preclude — intercept, prevent, obviate, hinder.

Predicament — condition, plight, position, situation.

Predict — prophesy, foretell.

Predominant — prevalent, overruling, controlling, supreme, prevailing.

Predominate — prevail, rule over.

Preference — advancement, priority, choice.

Prejudice — bias, injury, hurt, disadvantage.

Preliminary — previous, preparatory, introductory, antecedent.

Prepare — arrange, qualify, fit, equip, make ready.

Preposterous — impossible, ridiculous, absurd, foolish.

Prerogative — immunity, privilege.

Prescribe — dictate, ordain, appoint.

Preserve — uphold, maintain, protect, spare, save.

Pressing — urgent, emergent, important, crowding, squeezing, forcing.

Presume — guess, suppose, think, surmise, conjecture, believe.

Presuming — forward, arrogant, presumptuous.

Pretext — excuse, pretense, pretension.

Pretty — lovely, beautiful, fine, agreeable.

Prevailing — dominant, ruling, overcoming, prevalent, predominating.

Prevent — impede, obstruct, hinder, obviate, preclude.

Previous — before, prior, anterior, preliminary, introductory.

Price — value, worth, expense, cost.

Pride — self-esteem, arrogance, haughtiness, conceit, ostentation, loftiness, vanity.

Primary — elemental, first, original, pristine.

Principal — main, chief, capital, head, leading, important.

Principle — motive, tenet, constituent part, doctrine, element.

Print — impress, stamp, mark.

Prior — before, previous, former, antecedent, preceding, anterior.

Priority — preference, precedence, pre-eminence.

Pristine — original, first, primitive.

Privacy — seclusion, solitude, retirement, loneliness.

Privilege — prerogative, right, advantage, immunity, exemption.

Probability — supposition, likelihood, chance.

Probity — reliability, uprightness, honesty, integrity, veracity.

Proceed — progress, arise, issue, advance, emanate.

Proceeding — transaction, course, progression, work.

Proclaim — declare, publish, announce, tell, advertise, promulgate.

Proclivity — liking, tendency, inclination, proneness.

Procure — obtain, acquire, gain.

Prodigal — lavish, extravagant, wasteful.

Prodigious — great, astonishing, vast, large, amazing, monstrous.

Profane — secular, irreverent, impious, irreligious.

Profession — calling, employment, business, vocation, work, labor.

Proficiency — advancement, improvement, progress.

Profit — gain, advantage, benefit, emolument.

Profligate — depraved, wicked, corrupt, sinful, vicious, abandoned.

Profuse — lavish, wasteful, prodigal, extravagant.

Progeny — descendants, offspring, race, issue.

Project — invent, design, scheme, plan.

Prolific — productive, fruitful, fertile.

Prolix — tiresome, long, diffuse.

Prolong — extend, delay, protract, postpone, retard, procrastinate.

Prominent — eminent, conspicuous, distinguished.

Promise — agreement, assurance, engagement, declaration, pledge, word, obligation.

Promote — raise, encourage, forward, advance.

Prompt — quick, active, ready, assiduous.

Pronounce — say, speak, utter, declare, affirm, articulate, enunciate.

Proof — evidence, testimony, argument.

Propagate — multiply, increase, disseminate, diffuse, circulate, spread, extend.

Propensity — liking, inclination, proneness, tendency, bias.

Proper — fit, right, suitable, just, appropriate.

Propitious — favorable, auspicious.

Propitiate — conciliate, appease, reconcile.

Proportionate — equal, adequate, commensurate.

Propose — offer, apply, tender, intend, purpose, bid.

Prospect — view, landscape, survey.

Prospective — future, foreseeing, hereafter, forward.

Prosperous — fortunate, lucky, flourishing, successful.

Protect—uphold, guard, shield, maintain, defend, cherish, foster, patronize.

Protract—withhold, retard, prolong, delay, defer, postpone.

Proud—haughty, assuming, arrogant, lofty, vain, conceited.

Proverb—maxim, saying, adage.

Provide—procure, furnish, supply, prepare.

Provident—cautious, prudent, economical, careful.

Proviso—requirement, condition, stipulation.

Provoke—excite, irritate, enrage, aggravate, exasperate, tantalize.

Prudence—forethought, carefulness, wisdom, discretion, judgment.

Publish—announce, promulgate, proclaim, advertise, declare.

Puerile—infantile, boyish, childish, juvenile.

Pull—bring, haul, draw, drag.

Punctual — prompt, particular, exact.

Punish—whip, chastise, correct, discipline.

Pursue—follow, prosecute, chase, persist, continue, persevere.

Puzzle — confound, perplex, embarrass, bewilder, entangle.

Q

Quack—imposter, pretender, empiric, charlatan.

Qualified—capable, fit, adapted, competent.

Quarrel—fight, affray, riot, contest, battle, contention, altercation, dispute, tumult.

Query — question, interrogatory, inquiry.

Question—ask, examine, doubt, dispute, consider, inquire, interrogate.

Questionable—suspicious, doubtful.

Quick—rapid, active, lively, swift, prompt, expeditious, brisk.

Quiet—calm, repose, tranquillity, rest, ease, peaceable, placid, still.

Quit—depart, leave, resign, abandon, forsake, relinquish.

Quota—rate, share, proportion.

Quote—copy, relate, cite, adduce.

R

Race—lineage, family, breed, generation, course.

Radiance—light, glory, brightness, brilliancy.

Rage—indignation, anger, fury.

Raise—heighten, elevate, exalt, erect, collect, propagate.

Rank—class, degree, place, position.

Ransom—purchase, free, redeem.

Rapacious — voracious, greedy, ravenous.

Rapidity — swiftness, fleetness, celerity, speed, agility, velocity.

Rapture—joy, delight, transport, ecstasy.

Rare — scarce, uncommon, excellent, singular, unusual, incomparable, raw.

Rash — impulsive, hasty, violent, thoughtless, headstrong.

Rate—price, quota, proportion, ratio, value, degree, assessment.

Ravenous—voracious, rapacious, greedy.

Ray—dawn, beam, gleam, streak, glimmer.

Real—certain, true, genuine, positive, actual.

Realize—reach, procure, achieve, consummate, accomplish, effect.

Reason—purpose, proof, motive, argument, origin, understanding.

Reasonable—fair, probable, just, moderate, equitable, honest, rational.

Rebuke — reprimand, reproach, reproof, censure.

Recant—revoke, recall, renounce, withdraw, retract, abjure.

Recede—retire, retrograde, fall back, retreat.

Recite—repeat, rehearse.

Reckon — count, number, estimate, calculate, compute.

Reclaim—reform, recover, correct.

Recollection — memory, remembrance, reminiscence.

Recompense—satisfaction, pay, price, reward, equivalent, remuneration.

Reconcile—propitiate, conciliate.

Recruit—repair, retrieve, replace, recover.

Rectify—mend, improve, correct, amend, reform.

Redeem—restore, rescue, recover, ransom.

Redress—relief, remedy.

Refer—propose, suggest, allude, intimate, hint.

Refined — graceful, genteel, polished, polite, elegant.

Reform—correct, amend, rectify, improve, better.

Refractory—unmanageable, unruly, contumacious, perverse.

Refrain—forego, forbear, spare, abstain.

Regale—refresh, entertain, feast, gratify.

Regard—respect, esteem, value, reverence, mind, heed.

Regardless—careless, negligent, indifferent, unconcerned, unobservant, heedless.

Region—section, quarter, district, country.

Regret—sorrow, complaint, grief, lament.

Regulate—control, rule, direct, govern, dispose, adjust.

Rehearse—detail, repeat, recite, recapitulate.

Reject—refuse, deny, decline, repel.

Rejoinder—response, answer, reply.

Reliance — trust, belief, repose, confidence, dependence.

Believe—assist, help, succor, aid, alleviate, mitigate, support.

Religious—pious, devout, holy.

Remain — continue, stay, abide, tarry, sojourn.

Remainder—rest, residue, remnant.

Remark — comment, observation, note.

Reminiscence—recollection, remembrance.

Remiss—heedless, negligent, inattentive, careless, thoughtless.

Remit—send, transmit, liberate, abate, forgive, pardon, relax.

Remorse—penitence, contrition, distress.

Renew—revive, refresh, renovate.

Renounce — leave, resign, abdicate, abandon, forego, relinquish, quit.

Renown — reputation, celebrity, fame.

Repair — improve, retrieve, recover, restore.

Reparation—restitution, restoration, amends.

Repeal — cancel, annul, revoke, abolish, abrogate, destroy.

Repeat—detail, rehearse, recite.

Repetition—tautology, prolixity, iteration, reiteration.

Replenish—supply, fill, refill.

Repose—ease, sleep, rest, quiet.

Reproach—blame, reprove, censure, condemn, upbraid, reprimand.

Repugnance — aversion, abhorrence, antipathy, dislike, hatred.

Repugnant—hostile, adverse, opposite, contrary.

Reputation—repute, fame, character, honor, renown, credit.

Request — solicit, ask, demand, entreat, beg, beseech, implore.

Requisite—important, necessary, essential, expedient.

Research—investigation, study, examination, inquiry.

Resemblance — similarity, semblance, similitude, likeness.

Residence—home, abode, house, dwelling, domicile.

Residue — leavings, remainder, rest.

Resign—yield, abdicate, renounce, relinquish, forego.

Resignation — patience, endurance, submission, acquiescence.

Resist — endure, oppose, withstand.

Resolution—firmness, determination, fortitude, courage, decision.

Resort—visit, frequent, haunt.

Respect—esteem, regard, deference, attention, consideration, good-will, estimation.

Respectful—deferential, dutiful, obedient, civil.

Respite — delay, suspension, interval, reprieve.

Response — reply, answer, rejoinder.

Responsible—amenable, answerable, accountable.

Rest — quiet, ease, repose, intermission, stop, cessation, others, remainder.

Restore — cure, renew, return, repay, rebuild.

Restrain — confine, repress, restrict, coerce, limit, constrain.

Restrict — limit, circumscribe, bold, bind.

Result — effect, issue, ultimate, consequence, event.

Retain — hold, detain, keep, reserve.

Retard—hinder, defer, protract, postpone, delay, procrastinate, prolong, prevent, impede.

Retire — recede, withdraw, retreat, secede.

Retract — annul, take back, revoke, recant, recall.

Retrieve — renew, recover, regain.

Reveal—impart, divulge, communicate, disclose, expose.

Revenge—vindicate, avenge.

Revere — adore, worship, reverence, venerate.

Review — examine, survey, notice, revision.

Revive — enliven, renew, reanimate, refresh, renovate.

Revoke—cancel, annul, abolish, repeal, abrogate, efface, retract.

Reward—recompense, remuneration, compensation, satisfaction.

Riches — wealth, opulence, affluence.

Ridicule — deride, banter, laugh at.

Ridiculous—droll, absurd, ludicrous, preposterous, unreasonable, improbable.

Right — correct, just, honest, proper, privilege, claim, direct, straight, immunity.

Righteous—just, godly, upright, honest, incorrupt, virtuous.

Rite — form, custom, ceremony, observance.

Road—path, way, course, route.

Roam — wander, ramble, stroll, range, rove.

Room — chamber, space, place, apartment.

Rough—harsh, uncivil, rude, uncouth, unmannerly, unpolished, rugged, severe, stormy.

Round—globular, spherical, orb, circuit, tour.

Route—path, course, way, road.

Rude—rough, impertinent, coarse, impudent, unpolished, saucy, disagreeable, bold.

Rule—authority, law, regulation, government, custom, maxim, habit, precept, guide.

S

Sacred—holy, divine, devoted.

Sad — sorrowful, mournful, dejected, gloomy, melancholy.

Sagacity — perception, penetration, acuteness, discernment.

Salary—wages, pay, stipend, hire, reward, remuneration.

Sanction—maintain, sustain, uphold, countenance, ratify, support.

Sapient — discreet, wise, sage, sagacious.

Sarcasm—satire, irony, ridicule.

Satisfaction — compensation, remuneration, contentment, atonement, reward.

Saving—prudent, thrifty, frugal, economical, close, sparing, stingy, penurious.

Saying—adage, maxim, proverb, by-word, relating, speaking, uttering, communicating.

Scandal—disgrace, reproach, discredit, baseness, infamy.

Scarce — uncommon, unusual, singular, rare.

Scatter—disseminate, dissipate, spread, disperse.

Scent—odor, smell, perfume, fragrance.

Scoff—ridicule, sneer, jeer, jibe, belittle.

Scope — object, tendency, aim, drift.

Scruple — hesitate, doubt, fluctuate.

Scrupulous — truthful, upright, correct, careful, conscientious, cautious.

Scrutinize—search, examine, investigate.

Scurrilous—disgusting, abusive, offensive, insulting, insolent.

Search — inquiry, examination, scrutiny, pursuit, investigation.

Secede—withdraw, retire, recede.

Seclusion — quietude, privacy, solitude, retirement, loneliness.

Secondary — subordinate, inferior.

Secret—hidden, quiet, still, concealed, latent, mysterious, clandestine.

Secular—temporal, worldly.

Secure—safe, certain, confident, sure, procure, warrant.

Security — pledge, warranty, defense, guard, protection.

Sedate — serene, calm, unruffled, unconcerned, still, quiet, composed.

Seduce — decoy, betray, attract, allure.

See — examine, look, behold, observe, perceive, view.

Sense — idea, feeling, meaning, judgment, import, reason.

Sensitive—keen, susceptible, appreciative.

Sentence — mandate, judgment, decision, period, phrase, proposition.

Sentiment — expression, opinion, notion, feeling.

Separate — dissociate, detach, disengage.

Settle—determine, fix, establish, arrange, adjust, regulate.

Settled—conclusive, decided, confirmed, established.

Sever—separate, disjoin, divide, detach.

Several — sundry, different, various, diverse.

Severe—cold, stern, harsh, sharp, rigid, cruel, heartless, rough, strict, unyielding, austere, rigorous.

Shake — shiver, quiver, shudder, quake, agitate, totter.

Shame—dishonor, disgrace, ignominy.

Shameless — insolent, impudent, immodest, indelicate, indecent.

Shape—form, fashion, mould.

Share—divide, distribute, apportion, participate, partake.

Sharpness—shrewdness, penetration, keenness, acuteness, sagacity, cunning.

Shelter — shield, defend, screen, harbor, protect, cover.

Shine — illumine, glisten, gleam, glitter, glare.

Shining — bright, glittering, radiant, glistening, brilliant.

Shocking — disgusting, terrible, dreadful, horrible.

Short—brief, concise, scanty, defective, brittle.

Shorten—lessen, contract, reduce, abridge, curtail.

Show—display, exhibition, pomp, parade, representation, spectacle, sight.

Showy—grand, ostentatious, gay, gaudy, fine, sumptuous.

Shrewd—sharp, acute, keen, precise.

Shun—evade, avoid, elude.

Sickly—unwell, sick, ill, diseased, indisposed.

Sign—indication, omen, symptom, signal, note, mark, token.

Signify—imply, express, betoken, denote, declare, utter, intimate, testify.

Silence—quietude, stillness, muteness.

Silent — dumb, mute, speechless, still.

Silly—ridiculous, foolish, absurd, stupid, dull, weak, simple.

Similarity — resemblance, likeness, similitude.

Simple—weak, silly, artless, foolish, unwise, stupid, plain, single.

Simply—solely, merely, only.

Since—for, as, inasmuch, after.

Sincere—true, honest, frank, upright, incorrupt, plain.

Singular — particular, eccentric, odd, strange, remarkable, rare, scarce.

Situation — place, position, employment, site, locality, case, condition, plight.

Skilful — expert, adroit, adept, dexterous, accomplished.

Slander—defame, vilify, calumniate, detract.

Slavery — servitude, bondage, captivity.

Slender — slight, slim, fragile, thin.

Slow — tardy, dilatory, tedious, dull.

Small—little, minute, diminutive, narrow, infinitesimal.

Smooth—easy, mild, bland, even, level.

Smother — suffocate, stifle, suppress, conceal.

Snarling — snappish, waspish, surly.

Sober — grave, moderate, temperate, abstemious.

Social—sociable, companionable, convivial, familiar.

Society — fellowship, company, congregation, association, community.

Soft — flexible, ductile, yielding, pliant, mild, compliant.

Solicit—request, ask, entreat, implore, beg, beseech, supplicate, importune.

Solicitation — entreaty, invitation, importunity.

Solicitude — care, earnestness, anxiety.

Solid—enduring, firm, hard, substantial.

Solitary — sole, alone, desolate, only, lonely, remote, retired.

Soothe—quiet, compose, appease, calm, pacify, assuage, tranquilise.

Sorrow—trouble, grief, affliction.

Sort—order, kind, species.

Sound—tone, firm, whole, hearty, healthy, sane.

Sour — tart, acid, acrimonious, sharp.

Source—head, origin, fountain, cause, spring, reason.

Spacious — capacious, ample, large.

Sparkle—glitter, glisten, shine, glare, radiate, corruscate.

Speak — utter, talk, articulate, pronounce, converse, say, tell, recite, relate.

Species—order, kind, class, sort.

Specific—definite, particular, special.

Specimen — sample, model, pattern.

Spectator — beholder, observer, auditor.

Speech—oration, address, lecture, harangue, sermon.

Speechless—dumb, silent, mute.

Spend — expend, exhaust, dissipate, squander, waste.

Sphere—orb, circle, globe.

Spirited — quick, animated, ardent, vivacious, active.

Spiritual—ethereal, immaterial, unearthly, incorporeal.

Spite—pique, malice, grudge, malignity, hate.

Splendid — superb, magnificent, grand, sublime, heavenly.

Splendor — magnificence, luster, brightness, brilliancy.

Splenetic—peevish, melancholy, morose, sullen, gloomy, fretful.

Sport—play, game, amusement, pastime, diversion, recreation.

Spotless—faultless, unblemished, blameless, unsullied, clear, untarnished, pure, innocent, stainless.

Spread—distribute, diffuse, circulate, expand, disperse, disseminate, propagate, scatter, dispense, sow.

Spring—leap, arise, start, flow, proceed, emanate, jump, issue.

Sprinkle—bedew, water, scatter, besprinkle.

Sprout — vegetate, germinate, bud.

Stability — fixedness, continuity, steadiness, firmness.

Stain—mar, soil, tarnish, blemish, blot, flaw, spot, speck, tinge, color, discolor.

Stammer — hesitate, stutter, falter.

Stamp—mark, print, impress.

Standard—test, rule, criterion.

State—situation, condition, position, plight, predicament.

Station — place, situation, post, position.

Stay—dependence, reliance, staff, prop, abide, remain, continue, delay, hinder, support.

Sterility—barrenness, unfruitfulness.

Stern—unfeeling, severe, austere, strict, cold, rigid, rigorous.

Still—quiet, calm, silent, appease, assuage, lull, pacify.

Stimulate—arouse, excite, incite, urge, impel, encourage, instigate.

Stock — supply, collection, fund, accumulation, store, provision, cattle.

Stop—rest, intermission, vacation, cessation, delay, hinder, impede, check.

Story — tale, anecdote, incident, memoir.

Straight—direct, immediate.

Strange — unusual, curious, odd, singular, surprising, eccentric.

Stratagem—deception, cheat, artifice, fraud, trick, imposture, delusion.

Strength — potency, authority, force, force, might.

Strict—precise, exact, particular, accurate, nice, severe, harsh, rigorous, stern.

Strife—disagreement, dissension, discord, contest.

Strong — able, powerful, robust, stout, vigorous, firm, muscular, hardy.

Style — custom, mode, manner, phraseology, diction.

Subdue—vanquish, conquer, overcome, subjugate, subject, surmount.

Subject—control, liable, exposed, object, matter, material.

Subjoin—attach, connect, annex, affix.

Sublime—lofty, elevated, great, exalted, grand, magnificent.

Submissive — obedient, yielding, humble, compliant.

Subordinate — subject, subservient, inferior.

Subsistence — livelihood, living, sustenance, maintenance, support.

Substantial — reliable, strong, solid, stout, real, responsible.

Substitute — agent, representative, exchange, change.

Subtle—sly, artful, cunning, deceitful, crafty, wily, perfidious, insidious, arch, acute, fine.

Subtract—withdraw, deduct, take from.

Subvert — ruin, overthrow, reverse, controvert, invert, reverse.

Successful — prosperous, lucky, winning, fortunate.

Succession — series, order, continuance.

Succor—defend, help, aid, assist, relieve.

Sudden — unexpected, unlooked for, unanticipated, hasty.

Suffer—endure, tolerate, permit, bear, allow.

Suffocate—smother, choke, stifle.

Sufficient — plenty, abundance, enough, competent, adequate.

Suffrage—vote, ballot, aid, voice.

Suggest—propose, insinuate, hint, allude, intimate.

Suitable — appropriate, fit, becoming, agreeable, expedient.

Suitor—beau, wooer, lover, petitioner.

Summon—cite, call, invite, bid, convoke.

Sundry—several, various, diverse, different.

Superficial—flimsy, slight, shallow.

Supersede — supplant, overrule, displace.

Supplicate—solicit, entreat, beg, beseech, ask, implore.

Support—maintain, uphold, sustain, defend, encourage, second,

prop, protect, favor, forward, cherish, assist, endure.

Sure—reliable, confident, certain, infallible.

Surmise—presume, think, guess, suppose, believe, conjecture.

Surmount — subdue, overcome, vanquish, conquer.

Surpass — beat, outdo, outstrip, excel, exceed.

Surprise—astonishment, admiration, wonder, amazement.

Surrender — yield, resign, give up, deliver.

Surround — encompass, enclose, encircle, environ.

Survey—review, prospect, retrospect.

Suspense—hesitation, doubt, uncertainty.

Suspicion — distrust, jealousy, apprehension.

Sustain — carry, bear, support, uphold, maintain.

Sustenance — livelihood, living, maintenance, support.

Swiftness—speed, rapidity, velocity, fleetness, quickness, celerity.

Symbol—illustration, type, figure, emblem, metaphor.

Symmetry — harmony, proportion.

Sympathy — compassion, condolence, agreement, commiseration.

Symptom — evidence, indication, token, sign, mark, note.

System—order, method.

T

Talent — faculty, ability, gift, endowment, capability, intellectuality.

Talk—conference, discourse, chat, conversation, sermon, communication, lecture, dialogue, colloquy.

Tantalise—plague, tease, taunt, provoke, irritate, torment, aggravate.

Taste — perception, discernment, judgment, flavor, savor, relish.

Tax—duty, assessment, rate, toll, tribute, contribution, custom.

Tedious — wearisome, slow, tiresome, tardy.

Tell — inform, communicate, reveal, disclose, acquaint, impart, mention, state, talk, report.

Temper—mood, humor, temperament, disposition.

Temperate — moderate, sober, abstemious, abstinent.

Temporal — worldly, mundane, sublunary, secular.

Temporary—uncertain, fleeting, transitory, transient.

Tempt—allure, induce, entice, attract, decoy, seduce.

Tender—propose, offer, bid.

Tenderness—fondness, love, humanity, affection, benignity.

Tenet — belief, dogma, doctrine, principle, opinion, opinion.

Terms—conditions, words, expressions, language.

Terminate — close, finish, end, complete.

Terrible—awful, frightful, fearful, shocking, terrific, horrible.

Terror—alarm, fear, dread, consternation, apprehension, fright.

Test — experiment, proof, experience, trial, standard, criterion.

Testify — prove, declare, swear, signify, witness, affirm.

Testimony—proof, evidence.

Therefore — prove, declare, accordingly, then, hence, so, consequently.

Think—consider, deliberate, mediate, ponder, conceive, contemplate, imagine, surmise.

Though—allow, while, although.

Thought—contemplation, meditation, fancy, idea, supposition, reflection, conception, conceit.

Thoughtful — anxious, considerate, careful, attentive, discreet, contemplative.

Thoughtless — inconsiderate, indiscreet, careless, foolish, hasty, unthinking.

Throw—heave, cast, hurl, fling.

Time—period, season, age, date, duration, era, epoch.

Timely — opportune, seasonable, early.

Tired — wearied, fatigued, harassed.

Title—name, appellation, claim.

Token—emblem, sign, indication, symptom, mark, note.

Tolerate—permit, allow, suffer.

Tortuous—tormenting, crooked, twisted, winding.

Total — complete, whole, entire, gross, sum.

Touching—moving, pathetic, affecting.

Tour—round, circuit, jaunt, trip, journey, ramble, excursion.

Trace—clue, track, mark, vestige.

Trade — vocation, business, calling, labor, occupation, dealing, traffic.

Traduce—injure, condemn, censure, depreciate, degrade, decry, calumniate, detract.

Tranquillity— stillness, peace, quiet, calm.

Transact—manage, conduct, negotiate.

Transcend — surpass, excel, exceed, outdo.

Transparent — clear, pellucid, pervious, translucent.

Transient—brief, fleeting, short.

Transport — delight, rapture, ecstasy.

Treacherous — insidious, faithless, dishonest, perfidious, hearless.

Trepidation—palpitation, emotion, trembling, tremor, agitation.

Trespass — violation, transgression, offense, misdemeanor.

Trial—endeavor, attempt, effort, experiment, test, proof, temptation.

Trick — cheat, fraud, deception, artifice, imposture, stratagem, jugglery.

Trifling—insignificant, inconsiderable, unimportant, light, futile, petty, frivolous.

Trip—journey, jaunt, excursion, tour, ramble, voyage.

Trouble—anxiety, vexation, adversity, affliction, sorrow, distress.

Troublesome — annoying, disturbing, vexing, perplexing, irksome, teasing, harassing, importunate.

True—honest, candid, sincere, reliable, plain, upright.

Truth—fidelity, veracity, candor, faithfulness, honesty.

Try—endeavor, attempt.

Turbulent—raging, tumultuous, seditious, mutinous, riotous.

Turn—revolve, whirl, twist, circulate, wind, gyrate, contort, bend, distort, wheel.

Type—illustration, symbol, figure, emblem, mark.

U

Ultimate—latest, last, final, end.

Umpire—judge, arbitrator, arbiter.

Unbelief — incredulity, disbelief, skepticism, infidelity.

Unblemished — faultless, blameless, spotless, irreproachable, untarnished, stainless.

Unceasingly—eternally, perpetually, always, constantly, continually.

Unchangeable—unalterable, immutable.

Uncommon — singular, unusual, rare, unique, infrequent, choice, scarce.

Unconcerned—careless, regardless, uninterested, indifferent.

Uncover—reveal, expose, strip, discover.

Undaunted — courageous, bold, fearless, intrepid.

Undeniable — indisputable, incontrovertible, unquestionable.

Under — subordinate, lower, beneath, below, inferior, subject, subjacent.

Understanding—conception, intelligence, comprehension, sense, perception, faculty, reason, intellect.

Undetermined—uncertain, irresolute, hesitating, wavering, unsteady, doubtful, vacillating, fluctuating.

Unfaithful — untruthful, faithless, dishonest, disloyal, treacherous, perfidious.

Unfold—explain, divulge, reveal, unravel, develop, expand, open, display.

Unhandy — ungainly, awkward, uncouth, clumsy.

Unhappy—distressed, miserable, unfortunate, afflicted, wretched.

Uniform — even, alike, equal, same.

Unimportant — trivial, trifling, immaterial, insignificant, petty, inconsiderable.

Unlearned — uninformed, unlettered, ignorant, illiterate.

Unlike — distinct, dissimilar, different.

Unlimited — infinite, boundless, unbounded, illimitable.

Unquestionable — indubitable, undeniable, indisputable, incontrovertible.

Unravel — unfold, disentangle, extricate, reveal.

Unrelenting—unforgiving, hardhearted, inexorable, relentless.

Unruly — unmanageable, uncontrollable, refractory, ungovernable.

Unseasonable — ill-timed, unfit, untimely, unsuitable, late.

Unsettled — doubtful, wavering, undetermined, unsteady, vacillating.

Unspeakable — unutterable, inexpressible.

Unstable — inconstant, mutable, vacillating, changeable, wavering.

Untimely — inopportune, premature, unseasonable, unsuitable.

Unwilling—loth, backward, disinclined, disliking, averse, reluctant.

Upbraid — reprove, censure, reproach, blame.

Uproar—noise, confusion, bustle, tumult, disturbance.

Urbanity — courtesy, affability, suavity, civility.

Urge—press, incite, impel, instigate, stimulate, encourage, animate.

Urgent — importunate, pressing, earnest.

Usage — habit, fashion, custom, treatment, prescription.

Use—practice, custom, habit, service, usage, advantage, utility.

Usually—generally, commonly.

Utility—use, service, benefit, advantage, convenience, usefulness.

Utterly — perfectly, completely, fully.

V

Vacant—void, empty, devoid, unused.

Vague—unsettled, indefinite.

Vain—conceited, useless, fruitless, idle, ineffectual.

Valedictory — farewell, taking leave.

Valuable—expensive, costly, precious, useful, worthy, estimable.

Value—price, worth, rate, appreciation, estimation, account, appraise, assess, compute, regard, respect.

Vanity—pride, haughtiness, conceit, arrogance.

Vanquish — subdue, overcome, slay, conquer, confute, subjugate.

Variable—transitory, capricious, fickle, unsteady, changeable, versatile, wavering.

Variation — deviation, change, variety, vicissitude.

Variety—diversion, change, difference.

Various — sundry, different, diverse.

Vehement — hot, eager, ardent, fiery, passionate, violent, impetuous.

Velocity—speed, celerity, swiftness, fleetness, rapidity, quickness.

Venerate — worship, reverence, respect, adore.

Veracity—honesty, truth, integrity.

Verbal—oral, vocal.

Vestige — evidence, mark, trace, track.

Vexation — chagrin, uneasiness, trouble, sorrow, mortification.

Vicinity—locality, neighborhood, nearness, section.

View—picture, prospect, survey, landscape, see, look, behold.

Vigorous — robust, active, energetic, powerful, agile, forcible, potent.

Violent—turbulent, boisterous, impetuous, furious.

Virtue—chastity, purity, efficacy, goodness.

Visible — apparent, discernible, evident, plain, distinct, manifest, doubtless, obvious.

Visionary — fanatic, enthusiast, dreamer, imaginary, fanatical.

Volatility—lightness, flightiness, levity, giddiness, sprightliness, liveliness.

Vouch—assure, warrant, affirm, aver, protest, attest.

Vulgar—ordinary, common, low, mean.

W

Wages—stipulation, hire, salary, pay, allowance.

Wakeful—vigilant, attentive, observant, watchful.

Wander — roam, stroll, ramble, rove, range, journey.

Want—indigence, need, poverty, lack.

Wares—goods, merchandise, commodity.

Warlike—military, martial.

Warmth — fervor, ardor, cordiality, animation, heat, fervency, vigor, glow, zeal, vehemence.

Warning—notice, advice, monition, caution.

Wary—discreet, guarded, watchful, cautious, circumspect.

Waste — loose, dissipate, spend, expend, consume, lavish, squander.

Wasteful—profuse, extravagant, lavish, prodigal.

Watchful — cautious, observant, vigilant, careful, circumspect, attentive, wakeful.

Waver — hesitate, vacillate, fluctuate, scruple, to be undetermined.

Way—plan, method, course, manner, system, means, fashion, road, route.

Weak—infirm, feeble, unfeebled, debilitated, enervated.

Wealth—opulence, riches, affluence.

Weakness—debility, feebleness, frailty, infirmity, languor, failing, imbecility, silliness, folly.

Weariness — languor, lassitude, tediousness, fatigue.

Weary—annoy, distress, harass, jade, tire, vex, perplex, subdue.

Wedding—marriage, nuptials.

Weight—load, burden, heaviness, gravity, importance, signification.

Welcome — desirable, agreeable, grateful, acceptable.

Wherefore — consequently, accordingly, so, then, therefore, thence, hence.

Whiten—blanch, fade, bleach.

Whole—undivided, complete, entire, perfect, total, uninjured, sum.

Wicked—sinful, guilty, unjust, flagrant, impious, atrocious, villainous, criminal, depraved, outrageous.

Wily — cunning, artful, subtle, crafty.

Wisdom — foresight, prudence, knowledge, understanding.

Withdraw—retreat, recede, go back, retire, take back, retrograde.

Withhold — forbear, refrain, refuse, hinder, keep back.

Wonder—astonishment, marvel, surprise, admiration, amazement.

Wonderful — strange, curious, astonishing, surprising, marvelous, admirable.

Worthy — estimable, deserving, meritorious.

Wretched—unhappy, miserable.

Writer—author, scribe.

Y

Yearly—annually.

Yet—but, however, notwithstanding, still, nevertheless.

Yield—comply, conform, concede, allow, produce, permit, resign, surrender.

Z

Zeal—warmth, ardor, fervor, enthusiasm.

Zealous—concerned, earnest, ardent, fervent, anxious, warm, enthusiastic.

OU have thoughts that you wish to communicate to another through the medium of a letter. Possibly you have a favor to bestow. Quite as likely you have a favor to ask.

In either case you wish to write that letter in a manner such as to secure the respect and consideration of the person with whom you correspond.

The rules for the mechanical execution of a letter are few; understanding and observing the rules already considered for composition, the writer has only to study perfect naturalness of expression, to write a letter well.

Style and Manner.

The *expression* of language should, as nearly as possible, be the same as the writer would speak. A letter is but a talk on paper. The *style* of writing will depend upon the terms of intimacy existing between the parties. If to a superior, it should be respectful; to inferiors, courteous; to friends, familiar; to relatives, affectionate.

Originality.

Do not be guilty of using that stereotyped phrase,

Dear Friend;

    I now take my pen in hand to let you know that I am well, and hope you are enjoying the same great blessing.

Be original. You are not exactly like any one else. Your letter should be a representative of yourself, not of anybody else. The world is full of imitators in literature, who pass on, leaving no reputation behind them. Occasionally originals come up, and fame and fortune are ready to do them service. The distinguished writers of the past and present have gone aside from the beaten paths. Letter writing affords a fine opportunity for the display of originality. In your letter be yourself; write as you would talk.

* In the preparation of this chapter the author gathered many valuable suggestions from "Frost's Original Letter-Writer," and other works on epistolary correspondence, published by Dick & Fitzgerald, New York.

PARTS OF A LETTER.

> _Date._
>
> _Complimentary address._
>
> _Body of the Letter._
>
> _Complimentary closing._
>
> _Signature._
>
> _Name._
>
> _Address._

Purity of Expression.

Bear in mind the importance, in your correspondence, of using always the most chaste and beautiful language it is possible to command, consistent with ease and naturalness of expression. Especially in the long letters of friendship and love — those missives that reveal the heart—the language should show that the heart is pure. Let your letter be the record of the fancies and mood of the hour; the reflex of your aspirations, your joys, your disappointments; the faithful daguerreotype of your intellectuality and your moral worth.

You little dream how much that letter may influence your future. How much it may give of hope and happiness to the one receiving it. How much it may be examined, thought of, laughed over and commented on; and when you suppose it has long since been destroyed, it may be brought forth, placed in type, and published broadcast to millions of readers.

When, in after years, the letter you now write is given to the world, will there be a word, an expression, in the same that you would blush to see in print?

Write in the spirit of cheerfulness. It is unkind to the correspondent to fill the sheet with petty complainings, though there are occasions when the heart filled with grief may confide all its troubles and sorrows to the near friend, and receive in return a letter of sympathy and condolence, containing all the consolation it is possible for the written missive to convey.

The length of letters will depend upon circumstances. As a rule, however, business letters should be short, containing just what is necessary to be said, and no more.

Form.

To be written correctly according to general usage, a letter will embrace the following parts: 1st, the date; 2nd, complimentary address; 3rd, body of the letter; 4th, complimentary closing; 5th signature; 6th, superscription.

The above shows the position of the several parts of an ordinary letter.

Position of the Various Parts.

The following position of the several parts of a letter should be observed:

1. Write the date near the upper right hand corner of the sheet.
2. Commence the complimentary address on the line next beneath one inch from the left side of the sheet.
3. The body of the letter should be commenced nearly under the last letter of the complimentary address.
4. Begin the complimentary closing on the line next beneath the body of the letter, one half of the distance from the left to the right side of the page.
5. The center of the signature may be under the last letter of the complimentary closing.
6. The name and address of the person written to should come on the line beneath the signature, at the left of the sheet.

The Complimentary Address.

Of late years it has become common, in business letters, instead of giving name and address at the close, to write the same at the commencement; thus,

To the Business Man.

Mr. William B. Ashton,
Washington, D. C.
Dear Sir:
Your note of the 1st inst. received, etc.

To the Married Woman.

Mrs. Helen R. King,
Baltimore, Md.
Dear Madam:
Enclosed find check for, etc.

To the Unmarried Woman.

Miss Harriet A. Kendall,
Lowell, Mass.
In reply to your favor of the 4th ult., etc.

Note.—It is customary to address the married woman by the name which she uses on her cards. It is optional with the lady whether she uses her own name, "Mrs. Helen R. King," or that of her husband, "Mrs. Chas. H. King."

FORM OF A LETTER.

(Date.)
Olney, England, June 16, 1769.

(Complimentary Address.)
My Dear Friend:

(Body of the Letter.)
I am obliged to you for your invitation, but being long accustomed to retirement, which I was always fond of, I am now more than ever unwilling to visit those noisy scenes which I never loved, and which I now more than ever abhor. I remember you with all the friendship I ever professed, which is as much as I ever entertained for any man.

I love you and yours. I thank you for your continued remembrance of me, and shall not cease to be their and your

(Complimentary Closing.)
Affectionate Friend,

(Signature.)
William Cowper.

(Name.)
To Joseph Hill,

(Address.)
London.

Kinds of Paper to Use.

Be particular to use a sheet appropriate in shape to the purpose for which it is employed. Paper is now manufactured of every size adapted to the wants of any article written. The names of the various kinds of paper in general use are *Legal-cap, Bill-paper, Foolscap, Letter-paper, Commercial-note, Note-paper* and *Billet.*

In the writing of all *Legal Documents,* such as wills, taking of testimony, articles of agreement, etc., legal cap is generally used, characterized by a red line running from top to bottom of the sheet.

For *Bills,* paper is commonly ruled expressly for the purpose, and generally bears the name and business advertisement of the person using the same, at the top.

When writing *Notes, Orders, Receipts, Compositions, Petitions, Subscription Headings, etc.,* foolscap paper is used.

For the ordinary friendship letter or other

long letter, it is best to use letter paper, which in size is four-fifths the length of foolscap.

The common *Business Letter* should be so brief as generally to require but one page of commercial note, which is somewhat narrower and shorter than letter paper.

Note and billet paper are the smallest sheets made, being suitable for *Notes of Invitation, Parents' Excuses* for children to teachers, and other written exercises that are very brief.

Etiquette of Letter Writing.

As a rule, every letter, unless insulting in its character, requires an answer. To neglect to answer a letter, when written to, is as uncivil as to neglect to reply when spoken to.

In the reply, acknowledge first the receipt of the letter, mentioning its date, and afterwards consider all the points requiring attention.

If the letter is to be very brief, commence sufficiently far from the top of the page to give a nearly equal amount of blank paper at the bottom of the sheet when the letter is ended.

Should the matter in the letter continue beyond the first page, it is well to commence a little above the middle of the sheet, extending as far as necessary on the other pages.

It is thought impolite to use a half sheet of paper in formal letters. As a matter of economy and convenience for business purposes, however, it is customary to have the card of the business man printed at the top of the sheet, and a single leaf is used.

In writing a letter, the answer to which is of more benefit to yourself than the person to whom you write, enclose a postage stamp for the reply.

Letters should be as free from erasures, interlineations, blots and postscripts as possible. It is decidedly better to copy the letter than to have these appear.

A letter of introduction or recommendation, should never be sealed, as the bearer to whom it is given ought to know the contents.

Titles.

IT IS customary, in the heading of petitions to persons in official positions, in the complimentary address of a letter, and in superscriptions, to give each their proper title. These are divided into titles of respect, military, and professional titles.

Titles of respect are:—*Mr.*, from *Master*; *Mrs.*, from *Mistress*; *Miss*, from the French, *De-moi-selle*; *Esq.*, from *Esquire*, an English Justice of the Peace, or member of the legal profession, but applied very indiscriminately to males throughout this country generally.

Two titles of the same class should not be applied to the same name. Thus, in addressing John Smith, do not say *Mr.* John Smith, *Esq.*; though we may say *Mr.* John Smith, or John Smith, *Esq.*

If the profession of the person addressed be known, the professional title alone should be used. If the person be entitled to two titles the highest is given.

Titles of respect are usually placed before the name; as, *Mr.*, *Hon.*, *Rev.*, *Dr.*, and military titles.

Professional titles sometimes precede and sometimes follow the name: as, *Dr.* John Smith, or John Smith, *M. D.*; *Prof.* John Smith, or John Smith, *A. M.*

The following list illustrates the various titles used for the different ranks, among individuals, either in the complimentary address or superscription on the envelope.

To Royalty.
"*To the King's Most Excellent Majesty.*"
"*To the Queen's Most Excellent Majesty.*"
"*To his Royal Highness, Albert Edward, Prince of Wales.*"

In like manner all the other members, male and female, of the Royal family are addressed.

To Nobility.
"*To his Grace the Duke of Argyle.*"
"*To the Most Noble the Marquis of Westminster.*"
"*To the Right Honorable the Earl of Derby.*"
"*To the Right Honorable Lord Viscount Sidney.*"
"*To the Honorable Baron Cranworth.*"

The wives of noblemen have the same titles as their husbands; thus,

"*To her Grace the Duchess of Argyle.*"
"*To the Most Noble the Marchioness of Westminster.*"
"*To the Right Honorable the Countess of Derby.*"
"*To the Right Honorable the Viscountess Sidney.*"
"*To the Honorable the Baroness Cranworth.*"

The title of *Honorable*, in great Britain, is applied to the younger sons of noblemen (the elder son taking, by courtesy, the title next in rank below that of his father). It is also given to members of parliament and to certain persons holding positions of honor and trust.

To Baronets.
"*Sir Walter Scott, Bart.*"

To Knights.
"*Sir William Armstrong, Kt.*"

Ellsworth's "Text-Book on Penmanship" gives the following classification of the various titles used in the United States.

Titles of Honor, Profession and Respect.

"*His Excellency Richard Roe.*"	President of the United States, Governor of any State, or Minister to Foreign Countries.
"*Honorable Richard Roe.*"	Vice-President, Senators and Representatives of the U. S., Lieut.-Gov. of State, State Senators and Representatives, Judges, Mayors, Consuls, Ministers Abroad, and Heads of Executive Departments of the General Government.
"*Rev.* Richard Roe, D D."	Doctor of Divinity.
"Richard Roe, Ll. D."	Doctor of Laws.
"Richard Roe."	Minister of the Gospel.
"*Dr.* Richard Roe."	Physician and Surgeon.
"*Prof.* Richard Roe."	Professor or teacher of any art or science.
"Richard Roe, Esq."	Member of the legal Fraternity.
"*Mr.* Richard Roe."	Non-professional gentleman
"Richard Roe."	Plain signature.
"Richard X Roe."	Unable to write his own name.

Titles of the Dignitaries, Prelates, Clergy, and Other Officers of the Roman Catholic Church.

Of the Pope—*His Holiness* Pope Leo XIII.
Of a Cardinal—*His Eminence* John, Cardinal McCloskey.
Of an Archbishop—*Most Rev.* T. J. Burroughs, D.D.
Of a Bishop—*Rt. Rev.* Thomas Foley, D.D.
Of a Vicar-General—*Very Rev.* J. D. Halbert, D.D.
Of a Priest—*Rev.* Patrick Kelly, P.P.
Of Directors of Parish Schools—{ *Rev. Provincial* James Rice. / *Rev. Bro. Director* Henry Baker.
Of a Directress of a Seminary—*Madame* De Vincent.
Of a Teacher of a Seminary—*Sister Le Clerc.*
Of a Lady Superintendent of a Convent—*Sister Superior* Laflange.
Of a Lady Superintendent of a Catholic Orphan Asylum — *Mother Superior* St. Agnes.

Military Titles in the United States.

The following are addressed as *General, Colonel, Major, Captain, Lieutenant, Corporal,* or *Sergeant,* according to their rank:

COMMISSIONED OFFICERS.	
General of the Army.	Captain.
Lieutenant-General of the Army.	Chaplain.
Major-General.	Adjutant.
Adjutant-General.	First Lieutenant.
Inspector-General.	Second Lieutenant.
Quartermaster-General.	NON-COMMISSIONED OFFICERS.
Commissary-General.	Sergeant Major.
Paymaster-General.	Quartermaster-Sergeant.
Surgeon-General.	Sergeant.
Brigadier-General.	Corporal.
	Company Clerks.

Brigade-Inspector.	Drum-Major.
Colonel.	Fife-Major.
Lieutenant-Colonel.	Hospital-Stewards.
Major.	

Titles and Names of Naval Officers.

The only titles generally used among naval officers are those of *Admiral, Commodore, Captain* and *Lieutenant.*

Rear-Admiral.	Second Assistant-Engineer.
Vice-Admiral.	Third Assistant-Engineer.
Commodore.	Naval Constructor.
Captain.	Navy Agent.
Commander.	Purser, or Storekeeper.
Lieutenant-Commander.	Secretary to Commander.
First Lieutenant.	Navy-yard Clerks.
Second Lieutenant.	Bandmaster.
Master.	Musicians.
Ensign.	Mate—First, Second, and Third.
Midshipman.	Quartermaster.
Fleet Surgeon.	Master-at-Arms.
Ship's Surgeon.	Ship's Corporal.
Passed Surgeon.	Section Captain.
Assistant Surgeon.	Boatswain.
Retired Surgeon.	Coxswain.
Paymaster.	Carpenter.
Assistant Paymaster.	Sailmaker.
Chaplain.	Gunner.
Professor of Mathematics.	Armorer.
Engineer-in-Chief—on shore.	Quarter-Gunner.
Chief Engineer—on ship.	Seamen.
First Assistant-Engineer.	Marines.

Superscriptions.

NVELOPES that are perfectly plain, for ordinary letter writing, are regarded as in much the best taste. Ladies do well to use white. Buff, light straw color, or manila answer for business purposes, though it is always in good taste to use white.

The upper side of the envelope is that containing the flap. Care should be observed, in writing the superscription on the letter, to have the same right side up.

Extensive practice enables business men to write comparatively straight upon the envelope, without the aid of a line. The inexperienced penman may be aided in writing on the buff colored envelope by lead pencil lines, which should never be used, however, unless completely erased by rubber after the ink is dry.

Care should be taken to write upon the envelope very plainly, giving the full name and title of the person addressed, with place of residence written out fully, including town, county, State, and country if it goes abroad. The designation of the street, number, drawer, etc., when written upon the letter, is explained elsewhere.

For light colored envelopes, a piece of paper a little smaller than the envelope may be ruled with black ink over the blue lines, thus, and placed inside.

A scrap of paper, ruled like this, when placed
inside a light-colored envelope, will enable the
person writing on the same to trace distinctly
these lines, and thus write the superscription
straight.

In writing the superscription, commence the name a little to the left of the center of the envelope. The town, on a line beneath, should extend a little to the right of the name. The State, next below, should stand by itself still further to the right. The county may be on the same line with the State, towards the left side of the envelope; thus,

FORM OF SUPERSCRIPTION ON ENVELOPES.

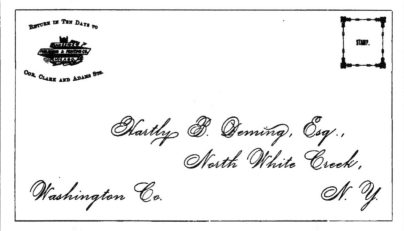

For the convenience of the mailing clerk in handling the letter, the postage stamp should be placed at the upper right hand corner of the envelope.

If the town is a large metropolis, the county may be omitted. In that event the street and number are usually given, or the post office box. Each should be written very conspicuously upon the envelope, for the convenience of the post office clerk and the mail carrier; thus,

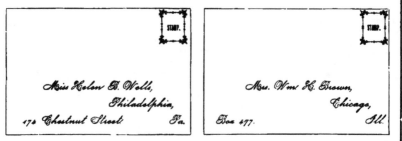

If written in the care of any one, the following may be the form :

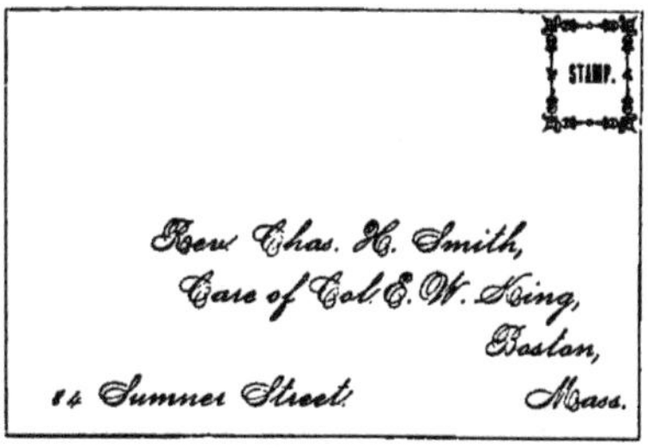

> STAMP.
>
> *Rev. Chas. H. Smith,*
> *Care of Col. E. W. King,*
> *Boston,*
> *14 Sumner Street.* *Mass.*

It is usually safest, in nearly all cases, to give the county, even if the town is well known; thus,

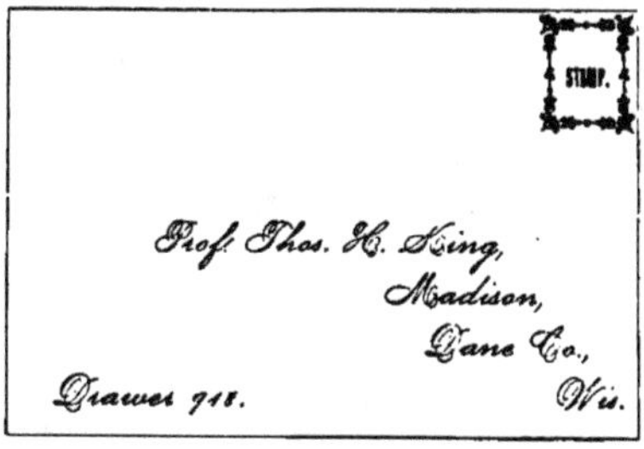

> STAMP.
>
> *Prof. Thos. H. King,*
> *Madison,*
> *Dane Co.,*
> *Drawer 918.* *Wis.*

If, after remaining in the office at its destination a certain length of time uncalled for, the writer is desirous of having the letter forwarded or returned, the same may be indicated upon the outside of the envelope ; thus,

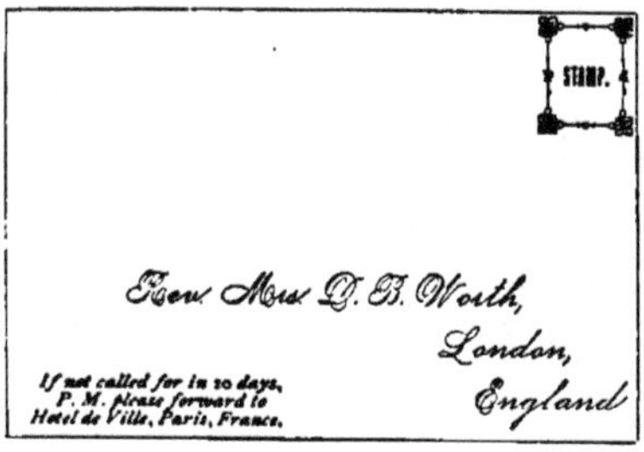

> STAMP.
>
> *Rev. Miss D. B. Worth,*
> *London,*
> *England*
>
> *If not called for in 10 days,*
> *P. M. please forward to*
> *Hotel de Ville, Paris, France.*

Tourists, when receiving letters abroad, frequently have their letters directed in the care of the bankers with whom they deal when on the continent, the form of superscription being thus :

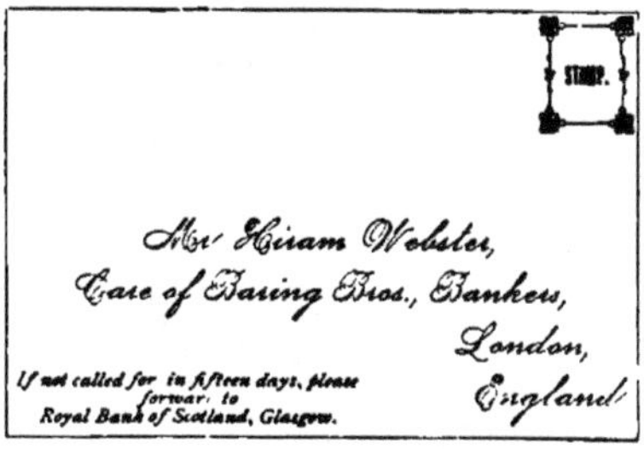

> STAMP.
>
> *Mr. Hiram Webster,*
> *Care of Baring Bros., Bankers,*
> *London,*
> *England*
>
> *If not called for in fifteen days, please*
> *forwar: to*
> *Royal Bank of Scotland, Glasgow.*

Letter Sent by a Private Party,
Acknowledging on the envelope obligation to the person carrying the same.

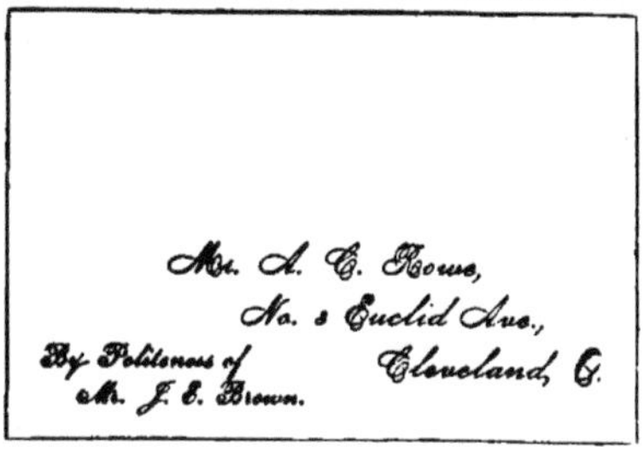

> *Mr. A. C. Rowe,*
> *No. 2 Euclid Ave.,*
> *Cleveland, O.*
> *By Politeness of*
> *Mr. J. E. Brown.*

Letter to a Person in the immediate Vicinity
Sent by carrier, but not through the mail.

> *Miss Lizzie Walker.*
> *Presented.*

Protect—uphold, guard, shield, maintain, defend, cherish, foster, patronise.

Protract—withhold, retard, prolong, delay, defer, postpone.

Proud—haughty, assuming, arrogant, lofty, vain, conceited.

Proverb—maxim, saying, adage.

Provide—procure, furnish, supply, prepare.

Provident—cautious, prudent, economical, careful.

Proviso—requirement, condition, stipulation.

Provoke—excite, irritate, enrage, aggravate, exasperate, tantalise.

Prudence—forethought, carefulness, wisdom, discretion, judgment.

Publish—announce, promulgate, proclaim, advertise, declare.

Puerile—infantile, boyish, childish, juvenile.

Pull—bring, haul, draw, drag.

Punctual—prompt, particular, exact.

Punish—whip, chastise, correct, discipline.

Pursue—follow, prosecute, chase, persist, continue, persevere.

Puzzle—confound, perplex, embarrass, bewilder, entangle.

Q

Quack—imposter, pretender, empiric, charlatan.

Qualified—capable, fit, adapted, competent.

Quarrel—fight, affray, riot, contest, battle, contention, altercation, dispute, tumult.

Query—question, interrogatory, inquiry.

Question—ask, examine, doubt, dispute, consider, inquire, interrogate.

Questionable—suspicious, doubtful.

Quick—rapid, active, lively, swift, prompt, expeditious, brisk.

Quiet—calm, repose, tranquillity, rest, ease, peaceable, placid, still.

Quit—depart, leave, resign, abandon, forsake, relinquish.

Quota—rate, share, proportion.

Quote—copy, relate, cite, adduce.

R

Race—lineage, family, breed, generation, course.

Radiance—light, glory, brightness, brilliancy.

Rage—indignation, anger, fury.

Raise—heighten, elevate, exalt, erect, collect, propagate.

Rank—class, degree, place, position.

Ransom—purchase, free, redeem.

Rapacious—voracious, greedy, ravenous.

Rapidity—swiftness, fleetness, celerity, speed, agility, velocity.

Rapture—joy, delight, transport, ecstasy.

Rare—scarce, uncommon, excellent, singular, unusual, incomparable, raw.

Rash—impulsive, hasty, violent, thoughtless, headstrong.

Rate—price, quota, proportion, ratio, value, degree, assessment.

Ravenous—voracious, rapacious, greedy.

Ray—dawn, beam, gleam, streak, glimmer.

Real—certain, true, genuine, positive, actual.

Realise—reach, procure, achieve, consummate, accomplish, effect.

Reason—purpose, proof, motive, argument, origin, understanding.

Reasonable—fair, probable, just, moderate, equitable, honest, rational.

Rebuke—reprimand, reproach, reproof, censure.

Recant—revoke, recall, renounce, withdraw, retract, abjure.

Recede—retire, retrograde, fall back, retreat.

Recite—repeat, rehearse.

Reckon—count, number, estimate, calculate, compute.

Reclaim—reform, recover, correct.

Recollection—memory, remembrance, reminiscence.

Recompense—satisfaction, pay, price, reward, equivalent, remuneration.

Reconcile—propitiate, conciliate.

Recruit—repair, retrieve, replace, recover.

Rectify—mend, improve, correct, amend, reform.

Redeem—restore, rescue, recover, ransom.

Redress—relief, remedy.

Refer—propose, suggest, allude, intimate, hint.

Refined—graceful, genteel, polished, polite, elegant.

Reform—correct, amend, rectify, improve, better.

Refractory—unmanageable, unruly, contumacious, perverse.

Refrain—forego, forbear, spare, abstain.

Regale—refresh, entertain, feast, gratify.

Regard—respect, esteem, value, reverence, mind, heed.

Regardless—careless, negligent, indifferent, unconcerned, unobservant, heedless.

Region—section, quarter, district, country.

Regret—sorrow, complaint, grief, lament.

Regulate—control, rule, direct, govern, dispose, adjust.

Rehearse—detail, repeat, recite, recapitulate.

Reject—refuse, deny, decline, repel.

Rejoinder—response, answer, reply.

Reliance—trust, belief, repose, confidence, dependence.

Relieve—assist, help, succor, aid, alleviate, mitigate, support.

Religious—pious, devout, holy.

Remain—continue, stay, abide, tarry, sojourn.

Remainder—rest, residue, remnant.

Remark—comment, observation, note.

Reminiscence—recollection, remembrance.

Remiss—heedless negligent, inattentive, careless, thoughtless.

Remit—send, transmit, liberate, abate, forgive, pardon, relax.

Remorse—penitence, contrition, distress.

Renew—revive, refresh, renovate.

Renounce—leave, resign, abdicate, abandon, forego, relinquish, quit.

Renown—reputation, celebrity, fame.

Repair—improve, retrieve, recover, restore.

Reparation—restitution, restoration, amends.

Repeal—cancel, annul, revoke, abolish, abrogate, destroy.

Repeat—detail, rehearse, recite.

Repetition—tautology, prolixity, iteration, reiteration.

Replenish—supply, fill, refill.

Repose—ease, sleep, rest, quiet.

Reproach—blame, reprove, censure, condemn, upbraid, reprimand.

Repugnance—aversion, abhorrence, antipathy, dislike, hatred.

Repugnant—hostile, adverse, opposite, contrary.

Reputation—repute, fame, character, honor, renown, credit.

Request—solicit, ask, demand, entreat, beg, beseech, implore.

Requisite—important, necessary, essential, expedient.

Research—investigation, study, examination, inquiry.

Resemblance—similarity, semblance, similitude, likeness.

Residence—home, abode, house, dwelling, domicile.

Residue—leavings, remainder, rest.

Resign—yield, abdicate, renounce, relinquish, forego.

Resignation—patience, endurance, submission, acquiescence.

Resist—endure, oppose, withstand.

Resolution—firmness, determination, fortitude, courage, decision.

Resort—visit, frequent, haunt.

Respect—esteem, regard, deference, attention, consideration, good-will, estimation.

Respectful—deferential, dutiful, obedient, civil.

Respite—delay, suspension, interval, reprieve.

Response—reply, answer, rejoinder.

Responsible—amenable, answerable, accountable.

Rest—quiet, ease, repose, intermission, stop, cessation, others, remainder.

Restore—cure, renew, return, repay, rebuild.

Restrain—confine, repress, restrict, coerce, limit, constrain.

Restrict—limit, circumscribe, hold, bind.

Result—effect, issue, ultimate, consequence, event.

Retain—hold, detain, keep, reserve.

Retard—hinder, defer, protract, postpone, delay, procrastinate, prolong, prevent, impede.

Retire—recede, withdraw, retreat, secede.

Retract—annul, take back, revoke, recant, recall.

Retrieve—renew, recover, regain.

Reveal—impart, divulge, communicate, disclose, expose.

Revenge—vindicate, avenge.

Revere—adore, worship, reverence, venerate.

Review—examine, survey, notice, revision.

Revive—enliven, renew, reanimate, refresh, renovate.

Revoke—cancel, annul, abolish, repeal, abrogate, efface, retract.

Reward—recompense, remuneration, compensation, satisfaction.

Riches—wealth, opulence, affluence.

Ridicule—deride, banter, laugh at.

Ridiculous—droll, absurd, ludicrous, preposterous, unreasonable, improbable.

Right—correct, just, honest, proper, privilege, claim, direct, straight, immunity.

Righteous—just, godly, upright, honest, incorrupt, virtuous.

Rite—form, custom, ceremony, observance.

Road—path, way, course, route.

Roam—wander, ramble, stroll, range, rove.

Room—chamber, space, place, apartment.

Rough—harsh, uncivil, rude, uncouth, unmannerly, unpolished, rugged, severe, stormy.

Round—globular, spherical, orb, circuit, tour.

Route—path, course, way, road.

Rude—rough, impertinent, coarse, impudent, unpolished, saucy, disagreeable, bold.

Rule—authority, law, regulation, government, custom, maxim, habit, precept, guide.

S

Sacred—holy, divine, devoted.

Sad—sorrowful, mournful, dejected, gloomy, melancholy.

Sagacity—perception, penetration, acuteness, discernment.

Salary—wage, pay, stipend, hire, reward, remuneration.

Sanction—maintain, sustain, uphold, countenance, ratify, support.

Sapient—discreet, wise, sage, sagacious.

Sarcasm—satire, irony, ridicule.

Satisfaction—compensation, remuneration, contentment, atonement, reward.

Saving—prudent, thrifty, frugal, economical, close, sparing, stingy, penurious.

Saying—adage, maxim, proverb, by-word, relating, speaking, uttering, communicating.

Scandal—disgrace, reproach, discredit, baseness, infamy.

Scarce—uncommon, unusual, singular, rare.

Scatter—disseminate, dissipate, spread, disperse.

Scent—odor, smell, perfume, fragrance.

Scoff—ridicule, sneer, jeer, gibe, belittle.

Scope—object, tendency, aim, drift.

Scruple—hesitate, doubt, fluctuate.

Scrupulous—truthful, upright, correct, careful, conscientious, cautious.

Scrutinise—search, examine, investigate.

Scurrilous—disgusting, abusive, offensive, insulting, insolent.

Search—inquiry, examination, scrutiny, pursuit, investigation.

Secede—withdraw, retire, recede.

Seclusion—quietude, privacy, solitude, retirement, loneliness.

Secondary—subordinate, inferior.

Secret—hidden, quiet, still, concealed, latent, mysterious, clandestine.

Secular—temporal, worldly.

Secure—safe, certain, confident, sure, procure, warrant.

Security—pledge, warranty, defense, guard, protection.

Sedate—serene, calm, unruffled, unconcerned, still, quiet, composed.

Seduce—decoy, betray, attract, allure.

See—examine, look, behold, observe, perceive, view.

Sense—idea, feeling, meaning, judgment, import, reason.

Sensitive—keen, susceptible, appreciative.

Sentence—mandate, judgment, decision, period, phrase, proposition.

Sentiment—expression, opinion, notion, feeling.

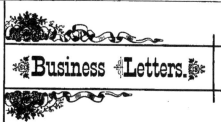

Business Letters.

 N letters of business, use as few words as possible.

2. Business letters should be promptly answered.

3. Use a clear, distinct writing, avoiding all flourish of penmanship or language.

4. Come at once to your subject, and state it so clearly that it will not be necessary to guess your meaning.

5. Give town, county, State and date explicitly. It is frequently of great importance to know *when* a letter was written.

6. Read your letter carefully when finished, to see that you have made no omissions and no mistakes. Also carefully examine your envelope, to see that it is rightly directed, with postage-stamp affixed.

7. Copy all business letters, of your own, by hand, or with the copying-press made for the purpose.

8. Send money by Draft, P. O. Money-Order, or Express, taking a receipt therefor; thus you have something to show for money, guarantying you against loss. Always state in your letter the amount of money you send, and by what means sent.

9. Write date, and by whom sent, across the end of each letter received, and file for future reference, fastening the letters together with rubber bands, or binding in a letter-file adapted to the purpose. The possession of a letter sometimes prevents litigation and serious misunderstanding.

Ordering Goods.

In ordering goods, state very explicitly the amount, kind, quality, color, shape, size, etc., and on what terms wanted. Whether you wish the same sent by freight or express, and *what* express. Much inconvenience is experienced among business men because of a neglect to designate explicitly what is wanted.

Should the writer wish to make suggestions, ask questions, or add other matter to the letter, which is foreign to the subject, such words should be placed entirely separate from the order. Of fifty or a hundred letters received to-day by the merchant, that one which is mixed up with complaints, enquiries, etc., will probably be laid over till to-morrow, or until time can be spared to read it through. Had the order been explicitly stated, and the suggestions placed elsewhere, the goods would have been forwarded immediately. It is, in fact, better to write the order on a separate sheet from the other matter.

Send your order, also, early enough to give yourself plenty of time in which to receive the goods before they are needed.

Books, being a common article ordered, may be taken as an example showing the importance of giving a careful description of the goods wanted. To illustrate: be explicit in giving name of book, name of author, by whom published, style of binding, price at which it is advertised, etc. Thus, a careless person, ordering of Harper & Brothers a United States History, will say, "Send me a United States History." Of course the first query of the shipping-clerk is, "*Whose* history?" There are many histories of the United States, published by as many different authors, and the clerk is liable to send the one not wanted; in which case the person ordering is very likely to unjustly blame Harper & Brothers.

If the writer should say, "Send me a copy of Willard's History of the United States, by Emma Willard, published by A. S. Barnes & Co., bound in cloth," there would be no liability to mistake. The following will serve as sample forms:

Form of Letter Ordering Books.

ROCKFORD, ILL., March 1, 18—.
MESSRS. JANSEN, MCCLURG & Co.,
Chicago, Ill.
Dear Sirs:
Enclosed find draft for $48.75, for which please send, by American Express,

10 Tennyson's Poems.	Published by Harper & Bros.	$1.25	$12.50
10 Thirty Years in the Harem.	" " "	1.50	15.00
10 Literature and Art, by M. Fuller.	" Fowler & Wells.	1.00	10.00
5 Getting on in the World, Mathews.	S. C. Griggs & Co.	2.25	11.25
			$48.75

Thanking you for the promptitude with which you have filled my orders heretofore, I am,
Very Respectfully,
CASH DOWN.

Form of an Order to a Dry-Goods Merchant.

April 5, 18—.
MESSRS. A. T STEWART & Co.,
New York.
Dear Sirs:
Enclosed find Post Office Order for $25, for which please send, by American Express, the following goods:

2 Lancaster Table spreads $3.50 .	$ 7 00
4 prs. Alexandre Kid Gloves $2.50 , No. 6 ., Brown, Green, Yellow, Black.	10 00
6 yds. Calico Brown, with small figure 25c \	2 00
12 " " White. " " pink dot "	3 00
2 Linen Handkerchiefs 50c .	1 00
4 prs. Ladies' Cotton Hose 50c ., No 9.	2 00
	$25 00

Direct to
MRS. MARY WILSON,
ELKHART, IND.

From a Young Man Commencing Business, to a Wholesale House, with Order.

RACINE, WIS., Aug. 10, 18—.
MESSRS. FIELD, LEITER & Co.,
Chicago, Ill.
Dear Sirs:
Having recently commenced business for myself, with fair prospects of success, I shall be pleased to open an account with your house, and trust it will be to our mutual advantage. Should you think favorably of the matter, you will please fill the accompanying order with the least possible delay, and on your best terms.
For testimonials, I refer you to Carson, Pirie, Scott & Co., of your city, by whom I have been, until recently, employed; but, as this is my first transaction with your house, upon forwarding me an invoice of goods, and deducting your usual discount for cash, I will remit a sight draft on the First National Bank of your city, for the amount, by return mail. Expecting your usual prompt attention, I am,
Yours Respectfully,
HENRY MAYNARD.

Reply from Wholesale House, with Invoice.

CHICAGO, Aug. 12, 18—.
MR. HENRY MAYNARD,
Racine, Wis.
Dear Sir:
We take pleasure in sending this day, by your order, the enclosed invoice of goods, amounting to $1,400, subject to 5 per cent discount for prompt cash.
Your references being entirely satisfactory, we have no hesitation in opening an account and allowing you our best terms. Trusting that the goods, which are shipped by express, will arrive safely and meet your favor, we are,
Yours Truly,
FIELD, LEITER & CO.

Requesting Information Concerning the Opening of a Store.

BOSTON, MASS., Sept. 18, 18—.
CHAS. H. WILLIAMS, Esq.,
Bennington, Vt.
Dear Sir:
My partner and myself being desirous of establishing a branch store in the clothing trade, I take the privilege of a friend in asking you to send me the number of clothing stores already in your village, and such other information as may be necessary, concerning the feasibility of establishing our business in your place. An early reply will greatly oblige,
Yours, Very Truly,
WM. B. HOPKINS.

Answer to the Foregoing.

BENNINGTON, VT., Sept. 20, 18—.
MR. WM. B. HOPKINS,
Boston, Mass.
Dear Sir:
I have taken occasion to enquire in relation to the extent and number of clothing stores in this place, and am happy to inform you that, while that department of trade is very fairly represented, there seems to be a good opening for a first-class store, such as your house would undoubtedly establish.
There is also a large store just vacated, in the center of the village, one of the best locations in the town, which can be had at reasonable rent. Hoping that you may carry out your design of locating here, and trusting that you may realize your expectations, I am,
Yours Truly,
CHAS. H. WILLIAMS.

Enquiry Concerning Real Estate.

SPRINGLAKE, MICH., Sept. 4, 18—.

MESSRS. S. TOWN & SON,
Aurora, Ill.,

Dear Sirs:
Having heard much said in praise of your beautiful city, particularly concerning railroad privileges, church and educational advantages, I have concluded to make your town my permanent place of abode, if I can locate myself aright, inasmuch as I have a large family of children to educate, and the numerous lines of railway radiating from your city will afford me the desired accommodations in my traveling agency.

My object in writing you at present is to learn your best terms for a residence containing not less than ten rooms, having from six to ten acres of land attached, situated not over a mile from the postoffice.

An immediate answer will oblige,
Your Obedient Servant,
HARVEY B. WILCOX.

Superintendent's Resignation.

GALESBURG, ILL., Sept. 1, 1878.

TO THE GENERAL SUPERINTENDENT OF THE C., B. & Q. R. R.,
Chicago, Ill.,

Dear Sir:
I herewith tender my resignation as local superintendent of the railroad repair works in this city, my labors in behalf of your company to cease October 1, 1878.

Respectfully Yours,
D. B. LAWSON.

Short Form of Resignation.

PITTSBURGH, PA., Dec. 2, 1879.

TO THE DIRECTORS OF THE PITTSBURGH GLASS WORKS,
Pittsburgh, Pa.,

Dear Sirs:
Please accept my immediate resignation as business manager of your manufactory.

Yours Respectfully,
WM. D. WEBSTER.

Clergyman's Resignation.

TO THE TRUSTEES OF FIRST BAPTIST CHURCH,
Pittsfield, Mass.,

Gentlemen:
It has now been seven years since the commencement of my pastoral connection with the First Baptist Church of this city. During this time the church society has grown in numbers, the sabbath school has been continually blessed by a large attendance, and the relations between pastor and congregation have always been of a most pleasant character. For these and other reasons it would be agreeable to continue my connection with the society longer; but other fields of labor affording wider and better opportunities, I feel it but just that I accept the privileges offered.

Thanking the congregation to whom I have ministered for their kind and unwavering support, and praying for your continued prosperity, I desire you to accept my resignation as pastor of your society, to take effect January 15, 1878.   Yours Very Respectfully,
CHAS. B. HANFORD.

Letter Complaining of Error in a Bill.

TROY, N. Y., June 10, 18—.

MESSRS. H. B. CLAFLIN & CO.,
New York,

Dear Sirs:
Upon examining bill accompanying your last lot of goods, I find that I am charged with four dozen pairs of cotton hose which I never ordered nor received. I enclose the bill and copy of the invoice of goods, that the error may be corrected. I am, gentlemen,
Yours Very Respectfully,
H. B. MOORE.

Answer to the Foregoing.

NEW YORK, June 11, 18—.

MR. H. B. MOORE,
Troy, N. Y.,

Dear Sir:
We regret that you were put to any trouble by the carelessness of a clerk, who, having proved himself incompetent, has left our service. We enclose the correct bill to you, and offer apologies for the error.   Truly Yours,
H. B. CLAFLIN & CO.

An Application for a Situation on a Railway.

DAVENPORT, IA., Jan. 15, 18—.

HON. B. C. SMITH,
Dear Sir:
Understanding that you are a shareholder in some of the principal railways, and on intimate terms with several of the directors, I venture to solicit your kind interest in behalf of my eldest son, William, now in his twentieth year. His education has been varied and useful, and his character, so far as I know, is above reproach.

For several years he has expressed a desire to enter the employ of a railroad company, and under the circumstances I venture to write to you, in the hope that, should you have it in your power to oblige me, you will kindly intercede in his favor. By doing so you will confer a lasting obligation both on him and me. I remain, sir,
Your Ob'd't Servant,

Recommending a Successor in Business.

MILWAUKEE, WIS., Dec. 24, 18—.

MESSRS. BELL & HARDY,
Dear Sirs:
We flatter ourselves that there are many friends among our connection who will regret that we are on the point of relinquishing business. In doing so our premises and stock of goods will be transferred to the hands of Messrs. Williams & Co., who will in future carry on the business on the same approved system and extensive scale as ourselves, provided they can rely upon receiving the patronage of our connection; in the hope of which, it is our pleasure and duty to present these gentlemen to your notice. We cannot speak too highly of the confidence we feel in their liberal mode of conducting mercantile transactions; and, in the hope that they may be honored with the same countenance received by ourselves from your respected firm, we beg to sign ourselves
Your Most Obedient Servants,
HOPE, GOOD & CO.

Notice of Having Forwarded Goods.

SOUTH HAVEN, MICH., Sept. 1, 18—.

MESSRS. HAGER, SPIES & CO.,
Chicago, Ill.,

Dear Sirs:
According to your order, I have shipped you this day, per Steamer Morning Star,

200 baskets Peaches,	(Marked H., S. & Co.)	
10 bbls. Sweet Potatoes,	"	" "
12 " Apples,	"	" "

Trusting that these will prove as satisfactory as those heretofore sent, and bring as good a price, I am
Respectfully Yours,
A. M. GOODFELLOW.

Requesting a Friend to Make Purchases.

KANKAKEE, ILL., Jan. 1, 18—.

DEAR MARY:
I am going to trespass on your kindness by asking you to make a few purchases for me. Enclosed find twenty dollars and a memorandum of what I want.

My household duties, combined with the objection I have to leaving my children at this season of the year in the care of servants, very closely confine me to my home, and are my excuse for troubling you.

We are in usual health, and I hope this note will find your family all well. With kind regards to Mr. Webster and love to children, I remain,

Your Sincere Friend,
HELEN D. WELLS.

To MRS. MAY BENSON,
— Michigan Ave., Chicago.

Requesting Settlement of Account.

MEMPHIS, TENN., Oct. 9, 18—

HIRAM BAXTER, Esq.,
Nashville, Tenn.

Sir:
I enclose your account. I shall feel obliged by your settlement at an early date, as I have several heavy payments to make. Trusting that you will excuse my troubling you, I am,

Yours Respectfully,
DELOS HARTWELL.

Reply to the Preceding.

NASHVILLE, TENN., Oct. 12, 18—

DELOS HARTWELL, Esq.,
Memphis, Tenn.

Sir:
As I am unable to send you the money for settlement of our account, without inconvenience, I enclose my acceptance for thirty days, which I trust you will be able to use.

Yours Truly,
HIRAM BAXTER.

Urging Payment of Rent.

COLUMBUS, O., March 11, 18—

MR. D. P. HOYT.
Dear Sir:
I have waited patiently for your convenience in the payment of rent for the house you are at present occupying. As, however, you have now been my tenant for four months without meeting any of the payments, which were to be made monthly, I feel obliged to remind you of the fact that there are now $80 due to me.

Trusting that you will give the subject your immediate attention, I am,

Yours Truly,
WEBSTER GREEN.

Letter to a Pioneer Settler in the West.

TOLEDO, OHIO, July 9, 18—

MR. MARTIN FULLER.
Dear Sir:
I take the liberty, though a stranger, of addressing you a few lines relative to the inducements for new settlers in your section of the country, having been recommended to do so through our mutual friend, Artemas Carter

As I have sold out my business in this city for ten thousand dollars, I am anxious to invest the proceeds in a large farm in a young State, feeling satisfied that a new country, like that you are now in, offers attractions for young and energetic men not found in the old cities.

You will much oblige me by giving information concerning climate, soil, water, timber, and other inducements for settling in your vicinity. Trusting that doing so will not seriously trouble you, and that I may hear from you soon, I remain,

Yours, Very Respectfully,
CHAS. W. CANFIELD.

Answer to the Foregoing.

BIG STRANGER, KANSAS, Aug. 15, 18—.

MR. CHAS. W. CANFIELD,
Toledo, Ohio.

Dear Sir:
Your welcome letter was received yesterday. I can assure you that I will be only too happy to furnish you all the information you desire relative to the prospects in this portion of Uncle Sam's domains.

I have now been two years in this place, and I can truly say that these years have been the happiest of my life. True, we have endured some hardships incident to pioneer life; but the glorious freedom from the frivolities of fashion and the formalities of aristocratic life, common to the old towns in the East, together with the pleasure one takes in making new improvements, all have combined to render our family perfectly delighted with the country.

For a quarter of the money in your possession, you can purchase all the land you will desire to cultivate; the remainder you can loan hereabouts, on bond and mortgage, at good interest.

The climate here is healthy and invigorating; the soil good, with running streams in sufficient abundance to water most of the farms. Plenty of building material and fuel can be had in the timber skirting the streams; and the prospect for the ultimate opening of the land in this section to a ready market, through several lines of railway now in contemplation, is very flattering. At present, however, the nearest station to my farm, on the stage route, is Chesterfield, thirty-four miles distant, at which place I will take great pleasure in meeting you, with my team, at any time you may appoint.

A very excellent farm, adjoining mine, can be bought for five dollars ($5) per acre. One corner of the land is crossed by a never-failing stream, with considerable timber along the same.

You will have to rough it for a little while after you arrive; but the neighbors will all turn out to aid in getting up your log house, after which you will be at home "under your own vine and fig-tree."

We have two rooms in our house, and, till your house is completed, we will give one of them to your family. It will seem a little odd, at first, for a fashionable family of six or eight persons to occupy one room, with wolf and deer skins for quilts and coverlets; but, by-and-by, when the young ladies find they are in just as good style as anybody else, they will dismiss their fastidiousness, and think it jolly fun. These privations that we at first endure are necessary, perhaps, to enable us to appreciate the fine homes which we all expect to have in the good time coming. Hoping to have the pleasure of welcoming yourself and family as neighbors, I am,

Yours, Very Truly,
MARTIN FULLER.

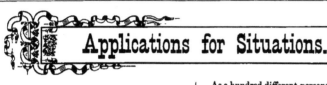

Applications for Situations.

Letters Answering Advertisements.

THE following advertisements, taken from metropolitan papers, are but samples of hundreds of such to be seen every day in the advertising columns of the leading daily newspapers in the great cities; showing that abundant opportunities . constantly offer for obtaining employment, the positions to be secured, however, by letters making application for them.

As a hundred different persons will sometimes make application for one position, which will be given to the individual writing the best letter, everything else being equal, this illustrates in a striking manner the importance of being able to write a letter elegantly and correctly.

Answer to an Advertisement for an Assistant Editor.

WANTED.

Miscellaneous.

WANTED—AN EDITORIAL ASSISTANT ON A literary paper. A thoroughly competent lady preferred. Address D 71, Herald office, New York.

WANTED—IN A GRAIN COMMISSION HOUSE, a smart lad for office work; must be a good penman. Address, in own handwriting, stating age and salary expected, W 32, Ledger office.

WANTED—A YOUNG LADY CLERK IN A DRY goods store. Must be accustomed to the business. Address, with reference, B 80, Picayune office.

WANTED—AN ASSISTANT BOOKKEEPER, one who writes neatly and rapidly; willing to work for a moderate salary, and who can bring A No. 1 recommendations. Address, stating experience and particulars, X. Y. Z., Bulletin office.

WANTED—AN EXPERIENCED BOOKKEEPER in a bank. Address, with reference, Z 61, Journal office.

WANTED—LADY COPYIST, ABLE TO WRITE A bold, distinct hand. Salary good. Address, in applicant's own handwriting, COPY, Republican office.

WANTED—A COMPETENT SALESMAN TO sell pianos—one who has experience and good references. Address, stating salary expected, PIANOS, Tribune office.

WANTED—AN ACCOMPLISHED, EDUCATED young lady as a companion, to travel for six months in Europe, with a gentleman, wife, and daughter. Must be a ready writer, a good conversationalist, and possess vivacity and pleasing manners. Wardrobe furnished, and money to pay all expenses. Address Z. B M., Commercial office, stating where an interview can be had.

Maplewood, Mass., April 1, 18—.

Dear Sir:

Observing the enclosed advertisement in this morning's "Herald," I improve the opportunity by writing you an application for the place, as I am at present disengaged.

I graduated four years ago at Mrs. Willard's Seminary, Troy, N. Y., since which time I conducted the literary department of Frank Leslie's "Magazine of Fashion" up to October last, when failing health, resulting from too much close confinement, compelled me to travel abroad, from which journey, principally through England and France, I have just returned, with health completely restored.

I beg to refer you to Mr. Leslie for testimonials. Being exceedingly fond of literary pursuits, I shall be happy to occupy the position you offer, if mutually agreeable.

Yours. Most Respectfully,

Harriet Sibley (May Myrtle)

General Directions.

Letters in reply to advertisements should be written immediately, else you may be too late.

Paste the advertisement at the head of your letter; thus it will be known exactly what your communication has reference to.

It is not necessary to speak much in praise of yourself, but you may state your reference, your experience, and qualifications fitting you for the position, the whole being told as briefly as possible.

Write your application yourself, your hand-writing and the manner of expressing yourself being the test by which the advertiser judges you. If you have written testimonials, copy the same, marking them as such, and enclose the copy.

From a Boy Applying for a Clerkship.

879 Market Street, Philadelphia, Pa., Nov. 4, 18—.

Dear Sir:

I notice in this morning's "Ledger" your advertisement of "a boy wanted in a grain commission house," which position I take the first opportunity to apply for.

I am fourteen years old, have been at school most of the time, winters, for the past seven years, and understand bookkeeping and conducting correspondence pretty well, having assisted my father much of the time while he was in the coal trade, which was about three years.

I am perfectly willing and ready to take my coat off and go right to work at handling grain or anything else in your line.

I refer you to Mr. Ira Belden, coal dealer, at 56 Benton street, who has always known me.

I will board at home, and will try to earn for you five dollars a week.

Very Respectfully Yours,

JOHN CLANCY.

From a Young Lady Applying for a Clerkship in a Store.

182 Murray St., Buffalo, N. Y., May 19, 18—.

Dear Sir:

I take the earliest opportunity of replying to the enclosed advertisement.

I have been for the past two years in the employ of Bennett & Hawley, dry-goods dealers, 492 Camden street, until the dissolution of their firm, about four weeks ago. I beg to refer you, for testimonials, to Mr. Chas. H. Bennett, of the firm of Snow, Williams & Bennett, 178 Harvard street, should you entertain my application.

Your Very Obedient Servant,

MARY H. BENSON.

Answering an Advertisement for a Bookkeeper.

1184 Longworth St., Cincinnati, O., May 1, 18—.

Dear Sir:

In reply to your advertisement in to-day's "Commercial" for a clerk or assistant bookkeeper, I beg to offer my services to your firm.

I have been in the employ of Mr. Wm. H. Wilson for the past four years, until he sold out his business a few days ago, having kept the books of his house during the time.

He permits me to refer to him for any testimonial of character or ability which you may require.

Should my application meet your views, it will be my earnest endeavor to faithfully and punctually fulfill the duties required. I have the honor to remain,

Yours, Very Respectfully,

HOMER BUXTON.

Answering an Advertisement for a Cook.

46 Wentworth Ave., Pittsburgh, Pa., March 17, 1873.

Mrs. D. N. Haskins.

Respected Madam:

Seeing an advertisement in this morning's "Press" for a good plain and fancy cook, I take the opportunity to apply for the situation.

I have been with my present mistress, Mrs. Burton, for three years, and only leave because she has rented her house for the summer, to make an extended visit among her relatives in New England.

I shall remain here until Tuesday next, unless I find a place sooner, and Mrs Burton will give you any information you may desire regarding my capacity.

I Remain, Very Respectfully,

SARAH E. WESTON.

Answer to an Advertisement for a Chambermaid.

(Advertisement pasted in.)

No. — St., Nashville, Tenn., Feb. 14, 18—.

Dear Madam:

In answer to the above advertisement, I beg to state that I am about to leave my present situation, as Mrs. Harrington, with whom I have been for the past six years, is about breaking up housekeeping; and I take the opportunity to apply for the position you offer.

Mrs. Harrington assures me that she will take pleasure in recommending me to any person who may apply to her concerning my industry and trustworthiness.

MARGARET BALLENTINE.

Application for a Situation as Gardener.

No. — 7th St., New York, June 10, 18—.

Dear Sir:

Understanding that you want a gardener, I beg to offer myself as a candidate to fill the place. I have had constant experience for ten years, both in nursery grounds and private gardens, and am thoroughly acquainted with the management of the greenhouse and hothouse.

The enclosed testimonials, from gentlemen for whom I have worked, will, I trust, prove satisfactory. My last employer, Mr. Snow, I would like to have you see personally concerning my fitness for the position. I am a married man, thirty-three years of age. If favorable to my application, please address as above, and oblige,

Your Obedient Servant,

JAMES H. HARPER.

Application for a Situation as Coachman.

178 —— St., Boston,
April 10, 18—.

Mr. John H. Williams.

Dear Sir:

Having been informed that you are in want of a coachman, I take the liberty of enclosing you the accompanying testimonials, to which I ask your attention. Though reared in Deerfield, I have been in Boston for the past fourteen years, having constantly had charge of horses during that time, as I did on the farm before leaving home.

As further evidence of my ability, I may mention that I had chief charge of the Tremont Street Livery Stable until the death of the owner, Mr. Paxton, after which the stock was sold and the stable closed.

Should my application meet your favor, I shall be glad to engage as your coachman, and will do all in my power to merit your approval.

Yours Respectfully,
HIRAM WILDER.

Application from a Governess Answering an Advertisement.

(Advertisement pasted in.)

No. 784 —— St., Troy, N. Y.,
July 18, 18—.

Mrs. C. B. Williams.

Dear Madam:

In answer to the above, I would say that I am seeking such a situation as you offer. My present term of teaching will close August 15th, at which time I would be ready to enter upon the work of superintending the education of your daughters.

I have, for several years, taught the higher English studies, besides German, Latin and drawing. For testimonials, I beg to refer you to the principal of my school, Rev. H. B. Watson.

Hoping that I may hear from you soon, and that we may make an arrangement mutually satisfactory, I remain,

Very Respectfully Yours,
HELEN B. CHANDLER.

Requesting the Character of a Governess.

No. 84 —— St., Troy, N. Y.,
July 19, 18—.

Rev. H. B. Watson,
Principal, Glenhaven Seminary.

My Dear Sir:

Having inserted an advertisement in the papers requiring the services of a governess competent to instruct my two daughters, I will esteem it a great favor if you will inform me concerning the ability of Miss Chandler to give instructions in the higher English studies, German and drawing, she having referred me to you.

I am especially desirous of securing the services of a young lady whose moral influence will guard my children from danger—one whose amiability of character will make her a pleasant companion as well as teacher. I am much pleased with the appearance of Miss Chandler, and, if your report is favorable, I shall not hesitate to perfect an engagement with her at once.

Yours, Very Respectfully,
CLARA B. WILLIAMS.

Favorable Reply to the Foregoing.

Glenhaven Seminary, N. Y.
July 21, 18—.

Mrs. Clara B. Williams.

Dear Madam:

Your letter of enquiry in regard to Miss Chandler is before me, in reply to which it affords me much pleasure to bear testimony to the high moral character, and superior intellectual culture, of which she is possessed. During five years' residence in our family she has ever been as one of our own household, and I can thus speak understandingly of her merits. She is thoroughly conversant with the higher English branches, and is quite fluent in Latin and German. Should you complete an engagement with her, I feel confident you will have every reason for being pleased with having done so.

Very Truly Yours,
HARVEY B. WATSON.

Unfavorable Reply to the Foregoing.

Glenhaven Seminary, N. Y.,
July 21, 18—.

Mrs. Clara B. Williams.

Dear Madam:

In reply to your polite inquiries, I am sorry to say that the educational acquirements of Miss Chandler, I fear, will not be up to the standard you require. While she has taught the higher English for some years, knowing, as I do, the proficiency of your daughters, I doubt if she is capable of advancing them in their studies. Another very unfortunate fault of which she is possessed, which causes me to dispense with her services at the close of the present term, is her failure to sufficiently command her temper. In other respects I have nothing to say to her prejudice.

Regretting that I cannot give a more favorable reply to your letter, I remain, Your Most Obedient Servant,
HARVEY B. WATSON.

Answering an Advertisement for an Apprentice to a Dressmaker.

(Advertisement pasted in.)

Mrs. Harriet Munson. Chicago, Ill., Aug. 1, 18—.

Dear Madam:

In answer to the above, I respectfully apply for the situation. Though I never took up the business as a trade, I have long been in the habit of doing all the dressmaking for our family, and feel myself competent to do all plainer kinds of sewing neatly and rapidly.

Having recently, by the death of an only brother, been thrown upon my own resources, I am thus induced to seek a position which I think I will enjoy.

Hoping that you will accept my services, I remain,

Very Respectfully Yours,
PAMELIA HARRISON.

Answer to an Advertisement for a Music-Teacher.

Walnut Grove Academy, Mass.,
June 9, 18—.

Col. H. B. Darling.

Dear Sir:

Seeing your advertisement in to-day's "Journal," I write to offer my services as music-teacher in your family.

I am a graduate of Music Vale Seminary, and have taught a music-class in this institution for the past three terms. My training has been with special reference to teaching the piano, the guitar, and vocal music.

I am permitted by Professor Weston, the teacher of music in the Academy, to refer to him for any testimonial of ability. I am,

Yours, Very Respectfully,
AMELIA D. PORTER.

Answering an Advertisement for an Apprentice to a Printer.

Troy Grove, Ill.,
Feb. 4, 18—.

Mr. A. B. Cook.

Dear Sir:

Having seen your advertisement in the last *Eagle*, I would respectfully apply for the position for my son Henry, who is anxious to learn printing. He is well versed in the common English branches, having been regular in attendance at the public school for the past seven years. He is now fifteen.

I would like to have you take him on trial for a few weeks, and, if he pleases you, will arrange to have him remain until he masters the trade. Respectfully Yours,
Z. K. HENDERSON.

Letters of Recommendation.

NOWLEDGE of persons recommended, of their fitness and capacity for the work they engage in, is always essential, before they can be conscientiously commended to others.

A letter of recommendation should be written in a plain hand, in as few words as can be used to express the idea distinctly.

A recommendation, after considering the moral character of the individual, should relate directly to the work of which the person makes a specialty.

An individual giving a recommendation is, in a certain sense, responsible for the character and ability of the person recommended; hence, certificates of character should be given with caution and care.

Recommending a Salesman.

SYRACUSE, N. Y., April 10, 18—.

MESSRS. DUTTON & BROWN.

Dear Sirs:

Your favor of the 4th inst., relative to the ability of Mr. Benjamin Walker, is received. We take great pleasure in testifying to his high moral worth and his business capacity. He was in our employ for four years, as a salesman, during which time his affability and uniform courtesy to customers, coupled with his truthful representations in regard to goods, made him a universal favorite.

Accurate in accounts, ready and graceful as a penman, attentive and kind to all, he is a most useful man in the counting-room; and the firm securing his services may be congratulated on their good fortune.

Very Truly Yours,
SMITH & PAXTON.

Recommending a Schoolmistress.

GLEN DALE SEMINARY,
March 1, 18—.

GEN. A. B. COTTRELL.

Dear Sir:

It gives me pleasure, in reply to your note of the 24th ult., to most cordially recommend Miss Fannie Chapman to the position of teacher of your village school.

As a graduate of this Seminary, and subsequently as a teacher, much of the time conducting the various classes alone, she has proven herself thoroughly competent to conduct a school under almost any circumstances.

Though very amiable, she is a strict disciplinarian, and thoroughly conversant with the ordinary branches of an English education.

Yours Respectfully,
DELOS SIMPSON,
Principal Glen Dale Seminary.

Recommending a Bookkeeper.

WHITEHALL, N. Y., Sept. 10, 18—.

Mr. Ransom Fellows having been in my employ for the past two years as a bookkeeper, it gives me great pleasure to testify to his ability. He is an upright, conscientious, exemplary young man, a good penman and accountant, and a most faithful clerk. He leaves my employ voluntarily, with my best wishes.

MARTIN BIGELOW.

Recommending a Waiter.

TREMONT HOUSE, CHICAGO,
Aug. 11, 18—.

Arthur Brooks, who has been in my employ for two years, has given entire satisfaction, both to myself and guests, as a table-waiter. Honest, obliging and neat, it affords me pleasure, as he now leaves my employ, to commend him as a first-class hotel waiter.

BROWN PORTER,
Steward, Tremont House.

Recommending a Cook.

HARRISBURG, PA., Dec. 20, 18—.

This is to certify that Catherine Miller did the cooking for my family some ten months, to my entire satisfaction, serving me both as a plain and fancy cook. She is very attentive to her work, and strictly honest and reliable.

MYRA D. ROWE.

Recommending a Washerwoman.

NEW ORLEANS, LA., May 7, 18—.

This certifies that Hannah Webber, who has been employed in my laundry for the past year, is an excellent washer and ironer, understanding fine starching, crimping, polishing, etc.

HELEN MAYDWELL.

Recommending a Porter.

CHARLESTON, S. C., Sept. 18, 18—.

Donald Kennedy, the bearer of this, has been in my employ, as a porter, for the last eighteen months. He is a strong, honest, reliable man, and always very punctual, careful, and faithful in the discharge of his duty.

JOHN H. BLISS.

Declining to Recommend a Cook.

SAVANNAH, GA., Oct. 10, 18—.

MRS. BALLARD:

In reply to your note of enquiry, I decline to recommend Bridget Mallory. She is both dishonest and addicted to intemperance.

HENRIETTA SANFORD.

EXPRESSIONS OF CONDOLENCE.

A LETTER of sympathy and condolence, though unpleasant to write, may afford inexpressible comfort to a friend in the hour of affliction.

Make your letter as brief, but earnest and sincere, as possible.

Do not commit the mistake of insinuating that the misfortune is the fault of your friend. Better leave the letter unwritten. Admit the loss. Do not attempt to make light of it. If you are satisfied that it will eventuate in a blessing, you may gently point the way, but with a full admission of the present deep affliction.

To a Friend, on the Death of a Husband.

NEWARK, O., Oct. 18, 18—.

DEAR FRIEND:

I know that no words can make amends for the great loss you have sustained. I deeply realize, from having passed through a similar bereavement, that expressions of condolence wholly fail to restore the loved and lost one, yet I cannot but hope that the heartfelt sympathy of a sincere friend will not be deemed intrusion on your grief.

It has been well said, that "we weep for the loved and lost because we know that our tears are in vain." I would ease your sorrow, and yet I know not how. We can only acknowledge that the affliction is God's will. Over in the beautiful land to which I trust your life-companion has gone, we may not doubt, he is free from the pains that he so long endured here; and when *we* gather at the river, is it not a sweet consolation to think that among the loved and lost he may meet you on the other side?

Commending you to Him who doeth all things well, I remain, in the tenderest friendship,

Your Sincere Friend,
WINFIELD BROWN.

To MRS. CLARA WAYLAND,
Columbus, O.

Reply to the Foregoing.

COLUMBUS, O., Oct. 20, 18—.

MY DEAR FRIEND:

I can scarcely express to you how grateful I am for your sympathizing letter, yet the loss of my husband has so prostrated me that I am hardly able to write this reply.

My friends assure me that time will reconcile me to my great bereavement. Yes, time, and the great consolation that you speak of, which comes from the hope that we will meet our friends in a world where partings are no more, will, I trust, enable me to bear my sorrow. God bless you for your thought of me in the dark hours, and your sweet words of consolation.

Your Friend,
CLARA WAYLAND.

To a Friend, on the Death of a Mother.

EVANSVILLE, TENN., Oct. 16, 18—.

FRIEND ALBERT:

I have just learned, on my return from a visit in the far West, of the death of your mother. Having suffered the loss of my mother when a child, I know how to sympathize with you in your affliction; though, fortunately for you, your mother lived to guide the footsteps of her boy till manhood's years had crowned his intellect with judgment and fixed moral principles. It can truly be said that, in the training of her family, in the church, in the social circle, she always did her duty nobly, and was an ornament to society. Ripened in years, and fully prepared for another state of existence, she passes on now to enjoy the reward of a life well spent on earth.

Restored to maidenhood prime, we cannot doubt that in the flowery walks of spirit life she is the same good woman that we knew so well here.

Truly Yours,
HARTLEY JONES.

To A. H. STEWART,
Belle Plain, Miss.

To a Friend, on the Death of a Brother.

LEXINGTON, MO., Dec. 10, 18—.

DEAR HENRY:

I have learned with profound regret of the death of your brother. I condole with you most sincerely on the sad event, and, if sympathy of friends can be any consolation under the trying circumstances, be assured that all who knew him share in your sorrow for his loss. There is, however, a higher source of consolation than earthly friendship, and, commending you to that, I remain,

Yours Faithfully,
SANFORD F. BARTON.

To a Friend, on the Death of a Wife.

BURLINGTON, IOWA, Nov. 10, 18—.

MY DEAR DELWIN:

    I know that this letter will find you filled with grief at the loss of your dear wife. You have, indeed, suffered a great affliction. A more faithful partner never lived, and few men, I venture to say, ever enjoyed more domestic tranquillity than yourself.

    A true wife, and a devoted mother! No higher eulogy can be pronounced upon any woman. How the little motherless children will miss her tender care! How those fragile little girls will miss her sweet presence at the evening hour, when she sat by the bedside and listened to their innocent prayers, soothing their little spirits as they dropped off to sleep! Truly the great central sun of your household has gone down, and I most truly, deeply sympathize with you in your affliction.

    Let us hope, however, in the language of Scripture, "I go to prepare a place for you," that, in the golden summer of another life, children, mother and father will gather again in a sweet reunion, where partings are unknown.

    Though the days are dark now, spring will come once more. Thus, I trust, pleasant days will come again for you and yours.

    Send both of the little girls to our home for a month's visit, and come yourself as soon as you can find time to do so. My previously arranged departure, to-morrow, prevents my visiting you.

Your Friend,
S. B. OSGOOD.

To D. B. MAXWELL,
    Henderson, Kentucky.

To a Friend, on the Death of a Sister.

AUBURN, N. Y., July 16, 18—.

DEAR FRIEND:

    I have learned, with sorrow, of the death of your sister Helen. Though I never knew her personally, I knew her so well through you, that it seems as if I, myself, had lost a very dear and intimate friend. I recollect her from that sweet face and gentleness of manner, as I saw her once in your company, that impressed me with the belief that she was one of the angelic ones of earth.

    I know how deeply you must have grieved at her death. No one could mourn her loss so truly as yourself. Younger than you, frail and delicate, her guardianship entrusted to yourself, confiding everything to you, it was natural that to a sister's affection should be added, also, almost a mother's love for your gentle sister Helen. She died, too, at a time when life was apparently all blossoming before her. How hard to reconcile ourselves to the loss of dear kindred, when their continued presence is so necessary to our happiness. But may we not hope that the same sweet voice, and gentle, confiding heart, that was so dear to sister and kindred here, is waiting for you in the summer land? "Not dead, but gone before."

    The loss of near friends thus calls for our contemplation of another life toward which we are all tending. You and I, dear M., have talked these matters over often. I know you expect to meet her on the other side; so do I. Believing that your faith in that golden, sunny Future, which you and I have so often considered, will sustain you, I am,

Your Ever Faithful Friend,
JAS. D. HENRY.

To a Friend, on the Death of a Daughter.

HARTFORD, CONN., Nov. 14, 18—.

MY DEAR FRIEND:

    It is with profound sorrow that I have heard of the death of dear Mary. While you have lost a dutiful and affectionate daughter, I have lost one of the dearest friends on earth. Outside of yourself, I am confident no one could more fully appreciate her loss than myself. We were so much together that I can hardly reconcile myself to the thought that I can no more meet her here. True, her death teaches us that, sooner or later, we must all make the journey across that mystic river. The angels called, and, in the ways of an all-wise Providence, it was best that she should go. We all have the ordeal to pass. Fortunate it would be if all could be as certain of being among the exalted angels as was our darling Mary. I will come and see you soon. *A propos*, I send you this little poem, "The Covered Bridge."

Your Friend,   MYRA.

THE COVERED BRIDGE.

BY DAVID BARKER.

Tell the fainting soul in the weary form,
  There's a world of the purest bliss,
That is linked, as the soul and form are linked,
  By a Covered Bridge, with this.

Yet to reach that realm on the other shore
  We must pass through a transient gloom,
And must walk, unseen, unhelped, and alone,
  Through that Covered Bridge—the tomb.

But we all pass over on equal terms,
  For the universal toll
Is the outer garb, which the hand of God
  Has flung around the soul.

Though the eye is dim, and the bridge is dark,
  And the river it spans is wide,
Yet Faith points through to a shining mount,
  That looms on the other side.

To enable our feet in the next day's march
  To climb up that golden ridge,
We must all lie down for one night's rest
  Inside of the Covered Bridge.

To a Friend, on the Death of an Infant.

PEMBERTON, Miss., Nov. 18, 18—.

MY DEAR FRIEND:

    I realize that this letter will find you buried in the deepest sorrow at the loss of your darling little Emma, and that words of mine will be entirely inadequate to assuage your overwhelming grief; yet I feel that I must write a few words to assure you that I am thinking of you and praying for you.

    If there can be a compensating thought, it is that your darling returned to the God who gave it, pure and unspotted by the world's temptations.

    The white rose and bud, I send, I trust you will permit to rest upon your darling's pillow.

    With feelings of the deepest sympathy, I remain, dear friend,

Yours, Very Sincerely,
MARION BRADSHAW.

To a Friend, on a Sudden Reverse of Fortune.

HANNIBAL, Mo., Aug. 16, 18—.

FRIEND STEWART:

    I regret to hear of your sudden and unexpected heavy loss, and hasten to offer you, not only my earnest sympathy, but aid in whatever way I can assist you.

    I know your energy and hopeful spirit too well to believe that you will allow this to depress or discourage you from further effort. Perhaps there is, somewhere, a blessing in this reverse. I have had my dark days, but I learned to trust the truth of that little stanza of Cowper:

"Judge not the Lord by feeble sense,
  But trust him for his grace;
Behind a frowning Providence
  He hides a smiling face."

    The child learns to walk after many falls, and many of our richest and most prosperous men have attained their eminence and wealth only by the experience resulting from failure.

    I predict that you will build on your ruins a brilliant future. How can I serve you? Let me know; by so doing, I shall understand that you have not ceased to value my friendship.

Sincerely Your Friend,
HERBERT D. WRIGHT.

To ROB'T H. STEWART,
    Singleton, Me.

Letters of Congratulation.

LETTERS of Congratulation are very properly written upon receiving intelligence of the sudden prosperity of a near and intimate friend.

They should be written as soon as possible after the occasion that calls them forth.

These letters will admit of an abundance of good-natured merriment.

Do not indulge in over-praise, or too much flowery exaggeration, lest your friend may doubt your sincerity.

No envy or discontent should show itself in such a letter. Nor should the same be marred by advice, bad news, the expression of any doubt, or any unfavorable prediction calculated to throw a cloud over the happiness of your friend.

Form of Letter Congratulating a Friend upon Election to Office.

Troy, N. Y., Feb. 1, 18—.

My Dear Friend Callie:

My newspaper informs me that the people of your County have shown their good judgment by selecting you to represent them as Superintendent of Public Schools. It affords me unfeigned pleasure to hear of the choice falling upon yourself. I am confident that no person in your district could fill the place more worthily.

Accept my congratulations.

Yours Truly,

S. C. Willing

To Miss Callie B. Spencer,
Cedar Grove, Ill.

Congratulating a Friend upon Receiving a Legacy.

APPLETON, WIS., Jan. 1, 18—.

FRIEND GEORGE:

I have learned to-day, through our friend Charlie Goodwin, of your good fortune in receiving a very material addition to your worldly possessions. Good! I congratulate you. I know of no one who more justly deserves good fortune, and of no person who will use it more worthily. You would be ever the same to me, whether good or ill success should attend your pathway. As it is, I take a friend's delight in congratulating you upon your fortune.

Your Friend,
DANIEL TEMPLETON.

Congratulating a Gentleman upon his Marriage.

KINGSTON, CANADA, April 4, 18—.

DEAR WILL:

I have just received a little missive, which informs me of two happy hearts made one. I wish you much joy. You have my earnest congratulations on the event, and good wishes for a long and serenely happy married life. May each succeeding year find you happier than the one before.

God bless you and yours, and surround you ever with his choicest blessings.

Your Friend,
JOHN K. BUEL.

Congratulating a Friend upon the Birth of a Son.

GRACELAND, FLA., Jan. 8, 18—.

DEAR CLARK:

Accept my warmest congratulations upon the birth of your son. May his years be long in the land which the Lord giveth him. May he honor his father and his mother, and be the blessing and support of their declining years. I anticipate holding the young gentleman on my knee, and will be over to see you in a few days.

My kindest regards to Mrs. Henry. I remain,

Faithfully Your Friend,
DEB. HARTWELL.

Congratulating a Friend upon the Twenty-fifth Anniversary of his Wedding Day.

DARTMOUTH, N. H., March 5, 18—.

MY DEAR MR. BANCROFT:

I acknowledge the receipt of a kind invitation to be present at the celebration of the twenty-fifth anniversary of your marriage. I have since learned that large numbers of your friends were present on the occasion, presenting you with an abundant and varied collection of silver, and other elegant and appropriate gifts.

I congratulate you and your good wife upon passing the signal-station indicating a quarter of a century of blissful wedded life. That you may both live to allow your friends to celebrate your golden and diamond weddings, is the hope of,

Your Sincere Friend,
PERRY OLMSTED.

Congratulating a Lady upon her Approaching Marriage.

BANGOR, ME., Dec. 2, 18—.

DEAR CATHERINE:

Two beautiful cards on my table advise me of your approaching nuptials. Allow me to congratulate you upon the choice of such a noble man, to whom you are to entrust your life's happiness. That the mid-day and evening of your married life may be as cloudless and beautiful as the morning, is the earnest wish of,

Your Loving Friend,
NELLIE GRANT.

Congratulating a Friend on Passing a Successful School Examination.

UTICA, N. Y., April 6, 18—.

DEAR HELEN:

I was greatly pleased to hear, through our friend Mary, that you had, through diligent application, passed through the prescribed course of study in the Aurora public schools, and had graduated with honors. Knowing how deeply interested your parents and relatives have been in your success, it is particularly gratifying to have you reward them by the achievement of such rapid progress. Accept my best wishes for your future success.

Your Friend,
DELLA MAYNARD.

Congratulating an Author upon the Success of his Book.

MARENGO, VA., May 7, 18—.

FRIEND KEMPLE:

I have just finished an attentive examination of your most valuable book, and cannot wonder, after a careful reading, that it is meeting so large a sale. The world is greatly indebted to you for presenting in such an attractive form the amount of useful information you have collected within its pages.

Thanking you for the benefit I have obtained from its perusal, I remain,

Yours Truly,
SILAS ACKLEY.

Congratulating a Friend upon Obtaining a Business Situation.

ASHBURY, PA., June 8, 18—.

FRIEND JOHN:

I am greatly pleased to learn that, notwithstanding the general dullness of business, you have succeeded in obtaining a clerkship. I doubt not your firm will regard themselves fortunate in securing your services. In the meantime, accept my congratulations upon your success.

Hoping that your stay may be permanent and prosperous, I am,

Yours Truly,
CHARLES BELSHAW.

JOHN BELDEN.

Letters of Introduction.

LETTERS of Introduction should be written very plainly, and should be brief, as the person introduced is compelled to wait while the letter is being read.

In introducing a person in a business capacity, state distinctly what is his business; if a professional man, his profession, and your knowledge or information of his ability.

The letter of introduction should be left unsealed. It would be a great discourtesy to prevent the bearer from seeing what you have written.

As in letters of recommendation, the person giving a letter of introduction is, in a measure, responsible for the character and ability of the person introduced. Hence, such letters should be guardedly written, or given with full knowledge of the person they introduce.

That the person receiving such a letter may know at a glance its character, the letter should, on the envelope, be addressed thus:

Chas. D. Kingsbury, Esq.,
Introducing *471 Broadway,*
Wm. H. Brown, *New York,*
of Cleveland, O.

Presenting the letter of introduction at the private house, send it by the servant to the person addressed, accompanied with your card.

At the business house, send the letter to the counting-room, accompanied by your card.

Introducing one Gentleman to Another.

NORWAY, MAINE, July 9, 18—.

FRIEND WILLIAM:

The bearer of this, Mr. Sterling Hepworth, is a dry-goods merchant in our town, who visits your city for the purpose of making purchases for his fall trade. Mr. H. is a heavy dealer in his line, pays cash for all he buys, and expects the discount accompanying cash payment. Any favor you can render him by introduction to your leading wholesale houses, or otherwise, will be appreciated by Mr. Hepworth, and acknowledged by,

Your Friend,
WALTER KIMBALL.

WILLIAM DARLING.

Introducing one Lady to Another.

ROME, GA., Aug. 10, 18—.

DEAR ANNABEL:

I take this occasion to introduce to you the bearer of this letter, Mrs. Pemberton, who is on a visit to her relatives in your city. Mrs. P. is my very dear friend, of whom you have often heard me speak. Believing that your acquaintance with each other would be mutually agreeable, I have urged her to call upon you during her stay. Any attention you may bestow upon her, during her visit, will be highly appreciated by,

Your Friend,
DELIA MAYBORNE.

Introducing a Young Musician to a Lady Friend.

SALEM, MASS., Sept. 12, 18—.

MRS. STEPHEN HAWKINS.
Dear Friend:

The bearer, Miss Serena Snow, visits your city for the purpose of pursuing a musical education, being as yet undetermined whom she will choose as an instructor. Any advice and assistance you may render will be highly appreciated by her, and duly acknowledged by her parents, who have great confidence in your judgment in matters pertaining to music.

Trusting that you will find it agreeable to aid my young friend, I remain,

Yours Sincerely,
MARY A. BARNET.

Introducing an Officer to a Brother-Officer.

HOLYOKE, MASS., Sept. 17, 18—.

DEAR CAPTAIN:

My old-time comrade, Capt. H. M. Benson, visits your town for the purpose of attending the Army Reunion on the 27th. As he will remain some little time, I commend him to your brotherly care. Believing that your acquaintance will be mutually agreeable, I remain,

Fraternally Yours,
T. M. SEYMOUR.

CAPT. A. M. BELLOWS.

Introducing a Gentleman Seeking a Clerkship.

DENVER, COL., Oct. 18, 18—.

FRIEND PATTERSON:

This letter will introduce to you my young friend, Morgan Hatfield, who has been in my employ as a clerk for the past eighteen months, and whom I would still retain, had not the disposing of a portion of my business rendered his services, with those of others of my clerks, unnecessary.

Believing that your wide influence would very materially aid him in securing a good position in the dry-goods trade in your city, I presume upon the acquaintance of an old friend in thus writing you. For reference you can use my name.

Believing that you will not afterwards regret any assistance you render the young man, I am,

Your Friend,
HERBERT HOPKINS.

A. B. PATTERSON, Esq.

Introducing a Sister to a Schoolmate.

SALEM, OREGON, Nov. 14, 18—.

DEAR FRIEND:

This will be brought you by my sister Callie, of whom you have heard me talk so much. No words of mine are necessary in introducing you. I have told you both so much of each other that you are already acquainted. I bid you love each other as well as I love you both.

Affectionately Yours,
JENNIE.

MISS LIZZIE BRATTON.

Introducing a Clerk to an Old Fellow-Clerk.

SILVER CITY, NEW MEXICO, Dec. 18, 18—.

DEAR HAL.:

My friend and fellow-clerk, Wm. Bell, will spend a week in your city, and wants to look at the desk where you and I stood, side by side, so long. You will find him a genial, friendly fellow, and will most assuredly not regret my sending him to you.

Ever Your Friend,
CON. BALDWIN.

HALBERT STEBBINS.

Introducing a Student to the Writer's Mother.

SAN FRANCISCO, CAL., Feb. 2, 18—.

DEAR MOTHER:

The bearer of this is my college chum, Harry Worthington. Being about to visit his parents at San Jose, I have persuaded him to stop over one train to see you and sister Kate. Harry is in the same class with myself, and is, I can assure you, a splendid fellow. Of course, you and Kate will treat him so finely as to make him, perhaps, stay longer than one day. He will tell you all the news.

Your Ever Affectionate Son,
SAMMY DOBBIN.

Introducing a Friend to a Member of Congress.

DOVER, DEL., Mar. 3, 18—.

HON. D. B. GRAHAM.

Respected Sir:

The bearer, Mr. D. H. Harmon, is the son of Mrs. Lieut. W. H. Harmon, of this town, whose husband was killed at the battle of Iuka, bravely defending the flag. This young man has just graduated from one of our best schools, and at my suggestion visits Washington, thinking to acquaint himself with the condition of things at the Capitol, and, if the same could be obtained, would gladly occupy a clerkship for a time. Should it be in your power to grant him such a favor, it will be warmly appreciated by his mother and myself. I remain,

Yours Respectfully,
V. H. MARTIN.

Introducing a Literary Lady to a Publisher.

BATON ROUGE, LA., March 4, 18—.

MR. WARREN H. WEBSTER.

Dear Sir:

The bearer, Mrs. Lydia Huntington, visits New York for the purpose of conferring with some publisher relative to introducing her first book to the public. She is a lady of well-known reputation and acknowledged talent throughout the South, and will, I feel sure, assume prominent rank ere long in the literary world. I take the liberty of an old friend to ask of you a consideration of her claims.

Yours, Very Respectfully,
B. H. CAMPBELL.

Introducing a Daughter About to Make a Visit.

CHARLESTON, S. C., May 6, 18—.

MY DEAR MRS. HAMILTON:

In compliance with your oft-repeated request, I send my daughter to spend a few weeks of her vacation in your delightful country home, trusting that her visit may be as delightful for her and yourself as mine was a year ago. Anticipating a visit from you all, ere the close of the present summer, I remain,

As Ever, Your Devoted Friend,
MARY DAVENPORT.

Letters of Advice.

Advising a Young Lady to Refuse Gifts from Gentlemen.

OUR life has been a success," said an individual to an old and prosperous business man. "To what do you attribute your success?" "To an admonition given me by my father, when a boy, which was this:

"First, to attend strictly to my own business. Second, to let other people's business alone. Observing this, I incurred no ill will by intermeddling with others, and I saved my time for the development and improvement of my own business."

Be very sparing of letters of advice. As a rule, you will have enough to do to attend to your own affairs; and, as a general thing, advice even when solicited is liable to give offence.

If, however, you are asked to give an opinion, you may plainly state it. Do not give it, however, as a law, nor feel offended if your advice is disregarded.

Beware of giving advice from selfishness. Sooner or later your motive will be discovered. Let your admonition be alone for the interest and welfare of your friend. If you expect, however, to be benefited by the course which you advise the person to pursue, you may frankly state the fact.

Monroeville, O., Feb. 2, 18—

My Dear Caroline:

Your letter of the 28th ult. is before me. I regret to learn that you accepted of a bracelet at the hands of Wm. Spencer. By all means return it. In its acceptance you place yourself under obligation to him, as you would to any one from whom you accept presents, unless you render an equivalent.

Nothing will more surely injure a young lady's reputation than the acceptance of many presents from different young men. When married, the gifts of your husband will come hallowed with his affection. Until then, refuse gifts from all gentlemen.

I am,

Your Sincere Friend,

Harriet McInhill

Letter Advising a Young Man to Beware of Bad Company.

WASHINGTON, D. C., Jan. 1, 18—.

MY DEAR YOUNG FRIEND:

I observe, by the tone of your last letter, that you are becoming very intimate with Henry Hubbard and Barney McIntosh. I need not tell you that your letter has given me much uneasiness. These young men are bad characters, and you cannot continue your association with them, without contaminating your morals.

I am an old man, and I write this, my boy, with a most earnest desire for your happiness. You have acquired a fine education, and have entered upon your profession with every prospect of success. You have a widowed mother to support, and an orphaned sister looking to you for guidance. It becomes you, therefore, to maintain a reputation unsullied, and obtain a good credit, which, to a young man in the commencement of a business career, is equal to a large capital of itself.

Association with these young men will certainly carry you downward. They are both without employment, they drive fast horses, they wear flash jewelry, they frequent gambling-houses, they both use intoxicating drink, chew tobacco, and talk profane language. What would you think of another that might be seen in their company? People will judge you as you would judge any one else. There is much truth in the old proverb, "A man is known by the company he keeps," and I would have your company such as will reflect the highest honor upon yourself.

I have written this letter earnestly and strongly, for I believe your good judgment will take it kindly; and I trust, when you sincerely reflect upon the matter, you will at once dismiss that class of associates from your company.

Your Earnest Well-Wisher
and Sincere Friend,
DAVID CLINE.

Advising a Young Man Against a Hurried Marriage.

RUTLAND, VT., April 5, 18—.

FRIEND CHARLES:

You ask me if you will not act the wiser part by marrying Miss Manchester at once, and settling yourself permanently; and yet you inform me that it has been but three weeks since you first made her acquaintance. You may possibly be in jest, and perhaps in earnest; in either case, as you ask my advice, I can but give it.

The choosing of a life-companion, dear Charles, is a too serious matter to be so hastily decided. The selection of a partner for a dance or a ride may be of little moment; the choice of an associate for business may be determined in a short time; but the acceptance of a partner for life requires the most serious deliberation. You should take ample time for the study of the character, temperament, disposition and accomplishments of the lady whom you choose to be the sharer of your labors, joys, sorrows, reverses and prosperity

Upon this step hangs a large share of your happiness in life. Do not act too hastily. Trusting, however, that I will some day see you happily married and settled, I am, as ever,

Your Most Sincere Friend,
GEORGE BATCHELDER.

Advice to a Gentleman on the Subject of Health.

BOSTON, MASS., May 6, 18—.

MY DEAR FRIEND:

Yours of the 2d inst. is before me. I am pleased with the prospect that you report in your business, but regret that you should be discouraged about your health. You ask me what you had better do; I will answer.

The first great secret of good health is good habits; and the next is *regularity* of habits. They are briefly summed up in the following rules:

1.—*Sleep.* Give yourself the necessary amount of sleep. Some men require five hours of the twenty-four; others need eight. Avoid feather beds. Sleep in a garment not worn during the day. To maintain robust health, sleep with a person as healthy as yourself, or no one.

2.—*Dress.* In cold weather, dress warmly with underclothing. Remove muffler, overcoat, overshoes, etc., when remaining any considerable length of time in a warm room. Keep your feet warm and dry. Wash them, in warm water, two or three times a week. Wear warm stockings, large boots, and overshoes when in the snow or wet. Wear a light covering on the head, always keeping it cool.

3.—*Cleanliness.* Have always a pint or quart of water in the sleeping room. In the morning, after washing and wiping hands and face, then wet, with the hands, every part of the body. Cold water will not be disagreeable when applying it with the bare hands. Wipe immediately; follow by brisk rubbing over the body. The whole operation need not take over five minutes. The result of this wash is, the blood is brought to the surface of the skin, and made to circulate evenly throughout the body. You have opened the pores of the skin, allowing impurities in the body to pass off, and have given yourself in the operation a good, vigorous morning exercise. Pursue this habit regularly, and you will seldom take cold.

4.—*Inflation of the Lungs.* Five minutes spent in the open air, after dressing, inflating the lungs by inhaling as full a breath as possible, and pounding the breast during the inflation, will greatly enlarge the chest, strengthen the lung power, and very effectually ward off consumption.

5.—*Diet.* If inclined to be dyspeptic, avoid mince pie, sausage and other highly seasoned food. Beware of eating too freely of soups; better to eat food dry enough to employ the natural saliva of the mouth in moistening it. If inclined to over-eat, partake freely of rice, cracked wheat, and other articles that are easily digested.

Eat freely of ripe fruit, and avoid excessive use of meats. Eat at regular hours, and lightly near the hour of going to bed. Eat slowly. Thoroughly masticate the food. Do not wash it down with continual drink while eating. Tell your funniest stories while at the table and for an hour afterwards. Do not engage in severe mental labor directly after hearty eating.

6.—*Exercise.* Exercise, not too violent, but sufficient to produce a gentle perspiration, should be had each day in the open air.

7.—*Condition of Mind.* The condition of the mind has much to do with health. Be hopeful and joyous. To be so, avoid business entanglements that may cause perplexity and anxiety. Keep out of debt. Live within your income. Attend church. Walk, ride, mix in jovial company. Do as nearly right as you know how. Thus, conscience will always be at ease. If occasionally disappointed, remember that there is no rose without a thorn, and that the darkest clouds have a silver lining; that sunshine follows storm, and beautiful spring follows the dreary winter. Do your duty, and leave the rest to God, who doeth all things well.

Hoping to hear of your continued prosperity and recovery of health, I am,

Your Very Sincere Friend,

ALLEN MATLOCK.   SIBLEY JOHNSON, M. D.

Advice to an Orphan Boy.

ARLINGTON, N. C., June 7, 18—.

MY DEAR CHARLES:

I received your letter last evening. I was greatly pleased to hear that you have secured a position with Colby, Henderson & Co., and that your sisters are comfortably situated in their new homes. You ask me for advice as to what you shall do to maintain the good opinion of your employers, and thus ultimately prosperously establish yourself.

This desire that you evince to please is one of the very best evidences that you *will* please. Your question is very commendable. How can you succeed? That should be the great question with all young men. It is best answered, perhaps, by the reply of the wealthy and honored old man, who gave this advice to his grandson:

"My boy, take the admonition of an old man who has seen every phase of human life.

"If I could give you but one precept to follow, it would be, *Keep good company.* But, adding more, I will say:

"Be truthful: you thus always have the confidence of others.

"Be temperate: thus doing, you preserve health and money.

"Be industrious: you will then be constantly adding to your acquisitions.

"Be economical; thus, you will be saving for the rainy day.

"Be cautious; you are not then so liable to lose the work of years.

"Be polite and kind; scattering words of kindness, they are reflected back upon yourself, continually adding to your happiness."

Observe these directions, and you will prosper. With many wishes for your success, remember I am always,

Your Friend,

ABEL MATTOCK.

Letters of Excuse.

ETTERS of Excuse should be written as promptly as may be.

Any damage that may have been caused by yourself, you should, if possible, repair immediately, with interest.

In apologizing for misconduct, failing to meet an engagement, or for lack of punctuality, always state the reason why.

By fulfilling every engagement promptly, discharging every obligation when due, and always being punctual, you thereby entirely avoid the necessity for an excuse.

Any article borrowed by measure, be certain to return in larger quantity and better quality, to make up the interest. To fail to make good that which has been borrowed is the certain loss of credit and business reputation in the neighborhood where you live. No letter of apology can make amends for neglecting to pay your debts.

Apologizing for a Broken Engagement.

FREDERICK, MD., July 18, 18—.

MY DEAR MISS MERTON:

I fear that you will feel injured at my failure to keep my appointment this evening. You will, however, I know, forgive me when I explain. When about to proceed to your residence, my horse, being very restive, became so frightened at an object by the roadside as to cause his runaway, throwing me violently to the ground, breaking an arm, and completely demolishing my carriage. Regretting my failure to keep my engagement, I am yet rejoiced that the accident occurred before you had entered the carriage.

Trusting that my excuse is a sufficient apology, I remain,

Your Faithful Friend,

ALBERT BIGBEE.

Apologizing for Failure to Pay Money Promptly.

DANBY, N. Y., July 11, 18—.

MR. D. B. FRISBIE.

Dear Sir:

I very much regret that the failure of H. Cole & Son will prevent my payment of your note on the 20th instant, without serious inconvenience to myself. I shall be able to pay it, however, promptly on the 25th. Should the five days' delay seriously incommode you, please write me at once, and I will aim to procure the money from another source.

Your Obedient Servant,

DANIEL FRAZIER.

Excuse to a Teacher for Non-Attendance of Child at School.

WEDNESDAY MORNING, Sept. 4, 18—.

MISS BLAKE:

You will please excuse Gertrude for non-attendance at school yesterday afternoon, she being detained in consequence of a severe headache.

Very Respectfully,

MARCIA BARROWS

Apology for Breaking a Business Engagement.

MONTICELLO, ILL., Oct. 15, 18—.

MR. PAUL D. WARREN,
Kensington.

Dear Sir:

I very much regret being compelled to apologize for not meeting you at the railroad meeting in Salem last Saturday, as I agreed to do. The cause of my detention was the sudden and severe illness of my youngest child, whose life for a time we despaired of. Please write me the result of the meeting. Hoping that the arrangements we anticipated were perfected, I am,

Yours Truly,

SOLOMON KING.

Apology for Delay in Returning a Book.

KENTLAND, IND., Nov. 19, 18—.

MY DEAR AMY:

You must excuse my long delay in returning your book. The truth is, it has been the rounds for several to read, though it has not been out of our house. When I had nearly finished its reading, Aunt Mary became interested in its contents and read it through. Her glowing description of the character of the work caused mother to peruse it; so that we have kept it from you several weeks. We feel very grateful to you, however, for furnishing us such an intellectual feast, and hope to have the pleasure of doing you a like favor.

Truly Your Friend,

LIZZIE BRAINARD.

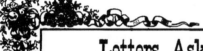

Letters Asking Favors.

IT is to be hoped that you will not often be compelled to write a letter asking a favor.

Do not urge your claims too strongly. Should you be refused, you will feel the more deeply humiliated.

In conferring a favor, avoid conveying the impression that the recipient is greatly under obligation to you. Rather imply that the granting and accepting of the favor is mutually a pleasure.

Letters refusing a favor should be very kindly worded, and, while expressing regret at your inability to comply with the request, state the reason why.

Requesting the Loan of a Book.

WEDNESDAY MORNING, JAN. 1, 18—.

DEAR BERTHA:

Will you be so kind as to loan me, for a few days, "How I Found Livingstone?" By so doing, you will greatly oblige,

Your Friend,
NANNIE WHITE.

Reply Granting the Favor.

WEDNESDAY MORNING, JAN. 1, 18—.

DEAR NANNIE:

I send you the book with pleasure, and hope you will enjoy its perusal as much as I did. I shall be over to see you next Thursday afternoon.

Affectionately Yours,
BERTHA.

Requesting a Loan of Money.

LISBON, ILL., Feb. 2, 18—.

FRIEND BAKER:

Will you do me the kindness to loan me one hundred dollars until Wednesday of next week. Having several large collections to make during the next three days, I may return the loan before then.

Yours Truly,
GEORGE HASKINS.

Answer Refusing the Request.

LISBON, ILL., Feb. 2, 18—.

FRIEND HASKINS:

I regret that all the money I have at liberty I am compelled to use this afternoon; else I would comply with your request with pleasure.

Respectfully,
JOHN BAKER.

Requesting a Letter of Introduction.

SPRINGFIELD, MASS., March 4, 18—.

FRIEND RICH:

I start for Boston to-morrow, to make arrangements for our excursion. I shall arrange to have the journey extend as far as the Holy Land. Be so kind, if you please, as to give me a letter of introduction to Prof. Wm. Kidder, whom I hope, also, to enlist in the scheme.

With warmest regards to your family, I remain,

Very Truly Yours,
HENRY FRENCH.

Reply Granting the Request.

SPARTA, R. I., March 6, 18—.

DEAR FRENCH:

I enclose, with pleasure, the letter to Prof. Kidder, who, I think, will be pleased to join us. Wishing you much success, I am,

Yours Truly,
BARTON RICH.

Requesting the Loan of an Opera Glass.

THURSDAY AFTERNOON, April 7, 18—.

DEAR MABEL:

Accompanied by cousin Fred and Jennie Masters, I am going to the theater to-night, and in behalf of Fred I wish you would loan me your opera-glass for the evening.

BECKIE HOWELL.

Answer Refusing the Request.

THURSDAY, April 7, 18—.

DEAR BECKIE:

Charlie Hackney called and borrowed my glass about an hour since; otherwise, I would take the greatest pleasure in granting your request. Wishing you a delightful evening, I am,

Your Devoted Friend,
MABEL GALE.

Requesting the Loan of a Pistol.

FRIDAY MORN., MAY 8, 18—.

FRIEND GODARD:

Please loan me your pistol this forenoon, and oblige

JOHN OGDON.

Reply Granting the Request.

FRIDAY, May 8, 18—.

FRIEND JOHN:

Accept the pistol. Beware that you do not get hurt. I shall want it to-morrow.

Truly Yours,
BEN GODARD.

Letters Accompanying Gifts.

Form of Letter Accompanying Photographs.

USALLY, in sending gifts, it is customary to accompany the same with a prettily written note. Such letters, with their answers, are very brief, and are usually written in the third person, unless among relatives or very intimate friends.

Though a reply should be given immediately, no haste need be made in repaying the gift, else it would seem that you feel the obligation, and will experience relief by paying the debt.

Accompanying a Betrothal Gift of a Ring.

No. 84 ELDRIDGE COURT, Jan. 1, 18—.
DEAR ANNIE:
 Will you accept the accompanying ring, and wear it as a pledge of the undying affection of,

  Yours Constantly,
   WILLIAM.

Reply to the Foregoing.

No. 8 ——— ST., Jan. 2, 18—.
DEAR WILLIAM:
 Your beautiful gift is on my finger, where it will be ever worn as a token of your love.
  Yours Truly,
   ANNIE.

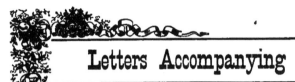

Rockland, Va., Oct. 20, 18—

Dear Helen.

 Will you accept the accompanying photographs of husband, May, Jennie, and your humble servant, in lieu of the visit that we anticipated making you this month?

 We want the photos of all your family to make our album complete, and I shall watch the mail, expecting to get them. Hoping to hear from you soon, I remain,

  Your Friend,

   Emily Berry.

To a Friend, on the Death of a Wife.

BURLINGTON, IOWA, Nov. 10, 18—.

MY DEAR DELWIN:

I know that this letter will find you filled with grief at the loss of your dear wife. You have, indeed, suffered a great affliction. A more faithful partner never lived, and few men, I venture to say, ever enjoyed more domestic tranquility than yourself. A true wife, and a devoted mother! No higher eulogy can be pronounced upon any woman. How the little motherless children will miss her tender care! How those fragile little girls will miss her sweet presence at the evening hour, when she sat by the bedside and listened to their innocent prayers, soothing their little spirits as they dropped off to sleep! Truly the great central sun of your household has gone down, and I most truly, deeply sympathize with you in your affliction.

Let us hope, however, in the language of Scripture, "I go to prepare a place for you," that, in the golden summer of another life, children, mother and father will gather again in a sweet reunion, where partings are unknown.

Though the days are dark now, spring will come once more. Thus, I trust, pleasant days will come again for you and yours.

Send both of the little girls to our home for a month's visit, and come yourself as soon as you can find time to do so. My previously arranged departure, to-morrow, prevents my visiting you.

Your Friend,
S. B. OSGOOD.

To D. B. MAXWELL,
Henderson, Kentucky.

To a Friend, on the Death of a Sister.

AUBURN, N. Y., July 16, 18—.

DEAR FRIEND:

I have learned, with sorrow, of the death of your sister Helen. Though I never knew her personally, I knew her so well through you, that it seems as if I, myself, had lost a very near and intimate friend. I recollect her from that sweet face and gentleness of manner, as I saw her once in your company, that impressed me with the belief that she was one of the angelic ones of earth.

I know how deeply you must have grieved at her death. No one could mourn her loss so truly as yourself. Younger than you, frail and delicate, her guardianship entrusted to yourself, confiding everything to you, it was natural that to a sister's affection should be added, also, almost a mother's love for your gentle sister Helen. She died, too, at a time when life was apparently all blossoming before her. How hard to reconcile ourselves to the loss of dear kindred, when their continued presence is so necessary to our happiness. But may we not hope that the same sweet voice, and gentle, confiding heart, that was so dear to sister and kindred here, is waiting for you in the summer land? "Not dead, but gone before."

The loss of near friends thus calls for our contemplation of another life toward which we are all tending. You and I, dear M., have talked these matters over often. I know you expect to meet her on the other side; so do I. Believing that your faith in that golden, sunny Future, which you and I have so often considered, will sustain you, I am,

Your Ever Faithful Friend,
JAS. D. HENRY.

To a Friend, on the Death of a Daughter.

HARTFORD, CONN., Nov. 14, 18—.

MY DEAR FRIEND:

It is with profound sorrow that I have heard of the death of dear Mary. While you have lost a dutiful and affectionate daughter, I have lost one of the dearest friends on earth. Outside of yourself, I am confident no one could more fully appreciate her loss than myself. We were so much together that I can hardly reconcile myself to the thought that I can no more meet her here. True, her death teaches us that, sooner or later, we must all make the journey across that mystic river. The angels called, and, in the ways of an all-wise Providence, it was best that she should go. We all have the ordeal to pass. Fortunate it would be if all could be as certain of being among the exalted angels as was our darling Mary. I will come and see you soon. A propos, I send you this little poem, "The Covered Bridge."

Your Friend, MYRA.

THE COVERED BRIDGE.

BY DAVID BARKER.

Tell the fainting soul in the weary form,
There 's a world of the purest bliss,
That is linked, as the soul and form are linked,
By a Covered Bridge, with this.

Yet to reach that realm on the other shore
We must pass through a transient gloom,
And must walk, unseen, unhelped, and alone,
Through that Covered Bridge—the tomb.

But we all pass over on equal terms,
For the universal toll
Is the outer garb, which the hand of God
Has flung around the soul.

Though the eye is dim, and the bridge is dark,
And the river it spans is wide,
Yet Faith points through to a shining mount,
That looms on the other side.

To enable our feet in the next day's march
To climb up that golden ridge,
We must all lie down for one night's rest
Inside of the Covered Bridge.

To a Friend, on the Death of an Infant.

PEMBERTON, Miss., Nov. 18, 18—.

MY DEAR FRIEND:

I realize that this letter will find you buried in the deepest sorrow at the loss of your darling little Emma, and that words of mine will be entirely inadequate to assuage your overwhelming grief; yet I feel that I must write a few words to assure you that I am thinking of you and praying for you.

If there can be a compensating thought, it is that your darling returned to the God who gave it, pure and unspotted by the world's temptations.

The white rose and bud, I send, I trust you will permit to rest upon your darling's pillow.

With feelings of the deepest sympathy, I remain, dear friend,

Yours, Very Sincerely,
MARION BRADSHAW.

To a Friend, on a Sudden Reverse of Fortune.

HANNIBAL, Mo., Aug. 16, 18—.

FRIEND STEWART:

I regret to hear of your sudden and unexpected heavy loss, and hasten to offer you, not only my earnest sympathy, but aid in whatever way I can assist you.

I know your energy and hopeful spirit too well to believe that you will allow this to depress or discourage you from further effort. Perhaps there is, somewhere, a blessing in this reverse. I have had my dark days, but I learned to trust the truth of that little stanza of Cowper:

"Judge not the Lord by feeble sense,
But trust him for his grace;
Behind a frowning Providence
He hides a smiling face."

The child learns to walk after many falls, and many of our richest and most prosperous men have attained their eminence and wealth only by the experience resulting from failure.

I predict that you will build on your ruins a brilliant future. How can I serve you? Let me know; by so doing, I shall understand that you have not ceased to value my friendship.

Sincerely Your Friend,
HERBERT D. WRIGHT.

To ROB'T H. STEWART,
Singleton, Me.

RITE letters to friends and relatives very often. As a rule, the more frequent such letters, the more minute they are in giving particulars; and the longer you make them, the better.

The absent husband should write a letter at least once a week. Some husbands make it a rule to write a brief letter home at the close of every day.

The absent child need not ask, "Do they miss me at home?" Be sure that they do. Write those relatives a long letter, often, descriptive of your journeys and the scenes with which you are becoming familiar. And, if the missive from the absent one is dearly cherished, let the relatives at home remember that doubly dear is the letter from the hallowed hearthstone of the home fireside, where the dearest recollections of the heart lie garnered. Do not fail to write very promptly to the one that is away. Give all the news. Go into all the little particulars, just as you would talk. After you have written up matters of general moment, come down to little personal gossip that is of particular interest. Give the details fully about Sallie Williams marrying John Hunt, and her parents being opposed to the match. Be explicit about the new minister, how many sociables you have a month, and the general condition of affairs among your intimate acquaintances.

Don't forget to be very minute about things at home. Be particular to tell of "bub," and "sis," and the baby. Even "Major," the dog, should have a mention. The little tid-bits that

Congratulating a Friend upon Receiving a Legacy.

APPLETON, WIS., Jan. 1, 18—.

FRIEND GEORGE:

I have learned to-day, through our friend Charlie Goodwin, of your good fortune in receiving a very material addition to your worldly possessions. Good! I congratulate you. I know of no one who are justly deserves good fortune, and of no person who will use it more worthily. You would be ever the same to me, whether good or ill success should attend your pathway. As it is, I take a friend's delight in congratulating you upon your fortune.

Your Friend,
DANIEL TEMPLETON.

Congratulating a Gentleman upon his Marriage.

KINGSTON, CANADA, April 4, 18—.

DEAR WILL:

I have just received a little missive, which informs me of two happy hearts made one. I wish you much joy. You have my earnest congratulations on the event, and good wishes for a long and serenely happy married life. May each succeeding year find you happier than the one before.

God bless you and yours, and surround you ever with his choicest blessings.

Your Friend,
JOHN K. BUEL.

Congratulating a Friend upon the Birth of a Son.

GRACELAND, FLA., Jan. 3, 18—.

DEAR CLARK:

Accept my warmest congratulations upon the birth of your son. May his years be long in the land which the Lord giveth him. May he honor his father and his mother, and be the blessing and support of their declining years. I anticipate holding the young gentleman on my knee, and will be over to see you in a few days.

My kindest regards to Mrs. Henry. I remain,

Faithfully Your Friend,
DEB. HARTWELL.

Congratulating a Friend upon the Twenty-fifth Anniversary of his Wedding Day.

DARTMOUTH, N. H., March 5, 18—.

MY DEAR MR. BANCROFT:

I acknowledge the receipt of a kind invitation to be present at the celebration of the twenty-fifth anniversary of your marriage. I have since learned that large numbers of your friends were present on the occasion, presenting you with an abundant and varied collection of silver, and other elegant and appropriate gifts.

I congratulate you and your good wife upon passing the signal-station indicating a quarter of a century of blissful wedded life. That you may both live to allow your friends to celebrate your golden and diamond weddings, is the hope of,

Your Sincere Friend,
PERRY OLMSTED.

Congratulating a Lady upon her Approaching Marriage.

BANGOR, ME., Dec. 3, 18—.

DEAR CATHERINE:

Two beautiful cards on my table advise me of your approaching nuptials. Allow me to congratulate you upon the choice of such a noble man, to whom you are to entrust your life's happiness. That the mid-day and evening of your married life may be as cloudless and beautiful as the morning, is the earnest wish of,

Your Loving Friend,
NELLIE GRANT.

Congratulating a Friend on Passing a Successful School Examination.

UTICA, N. Y., April 6, 18—.

DEAR HELEN:

I was greatly pleased to hear, through our friend Mary, that you had, through diligent application, passed through the prescribed course of study in the Aurora public schools, and had graduated with honors. Knowing how deeply interested your parents and relatives have been in your success, it is particularly gratifying to have you reward them by the achievement of such rapid progress. Accept my best wishes for your future success.

Your Friend,
DELLA MAYNARD.

Congratulating an Author upon the Success of his Book.

MARENGO, VA., May 7, 18—.

FRIEND KEMPLE:

I have just finished an attentive examination of your most valuable book, and cannot wonder, after a careful reading, that it is meeting so large a sale. The world is greatly indebted to you for presenting in such an attractive form the amount of useful information you have collected within its pages.

Thanking you for the benefit I have obtained from its perusal, I remain,

Yours Truly,
SILAS ACKLEY.

Congratulating a Friend upon Obtaining a Business Situation.

ASHBURY, PA., June 8, 18—.

FRIEND JOHN:

I am greatly pleased to learn that, notwithstanding the general dullness of business, you have succeeded in obtaining a clerkship. I doubt not your firm will regard themselves fortunate in securing your services. In the meantime, accept my congratulations upon your success.

Hoping that your stay may be permanent and prosperous, I am,

Yours Truly,
CHARLES BELSHAW.

JOHN BELDEN.

Answer of the Mother.

NEW YORK, Oct. 3, 18—.

MY DEAR CHILD:

I am sorry that you should urge me to grant you such an unreasonable request. Of course, nothing could please me better than to have my darling little Ella sitting on my lap at this very moment; but think how seriously the absence from your school, now, would derange all your recitations for this term. You must not think of it; recollect that all your brothers and sisters have been away at school, and always remained until the vacations. It is true that you, being the youngest, have been petted more than the rest, but it would be very unfortunate to have my indulgence interfere with your studies. You know that you are the idol of our hearts; for that very reason you should endeavor to become proficient in those branches of study that will render you an accomplished lady.

Believe me, my dear child, you will find school more pleasant every day, as you get better acquainted with your schoolmates; and, through improvement in your studies, you will steadily grow in favor with your teachers.

I will write Mrs. Mayhew to render your tasks as light as possible at first, and I have no doubt she will do all in her power to aid you.

Only a few weeks, remember, and you will be home for a long vacation, which will be all the more delightful for the privation you are at present undergoing. Your father, brothers and sisters all unite with me in sending you their love.

I remain, my dear child,

Your Affectionate Mother,

NANCY BENNETT.

To ELLA BENNETT,

Hopeville Female Seminary.

From an Absent Wife to her Husband.

ARGYLE, N. Y., March 2, 18—.

DEAREST LOVE:

I am at last safely under uncle's roof, having arrived here last evening, baby and myself both well, but really very tired. We had no delay, except about two hours at Buffalo. Uncle met me at the depot with his carriage, and, in fifteen minutes from the time of my arrival, I was cosily seated in my room, which was all in readiness for me.

Uncle and aunt seem greatly pleased with my coming, and both are loud in their praise of the baby. They very much regret that you could not have come with me, and say they intend to prevail on you to make them a visit when I am ready to go home.

Baby looks into my eyes once in a while and says, solemnly, "Papa, papa!" I do actually believe he is thinking about home, and wants to keep up a talk about you. Everybody thinks he looks like his papa.

By day after to-morrow I will write a long letter. I want you to get this by the first mail, so I make it short. With dearest love, I am,

Your Wife,

CAROLINE.

Answer to the Foregoing.

MICHIGAN CITY, IND., March 7.

DEAR WIFE:

I was indeed rejoiced to hear of your safe arrival, having felt no little anxiety for you, which is relieved by the receipt of your letter.

I miss you very much, the house looks so dreary without your loved presence; but I am, nevertheless, glad that you are making your visit, as the journey, I trust, will be beneficial to your health.

Kiss baby for me. Only by his absence do I know how much I have enjoyed my play with our little Charlie.

Don't take any concern about me. Enjoy your visit to the utmost extent. In one of my next letters I will write whether I can go East and return with you.

Remember me to uncle and aunt.

Your Ever-Faithful Husband,

ARCHIBALD.

From a Servant in the City, to her Parents in the Country.

NEW YORK, June 1, 18—.

MY DEAR PARENTS:

I take the first opportunity, since I arrived in the city, to write to you. It was a sore trial, I assure you, to leave home, but since coming here I have been quite contented, and I am getting so well accustomed to my work that I begin to like my place very much.

Mr. and Mrs. Benedict are both very kind to me. The family consists of father, mother and three children, the youngest being a little boy three years old—a beautiful little fellow, that always reminds me of brother James. Eliza, the oldest girl, is thirteen, and Martha is eleven. They are both very kind to me, and do so much about the house that it helps me very considerably.

Mr. Benedict is a clothing merchant in the city, and, I judge, is in very good circumstances. The girls are attending school at present. All the family are very regular in their attendance at church.

For the first few days here, everything seemed very strange. I hardly knew what to make of so much noise and so many people on the streets. I have now, however, become accustomed to the multitudes, and would, I presume, consider my native village very dull indeed, compared with the bustle and activity of the city.

I realize every day, dear parents, the worth of your good advice to me, which I never knew the value of so much before; thanking you for the same, I will always endeavor to follow it.

Give my love to Johnny, Mary, Jimmy and all inquiring friends. I shall anxiously look for a letter from you. Write me in the care of Solon Benedict, No.——Thirteenth Street.

Your Dutiful and Affectionate Daughter,

BETSEY ANN FAIRBANKS.

To MR. AND MRS. H. K. FAIRBANKS,

Swallow Hill, Pa.

The Mother's Reply.

SWALLOW HILL, PA., June 7, 18—.

DEAR BETSEY:

Your letter, which has been received, affords great pleasure and satisfaction to your father and myself. Nothing could give our hearts greater happiness than to know of your enjoyment and firm purpose to do right. Now that you are removed from all parental restraint, it is of the most vital importance that you implicitly rely upon the religious precepts which have been instilled into your mind, and that you daily pray to God for guidance and mercy.

We are greatly pleased that you are well situated with Mr. and Mrs. Benedict; in return for their kindness you must be honest, industrious, kind and obliging, always doing your duty faithfully, which will be a real satisfaction to yourself as well as to your employers.

Several of the neighbors, who have called, have wished to be remembered to you; Mary and Jimmy unite with you father and myself in sending you love.

We shall constantly pray for your continued protection and prosperity. I remain, dear Betsey,

Your Affectionate Mother,

HARRIET FAIRBANKS.

Letter from a Father, Remonstrating with his Son.

DANBURY, CONN., July 7, 18—.

MY DEAR SON:

I am sorry to learn that you are not inclined to be as strict in your line of duty as you should be. Remember, my son, that a down-hill road is before you, unless you rouse yourself and shake off immediately the habits of dissipation that are fastening themselves upon you. Be sure, dear boy, that nothing but sorrow and shame can come of bad company, late hours, neglect of duty, and inattention to the obligations of morality. I am willing to think that you have not given this matter sufficient thought heretofore; that your actions are the result of thoughtlessness, rather than a disposition to do wrong.

Congratulating a Friend upon Receiving a Legacy.

APPLETON, WIS., JAN. 1, 18—.

FRIEND GEORGE:
I have learned to-day, through our friend Charlie Goodwin, of your good fortune in receiving a very material addition to your worldly possessions. Good! I congratulate you. I know of no one who are justly deserves good fortune, and of no person who will use more worthily. You would be ever the same to me, whether good or ill success should attend your pathway. As it is, I take a friend's delight in congratulating you upon your fortune.

Your Friend,
DANIEL TEMPLETON.

Congratulating a Gentleman upon his Marriage.

KINGSTON, CANADA, April 4, 18—.

DEAR WILL:
I have just received a little missive, which informs me of two happy hearts made one. I wish you much joy. You have my earnest congratulations on the event, and good wishes for a long and serenely happy married life. May each succeeding year find you happier than the one before.

God bless you and yours, and surround you ever with his choicest blessings.

Your Friend,
JOHN K. BUEL.

Congratulating a Friend upon the Birth of a Son.

GRACELAND, FLA., JAN. 3, 18—.

DEAR CLARK:
Accept my warmest congratulations upon the birth of your son. May his years be long in the land which the Lord giveth him. May he honor his father and his mother, and be the blessing and support of their declining years. I anticipate holding the young gentleman on my knee, and will be over to see you in a few days.

My kindest regards to Mrs. Henry. I remain,

Faithfully Your Friend,
DEB. HARTWELL.

Congratulating a Friend upon the Twenty-fifth Anniversary of his Wedding Day.

DARTMOUTH, N. H., March 5, 18—.

MY DEAR MR. BANCROFT:
I acknowledge the receipt of a kind invitation to be present at the celebration of the twenty-fifth anniversary of your marriage. I have since learned that large numbers of your friends were present on the occasion, presenting you with an abundant and varied collection of silver, and other elegant and appropriate gifts.

I congratulate you and your good wife upon passing the signal-station indicating a quarter of a century of blissful wedded life. That you may both live to allow your friends to celebrate your golden and diamond weddings, is the hope of,

Your Sincere Friend,
PERRY OLMSTED.

Congratulating a Lady upon her Approaching Marriage.

BANGOR, ME., Dec. 2, 18—.

DEAR CATHERINE:
Two beautiful cards on my table advise me of your approaching nuptials. Allow me to congratulate you upon the choice of such a noble man, to whom you are to entrust your life's happiness. That the mid-day and evening of your married life may be as cloudless and beautiful as the morning, is the earnest wish of,

Your Loving Friend,
NELLIE GRANT.

Congratulating a Friend on Passing a Successful School Examination.

UTICA, N. Y., April 6, 18—.

DEAR HELEN:
I was greatly pleased to hear, through our friend Mary, that you had, through diligent application, passed through the prescribed course of study in the Aurora public schools, and had graduated with honors. Knowing how deeply interested your parents and relatives have been in your success, it is particularly gratifying to have you reward them by the achievement of such rapid progress. Accept my best wishes for your future success.

Your Friend,
DELLA MAYNARD.

Congratulating an Author upon the Success of his Book.

MARENGO, VA., May 7, 18—.

FRIEND KEMPLE:
I have just finished an attentive examination of your most valuable book, and cannot wonder, after a careful reading, that it is meeting so large a sale. The world is greatly indebted to you for presenting in such an attractive form the amount of useful information you have collected within its pages.

Thanking you for the benefit I have obtained from its perusal, I remain,

Yours Truly,
SILAS ACKLEY.

Congratulating a Friend upon Obtaining a Business Situation.

ASHBURY, PA., June 8, 18—.

FRIEND JOHN:
I am greatly pleased to learn that, notwithstanding the general dullness of business, you have succeeded in obtaining a clerkship. I doubt not your firm will regard themselves fortunate in securing your services. In the meantime, accept my congratulations upon your success.

Hoping that your stay may be permanent and prosperous, I am,

Yours Truly,
CHARLES BELSHAW.

JOHN BELDEN.

Returning, and looking through the house, I found almost everything changed. Two American and three Irish families had occupied it since we left, and they, evidently thinking that they would soon leave, did not pretend to make any improvements for their successors to enjoy. To sum up the description of the house — it has never been painted since we left; the dooryard fence is gone; the woodhouse has been removed; the outdoor cellar has caved in; the wagonhouse leans so badly it is liable to fall over at any time; the house itself, in a few years, will go the way of the fences; and most of the outbuildings are already gone. Nearly every American family that once lived here has gone West; the population of the vicinity, at the present time, being largely made up of Irish. Another generation, and, it is probable, scarcely an American will be left to tell the tale. Though sorrowing to see the wreck of our old home, I am greatly enjoying the visit. The scenery is truly beautiful; though, unfortunately, the people here know nothing of its beauties, and it takes us some years on the level plains of the West to learn to appreciate it.

One thing must be said of the people here, however, especially the Americans that are left — they take their full measure of enjoyment. With continuous snow four months in the year, the winter is made up of sleighriding to parties and festal occasions; the sunshine of spring is the signal for maple-sugar-making, and sugaring-off parties; the hard work of summer is broken up by fishing, berrying, and frequent excursions to various parts of the country; the fall is characterized by apple-parings and corn-huskings; so that, with their maple sugar, berries, cream, trout, honey and pumpkin pies, they are about the best livers and happiest people I ever met. I never knew, till I returned, that they enjoyed themselves so well.

I will continue the record of my visit in my next.

Yours Affectionately,
ALFRED T. WEEKS.

Descriptive Letter.
From a Young Lady Visiting Chicago, to her Parents in the East.

CHICAGO, ILL., June 1, 1873.

DEAR PARENTS:

Having been the rounds among our relatives here, I seat myself to give you something of an idea of this wonderful city — in many respects one of the most remarkable on the face of the earth, having a population to-day of over 300,000.

You have heard so much of the city that I must give you a brief sketch of its history.

The first white man ever known to have set foot on the spot where Chicago now stands, was a French Missionary, from Canada, named Pierre Jacques Marquette, who, with two others, having been on a missionary tour in the southern part of Illinois, when homeward bound was detained at this place in the fall of 1673, in consequence of the severe cold, until the following spring. That was two hundred years ago.

The first settler that came here was Point-au-Sable, a St. Domingo negro, who, in 1796, commenced a few improvements — seventy-seven years since. Au-Sable soon afterwards removed to Peoria, Ill., his improvements passing into the hands of one Le Mai, a Frenchman, who traded considerably with the Indians. The first permanent settler here was John Kinzie, who came over from St. Joseph, Michigan, and commenced his improvements in 1804 — sixty-nine years ago. Mr. Kinzie was, indeed, what Romulus was to Rome, the founder of the city. There was a fort built that year, a blockhouse made of logs, a few rods southwest of what is now known as Rush street bridge. Mr. Kinzie had a house near the south end of the bridge, which bridge, of course, had no existence in those days. An employe of Mr. Kinzie, named Ouilmette, a Frenchman, had a cabin a little west of Mr. Kinzie; and a little further west was the log cottage of one Burns, a discharged soldier. South of the fort, on the South Side, a Mr. Lee had a farm, in the low swamp lands, where now stands the heart of the business center of the city, and his cabin was a half mile or so down the river.

For a quarter of a century the growth of the village was remarkably slow, as shown by the fact that in 1830 there were but twelve houses in the village, with three suburban residences on Madison street, the entire population, whites, half-breeds and negroes, making about one hundred. That was forty years ago.

I should have told you that Chicago has a river, which is doubtless the cause of the wonderful commercial growth of the place of late years, which, at the time of its discovery, was two hundred feet wide, and twenty feet deep, with banks so steep that vessels could come up to the water's edge and receive their lading. A half mile or more from the mouth of the river, the stream divides: that portion north of the stream being known as the North Side; that between the forks, the West Side; and that south of the river, the South Side.

At that time, the North Side was covered with a dense forest of black walnut and other trees, in which were bears, wolves, foxes, wild cats, deer and other game in great abundance; while the South Side, now the business center, was a low, swampy piece of ground, being the resort of wild geese and ducks. Where the court house stands, was a pond, which was navigable for small boats. On the banks of the river, among the sedgy grass, grew a wild onion, which the Indians called Chikago, and hence the name of the city.

On a summer day, in 1831, the first vessel unloaded goods at the mouth of the river. In 1832, the first frame house was built, by Geo. W. Dole, and stood on the southeast corner of Dearborn and South Water streets. At an election for township trustees in 1833, — just forty-one years since — there were twenty-eight voters. In 1840, there were less than 5,000 people in the place. Thus you see this city, now the fifth in the order of the population in the United States, has grown from 5,000 to 300,000 in thirty-three years.

It is needless for me to describe the wonderfully rapid up-building of the city since the fire. You have heard all about it. What I want to tell you more especially is concerning our relatives. Uncles John, William and James, you recollect perhaps, all came here in 1836. They worked that summer for different parties, and until the next spring, when, in the summer of 1837, each of the men they had labored for failed. Uncle John had due him $150. Fortunately, as he thought, he was able to settle the claim at fifty cents on the dollar, and with $75 he left the place in disgust, and went to work for a farmer in Dupage County, a little distance west of Chicago. Uncle William could not get a cent. He even proposed to take $50 for the $175 that were due him, but cash could not possibly be obtained. He finally settled his claim by taking six acres of swampy land on the South Side, which he vainly tried to sell for several years that he might leave the city; but, unable to do so, he continued to work in Chicago. Uncle James took fifteen acres in the settlement of his claim, which he also found it impossible to sell, his experience being about the same as that of uncle William. Well, now the luck begins to come in. Uncle William got independent of his land by and by, but at last sold an acre for money enough to put up one of the most elegant residences you ever beheld. He sold afterwards another acre for money with which he bought a farm three miles from the court house, that is now worth $300,000. With two acres more, he got money enough to put up five business blocks, from which he gets a revenue, each year, sufficient to buy several farms.

Uncle James' experience is almost exactly similar to uncle William's. He has sold small portions of his land at various times, re-investing his money in real estate, until he is worth to-day about $2,000,000. Uncle William is said to be worth about the same amount. Uncle John came in from the country a few years ago, and, in various capacities, is working for his brothers around the city, being to-day a poor man; but will, I presume, be just as rich in eternity as uncles James and William.

All have interesting families of intelligent children, among whom I have almost terminated one of the most delightful visits I ever made. Such in brief is the history of Chicago, and a sketch of two of its sample rich men, who were made wealthy in spite of themselves.

In my next I will describe the parks and boulevards about the city. Till then, adieu.

Your Affectionate Daughter,
AMELIA SPARLAND.

Letters of Love.

F all letters, the love-letter should be the most carefully prepared. Among the written missives, they are the most thoroughly read and re-read, the longest preserved, and the most likely to be regretted in after life.

IMPORTANCE OF CARE.

They should be written with the utmost regard for perfection. An ungrammatical expression, or word improperly spelled, may seriously interfere with the writer's prospects, by being turned to ridicule. For any person, however, to make sport of a respectful, confidential letter, because of some error in the writing, is in the highest degree unladylike and ungentlemanly.

NECESSITY OF CAUTION.

As a rule, the love-letter should be very guardedly written. Ladies, especially, should be very careful to maintain their dignity when writing them. When, possibly, in after time the feelings entirely change, you will regret that you wrote the letter at all. If the love remains unchanged, no harm will certainly be done, if you wrote with judgment and care.

AT WHAT AGE TO WRITE LOVE-LETTERS.

The love-letter is the prelude to marriage — a state that, if the husband and wife be fitted for each other, is the most natural and serenely happy; a state, however, that none should enter upon, until, in judgment and physical development, both parties have completely matured. Many a life has been wrecked by a blind,

impulsive marriage, simply resulting from a youthful passion. As a physiological law, man should be twenty-five, and woman twenty-three, before marrying.

APPROVAL OF PARENTS.

While there may be exceptional cases, as a rule, correspondence should be conducted only with the assent and approval of the parents. If it is not so, parents are themselves generally to blame. If children are properly trained, they will implicitly confide in the father and mother, who will retain their love until they are sufficiently matured to choose a companion for life. If parents neglect to retain this love and confidence, the child, in the yearning for affection, will place the love elsewhere, frequently much too early in life.

TIMES FOR COURTSHIP.

Ladies should not allow courtship to be conducted at unseasonable hours. The evening entertainment, the walk, the ride, are all favorable for the study of each other's tastes and feelings. For the gentleman to protract his visit at the lady's residence until a late hour, is almost sure to give offence to the lady's parents, and is extremely ungentlemanly.

HONESTY.

The love-letter should be honest. It should say what the writer means, and no more. For the lady or gentleman to play the part of a coquette, studying to see how many lovers he or she may secure, is very disreputable, and bears in its train a long list of sorrows, frequently wrecking the domestic happiness for a life-time. The parties should be honest, also, in the statement of their actual prospects and means of support. Neither should hold out to the other wealth or other inducements that will not be realized, as disappointment and disgust will be the only result.

MARRYING FOR A HOME.

Let no lady commence and continue a correspondence with a view to marriage, for fear that she may never have another opportunity. It is the mark of judgment and rare good sense to go through life without wedlock, if she cannot marry from love. Somewhere in eternity, the poet tells us, our true mate will be found. Do not be afraid of being an "old maid." The disgrace attached to that term has long since passed away. Unmarried ladies of mature years are proverbially among the most intelligent, accomplished and independent to be found in society. The sphere of woman's action and work is so widening that she can to-day, if she desires, handsomely and independently support herself. She need not, therefore, marry for a home.

INTEMPERATE MEN.

Above all, no lady should allow herself to correspond with an intemperate man, with a view to matrimony. She may reform him, but the chances are that her life's happiness will be completely destroyed by such a union. Better, a thousand times, the single, free and independent maidenhood, than for a woman to trail her life in the dust, and bring poverty, shame and disgrace on her children, by marrying a man addicted to dissipated habits.

MARRYING WEALTH.

Let no man make it an ultimate object in life to marry a rich wife. It is not the possession, but the *acquisition*, of wealth, that gives happiness. It is generally conceded fact that the inheritance of great wealth is a positive mental and moral injury to young men, completely destroying the stimulus to advancement. So, as a rule, no man is permanently made happier by a marriage of wealth; while he is quite likely to

be given to understand, by his wife and others, from time to time, that, whatever consequence he may attain, it is all the result of his wife's money. Most independent men prefer to start, as all our wealthiest and greatest men have done, at the foot of the ladder, and earn their independence. Where, however, a man can bring extraordinary talent or distinguished reputation, as a balance for his wife's wealth, the conditions are more nearly equalized. Observation shows that those marriages prove most serenely happy where husband and wife, at the time of marriage, stand, socially, intellectually and pecuniarily, very nearly equal. For the chances of successful advancement and happiness in after life, let a man wed a woman poorer than himself rather than one that is richer.

POVERTY.

Let no couple hesitate to marry because they are poor. It will cost them less to live after marriage than before — one light, one fire, etc., answering the purpose for both. Having an object to live for, also, they will commence their accumulations after marriage as never before. The young woman that demands a certain amount of costly style, beyond the income of her betrothed, no young man should ever wed. As a general thing, however, women have common sense, and, if husbands will perfectly confide in their wives, telling them exactly their pecuniary condition, the wife will live within the husband's income. In the majority of cases where men fail in business, the failure being attributed to the wife's extravagance, the wife has been kept in entire ignorance of her husband's pecuniary resources. The man who would be successful in business, should not only marry a woman who is worthy of his confidence, but he should at all times advise with her. She is more interested in his prosperity than anybody else, and will be found his best counselor and friend.

CONFIDENCE AND HONOR.

The love correspondence of another should be held sacred, the rule of conduct being, to do to others as you wish them to do to you. No woman, who is a lady, will be guilty of making light of the sentiments that are expressed to her in a letter. No man, who is a gentleman, will boast of his love conquests, among boon companions, or reveal to others the correspondence between himself and a lady. If an engagement is mutually broken off, all the love-letters should be returned. To retain them is dishonorable. They were written under circumstances that no longer exist. It is better for both parties to wash out every recollection of the past, by returning to the giver every memento of the dead love.

HOW TO BEGIN A LOVE CORRESPONDENCE.

Some gentlemen, being very favorably impressed with a lady at first sight, and having no immediate opportunity for introduction, make bold, after learning her name, to write her at once, seeking an interview, the form of which letter will be found hereafter. A gentleman in doing so, however, runs considerable risk of receiving a rebuff from the lady, though not always. It is better to take a little more time, learn thoroughly who the lady is, and obtain an introduction through a mutual acquaintance. Much less embarrassment attends such a meeting; and, having learned the lady's antecedents, subjects are easily introduced in which she is interested, and thus the first interview can be made quite agreeable.

The way is now paved for the opening of a correspondence, which may be done by a note inviting her company to any entertainment supposed to be agreeable to her, or the further pleasure of her acquaintance by correspondence, as follows:

145 —— St., July 2, 18—.
Miss MYRA BRONSON:
Having greatly enjoyed our brief meeting at the residence of Mrs. Powell last Thursday evening, I venture to write to request permission to call on you at your own residence. Though myself almost entirely a stranger in the city, your father remembers, he told me the other evening, Mr. Williams of Syracuse, who is my uncle. Trusting that you will pardon this liberty, and place me on your list of gentleman acquaintances, I am,
Yours, Very Respectfully,
HARMON WILLIAMS.

Favorable Reply.

944 —— St., July 5, 18—.
MR. HARMON WILLIAMS.
Dear Sir:
It will give me much pleasure to see you at our residence next Wednesday evening. My father desires me to state that he retains a very favorable recollection of your uncle, in consequence of which he will be pleased to continue your acquaintance.
Yours Truly,
MYRA BRONSON.

Unfavorable Reply.

944 —— St., July 2, 18—.
Miss Myra Bronson, making it a rule to receive no gentleman visitors upon such brief acquaintance, begs to decline the honor of Mr. Williams' visits.
HARMON WILLIAMS, Esq.

An Invitation to a Place of Public Amusement.

462 —— St., April 4, 18—.
Miss FARRINGTON:
May I request the very great pleasure of escorting you to Barnum's Museum, at any time which may suit your convenience? To grant this favor will give me very much pleasure. No pains will be spared by myself to have you enjoy the occasion, and I will consult your wishes in every particular as to time of calling for you and returning. Waiting an early reply to this, I remain,
Most Sincerely,
CHAS. STEVENSON.

Reply Accepting.

876 —— St., April 7, 18—.
MR. STEVENSON.
Dear Sir: I thank you for your very kind invitation, which I am happy to accept. I will appoint next Monday evening, at which time, if you will call for me at our house, I will accompany you.
Yours Sincerely,
CLARA FARRINGTON.

Reply Refusing.

876 —— St., April 4, 18—.
MR. STEVENSON.
Dear Sir: I am grateful to you for your very polite invitation, but, as I should go only with my own family were I to attend any place of amusement, I am unable to avail myself of your kindness. Thanking you, I remain,
Yours Truly,
CLARA FARRINGTON.

Reply with Conditions.

876 —— St., April 4, 18—.
MR. STEVENSON.
Dear Sir: I shall be most happy to visit Barnum's Museum with you, but will prefer being one of a company in which yourself is included, such also being the wish of my mother, who sends her kind regards. A visit from you at our house, next Tuesday evening, will enable us to decide upon the time of going.
Very Sincerely,
CLARA FARRINGTON.

Love at First Sight.

96 — St., June 1, 18—.

DEAR MISS HAWLEY:

You will, I trust, forgive this abrupt and plainly spoken letter. Although I have been in your company but once, I cannot forbear writing to you in defiance of all rules of etiquette. Affection is sometimes of slow growth, but sometimes it springs up in a moment. I left you last night with my heart no longer my own. I cannot, of course, hope that I have created any interest in you, but will you do me the great favor to allow me to cultivate your acquaintance? Hoping that you may regard me favorably, I shall await with much anxiety your reply. I remain,

Yours Devotedly,

BENSON GOODRICH.

Unfavorable Reply.

694 — St., June 1, 18—.

MR. GOODRICH.

Sir! Your note was a surprise to me, considering that we had never met until last evening, and that then our conversation had been only on commonplace subjects. Your conduct is indeed quite strange. You will please be so kind as to oblige me by not repeating the request, allowing this note to close our correspondence.

MARION HAWLEY.

Favorable Reply.

694 — St., June 1, 18—.

MR. GOODRICH.

Dear Sir: Undoubtedly I ought to call you severely to account for your declaration of love at first sight, but I really cannot find it in my heart to do so, as I must confess that, after our brief interview last evening, I have thought much more of you than I should have been willing to have acknowledged had you not come to the confession first. Seriously speaking, we know but very little of each other yet, and we must be very careful not to exchange our hearts in the dark. I shall be happy to receive you here, as a friend, with a view to our further acquaintance. I remain, dear sir,

MARION HAWLEY.

A Lover's Good-bye Before Starting on a Journey.

104 — St., May 10, 18—.

MY DARLING MINNIE:

I go west, to-morrow, on business, leaving my heart in your gentle keeping. You need be at no expense in placing a guard around it, for I assure you that, as surely as the needle points towards the pole, so surely my love is all yours. I shall go, dearest, by the first train, hoping thereby to return just one train sooner, which means that not an hour, not a minute longer will I be absent from you, than is imperatively necessary. Like the angler, I shall "drop a line" frequently, and shall expect a very prompt response, letter for letter. No credit given in this case; business is business — I must have prompt returns.

Ever Faithfully Yours,

WINFIELD BAKER.

Reply to the Foregoing.

814 — St., May 10, 18—.

DEAR WINFIELD:

I have had my cry over your letter — a long, hard cry. Of course, I know that does not help the matter any. I suppose you must go, but I shall be so lonely while you are gone. However, you promise that you will return at the earliest moment, and that is one little ray of sunshine that lines the cloud. Shall we be enough happier after your return to pay for this separation? Thinking that we may be, I will let that thought sustain me. In the meantime, from this moment until your return I will think of you, just once — a long-drawn-out thought.

Yours Affectionately,

MINNIE LA SURE.

Letter Asking an Introduction through a Mutual Friend.

912 — St., April 2, 18—.

FRIEND HENRY:

I am very desirous of making the acquaintance of Miss Benjamin, with whom you are on terms of intimate friendship. Will you be so kind as to give me a letter of introduction to her? I am aware that it may be a delicate letter for you to write, but you will be free, of course, to make all needed explanations in your letter to her. I will send her your letter, instead of personally calling upon her myself, thus saving her from any embarrassment that may result from my so doing. By granting this favor, you will much oblige,

Yours, Very Respectfully,

WM. H. TYLER.

Reply.

117 — St., April 2, 18—.

FRIEND TYLER:

Enclosed, find the note you wish. As you will observe, I have acted upon your suggestion of giving her sufficient explanation to justify my letter. Your desire to please the lady, coupled with your good judgment, will, I doubt not, make the matter agreeable.

Truly Yours,

HENRY PARSONS.

LETTER OF INTRODUCTION.

DEAR MISS BENJAMIN: This will introduce to you my friend WM. Tyler, who is very desirous of making your acquaintance, and, having no other means of doing so, asks of me the favor of writing this note of introduction, which he will send you, instead of calling himself, thus leaving you free to grant him an interview or not. Mr. Tyler is a gentleman I very highly respect, and whose acquaintance, I think, you would not have occasion to regret. Nevertheless, you may not regard this a proper method of introduction, in which case, allow me to assure you, I will entertain the same respect for yourself, if you will frankly state so, though it would be gratifying to Mr. Tyler and myself to have it otherwise. With sincere respect, I am,

Very Respectfully,

HENRY PARSONS.

To the Father of the Lady.

BURLINGTON, IOWA, Jan. 1, 18—.

RESPECTED SIR:

I take this means of consulting you on a subject that deeply interests myself, while it indirectly concerns you; and I trust that my presentation of the matter will meet with your approval.

For several months your daughter Mary and myself have been on intimate terms of friendship, which has ripened into affection on my part, and I have reason to think that my attentions are not indifferent to her. My business and prospects are such that I flatter myself I can provide for her future, with the same comfort that has surrounded her under the parental roof. Of my character and qualifications, I have nothing to say; I trust they are sufficiently known to you to give confidence in the prospect of your child's happiness.

Believing that the parents have such an interest in the welfare of the daughter as makes it obligatory upon the lover to consult their desires, before taking her from their home, I am thus induced to request you to express your wishes upon this subject.

I shall anxiously await your answer.

Your Very Obedient Servant,

DANIEL HARRISON.

To WM. FRANKLIN, Esq.,

184 — St.

Favorable Reply.

184 —— St., Jan. 1, 18—.

My Dear Mr. Harrison:

I very highly appreciate the manly and honorable way in which you have addressed me in reference to my daughter Mary.

Believing you to be honest, industrious, ambitious to do well, and possessed of an excellent moral character, I unite with Mrs. Franklin in the belief that our darling child may very safely trust her happiness to your protecting care.

If agreeable and convenient to you, we shall be happy to have you dine with us to-morrow.

Very Sincerely Yours,

WM. FRANKLIN.

To Mr. Daniel Harrison.

Unfavorable Reply.

184 —— St.

Dear Sir:

Highly appreciating the straightforward and gentlemanly manner in which you have written me concerning a subject that every parent has an interest in, I am compelled to inform you that, though my daughter has treated you with much friendliness, as she is accustomed to with all her friends, she will be unable to continue with you a love acquaintance with a view to marriage, owing to a prior engagement with a gentleman of worth and respectability, which contract she has no occasion to regret.

Fully sensible of your most excellent qualities, and the compliment paid in your selection of her, my daughter unites with me in the wish that you may meet with a companion in every way calculated to ensure your happiness.

Yours, Very Respectfully,

WM. FRANKLIN.

To Mr. Daniel Harrison.

Reply to a Young Man that Uses Tobacco.

682 —— St., July 18, 18—.

Mr. Bannister.

Dear Sir:

I am in receipt of your courteous letter, containing a declaration of love. I will be frank enough with you to admit that, while I have been sensible of your affectionate regard for me for some months, I have also cherished a growing interest in you. In truth, to make a candid confession, I most sincerely love you. I should, perhaps, say no more, but I feel it due to you, as well as to myself, to be strictly honest in my expression, lest we foster this growing love, which, under present conditions, must be broken off.

I have always admired your natural ability; I appreciate you for your industry; I respect you for your filial conduct towards your parents. In fact, I consider you quite a model young man, were it not for one habit, which has always been, heretofore, a very delicate subject for me to speak of, fearing that it might give you offense. But believing it best that I be true to my convictions and state my objections plainly, I thus freely write them.

I have reference to the use of tobacco. Apparently, this is a little thing. I am aware that ladies generally consider it beneath their notice; but so thoroughly convinced am I that it is one of the most destructive habits, sapping the morality and vigor of our young men, that I could never consent to wed a man addicted to its use, my reasons being as follows:

It would impoverish my home. Only ten cents a day expended for a cigar, in a lifetime of forty years, with its accumulations of interest, amounts to over four thousand dollars! The little sum of eleven cents per day, saved from being squandered on tobacco, and properly put at interest, amounts in that time to $5,160! No wonder so many homes, the heads of which use tobacco, are without the comforts of life.

It might wreck my happiness. It is a well-known physiological fact that the use of tobacco deadens the sense of taste; that water and all common drinks become insipid and tasteless when tobacco is used, so that the person using the same involuntarily craves strong drink, in order to taste it. Therein lies the foundation of a large share of the drunkenness of the country. Observation proves that, while many men use tobacco that are not drunkards, almost every drunkard is a user of tobacco, having nearly always formed the habit from the use of this narcotic weed.

It would surround me with filth. To say nothing of the great drain on the physical health by the constant expectoration of saliva, thus ruining the health of many robust constitutions, I could not endure the fetid breath of the tobacco-user. I sicken at the sight of the brown saliva exuding from between the lips; physiology proving that, with tobacco-chewers, nearly all the waste fluids from the body pass through the mouth. I am immediately faint at the thought of dragging my skirts through spittle in a railway car, or any place where it is thrown upon the floor; I turn with disgust at the atmosphere—God's pure, fresh air—that is tainted with the stench of tobacco smoke.

It would corrupt my husband's morals. All the associations of tobacco are bad. It is true that many good men use tobacco. It is also a truth that nearly every man that is bad is addicted to its use. To smoke in peace, the man must resort to the place where others smoke. In that room are profanity, obscene language and every species of vulgarity. There may be occasionally an exception. The fact is patent, however, that, in the room in which vulgarity and obscenity prevail, there is always tobacco smoke in the air, and the vile spittle on the floor.

You will forgive me for speaking thus plainly. I love you too well to disguise my feelings on the subject. I could not possibly constantly love a tobacco-user, for the reasons that I have given.

While I devotedly love you, I cannot consent that you should bestow your affections upon a person that would instinctively repel you. Believing, therefore, under the circumstances, that our further correspondence should cease, I remain,

Your Friend and Well-Wisher,

MARIETTA WILCOX.

Letter to an Entire Stranger.

478 —— St., Jan. 1, 18—.

Miss Henderson:

I beg to apologise for addressing you thus, being an entire stranger; but having the misfortune to be unknown to you is my excuse for this strange proceeding, which, I am well aware, is entirely at variance with the rules of etiquette. I have for two sabbaths seen you at church, and I am frank to confess that your appearance has made so deep an impression upon me as to make me extremely desirous of forming your acquaintance. I am, at present, a clerk in the ribbon department at Smith & Brown's store. Will you do me the great favor of allowing this to commence a friendship, which, I trust, will never be regretted by yourself. Please deign to give me at least a single line in reply to this, and oblige,

Your Sincere Admirer,

WESLEY BARNUM.

Unfavorable Reply.

Mr. Barnum.

Dear Sir:

I considerably question whether it is due to propriety to answer your note at all. But as you might fear that your letter had miscarried, and thus be induced to write again, it is best, probably, for me to make an immediate reply, and thus settle the affair entirely, and relieve you, possibly, of further suspense. It will be impossible for me to recognize you, or to think under any circumstances of permitting an acquaintance to be commenced by such an introduction as you seem to deem sufficient. More especially should I regret allowing a friendship to be formed by recognitions in the hours of divine service in church, while the mind should be employed in religious observances. You will, therefore, please understand that I am not favorable to further recognition, nor to a continuance of correspondence.

AMELIA HENDERSON.

Reply More Favorable.

355 — St., June 10, 18—.

Mr. Barnum.

Dear Sir:

I am in receipt of your note, and must confess that I am surprised at your request. I am entirely opposed to commencing, on general principles, an acquaintance with such an introduction, and consider it very improper, especially to allow it to originate in church during the hours of divine service. Were it not that I think your meaning kind and your intentions good, I would return your letter unanswered. As it is, I will take your request under consideration, and, if I think best to grant it, you may know of the fact by my recognition at the close of the service in the Sabbath School.

Respectfully,
AMELIA HENDERSON.

An Advertisement in a Morning Paper.

PERSONAL.—Will the lady who rode up Broadway last Thursday afternoon, about two o'clock, in an omnibus, getting out at Stewart's, accompanied by a little girl dressed in blue suit, please send her address to D. B. M., Herald office?

REMARKS.

It is useless to advise people never to reply to a personal advertisement like the above. To do so is like totally refusing young people the privilege of dancing. People will dance, and they will answer personal advertisements. The best course, therefore, is to properly direct the dancers, and caution the writers in their answers to newspaper personals. If the eye of the young lady referred to meets the above advertisement, she will possibly be indignant at first, and will, perhaps, resolve to pay no attention to it. It will continue to occupy her attention so much, however, and curiosity will become so great, that, in order to ease her mind, she will at last give her address; in which case she makes a very serious mistake, as any lady replying to a communication of such a character, giving her name and residence to a stranger, places herself at a great disadvantage. Should her communication never be answered, she will feel mortified ever afterwards that she committed the indiscretion of replying to the advertisement at all; and, should the person she addresses prove to be some worthless fellow who may presume to press an acquaintance upon the strength of her reply, it may cause her very serious perplexity and embarrassment.

It is clearly evident, therefore, that she should not give her name and address as requested; and yet, as the advertisement may refer to a business matter of importance, or bring about an acquaintance that she will not regret, she may relieve her curiosity on the subject by writing the following note in reply:

THE REPLY.

(Advertisement pasted in.)

D. B. M.:

I find the above advertisement in the "Herald" of this morning. I suppose myself to be the person referred to. You will please state your object in addressing me, with references.

Address, A. L. K., Herald Office.

It is probable that the advertiser, if a gentleman, will reply, giving his reasons for requesting the lady's address, with references, upon receiving which, the lady will do as she may choose relative to continuing the correspondence; in either case, it will be seen that she has in no wise compromised her dignity, and she retains the advantage of knowing the motive and object that prompted the advertisement, while she is yet unknown to the advertiser.

Great caution should be exercised in answering personals. The supposition is, if the advertiser be a gentleman, that he will honorably seek an interview with a lady, and pay court as gentlemen ordinarily do. Still, an occasion may happen to a man, who is in the highest sense a gentleman, wherein he sees the lady that he very greatly admires, and can learn her address in no other way without rendering himself offensive and impertinent; hence, the apparent necessity of the above personal advertisement.

Instances have also occurred where gentlemen, driven with business, and having but little time to mingle in female society, or no opportunity, being strangers comparatively, desirous of forming the acquaintance of ladies, have honestly advertised for correspondence, been honestly answered, and marriage was the result.

Those advertisements, however, wherein Sammy Brown and Coney Smith advertise for correspondence with any number of young ladies, for fun, mutual improvement, "and what may grow out of it, photographs exchanged," etc., young ladies should be very wary of answering. Instances have been known where scores of young ladies, having answered such an advertisement, could they have looked in upon those young men, a week afterwards, would have seen them with a pile of photographs and letters, exhibiting them to their companions, and making fun of the girls who had been so foolish as to answer their advertisement.

It is true that no one but the meanest kind of a rascal would be guilty of such a disgraceful act as to advertise for and expose correspondence thus, and it is equally true that the young lady who gives the advertiser the opportunity to ridicule her shows herself to be very foolish.

Personal Advertisement.

PERSONAL.—A gentleman, a new comer in the city, having a sufficiency of this world's goods to comfortably support himself and wife, is desirous of making the acquaintance of a lady of middle years, with a view to matrimony. Address, in the strictest confidence, giving name, residence and photograph, H. A. B., Station H, Postoffice.

THE REPLY.

To H. A. B.

Sir:

I am led to suppose, from the reading of the above, that it is dictated in sincerity, by a desire to meet with a lady who would be treated with candor and respect. I have at present no acquaintance to whom I am inclined to give a very decided preference, nor have I ever had any very distinct ideas on the subject of marriage. I am free, however, to confess that, should circumstances favor my acquaintance with a gentleman whom I could honor and respect, I might seriously think of a proposal. Believing that you wish, as you intimate, this letter in confidence, I will say that I am — years old, am in receipt of —— annually, from property that is leased. I have been told that I was handsome, though others, probably, have a different opinion. Of that fact, you must be the judge. I am entirely free to select whomsoever I may choose. My social standing, I trust, would be satisfactory, and my accomplishments have not been neglected. It is not necessary that I should write more. I shall be happy to correspond with you with a view to better acquaintance, when, if mutually agreeable, an introduction may take place. You desire me to send name, address and photograph, which, I trust you will perceive, would be improper for me to do. It is due to myself, and, under certain circumstances, to you, that I should be very guarded as to the manner of my introduction. A letter addressed to M. A. L., Station A, Postoffice, will reach me.

I sign a fictitious name, for obvious reasons.

Respectfully,
NANCY HILLIS.

A Gentleman Makes a Frank Acknowledgment. — Gushing with Sentiment, and Running Over with Poetry.

WHITE MOUNTAINS, N. H., Oct. 1, 18—.

MY DEAR MARY:

One by one the brown leaves are falling, reminding us that the golden summer that we have so delightfully loitered through approaches its close. How thickly our pathway has been strewn with roses; how fragrant have been the million blossoms; how sweetly the birds have sung; how beautiful have been the sunny days; how joyous have been the starry nights! Dear M., I do not need to tell you that this delightful summer has been to me one grand Elysian scene. I have gazed on and dreamed of thy beauty. I have been fed by thy sparkling repartee and merriment; I have drank at the fountain of thy intellectuality; but the feast is ended, and gradually the curtain is falling. Dear, beautiful summer; so beautiful to me because of thy loved presence. And standing now on the threshold of a scene all changed, I take a last, fond, long, lingering look on the beautiful picture that will return to me no more; and yet, who knows, but on in that great eternity we may live again these Eden hours.

"Like a foundling in slumber, the summer day lay
    On the crimsoning threshold of even,
And I thought that the glow through the azure-arched way
        Was a glimpse of the coming of Heaven.
There together we sat by the beautiful stream;
    We had nothing to do but to love and to dream
In the days that have gone on before.
    These are not the same days, though they bear the same name,
With the ones I shall welcome no more.

"But it may be the angels are culling them o'er,
    For a Sabbath and Summer forever,
When the years shall forget the Decembers they wore,
    And the shroud shall be woven, no, never!
In a twilight like that, darling M. for a bride—
        Oh! what more of the world could one wish beside,
    As we gazed on the river unroll'd
        Till we heard, or we fancied, its musical tide,
Where it flowed through the Gateway of Gold?"

Dearest, you must forgive my ardent expressions in this letter. With a temperament gushing to the brim and overflowing with sentiment and rhapsody, I have passed the fleeting summer in thy charming presence in one continual dream of poesy. I cannot now turn back to the solemn duties before me, without telling you what trembled on my tongue a thousand times, as we gathered flowers together and wove our chaplets in the sunny days gone by. Dear, darling Mary, *I love you, I adore you.* How often in the beautiful moonlight nights, as we strolled among the lilacs and the primroses, have I been on the verge of clasping your jeweled hand and telling you all my heart. But, oh! I did not quite dare; the hours were so delightful, even as they were. Fearing that I might be repulsed, I chose to accept the joy even that there was, rather than run the risk of losing it all.

How many a morning have I arisen and firmly resolved that, ere another day, I would know my fate! But, ah! the twilight would fall, and the evening hour would pass by, and I never completely dared to risk the result of a declaration. The morrow I knew would be joyous if I bridled my impulse; it might not be if I made a mistake. But the dream has passed by. To-morrow, I bid adieu to these silvan groves, the quiet meadows and the gurgling brooks, to go back to the prose duties of business. And now, at the close of this festal season, as I am upon the verge of going, having nothing to lose and everything to gain, I have told you my heart. I have not the slightest idea what your reply will be. You have been to me one continual puzzle. If your answer is adverse, I can only entertain the highest respect for you ever in the future; and memory shall keep alive the recollection of the most blissful summer I have ever known. If your reply is favorable — dearest, may I fondly hope that it will be!— then opens before me a great volume of happiness, of which this joyous summer has been but the opening chapter.

Dear M., may I come again and see you, and address you henceforth as a lover? The messenger who brings you this will return again in an hour for your answer. I need not tell you what an hour of suspense this will be to me. Upon your reply hangs my future. If your reply is favorable, I shall tarry another day; and will you grant me a long interview, as I have much to talk over with you? If unfavorable, please return this letter with your note. Accept my warmest thanks for the entertainment which I, in common with others, have received at your hand in the past; and, if I may not sign myself your devoted lover, I shall at least, I trust, have ever the pleasure of subscribing myself,

Your Sincere Friend,
CLARENCE HARRINGTON.

Favorable Reply.

DEAR CLARENCE:
I shall not attempt in this to answer your missive with the same poetic fervor that colors your letter from beginning to end. While it is given you to tread the emerald pavements of an imaginative Eden, in my plainer nature I can only walk the common earth. I fully agree with you in your opinion of the beautiful summer just passed. Though in seasons heretofore many people have been here from the cities, I have never known a summer so delightful. Yes, Clarence, these three months have been joyous, because—shall I confess it?—because you have been here. I need not write more. You have agreed to stay another day; I shall be at home this afternoon, at two o'clock, and will be happy to see you.

Yours Very Truly,
MARY SINGLETON.

To a Lady, from a Gentleman Confessing Change of Sentiment.

844—St., April 2, 18—.
MISS MARION THORNTON:
Your note accusing me of coldness is before me. After spending several hours in a consideration of this subject, to determine what is my duty, I have concluded that it is decidedly best for me to be perfectly frank with you, and give my reasons for a change of sentiment.

I do not think we could live happily together if we were married, because, from disparaging remarks I have heard you make concerning people that are not wealthy, I think you would be entirely dissatisfied with my circumstances; and the further fact that you allow your mother to do all the drudgery of the household, you sitting in the parlor entertaining gentlemen, and affecting to have no knowledge of housekeeping, is proof that our tastes would not accord in home matters. I consider it just as honorable, and just as important, that young ladies should do something to support themselves, as that young men should. If the opportunities are not as great for them to go abroad, they can, at least while at home, learn to be good in sewing, cooking and housekeeping, and thus be prepared when opportunities offer, to make prudent, economical, tidy housewives. I do not under-value the importance of being proficient in the lighter accomplishments which go to make a lady at ease in society; but I vastly more prize the lady who knows how to get an excellent breakfast early in the morning, who is not only a model of neatness herself, but relieves her mother in household duties, keeping her younger brothers and sisters clean and orderly.

I have admired and loved you for your musical talent and your fine conversational powers, but, as I could not keep the necessary servants to enable you constantly to gratify those talents to the exclusion of the more substantial duties, I feel that our marriage would be a mistake for us both.

You asked my reason for my changing love: I have reluctantly, yet plainly, stated it. Hoping, however, that you may always be happy in life, I am,

Your Friend,
CLINTON HOLMES.

Reply to a Young Man Addicted to Intemperance.

669——St., Nov. 7, 18——

Mr. Spellman.

Dear Sir:

Your kind invitation to accompany you to the opera, to-morrow evening, is received. Under ordinary circumstances, I would be delighted to go with you, believing you at heart to be really a most excellent gentleman. I regret to add, however, that I have undoubted evidence of the fact that you are becoming addicted to the use of the wine-cup. I regard it entirely unsafe for any young lady to continue an intimacy with a young man upon whom is growing the habit of intemperance. With an earnest prayer for your reformation, ere it be too late, I beg you to consider our intimacy at an end.

Respectfully,
Helen Sanford

One Way of Breaking the Ice.

584 — St., July 1, 18—.

MY DEAR FRIEND CAROLINE:

I returned yesterday from a brief trip into Canada, my journey being most agreeable; only one little episode breaking the monotony, as I neared home, which was this: in the next seat behind me in the car sat a young couple, who were evidently regretting that their ride was so near an end. Though buried in my reading, I could not avoid hearing much that they said. One question asked by the young man made a striking impression on my mind. "Maggie," said he, "we have now been acquainted a good while; you know me, and I know you. I do not need to tell you that I love you with all my heart; now, do you love me?"

I knew the young fellow had taken that occasion, when the cars were thundering along, so that he might not be knocked down by the beating of his own heart. I confess to have been guilty of eavesdropping, then. I listened intently for the lady's answer, but just at that moment, as my ill luck would have it, another train came thundering by us, and her voice was drowned in the noise. I got to thinking like this: suppose you and I were riding thus, and I should ask precisely the same question; what would be your reply? I am very curious to know what your answer would be, and shall await a letter from you, with much anxiety.

Most Truly Yours,

ROLAND MILLS.

An Offer of Marriage.

248 — St., Dec. 10, 18—.

DEAREST BERTHA:

I have intended, oh, how many times! when we have been together, to put the simple question which I intend this note shall ask; but, although apparently a very easy matter to ask the hand in marriage of one I so deeply love as yourself, it is no easy task. I therefore write what I have never found courage in my heart to speak. Dearest, will you bestow upon me the great happiness of permitting me to call you mine? If I have spoken this too boldly, you will forgive; but I fondly hope that you will not be indifferent to my appeal. I trust, if you answer this in the affirmative, that you will never regret doing so. Anxiously awaiting your answer, I remain,

Yours Affectionately,

HARLAN DEMPSTER.

Favorable Reply.

897 — St., Dec. 10, 18—.

DEAR SIR:

Your proposal is quite unexpected to me, but it is made with such candor and frankness that I can take no offence. I cannot, in this note, give you a definite reply. Marriage is a very serious matter; and, while I regard you with the greatest favor, I desire to consult my near relatives, and consider the subject myself carefully for a few days, ere I give you a final answer. I think I can assure you, however, that you may hope.

Very Sincerely,

FANNIE KIMBALL.

Letter from a Young Man Who Proposes Marriage and Emigration.

482 — St., April 16, 18—.

DEAR CLARA:

You have doubtless heard of my intention to go West in the coming month. Though surrounded here with my relatives and all the many friends of my boyhood, I have an intense desire to try my fortune amid new scenes, feeling that the letters that now bind me and seem to hinder my upward progress will then be broken.

I shall sunder my ties with some regrets, but, to commence my business career as I am desirous of doing, I must make the sacrifice; in doing so, I do no more than thousands have done before me. In the great, broad fields of the growing West, a young man of resolution, ambition, honesty, temperance and perseverance cannot fail, I believe, to better his condition much more rapidly than he can here; you will, I think, coincide with me in this opinion.

Dear Clara, of all my farewells, none will be so sad to me as that I shall bid to you. Dear, dear Clara, you cannot be indifferent to the fact that I have long devotedly loved you; and, at the hour of parting, I may not have your love in return. And now, while I am asking, will you not take me and my heart, and in turn allow me to be your protector through life?

Dearest, I am going to press my suit still further. Will you not be mine before I go, and accompany me on my journey? I know this is asking a great deal of you. To accept of this proposition, is to take you from a home of affluence, where you are surrounded with every desired comfort. I have no right to ask the sacrifice; and yet I have resolved to make bold before I go, and tell you all. If you accept my offer, and will consent to cast your fortunes with me out in the great Sea of the Hereafter, I can assure you that no trouble or sorrow will come to you through me; and that, as you will be my dear, dear companion and sacred trust, so will I be to you all that a lover and husband can be.

Now, dearest, if you will accept my future as your own, and place yourself by my side, accepting the sorrow and partaking of the joy that is in store for me, you will make me the happiest of men. If you assent, God grant that you may never regret your faith. Do not decide the question hastily. The sacrifice is such, in leaving home and kindred, that you may not accept of my proposal even though you love. When you have fully determined, however, please send the answer, which I shall most anxiously await. Ever, Dear Clara,

Your Affectionate,

HENRY ADAMS.

Reply.

172 — St., April 16, 18—.

DEAR HENRY:

I can make a reply to your candid question at once. I do not need to deliberate upon it long. I love you; I confide in you. I will trust you; I will go with you; I will accept the love and the future you offer. You may have many joys; you may experience some sorrows: I will share and bear them all with you, trusting that patient, earnest, willing effort may crown our labors with success. Believing that God will guide and prosper us, I can only add, hoping to see you soon, that I am,

Ever yours,

CLARA DUNHAM.

Wedding Cards & Invitations.

WEDDING CARDS.

IF the lady who marries resides with her parents, with relatives, guardians, or friends, and the marriage receives the approval of those parties, the ceremony usually takes place at the residence of the bride, or at the church where she generally attends; a reception being held at her residence soon afterwards or upon the return from the bridal tour.

Some parties prefer to marry very quietly, having but few guests at the wedding. Others make more elaborate display, and observe the time as an occasion of general rejoicing. Where many guests are invited, it is customary to issue notes of invitation to those persons whose attendance is desired, accompanied by wedding cards bearing the name of the bride and groom. The form of wording such notes and cards has changed but little for several years, though the *style* in which such wording appears, changes frequently.

Two methods are pursued in preparing the invitations and cards: one being to have them neatly printed from type; the other, and more expensive manner, is to have them engraved and printed in the metropolis, by a card-engraver, who makes an exclusive business of preparing such cards.

The later style for cards and notes of invitation is to have the most of the wording in a light script, upon very fine, white, billet paper, and the cards upon thin bristol-board, sometimes long, and frequently nearly square, according to fancy.

The following cards and notes of invitation, while expressing the suitable wording, do not,

in all cases, represent the size of the card or note of invitation. They are of various sizes, according to fancy, and generally a little larger than here illustrated.

In sending the note of invitation, it is customary to inclose the cards in the same envelope. In cases where no guests are invited, yet it is desired to inform the acquaintances throughout the country of the marriage, it is usual to inclose the cards alone. Formerly, it was common to use but one card, having Mr. & Mrs. Chas. H. Smith in the center of the card, while the lady's maiden name was placed upon the lower left-hand corner. Of late, it is regarded more in style to use two cards, one considerably larger than the other; the larger bearing the names, Mr. & Mrs. Chas. H. Smith, the smaller, the lady's name alone, thus:

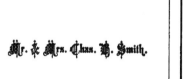

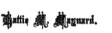

If it is definitely decided where the future permanent residence of the newly wedded couple is to be, it is proper to place the name of the town and state, at the lower left-hand corner of the larger card, as shown herewith.

Invitations to the Wedding.

THE following, are among the many of the various styles of notes of invitation to the wedding ceremony. The form shown here, is printed on paper about the width, but a little shorter than, commercial note paper, the wording being on the lower half of the sheet. In the center of the upper half of the sheet is the monogram, composed of the initial letters of the surnames of the bride and groom, blended together. This monogram is also printed upon the flap of the envelope containing the invitation and cards. The accompanying is the note of invitation issued by Mr. & Mrs. D Collins, on the occasion of the marriage of their daughter, M. Louise, to Jay H. Sabray; the ceremony taking place at their residence. Two cards accompany this note, one reading *Mr. & Mrs. Jay H. Sabray*, the other, *M. Louise Collins*.

Mr. & Mrs. Chas. B. Smith,

NEWARK, N J

Actual size of one form of Note of Invitation   This dotted line shows the fold.

Mr. & Mrs. D. Collins

Request the pleasure of your Company at the Marriage of their Daughter,

M. Louise to Jay H. Sabray,

Thursday, September 19th, '72, at 8 o'clock, P. M.

AT THEIR HOME, ATLANTA, GA.

If desirous of giving information of the time of return from the bridal tour, and an invitation to receptions afterwards, the address is omitted on the larger card, and a third card may accompany the other two, worded as follows:

Wednesdays and Fridays,

AFTER DECEMBER 14, 1872,

Cor. of Seventh and Clinton Sts.　　　MILWAUKEE, WIS.

This style of invitation, printed on a fine card about the size of a large envelope, is frequently employed. If desirous of using colored cardboard, a light olive or pink tint is sometimes admissible, though white is always in best taste.

THOS. H. CUMMINGS.　　　MARY C. BENHAM.

AT THE

Residence of Mr. & Mrs. G. Benham,

WEDNESDAY EVE'G, MAR. 10, 1872,

At Eight o'olook.

This style of invitation, requiring no cards, is frequently used:

FIRST BAPTIST CHURCH,

St. Paul, Minnesota.

CEREMONY

Thursday Evening, Dec. 27th, 1870,

AT 6 O'CLOCK.

GEORGE R. VANCE.　　　ALICE D. SPENCER.

The following note, announcing, "At Home," after October 15, requires no cards:

H. D. MILES.　　　MARY D. WILLIAMS.

CEREMONY.

Third Presbyterian Church

CHICAGO,

Monday, September 23d, 1872,

AT FOUR O'CLOCK, P. M.

At Home, after October 15th.　　　No. 12 Oakland Street.

The cards are often made in this proportion, and fastened with a ribbon, thus:

Not unfrequently the cards are fastened at the top, as shown in this illustration:

The following invitation is accompanied by the cards shown above, fastened by a ribbon in the center. The larger card bears the names of Mr. and Mrs. James Wilson; the other, the name of the bride, Angeline Sherman.

The succeeding invitation is issued by the parents of the bride, the reception taking place at their residence, after the ceremony at church. As with the other invitations, this is also accompanied by the monogram.

WEDDING CEREMONIES.
FOR
Notes of
INVITATION TO
WEDDINGS AND
PARTIES

Preceding Pages.

HAVING resolved upon marriage, the lady will determine when the ceremony shall take place.

No peculiar form of ceremony is requisite, nor is it imperative that it be performed by a particular person. In the United States, marriage is regarded as a civil contract, which may be entered into by a simple declaration of the contracting parties, made in the presence of one or more witnesses, that they, the said parties, do respectively contract to be husband and wife.

In consequence of the recognized vast importance of marriage to the parties contracting the same, long usage has established the custom, almost universally, of having the ceremony performed by, or in presence of, a clergyman or magistrate.

To be entitled to contract marriage, the following requisites are necessary: 1st, That they be willing to marry; 2d, That they be of sound mind; 3d, That they have arrived at the age allowed by law; 4th, That neither of the parties is married already to another who is living, and from whom such party has not obtained a divorce from the bonds of matrimony; and 5th, That the parties are not so nearly related by consanguinity, as to prohibit their marriage, by the laws of the State in which the marriage is contracted.

In most of the States, the common law requires that the male be fourteen and the female twelve years of age, before the marriage can take place. In certain States, seventeen for males and fourteen for females; in others, the age for males is eighteen, for females, fourteen.

Formerly in certain Eastern States, parties intending to marry were required by statute to record a notice of such intent with the town clerk for three weeks, at the expiration of which time, if no objection was interposed, the clerk was authorized to give a certificate to that effect, and the clergyman or magistrate was empowered to perform the ceremony. In various States, the law requires that parties intending marriage shall previously obtain from the city or town clerk, a certificate of their respective names, occupations, ages, birth-places, and residences upon receipt of which, any clergyman or magistrate is authorized to perform the ceremony.

In several States of the Union, the consent of the parents or guardians is required, before the proper officer can issue a license, if the male be under twenty-one years, or the female under eighteen

In some of the States, a license to marry must first be procured of the city, town, or county clerk, empowering the clergyman or magistrate to marry the contracting parties, which is worded as follows:

Marriage   License.

—State of—   —County of—

The people of the State of................................, to any person legally authorized to solemnize Marriage, GREETING: You are hereby authorized to join in the holy bonds of Matrimony, and to celebrate the rites and ceremonies of Marriage, between Mr.................................., and M................................, according to the usual custom and laws of the State of................................, and you are required to return this license to me within thirty days, from the celebration of such Marriage, with a Certificate of the same, appended thereto, and signed by you, under the penalty of One Hundred Dollars.

Witness................................, Clerk of our said Court and the Seal thereof, at his office, in................................, in said County, this day of................................, A. D.,................187....

Seal.

                                                 County Clerk.

State of................................ }
                     S.S.   I,................................, hereby certify that on
.... County.
the................................ day of................................, 187...., I joined in Marriage,
Mr................................, and M................................, agreeable to the authority given in the above License, and the customs and laws of this State.
Given under my hand and seal, this................................ day of................................, A. D., 187....

                                                 SEAL.

The Ceremony.

The license procured, the ceremony of marriage may take place wherever it best suits the convenience of the parties marrying, and may be performed by a clergyman, justice of the supreme court, judge of an inferior court, justice of the peace, or police justice; one or more witnesses being present to testify to the marriage. The clergyman or magistrate may visit the candidates for matrimony at a private residence, hotel, hall, church or other place; or the parties may call upon the clergyman at his residence, or visit the magistrate in his office, where the rite may be performed. When the ceremony is conducted by the magistrate, the following is the usual form.

Form of Marriage.

(The man and woman rising, the justice will say to the man:)

"Will you have this woman to be your wedded wife, to live together after God's ordinance, in the holy estate of Matrimony, to love her, comfort her, honor and keep her, in sickness and in health, and, forsaking all others, keep thee only unto her, so long as you both shall live?"

(Then, addressing the woman, the justice will say:)

"Will you have this man to be your wedded husband, to live together after God's ordinance, in the holy estate of Matrimony, to love, honor and keep him, in sickness and in health, and, forsaking all others, keep thee only unto him, so long as you both shall live?"

(The parties answering in the affirmative, the justice will then instruct to join hands, and say:)

"By the act of joining hands you take upon yourselves the relation of husband and wife, and solemnly promise and engage, in the presence of these witnesses, to love, honor, comfort and cherish each other as such, so long as you both shall live; therefore, in accordance with the laws of the State of —————, I do hereby pronounce you husband and wife."

Short Form of Marriage.

(The justice will instruct the parties to rise and join hands, and then say:)

"By this act of joining hands you do take upon yourselves the relation of husband and wife, and solemnly promise and engage, in the presence of these witnesses, to love and honor, comfort and cherish each other as such, as long as you both shall live; therefore in accordance with the laws of the State of —————, I do hereby pronounce you husband and wife."

The form used by clergymen is essentially the same, though the wording may vary slightly to suit the occasion and conform to the rites of the church under which the parties marry.

The marriage license is returned by the magistrate or clergyman to the clerk that granted it, for record. At the time of procuring the license, however, the bridegroom or other person should obtain a blank marriage certificate, usually furnished by the clerk, which should be filled by the clergyman or magistrate at the close of the ceremony, certifying to the marriage of the parties; which certificate should be always preserved by the husband and wife, as proof of marriage, if necessary, when they have removed to other parts of the country.

The following is the form of the marriage certificate:

Marriage Certificate.

State of —————————, ————— County.

THIS CERTIFIES

That .... of .... in the State of .... and .... of .... in the State of ....
were at .... in the said County, by me joined together in

HOLY MATRIMONY,

On the ...., day of ...., in the year of our Lord, One Thousand Eight Hundred and Seventy .....
In Presence of

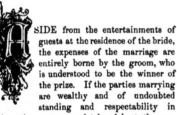SIDE from the entertainments of guests at the residence of the bride, the expenses of the marriage are entirely borne by the groom, who is understood to be the winner of the prize. If the parties marrying are wealthy and of undoubted standing and respectability in society, they can appropriately celebrate the nuptial ceremony in an expensive manner, the occasion being taken by the relatives and friends as an opportunity for the making of every description of present to the bride and groom. If, however, the parties move in the humbler walks of life, an expensive bridal tour, and very great display at the wedding, are not advisable. It is much better for the newly wedded couple to commence life in a manner so plain and modest that succeeding years cannot fail to steadily increase their wealth and give them better opportunities. People always more highly respect those persons who steadily go upward, no matter how slowly, than those that attempt a display beyond their ability honestly to maintain.

To legally marry in the United States, only a few incidental expenses are really necessary. Of these, the license costs, in different States, from one to two dollars, and the magistrate, for performing the ceremony, is allowed by law to charge two dollars. While no law regulates the price, it is customary to quietly present the clergyman five dollars or more, according to the ability and liberality of the groom. In giving notice of the marriage to the newspaper, it is courtesy always to enclose, with the same, a dollar bill.

The wording of the marriage notice will depend upon circumstances. If the parties have a large circle of acquaintance, to whom they desire to offer an apology for not having invited them to the wedding, they will announce, with the notice, that no general invitation was extended, thus:

MARRIED.

LEONARD—REYNOLDS.— In this city, at the residence of the bride's father, January 1, 1873, by the Rev. Chas. G. Robinson, rector of Christ Church. Mr. Theron D. Leonard and Mrs. A. B. Reynolds, daughter of Wm. Fairbanks, Esq., all of Philadelphia. No cards.

Other marriage notices, according to circumstances, will read as follows:

In this city, by the Rev. H. A. Henderson, CHARLES H. WILLIAMS and MYRA B. COOLEY, both of Chicago.

On Tuesday, the 7th inst., by the Rev. Dr. Belmont, at the residence of the bride's uncle, Harvey Baker, Esq., Cyrus E. Maynard, of New York, and Miss Lizzie H. Wentworth, of Cleveland, Ohio.

On Thursday, January 30th, at the residence of Mr. Asa Sprague, 144 Mayberry St., Anton D. Miller, of St. Joseph, Mich., and Harriet A. Sprague, of this city.
St. Joseph papers please copy.

At the Leland house, Springfield, Ill., January 30, by the Rev. J. L. Stoddard, Stephen M. Byron, of Detroit, Mich., and Carrie D. Paine, of Springfield, Ill.

On the evening of the 30th, at the Revere House, by Winfield Gardner, Miss Emma Brown to William Wedgewood, all of this city.

In this city, on Monday, at the residence of the bride's father, Mr. H. A. Waldron and Miss Agnes E. Willett.

The ceremonies took place at the residence of Henry Willett, Esq., on Beverly Place, yesterday morning at nine o'clock, only a select company of friends being present. The happy couple departed at once on their wedding tour, with New York as their main point of destination. Their visit will be protracted until the middle of next month, when, upon their return, Mr. Waldron will assume the secretaryship of the Great Western Mutual Insurance Company, of this city, to which position he has been recently called by the directors of the company.

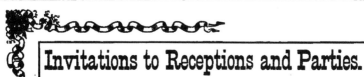

Invitations to Receptions and Parties.

PRINTED ON CARDS AND CIRCULARS.

Mr. & Mrs. Charles Simmonds,

RECEIVE FRIENDS,

Wednesday Evening, May 10th,

At 8 o'clock.

Mr. & Mrs. W. H. Bartlett,

BURLINGTON,

Friday Evening, Sept. 20th,

At 8 1-2 o'clock.

Dr. & Mrs. William Stewart,

Wednesday Eve'g, Nov. 10th, '71,

AT EIGHT O'CLOCK.

G.C.H.

GRAND CENTRAL HOTEL

Hop,

THURSDAY EVENING, JAN. 4TH, 1871.

COMPLIMENTARY.

Mr. _____

Yourself and Ladies are Cordially Invited.

Committee of Arrangements:

D. O. Lewis,   Wm. W. Brown,   D. B. Snow,
Hiram D. King,   Chas. Wilson,   H. E. Potwin.

Family Records.

How to Prepare the Register; giving Names of the Family, Births, Marriages and Deaths.

URING LIFE, a carefully prepared record of the family, which should be arranged by the head of the household, is of great convenience for reference. This register should contain the name, birth, marriage, and death of each member of the family. It may be kept in the Bible, on a paper prepared especially for the purpose, suitable for framing, or in any manner whereby the same may be preserved. It may also contain brief biographical sketches of members of the family.

N preparing the register, care should be taken to give the names of the family in full, the town and state where each was born, and date of birth; the state and town where each died, and date of death; town and state where each married, and date, together with the name of the officiating clergyman, or magistrate, and of one or more witnesses to the marriage. In proving claims to pensions, or heirship to estates, this is frequently of great importance. Observe carefully the form of record shown on the opposite page.

BIOGRAPHY OF CHILDREN.

UARDIANS and parents are also recommended to prepare in a book of blank pages, made for the purpose, a biographical sketch of each child under their charge, noting peculiarities of birth, attending physician, color of hair, eyes, &c., when born; strength of constitution, subsequent disposition, age at which the child first walks, talks, reads, writes, first attends school, and so on upwards until the child is able to take up the record itself.

HE child's record should be made very full and explicit for many reasons, the principal being that it may be of great service to the future biographer of the child, while the physiologist may draw an important lesson by a comparison between the habits of infancy and those of mature years. This record will certainly be a matter of value to the family, and like the infant-picture, it will be of especial interest to the man and woman as a daguerreotype of their early years.

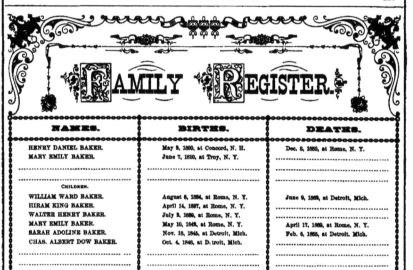

FAMILY REGISTER.

NAMES.	BIRTHS.	DEATHS.
HENRY DANIEL BAKER.	May 2, 1800, at Concord, N. H.	Dec. 8, 1850, at Rome, N. Y.
MARY EMILY BAKER.	June 7, 1810, at Troy, N. Y.	
CHILDREN.		
WILLIAM WARD BAKER.	August 6, 1834, at Rome, N. Y.	June 9, 1862, at Detroit, Mich.
HIRAM KING BAKER.	April 14, 1837, at Rome, N. Y.	
WALTER HENRY BAKER.	July 3, 1839, at Rome, N. Y.	
MARY EMILY BAKER.	May 10, 1842, at Rome, N. Y.	April 17, 1860, at Rome, N. Y.
SARAH ADOLINE BAKER.	Nov. 18, 1845, at Detroit, Mich.	Feb. 6, 1855, at Detroit. Mich.
CHAS. ALBERT DOW BAKER.	Oct. 4, 1848, at Detroit, Mich.	

MARRIAGES.

NAMES.	By Whom Solemnized.	Names of Witnesses.
HENRY DANIEL BAKER and MARY EMILY MUNSON.	By the Rev. A. H. Burline, June 2, 1831, At Troy, New York.	In Presence of A. D. Baker, Mary E. Sherman, Cynthia Benson.
CHILDREN.		
WILLIAM WARD BAKER and BERTHA JANE CORBETT.	By the Rev. D. P. Smith, Sept. 1, 1859, At Saratoga Springs, N. Y.	In Presence of Hannah E. Holmes, Thos. E. Andrews, W. H. Burton.
WALTER HENRY BAKER and ALICE ANN BAILEY.	By the Rev. Arthur Brown Sept. 4, 1865, At Rome, New York.	In Presence of D. R. Newell, Selden Marshall, Susan Maynard.
MARY EMILY BAKER and MYRON BURTON ELDRIDGE.	By the Rev. D. O. Smith, Aug. 16, 1865, At Detroit, Michigan.	In Presence of Capt. O. D. Kemple, Malvina Simpson, Harriet Putnam.
CHAS. A. D. BAKER and FLORENCE PERCY BRIGGS.	By Wm. M. Kellogg, J. P., March 4, 1872, At St. Louis, Missouri.	In Presence of Anna E. Moore, Chas. D. Wells, Abigail Minard.

Marriage Anniversaries.

GOLD, SILVER AND OTHER WEDDINGS.

ASHION has established the custom, of late years, of celebrating certain anniversaries of the marriage, these being named as follows:

The celebration at the expiration of the first year is called the COTTON wedding; at two years comes the PAPER; at three, the LEATHER; at the close of five years comes the WOODEN; at the seventh anniversary the friends assemble with the WOOLEN, and at ten years comes the TIN. At twelve years the SILK AND FINE LINEN; at fifteen the CRYSTAL wedding. At twenty, the friends gather with their CHINA, and at twenty-five the married couple, that have been true to their vows for a quarter of a century, are rewarded with SILVER gifts. From this time forward, the tokens of esteem become rapidly more valuable. At the thirtieth anniversary, they are presented with PEARLS; at the fortieth, come the RUBIES; and at the fiftieth, occurs the celebration of a glorious GOLDEN wedding. Beyond that time the aged couple are allowed to enjoy their many gifts in peace. If, however, by any possibility they reach the seventy-fifth anniversary, they are presented with the rarest gifts to be obtained, at the celebration of their DIAMOND wedding.

In issuing the invitations for celebrating these anniversaries, it is customary to print them on a material emblematical of the occasion. Thus, thin wood, leather, cloth, tin-foil, silk, silver and gold paper, and other materials are brought into use.

Of course, those who accept of such an invitation, and partake of the hospitalities of the host and hostess, are expected to contribute to the collection of gifts that will grace the occasion.

The form of invitation for such an anniversary is represented in the following:

Invitation to the Crystal Wedding.

CRYSTAL
1856.
WEDDING.
1873.

Mr. & Mrs. W. Stevens,

RECEPTION

*Thursday Evening, March 26, 1873,
at Four O'clock.*

ROME,   N. Y.

Invitation to the China Wedding.

China Wedding.

1850 1870.

Mr. & Mrs. B. Ring

WILL RECEIVE THEIR FRIENDS AT THE

TWENTIETH ANNIVERSARY

OF THEIR

MARRIAGE,

Tuesday Eve., June 14, 1870.

LONG BRANCH.

Invitation to the Silver Wedding.

MR. & MRS. H. R. MEAD,

*Cordially invite you to be present at their Twenty-
Fifth Wedding*

ANNIVERSARY,

On Monday Evening, June 16, 1873.

No. 700 Broadway, New York.   Ceremony at 8 o'Clock.

Invitation to the Golden Wedding.

1823   1873

Mr. & Mrs. T. Brown,

*Request the pleasure of your Com-
pany at the*

FIFTIETH

ANNIVERSARY,

OF THEIR MARRIAGE,

On Thursday Evening, Dec. 20, 1873,

174 MAYWOOD ST., CHICAGO.

Notes of Invitation to Parties
AND ELSEWHERE.

N OTES of invitation to a large party are usually printed and displayed in a style similar to the annexed, being always worded in the third person. If written, and among intimate friends, a more familiar style may be adopted.

Invitations should be written, or printed upon a whole sheet of small note-paper, and should be issued at least a week before the time appointed for the party, so that, if necessary, a suitable dress may be obtained. For a costume ball or masquerade, two weeks is the usual time allowed for preparation.

The letters R. S. V. P. are sometimes put at the end of a note. They stand for the French phrase, "*Rèpondez s'il vous plait*"—- answer, if you please. It is better, however, when an answer is particularly desired, to say, "An answer will oblige."

It is courtesy to reply promptly to a note of invitation requesting an answer.

If no reply is requested, and you send no regrets, it is understood that you accept the invitation.

Send invitations, to persons in your own city or neighborhood, by your own messenger. It is regarded a violation of etiquette to send them by mail.

Invitation to an Intimate Friend.

Mrs. Langford may write to her intimate friend, Miss Burling, as follows:

June 9th, 18—

Dear Lizzie:

We are to have a little social party on Wednesday evening next, which will be very incomplete without you. Please come, and bring your cousin with you. He will not, I trust, require a more formal invitation, as he knows he will be very welcome.

Your Friend,

Harriet Langford

Wednesday Evening.

Invitation to a Lawn Soiree.

MR. & MRS. HARRINGTON.

Mr. D. C. HARRINGTON.

Request the pleasure of your company, at a Lawn Soiree, Friday evening, from half-past seven to half-past ten o'clock, June 20th, 18—, weather permitting.

R. S. V. P.

Invitation to an Evening Party.

Mrs. Langford requests the pleasure of Mr. and Mrs. Bell's company on Thursday evening, 7th inst., at seven o'clock.

No. 7 —— St., Dec. 1st.

Answer Accepting the Invitation.

Mr. and Mrs. Bell accept, with pleasure, Mrs. Langford's kind invitation for Thursday evening, the 7th inst.

No. 8 —— St., Dec. 2d.

Answer Declining the Invitation.

Mr. and Mrs. Bell regret their inability to accept Mrs. Langford's kind invitation for Thursday evening, the 7th inst.

No. 8 —— St., Dec. 2d.

Invitation to a Dinner Party.

Mr. Conklin presents his warm regards to Mr. Belden, and requests the pleasure of his company to dinner, on Thursday next (18th) at 5 o'clock. Mr. Conklin expects the pleasure, also, of receiving Mr. Wilbur, of Buffalo.

An answer will oblige.

No. 44 —— St., June 16, 18—.

Answer Accepting the Invitation.

Mr. Belden presents his kind regards to Mr. Conklin, and accepts, with pleasure, his polite invitation for Thursday next.

No. 17 —— St., June 17, 18—.

Answer Declining the Invitation.

Mr. Belden regrets that a previously arranged business engagement will prevent his accepting Mr. Conklin's kind invitation for to-morrow. Mr. Belden has delayed answering until to-day, hoping to effect a change of appointment, but has learned this forenoon that no change can be made without serious disappointment to others.

No. 17 —— St., June 17, 18—.

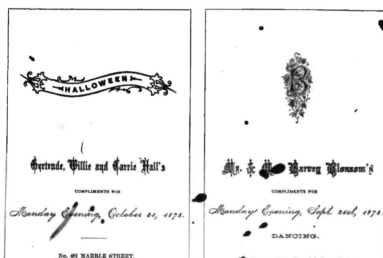

HALLOWEEN

Gertrude, Willie and Carrie Hall's

COMPLIMENTS FOR

Monday Evening, October 31, 1878.

No. 481 MARBLE STREET.

Mr. & Mrs. Harvey Blossom's

COMPLIMENTS FOR

Monday Evening, Sept. 24st, 1878.

DANCING.

Refreshments will be served at Ten o'Clock.

Familiar Invitation to a Wedding.

No.————St., Dec. 12, 18—.

DEAR HATTIE:

I have issued but few invitations for our Aggie's wedding, as we desire to be almost entirely private; but the presence of a few dear friends will give us all pleasure. Can we count you among those few? The ceremony will be at seven, on Tuesday evening next, December 18th, and at eight we will receive the other invited guests.

Hoping to see you early, I am,

Yours Affectionately,
BERTHA HANSON.

Answer Accepting the Invitation.

No.————St., Dec. 13, 18—.

MY DEAR BERTHA:

I accept with great pleasure your kind invitation to Aggie's wedding, and will be punctual. I most earnestly pray that she may be very happy in her new life and home. Please give her my kindest love and best wishes.

Your Friend,
HATTIE HARMON.

Answer Declining the Invitation.

No.————St., Dec. 13, 18—.

MY DEAR BERTHA:

My recent great bereavement must plead my excuse for not attending the wedding of your dear daughter Aggie. I would not cloud the festal scene by my heavy weeds of mourning, and I could not lay them aside, even for an hour, while the wound in my heart is so fresh with grief.

Deeply regretting that I cannot attend, I can only wish Aggie, in her new relations, the joyous life of happiness she so richly deserves.

Your Sincere Friend,
HATTIE HARMON.

The following exhibits the size of paper, and the wording of a Funeral Notice, in common use in the metropolitan cities, where it is impossible, frequently, for all the friends to know of the death.

Funeral Notice.

—

Yourself and family are respectfully invited to attend the funeral of

William Comstock,

from his late residence, on Oak Street, near Monroe, to-morrow afternoon, at three o'clock.

A discourse, by the Rev. A. W. Kendall, will be delivered, at the First Baptist Church, immediately before the funeral.

Pittsburgh, Nov. 7, 1874.

Invitation to a Picnic.

The Young Ladies of Mt. Hope Seminary Solicit the presence of Yourself and Friends AT THEIR **Annual Reunion and Picnic** ON THE GROUNDS OF HON. WM. STEVENSON, NEAR ELMWOOD, Friday Afternoon, Oct. 5th. AT TWO O'CLOCK.

Invitation to a Ball.

First Annual Ball OF **Philadelphian Society,** Wednesday Evening, Nov. 8, '74. AT CONTINENTAL HOTEL.

Invitation to a Festival.

Fête Champêtre, ON THE GROUNDS OF **Henry Mitchell, Esq.** SPRINGDALE, WEDNESDAY AFTERNOON, JUNE 10, 1874. Entrance Ticket, 50 Cents.

The above cards may be displayed in this manner, but for actual use should be about four times larger.

Visiting and Address Cards.

OUR kinds of cards are in general use, viz.: Wedding, Autograph or Visiting, Address, and Business cards. The wedding has already been described. The visiting card is used principally by the lady in her calls among acquaintances in the city. The address card is also frequently used for the same purpose, and is useful to present when it may be desired to open future correspondence. The business card is valuable for advertising and as being introductory to business acquaintance. In the autograph card, Chas. H. Briggs will write his name as follows:

Chas. H. Briggs.

His wife will write her name:

Mrs. Chas. H. Briggs.

His daughters will add Miss to their names, thus:

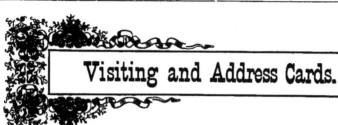

Miss Edith W Briggs.

Or the name may be without the Miss, thus:

Emily A. Briggs.

The address card may read thus:

Mrs. Chas. H. Briggs.
18 Beverly Place.

Or it may read thus:

Mrs. Chas. H. Briggs.
Appleton, Wis.

Autograph cards should be used only among those acquaintances to whom the residence is well known. Business cards should contain upon their face the name, business, address and references, if references are used.

NOTE.—A former rule of etiquette, not now so much observed, was for the eldest daughter, only, to prefix "Miss" to her name

Language and Sentiment of Flowers

A DICTIONARY OF THE LANGUAGE OF FLOWERS.

VERY charming and interesting method of communicating thought is by the aid of flowers, their language and sentiment being understood by the parties who present them. Although the following list is very complete, this vocabulary may be still enlarged by the addition of other definitions, the parties having an understanding as to what language the flower shall represent. Thus an extended and sometimes important correspondence may be carried on by the presentation of bouquets, single flowers and even leaves; the charm of this interchange of thought largely consisting in the romance attendant upon an expression of sentiment in a partially disguised and hidden language.

Of course much of the facility with which a conversation may be conducted, thus, will depend upon the intimate knowledge possessed of the language of flowers and the variety from which to select.

ILLUSTRATIONS.

A declaration of feeling between a lady and gentleman may be expressed by single flowers, as follows:

The gentleman presents a Red Rose—"I love you." The lady admits a partial reciprocation of the sentiment by returning a Purple Pansy—"You occupy my thoughts." The gentleman presses his suit still further by an Everlasting Pea—"Wilt thou go with me?" The lady replies by a Daisy, in which she says—"I will think of it." The gentleman, in his enthusiasm, plucks and presents a Shepherd's Purse—"I offer you my all." The lady, doubtingly, returns a sprig of Laurel—"Words, though sweet, may deceive." The gentleman still affirms his declaration by a sprig of Heliotrope—"I adore you." The lady admits a tenderness of sentiment by the Zinnia—"I mourn your absence."

LANGUAGE OF THE BOUQUET.

A collection of flowers in a bouquet may mean very much. Thus a Rose, Ivy and Myrtle will signify "Beauty, Friendship and Love." A Bachelor's Button "Hope," and a Red Rose "Love," will indicate that "I hope to obtain your love."

I DESIRE TO MARRY YOU.
Jonquil—Linden.

I HAVE SWEET MEMORIES IN MY SOLITUDE.
Periwinkle—Heath.

PRAY FOR ME IN MY ABSENCE.
White Verbena—Wormwood.

Thus longer and shorter sentences may be readily expressed by flower-language; and by agreement, if the variety of flowers is not sufficient, a change of definition may be given the more common blossoms and plants, whereby the language and correspondence may be conducted without inconvenience.

Flowers and their Sentiment.

Acacia, Rose..............Friendship.
Acanthus..............Art.
Adonis, Flos..............Painful recollections.
Agnus Castus..............Coldness; life without love.
Agrimony..............Gratitude.
Almonds..............Giddiness; heedlessness.
Aloe..............Bitterness.
Amaranth..............Immortality; Unfading.
Amaryllis..............Beautiful but timid.
Anemone, Garden..............Forsaken; Withered hopes; illness.
Amethyst..............Admiration.
Anemone, Windflower..............Desertion.
Angelica..............Inspiration.
Apple Blossom..............Preference.
Arbor Vitæ..............Unchanging Friendship.
Arbutus..............Thee only do I love.
Ash..............Grandeur.
Aspen..............Sighing.
Asphodel..............Remembered beyond the tomb.
Aster, Double German..Variety.
Aster, Large flowered....Afterthought; Love of variety.
Bachelors' Button........Hope; Single Blessedness.
Balm, Mint..............Pleasantry.
Balm of Gilead..............Healing; I am cured.
Balsamine..............Impatience.
Barberry..............Petulance; Ill temper.
Basil..............Give me your good wishes.
Bay Leaf..............I change but in death.
Beech..............Lovers' tryst; Prosperity.
Begonia..............Deformed.
Bindweed..............Humility; Night.
Birch..............Grace; Elegance.
Bittersweet Nightshade.Truth.
Blackthorn, or Sloe......Difficulties.
Bladder Tree..............Frivolous amusement

Blue Bell..............Constancy.
Blue Bottle..............Delicacy.
Borage..............Abruptness.
Box..............Stoicism.
Briers..............Envy.
Broom..............Neatness; Humility.
Bryony, Black..............Be my support.
Buckbean..............Calmness; Repose.
Bugloss..............Falsehood.
Bulrush..............Docility.
Burdock..............Touch me not; Importunity.
Buttercup..............Riches; Memories of childhood.
Cabbage..............Profit.
Calla..............Delicacy; Modesty.
Camillia..............Gratitude; Perfect Loveliness.
Camomile..............Energy in Adversity.
Candytuft..............Indifference; Architecture.
Canterbury Bell..............Constancy.
Cardinal Flower..............Distinction; Preferment.
Carnation..............Pure and deep love.
China Aster..............Love of variety.
Cedar Leaf..............I live for thee.
Cherry..............A good education.
Chestnut..............Do me justice.
Cereus, Night Blooming.Transient Beauty.
Chiccory..............Frugality; Economy.
Chrysanthemum..............A heart left to desolation.
Cinnamon Tree..............Forgiveness of injuries.
Cinquefoil..............A beloved daughter.
Cistus..............Surety.
Clover, Red..............Industry.
Clematis..............Mental Beauty; Artifice.
Clover, White..............I promise.
Clover, Four Leaved....Be mine.
Cockle..............Vain is beauty without merit.

Coltsfoot..............Justice shall be done you.
Columbine, Red..............Anxious and trembling.
Coreopsis..............Always cheerful.
Coriander..............Hidden merit.
Corn..............Riches; Abundance.
Cornelian, Cherry..............Continuance; Duration.
Cowslip..............Native grace; Pensiveness.
Coxcomb..............Foppery.
Crocus..............Cheerfulness.
Cresses..............Stability.
Crowfoot..............Ingratitude.
Currant..............Thy frown will kill me
Crown, Imperial..............Power; Pride of birth
Cucumber..............Criticism.
Cypress..............Despair; Mourning.
Dahlia..............Dignity and elegance.
Daffodil..............Unrequited love.
Daisy, Garden..............I share your feelings.
Daisy, Single Field......I will think of it.
Dandelion..............Oracle; Coquetry.
Datura..............Deceitful charms.
Dew Plant..............Serenade.
Dittany of Crete..............Birth.
Dodder..............Meanness; Baseness.
Ebony Tree..............Blackness.
Eglantine..............Poetry; I wound to heal.
Elder..............Compassion.
Elecampane..............Tears.
Everlasting..............Always remembered.
Everlasting Pea..............Wilt thou go with me?
Fennel..............Force; Strength.
Fern..............Sincerity.
Fir..............Elevation.
Flax..............I feel your benefits.
Flos, Adonis..............Painful recollections.
Forget-me-not..............Do not forget.
Foxglove..............Insincerity; Occupation.
Fraxinella..............Fire.
Fuchsia..............Taste; Frugality.

Gentian............Intrinsic worth.
Geranium, Ivy............I engage you for the next dance.
Geranium, Oak ....A melancholy mind.
Geranium, Rose ....I prefer you.
Geranium, Scarlet ......Silliness.
Gillyflower, Common ....Lasting Beauty.
Gillyflower, Stock......Promptness.
Gladiolus ....Ready armed.
Goats' Rue ....Reason.
Gold Basket ....Tranquility.
Gooseberry ....Anticipation.
Grape Vine..........Intemperance.
Grass..............Utility; Submission.
Greek Valerian......Rupture.
Golden Rod ....Encouragement.
Gorse, or Turse ......Anger.
Harebell............Retirement; Grief.
Hawthorn ....Hope.
Hazel..............Reconciliation.
Heath ....Solitude.
Heliotrope ....I adore you ; Devotion
Henbane............Blemish; Fault.
Hibiscus ....Delicate beauty.
Hoarhound ....Fire.
Holly ....Am I forgotten? Foresight.
Hollyhock ....Fecundity; Ambition.
Honey Flower........Sweet and secret love.
Honeysuckle ....Devoted love; Fidelity
Hop ....Injustice.
Hornbean............Ornament.
Horse Chestnut ......Luxury.
Houstonia ....Innocence; Content.
Houseleek ....Domestic economy.
Hyacinth ....Constancy; Benevolence.
Hydrangea ....Vain-glory; Heartlessness.
Ice Plant............Your looks freeze me.
Indian Plum..........Privation.
Iris, Common Garden...A message for thee.
Iris, German........Flame.
Ivy..............Friendship; Marriage
Jasmine, White ......Amiability.
Jasmine, Yellow ......Grace and elegance.
Jonquil ....Desire; Affection returned.
Juniper ....Asylum; Aid ; Protection.
Laburnum ....Pensive beauty.
Ladyslipper ....Capricious beauty.
Larch ....Boldness ; Audacity.
Larkspur, Pink......Lightness; Fickleness
Laurel, American......Words, though sweet, may deceive.
Lantana ....Rigor.
Laurel, Mountain......Glory; Victory; Ambition.
Laurestine..........I die if neglected.
Lavatera ....Sweet disposition.
Lavender ....Mistrust.
Lemon Blossom ......Prudence; Discretion.
Lettuce ....Cold hearted; Coolness.
Lichen..............Dejection.
Lilac, Purple ....First emotions of love
Lilac, White..........Youth.
Lily, Water ....Eloquence.
Lily, White..........Majesty; Purity.
Lily of the Valley......Return of happiness.
Linden, or Lime......Conjugal; Marriage.
Liverwort ....Confidence.
Locust Tree, Green......Love beyond the grave
Lotus Leaf ....Recantation.
Lucern ....Life.
Lupine ....Dejection.
Madder ....Calumny.
Magnolia ....Love of Nature.
Maiden Hair ....Discretion.
Marjoram ....Blushes.
Manchineel Tree......Falseness.
Mandrake ....Rarity.
Maple ....Reserve.
Marigold ....Sacred affection.
Marigold, Garden......Grief; Chagrin.
Marigold, Rainy......A storm.
Marigold and Cypress...Despair.
Marshmallow ......Beneficence.
Marvel of Peru........Timidity.
Mayflower..........Welcome.

Meadow Saffron......My best days are past
Mezereon............Desire to please.
Mignonette ....Your qualities surpass your charms.
Milfoil..............War.
Mint ....Virtue.
Milkweed ....Hope in misery.
Mistletoe ....I surmount everything
Mock Orange........Counterfeit; Uncertainty.
Monkshood ....Treachery; A foe is near.
Morning Glory........Coquetry; Affection.
Mountain Ash ......I watch over you.
Moss ....Maternal love.
Mourning Bride ......I have lost all.
Mugwort ....Good luck; Happiness
Mulberry, Black......I shall not survive you
Mulberry, White ......Wisdom.
Mullen ....Good nature.
Mushroom..........Suspicion.
Musk Plant..........Weakness.
Myrtle..............Love in Absence.
Myrrh ....Gladness.
Narcissus............Egotism; Self-Love.
Nasturtium ....Patriotism; Splendor
Nettle..............Cruelty.
Nightshade............Dark thoughts; Sorcery.
Oak ....Hospitality; Bravery.
Oleander ....Beware.
Olive ....Peace.
Orange Flower........Chastity.
Orchis, Bee..........Error.
Orchis, Spider ......Skill.
Osier ....Frankness.
Osmunda ....Reverie.
Oxalia ....Wood sorrel.
Pansy, Purple ......You occupy my thoughts.
Parsley..............Festivity; Banquet.
Passion Flower........Devotion; Religious fervor.
Peach Blossom ......I am your captive.
Peony ....O.entation; Anger.
Persimmons ....Bury me amid Nature's beauties.
Peppermint ....Warmth of feeling.
Pennyroyal ....Flee away.
Periwinkle ....Sweet memories.
Phlox..............Our hearts are united.
Pimpernel ....Rendezvous; Change.
Pine ....Pity; Endurance; Daring.
Pine Apple ....You are perfect.
Pink, Red ....Pure love.
Plane, or Platane......Genius.
Plum Tree..........Keep your promises.
Plum, Wild..........Independence.
Polyanthus ....Heart's mystery
Pomegranate ......Conceit.
Pompion or Pumpkin ...Grossness; Coarseness
Poplar, Black..........Courage.
Poplar, White ......Time.
Poppy, Corn..........Consolation.
Poppy, White ......Sleep; Oblivion.
Potatoe ....Benevolence.
Primrose ....Modest worth; Silent love.
Privit, or Prim......Prohibition.
Purple Scabious ......Mourning.
Queen of the Meadow...Uselessness.
Quince ....Temptation.
Ranunculus, Garden...You are radiant with charms.
Reeds ....Music.
Rest Harrow ....Obstacle.
Rhododendron........Agitation.
Rhubarb............Advice.
Rosebud..........Confession of love.
Rosebud, White ......Too young to love.
Rose, Cinnamon ......Without pretension.
Rose, Hundred leaved...The graces.
Rose, Austrian ......Thou art all that is lovely.
Rose Leaf..........I never trouble.
Rose, Monthly......Beauty ever new.
Rose, Moss..........Superior merit; Voluptuousness.
Rose, Musk..........Capricious beauty.
Rose, Red ....I love you.
Rose, White........Silence.

Rose, Wild, Single ......Simplicity.
Rose, Yellow ......Infidelity; Unfaithfulness.
Rosemary ....Remembrance; Your presence revives me
Rue.................Disdain.
Rush ....Docility.
Saffron, Meadow......My best days are past.
Saffron, Crocus......Do not abuse me.
Sage..............Domestic Virtue; Esteem.
St. John's Wort........Animosity.
Sardonia............Irony.
Satin Flower ......Forgetfulness.
Scratch Weed ....Roughness.
Scotch Thistle ......Retaliation.
Sensitive Plant......Sensitiveness; Modesty.
Serpent Cactus ......Horror.
Service Tree, or Sorb ...Prudence.
Shepherd's Purse......I offer you my all.
Silver Weed ....Naiveté.
Snapdragon..........Presumption.
Snowball ....Goodness ; Thoughts of Heaven.
Snowdrop ....Consolation; A friend in adversity.
Sorrel.............Parental Affection.
Speedwell ....Fidelity.
Spindle Tree..........Your charms are graven on my heart.
Star of Bethlehem......Reconciliation; Purity.
Straw, Broken........Quarrel.
Straw..............Agreement; United.
Strawberry ....Perfect excellence.
Sumach............Splendid misery.
Sunflower, Tall ......Lofty and wise thoughts.
Sunflower............False riches.
Sunflower, Dwarf......Adoration.
Sweet Flag ....Fitness.
Sweet Pea ....A meeting.
Sweet Sultan ......Happiness.
Sweet William ......Gallantry; Finesse; Dexterity.
Syringa.............Memory; Fraternal love.
Sycamore ....Curiosity.
Tare..............Vice.
Teasel ....Misanthropy.
Thistle ....Austerity.
Thorn Apple ....Disguise.
Thrift ....Sympathy.
Thyme ....Activity.
Tremella............Resistance.
Tube Rose............Dangerous Pleasure; Voluptuousness; Sweet voice.
Tulip, Variegated ......Beautiful eyes.
Tulip, Red............Declaration of love.
Valerian, Common......Accommodating disposition.
Valerian............Facility.
Venus's Looking Glass...Flattery.
Verbena............Sensibility; Sensitiveness.
Verbena, Purple ......I weep for you; Regret.
Verbena, White......Pray for me.
Vervain ....Enchantment.
Vernal Grass ......Poor, but happy.
Vetch ....I cling to thee.
Violet, Blue ......Faithfulness.
Violet, White......Purity; Candor; Modesty.
Volkamenia ....May you be happy.
Wall Flower ......Fidelity in misfortune.
Weeping Willow ......Melancholy.
Wheat..............Wealth.
Whortleberry ......Treachery.
Willow, Common......Forsaken.
Willow Herb..........Pretension.
Wood Sorrel..........Joy.
Woodbine ....Fraternal love.
Wormwood ....Absence.
Yarrow..............Cure for the heartache.
Yew.................Sadness.
Zinnia..............I mourn your absence.

VOCABULARY OF "GIVEN" NAMES, FOR REFERENCE.

Names of Men, Alphabetically Arranged.

Aaron.	Benjamin.	Ebenezer.	Frederick.	Isador.	Leander.	Nahum.	Raymond.	Theobald.
Abel.	Beriah.	Edgar.	Gabriel.	Isaiah.	Lemuel.	Nathan.	Reuben.	Theodore.
Abiel.	Bernard.	Edmund.	Gail.	Israel.	Leo.	Nathaniel.	Reuel.	Theodoric.
Abijah.	Bertram.	Edward.	Gaius.	Ivan.	Leon.	Neal.	Reynold.	Theophilus.
Abner.	Bertrand.	Edwin.	Gamaliel.	Jabez.	Leonard.	Nell.	Richard.	Theron.
Abraham.	Boniface.	Egbert.	Gardner.	Jacob.	Leonidas.	Nehemiah.	Robert.	Thomas.
Abram.	Burnell.	Elbert.	Garret.	Jairus.	Leopold.	Newton.	Roderic.	Thompson.
Adam.	Burton.	Elbridge.	George.	James.	Leroy.	Nicolas.	Roderick.	Timothy.
Addison.	Byron.	Eldred.	Gerald.	Japeth.	Levi.	Niles.	Rodman.	Titus.
Adelbert.	Cadwallader.	Eleazer.	Gerard.	Jared.	Lewis.	Noah.	Rodolph.	Tobias.
Adolphus.	Cæsar.	Eli.	Gershom.	Jason.	Lincoln.	Noel.	Rodolphus.	Tristram.
Adoniram.	Caleb.	Eliah.	Gideon.	Jasper.	Linus.	Norman.	Roger.	
Alanson.	Calvin.	Elias.	Gilbert.	Jay.	Lional.	Norton.	Roland.	Ulysses.
Alaric.	Casimir.	Elihu.	Giles.	Jean.	Llewelyn.		Rollo.	Umphrey.
Albert.	Cass.	Elijah.	Given.	Jedediah.	Loami.	Obadiah.	Romeo.	Uranus.
Alexander.	Casimer.	Eliphalet.	Goddard.	Jefferson.	Lorenzo.	Obed.	Roswell.	Urban.
Alexis.	Cecil.	Elisha.	Godfrey.	Jeffrey.	Lot.	Octavius.	Rowland.	Uriah.
Alfred.	Chauncey.	Elmer.	Gregory.	Jeremiah.	Louis.	Octavus.	Royal.	Urian.
Alias.	Charles.	Ellis.	Griffin.	Jeremy.	Lucian.	Oley.	Rudolph.	Uriel.
Alonzo.	Christian.	Ellsworth.	Gustavus.	Jerome.	Lucius.	Oliver.	Rudolphus.	
Alpheus.	Christopher.	Elmer.	Guy.	Jesse.	Ludovic.	Ona.	Rufus.	Valentine.
Alphonso.	Claudius.	Elmore.		Jethro.	Ludwig.	Orestes.	Rupert.	Vard.
Alvah.	Clarence.	Einathan.	Hannan.	Job.	Luke.	Orlando.		Verdemond.
Alvan.	Clark.	Emanuel.	Hanford.	Joel.	Luther.	Orrion.	Salem.	Verne.
Alvin.	Claude.	Emery.	Hannibal.	John.	Lycurgus.	Oscar.	Salmon.	Veronus.
Alwin.	Clement.	Emilius.	Harold.	Jonah.	Lyman.	Osmoud.	Samson.	Victor.
Amariah.	Columbus.	Emmerson.	Harris.	Jonas.	Lysander.	Oswald.	Sampson.	Vincent.
Amasa.	Conrad.	Emmery.	Harrison.	Jonathan.	Madoc.	Othello.	Samuel.	Virgil.
Ambrose.	Constant.	Emory.	Heman.	Joseph.	Madison.	Otto.	Saul.	Vivian.
Ammi.	Constantine.	Enoch.	Henry.	Josephus.	Mahlon.	Owen.	Seba.	
Amos.	Cornelius.	Enos.	Herbert.	Joshua.	Manasseh.	Patrick.	Sebastian.	Wade.
Andrew.	Cuthbert.	Ephraim.	Herman.	Josiah.	Mansfield.	Paul.	Sem.	Walter.
Anselm.	Cyprian.	Erasmus.	Hezekiah.	Josiae.	Marcelino.	Peleg.	Sereno.	Washington.
Anson.	Cyril.	Erastus.	Hiram.	Jotham.	Marcus.	Peregrine.	Serenus.	William.
Anthony.	Cyrus.	Eric.	Homer.	Joy.	Mark.	Peter.	Seth.	Willis.
Antony.	Dale.	Ernest.	Horace.	Judah.	Marmaduke.	Philander.	Shelden.	Winfield.
Archibald.	Dan.	Erving.	Horatio.	Julian.	Martin.	Philemon.	Sherman.	Winfred.
Artemas.	Dana.	Ethan.	Hosea.	Julius.	Marvin.	Philip.	Sigismund.	Winston.
Arthur.	Danforth.	Eugene.	Howard.	Justin.	Matthew.	Philo.	Silas.	
Asa.	Daniel.	Eustace.	Howe.	Justus.	Matthias.	Phineas.	Silvanus.	Zabdiel.
Asahel.	Darius.	Evan.	Howell.	Kenneth.	Maurice.	Pius.	Silvester.	Zaccheus.
Asaph.	David.	Everest.	Hubert.	King.	Melvin.	Pluto.	Simeon.	Zachary.
Asher.	Delos.	Ezekiel.	Hugh.	Kinnie.	Merton.	Pompey.	Simon.	Zadok.
Ashur.	Delwin.	Ezra.	Hugo.	Laban.	Merwin.	Pontus.	Solomon.	Zebadiah.
Augustin.	Demetrius.	Felix.	Humphrey.	Lambert.	Maximilian.	Queen.	Solon.	Zachariah.
Augustine.	Denis.	Ferdinand.	Ichabod.	Langdon.	Micah.	Quincy.	Stephen.	Zedekiah.
Austin.	Dennis.	Fernando.	Immanuel.	Lawrence.	Michael.	Quintin.	Steven.	Zelotes.
Augustus.	Derrick.	Festus.	Ingram.	Lawrence.	Miles.	Ralph.	Sylvan.	Zena.
Azariah.	Dionysius.	Fletcher.	Inigo.	Lafayette.	Milton.	Ransom.	Sylvanus.	Zenia.
Barnabas.	Donald.	Forrest.	Ira.	Lazarus.	Morgan.	Raphael.	Sylvester.	Zeno.
Barnard.	Earl.	Francis.	Irving.	Legrand.	Morris.	Ray.	Tamer.	Zenos.
Bartholomew.	Eben.	Frank.	Irwin.		Moses.		Taylor.	Zephaniah.
Barton.		Franklin.	Isaac.				Thaddus.	Zeri.
Basil.		Frederic.						Zerus.

Names of Women, Alphabetically Arranged.

Abigail.	Aurora.	Cornelia.	Ettie.	Hebe.	Katie.	Marianna.	Pauline.	Sophia.
Achsa.	Austin.	Cynthia.	Ethel.	Helen.	Katrina.	Marietta.	Penelope.	Sophronia.
Ada.			Ethelind.	Helena.	Keziah.	Marilla.	Pera.	Stella.
Adaline.	Barbara.	Darina.	Ethelinda.	Henrietta.	Kittie.	Marion.	Perabel.	Surelia.
Addie.	Beatrice.	Deborah.	Eudora.	Hessa.		Martha.	Perrine.	Susan.
Adela.	Beatrix.	Dela.	Eudosia.	Hester.	Larelda.	Mary.	Pettie.	Susanna.
Adelaide.	Belinda.	Delia.	Eugenia.	Heather.	Laura.	Mathilda.	Phebe.	Susannah.
Adelia.	Bella.	Della.	Eugenie.	Hilda.	Lauret.	Matilda.	Philip.	Sylvia.
Adelina.	Bertha.	Diana.	Eulice.	Honora.	Laurietta.	Maud.	Phœbe.	
Adeline.	Bessie.	Dinah.	Euphemia.	Honoria.	Laurinda.	May.	Phyllis.	Tabitha.
Adoline.	Betsey.	Dora.	Eva.	Hortensia.	Lavinia.	Maggie.	Pina.	Terine.
Agatha.	Beulah.	Dorcas.	Evangeline.	Huldah.	Lena.	Mehetabel.	Polly.	Theodora.
Agnes.	Blanch.	Dorinda.	Eve.		Leonora.	Mehitable.	Porcia.	Theodosia.
Alethea.	Blanche.	Dorothy.	Evelina.	Ida.	Letitia.	Melicent.	Priscilla.	Theresa.
Alexandra.	Bridget.	Doxie.		Imogene.	Lettice.	Melissa.		Thomasina.
Alexandrina.	Camilla.	Edessa.	Fanna.	Inez.	Lexie.	Meta.	Rachel.	Tilda.
Alice.	Capitola.	Edith.	Fanny.	Ionia.	Libbie.	Metta.	Rebecca.	Tillie.
Alicia.	Caroline.	Edna.	Fara.	Irene.	Lillian.	Mildred.	Rebekah.	Tina.
Almeda.	Carrie.	Effie.	Fatima.	Isabel.	Lillie.	Minnie.	Rena.	Tryphena.
Almira.	Cassandra.	Eleanor.	Faustina.	Isabella.	Lilly.	Miranda.	Revelia.	Ulrica.
Althea.	Cassie.	Electa.	Felicia.	Isadora.	Lois.	Miriam.	Rhoda.	Ureneo.
Alveretta.	Catharina.	Electra.	Fidelia.	Jane.	Lorana.	Morella.	Rosa.	Uretia.
Alsina.	Catharine.	Elfrida.	Flora.	Janet.	Lou.	Myra.	Rosabel.	Ursule.
Amabel.	Catherine.	Elinor.	Floralia.	Jean.	Louisa.	Nancy.	Rosalila.	Ursula.
Amanda.	Cecilia.	Elizabeth.	Florena.	Jeanne.	Louise.	Nannie.	Rosalie.	Valeria.
Amarilia.	Cecily.	Elizabeth.	Florence.	Jeannette.	Lucia.	Nanza.	Rosalind.	Valina.
Amelia.	Cedelia.	Ella.	Florenia.	Jemima.	Lucinda.	Naomi.	Rosamond.	Victoria.
Amy.	Celeste.	Ellen.	Frances.	Jennie.	Lucretia.	Nellie.	Rose.	Victorine.
Angelica.	Celestine.	Ellie.	Francelia.	Jenny.	Lucy.	Nina.	Rosella.	Vileeta.
Angelina.	Celia.	Eloisa.	Fredrica.	Jerusha.	Lulu.	Nora.	Rosetta.	Viola.
Angeline.	Charity.	Elsie.	Gabriella.	Jessie.	Lurelia.		Roxana.	Violet.
Ann.	Charlotte.	Elvira.	Genet.	Joan.	Lurelia.	Octavia.	Roxie.	Viorena.
Anna.	Chloe.	Eme.	Geneva.	Joanna.	Lureno.	Oliva.	Ruth.	Virginia.
Annabel.	Christina.	Emeline.	Genevieve.	Josepha.	Luretta.	Olivia.	Saloma.	Vivian.
Anne.	Cicely.	Emily.	Geneive.	Josephine.	Lydia.	Ophelia.	Samantha.	
Annette.	Clara.	Emma.	Georgiana.	Joyce.	Mabel.	Olympia.	Samima.	Welthy.
Antoinette.	Clarice.	Emmerett.	Geraldine.	Judith.	Madeline.	Ora.	Sara.	Wilhelmina.
Antonia.	Clarissa.	Eola.	Gertie.	Julia.	Maggie.	Orianna.	Sarah.	Winola.
Antonina.	Claudia.	Ercilla.	Gertrude.	Julianna.	Mahala.	Oriet.	Sarepta.	Winnie.
Arabella.	Clementina.	Ernestine.	Hagar.	Juliet.	Malvina.	Orlecta.	Selina.	
Ardelia.	Clementine.	Esmerelda.	Hadle.	Julietta.	Marcella.	Othalia.	Serena.	Zella.
Ariana.	Cleopatra.	Esther.	Hannah.	Junietta.	Maria.	Orlinda.	Sibyl.	Zella.
Aseneth.	Constance.	Estusia.	Harriet.	Katharine.	Maria.		Sibylla.	Zenobia.
Athena.	Cora.	Etta.	Harriot.	Katherine.	Maria.	Pansy.	Sonora.	
Augusta.	Cordelia.							
Aurelia.	Corinna.							

Selections for the Album.

THE individual is frequently called upon for his or her autograph. In complying, it is customary to couple with the same a sentiment, signing the name beneath. If the matter written is original, be it long or short, it is usually more highly valued. If a brief selection be made, some of the following quotations may be appropriate:

O NATURE! though blessed and bright are thy
    rays,
O'er the brow of creation enchantingly thrown,
Yet faint are they all to the luster that plays
In a smile from the heart that is dearly our
    own!

TAKE heart, nor of the laws of fate complain,
    Though now 'tis cloudy, 't will clear up again.

SO far is it from being true that men are naturally equal, that no two people can be half an hour together but one shall acquire evident superiority over the other.

IF others be as fair,
    What are their charms to me?
I neither know nor care,
For thou art all to me.

PURCHASE not friends by gifts; when thou ceasest to give, such will cease to love.

SMALL service is true service while it lasts;
    Of friends, however humble, scorn not one:
The daisy, by the shadow that it casts,
    Protects the lingering dew-drop from the sun.

OLD Time will end our story,
    But no time, if we end well, will end our glory.

THE most delicate, the most sensible of all pleasures, consists in promoting the pleasures of others.

AND what is fame? the meanest have their day;
    The greatest can but blaze and pass away.

AH! could you look into my heart
    And watch your image there!
You would own the sunny loveliness
    Affection makes it wear.

HE who labors with the mind governs others; he who labors with the body is governed by others.

THERE is pleasure in the pathless woods,
    There is rapture on the lonely shore,
There is society, where none intrudes,
    By the deep Sea, and music in its roar:
I love not Man the less, but Nature more.

HE who surpasses or subdues mankind,
    Must look down on the hate of those below.

LET us deal very gently with the erring. We should always remember that had we been born with a like unfortunate organization, and been trained amid as unfavorable circumstances, we would have done as badly ourselves.

I DEEMED that time, I deemed that Pride
    Had quenched at length my boyish flame;
Nor knew, till seated by thy side,
    My heart in all, save hope, the same.

EARTH holds no other like to thee,
    Or if it doth, in vain for me.

OH! many a shaft, at random sent,
    Finds mark the archer little meant;
And many a word, at random spoken,
    May soothe or wound a heart that 's broken.

THOSE who have finished by making others think with them, have usually been those who began by daring to think with themselves.

DESIRE not to live long, but to live well;
    How long we live, not years, but actions tell.

WHO does the best his circumstance allows,
    Does well, acts nobly; angels could do no more.

AH, well! for us all some sweet hope lies
    Deeply buried from human eyes;
And, in the hereafter, angels may
    Roll the stone from its grave away.

HE who sedulously attends, pointedly asks, calmly speaks, coolly answers, and ceases when he has no more to say, is in the possession of some of the best requisites of man.

SOMETIME, when all life's lessons have been learned,
    And sun and stars forever more have set,
The things which our weak judgments here have spurned,
    The things o'er which we grieved with lashes wet,
Will flash before us out of life's dark night,
    As stars shine most in deeper tints of blue;
And we shall see how all God's plans were right,
    And how what seemed reproof was love most true.

Peruse these simple rhymes,
   If ever you read any,
And think of me, sometimes,
   Among the many!

May you through life remain the same,
   Unchanged in all except your name.

Fond Memory, come and hover o'er
   This album page of my fair friend;
Enrich her from thy precious store,
   And happy recollections send.
If on this page she chance to gaze
   In years to come—where'er she be—
Tell her of earlier happy days,
   And bring her back one thought of me.

When I, poor elf, shall have vanished in vapor,
   May still my memory live—on paper.

As half in shade, and half in sun,
   This world along its path advances,
Oh! may that side the sun shines on
   Be all that ever meets thy glances;
May Time, who casts his blight on all,
   And daily dooms some joy to death,
On thee let years so gently fall
   They shall not crush one flower beneath.

As flowers bloom'd in Petrarch's favorite grove,
   So glows the heart beneath the smile of love.

Youngest joys won't last forever—
   Make the most of every day;
Youth and beauty Time will sever,
   But Content hath no decay.

I care not for beauty, but give me that heart
   Where truth has its dwelling, and goodness a part.

As o'er the cold, sepulchral stone
   Some name arrests the passer-by,
So, when thou view'st this page alone,
   Let mine attract thy pensive eye;
And when by thee that name is read,
   Perchance in some succeeding year,
Reflect on me as on the dead,
   And think my heart is buried here,

If Cupid be blind, as the ancients declare,
   'Tis strange he should always recognize the fair.

Had I the power to carve or print
   Thy future, my dear friend,
It would be fair and ever bright,
   Unclouded to the end.

Bright be the years before thee,
   Friend of my childhood days;
Peace weave her olive o'er thee,
   And joy attend thy ways.

When on this page you chance to look,
   Think of me and close the book.

Thy memory, as a spell
   Of love, comes o'er the mind;
As dew upon the purple bell,
   As perfume on the wind,
As music on the sea,
   As sunshine on the river,
So hath it always been to me,
   So shall it be forever.

Good sense and virtue must prevail
   O'er hearts where wit and beauty fail.

The changeful sand doth only know
   The shallow tide and latest;
The rocks have marked its highest flow,
   The deepest and the greatest:
And deeper still the flood-marks grow;—
   So, since the hour I met thee,
The more the tide of time doth flow,
   The less can I forget thee!

When you are gone, oh where has fled my rest?
   When you are near, I feel supremely bless'd.

Fair and flowery be thy way,
   The skies all bright above thee,
And happier every coming day
   To thee and those that love thee.

Sweet is the girl who reads this line;
   I wish her sweetness were all mine!

It may occur in after-life
   That you, I trust, a happy wife,
Will former happy hours retrace,
   Recall each well-remembered face.
At such a moment I but ask,
   I hope 'twill be a pleasant task,
That you'll remember as a friend
   One who'll prove true e'en to the end.

Most noble and generous, benevolent and free,
   My heart beats with affection and friendship for thee.

My Album's open! Come and see!
   What! won't you waste a line on me?
Write but a thought—a word or two,
   That Memory may revert to you.

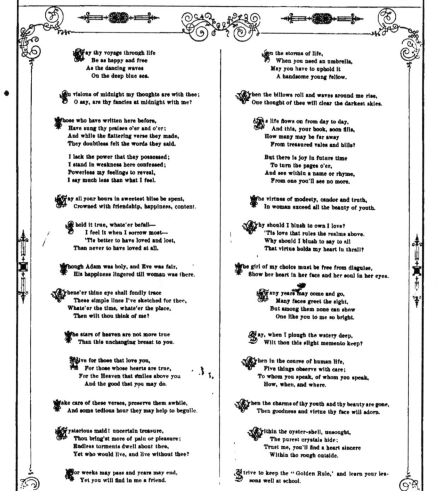

May thy voyage through life
Be as happy and free
As the dancing waves
On the deep blue sea.

In visions of midnight my thoughts are with thee;
O say, are thy fancies at midnight with me?

Those who have written here before,
Have sung thy praises o'er and o'er;
And while the flattering verse they made,
They doubtless felt the words they said.

I lack the power that they possessed;
I stand in weakness here confessed;
Powerless my feelings to reveal,
I say much less than what I feel.

May all your hours in sweetest bliss be spent,
Crowned with friendship, happiness, content.

I hold it true, whate'er befall—
I feel it when I sorrow most—
'Tis better to have loved and lost,
Than never to have loved at all.

Though Adam was holy, and Eve was fair,
His happiness lingered till woman was there.

Whene'er thine eye shall fondly trace
These simple lines I've sketched for thee,
Whate'er the time, whate'er the place,
Then wilt thou think of me?

The stars of heaven are not more true
Than this unchanging breast to you.

Live for those that love you,
For those whose hearts are true,
For the Heaven that smiles above you
And the good that you may do.

Take care of these verses, preserve them awhile,
And some tedious hour they may help to beguile.

Mysterious maid! uncertain treasure,
Thou bring'st more of pain or pleasure;
Endless torments dwell about thee,
Yet who would live, and live without thee?

For weeks may pass and years may end,
Yet you will find in me a friend.

On the storms of life,
When you need an umbrella,
May you have to uphold it
A handsome young fellow.

When the billows roll and waves around me rise,
One thought of thee will clear the darkest skies.

As life flows on from day to day,
And this, your book, soon fills,
How many may be far away
From treasured vales and hills?

But there is joy in future time
To turn the pages o'er,
And see within a name or rhyme,
From one you'll see no more.

The virtues of modesty, candor and truth,
In woman exceed all the beauty of youth.

Why should I blush to own I love?
'Tis love that rules the realms above.
Why should I blush to say to all
That virtue holds my heart in thrall?

The girl of my choice must be free from disguise,
Show her heart in her face and her soul in her eyes.

Many years may come and go,
Many faces greet the sight,
But among them none can show
One like you to me so bright.

Say, when I plough the watery deep,
Wilt thou this slight memento keep?

When in the course of human life,
Five things observe with care;
To whom you speak, of whom you speak,
How, when, and where.

When the charms of thy youth and thy beauty are gone,
Then goodness and virtue thy face will adorn.

Within the oyster-shell, unsought,
The purest crystals hide;
Trust me, you'll find a heart sincere
Within the rough outside.

Strive to keep the "Golden Rule,' and learn your lessons well at school.

A little health, a little wealth,
   A little house and freedom;
   A few good friends for certain ends,
   And little use to need them.

Some write for pleasure, some write for fame, but I
   write simply to sign my name.

May you live in bliss, from sorrow away,
   Having plenty laid up for a rainy day;
And when you are ready to settle in life,
May you find a good husband and make a good wife.

Count that day lost whose low descending sun, views
   from thy hand no worthy action done.

Think of me when you are happy,
   Keep for me one little spot;
In the depth of thine affection
   Plant a sweet " Forget-me-not. "

Meanness shun and all its train; goodness seek and
   life is gain.

These few lines to you are tendered,
   By a friend, sincere and true;
Hoping but to be remembered
   When I'm far away from you.

Is it vain in life's wide sea, to ask you to remember me?
   Undoubtedly it is my lot, just to be known and then
—forgot.

—————— is your name,
   And single is your station,
Happy will be the man
   Who makes the alteration.

In the golden chain of friendship regard me as a link.

Think of me in the hour of leisure,
   Think of me in the hour of care,
Think of me in the hour of pleasure,
   Spare me one thought in the hour of prayer.

Not to go back is somewhat to advance.

When far away by love you're carried,
   And to some little fellow married,
Remember me for friendship's sake,
   And send me a piece of wedding cake.

May happiness ever be thy lot
   Wherever thou shalt be,
And joy and pleasure light the spot
   That may be home to thee.

Remember me when "far, far off, where the wood-
   chucks die of whooping cough. "

Sweet ——————! could another ever share
   This wayward, loveless hea t, it would be thine;
But, check'd by every tie, I may not dare
   To cast a worthless offering at thy shrine.

He is a coward who will not turn back, when first he
   discovers he's on the wrong track.

May heaven protect and keep thee
   From every sorrow free,
And grant thee every blessing—
   My earnest wish for thee.

I thought, I thought, I thought in vain; at last I thought
   I would write my name.

When the golden sun is setting,
   And your heart from care is free,
When o'er a thousand things you're thinking,
   Will you sometimes think of me?

Within this book so pure and white, let none but
   friends presume to write; and may each line, with
friendship given, direct the reader's thoughts to heaven.

Though the lapse of years can change
   Cherished friendship to deceit,
After all, within its range,
   I'm your friend whene'er we meet.

Never trouble trouble, till trouble troubles you.

Oh, woman! Subtle, lovely, faithless sex!
   Born to enchant, thou studiest to perplex;
Ador'd as queen, thou play'st the tyrant's part,
And, taught to govern, would'st enslave the heart.

A smooth sea never made a skillful mariner.

May He, who clothes the lilies
   And marks the sparrow's fall,
Protect and save you, Bella,
   And guide you safe through all. "

THE LAWS of ETIQUETTE. WHAT TO SAY AND HOW TO DO.

PLEASANT WORDS AND AGREEABLE MANNERS.

O be loved is the instinctive desire of every human heart. To be respected, to be honored, to be successful, is the universal ambition. The ever constant desire of all is to be happy. This never varying instinct lies at the foundation of every action; it is the constantly propelling force in our every effort.

To be happy, we strive for the acquisition of wealth, for position and place, for social and political distinction. And when all is obtained, the real enjoyment in its possession comes from the thousand little courtesies that are exchanged between individuals — pleasant words and kindly acts, which the poor may enjoy as well as the rich.

In reality it need not take much to make one happy. Our real wants are very few. To be fed and clothed, and provided with comfortable shelter, are the prime necessities. Added to these are kindness and love from those with whom we associate. Given all these, with a contented spirit, and, however lowly our position, we may be very happy.

There is one perpetual law, however, running through all our intercourse with others, which is that we may rightly possess nothing without rendering therefor just compensation. This law is recognized in the commercial world, and it should be strictly observed in the etiquette of social life.

In short, in the many varied amenities of life, the fundamental rule of action should be the golden rule: "To do unto others as we would that others should do unto us."

We are at ease, we are made peaceful, satisfied and happy, by words and acts of kindly feeling extended to us; and in like manner we may strew the pathway of others with roses and sunshine, by courteous action, and kind, gentle and loving conduct; to do which may cost us no effort, but on the contrary may afford us real pleasure.

In a business, social and artistic view, it is of very great advantage to most people to be possessed of ease and grace of manner. By the possession of confidence and self-command, a single individual will oftentimes cause a large company, that otherwise would be socially very inharmonious, to be satisfied, composed and perfectly at ease; and in a thousand ways such a person will scatter happiness and blessings among those with whom he or she may come in contact.

Natural and Acquired Politeness.

To some, a pleasing manner comes very naturally. If born to the possession of an easy flow of language, agreeableness of address, poetical and imaginative power, and large knowledge of human nature, the whole accompanied by judicious training, good education and wide opportunities, such persons will most surely, without studied effort, be self-possessed and at ease in any company, upon any occasion.

On the contrary, if the natural advantages have been few, and the opportunities for acquiring polished deportment limited, then we may very appropriately make a study of the subject of how to please; and hence the necessity for special instruction on the subject of Etiquette.

It is of the utmost importance, however, that there be no labored effort to behave by rule, and that the forms of etiquette be not carried too far. The law of common sense should rest at the basis of our intercourse with society, and a kindly desire to make happy everybody with whom we come in contact, should actuate our conduct. Still, with all this, there are thousands of people of the kindest intentions, with much breadth of intellect, who continually violate the common usages of society, and who are liable to do the wrong thing at important times, and thus embarrass their warmest friends. Hence, the need of a treatise on general conduct is evidently as much a necessity as is the text-book on grammar, penmanship or mathematics.

If the soldier is more efficient by drill, the teacher more competent by practice, the parliamentarian more influential by understanding the code of parliamentary law, then equally is the general member of society more successful by an understanding of the laws of etiquette, which teach how to appear, and what to do and say in the varied positions in which we may be placed.

In the study of etiquette, much may be learned by observation, but much more is learned by practice. We may listen to the finest oratory for a dozen years, and yet never be able to speak in public ourselves; whereas, by practice in the art of declamation, with passable talent, we may become quite proficient in half that time. We may thoroughly study the theory and art of language for twenty years, and yet be very poor talkers. We may practice the art of conversation by familiar and continuous intercourse with the cultured and refined, and become fluent and easy in communicating thought in a few years.

Such is the difference between theory and practice. Both are necessary—the former in pointing the way; the latter by making use of theory in practical application. Thus we may acquire ease and grace of manner: First, by understanding the regulations which govern social etiquette; and secondly, by a free intermingling in society, putting into continual practice the theories which we understand. To avail ourselves, however, to the fullest extent of society advantages, we must have acquaintance; and hence, we introduce the rules of etiquette by a chapter on the forms of presentation—the art of getting acquainted.

Etiquette of Introductions.

THERE are various forms of introduction to be used, each depending on particular circumstances. Thus, when introducing a gentleman to a lady, the party introducing them will say, however, ing to each as the name of each is pronounced, "Miss Williamson, allow me to introduce to you my friend Mr. Grant; Mr. Grant, Miss Williamson."

Some prefer the word "present" instead of the word "introduce." The words are not very material. The form is all that is essential.

Of two gentlemen being introduced, one of whom is more eminent in position, look first at the elder or superior, with a slight bow, saying, "Mr. Durham, I make you acquainted with Mr. Stevens; Mr. Stevens, Mr. Durham."

The last clause repeating the names, "Mr. Stevens, Mr. Durham," may be justly regarded a useless formality, and is not necessary unless for the purpose of making the names more distinct by their repetition.

Parties being introduced have an opportunity for conversation, and are immediately set at ease by the person introducing giving the place of residence and the business of each, with the introduction, thus: "Mr. Snow, allow me to make you acquainted with Mr. Burton. Mr. Burton is extensively engaged in mining in Colorado. Mr. Snow is one of our lawyers in this city." He may still continue, if he wishes to aid the parties he is introducing, by saying, "Mr. Burton comes East for the purpose of disposing of mining stock to some of our capitalists, and it is possible, Mr. Snow, that with your large acquaintance you can give him some information that will aid him." Such an introduction will immediately lead to a general conversation between the parties, and the person having introduced them can then retire if he desires.

It is always gratifying to anyone to be highly esteemed, hence you will confer pleasure by always conveying as favorable an impression as possible when giving the introduction.

Always apply the titles when making introductions, where the parties are entitled to them, as Honorable, Reverend, Professor, etc. Thus, in introducing a clergyman to a member of the legislature, it is etiquette to say: "Mr. Shelden, permit me to present to you the Reverend Mr. Wing." Addressing Mr. Shelden, he says: "Mr. Wing is the pastor of the First Presbyterian church at Troy, New York." Addressing Mr. Wing, he continues: "Mr. Shelden is at present our representative in the State Legislature, and author of the "Shelden Letters" which you have so much admired."

If there are many introductions to be made, the simple words, "Mr. Smith, Mr. Jones," will serve the purpose. Mr. Smith and Mr. Jones will then take up the weather or some other topic, and proceed with their conversation. A very proper reply for either party to make when introduced is, "I am glad to meet you," or, "I am happy to make your acquaintance."

If several persons are introduced to one, mention the name of the single individual but once, as follows: "Mr. Belden, allow me to introduce Mr. Maynard, Mr. Thompson, Miss Hayward, Mrs. Rice, Mr. Harmon, Mr. Brown," bowing to each as the name is mentioned.

When introducing a couple that may be somewhat diffident, the parties will be materially aided in becoming sociable and feeling at ease, by a very full introduction, thus: "Miss Kennicott, allow me to present to you my friend Miss Swift. Miss Kennicott is from the far-famed city of New Haven, Connecticut; and, upon the close of her visit here, is going to California for a visit of a year. Miss Swift is from Buffalo, New York, and is attending Hopedale Seminary in this city."

General Suggestions About Introductions.

Ladies being introduced should never bow hastily, but with slow and measured dignity.

The inferior is to be introduced to the superior; the younger to the older; the gentleman to the lady.

It is the lady's privilege to recognize the gentleman after an introduction, and his duty to return the bow.

Introductions on the streets or in public places should be made so quietly as not to attract public attention.

Perfect ease and self-possession are the essentials to the making and receiving of graceful and happy introductions.

Etiquette requires that a gentleman always raise his hat (Fig. 2) when introduced to either a lady or gentleman on the street.

Introduce to each other only those who may find acquaintance agreeable. If any doubt exists on the subject, inquire beforehand.

When introducing parties, pronounce the names distinctly. If you fail to understand the name when introduced, feel at liberty to inquire.

One of the duties of the host and hostess of a private party is to make the guests acquainted with each other. Guests may, however, make introductions.

Introductions are often dispensed with at a private ball, it being taken for granted that only those are invited who ought to be acquainted. Thus acquaintance may begin without formal introduction.

Fig. 2. Introduction on the Street.

... to make examination with a new ..., ... on any occasion perfectly frank. There is no necessity for practicing deceit.

The rule should be to pay for goods when you buy them. If, however, ... should be very particular to courtesy requires that you salute him, or her, and give no sign of illfeeling while you are the guest of your friend.

If casually introduced to a stranger, when making a call at the house of a friend, etiquette does not require a subsequent recognition. It is optional with the parties whether the acquaintance be continued or not after such accidental meeting and introduction.

Always pronounce the surname when giving the introduction. To be introduced to "my cousin Carrie" leaves the stranger at a loss how to address the lady. In introducing a relative, it is well to say, "My brother, Mr. Wells;" "My mother, Mrs. Briggs," etc.

To shake hands when introduced, is optional; between gentlemen it is common, and oftentimes between an elderly and a young person. It is not common between an unmarried lady and a gentleman, a slight bow between them when introduced being all that etiquette requires. The married lady will use her discretion when introduced to gentlemen.

Two parties meeting on the street, accompanied by friends, may stop and speak to each other without the necessity of introducing their friends, though, when parting, it is courtesy for each to give a parting salutation as though acquaintance had been formed.

Parties who may meet by chance at your house, when making calls, need not necessarily be introduced to each other. If, however, they continue their calls together, it may be agreeable to make them acquainted in order to more pleasantly carry forward conversation.

If you are a gentleman, do not let the lack of an introduction prevent you from rendering services to any unattended lady who may need them. Politely offer your protection, escort or assistance, and, when the service has been accomplished, politely bow and retire.

A visitor at your house should be introduced to the various callers, and the acquaintance should continue while the friend remains your guest. All callers should aim to make the visit of the friend as pleasant as possible, treating the guest as they would wish their friends to be treated under similar circumstances.

If thrown into the company of strangers, without the formality of an introduction, as is often the case when traveling and at other times, acquaintance may be formed between gentlemen and ladies, with proper reserve, but duty requires that the slightest approach toward undue familiarity should be checked by dignified silence.

Persons who have been properly introduced have claims upon the acquaintance of each other which should call for at least a slight recognition thereafter, unless there be very decided reasons for cutting the acquaintance entirely. To completely ignore another to whom you have been rightly introduced, by meeting the person with a vacant stare, is a mark of ill-breeding.

Introductions at Court and Presidential Receptions.

In paying your respects to the President of the United States, you will be introduced by the master of ceremonies on public occasions. At other times, to send in your card will secure you audience, although the better way is to be introduced by a mutual acquaintance, or a member of Congress. Introductions at Court in foreign countries are accompanied by a good deal of formality. At the English Court, the stranger, having the credential of the American Ambassador, will be introduced, if a lady, by a lady; if a gentleman, by a gentleman. Elsewhere abroad the proper method in each case can be best learned from our national representative at each capital. Court etiquette requires that the lady appear in full dress, and the gentleman in black suit, with white vest, gloves and necktie.

 # FORMS OF SALUTATION.

SUGGESTIONS CONCERNING THE BOW.

COMMON forms of salutation, in America, are the bow, the kiss, words of address, and shaking hands.

Acquaintances are usually entitled to the courtesy of a bow. It is poor policy to refuse recognition because of a trifling difference between parties.

The young lady should show a similar deference to an elderly lady, or to one in superior position, that a gentleman does to a lady.

A gentleman who may be smoking when he meets a lady, should in bowing remove the cigar from his mouth and from her presence.

When bowing to ladies, it is etiquette for the gentleman to raise his hat from his head. If passing on the street, the hat should be raised and salute given with the hand farthest from the person addressed.

A bow or graceful inclination should be made by ladies when recognizing their acquaintances of the opposite sex. It is the privilege of the lady to bow first.

On the contrary, if the natural advantages

To a casual acquaintance you may bow without speaking; but to those with whom you are well acquainted, greater cordiality is due. A bow should always be returned; even to an enemy it is courtesy to return the recognition.

When a gentleman, accompanied by a friend, meets a lady upon the street, it is courtesy, in the salutation, for the gentleman's friend to bow slightly to the lady also, as a compliment to his companion, even though unacquainted with the lady.

On meeting a party, some of whom you are intimately acquainted with, and the others but little, the salutation should be made as nearly equal as possible. A slight recognition of some, and great demonstration of pleasure toward others, is a violation of etiquette.

A gentleman should return a bow made him upon the street, even if the one making the same is not recognized. The person may possibly be a forgotten acquaintance; but, even if a mistake has been made, there will be less embarrassment if the bow is returned.

A gentleman should not bow from a window to a lady on the street, though he may bow slightly from the street upon being recognized by a lady in a window. Such recognition should, however, generally be avoided, as gossip is likely to attach undue importance to it when seen by others.

A warm cordiality of manner, and a general recognition of acquaintances, without undue familiarity, is the means of diffusing much happiness, as well as genial and friendly feeling. In thinly settled localities, the habit of bowing to every one you meet is an excellent one, evincing, as it does, kindliness of feeling toward all.

When meeting a lady who is a stranger, in a hallway, upon a staircase, or in close proximity elsewhere, courtesy demands a bow from the gentleman. In passing up a stairway, the lady will pause at the foot and allow the gentleman to go first; and at the head of the stairway he should bow, pause, and allow her to precede him in the descent.

How to Address Others.—Nicknames.

Use the title, when speaking to others, whenever possible. Thus, addressing John Brown, a Justice of the Peace, say, "Squire;" Dr. Bell, you will address as "Doctor;" Mayor Williams, as "Mayor;" Senator Snow, as "Senator;" Governor Smith, as "Governor;" Professor Stevens, as "Professor," etc.

Before all public bodies, take pains to address those in authority very respectfully, saying to the presiding officer, "Mr. President," or if he be a Mayor, Judge, or Justice, address him as "Your Honor," etc.

When stopping at the house of a friend, ascertain the Christian names of all the children, and of those servants that you frequently have to address; and then always speak respectfully to each, using the full Christian name, or any pet name to which they are accustomed.

To approach another in a boisterous manner, saying, "Hello, Old Fellow!" "Hello Bob!" or using kindred expressions, indicates ill-breeding. If approached, however, in this vulgar manner, it is better to give a civil reply, and address the person respectfully, in which case he is quite likely to be ashamed of his own conduct.

Husbands and wives indicate pleasant conjugal association existing where they address each other in the family circle by their Christian names, though the terms of respect, "Mr." and "Mrs.," may be applied to each among strangers. When speaking of each other among near and intimate relatives, they will also use the Christian name; but among general acquaintances and strangers, the surname.

Never call anyone by a nickname, or a disrespectful name. Treat all persons, no matter how lowly, in addressing them, as you would wish to be addressed yourself. You involuntarily have more respect for people, outside of your family or relatives, who call you "Mr. Smith," or "Mr. Jones," than for those who call you "Jack," or "Jim." Hence, when you speak to others, remember that you gain their favor by polite words of address.

When speaking to a boy, under fifteen years of age, outside of the circle of relatives, among comparative strangers, call him by his Christian name, as "Charles," "William," etc. Above that age, if the boy has attained good physical and intellectual development, apply the "Mr." as "Mr. Brown," "Mr. King," etc. To do so will please him, will raise his self-respect, and will be tendering a courtesy which you highly valued when you were of the same age.

It is an insult to address a boy or girl, who is a stranger to you, as "Bub" or "Sis." Children are sometimes very sensitive on these points, resenting such method of being addressed, while they very highly appreciate being spoken to respectfully. Thus, if the child's name is unknown, to say "My Boy," or "My Little Lad," "My Girl," or "My Little Lady," will be to gain favor and set the child a good example in politeness. Children forever gratefully remember those who treat them respectfully. Among relatives, nicknames should not be allowed. Pet names among the children are admissible, until they outgrow them, when the full Christian name should be used.

THE PRACTICE OF KISSING.

Upon the meeting of intimate friends among ladies, at the private house, the kiss as a mode of salutation is yet common; but even there it is not as customary as formerly. The custom ought to be abolished for physiological and other reasons.

Upon the meeting or departure of a young person, as between parents and children, or guardians and wards, the kiss is not inappropriate in public. Between all other parties it is a questionable propriety in public places, it being etiquette to avoid conduct that will attract the attention of strangers.

ETIQUETTE OF SHAKING HANDS.—SUGGESTIONS ABOUT SHOPPING.

WAYS OF CLASPING HANDS.

ACCOMPANYING the salutation of hand-shaking, it is common, according to the customs of English-speaking people, to inquire concerning the health, the news, etc.

Offer the whole hand. It is an insult, and indicates snobbery, to present two fingers (Fig. 3) when shaking hands. It is also insulting to return a warm, cordial greeting with a lifeless hand (Fig. 4), and evident indifference of manner, when hand-shaking. Present a cordial grasp (Fig. 5) and clasp the hand firmly, shaking it warmly for a period of two or three seconds, and then relinquish the grasp entirely. It is rude to grasp the hand very tightly or to shake it over-vigorously. To hold it a long time is often very embarrassing, and is a breach of etiquette. It is always the lady's privilege to extend the hand first. In her own house a lady should give her hand to every guest.

Fig. 3. The snob that sticks out two fingers when shaking hands.

If both parties wear gloves, it is not necessary that each remove them in shaking hands; if one, however, has ungloved hands, it is courtesy for the other to remove the glove, unless in so doing it would cause an awkward pause; in which case apologize for not removing it, by saying, "Excuse my glove." The words and forms will always very much depend upon circumstances, of which individuals can themselves best judge. Kid and other thin gloves are not expected to be removed in hand-shaking; hence, apology is only necessary for the non-removal of the thick, heavy glove.

Fig. 4. The cold-blooded, languid person, that exhibits only indifference as you shake the hand.

As a rule in all salutations, it is well not to exhibit too much haste. The cool, deliberate person is much the most likely to avoid mistakes. The nervous, quick-motioned, impulsive individual will need to make deliberation a matter of study; else, when acting on the spur of the moment, with possibly slight embarrassment, ludicrous errors are liable to be made. In shaking hands, offer the right

Fig. 5. The generous, frank, whole-souled individual, that meets you with a warm, hearty grasp.

hand, the same be engaged; in which case, apologize, by saying "Excuse my left hand." It is the right hand that carries the sword in time of war, and its extension is emblematic of friendliness in time of peace.

CONDUCT IN THE STORE.

PURCHASERS should, as far as possible, patronize the merchants of their own town. It is poor policy to send money abroad for articles which can be bought as cheaply at home.

Do not take hold of a piece of goods which another is examining. Wait until it is replaced upon the counter before you take it up.

Injuring goods when handling, pushing aside other persons, lounging upon the counter, whispering, loud talk and laughter, when in a store, are all evidences of ill-breeding.

Never attempt to "beat down" prices when shopping. If the price does not suit, go elsewhere. The just and upright merchant will have but one price for his goods, and he will strictly adhere to it.

It is an insult to a clerk or merchant to suggest to a customer, about to purchase, that he may buy cheaper or better goods elsewhere. It is also rude to give your opinion, unasked, about the goods that another is purchasing.

Never expect a clerk to leave another customer to wait on you; and when attending upon you, do not cause him to wait while you visit with another. When the purchases are made, let them be sent to your home, and thus avoid loading yourself with bundles.

Treat clerks, when shopping, respectfully, and give them no more trouble than is necessary. Ask for what is wanted, explicitly, and if you wish to make examination with a view to future purchase, say so. Be perfectly frank. There is no necessity for practicing deceit.

The rule should be to pay for goods when you buy them. If, however, you are trusted by the merchant, you should be very particular to pay your indebtedness when you agree to. By doing as you promise, you acquire habits of promptitude, and at the same time establish credit and make reputation among those with whom you deal.

It is rude in the extreme to find fault and to make sneering remarks about goods. To draw unfavorable comparisons between the goods and those found at other stores does no good, and shows want of deference and respect to those who are waiting upon you. Politely state that the goods are not what you want, and, while you may buy, you prefer to look further.

If a mistake has been made whereby you have been given more goods than you paid for, or have received more change than was your due, go immediately and have the error rectified. You cannot afford to sink your moral character by taking advantage of such mistakes. If you had made an error to your disadvantage, as a merchant, you would wish the customer to return and make it right. You should do as you would be done by. Permanent success depends upon your being strictly honest.

Etiquette of Calling.

THE morning call should be very brief. This formal call is mainly one of ceremony, and from ten to twenty minutes is a sufficient length of time to prolong it. It should never exceed half an hour.

In making a formal call, a lady does not remove her bonnet or wraps.

Unless there be a certain evening set apart for receiving, the formal call should be made in the morning.

It is customary, according to the code of etiquette, to call all the hours of daylight morning, and after nightfall evening.

Calls may be made in the morning or in the evening. The call in the morning should not be made before 12 M., nor later than 5 P. M.

A gentleman, making a formal call in the morning, must retain his hat in his hand. He may leave umbrella and cane in the hall, but not his hat and gloves. The fact of retaining hat indicates a formal call.

When a gentleman accompanies a lady at a morning call (which is seldom), he assists her up the steps, rings the bell, and follows her into the reception-room. It is for the lady to determine when they should leave.

All uncouth and ungraceful positions are especially unbecoming among ladies and gentlemen in the parlor. Thus (Fig. 6), standing with the arms akimbo, sitting astride a chair, wearing the hat, and smoking in the presence of ladies, leaning back in the chair, standing with legs crossed and feet on the chairs — all those acts evince lack of polished manners.

If possible, avoid calling at the lunch or dinner hour. Among society people the most fashionable hours for calling are from 12 M. to 3 P. M. At homes where dinner or lunch is taken at noon, calls may be made from 2 to 5 P. M.

Should other callers be announced, it is well, as soon as the bustle attending the new arrival is over, to arise quietly, take leave of the hostess, bow to the visitors, and retire, without apparently doing so because of the new arrivals. This saves the hostess the trouble of entertaining two sets of callers.

To say bright and witty things during the call of ceremony, and go so soon that the hostess will desire the caller to come again, is much the more pleasant. No topic of a political or religious character should be admitted to the conversation, nor any subject of absorbing interest likely to lead to discussion.

A lady engaged upon fancy sewing of any kind, or needlework, need not necessarily lay aside the same during the call of intimate acquaintances. Conversation can flow just as freely while the visit continues.

FIG. 6. UNGRACEFUL POSITIONS.

No. 1. Stands with arms akimbo.
" 2. Sits with elbows on the knees.
" 3. Sits astride the chair, and wears his hat in the parlor.
" 4. Stains the wall paper by pressing against it with his hand; eats an apple alone, and stands

with his legs crossed.
No. 5. Rests his foot upon the chair-cushion.
" 6. Tips back his chair, soils the wall by resting his head against it, and smokes in the presence of ladies.

During the visits of ceremony, however, strict attention should be given to entertaining the callers.

Gentlemen may make morning calls on the following occasions: To convey congratulations or sympathy and condolence, to meet a friend who has just returned from abroad, to inquire after the health of a lady who may have accepted his escort on the previous day. (He should not delay the latter more than a day.) He may call upon those to whom letters of introduction are given, to express thanks for any favor which may have been rendered him, or to return a call. A great variety of circumstances will also determine when at other times he should make calls.

Evening Calls.

Evening calls should never be made later than 9 P. M., and never prolonged later than 10 P. M.

In making a formal call in the evening, the gentleman must hold hat and gloves, unless invited to lay them aside and spend the evening.

In making an informal call in the evening, a gentleman may leave hat, cane, overshoes, etc., in the hall, provided he is invited to do so, and the lady may remove her wraps.

The evening call should not generally be prolonged over an hour. With very intimate friends, however, it may be made a little longer; but the caller should be very careful that the visit be not made tiresome.

General Suggestions.

Calls from people living in the country are expected to be longer and less ceremonious than from those in the city.

When it has been impossible to attend a dinner or a social gathering, a call should be made soon afterwards, to express regret at the inability to be present.

A gentleman, though a stranger, may with propriety escort an unattended lady to the carriage, and afterwards return and make his farewell bow to the hostess.

Should a guest arrive to remain for some time with the friend, those who are intimate with the family should call as soon as possible, and these calls should be returned at the earliest opportunity.

Unless invited to do so, it is a violation of etiquette to draw near the fire for the purpose of warming one's self. Should you, while waiting the appearance of the hostess, have done so, you will arise upon her arrival, and then take the seat she may assign you.

When a lady has set apart a certain evening for receiving calls, it is not usual to call at other times, except the excuse be business reasons.

THE USE OF CARDS WHEN CALLING.

The gentleman's card should bear nothing but the name and address of the caller, in small script or card text. In addition, the lady's card may bear the "Mrs." or the "Miss," thus:

CHARLES BELDEN
Cambridge, Mass.

MRS. H. B. KING,
17 Belmont Place.
At Home Thursday Evenings.

The eldest daughter and unmarried sisters often adopt the following:

MISS CLARA D. WELLS,
No. 44 Birch Street.

THE MISSES HAMMOND,
No. 1 Day Street.

The physician may have his professional title, as

DR. ROBERT HOLLAND, or ROBERT HOLLAND, M. D.
No. 70 Henderson St.   *No. 70 Henderson St.*

The officers of the army and navy may have their titles thus:

LIEUT. HENRY H. WEBSTER, U. S. A.
LIEUT. HARVEY B. SNOW, U. S. N.

A card left, during your illness, should be answered by a call as soon as your health will permit.

The honorary titles of Prof., Hon., Esq., etc., are not allowable upon the calling card in the United States.

When about leaving town, the card which is left will bear on the lower left-hand corner the letters "P. P. C."—"Presents parting compliments," from the French "*Pour Prendre Congé*"—to take leave. The card may also be sent by mail or private carrier, the latter mode of conveyance showing most respect. *

A card sent to a person who is ill or in affliction, from the loss of a relative, should be accompanied by verbal inquiries regarding the person's health.

Cards may be left immediately where a death is known, but a call of sympathy and condolence is not usually made within a week after the bereavement.

The lady in mourning who may not desire to make calls, will send mourning cards instead of making calls for such period of time as she may not desire to mingle in general society.

Should the servant reply to a gentleman that the lady of the house, to whom the call is made, is not at home, but the daughter is, he should send in his card, as it is not usual for young ladies to receive calls from gentlemen unless they are quite intimate friends.

It is well to have cards in readiness at every call. If a servant meets you at the door, to send up a card will save mispronouncing your name, and if the lady is not at home it will show that you have called. Should there be two or more ladies in the household, to turn down one corner of the card will signify that the call was designed for all the family.

The handsomest style of card is that which is engraved; next is that which is prettily written. Succeeding, comes the printed card, which, with some of the modern script or text types, makes a most beautiful card if neatly printed. Extra ornament is out of place.

When desirous of seeing anyone at a hotel or parlor, send up your card by the waiter, while you wait in the reception-room or office.

The hostess should, if not desiring to see anyone, send word that she is "engaged" when the servant first goes to the door, and not after the card has been sent up. Should she desire certain persons only to be admitted, let the servant understand the names definitely.

* P. P. C. cards are no longer left when leaving home to be absent a few months.

FIG. 7. GENTILITY IN THE PARLOR.

The figures in the above illustration represent graceful postures to be assumed by both ladies and gentlemen in the parlor. As will be seen, whether holding hat or fan, either sitting or standing, the positions are all easy and graceful.

To assume an easy, genteel attitude, the individual must be self-possessed. To be so, attention must be given to easy flow of language, happy expression of thought, study of cultured society and the general laws of etiquette.

WHAT SHOULD BE AVOIDED WHEN CALLING.

Do not stare around the room.

Do not take a dog or small child.

Do not linger at the dinner-hour.

Do not lay aside the bonnet at a formal call.

Do not fidget with your cane, hat or parasol.

Do not make a call of ceremony on a wet day.

Do not turn your back to one seated near you.

Do not touch the piano, unless invited to do so.

Do not handle ornaments or furniture in the room.

Do not make a display of consulting your watch.

Do not go to the room of an invalid, unless invited.

Do not remove the gloves when making a formal call.

Do not continue the call longer when conversation begins to lag.

Do not remain when you find the lady upon the point of going out.

Do not make the first call if you are a new-comer in the neighborhood.

Do not open or shut doors or windows or alter the arrangement of the room.

Do not enter a room without first knocking and receiving an invitation to come in.

Do not resume your seat after having risen to go, unless for important reasons.

Do not walk around the room, examining pictures, while waiting for the hostess.

Do not introduce politics, religion or weighty topics for conversation when making calls.

Do not prolong the call if the room is crowded. It is better to call a day or two afterwards.

Do not call upon a person in reduced circumstances with a display of wealth, dress and equipage.

Do not tattle. Do not speak ill of your neighbors. Do not carry gossip from one family to another.

Do not, if a gentleman, seat yourself upon the sofa beside the hostess, or in near proximity, unless invited to do so.

Do not, if a lady, call upon a gentleman, except officially or professionally, unless he may be a confirmed invalid.

Do not take a strange gentleman with you, unless positively certain that his introduction will be received with favor.

Do not, if a gentleman, leave the hat in the hall when making merely a formal call. If the call is extended into a visit, it may then be set aside. Whether sitting or standing (Fig. 7), the hat may be gracefully held in the hand.

Duty of the Hostess.

She should greet each guest with quiet, easy grace.

She should avoid leaving the room while guests are present.

She should furnish refreshments to those callers who come a long distance to see her.

She should be aided, upon important occasions, by a gentleman, in the reception of guests.

She should avoid speaking disrespectfully of those who have previously called upon her; she should equally divide her attentions among the several callers, that none may feel slighted.

Etiquette of Conversation.

HOW, WHEN AND WHERE TO SPEAK.

TO ACQUIRE the art of conversation in a superior degree, there must be intimacy with those who possess refinement and general information. There must also be observed certain general rules in order to accomplish the best results, prominent among which are the following·

In the first place, in order to converse well, there must be knowledge; there must be a command of language, assisted by imagination; there must be understanding of the rules of construction, to frame sentences aright; there must be confidence and self-possession, and there must be courage to overcome failure.

To be an excellent conversationalist is a very desirable accomplishment. We talk more than we do anything else. By conversation we may make friends, we may retain them, or we may lose them. We may impart information; we may acquire it. We may make the company with whom we associate contented with itself, or we can sow inharmony and discord. Our success in life largely rests upon our ability to converse well; therefore the necessity of our carefully studying what should and what should not be said when talking.

How to Please in Conversation.

Use clear, distinct words to express your ideas, although your voice should be low.

Be cool, distinct and self-possessed, using respectful, chaste and appropriate language.

Always defend the absent person who is being spoken of, as far as truth and justice will permit.

Allow people that you are with to do their full share of the talking if they evince a willingness to converse.

Beware of talking much about yourself. Your merits will be discovered in due time, without the necessity of sounding your own praises.

Show the courtesy, when another person joins the group where you are relating an incident, of recapitulating what has been said, for the advantage of the newcomer.

Recollect that the object of conversation is to entertain and amuse; the social gathering, therefore, should not be made the arena of dispute. Even slight mistakes and inaccuracies it is well to overlook, rather than to allow inharmony to present itself.

Aim to adapt your conversation to the comprehension of those with whom you are conversing. Be careful that you do not undervalue them. It is possible that they are as intelligent as yourself, and their conversation can, perhaps, take as wide a range as your own.

Remember that the person to whom you are speaking is not to blame for the opinion he entertains. Opinions are not made by us, but they are made for us by circumstances. With the same organization, training and circumstances around us, we would have the same opinions ourselves.

Remember that people are fond of talking of their own affairs. The mother likes to talk of her children, the mechanic of his workmanship, the laborer of what he can accomplish. Give everyone an opportunity, and you will gain much valuable information besides being thought courteous and well-bred.

Be patient. The foreigner cannot, perhaps, recall the word he desires; the speaker may be slow of speech; you may have heard the story a dozen times; but even then you must evince interest, and listen patiently through. By so doing, you gain the esteem of the person with whom you are conversing.

What to Avoid in Social Conversation.

Do not manifest impatience.

Do not engage in argument.

Do not interrupt another when speaking.

Do not find fault, though you may gently criticise.

Do not talk of your private, personal and family matters.

Do not appear to notice inaccuracies of speech in others.

Do not allow yourself to lose temper or to speak excitedly.

Do not allude to unfortunate peculiarities of anyone present.

Do not always commence a conversation by allusion to the weather.

Do not, when narrating an incident, continually say, "you see," "you know," etc.

Do not introduce professional or other topics that the company generally cannot take an interest in.

Do not talk very loud. A firm, clear, distinct, yet mild, gentle and musical voice has great power.

Do not be absent-minded, requiring the speaker to repeat what has been said that you may understand.

Do not speak disrespectfully of personal appearance when anyone present may have the same defects.

Do not try to force yourself into the confidence of others. If they give their confidence, never betray it.

Do not use profanity, vulgar terms, slang phrases, words of double meaning, or language that will bring the blush to anyone.

Do not intersperse your language with foreign words and high sounding terms. It shows affectation, and will draw ridicule upon you.

Do not carry on a conversation with another in company about matters which the general company knows nothing of. It is almost as impolite as to whisper.

Do not allow yourself to speak ill of the absent one if it can be avoided; the day may come when some friend will be needed to defend you in your absence.

Do not speak with contempt and ridicule of a locality where you may be visiting. Find something to truthfully praise and commend; thus make yourself agreeable.

Do not make a pretense of gentility, nor parade the fact that you are a descendant of any notable family. You must pass for just what you are, and must stand on your own merit.

Do not contradict. In making a correction say, "I beg your pardon, but I had an impression that it was so and so." Be careful in contradicting, as you may be wrong yourself.

Do not be unduly familiar; you will merit contempt if you are. Neither should you be dogmatic in your assertions, arrogating to yourself much consequence in your opinions.

Do not be too lavish in your praise of various members of your own family when speaking to strangers; the person to whom you are speaking may know some faults that you do not.

Do not feel it incumbent upon yourself to carry your point in conversation. Should the person with whom you are conversing feel the same, your talk will lead into violent argument.

Do not allow yourself to use personal abuse when speaking to another, as in so doing you may make that person a life-long enemy. A few kind, courteous words might have made him a lifelong friend.

Do not discuss politics or religion in general company. You probably would not convert your opponent, and he will not convert you. To discuss those topics is to arouse feeling without any good result.

Do not make a parade of being acquainted with distinguished or wealthy people, of having been to college, or of having visited foreign lands. All this is no evidence of any real genuine worth on your part.

Do not use the surname alone when speaking of your husband or wife to others. To say to another, that "I told Jones,' referring to your husband, sounds badly. Whereas, to say, "I told Mr. Jones," shows respect and good breeding.

Do not yield to bashfulness. Do not isolate yourself, sitting back in a corner, waiting for some one to come and talk with you. Step out; have something to say. Though you may not say it very well, keep on. You will gain courage and will improve. It is as much your duty to entertain others as theirs to amuse you.

Do not attempt to pry into the private affairs of others by asking what their profits are, what things cost, whether Melissa ever had a beau, and why Amarette never got married. All such questions are extremely impertinent, and are likely to meet with rebuke.

Do not whisper in company; do not engage in private conversation; do not speak a foreign language which the general company present may not understand, unless it is understood that the foreigner is unable to speak your own language.

Do not take it upon yourself to admonish comparative strangers on religious topics; the persons to whom you speak may have decided convictions of their own in opposition to yours, and your over-zeal may seem to them an impertinence.

Do not aspire to be a great story-teller; an inveterate teller of long stories becomes very tiresome. To tell one or two witty, short, new stories, appropriate to the occasion, is about all that one person should inflict on the company.

Do not indulge in satire; no doubt you are witty, and you could say a most cutting thing that would bring the laugh of the company upon your opponent, but you must not allow it, unless to rebuke an impertinent fellow who can be suppressed in no other way.

Do not spend your time in talking scandal; you sink your own moral nature by so doing, and you are, perhaps, doing great injustice to those about whom you talk. You probably do not understand all the circumstances. Were they understood, you would doubtless be much more lenient.

Do not flatter; in doing so you embarrass those upon whom you bestow praise, as they may not wish to offend you by repelling it, and yet they realize that if they accept it they merit your contempt. You may, however, commend their work whenever it can truthfully be done; but do not bestow praise where it is not deserved.

NEW YEAR'S CALLING.

OF LATE years it has become fashionable, for ladies in many cities and villages, to announce in the newspapers the fact of their intention to receive calls upon New Year's day, which practice is very excellent, as it enables gentlemen to know positively who will be prepared to receive them on that occasion; besides, changes of residence are so frequent in the large cities as to make the publication of names and places of calling a great convenience.

The practice of issuing personal notes of invitation, which is sometimes done, to a list of gentleman acquaintances, stating that certain ladies will receive on New Year's day, is not to be commended. It looks very much like begging the gentlemen to come and see them; besides, should this practice generally prevail, it would, in a brief time, abolish New Year's calls altogether, as gentlemen would not feel at liberty to make calls unless personally invited; and thus the custom would soon go into disuse.

Upon calling, the gentlemen are invited to remove overcoat and hat, which invitation is accepted unless it is the design to make the call very brief. If refreshments are provided, the ladies will desire to have the gentlemen partake of them, which cannot conveniently be done in overcoat, with hat in hand. Gloves are sometimes retained upon the hand during the call, but this is optional. Cards are sent up, and the gentlemen are ushered into the reception-room. The call should not exceed ten or fifteen minutes, unless the callers are few and it should be mutually agreeable to prolong the stay.

Fig. 8. Gentlemen Making New Year's Calls.

Best taste will suggest that a lady having the conveniences shall receive her guests at her own home, but it is admissible and common for several ladies to meet at the residence of one, and receive calls together. Whether ladies make announcement or not, however, it will be usually safe for gentlemen to call on their lady friends on New Year's, as the visit will be generally received with pleasure.

It is customary for the ladies who announce that they will receive, to make their parlors attractive on that day, and present themselves in full dress. They should have a bright, cheerful fire if the weather be cold, and a table, conveniently located in the room, with refreshments, consisting of fruits, cakes, bread and other food, such as may be deemed desirable, with tea and coffee. No intoxicating drinks should be allowed. Refreshments are in no case absolutely essential. They can be dispensed with if not convenient.

Ladies expecting calls on New Year's should be in readiness to receive from 10 A. M. to 9 P. M. It is pleasant for two or more ladies to receive calls together on that occasion, as several ladies can the more easily entertain a party of several gentlemen who may be present at one time. While gentlemen may go alone, they also frequently go in pairs, threes, fours (Fig 8) or more. They call upon all the ladies of the party, and where any are not acquainted, introductions take place, care being taken that persons do not intrude themselves where they would not be welcome. Each gentleman should be provided with a large number of cards, with his own name upon each, one of which he will present to every lady of the company where he calls.

The ladies keep these cards for future reference, it being often pleasant to revive the incidents of the day by subsequent examination of the cards received upon that occasion.

An usher should be present wherever many calls are expected, to receive guests, and care for hats and coats. The calls are necessarily very brief, and are made delightfully pleasant by continual change of face and conversation. But, however genial and free may be the interchange of compliments upon this occasion, no young man who is a stranger to the family should feel at liberty to call again without a subsequent invitation.

The two or three days succeeding New Year's are the ladies' days for calling, upon which occasion they pass the compliments of the season, comment upon the incidents connected with the festivities of the holiday, the number of calls made, and the new faces that made their appearance among the visitors. It is customary upon this occasion of ladies' meeting, to offer refreshments and to enjoy the intimacy of a friendly visit. This fashion of observing New Year's day is often the means of commencing pleasant friendships which may continue through life.

Etiquette of the Party and Ball.

THE DANCE---RULES THAT SHOULD GOVERN IT.

YOU purpose giving a larger entertainment than the dinner party—one to which you will invite a greater number of your friends and associates—so great a number, indeed, of young and middle-aged people, that the serious question is, how they shall be entertained; you conclude that you will allow them to dance, and you will name your entertainment a ball.

In this connection we will express no opinion concerning the propriety or the impropriety of dancing. In the simple act of passing through the figures of the dance, there need be no wrong committed; but, as the ball is often conducted, very serious and unfortunate results follow.

Evils of the Ball.

For the company to assemble at a late hour and engage in unusual, exciting and severe exercise throughout the entire night, is often too great a tax upon the physical system. To dress too thinly, and in a state of perspiration to be exposed, as ladies at the ball frequently are, to draughts of cold, is oftentimes to plant the seeds of a disease from which they never recover. Again, to come in contact, as ladies are liable to, more especially at the public ball, with disreputable men, is sometimes to form alliances that will make a lifetime of sorrow.

Well may the watchful parent look with anxiety and suspicion upon the ball, because its associations are so frequently dangerous. If in this chapter we may give admonitions and suggestions that shall tend to correct some of the evils of the dance, our labors will not be in vain.

The dancing-master should be in the highest sense of the term a gentleman; he should be thoroughly schooled in the laws of etiquette; he should be a man of good moral character; he should be a physiologist; he should be a reformer. Such a man at the head of a dancing-school would be of infinite assistance to the young men and women coming upon the stage of action. In his class he would teach his pupils the laws of good behavior; he would warn them concerning the evils of bad association; he would instruct them in the importance of regularity of habit and of keeping proper hours: with which instruction he would reform many abuses that now exist at public entertainments.

Fortunately we have some instructors who appreciate the importance of their work, and are thus instrumental in doing a great amount of good to those who are so favored as to attend their classes.

How to Conduct the Ball.

The management of the ball will largely depend upon whether it is a public or private entertainment. If public, it will be under the control of managers who will send out tickets to those likely to attend, often several weeks before the ball is given. These tickets are sent only to gentlemen who invite such ladies to attend the ball with them as they may choose.

In tendering the invitation, the gentleman frequently visits the lady personally. If he sends a written note of invitation, the form may be as follows:

Wednesday, Oct. 10.

Miss Hammond:

May I have the pleasure of your company to the ball at the Grand Central Hotel, in New York, on the evening of October 25th, at eight o'clock?   *Very Respectfully,*

W. H. SIMPSON.

The following may be the reply:

Thursday, Oct. 11.

Mr. W. H. Simpson:

I shall be happy to accompany you to the ball at the Grand Central, on the evening of October 25th.

CARRIE D. HAMMOND.

Or, if the invitation is declined, the note may have this form·

Thursday, Oct. 11.

Mr. W. H. Simpson:

I regret that absence from the city, (or assign such other cause as may occasion the refusal) *will deprive me of the pleasure of accompanying you to the ball at the Grand Central, on the evening of October 25th.*

CARRIE D. HAMMOND.

If the ball is to be given at a private residence, the notes of invitation should be sent by messenger or post, to each guest, two or three weeks before the dance, and will read as follows:

Mrs. Conklin's compliments to Miss Henry, requesting the pleasure of her company at a ball on Thursday evening, April 12th, at eight o'clock.

This should invariably be answered within a day or two, and, if accepted, the reply may read in the following form:

Miss Henry's compliments to Mrs. Conklin, accepting with pleasure her kind invitation for Thursday evening, April 12th.

If declined, the answer may be—

Miss Henry's compliments to Mrs. Conklin, regretting that the recent death of a relative (or assign such other cause as may occasion the refusal) *will prevent her acceptance of the kind invitation for the evening of April 12th.*

Invitations to all the Family.

In sending invitations to a family where there are parents, sons and daughters, all of whom you desire to invite, enclose an invitation full and complete to the heads of the family, one to the daughters, and one to the sons. Should there be a visitor staying with the family, a distinct card must be sent, but all can be enclosed in one envelope, and addressed to the lady of the house. The invitations to each may read as follows:

(To the Parents.)

Mrs. Hobart's compliments to Mr. and Mrs. Hanson, requesting the pleasure of their company at a ball on the evening of Sept. 8th, at 8 o'clock.

R. S. V. P.*

(To the Daughters.)

Mrs. Hobart's compliments to Misses Ruth and Mary Hanson, requesting the pleasure of their attendance at a ball, Sept. 8th, at 8 o'clock.

R. S. V. P.†

(To the Sons.)

Mrs. Hobart's regards to Messrs. Robert D., Henry H. and Chas. C. Hanson, soliciting their company at a ball on the evening of Sept. 8th, at 8 o'clock.

R. S. V. P.

* R. S. V. P. From the French, "Repondes s'il vous plait." Answer if you please.
† R. S. V. P. may be considered unnecessary, as a reply should always be made.

(To the Visitor.)

Mrs. Hobart's respects to Miss Williamson, desiring the pleasure of her company at a ball on the evening of Sept. 5th, at 8 o'clock.

R. S. V. P.

The acceptance or regrets from each party invited should be enclosed in one envelope, and directed to the hostess, being sent by a messenger within from one to three days from the time the invitations are received.

The hostess having considered how many sets may be accommodated in the dancing-room, it may be well to invite twice that number to the entertainment, thus allowing for those who will decline and for those who will desire to rest while the others are engaged in the dance.

The requisites of a room suitable for dancing purposes are a smooth floor and good ventilation; added to these, an elaborate trimming of the room with various decorations will be appropriate. Floral embellishment gives much attraction, and if an abundance of flowers, shrubbery and evergreens are about the music-stand, concealing the musicians from view, the effect will be all the more charming.

The dressing-room should be provided with servants to receive the wraps, to each of which a card should be attached bearing the name of the owner, or checks may be provided and the same system pursued as is ordinarily observed in checking baggage.

A dressing-table in the ladies' room should be supplied with soap, water, towels, brushes, combs, pomade, face-powder, cologne, needles, thread, pins, etc.; while water, soap, towels, brush-broom, comb, hairbrush, bootjack, and blacking-brush with a box of blacking, should be in the gentlemen's dressing apartment.

Unlike the dinner-party, it is not absolutely necessary that each guest come promptly at a certain time; still, for the sake of regularity of sleep, it is well for each to go early and retire early, though it will be allowable to go somewhat later than the hour appointed.

The host and hostess should be near the door to welcome arrivals, occupying any unused time in making the guests acquainted with each other by introductions. Other members of the family will also intermingle with the company, making introductions and seeing that all are provided with partners for dancing.

It is expected that those who accept an invitation to a ball are able to dance; otherwise it is better to decline, as the wall-flower serves but to embarrass the hostess and other members of the company.

A gentleman, having arranged to accompany a lady to a ball, may very appropriately send her a bouquet of flowers in the afternoon, and in the evening he should call promptly with his carriage at the appointed hour. Upon reaching the house where the entertainment is given, he will conduct the lady immediately to the ladies' dressing-room; when, retiring to the gentlemen's apartment and putting his own toilet in order, he will return to the door of the ladies' room, meet his charge, and conduct her to the ball-room and the hostess.

Etiquette requires that the lady dance first with her escort, and afterwards he should see that she is provided with partners, and that she enjoys herself, though she may dance with whom she pleases. He should conduct her to supper, and will hold himself in readiness to escort her home whenever she desires to go.

In inviting a lady to dance, various forms of invitation may be used to avoid repetition, as, "Will you honor me with your hand for the quadrille?" "May I have the honor of dancing this set with you?" "May I have the pleasure?" "Will you give me the pleasure?" etc.

A gentleman who may be at the party unattended, will invite one of the ladies of the house for the first dance, but she, possibly being otherwise occupied or engaged, will quite likely introduce him to another lady, whom he must accept.

The music will first play a march, then a quadrille, a waltz, a polka, a galop, etc., interspersed with several round dances to each quadrille, usually ending with a march, prior to supper, when the gentleman, presenting his arm to the lady he is dancing with at the time, unless she has come with another gentleman, will proceed to the table, where possibly a little more freedom will prevail than at the dinner-party, though essentially the same etiquette will govern it.

If any lady is without an attendant, it should be the duty of the lady of the house to see that she is provided with an escort. After supper,

several dances will follow, the company dispersing, let us hope, at an early, temperate hour.

Each dancer should be provided with a ball-card bearing a printed programme of the dances, having a space for making engagements upon the same, with a small pencil attached. Much care should be taken to keep each engagement. It is a great breach of etiquette to invite a lady to dance, and then fail to remind her of her promise when the time comes for its fulfillment.

It is customary for the lady and gentleman, who accompany each other to the ball, to dance together once or twice only; to dance as partners oftener is likely to excite remark, though, if the parties be indifferent to comment, no harm will be done. To dance together continually is impolite, and will deservedly provoke severe criticism.

While upon the floor, awaiting the music, a lady and gentleman should avoid long conversations, as they are likely to interfere with the dance; but a pleasant word or two in light conversation will be appropriate if the parties are acquainted; if not, they may quietly wait. The bow should be given at the commencement and close of each dance.

General Suggestions to those who Attend Balls.

When all the ladies are provided for at the table, then the gentlemen may think of their own supper.

Ladies will consult their own pleasure about recognizing a ball-room acquaintance at a future meeting.

Gently glide in the dance, wearing a pleasant expression. "Bow the head slightly as you touch hands lightly."

Should you make a mistake in taking a position, apologize to the party incommoded, and take another place in the set.

Any difficulty or misunderstanding at a public ball should be referred to the master of ceremonies, whose decision should be deemed final.

In tendering an invitation to the lady to dance, allow her to designate what set it shall be, and you are expected to strictly fulfill the engagement.

A gentleman who goes to a ball should dance frequently; if he does not, he will not receive many invitations afterwards; he is not invited to ornament the wall and "wait for supper."

After dancing, a gentleman should conduct the lady to a seat, unless she otherwise desires; he should thank her for the pleasure she has conferred, but he should not tarry too long in intimate conversation with her.

A gentleman having taken a lady's seat during a dance, must rise as soon as it is over, and invite her to come and take it again. It is not necessary to bow more than once, though you frequently meet acquaintances upon the promenade; to bow every time would be tiresome.

What Conduct to Avoid at the Ball.

A ball-room engagement should not be broken.

A lady should not enter or cross the hall unattended.

No gentleman should enter the ladies' dressing-room at a ball.

No evidence of ill-nature should ever show itself at the ball.

Never lead a lady in the hall by the hand; always offer the arm.

Guests should remain at the supper-table no longer than is necessary.

A couple should not engage in a long, private, confidential talk in a ball-room.

While one dance is in progress, it is not in good taste to be arranging for another.

Do not engage yourself for the last two or three dances; it may keep you too late.

Neither married nor unmarried ladies should leave a ball-room assemblage unattended.

A gentleman should not wait until the music has commenced, before selecting his partner.

Do not aim to put in all the steps in the quadrille. The figures are now executed in a graceful walk.

A gentleman should not insist upon a lady continuing to dance, when she has expressed a desire to sit down.

Excepting the first set, it is not etiquette for married people to dance together at either a public or private ball.

Do not contend for a position in the quadrille at either head or sides. It indicates frivolity. You should be above it.

A gentleman should not take a vacant seat beside a lady, without asking permission, whether he is acquainted or not.

The lady should never accept of an invitation to dance with one gentleman immediately after having refused another.

No lady at a ball should be without an escort at the supper-table. The hostess should see that she is provided with one.

A gentleman should never presume upon the acquaintance of a lady after a ball; ball-room introductions close with the dancing.

Ladies should not boast to others, who dance but little, of the great number of dances for which they are engaged in advance.

No gentleman should use his bare hand to press the waist of a lady in the waltz. If without gloves, carry a handkerchief in the hand.

A lady should not select a gentleman to hold her bouquet, fan and gloves during the dance, unless he be her husband, escort or a relative.

Gentlemen should never forget that ladies are first to be cared for, to have the best seats, and to always receive the most courteous attention.

A gentleman in waltzing should not encircle the waist of a lady until the dancing commences, and he should drop his arm when the music ceases.

No gentleman whose clothing or breath is tainted with the fumes of strong drink or tobacco, should ever enter the presence of ladies in the dancing-room.

When the company has been divided into two different sets, you should not attempt to change from one to the other, except by permission of the master of ceremonies.

A lady should not refuse to be introduced to a gentleman at a private ball. At a public ball she will use her discretion, and she can with propriety refuse any introduction.

Never eat your supper in gloves. White kids should be worn at other times throughout the dancing. It is well to have two pairs, one before supper, the other afterwards.

Ladies should not be allowed to sit the evening through without the privilege of dancing. Gentlemen should be sufficiently watchful to see that all ladies present are provided with partners.

Do not, unless for very urgent reasons, withdraw from a quadrille or a set where your assistance is required. Even then you should inform the master of ceremonies, that he may find a substitute.

A gentleman should not invite a lady to be his partner in a dance with which he is not perfectly familiar. It is tiresome and embarrassing to a lady to have a partner who appears awkward.

No gentleman should play the clown in the ball-room. Dancing a break-down, making unusual noise, dressing in a peculiar style, swaggering, swinging the arms about, etc., are simply the characteristics of the buffoon.

The lady is not obliged to invite her escort to enter the house when he accompanies her home, and if invited he should decline the invitation. But he should request permission to call the next day or evening, which will be true politeness.

No display should be made when leaving the ball. Go quietly. It is not necessary to bid the host and hostess good-bye. To do so may cause others to think it later than it is, and thus the ball may be broken up sooner than the hostess might desire.

A lady may not engage herself to two gentlemen for the same dance, excepting the waltz, the first of which may be danced with one and the last with another, she explaining the matter to her first partner, that he may not be offended when she leaves him for the other.

The members of the family where the ball is given should not dance too frequently. It is possible that others may desire to fill their places, and they should have the opportunity. It is the duty of the family to entertain the guests, and not usurp their opportunities.

A gentleman should not be offended if a lady that has declined an invitation from him is seen dancing with another. Possibly she did not despise the one, but she preferred the other, or she may have simply redeemed a forgotten promise. Special evidences of partiality should, however, as much as possible be avoided at places where all should be courteous to each other.

 # ETIQUETTE OF A SOCIAL GAME.

The topics of conversation have become exhausted at the party; you have no musicians in the company, possibly, or if you have music, it no longer entertains. Under the circumstances, you bethink yourself of some light, pleasant indoor game that nearly all can play, and very likely you may select cards, about which the following suggestions may be appropriate:

Should you engage in the game, do so simply for recreation and sociability. Never bet on cards. Like all bets, it leads to demoralization. If you cannot play without gambling and spending too much time, then dismiss the game from your mind. In the simple matter of playing cards there is no harm, but in the abuse of the game there is very much injury.

It is the province of the hostess, not of the guests, to introduce the game. New, bright, clean cards should be kept in readiness for occasions like the evening party.

In taking a seat at the table, where there may be a choice, the elder and married ladies take precedence over the younger members of the company, only those persons being urged to join in the game who have no conscientious scruples against playing.

Rules of the Game.

Do not remove the cards from the table until all are dealt.

Partners should give no appearance of an understanding between themselves by signals of any kind.

Never play with an air of indifference. If tired, you will ask to be excused, and retire; but evince interest while you play.

It is a violation of etiquette to converse upon other topics while playing the game, especially if at the table there are those who are interested, and desire to confine their attention to the play.

It is not courtesy to hurry others when playing. It is very annoying to have an opponent, or even a partner, continually saying, "Come, hurry up!" "We are waiting!" "Any time to-day!" etc.

The object of the game is to give rest. Therefore all topics liable to lead to long argument should be avoided when conversing in the pauses of the play. Small talk, that requires no mental effort, is all that should be indulged in while at the game.

If possible, never violate the rules of the game, and never be guilty of cheating. Should you observe any one doing so, quietly and very politely call their attention to the fact, and be careful that you do not get excited. People who lose patience, and experience ill-feeling at the game, should avoid playing.

It is unkind in those who may have continued success to irritate the opponent; and, whatever may be the ill luck, it is a serious breach of etiquette to lose temper. Neither should there be reflections made upon the playing of the partner nor criticisms upon the opponents.

It is the duty of those who play to make themselves proficient in the game, and thus not embarrass a partner when playing; and courtesy requires that those who play much together should not play with each other in general company, as they would thus be taking unfair advantage of their opponents.

Etiquette of the Table.

THE TABLE--HOW TO SET AND ARRANGE IT.

THE dinner-hour will completely test the refinement, the culture and good breeding which the individual may possess. To appear advantageously at the table, the person must not only understand the laws of etiquette, but he must have had the advantage of polite society. It is the province of this chapter to show what the laws of the table are. It will be the duty of the reader, in the varied relations of life, to make such use of them as circumstances shall permit.

Rules to be Observed.

Sit upright, neither too close nor too far away from the table.

Open and spread upon your lap or breast a napkin, if one is provided—otherwise a handkerchief.

Do not be in haste; compose yourself; put your mind into a pleasant condition, and resolve to eat slowly.

Keep the hands from the table until your time comes to be served. It is rude to take knife and fork in hand and commence drumming on the table while you are waiting.

Possibly grace will be said by some one present, and the most respectful attention and quietude should be observed until the exercise is passed.

It is the most appropriate time, while you wait to be served, for you to put into practice your knowledge of small talk and pleasant words with those whom you are sitting near. By interchange of thought, much valuable information may be acquired at the table.

Do not be impatient to be served. With social chit chat and eating, the meal-time should always be prolonged from thirty minutes to an hour.

Taking ample time in eating will give you better health, greater wealth, longer life and more happiness. These are what we may obtain by eating slowly in a pleasant frame of mind, thoroughly masticating the food.

If soup comes first, and you do not desire it, you will simply say, "No, I thank you," but make no comment; or you may take it and eat as little as you choose. The other course will be along soon. In receiving it you do not break the order of serving; it looks odd to see you waiting while all the rest are partaking of the first course. Eccentricity should be avoided as much as possible at the table.

The soup should be eaten with a medium-sized spoon, so slowly and carefully that you will drop none upon your person or the table-cloth. Making an effort to get the last drop, and all unusual noise when eating, should be avoided.

Fig. 9. The general arrangement of the table set for a party of twelve persons. The plates are often left off, and furnished by the waiter afterwards.

Fig. 10. Relative position of plate, napkin, goblet, salt-cup, knife and fork, when the table is set.

If asked at the next course what you desire, you will quietly state, and upon its reception you will, without display, proceed to put your food in order for eating. If furnished with potatoes in small dishes, you will put the skins back into the dish again; and thus where there are side-dishes all refuse should be placed in them—otherwise potato-skins will be placed upon the table-cloth, and bones upon the side of the plate. If possible, avoid putting waste matter upon the cloth. Especial pains should always be taken to keep the table-cover as clean as may be.

Eating with the Fork.

Fashions continually change. It does not follow, because he does not keep up with them, that a man lacks brains; still to keep somewhere near the prevailing style, in habit, costume and general deportment, is to avoid attracting unpleasant attention.

Fashions change in modes of eating. Unquestionably primitive man conveyed food to his mouth with his fingers. In process of time he cut it with a sharpened instrument, and held it, while he did so, with something pointed. In due time, with the advancement of civilization, there came the two-tined fork for holding and the broad-bladed knife for cutting the food and conveying it to the mouth. As years have passed on, bringing their changes, the three and four-tined forks have come into use, and the habit of conveying food with them to the mouth; the advantage being that there is less danger to the mouth from using the fork, and food is less liable to drop from it when being conveyed from the plate. Thus the knife, which is now only used for cutting meat, mashing potatoes, and for a few other purposes at the table, is no longer placed to the mouth by those who give attention to the etiquette of the table.

Set the table as beautifully as possible. Use only the snowiest of linen, the brightest of cutlery, and the cleanest of china. The setting of the table (Fig. 9) will have fruit-plates, castors and other dishes for general use, conveniently placed near the center. The specific arrangement (Fig. 10) of plate, knife, fork, napkin, goblet and salt-cup, is shown in the accompanying illustration.

It is customary for the gentleman who is the head of the household, in the ordinary family circle, to sit at the side of the table, in the center, having plates at his right hand, with food near by. When all the family are seated, and all in readiness, he will serve the guests who may be present; he will next serve the eldest lady of the household, then the ladies and gentlemen as they come in order. The hostess will sit opposite her husband, and preside over the tea, sauces, etc.

ERRORS TO BE AVOIDED.

DO NOT speak disrespectfully to the waiters, nor apologize to them for making them trouble; it is their business to bring forward the food called for.

It is courtesy, however, when asked if you desire a certain article, to reply, "If you please;" "Not any, I thank you," etc.; when calling for an article, to say, "Will you please bring me," etc.; and when the article has been furnished, to say, "Thank you."

Never eat very fast.

Never fill the mouth very full.

Never open your mouth when chewing.

Never make noise with the mouth or throat.

Never attempt to talk with the mouth full.

Never leave the table with food in the mouth.

Never soil the table-cloth if it is possible to avoid it.

Never carry away fruits and confectionery from the table.

Never encourage a dog or cat to play with you at the table.

Never use anything but fork or spoon in feeding yourself.

Never explain at the table why certain foods do not agree with you.

Never introduce disgusting or unpleasant topics for conversation.

Never pick your teeth or put your hand in your mouth while eating.

Never cut bread; always break it, spreading with butter each piece as you eat it.

Never come to the table in your shirt-sleeves, with dirty hands or disheveled hair.

Never express a choice for any particular parts of a dish, unless requested to do so.

Never hesitate to take the last piece of bread or the last cake; there are probably more.

Never call loudly for the waiter, nor attract attention to yourself by boisterous conduct.

Never hold bones in your fingers while you eat from them. Cut the meat with a knife.

Never use your own knife when cutting butter. Always use a knife assigned to that purpose.

Never pare an apple, peach or pear for another at the table without holding it with a fork.

Never wipe your fingers on the table-cloth, nor clean them in your mouth. Use the napkin.

Never allow butter, soup or other food to remain on your whiskers. Use the napkin frequently.

Never wear gloves at the table, unless the hands from some special reason are unfit to be seen.

Never, when serving others, overload the plate nor force upon them delicacies which they decline.

Never pour sauce over meat and vegetables when helping others. Place it at one side, on the plate.

Never make a display of finding fault with your food. Very quietly have it changed if you want it different.

Never pass your plate with knife and fork on the same. Remove them, and allow them to rest upon a piece of bread.

Never make a display when removing hair, insects or other disagreeable things from your food. Place them quietly under the edge of your plate.

Never make an effort to clean your plate or the bones you have been eating from too clean; it looks as if you left off hungry.

Never tip back in your chair or lounge upon the table; neither assume any position that is awkward or ill-bred.

Never, at one's own table or at a dinner-party elsewhere, leave before the rest have finished without asking to be excused. At a hotel or boarding house this rule need not be observed.

Never feel obliged to cut off the kernels with a knife when eating green corn; eaten from the cob, the corn is much the sweetest.

Never eat so much of any one article as to attract attention, as some people do who eat large quantities of butter, sweet cake, cheese or other articles.

Never expectorate at the table; also avoid sneezing or coughing. It is better to arise quietly from the table if you have occasion to do either. A sneeze is prevented by placing the finger firmly on the upper lip.

Never spit out bones, cherry pits, grape skins, etc., upon your plate. Quietly press them from your mouth upon the fork, and lay them upon the side of your plate.

Never allow the conversation at the table to drift into anything but chit-chat; the consideration of deep and abstruse principles will impair digestion.

Never permit yourself to engage in a heated argument at the table. Neither should you use gestures, nor illustrations made with a knife or fork on the table-cloth. The accompanying engraving (Fig. 11) very forcibly illustrates several faults to which many people are addicted.

FIG. 11. BAD MANNERS AT THE TABLE.

No. 1. Tips back his chair.
" 2. Eats with his mouth too full.
" 3. Feeds a dog at the table.
" 4. Holds his knife improperly.
" 5. Engages in violent argument at the meal-time.
" 6. Lounges upon the table.
" 7. Brings a cross child to the table.

No. 8. Drinks from the saucer, and is, at with his tongue the last drop from the plate.
" 9. Comes to the table in his shirt-sleeves, and puts his feet beside his chair.
" 10. Picks his teeth with his fingers.
" 11. Scratches her head and is frequently unnecessarily getting up from the table.

Never pass forward to another the dish that has been handed to you, unless requested to do so; it may have been purposely designed for you, and passing it to another may give him or her what is not wanted.

Never put your feet so far under the table as to touch the person on the opposite side; neither should you curl them under nor at the side of your chair.

Never praise extravagantly every dish set before you; neither should you appear indifferent. Any article may have praise.

POLITENESS AT THE TABLE.

ROPERLY conducted, the dinner-party should be a pleasant affair; and if rightly managed, from the beginning to the end, it may prove a very enjoyable occasion to all in attendance, the dinner being from 5 to 8 P. M., the guests continuing at the table from one to two hours.

For a very pleasant social affair the rule is not to have the company when seated exceed twelve in number. With a party of that size the conversation can be general, and all are likely to feel more at ease than if the number be larger, provided a selection of guests is made that are congenial to each other. None of them should be conspicuously superior to the others, and all should be from the same circle of society.

Having determined upon the number of guests to be invited, the next thing in order will be the issuing of notes of invitation, by special messenger, which should be sent out ten or twelve days before the dinner is given. Their form will be—

Mr. and Mrs. L—— request the pleasure of the company of Mr. and Mrs. T—— at dinner on Wednesday, the 10th of March, at six o'clock P. M.

R. S. V. P.

The answer accepting the invitation may read—

Mr. and Mrs. T—— accept with much pleasure Mr. and Mrs. L——'s invitation for dinner on the 10th of March.

If declined, the form may be as follows:

Mr. and Mrs. T—— regret that a previous engagement (or for other reasons which may be given) *will prevent their accepting Mr. and Mrs. L——'s kind invitation for dinner on the 10th of March.*

Should the invitation be declined, the declination, which should state the reason for non-acceptance of the invitation, should be sent immediately by a messenger, that the hostess may have an opportunity for inviting other guests in the place of those who decline.

Should the invitation be accepted, nothing but serious difficulty should prevent the appointment being fulfilled. Should anything happen to prevent attendance, notification should be given the hostess immediately.

It is of the utmost importance that all of the company be punctual, arriving from ten to fifteen minutes before the appointed time. To be ten minutes late, keeping the dinner waiting, is a serious offense which no one should be guilty of.

The host, hostess and other members of the family should be early in the drawing-room to receive guests as they arrive, each of whom should be welcomed with a warm greeting.

The hostess having determined who shall accompany each other to the table, each gentleman should be informed what lady he is expected to escort. The hour having arrived, the host offers his right arm to the most honored or possibly the eldest lady guest, and the gentleman most distinguished will escort the lady of the house.

Proceeding to the dining-room when all is in readiness, the host will take his seat at the foot of the table, and the hostess at the head, the lady escorted by the host taking her seat at his right, and the escort of the hostess sitting also at *her* right. The next most honored seat is at the *left* of the hostess. The illustration (Fig. 12) upon this page shows a company thus seated.

It is fashionable to have cards laid upon the table, bearing the name, sometimes printed very beautifully upon silk, indicating where each guest shall sit, which saves confusion in being seated. The ladies having taken their places, the gentlemen will be seated, and all is in readiness for the dinner to be served, unless grace be said by a clergyman present or by the host.

Let us hope if there is any carving, it will be done before the meat is brought to the table, and the time of the company saved from this sometimes slow and tedious work. Should soup be passed, it is well for each one to take it, and also the various courses as they are served, making no special comment on the food.

The gentleman will, when a dish is brought, having seen the lady he escorted provided for, help himself and pass it on; he will pay no attention to the other lady near him, but will leave that to her escort. In all cases he will be careful and attentive to the wants of the lady in his charge, ascertaining her wishes and issuing her orders to the waiters.

No polite guest will ever fastidiously smell or examine any article of food before tasting it. Such conduct would be an insult to those who have invited him; neither will the host or hostess apologize for the cooking or find fault with each other, the cook or the waiters; all having done the best they could, there is nothing left to do but to make the best of everything that is provided.

Especial pains should be taken by the host and hostess, as well as all the company, to introduce topics of conversation that shall be agreeable and pleasing, that the dinner hour may be in the highest degree entertaining. When all the guests have finished their eating, the hostess, with a slight nod to one of the leading members of the party, will rise, as will all the company, and repair to the drawing-room, where, in social converse, the time should be spent for the next two or three hours. Etiquette demands that each member of the company remain at least an hour after the dinner is finished, it being impolite to hurry away immediately after rising from the table. Should he do so, however, he will ask to be excused.

Fig. 12. GENTILITY IN THE DINING-ROOM.

The evidences of good breeding with a party of ladies and gentlemen seated about a table, who are accustomed to the usages of polite society, are many. Among these will be the fact that the table is very beautifully and artistically spread. This need not require much wealth, but good taste is necessary to set it handsomely.

Again, the company evince gentility by each assuming a genteel position while eating. It is not necessary that an elaborate toilet be worn at the table, but careful attention should always be given to neatness of personal appearance, however plain may be the dress which is worn.

Another evidence of good manners is the self-possession with which the company deport themselves throughout the meal.

CORRECT AND INCORRECT POSITIONS.

HEREWITH is shown a fault common with many people of holding knife and fork above the hand (Fig. 13) when mashing potatoes, cutting meat, etc. The position is not only unfavorable for obtaining a good command of knife and fork, but it is likewise ungraceful. The contrasting illustration (Fig. 14) represents an easy, graceful posture for hands, when

Fig. 13. Incorrect Position for Holding Knife and Fork.

eating. The habit of holding the hands thus in correct positions can be acquired as easily as any other.

It is well to become accustomed to eating with the left hand, so as to avoid the necessity of changing the fork from the left to the right hand frequently when eating meat. When no knife is required for spreading, mashing or cutting, lay it aside entirely and eat only with the fork, holding it with the right hand.

Drinking from the Teacup.

Formerly it was the fashion to pour tea into the saucer; not so now. Tea should be gently sipped from the spoon or cup, taking cup and spoon in hand (Fig. 15) when drinking, as shown in the accompanying diagram.

The spoon should never be removed from the cup when the guest is satisfied with its contents. Should the cup be empty, and more be desired, to take the spoon out and place it beside the cup in the saucer is an intimation to the waiter to have it refilled. If not empty, and the spoon is placed thus beside the cup, it is an intimation to the waiter that you want the tea or coffee changed. Do not call for "milk;" call for and speak only of "cream." Never set your teacup upon the table-cloth. In taking sugar, use only the sugar-spoon.

Fig. 14. Correct Position for Holding Knife and Fork.

As in all the affairs of life, common sense must always rise superior to fashion or forms of etiquette. In this chapter on "The Table" we have aimed to give the leading outlines which should govern conduct in the dining-room. Much judgment will be required to always understand where these rules should be applied. Certainly to meet a company of people at the table, appear to advantage, carry forward an intelligent conversation, be agreeable and finish the meal, having eaten, in kind and quantity, sufficient to preserve health and vigor, requires much wisdom and experience.

Fig. 15. Position for Holding Cup and Spoon. ●

● The cup with handle, or of unusual size, may be held differently.

Etiquette of Parties in General.

Sociables, Tea-Parties, Private Theatricals, Picnics, Etc.

THERE are many other kinds of gatherings, aside from the formal dinner-party and the ball, where less formality is required, but where the rules of etiquette, nevertheless, must be continually brought into service. These comprise conversations, or sociables, private concerts, readings, tea-parties, private theatricals, card-playing, etc. At these entertainments some prefer dancing, some music, some conversation, and some the playing of games.

Whatever may be the nature of the entertainment, it is well to specify it in the invitation. Thus, for a large, full-dress party, the invitation will read:

Miss J——'s compliments to Miss H——, requesting the pleasure of her company for Friday evening, March 10, at eight o'clock.

For the small party meeting for a specific purpose, the invitation will read thus:

Miss B—— requests the pleasure of Miss K——'s company on Friday evening next at 8 o'clock, to meet the members of the Salem Literary Club, to which Miss B—— belongs.

Or,

Miss B—— would be happy to have Miss K—— take part in an entertainment consisting of readings and recitations, at her residence, on Wednesday evening, March 15th, at eight o'clock.

Like the dinner-party and ball, an answer should be promptly returned. The reply may read:

Miss K—— accepts with pleasure Miss B——'s kind invitation for next Wednesday evening.

Unable to accept the invitation, the reply may read as follows:

Miss K—— regrets that a previous engagement (or other reason) will prevent her accepting Miss B——'s kind invitation for Wednesday evening next.

Should there be any probability of mistake as to time, and identity of the person sending the invitation, the date should be explicitly given in the body of the note, and the full name and address may be placed in the lower left-hand corner.

As upon other occasions, it is the duty of the host and hostess to welcome arrivals and make all the guests feel at ease. To do this, much depends upon the hostess, who, by self-possession, geniality and continual movement among the guests, will make all feel at home. More especially if the entertainment par[?]es of the character of a sociable, much tact is necessary upon the part [?] the family to have the gathering entertained.

To keep the attention of the company occupied, as many rooms should be thrown open as possible, and many objects of interest should be scattered around the apartments to interest, amuse and instruct.

If among the company there are those particularly eminent, there should be also other notables, that attention may not be entirely concentrated upon the few.

Special pains should be taken that the party does not divide itself up into cliques, twos, threes or more, leaving a number out who seem to possess no power to get into conversation.

While it is not always advisable to break up a pleasant conversation going forward between two, three or four, care must be exercised that those inclined to drop aside and spend the time in conversing with each other are prevented by the hostess as much as possible from so doing, as the best conversationalists, thus going by themselves, would cause the remainder of the company to be wanting in spirit and animation. The introduction of others into the group, the calling for a story, the reading of a poem, the singing of a song, with instrumental music, will thus effectually break up the monotony.

Piano-Playing.

Should dancing form a principal feature of the entertainment, and the piano be used to furnish music, the hostess or one of the family should play the instrument. One of the guests should not be depended upon to furnish all of the music. If the hostess cannot play, a pianist for the occasion should be engaged. Either a lady or gentleman-guest may with propriety volunteer to play, if they choose; but the hostess cannot expect that music, thus voluntarily offered, will be cheerfully furnished for more than one dance.

It is courtesy, while anyone is playing an instrument, or singing, to preserve as much stillness as possible. Should you converse, do it so quietly as not to be heard by those near the piano. Should your conversation be animated, it is well to retire to another room.

Amateur performers upon the piano should thoroughly commit to memory a few pieces to play independently of notes, as to take sheet-music to a party is a hint that they expect to be invited to play. If possible, have the voice in good condition also, so as not to be obliged to complain of a cold. To eat a small amount of horse-radish just previous to reading, singing or speaking, will quite effectually remove hoarseness.

Any lady-guest being invited to play the piano, it is courtesy for the gentleman nearest her to offer his arm and escort her to the instrument. While she is playing he will hold her bouquet, fan and gloves, and should also turn the leaves if he can readily read music, but he should not attempt it otherwise.

When a guest is invited by another guest to play the piano, it will be well to wait until the request is seconded by others; and even then the guest may not play unless it should meet the favor of the hostess, and it is believed to be the pleasure of the majority of the company. If certain that the playing will be acceptable, it is well to suggest to the hostess to invite your friend.

It is very impolite to speak disparagingly of the piano, however much it may be out of tune, or however inferior it may be. More especially is it a breach of etiquette to draw unfavorable comparisons between the instrument and another elsewhere.

How to Entertain the Party.

If it happens to be stormy on the evening of your party, an awning erected from the carriage-landing to the house, or a large umbrella carried by a servant, will be a kind provision for the comfort of the guests as they alight from their carriages.

Suppers have wisely been dispensed with of late years at the ordinary evening party. To furnish a full, late supper is a piece of folly for various reasons; among them being the fact that it is positively injurious to the health of the company to eat it. The majority of the party, in all probability, do not desire it; and consequently it is time, labor and expense, upon the part of the hostess, worse than thrown away. She should have all of her time to ... o her company; to do which, she can provide only light refreshments, which may be passed around.

Among the methods of entertainment resorted to, aside from conversation and dancing, may be those of a literary character. Thus a debatable question may be propounded, a presiding officer selected, assisted by two, four or six others, two leading disputants appointed, debaters chosen upon each side, and the speakers given each two, three or five minutes to talk; the president and board of arbitration to decide the question according to the weight of argument. This is a pleasant and profitable way of spending the evening, if all can be enlisted and be interested in listening or have something to say.

Another intellectual and pleasant mode of spending an evening is for each member of the company to read or recite something that shall interest, amuse, instruct and entertain the audience. To do this rightly, some one should be appointed to act as master of ceremonies for the evening, being assisted by two or three others, who will make suggestions. It will be the duty of the presiding officer, at these parlor recitations, to ascertain in the beginning what each one will recite, make out a programme, and then announce the various readers and speakers of the evening, as they come in turn, having the exercises suitably interspersed with music. The pleasure of the occasion will much depend upon having every piece upon the programme short, and clearly announced by the presiding officer.

Parlor-theatricals and parlor-concerts are a pleasant means of entertaining an evening gathering — a company of six, eight, or more, thoroughly mastering a play and giving it to an audience that may assemble in the parlors. To have an entertainment of this kind pass smoothly through, some competent person must take upon himself or herself the duties of manager. Each player should be consulted before parts are assigned, and it is of the utmost importance that the players be each prompt in rendering their parts. It is the province of the hostess to act the part of stage-manager, unless she appoints some one from the audience to conduct the exercises.

Croquet parties are very fashionable, and are a healthful, pleasant means of diversion. The essentials necessary to make the game pleasant are good grounds that can be shaded, and clean, comfortable, cool seats. A table may be set in the shade, and refreshments served thereon; or they may be passed to the guests as they sit in their seats.

On all occasions when a number of people convene together, whether indoors or out, the laws of courtesy should be obeyed. It is the duty of the gentlemen to be ever attentive to the ladies. If it be a picnic, the gentlemen will carry the luncheon, erect the swings, construct the tables, bring the water, provide the fuel for boiling the tea, etc. On the fishing excursion they will furnish the tackle, bait the hooks, row the boats, carry the fish, and furnish comfortable seats for the ladies. In gathering nuts, they will climb the trees, do the shaking, carry the nuts, and assist the ladies across the streams and over the fences. If possible, in crossing the fields, go through the bars or gateway, and avoid the necessity of compelling the ladies to clamber over the fences. Should it be necessary to climb them, it is etiquette for the gentleman to go over first, and when the lady is firmly on the top, he will gently help her down.

It should ever be the rule, with both ladies and gentlemen, upon all such occasions, to render every assistance possible to entertain the company. Self should be forgotten. More or less assistance is all the time required by the managers of the outdoor gatherings, and labor is continually necessary to make the occasion pleasant. To aid in rendering the affair agreeable by needed assistance will very likely give you more pleasure than to be entertained yourself.

Etiquette for Public Places.

It is not etiquette for a young lady to visit a place of public amusement with a gentleman, alone, with whom she is but slightly acquainted. Her escort should the first time invite another member of the family to accompany her.

The gentleman should make a point of extending his invitation to the lady long enough before the entertainment to be able to secure desirable seats. Most of the pleasure of the occasion will depend upon being so seated as to be able to witness the performance to advantage.

The lady having received a note of invitation, she should reply to the same immediately, that the gentleman may make his arrangements accordingly.

Should the weather be stormy, and for other reasons, it will be a very graceful way of complimenting the lady to provide a carriage for the occasion.

Seats having been secured, it is not necessary to arrive until about five minutes before the commencement of the performance. It is bad manners to go late to a public entertainment; the bustle and noise incident to the late arrival is often a serious interference with the exercises of the occasion.

Upon entering the hall, secure a programme for each member of your party, and follow the usher to the designated seats. The gentleman will go first, and pause at the entrance, allowing the lady to pass into the seat, when he will follow.

Etiquette of Visiting.

WHEN, WHERE AND HOW TO VISIT.

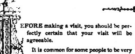

EFORE making a visit, you should be perfectly certain that your visit will be agreeable.

It is common for some people to be very cordial, and even profuse in their offers of hospitality. They unquestionably mean what they say at the time, but when they tender you an invitation to come and tarry *weeks*, it may seriously incommode them if you should pay them a visit of even a few *days*.

As a rule, a visit should never be made upon a general invitation. Should you visit a city where a friend resides, it will be best to go first to the hotel, unless you have a special invitation from the friend. From the hotel you will make a polite call, and if then you are invited, you can accept of the hospitality.

In all cases when you contemplate a visit, even with relatives, it is courtesy to write and announce your coming, giving, as nearly as possible, the day and exact time of your arrival.

An invitation to visit a friend should be answered as soon as may be; stating definitely when you will come, and how long you intend to stay.

When near your destination, it is well to send a prepaid telegram, stating upon what train you will arrive. As a reward for this forethought, you will probably find your friends waiting for you at the depot, and the welcome will be very pleasant.

What is Expected of the Guest when Visiting.

You are expected to pleasantly accept such hospitality as your friends can afford.

If no previous understanding has been had, the visit should be limited to three days, or a week at most.

You should make your visit interfere as little as possible with the routine work of the household in which you are a guest.

You should aim to conform your action, as much as may be, to the rules of the house, as to times of eating, retiring to rest, etc.

You should state upon your arrival how long you intend to stay, that your friends may arrange their plans to entertain accordingly.

Letters and papers being received in the presence of the host, hostess and others, the guest should ask to be excused while reading them.

Furnish your own materials in doing work for yourself when you are visiting, as much as possible, and never depend upon your entertainers.

A kind courtesy, while you remain, will be to execute some work representing your own skill, to be given the hostess as a memento of the occasion.

You should in shopping or transacting business, when you desire to go alone, select the hours of the day when your friends are engaged in their own duties.

The guest should beware of making unfavorable comment about the friends of the host and hostess, or of offering unfavorable criticism upon what they are known to favor or admire.

Should you happen to injure any article or other property while visiting, you should have the same immediately repaired, and, if possible, the article put in better condition than it was before.

You should not treat your friend's house as if it was a hotel, making your calls, visiting, transacting business about the town, and coming and going at all hours to suit your own convenience.

Never invite a friend who may call upon you to remain to dinner or supper. This is a right which belongs to the hostess, and it is for her to determine whether she wishes your guest to remain or not.

The guest should aim to render efficient assistance in case of sickness or sudden trouble at the house where the visit may be made. Oftentimes the best service will be rendered by considerately taking your leave.

Invitations accepted by the lady-guest should include the hostess, and those received by the hostess should include the guest. Thus, as much as possible, at all places of entertainment hostess and guest should go together.

While husbands and wives are always expected to accompany each other, where either may be invited, it is a trespass upon the generosity of the friend to take children and servants unless they are included in the invitation.

Never invite a friend who calls upon you into any other room than the parlor, unless it is suggested by the hostess that you do so. While you may have the right to enter various rooms, you have no authority for extending the privilege to others.

Immediately upon the return to your home, after paying a visit, you should write to your hostess, thanking her for hospitality and the enjoyment you received. You should also ask to be remembered to all of the family, mentioning each one by name.

Expenses which the friends may incur in removal and care of baggage, in repairs of wardrobe, or any other personal service requiring cash outlay, the guest should be careful to have paid. Washing and ironing should be sent elsewhere from the place where the guest is visiting.

The lady-guest should beware of receiving too many visits from gentlemen, and if invited to accompany them to places of amusement or on rides, she should consult with the hostess and learn what appointments she may have, and whether the going with others will be satisfactory to her.

Should a secret of the family come into your possession while on a visit, you should remember that the hospitality and privileges extended should bind you to absolute secrecy. It is contemptibly mean to become the possessor of a secret thus, and afterwards betray the confidence reposed in you.

Be careful that you treat with kindness and care servants, horses, carriages and other things at your friend's house which are placed at your disposal. To pluck choice flowers, to handle books roughly, to drive horses too fast, to speak harshly to servants—all this indicates selfishness and bad manners.

The visitor should beware of criticism or fault-finding with the family of the hostess. It is also in extremely bad taste for the guest to speak disparagingly of things about the home or the town where the visit is being made, being at the same time enthusiastic in praise of people and places elsewhere.

When a child is taken along, the mother should be very watchful that it does no injury about the house, and makes no trouble. It is excessively annoying to a neat housekeeper to have a child wandering about the rooms, handling furniture with greasy fingers, scattering crumbs over the carpets, and otherwise making disturbance.

The gentleman visitor should be certain that smoking is not offensive to the various members of the family, before he indulges too freely in the pipe and cigar about the house. For the guest, without permission, to seat himself in the parlor (Fig. 16), and scent the room with the fumes of tobacco, is a serious impoliteness.

When you can at times render assistance to those you are visiting, in any light work, you will often make your visit more agreeable. A lady will not hesitate to make her own bed if there be few or no servants, and will do anything else to assist the hostess. If your friend, however, declines allowing you to assist her, you should not insist upon the matter further.

Guests should enter with spirit and cheerfulness into the various plans that are made for their enjoyment. Possibly some rides will be had, and some visits made, that will be tiresome, but the courteous guest should find something to admire everywhere, and thus make the entertainers feel that their efforts to please are appreciated.

Of various persons in the family where the guest may be visiting, gifts may most appropriately be given to the hostess, and the baby or the youngest child. If the youngest has reached its teens, then it may be best to give it to the mother. The visitor will, however, use discretion in the matter. Flowers and fancy needle-work will always be appropriate for the lady. Confectionery and jewelry will be appreciated by the children. Small articles of wearing apparel or money will be suitable for servants who have been particularly attentive to the guest.

Special pains should be taken by guests to adapt themselves to the religious habits of those with whom they are visiting. If daily prayers are had, or grace is said at meals, the most reverent attention should be given; though when invited to participate in any of these exercises, if unaccustomed to the same, you can quietly ask to be excused. As a rule, it is courtesy to attend church with the host and hostess. Should you have decided preferences, and go elsewhere, do so quietly and without comment, and under no circumstances should there be allowed religious discussion afterwards. You visit the home of your friends to entertain and be entertained. Be careful that you so treat their opinions that they will wish you to come again.

Hints to the Host and Hostess.

Take the baggage-checks, and give personal attention to having the trunks conveyed to your residence, relieving the guest of all care in the matter.

Having received intelligence of the expected arrival of a guest, if possible have a carriage at the depot to meet the friend. Various members of the family being with the carriage will make the welcome more pleasant.

Have a warm, pleasant room especially prepared for the guest, the dressing-table being supplied with water, soap, towel, comb, hair-brush, brush-broom, hat-brush, pomade, cologne, matches, needles and pins. The wardrobe should be conveniently arranged for the reception of wearing apparel. The bed should be supplied with plenty of clothing, a side-table should contain writing materials, and the center-table should be furnished with a variety of entertaining reading matter.

Arrange to give as much time as possible to the comfort of the guest, visiting places of amusement and interest in the vicinity. This should all be done without apparent effort on your part. Let your friends feel that the visit is a source of real enjoyment to you; that through their presence and company you have the pleasure of amusements and recreation that would, perhaps, not have been enjoyed had they not come. Treat them with such kindness as you would like to have bestowed upon yourself under similar circumstances.

At the close of their stay, if you would be happy to have the visitors remain longer, you will frankly tell them so. If they insist upon going, you will aid them in every way possible in their departure. See that their baggage is promptly conveyed to the train. Examine the rooms to find whether they have forgotten any article that they would wish to take. Prepare a lunch for them to partake of on their journey. Go with them to the depot. Treat them with such kindness and cordiality to the close that the recollection of their visit will ever be a bright spot in their memory. Remain with them until the train arrives. They would be very lonely waiting without you. You will ever remember with pleasure the fact that you made the last hours of their visit pleasant. And thus, with the last hand-shaking, and the last waving of adieu, as the train speeds away, keep up the warmth of hospitality with your guests to the very end. It is, perhaps, the last time you will ever see them.

CONDUCT AT PLACES OF PUBLIC AMUSEMENT.

While a quiet conversation is allowable in the intervals after the opening of the performance, close attention should be given to the stage. Should it be a concert, the utmost stillness should be observed, as the slightest whisper will disturb the singers. This considerate attention should be given to the very end. It is in exceedingly bad taste, near the close of the last act, for the audience to commence moving about, putting on wraps and outer clothing, preparatory to leaving. Those who do so, lose the choicest part of the entertainment; they distract others who wish to be attentive, and they advertise the fact that they have no private carriage of their own, but on the contrary go by some public conveyance, and with characteristic selfishness they intend to rush out first and secure the best seats.

Fig. The Visitor who Converts the Parlor into a Smoking-Room.

If the entertainment be a fancy fair, where goods which have been manufactured by a company of ladies are sold for church or charitable purposes, good sense will immediately suggest that as large a price should be realized as possible, and hence it is not etiquette for the purchaser to attempt to buy under price. It is also courtesy for the saleswoman, when a larger sum is presented than is charged, to deduct the price and promptly return the change, unless the surplus be donated to the charity.

Bad Manners.

Do not forget, while you make yourself comfortable, that others have rights which should be always considered.

Do not talk loudly, laugh boisterously, or make violent gestures.

Do not talk or whisper so loudly during the entertainment as to disturb those sitting near you.

Do not make a display of secrecy, mystery, or undue lover-like affection with your companion.

Do not prevent your companion from giving attention to the exercises, even though they may be without interest to yourself.

Do not, in a picture-gallery, stand conversing too long in front of pictures. Take seats, and allow others to make examination.

Do not, if a lady, allow a gentleman to join you, and thus withdraw your attention from your escort. And do not, if a gentleman, allow your attention to be taken up, to any great extent, with a lady other than the one you have in charge.

Do not, if a gentleman, be continually going from the hall between the acts of the play. To be passing up and down the aisle, eating peppers and cardamom seeds, advertises the fact that you are addicted to the too frequent use of liquors.

Do not join a party about to visit a place of amusement unless invited to do so. Should the party consist of one gentleman and two ladies, a gentleman, if well acquainted, may ask the privilege of attending one of the ladies. Should a ticket be furnished him, he should return the favor by an equal politeness bestowed upon the party, if possible, during the evening.

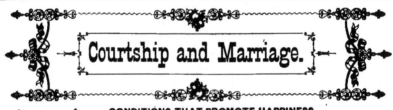

Courtship and Marriage.

CONDITIONS THAT PROMOTE HAPPINESS.

HE happiness of married life comes from pleasant, harmonious relations existing between husband and wife. If rightly mated in the conjugal state, life will be one continual joy. If unhappily wedded, the soul will be forever yearning, and never satisfied; happiness may be hoped for, may be dreamed of, may be the object ever labored for, but it will never be realized.

In view, therefore, of the great influence that marriage has upon the welfare and happiness of all those who enter the conjugal relation, it becomes the duty of everyone to study the laws which make happy, enduring companionships between husbands and wives. It is a duty which not only the unmarried owe themselves, but it is an obligation due to society, as the well-being of a community largely rests upon the permanent, enduring family relation.

Very properly does the highest civilization not only recognize one woman for one man, and one man for one woman, but it ordains that marriage shall be publicly solemnized; and in view of its sacred nature and its vast influence on the welfare of society, that its rights shall be jealously guarded, and that a separation of those who pledge themselves to each other for life shall be as seldom made as possible.

The young should, therefore, be thoroughly imbued with the idea that the marriage state may not be entered upon without due and careful consideration of its responsibilities, as explained in the introductory remarks found in the department devoted to "Love Letters."

The province of this chapter is to consider the etiquette of courtship and marriage, not its moral bearings; and yet we may in this connection very appropriately make a few suggestions.

Whom to Marry.

There are exceptions to all rules. Undoubtedly parties have married on brief acquaintance, and have lived happily afterwards. It is sometimes the case that the wife is much older than the husband, is much wiser, and much his superior in social position, and yet happiness in the union may follow. But, as a rule, there are a few fundamental requisites, which, carefully observed, are much more likely to bring happiness than does marriage where the conditions are naturally unfavorable.

Of these requisites, are the following:

Marry a person whom you have known long enough to be sure of his or her worth—if not personally, at least by reputation.

Marry a person who is your equal in social position. If there be a difference either way, let the husband be superior to the wife. It is difficult for a wife to love and honor a person whom she is compelled to look down upon.

Marry a person of similar religious convictions, tastes, likes and dislikes to your own. It is not congenial to have one companion deeply religious, while the other only ridicules the forms of religion. It is not pleasant for one to have mind and heart absorbed in a certain kind of work which the other abhors; and it is equally disagreeable to the gentle, mild and sweet disposition to be united with a cold, heartless, grasping, avaricious, quarrelsome person. Very truthfully does Lena S. Peck, in the "Vermont Watchman," describe one phase of inharmony, in the following poem:

MISMATED.

HAWK once courted a white little dove,
　With the softest of wings and a voice full of love;
　And the hawk — O yes, as other hawks go—
　Was a well-enough hawk, for aught that I know.
　　　But she was a dove,
　　　And her bright young life
　　　Had been nurtured in love,
　　　Away from all strife.

Well, she married the hawk. The groom was delighted;
A feast was prepared, and the friends all invited.
(Does anyone think that my story's not true?
He is certainly wrong — the facts are not new.)
　　　Then he flew to his nest,
　　　With the dove at his side,
　　　And soon all the rest
　　　Took a squint at the bride.

A hawk for his father, a hawk for his mother,
A hawk for his sister, and one for his brother,
And uncles and aunts there were by the dozens,
And oh, such a number of hawks for his cousins!
　　　They were greedy and rough—
　　　A turbulent crew,
　　　Always ready enough
　　　To be quarrelsome, too.

To the dove all was strange; but never a word
In resentment she gave to the wrangling she heard.
If a thought of the peaceful, far-away nest
Ever haunted her dreams, or throbbed in her breast,
　　　No bird ever knew;
　　　Each hour of her life,
　　　Kind, gentle and true
　　　Was the hawk's dove-wife.

But the delicate nature too sorely was tried;
With no visible sickness, the dove drooped and died;
Then loud was the grief, and the wish all expressed
To call the learned birds, and hold an inquest.
　　　So all the birds came,
　　　But each shook his head:
　　　No disease could he name
　　　Why the dove should be dead,

'Till a wise old owl, with a knowing look,
Stated this· "The case is as clear as a book;
The cause of her death was too much hawk!
Hawk for her father, and hawk for her mother,
Hawk for her sister, and hawk for her brother;
Was more than the delicate bird could bear;
She hath winged her way to a realm more fair!
　　　She was nurtured a dove;
　　　Too hard the hawk's life—
　　　Void of kindness and love,
　　　Full of hardness and strife."

And when he had told them, the other birds knew
That this was the cause, and the verdict was true!

Natural Selection.

In the first place, observation proves that selections made in nature by the beasts of the field and fowls of the air, of couples which pair, the male is always the strongest, generally the largest, the most brave, and always the leader. The female follows, trusting to her companion, leaving him to fight the heavy battles, apparently confident in his bravery, strength and wisdom.

If nature teaches anything, it is what observation and experience in civilized life has also proved correct, that of husband and wife, rightly mated, the husband should represent the positive — the physical forces, the intellectual and the strongly-loving; while the wife will represent the negative — the sympathetic, the spiritual, and the affectional. The husband should be so strong as to be a natural protector to his family. He should be brave, that he may defend his companion. He should be wise, and he should be so thoroughly true and devoted to his wife that he will delight in being her guardian and support.

The wife, confident in the husband's strength and wisdom, will thus implicitly yield to his protecting care. And thus both will be happy — he in exercising the prerogatives which belong naturally to the guardian and protector; and she in her confidence, love and respect for her companion, whom she can implicitly trust.

Peculiarities Suitable for Each Other.

Those who are neither very tall nor very short, whose eyes are neither very black nor very blue, whose hair is neither very black nor very red, — the mixed types — may marry those who are quite similar in form, complexion and temperament to themselves.

Bright red hair and a florid complexion indicate an excitable temperament. Such should marry the jet-black hair and the brunette type.

The gray, blue, black or hazel eyes should not marry those of the same color. Where the color is very pronounced, the union should be with those of a decidedly different color.

The very corpulent should unite with the thin and spare, and the short, thick-set should choose a different constitution.

The thin, bony, wiry, prominent-featured, Roman-nosed, cold-blooded individual, should marry the round-featured, warm-hearted and emotional. Thus the cool should unite with warmth and susceptibility.

The extremely irritable and nervous should unite with the lymphatic, the slow and the quiet. Thus the stolid will be prompted by the nervous companion, while the excitable will be quieted by the gentleness of the less nervous.

The quick-motioned, rapid-speaking person should marry the calm and deliberate. The warmly impulsive should unite with the stoical.

The very fine-haired, soft and delicate-skinned should not marry those like themselves; and the curly should unite with the straight and smooth hair.

The thin, long-face should marry the round-favored; and the flat nose should marry the full Roman. The woman who inherits the features and peculiarities of her father should marry a man who partakes of the characteristics of his mother; but in all these cases where the type is not pronounced, but is, on the contrary, an average or medium, those forms, features and temperaments may marry either.

Etiquette of Courtship.

But however suitable may be the physical characteristics, there are many other matters to be considered before a man and woman may take upon themselves the obligation to love and serve each other through life, and these can only be learned by acquaintance and courtship, concerning which the following suggestions may be appropriate:

Any gentleman who may continuously give special, undivided attention to a certain lady, is presumed to do so because he prefers her to others. It is reasonable to suppose that others will observe his action. It is also to be expected that the lady will herself appreciate the fact, and her feelings are likely to become engaged. Should she allow an intimacy thus to ripen upon the part of the gentleman, and to continue, it is to be expected that he will be encouraged to hope for her hand; and hence it is the duty of both lady and gentleman, if neither intends marriage, to discourage an undue intimacy which may ripen into love, as it is in the highest degree dishonorable to trifle with the affections of another. If, however, neither has objections to the other, the courtship may continue.

The Decisive Question.

At length the time arrives for the gentleman to make a proposal. If he is a good judge of human nature, he will have discovered long ere this whether his favors have been acceptably received or not, and yet he may not know positively how the lady will receive an offer of marriage. It becomes him, therefore, to propose.

What shall he say? There are many ways whereby he may introduce the subject. Among these are the following:

He may write to the lady, making an offer, and request her to reply. He may, if he dare not trust to words, even in her presence write the question on a slip of paper, and request her laughingly to give a plain "no" or "yes." He may ask her if in case a gentleman very much like himself was to make a proposal of marriage to her, what she would say. She will probably laughingly reply that it will be time enough to tell what she would say when the proposal is made. And so the ice would be broken. He may jokingly remark that he intends one of these days to ask a certain lady not a thousand miles away if she will marry him, and asks her what answer she supposes the lady will give him; she will quite likely reply that it will depend upon what lady he asks. And thus he may approach the subject, by agreeable and easy stages, in a hundred ways, depending upon circumstances.

Engaged.

An engagement of marriage has been made. The period of courtship prior to marriage has been passed by the contracting parties, doubtless pleasantly, and we trust profitably.

Let us hope that they have carefully studied each other's tastes, that they know each other's mental endowments, and that by visits, rides and walks, at picnics, social gatherings and public entertainments, they have found themselves suited to each other.

Upon an engagement being announced, it is courtesy for various members of the gentleman's family, generally the nearest relatives, to call upon the family of the lady, who in turn should return the call as soon as possible. Possibly the families have never been intimate; it is not necessary that they should be so, but civility will demand the exchange of visits. If the betrothed live in different towns, an exchange of kind and cordial letters between the families is etiquette, the parents or near relatives of the gentleman writing to the lady or her parents.

A present of a ring to the lady, appropriately signalizes the engagement of marriage. This is usually worn on the fore-finger of the left hand. If the parties are wealthy, this may be set with diamonds; but if in humble circumstances, the gift should be more plain. Other presents by the gentleman to the lady, of jewelry, on birthdays, Christmas or New Year's, will be very appropriate; while she, in turn, may reciprocate by gifts of articles of fancy-work made with her own hands.

Aside from the engagement-ring, a gentleman should not, at this period of acquaintance, make expensive presents to his intended bride. Articles of small value, indicative of respect and esteem, are all that should pass between them. Should the marriage take place, and coming years of labor crown their efforts with success, then valuable gifts will be much more appropriate than in the earlier years of their acquaintance.

Arrangements for a Permanent Home.

It remains to be seen whether the intended husband will prove a financial success or not. He may be over benevolent; he may be too ready to become security for others; he may prove a spendthrift; he may lose his property in a variety of ways. It is therefore wise for the lady and her friends to see that, previous to the marriage, if she have money in her own right, a sufficient sum should be settled upon her to provide for all contingencies in the future. This is a matter that the gentleman should himself insist upon, even using his own money for the purpose, as many a man has found, when his own fortune was wrecked, the provision made for his wife to be his only means of support in declining years.

Conduct During the Engagement.

An engagement having been made, it is desirable that it be carried to a successful termination by marriage. To do this, considerable depends upon both parties.

The gentleman should be upon pleasant terms with the lady's family, making himself agreeable to her parents, her sisters and her brothers. Especially to the younger members of her family should the gentleman render his presence agreeable, by occasional rides and little favors, presents of sweetmeats, etc.

He should also take pains to comply with the general regulations of the family during his visits, being punctual at meals, and early in retiring; kind and courteous to servants, and agreeable to all.

He should still be gallant to the ladies, but never so officiously attentive to anyone as to arouse uneasiness upon the part of his affianced. Neither should he expect her to eschew the society of gentlemen entirely from the time of her engagement.

The lady he has chosen for his future companion is supposed to have good sense, and while she may be courteous to all, receiving visits and calls, she will allow no flirtations, nor do anything calculated to excite jealousy on the part of her fiancé.

The conduct of both after the engagement should be such as to inspire in each implicit trust and confidence.

Visits should not be unduly protracted. If the gentleman makes them in the evening, they should be made early, and should not be over two hours in length. The custom of remaining until a late hour has passed away in genteel society. Such conduct at the present time, among the acquaintance of the lady, is certain to endanger her reputation.

For the gentleman and lady who are engaged to isolate themselves from others when in company, or do anything that shall attract the attention of the company to themselves, is in bad taste. Such conduct will always call forth unfavorable comments. The young ladies will sneer at it from jealousy, the young men will pronounce it foolish, and the old will consider it out of place.

And yet, by virtue of engagement, the gentleman should be considered the rightful escort, and upon all occasions the lady will give him preference; and he will especially see, however thoughtful he may be of others, that her wants are carefully attended to.

Should a misunderstanding or quarrel happen, it should be removed by the lady making the first advances towards a reconciliation. She thus shows a magnanimity which can but win admiration from her lover. Let both in their conduct towards the other be confiding, noble and generous.

The Wedding.

The wedding-day having arrived, the presents for the bride, if there be any, which may be sent at any time during the previous week, will be handsomely displayed before the ceremony. The presents, which have the names of the donors attached, are for the bride — never the bridegroom, although many of them may be sent by friends of the latter.

The form and ceremony of the wedding will be as various as are the peculiarities of those who marry, and comprise every description of display, from the very quiet affair, with but a few friends present, to the elaborate occasion when the church is filled to repletion, or in the palatial residence of the father of the bride, "the great house filled with guests of every degree."

We will suppose that the parties desire a somewhat ostentatious wedding, and the marriage takes place in church. In arranging the preliminaries, the bride may act her pleasure in regard to bridesmaids. She may have none; she may have one, two, three, four, six or eight; and, while in England it is customary to have but one groomsman, it is not uncommon in the United States to have one groomsman for every bridesmaid.

The bridegroom should make the first groomsman the manager of affairs, and should furnish him with money to pay necessary expenses.

Ushers are selected from the friends of the bride and groom, who, designated by a white rosette worn on the left lapel of the coat, will wait upon the invited guests at the door of the church, and assign them to their places, which will be a certain number of the front seats.

The bridegroom should send a carriage at his expense for the officiating clergyman and his family. He is not expected to pay for the carriage of the parents of the bride, nor for those occupied by the bridesmaids and groomsmen.

The latter will furnish the carriages for the ladies, unless otherwise provided. The invited guests will go in carriages at their own expense.

The clergyman is expected to be within the rails, and the congregation promptly in their seats, at the appointed hour. The bridegroom will proceed to the church, accompanied by his near relatives, and should precede the bride, that he may hand her from the carriage, if not waited upon by her father or other near relative.

The bride goes to the church in a carriage, accompanied by her parents, or those who stand to her in the relation of parents (as may other relatives, or legal guardian), or she may be accompanied by the bridesmaids.

When the bridal party is ready in the vestibule of the church, the ushers will pass up the center aisle, the first groomsman, accompanied by the first bridesmaid, coming next, the others following in their order. The groom walks next with the bride's mother upon his arm, followed by the father with the bride. At the altar, as the father and mother step back, the bride takes her place upon the left of the groom.

Another mode of entering the church is for the first bridesmaid and groomsman to lead, followed by the bride and groom. When in front of the altar, the groomsman turns to the right, the bridesmaid to the left, leaving a space in front of the minister for the bride and groom; the near relatives and parents of the bride and groom follow closely, and form a circle about the altar during the ceremony.

The former mode is, however, established etiquette. At the altar the bride stands at the left of the groom, and in some churches both bride and groom remove the right-hand glove. In others it is not deemed necessary. When a ring is used, it is the duty of the first bridesmaid to remove the bride's left-hand glove. An awkward pause is, however, avoided by opening one seam of the glove upon the ring finger, and at the proper time the glove may be turned back, and the ring thus easily placed where it belongs, which is the third finger of the left hand.

The responses of the bride and groom should not be too hastily nor too loudly given.

Following the ceremony, the parents of the bride speak to her first, succeeded by the parents of the groom before other friends.

Essentially the same ceremonies will be had, the same positions will be assumed, and the same modes of entering will be observed, in the parlors at the residence, as at the church.

The bride and groom, after the ceremony, will go in the same carriage from the church to the home or to the depot.

Should a breakfast or supper follow the ceremony, the bride will not change her dress until she assumes her traveling apparel. At the party succeeding the ceremony, the bridesmaids and groomsmen should be invited, and all may, if they prefer, wear the dresses worn at the wedding.

The Wedding Trousseau.

It is customary, at the wedding, for the young bride to wear only pure white, with a wreath of orange flowers to adorn the full veil of lace. The widow or elderly lady will wear pearl color or tinted silk, without wreath or veil. The bridesmaid of the youthful bride may wear colors, but a very beautiful effect is produced by pure white, with colored trimmings. In some cases, one-half of the bridesmaids will wear one color, and the other half another color. No black dresses should be worn by the guests. Any in mourning may, for the time, wear purple, lavender, iron-gray and other quiet colors.

The bridegroom and groomsmen will wear white gloves, vest and neckties.

The bride's traveling dress should be very quiet and modest, and not such as in any way to attract

Only the bridegroom is congratulated at the wedding; it is he who is supposed to have won the prize. Acquaintances of both should speak to the bride first; but if acquainted with but one, they will address that one first, when introductions will take place.

At the wedding breakfast or supper the bride sits by the side of her husband, in the center of the table, at the side; her father and mother occupy the foot and head of the table, and do the honors of the occasion, as at the dinner-party.

The festivities of the occasion being over, and the hour of departure having arrived, the guests disperse, it being etiquette for them to make a formal call on the mother of the bride in the succeeding two weeks.

Etiquette Between Husbands and Wives.

Let the rebuke be preceded by a kiss.

Do not require a request to be repeated.

Never should both be angry at the same time.

Never neglect the other, for all the world beside.

Let each strive to always accommodate the other.

Let the angry word be answered only with a kiss.

Bestow your warmest sympathies in each other's trials.

Make your criticism in the most loving manner possible.

Make no display of the sacrifices you make for each other.

Never make a remark calculated to bring ridicule upon the other.

Never deceive; confidence, once lost, can never be wholly regained.

Always use the most gentle and loving words when addressing each other.

Let each study what pleasure can be bestowed upon the other during the day.

Always leave home with a tender good-bye and loving words. They may be the last.

Consult and advise together in all that comes within the experience and sphere of each individually.

Never reproach the other for an error which was done with a good motive and with the best judgment at the time.

The Wife's Duty.

Never should a wife display her best conduct, her accomplishments, her smiles, and her best nature, exclusively away from home.

Be careful in your purchases. Let your husband know what you buy, and that you have wisely expended your money.

Let no wife devote a large portion of her time to society-work which shall keep her away from home daytimes and evenings, without the full concurrence of her husband.

Beware of entrusting the confidence of your household to outside parties. The moment you discuss the faults of your husband with another, that moment an element of discord has been admitted which will one day rend your family circle.

If in moderate circumstances, do not be over ambitious to make an expensive display in your rooms. With your own work you can embellish at a cheap price, and yet very handsomely, if you have taste. Let the adornings of your private rooms be largely the work of your own hands.

Beware of bickering about little things. Your husband returns from his labors with his mind absorbed in business. In his dealings with his employes, he is in the habit of giving commands and of being obeyed. In his absent-mindedness, he does not realize, possibly, the change from his business to his home, and the same dictatorial spirit may possess him in the domestic circle. Should such be the case, avoid all disputes. What matters it where a picture hangs, or a flower-vase may sit. Make the home so charming and so wisely-ordered that your husband will gladly be relieved of its care, and will willingly yield up its entire management to yourself.

Be always very careful of your conduct and language. A husband is largely restrained by the chastity, purity and refinement of his wife.

A lowering of dignity, a looseness of expression and vulgarity of words, may greatly lower the standard of the husband's purity of speech and morals.

Whatever may have been the cares of the day, greet your husband with a smile when he returns. Make your personal appearance just as beautiful as possible. Your dress may be made of calico, but it should be neat. Let him enter rooms so attractive and sunny that all the recollections of his home, when away from the same, shall attract him back.

Be careful that you do not estimate your husband solely by his ability to make display. The nature of his employment, in comparison with others, may not be favorable for fine show, but that should matter not. The superior qualities of mind and heart alone will bring permanent happiness.

To have a cheerful, pleasant home awaiting the husband, is not all. He may bring a guest whom he desires to favorably impress, and upon you will devolve the duty of entertaining the visitor so agreeably that the husband shall take pride in you. A man does not alone require that his wife be a good housekeeper. She must be more; in conversational talent and general accomplishment she must be a companion.

The Husband's Duty.

A very grave responsibility has the man assumed in his marriage. Doting parents have confided to his care the welfare of a loved daughter, and a trusting woman has risked all her future happiness in his keeping. Largely will it depend upon him whether her pathway shall be strewn with thorns or roses.

Let your wife understand fully your business. In nearly every case she will be found a most valuable adviser when she understands all your circumstances.

Do not be dictatorial in the family circle. The home is the wife's province. It is her natural field of labor. It is her right to govern and direct its interior management. You would not expect her to come to your shop, your office, your store or your farm, to give orders how your work should be conducted; neither should you interfere with the duties which legitimately belong to her.

If a dispute arises, dismiss the subject with a kind word, and do not seek to carry your point by discussion. It is a glorious achievement to master one's own temper. You may discover that you are in error, and if your wife is wrong, she will gladly, in her cooler moments, acknowledge the fault.

Having confided to the wife all your business affairs, determine with her what your income will be in the coming year. Afterwards ascertain what your household expenses will necessarily be, and then set aside a weekly sum, which should regularly and invariably be paid the wife at a stated time. Let this sum be even more than enough, so that the wife can pay all bills, and have the satisfaction besides of accumulating a fund of her own, with which she can exercise a spirit of independence in the bestowal of charity, the purchase of a gift, or any article she may desire. You may be sure that the wife will very seldom use the money unwisely, if the husband gives her his entire confidence.

Your wife, possibly, is inexperienced; perhaps she is delicate in health, also, and matters that would be of little concern to you may weigh heavily upon her. She needs, therefore, your tenderest approval, your sympathy and gentle advice. When her efforts are crowned with success, be sure that you give her praise. Few husbands realize how happy the wife is made by the knowledge that her efforts and her merits are appreciated. There are times, also, when the wife's variable condition of health will be likely to make her cross and petulant; the husband must overlook all this, even if the wife is at times unreasonable.

Endeavor to so regulate your household affairs that all the faculties of the mind shall have due cultivation. There should be a time for labor, and a time for recreation. There should be cultivation of the social nature, and there should be attention given to the spiritual. The wife should not be required to lead a life of drudgery. Matters should be so regulated that she may early finish her labors of the day; and the good husband will so control his business that he may be able to accompany his wife to various places of amusement and entertainment. Thus the intellectual will be provided for, and the social qualities be kept continually exercised.

The wise husband will provide for the moral and spiritual growth of his family by regular attendance at church; the spiritual faculties of our nature are given for a beneficent purpose; their exercise and cultivation leads up into the higher and the better; one day in seven, at least, should therefore be set apart for the spiritual improvement of the family. Select a church, the religious teaching in which is nearest in accord with the views of yourself and wife, and be regular in your attendance; accompany your wife; give her the pleasure of your escort; see that she is provided with a good seat and all the advantages which the church has to give; enter fully and freely into the religious work of your church, and your family will be blessed in consequence.

Give your wife every advantage which it is possible to bestow. Shut up with her household duties, her range of freedom is necessarily circumscribed, and in her limited sphere she is likely to remain stationary in her intellectual growth. Indeed, oftentimes, if her family be large and her husband's means are limited, in her struggle to care for the family she will sacrifice beauty, accomplishments, health — life, almost — rather than that her husband shall fail. In the meantime, with wide opportunities and intellectual advantages, he will be likely to have better facilities for growth and progression. There is sometimes thus a liability of the husband and wife growing apart, an event which both should take every pains to avert. In avoiding this, much will depend upon the wife. She must resolutely determine to be in every way the equal of her companion. Much also will depend upon the husband. The wife should have every opportunity whereby she may keep even pace with him.

Possibly the wife in social position, intellectual acquirement, and very likely in moral worth, may be superior to her husband. It is equally necessary, therefore, that the husband put forth every effort to make himself worthy of his companion. It is a terrible burden to impose on a wife to compel her to go through life with a man whom she cannot love or respect.

ETIQUETTE OF TRAVELING.

THE reader will call to mind people who always appear at ease when they are traveling. Investigation will prove that these individuals have usually had a wide experience in journeying, and an extensive acquaintance with the world. The experienced traveler has learned the necessity of always being on time, of having baggage checked early, of purchasing a ticket before entering the cars, and of procuring a seat in a good location before the car is full.

The inexperienced traveler is readily known by his flurry and mistakes. He is likely to be behind time, and he is likely to be an hour too early. For want of explicit direction, his baggage often fails to reach the train in time, or does not come at all. His trunks, from lack of strength, are liable to be easily broken. In his general confusion, when he buys a ticket he neglects to place it where it will be secure, and consequently loses it. He forgets a portion of his baggage, and thus in a dozen ways he is likely to be in trouble.

If the person be a lady who is unacquainted with travel, she reveals the fact by a general impatience, restlessness, and absent-mindedness. In her want of self-possession she forgets several things she had intended to bring, and her continual fault-finding at flies, dust, heat, delay and other trials, all betray the fact that she has not heretofore been accustomed to these difficulties.

The following suggestions relating to railway traveling may be of service:

Whenever you contemplate a journey, consider carefully what route you want to take, and decide it definitely. Learn accurately what time the train leaves, and provide yourself with a table giving the running time of the road, stations on the way, etc., which will save you the trouble of asking many questions.

If you desire to ride in a sleeping-car, secure your berth a day or two previous to the time of going, in order that you may be in time to take your choice. The most desirable sections are in the center of the car, away from the annoyance of dust, drafts of air and sudden noises resulting from opening and closing doors.

At least a day before you go, consider carefully what baggage you need to take, and have it packed. Take just as little as possible. Have your trunks very secure, and pack all articles of baggage in such a manner that they cannot shake and thus be broken.

Provide among your baggage necessary toilet articles — a linen wrap to exclude the dust from your finer clothing, and a small amount of reading-matter with very coarse type. See that your baggage is perfectly in order, and an hour before you start engage an authorized expressman to take your baggage to the depot. State very distinctly where you want the baggage taken, and for what train. It is also a wise provision to have your trunk labeled with a card bearing your name and destination.

Take the number of the expressman, ascertain his charge, and withhold payment until he has assisted in finding baggage, and has aided in getting it checked at the depot. Be very sure that your watch or clock is perfectly correct with railroad time, and that you, half an hour before the starting time of the train, arrive at the depot, buy a ticket, and take your seat in the car. You are probably early enough to take your choice of location in the seats.

If in the summer time, and the train runs east or west, the north side will probably be most pleasant. Seats midway in the car are easiest to ride in, and the left side is freest from sudden gusts of wind which may come in at the open doors.

Having selected a seat, it is customary to deposit the satchel, umbrella or some article of wearing-apparel in the same, should you not be ready to occupy it; and it is etiquette for anyone finding a seat so occupied to look further.

You should carry just as little baggage into the car as possible, and all separate pieces should have your name plainly written or printed upon them, which will secure their being forwarded to you in case they are left upon the seat.

Having paid for one ticket, you are entitled to only one seat. It shows selfishness, therefore, when the coach is quite full to deposit a large amount of baggage in the surrounding seats and occupy three or four, and engage in reading, while others look in vain for a place to sit down.

Fig. 11.   The couple that make themselves appear ridiculous when traveling.

It is courtesy for a gentleman when sitting alone to offer the vacant seat beside himself to a lady who may be unattended. He will also give his seat to two ladies, or a lady and gentleman who desire to sit together, and take a seat elsewhere. Such attention will often be a great kindness, while the individual bestowing it may suffer but very little inconvenience.

The true lady or gentleman will always consult the convenience of others when traveling. Thus, care should be exercised that no one be incommoded by your opening doors or windows in a railway coach. If possible, so arrange that the air of a window that you may open shall strike full upon yourself, and not upon those in the rear; certainly not if it is unpleasant to them.

What to Avoid when Traveling.

A lady and gentleman should avoid evidences of undue familiarity in the presence of strangers. Couples who may evince a silly affection by overfondling of each other in public (Fig. 17) make themselves appear extremely ridiculous to all who may see them.

People with weak eyes should avoid reading on the train, and those having weak lungs should avoid much talking, as an undue effort will be required to talk above the noise of the train.

Passengers should avoid eating at irregular times on the journey, and gentlemen should avoid smoking in the presence of those to whom it may be offensive.

Avoid leaving the pockets so open and money so exposed that thieves may steal your effects. In the sleeping-car the valuables should be put in some article of wearing-apparel and placed under the pillow.

Avoid undue haste and excitement when traveling, by forethought. Have a plan matured, and when the time comes to act you will know what to do, and with self-possession you accomplish your work very much better.

Avoid wearing laces, velvets, or any articles that naturally accumulate and hold dust. Excessive finery or a lavish display of jewelry are in bad taste on extended journeys. Before commencing a journey, consider carefully what will be most suitable to wear, and study how little baggage may be taken.

CONDUCT FOR GENTLEMEN

WHEN

TRAVELING WITH LADIES.

If the gentleman is an authorized escort he will, if an old acquaintance, accompany the lady in his charge from her residence to the depot. If the acquaintance is of short duration, it will be sufficient to meet her at the depot in ample time to purchase tickets and see that her baggage is checked, while she remains in the sitting-room at the station.

Arrangements being made, he will secure her a seat upon the train, will find a place for packages, will attend to her wants in adjusting the window, and will aim to put her entirely at ease.

In getting on and off the train, the gentleman will care for all parcels and see that nothing is left. He will assist the lady into the coach or omnibus before getting in himself, and in getting out he will precede her, and afterwards turn and help her carefully down.

If requested by the lady to defray her expenses from her purse, the gentleman may take the same and keep it the entire journey, or he may pay from his own pocket and keep an account of expenses which she will refund at the end of the journey.

He should purchase the needed confections or literature on the train. He should be fruitful in the introduction of topics that will enliven, amuse and instruct the lady, if she is inclined to be reticent; and at her journey's end he should go with her to her home, or the place where she is to stop. He may call next day, and if the acquaintance seems desirable it may be continued. The gentleman should be very careful not to continue his visits unless certain that they are acceptable.

If a hotel be the point of destination, the gentleman will accompany the lady to the parlor. He will then secure for her a room, and leave her in care of a waiter; her desire being probably to proceed to her apartments at once, where she will remove the dust and travel stains of the journey, and meet him again at a concerted hour in the parlor.

Ladies and gentlemen who are strangers, being thrown into the company of each other for a long journey, need not necessarily refuse to speak to each other. While the lady should be guarded, acquaintance may be made with certain reserve.

THE HORSEBACK RIDE,

AND THE

RULES THAT GOVERN IT.

A gentleman who may act as escort for a lady when riding should be very careful that the horse selected for her is entirely reliable and gentle. If he has no horse of his own, and she has none to which she is accustomed, he must understand that there is considerable danger in allowing her to use a horse that has not been tried, no matter what may be the representations of the liverymen or servant.

A trustworthy horse having been secured for the lady, it is the gentleman's duty before mounting to give a very thorough examination of the saddle and bridle, to see that all are secure. It will not do to leave this matter to the stablemen. They are accustomed to such continuous handling of harness that they become careless, and are liable to overlook defects in buckles, girths, etc., that might cause a severe accident.

FIG. 18. THE RIDE ON HORSEBACK.
The gentleman takes his position at the right of the lady.

When all is in readiness, it is the gentleman's province to assist the lady in mounting. To do this, it is well to have some one hold the horse, otherwise he holds the bridle with his left hand. The lady, then, with her skirt in her left hand, will take hold of the pommel of the saddle with her right, her face turned towards the horse's head. The gentleman will stand at the horse's shoulder, facing the lady, and stoop, allowing her to place her left foot in his right hand. She will then spring, while he lifts her gently and steadily into her seat, following which he will place her left foot in the stirrup and arrange her riding habit.

After the lady is in position, the gentleman will still remain with her until she has whip and reins properly in hand and is securely in her seat, when he will mount his horse and take his place (Fig. 18) upon her right, as shown in the accompanying illustration.

Should there be two ladies on horseback, the gentleman should ride to the right of both of them, unless they may need his assistance, in which case he will ride between them.

In dismounting, the gentleman should take the lady's left hand in his right, remove the stirrup and take her foot in his left hand, lowering her gently to the ground.

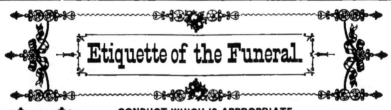

CONDUCT WHICH IS APPROPRIATE.

HOULD there be no competent, near friend of the family to take charge of the funeral, then its management should devolve upon the sexton of the church, the undertaker, or other suitable person.

It is the duty of the person having the funeral in charge to have one interview with the nearest relatives as to the management, after which they should be relieved of all care in the matter.

The expense of the funeral should be in accordance with the wealth and standing of the deceased, both ostentation and parade being avoided, as should also evidences of meanness and parsimony. It is well, in the interview between the manager and the relatives to have a definite understanding as to the expense that should be incurred.

In the large city, where many friends and even relatives may not hear of the death, it is common to send invitations to such friends as might not otherwise hear of the fact, worded somewhat as follows:

Yourself and family are respectfully invited to attend the funeral of H. H. B——, on Thursday, the 27th of June, 1878, at 2 o'clock P. M., from his late residence, No. 16, —— street, to proceed to Rosehill Cemetery.

Or, if the services are conducted at a church:

Yourself and family are respectfully invited to attend the funeral of H. H. B——, from the church of the Redeemer, on Thursday, the 27th of June, 18—, at 2 o'clock P. M., to proceed to Rosehill Cemetery.

It is customary to have these invitations printed according to the forms shown elsewhere under the head of "notes of invitation," and to send them by private messenger. The list of invited persons should be given to the manager, that he may provide a suitable number of carriages for the invited friends who may be likely to attend. It is a breach of etiquette for any who have been thus personally invited not to attend.

Persons attending a funeral are not expected to be present much before the hour appointed. Previous to this time it is well for the family of the deceased to take their last view of the remains, and thus avoid confusion.

In assembling at the house, it is customary for some near relative, but not of the immediate family, to act as usher in receiving and seating the people. The ladies of the family are not expected to notice the arrival of guests. With gentlemen it is optional whether they do so or not.

The clergyman, or person chosen to make remarks upon the funeral occasion, should be one whose religious views would be most nearly in accord with those entertained by the deceased. But even if the deceased had no religious convictions, and a clergyman of any denomination may be chosen, he should use the courtesy of saying nothing in his discourse which could in the least offend the mourners.

The remains should be so placed, either in the house or church, that when the discourse is finished, if the corpse is exposed to view, the assembled guests may see the same by passing in single file past the coffin, going from foot to head, up one aisle and down another.

While in the house of mourning, the hat should be removed from the head of the gentlemen, and not replaced again while in the house.

Loud talk or laughter in the chamber of death would be a great rudeness. All animosities among those who attend the funeral should be forgotten, and interviews with the family at the time should not be expected.

The exercises at the house or church being finished, the clergyman enters a carriage, which heads the procession. The coffin being placed in the hearse, the bearers, who are usually six in number, will go in threes, on each side of the hearse, or in a carriage immediately before, while the near relatives directly follow the hearse, succeeded by those more distantly connected. As the mourners pass from the house to the carriages, no salutations are expected to take place, the gentlemen among the guests in the meantime standing with uncovered heads, as they do also when the coffin is carried from the house to the hearse.

The master of ceremonies should precede the mourners to the carriages, see that the proper carriages are in attendance, assist the ladies to their place, and signal the drivers to pass forward as their carriages are filled. Should the attending physician be present, he will occupy the carriage immediately following the near relatives of the deceased.

The pall-bearers are selected from among the immediate friends of the deceased, and should be as near as possible of corresponding age, worth and intelligence.

It is common, upon the coffin of the infant or young person, to lay a wreath of white flowers, and upon that of a married person a cross of white blossoms. Upon the coffin of a navy or army officer, the hat, epaulets, sash, sword and the flag may be borne; while his horse, if a mounted officer, will, without a rider, be led behind the hearse. It is sometimes the case that the private carriage of the deceased, with no occupant save the driver, follows the hearse in the procession.

Arriving at the cemetery, the clergyman will precede the mourners to the grave; when gathered around, the bearers will place the coffin in its last resting place, and the final prayer will be said. This done, the guests will depart for their several homes, each informing the drivers where they desire to be left.

With the more hopeful view of death which comes with the Christian belief, there is less disposition to wear evidences of mourning. It is well, however, to drape the door-knob, especially of the residence, with crape, during the days between the death and the funeral; and the family should go out as little as possible during that time. The dress of all guests at the funeral should be of subdued and quiet colors, and, while for the young person it is customary to trim the hearse in white, it is common to drape it in dark, with black plumes, for the person of mature years.

Should the deceased have been a member of an organization that might desire to conduct the funeral, immediate notification of his death should be sent to the organization, that its members may have time to make arrangements for attending the funeral.

Etiquette of Carriage-Riding.

PRECAUTIONS AGAINST ACCIDENTS.

THE mode of entering a carriage will depend somewhat upon circumstances. Should the team be very restive, and the gentleman remain in the carriage the better to control his horses, the lady will enter upon the left side, the gentleman assisting her by the hand. While circumstances may sometimes prevent, it is always etiquette for the gentleman to see that the lady enters the carriage first. To aid in entering and alighting from a carriage easily and safely, every residence should be provided with an elevated platform near the walk, beside which the vehicle may be driven, as represented in the illustration.

Of two seats in the carriage facing each other, that in the rear, and facing the horses, is the most desirable; the place of honor being the right side of this seat, which should be given to any elderly person, an honored guest or ladies, during the carriage ride.

The ladies being in place, the gentlemen will take the seat with their backs to the horses, care being observed that dresses and shawls are not shut in the door when it is closed. The

Fig. 19. Assisting the lady into the carriage.

gentleman last in will sit on the right, and upon him should devolve the giving of orders to the driver, and any other directions which the company may determine upon.

At the close of the ride, the gentlemen will dismount first, and afterwards help the ladies carefully from the carriage, taking care to keep their dresses from being soiled upon the wheels.

The single carriage should be driven as near the curbstone as possible, on the right side. The driver, having the top of the carriage down, should then turn the horses to the left, spreading the wheels on the right side, giving an opportunity for the lady to get into the carriage without soiling her dress upon the wheels. The lady should have both of her hands free to assist herself, while the gentleman (Fig. 19) should aid her, as shown in the illustration. The lady being in her place, her escort will take his seat upon the right side, will spread a lap-robe in front of the lady and himself to ward off dust and mud, and all is in readiness for the ride.

In getting from the carriage, the gentleman should alight first. He should quiet the team, and turn them, that the wheels may spread apart, retaining the reins in his hand, that he may hold the horses in case of

fright. The lady should then place her hands upon the gentleman's shoulders (Fig. 20), while her escort, taking her by the elbows, will assist her carefully to the ground. Being aided thus in safely alighting, a lady will, oftentimes, be saved from severe injury.

The gentleman on the pleasure ride should not drive so fast as to throw mud upon the occupants of the carriage. He should avoid fast driving if the lady is timid, and at the close of the ride he should take the friend to his or her residence.

Horses should not have their heads checked painfully high. They will be less shy if trained and driven without blinds. They should be driven with tight rein, and care should be observed to avoid accidents.

Ladies Unattended.

For the advantage of the unattended lady who may be stopping at a hotel, the following suggestions are made.

The lady should enter a hotel by the ladies' entrance. When in the parlor, she should send for the proprietor or clerk, present her card, and state the length of time that she designs to remain.

By requesting the waiter to do so, he will meet the lady at the entrance to the dining-room and conduct her to a seat; thus saving her the necessity of crossing the room without an escort.

Meeting friends at the table, the lady should converse in a voice so low and quiet as not to attract attention from strangers. Particularly should she avoid loud laughter or any conspicuous evidence of commenting upon others.

To make the time spent at the hotel pass agreeably, care should be taken to obtain a pleasant room that will allow the entrance of sunshine and fresh air.

Orders at the table should be given in a low, yet clear, distinct voice. In the interval while waiting to be served, it is allowable to read a paper. Staring about the room, handling of the knife, spoons, or other articles upon the table, should be avoided.

Do not point to a dish wanted. A look in the direction of the article desired, and a request to the waiter that it be passed, will secure the dish without trouble.

The lady in the dining-room, unless accompanied by an escort, should avoid dressing ostentatiously. A very modest dress is in best taste.

The lady should not take her supper very late in the evening, in the dining-room, without an escort. It is in better taste to have the meal sent to her room. A lady should also avoid loitering in the halls or standing alone at the hotel-windows.

Unless invited, a lady should not play upon the piano in the hotel-parlor nor sing if there are others in the room, neither should she sing or hum tunes when passing through the halls.

Trunks and rooms should be carefully locked when leaving them, and valuables should be given into the hands of the proprietor for deposit in the safe, the guest ringing whenever she may require them during her stay.

The lady in her unattended condition will probably require considerable assistance from some one of the waiters, who should be suitably remunerated when she leaves.

Instead of scolding at servants who are neglectful of their duty, complain to the housekeeper or proprietor. Polite requests of the servants will, however, usually secure an immediate and pleasant response.

When intending to leave upon a special train, care should be had that trunks are packed, tickets purchased and all arrangements made sufficiently long before the time of starting to avoid hurry and mistakes.

ETIQUETTE IN CHURCH.

CHURCH should be entered with a most reverent feeling. The object of attending divine service is to improve the spiritual nature, and hence business and everything of a secular character should be left behind when you enter the church portals.

If a stranger, you will wait in the vestibule until the arrival of the usher, who will conduct you to a seat.

Enter the church quietly, removing the hat, and never replacing it until the door is reached again at the close of the service.

If a stranger, and accompanied by a lady, you will precede her, and follow the usher up the aisle until the pew is reached, when you will pause, allow her to pass in, and you will follow, taking seats at the further end if you are first, so that you will not be disturbed by later arrivals. It is no longer a custom, as formerly, for the gentleman to step into the aisle and allow ladies that are strangers to pass to the inside.

The gentleman will place his hat, if possible, under the seat, and while in church the occupant should avoid making a noise, staring around the building, whispering, laughing or nodding to others.

All greetings, recognitions and conversation should be conducted in the vestibule after service. While in church, the passage of a fan or hymn-book to another should be recognized by merely a quiet bow.

Should you see a stranger waiting, you may invite him to enter your pew. No speaking is necessary then, nor when you open the book and point out the service.

If a stranger, it is best to conform to the rules of the service, rising and sitting down with the congregation; and, although the forms may be radically different from what you are accustomed to, you should comport yourself with the utmost attention and reverence.

Avoid making a noise when you enter a church after the services have commenced. It is disrespectful to come late, and shows bad manners to leave before the service is through. You should wait until the benediction is pronounced before you commence putting your articles in order for leaving.

It is a breach of etiquette for a number of young men to congregate in the vestibule, and there carry forward a conversation, commenting upon the services and various members of the congregation present.

If a member of a church, you should be regular in attendance. While the pastor has put forth, possibly, extra effort to prepare an effective sermon, it is poor encouragement to find members of the congregation absent because of a trivial storm, or away upon the pleasure drive.

ETIQUETTE IN THE SCHOOL.

THE following are the requisites for successful management in the schoolroom:

The teacher must be a good judge of human nature. If so, his knowledge will teach him that no two children are born with precisely the same organization. This difference in mentality will make one child a natural linguist, another will naturally excel in mathematics, another will exhibit fondness for drawing, and another for philosophy. Understanding and observing this, he will, without anger or impatience, assist the backward student, and will direct the more forward, ever addressing each child in the most respectful manner.

As few rules as possible should be made, and the object and necessity for the rule should be fully explained to the school by the teacher. When a rule has been made, obedience to it should be enforced. Firmness, united with gentleness, is one of the most important qualifications which a teacher can possess.

Everything should be in order, and the exercises of the day should be carried forward according to an arranged programme. The rooms should be swept, the fires built, and the first and second bells rung, with exact punctuality. In the same manner each recitation should come at an appointed time throughout the school hours.

The programme of exercises should be so varied as to give each pupil a variety of bodily and mental exercise. Thus, music, recreation, study, recitation, declamation, etc., should be so varied as to develop all the child's powers. Not only should boys and girls store their minds with knowledge, but they should be trained in the best methods of writing and speaking, whereby they may be able to impart the knowledge which they possess.

The teacher should require the strictest order and neatness upon the part of all the students. Clean hands, clean face and neatly combed hair should characterize every pupil, while a mat in the doorway should remind every boy and girl of the necessity of entering the schoolroom with clean boots and shoes. Habits of neatness and order thus formed will go with the pupils through life.

At least a portion of each day should be set apart by the teacher, in which to impart to the pupils a knowledge of etiquette. Students should be trained to enter the room quietly, to always close without noise the door through which they pass, to make introductions gracefully, to bow with ease and dignity, to shake hands properly, to address others courteously, to make a polite reply when spoken to, to sit and stand gracefully, to do the right thing in the right place, and thus, upon all occasions, to appear to advantage.

All the furnishings of the schoolroom should be such as to inspire the holiest, loftiest and noblest ambition in the child. A schoolroom should be handsomely decorated. The aquarium, the trailing vine, the blossom and the specimens of natural history should adorn the teacher's desk and the windows, while handsome pictures should embellish the walls. In short, the pupils should be surrounded with such an array of beauty as will constantly inspire them to higher and nobler achievements.

Boys and girls should be taught that which they will use when they become men and women. In the first place they will talk more than they will do anything else. By every means possible they should be trained to be correct, easy, fluent and pleasant speakers; and next to this they should be trained to be ready writers. To be this, they should be schooled in penmanship, punctuation, capitalization, composition and the writing of every description of form, from the note of invitation to an agreement, from the epistle to a friend to the promissory note, from the letter of introduction to the report of a meeting.

Above all, the teacher should be thoroughly imbued with the importance of inculcating in the mind of the student a knowledge of general principles. Thus, in the study of geography, the pupil should be taught that the earth is spherical in form; that its outer surface is divided into land and water; that the land is divided into certain grand divisions, peopled with different races of human beings, who exhibit special characteristics. That civilization is the result of certain causes, and progress in the human race arises from the inevitable law of nature that everything goes from the lower steadily toward the higher. A study of the causes which make difference in climate, difference in animals, difference in intellectual and moral developments among the races—a general study of causes thus will make such an impression upon the child's mind as will never be effaced; while the simple study of facts, such as loud the mind with names of bays, islands, rivers, etc., is the crowding of the memory with that which is likely, in time, to be nearly all forgotten.

Thus, in the study of history, dates will be forgotten, while the outlines of the rise and fall of kingdoms, and the causes which produced the same, if rightly impressed by the teacher, will be ever stored in the mind of the pupil.

So should the teacher instruct the student in every branch of study, remembering that facts are liable to be forgotten, but fundamental principles and causes, well understood, will be forever remembered.

It is of the utmost importance, also, that the teacher continuously and persistently keep before the student the importance of temperance, justice and truth; as without these, however superior the education, the individual is entirely without balance, and is always liable to fall. The teacher should never relax his efforts in this direction.

The good teacher will be a living example in all that he teaches to others. If wise, he will seldom if ever resort to the infliction of corporal pain on the pupil, although if a law or rule be violated, it is of the utmost importance that a just punishment follow the violation, but this should never be such as will destroy the child's self-respect.

Duty of the Pupil.

It should be the aim of the student to be punctual in attendance at school, to be thorough in study, and good in the recitation. The boy or girl who would be successful in after life must lay the foundation of success in youth. They should fully understand the importance of improving their school-days for this purpose.

The student that seeks every opportunity to idle away his time in making sport and amusement for himself and fellow-students, will live to regret that he thus wasted his time. The happy, sportive, joyous, laughing boy and girl shed happiness wherever they go, if they are careful to control their gayety, and allow its flow only in the proper place; but they should never permit the love of the mirthful to infringe on the rules of the schoolroom or the laws of etiquette. On the contrary, true courtesy should teach them to use every endeavor to aid the teacher in his work, as in so doing they are themselves reaping the benefit.

The boy and the girl at school foretell the future man or woman. Those who are prompt, punctual and orderly, will be so in after life. Those who are truthful, reliable and honest in childhood, will be trusted in position and place in after years; and those who store the mind in youth with valuable knowledge, will possess that which can never be lost, but on the contrary will always be a means by which they may procure a livelihood; and, if united with energy and perseverance, will be sure to give them reputation, eminence of position, and wealth.

The boy should never take pride in disobedience to the rules of school. To be a truant, to be indolent, to be working mischief, evinces no talent; any rowdy could do this; most worthless men did this when they attended school. It requires effort to be a good scholar; it evinces brain-power to be a good student.

The youth should earnestly resolve to achieve an honorable and noble position in life. With the wide opportunities which open to the ambitious and the enterprising in this age of progression, there is no limit to the greatness which the thoroughly earnest student may attain. The idle and the dissolute will naturally, of their own weight, drop out by the wayside and sink from sight. The plodder who is content to go the dull, daily round in the same narrow rut will get the reward of his labor, though he never betters his condition. But the earnest, original, aspiring, energetic, intelligent worker, can always be sure of new fields to enter, nobler victories to gain, and grander work to be accomplished.

ETIQUETTE IN THE HOME.

PARENTS AND CHILDREN.

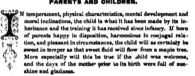

IN temperament, physical characteristics, mental development and moral inclinations, the child is what it has been made by its inheritance and the training it has received since infancy. If born of parents happy in disposition, harmonious in conjugal relation, and pleasant in circumstances, the child will as certainly be sweet in temper as that sweet fluid will flow from a maple tree. More especially will this be true if the child was welcome, and the days of the mother prior to its birth were full of sunshine and gladness.

If, on the contrary, a badly-developed and unhappy parentage has marked the child, then a correspondingly unfortunate organization of mind and unhappy disposition will present itself for discipline and training.

Fortunate is it for the parent who can understand the cause of the child's predilections thus in the beginning. As with the teacher, when the causes that affect the child's mind are understood, the correct system of government to be pursued is then more easily comprehended. The result of this early appreciation of the case is to teach the parent and teacher that, whatever may be the manifestation of mind with the child, it should never be blamed. This is a fundamental principle necessary to be understood by any person who would be successful in government.

When thoroughly imbued with that understanding, kindness and love will take the place of anger and hatred, and discipline can be commenced aright.

One of the first things that the child should understand is that it should implicitly obey. The parent should therefore be very careful to give only such commands as should be observed, and then the order should be firmly but kindly enforced.

To always secure obedience without trouble, it is of the utmost importance that the parent be firm. For the parent to refuse a request of a child without due consideration, and soon afterward, through the child's importunities, grant the request, is to very soon lose command. The parent should carefully consider the request, and if it be denied the child should feel that the denial is the result of the best judgment, and is not dictated by momentary impatience or petulance. A child soon learns to discriminate between the various moods of the fickle parent, and very soon loses respect for government that is not discreet, careful and just.

If a command is disobeyed, parents should never threaten what they will do if the order is disobeyed again, but at once withhold, quietly, yet firmly and pleasantly, some pleasure from the child in consequence of the disobedience. The punishment should be very seldom, if ever, the infliction of bodily pain. A slight deprivation of some pleasure—it may be very slight, but sufficient to teach the child that it must obey—will be of great service to its future discipline and government by the parent. Commencing thus when the child is very young, treating it always tenderly and kindly, with mild and loving words, the child will grow to womanhood or manhood an honor to the parents.

What Parents Should Never Do.

Never speak harshly to a child.

Never use disrespectful names.

Never use profane or vulgar words in the presence of a child.

Do not be so cold and austere as to drive your child from you.

Never misrepresent. If you falsify, the child will learn to deceive also.

Never withhold praise when the child deserves it. Commendation is one of the sweetest pleasures of childhood.

Never waken your children before they have completed their natural slumbers in the morning. See that they retire early, and thus get the requisite time for sleep. Children require more sleep than older persons. The time will come soon enough when care and trouble will compel them to waken in the early morning. Let them sleep while they can.

Do not reproach a child for a mistake which was done with a good motive at the time. Freely forgive, wisely counsel, and the child will thus be taught that there is no danger in telling the truth.

Never give your children money indiscriminately to spend for their own use. However wealthy you may be, teach the child the value of money by requiring it to earn it in some manner. Commencing young, let the child perform simple duties requiring labor, which the parent may reward by pennies and very small sums. Let the child thus spend only money of its own earning. The boy who thus early learns by labor the value of a dollar, knows how to accumulate the same in after-life, and how to save it.

Never demean yourself by getting angry and whipping a child. The very fact of your punishing in anger arouses the evil nature of the child. Some day this punishment thus inflicted will react upon yourself.

What Parents Should Do.

Always speak in a pleasant voice.

Teach your children how to work; how to obtain a living by their own efforts. Teach them the nobility and the dignity of labor, that they may respect and honor the producer.

Explain the reason why. The child is a little walking interrogation point. To it all is new. Explain the reason. Your boy will some day repay this trouble by teaching some other child.

Teach your children the evil of secret vice, and the consequences of using tobacco and spirituous liquors; teach them to be temperate, orderly, punctual, prompt, truthful, neat, faithful and honest.

Encourage your child to be careful of personal appearance; to return every tool to its place; to always pay debts promptly; to never shirk a duty; to do an equal share, and to always live up to an agreement.

Teach your children to confide in you, by conference together. Tell them your plans, and sometimes ask their advice; they will thus open their hearts to you, and will ask your advice. The girl who tells all her heart to her mother has a shield and a protection about her which can come only with a mother's advice and counsel.

Give your children your confidence in the affairs of your business. They will thus take interest, and become co-workers with you. If you enlist their respect, then their sympathy and coöperation, they will quite likely remain to take up your work when you have done, and will go ahead perfecting what you have commenced.

If you are a farmer, do not overwork your children, and thus by a hard and dreary life drive them off to the cities. Arise at a reasonable hour in the morning, take an hour's rest after meals, and quit at five or six o'clock in the afternoon. Let the young people, in games and other amusements, have a happy time during the remainder of the day. There is no reason why a farmer's family should be deprived of recreation and amusement, any more than others.

Teach your child the value of the Sabbath as a day for the spiritual improvement of the mind; that on the Sabbath morn the ordinary work of the week should not be resumed if it is possible to avoid it; that the day should be passed in attendance upon religious service of some kind, or exercises that will ennoble and spiritualize the nature. While rest and recreation may be a part of the day's programme, true philosophy dictates that the spiritual faculties of the nature should be cultivated by setting apart a portion of the time for their improvement.

Teach your children those things which they will need when they become men and women. As women they should understand how to cook, how to make a bed, how to preserve cleanliness and order throughout the house, how to ornament their rooms, to renovate and preserve furniture and clothing, how to sing, and play various games, that they may enliven the household. They should be taught how to swim, how to ride, how to drive, how to do business, and how to preserve health. The mother should early intrust money to the girl, with which to buy articles for the household, that she may learn its value. Think what a man and woman need to know in order to be healthy, happy, prosperous and successful, and teach them that.

SAY "NO" POLITELY.

COMMON saying is, "A man's manners make his fortune." This is a well-known fact, and we see it illustrated every day. The parents who considerately train a child amid kindness and love, rear a support for their declining years. The teacher that rules well and is yet kind, is beloved by his pupils. The hotel proprietor, by affability and an accommodating spirit, may fill his hotel with guests. The railway conductor, who has a pleasant word for the lonely traveler, is always remembered with favor. The postoffice clerk who very carefully looks through a pile of letters and says, "not any," very gently, pleasantly adding a word of hope by saying, "it may come on the afternoon train," we always gratefully recollect. When the time comes that we can return the kindness, we take great pleasure in doing so.

The man who shows himself to be a gentleman, even though he may not buy what we have to sell when we solicit him, we always know will get his reward. His affability, when he declined, demonstrated that he could say "no" with a pleasant word. The very fact of impressing us so favorably, even when he did not purchase, clearly indicated that he was thoroughly schooled in the ways of politeness, and that he lived up to the golden rule of doing to others as he desired others to do to him.

Thus every day, in the multifarious relations of life, it is in the power of persons to grant favors by at least kind words. And when pleasant manners are exhibited, how strongly these stand out in contrast with the short, curt, rough, uncouth manner which so frequently accompanies the refusal of a favor. We realize, as we see the contrast, that no one can be a gentleman who ignores the laws of etiquette.

TREATMENT OF EMPLOYES.

T takes every grade of society to make the complete whole. One class is just as necessary as the other. In carrying forward great enterprises, how plainly do we see this manifested. Take the building of a railroad as an illustration:

A certain grade of mind is essential to prepare the road-bed and lay the track. This class of men must have strong physical natures, and the qualities that give the necessary force and energy to hew down rocks, tunnel mountains and remove all obstructions. Another class will act as foremen of the laborers, another will serve as engineers, another is fitted to act as officers, while still another grade of mind projected the enterprise and furnished the means for carrying it to a successful conclusion.

As in the materials that enter into the erection of the building, the foundation stones that support the superstructure down deep in the earth, while they are never seen, are nevertheless just as essential to the completion of the building as are the ornamental capstones above the windows; so, in associated labor, each grade of mind does its appropriate work. We could not dispense with either, and all should have due praise.

Each class being thus dependent, one upon the other, all should labor in harmony together. The workman should guard his employer's interest. He should always be promptly on time and faithful to the last hour. He should make his work a study; he should give it thought, as thereby he renders his services so much the more valuable, and his compensation in the end so much better. Probably, if faithful, he may succeed to the business of his employer, or may enter a separate field. It is certain, at any rate, if he proves himself a competent assistant he is the more likely, in time, himself to become a manager of others.

The employer, through kind and pleasant manner, may do much toward making the subordinate worthy and competent. The workman should thoroughly understand what the duty is which he is expected to perform, and he should be required pleasantly yet firmly to execute it to the letter. When once there is a definite understanding on his part as to what is explicitly required, it is not necessary that an employer use harsh means or a manner in any way discourteous in order to secure obedience to his commands.

ELEMENTS OF THE BEAUTIFUL.

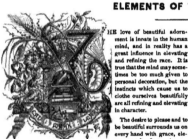

HE love of beautiful adornment is innate in the human mind, and in reality has a great influence in elevating and refining the race. It is true that the mind may sometimes be too much given to personal decoration, but the instincts which cause us to clothe ourselves beautifully are all refining and elevating in character.

The desire to please and to be beautiful surrounds us on every hand with grace, elegance and refinement.

The person who cares nothing for personal appearance is a sloven. Were all to be thus, the human race would rapidly degenerate toward barbarism. The person who is careless of dress is likely to be equally regardless concerning purity of character.

The little girl that studies her features in the mirror, while she evinces possibly a disposition to be vain, nevertheless in this act shows herself to be possessed of those instincts of grace which, rightly directed, will beautify and embellish all her surroundings through life.

The boy that cares nothing for personal appearance, that does not appreciate beauty in others, is likely to develop into the man who will be slovenly in habits, whose home will quite probably be a hovel, and himself very likely a loafer or a tramp. But the boy — the rollicsome, frolicsome boy, ready to roll in the dirt, possibly — who, under all this, aspires to appear handsome, who desires a clean face, clean hands and a clean shirt, who admires a well-dressed head of hair and a good suit of clothes — that boy possesses the elements which in the man, in an elegant home, will surround him with the artistic and the charming.

The love of the beautiful ever leads to the higher, the grander and the better. Guided by its impulses, we pass out of the hut into the larger and better house; into the charming and elegantly-adorned mansion. Actuated by its influence, we convert the lumbering railway carriage into a palace-car, the swamp into a garden, and the desolate place into a park, in which we wander amid the trees, the streams of limpid water, and the fragrance of beautiful flowers.

All along the world's highway are the evidences, among the most elevated and refined, of the love of the beautiful, which, perhaps more than in any other manner, finds expression in dress.

This love of personal adornment being an inherent, desirable, refining element of character, it does not, therefore, become us to ignore or to suppress it. On the contrary, it should be our duty to cultivate neatness of appearance and artistic arrangement in dress, the whole being accompanied by as much personal beauty as possible.

In the cultivation of beauty in dress, it will become necessary to discriminate between ornament as displayed by the savage, and the science of beauty as observed in a more highly civilized life. Ornament is one thing; beauty is quite another.

To develop beauty, it is necessary to understand that the combination of a few fundamental principles forms the basis in the construction of all that we admire as beautiful. Of these are —

1. CURVED LINES. 2. SYMMETRY. 3. CONTRAST. 4. HARMONY OF COLOR. 5. HARMONY OF ASSOCIATION.

The Curved Line.

A prominent feature of beauty everywhere is the curved line. The winding pathway, the graceful outline of tree, cloud and mountain in the distance, the arched rainbow, the well-trimmed shrub, the finely-featured animal, the rounded form of everything that is beautiful — all illustrate this principle. The delicately, finely rounded face, hands and general features, are essential to the highest forms of beauty in the person, and the same principles apply in the manufacture of dress. Every line and seam should run in curves.

Symmetry of Proportion.

As harmonious proportions always please the eye in every object, so we are pleased with the symmetry displayed in the human form and features. Thus symmetry will give a well-shaped head, a moderate length of neck, a clearly-defined nose, mouth not too large, shoulders of even height, and all parts of the body of proportionate length and size. The clothing should be made to set off the natural features of the body to the best advantage. Thus the coat should be so cut as to make the shoulders of the man look broad. The dress should be so fitted as to cause the shoulders of the woman to appear narrow and sloping.

Long garments will make the individual appear taller. Short garments will cause the person to seem shorter. Lines that run perpendicularly add to the apparent height; horizontal lines shorten it.

Contrast.

Another feature of beauty in personal appearance is contrast, or those qualities which give animated expression and vivacity of manner. Thus the sparkling eye, clear-cut features, a color of hair that contrasts with the skin; happy, lively expression of face; graceful, animated movement of body; interesting conversational powers — all these make the face attractive by variety and contrast.

The lady's dress is relieved by flounce, frill, and various other trimmings, with colors more or less pronounced, according to the complexion of the wearer. The gentleman's dress, as now worn, does not admit of so great variety.

Harmony.

The harmony of colors suitable for various complexions is quite fully detailed elsewhere. Harmony of association will include those principles that derive their beauty chiefly from their association with other objects. Thus the best height and form for man or woman will be the average form of men and women with whom they associate. Anything unusual will detract from this beauty.

Any article of jewelry or dress which may appear out of place for the occasion, or not appropriate with the other articles worn, is also included under this head.

CARE OF THE PERSON.

It is assumed that the reader desires health and beauty, and is willing to govern habits accordingly. Observe then the following regulations:

Retire sufficiently early to get the necessary rest and sleep, that you may arise early in the morning.

Be sure that plenty of fresh air is admitted to the room throughout the night, by the opening of windows. Avoid feathers. A perfectly clean, moderately hard bed is best for health.

The Bath.

Upon arising, take a complete bath. A simple washing out of the eyes is not sufficient. The complete bathing of the body once each day is of the utmost importance to health and beauty. Not more than a quart of water is necessary. Use the hands the same as you do upon the face. No sponge is required, and water is more agreeable to the skin when applied with the bare hand. Use rainwater; and, for a healthy person, the temperature of that which has been in the room throughout the night is about right. Use plenty of soap, and wash quickly. Follow by wiping the skin perfectly dry with a soft towel, and afterward give the body and limbs a thorough rubbing. The glow that is diffused throughout the face and body by this exercise is worth more in giving a ruddy, beautiful complexion, than all the rouge and powder in the world.

The arrangements for this bath are very simple. There is nothing required but a small amount of soft water, a piece of soap, and a towel. No elaborately-fitted-up bathroom is necessary. We have detailed all the appliances that are essential, and they are so simple that the laboring classes and the poor can have them, and be clean, as well as the rich. Occasionally, warm water, with sponge, may be necessary to remove completely all the oily exudations from the body, but for the ordinary bath this is not essential.

The sun and air bath is very excellent for health; therefore to leave the body exposed in the sun for a short time previous to dressing is very invigorating.

Before the breakfast hour the lungs should be completely inflated with fresh air. The meals should be partaken of with regularity, while more or less of fruit, oatmeal, rice, cracked wheat, graham bread, etc., will be found necessary as a diet, in order to keep the skin clear.

The Breath.

The breath should be watched, lest it become offensive. Unfortunately, it is one of the troubles which we may not be aware of, as our friends may not feel at liberty to inform us of the difficulty. Offensive breath may arise from the stomach, the teeth, the lungs, or catarrhal affection of the throat and nose.

Unquestionably, the best remedy for bad breath is a system of diet and treatment that shall remove the cause. As a temporary expedient, when offensiveness arises from a peculiar food or drink which has been partaken of, a few grains of coffee, or cassia buds, cloves, cardamom seeds or allspice, may be used; although if the breath be very strong these will not always prove effective. It is better to remove the cause.

The following remedies for offensive breath are commended by those who have had experience in testing the matter:

Powdered sugar, ¼ ounce; vanilla, ¼ ounce; powdered charcoal, ¼ ounce; powdered coffee, 1½ ounces; gum arabic, ¼ ounce. Make into pellets of 18 grains each, and take six a day. Bad breath will disappear.

Disagreeable breath arising from decay or secretions about the teeth may be removed by the following:

Rose-water, 1 ounce, and permanganate of potash, 1 grain. Rinse the mouth every three hours.

To remove catarrh, the following is highly commended:

In a pint of water put two tablespoonfuls of common fine table salt. Heat the water in a tin cup. With the aid of a nasal douche, obtained at the drugstore, or even without that, snuff about a teaspoonful of the brine up each nostril, requiring it to pass into the mouth. Use twice a day—morning and night.

For offensive breath arising from foul stomach, the following is recommended:

To a wine-glass of water add 3 grains of chloride of lime. Take a tablespoonful three times a day, before the meal, and eat of simple food which is easily digested.

Another remedy for foul breath is powdered charcoal, half a teaspoonful, spread on a piece of bread, and eaten once a day for two or three days. Another is a drink of pure water, taken twice a day, containing each time 20 grains of bisulphate of soda. The taste is made pleasant by a few drops of peppermint essence.

The following is recommended as beneficial for the teeth, and effective in removing the acidity of the stomach:

Take of gum arabic 5 drachms; vanilla sugar, 3 drachms; chlorate of lime, 7 drachms, and mix with water to a stiff paste. Roll and cut into the ordinary-sized lozenge, and eat six each day.

The Skin.

Beware of exterior application of cosmetics for the purpose of beautifying the skin. The greatest beautifiers in existence are plenty of exercise in the fresh air, the keeping of the pores of the skin completely open by bathing, the feeding of the body with a sufficiency of simple, healthy food, and the obtaining of the requisite amount of sleep.

It is true that sometimes a slight touch of art may improve the personal appearance. The very sallow complexion may be improved by a small amount of color applied; the hair, if naturally dry and stiff, may be kept in place by a simple hair preparation, and a white eyebrow may be brought into harmonious color with the hair of the head by a dye; all this being done so adroitly that the external application cannot be detected. But, as a rule, greatest beauty is obtained by a strict observance of the laws of health.

The following preparations, culled from De la Banta's "Advice to Ladies," are recommended for improving the complexion:

Take a teaspoonful of powdered charcoal (kept by druggists), mixed with sweetened water or milk, for three nights successively. This should be followed by a gentle purge afterwards, to remove it from the system. Taken once in two or three months, this remedy will prove efficacious in making the complexion clear and transparent.

ANOTHER.

Tincture of balsam of Peru, 2 drachms; tincture of tolu, 2 drachms; tincture of benzoin, 2 drachms. Mix with one gill of distilled water, and take of melted white wax, 1 ounce; spermaceti, ¼ ounce; sweet almond oil, 8 drachms, and rose-water, 1 ounce. Mix all the ingredients together, and beat thoroughly, applying to the skin with a sponge.

This may be used with benefit where the skin presents a greasy appearance:

To ½ pint of rose-water, add chlorate of potash, 18 grains; glycerine, 1 ounce. Mix carefully, and use in a pure state. Apply with a sponge or linen cloth. Should it irritate the skin, dilute with more water. These lotions should be applied with care, and are best used at night.

The greasy skin, inclined to pimples, is benefited by the following preparation:

Bicarbonate of soda, 18 grains; essence of Portugal, 6 drops, distilled water, ½ pint. Mix, and bathe the face.

The shiny, polished skin, which is caused by fatty secretions beneath it, may have the difficulty removed by this preparation:

Take 1 quart of camphor water, pure glycerine 1 ounce, and ¼ ounce of powdered borax. Mix, and bathe the face. Let it dry and remain a few minutes after applying it, then wash the face thoroughly with soft water.

If the skin is very pallid, it is improved by the bath in lukewarm water, followed by brisk rubbing with a coarse towel, and exercise in the air and sun. The pale skin is improved also by the sunshine. The rough skin is made smooth by the application of glycerine at night, followed by its removal with water and fine soap in the morning.

The skin may be whitened by the following prescription:

To one pint of water add 1 wineglass of fresh lemon juice, and 10 drops of attar of roses. Mix, and keep in a well corked bottle. Use once a day.

The sallow and muddy skin is improved by this preparation.

To one pint of water add 2 drachms of iodide of potassium and 1 ounce of glycerine. Mix, and apply with a sponge once a day.

To keep the skin clear, beware of pork, cheese and other substances containing much grease. Also avoid alcoholic drinks. Keep the bowels loose by fruit and a sufficiency of coarse food. Take exercise sufficient, if possible, to produce a gentle perspiration each day; bathe daily, and get into the sunshine and open air.

The Hand.

Various are the recipes for keeping the hand beautiful. If not engaged in hard manual labor, and it is very desirable to make the hands present as handsome an appearance as possible, there are a few directions necessary to keep them well preserved. Among these is perfect cleanliness, which is produced by a thorough washing, using an abundance of good toilet soap, and frequently a nail-brush.

Should the hands be inclined to chap, they will be relieved of the difficulty by washing them in glycerine before going to bed. In the winter season, to wash them in snow and soap will leave them smooth and soft.

To make the hands very white and delicate, the person is assisted by washing them several times for two or three days in milk and water, and, upon retiring to rest, bathing in palm oil, and encasing them in a pair of woolen gloves, cleaning with warm water and soap the next morning. They should be thoroughly rubbed to promote circulation, and a pair of soft leather gloves should be worn during the day.

Should the hands become sunburned, the tan may be removed by using lime-water and lemon-juice.

Should warts make their appearance, they may be removed by paring them on the top and applying a small amount of acetic acid on the summit of the wart, with a camel's hair brush, care being taken that none of the acid gets upon the surrounding skin. To prevent this, wax may be placed upon the finger or hand during the operation, or an old kid glove may be used, the wart being allowed to project through.

The nails should be cut about once a week, directly after a bath, and should never be bitten. In rough, hard labor, if it is desired to protect the hands, gloves should be worn.

But however beautiful it may be, the hand should do its full share of work. The hand that is beautiful from idleness is to be despised.

The Feet.

Much care should be taken to keep the feet in good condition. The first important consideration in their management is perfect cleanliness. Some people find it necessary to wash the feet morning and evening. Many find it indispensably necessary to wash them once a day, and no one should fail of washing them at least three times a week, and the stockings should be changed as frequently if much walking be done.

Without washing, the feet are liable to become very offensive to others in a short time. The feet of some persons will become disagreeably so sometimes within a week if they are not washed, more especially if they perspire freely.

A foot bath, using warm water, followed by wiping the feet completely dry, and afterward putting on clean stockings, is very invigorating after a long walk, or when the feet are damp and cold.

To escape chilblains, avoid getting the feet wet. Should they become damp, change shoes and stockings at once. Wear woolen stockings, and do not toast the feet before the fire. The approach of the chilblain is frequently prevented by bathing the feet in a strong solution of alum.

With the first indications of chilblains, as revealed by the itching sensation, it is well to rub them with warm spirits of rosemary, adding to the same a little turpentine. Lint, soaked in camphorated spirits, opodeldoc, or camphor liniment, may be applied and retained when the part is affected.

It is claimed also that chilblains may be cured by bathing the feet in water in which potatoes have been boiled.

Wear boots and shoes amply large for the feet, but not too large, and thus escape corns. A broad heel, half an inch in height, is all that comfort will allow to be worn.

The Hair.

The head should be washed occasionally with soap and water. Follow by wiping perfectly dry, and afterward brush the hair and scalp with a hairbrush of moderate hardness. When the hair is inclined to be harsh and dry, a moderate supply of olive oil, bear's grease or other dressing may be used. With many heads no oil is necessary, and with any an over-abundance is to be avoided. Frequent brushing with a perfectly clean brush is of great service in giving a glossy, beautiful appearance to the hair. The brush may be kept clean by washing every day or two in warm water and soda, or in diluted ammonia.

For removing dandruff, glycerine diluted with a little rosewater is recommended. Rosemary in almost any preparation is a very cleansing wash.

The yolk of an egg, beaten up in warm water, makes an excellent application for cleansing the scalp.

To clip the ends of the hair occasionally is an excellent plan for ladies, as it prevents the hair from splitting.

It is doubtful if a hair-dye is ever advisable, though an eyebrow is sometimes improved by a light application, to bring it into harmonious color with the hair, as is also hair which grows white in patches. There is no objection to the hair growing gray. Indeed the gray is often fully as beautiful as the former color.

Baldness is usually avoided by keeping the head cool. Women seldom have bald heads, but men often do, the baldness commencing upon the head at a point which is covered by the hat. In order to preserve the hair, gentlemen must avoid warm hats and caps, and whatever is worn must be thoroughly ventilated by apertures sufficient in quantity and size to allow all the heated air to escape. The silk hat should have at least twenty holes punched in the top to afford sufficient ventilation.

The beard is nature's badge to indicate manhood. It was an unwise fashion that ordained that the face should be shaved. Gradually men begin to learn that health, comfort and improved appearance come with the full beard, and in later years the beard is acquiring the prestige it held in olden times. Care should be taken to keep the beard and hair so cut and trimmed that they may present a handsome appearance.

The Teeth.

The teeth should be thoroughly cleaned with a toothbrush each morning after breakfast. Some persons clean the teeth after every meal, which is a most excellent habit. By cleaning the teeth regularly, no washes are necessary, though occasionally castile soap will be beneficial. Should tartar collect in such quantity as to be difficult to remove, the dentist should be consulted. Should the teeth begin to decay, they should be immediately cared for by the dentist. Powdered charcoal easily removes stains, and makes the teeth white.

The following also is an excellent wash for the teeth:

Tincture of myrrh, 1 ounce; compound tincture of cinchona, 1 ounce; water, 1 ounce. Put five drops on the toothbrush, dip the brush then in water, and wash the teeth.

Keep the teeth clean. They look badly if not perfectly white and clean.

Ears, Eyes and Nose.

In the daily bath, all the crevices of the ears should be thoroughly cleaned, and the earwax carefully removed whenever it shows itself.

Special pains should be taken to keep the eyes clean. It shows filthy habits to see matter gathered in the corners. If dirt accumulates between washings, the eyes should be carefully wiped with a soft handkerchief.

Keep the nasal passages perfectly clear. If there is an inclination for accumulations to stop there, snuff water up the nose, and afterward blow it, placing the thumb on one side while you blow the other. Keep the nose so clear that you can breathe through it with ease, and avoid the coarse habit of picking it.

Regularity of Habits.

It is of the utmost importance, if the individual would enjoy health and possess beauty, that all the personal habits be perfectly regular, and that attention be given to these each twenty-four hours at a regular time.

Do not let visiting, traveling or business interfere with them. You must be regular in sleep, in evacuation of the bowels, in bathing and in eating. Nature will not be cheated. She requires perfect attention to certain duties. If you attempt to violate her requirements, you will be certainly punished.

Whenever the person complains of sickness, he confesses to a violation, consciously or unconsciously, unavoidably or otherwise, of some of nature's requirements. (See remarks on "Health," in the "Letters of Advice," elsewhere in this volume.)

WHAT COLORS MAY BE WORN.

Nature has her peculiar shades and contrasts, with which she embellishes all her works.

Over the retreating dark gray cloud in the east does the rainbow show itself, strong by contrast, and beautiful in the harmony of its surroundings. Surpassingly lovely are the brilliant rays of the golden sunset, as they lie reflected upon the fleecy clouds at eventide, their charm coming from their surroundings of the gray and azure blue. Dazzlingly bright are the twinkling stars as they smile upon us in their bed of cerulean blue; and very beautiful is the rose, as it perfumes the air and charms the eye amid its accompaniments of green.

Nature thus robes all her works with shades that complement and harmonize; the result being to show the object to the best advantage.

In the higher civilization, men have donned the conventional suit of black, and have abandoned the domain of color to woman, who with her keenly æsthetic nature can never be induced to forego the pleasure that comes from brilliant and harmonious hues. Alive as woman is, therefore, to the principles that make beauty, it becomes us to investigate the subject of personal appearance as affected by color.

Colors that Suit Different Complexions.

Two distinct types of complexion exist among the white race, namely, the light-haired, fair and ruddy complexions, termed Blondes; and the dark-haired and dark-skinned, called Brunettes.

Between these are several intermediate tints and shades, all requiring much close observation to fully discriminate as to the colors most suitable to be worn, to harmonize with the different shades of complexion.

Investigation has proven that the light-haired and rosy-cheeked, with red or golden hair and ruddy complexion, require certain colors in headdress and drapery to harmonize; and the same is true of the dark complexion, with dark hair and eyebrows.

The Shades that Blondes May Wear.

Dark violet, intermixed with lilac and blue, give additional charms to the fair-haired, ruddy blonde. Green, also, with lighter or darker tints, is favorable. With the very ruddy, the blue and green should be darker rather than lighter. An intermixture of white may likewise go with these colors.

The neutral colors are also suitable to the ruddy blondes. Of these are the russet, slate, maroon, and all the hues of brown. Light neutral tints are also pleasing, such as gray, drab, fawn and stone colors.

Transparent and delicate complexions, with light, chestnut or brown hair, should have the same set off by contrast. Thus blue, pale yellow, azure, lilac and black, trimmed with rose or pink, are suitable, as are also the various shades of gray.

Colors that become the Brunette.

Glossy black becomes the brunette; so do white, scarlet, orange and yellow. The scarlet blossom in the hair, gold-colored ribbon and poppy colors, deftly but not too conspicuously woven about the neck and breast, will display the face to fine advantage. Green also befits the dark complexion.

The sallow complexion is improved by the different shades of dark green and red. A yellow complexion is made handsomer by the reflection of yellow about it; especially if relieved by poppy colors or black.

The red and yellow face is benefited by coming in contact with blue or orange. The red face is improved by red around it, red and blue tints being developed thereby. Red and blue are relieved by purple, and the blue and yellow by green. White and black become the pale face, but red and blue become it better. Light colors harmonize with and befit the pale skin, while the dark skin is improved by the darker tints.

Colors in Bonnets.

Black Bonnets, with white, pink or red flowers and white feathers, become the fair complexion. They also become the black-haired type when trimmed with white, red, orange or yellow.

White Bonnets, made of lace, muslin or crape, suit all complexions, though not so becoming to the rosy complexion as other colors. A white bonnet may be trimmed with white or pink, but with the blonde is handsomest when trimmed with blue flowers. For the brunette, preference should be given to trimmings of red, pink, orange and yellow — never blue.

Blue Bonnets are suitable only for fair or light, rosy complexions. They should never be worn by the brunette.

Yellow and Orange Bonnets suit the brunette, their appropriate trimming being poppy colors, scarlet, white and black, black and scarlet, black, scarlet and yellow.

Light Blue Bonnets are very suitable for those having light hair. They may be trimmed with white flowers, and in many cases with orange and yellow.

Green Bonnets best become the fair and rosy complexion. White flowers will harmonize in the trimmings, but pink is preferable.

Colors Suitable for the Different Seasons.

Red, in its various tints, being a warm color, when worn in dress, has a pleasing effect in winter.

Purple is appropriate in winter, spring and autumn.

Green is becoming in late summer and in autumn, by contrast with the general somber appearance of dead foliage at that season of the year.

White and light tints in clothing give an appearance of coolness and comfort in summer.

Black and dark colors are appropriate at all seasons.

Colors We See First.

Of a variety of colors to be seen, the white or light-colored will usually attract attention first and farthest, from the fact that, most objects being of dark shades of color, it is strongest in contrast. Next to white comes the scarlet red, which, close by, is one of the most brilliant and attractive colors. Yellow is one of the most noticeable, succeeded by the orange, crimson, blue and purple.

Colors in Dress Most Beautiful at Night.

A dress of a color that may be beautiful during the day, may be lacking in beauty at night, owing to the effect of gaslight; and another, most charming in the evening, may possess little beauty in the daytime. Thus, crimson, which is handsome in the evening, loses its effect upon the complexion in the daytime. So white and yellow, that add beauty at night, are unbecoming by day.

The scarlet, orange and the light brown are also most charming at night.

Colors Most Beautiful by Daylight.

Pale yellow, which is handsome by day, is muddy in appearance by gaslight. So purple and orange, that harmonize and are beautiful by daylight, lose their charm at night.

The beauty of rose color disappears under the gaslight; and all the shades of purple and lilac, the dark blues and green lose their brilliancy in artificial light. Ordinarily, the complexion will bear the strongest color at night.

Apparent Size Affected by Color.

The apparent size is affected by colors. As white upon the building will make it appear larger, so a light-colored dress will have the same effect upon the person. Thus the large figure will appear best in close-fitting black, and next best in the sober hues. The smaller figure will show to advantage in the light colors. Black, however, for a person of any size, is the most suitable color for nearly all occasions; and, handsomely made, well fitted, artistically trimmed, and suitably relieved at throat and bodice with ribbons, lace and flowers corresponding with the complexion, makes always a most beautiful costume.

Persons whose resources are limited and who cannot afford a varied wardrobe should by this fact be guided to a constant preference for black.

Colors that Contrast and Harmonize.

The object of two or more different tints in dress is to obtain relief by variety, and yet the two shades brought thus in contrast should harmonize, else the beauty of each will be lessened. Thus, a lady with a blue dress would greatly injure its effect by wearing a crimson shawl; as she would also a lilac-colored dress by trimming it with a dark brown.

That the reader may understand the colors that will contrast and yet blend, the following list of harmonizing colors is given:

Blue and gold; blue and orange; blue and salmon color; blue and drab; blue and stone color; blue and white; blue and gray; blue and straw color; blue and maize; blue and chestnut; blue and brown; blue and black; blue and white; blue, brown, crimson and gold.

Black and white; black and orange; black and maize; black and scarlet; black and lilac; black and pink; black and slate color; black and buff; black, white, yellow and crimson; black, orange, blue and yellow.

Crimson and gold; crimson and orange; crimson and maize; crimson and purple; crimson and black; crimson and drab.

Green and gold; green and yellow; green and orange; green and crimson; green, crimson and yellow; green, scarlet and yellow.

Lilac and gold; lilac and maize; lilac and cherry; lilac and scarlet; lilac and crimson; lilac, scarlet, white and black; lilac, gold and chestnut; lilac, yellow, scarlet and white.

Orange and chestnut; orange and brown; orange, lilac and crimson; orange, red and green; orange, blue and crimson; orange, purple and scarlet; orange, blue, scarlet, green and white.

Purple and gold; purple and orange; purple and maize; purple, scarlet and gold color; purple, white and scarlet; purple, orange, blue and scarlet; purple, scarlet, blue, yellow and black.

Red and gold; red, white or gray; red, green and orange; red, black and yellow; red, yellow, black and white.

Scarlet and purple; scarlet and orange; scarlet and blue; scarlet and slate color; scarlet, black and white; scarlet, white and blue; scarlet, gray and blue; scarlet, yellow and blue; scarlet, blue, yellow and black.

Yellow and red; yellow and brown; yellow and chestnut; yellow and violet; yellow and blue; yellow and purple; yellow and crimson; yellow and black; yellow, purple and crimson; yellow and scarlet.

FASHION--WHY DOES IT CHANGE?

Because change is one of nature's laws. If there was no change, there would be no motion; and without motion there would be no life.

Change is ever going forward in nature. To-day it is spring, and all nature is waking to new life. A few weeks hence, and every tree and shrub will be clothed in a garb of green, sprinkled with blossoms. Later, the green of various shades will merge into the autumn tints; and later still, nature will doff her garb entirely, only to clothe herself in the coming years again with various changes, according to the seasons.

So mankind instinctively changes in style of costume, oftentimes for better, and sometimes, it must be admitted, for the worse. But the change ever goes forward, fashion repeating itself within the century, often within a generation, almost as certainly as the seasons do within the year.

There is no use, therefore, in issuing a fiat against changes of fashion. Best judgment is shown in accepting of the inevitable and adapting ourselves to the circumstances.

Hints to Gentlemen.

It is best taste to conform to fashion, avoiding extremes.

While it is well to guard against the adoption of a decidedly unwise fashion, it is well also to avoid an oddity in dress.

Well dressed gentlemen wear dark clothing cut and made to measure. Watch-chain, one ring, shirt-stud and sleeve-buttons are all the jewelry allowable for the gentleman.

Other colors than black will be appropriate in their season and for various kinds of employment.

Hints to Parents.

Give the boy a good suit of clothes, if you wish him to appear manly. An ill-fitting, bad-looking garment destroys a boy's respect for himself.

To require the boy to wear men's cast-off clothing, and go shambling around in a large pair of boots, and then expect him to have good manners, is like giving him the poorest of tools, because he is a boy, and then expecting him to do as fine work with them as a man would with good tools.

Like the man or woman, the boy respects himself, and will do much more honor to his parents, when he is well dressed in a neatly fitting suit of clothes. Even his mother should relinquish her rights, and let the barber cut his hair.

As a rule, well dressed children exhibit better conduct than children that are careless in personal appearance. While vanity should be guarded against, children should be encouraged to be neat in person and dress.

The mother should strive also to make her boy manly. Possibly, as a pet, her boy has in infancy had his hair curled. Even now, when he is six or eight years of age, the curls look very pretty. But the mother must forego her further pleasure in the curls; for the boy, to take his place along with the others, to run and jump, to grow manly and strong, must wear short hair. His mother can no longer dress it like a girl's. It will be necessary and best to cut off his curls.

Hints to Ladies.

Best taste will dictate an observance of fashion, avoiding extremes.

Dress the hair so that it will exhibit variety and relief, without making the forehead look too high.

Have one pronounced color in the dress, all other colors harmonizing with that. See "Harmony of Colors."

A dress should fit the form. Well fitted and judiciously trimmed, a calico dress is handsomer than an ill-fitting silk dress.

To present a handsome appearance, all the appurtenances of the lady's dress should be scrupulously neat and clean. Every article that is designed to be white should be a pure white, and in perfect order.

Much taste may be displayed in dress about the neck, and care should be observed not to use trimmings that will enlarge the appearance of the shoulders. The dress should be close-fitting about the waist and shoulders, though the lady should not lace too tightly.

As with the gentleman, quiet colors are usually in best taste. Heavy, rich, dark materials best suit the woman of tall figure; while light, full draperies should be worn only by those of slender proportions. Short persons should beware of wearing flounces, or horizontal trimmings that will break the perpendicular lines, as the effect is to make them appear shorter.

Care should be taken to dress according to the age, the season, the employment and the occasion. As a rule, a woman appears her loveliest when, in a dress of dark color, we see her with the rosy complexion of health, her hair dressed neatly, her throat and neck tastefully cared for, her dress in neither extreme of fashion, while the whole is relieved by a moderate amount of carefully selected jewelry.

We have aimed, in this chapter on the toilet, to present the scientific principles of dress -- principles that can be applied at all times, whatever may be the fashion. It will now become the reader to study these principles, and apply them in accordance with the rules of common sense and the fashions as they may prevail.

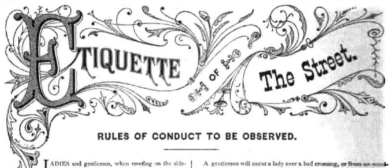

ETIQUETTE of The Street.

RULES OF CONDUCT TO BE OBSERVED.

LADIES and gentlemen, when meeting on the sidewalk, should always pass to the right. Should the walk be narrow or dangerous, gentlemen will always see that ladies are protected from injury.

Ladies should avoid walking rapidly upon the street, as it is ungraceful and unbecoming.

Running across the street in front of carriages is dangerous, and shows want of dignity.

The gentleman should insist upon carrying any package which the lady may have, when walking with her.

Before recognizing a lady on the street, the gentleman should be certain that his recognition will meet with favor.

No gentleman should stand on the street-corners, steps of hotels, or other public places, and make remarks about ladies passing by.

A gentleman may take two ladies upon his arms, but under no circumstances should the lady take the arms of two gentlemen.

Upon the narrow walk, for her protection, the gentleman should generally give the lady the inside of the walk (Fig. 21), passing behind her when changing at corners.

Allowing a dress to trail on the street is in exceedingly bad taste. Such a street costume simply calls forth criticism and contempt from the more sensible people.

A gentleman walking with a lady should accommodate his step and pace to hers. For the gentleman to be some distance ahead, presents a bad appearance.

Should protection on the street be necessary, it is customary for the gentleman to give his right arm to the lady; but if more convenient, he may give the left.

It is courtesy to give silent, respectful attention as a funeral procession passes. It shows want of respect to pass between the carriages while the procession is moving.

Staring at people, spitting, looking back after they pass, saluting people across the street, calling out loudly or laughing at people as they go by, are all evidences of ill-breeding.

The gentleman accompanying a lady should hold the door open for the lady to enter first. Should he be near the door when a lady, unattended, is about to enter, he will do the same for her.

In the evening, or whenever safety may require, a gentleman should give a lady his arm. It is not customary in other cases to do so on the street, unless with an elderly lady, or the couple be husband and wife.

Fig 21. The street-promenade. The gentleman gives the lady the inside of the walk. *

A gentleman will assist a lady over a bad crossing, or from an omnibus or carriage, without waiting for the formality of an introduction. When the service is performed, he will raise his hat, bow, and pass on.

In a street car or an omnibus, the passengers who are seated should strive to give seats to those who are standing, rendering such accommodation as they would themselves desire under similar circumstances.

When crossing the pavement, the lady should raise her dress with the right hand, a little above the ankle. To raise the dress with both hands, is vulgar, and can be excused only when the mud is very deep.

No gentleman will smoke when walking with, or standing in the presence of, a lady on the street. He should remove the cigar from her presence entirely, even though permission be granted to continue the smoking.

A gentleman should give his seat to any lady who may be standing in a public conveyance. For this favor she should thank him, which courtesy he should acknowledge by a slight bow. In an omnibus he will pass up the ladies' fares.

A true lady will go quietly and unobtrusively about her business when on the street, never seeking to attract the attention of the opposite sex, at the same time recognizing acquaintances with a courteous bow, and friends with pleasant words of greeting.

Swinging the arms when walking, eating upon the street, sucking the parasol handles, pushing violently through a crowd, very loud and boisterous talking and laughing on the streets, and whispering in public conveyances, are all evidences of ill-breeding in ladies.

A lady should have the escort of a gentleman in the evening. A gentleman at the house where she may call may return with her if she goes unattended; gossip and scandal are best avoided, however, if she have some one from her home call for her at an appointed hour.

On the narrow street-crossing the gentleman will allow the lady to precede him, that he may see that no injury befalls her.

Should a lady stop in the street, when meeting a gentleman, it is courtesy for him to stop also. Should his business be urgent, he will apologize for not continuing the conversation, and ask to be excused. Should it be desirable to lengthen the interview, and the lady reserves her walk in the midst of her conversation, it is courtesy for him to turn and accompany her. Should she desire to end the conversation, a slight bow from her will indicate the fact, when he should bid her " good day " and take his leave.

* Some authorities claim that it is most sensible for the lady to walk always at the right of the gentleman, whether on the street or indoors; her right hand being thus free to hold trail, fan, or parasol.

Unclassified LAWS OF Etiquette.

IMPORTANT RULES OF CONDUCT.

NEVER exaggerate.

Never point at another.

Never betray a confidence.

Never wantonly frighten others.

Never leave home with unkind words.

Never neglect to call upon your friends.

Never laugh at the misfortunes of others.

Never give a promise that you do not fulfill.

Never send a present, hoping for one in return.

Never speak much of your own performances.

Never fail to be punctual at the time appointed.

Never make yourself the hero of your own story.

Never pick the teeth or clean the nails in company.

Never fail to give a polite answer to a civil question.

Never question a servant or a child about family matters.

Never present a gift saying that it is of no use to yourself.

Never read letters which you may find addressed to others.

Never fail, if a gentleman, of being civil and polite to ladies.

Never call attention to the features or form of anyone present.

Never refer to a gift you have made, or favor you have rendered.

Never associate with bad company. Have good company, or none.

Never look over the shoulder of another who is reading or writing.

Never appear to notice a scar, deformity, or defect of anyone present.

Never arrest the attention of an acquaintance by a touch. Speak to him.

Never punish your child for a fault to which you are addicted yourself.

Never answer questions in general company that have been put to others.

Never, when traveling abroad, be over boastful in praise of your own country.

Never call a new acquaintance by the Christian name unless requested to do so.

Never lend an article you have borrowed, unless you have permission to do so.

Never attempt to draw the attention of the company constantly upon yourself.

Never exhibit anger, impatience or excitement, when an accident happens.

Never pass between two persons who are talking together, without an apology.

Never enter a room noisily; never fail to close the door after you, and never slam it.

Never forget that, if you are faithful in a few things, you may be ruler over many.

Never exhibit too great familiarity with the new acquaintance; you may give offense.

Never will a gentleman allude to conquests which he may have made with ladies.

Never be guilty of the contemptible meanness of opening a private letter addressed to another.

Never fail to offer the easiest and best seat in the room to an invalid, an elderly person, or a lady.

Never neglect to perform the commission which the friend entrusted to you. You must not forget.

Never send your guest, who is accustomed to a warm room, off into a cold, damp, spare bed, to sleep.

Never enter a room filled with people, without a slight bow to the general company when first entering.

Never fail to answer an invitation, either personally or by letter, within a week after the invitation is received.

Never accept of favors and hospitalities without rendering an exchange of civilities when opportunity offers.

Never cross the leg and put out one foot in the street-car, or places where it will trouble others when passing by.

Never fail to tell the truth. If truthful, you get your reward. You will get your punishment if you deceive.

Never borrow money and neglect to pay. If you do, you will soon be known as a person of no business integrity.

Never write to another asking for information, or a favor of any kind, without inclosing a postage stamp for the reply.

Never fail to say kind and encouraging words to those whom you meet in distress. Your kindness may lift them out of their despair.

Never refuse to receive an apology. You may not revive friendship, but courtesy will require, when an apology is offered, that you accept it.

Never examine the cards in the card-basket. While they may be exposed in the drawing-room, you are not expected to turn them over unless invited to do so.

Never, when walking arm in arm with a lady, be continually changing and going to the other side, because of change of corners. It shows too much attention to form.

Never should the lady accept of expensive gifts at the hands of a gentleman not related or engaged to her. Gifts of flowers, books, music or confectionery may be accepted.

Never insult another by harsh words when applied to for a favor. Kind words do not cost much, and yet they may carry untold happiness to the one to whom they are spoken.

Never fail to speak kindly. If a merchant, and you address your clerk; if an overseer, and you address your workmen; if in any position where you exercise authority, you show yourself to be a gentleman by your pleasant mode of address.

Never attempt to convey the impression that you are a genius, by imitating the faults of distinguished men. Because certain great men were poor penmen, wore long hair, or had other peculiarities, it does not follow that you will be great by imitating their eccentricities.

Never give all your pleasant words and smiles to strangers. The kindest words and the sweetest smiles should be reserved for home. Home should be our heaven.

"We have careful thought for the stranger,
　And smiles for the sometimes guest;
But oft for our own the bitter tone,
　Though we love our own the best.
Ah! lips with the curl impatient—
　Ah! brow with the shade of scorn,
'T were a cruel fate were the night too late
　To undo the work of the morn."

Kindness to the Erring.

A PLEA FOR THE UNFORTUNATE.

AN officer of the law you may be, and it becomes you to care for the prisoner in your charge. While law should be enforced, for the good of the criminal as well as the protection of society, it does not become you to be unkind. Perhaps investigation may prove that your prisoner is innocent and has been wrongly arrested. But if guilty, at most he is simply unfortunate. He had no power to say what qualities of mind he should inherit, what his temperament should be, or what training he should receive in infancy, all of which are usually determining causes that fix men's destiny in after-life.

He stands before you largely the victim of unfortunate circumstances. He lacks the moral strength which others possess, and hence his weakness and his errors. True, he must pay the penalty of his transgression, but you can temper the administration of your government with such justice as will tend to the improvement and, possibly, the reformation of the criminal. Whatever the conduct of the prisoner, you should always rise superior to the feelings of passion or revenge.

In a thousand ways our paths in life will be crossed by those who commit errors. It will be easy to find fault; it will be natural to blame. But we must never forget that further back, far beyond our sight, lie causes that tended to produce these results.

Well may the mother look with deep anxiety upon the infant, wondering what destiny lies before it. Alas! that a mother's hopes and prayers often do not avail. Drifted away from parental control, the footsteps fall amid temptation, and a life of sorrow is the result.

We should never forget, in our treatment of the erring, that, were the mother present, she would plead with us to deal gently with her child. Very touchingly does the following poem ask that we be lenient for her sake:

Some Mother's Child.

AT home or away, in the alley or street,
Whenever I chance in this wide world to meet
A girl that is thoughtless, or a boy that is wild,
My heart echoes sadly, "'T is some mother's child!"

And when I see those o'er whom long years have rolled,
Whose hearts have grown hardened, whose spirits are cold—
Be it woman all fallen, or man all defiled,
A voice whispers sadly, "Ah! some mother's child!"

No matter how far from the right she hath strayed;
No matter how deep inroads dishonor hath made;
No matter what element cankered the pearl—
Though tarnished and sullied, she's some mother's girl.

No matter how wayward his footsteps have been;
No matter how deep he is sunken in sin;
No matter how low is his standard of joy—
Though guilty and loathsome, he's some mother's boy.

That head hath been pillowed on tenderest breast;
That form hath been wept o'er, those lips have been pressed;
That soul hath been prayed for in tones sweet and mild;
For her sake deal gently with "some mother's child."

WHILE error must be deplored and virtue ever commended, we should deal carefully and considerately with the erring, ever remembering that a myriad of untoward circumstances are continually weaving a network around the individual, fettering and binding a soul that otherwise would be white and pure.

It is a most fortunate circumstance for the child to be born of an excellent parentage, to be reared amid kindness, and to be guided in youth by wise counsels. Given all these favoring circumstances, and the chances are that the pathway in life will be honorable. Deprived of these advantages, the individual is likely to fall short in excellence in proportion as the circumstances have been unfavorable.

There are those who seemingly have only a smooth pathway in life. They were so fortunate as to be born with an excellently balanced organization of mind. They have no passion unduly in excess. They have no abnormal longings, no eccentricities, no weaknesses. Roses strew their way, and they live a life well rounded out and full of honor.

But while there are those who are apparently exempt from temptation, all are not so fortunate in ability, in strength of purpose and in power of will which may enable them to resist evil. Some are liable to easily err, and it will take, possibly, but a trivial circumstance to carry them aside. In the transgression they will get their punishment—they will suffer sufficiently. It does not become the more fortunate, therefore, to take too much credit to themselves for being virtuous and free from error. It is vastly more noble and charitable to extend sympathy and compassion. This sentiment is well expressed in the following poem, by Millie C. Pomeroy.

You Had a Smooth Path.

ONE morning, when I went to school,
In the long-vanished Yesterday,
I found the creek had burst its banks,
And spilled its waters o'er my way.
The little path was filled with mud;
I tried to cross it on a log;
My foot slipped, and I, helpless, fell
Into a mass of miry bog.

My clothes were pitiful to see;
My hands and face were covered quite.
The children laughed right heartily,
And jeered me when I came in sight.
Sweet Jessie Brown, in snow-white dress,
Stood, smiling, by the teacher's desk,
The while he, gravely as he might,
Inquired the secret of my plight.

Then Jessie shook her snow-white dress,
And said, "What will you give to me
For coming here so nice and clean?
My very shoes from dirt are free."
The tutor frowned, and answered her,
"You merit no reward to-day;
Your clothes and hands are clean, because
You had a smooth path all the way."

And so, I think, when children grown
Are white in grace or black with sin,
We should not judge until we know
The path fate had them travel in;
For some are led on sunny heights,
Beyond the power of Sin to sway;
While others grope in darksome paths,
And face temptation all the way.

Charming, Beautiful Homes.

BARRIERS BETWEEN NEIGHBORS REMOVED.

THE fences shown upon the opposite page, separating houses and lots, often prevent acquaintance with neighbors being made. The result of this non-intercourse is usually a suspicion that the neighbor is unworthy of confidence, an opinion which is never overcome except by interchange of civilities which would show each the worth of the other.

Unacquainted with his neighbors, the resident, ceasing to consider their rights, grows careless of his obligations toward others, and consequently becomes a less worthy citizen.

The illustration upon this page (Fig. 23) represents the scene very much changed. Again we have the same residences, and the same neighbors, who have become acquainted and have learned to value each other. The result of this social intercourse and evident observance of the rights of others has wrought a vast change in the appearance of the homes, which is manifest at a glance.

It is plainly apparent in the scene that a higher civilization pervades the neighborhood. The animals, that broke down the trees and devastated the sidewalks and grounds, have been withdrawn by their owners, and sent to pastures, where they belong. This of itself is evidence of decided advancement.

Examine the scene further. The fences have disappeared, save a low coping that determines the outer edge of the lot. In this alone a heavy item of expense has been removed, while with it has come the enlargement of grounds, which, studded with finely trimmed trees, and intersected with winding pathways, surround every residence with a most elegant park. That this improvement is enjoyed, is shown in the congregating of the neighbors together in the shady nook, the gambols of the children on the lawn, and the promenade of the ladies and gentlemen throughout the beautifully embellished grounds. All delight in the scene, and all are made better by it. While the resident could be coarse and selfish in his own little lot, he is now thrown upon his good behavior as he mingles with others on the beautiful grounds, and thus

all are improved. Even the cat and dog that quarrelled in the former scene are now acquainted with each other, and happily play together.

To maintain pleasant relations among neighbors, there are a few things which the citizen must avoid. Among these are the following:

Never allow children to play upon a neighbor's grounds or premises unless they are invited and made perfectly welcome by the neighbor.

Never allow fowls or animals of any kind, which you have control over, to trespass upon the premises or rights of other people.

Never borrow of neighbors if it be possible to avoid it. It is better to buy what you need than to frequently borrow. There are a few things which a neighbor should never be expected to lend. Among these are fine-edged tools, delicate machinery, and any article liable to easily get out of order. The less business relations among neighbors, the better.

Never fail to return, with thanks, any article borrowed, as soon as you have finished using it, and see that it is in as good or better condition than when you received it.

Articles of provisions which may be borrowed should be very promptly returned in larger quantity, to pay interest, and better in quality if possible. In no way can a neighbor lose character more effectually in business dealing than by the petty meanness of borrowing and failing to pay, or by paying with a poorer quality and in less amount.

Avoid speaking evil of your neighbor. As a rule it is only safe to compliment and praise the absent one.

FIG. 23.   THE NEIGHBORHOOD WHERE PEOPLE LIVE IN HARMONY.

This illustration represents a neighborhood where the people evidently do unto others as they wish others to do unto them. They trust each other. The barriers between them are removed. No animal is allowed to do injury. Enjoying peace and beauty they evidently desire that the neighbor shall share the same. This co-operation, kindness and regard for all, give the beauty, the harmony, the peace, and the evident contentment which are here presented.

If any misunderstanding arises between yourself and a neighbor, endeavor to effect a reconciliation by a full explanation. When the matter is fully understood you will very likely be better friends ever afterwards.

Never fail, if the grounds run together, to keep your premises in as good order as your neighbor's. Should you own the house and grounds, and others occupy the same, you will do well to arrange to keep the exterior of the premises in order at your own expense, as tenants have not the same interest. The improvements of grounds among neighbors thus will always be kept up; you will be compensated by securing the best class of tenants, and the neighborhood will be greatly improved.

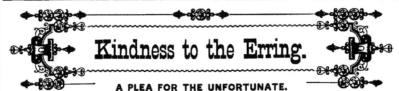

Kindness to the Erring.

A PLEA FOR THE UNFORTUNATE.

AN officer of the law you may be, and it becomes you to care for the prisoner in your charge. While law should be enforced, for the good of the criminal as well as the protection of society, it does not become you to be unkind. Perhaps investigation may prove that your prisoner is innocent and has been wrongly arrested. But if guilty, at most he is simply unfortunate. He had no power to say what qualities of mind he should inherit, what his temperament should be, or what training he should receive in infancy, all of which are usually determining causes that fix man's destiny in after-life.

He stands before you largely the victim of unfortunate circumstances. He lacks the moral strength which others possess, and hence his weakness and his errors. True, he must pay the penalty of his transgression, but you can temper the administration of your government with such justice as will tend to the improvement and, possibly, the reformation of the criminal. Whatever the conduct of the prisoner, you should always rise superior to the feelings of passion or revenge.

In a thousand ways our paths in life will be crossed by those who commit errors. It will be easy to find fault; it will be natural to blame. But we must never forget that further back, far beyond our sight, lie causes that tended to produce these results.

Well may the mother look with deep anxiety upon the infant, wondering what destiny lies before it. Alas! that a mother's hopes and prayers often do not avail. Drifted away from parental control, the footsteps fall amid temptation, and a life of sorrow is the result.

We should never forget, in our treatment of the erring, that, were the mother present, she would plead with us to deal gently with her child. Very touchingly does the following poem ask that we be lenient for her sake:

Some Mother's Child.

AT home or away, in the alley or street,
Whenever I chance in this wide world to meet
A girl that is thoughtless, or a boy that is wild,
My heart echoes sadly, "T is some mother's child!"

And when I see those o'er whom long years have rolled,
Whose hearts have grown hardened, whose spirits are cold—
Be it woman all fallen, or man all defiled,
A voice whispers sadly, "Ah! some mother's child!"

No matter how far from the right she hath strayed;
No matter what inroads dishonor hath made;
No matter what element cankered the pearl—
Though tarnished and sullied, she's some mother's girl.

No matter how wayward his footsteps have been;
No matter how deep he is sunken in sin;
No matter how low is his standard of joy —
Though guilty and loathsome, he's some mother's boy.

That head hath been pillowed on tenderest breast;
That form hath been wept o'er, those lips have been pressed;
That soul hath been prayed for in tones sweet and mild;
For her sake deal gently with "some mother's child."

WHILE error must be deplored and virtue ever commended, we should deal carefully and considerately with the erring, ever remembering that a myriad of untoward circumstances are continually weaving a network around the individual, fettering and binding a soul that otherwise would be white and pure.

It is a most fortunate circumstance for the child to be born of an excellent parentage, to be reared amid kindness, and to be guided in youth by wise counsels. Given all these favoring circumstances, and the chances are that the pathway in life will be honorable. Deprived of these advantages, the individual is likely to fall short in excellence in proportion as the circumstances have been unfavorable.

There are those who seemingly have only a smooth pathway in life. They were so fortunate as to be born with an excellently balanced organization of mind. They have no passion unduly in excess. They have no abnormal longings, no eccentricities, no weaknesses. Roses strew their way, and they live a life well rounded out and full of honor.

But while there are those who are apparently exempt from temptation, all are not so fortunate in ability, in strength of purpose and in power of will which may enable them to resist evil. Some are liable to easily err, and it will take, possibly, but a trivial circumstance to carry them aside. In the transgression they will get their punishment—they will suffer sufficiently. It does not become the more fortunate, therefore, to take too much credit to themselves for being more virtuous and free from error. It is vastly more noble and charitable to extend sympathy and compassion. This sentiment is well expressed in the following poem, by Millie C. Pomeroy.

You Had a Smooth Path.

ONE morning, when I went to school,
In the long-vanished Yesterday,
I found the creek had burst its banks,
And spilled its waters o'er my way.
The little path was filled with mud;
I tried to cross it on a log;
My foot slipped, and I, helpless, fell
Into a mass of miry bog.

My clothes were pitiful to see;
My hands and face were covered quite.
The children laughed right heartily,
And jeered me when I came in sight.
Sweet Jessie Brown, in snow-white dress,
Stood, smiling, by the teacher's desk,
The while he, gravely as he might,
Inquired the secret of my plight.

Then Jessie shook her snow-white dress,
And said, "What will you give to me
For coming here so nice and clean?
My very shoes from dirt are free."
The tutor frowned, and answered her,
"You merit no reward to-day;
Your clothes and hands are clean, because
You had a smooth path all the way."

And so, I think, when children grown
Are white in grace or black with sin,
We should not judge until we know
The path fate had them travel in;
For some are led on sunny heights,
Beyond the power of Sin to sway;
While others grope in darksome paths,
And face temptation all the way.

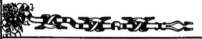

Commercial Forms.

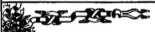

NOTES, BILLS, ORDERS, CHECKS, DRAFTS, RECEIPTS, Etc., Etc.

IN the transaction of business, it becomes necessary for all persons to occasionally write various business forms. Among those in most frequent use are Receipts, Orders, Bills of Articles Purchased, Promissory Notes, Checks, Drafts, etc.

To better understand these, it is well to be acquainted with the meaning of the various commercial terms to be constantly seen in our general reading.

Definition of Commercial Terms.

$——— means *dollars*, being a contraction of U. S., which was formerly placed before any denomination of money, and meant, as it means now, United States Currency.

£——— means *pounds*, English money.

@ stands for *at* or *to*. ℔ for *pound*, and bbl. for *barrel;* ℔ for *per* or *by the.* Thus, Butter sells at 20@30c ℔ ℔, and Flour at $8@12 ℔ bbl.

% for *per cent* and # for *number.*

May 1.— Wheat sells at $1.20@1.25, "seller June." *Seller June* means that the person who sells the wheat has the privilege of delivering it at any time during the month of June.

Selling *short*, is contracting to deliver a certain amount of grain or stock, at a fixed price, within a certain length of time, when the seller has not the stock on hand. It is for the interest of the person selling "short," to depress the

market as much as possible, in order that he may buy and fill his contract at a profit. Hence the "shorts" are termed "bears."

Buying *long*, is to contract to purchase a certain amount of grain or shares of stock at a fixed price, deliverable within a stipulated time, expecting to make a profit by the rise of prices. The "longs" are termed "bulls," as it is for their interest to "operate" so as to "toss" the prices upward as much as possible.

Promissory Notes.

A promissory note is a promise or engagement in writing to pay a specified sum at a time therein limited, or on demand, or at sight, to a person therein named, or his order or assigns, or to the bearer. The person making the note is called the drawer or maker.

A note is void when founded upon fraud. Thus, a note obtained from a person when intoxicated, or obtained for any reason which is illegal, cannot be collected.* A note given upon Sunday is also void in some States.

Notes bear interest only when it is so expressed; after they become due, however, they draw the legal rate of the State. † Notes payable on demand or at sight, draw no interest until after presentation or demand of the same has

---

* If, however, the note is transferred to an innocent holder, the claim of fraud or no value received will not avail. The party holding the note can collect it if the maker is able to pay it.

† If it is intended to have the note draw more than the legal rate of interest, after maturity, the words should so specify in the body of the note as follows: "with interest at the rate of ——— per cent until paid.

been made, unless they provide for interest from date on their face; they then draw the legal rate of interest of the State.

If "with interest" is included in the note, it draws the legal rate of the State where it is given, from the time it is made.

If the note is to draw a special rate of interest higher than the legal, but not higher than the law allows, the rate must be specified.

If the note is made payable to a person or order, to a person or bearer, to a person or his assigns, or to the cashier of an incorporated company or order, such notes are negotiable.

When transferring the note, the indorser frees himself from responsibility, so far as the payment is concerned, by writing on the back, above his name, "Without recourse to me in any event." *

When a note is made payable at a definite period after date, three days beyond the time expressed on the face of the note (called days of grace) are allowed to the person who is to pay the same, within which to make such payment. Notes payable on demand are not entitled to days of grace.

If a note is payable at a bank, and is held there on the day upon which it falls due, until the usual hour for closing, ready for receiving payment thereon, no further demand upon the maker is necessary, in order to charge the indorser. The demand must, in all cases, be made upon the last of the days of grace; a demand

before that time passing for nothing as against the indorser.

The days of grace, which must be computed according to the laws of the State where the note is payable, are to be reckoned exclusive of the day when the note would otherwise become due, and without deduction for Sundays or holidays; in which latter case, by special enactments in most of the States, notes are deemed to become due upon the secular day next preceding such days. Thus, a note, due upon the twenty-fifth day of December, is payable on the twenty-fourth, as the day when due is Christmas day; if the twenty-fourth chance to be Sunday, it is due upon the twenty-third.

In order to charge an indorser, the note, if payable at a particular place, must be presented for payment at the place upon the very day it becomes due; if no place of payment be named, it must be presented, either to the maker personally, or at his place of business, during business hours, or at his dwelling house, within reasonable hours; if payable by a firm, a presentment may be made to either of the partners, or at the firm's place of business; if given by several persons jointly, not partners, the demand must be made upon all. If the note has been lost, mislaid, or destroyed, the holder must still make a regular and formal demand, offering the party, at the same time, a sufficient indemnity in the event of his paying the same

---

* The simple indorsement of the name of the person selling the note, which serves as a transfer, upon the back of the same, is not in some States a guarantee for the payment of the note at maturity. When it is designed particularly to be so stated on the back of the note, as follows:

RICHARD ROE.

"For value received, I (or we) hereby guarantee the payment of the within note at maturity, or at any time thereafter, with interest at —— per cent. until paid; and agree to pay all costs or expenses paid or incurred in collecting the same."

RICHARD ROE.

To avoid the danger of the signer of the guarantee claiming at a future time that said guarantee was written above his name without his knowledge, it is best to have his signature written twice, once above the guarantee, to serve as a transfer, and once below to serve as the guarantee, as shown above.

Negotiable Note.

With interest at legal rate per cent. from date.

$500.   CHICAGO, ILL., Jan. 1, 18—.

Three months after date, for value received, I promise to pay Charles Mix, or order, Five Hundred dollars, with interest.

ORSON KENDALL.

Negotiable Note.

With interest at ten per cent. after maturity, until paid.

$100.   DES MOINES, IA., April 2, 18—.

For value received, ninety days after date, I promise to pay Orlando Warner, or order, One Hundred dollars, with interest at ten per cent. after maturity, until paid.

CHESTER BUTTERFIELD.

COMMERCIAL AND BUSINESS FORMS.   185

Form for Pennsylvania.

$200.   *Philadelphia, Pa., July 2, 18___.*

For value received, I promise to pay to the order of Arthur Bennett, Two Hundred dollars, ninety days after date, without defalcation.

        Hiram Wentworth

Note not Negotiable.

$500.   *Buffalo, N. Y., Oct. 2, 18___.*

Nine months after date, for value received, I promise to pay Harvey Baldwin, Five Hundred dollars.

        Barton King

Note for Two or More Persons.

$1,000.   *Clinton, Ia., April 4, 18___.*

We, or either of us, promise to pay to the order of Winfield Judson, One Thousand dollars, for value received.

        Thos. Armstrong,
        John A. Bruce.

Note on Demand.

$100.

NORTHAMPTON, MASS., March 1, 18—.

On demand, I promise to pay Clinton Briggs, or order, One Hundred dollars, value received, with interest.

     McREA BROWN.

Married Woman's Note in New York.

$50.   ROCHESTER, N. Y., April 10, 18—.

For value received, I promise to pay A. B. Smith, or order, Fifty dollars, one year from date, with interest. And I hereby charge my individual property and estate with the payment of this note.

     MARY H. WILLIAMS.

Note Payable by Installments.

$700.   NASHVILLE, TENN., Feb. 10, 18—.

For value received, I promise to pay to Simon Butterfield, or order, Seven Hundred dollars, in manner following, to-wit: Two Hundred dollars in one month from date; Two Hundred dollars in two months; and Three Hundred dollars in three months, with interest on the several sums as they become due.   CALEB PRINDLE.

Judgment Note.

$999.99/100   CHICAGO, ILL., Oct. 1, 1878.

Ninety days after date, we promise to pay to the order of The Merchants' Savings, Loan and Trust Co. of Chicago, at its office, Nine Hundred, Ninety-Nine and 99-100 dollars, for value received, with interest at the rate of ten per cent. per annum, after due.

CLARK D. BROWN.   [SEAL.]
SOLON P. WELLS.   [SEAL.]

Know all Men by these Presents, That we, the subscribers, are justly indebted to The Merchants' Savings, Loan and Trust Co., of Chicago, upon a certain Promissory Note, bearing even date herewith, for the sum of Nine Hundred, Ninety-Nine and 99-100 dollars, with interest at the rate of ten per cent. per annum, after due, and payable ninety days after date.

Now, therefore, in consideration of the premises, we do hereby make, constitute and appoint Wm. H. King, or any Attorney of any Court of Record, to be our true and lawful Attorney, irrevocably, for us and in our names, place and stead, to appear in any Court of Record, in term time or vacation, in any State or Territory of the United States, at any time before or after said note becomes due, to waive the service of process, and confess a judgment in favor of The Merchants' Savings, Loan and Trust Co., of Chicago, or its assign or assigns, upon the said Note, for the amount thereof, and interest, together with costs, and ten dollars Attorney's fees, and also to file a cognovit for the amount thereof, with an agreement therein that no writ of error or appeal shall be prosecuted upon the judgment entered by virtue hereof, nor any bills in equity filed to interfere in any manner with the operation of said judgment, and to release all errors that may intervene in the entering up of such judgment, or issuing the execution thereon; and also to waive all benefit or advantage to which we may be entitled by virtue of any Homestead or other exemption law now or hereafter in force, in this or any other State or Territory, where judgment may be entered by virtue hereof. Hereby ratifying and confirming all that our said attorney may do by virtue hereof.

Witness our hands and seals this first day of October, A. D. 1878.

IN PRESENCE OF   CLARK D. BROWN.   [SEAL.]
NATHAN WHITMAN.   SOLON P. WELLS.   [SEAL.]

Note in Missouri.

$400.   ST. JOSEPH, MO., June 1, 18—.

Three months after date, I promise to pay to Orson Barber, Four Hundred dollars, for value received; negotiable and payable, without defalcation or discount.   MURRAY SIMPSON.

Note Payable in Merchandise.

$1,500.   CHESTER, VT., July 14, 18—.

For value received, on or before the first day of October next, we promise to pay H. Miller & Co., or order, Fifteen Hundred dollars, in good merchantable White Wheat, at our warehouse in this city, at the market value, on the maturity of this note.

ARMSTRONG & PHELPS.

Joint Note.

$900.00/100   SPRINGFIELD, ILL., May 10, 18—.

One year after date, we jointly and severally promise to pay Smith Fairbanks, or order, Nine Hundred and 50-100 dollars, for value received, with interest at ten per cent.

PAUL KENYON.
JACOB HAWKINS.

Form of a Note for Indiana.

$100.00/100   INDIANAPOLIS, IND., March 1, 18—.

On demand for value received, I promise to pay Clinton Briggs, or order, One Hundred and 50-100 dollars, with interest; payable without any relief whatever from valuation or appraisement.

DANIEL BURLINGAME.

Form of Guarantee.

For and in consideration of One Dollar, to me paid by H. B. Claflin & Co., of New York, who, at my request, purpose opening a credit with John Smith, of Aurora, Ill., I do hereby guarantee the payment to H. B. Claflin & Co., their successors and assigns, of all indebtedness which said John Smith has incurred or may incur for goods and merchandise sold to him, or delivered at his request, by said H. B. Claflin & Co., their successors and assigns, upon credit or for cash, or on note, or otherwise, without requiring any notice in respect thereto.

This guarantee to be open and continuing, covering all interest on any such indebtedness, and also any costs and expenses which may be incurred by H. B. Claflin & Co., their successors and assigns, in collecting.

Further, it shall remain in full force until revoked by a written notice from me, provided, however, that my liability hereunder for purchases made shall not at any time exceed $5,000.

Witness my hand and seal, }
New York, Jan. 1, 1878.   }   WM. H. HAWKINS.

DUE-BILLS.

Form of Due-Bill Payable in Money.

$100.   ROCHESTER, N. Y., Oct. 2, 18—.

Due Walter P. Kimball, or order, on demand, One Hundred dollars, value received.   C. T. MARSH.

Payable in Flour.

$400.   KALAMAZOO, MICH., Feb. 1, 18—.

Due on demand, to Sanford Burton, Four Hundred dollars, in Flour, at the market value when delivered.   Value received.

CHAS. H. WALKER.

Payable in Money and Merchandise.

$200.   KEOKUK, IOWA, May 19, 18—.

Due, on the 10th of June next, to A. B. Condit, or order, One Hundred dollars in cash, and One Hundred dollars in merchandise from our store.   BELDEN, GREEN & CO.

Payable in Merchandise.

$20.   WEST ARLINGTON, VT., April 9, 18—.

Due Wright Marsh, Twenty Dollars, in merchandise from our store.   R. T. HURD & CO.

STATE LAWS RELATING TO RATES OF INTEREST, AND PENALTIES FOR USURY.

States and Territories.	Legal Rate of Interest	Rate allowed by Contract.	Penalties for Usury.	States and Territories.	Legal Rate of Interest	Rate allowed by Contract.	Penalties for Usury.
	per cent	per cent.			per cent	per cent.	
Alabama	8	8	Forfeiture of entire interest.	Montana	10	Any rate.	
Arizona	10	Any rate.		Nebraska	7	10	Forfeiture of entire interest.
Arkansas	6	10	Forfeiture of prin'l and int.	Nevada	10	Any rate.	
California	7	Any rate.		New Hampshire	6	6	For. of thrice the ex. & costs
Colorado	10	Any rate.		New Jersey	6	6	Forfeiture of int. and costs.
Connecticut	6	Any rate.		New Mexico	6	12	Forfeiture of excess of int.
Dakota	7	12	Forfeiture of entire interest.	New York	6	6	Forfeiture of contract.
Delaware	6	6	Forfeiture of principal.	North Carolina	6	8	Forfeiture of entire interest.
Dist. of Columbia	6	10	Forfeiture of entire interest.	Ohio	6	8	For. of excess above 6%.
Florida	8	Any rate.		Ontario, Canada	6	Any rate.	
Georgia	7	8	Forfeiture of excess of int.	Oregon	8	10	For. of principal and int.
Idaho	10	18	Fine and imprisonment.	Pennsylvania	6	6	Forfeiture of excess of int.
Illinois	6	8	Forfeiture of entire interest.	Quebec, Canada	6	Any rate.	
Indiana	6	8	Forfeiture of excess of int.	Rhode Island	6	Any rate.	
Iowa	6	10	Ten pr ct. on entire contract.	South Carolina	7	7	Forfeiture of entire interest.
Kansas	7	12	For. of ex. of int. above 12%.	Tennessee	6	6	Forfeiture of excess of int.
Kentucky	6	6	Forfeiture of excess of int.	Texas	8	12	Forfeiture of all interest.
Louisiana	5	8	Forfeiture of entire interest.	Utah	10	Any rate.	
Maine	6	Any rate.		Vermont	6	6	Forfeiture of excess of int.
Maryland	6	6	Forfeiture of excess of int.	Virginia	6	6*	Forfeiture of entire interest.
Massachusetts	6	Any rate.		Wash. Territory	10	Any rate.	
Michigan	7	10	For. of ex. of int. above 7%.	West Virginia	6	6*	Forfeiture of excess of int.
Minnesota	7	10	Forfeiture of entire int.	Wisconsin	7	10	Forfeiture of entire interest.
Mississippi	6	10	Forfeiture of entire int.	Wyoming	12	Any rate.	
Missouri	6	10	Forfeiture of entire interest.				

* Except in cases defined by Statutes of the State.

STATE LAWS RELATING TO LIMITATION OF ACTIONS.

LIMIT OF TIME IN WHICH ACTION MAY BE BROUGHT ON THE FOLLOWING:

States and Territories.	Assault and slander.	Open Acc'ts.	Notes.	Judg-ment.	Sealed and witnessed Instruments.	States and Territories.	Assault and slander.	Open Acc'ts.	Notes.	Judg-ment.	Sealed and witnessed Instruments.
	Years.	Years.	Years.	Years.	Years.		Years.	Years.	Years.	Years.	Years.
Alabama	1	3	6	20	10	Montana	2	2	6	6	6
Arkansas	1	3	5	10	10	Nebraska	1	4	5	5	10
California	1	2	4	5	5	Nevada	2	4	4	5	4
Colorado	1	6	6	6	6	New Hampshire	2	6	6	20	20
Connecticut	1	6	6		17	New Jersey	2§	6	6	20	16
Dakota	2	6	6	20	20	New Mexico	3	4	6	13	6
Delaware	8	3	6	20	20	New York	2	6	6	20	20
District of Columbia	1	3	3	12	12	North Carolina	1†	3	3	10	10
Florida	2	8	5	20	20	Ohio	1	6	15	21	15
Georgia	1	4	6	7	20	Ontario (U. Canada)	2	6	6	10	10
Idaho	8	4	5	6	5	Oregon	2	6	6	10	10
Illinois	1	5	10	20	10	Pennsylvania	2	6	6	20	20
Indiana	2	6	10	10	10	Quebec (L. Canada)	1, 2	5	5	30	30
Iowa	2	5	10	20	10	Rhode Island	1	6	6	20	20
Kansas	1	3	5	5	15	South Carolina	2	6	6*	20	20
Kentucky	1	2	15	15	15	Tennessee	1	6	6	10	6
Louisiana	1	3	5	10	10	Texas	1	2	4	10	4‡
Maine	2	6	20*	20	20	Utah	1	2	4	5	4
Maryland	3	3	3	12	12	Vermont	1	6	14*	8	8
Massachusetts	2	6	20*	20	20	Virginia	5	5‡	5	10	20
Michigan	2	6	6	10		Washington Territory	2	3	6	6	6
Minnesota	2	6	6	10	6	West Virginia	1	5‖	10	10	10
Mississippi	1	3	6	7	6	Wisconsin	2	6	6	20	20
Missouri	2	5	10	20 ¶	10	Wyoming	1	4	5	5	5

* Promissory notes in Massachusetts, Maine, South Carolina and Vermont barred in six years, unless signed by attesting witnesses.
† Slander, 6 months.   § Assault. 4 years.   ‖ Store accounts, 2 years.
‡ Seals abolished.   ¶In certain courts, 20 years.   ‖ Store accounts, 3 years.

Rates of Interest.

Showing Accumulations of Interest on Moneys for Days, Months and Years.

HOW TO COMPUTE INTEREST ON ANY AMOUNT OF MONEY AT ANY RATE PER CENT.

On the following page will be found several valuable Interest Tables, giving the principal legal rates of interest as adopted by the various States in the Union, and the means by which the interest, at any rate, on any amount of money, can be almost instantly computed.

Explanation of Interest Tables.

By reference to the table on the following page, the *time* or number of days, months, and years, will be found at the top of the columns; and the *amount* of money upon which interest is computed, in the left hand column.

Thus: If we wish to find the interest on $1,108 for one year, 8 months, and 29 days, at 7 per cent we trace from *amounts* towards the right, and from *time*, downwards; resulting as shown in the accompanying example.

EXAMPLE.

Inter'st on $1000 for 1 year at 7 per cent.			$70.00
" " 100 " " " 7 " "			7.00
" " 8 " " " 7 " "			.56
" " 1000 " 8 m'hs " 7 " "			17.50
" " 100 " 8 " " 7 " "			1.75
" " 8 " 8 " " 7 " "			.14
" " 1000 " 29 days " 7 " "			5.64
" " 100 " 29 " " 7 " "			.56
" " 8 " 29 " " 7 " "			.05
Interest on the Amount............			$103.20

To find the interest for more than one year multiply by the number of years. For $20, $40, $60, etc., multiply the interest on $10, by 2, 4, and so on. The same rule applies for hundreds or thousands. The interest at five per cent is one-half of ten per cent; hence, divide by 2. The interest at 12 per cent is double 6 per cent; hence, multiply by 2. Other rates will be found thus by division and multiplication.

TABLES OF INTEREST.

INTEREST AT SIX PER CENT.

INTEREST AT SEVEN PER CENT.

INTEREST AT EIGHT PER CENT.

INTEREST AT TEN PER CENT.

BANK FORMS.

Importance of Keeping a Bank Account.

O business men or women, the keeping of a bank account is a matter of very considerable convenience, as well as pecuniary benefit. If much business is done, money is constantly accumulating, which is easily deposited, and is usually more secure from burglary in a reliable bank than elsewhere. It is true that money will sometimes be lost, through the robbery or failure of a bank; but of all the chances for loss which business people have to contend with, that by failure of banks is the least; while it is found that the practice of depositing each day's accumulations in a bank, having the same in readiness to draw whenever wanted, as a whole, works greatly to the advantage of people doing a large amount of business.

Of course, where the deposits are large, and the rates of interest are good, the banker is considerably benefited by having the use of the money. Bankers, however, realize their indebtedness to the customer, and in various ways, through their acquaintance and influence with wealthy men, often render such aid to their patrons in a time of need, as enables them to carry forward certain enterprises that would be found oftentimes very difficult to accomplish without such aid.

If it is intended, when depositing money in a bank, to allow the same to remain for several weeks or months, the banker will usually give the person so depositing a "Certificate of Deposit;" if, however, it is desired to draw the money out frequently, while daily, perhaps, adding more, the banker will present the depositor with a Pass Book, a Check Book, and Deposit Tickets. The Deposit Ticket is a blank form, which the customer will fill up, indicating when, as well as the amount, and kind of funds deposited. The following exhibits the form of a deposit ticket. That printed in Roman type represents the printed matter on the same; the wording in script illustrates what is written by the depositor, thus:

Deposit Ticket.

Deposited in THIRD NATIONAL BANK,		
By *George Smith*		
NEW YORK, *June 1*, 1873.		
Currency		*$5,500*
Checks		
	2,000	
	500	*2,500*
		$8,000

The Pass Book.

The Pass Book is a memorandum book, in which the receiving teller of a bank enters the date and amount of deposits. On the opposite page is shown the amounts drawn out. From time to time a balance is struck, showing the amount of deposits then in bank. The following shows the ordinary form of keeping the bank account:

Dr. THIRD NATIONAL BANK IN ac.		WITH GEORGE SMITH.		Cr.
1873.		1873.		
June 8 To Cash	8,000			800 10
" 10 "	1,400			400 15
" 15 "	800			840
July 7 "	150			1,010
" 30 "	5,000			3,000
				8,079 75
		Aug. 7 Balance		
	14,850	8 Vouch's rec'd	14,850	
Aug. 7 Balance	9,079 75			

The Check Book is a book of blank orders, or checks as they are called, with a margin on which to make a memorandum of date, amount, and to whom the check is given. When the check is filled, it goes to the bank where the individual giving the check deposits money, while the memorandum remains in the book. An idea of the check book may be obtained from the following:

Form of a Check Book.

No. 1.		
A. D. Brown,		
Clerk Hire.		
June 16, 1878.	800	10

No. 1. New York, *June 16*, 1873.

THIRD NATIONAL BANK,

Pay to *A. D. Brown,* or Order,

Eight Hundred .... $\frac{1}{100}$ Dollars,

800\frac{1}{100}$ *George Smith.*

No. 2.		
N. Y. Independent,		
for Advertising.		
July 1, 1878.	400	15

No. 2. New York, *July 1*, 1873.

THIRD NATIONAL BANK,

Pay to *New York Independent,* or Order,

Four Hundred .... $\frac{1}{100}$ Dollars,

400\frac{1}{100}$ *George Smith.*

No. 3.	
Am. Ex. Company,	
Freight acc.	
July 8, 1878.	560

No. 3. New York, *July 8*, 1873.

THIRD NATIONAL BANK,

Pay to *American Express Co.,* or Order,

Five Hundred and Sixty $\frac{00}{100}$ Dollars,

$560. *George Smith.*

No. 4.	
Brown & Jones,	
Ribbons and Laces,	
July 21, 1878.	1,010

No. 4. New York, *July 21*, 1873.

THIRD NATIONAL BANK,

Pay to *Brown & Jones,* or Order,

One Thousand and Ten $\frac{00}{100}$ Dollars,

$1,010. *George Smith.*

No. 5.	
Williams & Kent,	
Silks.	
August 7, 1878.	3,000

No. 5. New York, *August 7*, 1873.

THIRD NATIONAL BANK,

Pay to *Williams & Kent,* or Order,

Three Thousand .... $\frac{00}{100}$ Dollars,

$3,000. *George Smith.*

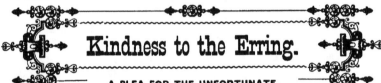

Kindness to the Erring.

A PLEA FOR THE UNFORTUNATE.

AN officer of the law you may be, and it becomes you to care for the prisoner in your charge. While law should be enforced, for the good of the criminal as well as the protection of society, it does not become you to be unkind. Perhaps investigation may prove that your prisoner is innocent and has been wrongly arrested. But if guilty, at most he is simply unfortunate. He had no power to say what qualities of mind he should inherit, what his temperament should be, or what training he should receive in infancy, all of which are usually determining causes that his man's destiny in after-life.

He stands before you largely the victim of unfortunate circumstances. He lacks the moral strength who others possess, and hence his weakness and his errors. True, he must pay the penalty of his transgression, but you can temper the administration of your government with such justice as will tend to the improvement and, possibly, the reformation of the criminal. Whatever the conduct of the prisoner, you should always rise superior to the feelings of passion or revenge.

In a thousand ways our paths in life will be crossed by those who commit errors. It will be easy to find fault; it will be natural to blame. But we must never forget that further back, far beyond our sight, lie causes that tended to produce these results.

Well may the mother look with deep anxiety upon the infant, wondering what destiny lies before it. Alas! that a mother's hopes and prayers often do not avail. Drifted away from parental control, the footsteps fall amid temptation, and a life of sorrow is the result.

We should never forget, in our treatment of the erring, that, were the mother present, she would plead with us to deal gently with her child. Very touchingly does the following poem ask that we be lenient for her sake:

Some Mother's Child.

AT home or away, in the alley or street,
Whenever I chance in this wide world to meet
A girl that is thoughtless, or a boy that is wild,
My heart echoes sadly, "'T is some mother's child!"

And when I see those o'er whom long years have rolled,
Whose hearts have grown hardened, whose spirits are cold—
Be it woman all fallen, or man all defiled,
A voice whispers sadly, "Ah! some mother's child!"

No matter how far from the right she hath strayed;
No matter what inroads dishonor hath made;
No matter what element cankered the pearl—
Though tarnished and sullied, she's some mother's girl.

No matter how wayward his footsteps have been;
No matter how deep he is sunken in sin;
No matter how low is his standard of joy—
Though guilty and loathsome, he's some mother's boy.

That head hath been pillowed on tenderest breast;
That form hath been wept o'er, those lips have been pressed;
That soul hath been prayed for in tones sweet and mild;
For her sake deal gently with "some mother's child."

WHILE error must be deplored and virtue ever commended, we should deal carefully and considerately with the erring, ever remembering that a myriad of untoward circumstances are continually weaving a network around the individual, fettering and binding a soul that otherwise would be white and pure.

It is a most fortunate circumstance for the child to be born of an excellent parentage, to be reared amid kindness, and to be guided in youth by wise counsels. Given all these favoring circumstances, and the chances are that the pathway in life will be honorable. Deprived of these advantages, the individual is likely to fall short in excellence in proportion as the circumstances have been unfavorable.

There are those who seemingly have only a smooth pathway in life. They were so fortunate as to be born with an excellently balanced organization of mind. They have no passion unduly in excess. They have no abnormal longings, no eccentricities, no weaknesses. Roses strew their way, and they live a life well rounded out and full of honor.

But while there are those who are apparently exempt from temptation, all are not so fortunate in ability, in strength of purpose and in power of will which may enable them to resist evil. Some are liable to easily err, and it will take, possibly, but a trivial circumstance to carry them aside. In the transgression they will get their punishment—they will suffer sufficiently. It does not become the more fortunate, therefore, to take too much credit to themselves for being more virtuous and free from error. It is vastly more noble and charitable to extend sympathy and compassion. This sentiment is well expressed in the following poem, by Millie C. Pomeroy.

You Had a Smooth Path.

ONE morning, when I went to school,
In the long-vanished Yesterday,
I found the creek had burst its banks,
And spilled its waters o'er my way.
The little path was filled with mud;
I tried to cross it on a log;
My foot slipped, and I, helpless, fell
Into a mass of miry bog.

My clothes were pitiful to see;
My hands and face were covered quite.
The children laughed right heartily,
And jeered me when I came in sight.
Sweet Jessie Brown, in snow-white dress,
Stood, smiling, by the teacher's desk,
The while he, gravely as he might,
Inquired the secret of my plight.

Then Jessie shook her snow-white dress,
And said, "What will you give to me
For coming here so nice and clean?
My very shoes from dirt are free."
The tutor frowned, and answered her,
"You merit no reward to-day;
Your clothes and hands are clean, because
You had a smooth path all the way."

And so, I think, when children grown
Are white in grace or black with sin,
We should not judge until we know
The path fate had them travel in;
For some are led on sunny heights,
Beyond the power of Sin to sway;
While others grope in darksome paths,
And face temptation all the way.

large city, can generally buy, of their home bank, drafts, thus, on the nearest metropolis, by the payment of the exchange.

The object in purchasing a draft is to avoid the danger of loss when sending money from one part of the country to another. Such form is worded as follows, and is known as a bank draft.

Form of a Bank Draft.

$150. 251537 No. 84.

First National Bank,

Aurora, Ill., May 6, 187 .

Pay to the order of Allen C. Green,

One Hundred and Fifty Dollars

DUPLICATE UNPAID.

E. A. Bradley, Cashier.

To Union Nat'. Bank, Chicago.

In making collections of money, drafts are frequently used, which are usually sent through the banks. A sight draft is used where the person upon whom it is drawn is expected to pay the debt immediately. In the time draft the same is made payable in a certain number of days.

Sight Draft.

$400.   CINCINNATI, O., June 10, 18—.
       At sight, pay to the order of Higgins & Co., Four Hun-
dred Dol' rs, value received, and charge the same to our account.
To B. L. SMITH, Milwaukee, Wis.   POLLOK BROS. & CO.

Time Draft.

$50.   MEMPHIS, TENN., April 4, 18—.
       Thirty days after date, pay to the order of Cobb & Co.,
Fifty Dollars, value received, and charge to our account.
To HARMON, MOSHER & Co.,   A. B. MOORE & CO.
       Buffalo, N. Y

Acceptance.

The acceptance of a draft is effected by the drawee, or the person upon whom the same is drawn, if he consents to its payment, writing across the face of the draft, thus: "Accepted, June 12, 1873. B. L. Smith."

LAWS OF GRACE ON SIGHT DRAFTS.

Grace on Sight Drafts is ALLOWED in the following States:

Alabama,	Nebraska,
Arkansas,	New Hampshire,
Dakota,	New Jersey,
Indiana,	North Carolina,
Iowa,	Oregon,
Kentucky,	Rhode Island,
Maine,	South Carolina,
Massachusetts,	Utah,
Michigan,	Wisconsin,
Minnesota,	Wyoming,
Mississippi,	Canada.
Montana,	

Grace on Sight Drafts is NOT ALLOWED in the following States:

California,	Maryland,
Colorado.	Missouri,
Connecticut,	Nevada,
Delaware,	New York,
District of Columbia,	Ohio,
Florida,	Pennsylvania,
Georgia,	Tennessee,
Idaho,	Texas,
Illinois,	Vermont,
Kansas,	Virginia,
Louisiana,	West Virginia.

Forms of Book-Keeping.

RULES, DIRECTIONS, AND FORMS FOR KEEPING BOOKS OF ACCOUNT.

EVERY person having occasion to keep an account with others, is greatly benefited by a knowledge of book-keeping. There are two systems of keeping books in use: one known as SINGLE ENTRY; the other, as DOUBLE ENTRY.

In this chapter it is the design to give simply an outline of Single Entry, a method of keeping books which answers every purpose with the majority of people, besides being a system so plain and simple as to be readily comprehended.

The books used in Single Entry are generally a Day-book, in which are recorded each day's sale of goods, or labor performed, and money, service, or goods received; and a Ledger, in which the sum total of each transaction is put in its proper place, so arranged as to show, on a brief examination, how the account stands. These books, of different sizes, may be found at the bookstores; though, in case of necessity, they can easily be made with a few sheets of foolscap paper, ruled as hereafter shown.

Persons having many dealings with customers should use a Day-book, in which is written each transaction; these being afterwards transferred to the Ledger. Where, however, accounts are few, the account may be made complete in the Ledger, as shown in several forms on the following page.

In making charges in a book and giving credit, it is necessary to keep clearly in mind whether the person of whom we write *gives* or *receives*. If the individual *gives* he is a *creditor*, which is designated by the abbreviation, **Cr.** If the person receives, he is a *Debtor*, the sign for which is **Dr.** In the passage from the creditor *to* the debtor of any article, we get the word "**To**," with which the creditor commences the account. In the reception *by* a debtor of an article from a creditor, we get the word "**By**."

The following forms show the manner of keeping an account by Arthur Williams, a merchant, with Chas. B. Strong, a farmer, who buys goods and settles his bills, usually, at the end of every month; in the meantime taking to the store various kinds of produce, for which the merchant gives credit according to the market value. Mr. Williams keeps two books, a Day-book and Ledger.

DAY BOOK.

Saturday, July 10, 1875. 14

66	Chas. B. Strong,	**Dr.**		
	To 1 lb. Tea,	$1.25		
	" 10 " Sugar, 10c.	1.00	2	25

Monday, July 19, 1875. 38

66	Chas. B. Strong,	**Dr.**		
	To 20 Yds. Calico, 10c.	2.00		
	" 1 Scoop Shovel,	1.25	3	25
	Cr.			
66	By 2 Bu. Potatoes, 80c.	1.60		
	" 10 Lbs. Butter, 25c.	2.50	4	10

Saturday, July 24, 1875. 80

66	Chas. B. Strong,	**Dr.**		
	To 1 Pr. Rubber Boots,			
	Per D. Wilcox,	7.00	7	00

Friday, July 30, 1875. 84

66	Chas. B. Strong,	*Cr.*		
	By Cash, to Balance Account,		8	40

LEDGER.

Dr.		Charles B. Strong.				**Cr.**	66

1875						1875				
July	10	To D	14	2	25	July	19	By D	38	4	10
"	19	" "	38	3	25	"	30	" "	84	8	40
"	24	" "	80	7	00						
				12	50					12	50

Remarks Concerning the Ledger.

AS will be seen by the example in the Ledger, the first column contains months; second, day of the month; third, "To D" means To Day-book. In the fourth column, the 14, 38, and 80 refer to the No. of the page in the Day-book which by reference fully explains the transaction. The fifth and sixth columns contain the totals of each purchase or sale as recorded in the Day-book. The Ledger should have an index in the first part which, under the head of S, will contain "*Strong, Chas. B.,*" opposite which is the number 66, showing that Strong's account may be found on page 66 of the Ledger. When the account is balanced and closed, a sloping line is drawn down the space containing the least writing and double lines are made beneath the totals, indicating that the account is "closed."

The Day-Book.

In the foregoing example only Chas. B. Strong's account is shown on a page of the Day-book. This is, however, a long book usually, each page being of sufficient length to contain the accounts of several customers. At the top of each page, the day of the week, day of the month, and year, should always be written. If the day's entries commence in the middle of the page, write the day of the week and day of the month distinctly above the first, and thus at the beginning of each day's entries.

When the total of the entry on the Day-book is transferred to the Ledger, the No. of the page in the Ledger where the account is kept, is placed beside the entry in the Day-book, which shows that the account has been "posted" to the Ledger.

Importance of Book-Keeping.

TRANGE as it may seem, there are but very few people who can keep the simplest form of account correctly. Most individuals are evidently deterred from learning correct forms, from the supposition that the art of book-keeping is difficult to master. The fact is, however, all the book-keeping necessary to be understood by people having few accounts, is very easily learned, as will be seen by studying, for a little time, the accompanying forms.

The importance of this knowledge cannot be over-estimated.

THE MERCHANT

who is successful in business, keeps his accounts in a form so condensed and clear, that his assets and liabilities can be determined in a few minutes of examination.

THE FARMER

who would be prosperous keeps his books in such a manner, that he can tell at a glance what product is most profitable to raise, what he owes, and what is due him from any source.

THE MECHANIC

who keeps himself free from litigation, and conducts his business successfully, has his dealings all clearly expressed in his accounts, and settles with his customers, if possible, once a month.

THE TREASURER

of an association, whose accounts are clear, explicit, and correct, is justly appreciated for the evident honesty of the financial exhibit, and is selected for other places of responsibility and trust.

THE HOUSEKEEPER

who avoids misunderstandings with her servants, has her account written so clearly that no mistake is made, and no ill feeling is thus engendered in her settlements.

ALL PERSONS,

in short, who have occasion to keep accounts with others, should have a plain condensed form, which will show at a glance how the account stands.

The accompanying forms show the correct methods of keeping accounts in the Ledger, according to the established principles of book-keeping by Single Entry.

Farmer's Account with the Merchant.—Chas. B. Strong, having but few accounts, requires only the Ledger in which to keep them. He records his transactions with the merchant as follows:

Dr.			ARTHUR WILLIAMS.				Cr.		
1875						1875			
July	19	To 2 Bu. Potatoes, 80c.	1	60	July	10	By 1 Lb. Tea,	1	25
"	19	" 10 Lbs. Butter, 25c.	2	50	"	10	" 10 " Sugar, 10c.	1	00
"	30	" CASH, TO BALANCE.	8	40	"	19	" 20 Yds. Calico, 10c.	2	00
					"	19	" 1 Scoop Shovel,	1	25
					"	24	" 1 Pair Rubber Boots,	7	00
			12	50				12	50

Farmer's Account with Hired Man.—A Memorandum in the back part of the Ledger should state the contract between the farmer and hired man. The Ledger shows how the account stands.

Dr.			HENRY WELLS.				Cr.		
1875						1875			
April	4	To 1 Pair of Boots.	17	50	July	8	By 4 Months Labor at 16.00	64	00
"	24	" Wm. Wells, for Clothing,	11	00	Aug.	31	" 3 " " " 10.00	30	00
May	18	" R. R. Ticket to Boston,	6	00	Sept.	8	" 8 Days " " 1.00	8	00
July	4	" Cash,	8	00					
Sept.	30	" NOTE AT 3 MOS. TO BAL.	50	00					
			92	00				92	00

Farmer's Account with Crops.—That the farmer may know the profit on any of his crops, he may keep an account as follows. In like manner, an account may be kept with any enterprise.

Dr.			Aco't with Cornfield ; 16 Acres.				Cr.		
1876.						1876.			
May	4	To 6 Days Plowing, 2.50	15	00	Oct.	12	By Stalks for Fodder,	30	00
"	10	" 4 " Harrowing, 2.00	8	00	"	16	" Husks for Beds,	20	00
"	14	" 2 " Planting, 1.00	2	00	1877.	90	" " " Mats,	8	00
"	14	" 4 Bu. Seed Corn,	4	00	Mar.	15	" 800 Bushels Corn, 50c.	400	00
"	25	" 3 Days Cultivating, 2.00	6	00					
June	10	" 3 " 3.00	9	00					
Sept.	12	" 10 " Cutting, 1.00	10	00					
Nov.	3	" Husking and Cribbing,	30	00					
1877.									
Mar.	4	" Shelling 800 Bushels,	22	00					
"	15	" Cost of Taking to Market,	38	00					
May	4	" Interest on the Land,	51	00					
"	4	" PROFITS ON THE CROP,	270	00					
			458	00				458	00

Blacksmith's Account with Farmer where Day-book and Ledger are Kept.
When the account is not settled at the end of the month, it may be "closed," and the balance carried over into the next month, as follows:

Dr.			JAMES H. WATSON.					Cr.		
1874.						1874.				
Aug.	12	To Shoeing 2 Horses.	7	4	00	Aug.	12	By 8 Bu. Potatoes, 80c.	7	3	40
"	18	" Repairing Wagon,	11	10	00	"	20	" 6 " Apples, 50c.	14	3	00
"	22	" Shoeing Horse,	12	2	00	"	24	" 1 Ton Hay,	15	9	00
"	24	" Mending Shovel,	12		50	Sept.	1	" BAL. TO NEW ACC.		1	10
				16	50					16	50
Sept.	1	To BAL. BRO'T DOWN,		1	10	Sept.	1	By 30 Lbs. Butter, 20c.	29	4	00
"	8	" Repairing Reaper,	30	8	00	"	17	" 2 Cds. Wood, 7.00	34	14	00
"	15	" Ironing Wagon,	42	17	00	"	30	" CASH, TO BALANCE,	50	11	10
				26	10					29	10

* The figures in this column refer to the number of the page in the Day-book ; a book in which should be fully recorded each day's transactions.

Book-Keeping for Housekeepers.—The following form of account, with the servant, is applicable to all domestic affairs; such as accounts with grocerymen, boarders, etc.

Dr.			MRS. ELLEN STRONG.				Cr.		
1873.						1873.			
June	17	To 8 Yds. Cotton Cloth, 10c.		80	June	8	By Washing and Ironing,	1	50
"	24	" Cash,		75	"	14	" Washing and Cleaning,	2	00
"	27	" 4 pairs Stockings, 25c.	1	00	"	21	" Cleaning Windows,	3	00
"	28	" CASH, TO BALANCE,	5	45	"	28	" Washing and Ironing,	1	50
			8	00				8	00

Book-Keeping for Treasurers and Others.—Treasurers of Societies are shown the correct method of keeping their accounts in the following form:

Dr.			Salem Lyceum in Aco't with Wm. Brown.				Cr.		
1872.						1872.			
Jan'y	1	To 6 Months Rent of Hall,	50	00	Jan.	1	By Cash from Last Year,	84	50
Mar.	6	" 2 Tons of Coal, 10.00	20	00	Mar.	10	" Dues,	140	00
April	10	" Lecture by J. Webb,	25	00	Nov.	10	" Initiation Fees,	44	00
Dec.	5	" Gas,	10	00	Dec.	1	" Dues	70	00
"	31	" 6 Months Rent of Hall,	50	00					
"	31	" BALANCE ON HAND,	183	50					
			338	50				338	50

ORDERS.

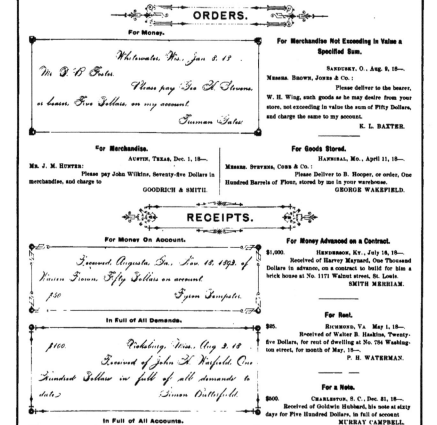

For Money.

Whitewater, Wis., Jan. 8, 18 .

Mr. P. B. Foster.

Please pay Geo. H. Stevens,
or bearer, Five Dollars, on my account.

Truman Gates.

For Merchandise Not Exceeding in Value a Specified Sum.

SANDUSKY, O., Aug. 9, 18—.

MESSRS. BROWN, JONES & CO.:

Please deliver to the bearer,
W. H. Wing, such goods as he may desire from your
store, not exceeding in value the sum of Fifty Dollars,
and charge the same to my account.

K. L. BAXTER.

For Merchandise.

AUSTIN, TEXAS, Dec. 1, 18—.

MR. J. M. HUNTER:

Please pay John Wilkins, Seventy-five Dollars in
merchandise, and charge to

GOODRICH & SMITH.

For Goods Stored.

HANNIBAL, MO., April 11, 18—.

MESSRS. STEVENS, COBB & CO.:

Please Deliver to B. Hooper, or order, One
Hundred Barrels of Flour, stored by me in your warehouse.

GEORGE WAKEFIELD.

RECEIPTS.

For Money On Account.

Received, Augusta, Ga., Nov. 18, 1893, of
Warren Flown, Fifty Dollars on account.

$50

Tyson Tempster.

For Money Advanced on a Contract.

$1,000.   HENDERSON, KY., July 16, 18—.

Received of Harvey Maynard, One Thousand
Dollars in advance, on a contract to build for him a
brick house at No. 1171 Walnut street, St. Louis.

SMITH MERRIAM.

In Full of All Demands.

$100.   Vicksburg, Miss., Aug. 3, 18

Received of John H. Warfield, One
Hundred Dollars in full of all demands to
date.

Simon Butterfield.

For Rent.

$25.   RICHMOND, VA. May 1, 18—.

Received of Walter B. Haskins, Twenty-
five Dollars, for rent of dwelling at No. 784 Washington street, for month of May, 18—.

P. H. WATERMAN.

For a Note.

$500.   CHARLESTON, S. C., Dec. 81, 18—.

Received of Goldwin Hubbard, his note at sixty
days for Five Hundred Dollars, in full of account

MURRAY CAMPBELL.

In Full of All Accounts.

$160.   Little Rock, Ark., Nov. 10, 18

Received of Barnard Rathbone, One
Hundred and Sixty Dollars in full of all
accounts

Smith, Steele & Co.

For a Note of Another Person.

$200.   PENSACOLA, FLA., May 2, 18—.

Received of Herbert Spencer, a note of
Robt. Hatfield, for the sum of Two Hundred Dollars,
which, when paid, will be in full of all demands to
date.

SAMPSON & COLLINS.

BILLS OF PURCHASE.

A Bill of Purchase is a statement of goods or wares bought at one time, embracing both the quantity and price of each article and the amount of the whole. If paid at the time of purchase, it should be receipted by the seller, as in the first of the following examples; if settled "by note" as in the second example, or if "charged on acc't," it may be so stated.

Forms of Bills of Purchase.

Racine, Wis., January 2, 1873

Mrs. Charles R. Smith,

     Bought of Mary A. Cummings,

2 Leghorn Hats,	@ $1.37,	$8.74
2 Pair Gloves,	" 1.62,	3.24
2 Pair Silk Hose,	" 1.00,	2.00
		$8.98

    Received Payment,

       Mary A. Cummings.

Danbury, Ct., Dec. 2, 1872.

Mr. Wm. W. Wells,

     Bought of David C. Hoyt,

24 Seamless Bags,	at .31,	$7.44
20 lbs. Brown Sugar,	" .07,	1.40
14 " Rice,	" .05,	.70
1 " Black Tea,	"	.75

Received Payment, by Note at 30 days. $10.29

     David C. Hoyt,

       per Wilder.

STATE CAPITOL BUILDING,
SPRINGFIELD, ILL.

Including Agreements, Arbitrations, Assignments, Affidavits, Acknowledg-
ments, Bills of Sale, Bills of Lading, Bonds, Corporation Charters,
Deeds, Guaranty, Leases, Licenses, Mortgages, Patents,
Pensions, Wills, Etc.,

Carefully Selected to the Latest Dates, Critically Examined by
the Best Legal Talent, and Adapted to the Requirements
of People in all Regions of the Country.

Forms of Agreements and Contracts.

An agreement is virtually a contract by which individuals, singly or collectively, agree to perform certain duties within a specified time.

It is of much importance, in all matters upon which may arise a difference of opinion or misunderstanding, that contracts be reduced very explicitly to writing, thereby frequently saving the parties to the contract a long and expensive law-suit.

Agreements should show that they are made for a lawful consideration, else they are void in law.

It is well to have a written agreement signed by a witness, though the witness need not know the contents of the document.

While a signature, or mark, written with a pencil, if proven by witnesses, is good in law, it is always safest to execute the contract with pen and ink.

A discovery of fraud, or misrepresentation by one party to the agreement, or changing of the date, renders the contract void.

Every agreement should state most distinctly the time within which its conditions are to be complied with.

Copies of an agreement should always be prepared in duplicate, and each party to the agreement should retain a copy.

General Form of Agreement.

THIS AGREEMENT, made the first day of August, 18—, between Isaac E. Hill, of Tarkio, county of Atchison, State of Missouri, of the first part, and Vardemon Blevins, of Fairfax, Mo., of the second part:

WITNESSETH, that the said Isaac E. Hill, in consideration of the agreement of the party of the second part, hereinafter contained, con-

tracts and agrees to and with the said Vardemon Blevins, that *he will deliver, in good and marketable condition, at the village of Corning, Mo., during the month of September, of this year, one hundred tons of prairie hay, in the following lots, and on the following specified terms; namely, twenty-five tons by the seventh of September, twenty-five tons additional by the fourteenth of the month, twenty-five tons more by the twenty-first, and the entire one hundred tons to be all delivered by the thirtieth of September.*

And the said Vardemon Blevins, in consideration of the prompt fulfillment of this contract, on the part of the party of the first part, contracts to and agrees with the said Isaac E. Hill, *to pay for said hay Six Dollars per ton, for each ton as soon as delivered.*

In case of failure of agreement by either of the parties hereto, it is hereby stipulated and agreed that the party so failing shall pay to the other *One Hundred Dollars* as fixed and settled damages.

In witness whereof, we have hereunto set our hands the day and year first above written.

ISAAC E. HILL,
VARDEMON BLEVINS.

Agreement to Convey Land By Deed.

ARTICLES OF AGREEMENT, made this seventh day of June in the year of our Lord one thousand eight hundred and seventy-three, between Luther Henderson, of Sandy Hill, Washington county, State of New York, party of the first part, and William W. Stewart, of Jamaica, county of Windham, State of Vermont, party of the second part:

WITNESSETH, that said party of the first part hereby covenants and agrees, that if the party of the second part shall first make the payment and perform the covenants hereinafter mentioned on his part to be made and performed, the said party of the first part will convey and assure to the party of the second part, in fee simple, clear of all incumbrances whatever, by a good and sufficient warranty deed, the following lot, piece, or parcel of ground, viz. : The west fifty-five (55) feet of the north half of lot number six (6) in block number three (3) Whitford's addition to Chicago, as recorded at Chicago, Cook county, Illinois.

And the said party of the second part hereby covenants and agrees to pay to said party of the first part the sum of One Thousand Dollars, in the manner following: Three Hundred Dollars, cash in hand paid, the receipt whereof is hereby acknowledged, and the balance in three annual payments, as follows, viz. : Two Hundred Dollars, June 7, 1874; Two Hundred Dollars, June 7, 1875; and Three Hundred Dollars, June 7, 1876; with interest at the rate of ten per centum per annum, payable on the dates above specified, annually, on the whole sum remaining from time to time unpaid, and to pay all taxes, assessments, or impositions that may be legally levied or imposed upon said lands subsequent to the year 1873. And in case of the failure of the said party of the second part to make either of the payments, or perform any of the covenants on his part hereby made and entered into, this contract shall, at the option of the party of the first part, be forfeited and determined, and the party of the second part shall forfeit all payments made by him on this contract, and such payments shall be retained by the said party of the first part, in full satisfaction and in liquidation of all damages by him sustained, and he shall have the right to re-enter and take possession of the premises aforesaid, with all the improvements and appurtenances thereon, paying said Wm. W. Stewart the appraised value of said improvements and appurtenances; said appraisement to be made by three arbitrators, one being chosen by each of the parties, the other being chosen by the first two.

It is mutually agreed that all the covenants and agreements herein contained shall extend to and be obligatory upon the heirs, executors, administrators and assigns of the respective parties.

In witness whereof, the parties to these presents have hereunto set their hands and seals, the day and year first above written.

Signed, sealed and delivered in presence of

HARTLY D. WELLS.

LUTHER HENDERSON, [L. S.]

WM. W. STEWART. [L. S.]

Agreement with Clerk for Services.

THIS AGREEMENT, made this fourteenth day of April, one thousand eight hundred and seventy-one, between Thomas Babcock, of Ohio City, county of Cuyahoga, State of Ohio, party of the first part, and Perley White, of Cleveland, county of Cuyahoga, State of Ohio, party of the second part:

WITNESSETH, that said Perley White agrees faithfully and diligently to work as clerk and salesman for the said Thomas Babcock, for and during the space of one year from the date hereof, should both live such length of time, without absenting himself from his occupation; during which time, he, the said White, in the store of said Babcock, of Ohio City, will carefully and honestly attend, doing and performing all duties as clerk and salesman aforesaid, in accordance and in all respects as directed and desired by the said Babcock.

In consideration of which services, so to be rendered by the said White, the said Babcock agrees to pay to said White the annual sum of Twelve Hundred Dollars, payable in twelve equal monthly payments each upon the last day of each month; provided that all dues for days of absence from business by said White shall be deducted from the sum otherwise by this agreement due and payable by the said Babcock to the said White.

Witness our hands.

THOMAS BABCOCK,
PERLEY WHITE.

Agreement for Building a House.

THIS AGREEMENT, made the tenth day of April, one thousand eight hundred and seventy-two, between Jesse Perry, of Germantown, county of Philadelphia, State of Pennsylvania, of the first part, and Abijah Howe, of the same town, county and State, of the second part:

WITNESSETH, that the said Jesse Perry, party of the first part, for considerations hereinafter named, contracts and agrees with the said Abijah Howe, party of the second part, his heirs, assigns and administrators, that he, the said Perry, will, within one hundred and twenty days, next following this date, in a good and workmanlike manner, and according to his best skill, well and substantially erect and finish a dwelling-house on lot number six, in block number nine, in Solomon's addition to Germantown, facing on Talpehocken street, which said house is to be of the following dimensions, with brick, stone, lumber and other materials, as are described in the plans and specifications hereto annexed.

[*Here describe the house, material for construction, and plans in full.*]

In consideration of which, the said Abijah Howe does, for himself and legal representatives, promise to the said Jesse Perry, his heirs, executors and assigns, to pay, or cause to be paid, to the said Perry, or his legal representatives, the sum of Seven Thousand Dollars, in manner as follows, to wit: One Thousand Dollars at the beginning of said work, One Thousand Dollars on the fifteenth day of May next, One Thousand Dollars on the first day of June next, Two Thousand Dollars on the first day of July next, and the remaining Two Thousand Dollars when the work shall be fully completed.

It is also agreed that the said Jesse Perry, or his legal representatives, shall furnish, at his or their own expense, all doors, blinds, glazed sash and window frames, according to the said plan, that may be necessary for the building of said house.

It is further agreed that in order to be entitled to said payments (the first one excepted, which is otherwise secured), the said Jesse Perry, or his legal representatives, shall, according to the architect's appraisement, have expended, in labor and material, the value of said payments, on the house, at the time of payment.

For failure to accomplish the faithful performance of the agreement aforesaid, the party so failing, his heirs, executors and assigns, agrees to forfeit and pay to the other party, or his legal representatives, the penal sum of Fifteen Hundred Dollars, as fixed and settled damages, within one month from the time of so failing.

In witness whereof, we have hereunto set our hands the year and day first above written.

JESSE PERRY,
ABIJAH HOWE.

Agreement for Sale and Delivery of Personal Property.

ARTICLES OF AGREEMENT, made this eighteenth day of June, in the year of our Lord one thousand eight hundred and seventy-three, between Arthur Belden, of Salem, Washington county, New York, party of the first part, and Lemuel Baldwin, of Jackson, Washington county, New York, party of the second part:

WITNESSETH, that the said party of the first part hereby covenants and agrees, that if the party of the second part shall first make the payments and perform the covenants hereinafter mentioned on his part to be made and performed, the said party of the second part will, on or before the first day of August next, deliver, in a clean and marketable condition, twelve hundred pounds of wool, of his own production, at the wool-house of Barnard & Cline, in Albany, New York. And the said party of the second part hereby covenants and agrees to pay to said party of the first part the sum of fifty-five cents per pound, in the manner following: One Hundred Dollars cash in hand paid, the receipt whereof is hereby acknowledged, and the balance at the time of delivery of said wool. And in case of the failure of the said party of the second part to make either of the payments, or perform any of the covenants on his part hereby made and entered into, this contract shall, at the option of the party of the first part, be forfeited and determined, and the party of the second part shall forfeit all payments made by him on this contract, and such payments shall be retained by the said party of the first part in full satisfaction and in liquidation of all damages by him sustained, and he shall have the right to take possession of said wool, remove, and sell the same elsewhere, as he may deem for his interest.

It is mutually agreed that all the covenants and agreements herein contained shall extend to and be obligatory upon the heirs, executors, administrators and assigns of the respective parties.

In witness whereof, the parties to these presents have hereunto set their hands the day and year first above written.

ARTHUR BELDEN,
LEMUEL BALDWIN.

ACKNOWLEDGMENTS.

TO ACKNOWLEDGE anything is to admit of its existence, whether it be any known fact or circumstance, or the confession of any sentiment or act known only to ourselves.

In law, an acknowledgment is the assent of any individual, in writing, made before a competent legal authority, that any document to which it is appended is true in fact, or that it is a voluntary act on the part of a person in transferring property or any personal right to another.

The law makes it necessary that persons who execute deeds for lands, or mortgages covering any property, should acknowledge the execution of the paper in order that it may be recorded.

An unmarried person's acknowledgment alone is sufficient on any legal document; but, if married, both husband and wife must sign the acknowledgment jointly, and the wife must also, in some States, make her voluntary and separate acknowledgment apart from her husband, wherever the sale or mortgaging of land is effected.

The forms of acknowledgments closely resemble each other, and but a few of them are here introduced as examples.

Examining Witnesses to a Deed, on Oath.

UPON THE BIBLE:

You do solemnly swear that you will true answers make to such questions as shall be put to you in regard to the parties to the deed here shown to you, and the execution thereof; so help you God.

HOLDING UP THE RIGHT HAND:

You do swear, in the presence of the everliving God, that you will true answers make to such questions as shall be put to you touching the parties to the deed here shown to you, and the execution thereof.

A Single Grantor's Acknowledgment.

STATE OF ILLINOIS, } ss.
County of Cook,

I, Martin Stone, a notary public for and within said county, in the State aforesaid, do hereby certify that Lewis Nott, personally known to me as the real person whose name is subscribed to the foregoing deed as having executed the same, appeared before me in person and acknowledged that he signed, sealed and delivered the said instrument of writing as his free and voluntary act, for the uses and purposes therein set forth.

Given under my hand and seal of office, this tenth day of December, A.D. 1882.

MARTIN STONE,
Notary Public.

[NOTARIAL SEAL]

Joint and Separate Acknowledgment of a Deed by Husband and Wife.

STATE OF ILLINOIS, } ss.
County of Cook,

Before me, Martin Stone, a notary public for and within said county, in the State aforesaid, appeared the above-named Elias Robinson and Rhoda E., his wife, both personally known to me as the real persons whose names are subscribed to the annexed deed, as having executed the same, and acknowledged that they signed, sealed and delivered the said instrument of writing as their free and voluntary act, for the use and purposes therein set forth.

And the said Rhoda E., wife of the said Elias Robinson, having been by me examined, separate and apart, and out of the hearing of her husband, and the contents and meaning of the said instrument of writing having been by me fully made known and explained to her; and she also by me being fully informed of her rights under the homestead laws of this State, acknowledged that she had freely and voluntarily executed the same, and relinquished her dower to the lands and tenements therein mentioned, and also all the rights and advantages under and by virtue of all laws of this State relating to the exemption of homesteads, without compulsion of her husband; and that she does not wish to retract the same.

Given under my hand and seal of office, this twelfth day of November, A.D. 1882.

MARTIN STONE,
Notary Public.

[NOTARIAL SEAL]

AFFIDAVITS.

AFFIDAVITS are of a confirmatory nature, and consist of written statements of facts, signed and sworn to (or affirmed) as true by the persons who make them. The cases in which they are used are numerous.

In courts of law or equity they are not testimony, because the makers of them (called affiants) are not cross-examined; but a false affiant may be punished as a perjurer, when the affidavit is required by law.

A Common Form of Affidavit, Attached to a Declaration of Any Kind.

STATE OF ILLINOIS, } ss.
County of Cook, }   CHICAGO, November 6, 1882

Then the above-named Jesse James personally appeared and made oath (or solemnly affirmed) that the foregoing declaration, by him subscribed, is true. Before me,

             GEORGE MOORE, Justice of the Peace.

Form of Affidavit of Publication of a Legal Notice.

STATE OF ILLINOIS, } ss.
County of Cook, }

FRITZ METER } In the Superior Court of the City of Chicago,
    vs. } Illinois, of November term, 1882.
GEORGE C. LOWE. }

Frank Smith, being duly sworn (or affirmed) according to law, says that he is the publisher of a weekly newspaper in the city of Chicago, in the county of Cook, and State of Illinois, called the *Chicago Clarion*, and that the above notice was published in his said newspaper for six consecutive weeks, the last publication of it being upon Saturday, November 18, A. D. 1882.

Sworn to (or affirmed) and subscribed before me, this twentieth day of November, A. D. 1882.

             MOSES WILLETT, Justice of the Peace.

Affidavit Requiring a Debtor to be Held to Bail.

STATE OF OHIO, } ss.
Cuyahoga County, }

EDWARD PLACE } In the Court of Common Pleas of Cleveland,
    vs. } of November term, A. D. 1882. No. 283.
ROBERT GRIMES. }

Edward Place, of Cleveland, in said county, butcher, on oath declares that he has a demand against the within-named Robert Grimes, upon the cause of action stated in the within writ, which he believes to be justly due, and upon which he expects that he will recover Twelve Dollars and fifty-three cents, or upwards; and that he

has reasonable cause to believe that the said Robert Grimes is about to depart beyond the jurisdiction of the court to which said writ is returnable, and not to return until after judgment may probably be recovered in said suit, so that he cannot be arrested on the first execution (if any) which may issue in said suit.

             EDWARD PLACE.

Subscribed and sworn to this twenty-second day of November, A. D. 1882. Before me,

             JOHN BROWN, Justice of the Peace.

Affidavit of a Creditor's Attorney, Requiring a Debtor to be Held to Bail.

STATE OF OHIO, } ss.
Cuyahoga County, }

EDWARD PLACE } In the Court of Common Pleas of Cleveland,
    vs. } of November term, A. D. 1882. No. 282
ROBERT GRIMES. }

George Phillips, of Cleveland, in said county, a lawyer and attorney of Edward Place, of said city, county and State, butcher, on oath declares that the said Edward Place has a demand against the within-named Robert Grimes, upon the cause of action stated in the within writ, which this deponent believes to be justly due, and upon which he expects that the said Edward Place will recover Twelve Dollars and fifty-three cents, or upwards; and that this deponent has reasonable cause to believe that the said Robert Grimes is about to depart beyond the jurisdiction of the court to which said writ is returnable, that is to say, into the Province of Ontario, Canada, and not to return till after judgment may probably be recovered in said suit, so that he cannot be arrested on the first execution (if any) which may issue in said suit.

             GEORGE PHILLIPS.

Subscribed and sworn to this twenty-third day of November, A. D. 1882. Before me,

[NOTARIAL SEAL]   QUARTUS K. RICE, Notary Public.

APPRENTICE FORMS.

AN APPRENTICE may be either a boy or a girl, usually not younger, if a lad, than fourteen years of age.

No child can be apprenticed for a term extending beyond his twenty-first birthday.

The usual motive for apprenticing children is that they may be thoroughly taught some honorable trade or calling, becoming perfectly familiar

with which, they may always be able to earn a livelihood and acquire wealth.

The methods of apprenticing children and for protecting their rights and interests are generally provided for in the laws of the several States. These methods differ but little, however, in any of the States.

No minor can alone bind himself or herself

to learn any trade or calling. The parents, guardians, or overseers of the poor must give their consent, and the child must be willing to be bound.

Any act or habit of the master that may be injurious to the morals or intellect of the apprentice is a sufficient cause for the proper authorities to dissolve the contract of apprenticeship. No apprentice, for instance, can be compelled to

work on Sundays, except in a case of absolute necessity.

Should the master die before the expiration of the apprenticeship, unless the contract includes the master's "executors and administrators," the apprentice is free to seek a new master.

The following forms will serve to indicate what is particularly expected of parents, children and masters.

Binding an Apprentice—A General Form.

THIS AGREEMENT, made this twenty-second day of November, A. D. 1882, between Parker Ellis, the father, and Allen Ellis, his son, aged fourteen years, both of Pittsburgh, in Allegheny county, and State of Pennsylvania, of the one part, and Marcus Moran, blacksmith, of the same place, of the other part, witnesseth:

That the said Allen Ellis, with the consent of his father, Parker Ellis, does by these presents bind himself out as an apprentice to the said Marcus Moran, to be taught and exercise and employ himself in the trade of a blacksmith, in which the said Marcus Moran is now engaged, and to live with and serve as an apprentice until the expiration of six years, ten months and four days from the date hereof. That during said time said Allen Ellis shall and will, to his best and utmost ability, skill and knowledge, intelligently and faithfully serve, and be just and true to his said master, keep his secrets and counsel, and everywhere, and at all times, shall obey his lawful commands. That he shall do and attempt no hurt to his said master, in person, goods, estate, or otherwise, nor willingly suffer injury to the same to be done by others, but forthwith give his said master notice when he shall have any knowledge of such injury done or about to be done. That he shall not convert to his own use or waste his said master's goods or money, nor suffer the same to be done by others. That he will not lend his master's goods or effects to any person or persons whomsoever, nor allow any one else to do so without his master's consent. That he will not buy or sell any merchandise of his own or of others, during his term of apprenticeship, without his master's permission. That he shall not play with cards or dice, nor take part in any unlawful games of skill or chance, whereby his master shall suffer loss or damage. That he shall not loiter about or in play-houses, theaters, saloons, or other disreputable resorts, nor visit them, except the business of his master shall require him to do so. That he shall not, at any time, willfully absent himself from his master's premises or service without leave. That in all things he will behave as a faithful apprentice ought to do throughout his term of service.

And the said Marcus Moran, in consideration of these premises and the sum of Twenty Dollars, the receipt whereof is hereby

acknowledged, does hereby promise, covenant and agree: That he will comfortably clothe and provide for the said Allen Ellis, his apprentice, and in sickness and in health supply him with sufficient and suitable food, lodging and medicine; and will instruct and teach his said apprentice, either by himself or others, whatever may be learned of the trade and mystery of blacksmithing during his said term of service. That he shall cause his said apprentice to be taught to read and write, and the elementary and compound rules of arithmetic and the rule of three. That he will, when the said term of apprenticeship shall legally expire, give the said Allen Ellis, over and above the clothing he shall then possess, the following articles of apparel (name them here particularly), of quality, fit, and suitable for his condition in life.

And for the true performance of all and singular the covenants and agreements aforesaid, the said parties bind themselves each to the other firmly by these presents.

In witness whereof the parties aforesaid have hereunto interchangeably set their hands the day and year first above written.

                                 (Apprentice) ALLEN ELLIS,
                                 (Master) MARCUS MORAN,
Witnesses, { SARAH ELLIS,   (Parent) PARKER ELLIS.
           { JOSEPH MORAN.

Consent of a Parent, indorsed on indentures of Apprenticeship.

I do hereby consent to, and approve of, the binding of my son, William Blair, as in the within indenture mentioned. Dated the twenty-second day of November, A. D. 1882.
                                           LOIS BLAIR.

Certificate of a Justice as to Death of the Father of an Apprentice.

I, Matthew Marr, a justice of the peace within and for the county of Cook and State of Illinois, residing in the town of Lake, in said county, do hereby certify that Thomas Blair, the father of the infant named in the within indenture, is dead (or has abandoned, and neglects to provide for, his family). Dated this twenty-second day of November, A. D. 1882.
                          MATTHEW MARR, Justice of the Peace.

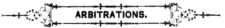

ARBITRATIONS.

THE SUBMISSION of any question concerning the rights of persons or personal property, by parties in dispute, to the decision of one or more disinterested individuals, mutually agreed upon, instead of taking the controversy before a court of law, is called an arbitration.

Both parties may have sufficient confidence in some one person to abide by his single decision. Usually, however, each party selects one individual, and the two thus appointed choose a third one, who is called the umpire, to assist them in forming their judgment. In such a case the decision is made either by all agreeing, or the agreement of two against the other, as may be provided in the submission.

The parties engaged in determining disputes in this manner are known as arbitrators.

The decision of the arbitrators is called an award.

Arbitrations, and their determination of cases, are sometimes regulated by the laws of the State in which they occur.

Arbitrations are not always voluntary on the part of the persons in dispute, for in some States one party may compel the other to refer the case to arbitrators, if he refuses to do so. This is called a reference.

The courts may also sometimes order a disputed case to be settled in this manner, with the consent of both parties.

A party cannot be compelled to agree to arbitrate, nor after he has signed the agreement can he, as a general rule, be compelled to select his arbitrators, nor after the arbitrators are appointed can he be compelled to submit his side of the case. But after a valid award has been made the courts will enforce it. Either party may recall his submission to arbitration, how-ever, at any time before the award is written out; but the party who thus recalls the arbitration is responsible for all the costs and damages that have accrued in consequence of his previous consent to submit his case to arbitrators.

If an award is illegal, unreasonable, incapable of being executed, or indecisive of any or all matters submitted to the arbitrators, it is not binding.

Beside the agreement to submit the questions in dispute, called a submission, the parties usually execute to each other, with sureties, a bond to abide by and perform the award, on which also a suit can be brought, if the award is not performed.

Arbitrations are customary in disputes relating to wages for services, current accounts, failures to fulfill contracts, partnerships, annuities in lieu of dower, land titles, boundaries and trespasses.

Awards may cover the payment of moneys, the fulfillment of agreements, the delivery of goods or writings, the assignment of mortgages and leases, and the specific conveyance of land, but not as to the title to land.

Form of Submission to Arbitration.

The following is the general form to be used in referring all matters in dispute between the parties at issue; the special form is used where the controversy is confined to one or two particular disagreements:

KNOW ALL MEN BY THESE PRESENTS, That we, the undersigned, hereby mutually agree to submit all the matters in difference between us, of every kind, name and nature, to the determination and award of Edward Blair, Edward R. Stimpson and Robert Merritt, of Villisca, Montgomery county, Iowa, as arbitrators. That said arbitrators, or any two of them, shall hear and determine the matters in dispute between us, and award the payment of all the costs and expenses incurred in such arbitration. That the said arbitrators shall make their award in writing on or before the tenth day of January, A. D. 1883. Done at Villisca, Iowa, December 1, A. D. 1882.

JOHN CLEVER, } Witnesses. T. S. WALLEY. }	MERRICK WELCH, SIMON J. GROVER.

Form for Special Arbitration.

KNOW ALL MEN BY THESE PRESENTS, That we, the undersigned, are partners doing business under the firm-name of Welch & Grover, at Villisca, Iowa, and are about to dissolve our partnership. That a controversy exists between us concerning the settlement of the firm business, and the business transactions and claims by and between us, subsequent to the twelfth day of June, A. D. 1882. That we hereby mutually agree to submit these matters in difference between us to the determination and award of, etc. (As in the form of general submission, to the end.)

[Other special grievances may be embodied in a similar form.]

Bond for Submission to Arbitration.

Each party in dispute executes this bond to the other, so that both are equally bound to submit to the award of their chosen arbitrators.

KNOW ALL MEN BY THESE PRESENTS, That I, Merrick Welch (or Simon J. Grover), of the town of Villisca, in the county of Montgomery, and State of Iowa, am held and firmly bound to Simon J. Grover (or Merrick Welch) in the sum of Two Thousand Dollars, for the payment of which I bind myself and my legal representatives by these presents.

The condition of this obligation is: That if the above bounden Merrick Welch (or Simon J. Grover), or his legal representatives shall submit, perform, and comply with the award, determination, judgment and orders of Edward Blair, Edgar R. Stimpson and Robert Merritt, the arbitrators named and selected by the said Merrick Welch and Simon J. Grover to award, determine, judge and order of and concerning the controversy existing between them, as partners, as to the settlement of the firm business and the business transactions and claims by and between them subsequent to the twelfth day of June, A. D. 1882 (with power to award payment of costs and expenses incurred in said arbitration), then this obligation shall be void; otherwise it shall remain in full force.

Sealed with my seal and dated this first day of December, 1882.

JOHN CLEVER, } Witnesses. T. S. WALLER, }	MERRICK WELCH, (Or SIMON J. GROVER.)

Sometimes the limitations of the time in which the arbitration award shall be made is embodied in the bond, as well as in the agreement of submission to the arbitration.

Form of Notice to Arbitrators.

EDWARD BLAIR, EDGAR R. STIMPSON and ROBERT MERRITT:

GENTLEMEN—You have been chosen arbitrators on behalf of the undersigned, to arbitrate and award between them, in such matters and things as set forth in their submission, which will be open to your inspection when you meet at the Runals House, in the village of Villisca, Iowa, on the second day of January, A. D. 1883, at ten o'clock in the forenoon, to hear the allegations and proofs of

Yours, etc.,

MERRICK WELCH,
SIMON J. GROVER.

Dated at Villisca, Iowa, this fifteenth day of December, A. D. 1882.

From of Subpœna of Witness.

The people of the State of Iowa, to Edmund W. Thomas and Samuel M. West: You, and each of you, are commanded personally to appear and attend at the Runals house, in the village of Villisca, in Montgomery county, Iowa, on the second day of January, A. D. 1883, at ten o'clock in the forenoon, before Edward Blair, Edgar R. Stimpson and Robert Merritt, of Villisca, arbitrators chosen to determine a controversy between Merrick Welch and Simon J. Grover, then and there to testify as a witness in relation thereto, before said arbitrators, on the part of the said Merrick Welch. Hereof fail not at your peril. Given under my hand, this twenty-sixth day of December, A. D. 1882.

ERICK LARSON, Justice of the Peace.

It is customary to allow fees to arbitrators for their services equal to those given referees appointed by courts of law to determine cases.

Form of Arbitrators' Oath.

Before entering upon their duties, the arbitrators should, if required by law or the submission, go before a judge of some court of record, or a justice of the peace, and make oath as follows:

You do severally swear, faithfully and fairly to hear and examine the matters in controversy between Merrick Welch, of the one part, and Simon J. Grover, of the other part, and to make a just award according to the best of your understanding. So help you God.

The arbitrators can administer the oath to witnesses before them, in the usual form of courts of law, when they are acting under the order of a court or statute.

General Form for the Arbitrators' Award.

KNOW ALL MEN BY THESE PRESENTS, that we, the undersigned, arbitrators of all matters in difference, of every kind, name and nature, between Merrick Welch and Simon J. Grover, by virtue of their agreement of submission of said matters, dated at Villisca, Iowa, on the first day of December, A. D. 1882, do award, order, judge and determine of and concerning the same as follows:

1. That, etc. } Plainly setting forth each point of difference be-
2. That, etc. } tween the parties, and the decision reached by the
3. That, etc. } arbitrators on each item, in accordance with law
4. That, etc. } and equity, and with the testimony presented.

In witness whereof, we have, in the presence of each other, here-unto set our hands this third day of January, A. D. 1883.

EDWARD BLAIR,
ROBERT MERRITT,
EDGAR R. STIMPSON.

Special Form of the Arbitrators' Award.

KNOW ALL MEN BY THESE PRESENTS, that we, the undersigned, arbitrators of the controversy existing between Merrick Welch and Simon J. Grover, partners, doing business at Villisca, Montgomery county, Iowa, under the firm-name of Welch & Grover, relative to a settlement of their firm business, and especially of the business transactions by and between them since the twelfth day of June, A. D. 1882, by virtue of their submission to us of the settlement of said matters, dated at Villisca, Iowa, on the first day of December, A. D. 1882, do award, judge and determine of and concerning the same as follows:

1. That the said partners are each equally liable for one-half of the indebtedness of said firm.

2. That each of ld partners is fully entitled to receive one-half of all profits accruing to their said business, if any there be, since the twelfth day of June, A. D. 1882.

3. That the copartnership heretofore existing between the said Welch and Grover be, and hereby is, fully dissolved from and after the date hereof.

4. That John Allen, of Villisca, Iowa, merchant, is hereby appointed and confirmed a receiver to take charge of all accounts and evidences of debt of said firm, and to sell to the best advantage, for cash, within one year, all the real estate and personal property of every kind, held and owned by said partners.

5. That the money realized from the sales of the said property by the receiver of the said firm shall be discreetly used only for the payment of the indebtedness of said firm of Welch & Grover, until the expiration of two years from this date, at which time the surplus funds arising from such sales, and remaining after the indebtedness of the said firm, is all paid (if any such surplus shall exist), shall be equally divided between said partners by the said receiver.

6. That the promissory note executed June 15, A. D. 1882, by the said Merrit Welch to the said Simon J. Grover, for the sum of One Thousand Dollars, which was given as a collateral security in a contingency which we, the said arbitrators, find did never exist, is declared void and uncollectable for want of a proper consideration therefor.

In witness whereof, we have, in the presence of each other, here-unto set our hands this third day of January, A. D. 1883.

EDWARD BLAIR,
EDGAR R. STIMPSON,
ROBERT MERRITT.

ASSIGNMENTS.

AN ASSIGNMENT is the act which transfers the title to a right of property. The act may be by words, accompanied by delivery of the thing assigned, or may be in writing.

Corporations, legally existing, may lawfully assign their interest in papers or property to other corporations, or to individuals.

The writing by which ownership is thus transferred is called an assignment.

An assignor is one who transfers his interest, right or title to another.

An assignee is one to whom a transfer is made.

Certain assignments must be in writing, as transfers of real estate.

All assignments relating to lands and tenements must be properly signed, sealed, acknowledged and recorded, like a deed.

The usual phrase in making an assignment is "assign, transfer and set over;" but the words, "give, grant, bargain and sell," will constitute an assignment.

Where property of any kind is assigned for the benefit of creditors, its immediate delivery to the assignee is required.

An assignment may convey the whole property absolutely, or in trust, or only an equitable right to the benefit of it, the legal title remaining in the assignor.

An assignment for the benefit of creditors may be at common law, or under a statute. At common law the assignor may prefer creditors. By statute he can not.

An assignment for the benefit of creditors must provide that the property be turned into cash and divided amongst creditors, and must not reserve any benefit to the assignor. Such an assignment should be of all the assignor's property liable to and not exempt from execution.

Under some insolvent and bankrupt acts, the adjudication itself that a person is a bankrupt transfers his property to the assignee.

When insured property is sold, the policy should be assigned to the purchaser. This can only be done with the consent of the insurer, to be indorsed on the policy. Forms for transfer of the policy and assent are usually printed on the policies.

No one except the person owning insured property at the time of the assignment can legally become the assignee of an insurance policy covering it, and then the consent of the insurers to the transfer must be obtained. Legal assignments can be made of copyrights, contracts, deeds, mortgages, bonds, leases, notes, drafts, accounts, judgments, all claims for money or wages, insurance, corporation shares, etc.

All property assigned must be distinctly described in the assignment, or the schedule attached thereto.

Stock in incorporated companies is assigned by an assignment on the back of the certificate, and by a transfer on the stock-book. Forms for this purpose are usually printed on the back of the certificate.

All assignments, except statutory, are contracts, and subject to the same law.

Thus, an assignment at common law for the benefit of creditors needs the assent of the creditors to make it valid.

Assignments for the benefit of creditors are now regulated by statute law in nearly every State.

An assignment of a debt or note carries with it all collaterals and securities.

A mortgage cannot be assigned without a transfer, at the same time, of the debt, note or bond. In addition, in some States, the land also should be conveyed as in the form below.

A Simple Assignment.

For value received, I hereby assign all my right, title and interest in the within contract to John Doe. Dated Chicago, November 17, A. D. 1882.

RICHARD ROE.

Assignment of Wages.

KNOW ALL MEN BY THESE PRESENTS, That I, Myrick J. Lasley, of Riverside, Cook county, and State of Illinois, in consideration of Fifty Dollars, the receipt of which I acknowledge, do hereby assign, transfer and set over to George Z. Bassett, of the same place, all claims and demands which I now have, and all which at any time between the date hereof and the seventeenth day of January next, A. D. 1883, I may or shall have against Cooper Donelson for all sums of money due, or to become due to me, as engineer in his factory; that I do hereby appoint and constitute said George Z. Bassett, and his assigns, my attorney irrevocable, to do and perform all acts, matters and things in the premises in like manner, and to all intents and purposes, as I could if personally present.

In witness whereof I have hereunto set my hand this seventeenth day of November, A. D. 1882.

F. O. BUCK, Witness.   MYRICK J. LASLEY.

[*The above form is proper for all assignments of rights.*]

Form of Assignment of a Mortgage.

KNOW ALL MEN BY THESE PRESENTS, That whereas Donald Cooper, of the town of Aurora, in Kane county, and State of Illinois, on the fifth day of August, A. D. 1881, by his deed of mortgage of that date, for the consideration of One Thousand Dollars, did grant, bargain, sell and convey unto me, Cameron Smith, of Chicago, in Cook county and State of Illinois, my heirs and assigns, all and singular the real estate (minutely described); to have and to hold the same to me, the said Cameron Smith, my heirs and assigns, forever, upon condition (here insert the conditions of the mortgage). Now, therefore, I, the said Cameron Smith, in consideration of the sum of One Thousand Dollars, to me in hand paid before the ensealing hereof, do by these presents sell, assign, transfer, and set over unto William Anderson, of Aurora, in Kane county and State of Illinois, his heirs and assigns, forever, the mortgage, debt, notes, and bonds, and the said (premises or property), to have and to hold the same to him, the said William Anderson, his heirs and assigns, forever, as fully, and in as ample a manner as I, the said Cameron Smith, my heirs or assigns, might hold and enjoy the same by virtue of the mortgage deed aforesaid, and not otherwise.

And I do, for myself, my heirs, executors, and administrators, hereby authorize and empower the said William Anderson, his heirs, executors, and administrators, to receive to his and their own use the sum or sums mentioned in the condition of said deed whenever the same shall be tendered or paid to him, or them, by the said Donald Cooper, his heirs, executors, or administrators, agreeably thereto, and to discharge the said mortgage, or to take and pursue such other steps and means for recovery of the said sum or sums, with the interest, by the sale of the said mortgaged premises, or otherwise, as by law are provided, as fully to all intents and purposes as I, the said Cameron Smith, my heirs, executors, or administrators, might or could do.

And I do, for myself, my heirs, executors, and administrators, covenant with the said William Anderson, his heirs and assigns, that I have good right to assign the said mortgage, debt, and premises as aforesaid, that there is now due thereon ——Dollars; and that he, the said William Anderson, shall and may have, hold, occupy, possess, and enjoy the same (subject, however, to the right of redemption, as by law in such cases is provided), against the lawful claim of all persons.

In witness whereof I have hereunto set my hand and seal this eighteenth day of November, A. D. 1882.

In presence of   }
JOHN JONES,   }   CAMERON SMITH. [L. S.]
GEORGE DAVIS.   }

[*The above should be acknowledged the same as a deed.*]

Form of Assignment of a Lease.

KNOW ALL MEN BY THESE PRESENTS, That I, Jacob Spencer, of Chicago, in Cook county, and State of Illinois, for and in consideration of Two Hundred Dollars, to me duly paid by George J. Watson, of the same city, county and State, do by these presents grant, convey, assign, transfer and set over unto said George J. Watson a certain instrument of lease, bearing date the first day of May, A. D. 1882, executed by Andrew Knox, of the same city, county and State, to me for a term of two years, reserving unto said Andrew Knox the yearly rent of One Hundred and Eight Dollars, payable monthly.

That this assignment shall take effect on the first day of November, A. D. 1882, to continue during all the remainder of said term of two years, subject, nevertheless, to the rents, covenants, conditions and provisions in said lease mentioned.

That I do covenant, promise and agree, that I, Jacob Spencer aforesaid, am now in the full enjoyment and possession of said premises, and that they are now free and clear of all assessments, assignments, back-rents, bargains, demands, taxes, and all other encumbrances tending to disturb the peaceful enjoyment of said premises by the said George J. Watson during the unexpired term of this said lease.

In witness whereof I have hereunto set my hand and seal this eighteenth day of September, A. D. 1882.

In presence of   }
ROBERT SCOTT,   }   JACOB SPENCER. [L. S.]
MICHAEL KANE.   }

Assignment of an Insurance Policy.

KNOW ALL MEN BY THESE PRESENTS, That having sold and conveyed the insured property within mentioned to George M. Porter, of Evanston, Cook county and State of Illinois, his heirs and assigns forever, I do hereby, for and in consideration of the sum of One Dollar, to me in hand paid by the said George M. Porter, assign and transfer the within policy of insurance to him, his executors, administrators, and assigns; and the said George M. Porter, by subscribing this assignment, makes himself responsible for all the agreements to which I have bound myself by the within policy.

Witness our hands and seals, at Chicago, Cook county and State of Illinois, this twenty-first day of November, A. D. 1882.

Signed, sealed and delivered }
in presence of   }   HENRY SILL. —(SEAL)—
BARTLETT C. CHAUNCEY,   }   GEORGE M. PORTER. —(SEAL)—
THOMAS W. EDMUNDS.   }

Assignment of Stock of Railroad and Other Corporations.

KNOW ALL MEN BY THESE PRESENTS, That I, Charles Ross, of Sycamore, De Kalb county, and State of Illinois, for and in consideration of Ten Thousand Dollars, to me duly paid by Mortimer M. Elliott, of Aurora, Kane county, and State of Illinois, do hereby assign, convey, transfer and set over unto said Mortimer M. Elliott all my right, title and interest in the shares, scrip and capital stock and property of the corporation and concern known as the Pullman & Burlington Railroad company, which company has its place of business at Chicago, in Cook county, and State of Illinois. And I further covenant and agree to and with the said Mortimer M. Elliott, his executors, administrators, and assigns, that, at the request of him or them, I and my executors, administrators and assigns, shall and will at all times hereafter execute any instrument that may be necessary to vest completely in him or them all my rights, title and interest to said property, scrip and stock, and to enable him or them to possess, control, enjoy and transfer all the property and choses in action herein assigned, or intended to be assigned.

In witness whereof, I hereunto affix my hand and seal, at Sycamore, De Kalb county, and State of Illinois, this twenty-first day of November, A. D. 1883.

Signed, sealed and delivered }
in presence of   }   CHARLES ROSS. [L. S.]
ROBERT FLAGG,   }
WILLIAM B. SMITH.   }

Form of Assignment of a Patent.

KNOW ALL MEN BY THESE PRESENTS, That in consideration of One Thousand Dollars, to me in hand paid by Norman Endicott, of the city of Rochester, in the county of Genesee, and State of New York, I do hereby sell and assign to the said Norman Endicott all my right, title and interest in and to the letters patent of the United States, No. 100,000, for an improvement in hydraulic engines, granted to me September twenty-one, A. D. 1882, the same to be held and enjoyed by the said Norman Endicott to the full end of the term for which said letters patent are granted, as fully and entirely as the same would have been held and enjoyed by me if this assignment and sale had not been made.

Witness my hand and seal this twenty-first day of November, A. D. 1882, at the city of Buffalo, in the county of Erie, and State of New York.

In presence of   }
SILAS W. JONES,   }   SOLOMON TIBBS. [L. S.]
ROBERT SCOTT.   }

Form of Assignment of the Copyright of a Book.

KNOW ALL MEN BY THESE PRESENTS, That in consideration of the sum of Three Thousand Dollars, to me in hand paid by Josiah Allen and Joshua Billings, partners and publishers, doing business at Boston, in the county of Suffolk, and State of Massachusetts, I do hereby sell and assign the copyright heretofore taken out by me for the book entitled "Cottage Papers: A Literary Miscellany for All Ages," of which I am the author and proprietor, the certificate of which copyright is annexed to this assignment, with all my literary property, right, title and interest in and to said book, and all the profit, benefit, or advantage that shall or may arise from printing, publishing and vending the same in all the States and Territories of the United States of America, to hold and enjoy the same during the full end and term for which the said copyright has been issued.

In witness whereof, at Chicago, in Cook county, and State of Illinois, I have hereunto affixed my hand and seal this twenty-first day of November, A. D. 1882.

In presence of }
ROGER RIDERHOOD, }   MATTHEW HAWTHORN. [L. S.]
JOHN HARMON. }

NOTE.—To the foregoing assignment must be securely fastened either the original, or a properly certified copy, of the certificate of copyright for said book, issued by the librarian of Congress at Washington.

Assignments of patent and copyrights should be acknowledged and recorded in the patent office, Washington, D. C.

Assignment by a Debtor, for the Benefit of His Creditors.

KNOW ALL MEN BY THESE PRESENTS, that this assignment, made this twenty-first day of November, A. D. 1882, by Norton Norris, of Salamanca, in the county of Gregory, and State of Tennessee, dealer in general merchandise, of the first part, and Hiram Hunt, of the same place, of the second part, and the several persons, creditors of the said party of the first part, who have executed or shall hereafter execute or accede to these presents, of the third part, witnesseth:

That whereas the said party of the first part is justly indebted in considerable sums of money, and has become unable to pay and discharge the same with punctuality, or in full; and that he, the said Norris Norton, is now desirous of making a fair and equitable distribution of his property and effects among his creditors: Now, therefore, the said party of the first part, in consideration of the premises, and of the sum of One Dollar, to him in hand paid by the party of the second part, the receipt whereof is hereby acknowledged, has bargained, granted and sold, released, assigned, transferred, and set over and by these presents does grant, bargain and sell, release, assign, transfer, and set over unto the said party of the second part, and to his heirs and assigns forever, all and singular, his lands tenements, hereditaments, goods, chattels and choses in action, of every name, nature and description, wheresoever the same may be, more particularly enumerated and described in the schedule hereunto annexed, marked "Schedule 1," excepting and reserving such property only as is exempted by law from attachment; to have and to hold the same unto the said party of the second part, his heirs and assigns; but in trust and confidence, nevertheless, to sell and dispose of the said real and personal estate, and to collect the said choses in action, and sell and dispose of the same for cash upon such terms and conditions as in his judgment may appear best, and most for the interest of the parties concerned, making sales thereof for cash or on credit, at public auction, or by private contract, and with the right to compound for the said choses in action, accepting a part of the value thereof for the whole, where the trustee shall deem it expedient so to do; and then, *in trust*, to dispose of the proceeds of the said property in the manner following, to wit:

First. To pay all such debts as by the laws of the United States are entitled to a preference in such cases.

Second. To pay and discharge all the just and reasonable expenses, costs and charges of executing this assignment, and of carrying into effect the trust hereby created, including the lawful commissions of the party of the second part for his services in executing the said trust.

Third. To distribute and pay the remainder of said proceeds to the creditors of the said party of the first part, for all debts and liabilities which he may owe, or for which he may lawfully be held responsible, to any person whomsoever; provided, that should the proceeds arising from the sale of his assets not be sufficient to pay all his indebtedness, then the said debts are to be paid ratably and in proportion.

Fourth. The residue and remainder of the proceeds of said sales and disposal of the assets of the party of the first part, if any there be, after paying all his debts in full, shall be repaid to him, the said party of the first part, his executors, administrators or assigns.

And the said party of the first part, for the better execution of these presents, and of the several trusts hereby reposed, does hereby make, nominate and appoint the said party of the second part, and his executors, administrators and assigns, his true and lawful attorney irrevocable, with full power and authority to do, transact and perform all acts, deeds, matters and things which can or may be necessary in the premises, as fully and completely as the said party of the first part might or could do, were these presents not executed; and also for the purposes aforesaid, or for any of them, to make, constitute and appoint one or more attorneys under him, and at his pleasure to revoke the same; hereby ratifying and confirming whatever the said party of the second part, or his substitute, shall lawfully do in the premises.

And the party of the second part, hereby accepting these trusts, covenants to and with each of the other parties hereto, to execute the same faithfully; and that this covenant shall be as binding upon his executors, administrators and assigns as it is upon himself.

In witness whereof the parties to these presents have hereunto set their hands and seals the day and year first above written.

In presence of }
URIAH WELCH, }   NORTON NORRIS,-(SEAL)-
DAVID T. ELLIS. }   HIRAM HUNT,-(SEAL)-

Creditors assent by proving their debts or filing the same with the assignee As it conveys real estate, it should be acknowledged and recorded as a deed.

BAIL.

THE WORD BAIL, in law, has very much the same meaning as "guaranty," and is a voucher by a competent person, or persons, that another person will perform a duty required by the civil authority.

The effect of such a voucher, or guaranty, is to temporarily set free, liberate, or release from custody a person, or persons, charged with the infraction of some public law.

In law, such a guaranty is called a recognizance, the surety being the bailor, and the prisoner the bailee.

The bailor usually engages, under the penalty of paying a certain sum of money, in case of forfeiture, that the bailee will be present and submit himself peaceably to the court whenever his trial or examination is appointed, and patiently abide the issue thereof.

In case a prisoner who has been bailed out of custody does not appear for trial at the time specified in the bail-bond, the surety forfeits whatever sum is thereby pledged.

Bail in civil transactions is seldom required. Guaranty Forms and Letters of Credit, elsewhere explained, appear to have superseded the necessity and practice of these obligations.

Recognizance for Further Examination.

STATE OF ILLINOIS, } *ss.*
County of Cook, } This day personally appeared before the undersigned, a justice of the peace in and for said county, Henry Carter, George R. Brown and James T. White, all of Chicago, in said county and State, and jointly and severally acknowledged themselves to be indebted unto the people of the State of Illinois, in the sum of Five Hundred Dollars, to be levied of their goods and chattels, lands and tenements.

WHEREAS, the above bounden Henry Carter, on the thirtieth day of December, A. D. 1882, was brought and examined by and before Horace Donohue, a justice of the peace in and for the county aforesaid, on a charge preferred against the said Henry Carter, for stealing Fifty Dollars from the store of Julius Wright, in said county, and the further examination of said Henry Carter having been continued to the tenth day of January, A. D. 1883, at ten o'clock A. M., and the said Henry Carter having been adjudged and required by the said justice to give bonds, as required by the statute in such case made and provided, for his appearance to answer to said charge. Now the condition of this recognizance is such that if the above-bounden Henry Carter shall be and appear before the undersigned, at the Third District Police court-room, in the city of Chicago, in said county, on the tenth day of January, A. D. 1883, at ten o'clock A. M., then and there to answer to the said people of the State of Illinois, on said charge, and abide the order and judgment of said court, and not depart the same without leave, then and in that case this recognizance to become void, otherwise to be and remain in full force and virtue.

As witness our hands and seals this thirtieth day of December, A. D. 1882.

Taken, entered into and acknowledged before me, this thirtieth day of December, 1882.
HORACE DONOHUE,
     Justice of the Peace.

HENRY CARTER,   —(SEAL)—

GEORGE R. BROWN,   —(SEAL)—

JAMES T. WHITE.   —(SEAL)—

BILLS OF SALE.

BILLS OF SALE are written evidences of agreements by which parties transfer to others, for a consideration, all their right, title and interest in personal property.

The ownership of personal property, in law, is considered changed by the delivery of such property to the purchaser; though in some States, without delivery, a bill of sale is good evidence of ownership, even against creditors, provided the sale was not fraudulently made for the purpose of avoiding the payment of debts

Juries have power to determine the fairness or unfairness of a sale, and upon evidence of fraud such bill of sale will be ignored and declared void.

Any form of words, importing that the seller transfers to the buyer the title to personal property, is a bill of sale.

Common Form of Bill of Sale.

KNOW ALL MEN by this instrument, that I, Philetus Howe, of Middlebury, Vermont, of the first part, for and in consideration of Four Hundred and Fifty Dollars, to me paid by Charles Rose, of the same place, of the second part, the receipt whereof is hereby acknowledged, have sold, and by this instrument do convey unto the said Rose, party of the second part, his executors, administrators and assigns, my undivided half of twenty acres of grass, now growing on the farm of Lorenzo Pease, in the town above mentioned: one pair of mules, ten swine, and three cows, belonging to me and in my possession at the farm aforesaid: to have and to hold the same unto the party of the second part, his executors and assigns, forever. And I do, for myself and legal representatives, agree with the said party of the second part, and his legal representatives, to warrant and defend the sale of the afore-mentioned property and chattels unto the said party of the second part, and his legal representatives, against all and every person whatsoever.

In witness whereof, I have hereunto affixed my hand this tenth day of June, one thousand eight hundred and seventy.
PHILETUS HOWE.

Bill of Sale of Personal Property.

KNOW ALL MEN by these presents, that I, John T. Hall, of Montgomery, Alabama, planter, in consideration of Six Hundred and Seventy-Five Dollars ($675) to me in hand paid by Oscar D. Scott, of Montgomery, Albany, the receipt whereof is hereby acknowledged, do hereby bargain, sell, and deliver unto the said Oscar D. Scott the following property, to wit:

Four mules .... @ $125 ....$500
Two sets Harness.......... @ 20 40
Two Farm Wagons..........@ 35 70
One Corn-Planter .... @ 20 20
Three Plows .... @ 15 45

Total.....................................$675

To have and to hold the said goods and chattels unto the said Oscar D. Scott, his executors, administrators, and assigns, to his own proper use and benefit, forever. And I, the said John T. Hall, do avow myself to be the true and lawful owner of said goods and chattels; that I have full power, good right, and lawful authority to dispose of said goods and chattels in manner as aforesaid; and that I will, and my heirs, executors, and administrators shall warrant and defend the said bargained goods and chattels unto the said Oscar D. Scott, his executors, administrators, and assigns, from and against the lawful claims and demands of all persons.

In witness whereof, I, the said John T. Hall, have hereto set my hand this first day of April, in the year of our Lord eighteen hundred and seventy-three.

JOHN T. HALL.

BILLS OF LADING.

BILLS OF LADING are accounts in writing of merchandise shipped from one place to another, by any person, on board of an ocean or lake vessel, or on a railroad car, signed by the master of the vessel, or an officer of a freight line or a railroad company, who thus acknowledges the receipt of the goods, and agrees to deliver them safely at the place to which they are sent. One bill of lading is kept by the shipper, one by the party transporting the goods, and one is sent to the person to whom the goods are directed. The following shows form of bill:

★ UNION LINE.

THROUGH FREIGHT LINE, OWNED AND OPERATED BY THE PENNSYLVANIA COMPANY, VIA P. F. & C. R. R.

GEO. B. EDWARDS, Eastern Manager, Pittsburgh, Pa.
W. W. CHANDLER, General Agent, - - - - - -

D. S. GRAY, Western Manager, Columbus, Ohio.
N. W. Corner Dearborn and Washington Streets, Chicago, Ill.

MARKS.

B

New York.

This Bill of Lading
FROM
Chicago, Ill.,
TO
New York

The Rate of Freight Through is to be
$1.00 per 100 lbs.

No. *4846.* Chicago, Ill., *June 28,* 1882

Received from *A. H. Standard B. & Co.*

the following packages (contents and value unknown,) in apparent good order, viz.:

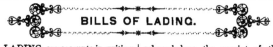

Five Bx. Books.   *1250 lbs.*

Marked and numbered as in the margin, to be transported by the Union Line, and the steamboats, railroad companies and forwarding lines with which it connects, on the following terms and conditions, viz.:

It being expressly understood and agreed, That the Union Line reserves the right, in consideration of issuing a through bill of lading, and guaranteeing a through rate, to forward said goods by any railroad line between points of shipment and destination.

It is further agreed That the rates given on bulk freight are given on the understanding that not less than 24,000 pounds will be loaded in each car, and that such minimum weight may, at the option of this line, be charged for, whether that quantity is placed in the car or not.

It is further agreed That all weight in excess of 30,000 lbs. per car will be charged double the rate named in this bill of lading.

It is further agreed That the said Union Line, and the steamboats, railroad companies and forwarding lines with which it connects, and which receives said property, shall not be liable for leakage of oils or any kind of liquids; breakage of any kind of glass, earthen or queensware, carboys of acids, or articles packed in glass, stoves and stove furniture, castings, machinery, carriages, furniture, musical instruments of any kind, packages of eggs; or for rust of iron and iron articles; or for loss or damage by wet, dirt, fire or loss of weight; or for condition of baling in hay, hemp or cotton; nor for loss or damage of any kind on any articles whose bulk requires it to be carried on open cars; nor for damage to perishable property of any kind, occasioned by delays from any cause, or by change of weather; nor for loss or damage on any article of property whatever, by fire or other casualty, while in transit, or while in depots or places of transhipment, or at depots or landings at point of delivery; nor for loss or damage by fire, collision, or the dangers of navigation while on seas, rivers, lakes or canals. All goods or property under this bill of lading will be subject, at its owner's cost, to necessary cooperage or baling, and is to be transported to the depots of the companies or landing of the steamboats or forwarding lines, at the point receipted to, for delivery.

It is further agreed That unless this bill of lading, properly indorsed, be delivered to the agent of the Union Line at destination, on or before the arrival there of the herein-above-described property, the said line is authorized to deliver the said property to the consignee, or to the party to whose care it is, by this bill of lading, consigned; and after such delivery, the said line shall be no longer responsible for or on account of any assignment or transfer thereof.

[*The claims relating to the time when the liability of the Union Line ceases, and the responsibility of shippers as to costs and charges, omitted.*]

It is further stipulated and agreed That in case of any loss, detriment, or damage, done to or sustained by any of the property herein receipted for during such transportation, whereby any legal liability or responsibility shall or may be incurred, that company alone shall be held answerable therefor in whose actual custody the same may be at the time of the happening of such loss, detriment, or damage, and the carrier so liable shall have the full benefit of any insurance that may have been effected upon or on account of said goods.

And it is further agreed That the amount of the loss or damage so accruing, so far as it shall fall upon the carriers above described, shall be computed at the value or cost of said goods or property at the place and time of shipment under this bill of lading, unless the value of the articles has been agreed upon with the shipper, or so determined by the classification upon which the rates are based.

It is further agreed That all weights furnished by shippers are subject to corrections.

This contract is executed and accomplished, and the liability of the companies, as common carriers thereunder, terminates on the arrival of the goods or property at the station or depot of delivery (and the companies will be liable as warehousemen only thereafter), and unless removed by the consignee from the stations or depots of delivery within twenty-four hours of their said arrival, they may be removed and stored by the companies, at the owner's expense and risk.

NOTICE—In accepting this bill of lading, the shipper or other agent of the owner of the property carried, expressly accepts and agrees to all its stipulations, exceptions and conditions.

W. W. CHANDLER, Agent.

BONDS.

BOND is a written admission of an obligation on the part of the maker, whereby he pledges himself to pay a certain sum of money to another person or persons, at a certain specified time, for some real consideration.

The person giving the bond is termed the obligor; the person receiving the same is called the obligee.

A bond, as defined above, is a single bond; but generally conditions are added to the bond, whereby the person giving the same must perform some specific act or acts, in which case the bond becomes void; otherwise it remains in full force and effect.

The penalty attached to the bond is usually sufficient to cover debt, interest, and costs, being generally placed at a sum twice the amount of the real debt, the fact being stated that such penalty is the sum fixed upon as liquidated or settled damages, in event of failure to meet payments according to the conditions of the bond.

The bond may be so drawn as to have the penalty attach and appertain to either the obligor or obligee.

Though, under ordinary circumstances, the bond is in full effect, yet an act of Providence, whereby its accomplishment is rendered impossible, relieves the party obligated from an enforcement of the penalty.

Action on such instrument must be brought within twenty years after right of action accrues, or within such time as provided by the statutes of the different States.

Common Form of Bond.

KNOW ALL MEN by this instrument, that I, Jonas Clayton, of Wilmington, Hanover County, State of North Carolina, am firmly bound unto Henry Morse of the place aforesaid, in the sum of One Thousand Dollars, to be paid to the said Henry Morse, or his legal representatives; to which payment, to be made, I bind myself or my legal representatives, by this instrument.

Sealed with my seal, and dated this first day of July, one thousand eight hundred and seventy-three.

The condition of this bond is such that, if I, Jonas Clayton, my heirs, administrators, or executors, shall promptly pay the sum of five hundred dollars in three equal annual payments from the date hereof, with annual interest, then the above obligation to be of no effect; otherwise to be in full force and valid.

Signed, sealed and delivered in presence of }
   GEORGE DOWNING.   JONAS CLAYTON. [L. S.]

Bond of Cashier of a Bank.

KNOW ALL MEN by this instrument, that I, Nathaniel Howard, of San Antonio, County of Bexar, and State of Texas, am firmly bound to the First National Bank corporation of said town, county, and State, in the sum of One Hundred Thousand Dollars, to be paid to the First National Bank corporation, or assigns, aforementioned: for which payment I bind myself, my heirs, executors, and administrators by this instrument.

Sealed with my seal, and dated this third day of February, one thousand eight hundred and seventy-two.

Whereas, the above bounden Nathaniel Howard has been appointed cashier of the First National Bank of San Antonio, aforementioned, by reason whereof various sums of money, goods, valuables, and other property, belonging to said Bank corporation, will come into his custody;

Therefore, the condition of the above bond is such, that, if the said Nathaniel Howard, his executors or administrators, at the expiration of his time of service to said bank, upon request to him or them made, shall deliver unto the said bank corporation or their agent, or their attorney, a correct account of all sums of money, goods, valuables, and other property, as it comes into his custody, as cashier of said bank, and shall pay and deliver to his successor in office, or any other person authorized to receive the same, all balances, sums of money, goods, valuables, and other property, which shall be in his hands, and due by him to said bank corporation; and if the said Nathaniel Howard shall justly, honestly, and faithfully, in all matters, serve the said bank corporation as cashier, during his continuance in such capacity, then the above obligation to be of no effect; otherwise to remain valid and in full force.

Signed, sealed and delivered in presence of }
   JOHN STODDARD.   NATHANIEL HOWARD.

Bond to a Corporation.

KNOW ALL MEN BY THESE PRESENTS, that I, Cornelius Burr, of West Chester, Chester county, State of Pennsylvania, am firmly bound unto the Chester County Beet-Sugar Manufacturing Company, in the sum of Twenty Thousand Dollars, to be paid to the said company, or their assigns, for which payment to be made, I bind myself and representatives firmly by these presents,

Sealed with my seal, and dated this first day of August, eighteen hundred and seventy.

The condition of the above bond is such that, if I, the said Cornelius Burr, my heirs, administrators, or assigns, shall pay unto the said Chester County Beet-Sugar Manufacturing Company, or assigns, Ten Thousand Dollars, in two equal payments, viz.: Five Thousand Dollars January first, eighteen hundred and seventy-one, and Five Thousand Dollars July first next following, with accrued interest, then the above to be void; otherwise to remain in full force and effect.

Signed, sealed and delivered in presence of }
   CHARLES ROYCE.   CORNELIUS BURR. [L. S.]

The printed forms contain in addition to all these matters, which are essential, the following notes, which are important for the saving of time and trouble in the public office concerned, and to the incorporators.

The Constitution provides that all fees shall be paid in advance into the State treasury.

Fee for filing statement and issuing license, $3.50; fee for filing report of commissioners and issuing certificate, $3.50.

Blanks furnished on application.

The Secretary of State replies to the application, if accompanied by the fee indicated, forwarding the required license.

Form of State License for Incorporating.

STATE OF ILLINOIS, }
Department of State. } ——, Secretary of State.

To all to whom these Presents shall come, Greeting:

Whereas, it being proposed by the persons hereinafter named to form a corporation, under an act of the General Assembly of the State of Illinois, entitled "An Act Concerning Corporations," approved April 18, 1872, the object and purposes of which corporation are set forth in a statement, duly signed and acknowledged according to law, and filed this day in the office of the Secretary of State.

Now, therefore, I, ——, Secretary of State of the State of Illinois, by virtue of the powers and duties vested in me by law, do hereby authorize, empower and license George C. Anderson, Rudolph S. Schenck, and Jonathan Bigelow, the persons whose names are signed to the before-mentioned statement, as commissioners to open books for subscription to the capital stock of the Metropolitan Boot and Shoe Manufacturing Company, such being the name of the proposed corporation, as contained in the statement, at such times and places as the said commissioners may determine.

In testimony whereof, I hereto set my hand and cause to be affixed the great seal of State. Done at the city of Springfield this sixth day of December, in the year of our Lord one thousand eight hundred and eighty-one, and of the independence of the United States the one hundred and sixth.

——, Secretary of State.

The incorporators, thus empowered, proceed with the work of incorporation, and having allotted the capital stock of the company, report as follows, on another printed form prepared for such occasions:

Form of Incorporator's Report.

To Hon. ——, Secretary of State of the State of Illinois:

The commissioners duly authorized to open books for subscription to the capital stock of the Metropolitan Boot and Shoe Manufacturing Company, pursuant to license heretofore issued bearing date the sixth day of December, A. D. 1881, do hereby report that they opened books for subscription to the capital stock of the said company, and that the said stock was fully subscribed; that the following is a true copy of such subscription, viz.: We, the undersigned, hereby severally subscribe for the number of shares set opposite our respective names to the capital stock of the Metropolitan Boot and Shoe Manufacturing Company, and we severally agree to pay the said company, on each share, the sum of One Hundred Dollars.

NAMES.	SHARES.	AMOUNT.
George C. Anderson	2,000	$200,000
Rudolph S. Schenck	2,000	200,000
Jonathan Bigelow	1,000	100,000
	5,000	$500,000

That on the twentieth day of December, A. D. 1881, at the offices of the company in Chicago, at the hour of ten o'clock A. M., they convened a meeting of the subscribers aforesaid, pursuant to notice required by law, which said notice was deposited in the post-office, properly addressed to each subscriber, ten days before the time fixed therefor, a copy of which said notice is as follows, to wit:

To ——

You are hereby notified that the capital stock of the Metropolitan Boot and Shoe Manufacturing Company has been fully subscribed, and that a meeting of the subscribers of such stock will be held at the offices of the company, 209 Wabash avenue, Chicago, on the twentieth day of December, A. D. 1881, at ten o'clock A. M., for the purpose of electing a board of directors for said company, and for the transaction of such other business as may be deemed necessary.

GEORGE C. ANDERSON, }
RUDOLPH S. SCHENCK, } Commissioners.
JONATHAN BIGELOW, }

That said subscribers met at the time and place in said notice specified, and proceeded to elect directors, and that the following persons were duly elected for the term of one year, as follows: George C. Anderson, Rudolph S. Schenck, Jonathan Bigelow.

Signed,   GEORGE C. ANDERSON, }
RUDOLPH S. SCHENCK, } Commissioners.
JONATHAN BIGELOW, }

Notarial Endorsement.

The notarial endorsement is once more demanded to attest the regularity of the foregoing proceedings, and it is given on the back of the form last supplied, as follows:

STATE OF ILLINOIS, } s.
County of Cook, }

On this twentieth day of December, A. D. 1881, personally appeared before me, a notary public in and for said county, in said State, George C. Anderson, Rudolph S. Schenck, and Jonathan Bigelow, and made oath that the foregoing report by them subscribed is true in substance and in fact.

——, Notary Public.

Charter of an Organized Company.

The papers are then all returned to the Secretary of State, except the license to act as commissioners, and subsequently that officer informs the incorporators that the certificate of organization has been issued, the final fee of $3.50 having been forwarded with the document last mentioned. The certificate, which places the company on a basis to commence business as a corporation, is an elegant compendium of all the papers that have theretofore been issued, tied with ribbon and bearing the great seal of State, comprising the following statement in due form, properly attested:

STATE OF ILLINOIS, } ——, Secretary of State.
Department of State. }

To all to whom these Presents shall come, Greeting:

Whereas, a statement, duly signed and acknowledged, has been filed in the office of the Secretary of State, on the thirtieth day of November, A. D. 1881, for the organization of the Metropolitan Boot and Shoe Manufacturing Company, under and in accordance with the provisions of "an act concerning corporations," approved April 18, 1872, and in force July 1, 1872, and all acts amendatory thereof, a copy of which statement is hereto attached;

And whereas, a license having been issued to George C. Anderson, Rudolph S Schenck, and Jonathan Bigelow, as commissioners to open books for subscription to the capital stock of the said company;

And whereas, the said commissioners having, on the twentieth day of December, A. D. 1881, filed in the office of the Secretary of State a report of their proceedings under the said license, a copy of which report is hereto attached;

The federal laws provide that all valuable mineral deposits in lands belonging to the United States, whether previously surveyed or not, are free and open to exploration and purchase; that the land in which these mineral deposits are found may be occupied and purchased by citizens of the United States, or those who have declared their intention to become such, under regulations provided in such cases by law and the local customs or rules of miners in the several mining districts, wherever they are applicable and consistent with the federal laws; and that in the case of an association of persons unincorporated, proof of citizenship of the parties may be given by the affidavit of their authorized agent, made on his own knowledge, information or belief; while in the case of a corporation organized under the federal laws, or the laws of any State or Territory, the filing of a certified copy of their charter, or certificate of incorporation, is sufficient evidence.

HOW TO ORGANIZE A COMPANY.

To illustrate the various steps to be taken in organizing a company, the following forms, as used in Illinois, accompanied by suggestions, will give the reader an idea of the methods of general procedure, subject to slight modifications, of a local character in different States.

The statutes of Illinois provide for the licensing of associations for pecuniary profit; not for pecuniary profit; religious purposes; moral purposes, etc.

Of these associations for banking, insurance, real-estate brokerage, the operating of railroads, and money loaning, require to be licensed under the general law of the United States. Companies organized to conduct horse and dummy railways, and sales of land for burial purposes, however, have permission to incorporate under the laws of the State.

THE APPLICATION.

When three and not more than seven persons propose to form a corporation they must file with the Secretary of State a statement setting forth the objects of the association, the amount of its capital stock, the number of shares into which it is divided, the location of the principal office, and the duration of the corporation, which may not, however, exceed ninety-nine years; this statement must be signed and duly acknowledged before a proper officer by the proposed incorporators. Thereupon the Secretary of State issues to such persons a license as commissioners to open books for subscriptions to the capital stock of such corporation at set times and places. No two companies of the same name may be licensed.

Form of Application for Incorporation.

STATE OF ILLINOIS, } ss.
County of Cook,

To —— SECRETARY OF STATE:

We, the undersigned, George C. Anderson, Rudolph S. Schenck, and Jonathan Bigelow, propose to form a corporation under an act of the general assembly of the State of Illinois, entitled, "An Act Concerning Corporations," approved April 18, 1872, and all acts amendatory thereof; and that for the purposes of such organization we hereby state as follows, to wit:

1. The name of such corporation is the Metropolitan Boot and Shoe Manufacturing Company.

2. The object for which it is formed is to carry on the business of manufacturing boots and shoes, in all its branches, and to sell the goods so manufactured in the best markets obtainable.

3. The capital stock shall be five hundred thousand ($500,000) dollars.

4. The amount of each share is one hundred ($100) dollars.

5. The number of shares five thousand (5,000).

6. The location of the principal office is in Chicago, in the county of Cook, State of Illinois.

7. The duration of the corporation shall be eighty (80) years.

GEORGE C. ANDERSON,
RUDOLPH S. SCHENCK,
JONATHAN BIGELOW.

The document must bear the following

Endorsement on the Back.

STATE OF ILLINOIS, } ss.
County of Cook,

I, ——, a notary public in and for the said Cook county, and State aforesaid, do hereby certify that on this thirtieth day of November, A. D 1881, personally appeared before me George C. Anderson, Rudolph S. Schenck, and Jonathan Bigelow, to me personally known to be the same persons who executed the foregoing statement, and severally acknowledged that they executed the same for the purposes therein set forth.

In witness whereof I have hereunto set my hand and seal the day and year above written.

——, Notary Public.

A descriptive endorsement will also be made as follows:

Corporation for Pecuniary Profit.

Statement of incorporation of the Metropolitan Boot and Shoe Manufacturing Company. Location, Chicago, Cook county, State of Illinois. Capital stock, $500,000. Object, manufacture and sale of boots and shoes. Duration, eighty years.

The printed forms contain in addition to all these matters, which are essential, the following notes, which are important for the saving of time and trouble in the public office concerned, and to the incorporators.

The Constitution provides that all fees shall be paid in advance into the State treasury.

Fee for filing statement and issuing license, $2.50; fee for filing report of commissioners and issuing certificate, $3.50.

Blanks furnished on application.

The Secretary of State replies to the application, if accompanied by the fee indicated, forwarding the required license.

Form of State License for Incorporating.

STATE OF ILLINOIS, }
Department of State. } ———, Secretary of State.

To all to whom these Presents shall come, Greeting:

Whereas, it being proposed by the persons hereinafter named to form a corporation, under an act of the General Assembly of the State of Illinois, entitled "An Act Concerning Corporations," approved April 18, 1872, the object and purposes of which corporation are set forth in a statement, duly signed and acknowledged according to law, and filed this day in the office of the Secretary of State.

Now, therefore, I, ———, Secretary of State of the State of Illinois, by virtue of the powers and duties vested in me by law, do hereby authorize, empower and license George C. Anderson, Rudolph S. Schenck, and Jonathan Bigelow, the persons whose names are signed to the before-mentioned statement, as commissioners to open books for subscription to the capital stock of the Metropolitan Boot and Shoe Manufacturing Company, such being the name of the proposed corporation, as contained in the statement, at such times and places as the said commissioners may determine.

GREAT
SEAL.

In testimony whereof, I hereto set my hand and cause to be affixed the great seal of State. Done at the city of Springfield this sixth day of December, in the year of our Lord one thousand eight hundred and eighty-one, and of the independence of the United States the one hundred and sixth.

———, Secretary of State.

The incorporators, thus empowered, proceed with the work of incorporation, and having allotted the capital stock of the company, report as follows, on another printed form prepared for such occasions:

Form of Incorporator's Report.

To Hon. ———, Secretary of State of the State of Illinois:

The commissioners duly authorized to open books for subscription to the capital stock of the Metropolitan Boot and Shoe Manufacturing Company, pursuant to license heretofore issued bearing date the sixth day of December, A. D. 1881, do hereby report that they opened books for subscription to the capital stock of the said company, and that the said stock was fully subscribed; that the following is a true copy of such subscription, viz.: We, the undersigned, hereby severally subscribe for the number of shares set opposite our respective names to the capital stock of the Metropolitan Boot and Shoe Manufacturing Company, and we severally agree to pay the said company, on each share, the sum of One Hundred Dollars.

NAMES.	SHARES.	AMOUNT.
George C. Anderson	2,000	$200,000
Rudolph S. Schenck	2,000	200,000
Jonathan Bigelow	1,000	100,000
	5,000	$500,000

That on the twentieth day of December, A. D. 1881, at the offices of the company in Chicago, at the hour of ten o'clock A. M., they

convened a meeting of the subscribers aforesaid, pursuant to notice required by law, which said notice was deposited in the post-office, properly addressed to each subscriber, ten days before the time fixed therefor, a copy of which said notice is as follows, to wit :

To ———

You are hereby notified that the capital stock of the Metropolitan Boot and Shoe Manufacturing Company has been fully subscribed, and that a meeting of the subscribers of such stock will be held at the offices of the company, 209 Wabash avenue, Chicago, on the twentieth day of December, A. D. 1881, at ten o'clock A. M., for the purpose of electing a board of directors for said company, and for the transaction of such other business as may be deemed necessary.

GEORGE C. ANDERSON, }
RUDOLPH S. SCHENCK, } Commissioners.
JONATHAN BIGELOW, }

That said subscribers met at the time and place in said notice specified, and proceeded to elect directors, and that the following persons were duly elected for the term of one year, as follows: George C. Anderson, Rudolph S. Schenck, Jonathan Bigelow.

Signed, GEORGE C. ANDERSON, }
RUDOLPH S. SCHENCK, } Commissioners.
JONATHAN BIGELOW, }

Notarial Endorsement.

The notarial endorsement is once more demanded to attest the regularity of the foregoing proceedings, and it is given on the back of the form last supplied, as follows:

STATE OF ILLINOIS, }
County of Cook, }

On this twentieth day of December, A. D. 1881, personally appeared before me, a notary public in and for said county, in said State, George C. Anderson, Rudolph S. Schenck, and Jonathan Bigelow, and made oath that the foregoing report by them subscribed is true in substance and in fact.

———, Notary Public.

Charter of an Organized Company.

The papers are then all returned to the Secretary of State, except the license to act as commissioners, and subsequently that officer informs the incorporators that the certificate of organization has been issued, the final fee of $3.50 having been forwarded with the document last mentioned. The certificate, which places the company on a basis to commence business as a corporation, is an elegant compendium of all the papers that have theretofore been issued, tied with ribbon and bearing the great seal of State, comprising the following statement in due form, properly attested:

STATE OF ILLINOIS, }
Department of State. } ———, Secretary of State.

To all to whom these Presents shall come, Greeting:

Whereas, a statement, duly signed and acknowledged, has been filed in the office of the Secretary of State, on the thirtieth day of November, A. D. 1881, for the organization of the Metropolitan Boot and Shoe Manufacturing Company, under and in accordance with the provisions of "an act concerning corporations," approved April 18, 1872, and in force July 1, 1872, and all acts amendatory thereof, a copy of which statement is hereto attached;

And whereas, a license having been issued to George C. Anderson, Rudolph S. Schenck, and Jonathan Bigelow, as commissioners to open books for subscription to the capital stock of the said company;

And whereas, the said commissioners having, on the twentieth day of December, A. D. 1881, filed in the office of the Secretary of State a report of their proceedings under the said license, a copy of which report is hereto attached;

Now, therefore, I, ———, Secretary of State of the State of Illinois, by virtue of the powers and duties vested in me by law, do hereby certify that the said "Metropolitan Boot and Shoe Manufacturing Company," is a legally organized corporation under the laws of this State.

In testimony whereof, I hereunto set my hand and cause to be affixed the great seal of State.

Done at the city of Springfield, this tenth day of January, in the year of our Lord one thousand eight hundred and eighty-two, and of the independence of the United States the one hundred and seventh.

———, Secretary of State.

Charter to be Recorded.

It then only remains for the corporation to take their certificate, etc., to the office of the recorder, the fact of record being endorsed on the back of the completed issue, thus:

Metropolitan Boot and Shoe Manufacturing Company
No. ———,

State of Illinois, } ss.
County of Cook, }

Recorded, January 20, 1882, at two P. M.

Book —— of Corporations, Page ——.

———, Recorder.

What it Costs to Organize a Company.

The actual cost of the organization of the company is thus ascertained to be in fees to the office of the Secretary of State $6.00, notarial fees, postage and forms about $1. And when any doubt arises in the minds of corporators that cannot be removed by the perusal of the revised statutes touching corporations, a fee may be paid to counsel for advice.

After or during incorporation, any number of members may be added, by subscription for shares in capital stock or subsequent purchase, in accordance with the conditions of the certificate. The law does not recognize young men or women who have not attained their majority, but in practice it is well known that minors in many companies hold stock.

When the capital stock has all been subscribed, the commissioners, after at least ten days' personal notice, convene the subscribers at some specified time and place to elect as many directors or managers of such corporation as may be agreed upon. Each subscriber or stockholder, in person or by proxy, casts as many votes as he owns shares for as many persons as are to be elected managers or directors; or he may give one candidate as many votes as the number of directors or managers multiplied by the number of his shares of stock shall equal; or distribute his votes on the same principle among as many candidates as he may choose; and no directors or managers can be elected in any other way.

Voting by Proxy.

Voting by proxy, referred to above, is where a stockholder gives a written authority to some other stockholder to vote for him at the election of managers, if not himself able to be present at the election. The following is the form for such authority:

KNOW ALL MEN BY THESE PRESENTS, That I, Eben C. West, of Chicago, Ill., owner of one hundred shares in the Metropolitan Boot and Shoe Manufacturing Company, do hereby constitute and appoint Roswell Jones, of the same place, and also a shareholder in the said company, an attorney and agent for me and in my name, place and stead to vote as my proxy at an election of directors of said company, to be holden at No. —— Clark street, Chicago, December 7, A. D. 1882, according to the number of votes that I should be entitled to vote if then personally present, with power of substitution in case he cannot be present at the election.

In witness whereof, I have hereunto set my hand and seal this first day of December, one thousand eight hundred and eighty-two.

Witness:
ROBERT D. TWEED.   EBEN C. WEST. [L. s.]

Completing the Organization of a Company.

After their election the board of managers or directors may be divided by such corporation into three classes, the first of whose term of office shall expire at the next annual election; that of the second-class at the second annual election, and that of the third-class at the third annual election, the vacancies being filled at each annual election at which they occur.

To complete the organization the commissioners file in the office of the Secretary of State a full report of their proceedings, as set forth above, with copies of the election notice sent to subscribers, the subscription list, and the list of the elected managers or directors, with the length of their respective terms of office; the whole sworn to by a majority or all of the commissioners. The Secretary of State then issues his certificate of the complete organization of the corporation under his hand and seal of State and records it in the office of the Recorder of Deeds of the county in which the corporation is located. The organization is then ready for business, which it must commence within two years or forfeit its license.

Such a corporation may have a common seal, may sue and be sued, and possess such amounts of real estate as will enable it to carry on its business and dispose of it at will; but no other real estate acquired by the corporation in the way of business can be retained by it, but must be sold at auction, after due advertisement, for the benefit of the organization, at least once a year.

Officers of a Company.

The officers of such a corporation consist of a president, secretary and treasurer, and such other official personages as may be determined by the board of directors or managers, who may also require the officers or agents of the organization to give proper bonds for the performance of their duties and make by-laws for the government and continuance in office of all connected with the corporation.

Shares of stock cannot be less than $10, nor more than $100 each, and are classed as personal property and transferable under certain restrictions and regulations. Correct accounts of all its business are required to be kept by each corporation, and these accounts are open to inspection by every stockholder in the organization, or his attorney, at reasonable hours.

Should any corporation perform or neglect any act in such a manner as to forfeit its license to organize, all its subscribers may personally be sued for the indebtedness of the defunct organization, provided that its company assets are not sufficient to cancel its obligations. Officers and directors are liable, personally, if they permit the debts of the corporation to exceed the amount of its capital stock.

Corporations for Social and Benevolent Purposes.

ANY three or more persons, who are citizens of the United States, may apply to the Secretary of State in a manner similar to money-making corporations for license to organize for other purposes, filing with him a duly acknowledged statement in writing of the name and particular business or objects of such association, the number of its trustees, directors or managers, and the names of those officials selected to serve during the first year. The Secretary of State may then issue his certificate of the organization of such corporation, and when this certificate is duly recorded in the office of the recorder of deeds in the county where the association is located, the incorporators may proceed to transact business. Such corporations may sue and be sued; may make and enforce contracts in relation to their legitimate business; may have a common seal; may purchase, hold and dispose of real and personal estate for purposes of their respective organizations; make by-laws for their own government not inconsistent with general laws; may elect trustees, managers or directors to control the affairs and funds of the corporation; may borrow money for the purposes of the organization and pledge its property for the payment thereof; may register the names of its officers in the county where it is located, and when its debts are paid may dissolve the corporation, distribute the property among its members, and register its dissolution papers in the county recorder's office.

Corporations for Religious Purposes.

ANY church, congregation or society formed for the purpose of religious worship may be incorporated as follows: By electing or appointing, at any meeting of its members held for that purpose, two or more members as trustees, wardens and vestrymen, or other such officers with powers and duties equivalent to those of trustees, as shall be in accordance with the customs and usages of such congregation, church or society; may adopt a corporate name; and may make and file, by the chairman or secretary of such meeting, a sworn affidavit setting forth the details of the business transacted at such meeting, in the office of the recorder of deeds of the county where the said church, congregation or society is located. The church, congregation or society, thus incorporated, may adopt by-laws and regulations for the government of its own members, the election of its own officers, filling vacancies therein, removing trustees for immoral or other causes; may hold and control personal property, borrow money and pledge such property for its payment; may own and use land acquired by gift, devise or purchase, not exceeding ten acres; may build houses or other buildings, lay out burial grounds, etc., for the use of the church, congregation or society thus organized; may improve or repair or alter such buildings at will; may own camp-meeting grounds, not exceeding forty acres, acquired by grant, devise or bequest, and fit them up for the comfort and convenience of worshipers, and may publish books, periodicals, tracts, etc.

The statutes prescribe numerous regulations and provisions, aside from the foregoing, for the control of incorporated associations, relative to compulsory payments of stock instalments and the transfer of stock; powers and rights after the expiration of charters; inspection of accounts; the liability of directors and officers for corporation debts; annual statements of acquired real estate; the penalties for rendering false official reports; the legal powers of official meetings of directors or stockholders; the change of articles of association, name and place of business of the organization; the increase or decrease of capital stock and number of directors; the consolidation of associations; the holding of special meetings of stockholders, etc.

Special provisions are also made for action by attorneys of corporations; loans of money on real estate securities by foreign corporations; the building of elevated railways and conveyors; the formation of total abstinence societies; the licensing of homestead loan associations and the regulation thereof.

DEEDS.

AN INSTRUMENT in writing, by which lands and appurtenances thereon are conveyed from one person to another, signed, sealed, and properly witnessed, is termed a deed. A deed may be written or printed on parchment or paper, and must be executed by parties competent to contract.

The law provides that an acknowledgment of a deed can only be made before certain persons authorized to take the same; these including, in different States, justices of the peace, notaries, masters in chancery, judges and clerks of courts, mayors of cities, commissioners of deeds, etc. In some States one witness, in some two, and in some none are required.

To render a deed valid, there must be a realty to grant, and a sufficient consideration.

To enable a person legally to convey property to another, the following requisites are necessary: First, he or she must be of sane mind; second, of age; and third, the rightful owner of the property.

The maker of the deed is called the grantor; the person or party to whom the deed is delivered, the grantee. The wife of the grantor, in the absence of any statute regulating the same, must execute the deed, or else, after the death of her husband, she will be entitled to a one-third interest in the property, as dower, during her life. A deed of a homestead not executed by the wife is void. Her acknowledgment of the deed must be of her own free will and accord, and the commissioner, or other officer, before whom the acknowledgment is taken, must certify to the fact that her consent was without compulsion.

Special care should be taken to have the deed properly acknowledged and witnessed, and the proper seal attached.

The deed takes effect upon its delivery to the person authorized to receive it.

Any alterations or interlineations in the deed should be noted at the bottom of the instrument, and properly witnessed. After the acknowledgment of the deed, the parties may not make the slightest alteration. An alteration after the delivery, in favor of the grantee, vitiates the deed.

By a general warranty deed, the grantor agrees to warrant and defend the property conveyed against all persons whatsoever. A quit-claim deed releases what interest the grantor may have in the land, but does not warrant and defend against others.

Deeds, upon their delivery, should be recorded in the recorder's office without delay.

Warranty Deed, with Covenants.

This INDENTURE, made this eighteenth day of March, in the year of our Lord one thousand eight hundred and seventy-three, between Henry Botsford, of Lee, county of Berkshire, State of Massachusetts, and Mary, his wife, of the first part, and Calvin Daggett, of the same place, of the second part:

WITNESSETH, that the said party of the first part, for and in consideration of the sum of Three Thousand Dollars in hand paid by the said party of the second part, the receipt whereof is hereby acknowledged, have granted, bargained, and sold, and by these presents do grant, bargain, and sell, unto the said party of the second part, his heirs and assigns, all the following-described lot, piece, or parcel of land, situated in the town of Lee, in the county of Berkshire, and State of Massachusetts, to wit:

[Here describe the property.]

Together with all and singular the hereditaments and appurtenances thereunto belonging or in any wise appertaining, and the reversion and reversions, remainder and remainders, rents, issues, and profits thereof; and all the estate, right, title, interest, claim, and demand whatsoever, of the said party of the first part, either in law or equity, of, in, and to the above bargained premises, with the hereditaments and appurtenances: To have and to hold the said premises above bargained and described, with the appurtenances, unto the said party of the second part, his heirs and assigns, forever. And the said Henry Botsford and Mary Botsford, his wife, party of the first part, hereby expressly waive, release, and relinquish unto the said party of the second part, his heirs, executors, administrators, and assigns, all right, title, claim, interest, and benefit whatever, in and to the above-described premises, and each and every part thereof, which is given by or results from all laws of this State pertaining to the exemption of homesteads.

And the said Henry Botsford and Mary Botsford, his wife, party of the first part, for themselves and their heirs, executors, and administrators, do covenant, grant, bargain, and agree, to and with the said party of the second part, his heirs and assigns, that at the time of the ensealing and delivery of these presents they were well seized of the premises above conveyed, as of a good, sure, perfect, absolute, and indefeasible estate of inheritance in law, and in fee simple, and have good right, full power, and lawful authority to grant, bargain, sell, and convey the same, in manner and form aforesaid, and that the same are free and clear from all former and other grants, bargains, sales, liens, taxes, assessments, and encumbrances of what kind or nature soever; and the above-bargained premises in the

quiet and peaceable possession of the said party of the second part, his heirs and assigns, against all and every person or persons lawfully claiming or to claim the whole or any part thereof, the said party of the first part shall and will warrant and forever defend.

In testimony whereof, the said parties of the first part have hereunto set their hands and seals the day and year first above written.

Signed, sealed and delivered in the presence of   HENRY BOTSFORD.—(SEAL)—
ABIAL KETCHUM.   MARY BOTSFORD. —(SEAL)—

[The foregoing should be acknowledged before a legally authorized officer. See "Acknowledgments."]

Quit-Claim Deed.

This INDENTURE, made the fourth day of July, in the year of our Lord one thousand eight hundred and seventy-one, between Oscar Joy, of Nashville, county of Davidson, State of Tennessee, party of the first part, and Lorenzo Fisher, of the same place, party of the second part.

WITNESSETH, that the said party of the first part, for and in consideration of Eight Hundred Dollars in hand paid by the said party of the second part, the receipt whereof is hereby acknowledged, and the said party of the second part forever released and discharged therefrom, has remised, released, sold, conveyed and quit-claimed, and by these presents does remise, release, sell, convey, and quit-claim, unto the said party of the second part, his heirs and assigns, forever, all the right, title, interest, claim, and demand, which the said party of the first part has in and to the following-described lot, piece, or parcel of land, to wit:

[Here describe the land.]

To have and to hold the same, together with all and singular the appurtenances and privileges thereunto belonging, or in anywise thereunto appertaining, and all the estate, right, title, interest, and claim whatever, of the said party of the first part, either in law or equity, to the only proper use, benefit, and behoof of the said party of the second part, his heirs and assigns forever.

In witness whereof, the said party of the first part hereunto sets his hand and seal the day and year above written.

Signed, sealed and delivered in presence of   OSCAR JOY. [L. S.]
AZRO HOLLIS.

[The above should be duly acknowledged.]

Long Form Quit-Claim Deed---Homestead Waiver.

THIS INDENTURE, made the fourteenth day of October, in the year of our Lord one thousand eight hundred and seventy-two, between Park Converse, of Burlington, county of Des Moines, State of Iowa, party of the first part, and Elbridge Robinson, of the same place, party of the second part,

WITNESSETH, that the said party of the first part, for and in consideration of Four Thousand Dollars in hand paid by the said party of the second part, the receipt whereof is hereby acknowledged, and the said party of the second part forever released and discharged therefrom, has remised, released, sold, conveyed, and quit-claimed, and by these presents does remise, release, sell, convey, and quit-claim, unto the said party of the second part, his heirs and assigns, forever, all the right, title, interest, claim, and demand which the said party of the first part has in and to the following described lot, piece, or parcel of land, to wit:

[*Here describe the land.*]

To have and to hold the same, together with all and singular the appurtenances and privileges thereunto belonging, or in any wise thereunto appertaining; and all the estate, right, title, interest, and claim whatever, of the said party of the first part, either in law or equity, to the only proper use, benefit, and behoof of the said party of the second part, his heirs and assigns forever.

And the said Park Converse, party of the first part, hereby expressly waives, releases, and relinquishes unto the said party of the second part, his heirs, executors, administrators, and assigns, all right, title, claim, interest, and benefit whatever, in and to the above-described premises, and each and every part thereof, which is given by or results from all laws of this State pertaining to the exemption of homesteads.

And the said party of the first part, for himself and his heirs, executors, and administrators, does covenant, promise and agree, to and with the said party of the second part, his heirs, executors, administrators, and assigns, that he hath not made, done, committed, executed, or suffered, any act or acts, thing or things, whatsoever, whereby, or by means whereof, the above-mentioned and described premises, or any part or parcel thereof, now are, or any time hereafter, shall or may be impeached, charged, or incumbered, in any way or manner whatsoever.

In witness whereof, the said party of the first part hereunto sets his hand and seal the day and year first above written.

Signed, sealed and delivered in presence of }   PARK CONVERSE. [L.S.]
GERRY HOBBS.

Acknowledgment Before a Justice of the Peace.

STATE OF IOWA, } *ss.*
County of Des Moines, }   I, Gerry Hobbs, a justice of the peace in and for the said county, in the State aforesaid, do hereby certify that Park Converse, who is personally known to me as the same person whose name is subscribed to the foregoing instrument, appeared before me this day in person, and acknowledged that he signed, sealed and delivered the said instrument as his free and voluntary act, for the uses and purposes therein set forth, including the release and waiver of the right of homestead.

Given under my hand and seal, this fourteenth day of October, A. D. 1872.   GERRY HOBBS,
             Justice of the Peace. [L.S.]

EXTRADITION.

THE SIGNIFICATION of the word "extradition" is delivery out of, or up from, and has been adopted by various States and nations to express the return from one to the other of fugitives from justice, for punishment in the place where the crime was committed.

The constitution of the United States declares that "a person charged in any State with treason, felony, or other crime, who shall flee from justice, and be found in another State, shall, on demand of the executive authority of the State from which he fled, be delivered up, to be removed to the State having jurisdiction of the cause."

Extradition between the several States is regulated by the laws of the United States, and between foreign States by treaties. Still, a foreign State sometimes extradites without a treaty, as was done by us in the case of a Cuban slave-trader, in 1863.

The surrender of fugitives from justice having been abused for private purposes, governors of States from which the fugitives fled, in addition to the usual papers, require an affidavit asserting that the application is made for the purpose of public justice, and not for private gain.

The usual papers are a duly certified copy of the indictment, and an affidavit showing that the criminal was within the State when the crime was committed, and fled therefrom after the crime to the State on which the demand is to be made. If there is not time to wait for an indictment, a duly certified copy of the complaint to the magistrate and his warrant are sent.

If the papers satisfy the governor, he issues a requisition on the other governor for the fugitive. A requisition is a request to have the criminal arrested and delivered to the person named in the requisition. With the requisition are sent copies of the indictment, or complaint, and the warrant.

If the governor is satisfied with the papers, he issues a warrant to an officer of his State to arrest the criminal and deliver him to the person named in the requisition. If the governor refuses to issue the warrant, he may, in a proper case, be compelled to do so by a mandamus from the United States Circuit Court.

The proceedings in the case of foreign States are substantially similar.

The Secretary of State of each State, and of the United States, will furnish forms and instructions on application.

Treaties with other nations also specify the forms in which the extradition laws may be mutually enforced. In some countries extradition is more difficult, and the methods more complicated than in others.

The following forms are those in substance, that regulate our inter-state system of returning criminals :

Philip Maxwell has been robbed by a well-known thief, at Hannah, Ga., and the robber has escaped to Wisconsin, beyond the jurisdiction of the State. Maxwell therefore goes before a magistrate, and makes the following affidavit :

Affidavit.

STATE OF GEORGIA, } ss.
County of Harris, }

Philip Maxwell, of Hannah, Harris county, and State of Georgia, being duly sworn, says:

First—That Robert Thorsen, *alias* "Big Bob," is a fugitive from justice from the State of Georgia, where he stands charged on oath with felony, committed in this State, viz. : With having, on the night of June 6, A. D. 1882, between the hours of eleven and twelve o clock, midnight, brutally assaulted the said Philip Maxwell, knocking him senseless with a wooden club believed to be three feet long and one and one-half inches thick; and with having then and there robbed the said Philip Maxwell, while he lay unconscious, of a silver watch and gold chain, of the value of Fifty Dollars, and of money, in greenbacks, gold and silver coins, of the value of One Hundred and Forty-three Dollars and sixty-five cents, lawful currency of the United States; which said acts are by the law of the said State of Georgia a crime.

Second—That the said charge was made on or about the seventh day of June, A. D. 1882, by the said Philip Maxwell, testifying under oath before the Hannah Police-court, in Harris county, Georgia, as to the facts above set forth, with such other details of the crime as he could remember.

Third—That the said Robert Thorsen, *alias* "Big Bob," has fled from the said State last aforesaid and has taken refuge in the State of Wisconsin, from the laws and justice of the State of Georgia.

AND DEPONENT PRAYS that the said Robert Thorsen, *alias* "Big Bob," may be arrested and held in custody by the proper authorities of the State of Wisconsin until the proper authorities of the said State of Georgia shall have sufficient time to require, in manner and form as the law directs, the body of said Robert Thorsen, *alias* "Big Bob," from the executive and authorities of the State of Wisconsin, and until the said executive of said last above-named State shall make his warrant for the surrender of the body of said Robert Thorsen, *alias* "Big Bob," to the end that he may be brought to the State of Georgia and dealt with as law and justice shall require.

And this deponent further says, upon his oath, that this affidavit is made in order that the ends of public justice may be served, and not from motives of private gain or malice.

PHILIP MAXWELL.

Sworn before me, this twelfth day of July, A. D. 1882, at Hannah, Harris county, Georgia.

JESSE SMITH,
Clerk of the Criminal Court of said County.

This affidavit, upon which the requisition of the governor of Georgia for the return of the criminal is based, having been taken by a police or sheriff's officer to the governor of Wisconsin, the latter proceeds to issue the following warrant for the surrender of the criminal, if found within his State, to the authorities of the State of Georgia:

The Order for Surrender.

——, governor of the State of Wisconsin, to the sheriffs of the county of Dane, and the sheriffs, constables and other peace-officers of the several counties in said State:

WHEREAS, it has been represented to me by the governor of the State of Georgia, that Robert Thorsen (also well-known as "Big Bob"), late of Hannah, in said State, has been guilty of assault and robbery upon the highway upon the person of Philip Maxwell, of the same place, which said acts are made criminal by the laws of that State; and that he has fled from justice in that State, and has taken refuge in the State of Wisconsin; and that said governor of Georgia has, in pursuance of the constitution and laws of the United States, demanded of me that I should cause the said Robert Thorsen to be arrested and delivered into the custody of ——, sheriff of the county of Harris, in said State, who is duly authorized to receive him into his custody, and to convey him back to the said State of Georgia; and whereas the said representation and demand is accompanied by an affidavit taken before the clerk of the circuit court of the county of Harris in the said State of Georgia, whereby the said Robert Thorsen is charged with the said crime, which affidavit is certified by the said governor of Georgia to be duly authenticated: You are therefore required to arrest the said Robert Thorsen wherever he may be found within this State, and to deliver him into the custody of the said ——, sheriff of said county of Harris, to be taken back to the said State from which he fled, pursuant to the said requisition.

Given under my hand and the privy seal of the State of Wisconsin, at the city of Madison, this sixteenth day of July, one thousand eight hundred and eighty-two.

PRIVY
SEAL OF
STATE.

——
Governor.

Fugitives from Justice in Foreign Lands.

After the preliminary affidavit and order of surrender have been properly made out, as above designated, it is usual for some police-officer, or other authorized person, to visit the country where the fugitive has taken refuge, and, with the aid of the United States minister to that government, secure the criminal and bring him back to the State where the crime was committed, for trial. The expenses are to be borne by the party who makes the requisition for his return.

GUARDIANS AND MINOR CHILDREN.

MINOR is a person under twenty-one years of age, or, in some States, a maiden under eighteen years old. In England, and in many of the United States, sex makes no difference.

The legal term for a minor is "infant." The legal consequences of infancy are: First, inability to commit crime until of a certain age; secondly, inability to consent until a certain age; third, inability to make a contract of any kind except marriage; and, fourth, inability to sue or be sued, except by guardians.

Infants may own and hold all kinds of property.

Infants should have guardians of their persons and property.

The parents are the guardians of the person. Courts of probate appoint suitable persons for guardians of their property. At fourteen the infant may select his or her guardian of his or her property.

Infants whose parents are unfit to be guardians, or who suffer them to become a public charge, may have guardians of their persons appointed by some public officer.

The parties so chosen are called guardians, and the infants wards.

Thus the guardians of the person must supply the ward with necessaries and instruction, and the guardian of the property must preserve it, and cannot expend it or change it from real to personal property without the order of the court.

The laws relating to the rights and duties of guardians vary in different States, but in essential particulars resemble each other.

Petition to Have a Guardian Appointed, Made by a Friend.

To the Surrogate of the County of ——, State of ——:

OR

To the County Court of the County of ——, State of ——:

The petition of William J. Erskine, of the city of Milwaukee, Wis., respectfully shows that Moses Erskine is a resident of the county of Milwaukee, and is a minor over fourteen years of age, and was fifteen years of age on the twelfth day of September last past. That he is entitled to certain property and estate, to wit, two building-lots at the northwest corner of Sholto and Schiller streets, in said city, and that to protect and preserve the legal rights of said infant it is necessary that some proper person should be duly appointed the guardian of his estate during his minority. Wherefore, your petitioner nominates, subject to the approbation of the (surrogate or county court of the county of ——), George V. Norcott, of the city of Milwaukee, Wisconsin, merchant, to be such guardian, and prays his appointment accordingly, pursuant to the statute in such case made and provided.

WILLIAM J. ERSKINE.

MILWAUKEE, Wis., November 1, 1882.

To the bottom of this petition the merchant may add:

I, George V. Norcott, of the city of Milwaukee, Wis., merchant, hereby consent to be appointed the guardian of the person and estate of the above-named minor during his minority.

GEORGE V. NORCOTT.

MILWAUKEE, Wis., November 1, 1882.

Form of Bond of Guardian.

KNOW ALL MEN BY THESE PRESENTS, That we, George V. Norcott, of the city of Milwaukee, Wis., merchant, and Samuel Finch, provision packer, of the same city, are held and firmly bound unto (either the State, or the probate or county judge, as the law declares), in the sum of Four Thousand Dollars, lawful money of the United States, to be paid to the said (State or judge), his executors, administrators, or assigns; to which payment, well and truly to be made, we bind ourselves, and heirs (and each of them), and our executors and administrators, jointly and severally, firmly by these presents.

Sealed with our seals. Dated the fourth day of November, A. D. one thousand eight hundred and eighty-two.

The condition of this obligation is such, that if the above bounden George V. Norcott shall and will faithfully, in all things, discharge the duty of a guardian to the said minor, according to law, and render a true and just account of all the property and moneys received by him, and of the application thereof, and of his guardianship in all respects, to any court having cognizance thereof, when thereunto required, then this obligation to be void; otherwise to remain in full force and virtue.

Signed, sealed and deliv-
ered
in presence of
J. T. BROWN,   GEORGE V. NORCOTT,—{SEAL}—
W. M. SMITH.   SAMUEL FINCH,—{SEAL}—

The obligee of the bond is sometimes the State, and sometimes the judge.

GUARANTY.

GUARANTY (sometimes spelled guarantee) is a written promise that a person will do as he has promised, or that on his default, the guarantor will pay all damages.

The person who guarantees the performance of another is called the guarantor. The person to whom the pledge is made is called the guarantee.

The liability, in such a case, first rests upon the person who is guaranteed by another; and,

secondly, if the first person fails, the individual who gives the guaranty is held to the same extent as the other. The consideration for giving the pledge should be either named or expressed as "for value received."

The laws recognize guarantees of any contract that may be legally made, and aid in enforcing them.

The following forms will serve to show how they may be drawn, and some of their uses.

Form of Guaranty on the Back of a Note.

For value received, I hereby guarantee the payment of the within note.

FORT WAYNE, IND., May 20, 1868.   JOHN HOOVER.

A Father's Guarantee of His Son's Fidelity as an Apprentice.

(*Written on the back of the Contract of Apprenticeship.*)

In consideration of the performance of the agreements and covenants specified in the within indenture (or agreements) by Marcus Moran with my son, Allen Ellis, I do hereby bind myself to the said Marcus Moran for the true and faithful observation and performance of all matters and things by the said Allen Ellis agreed and covenanted therein, and that he shall well and truly serve the said Marcus Moran.

Witness my hand this twenty-second day of November, A.D. 1882.

PARKER ELLIS.

Guarantee for the Performance of a Contract for Labor.

For a good and valuable consideration by us received, we, the undersigned, do hereby guarantee a faithful compliance with the terms of the above (or within) agreement, upon the part of the said contractor, William Hawkins. Done at Kenosha, Kenosha county, and State of Wisconsin, this tenth day of December, A.D. 1882.

Signed, sealed and delivered in presence of
RICHARD SLOAN,
MARY ANN SLOAN.
}
ROBERT N. MORRIS,-(SEAL)-
THOMAS WILMOT.-(SEAL)-

INSURANCE.

INSURANCE is a guarantee of protection against loss by fire, tempests, disease, death or other calamity common to all men, by individuals or corporations possessing large amounts of money, upon payment, by the insured, of a stipulated sum at set times agreed upon between the insurer and insured.

Insurance is classed under the heads of fire, marine, accident and life.

Fire insurance extends to stores, dwellings, barns, offices, out-buildings, manufactories and other structures, together with their contents. The more combustible the property is, or the more it is exposed to danger from neighboring buildings, etc., the greater the hazard and the larger the premium (a sum paid by the insured) will be.

Marine insurance includes the hulks, sails, rigging and fittings of vessels or steamers in

port or at sea, and the cargoes which are carried by them.

Accident insurance covers the casualties to which travelers by land or sea are commonly exposed without undue carelessness on their part; and if loss of limb or health results therefrom, the insurer agrees to pay a stipulated sum to the insured, proportionate to the premium paid.

Life insurance extends to all persons in good health, and is founded upon the established death-rate among such persons at all ages from youth to elderly manhood. The premium is regulated by the age of the insured at the time when the insurance is applied for, the prospect of long life, and the amount for which the policy is issued.

An insurance broker is the agent of an insurance company to effect insurance with the people upon their property, and cannot change the restrictions of his company or the privileges allowed by it.

Insurance companies and agents are governed by the laws of the several States, so as to prevent frauds from being perpetrated upon the insured. The insurance companies are also protected by State laws against frauds by the persons insured. The policy is the contract given by the insurer to the insured. The following is the general form of an insurance policy:

Form of Fire Insurance Policy.

No. 102,567. Cash Capital $2,000,000. $5,000.00.

THE

SEWARD INSURANCE COMPANY,

Incorporated 1864. OF HARTFORD, CONN. Stock Policy.

In Consideration of Seventy Dollars, do insure Harry J. Wettzel against loss or damage by fire, to the amount of Five Thousand Dollars; $3,000 on his two-story and basement brick dwelling house, situate No. 976 Ericcson street, Albany, N. Y.; $1,000 on his brick barn in rear of above dwelling: $1,000 on his household furniture, useful and ornamental, beds, bedding, linen, family wearing apparel, printed books and music, silver plate and plated ware, paintings, engravings, and their frames, at not exceeding their cost, piano, sewing-machine, fuel and family stores contained in above brick dwelling house and barn, for one year, to wit: from the twenty-third day of November, 1881, at 12 o'clock noon, to the twenty-third day of November, 1882, at 12 o'clock noon.

1. **Warranty of the assured** — The assured by the acceptance of this policy hereby warrants that any application, survey, plan, statement or description, connected with procuring this insurance, or contained in, or referred to in this policy, is true, and shall be a part of this policy; that the assured has not overvalued the property herein described, nor omitted to state to this company any information material to the risk; and this company shall not be bound under this policy by any act of, or statement to, or by any agent or other person, which is not contained in this policy or in any written paper above mentioned.

It is also a part of this warranty that if the policy shall be continued by renewal, it shall be considered as continued under the original representations; and that any change in the risk, not made known to this company at the time it is so continued, shall render this policy void.

2. **Why this policy will become void** — This policy shall become void, unless consent in writing is endorsed by the company hereon, in each of the following instances, viz.: If the assured is not the sole and unconditional owner of the property; or the building herein described stand on ground not owned in fee simple by the assured; or if the interest of the assured in the property, whether as owner, trustee, consignee, factor, agent, mortgagee, lessee, or otherwise, is not truly stated in this policy; or if any change take place in the title, interest, location or possession of the property (except in case of succession by reason of the death of the assured), whether by sale, transfer or conveyance, in whole or in part, or by legal process or by judicial decree, or the title or possession be now or hereafter become involved in litigation, or if this policy be assigned or transferred before a loss.

2. If the assured have or shall hereafter obtain any other policy or agreement for insurance, whether valid or not, on the property above mentioned, or any part thereof.

3. If the risk be increased by any change in the occupation of the building or premises herein described, or by the erection or occupation of adjacent buildings; or by any means whatever within the knowledge of the assured.

4. If any building herein described be or become vacant or unoccupied for the purposes indicated in this contract.

5. If the property herein described, being a manufacturing establishment, shall be run at night or overtime, or shall cease to be operated.

6. Or if any of the following-named articles be kept, stored or used in or on the premises herein described, any custom or usage of trade or manufacture to the contrary notwithstanding, viz.: benzine, benzole, benzine, varnish, burning fluid, chemical oils, fire-works, gasoline, gunpowder, naphtha, nitro-glycerine, nitrate of soda, oily waste, petroleum and products, phosphorus, rubber cement, saltpetre, spirit-gas, or any articles subject to legal restriction.

3. **What this company is liable for** — This company shall not be liable under this policy for loss or damage by fire in any of the following instances, viz.:

1. If caused directly or indirectly by means or in consequence of an invasion, insurrection, riot, civil war or commotion, or military power, or by order of any military or civil authority, or in consequence of any neglect or violation of any law or ordinance, or by the fraudulent act or procurement of the assured.

2. If caused by lightning or explosion of any kind, unless fire ensues, and then for the loss by fire only.

3. If the building herein described or any part thereof fall, except the fall is the result of fire.

4. If caused by neglect of the assured to use all practicable means to save and protect the property at and after the fire, or when the property is endangered by a fire in neighboring premises.

5. For loss of accounts, bills, notes, deeds, manuscripts, evidences of debt or securities of property of any kind, or for loss by theft at or after the fire.

4. For any consequential or constructive loss or damage, beyond the actual damage by fire to the property, whether such loss or damage be occasioned by any ordinances or law regulating the construction or repair of buildings or otherwise.

4. **What is not insured** — This insurance does not cover any of the following named articles or goods, unless separately and specifically mentioned in writing in the policy, viz. Money or bullion, drawings, models, patterns, tools, implements, paintings, sculpture, medals, casts, curiosities, jewels, watches, scientific apparatus, store furniture and fixtures, awnings, signs, yard fixtures, nor goods held on storage.

5. **General privileges** — 1. Kerosene or refined petroleum oil of the legal standard may be used for lights only, lamps to be filled and trimmed by daylight and not within ten feet of artificial light.

2. Mechanics are allowed to make ordinary alterations and repairs to buildings not exceeding fifteen days in each year of this insurance, without notice to the company. Any extension of this privilege must be previously consented to in writing on this policy.

3. Plate-glass, frescoes and wall decorations are covered by insurance on the building; but if there shall be any other insurance on the building, this company shall be liable only for such proportion of the loss on said plate-glass, frescoes and decorations as the amount hereby insured shall bear to the whole insurance on the building, whether such other insurance applies to said glass, frescoes and decorations or not.

6. **Cancellation of policy** — 1. If any broker or other person than the assured have procured this policy, or any renewal thereof, or any endorsement thereon, he shall be deemed to be the agent of the assured, and not of this company, in any transaction relating to this insurance, including the delivering of this policy and payment of the premium.

2. This insurance may be terminated at any time by request of the assured, or by the company, on giving notice to that effect. On surrender of the policy, the company shall refund any premium that may have been paid, reserving the usual short rates in the first case, and pro rata rates in the other case.

Agreement as to loss — The amount of sound value and of damage to the property may be determined by mutual agreement between the company and the assured, or failing to agree, the same shall then, at the written request of either party, be ascertained by an appraisal of each article of personal property, or by an estimate in detail of the building, by competent and impartial appraisers, one to be selected by each party, and the two so chosen shall first select an umpire to act with them in case of their disagreement, and, if the said appraisers fail to agree, they shall refer the differences to each umpire; and the award of any two, in writing, under oath, shall be binding and conclusive as to the amount of such loss or damage, but shall not decide as to the validity of the contract or any other question except the amount of such loss or damage. Each party shall pay their own appraiser and one-half the umpire's fee. It shall be optional with this company to take the whole or any part of the articles at their appraised value, and also to repair, rebuild or replace the property lost or damaged with other of like kind and quality within a reasonable time, giving notice of their intention so to do within thirty days after completion of the proofs herein required.

[*Suggestions as to particular statement relative to property here omitted.*]

Any fraud or attempt at fraud, or any misrepresentation in any statement touching the loss, or any false swearing on the part of the assured or his agent, in any examination or in the proofs of loss or otherwise, shall cause a forfeiture of all claim on this company under this policy; and in such case, this company shall have the right at any time to require the same to be delivered up to be canceled.

[*What the Company is not liable for and other conditions are here omitted.*]

In Witness Whereof the Seward Insurance Company on its part, has caused these presents to be signed by its President or Vice-President, and attested by its Secretary, in the city of Hartford. But this policy shall not be valid unless countersigned by Hiram Hankins, agent of said Seward Insurance Company, at Albany, N. Y.

SMITH C. WATKINS, Secretary.   HENRY K. WILLIAMS, President.

HIRAM HANKINS, Agent.

LIFE INSURANCE.

That our readers may understand the condition of insurance upon life, we present herewith the questions asked of an applicant, and the form of life insurance policy.

Application for Assurance

To the Home Life Insurance Company, Brooklyn and New York.

The applicant is expected and required to answer all the following questions definitely and fully. *Notice to applicants.* It is desirable that the answer be written by the hand of the applicant; if written by the agent, it will be at the request of and as the *amanuensis* of the applicant.

1. For whose benefit is the insurance to be effected?
2. Whose life to be insured?
3. Amount of assurance?
4. How do you wish to pay the premium?
5. When and where was the party to be insured born?
6. Is the party in good health, and free from any symptom of disease?
7. Is the party whose life is to be insured married?
8. Has the party been vaccinated, or had the small-pox, or varioloid?
9. Are the habits of the party uniformly and strictly sober and temperate?
10. Has the party ever been addicted to the excessive or intemperate use of any alcoholic stimulants or opium? Does the party use, habitually, intoxicating drinks as a beverage? Does the party practice any bad or vicious habit that tends to the shortening of life?
11. What employments has the party been engaged in? Has the health of the party suffered thereby? Has the party been engaged or employed in the manufacture or sale of intoxicating liquors? If so, in what way and when?
12. Is the party now deaf, dumb, blind, or crippled in any way.
13. Has the party ever had any of the following diseases, or any symptoms thereof? (Here follows a long list of well-known, ordinary maladies.) If the party has had one or more of these diseases, please state particularly which.
14. Has the party had inflammatory rheumatism? If so, when and how often?
15. Has the party ever had disease of any vital organ? If so, what was it, and when?
16. Is the party subject to dyspepsia, diarrhœa, or vertigo?
17. Has the party ever had an habitual cough? Has he ever spit blood?
18. Has the party ever met with any severe personal injury? If so, what?
19. Has the party had, during the past ten years, any sickness or disease? If so, state the particulars of each and every such sickness or disease, and the name of each and every physician or physicians who prescribed or were consulted?
20. Have the ancestors of the party generally reached old age?
21. Have the parents, uncles, aunts, brothers or sisters of the party been, or are any of them now afflicted with insanity, fits, cancer, dropsy, or chronic disease of brain, lungs, heart, kidneys, or liver? If so, state explicitly how many and who?
22. Are the parents of the party living?
23. Are the parents of the party dead?
24. How many brothers has the party had? How many sisters? How many are living, and their names? At what ages? What is the state of their health respectively? How many have died, and their names? At what age? Of what disease did they die?
25. Has the party employed or consulted any physician for self or family? Please answer this, Yes or no. If Yes, give name or names of each and every such physician, and residence.
26. Name and residence of an intimate friend to whom the party refers as competent and authorized to answer such questions as may be asked by the company relating to him or her.
27. What amount is now assured on the life of the party, and in what company or companies?
28. Has application ever been made to this or any other company for insurance on the life of the party, which was not granted? If so, what company, when, and for what reason?
29. Have you read the " Notice to Applicants" at the head of this page, and have you duly considered your answers to all the foregoing questions? Do they definitely express what you intend to say, and are you aware that any untrue, evasive or fraudulent answer to the above queries, or any suppression or misstatement of facts in these answers in regard to the health, habits, or circumstances of the party, or of the family relations of the party, will vitiate the policy, and forfeit all payments thereon?

[*The party insured here affirms that he has truly answered the above, which affirmation is duly attested by a competent witness.*]

The Life Insurance Policy.

The foregoing questions being answered to the satisfaction of the company, a policy is issued to the party insured in the following form:

No. 316,725.   ◆THE◆ $2,000.00.

HOME LIFE INSURANCE COMPANY,
OF BROOKLYN AND NEW YORK,

Premium, $80.00.   **Age, 49 Years.**

In consideration of the representations and agreements contained in the application therefor, and of the payment of two-thirds of the amount per annum of Eighty Dollars, and the interest on one-third of the said annual premium which there is a loan secured by this policy, to be liquidated as hereinafter stated, by Edward G. Martell,

Does assure the life of Edward G. Martell, of Fleming, in the county of Cox, State of New Jersey, in the sum of Two Thousand Dollars for the term of life with participation in profits. And the said Home Life Insurance Company does hereby promise and agree to and with the said Edward G. Martell to pay the sum assured, less the balance of the year's premium, if any, and any indebtedness to the company on account of this contract, or for any loan made on all policies at its offices in this city, to his wife, Mary Louise Martell, within sixty days after due notice and satisfactory proof of death, and interest in accordance with the terms of this contract.

Provided always, and it is hereby declared to be the true intent and meaning of this policy, and the same is granted by this company, and accepted by the said Edward G. Martell upon these express conditions, that if the statements made for or for him, contained in the application bearing date the tenth day of January, 188-, upon the faith of which this policy is made which statements he makes his own, and warrants to be full, correct and true, or any part thereof shall be found untrue, incomplete or deceptive in any respect, or in case the said Edward G. Martell shall not actually pay the first premium as aforesaid, before the delivery of this policy, and while the

said Edward G. Martell is in good health, or shall not pay, or cause to be paid to this company, at its office in the city of New York on or before the seventeenth day of January, at 12 o'clock, noon, in each and every year during the continuance of this policy, the said two-thirds of the annual premium of eighty dollars, to wit, the sum of fifty-three dollars and thirty-three cents, and annually in advance during the continuance of this policy, the interest on one-third of the annual premiums which may have loaned to the assured from year to year, or so much thereof as may remain unpaid, or in case the said Edward G. Martell shall not pay, or cause to be paid, any note or notes which may be given to and received by said company, in part payment of any premium, on the day or days when the same shall become due;

Or in case the said Edward G. Martell shall, without the written consent of this company, previously obtained, engage as mariner, engineer, fireman, conductor, agent, messenger, laborer or servant in any capacity, in service on any sea, sound, inlet, river, lake or railroad, or in the manufacture of any explosive substance, or of any article of which any explosive substance or compound forms a component part, or in submarine operations or mining, or shall enter upon or engage in any aerial voyage, or in any military or naval service whatsoever (the militia not in actual service excepted):

Or in case the said Edward G. Martell shall die in consequence of a duel, or of the violation of law, then, and in every such case, the said company shall not be liable for the payment of the sum assured, or any part thereof, and this policy shall cease, and be null, void and of no effect.

[*Provisions restricting the assured to moderation in living, avoiding hurtful business and non-payment of premiums, etc., are omitted.*]

In Witness Whereof, The Home Life Insurance Company has, by its president and secretary, signed and delivered this contract at the city of New York, in the State of New York, this seventeenth day of January, one thousand eight hundred and eighty-one.

——————, Secretary.   ——————, President.

MARGINAL NOTE.—*Notice to the Holder of this Policy:* No agent of this company is authorised or permitted to waive, alter or change any of the conditions of this policy, or agree to any terms not herein distinctly stated, nor to collect or receive any premiums which may become due and payable under it, without producing and delivering to the insured a receipt for said premium, signed by the president or secretary of this company.

LEASES.

PERSON leasing real estate to another is termed a landlord; the person occupying such real estate is known as a tenant. The person making the lease is known in law as the lessor; the person to whom the lease is made, as the lessee. No particular form of wording a lease is necessary. It is important, however, that the lease state, in a plain, straightforward manner, the terms and conditions of the agreement, so that there may be no misunderstanding between the landlord and tenant.

It is essential that the lease state all the conditions, as additional verbal promises avail nothing in law. It is held, generally, that a written instrument contains the details, and states the bargain entire, as the contracting parties intended.

The tenant can sub-let a part, or all, of his premises, unless prohibited by the terms of his lease.

A lease by a married woman, even if it be upon her own property, at common law, is not valid; but, by recent statutes, she, in many States, may lease her own property and have full control of the same; neither can the husband effect a lease that will bind her after his death. His control over her property continues only so long as he lives.

Neither a guardian nor a minor can give a lease, extending beyond the ward's majority, which can be enforced by the lessee; yet the latter is bound unless the lease is annulled.

If no time is specified in a lease, it is generally held that the lessee can retain possession of the real estate for one year. A tenancy at will, however, may be terminated in the eastern States by giving three months' notice in writing; in the middle and southern States, six months; and in the western States, one month; though recent statutes, in some States, have somewhat modified the above.

The lease that specifies a term of years without giving the definite number is without effect at the expiration of two years. A lease for three or more years, being acknowledged and recorded in the recorder's office, is an effectual bar to the secret or fraudulent conveyance of such leased property; and it further obviates the necessity of procuring witnesses to authenticate the validity of the lease.

Duplicate copies of a lease should always be made, and each party should retain a copy of the same.

A new lease to the same person invalidates an old one.

A lease on property that is mortgaged ceases to exist when the person holding such mortgage forecloses the same if it is prior to the lease.

A landlord, consenting to take a substitute, releases the first tenant

Where there is nothing but a verbal agreement the tenancy is understood to commence at time of taking possession. When there is no time specified in the lease, tenancy is regarded as commencing at the time of delivering the writings.

If it is understood that the tenant is to pay the taxes on the property he occupies, such fact must be distinctly stated in the lease, as a verbal promise is of no effect.

Short Form of Lease for a House.

THIS INSTRUMENT, made the first day of May, 1872, witnesseth that Theodore Shonts, Ashville, County of Buncombe, State of North Carolina, hath rented from Tilgham Schnee, of Ashville, aforesaid, the dwelling and lot No. 46 Broadway, situated in said town of Ashville, for four years from the above date, at the yearly rental of Two Hundred and Forty Dollars, payable monthly, on the first day of each month, in advance, at the residence of said Tilgham Schnee.

At the expiration of said above-mentioned term, the said Shonts agrees to give the said Schnee peaceable possession of the said dwelling, in as good condition as when taken, ordinary wear and casualties excepted.

In witness whereof, we place our hands and seals the day and year aforesaid.

Signed, sealed and delivered in presence of
JOHN EDMINSTER,
Notary Public.

THEODORE SHONTS,—(SEAL)—
TILGHAM SCHNEE.—(SEAL)—

Lease of Dwelling-House for a Term of Years, with a Covenant not to Sub-let.

THIS INDENTURE, made this first day of May, 1873, between Hiram Wilcox, of Oxford, county of Benton, and State of Alabama, party of the first part, and Barton D. Maynard, of the same town, county and State, party of the second part:

WITNESSETH, that the said party of the first part, in consideration of the covenants of the said party of the second part, hereinafter set forth, does by these presents lease to the said party of the second part the following-described property, to wit: The dwelling-house and certain parcel of land, situated on the south side of Main street, between Spring and Elm streets, known as No. 82 Main street.

To have and to hold the same to the said party of the second part, from the first day of May, 1873, to the thirtieth day of April, 1875. And the said party of the second part, in consideration of the leasing the premises as above set forth, covenants and agrees with the party of the first part to pay the said party of the first part, as rent for the same, the sum of One Hundred and Eighty Dollars per annum, payable quarterly in advance, at the residence of said party of the first part, or at his place of business.

The said party of the second part further covenants with the party of the first part, that at the expiration of the time mentioned in this lease, peaceable possession of the said premises shall be given to said party of the first part, in as good condition as they now are, the usual wear, inevitable accidents, and loss by fire, excepted; and that upon the non-payment of the whole or any portion of the said rent at the time when the same is above promised to be paid, the said party of the first part may, at his election, either distrain for said rent due, or declare this lease at an end, and recover possession as if the same were held by forcible detainer; the said party of the second part hereby waiving any notice of such election, or any demand for the possession of said premises.

And it is further covenanted and agreed, between the parties aforesaid, that said Barton D. Maynard shall use the above-mentioned dwelling for residence purposes only, and shall not sub-let any portion of the same to others, without permission from said Hiram Wilcox.

The covenants herein shall extend to and be binding upon the heirs, executors and administrators of the parties to this lease.

Witness the hands and seals of the parties aforesaid.

HIRAM WILCOX,-(SEAL)-
BARTON D. MAYNARD.-(SEAL)-

Lease of Farm and Buildings Thereon.

THIS INDENTURE, made this first day of March, 1873, between Moses Waite, of the town of Doyleston, State of Pennsylvania, of the first part, and Abijah Hazelton, of the same place, of the second part:

WITNESSETH, that the said Moses Waite, for and in consideration of the covenants hereinafter mentioned and reserved, on the part of the said Abijah Hazelton, his executors, administrators and assigns, to be paid, kept and performed; hath let, and by these presents doth grant, demise and let, unto the said Abijah Hazelton, his executors, administrators and assigns, all that parcel of land situate in Doyleston aforesaid, bounded and described as follows, to wit:

[*Here describe the land.*]

Together with all the appurtenances appertaining thereto. To have and to hold the said premises, with appurtenances thereto belonging, unto the said Hazelton, his executors, administrators and assigns, for the term of five years from the first day of April next following, at a yearly rent of Eight Hundred Dollars, to be paid in equal payments, semi-annually, as long as said buildings are in good tenantable condition.

And the said Hazelton, by these presents, covenants and agrees to pay all taxes and assessments, and keep in repair all hedges, ditches, rail, and other fences (the said Moses Waite, his heirs, assigns and administrators, to furnish all timber, brick, tile and other materials necessary for such repairs.)

Said Hazelton further covenants and agrees to apply to said land, in a farmer-like manner, all manure and compost accumulating upon said farm, and cultivate all the arable land in a husband-like manner, according to the usual custom among farmers in the neighborhood; he also agrees to trim the hedges at a seasonable time, preventing injury from cattle to such hedges, and to all fruit and other trees on the said premises. That he will seed down with clover and timothy seed twenty acres yearly of arable land, ploughing the same number of acres each spring of land now in grass, and hitherto unbroken.

It is further agreed, that if the said Hazelton shall fail to perform the whole or any one of the above-mentioned covenants, then and in that case the said Moses Waite may declare this lease terminated, by giving three months' notice of the same, prior to the first of April of any year, and may distrain any part of the stock, goods or chattels, or other property in possession of said Hazelton, for sufficient to compensate for the non-performance of the above-written covenants, the same to be determined, and amounts so to be paid to be determined by three arbitrators, chosen as follows: Each of the parties to this instrument to choose one, and the two so chosen to select a third; the decision of said arbitrators to be final.

In witness whereof, we have hereto set our hands and seals.

Signed, sealed and delivered in presence of
HARRY CRAWLEY.

MOSES WAITE,-(SEAL)-
ABIJAH HAZELTON.-(SEAL)-

Landlord's Agreement.

THIS CERTIFIES that I have let and rented, this first day of May, 1872, unto Dennis Holden, my house and lot, No. 18, North Front street, in the city of Philadelphia, State of Pennsylvania, and its appurtenances; he to have the free and uninterrupted occupation thereof for one year from this date, at the yearly rental of Twelve Hundred Dollars, to be paid monthly in advance; rent to cease if destroyed by fire, or otherwise made untenantable.

JONAS WHEELOCK.

Tenant's Agreement.

THIS CERTIFIES that I have hired and taken from Jonas Wheelock, his house and lot, No. 18 North Front street, in the city of Philadelphia, State of Pennsylvania, with appurtenances thereto belonging, for one year, to commence this day, at a yearly rental of Twelve Hundred Dollars, to be paid monthly in advance; unless said house becomes untenantable from fire or other causes, in which case rent ceases; and I further agree to give and yield said premises one year from this first day of May, 1873, in as good condition as now, ordinary wear and damage by the elements excepted.

Given under my hand this day.

DENNIS HOLDEN.

Notice to Quit.

To CHANDLER PECK,

Sir:—Please observe that the term of one year, for which the house and land, situated at No. 14 Elm street, and now occupied by yourself, were rented to you, expired on the first day of May, 1873, and as I desire to repossess said premises, you are hereby requested and required to vacate the same.

Respectfully Yours,
NEWTON, MASS., May 4, 1873.　　　DENSLOW MOORE.

Tenant's Notice of Leaving.

Dear Sir:—The premises I now occupy as your tenant, at No. 14 Elm street, I shall vacate on the first day of May, 1873. You will please take notice accordingly.

Dated this first day of February, 1873.

To DENSLOW MOORE, Esq.　　　CHANDLER PECK.

LETTERS OF CREDIT.

ETTERS OF CREDIT are written papers authorizing credit to the amount named to the persons bearing them.

Such a letter is usually given by a banker, merchant, or other responsible man, to a distant banker or wealthy friend. The person bearing it may leave an equivalent with the party giving it, as a deposit of money, bonds, mortgages or stocks; or no security may be required, as in the case of a son or other near relative, or of a very intimate friend. It must have the written signature of the person sending it, and be guarded in other ways, as are drafts, checks, etc. A copy of the letter, with a description of the person named, is also sent to the correspondent addressed, by mail, in order to make the recognition of the person to be credited the more certain.

The person presenting the letter of credit, having been fully identified by the party to whom it is sent, must comply freely with any conditions stated in the letter before receiving the money.

If the money to be received on the letter of credit is to be used in paying a debt owing by the bearer of it to another party, the fact should be stated in the letter.

Should the letter not be accepted by the person to whom it is directed, the bearer of it should at once notify the writer of it, and state the ostensible reason for not honoring it.

A gentleman of means may obtain from another, in similar circumstances, a letter to a business house where the latter is well known and the former is not, reciting the financial ability of the applicant for credit, and guaranteeing the payment of any indebtedness incurred by him within a certain limit. The person of the strange gentleman must be so described in the letter that the business firm to whom it is addressed may readily recognize him as the person entitled to present it.

Or, if one gentleman has already incurred a debt, the letter of credit may guarantee the payment of the amount due within a specified time.

The gentleman who signs either letter is holden for the amount involved, provided the business house accepts the guarantee as soon as it is received.

Form of Letter of Credit.

14 Soho Square, Beaver Street, LONDON, ENG., Dec. 4, 1882.
Messrs. DREXEL, MORGAN & CO.,
New York City, U. S. A.

Dear Sirs:

I take pleasure in introducing to you Mr. George W. Hopkins, of Belgrave Terrace, Newton street, London, C.W., who visits the United States for the purpose of investing in manufacturing property in the city or vicinity of Philadelphia, Pa., and desires to open a credit with you of Ten Thousand Dollars during each of the months of May, June and July, of 1883. I hereby authorize you to honor his drafts to an amount not exceeding in the aggregate the above-named sum, and charge the same to me.

The signature of Mr. Hopkins accompanies this.

Yours Very Respectfully,
MOSES BRANDENBERG.
Signature of GEORGE W. HOPKINS

Mr. Brandenberg's Letter Sent by Mail.

14 Soho Square, Beaver Street, LONDON, ENG., Dec. 4, 1882.
Messrs. DREXEL, MORGAN & CO.,
New York City, U. S. A.

Gentlemen:

We have to-day granted a letter of credit on your house (as per enclosed duplicate) to Mr. George W. Hopkins, for Thirty Thousand Dollars.

Mr. Hopkins is fifty-one years of age, six feet and one inch tall; has a dark complexion, with dark hair and eyes, and is slightly lame in his right foot.

Respectfully Yours,
MOSES BRANDENBERG.

A Guarantee Letter of Credit.

NEW ORLEANS, LA., May 3, 1882.
Mr. ROBERT FLEMING,
St. Louis, Mo.

Dear Sir:

Mr. Asahel T. Cox, the bearer of this letter, is an extensive dealer in hardware, stoves and tinners' stock, at Baton Rouge, La., who is now about visiting your city for the first time, with a view of purchasing large additions to his stock of merchandise. We have reason to know the condition of his financial ability, his character for fair dealing and his promptness in meeting his liabilities. We, therefore, do not hesitate to guarantee the payment of any indebtedness that he may contract with your house not exceeding Ten Thousand Dollars, on not less time than sixty days.

Very Respectfully Yours,
GEORGE PROBITY & CO.,
104 Breadalbane Street.

The Letter Sent by Mail.

104 Breadalbane street, NEW ORLEANS, LA., May 5, 1882.

Mr. ROBERT FLEMING,

St. Louis, Mo.

Dear Sir:

We have to-day given a guarantee letter of credit upon you for Ten Thousand Dollars in merchandise, to be paid within sixty days after your receipt of this. The bearer of our letter of credit is Mr. Asahel T. Cox, an acquaintance of long standing and a prosperous hardware merchant at Baton Rouge, La.

Mr. Cox is twenty-nine years old, five feet four inches tall, with blue eyes, light hair, side whiskers of a darker shade, and has a hair-mole on his left cheek. We commend him to your kind consideration.

Yours Very Respectfully,
GEORGE PROBITY & CO.

LICENSE.

LICENSE is a paper permitting a proper person, or persons, to sell certain merchandise, or transact other lawful and specific business with the public, within certain prescribed districts, on payment of a special tax or premium for such privilege.

Licenses may be issued, respectively, by national, State, county, or municipal governments, or by others in authority.

Licenses cover an indefinite number of objects, trades and professions, and are regulated by statutes and ordinances, providing restrictions and inflicting penalties for misrepresentations and other fraudulent practices.

Licenses are liable to be recalled, or annulled, by the parties who issue them, whether of a public or private nature, either by agreement at a particular date, or on account of some violation of good faith on the part of the licensed person.

A license may exist if only framed in words, without a writing, but in such a case it should only be uttered in the presence of competent witnesses.

The following are the forms of license, issued by the municipal authority, and are good general forms for use anywhere:

Form of Peddler's License.

By authority of the city of Buffalo, permission is hereby given to John Ryan to peddle green fruit, numbered 872, from the date hereof until the first day of May next, in said city, subject to the ordinances of said city in such cases made and provided, and to revocation by the Mayor at any time, at his discretion.

[CITY SEAL] Witness the hand of the Mayor of said city, and the corporate seal thereof, this twenty-second day of May, 1882.

H. H. CARTER, Mayor.

Attest: JOHN SMITH, City Clerk.

On the back of this license is printed the following:

LICENSE NO. 872.

TO PEDDLERS: Your attention is directed to the following section from the ordinance relating to peddlers:

SECTION 5. -- Any person who shall exercise the vocation of peddler, by means of a wagon, cart or other vehicle, shall cause his name, together with the number of his license, to be painted on the outside of his vehicle, the letters and figures not less than one inch in length. Any violation of this section shall subject the offender to a fine of not less than Five Dollars, and not more than Fifty Dollars.

Licenses for other purposes, including taverns, saloons, etc., may be issued by the presidents and common councils of villages, supervisors of towns, or mayors and aldermen of cities, in States where such governments are permitted by the State and municipal laws, to license such business, within their limits.

Druggist's License from the Government to Retail Ardent Spirits.

$25.00.   Series of 1881.   No. 2071654.   United States stamp for special tax.   Internal revenue.

Received from George T. Meriton the sum of Twenty-five Dollars, for special tax on the business of retail liquor dealer, to be carried on at Freeport, State of Pennsylvania, for the periods represented by [U. S. REV. SEAL] the coupon or coupons hereto attached. Dated at Philadelphia, 23 April, 1881.

THOMAS B. SMITH,
Collector 1st Dist., State of Pennsylvania.

Severe penalties are imposed for neglect or refusal to place and keep this stamp conspicuously in your establishment or place of business.

Form of License to Sell Tobacco and Cigars.

$5.00.   Series of 1882.   No. 6521075.   United States stamp for special tax.   Internal revenue.

Received from Andrew R. Phillips, the sum of Five Dollars, for special tax on the business of retail tobacco dealer, to be carried on at Albany, State of New York, for the period represented by [U. S. REV. SEAL] the coupon or coupons hereto attached. Dated at Albany, N. Y., 6 June, 1882.

ARTHUR KELLEY,
Collector 3d Dist., State of New York.

Severe penalties are imposed for neglect or refusal to place and keep this stamp conspicuously in your establishment or place of business.

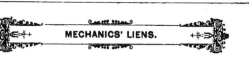

MECHANICS' LIENS.

IEN-LAWS establish a right to retain possession of personal property until the payment is made for services in respect to it.

A lien is lost by the voluntary surrender of the property to the owner or his agent.

There is no common law lien without possession. It is a right created by law in favor of the tavern-keepers, livery-men, pasturers, carriers and mechanics. It may be created by contract between the parties, as in a lease.

Whatever is affixed to land belongs to the owner of the land, except in a few cases. Hence, carpenters who built houses on the land of others had no lien. But as the principle is just, and the practice beneficial, States have, by law, given builders and persons who furnish material a lien on the land and building, if claimed within a limited time. Under this kind of mechanics' lien, no possession is required. The right to pay the charge and take the property is a right of redemption which is lost by a public sale of the property. The surplus, if any, is paid to the owner.

Liens by State law are generally foreclosed in a court, upon a petition for that purpose. By its decree the property is sold and the proceeds divided according to the rights of the parties.

Liens may, in certain States, be enforced against vessels and wharves as well as buildings, for construction, alteration or repairs. In most States, while the same general principle is maintained, the modes of procedure vary.

A workman desiring the protection of the law for the security of his wages, may draw up a paper, addressed to the county clerk of the county where the work was done, filled up in a manner similar to the following form, setting forth all the circumstances of the work done, his bargain with the contractor, the failure to receive his pay and his fears that he will lose all if his lien is not made. This paper, sworn to before a justice or notary public, as true, is filed in the county clerk's office and becomes a cloud upon the building, which the owner is only too glad, frequently, to remove by paying the debt himself and taking it out of the contractor's bill. In either event the owner or contractor must pay the debt if it is an honest one.

Notice to the County Clerk.

To Philip Best, clerk of the city and county of New York, in the State of New York:

Sir: Please to take notice that I, James Van Horn, residing at No. 45 Conkling avenue, in the city of New York, in said county, have a claim against William Y. Heath, owner (or only contractor, as the case may be), of a new two-story brick dwelling-house, amounting to Nineteen Hundred and Sixty-two Dollars and forty cents, now due to me, and that the claim is made for and on account of brick furnished and labor done before the whole work on said building was completed, and which labor and materials were done and furnished within three months of the date of this notice; and that such work and brick were done and furnished in pursuance of a contract for twenty thousand serviceable brick and the mason work of putting up the outer walls of said new building, between the undersigned and the said William Y. Heath, which building is situated on lot ——, in block ——, in Wetzel's addition to the city of New York, on the west side of Salina avenue, and is known as No. 432 of said avenue. The following is a diagram of said premises.

[*Insert diagram.*]

And that I have and claim a lien upon said dwelling-house and the appurtenances and lot on which the same stands, pursuant to the provisions of an act of the legislature of the State of New York, entitled "An act to secure the payment of mechanics, laborers and persons furnishing material toward the erection, altering or repairing of buildings in the city of New York," passed ——, 18—, and of the acts amending the same.

New York, December 1, 1882.　　JAMES VAN HORN.

James Van Horn, being duly sworn, says that he is the claimant mentioned in the foregoing notice of lien; that he has read the said notice, and knows the contents; and that the same is true to his own knowledge, except as to the matters therein stated on information and belief, and as to those matters he believes it to be true.

JAMES VAN HORN.

Sworn before me this first day of December, A. D. 1882.

J. L. LESLIE, Police Justice.

The lien-laws of certain States provide that any person who shall either labor himself, or furnish laborers or materials for constructing, altering, or repairing any building, shall have a lien therefor upon such building and the specific lot or tract of land on which it is located; but a suit to enforce the payment of said claim must begin within six months from the time the last payment therefor is due. Landlords, also, may enforce a lien for arrears of rent, upon all crops of their tenants, whether growing or matured.

MINING AND MINERS' FORMS.

THE PERSON who proposes to visit a mining region with a view to prospecting, discovering, and extracting from the earth precious metals, should first study the geography of the country in which he expects to operate.

Second, he should read all available matter relating to the region and the subject of mining.

Third, he should, if possible, make the acquaintance of those who have traveled in that portion of the country, and thus avail himself of their experience.

Fourth, he should then proceed to a "School of Mines," one or more of which may usually be found in the immediate vicinity of all rich mining regions, and there spend a few days or weeks in receiving instruction from competent instructors as to the means by which rich ores may be known when found, methods of testing ores, processes of reduction, assaying, smelting, taking out of ore, and much other useful information which will be of service to the prospector.

Experience has shown that a company of three, each provided with a mule or small horse, if this convenience can be afforded, make the number best calculated to prospect together, especially in the mountainous regions of America, the advantage of this number being that while one cares for baggage, mules, washing, cooking, etc., the others are free to engage in exploration.

Having found, outside of property owned by anybody else, evidence of mineral in such quantity and richness as to make it desirable to locate a claim, the miner will proceed to stake off the amount of land to which he is entitled by law, on each side of the nearest place where he intends to sink an opening into the earth in search of ore.

The law of most of the mining regions in the Rocky Mountains permits the miner to claim 750 feet in each direction from the discovery shaft in the line that the vein of ore is supposed to run, and 150 feet on each side, so that when the claim is staked off it will be in shape as follows:

Prospecting Miner's Claim.

1,500 FEET LONG.

| 300 feet wide. | Discovery O Shaft. | 300 feet wide. |

1,500 FEET LONG.

The law of different mining localities is liable to change, however, so that it may be necessary for the miner to provide himself with the various pocket manuals containing the law of his locality in order to know how much land he is actually entitled to claim, as the law frequently differs in different portions of a State.

A prospector, holding a discovery claim, is allowed sixty days in which to sink his discovery shaft the distance of ten feet. At the place where the discovery of a vein has been made, it is customary to post a notice in substance as follows:

Coming-Day Lode.

The undersigned claim sixty days to sink discovery shaft and three months to record on this vein.

May 6, 1880.   FRANKLIN ALLEN,
WALTER B. SMITH, } Discoverers.
JOHN JOHNSON,

This notice is not a necessity, but simply a warning to other prospectors that the vein is to be claimed. The sixty days begin when the vein is discovered, and cannot be extended beyond that number.

Having sunk his discovery shaft to a depth of ten feet, the miner should, if possible, procure the services of a surveyor, who will make a competent and lawful survey. But even without a surveyor the claim, if definitely marked off by stakes driven into the ground, or supported by a pile of stone around each, will be sufficiently well defined to enable a record to be made of the same

Having sunk a discovery shaft, and having an accurate description by a surveyor or otherwise, the next step is to have a record made of the same in the recorder's office of that county as follows:

Certificate of Mining Location.

KNOW ALL MEN BY THESE PRESENTS, That we, Franklin Allen, Walter B. Smith and John Johnson, of the county of Clear Creek, State of Colorado, claim by right of discovery and location fifteen hundred feet linear and horizontal measurement, on the Coming Day lode, along the vein thereof, with all its dips, variations and angles; together with one hundred and fifty feet in width on each side of the middle of said vein at the surface; and all veins, lodes, ledges, deposits and surface ground within the lines of said claim; seven hundred and fifty feet on said lode, running east fifteen degrees north from the center of the discovery shaft, and seven hundred and fifty feet running west fifteen degrees south from said center of discovery shaft.

Said claim is on the eastern slope of Democrat mountain, in Griffith mining district, county of Clear Creek, State of Colorado, and is bounded and described as follows: Beginning at corner No. 1, from which deep shaft on Famine lode bears west three degrees, south 180 feet, and chiseled on prominent ledge of rock, bears east twenty degrees, north 290 feet, and running thence west fifteen degrees, north 750 feet to east center stake, thence same course 750 feet to corner No. 2; thence (etc., going all around the claim in the same manner). Discovery shaft bears west forty-nine degrees, north 100 feet from corner No. 1 of survey lot No. 777.

Said lode was discovered on the 6th day of May, 1882. Date of location, July 15, 1882. Date of this certificate, August 6, 1882.

FRANKLIN ALLEN,
WALTER B. SMITH,
JOHN JOHNSON.
Attest: FRANCIS FRENCH.

Annual Labor to Hold a Claim.

The law makes it necessary that at least Five Hundred Dollars' worth of labor shall be performed upon the claim before a patent will be granted by the government to the person who may desire to buy the land, and of this labor at least One Hundred Dollars' worth shall be done each year in order to hold the claim.

Where annual labor is performed for the purpose of holding a claim, affidavit must be made of that fact before a legally constituted authority, as shown in the following:

Form of Affidavit of Labor Performed.

STATE OF COLORADO, } ss.
County of Clear Creek, }

Before me, the subscriber, personally appeared Franklin Allen, Walter B. Smith, and John Johnson. who, being duly sworn, say that at least one hundred dollars' worth of labor or improvement was done or made upon the Coming-Day lode, situate on Democrat mountain, in the Griffith mining district, county of Clear Creek, State of Colorado. Said expenditure was made by or at the expense of Frederick Allen, Walter B. Smith and John Johnson, principal owners of said claim, for the purpose of holding said claim for the annual period expiring on the thirtieth day of June, A. D. 1881.

FRANKLIN ALLEN,
WALTER B. SMITH,
JOHN JOHNSON.
Sworn and subscribed before me this first day of May, A.D. 1881.
[NOTARIAL SEAL.]   JAPHETH E. COX, Notary Public.

In order to keep a claim good as against others entering upon the land, the discoverers, their heirs or assigns, must perform One Hundred Dollars' worth of work upon the mine each year. If one or more of the co-owners neglect or refuse to contribute their portion of the annual assessment, they thereby forfeit their ownership, which notice of forfeiture will be published in the nearest newspaper thirteen successive weeks, and will read as follows:

Notice of Forfeiture of Claim.

GEORGETOWN, COL., May 6, 1882.
To JOHN JOHNSON:
You are hereby notified that we have, during the year just past, ending this day, expended One Hundred Dollars in labor and improvements upon the Coming-Day lode, situate

upon Democrat mountain, in the Griffith mining district, county of Clear Creek, and State of Colorado, of which the location certificate is found on record in book 35, page 301, in the office of the recorder of said county, in order to hold said claim under the provisions of sections 2,324 of the Revised Statutes of the United States, and the amendments thereto approved January 22, 1880, concerning annual labor upon mining claims, being the amount required to hold said lode for the period ending on May 6, A. D. 1882. And if, within ninety days from the service of this notice (or, within ninety days after this notice by publication) you fail or refuse to contribute your proportion of such expenditure as a co-owner, your interest in the claim will become the property of the subscribers by the terms of said section.

FRANKLIN ALLEN,
WALTER B. SMITH.

The forfeiture notice being personally served upon the delinquent co-owner, and he paying no attention to the same, the forfeiture is considered complete at the expiration of ninety days from the time the notice was served.

In the meantime Franklin Allen and Walter B. Smith having hired Granville Smith and Philip H. Cooper to perform the assessment work, and, neglecting to pay them for their services, said workmen file a lien against the Coming-Day mining claim, which reads as follows, Twenty-five Dollars being the lowest amount for which a lien can be allowed, which claim must be made within six months from the time the labor was performed.

Notice of Miners' Lien for Labor.

GRIFFITH MINING DISTRICT, Clear Creek County,
Colorado, September 6, 1882.
To FRANKLIN ALLEN, WALTER B. SMITH and JOHN JOHNSON:
You are indebted to us in the sum of One Hundred Dollars for work done by us, under a contract with you on the Coming-Day mining claim, recently worked by you, on Democrat mountain, in this mining district, in said county, for which sum we claim a lien on said mining claim.

GRANVILLE SMITH,
PHILIP H. COOPER.
STATE OF COLORADO, } ss.
Clear Creek County, }
Granville Smith and Philip H. Cooper, being this day sworn by me, deposed and said that the sum of money mentioned in the foregoing statement is justly due to them from said Frederick Allen, Walter B. Smith and John Johnson.
[NOTARIAL SEAL.]   PETER BEASLEY, Notary Public.
September 6, 1882.

How to Secure a Mine From Government.

The foregoing claim for miners' lien having been paid, and the owners being desirous of securing absolute ownership of the land and mine from government, now observe the following directions from the United States statutes relating to mining and mining claims.

Section 2,325.—Any person, association or corporation authorized to locate a claim under this chapter, having claimed and located a piece of land for such purposes, who has or have, complied with the terms of this chapter, may file in the proper land office an application for a patent, under oath, showing such compliance, together with a plat and field notes of the claim or claims in common, made by or under the direction of the United States Surveyor-General, showing accurately the boundaries of the claim or claims, which shall be distinctly marked by monuments on the ground, and shall post a copy of such plat together with a notice of such application for a patent, in a conspicuous place on the land embraced in such plat previous to the filing of the application for a patent, and shall file an affidavit of at least two persons that such notice has been duly posted, and shall file a copy of the notice in such land office, and shall thereupon be entitled to a patent for the land, in the manner following The register of the land office, upon the filing of such application, plat, field notes and affidavits, shall publish a notice that such application has been made, for the period of sixty days, in a newspaper to be by him designated as published nearest to such claim, and he shall also post such notice in his office for the same period. The claimant at the time of filing this application or at any time thereafter, within the sixty days of publication, shall file with the register a certificate of the United States Surveyor General that Five Hundred Dollars worth of labor has been expended or improvements made upon the claim by himself or grantors; that the plat is correct, with such further description by such reference to natural objects or permanent monuments as shall identify the claim and furnish an accurate description, to be incorporated in the patent. At the expiration of the sixty days of publication the claimant shall file his affidavit, showing that the plat and notice have been posted in a conspicuous place on the claim during such period of publication. If no adverse claim (by other parties) shall have been filed with the register and the receiver of the proper land office at the expiration of the sixty days of publication, it shall be assumed that the applicant is entitled to a patent upon the payment to the proper officer of Five Dollars per acre, and that no adverse claim exists, and thereafter no objection from third parties to the issuance of a patent shall be heard except it be shown that the applicant has failed to comply with the terms of this chapter: Provided, that where the claimant for a patent is not a resident of or within the land district wherein the vein, lode, ledge or deposit sought to be patented is located, the application for patent and the affidavit required to be made by this section by the claimant for such patent may be made by his, her or its authorized agent, where said agent is conversant with the facts sought to be established by said affidavits.

Afterward for a time the owners lease the mine, the following being the form of paper drawn for that purpose:

Form of Lease of a Mine.

THIS INDENTURE, made this first day of July, in the year of our Lord one thousand eight hundred and eighty-three, between Franklin Allen and Walter B. Smith, of the county of Clear Creek, and State of Colorado, lessors, and Nestor P. Robbins, of the same place, lessee;

WITNESSETH, that the said lessors, for and in consideration of the rents, royalties, covenants and agreements hereinafter mentioned, reserved and contained, and by the said lessee, his executors, administrators, and assigns, to be paid, kept and performed, do lease and convey to said lessee, his heirs, executors, administrators, and assigns, the right of entering in upon the following lands, situated (*here insert the description of the mining claim, as set forth in the previous form of "Certificate of Mining Location,"*) for the purpose of searching for mineral and fossil substances, and of conducting mining and quarrying to any extent that he may deem advisable; for the term of two years from the first day of July, A. D. 1883, (but not to hold possession of any part of said lands for any other purpose whatsoever,) paying for the site of buildings (or designate any specific works or machinery) necessary thereto, a reasonable rent.

And the lessee hereby agrees that he, his heirs, executors, administrators or assigns, will pay or cause to be paid to the said lessors, their heirs or assigns, as follows: Two Thousand Dollars semi-annually, on each first day of January and July of each year during the continuance of this lease, at the First National Bank of Denver, at the city of Denver, in the State of Colorado.

And the said lessee covenants that no damage shall be done to or upon said lands and premises, other than may be necessary in conducting his said mining and quarrying operations.

And the lessors and the lessee, each for themselves, their heirs, executors, administrators, and assigns, covenant and agree, and this indenture is made with this express proviso, that if no mineral or fossil substance be mined or quarried, as now contemplated by said parties, within the period of one year from and after the first day of July, A. D. 1883, then these presents, and everything contained herein, shall cease and be forever null and void.

In witness whereof the lessors and lessee have hereunto set their hands and seals the day and year first above written.

Executed in pres- } FRANKLIN ALLEN, –(SEAL)–
ence of   } WALTER B. SMITH, –(SEAL)–
CHARLES DANE.   } NESTOR P. ROBBINS. –(SEAL)–

These parties also arrange with Peter Conant and Simon D. Thompson to prospect for them, making with them the following agreement:

Form of Agreement for Prospecting.

In consideration of provisions advanced to us by Franklin Allen and Walter B. Smith, and of their agreement to supply us from time to time, as we may reasonably demand them, with tools, food

and mining outfit generally, and the sum of One Hundred Dollars in hand paid, we agree to prospect for lodes and deposits in the county of Boulder, and State of Colorado, and to locate all discoveries which we may consider worth the expenditure, and record the same in the joint names of said outfitters and ourselves, and in our names only as equal owners. Our time and labor shall stand against money, provisions, etc., as aforesaid. All expenses of survey and record shall be paid by the outfitters, and we agree to make no debts on account of this agreement. Work done on claim after record and before the expiration of this contract, shall be considered as done under this contract, and no charge for labor or time shall be made for the same. This contract shall stand good during the whole of the summer and fall of 1883, and during all that period we will not work or prospect on our own account, or for parties other than said outfitters.   PETER CONANT,
Dated, Boulder, Col., July 1, 1883.   SIMON D. THOMPSON.
We agree to the terms above stated.

                                        FRANKLIN ALLEN,
                                        WALTER B. SMITH.

In the prospecting tour Conant and Thompson find an abandoned mining claim which they are satisfied from indications can be made profitable to work. Learning that assessments have not been kept up on the same, and that they are free to relocate this claim, they proceed to take possession in the following form:

Form for Relocating a Mine.

KNOW ALL MEN BY THESE PRESENTS, that we, Franklin Allen, Walter B. Smith, Peter Conant and Simon D. Thompson, of the town of Boulder, in the county of Boulder, and State of Colorado, claim, by right of relocation, fifteen hundred feet, linear and horizontal measurement, on the Tennessee lode, along the vein thereof, with all its dips, variations and angles; together with seventy-five feet in width on each side of the middle of said vein at the surface; and all veins, lodes, ledges and surface-ground within the lines of said claim: seven hundred and fifty feet on said lode running west, ten degrees north from the center of the discovery shaft, and seven hundred and fifty feet running east, ten degrees south from said center of discovery shaft; said discovery shaft being situate upon said lode, within the lines of said claim, in Merton mining district, county of Boulder, State of Colorado; said claim being bounded and described as follows: Beginning at corner No. 1, (here follow the description in the original location); being the same lode originally located on the tenth day of June, A. D. 1880, and recorded on the twenty-fifth day of June, A. D. 1880, in book R, page 106, in the office of the recorder of said county;—this further certificate of location being made without waiver of any previous rights, but to correct any error in prior location or record, to secure all abandoned overlapping claims, and to secure all the benefits of section 1823 of the general laws of Colorado. Date of relocation, December 10, A. D. 1883. Date of certificate, December 11, A. D. 1883.

Attest: G. W. FLINT.   FRANKLIN ALLEN,
                                         WALTER B. SMITH,
                                         PETER CONANT,
                                         SIMON D. THOMPSON.

The claim which has been relocated the new owners conclude to sell, and in doing so execute only a quit-claim deed. This differs very little in any essential point from common quit-claim deeds, (see "Deeds," on a previous page), in form. The description of the property is worded minutely, so that its location and dimensions are clearly defined.

Description of Quit-Claim Deed.

"Situate in Merton mining district, in the county of Boulder, and State of Colorado, to wit: The Brilliant mining claim, on the Tennessee lode, known as survey 888, being fifteen hundred feet in length and three hundred feet in width, together with all and singular the lodes and veins within the lines of said claim, and the dips, spurs, mines, minerals, easements, mining fixtures, improvements, rights, privileges and appurtenances thereunto in anywise pertaining."

This must be acknowledged before a proper officer, like other deeds.

Allen and Smith being satisfied with their original claim, and the term for which it was leased having expired, propose to work it yet more vigorously, and to that end, with a view to getting more capital, they organize a stock company, the articles and forms of incorporation of which are shown in the following:

Articles Incorporating a Company for Mining.

WHEREAS Franklin Allen, Walter B. Smith and Granville Smith, of the county of Clear Creek, and State of Colorado, have associated themselves together for purposes of incorporation under the General Incorporation Acts of the State of Colorado, they do therefore make, sign and acknowledge these duplicate certificates in writing, which, when filed, shall constitute the articles of incorporation of the "Coming-Day Mining Company."

Article I.—The name of said company shall be the "Coming-Day Mining Company."

Article II.—The objects for which said company is created, are to acquire and operate mines of silver-bearing ore, in said county of Clear Creek, and to do all things incident to the general object of mining.

Article III.—The term of existence of said company shall be fifteen years.

Article IV.—The capital stock of said company shall be Seven Hundred and Fifty Thousand Dollars, divided into seven thousand five hundred shares of One Hundred Dollars each.

Article V.—The number of directors of said company shall be three, and the names of those who shall manage the affairs of the company for the first year of its existence are Franklin Allen, Walter B. Smith, and Granville Smith.

Article VI.—The principal office of said company shall be kept at Idaho Springs, in said county; and the principal business of said

company shall be carried on in said county of Clear Creek; but a part of the business may be transacted in the county of Arapahoe, at the city of Denver, in this State.

Article VII.—The stock of said company shall be non-assessable.

Article VIII.—The directors shall have power to make such prudential by-laws as they may deem proper for the management of the affairs of the company, not inconsistent with the laws of this State, for the purpose of carrying on all kinds of business within the objects and purposes of said company.

IN WITNESS WHEREOF the said incorporators have hereunto set their hands and seals this first day of January, A. D. 1883.

FRANKLIN ALLEN, –(SEAL)–
WALTER B. SMITH, –(SEAL)–
GRANVILLE SMITH. –(SEAL)–

STATE OF COLORADO, } ss.
County of Clear Creek,   I, Nicholas Welch, a notary public in and for said county, do hereby certify that Franklin Allen, Walter B. Smith and Granville Smith, who are personally known to me to be the same persons described in, and who executed the within duplicate articles, appeared before me this day and personally acknowledged that they signed, sealed and delivered the same as their free and voluntary act and deed. Witness my hand and notarial seal this first day of January, A. D. 1883.

[NOTARIAL SEAL]

NICHOLAS WELCH,
Notary Public.

These articles of agreement are made in duplicate copies. One is filed with the recorder, or register of deeds, of the county where the company is formed. In the above case, as part of the business of the company is to be done at Denver, a copy of the articles of association must be filed with the recorder of Arapahoe county; and another copy is filed with the Secretary of State. This last copy is not called a duplicate, but is known as the *original* of the document. The Secretary of State issues a certified copy of the articles, thus giving them his official approval.

The number of directors in such a company—sometimes they are called trustees—must not exceed nine, nor be less than three.

Facts Which Miners Should Understand.

Right of Way.—Miners have the right of way across any claim when hauling quartz.

Liability of Stockholders.—Stockholders are liable only for debt to the amount of unpaid stock held by them.

Number to Form Company.—Any three or more persons can form a company for tunnel, ditch or mining purposes.

Alkaline Waters.—A few drops of lemon juice will remove the alkali from water, which otherwise is hurtful for miners to drink.

Caution.—Miners in high altitudes should be protected with warm woolen garments, extra clothing in case of sudden changes, and material to keep themselves dry.

Sizes in Feet.—Forty-three thousand five hundred and sixty square feet equal one acre of land. A square, 208 71-100 feet in length and width contains one acre.

Water Rights.—Water may be brought across any claim, road, ditch or other mining improvement, provided it is so guarded that it does not interfere with the prior rights of another.

Annual Assessment of Placer Claims.—The law requires that $12 worth of work shall be done each year on a placer claim of 20 acres or under, and $100 worth on a 160 acre tract, in order to hold it.

Amount of Land in Placer Claims.—In locating a placer (that is surface, or loose dirt) claim, the amount of land is limited to 20 acres to one person. An association of eight persons may locate 160 acres.

Things that Seldom Happen.—That a miner given to strong drink ever goes back rich to his old home; that a miner that gambles ever saves any money; that a miner that attempts to get rich by dishonesty ever permanently prospers.

Cooking.—Boiling provisions in the high altitudes require thrice the time that it does in the lower regions.

Duration of Charter.—The term of existence of a mining tunnel, ditch or mining company cannot exceed twenty years.

Cannot Mine Under Another.—No miner has a right to mine under the improvements of another, except by legal permission.

Test for Copper.—Immerse ore in hot vinegar, remove and expose to the air. If green or blue appears on its surface, it contains copper.

Must be a Citizen.—To secure claims from government the miner must be a citizen of the United States, or have legally declared his intention to become such.

Where Law is Found.—A copy of the laws relating to mining in each district will be found at the office of the county clerk in the district where the mine is located.

Penalty for False Weights.—Any person using scales that improperly weigh gold dust or other commodity for others is subject to a fine of $500 and imprisonment for six months.

Penalty for Destroying Claim Marks.—Any person who shall destroy or remove location stakes, except on abandoned property, shall be liable to a fine of $1,000 and one year's imprisonment.

Penalty for Taking Another's Claim.—The person jumping a claim owned by another, and gaining the same by threats or violence, shall be liable to a fine of $250 and imprisonment in the county jail six months.

Amount of Land for Mill Sites.—The United States law allows five acres to be taken as a claim for a mill site, but the site must not be upon known mineral lands. Sometimes the district regulations restrict the amount to much less dimensions.

Test for Silver.—To a quantity of ore add one-third the quantity of salt. Reduce to a powder, and bake in a clay-pipe bowl. Cool and add a little water, heat again and stir. Insert a piece of bright copper, and it will become coated if any silver is present.

Penalty for Misrepresenting.—Any person engaged in milling, sampling, reducing, shipping or purchasing ores, who shall knowingly change the true value of the same, whereby the owner of such ore shall not obtain its true value, shall be liable to a fine of $1,000 and one year's imprisonment.

Principal Points in Locating a Claim.—When locating a claim the certificate of such location should contain the name of the lode, name of the locators, date of location, description such as will clearly identify the claim, and the requisite amount of land, not to exceed the amount allowed by the district rules of the locality.

Testing for Gold.—In certain kinds of quartz gold is readily distinguished. In others, though present, it cannot be seen. Of the numerous ways of discovering it, scientific and otherwise, one of the simplest is to grind the ore fine, place in a cup, and add water. Stir well, and pour off the top water. Add more ore and repeat. In time, gold, if there be any, will appear. A further test is to add a little mercury to the sediment, and heat in an iron spoon. The mercury evaporates, and gold, if there is any, appears. If still unsatisfied, add a small quantity of lead to the metal left in the spoon and melt together. Place the compound in nitric acid, and the gold, undissolved, will show itself when rubbed with a polished instrument.

Values and Weights of Gold and Silver.—A pound of silver is worth about $13.11. A pound of gold is worth $248.04. Gold is almost twice as heavy as silver, as shown in the fact that a cubic foot of gold weighs 1,203, while a cubic foot of silver weighs 625 pounds. A ton of gold is worth $602,799, and a ton of silver is worth $37,704. When the teamster has a load of pure gold which weighs 3,685 pounds avoirdupois, he has $1,000,000; but while one team could draw this, it would require over thirty teams to draw the same value in silver, allowing nearly two tons to the team, as it takes 58,929 pounds of silver to make $1,000,000. Since 1792 California has produced up to June 30, 1881, $709,024,000 of gold, and Nevada, in the same length of time, yielded $77,435,000 in silver. Among the people in the United States there are about $470,000,000 of gold in circulation and $181,000,000 of silver, making about $12 in specie to each man, woman and child in the country. The largest nugget of gold on record was found in the Ballarat Diggings, Victoria, Australia, in 1858. It weighed 2,166 ounces, and was sold for $41,580. Silver bullion fluctuates in value. At the present writing, in 1883, it is worth $1.00¼ per ounce. Gold bullion has remained at the same value for many years, being worth $20.67 per ounce.

Penalty for Putting Foreign Ore in a Claim.—"Salting" a claim, that is, taking ore from another mine and placing it in the one that is to be sold, thereby deceiving the purchaser, is punishable by a fine of $1,000 and confinement in the State prison fourteen years.

Gold Nuggets Found in Montana.—A nugget of gold found on the claim of Detrick & Brother, in Rucker Gulch, sold for $1,800. One found in Nelson Gulch, in 1865, brought $2,073; and another taken out of Snowshoe Gulch, in 1865, weighed fourteen pounds and ten ounces troy, and sold for $3,300.

Penalty for False Count.—The superintendent, manager or owner of a quartz-mill, mill-furnace or cupel, engaged in extracting ore, who shall neglect or refuse to account for and pay to the owner of the quartz or mineral all sums which shall be due, except such as may be retained for services, shall be liable to a fine of $1,000 and imprisonment not exceeding one year.

Number of Feet that Make Acres.—A claim 2,640 by 2,640 feet contains 160 acres. A claim 1,320 by 1,320 feet contains 40 acres. A claim 933¼ by 933¼ feet contains 20 acres. A claim 800 by 1,089 feet contains 20 acres. A claim 1,320 by 660 feet contains 20 acres. A claim 660 by 660 feet contains 10 acres. A claim 500 by 500 feet contains 5 75-100 acres. A claim 660 by 330 feet contains five acres.

Camp Outfit.—Pomeroy's "Mining Manual" gives the following as a suitable camp outfit for three persons: One tent, two or more woolen blankets each; one rubber blanket each; two pairs of rubber boots with high tops, for wading streams; one folding camp-table; three folding camp-stools; one iron frying-pan; one bake-oven; one granite coffee-pot, six granite plates; six granite cups; two granite kettles, one granite bucket, six tin spoons (three large and three small), three knives and three forks, one butcher-knife; one coffee-mill; needles, thread and buttons; can-opener, cork-screw, fishing-hooks and lines; one field-glass, for examining inaccessible mountain formations; one pocket-lens; one pocket-compass; one tape-line; one axe; two prospecting-picks; one drilling-hammer, and sledge, two long-handled shovels; one driller's spoon; three drills of Jessop's steel, one eighteen inches, one twenty-six inches, and one thirty-six inches long, five pounds giant powder; one box of caps and necessary fuse; one blow-pipe, soda, candles, charcoal, coffee, tea, sugar, flour, corn meal, onions, bacon or ham, dried apples, dried beef, pepper, salt, condensed milk, beans, dried peas, crackers, cheese, soap, molasses, baking-powder, all the canned goods that may be suited to the liking of the prospectors, the necessary means of protecting life from danger, and an equipment for testing ores.

MORTGAGES.

THE LAW defines a mortgage as a conveyance of property, personal or real, given to secure the payment of a debt, or as a guaranty for the performance of some special duty. As soon as the debt is paid, or the duty is performed, the mortgage is void and of no value.

The meaning of the word mortgage is a "dead pledge," because the property pledged becomes lost or dead to the person who executed the mortgage if he fails to fulfill the conditions necessary to prevent such loss.

The party who mortgages his property is called the mortgagor, and the person to whom the mortgage is given is the mortgagee.

Where real estate is mortgaged, unless otherwise provided, the mortgagor retains possession of the property, and receives its rents and other profits, paying all taxes, insurance, repairs and liens upon it.

In case real estate is pledged, the mortgage must be properly acknowledged, like a deed, before a notary public or other legal officer. See "Acknowledgments," on a previous page.

Personal property may pass into possession of the mortgagee, if such is the contract, or the mortgagor may continue to hold and use it, if it is so agreed.

Mortgages must be in writing, contain a redemption clause, be signed and sealed by the mortgagor, properly witnessed, and recorded in the office of the county clerk or of the register of deeds, as State laws may require.

The times of payment of the interest and of the principal sum must be distinctly stated in the mortgage, and the property carefully described, with its location.

A mortgage may contain a clause permitting the sale of the property, if forfeited, without a decree of the court, or otherwise. as the several State laws determine, or by agreement of the parties.

A mortgage may be drawn so that a single failure to pay the interest at the stated time may render due the whole sum, principal and interest, and permit the mortgagee to sell the property upon taking the necessary legal steps, long before the date of its maturity.

The foreclosure of a mortgage is a legal declaration that the property has been forfeited and must be sold.

A mortgage may be assigned by the mortgagee to some other person for a valuable consideration.

If a mortgage is given to secure the payment of a certain note, the note must be transferred to the party to whom the mortgage is assigned.

When forfeited property is sold upon a mortgage, should it bring more money than is necessary to pay the debt, interest, costs and charges, the surplus funds must be paid to the mortgagor or his representatives.

Form of a Note Secured by Mortgage.

$10,000.　　CHAMPAIGN, Ill., February 4, 1881.

For value received, on the fourth day of February, A. D. 1884, I promise to pay to Robert Fairchild, or his order, at the First National Bank, in Champaign, in the State of Illinois, the sum of Ten Thousand Dollars ($10,000), with interest at eight per cent. per annum, said interest to be paid without grace semi-annually, to wit: On the fourth day of August, 1881, the fourth day of February, 1882, the fourth day of August, 1882, the fourth day of February, 1883, the fourth day of August,* 1883, and the fourth day of February, 1884, in accordance with the requirements of six coupon notes, bearing even date herewith, for Four Hundred Dollars ($400) each, payable respectively upon the days above named, at such place in the city of Champaign, in the State of Illinois, as he, his executors, administrators or assigns may appoint in writing, and in default of such appointment, then at the First National Bank, in said city of Champaign, with interest upon each coupon note after due until paid, at eight per cent. per annum.

　　　　　　　　　　　　　　BENJAMIN HARRISON.

Caution to Persons Loaning Money.

Before Mr. Fairchild gives the money to Mr. Harrison, as specified in the above note, he should require that an abstract of title to the land be made from the records, at the recorder's office, of the property upon which it is proposed to place a mortgage. This abstract, which is made by a person duly authorized to make the same at the county seat, should show, and it will if lawfully made, whether there is an incumbrance, such as a deed, previous mortgage, or tax lien, upon the property or not.

If Harrison has borrowed money heretofore, and given a previous mortgage to any one, then the person who holds the first mortgage will have the first claim in case the property mortgaged by Harrison has to be sold.

Should the property when sold bring only enough to pay the first mortgage, then Fairchild would have no security whatever. Should it bring more than is required to pay the first claim, then the surplus will go to Fairchild, if his is the second mortgage; and should there be more than enough to pay a first and second mortgage, the surplus will go toward the payment of a third mortgage if there be such upon the property.

The person loaning an amount of money which it is desired to have

absolutely secured by mortgage, should first ascertain from the county records, through an absolutely responsible person, that the property is perfectly free from incumbrance. Second, he should, as soon as he gets the mortgage, have it recorded. This applies equally to all mortgages, whether upon real estate or personal property.

The following shows the mortgage taken by Fairchild from Harrison, upon property which is found to be, upon investigation, absolutely free from incumbrance. As will be seen by examination, in case the note is not paid when due, this mortgage provides that the property shall be forfeited and sold at public auction, according to the legal forms of foreclosing a mortgage.

Real-Estate Mortgage to Secure Payment of Above Note.

THIS INDENTURE, made this fourth day of February, in the year of our Lord one thousand eight hundred and eighty-one, between Benjamin Harrison, of Urbana, county of Champaign, and State of Illinois, and Helen, his wife, party of the first part, and Robert Fairchild, party of the second part:

Whereas, the said party of the first part is justly indebted to the said party of the second part in the sum of Ten Thousand Dollars, secured to be paid by a certain promissory note, bearing even date herewith, due and payable at the First National Bank in Champaign, Ill., with interest, on the fourth day of February, in the year one thousand eight hundred and eighty-four:

Now, therefore, this indenture witnesseth, that the said party of the first part, for the better securing the payment of the money aforesaid, with interest thereon, according to the tenor and effect of the said promissory note above mentioned; and, also, in consideration of the further sum of One Dollar to them in hand paid by the said party of the second part, at the delivery of these presents, the receipt whereof is hereby acknowledged, have granted, bargained, sold and conveyed, and by these presents do grant, bargain, sell, and convey, unto the said party of the second part, his heirs and assigns, forever, all that certain parcel of land, situate, etc.

[Describing the premises.]

To have and to hold the same, together with all and singular the tenements, hereditaments, privileges and appurtenances thereunto belonging or in any wise appertaining. And, also, all the estate, interest, and claim whatsoever, in law as well as in equity, which the party of the first part have in and to the premises hereby conveyed unto the said party of the second part, his heirs and assigns, and to his only proper use, benefit and behoof. And the said Benjamin Harrison, and Helen, his wife, party of the first part, hereby expressly waive, relinquish, release, and convey unto the said party of the second part, his heirs, executors, administrators, and assigns, all right, title, claim, interest, and benefit whatever, in and to the above-described premises, and each and every part thereof, which is given by or results from all laws of this State pertaining to the exemption of homesteads.

Provided always, and these presents are upon this express condition, that if the said party of the first part, their heirs, executors, or administrators, shall well and truly pay, or cause to be paid, to the said party of the second part, his heirs, executors, administrators, or assigns, the aforesaid sum of money, with such interest thereon, at the time and in the manner specified in the above-mentioned promissory note, according to the true intent and meaning thereof, then and in that case, these presents, and everything herein expressed, shall be absolutely null and void.

But if default shall be made in the payment of the said sum of money mentioned in the note aforesaid, or the interest that may become due thereon, or of any part thereof, then and from thenceforth it shall be lawful for the said party of the second part, his heirs, executors, administrators or assigns, to enter into and upon all and singular the premises hereby granted, or intended so to be, and to sell and dispose of the same, and all benefit and equity of redemption of the said party of the first part, his heirs, executors, administrators, or assigns therein, at public auction, to the highest and best bidder, according to the act in such case made and provided.

In witness whereof, the said party of the first part hereunto set their hands and seals, the day and year first above written.

Signed, sealed and de- ⎫   BENJAMIN HARRISON, [L.s.]
livered in presence of ⎬   HELEN HARRISON. [L.s.]
OTIS OBER,   ⎭
ANDREW AUSTIN.

The foregoing note being paid as was agreed, Fairchild gives a release of mortgage to Harrison, which, like all releases and mortgages should be recorded, to show that there is now no incumbrance on the property.

A release is simply a setting free, or the relinquishment of an established interest in property, real or personal, belonging to another party; as, where chattels or lands have been mortgaged, and the mortgage has been duly paid, the mortgagee gives his written acknowledgment that he is satisfied and has no longer any claim upon the mortgagor, as shown in the following:

Form of Release of Mortgage When Note is Paid.

For and in consideration of the fulfillment of all the covenants contained in a certain mortgage bearing date the fourth day of February, A. D. 1881, made and executed by Benjamin Harrison, of Urbana, Champaign county, and State of Illinois, and Helen, his wife, to secure the payment to me, Robert Fairchild, of the same place, of his note for Ten Thousand Dollars, with interest bearing even date with said mortgage, which said mortgage was duly recorded in the recorder's office of said Champaign county, Illinois, on the fourth day of February, A D. 1881, I declare the said mortgage fully satisfied, and consent that the same may be discharged of record.

Dated at Urbana, Champaign county, and State of Illinois, February 5, 1884.

In presence of   ⎫   ROBERT FAIRCHILD, [L.s.]
WILLIAM DORUS,   ⎬   Mortgagee.
TIMOTHY Y. CASS. ⎭

[The above release should be recorded the same as the mortgage.]

Second Form of Release.

[Endorsed on the margin of the mortgage in the recorder's book.]

URBANA, Champaign County. State of Illinois, Feb. 5, 1884. $10,000.

Received of Benjamin Harrison, the within-named mortgagor, the sum of Ten Thousand Dollars, in full satisfaction of the within mortgage.

WM. DORUS, ⎫ Witnesses.   ROBERT FAIRCHILD, [L.s.]
T. Y. CASS, ⎭   Mortgagee.

Third Form of Release.

KNOW ALL MEN BY THESE PRESENTS, That the whole debt secured by mortgage upon the following-described real estate, situate in the county of Champaign, and State of Illinois, to wit:

[Here describe the premises.]

Wherein Benjamin Harrison is grantor, and Robert Fairchild is grantee, and dated February 4, A. D. 1881, a transcript of which is recorded in vol. iv. p. 73, in the office of the register of deeds of said county, has been fully satisfied; in consideration of which said mortgage is hereby released. Witness my hand and seal at Urbana, Champaign county, State of Illinois, February 5, A. D. 1884.

MARY REESE, ⎫ Witnesses.   ROBERT FAIRCHILD, [SEAL.]
CLARA BELL, ⎭   Grantee.

[The above release should be recorded the same as the mortgage.]

How to Foreclose a Mortgage.

Methods of foreclosure vary in different States, but possess some general features, thus:

Application to a court of chancery for authority to foreclose; notification to the mortgagor; hearing of the parties; reference to a master in chancery; advertising the property; selling it at a specified time to the highest bidder at auction; deeding it to the purchaser, and paying over any surplus funds remaining from the sale to the mortgagor. To illustrate:

Joseph Lacy and his wife, owning certain lands in Cumberland county, Tennessee, and needing money to use in establishing a small mercantile business at Nashville, borrow $1,500 of Robert Jones, their neighbor, and give him a mortgage for the amount, on certain real estate in Cumberland county, valued at from $2,500 to $3,000, bearing even date with Lacy's promissory note, due at the end of three years, at six per cent. interest per annum, the interest to be paid every six months. Two years elapse, and Lacy neglects to pay interest on his note after the first six months. Robert Jones, having therefore decided to foreclose the mortgage on account of this default, gives notice thereof in form following, by publishing it in some newspaper in the county where the land is located, twelve weeks or as long as the State laws require:

Notice of Intended Sale of Mortgaged Property.

MORTGAGEE'S SALE.—WHEREAS, Joseph Lacy, and Emily Lacy, his wife, did, by their certain mortgage, dated the third day of July, 1874, and recorded in the recorder's office of Cumberland county, Tennessee, in book 74 of records, at p. 307, convey to the undersigned as mortgagee the real estate hereinafter described, to secure the payment of the certain promissory note of said Joseph Lacy, of even date with said mortgage, for the sum of $1,500, payable on or before three years after the date thereof, to the order of Robert Jones, the undersigned, with interest, at the rate of six per cent. per annum

And, whereas, default has been made in the payment of said promissory note and the interest accruing thereon since one year and six months from the date thereof;

Now, therefore, I, Robert Jones, as mortgagee, under the powers vested in me by said mortgage, and for the purposes expressed therein, will, by M. M. Wells, my attorney in fact, duly constituted therefor, on the 20th day of January, 1877, at nine o'clock in the forenoon, at the east door of the court-house at Crossville, in the county of Cumberland, in the State of Tennessee, sell at public auction, to the highest and best bidder for cash, the premises hereinafter described, and all the right, title, benefit and equity of redemption of the said Joseph Lacy, and Emily Lacy, his wife, their heirs and assigns therein, to wit: Lot seventy (70), division four (4), of the eastern subdivision in the northwest fractional quarter of section thirty-one (31), township thirty-eight (38) north, range fifteen (15) east, of the 3d P. M., in the county of Cumberland, and State of Tennessee, said lot having a frontage of 100 feet by a depth of 370 feet.

The amount claimed to be due upon the note described in said mortgage at the date of sale is $1,585.

Dated Crossville, October 7, 1876.

ROBERT JONES, Mortgagee.

When the foregoing notice has been printed the requisite number of times, the publisher of the newspaper in which it appeared, or the foreman of the printing-office from which the newspaper was issued, or the clerk of the publisher, must make an affidavit with printed copy of the mortgagee's notice of foreclosure and sale pasted beside the affidavit, as follows:

Affidavit that Notice of Sale Has Been Published.

STATE OF TENNESSEE,
County of Cumberland, } ss.   Martin Newman, of the city of Crossville, in said county and State, being duly sworn, says that he is the printer and publisher of the *Weekly Budget*, a newspaper published at Crossville, in Cumberland county, and State of Tennessee, aforesaid; and that the annexed notice of mortgage sale has been published in the said newspaper twelve weeks successively, at least once in each week, the said publication beginning on the seventh day of October, A. D. 1876, and ending on the eighth day of January, A. D. 1877.

Sworn before me this twelfth day
of January, A. D. 1877,   } MARTIN NEWMAN.
GORHAM T. STILES, J. P.

The publisher or mortgagee also makes an affidavit, to which a copy of the mortgagee's printed notice of sale is attached, that he delivered a copy of such notice to the county clerk for filing in his office.

The publisher or mortgagee also makes a similar affidavit, to which a printed copy of the mortgagee's notice of sale is attached, that he has posted a copy of said notice on the outer door of the county court-house.

The mortgagee, or some proper officer, also makes a similar affidavit, to which a printed copy of the mortgagee's notice of sale is attached, that he delivered "a true copy of said notice to the wife" (son or daughter of a competent age) "of the said Joseph Lacy, at his usual place of residence, No.— Blank street, he being absent therefrom at the time;" or that "he served the said Joseph Lacy and Emily Lacy, his wife, by delivering a copy of said notice to each of them individually, and leaving the same with them;" or "served Joseph Lacy with a notice of sale, of which the annexed printed notice is a copy, by depositing a copy of said notice in the post-office in Crossville, Tennessee, properly folded, and enclosed in a sealed envelope, and directed to him at his place of residence, No.— Blank street."

A printed copy of the mortgagee's advertisement of foreclosure and sale should be attached to the following notice, in all cases:

The Auctioneer's Affidavit of the Sale of the Mortgaged Property.

STATE OF TENNESSEE,
County of Cumberland, } ss.   Richard Tennyson of Crossville, in said county and State, being duly sworn, says that he sold the premises described in the annexed printed notice, by public auction, at the time and place of sale therein mentioned, to wit: On the twentieth day of January, A. D. 1877, at nine o'clock in the forenoon, at the east door of the court-house, in the city of Crossville, in said county and State, and that Thomas Paine then and there purchased the same, for the price of Twenty-Five Hundred Dollars, he being the highest bidder, and that being the greatest sum bidden for the same.

And this deponent further says that said sale was made in the daytime, and, in all respects, honestly, fairly and legally conducted, according to his best knowledge and belief; and, also, that the said Thomas Paine purchased the said premises fairly and in good faith, as he verily believes.

RICHARD TENNYSON.

Sworn before me this twentieth day of January, A. D. 1877.
GORHAM T. STILES, Justice of the Peace.

It now remains for the person holding the mortgage to figure up the principal and interest actually due upon the mortgage at the time of sale, adding to that amount all fees to legal officers, cost of advertising, and other necessary expenditures attending the foreclosure, to deduct the total sum from the $2,500 for which the property was sold, and to pay the surplus to the one who gave the mortgage.

This having been done, the sheriff of the county proceeds to give a deed of the property sold to the one who buys it. This deed sets forth the circumstances of the indebtedness, the foreclosure of the mortgage, the advertising and the sale, and transfers the ownership to the purchaser in the usual form of a deed.

Usually there is a fixed time and method for the redemption of his forfeited real estate by the one who gave the mortgage, but the laws of the several States differ in this direction. Thus in North Carolina there is no redemption; in California six months are allowed for redemption upon repayment of the money for which the property was sold and two per cent. interest per month on the amount; in Arkansas, one year, with costs and 10 per cent. interest per annum; and in Alabama, two years, under the same conditions.

Form of Chattel Mortgage.

THIS INDENTURE, made and entered into this tenth day of March, in the year of our Lord one thousand eight hundred and seventy-two, between Amos W. Barber, of the town of Waukegan, of the county of Lake, and State of Illinois, party of the first part, and Alonzo W. King, of the same town, county, and State, of the second part:

WITNESSETH, that the said party of the first part, for and in consideration of the sum of Six Hundred Dollars in hand paid, the receipt whereof is hereby acknowledged, does hereby grant, sell, convey, and confirm unto the said party of the second part, his heirs and assigns forever, all and singular, the following described goods and chattels, to wit:

Two four-year-old cream-colored horses, one Chickering piano, No. 6132, one tapestry carpet, 16x18 feet in size, one marble-top center-table, one Stewart cooking-stove, No. 4½, one black-walnut bureau with mirror attached, one set of parlor chairs (six in number), upholstered in green rep, with lounge corresponding with same in style and color of upholstery, now in possession of said Barber, at No. 8 State street, Waukegan, Ill. ;

Together with all and singular the appurtenances thereunto belonging, or in any wise appertaining; to have and to hold the above-described goods and chattels unto the said party of the second part, his heirs and assigns, forever.

Provided, always, and these presents are upon this express condition, that if the said Amos W. Barber, his heirs, executors, administrators, or assigns, shall, on or before the tenth day of March, A. D. one thousand eight hundred and seventy-three, pay or cause to be paid to the said Alonzo W. King, or his lawful attorney or attorneys, heirs, administrators, or assigns, the sum of Six Hundred Dollars, together with the interest that may accrue thereon, at the rate of ten per cent per annum, from the tenth day of March, A. D. one thousand eight hundred and seventy-two until paid, according to the tenor of one promissory note bearing even date herewith for the payment of said sum of money, that then and from thenceforth, these presents, and everything herein contained, shall cease, and be null and void, anything herein contained to the contrary notwithstanding.

Provided, also, that the said Amos W. Barber may retain the possession of and have the use of said goods and chattels until the day of payment aforesaid; and also, at his own expense, shall keep said goods and chattels; and also at the expiration of said time of payment, if said sum of money, together with the interest as aforesaid, shall not be paid, shall deliver up said goods and chattels, in good con-

dition, to said Alonzo W. King, or his heirs, executors, administrators, or assigns.

And provided, also, that if default in payment as aforesaid, by said party of the first part, shall be made, or if said party of the second part shall at any time before said promissory note becomes due, feel himself unsafe or insecure, that then the said party of the second part, or his attorney, agent, assigns, or heirs, executors, or administrators, shall have the right to take possession of said goods and chattels, wherever they may or can be found, and sell the same at public or private sale, to the highest bidder for cash in hand, after giving ten days' notice of the time and place of said sale, together with a description of the goods and chattels to be sold, by at least four advertisements, posted up in public places in the vicinity where the said sale is to take place, and proceed to make the sum of money and interest promised as aforesaid, together with all reasonable costs, charges, and expenses in so doing; and if there shall be any overplus, shall pay the same without delay to the said party of the first part, or his legal representatives.

In testimony whereof, the said party of the first part has here unto set his hand and affixed his seal, the day and year first above written.

Signed, sealed and deliv- }
ered in presence of   }   AMOS W. BARBER. [L.S.]
ROBERT KENDALL.   }

NATURALIZATION.

FOREIGNERS, before they become citizens of the United States, as set forth in the following forms and explanations, are called aliens, and owe no allegiance to the State in which they reside.

Aliens do not possess the right to vote for the election of any officer of the government, town, municipal, county, State or national; nor can they hold public offices until they are naturalized or have declared their intentions to become citizens.

Their personal and property rights while aliens are, however, respected and protected by all branches of our government.

Comparing individuals with governments, the alien seems to bear about the same relation to citizenship that the Territories of the United States do to the Union—protected, but with certain privileges withheld.

The laws by which an alien is transformed into a citizen, and is endowed with all a citizen's rights and privileges, are established by the general government.

The United States laws require the applicant for naturalization to be an individual who

has lived within its territory for five years immediately before and up to the time of his application. He must also have resided during one year of the five in the State or Territory in which he makes his application. Two years before he can legally be naturalized, he must go before a federal court, or some local court of record, or the clerk of either of such courts, and make an affidavit that he proposes to become a full citizen of the United States at the proper time, and to renounce his allegiance to all other governments, princes or potentates, and, particularly, the sovereignty of the country from which he emigrated. In most States this declaration entitles him to vote. If an alien has served in the army or navy of the United States, and has been honorably discharged from such service, he may be naturalized after one year's residence in any State or Territory. Such residence must, however, be definitely proven before the court

The first step in the process of legal naturalization, the applicant having duly shown that he is entitled to become a citizen, is to file in court a declaration of his intentions as follows:

Form of Declaring Intention to Become a Citizen.

I, Gustave Baum, do declare on oath (or do affirm), that it is really my intention to become a citizen of the United States, and to renounce forever all allegiance and fidelity to all and any foreign prince, potentate, State and sovereignty whatever, and particularly to William, Emperor of the German confederation.

GUSTAVE BAUM.

Sworn (or affirmed) in open court, at Loredo, Webb county, State of Texas, this sixteenth day of January, A. D. 1881.

SIMON R. PETERSON, Clerk.

The Clerk's Certificate.

The following is annexed to the declaration of intentions:

STATE OF TEXAS, } ss.
County of Webb, }   I, Simon R Peterson, clerk of the circuit court of said county, do certify that the above is a true copy of the original declaration of intention of Gustave Baum to become a citizen of the United States, remaining on record in my office.

In testimony whereof I have hereunto subscribed my name and affixed the seal of said court, the sixteenth day of January, one thousand eight hundred and eighty-one.

| SEAL OF |
| CLERK OF |
| CIRCUIT |
| COURT. |

SIMON R. PETERSON, Clerk.

Two years after filing his declaration of intention to become a citizen, the alien, having been a resident of the United States for five years, goes into the court again, bearing the written proof that he has been sufficiently long in the United States to become a citizen, and there makes oath of his allegiance as a citizen in the following forms:

Proof of an Alien's Residence and Moral Character.

CIRCUIT COURT, }
COUNTY OF WEBB, } ss.
STATE OF TEXAS, }   Robert Morris, of Loredo, being duly sworn (or affirmed) says that he is a citizen of the United States, and is, and has been during the last past five years, well acquainted with Gustave Baum, now present; that said Gustave Baum has resided within the United States for at least five years last past, and for one year last past within the State of Texas: and that during that time the said Gustave Baum has behaved as a man of good moral character, attached to the principles of the constitution of the United States, and well disposed to the good order and happiness of the same.

ROBERT MORRIS.

Sworn (or affirmed) in open court the twenty-fifth day of January, A. D. 1883.

SIMON R. PETERSON, Clerk.

The Applicant's Oath of Allegiance Accompanying the Foregoing Proof.

CIRCUIT COURT, }
County of Webb, } ss.
STATE OF TEXAS, }   I, Gustave Baum, do swear (or affirm) that the contents of my petition are true; that I will support the constitution of the United States, and I now renounce and relinquish any title or order of nobility to which I am now or may hereafter be entitled; and I do absolutely and entirely renounce and abjure all allegiance and fidelity to any foreign prince, potentate, State, or sovereignty whatever, and particularly to William, Emperor of the German confederation, of whom before I was a subject.

GUSTAVE BAUM.

Sworn (or affirmed) in open court, this twenty-fifth day of January, A. D. 1883.

SIMON R. PETERSON, Clerk.

The applicant for citizenship having now complied with all the requirements of the naturalization law, by properly declaring his intentions, and proving his eligibility to become a citizen, and having taken the oath of allegiance to the United States government and renounced the claims of any other government upon him to the satisfaction of the court, is now entitled to receive the final certificate that he is a citizen of the United States. The form of the certificate is as follows:

Certificate of Citizenship After Having Been Fully Naturalized.

UNITED STATES OF AMERICA, }
STATE OF TEXAS, } ss.
County of Webb, }   Be it remembered that on the twenty-fifth day of January, in the year of our Lord one thousand eight hundred and eighty-three, Gustave Baum, formerly of Berlin, in the empire of Germany, now of Loredo, Webb county, in the State of Texas, appeared in the circuit court (the said court being a court of record, having common-law jurisdiction, and a clerk and seal), and applied to the said court to be admitted to become a citizen of the United States of America, pursuant to the provisions of the several acts of Congress of the United States of America, for that purpose made and provided. And the said applicant having produced to the court such evidence, made such declaration and renunciation, and taken such oaths as are by the said acts required, it was ordered by the said court that the said applicant be admitted, and he was accordingly admitted by said court, to be a citizen of the United States of America.

In testimony whereof the seal of the said court is hereunto affixed this twenty-fifth day of January, in the year of our Lord one thousand eight hundred and eighty-three, and in the year of our independence one hundred and seven.

| SEAL |
| OF THE |
| COURT. |

By the Court,
SIMON R. PETERSON, Clerk.

If any alien die after declaring his intention to become a full citizen, and before he can legally do so, his widow and children are entitled to all the rights and privileges of citizens upon taking the oath of allegiance to this government.

Minor Aliens.

Alien parents coming to this country bring male children under eighteen years of age. These boys, residing here continuously for five or more years, become of age. Then they are eligible to naturalization, and are not required to make the formal declaration of intention two years before applying for citizenship, as in other cases. But when they appear before the proper court to apply for citizenship they must make the declaration, and swear (or affirm) that for the three years immediately preceding their application such has been their intention, and in all other respects must comply with the naturalization laws.

Proof of a Minor Alien's Residence and Good Character.

CIRCUIT COURT, }
County of Oswego, } ss.
STATE OF NEW YORK, }   Thomas G. Magill, of Oswego, N. Y., being duly sworn (or affirmed), says that he is a citizen of the United States, and is, and has been during the last past five years, well acquainted with Saunders McCarty, now present; that said Saunders McCarty has resided within the United States for at least five years last past, and for one year last past within the State of New York; that during that time the said Saunders McCarty has behaved as a man of good moral character, attached to the principles of the constitution of the United States; that said Saunders McCarty

became of the age of twenty-one years on the tenth day of December, A. D. 1882; and that he resided within the United States at least three years next previous to his becoming twenty-one years of age.

THOMAS G. MAGILL.

Sworn (or affirmed) in open court this first day of April, A. D. 1883.   ALISON M. BARBER, Clerk.

Oath of Recently Minor Alien for Naturalization.

CIRCUIT COURT,
County of Oswego, } ss.
STATE OF NEW YORK,   I, Saunders McCarty, do swear (or affirm) that the contents of my petition are true; that I will support

the constitution of the United States; and I now renounce and relinquish any title or order of nobility to which I am now or may hereafter be entitled; and I do absolutely and entirely renounce and abjure all allegiance and fidelity to any foreign prince, potentate, State, or sovereignty whatever, and particularly to Victoria, Queen of Great Britain and Ireland, of whom before I was a subject (or citizen): And I do also swear (or affirm) that it is really my intention, and has been for the last three years, to become a citizen of the United States.

SAUNDERS McCARTY.

Sworn (or affirmed) in open court this first day of April, A. D. 1883.   ALISON M. BARBER, Clerk.

PARTNERSHIP.

AN agreement between two or more persons to invest their labor, time and means together, sharing in the loss or profit that may arise from such investment, is termed a partnership.

This partnership may consist in the contribution of skill, extra labor, or acknowledged reputation upon the part of one partner. while the other, or others, contribute money, each sharing equally, or in fixed proportion, in the profits. Or an equal amount of time, labor and money may be invested by the partners and the profits equally divided; the test of partnership being the joint participation in profit and joint liability to loss.

A partnership formed without limitation is termed a general partnership. An agreement entered into for the performance of only a particular work, is termed a special partnership; while the partner putting in a limited amount of capital, upon which he receives a corresponding amount of profit, and is held correspondingly responsible for the contracts of the firm, is termed a special partner. The conditions of such a partnership, are regulated by law in different States.

Negotiable paper of the firm, even though given on private account by one of the partners, will hold all the partners of the firm when it passes into the hands of holders who were ignorant of the facts attending its creation.

Partnership effects may be bought and sold by a partner; he may make contracts; may receive money; endorse, draw and accept bills and notes; and while this may be for his own private account, if it apparently be for the use of the firm, his partners will be bound by his action, provided the parties dealing with him were ignorant of the transaction being on his private account; and thus representation or misrepresentation of a partner having relation to business of the firm, will bind the members in the partnership.

An individual lending his name to a firm, as partner or allowing the same to be used after he has withdrawn from the same, is still responsible to third persons as a partner.

A partnership is presumed to commence at the time articles of copartnership are drawn, if no stipulation is made to the contrary, and the same can be discontinued at any time, unless a specified period of partnership is designated in the agreement; and even then he may withdraw by giving previous notice of such withdrawal from the same, being liable, however, in damages, if such are caused by his withdrawal.

Should it be desired that the executors and representatives of the partner continue the business in the event of his death, it should be so specified in the articles, otherwise the partnership ceases at death. Should administrators and executors continue the business under such circumstances, they are personally responsible for the debts contracted by the firm.

If it is desired that a majority of the partners in a firm have the privilege of closing the affairs of the company, or in any way regulating the same, such fact should be designated in the agreement; otherwise such right will not be presumed.

Partners may mutually agree to dissolve a partnership, or a dissolution may be effected by a decree of a court of equity. Dissolute conduct, dishonesty, habits calculated to imperil the business of a firm, incapacity, or the necessity of partnership no longer continuing, shall be deemed sufficient causes to invoke the law in securing a dissolution of partnership, in case the same cannot be effected by mutual agreement.

After dissolution of certain kinds of partnership, notice of the same should be given in the most public newspapers, and a notice likewise should be sent to every person having special dealings with the firm. These precautions not being taken, each partner continues liable for the acts of the others to those persons pecuniarily interested who have no knowledge of the dissolution and have had previous dealings with the firm.

Form of Partnership Agreement.

THIS AGREEMENT made this tenth day of June, A. D. one thousand eight hundred and seventy one, between Charles R. Field, of Salem, Washington county, New York, of the one part, and David G. Hobart, of the same place, of the other part, witnesseth:

The said parties agree to associate themselves as copartners, for a period of five years from this date, in the business of buying and selling hardware and such other goods and commodities as belong in that line of trade; the name and style of the firm to be "Field & Hobart."

For the purpose of conducting the business of the above-named partnership, Charles R. Field has, at the date of this writing, invested Five Thousand Dollars as capital stock, and the said David G. Hobart has paid in the like sum of Five Thousand Dollars, both of which amounts are to be expended and used in common, for the mutual advantage of the parties hereto, in the management of their business.

It is hereby also agreed by both parties hereto, that they will not, while associated as copartners, follow any avocation or trade to their own private advantage; but will, throughout the entire period of copartnership, put forth their utmost and best efforts for their mutual advantage and the increase of the capital stock.

That the details of the business may be thoroughly understood by each, it is agreed that during the aforesaid period accurate and full book-accounts shall be kept, wherein each partner shall record, or cause to be entered and recorded, full mention of all moneys received and expended, as well as every article purchased and sold belonging to, or in any wise appertaining to such partnership; the gains, profits, expenditures and losses being equally divided between them.

It is further agreed, that once every year or oftener, should either party desire, a full, just and accurate exhibit shall be made to each other, or to their executors, administrators, or representatives, of the losses, receipts, profits and increase made by reason of, or arising from such copartnership. And after such exhibit is made, the surplus profit, if such there be resulting from the business, shall be divided between the subscribing partners, share and share alike.

Either party hereto shall be allowed to draw a sum, the first year, not exceeding Six Hundred Dollars per annum, from the capital stock of the firm, in monthly installments of Fifty Dollars each; which amount may be increased by subsequent agreement.

And further, should either partner desire, or should death of either of the parties, or other reasons, make it necessary, they, the said copartners, will each to the other, or, in case of either, the surviving party to the executors or administrators of the party deceased, make a full, accurate and final account of the condition of the partnership as aforesaid, and will, fairly and accurately, adjust the same. And also, upon taking an inventory of said capital stock, with increase and profit thereon, which shall appear or is found to be remaining, all such remainder shall be equally apportioned and divided between them, the said copartners, their executors or administrators, share and share alike.

It is also agreed that in case of a misunderstanding arising with the partners hereto, which cannot be settled between themselves, such difference of opinion shall be settled by arbitration, upon the following conditions, to wit: Each party to choose one arbitrator, which two thus elected shall choose a third; the three thus chosen to determine the merits of the case, and arrange the basis of a settlement.

In witness whereof the undersigned hereto set their hands the day and year first above written.

CHARLES R. FIELD,
DAVID G. HOBART.

Signed in presence of
ABEL SMITH,
MYRON BROWN.

Dissolution of a Firm.

A silent partner withdrawing from the firm, a majority of the creditors not knowing of his interest in the business, a public announcement of his retirement is not deemed necessary. But if his name has been prominently associated in the partnership, a notice of the dissolution is published in some newspaper within the county where the business was transacted, in the following form:

Notice of Dissolution of Partnership.

The partnership heretofore existing under the name of Beecher, Moulton & Tilton, wherein John L. Beecher and Richard T. Moulton, both of the city of Huntsville, in the county of Butler and State of Kentucky, were general partners, and Frederick W. Tilton, of the city of St. Louis, in the county of St. Louis and State of Missouri, was a special partner, is this, the twenty-seventh day of January, A. D. 1883, dissolved by mutual consent.

JOHN L. BEECHER,
RICHARD T. MOULTON,
FREDERICK W. TILTON.

The business will be continued at Huntsville, Ky., by John L. Beecher, who alone is authorized to settle the affairs of the said firm.

HUNTSVILLE, Ky., January 27, 1883.

PASSPORTS.

PASSPORTS are written permits, furnished without charge, to citizens of this country to travel unmolested in European or other dominions, virtually commending them to the protection of the foreign governments which they may visit. The Secretary of State of the United States at Washington, is alone authorized to grant and issue passports; but the ministers and other diplomatic representatives of our government abroad may also grant, issue and verify passports. None but citizens of the United States can receive passports, and they are only issued under such rules as the President of the United States prescribes. The unlawful granting or verifying of a passport by any officer of the United States subjects him to punishment by fine or imprisonment. Collectors of customs may also issue passports to United States vessels visiting foreign ports, and the master of the vessel is punished if he sails from an American port to a foreign country without one.

The name, age and residence of the individual applying for a passport, with a description of his person and appearance, are entered in it, for the purpose of properly identifying him. Though passports possess less importance now than formerly, it is well for the traveler abroad to always procure one before commencing a foreign journey.

Passports are engraved and printed, in large letters and open lines, on parchment. The following is the form:

Form of Passport for Citizen of the United States when Traveling Abroad.

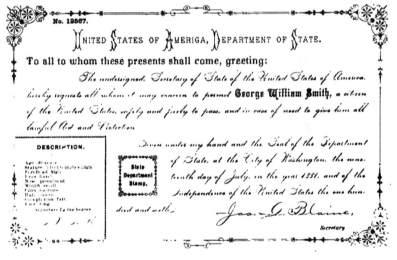

PATENTS.

PATENTS are granted in the United States, giving the exclusive right to the inventor, his heirs and assigns, to make, use and sell the invention or discovery throughout the United States and the Territories thereof for a term of seventeen years.

Before any inventor or discoverer can receive a patent he must make a written application for it, addressed to the commissioner of patents, and file in the patent-office a written description of his invention or discovery, giving details of its various parts, the materials used, how constructed or compounded, the manner of operating it, and the results proposed to be accomplished by its use; all expressed in such full, clear, concise and exact language that any person, familiar with the art or science which the invention is designed to benefit or illustrate, may be enabled to make, construct, compound and use it. If it is a machine, the principle on which it performs its work must be explained, as well as the best methods of applying it to the objects of the invention. This is required to distinguish it from other machines. Every part, improvement or combination of the invention which the applicant claims as original with himself, must be particularly pointed out.

The specifications must be signed by the inventor and be attested by two witnesses.

When the character of the application requires drawings of machinery, or parts thereof, the applicant must furnish one copy of each drawing, signed by the inventor or his attorney in fact, with two witnesses. This copy is filed in the patent-office, and the government officials attach another copy to the patent as a part of the specifications.

If the article to be patented is compounded of several ingredients, specimens of the materials used in making it, and of the whole composition, must be forwarded with the application, in such quantities that experiments can be made according to the specifications by the official examiners.

Where a machine for which a patent is asked can be illustrated by a working model thereof, the commissioner may require the applicant to furnish such model, in order to show how all parts of the invention are to be operated. The model must not exceed one square foot in size.

An applicant for a patent-right must swear (or affirm) that he is, or believes himself to be the first, or original, inventor or discoverer of the art, machine, manufacture, composition or improvement which he desires to patent; that he does not know, and does not believe, that the same was ever before known or used; and must tell of what country he is a citizen. This affidavit may be made before any person authorized to administer oaths in the United States; or, if the applicant is a resident of a foreign government, he may take this oath before an American minister, consul or a notary public of the foreign country where he resides.

Application for a Patent.

To the Commissioner of Patents, Washington, D. C.:

The petition of Joel Rice, of Florence, in the county of Erie, and State of Ohio, respectfully represents:

That your petitioner has invented a new and improved mode of creating steam-power for the operation of machinery, propulsion of vehicles on common roads, and of all kinds of crafts upon navigable waters, which he verily believes has not been known or used prior to the invention thereof by your petitioner. He therefore prays that letters-patent of the United States may be granted to him therefor, vesting in him and his legal representatives the exclusive right to the same, upon the terms and conditions expressed in the acts of Congress in that case made and provided; he having paid Fifteen Dollars into the treasury, and complied with the other provisions of the said acts.

JOEL RICE.

Form of Specifications for a New Method of Creating Steam-Power.

BE IT KNOWN, that I, Joel Rice, of Florence, in the county of Erie, and State of Ohio, have invented a new and useful machine for the purpose of creating steam-power for the operating of machinery, the propulsion of vehicles on common roads, and of all kinds of crafts upon navigable waters; and I do hereby declare that the following is a full, clear and exact description of the construction and operation of the same; reference being had to the annexed drawings, making a part of this specification, in which figure one is a general view, in perspective, of the complete machine attached to an ordinary steam-engine; figure two is an ordinary fire-arch, surmounted by a semi-globular iron kettle, with a flat, iron top, closely fitted to the entire upper rim of the kettle, and fastened tightly down thereto by four separate hasps attached to said cover, staples and keys, all of iron, as shown in the working model accompanying this application; figure three is an iron pipe (*a*) three-fourths of an inch in diameter, the upper end of which passes diagonally into the lower part of the right side of the kettle, and the other end is attached to a tank of water (*b*) placed upon a standard (*c*) above the top of the kettle and one side thereof, so that by a hydraulic pressure, regulated by an automatic valve (*d*) within said pipe, and a small syphon (*e*) extending from the tank to said pipe outside of said kettle, a supply of water equal to half a gill is ejected into the kettle through the pipe every thirty seconds; figure four is a pipe (*f*) of similar size and construction, passing directly from the inside of the kettle, outwardly, to the steam-chest of the engine, for the purpose of conveying steam from the kettle to the engine as a motive power for the propulsion of said engine. What I claim as my invention and discovery, and desire to secure by letters-patent, is the production of superheated steam by the injection of half a gill of cold water, every thirty seconds, into the red-hot kettle, and the passage of the superheated steam directly to the engine to supply it with power, to perform any work that any steam-engine may perform, increasing the ordinary force of common steam from two to fifteen-horse power by my invention, and the use of superheated steam created by the process above described. I also claim the right to patent, as my discovery and method of application, the use of superheated steam as a motor in the propulsion of all machinery to which it can be applied by ordinary steam-engines.

PETER M. RICE, } Witnesses.
WILLIAM T. PETRIE, }   JOEL RICE.

The Inventor's Oath Accompanying his Application.

STATE OF OHIO, } *ss.*
County of Erie, }   On this tenth day of July, 1882, before me, the subscriber, a notary public, appeared the within-named Joel Rice, and made solemn oath (or affirmation) that he verily believes himself to be the original and first inventor of the mode herein described for creating and applying superheated steam as a propelling power to ordinary steam-engines, and the propulsion of all kinds of machinery; and that he does not know or believe the same was ever before known or used; and that he is a citizen of the United States.

[NOTARIAL SEAL.]   EBEN TATTERSALL,
                                                Notary Public.

Petition for a Patent with Power of Attorney.

To the Commissioner of Patents:
Your petitioner, a resident of the city of Raleigh, in the State of North Carolina, requests that letters-patent may be granted to him for the invention set forth in the annexed specification; and he hereby appoints Charles S. Dixon, of the city of Charleston, in the State of South Carolina, his attorney, with full power of substitution and revocation, to prosecute this application, to make alterations and amendments therein, to receive the patent and to transact all business in the patent-office connected therewith
Signed at Charleston, in the State of South Carolina, this seventeenth day of October, 1882.   ELLIOTT WELLS.

Petition for a Patent for a Design.

To the Commissioner of Patents:
Your petitioner, residing in Noel county, South Carolina, requests that letters-patent may be granted to him for the term of seven years for the new and original design set forth in the annexed specification.   GEORGE S. STEELE.

Here follow the specifications of the design (for emblems of civic or military societies, carpets, home ornaments, etc.), carefully described in detail, and ending: "What I claim as my invention, and desire to secure by letters-patent, is the design or pattern for (naming the article) herein set forth."

Petition for the Registration of a Trade-Mark.

To the Commissioner of Patents:
Your petitioners respectfully represent that the firm of Lancaster, Berkshire & Kent is engaged in the packing of pork, for European markets, at the city of St. Louis, in the county of St. Louis, and the State of Missouri, and at the city of Cincinnati, in the county of Hamilton, and State of Ohio, and that the said firm is entitled to the exclusive use, upon the packages of the goods that they sell, of the trade-mark described in the annexed statement or specification, as shown more clearly in the accompanying specimen of said trade-mark. They therefore request that they may be permitted to obtain protection for such trade-mark under the law in such cases made and provided.   LANCASTER, BERKSHIRE & KENT.
                                         By J. B. LANCASTER.

Transfer of a Trade-Mark.

We, J. B. Lancaster, Robert Berkshire and L. W. Kent, of the city and county of St. Louis, in the State of Missouri, and the city of Cincinnati, county of Hamilton, and State of Ohio, partners, under the firm-name of Lancaster, Berkshire & Kent, in consideration of Six Hundred Dollars to us paid by Roswell Jones, of the city and county of St. Louis, in the State of Missouri, do hereby sell, assign and transfer to the said Roswell Jones and his assigns the exclusive right to use, in the business of packing pork for exportation, a certain trade-mark for packages of pork, deposited by us in the United States patent-office, and recorded therein January 15, 1883; the same to be held, enjoyed and used by the said Roswell Jones as fully and entirely as the same would have been held and enjoyed by us if this grant had not been made.
Witness our hands this fifteenth day of January, 1883.
                                         J. B. LANCASTER,
                                         ROBERT BERKSHIRE,
                                         L. W. KENT.

Petition for a Caveat.

To the Commissioner of Patents:
The petition of Michael Harris, of the town of Ralston, county of Vesper, and State of Virginia, respectfully represents:
That he has made certain improvements in the sawing of lumber with upright and circular saws, and that he is now engaged in testing the same, preparatory to applying for letters-patent therefor. He therefore requests that the subjoined description of his invention may be filed as a caveat in the confidential archives of the patent-office.   MICHAEL HARRIS.
[*Here follows the specification, in which the invention is clearly and fully explained.*]

License to Use a Patent by Paying a Royalty Thereon.

THIS AGREEMENT, made this sixteenth day of January, A. D. 1881, between John L. Palmer, of Knoxville, in the county of Knox, and State of Tennessee, party of the first part, and Jerome I. Case, of the city of Racine, in the county of Racine, and State of Wisconsin, party of the second part:
WITNESSETH, That whereas letters-patent of the United States for an improvement in the grain-separators of thrashing-machines were granted to the said party of the first part, November 6, A. D. 1879; and whereas the party of the second part is desirous of making thrashing-machines containing said patented improvement: Now, therefore, the parties hereto have agreed as follows:

1. The party of the first part hereby licenses and empowers the party of the second part to manufacture, subject to the conditions hereinafter named, at his factory in Racine, in the State of Wisconsin, and in no other place or places, to the end of the term for which said letters-patent were granted, grain-separators for thrashing-machines containing said patented improvements, and to sell the same within the United States.

2. The party of the second part agrees to make full and true returns to the party of the first part, under oath, upon the first days, respectively, of January and July in each year, of all grain-separators containing said patented improvements manufactured by him.

3. The party of the second part agrees to pay to the party of the first part Five Dollars, as a license-fee, upon every grain-separator manufactured by said party of the second part containing said patented improvements; *provided*, that if the said fee be paid upon the days specified herein for semi-annual returns, or within ten days thereafter, a discount of twenty per cent. shall be made from said fee for prompt payment.

4. Upon a failure of the party of the second part to make returns, or to make payment of license-fees, as herein provided, for thirty days after the days herein named, the party of the first part may terminate this license by serving a written notice upon the party of the second part; but the party of the second part shall not thereby be discharged from any liability to the party of the first part for any license-fee due at the time of the service of the said notice.

IN WITNESS WHEREOF the parties above named have hereunto set their hands the day and year first above written.

In presence of } JOHN L. PALMER,
THOMAS LAY.   } JEROME I. CASE.

License Granted to Use a Patent in a Mechanic's Shop.

KNOW ALL MEN BY THESE PRESENTS, That in consideration of the payment to me of the sum of Sixty Dollars, by John Scott, of the village of Trenton, in the county of Yell, and State of Arkansas, the receipt of which I hereby acknowledge, I do hereby license and empower the said John Scott to manufacture, at one blacksmith shop in the village of Trenton aforesaid, my improved rotary horseshoe, for which letters-patent of the United States, No. 81,265, were granted to me December 6, 1861, and to use and sell the said rotary horseshoes, in his business of blacksmithing, for two years from and after this date.

Witness my hand and seal this third day of April, A. D. 1882.

ASAHEL MERRITT. [L.S.]

Territory Assigned to the Purchaser of the Right to Sell a Patent.

KNOW ALL MEN BY THESE PRESENTS, That in consideration of the sum of Fifteen Hundred Dollars, to me in hand paid by George M. Van Cleve, of the city of Syracuse, in the county of Onondaga, and State of New York, the receipt whereof is hereby acknowledged, I do hereby grant and convey to the said George M. Van Cleve the exclusive right to make, use and vend, within the State of Delaware, and in no other place or places, the improvement in thrashing-machines for which letters-patent of the United States, dated July 5, 1882, were granted to me, the same to be held and enjoyed by the said George M. Van Cleve as fully and entirely as the same would have been held and enjoyed by me if this grant had not been made.

Witness my hand and seal this fifteenth day of January, A. D. 1883.

ROMEO KENDALL. [L.S.]

Facts Which Patentees Should Understand.

Tax on Patents.—A patent is not subject to either local, State or national taxes.

Can Be Assigned.—Patents can be assigned like other written evidence of proprietorship. (See ASSIGNMENTS.)

Aliens and Minors.—Patents are granted to aliens, minors or women; also to administrators and executors of deceased inventors.

Assignees.—Patents may be granted and also re-issued to the assignee of the inventor or discoverer; but the assignment must first be recorded in the patent-office.

The Name of the Inventors and that of the assignee, if it be assigned, together with the title of the invention, must be permanently affixed to the model.

Patents in Great Britain.—Patent covers England, Wales, Scotland and Ireland. No model required. Patent good for fourteen years. Fees from £200 to £300.

Appeals.—When an examiner rejects a case, appeal is made to the examiner-in-chief, next to the commissioner of patents, and lastly to the supreme court of the district.

Patent Papers are not prepared at the patent-office at Washington, but should be prepared and all in readiness for examination before sending the model and papers to Washington.

Public Property.—The commissioner of patents has no power to renew a patent. The monopoly on the same expires at the end of seventeen years and it then becomes public property.

Other Countries.—Patents in Spain extend for twenty years; Italy, fifteen years; Russia, ten years; Australian colonies, fourteen years. Fees for the entire term in foreign countries will be from $200 to $500.

Interference.—A disagreement as to who is the first to produce a certain invention is termed an interference. In such case a trial is had before the examiner, each contestant being represented by a competent person to present the merits of the case fully.

Order of Examination.—The case of a patent passes into its regular class, and is taken up for examination with others in its regular rotation. Exception to this is made in cases of re-issue, in foreign patents, and patents which are of especial importance to the public service.

The Inventor of a patent must apply for the same in his own name, over his own signature. An attorney cannot sign for the inventor; and yet, in many cases, the inventor may find it most convenient and economical to employ a patent-solicitor of experience to care for his legal work.

Legibility.—The law requires that all papers deposited at the patent-office shall be correctly and legibly written.

Patents in Germany.—Good for fifteen years. Patent may be taken for one year and extended by payment of annual tax.

Foreign Inventors must have their patented article in use or for sale in the United States within eighteen months from date of patent.

Patents in France.—Patent good for fifteen years. No model required. Annual tax on patent of $20. Patent ceases if tax unpaid. Fees from $100 to $150.

Infringement.—An invention which is an improvement on a previous patent is not an infringement, unless to produce the improvement the previous patent be used.

Assignments, agreements, contracts, and all important papers relating to change of ownership should be recorded at Washington, the same as the original patent papers.

Patents in Belgium.—Patent allowed for twenty years, except where first issued in another country, in which case patent expires according to the law where it was first issued.

In Case of Death.—If a person entitled to receive a patent should die before it is granted, his executors or administrators may receive it in trust for his heirs upon the same condition.

If Not Patented.—If an inventor makes and sells any newly invented machine before it is patented, the purchaser of it shall have the right to sell it to another person to be used without liability therefor.

Original Papers relating to a patent, when decided, are retained at the patent-office. Copies of the same are sent to the patentee at the usual costs. Though patent be denied, the money paid on the application cannot be withdrawn.

When Finished.—All applications for patents must be completed and prepared for examination within two years after the application is first filed in the patent-office, or be considered as abandoned, unless some satisfactory reason for the long delay is given.

New Designs.—Patents are granted for new designs of ornamental character for three-and-a-half years, or seven and fourteen years, as may be desired in the application. The patent expires at the expiration of the time for which application was made, and no extension is granted.

Foreign Patents.—A patent procured in the United States, for which the owner desires a patent in a foreign country, may remain in the secret archives of the patent-office at Washington for a period not exceeding six months, in order to give opportunity to arrange for patents abroad.

Re-Issue.—Whenever a mistake has been made in the claims or specifications of a patent a petition may be made for a re-issue, the petition to be accompanied by new drawings and corrected specifications. A new and corrected patent will thereupon be issued, and the former patent will be cancelled.

Marked "Patented."—All patented articles must be marked "patented" before being sold or used. It is a punishable offense to put the word "patented" upon any article for which a patent has not been issued. The penalty is a fine of not less than $100, with costs; one-half of the fine, when collected, to be paid to the person who prosecutes the guilty party, and the other half to the United States.

Patents in Canada.—The patent must be applied for within one year after the patent was allowed in the United States, by an American wishing a patent in Canada, else it is refused. Model required, and patent good for fifteen years. May import the article ready-made during the first year, but within two years must begin to manufacture the article on Canadian soil, or else arrange a definite place where the same may be obtained. Fees from $50 to $100.

Selling Patents.—Of the various methods for disposing of patents, there is, first, the selling of the patent entire to others, without reserving any rights; second, selling the patent on condition of receiving a royalty on each article manufactured where the patent is used; third, selling the right to manufacture, receiving a royalty for a certain length of time; fourth, selling the exclusive right to manufacture in certain territory on a royalty or not as may be agreed; fifth, selling the right to use in certain localities, or the right to manufacture in certain shops.

Official Fees.—Sec. 4934. The following shall be the rate for patent fees: On filing each original application for a patent, except in design cases $15. On issuing each original patent, except in design cases, $20. In design cases: For three years and six months, $10; for seven years, $15; for fourteen years, $30. On filing each caveat, $10. On every application for the re-issue of a patent, $30. On filing each disclaimer, $10. On every application for the extension of a patent, $50. On the granting of every extension of a patent, $50. On an appeal for the first time from the primary examiners to the examiners-in-chief, $10. On every appeal from the examiners-in-chief to the commissioner, $20. For certified copies of patents and other papers, including certified printed copies, ten cents per hundred words. For recording every assignment, agreement, power of attorney, or other paper of three hundred words or under, $1; of over three hundred and under one thousand words, $2; of over one thousand words, $3. For copies of drawings, the reasonable cost of making them. Sec. 4935. Patent fees may be paid to the commissioner of patents, or to the treasurer or any of the assistant

treasurers of the United States, or to any of the designated depositaries, national banks, or receivers of public money, designated by the secretary of the treasury for that purpose; and such officer shall give the depositor a receipt or certificate of deposit therefor. All money received at the patent office, for any purpose, or from any source whatever, shall be paid into the treasury as received, without any deduction whatever. Sec. 4936. The treasurer of the United States is authorized to pay back any sum or sums of money to any person who has through mistake paid the same into the treasury, or to any receiver or depositary, to the credit of the treasury, as for fees accruing at the patent-office, upon a certificate thereof being made to the treasurer by the commissioner of patents.

Models Required.—While a complete model is required not exceeding one foot square for a new invention, in case of an improvement upon a machine only a model of such improvement is required. A model may be made of wood or metal as best suits the convenience of the inventor, its simple purpose being to illustrate the working of the improvement or invention.

Drawings.—Paper must be used stiff enough to be stowed away in the portfolios; must be calendered and smooth. India ink, or other article giving a clear black mark, must be used. Size of the sheet should be exactly 10 by 15 inches, and one inch from its edge a single marginal line should be drawn, leaving the space for drawing exactly 8 by 13 inches. As much care is to be exercised in producing the drawings and specifications, the inventor should avail himself of the experience of some competent person in their preparation.

Caveats give inventors time to test and perfect their discoveries, running for one year, and can be extended from year to year. They can only be filed by citizens of the United States and foreigners who have resided here one year and have declared their intention to become citizens. A caveat is secret, and the caveator can use the stamp "caveat filed." No model required for a caveat. The caveat does not secure exclusive right of sale—a patent does. A caveat consists of a petition, specification, drawing and affidavit of invention.

Trade-Marks may be registered, giving person, firm or corporation exclusive right to use the same. Trade-marks remain in use for thirty years and may be renewed for thirty years more. No one may use the patented trade-mark of another on a similar class of goods calculated to deceive, but the same mark may be used on another class of goods to another line of trade without infringement. Where the word "star" is used by a certain maker, to illustrate, on shirts, it would not be lawful to use the figure of a star on a competing shirt, as the purpose in this case would be to deceive. Neither can a word similar in pronunciation be used as the words "royal" and "loyal."

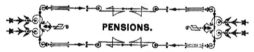

PENSIONS.

INDIVIDUALS entitled to obtain pensions from the United States government for wounds or injuries to their persons or health, received in the line of duty, so that they are incapacitated for active service or for earning their own support, are the following:

Any officer of the army, in either division, and any officer of the navy or marine corps.

Any enlisted man, however employed, in the military or naval service of the United States.

Any master serving on a government gun-boat, or any pilot, engineer, sailor, or other person not regularly mustered into the naval service.

Any person not enlisted in the army, but who has served as a volunteer soldier or militiaman in any regularly organized military or naval force.

Any assistant or contracting army surgeon,

or provost-marshal, deputy provost-marshal, or enrolling officer.

The following are the pensions per month, allowed for total disability in the army and navy, payable every six months:

Army Pension.—Lieutenant-colonels, and all above that rank, $30; major, $25; captain, $20; first lieutenant, $17; second lieutenant, $15; non-commissioned officers, musicians and private soldiers, $8.

Navy Pension.—Captain, commander, surgeon, paymaster and chief-engineer (by law ranking as commanders), lieutenant-commanding and master-commanding, $30; lieutenant, surgeon, paymaster and chief-engineer (by law ranking as lieutenants), and passed assistant-surgeon, $25; professor of mathematics, master, assistant-surgeon, assistant-paymaster and chaplain, $20; first assistant-engineers and pilots, $15; passed midshipman, midshipman, captain's and paymaster's clerks, second and third assistant-engineers, master's-mate and all warrant officers, $10; all petty officers, and all other persons not named above, but employed in the naval service, $8.

PENSIONS TO RELATIVES.

Only one full pension can be claimed by the relatives of a deceased officer, soldier or seaman, and these are classified, in order of precedence, as follows: Widows of officers, soldiers and seamen; children under sixteen years of age, if the widow is dead, or from the date of her remarriage, when her pension ceases; mothers of officers, soldiers and seamen, dependent upon the deceased for support, or where the deceased leaves neither widow nor children under sixteen years of age; sisters of the deceased, under sixteen years of age, or who were dependent upon their brothers for support, provided that none of the other above-named relatives are living. When more than one minor child or orphan sister become entitled to the pension, it must be equally divided between them.

WHEN PENSIONS BEGIN.

Invalid pensions to officers, soldiers and seamen begin from the date of the pensioner's discharge from the service, if claimed within a year afterward; if it is not, the pension must commence from the date of the application. The pensions of relatives begin at the date of the death of the pensioner.

It will be noticed in the following declarations —and this the government laws require—that the identity of the claimant is established by the oaths of two witnesses, certified by a proper officer to be respectable and truthful, who are present and testify to the signature of the claimant.

Applicants for invalid pensions must, if possible, produce certificates from the captains or some other commissioned officers under whom they served, distinctly stating the times and places when and where the applicants were disabled or seriously wounded, and the nature of the disability, and that this occurred while the claimant was actually in the service of the United States and performing his duty.

Should the proper officer be dead or beyond reach, the applicant must swear to that fact, and produce the testimony of two credible witnesses upon the subject; and the good character of these witnesses must be vouched for by some judicial officer, or by some one well known at the treasury department at Washington. The testimony of these witnesses must be minute in detail, and they must show on what their knowledge of the facts is founded.

The personal habits of the applicant and his occupation, after having been discharged from the service, must also be verified by the testimony of two trustworthy witnesses.

The counsel of an intelligent lawyer, when applying for a pension, will greatly aid the claimant in establishing his rights.

The fees of agents to obtain pensions are Five Dollars.

THE FIRST STEP.

The first thing to be done by the claimant for a pension is to make out, sign and verify by oath and proper witnesses, the following declaration— if formerly in the army:

Applicant's Declaration.

STATE OF OHIO,
County of Cuyahoga, } ss.   On this first day of April, A. D. 1865, personally appeared before me, a justice of the peace in and for said county, Jonas Allen, a resident of the city of Toledo, Miami county, and State of Ohio, aged twenty-seven years, who, being first duly sworn, according to law, declares that he is the identical Jonas Allen who enlisted in the service of the United States at Toledo, Miami county, in the State of Ohio, on the twelfth day of October, A. D. 1861, as a private soldier, in company C, commanded by Captain Robert Bell, in the Seventieth Regiment of Ohio Volunteer Infantry, in the war of 1861, and was honorably discharged on the seventeenth day of July, A. D. 1864. That while in the service aforesaid, and in the line of his duty on or about the tenth day of June, A. D. 1864, he received the following wound, to wit, a bullet three-eighths of one inch in diameter passing into the front part of his right leg, two inches above the knee, passing downward and into the cap of said right knee, shattering it, and passing out of the hinder part of his said right leg, about two inches below the knee-joint thereof, producing permanent lameness of the said right leg; from which wound he is now a sufferer and incapacitated for military duty and earning a livelihood by his trade as a stonemason. That at the time the wound above described was received he was engaged with his company and regiment in repulsing an assault by confederates at Honey Creek, in the State of Missouri. That he languished in the military hospital at Nero in said State of Missouri, in consequence of said wound, unable to perform any active duty, for six weeks and three days. That when discharged from said military hospital, he returned to Toledo, Miami county, and State of Ohio, where he has ever since resided, and that since his return home he has followed the occupation of a clerk in a lawyer's office at Toledo aforesaid. He makes this application for a pension, provided by the act of Congress, approved July 14, A. D. 1862. My post-office address is as follows: Box 6,000, Toledo, Miami county, Ohio.

JONAS ALLEN.

Also personally appeared before me Edward C. Thomas and Bartlett Chauncey, residents of the city of Toledo, in the county of Miami, and State of Ohio, to me well known as credible persons, who, being duly sworn, declare that they were present and saw said Jonas Allen sign his name to the foregoing declaration, and that they believe, from the appearance of the applicant and their acquaintance with him, that he is the identical person he represents himself to be, that his habits and character are good, and that his occupation is that of a lawyer's clerk; and they further state that they have no interest in the prosecution of this claim.

EDWARD C. THOMAS,
BARTLETT CHAUNCEY.

Sworn to and subscribed before me this first day of April, A. D. 1865; and I hereby certify that I have no interest, direct or indirect, in the prosecution of this claim.

HIRAM COE, Justice of the Peace.

The Widow's Application.

The widow of a soldier, who died while in the line of his duty and is entitled to a pension under the laws of the United States, must execute an affidavit similar to the foregoing, setting forth that she

Doth on her oath make the following declaration in order to obtain the benefits of the provision made by the act of Congress, approved July 14, 1862, granting pensions; that she is the widow of Charles James Fox, late of the county of Oswego, and State of New York, who was a corporal in Company M, commanded by Captain Martin Roy, in the Ninety-third Regiment of New York Volunteer Infantry, mustered into the service of the United States, from the State of New York, in the war of 1861, and who was killed at the first battle of Bull Run, on the twenty-first day of July, A. D. 1861, as this deponent verily believes. She further declares that she was lawfully married to the said Charles James Fox, at Oswego, in the State of New York,

by the Rev. William Pitt, a clergyman of the Congregational church, on the fourth day of February, A. D. 1856; that her husband, the aforesaid Charles James Fox, died on the day above mentioned, as she verily believes, and she remained his faithful wife until his decease. She further declares that she has remained his widow ever since the death of her said husband. She further declares that she had by her said deceased husband one child, a boy, now living, under the age of sixteen years, named Ebon Fox, aged eight years, and residing with her at Oswego, in the State of New York; and that she has not, in any manner, been engaged in, or aided or abetted, the rebellion in the United States, and that her maiden name was Stella Swift. My post-office address is 750 Fifth street, Oswego, Oswego county, State of New York.   STELLA FOX.

Also personally appeared Mary Rose and Hermann Lange, residents of Oswego, in the county of Oswego, and State of New York, persons whom I certify to be respectable and entitled to credit, and who, being by me duly sworn, say that they were present and saw Stella Fox sign her name to the foregoing declaration; and they further swear that they have known the parties above described to have lived together as husband and wife five years previous to and up to the time of deceased going into the aforesaid service of the United States, and that they have every reason to believe, from the appearance of the applicant, and their acquaintance with her, that she is the identical person she represents herself to be; and that they have no interest in the prosecution of this claim.

[*Sworn to and subscribed as in the declaration preceding.*]

PROCLAMATIONS.

PROCLAMATIONS are either verbal or written public announcements, from an official personage, relating to some especial exigency or a particular occasion. They may be addressed to a class or certain classes of people, or to all the citizens of a nation or State.

They possess the character of a law, because they require obedience or co-operation of action in those to whom they are addressed, although no penalty attaches to their infraction, except in time of war, invasion or insurrection, when offenders are punished by the ruling authorities, whether civil or military.

The most of the following forms show proclamations which have been actually issued upon important occasions by government officials.

President Buchanan's Proclamation for a Fast-Day in 1860.

Numerous appeals have been made to me by pious and patriotic associations and citizens, in view of the present distracted and dangerous condition of our country, to recommend that a day be set apart for humiliation, fasting and prayer throughout the Union. In compliance with their request, and my own sense of duty, I designate Friday, the fourth day of January, 1861, for this purpose, and recommend that the people assemble on that day, according to their several forms of worship, to keep it as a solemn fast.

The Union of the States is at the present moment threatened with alarming and immediate danger—panic and distress of a fearful character prevail throughout the land—our laboring population are without employment, and consequently deprived of the means of earning their bread—indeed hope seems to have deserted the minds of men. All classes are in a state of confusion and dismay; and the wisest counsels of our best and purest men are wholly disregarded.

In this, the hour of our calamity and peril, to whom shall we resort for relief but to the God of our fathers? His omnipotent arm only can save us from the awful effects of our crimes and follies—our own ingratitude and guilt towards our Heavenly Father.

Let us, then, with deep contrition and penitent sorrow, unite in humbling ourselves before the Most High, in confessing our individual and national sins, and in acknowledging the justice of our punishment. Let us implore Him to remove from our hearts that false pride of opinion which would impel us to persevere in wrong for the sake of consistency, rather than yield a just submission to the unforeseen exigencies by which we are now surrounded. Let us, with deep reverence, beseech Him to restore the friendship and good-will which prevailed in former days among the people of the several States, and, above all, to save us from the horrors of civil war and "blood-guiltiness." Let our fervent prayers ascend to His throne, that He would not desert us in this hour of extreme peril, but remember us as He did our fathers in the darkest days of the Revolution, and preserve our constitution and our Union—the work of their hands—for ages yet to come. An Omnipotent Providence may overrule existing evils for permanent good. He can make the wrath of man to praise Him, and the remainder of wrath He can restrain. Let me invoke every individual, in whatever sphere of life he may be placed, to feel a personal responsibility to God and his country for keeping this day holy, and for contributing all in his power to remove our actual and impending difficulties

JAMES BUCHANAN.

WASHINGTON, D. C., December 14, 1860.

Emancipation Proclamation by President Lincoln.

WHEREAS, on the twenty-second day of September, in the year of our Lord one thousand eight hundred and sixty-two, a proclamation was issued by the President of the United States, containing, among other things, the following, to wit:

"That on the first day of January, in the year of our Lord one thousand eight hundred and sixty-three, all persons held as slaves within any State or designated part of a State, the people whereof shall then be in rebellion against the United States, shall be then, thence forward, and forever, free; and the executive government of the United States, including the military and naval authority thereof, will recognize and maintain the freedom of such persons, and will do no act or acts to repress such persons, or any of them, in any efforts they may make for their actual freedom.

"That the executive will, on the first day of January aforesaid, by proclamation, designate the States and parts of States, if any, in which the people thereof, respectively, shall then be in rebellion against the United States; and the fact that any State, or the people thereof, shall on that day be in good faith represented in the Congress of the United States, by members chosen thereto at elections wherein a majority of the qualified voters of such States shall have participated, shall, in the absence of strong countervailing testimony, be deemed conclusive evidence that such State, and the people thereof, are then in rebellion against the United States."

Now, therefore, I, Abraham Lincoln, President of the United States, by virtue of the power in me vested as commander-in-chief of the army and navy of the United States, in time of actual armed rebellion against the authority and government of the United States, and as a fit and necessary war measure for suppressing said rebellion, do, on this first day of January, in the year of our Lord one thousand eight hundred and sixty-three, and in accordance with my purpose so to do, publicly proclaimed for the full period of one hundred days from the day first above mentioned, order and designate as the States and parts of States wherein the people thereof, respectively, are this day in rebellion against the United States, the following, to wit:

Arkansas, Texas, Louisiana (except the parishes of St. Bernard, Plaquemines, Jefferson, St. John, St. Charles, St. James, Ascension, Assumption, Terre Bonne, Lafourche, St. Mary, St. Martin and Orleans, including the city of New Orleans), Mississippi, Alabama, Florida, Georgia, South Carolina, North Carolina and Virginia (except the forty-eight counties designated as West Virginia, and also the counties of Berkeley, Accomac, Northampton, Elizabeth City, York, Princess Ann and Norfolk, including the cities of Norfolk and Portsmouth), and which excepted parts are for the present left precisely as if this proclamation were not issued.

And by virtue of the power and for the purpose aforesaid, I do order and declare that all persons held as slaves within said designated States and parts of States are, and henceforward shall be, FREE; and that the executive government of the United States, including the military and naval authorities thereof, will recognize and maintain the freedom of said persons.

And I hereby enjoin upon the people so declared to be free to abstain from all violence, unless in necessary self-defense; and I recommend to them that, in all cases when allowed, they labor faithfully for reasonable wages.

And I further declare and make known that such persons, of suitable condition, will be received into the armed service of the United States to garrison forts, positions, stations and other places, and to man vessels of all sorts in said service.

And upon this act, sincerely believed to be an act of justice, warranted by the constitution upon military necessity, I invoke the considerate judgment of mankind and the gracious favor of Almighty God.

In witness whereof I have hereunto set my hand and caused the seal of the United States to be affixed.

Done at the city of Washington, this first day of January, in the year of our Lord one thousand eight hundred and sixty-three, and of the independence of the United States of America the eighty-seventh.

UNITED
STATES
SEAL.

ABRAHAM LINCOLN.

By the President:

WILLIAM H. SEWARD,
Secretary of State.

Proclamation at the Time of the Chicago Fire.

WHEREAS, in the providence of God, to whose will we humbly submit, a terrible calamity has befallen our city, which demands of us our best efforts for the preservation of order and the relief of the suffering.

Be it known that the faith and credit of the city of Chicago is hereby pledged for the necessary expenses for the relief of the suffering. Public order will be preserved. The police, and special police now being appointed, will be responsible for the maintenance of the peace and the protection of property. All officers and men of the fire department and health department will act as special policemen without further notice. The mayor and comptroller will give vouchers for all supplies furnished by the different relief committees. The head-quarters of the city government will be at the Congregational church, corner of West Washington and Ann streets. All persons are warned against any acts tending to endanger property. All persons caught in any depredation will be immediately arrested.

With the help of God, order and peace and private property shall be preserved. The city government and the committees of citizens pledge themselves to the community to protect them and prepare the way for a restoration of public and private welfare.

It is believed the fire has spent its force, and all will soon be well.

R. B. MASON, Mayor.
GEORGE TAYLOR, Comptroller.
T. B. BROWN, President Board of Police.
CHARLES C. P. HOLDEN, President Common Council.
CHICAGO, October 9, 1871.

Chicago Fire Proclamation in New York.

MAYOR'S OFFICE, NEW YORK,
Afternoon of October 9, 1871.

A disaster has fallen on the great city of Chicago, which not only has destroyed the best part of its dwellings, and paralyzed its industry and its business, but threatens the gravest consequences to the commerce and prosperity of our country. It has also reduced thousands of people to houselessness and privation. A dispatch from the mayor of Chicago comes in these words: "Can you send us some aid for a hundred thousand houseless people? Army bread and cheese desirable." I have responded that New York will do everything to alleviate this disaster; and I now call upon the people to make such organization as may be speediest and most effective for the purpose of sending money and clothing and food. I would recommend the immediate formation of general relief committees, who would take charge of all contributions, in order that no time may be lost in carrying relief to those of our fellow-citizens who have fallen under this dispensation of Providence. I suggest that the Chamber of Commerce, the Produce Exchange, the Board of Brokers, and the united presidents of the banks, and all religious and charitable associations immediately call a meeting of their respective members, and from them select independent relief committees, who shall solicit subscriptions of money, food and clothing within their appropriate spheres of action. In the meantime I am authorized to state that contributions of food and clothing sent to the depots of the Erie and Hudson and Central railroads (under early and spontaneous offers of Jay Gould and William H. Vanderbilt), in even small quantities, from individuals or business sources, will be at once forwarded through to Chicago free of expense. I cannot too strongly urge upon our citizens immediate attention to this subject.

                              A. OAKEY HALL, Mayor.

President's Proclamation for Thanksgiving.

By the President of the United States of America—a Proclamation:

In conformity with custom, the annual observance of which is justly held in honor by this people, I, Chester A. Arthur, President of the United States, do hereby set apart Thursday, the thirtieth day of November next, as a day of public thanksgiving.

The blessings demanding our gratitude are numerous and varied; for the peace and amity which subsist between this republic and all nations of the world; for freedom from internal discord and violence; for increasing friendliness between the different sections of this land of liberty, justice and constitutional government; for the devotion of our people to our free institutions, and their cheerful obedience to mild laws; for the constantly increasing strength of the republic, while extending its privileges to fellow-men who come to us; for the improved means of internal communication and the increased facilities of intercourse with other nations; for the general prevailing health of the year; for the prosperity of all our industries—a liberal return for the mechanic's toil, affording a market for the abundant harvests of the husbandmen; for the preservation of the national faith and credit; for the wise and generous provision to effect the intellectual and moral education of our youth; for the influence upon conscience of restraining and transforming religion, and for the joys of home; for these and for many other blessings we should give thanks.

WHEREFORE, I do recommend that the day above designated be observed throughout the country as a Day of National Thanksgiving and Prayer, and that the people, ceasing from their daily labors, and, meeting in accordance with their several forms, worship and draw near to the Throne of Almighty God, offering to Him praise and gratitude for the manifold good which He has vouchsafed to us, and praying that His blessings and mercies may continue.

And I do further recommend that the day thus appointed may be made the special occasion for deeds of kindness and charity to the suffering and needy, so that all who dwell within the land may rejoice and be glad in this season of national thanksgiving.

IN WITNESS WHEREOF I have hereunto set my hand, and caused the seal of the United States to be affixed.

[UNITED STATES SEAL.] Done at the City of Washington, this twenty-fifth day of October, in the year of our Lord one thousand eight hundred and eighty-two, and of the independence of the United States the one hundred and seventh.

                              CHESTER A. ARTHUR.

By the President:

        FREDERICK T. FRELINGHUYSEN,
                              Secretary of State.

Proclamation Concerning Mad Dogs.

WHEREAS, it has been officially reported to me that mad dogs have recently bitten certain dogs and other animals within this corporation, thereby endangering their lives and the lives of our citizens:

Therefore, in order to preserve the lives and peace of our citizens and their animals, I do hereby order that from and after the date hereof, for the next sixty days, any dog found running at large, without having a substantial wire muzzle securely fastened over its month, shall be shot by the city marshal or officers under his charge.

IN WITNESS WHEREOF I have affixed my signature and the official seal of the city of Herman, in the county of Grant, and State of Minnesota, this thirty-first day of June, A. D. [CITY SEAL.] 1880.   PHILO STEPHENS, Mayor.

Attest: ELI M. PAGE, City Clerk.

SUBSCRIPTION PAPER.

A SUBSCRIPTION heading should be written very plainly and as briefly as may be, and express the object for which the money is subscribed. The following, with variations to suit the circumstances, will give the reader a general idea of the manner of preparing such a form:

Form of a Subscription Heading.

(Here Give Town, State, and Date.)

We, the undersigned, agree to pay the sums set opposite our names, to John Jones, for the purpose of defraying the expenses necessary to the appropriate celebration, in this city, of our National Independence, on the coming Fourth of July.

Names.		Names.	
William S. Tinckerbroker.	$50 00	Daniel F. Cunningham.	$25 00

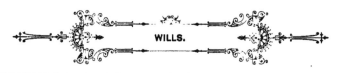

WILLS.

THE LEGAL declaration of what a person determines to have done with his property after death, is termed a will.

All persons of lawful age, possessed of sound mind, excepting married women in certain States, are entitled to dispose of their property by will.

No exact form of words is necessary in order to make a will good at law; though much care should be exercised to state the provisions of the will so plainly that its language may not be misunderstood.

The person making the will is termed the testator (if a female, testatrix).

A will is of no force and effect until the death of the testator, and can be cancelled or modified at any date by the maker.

The last will made annuls the force of all preceding wills, if not an addition to them.

The law regards marriage, and offspring resulting, as good evidence of revocation of a will made prior to such marriage, unless the wife and children are provided for by the husband in some other manner, in which case the will remains in full force.

To convey real estate by will, it must be done in accordance with the law of the State or country where such land is located; but personal property is conveyed in harmony with the law that obtains at the place of the testator's residence.

There are two kinds of wills, namely, written and verbal, or nuncupative. The latter, or spoken wills, depending upon proof of persons hearing the same, generally relate to personal property only, and are not recognized in all the States, unless made within ten days previous to the death, or by persons in the military or naval service. Verbal or unwritten wills are usually unsafe, and, even when well authenticated, often make expensive litigation; hence the necessity of having the wishes of the testator fully and clearly defined in a written will.

To give or make a devise of property by will and subsequently dispose of the same, without altering the will to conform to such sale, destroys the validity of the devise.

A will made by an unmarried woman is legally revoked by marriage; but she can take such legal steps in the settlement of her property before marriage as will empower her to dispose of the same as she may choose, after marriage.

No husband can make a will that will deprive the wife of her right of dower in the property; that is, her right to the proceeds of one-third of the real estate and appurtenances, as long as she may live. But the husband can will the wife a certain amount in lieu of her dower, stating it to be in lieu thereof. Such bequest, however, will not exclude her from her dower, provided she prefers it to the bequest made in the will. Unless the husband states distinctly that the bequest is in lieu of dower, she is entitled to both.

Property bequeathed must pay debts and incumbrances upon the same before its distribution can be made to the legatees of the estate.

Though property may be willed to a corporation, the corporation cannot accept such gift unless provision is made for so doing in its charter.

A will may be revoked by marriage, a codicil, destruction of the will, disposing of property devised in a will, or by the execution of another will.

The person making a will may appoint his executors, but no person can serve as such executor if, at the time of the proving of the will, he be under twenty-one years of age, a convict, a thoroughly confirmed drunkard, a lunatic, or an imbecile. No person appointed as an executor is obliged to serve, but may renounce his appointment by legal written notice signed before two witnesses, which notice must be recorded by the officer before whom the will is proved.

The person named in the will by the testator to administer the same is termed an executor. The individual appointed by a court is known as an administrator. The duties of each, in the settlement of an estate, are essentially the same.

In case a married woman possesses property, and dies without a will, her husband is entitled to administer upon such property in preference to any one else, provided he be of sound mind.

Any devise of property made to a subscribing witness is invalid, although the integrity of the will in other respects is not affected.

In all wills the testator's full name should be written at the end of the will. If he be unable to write, he may have his hand guided in making a mark against the same. If he possesses a sound mind, and is conscious at the time of the import of his action, such mark renders the will valid.

Witnesses should always write their respective places of residence after their names, their signatures being written in the presence of each other, and in the presence of the testator.

Different States require a different number of witnesses. To illustrate: Missouri, Illinois, Ohio, Kentucky, North Carolina, Tennessee, Iowa, Utah, Texas, California, New Jersey, Delaware, Indiana, Virginia, Oregon, Minnesota, Michigan, Wisconsin, Rhode Island, Louisiana and New York require two witnesses.

The States of Florida, Mississippi, Maryland, Georgia, South Carolina, Massachusetts Connecticut, Maine, New Hampshire and Vermont demand THREE witnesses to authenticate a will.

Witnesses are not required to know the contents of a will. They have simply to know that the document is a will, and witness the signing of the same by the testator, or he to witness their signing.

Proof of signature of the testator by the oath of two reputable witnesses, is sufficient to establish the validity of a will in the State of Pennsylvania; no subscribing witnesses being absolutely demanded.

CODICILS.

An addition to a will, which should be in writing, is termed a codicil, and executed like a will.

A codicil is designed to explain, modify, or change former bequests made in the body of the will. It should be done with the same care and precision as was exercised in the making of the will itself.

General Form of Will for Real and Personal Property.

I, Warren P. Holden, of the town of Bennington, county of Bennington, State of Vermont, being aware of the uncertainty of life, and in failing health, but of sound mind and memory, do make and declare this to be my last will and testament, in manner following, to wit:

First. I give, devise and bequeath unto my oldest son, Lucius Denne Holden, the sum of One Thousand Dollars, of bank stock, now in the First National Bank of Troy, New York, and the farm owned by myself in the town of Arlington, consisting of one hundred and forty acres, with all the houses, tenements, and improvements thereunto belonging; to have and to hold unto my said son, his heirs and assigns, forever.

Second. I give, devise and bequeath to each of my daughters, Fanny Almira Holden and Hannah Oriana Holden, each One Thousand Dollars in bank stock, in the First National Bank of Troy, N. Y., and also each one quarter-section of land, owned by myself, situated in the town of Mount Pleasant, Iowa, and recorded in my name in the recorder's office in the county where such land is located. The north one hundred and sixty acres of said half-section is devised to my eldest daughter, Fanny Almira.

Third. I give, devise and bequeath to my son, Emory Randor Holden, five shares of railroad stock in the Troy and Boston Railroad, and my one hundred and sixty acres of land and saw-mill thereon, situated in Muskegon, Michigan, with all the improvements and appurtenances thereunto belonging, which said real estate is recorded in the county where situated.

Fourth. I give to my wife, Mary Leffenwell Holden, all my household furniture, goods, chattels and personal property, about my home, not hitherto disposed of, including Six Thousand Dollars of bank stock, in the First National Bank of Troy, New York, fifteen shares in the Troy and Boston Railroad, and the free and unrestricted use, possession and benefit of the home-farm, so long as she may live, in lieu of dower, to which she is entitled by law, said farm being my present place of residence.

Fifth. I bequeath to my invalid father, Walter B. Holden, the income from rents of my store building, at 144 Water street, Troy, New York, during the term of his natural life. Said building and land therewith to revert to my said sons and daughters in equal proportion, upon the demise of my said father.

Sixth. It is also my will and desire that, at the death of my wife, Mary Leffenwell Holden, or at any time when she may arrange to relinquish her life interest in the above-mentioned homestead, the same may revert to my above-named children, or to the lawful heirs of each.

And lastly. I nominate and appoint as executors of this my last will and testament, my wife, Mary Leffenwell Holden, and my eldest son, Lucius Denne Holden.

I further direct that my debts and necessary funeral expenses shall be paid from moneys now on deposit in the Savings Bank of Bennington, the residue of such moneys on deposit to revert to my wife, Mary Leffenwell Holden, for her use forever.

In witness whereof, I, Warren P. Holden, to this my last will and testament have hereunto set my hand and seal, this tenth day of September, one thousand eight hundred and sixty-seven.

Signed, sealed and declared by Warren P. Holden, as and for his last will and testament, in the presence of us, who, at his request, and in his presence, and in the presence of each other, have subscribed our names hereunto as witnesses thereof.

WARREN P. HOLDEN. [L. S.]

LUTHER O. WESTCOTT,
        Manchester, Vermont.
HARTLEY B. HAWLEY,
        Bennington, Vermont.
DANIEL R. BOTTOM,
        Bennington, Vermont.

Codicil.

Whereas I, Warren P. Holden, did, on the tenth day of September, one thousand eight hundred and sixty-seven, make my last will and testament, I do now, by this writing, add this codicil to my said will, to be taken as a part thereof.

Whereas, by the dispensation of Providence, my daughter, Fanny Almira, has deceased, the third day of February, A. D. 1868, and whereas, a son has been born to me, which son is now christened Francis Allen Holden, I give and bequeath unto him my gold watch, and all right, interest, and title in lands and bank stock and chattels bequeathed to my deceased daughter, Fanny Almira, in the body of this will.

In witness whereof, I hereunto place my hand and seal, this first day of January, one thousand eight hundred and seventy.

Signed, sealed, published and declared to us by the testator, Warren P. Holden, as and for a codicil to be annexed to his last will and testament. And we, at his request, and in his presence, and in the presence of each other, have subscribed our names as witnesses thereto, at the date hereof.

WARREN P. HOLDEN [L. S.]

HARTLEY B. HAWLEY,
        Bennington, Vermont.
SAMUEL M. WEST,
        Arlington, Vermont.
DANIEL R. BOTTOM,
        Bennington, Vermont.

Shorter Form of Will.

I, Alvin B. Adams, of the city of Pittsburg, in the county of Alleghany, and State of Pennsylvania, being of sound mind, memory and understanding, do make my last will and testament in manner and form following:

First. I give, devise and bequeath to my wife, Mary, her heirs and assigns forever, one-half of all my property, real, personal and mixed, of what nature and kind soever, and wheresoever the same shall be at the time of my death; the same to be in lieu of her dower at common law.

Second. I give, devise and bequeath unto such of my children as may be living at the time of my death, one-half of all my property, real, personal and mixed, of what nature and kind soever, and wheresoever the same shall be at the time of my death, to be divided among them share and share alike.

Third. I hereby direct and empower my executor to sell and dispose of all my personal property to the highest bidder at auction, as soon as practicable after my decease, and to sell my real estate at auction or private sale, as it may in his judgment seem most advantageous, or for the interest of my said devisees.

Fourth. I direct that the net avails of my real and personal property, so disposed of as aforesaid, and converted into money, shall be divided and paid to my said devisees within one year after my decease.

Fifth. I hereby appoint my wife, Mary, guardian of the person and estate of such of my children as may be minors at the time of my death.

Sixth. I hereby appoint William H. Adams executor of this my last will and testament.

In witness whereof, I, Alvin B. Adams, the testator, have, to this my last will and testament, set my hand and seal this tenth day of April, A. D. 1865.

Signed, sealed, published and declared by the above-named Alvin B. Adams, as and for his last will and testament, in the presence of us, who have hereunto subscribed our names at his request, as witnesses thereto, in the presence of the said testator and of each other.

ALVIN B. ADAMS. [L. S.]

WINFIELD D. BROWN,
        Pittsburg, Pa.
CHARLES CAMPBELL,
        Pittsburg, Pa.
JOHN DOE,
        Pittsburg, Pa.

Form of Will Where Property is Left to Wife Absolutely.

This is the last will and testament of me, Thomas Wedgewood, made this eighteenth day of September, A. D. 1872, in Chicago, county of Cook, and State of Illinois, as follows:

I bequeath all my lands, tenements and hereditaments, and all my household furniture, ready money, securities for money, money secured by life assurance, goods and chattels, and all other parts of my real and personal estate and effects whatsoever and wheresoever, unto my wife, Clara Wedgewood, her heirs, administrators and assigns, to and for her and their absolute use and benefit, according to the nature and quality thereof respectively, subject only to the payment of my just debts, funeral and testamentary expenses, and the charge of proving and registering this my will. And I appoint my said wife executrix of this my will, and hereby revoke all other wills.

In witness whereof, I hereunto set my hand and seal, the day and year above mentioned.

Signed, sealed, published and acknowledged by the said Thomas Wedgewood, as and for his last will and testament, in the presence of us, who, in his presence, and at his request, and in the presence of each other, have subscribed our names hereunto as witnesses thereof.

THOMAS WEDGEWOOD. [L. S.]

SOLON W. WATSON,
        Chicago, Ill.
CHARLES D. SNYDER,
        Chicago, Ill.

Form of Will with Entire Property Left to Wife, for Life or Widowhood, with Disposition of the Same After Her Marriage or Death, Provision Being Made for Maintaining Children, Legacies to Executors, etc.

Realizing the uncertainty of life, I, Charles W. Freeman, of Kenosha, in the county of Kenosha, and State of Wisconsin, make this last will and testament, while in the possession of sound mind and memory, this fourteenth day of August, A. D. 1870.

I give, devise and bequeath unto my executors, hereafter named, all my estate and effects that I may die possessed of or entitled to, upon trust, to be, as soon as conveniently can be, after my decease, sold and converted into money, and the proceeds invested in one or other of the public funds, and the dividends arising therefrom to be paid yearly, each and every year, unto my wife, Harriet D. Freeman, during the term of her natural life, should she so long continue my widow; the first yearly payment thereof to commence and be payable at the expiration of the first year after my decease, if my wife remains a widow.

Upon her second marriage, I direct that one-third of all moneys from my estate, set apart for her use by my executors, be given her for her use and behoof forever, to control as she may choose, and the remaining two-thirds I will to be given to my children, to be divided equally among all my children by my said wife, the share of each child to be paid on his or her respectively attaining the age of lawful majority; and I direct that the dividends arising therefrom shall be applied, at the discretion of my executors, toward the maintenance and education of my said children, until they shall severally and respectively attain the said age. And in case any or either of my said children shall happen to die under lawful majority, then I give and bequeath the share or shares of him, her, or them, so dying, unto the survivor or survivors of them.

And I nominate and appoint my wife, Harriet D. Freeman, my eldest son, Clinton W. Freeman, and Walter C. Kimball, and the survivor of them, and the executors or administrators of such survivor, to be the executors of this my will, and in consideration of the trouble thus imposed on them, I do hereby give and bequeath unto each of my said executors the legacy or sum of Five Hundred Dollars, free of legacy duty and all other deductions. And hereby revoking all former or other wills by me at any time made, I, the said Charles W. Freeman, to this which I declare to be my last will and testament, set my hand and seal.

Signed by the said testator, Charles W. Freeman, and acknowledged by him to be his last will and testament, in the presence of us, present at the same time, and subscribed by us in the presence of the said testator and of each other.   CHARLES W. FREEMAN [SEAL]
BARNARD McDOLE, Kenosha, Wis.
HIRAM FLEMING, Kenosha, Wis.
RICHARD WILSON, Kenosha, Wis.

Nuncupative Will.

In the matter of nuncupative will of Jonas Lyman, deceased.

On the first day of July, in the year one thousand eight hundred and seventy-one, Jonas Lyman, being in his last sickness, in his dwelling, situate in Burlington, Iowa, at 84 Huron street, in the presence of the subscribers, did declare his last will and wishes concerning the disposition of his property, in the following words, viz.:

He desired that his Seven Hundred Dollars in the First National Bank of Burlington, and Two Hundred Dollars in the hands of Silas Holmes, should be given to his mother. He also expressed a desire to have Silas Holmes act as his executor, to collect the same as soon as possible, with interest due, paying the entire amount, when collected, to his mother. He also said, "All my other property I want my mother to have for her separate use, except my house and lot where I live, which I will to my sister Mary."

At the time the said Jonas Lyman stated the foregoing as his will, he was of sound mind and memory, and desired us to bear witness that such was his wish and desire.

Reduced to writing by us, this tenth day of July, in the year one thousand eight hundred and seventy-one.

ABIAL GOODING,
ARTEMAS WHITE,
PETER H. SMITH.

Affidavit to the Foregoing.

STATE OF IOWA, } ss.
County of Lee, }   Personally appeared before me, George Hartwell, clerk of the court of probate for said county, Abial Gooding, Artemas White, and Peter H. Smith, who deposed that they were present on the first day of July, A. D. 1871, at the dwelling of the said Jonas Lyman, situate at 84 Huron street, Burlington, Iowa, and did hear Jonas Lyman utter what is specified in the foregoing writing; that he wished them to witness that it was his last will; and that at the time he was of sound mind and memory, to the best of their knowledge and belief.

Sworn and subscribed before me, this twelfth day of July, A. D. 1871.   GEORGE HARTWELL, Clerk.

A Short Form of Will, Conveying the Entire Real and Personal Property to the Wife of the Testator.

A will which bequeaths all the property of the testator, real and personal, wheresoever it may be, carries with it property acquired after its publication, without a repetition of any formalities.

The question in relation to a bequest in such cases is one of intention, not of power. The following will of Onslow Peters, the legality of which was tested and sustained by the courts, was found to be amply sufficient in length for the purpose for which it was designed. It read as follows:

I, Onslow Peters, do make and publish this my last will and testament, hereby revoking all former wills by me made.

I bequeath all my property, real and personal, wheresoever the same may be, to my beloved wife, Hannah P. Peters.

I appoint my said wife the executrix of this my last will and testament. My will is that my said wife shall not be required to give any bonds or security to the judge of probate for the faithful execution of the duties of executrix.

In witness whereof I have hereunto set my hand and seal this thirteenth day of September, one thousand eight hundred and thirty-eight.

CLAUSES FOR INSERTION IN WILLS.

Cancelling Debts That Are, or May Be, Due.

Whereas, there are certain sums of money due me, upon mortgages, bills, and otherwise, from persons hereafter named (naming them), it is my will that such indebtedness, immediately after my death, shall be cancelled by my executors. And I do hereby release those persons aforesaid from the payment of all debts due.

Desiring that Difference of Opinion about Provisions of the Will be Settled by Arbitrators.

It is my desire, that if any dispute, question or controversy shall happen concerning any bequest or other matter in this my will, such question shall be referred to the arbitration of my friends, A. D and C. L., with provision for them to choose an umpire, but should they not be able to act in the matter, then I desire that my wife and eldest son each appoint an arbitrator or arbitrators, with the power of choosing a third arbitrator; and what a majority of them shall determine therein shall be binding upon all and every person or persons therein concerned.

Providing that the Wife Shall Have the Custody of the Children, and Appointing a Guardian in Case of Her Death.

And in case I shall leave any child or children at the time of my death, my will is that my wife shall have the guardianship of them during their minority; and in the case of her death, during the minority of said children, then I desire that my friend, D. M., shall have the guardianship of them during their minority; should he refuse, I will that A. J. shall take such supervision and guardianship.

DUTIES OF ADMINISTRATORS AND METHODS OF PROCEDURE IN SETTLING ESTATES.

HAVING made a will, the testator should recollect that marriage, birth of children, death, or the purchase or sale of real estate may affect the will. So the death or removal of executors may require a change. These alterations may be made by a codicil, which must be executed and witnessed the same as a will.

The will, enclosed in a sealed envelope, indorsed "Will of A. B.," should be kept in safe custody under the control of the testator. It should not be placed for safe keeping in the hands of interested parties, nor beyond the reach of the testator. It should also be placed where it will be absolutely forthcoming in case of the testator's sudden demise.

After the death of the testator the will should be taken to the court, unopened, and there filed with an affidavit as to the custody of it and death of the testator.

The judge having opened it, orders that publication be made according to law, that on a certain day it will be offered for proof, and causes notice to be given the heirs at law of the deceased and the executors named, if any, in the will.

At the time appointed the widow, if there is one, some of the heirs, and one or more of the executors, appear in court, with the witnesses to the will. To enable the will to be probated the witnesses must swear the testator executed it as and for his last will, and was then of a sound and disposing mind and memory. At this period any party interested in the estate may contest the will before the court.

Both husbands and wives are entitled to an interest in their joint estate, termed right of dower, which is not affected by wills, so that where it appears by the will that the provision is made by devise or legacy, in lieu of dower, the husband or wife must be called into court to accept or waive the provisions in the will.

If the judge thinks the will properly proved, he orders it recorded and issues letters of administration to the executors. A certified copy of the will and above order should be recorded in the registry of deeds of every county in which there is land devised by the will.

If the executors named do not wish to act, they file a disclaimer, and the judge then appoints an administrator with the will annexed. If an administrator dies before he has settled the estate, the court appoints his administrator to settle it, who is called administrator of estate yet to be settled. Persons administering on estate are by law required to give a bond with sureties in double the sworn value of the personal estate. This may be waived by the will.

The law vests the personal estate in the executor or administrators from the death of the testator, and the real estate in the heirs at law. These latter enter into possession at once, by descent or will, but their rights are subject to the widow's privilege of residing in her husband's home for forty days after his death, and all homestead laws.

In every State a widow has first, in preference to creditors, an allowance for the support of the family, or an award. Except in this respect all property is subject to the debts of the deceased.

In many respects the work of administrators appointed by the court, in case there is no will, is similar to that of executors when there is a will.

In case the deceased dies intestate (that is, leaving no will), then the widow, or the nearest heir to the estate, at once petitions the probate court for letters of administration to issue to some suitable person for its settlement, the following being the form of petition:

Heir's Petition to Have Administrator Appointed.

To the County Court of Kane county, in the State of Illinois:

The petition of Raymond Scott, the oldest surviving son of Willard J. Scott, late of said county, deceased, respectfully showeth: That on the eighteenth day of December, A. D. 1882, the said Willard J. Scott died, leaving goods, chattels, rights, credits and real estate in the county aforesaid; that, at the time of his decease, the said Willard J. Scott was a widower, his wife having died at St. Charles, in said county, as can be duly verified, on the tenth day of May, A. D. 1881; that, to the best of the knowledge and belief of your petitioner, no last will and testament was left by the said Willard J. Scott, deceased; that he has left, as heirs to his estate, two children, one (the undersigned) aged twenty-seven years, and a girl, Mary, now in the fourteenth year of her age; and that the deceased was, at and immediately prior to his death, a resident of the said county of Kane. Your petitioner, therefore, prays that letters of administration may be granted on the estate of the deceased, and that he may be appointed the administrator thereof. RAYMOND SCOTT.

Dated this twenty-first day of December, A. D. 1882, at St. Charles, in said county of Kane, and State of Illinois.

(An affidavit is required of the petitioner to verify the facts as stated in his petition. See AFFIDAVITS.)

Bond Required of the Administrator.

The petition of the nearest heir (whether widow or child) having been granted by the court, the administrator must execute a good and sufficient bond, in form following, in order to secure the estate from loss by carelessness or roguery.

KNOW ALL MEN BY THESE PRESENTS, that we, Raymond Scott, as principal, and Edward Poor and David T. Rich, as sureties, all being residents of Kane county, in the State of Illinois, are held and firmly bound unto Roswell C. Otis, judge of the county court in and for said county, in the penal sum of Thirty Thousand Dollars, to be paid to said judge and his successors in said office; to the true payment whereof we bind ourselves and each of us, one and each of our heirs, executors and administrators, jointly and severally, firmly by these presents. Sealed with our seals and dated the first day of January, A. D. 1883.

The condition of this obligation is, that if the above-bounden Raymond Scott, administrator of all and singular the goods, chattels and credits of Willard J. Scott, deceased, do make, or cause to be made, a true and perfect inventory of all and singular the goods, chattels and credits of the said deceased, which have or shall come to the hands, possession or knowledge of him the said Raymond Scott, or into the hands and possession of any other person, or persons, for him, and the same so made do exhibit, or cause to be exhibited into the county clerk's office of Kane, in the State of Illinois, within thirty days from the date hereof; and the same goods, chattels and credits and all other the goods, chattels and credits of the said deceased at the time of his death, or which at any time after shall come to the hands and possession of the said Raymond Scott, or into the hands and possession of any other person or persons for him, do well and truly administer according to law; and further do make, or cause to be made, a just and true account of his said administration within ninety days from the date hereof, or when thereunto legally required; and all the rest and residue of the said goods, chattels and credits which shall be found remaining upon the said administrator's account, the same being first examined and allowed by the county (or probate) court of the county having jurisdiction, shall deliver and pay unto such person or persons as the said court, by their decree or sentence, pursuant to law, shall limit and appoint; and shall well and truly comply with the law of this State relating to inheritances; and if it shall hereafter appear that any past will and testament was made by the said deceased, and the same shall be proved according to law, if the said Raymond Scott, being thereto required, do surrender the said letters of administration into the office of the clerk of said county (or probate) court of Kane county, as aforesaid, then this obligation to be void, otherwise to remain in full force and virtue.

Signed, sealed and delivered in the presence of
DANIEL J. SINCLAIR,
GEORGE W. DEAN.

RAYMOND SCOTT, –(SEAL)–
EDWARD POOR, –(SEAL)–
DAVID T. RICH. –(SEAL)–

Administrator's Advertisement Calling for Settlement.

The preliminaries being arranged, the administrator inserts the following notice in a local newspaper several times, which notice he posts on the court-house door, and in two other prominent places in the county.

NOTICE.—Whereas letters of administration upon the estate of Willard J. Scott, late of St. Charles, in this county, have been granted to the subscriber, all persons indebted to the said estate are requested to make immediate payment, and those having claims or demands against the same will present them without delay to
RAYMOND SCOTT, Administrator.
GENEVA, Kane county, Illinois, January 1, A. D. 1888.

The Work of Settling the Estate.

The administrator is now ready to begin the work of administration, under the sanction and restraint of the State laws upon this subject, using the first ready money realized from the estate (in most States) to pay the funeral expenses of the deceased, the bills for nurses and medical attendance in his last illness, and the probate fees of the court; debts (if any) due to the United States; debts (if any) due to the State in which he lived; all liens that may exist upon and encumber any of his property, and, then, debts due to all other creditors. The administrator has no power outside of the State in which he acts in that capacity.

The first work to be done, however, is to search for and gather up all the personal property and real estate owned by the deceased. This must be carefully inventoried and classified. In some States the inventory is submitted to two or more appraisers, in order to obtain the real value of the listed property, who bring in a report worded as follows:

Inventory of Property of Willard J. Scott.

A true and perfect inventory and just appraisement of all and singular the goods and chattels, rights and credits which were of Willard J. Scott, late of the county of Kane, and State of Illinois, deceased, at the time of his death, to wit:
[*Here follows the list of property, the personal (including the bonds, notes, book-accounts, classified as "good," "doubtful" ,or "worthless," as the case may be) in one column, and the real estate in another—the footing of each being noted separately*].
Taken and appraised by us, the third and fourth days of January, A. D. 1888.
GEORGE ERICKSON,
THOS. B. WELLS.

STATE OF ILLINOIS }
County of Kane, } ss.
Personally appeared before me, a notary public in and for the county of Kane, and State of Illinois, the above-named George Erickson and Thomas B. Wells, who solemnly swear (or affirm) that at the request of Raymond Scott, administrator, they did well and truly, and without prejudice or partiality, value and appraise the goods, chattels and credits which were of Willard J. Scott, deceased, as set forth in the foregoing inventory, and in all respects perform their duties as appraisers, to the best of their skill and judgment.
GEORGE ERICKSON,
THOS. B. WELLS.
Sworn (or affirmed) and subscribed this fifth day of January, A. D. 1888, before me.
[NOTARIAL SEAL.]
NELSON DODGE, Notary Public.

If sufficient property belonging to the deceased cannot be found to pay off his indebtedness, under ordinarily careful management, the administrator should at once notify the county (or probate) court that the estate is insolvent, and proceed according to the laws of the State in which he lives concerning insolvent debtors.

Administrator's Accounts.

The administrator charges himself with whatever property of the deceased comes into his hands, valued at the sworn appraisement, and all moneys received on accounts, notes, bonds, mortgages and from all other resources of the estate; and credits himself with all moneys and effects paid out and bestowed upon creditors and heirs of the estate, together with his fees and commissions as administrator; and when the estate is fully settled he renders to the county or probate court, in the following form, his account, duly sworn to:

Account of Raymond Scott with Estate of Willard J. Scott.

The account of Raymond Scott, administrator of all and singular the goods and chattels, rights and credits which were possessed by Willard J. Scott, late a citizen of Kane county, in the State of Illinois, deceased:

RAYMOND SCOTT, ADMINISTRATOR,
In account with
ESTATE OF WILLARD J. SCOTT, DECEASED.

Debits. Carefully itemized.	Credits. Carefully itemized.
Total.......... $	Total................. $
	Balance in favor of the estate.............$
	(Signed) RAYMOND SCOTT.

STATE OF ILLINOIS, }
County of Kane, } ss.
Before me, a justice of the peace for and within said county, personally appeared Raymond Scott, administrator aforesaid, who doth depose and say that the accompanying account is just and true, to the best of his knowledge and belief.
Sworn (or affirmed) and subscribed this fifteenth day of November, A. D. 1888.
WILLIAM H. WHITING, Justice of the Peace.

The balance derived from the estate, after paying all costs, charges and expenses that have accrued or stand against it, is distributed among the heirs by the judge of the court according to law and equity. The judge then formally discharges the administrator from all further responsibility and care of the estate.

SUMMARY OF STATE LAWS RELATING TO WRITTEN WILLS.

Age at which Testators can Make Wills, Rights of Married Women, Number of Witnesses Required, Courts that have Jurisdiction, Etc.

Alabama.—All persons twenty-one years of age may devise real estate by will, and at eighteen or over may dispose of personal property. Two witnesses are required. Married women may bequeath their separate estates. Wills are recorded in the probate judge's office.

Arizona Territory.—Testators, male or female, must be twenty-one years old. Two witnesses are required. Married women may devise their separate property.

Arkansas.—Must be twenty-one years of age to devise real estate, and eighteen to devise personal property. Three witnesses are required. Wills are recorded in the probate court of the county where most of the bequeathed land is situated; but if only personal property is devised, then in the county where the testator died. Married women devise their separate property as they please.

California.—At eighteen or over testators may devise real or personal property. Married women may dispose, by will, of their separate estate without the consent of their husbands. Two witnesses are required for all written wills.

Colorado.—The testator, if male, must be twenty-one; if female, eighteen. Either male or female may will personal property at seventeen. Neither husband nor wife can deprive the other of one-half the property by will, except wife may do so with written consent of husband. Two witnesses are required. Wills are recorded in county courts, where letters of administration are issued; also with the recorder in counties where the testator owned real estate.

Connecticut.—All persons over eighteen can dispose of their property by will, either real or personal. Three witnesses are required. Ten years are allowed, after the testator's death, in which to probate his will. Wills are recorded in the probate courts.

Dakota Territory.—At eighteen persons may devise both their personal and real property. Two witnesses are necessary. Married women may dispose of their separate estates without the consent of their husbands. A will made by an unmarried woman is revoked by her marriage, and not revived by the death of her husband.

Delaware.—The testator must be twenty-one years old. Two witnesses are required. Married women, with the written consent of their husbands, given under their hands and seals, in presence of two witnesses, may dispose of their property by will.

District of Columbia.—Male testators must be twenty-one years old; females, eighteen. Three witnesses are required to testator's signature. Married women will their separate property to whom they please. Wills are recorded in the registry of wills.

Florida.—Required age, twenty-one. Three witnesses.

Georgia.—Testator must be twenty-one. Three witnesses required. Recorded in the court of ordinary.

Idaho Territory.—Testator must be twenty-one. Husband must leave wife one-half of common property. At eighteen can dispose of goods and chattels. Married woman may dispose of her separate estate. Two witnesses required. Will first recorded in the probate court, and afterward in all counties where real estate is located.

Illinois.—Males must be twenty-one; females, eighteen. Two witnesses necessary. Wills filed in probate court and originals remain there.

Indiana.—Testator must be twenty-one. Two witnesses.

Iowa.—Must be twenty-one years old. Two witnesses.

Kansas.—Testator required to be twenty-one years old. Two witnesses.

Kentucky.—Testator must be twenty-one. If written by testator himself, one witness only required; if written by other than the testator, two witnesses necessary. A married woman may dispose of her separate estate by will.

Louisiana.—Must be twenty-one. Two male witnesses required over the age of sixteen.

Maine.—Men and women alike may devise their property, real and personal. Three witnesses necessary. Wills, transferring real estate, are recorded like deeds. Estates are settled in the probate court.

Maryland.—Men must be twenty-one; women, eighteen. Three witnesses necessary. Wills of personal property do not require witnesses. Wills must be proven in the orphans' court of each county, or before the register of wills.

Massachusetts.—Any person may will real or personal property. A husband cannot be deprived of one-half of his wife's personal property or a life interest in her real estate by her will, unless he consents to the devise. Three witnesses required to signature of testator. Wills are recorded in the office of register of probate.

Michigan.—Testator must be twenty-one. Two witnesses. Copies of the wills must be recorded in the county registers' offices where the lands are located.

Minnesota.—Men must be twenty-one; women, eighteen. Two witnesses. Estates are settled in probate courts, where wills are recorded. Copies are recorded in counties where devised real estate is located.

Mississippi.—Testators must be twenty-one, male or female. Three witnesses required. Probate is made in the court of chancery, or by the clerk thereof, and recorded in his office.

Missouri.—Must be twenty-one to devise real estate, and eighteen to bequeath personal property. Married women may devise real estate at the age of eighteen. Two witnesses. After probate, wills are recorded in the office of the register of deeds.

Montana Territory. — Every person, at eighteen, may devise any kind of property in writing. Two witnesses.

Nebraska Territory. — Two witnesses. Wills may be recorded in the office of the clerk of the county where bequeathed real estate is located.

Nevada. — Testators over eighteen years of age may dispose of any of their property after payment of debts is provided for. Married woman may devise her separate estate without husband's consent. Wills must be recorded in the courts where they are admitted to probate.

New Hampshire. — Must be twenty-one years old. Three witnesses. Wills are recorded in the office of the register of probate, and proved in probate courts.

New Jersey.—Must be twenty-one years old. Married woman cannot will away her husband's interest in her real estate. Two witnesses. They are proved and recorded in the office of the surrogate of the county.

New Mexico. — Males over fourteen years and females over twelve years of age, if of sound mind, may execute wills, unless known to be prodigals. Verbal wills require five witnesses, and all must testify clearly as to every part of the will. Written wills need three or more witnesses. Probate judges approve of wills or reject them. Appeals are taken to the district court.

New York.—Wills must be signed by testators at the end, but need not be sealed. Males can bequeath personal property when eighteen, and females at sixteen. Two witnesses to the signature of the testator and his acknowledgment of the document are required to be affixed to the will, which is proven in the office of the surrogate of the county where the testator lived.

North Carolina.—Wills have two witnesses. Married women devise their separate estates. Wills must be recorded in the probate court of the county where the testator lived.

Ohio.—Must be twenty-one years old. Two witnesses. Wills are admitted to probate or record in the office of the probate judge.

Oregon.—Testators must be twenty-one years old in order to devise real estate, but may bequeath personal property if over eighteen years of age. Married women devise real estate subject to their husbands' interest in it. Two witnesses.

Pennsylvania.—Testators must be twenty-one years old. Two witnesses necessary, who,

however, are not required to place their signatures to the will. A husband is not competent as a witness to his wife's will.

Rhode Island.—Real estate may be devised by persons twenty-one years old, and personal property by those over eighteen years. Two witnesses. Probate courts are located at Newport and Providence, where wills are recorded. In other places they are recorded by town-clerks.

South Carolina.—Wills devising both real estate and personal property must be executed in the presence of three or more subscribing witnesses, and recorded in the probate court of the county where the testator resided.

Tennessee.—Where only personal property is devised the witnesses need not subscribe their names to the will. Married women can devise their separate property, unless they hold it under previous restraint. County courts are courts of probate.

Texas.—All persons, twenty-one years old, may devise their real and personal estate. Two witnesses necessary. Wills are admitted and proved in county courts, if presented for probate within four years after the death of the testator. Devises of real estate must be confined to written wills.

Utah Territory.—Testators, male and female, may devise their real and personal property by will when eighteen years old. This includes the separate property of married women. Two witnesses required.

Vermont.—Three witnesses. Real and personal property of a married woman may be devised by her will. Estates are settled in probate courts. Wills may be recorded either in probate courts or in town-clerk's office wherever the devised real estate is located.

Virginia.—Persons of sound mind may devise their real estate by will after they become twenty-one years of age, and their personal property at the age of eighteen years. This includes the separate property of married women. Two witnesses. Estates are settled in either corporation, county or circuit courts, in the county or corporation where the testator lived, or where his real estate is located.

Washington Territory.—Two witnesses. Males must be twenty-one years old, and females eighteen years, devising both real and personal estate. Married women are restricted in this respect by their husbands' claims upon their property.

West Virginia.—All persons of twenty-one years old, may devise their real and personal estate by a written will, duly attested. Two witnesses.

Wisconsin.—Wills, including those of married women, must be in writing, and signed in the presence of two or more subscribing witnesses. Wills are proved and admitted to probate in county courts.

Wyoming Territory.—There being no territorial laws on the subject, the usages of common law regulate the execution and proof of wills. They are proved and admitted to settlement in the probate courts. Married women are at liberty to devise their separate property as they please.

Canadian Wills.

Quebec.—All persons twenty-one years old and of sound mind may devise their real and personal property by will. Wills are of three kinds. The French will is made before two notaries, or one notary and two witnesses, the English, signed by the testator in presence of two subscribing witnesses, and the olograph, written and signed by the testator's hand, which requires neither the presence of a notary or subscribing witnesses. The English and olograph wills require to be probated. Married women cannot devise their estates without their husbands' consent.

Ontario.—Married women may bequeath their separate estate to whom they wish. Wills must be in writing, the signature of the testator being attested by two subscribing witnesses in the presence of the testator and each other. An executor is a competent witness to the will.

Parliament Buildings, Ottawa, Canada.

THE CANADIAN DOMINION.

An Outline of its History, its Government, its Resources, with Other Material Facts, and its Forms for the Transaction of Business.

The history of Canada, so named from the Indian word "kanata," which signifies a number of huts, is briefly sketched in the following:

Newfoundland was discovered in 1497, by Sebastian Cabot, and subsequently, in 1534, Canada proper was discovered by Jacques Cartier, who sailed up the river St. Lawrence to the point where now stands Montreal.

The foundation of Quebec was laid by Samuel Champlain, in 1608; following which a French expedition was formed in 1617, to explore the unknown domains of Canada, an enterprise which was entered upon still later by the English, in 1689, and prosecuted with some advantage for the next twelve years.

In 1754 a contest for ownership of the country broke out between the French and the English, which resulted in a five years' war and the triumph of the English, who came into possession by the treaty of Paris in 1763. Among the chief events of this war was the taking of Quebec in 1759, at which time Montcalm, the French general, and Wolfe, the English chieftain, both lost their lives.

In 1791 an act of parliament divided Canada into two provinces—Upper and Lower Canada. By an act of the imperial parliament, in 1867, these two divisions became known as the provinces of Ontario and Quebec; and, together with Nova Scotia and New Brunswick, were constituted the Dominion of Canada. In 1870 the province of Manitoba was formed, and, with the remainder of the Hudson Bay Territory, now known as the Northwest Territory, admitted into the Dominion. British Columbia and Vancouver Island followed in 1871, and Prince Edward Island in 1873.

Of Canada proper, Ontario comprises the upper and western portion, whose inhabitants are principally English. Quebec includes the lower and eastern portion, the people in which are mostly of French descent, who retain their original language, religion and customs.

The timber trade, from the first settlement of Canada, has ever been the principal industry of the people, which, as the country is cleared of its forests, is being followed by the raising of cattle and the cultivation of the soil.

The executive authority of the country is vested in the sovereign of Great Britain, and is represented at the capital of the Dominion by a governor-general, assisted by a privy council.

The legislative power is a parliament consisting of an upper house, styled the senate, and a house of commons; the seat of government for the Dominion being at Ottawa.

The details for the government of the Canadian Dominion are clearly set forth in the following constitution, being the imperial act of 1867:

CONSTITUTION FOR THE GOVERNMENT OF CANADA,

Entitled An Act for the Union of Canada, Nova Scotia and New Brunswick, and the Government Thereof, and for Purposes Connected Therewith, which Took Effect March 29, 1867.

WHEREAS the Provinces of Canada, Nova Scotia, and New Brunswick have expressed their desire to be federally united into One Dominion under the crown of the United Kingdom of Great Britain and Ireland, with a constitution similar in principle to that of the United Kingdom:

And whereas such a union would conduce to the welfare of the provinces and promote the interests of the British empire:

And whereas on the establishment of the union by authority of parliament it is expedient, not only that the constitution of the legislative authority in the Dominion be provided for, but also that the nature of the executive government therein be declared:

And whereas it is expedient that provision be made for the eventual admission into the union of other parts of British North America:

Be it therefore enacted and declared by the queen's most excellent majesty, by and with the advice and consent of the lords spiritual and temporal, and commons, in this present parliament assembled, and by the authority of the same, as follows:

Preliminary.

1. This act may be cited as The British North America act, 1867.

2. The provisions of this act referring to her majesty the queen extend also to the heirs and successors of her majesty, kings and queens of the United Kingdom of Great Britain and Ireland.

Union of Different Provinces.

3. It shall be lawful for the queen, by and with the advice of her majesty's most honorable privy council, to declare by proclamation that, on and after a day therein appointed, not being more than six months after the passing of this act, the provinces of Canada, Nova Scotia and New Brunswick shall form and be one Dominion under the name of Canada; and on and after that day those three provinces shall form and be one Dominion under that name accordingly.

4. The subsequent provisions of this act shall, unless it is otherwise expressed or implied, commence and have effect on and after the union, that is to say, on and after the day appointed for the union taking effect in the queen's proclamation; and in the same provisions, unless it is otherwise expressed or implied, the name Canada shall be taken to mean Canada as constituted under this act.

5. Canada shall be divided into four provinces, named Ontario, Quebec, Nova Scotia and New Brunswick.

6. The parts of the province of Canada (as it exists at the passing of this act) which formerly constituted respectively the provinces of Upper Canada and Lower Canada shall be deemed to be severed, and shall form two separate provinces. The part which formerly constituted the province of Upper Canada shall constitute the province of Ontario; and the part which formerly constituted

the province of Lower Canada shall constitute the province of Quebec.

7. The provinces of Nova Scotia and New Brunswick shall have the same limits as at the passing of this act.

8. In the general census of the population of Canada, which is hereby required to be taken in the year one thousand eight hundred and seventy-one, and in every tenth year thereafter, the respective populations of the four provinces shall be distinguished.

Executive Power Vested in the Queen.

9. The executive government and authority of and over Canada is hereby declared to continue and be vested in the queen.

10. The provisions of this act referring to the governor-general extend and apply to the governor-general for the time being of Canada, or other chief executive officer or administrator for the time being carrying on the government of Canada on behalf and in the name of the queen, by whatever title he is designated.

11. There shall be a council to aid and advise in the government of Canada, to be styled the queen's privy council for Canada; and the persons who are to be members of that council shall be from time to time chosen and summoned by the governor-general and sworn in as privy councillors; and members thereof may be from time to time removed by the governor-general.

12. All powers, authorities, and functions which under any act of the parliament of Great Britain, or of the parliament of the United Kingdom of Great Britain and Ireland, or of the legislature of Upper Canada, Lower Canada, Canada, Nova Scotia, or New Brunswick, are at the union vested in or exercisible by the respective governors or lieutenant-governors of those provinces, with the advice or with the advice and consent of or in conjunction with the queen's privy council for Canada, or any members thereof, or by those governors or lieutenant-governors individually, shall, as far as the same continue in existence and capable of being exercised after the union in relation to the government of Canada, be vested in and exercisible by the governor-general, with the advice or with the advice and consent of or in conjunction with the queen's privy council for Canada, or any members thereof, or by the governor-general individually, as the case may require, subject nevertheless (except with respect to such as exist under acts of the parliament of Great Britain or of the parliament of the United Kingdom of Great Britain and Ireland) to be abolished or altered by the parliament of Canada.

13. The provisions of this act referring to the governor-general in council shall be construed as referring to the governor-general acting by and with the advice of the queen's privy council for Canada.

14. It shall be lawful for the queen, if her majesty thinks fit, to authorize the governor-general from time to time to appoint any person or any persons jointly or severally to be his deputy or deputies within any part or parts of Canada, and in that capacity to exercise during the pleasure of the governor-general such of the powers, authorities and functions of the governor-general, as the governor-general deems it necessary or expedient to assign to him or them, subject to any limitations or directions expressed or given by the queen; but the appointment of such a deputy or deputies

shall not affect the exercise by the governor-general himself of any power, authority or function.

15. The commander-in-chief of the land and naval militia, and of all naval and military forces, of and in Canada, is hereby declared to continue and be vested in the queen.

16. Until the queen otherwise directs, the seat of government of Canada shall be Ottawa.

Legislative Power.

17. There shall be one parliament for Canada, consisting of the queen, an upper house styled the senate, and the house of commons.

18. The privileges, immunities and powers to be held, enjoyed and exercised by the senate and by the house of commons and by the members thereof respectively shall be such as are from time to time defined by act of the parliament of Canada, but so that the same shall never exceed those at the passing of this act held, enjoyed and exercised by the commons house of parliament of the United Kingdom of Great Britain and Ireland and by the members thereof.

19. The parliament of Canada shall be called together not later than six months after the union.

20. There shall be a session of the parliament of Canada once at least in every year, so that twelve months shall not intervene between the last sitting of the parliament in one session and its first sitting in the next session.

The Senate: Qualification of Senators.

21. The senate shall, subject to the provisions of this act, consist of seventy-two members, who shall be styled senators.

22. In relation to the constitution of the senate Canada shall be deemed to consist of three divisions:

1. Ontario;
2. Quebec;
3. The maritime provinces, Nova Scotia and New Brunswick; which three divisions shall (subject to the provisions of this act) be equally represented in the senate as follows: Ontario by twenty-four senators; Quebec by twenty-four senators; and the maritime provinces by twenty-four senators, twelve thereof representing Nova Scotia and twelve thereof representing New Brunswick.

In the case of Quebec each of the twenty-four senators representing that province shall be appointed for one of the twenty-four electoral divisions of Lower Canada specified in schedule A. to chapter one hundred and three of the consolidated statutes of Canada.

23. The qualification of a senator shall be as follows:

(1.) He shall be of the full age of thirty years;

(2.) He shall be either a natural-born subject of the queen, or a subject of the queen naturalized by an act of the parliament of Great Britain, or of the parliament of the United Kingdom of Great Britain and Ireland, or of the legislature of one of the provinces of Upper Canada, Lower Canada, Canada, Nova Scotia, or New Brunswick, before the union, or of the parliament of Canada after the union;

(3.) He shall be legally or equitably seized as of freehold for his own use and benefit of lands or tenements held in free and common socage, or seized or possessed for his own use and benefit of lands or tenements held in franc-alleu or in roture, within the province for which he is appointed, of the value of four thousand dollars, over and above all rents, dues, debts, charges, mortgages, and incumbrances due or payable out of or charged on or affecting the same

(4.) His real and personal property shall be together worth four thousand dollars over and above his debts and liabilities

(5.) He shall be resident in the province for which he is appointed.

(6.) In the case of Quebec he shall have his real property qualification in the electoral division for which he is appointed, or shall be resident in that division.

24. The governor-general shall from time to time, in the queen's name, by instrument under the great seal of Canada, summon qualified persons to the senate; and, subject to the provisions of this act, every person so summoned shall become and be a member of the senate and a senator.

25. Such persons shall be first summoned to the senate as the queen by warrant under her majesty's royal sign-manual thinks fit to approve, and their names shall be inserted in the queen's proclamation of union.

26. If at any time on the recommendation of the governor-general the queen thinks fit to direct that three or six members be added to the senate, the governor-general may by summons to three or six qualified persons (as the case may be), representing equally the three divisions of Canada, add to the senate accordingly.

27. In case of such addition being at any time made the governor-general shall not summon any person to the senate, except on a further like direction by the queen on the like recommendation, until each of the three divisions of Canada is represented by twenty-four senators and no more.

Number of Senators Allowed.

28. The number of senators shall not at any time exceed seventy-eight.

29. A senator shall, subject to the provisions of this act, hold his place in the senate for life.

30. A senator may by writing under his hand addressed to the governor-general resign his place in the senate, and thereupon the same shall be vacant.

31. The place of a senator shall become vacant in any of the following cases

(1.) If for two consecutive sessions of the parliament he fails to give his attendance in the senate:

(2.) If he takes an oath or makes a declaration or acknowledgment of allegiance, obedience, or adherence to a foreign power, or does an act whereby he becomes a subject or citizen, or entitled to the rights or privileges of a subject or citizen, of a foreign power

(3.) If he is adjudged bankrupt or insolvent, or applies for the benefit of any law relating to insolvent debtors, or becomes a public defaulter:

(4.) If he is attainted of treason or convicted of felony or of any infamous crime:

(5.) If he ceases to be qualified in respect of property or of residence; provided, that a senator shall not be deemed to have ceased to be qualified in respect of residence by reason only of his residing at the seat of the government of Canada while holding an office under that government requiring his presence there.

32. When a vacancy happens in the senate by resignation, death, or otherwise, the governor-general shall by summons to a fit and qualified person fill the vacancy.

33. If any question arises respecting the qualification of a senator or a vacancy in the senate the same shall be heard and determined by the senate.

34. The governor-general may from time to time, by instrument under the great seal of Canada, appoint a senator to be speaker of the senate, and may remove him and appoint another in his stead.

35. Until the parliament of Canada otherwise provides, the presence of at least fifteen senators, including the speaker, shall be necessary to constitute a meeting of the senate for the exercise of its powers.

36. Questions arising in the senate shall be decided by a majority of voices, and the speaker shall in all cases have a vote, and when the voices are equal the decision shall be deemed to be in the negative.

The House of Commons.

37. The house of commons shall, subject to the provisions of this act, consist of one hundred and eighty-one members, of whom eighty-two shall be elected for Ontario, sixty-five for Quebec, nineteen for Nova Scotia, and fifteen for New Brunswick

38. The governor-general shall from time to time, in the queen's name, by instrument under

the great seal of Canada, summon and call together the house of commons.

39. A senator shall not be capable of being elected or of sitting or voting as a member of the house of commons.

40. Until the parliament of Canada otherwise provides, Ontario, Quebec, Nova Scotia, and New Brunswick shall, for the purposes of the election of members to serve in the house of commons, be divided into electoral districts as follows

1.---Ontario.

Ontario shall be divided into the counties, ridings of counties, cities, parts of cities, and towns enumerated in the first schedule to this act, each whereof shall be an electoral district, each such district as numbered in that schedule being entitled to return one member.

2.---Quebec.

Quebec shall be divided into sixty-five electoral districts, composed of the sixty-five electoral divisions into which Lower Canada is at the passing of this act divided under chapter two of the consolidated statutes of Canada, chapter seventy-five of the consolidated statutes for Lower Canada, and the act of the province of Canada of the twenty-third year of the queen, chapter one, or any other act amending the same in force at the union, so that each electoral division shall be for the purposes of this act an electoral district entitled to return one member.

3.---Nova Scotia.

Each of the eighteen counties of Nova Scotia shall be an electoral district. The county of Halifax shall be entitled to return two members, and each of the other counties one member.

4.---New Brunswick.

Each of the fourteen counties into which New Brunswick is divided, including the city and county of St. John, shall be an electoral district, the city of St. John shall also be a separate electoral district. Each of those fifteen electoral districts shall be entitled to return one member.

41. Until the parliament of Canada otherwise provides, all laws in force in the several provinces at the union relative to the following matters or any of them, namely,—the qualifications and disqualifications of persons to be elected or to sit or vote as the members of the house of assembly or legislative assembly in the several provinces, the voters at elections of such members, the oaths to be taken by voters, the returning officers, their powers and duties, the proceedings at elections, the periods during which elections may be continued, the trial of controverted elections and proceedings incident thereto, the vacating of seats of members, and the execution of new writs in case of seats vacated otherwise than by dissolution,—shall respectively apply to elections of members to serve in the house of commons for the same several provinces.

Provided that, until the parliament of Canada otherwise provides, at any election for a member of the house of commons for the district of Algoma, in addition to persons qualified by the law of the province of Canada to vote, every male British subject, aged twenty-one years or upwards, being a householder, shall have a vote.

42. For the first election of members to serve in the house of commons the governor-general shall cause writs to be issued by such person, in such form, and addressed to such returning officers as he thinks fit.

The person issuing writs under this section shall have the like powers as are possessed at the union by the officers charged with the issuing of writs for the election of members to serve in the respective house of assembly or legislative assembly of the province of Canada, Nova Scotia, or New Brunswick; and the returning officers to whom writs are directed under this section shall have the like powers as are possessed at the union by the officers charged with the returning of writs for the election of members to serve in the same respective house of assembly or legislative assembly.

43. In case a vacancy in the representation in the house of commons of any electoral district happens before the meeting of the parliament, or after the meeting of the parliament, before provision is made by the parliament in this behalf, the provisions of the last foregoing section of this act shall extend and apply to the issuing and returning of a writ in respect of such vacant district.

Election of Speaker in the House of Commons.

44. The house of commons on its first assembling after a general election shall proceed with all practicable speed to elect one of its members to be speaker

45. In case of a vacancy happening in the office of speaker by death, resignation, or otherwise, the house of commons shall with all practicable speed proceed to elect another of its members to be speaker.

46. The speaker shall preside at all meetings of the house of commons.

47. Until the parliament of Canada otherwise provides, in case of the absence for any reason of the speaker from the chair of the house of commons for a period of forty-eight consecutive hours, the house may elect another of its members to act as a speaker, and the member so elected shall, during the continuance of such absence of the speaker, have and execute all the powers, privileges and duties of speaker.

48. The presence of at least twenty members of the house of commons shall be necessary to constitute a meeting of the house for the exercise of its powers; and for that purpose the speaker shall be reckoned as a member.

49. Questions arising in the house of commons shall be decided by a majority of voices other than that of the speaker, and when the voices are equal, but not otherwise, the speaker shall have a vote.

50. Every house of commons shall continue for five years from the day of the return of the writs for choosing the house (subject to be sooner dissolved by the governor-general), and no longer

51. On the completion of the census in the year one thousand eight hundred and seventy-one, and of each subsequent decennial census, the representation of the four provinces shall be readjusted by such authority, in such manner, and from such time, as the parliament of Canada from time to time provides, subject and according to the following rules

(1.) Quebec shall have the fixed number of sixty-five members:

(2.) There shall be assigned to each of the other provinces such a number of members as will bear the same proportion to the number of its population (ascertained at such census) as the number sixty-five bears to the number of the population of Quebec (so ascertained):

(3.) In the computation of the number of members for a province a fractional part not exceeding one-half of the whole number requisite for entitling the province to a member shall be disregarded; but a fractional part exceeding one-half of that number shall be equivalent to the whole number:

(4.) On any such re-adjustment the number of members for a province shall not be reduced unless the proportion which the number of the population of the province bore to the number of the aggregate population of Canada at the then last preceding re-adjustment of the number of members for the province is ascertained at the then latest census to be diminished by one-twentieth part or upwards:

(5.) Such re-adjustment shall not take effect until the termination of the then existing parliament.

52. The number of members of the house of commons may be from time to time increased by the parliament of Canada, provided the proportionate representation of the provinces prescribed by this act is not thereby disturbed.

The Raising and Distribution of Money.

53. Bills for appropriating any part of the public revenue, or for imposing any tax or impost, shall originate in the house of commons.

54. It shall not be lawful for the house of commons to adopt or pass any vote, resolution, address, or bill for the appropriation of any part of the public revenue, or of any tax or impost, to any purpose that has not been first recommended to that house by message of the governor-general in the session in which such vote, resolution, address, or bill is proposed.

55. Where a bill passed by the houses of the parliament is presented to the governor-general for the queen's assent, he shall declare, according to his discretion, but subject to the provisions of this act, and to her majesty's instructions, either that he assents thereto in the queen's name, or that he withholds the queen's assent, or that he reserves the bill for the signification of the queen's pleasure.

56. Where the governor-general assents to a bill in the queen's name, he shall by the first convenient opportunity send an authentic copy of the act to one of her majesty's principal secretaries of state, and if the queen in council within two years after receipt thereof by the secretary of state thinks fit to disallow the act, such disallowance, with a certificate of the secretary of state of the day on which the act was received by him being signified by the governor-general by speech or message to each of the houses of the parliament or by proclamation, shall annul the act from and after the day of such signification.

57. A bill reserved for the signification of the queen's pleasure shall not have any force unless and until within two years from the day on which it was presented to the governor-general for the queen's assent, the governor-general signifies, by speech or message to each of the houses of the parliament, or by proclamation, that it has received the assent of the queen in council.

An entry of every such speech, message or proclamation shall be made in the journal of each house, and a duplicate thereof, duly attested, shall be delivered to the proper officer to be kept among the records of Canada.

Executive Power in Each Province.

58. For each province there shall be an officer, styled the lieutenant-governor, appointed by the governor-general in council by instrument under the great seal of Canada.

59. A lieutenant-governor shall hold office during the pleasure of the governor-general; but any lieutenant-governor appointed after the commencement of the first session of the parliament of Canada shall not be removable within five years from his appointment, except for cause assigned, which shall be communicated to him in writing within one month after the order for his removal is made, and shall be communicated by message to the senate and to the house of commons within one week thereafter if the parliament is then sitting, and if not, then within one week after the commencement of the next session of the parliament.

60. The salaries of the lieutenant-governors shall be fixed and provided by the parliament of Canada.

61. Every lieutenant-governor shall, before assuming the duties of his office, make and subscribe before the governor-general or some person authorised by him, oaths of allegiance and office similar to those taken by the governor-general.

62. The provisions of this act, referring to the lieutenant-governor, extend and apply to the lieutenant-governor for the time being of each province or other the chief executive officer or administrator for the time being carrying on the government of the province, by whatever title he is designated.

63. The executive council of Ontario and of Quebec shall be composed of such persons as the lieutenant-governor from time to time thinks fit, and in the first instance of the following officers, namely,—the attorney-general, the secretary and registrar of the province, the treasurer of the province, the commissioner of crown lands, and the commissioner of agriculture and public works, with, in Quebec, the speaker of the legislative council and the solicitor-general.

64. The constitution of the executive authority in each of the provinces of Nova Scotia and New Brunswick shall, subject to the provisions of this act, continue as it exists at the union until altered under the authority of this act.

65. All powers, authorities and functions which, under any act of the parliament of Great Britain, or of the parliament of the United Kingdom of Great Britain and Ireland, or of the legislature of Upper Canada, Lower Canada, or Canada, were or are before or at the union vested in or exercisable by the respective governors or lieutenant-governors of those provinces, with the advice, or with the advice and consent, of the respective executive councils thereof, or in conjunction with those councils, or with any number of members thereof, or by those governors or lieutenant-governors individually, shall, as far as the same are capable of being exercised after the union in relation to the government of Ontario and Quebec respectively, be vested in and shall or may be exercised by the lieutenant-governor of Ontario and Quebec respectively, with the advice or with the advice and consent of or in conjunction with the respective executive councils, or any members thereof, or by the lieutenant-governor individually, as the case requires, subject nevertheless (except with respect to such as exist under acts of the parliament of Great Britain, or of the parliament of the United Kingdom of Great Britain and Ireland) to be abolished or altered by the respective legislatures of Ontario and Quebec.

66. The provisions of this act referring to the lieutenant-governor in council shall be construed as referring to the lieutenant-governor of the province acting by and with the advice of the executive council thereof

67. The governor-general in council may from time to time appoint an administrator to execute the office and functions of lieutenant-governor during his absence, illness or other inability.

68. Unless and until the executive government of any province otherwise directs with respect to that province, the seats of government of the provinces shall be as follows, namely,—of Ontario, the city of Toronto; of Quebec, the city of Quebec;

of Nova Scotia, the city of Halifax; and of New Brunswick, the city of Fredericton.

Legislative Power in Ontario.

69. There shall be a legislature for Ontario, consisting of the lieutenant-governor and of one house, styled the legislative assembly of Ontario.

70. The legislative assembly of Ontario shall be composed of eighty-two members, to be elected to represent the eighty-two electoral districts set forth in the first schedule to this act.

Legislative Power in Quebec.

71. There shall be a legislature for Quebec, consisting of the lieutenant-governor and of two houses, styled the legislative council of Quebec and the legislative assembly of Quebec.

72. The legislative council of Quebec shall be composed of twenty-four members, to be appointed by the lieutenant-governor in the queen's name, by instrument under the great seal of Quebec, one being appointed to represent each of the twenty-four electoral divisions of Lower Canada in this act referred to, and each holding office for the term of his life, unless the legislature of Quebec otherwise provides under the provisions of this act.

73. The qualifications of the legislative councillors of Quebec shall be the same as those of the senators for Quebec.

74. The place of a legislative councillor of Quebec shall become vacant in the cases *mutatis mutandis*, in which the place of senator becomes vacant.

75. When a vacancy happens in the legislative council of Quebec by resignation, death, or otherwise, the lieutenant-governor, in the queen's name, by instrument under the great seal of Quebec, shall appoint a fit and qualified person to fill the vacancy.

76. If any question arises respecting the qualification of a legislative councillor of Quebec, or a vacancy in the legislative council of Quebec, the same shall be heard and determined by the legislative council.

77. The lieutenant-governor may from time to time, by instrument under the great seal of Quebec, appoint a member of the legislative council of Quebec to be speaker thereof, and may remove him and appoint another in his stead.

78. Until the legislature of Quebec otherwise provides, the presence of at least ten members of the legislative council, including the speaker, shall be necessary to constitute a meeting for the exercise of its powers.

79. Questions arising in the legislative council of Quebec shall be decided by a majority of voices, and the speaker shall in all cases have a vote, and when the voices are equal the decision shall be deemed to be in the negative.

80. The legislative assembly of Quebec shall be composed of sixty-five members, to be elected to represent the sixty-five electoral divisions or districts of Lower Canada in this act referred to, subject to alteration thereof by the legislature of Quebec: Provided that it shall not be lawful to present to the lieutenant-governor of Quebec for assent any bill for altering the limits of any of the electoral divisions or districts mentioned in the second schedule to this act, unless the second and third readings of such bill have been passed in the legislative assembly with the concurrence of the majority of the members representing all those electoral divisions or districts, and the assent shall not be given to such bill unless an address has been presented by the legislative assembly to the lieutenant-governor stating that it has been so passed.

The Legislatures of Ontario and Quebec.

81. The legislatures of Ontario and Quebec respectively shall be called together not later than six months after the union.

82. The lieutenant-governor of Ontario and of Quebec shall from time to time, in the queen's name, by instrument under the great seal of the province, summon and call together the legislative assembly of the province.

83. Until the legislature of Ontario or of Quebec otherwise provides, a person accepting or holding in Ontario or in Quebec any office, commission or employment, permanent or temporary, at the nomination of the lieutenant-governor, to which an annual salary, or any fee, allowance, emolument, or profit of any kind or amount whatever from the province is attached, shall not be eligible as a member of the legislative assembly of the respective province, nor shall he sit or vote as such; but nothing in this section shall make ineligible any person being a member of the executive council of the respective province, or holding any of the following offices that is to say, the offices of attorney-general, secretary and registrar

of the province, treasurer of the province, commissioner of crown lands, and commissioner of agriculture and public works, and in Quebec solicitor-general, or shall disqualify him to sit or vote in the house for which he is elected, provided he is elected while holding such office.

84. Until the legislatures of Ontario and Quebec respectively otherwise provide, all laws which at the union are in force in those provinces respectively, relative to the following matters, or any of them, namely,—the qualifications and disqualifications of persons to be elected or to sit or vote as members of the assembly of Canada, the qualifications or disqualifications of voters, the oaths to be taken by voters, the returning officers, their powers and duties, the proceedings at elections, the periods during which such elections may be continued, and the trial of controverted elections and the proceedings incident thereto, the vacating of the seats of members and the issuing and execution of new writs in case of seats vacated otherwise than by dissolution, shall respectively apply to elections of members to serve in the respective legislative assemblies of Ontario and Quebec.

Provided that until the legislature of Ontario otherwise provides, at each election for a member of the legislative assembly of Ontario for the district of Algoma, in addition to persons qualified by the law of the province of Canada to vote, every male British subject, aged twenty-one years or upwards, being a householder, shall have a vote.

85. Every legislative assembly of Ontario and every legislative assembly of Quebec shall continue for four years from the day of the return of the writs for choosing the same (subject nevertheless to either the legislative assembly of Ontario or the legislative assembly of Quebec being sooner dissolved by the lieutenant-governor of the province), and no longer.

86. There shall be a session of the legislature of Ontario and of that of Quebec once at least in every year, so that twelve months shall not intervene between the last sitting of the legislature in each province in one session and its first sitting in the next session.

87. The following provisions of this act respecting the house of commons of Canada shall extend and apply to the legislative assemblies of Ontario and Quebec, that is to say,—the provisions relating to the election of a speaker originally and on vacancies, the duties of the speaker, the absence of the speaker, the quorum, and the mode of voting, as if those provisions were here re-enacted and made applicable in terms to each such legislative assembly.

Nova Scotia and New Brunswick.

88. The constitution of the legislature of each of the provinces of Nova Scotia and New Brunswick shall, subject to the provisions of this act, continue as it exists at the union until altered under the authority of this act; and the house of assembly of New Brunswick existing at the passing of this act shall, unless sooner dissolved, continue for the period for which it was elected.

Ontario, Quebec and Nova Scotia.

89. Each of the lieutenant-governors of Ontario, Quebec and Nova Scotia shall cause writs to be issued for the first election of members of the legislative assembly thereof in such form and by such person as he thinks fit, and at such time and addressed to such returning officer as the governor-general directs, and so that the first election of member of assembly for any electoral district or any subdivision thereof shall be held at the same time and at the same place as the election for a member to serve in the house of commons of Canada for that electoral district.

The Four Provinces.

90. The following provisions of this act respecting the parliament of Canada, namely,—the provisions relating to appropriation and tax bills, the recommendation of money votes, the assent to bills, the disallowance of acts, and the signification of pleasure on bills reserved, shall extend and apply to the legislatures of the several provinces as if those provisions were here re-enacted and made applicable in terms to the respective provinces and the legislatures thereof, with the substitution of the lieutenant-governor of the province for the governor-general, of the governor-general for the queen and for a secretary of state, of one year for two years, and of the province for Canada.

Powers of the Canadian Parliament.

91. It shall be lawful for the queen, by and with the advice and consent of the senate and house of commons, to make laws for the peace, order and good government of Canada, in relation to all matters not coming within the classes of subjects by this act assigned exclusively to the legislatures of the provinces, and for greater certainty, but not so as to restrict the generality of the foregoing terms of this section, it is hereby declared that (notwithstanding anything in this act) the exclusive legislative authority of the parliament of Canada extends to all matters coming within the classes of subjects next hereinafter enumerated; that is to say:

1. The public debt and property.
2. The regulation of trade and commerce.
3. The raising of money by any mode or system.
4. The borrowing of money on the public credit.
5. Postal service.
6. The census and statistics.
7. Militia, military and naval service and defense.
8. The fixing of and providing for the salaries and allowances of civil and other officers of the government of Canada.
9. Beacons, buoys, lighthouses and Sable Island.
10. Navigation and shipping.
11. Quarantine and the establishment and maintenance of marine hospitals.
12. Sea-coast and inland fisheries.
13. Ferries between a province and any British or foreign country or between two provinces.
14. Currency and coinage.
15. Banking, incorporation of banks and the issue of paper money.
16. Savings banks.
17. Weights and measures.
18. Bills of exchange and promissory notes.
19. Interest.
20. Legal tender.
21. Bankruptcy and insolvency.
22. Patents of invention and discovery.
23. Copyrights.
24. Indians and lands reserved for the Indians.
25. Naturalization and aliens.
26. Marriage and divorce.
27. The criminal law, except the constitution of courts of criminal jurisdiction, but including the procedure in criminal matters.
28. The establishment, maintenance and management of penitentiaries.
29. Such classes of subjects as are expressly excepted in the enumeration of the classes of subjects by this act assigned exclusively to the legislatures of the provinces.

And any matter coming within any of the classes of subjects enumerated in this section shall not be deemed to come within the class of matters of a local or private nature comprised in the enumeration of the classes of subjects by this act assigned exclusively to the legislatures of the provinces.

Exclusive Powers of Provincial Legislatures.

92. In each province the legislature may exclusively make laws in relation to matters coming within the classes of subjects next hereinafter enumerated; that is to say:

1. The amendment from time to time, notwithstanding anything in this act, of the constitution of the province, except as regards the office of lieutenant-governor.
2. Direct taxation within the province in order to the raising of a revenue for provincial purposes.
3. The borrowing of money on the sole credit of the province.
4. The establishment and tenure of provincial offices and the appointment and payment of provincial officers.
5. The management and sale of the public lands belonging to the province and of the timber and wood thereon.
6. The establishment, maintenance and management of public and reformatory prisons in and for the province.
7. The establishment, maintenance and management of hospitals, asylums, charities and eleemosynary institutions in and for the province, other than marine hospitals.
8. Municipal institutions in the province.
9. Shop, saloon, tavern, auctioneer and other licenses in order to the raising of a revenue for provincial, local or municipal purposes.
10. Local works and undertakings other than such as are of the following classes:
    a. Lines of steam or other ships, railways, cannals, telegraphs and other works and undertakings connecting the province with any other or others of the provinces, or extending beyond the limits of the province:
    b. Lines of steamships between the province and any British or foreign country:
    c. Such works as, although wholly situate within the province, are before or after their execution declared by the parliament of Canada to be for the general advantage of Canada or for the advantage of two or more of the provinces.
11. The incorporation of companies with provincial objects.
12. The solemnization of marriage in the province.
13. Property and civil rights in the province.
14. The administration of justice in the province, including the constitution, maintenance and organization of provincial courts, both of civil and of criminal jurisdiction, and including procedure in civil matters in those courts.
15. The imposition of punishment by fine, penalty or imprisonment for enforcing any law of the province made in relation to any matter coming within any of the classes of subjects enumerated in this section.
16. Generally all matters of a merely local or private nature in the province.

What Shall be Done for Schools.

93. In and for each province the legislature may exclusively make laws in relation to education, subject and according to the following provisions:

1. Nothing in any such law shall prejudicially affect any right or privilege with respect to denominational schools which any class of persons have by law in the province at the union.
2. All the powers, privileges and duties at the union by law conferred and imposed in Upper Canada on the separate schools and school trustees of the queen's Roman Catholic subjects shall be and the same are hereby extended to the dissentient schools of the queen's Protestant and Roman Catholic subjects in Quebec:
3. Where in any province a system of separate or dissentient schools exists by law at the union or is thereafter established by the legislature of the province, an appeal shall lie to the governor-general in council from any act or decision of any provincial authority affecting any right or privilege of the Protestant or Roman Catholic minority of the queen's subjects in relation to education:
4. In case any such provincial law as from time to time seems to the governor-general in council requisite for the due execution of the provisions of this section is not made, or in case any decision of the governor-general in council on any appeal under this section is not duly executed by the proper provincial authority in that behalf, then and in every such case, and as far only as the circumstances of each case require, the parliament of Canada may make remedial laws for the due execution of the provisions of this section and of any decision of the governor-general in council under this section.

Uniformity of Laws in the Provinces.

94. Notwithstanding anything in this act, the parliament of Canada may make provision for the uniformity of all or any of the laws relative to property and civil rights in Ontario, Nova Scotia and New Brunswick, and of the procedure of all or any of the courts in those three provinces, and from and after the passing of any act in that behalf the power of the parliament of Canada to make laws in relation to any matter comprised in any such act shall, notwithstanding anything in this act, be unrestricted; but any act of the parliament of Canada making provision for such uniformity shall not have effect in any province unless and until it is adopted and enacted as law by the legislature thereof.

Agriculture and Immigration.

95. In each province the legislature may make laws in relation to agriculture in the province, and to immigration into the province, and it is hereby declared that the parliament of Canada may from time to time make laws in relation to agriculture in all or any of the provinces, and to immigration into all or any of the provinces; and any law of the legislature of a province relative to agriculture or to immigration shall have effect in and for the province as long and as far only as it is not repugnant to any act of the parliament of Canada.

Appointment of Judges.

96. The governor-general shall appoint the judges of the superior, district and county courts in each province, except those of the courts of probate in Nova Scotia and New Brunswick.

97. Until the laws relative to property and civil rights in Ontario, Nova Scotia and New Brunswick, and the procedure of the courts in those provinces, are made uniform, the judges of the courts of those provinces appointed by the governor-general shall be selected from the respective bars of those provinces.

98. The judges of the courts of Quebec shall be selected from the bar of that province.

99. The judges of the superior courts shall hold office during good behavior, but shall be removable by the governor-general on address of the senate and house of commons.

100. The salaries, allowances and pensions of the judges of the superior, district and county courts (except the courts of probate in Nova Scotia and New Brunswick) and of the admiralty courts in cases where the judges thereof are for the time being paid by salary, shall be fixed and provided by the parliament of Canada.

101. The parliament of Canada may, notwithstanding anything in this act, from time to time provide for the constitution, maintenance and organization of a general court of appeal for Canada, and for the establishment of any additional courts for the better administration of the laws of Canada.

Revenues, Debts, Assets, Taxation.

102. All duties and revenues over which the respective legislatures of Canada, Nova Scotia and New Brunswick before and at the union had and have power of appropriation, except such portions thereof as are by this act reserved to the respective legislatures of the provinces, or are raised by them in accordance with the special powers conferred on them by this act, shall form one consolidated revenue fund, to be appropriated for the public service of Canada in the manner and subject to the charges in this act provided.

103. The consolidated revenue fund of Canada shall be permanently charged with the costs, charges and expenses incident to the collection, management and receipt thereof, and the same shall form the first charge thereon, subject to be reviewed and audited in such manner as shall be ordered by the governor-general in council until the parliament otherwise provides.

104. The annual interest of the public debts of the several provinces of Canada, Nova Scotia and New Brunswick at the union shall form the second charge on the consolidated revenue fund of Canada.

Salary of the Governor-General.

105. Unless altered by the parliament of Canada, the salary of the governor-general shall be ten thousand pounds sterling money of the United Kingdom of Great Britain and Ireland, payable out of the consolidated revenue fund of Canada, and the same shall form the third charge thereon.

106. Subject to the several payments by this act charged on the consolidated revenue fund of Canada, the same shall be appropriated by the parliament of Canada for the public service.

107. All stocks, cash, bankers' balances and securities for money belonging to each province at the time of the union, except as in this act mentioned, shall be the property of Canada, and shall be taken in reduction of the amount of the respective debts of the provinces at the union.

108. The public works and property of each province, enumerated in the third schedule to this act, shall be the property of Canada.

109. All lands, mines, minerals and royalties belonging to the several provinces of Canada, Nova Scotia and New Brunswick at the union, and all sums then due or payable for such lands, mines, minerals or royalties shall belong to the several provinces of Ontario, Quebec, Nova Scotia and New Brunswick, in which the same are situate or arise, subject to any trusts existing in respect thereof, and to any interest other than that of the province in the same.

110. All assets connected with such portions of the public debt of each province as are assumed by that province shall belong to that province.

111. Canada shall be liable for the debts and liabilities of each province existing at the union.

112. Ontario and Quebec conjointly shall be liable to Canada for the amount (if any) by which the debt of the province of Canada exceeds at the union sixty-two million five hundred thousand dollars, and shall be charged with interest at the rate of five per centum per annum thereon.

113. The assets enumerated in the fourth schedule to this act belonging at the union to the province of Canada shall be the property of Ontario and Quebec conjointly.

114. Nova Scotia shall be liable to Canada for the amount (if any) by which its public debt exceeds at the union eight million dollars, and shall be charged with interest at the rate of five per centum per annum thereon.

115. New Brunswick shall be liable to Canada for the amount (if any) by which its public debt exceeds at the union seven million dollars, and shall be charged with interest at the rate of five per centum per annum thereon.

116. In case the public debts of Nova Scotia and New Brunswick do not at the union amount to eight million and seven million dollars respectively, they shall respectively receive by half-yearly payments in advance from the government of Canada interest at five per centum per annum on the difference between the actual amounts of their respective debts and such stipulated amounts.

117. The several provinces shall retain all their respective public property not otherwise disposed of in this act, subject to the right of Canada to assume any lands or public property required for fortifications or for the defense of the country.

Money for the Support of Government.

118. The following sums shall be paid yearly by Canada to the several provinces for the support of their governments and legislatures: Ontario, eighty thousand dollars; Quebec, seventy thousand; Nova Scotia, sixty thousand, New Brunswick, fifty thousand; total, two hundred and sixty thousand dollars; and an annual grant in aid of each province shall be made, equal to eighty cents per head of the population as ascertained by the census of one thousand eight hundred and sixty-one, and in the case of Nova Scotia and New Brunswick, by each subsequent decennial census until the population of each of those two provinces amounts to four hundred thousand souls, at which rate such grant shall thereafter remain. Such grants shall be in full settlement of all future demands on Canada, and shall be paid half-yearly in advance to each province; but the government of Canada shall deduct from such grants, as against any province, all sums chargeable as interest on the public debt of that province in excess of the several amounts stipulated in this act.

119. New Brunswick shall receive by half-yearly payments in advance from Canada for the period of ten years from the union an additional allowance of sixty-three thousand dollars per annum; but as long as the public debt of that province remains under seven million dollars, a deduction equal to the interest at five per centum per annum on such deficiency shall be made from that allowance of sixty-three thousand dollars.

120. All payments to be made under this act, or in discharge of liabilities created under any act of the provinces of Canada, Nova Scotia and New Brunswick respectively, and assumed by Canada, shall, until the parliament of Canada otherwise directs, be made in such form and manner as may from time to time be ordered by the governor-general in council.

121. All articles of the growth, produce or manufacture of any one of the provinces shall, from and after the union, be admitted free into each of the other provinces.

122. The customs and excise laws of each province shall, subject to the provisions of this act, continue in force until altered by the parliament of Canada.

Exports and Imports Between Provinces.

123. Where customs duties are, at the union, leviable on any goods, wares or merchandises in any two provinces, those goods, wares and merchandises may, from and after the union, be imported from one of those provinces into the other of them on proof of payment of the customs duty leviable thereon in the province of exportation, and on payment of such further amount (if any) of customs duty as is leviable thereon in the province of importation.

124. Nothing in this act shall affect the right of New Brunswick to levy the lumber dues provided in chapter fifteen of title three of the revised statutes of New Brunswick, or in any act amending that act before or after the union, and not increasing the amount of such dues; but the lumber of any of the provinces other than New Brunswick shall not be subject to such dues.

125. No lands or property belonging to Canada or any province shall be liable to taxation.

126. Such portions of the duties and revenues over which the respective legislatures of Canada, Nova Scotia and New Brunswick had before the union power of appropriation as are by this act reserved to the respective governments or legislatures of the provinces, and all duties and revenues raised by them in accordance with the special powers conferred upon them by this act, shall in each province form one consolidated revenue fund to be appropriated for the public service of the province.

127. If any person, being at the passing of this act a member of the legislative council of Canada, Nova Scotia or New Brunswick, to whom a place in the senate is offered, does not within thirty days thereafter, by writing under his hand addressed to the governor-general of the province of Canada or to the lieutenant-governor of Nova Scotia or New Brunswick (as the case may be), accept the same, he shall be deemed to have declined the same; and any person who, being at the passing of this act a member of the legislative council of Nova Scotia or New Brunswick, accepts a place in the senate shall thereby vacate his seat in such legislative council.

Must Take the Oath of Allegiance.

128. Every member of the senate or house of commons of Canada shall, before taking his seat therein, take and subscribe before the governor-general or some person authorized by him, and every member of a legislative council or legislative assembly of any province shall, before taking his seat therein, take and subscribe before the lieutenant-governor of the province or some person authorised by him, the oath of allegiance contained in the fifth schedule to this act; and every member of the senate of Canada and every member of the legislative council of Quebec shall also, before taking his seat therein, take and subscribe before the governor-general or some person authorized by him, the declaration of qualification contained in the same schedule.

129. Except as otherwise provided by this act, all laws in force in Canada, Nova Scotia or New Brunswick at the union, and all courts of civil and criminal jurisdiction and all legal commissions, powers and authorities, all officers, judicial, administrative and ministerial, existing therein at the union, shall continue in Ontario, Quebec, Nova Scotia and New Brunswick respectively, as if the union had not been made; subject nevertheless, except with respect to such as are enacted by or exist under acts of the parliament of Great Britain or of the parliament of the United Kingdom of Great Britain and Ireland, to be repealed, abolished or altered by the parliament of Canada, or by the legislature of the respective province, according to the authority of the parliament or of that legislature under this act.

130. Until the parliament of Canada otherwise provides, all officers of the several provinces having duties to discharge in relation to matters other than those coming within the classes of subjects by this act assigned exclusively to the legislatures of the provinces shall be officers of Canada, and shall continue to discharge the duties of their respective offices under the same liabilities, responsibilities and penalties as if the union had not been made.

131. Until the parliament of Canada otherwise provides, the governor-general in council may from time to time appoint such officers as the governor-general in council deems necessary or proper for the effectual execution of this act.

132. The parliament and government of Canada shall have all powers necessary or proper for performing the obligations of Canada or of any province thereof, as part of the British empire, toward foreign countries, arising under treaties between the empire and such foreign countries.

English and French in Parliament.

133. Either the English or the French language may be used by any person in the debates of the houses of the parliament of Canada and of the houses of the legislature of Quebec; and both those languages shall be used in the respective records and journals of those houses; and either of those languages may be used by any person or in any pleading or process in or issuing from any court of Canada established under this act, and in or from all or any of the courts of Quebec.

The acts of the parliament of Canada or of the legislature of Quebec shall be printed and published in both those languages.

134. Until the legislature of Ontario and of Quebec otherwise provides, the lieutenant-governors of Ontario and Quebec may each appoint under the great seal of the province the following officers, to hold office during pleasure, that is to say,—the attorney-general, the secretary and registrar of the province, the treasurer of the province, the commissioner of crown lands, and the commissioner of agricultural and public works, and in the case of Quebec the solicitor-general; and may, by order of the lieutenant-governor in council, from time to time prescribe the duties of those officers and of the several departments over which they shall preside or to which they shall belong, and of the officers and clerks thereof; and may also appoint other and additional officers to hold office during pleasure, and may from time to time prescribe the duties of those officers, and of the several departments over which they shall preside or to which they shall belong, and of the officers and clerks thereof.

Powers and Duties of Executive Officers.

135. Until the legislature of Ontario or Quebec otherwise provides, all rights, powers, duties, functions, responsibilities or authorities at the passing of this act vested in or imposed on the attorney-general, solicitor-general, secretary and registrar of the province of Canada, minister of finance, commissioner of crown lands, commissioner of public works and minister of agriculture and receiver-general, by any law, statute or ordinance of Upper Canada, Lower Canada, or Canada, and not repugnant to this act, shall be vested in or imposed on any officer to be appointed by the lieutenant-governor for the discharge of the same or any of them; and the commissioner of agriculture and public works shall perform the duties and functions of the office of minister of agriculture at the passing of this act imposed by the law of the province of Canada, as well as those of the commissioner of public works.

136. Until altered by the lieutenant-governor in council, the great seals of Ontario and Quebec respectively shall be the same, or of the same design, as those used in the provinces of Upper Canada and Lower Canada respectively before their union as the province of Canada.

137. The words "and from thence to the end of the then next ensuing session of the legislature," or words to the same effect, used in any temporary act of the province of Canada not expired before the union, shall be construed to extend and apply to the next session of the parliament of Canada, if the subject matter of the act is within the powers of the same, as defined by this act, or to the next sessions of the legislatures of Ontario and Quebec respectively, if the subject matter of the act is within the powers of the same as defined by this act.

138. From and after the union the use of the words "Upper Canada" instead of "Ontario," or "Lower Canada" instead of "Quebec," in any deed, writ, process, pleading, document, matter or thing, shall not invalidate the same.

Concerning Proclamations.

139. Any proclamation under the great seal of the province of Canada issued before the union to take effect at a time which is subsequent to the union, whether relating to that province, or to Upper Canada, or to Lower Canada, and the several matters and things therein proclaimed shall be and continue of like force and effect as if the union had not been made.

140. Any proclamation which is authorized by any act of the legislature of the province of Canada to be issued under the great seal of the province of Canada, whether relating to that province, or to Upper Canada, or to Lower Canada, and which is not issued before the union, may be issued by the lieutenant-governor of Ontario or of Quebec, as its subject matter requires, under the great seal thereof and from and after the issue of such proclamation the same and the several matters and things therein proclaimed shall be and continue of the like force and effect in Ontario or Quebec as if the union had not been made.

141. The penitentiary of the province of Canada shall, until the parliament of Canada otherwise provides, be and continue the penitentiary of Ontario and Quebec.

142. The division and adjustment of the debts, credits, liabilities, properties and assets of Upper Canada and Lower Canada shall be referred to the arbitrament of three arbitrators, one chosen by the government of Ontario, one by the government of Quebec and one by the government of Canada; and the selection of the arbitrators shall not be made until the parliament of Canada and the legislatures of Ontario and Quebec have met; and the arbitrator chosen by the government of Canada shall not be a resident either in Ontario or in Quebec.

143. The governor-general in council may from time to time order that such and so many of the records, books and documents of the province of Canada as he thinks fit shall be appropriated and delivered either to Ontario or to Quebec, and the same shall thenceforth be the property of that province; and any copy thereof or extract therefrom, duly certified by the officer having charge of the original thereof, shall be admitted as evidence.

144. The lieutenant-governor of Quebec may from time to time, by proclamation under the great seal of the province, to take effect from a day to be appointed therein, constitute townships in those parts of the province of Quebec in which townships are not then already constituted, and fix the metes and bounds thereof.

145. Inasmuch as the provinces of Canada, Nova Scotia and New Brunswick have joined in a declaration that the construction of the intercolonial railway is essential to the consolidation of the union of British North America, and to the assent thereto of Nova Scotia and New Brunswick, and have consequently agreed that provision should be made for its immediate construction by the government of Canada: Therefore, in order to give effect to that agreement, it shall be the duty of the government and parliament of Canada to provide for the commencement, within six months after the union, of a railway connecting the river St. Lawrence with city of Halifax in Nova Scotia, and for the construction thereof without intermission and the completion thereof with all practicable speed.

Admission of Other Colonies.

146. It shall be lawful for the queen, by and with the advice of her majesty's most honorable privy council, on addresses from the houses of the parliament of Canada, and from the house of the respective legislatures of the colonies or provinces of Newfoundland, Prince Edward Island and British Columbia, to admit those colonies or provinces, or any of them, into the union, and on address from the houses of the parliament of Canada to admit Rupert's Land and the Northwestern Territory, or either of them, into the union, on such terms and conditions in each case as are in the addresses expressed and as the queen thinks fit to approve, subject to the provisions of this act; and the provisions of any order in council in that behalf shall have effect as if they had been enacted by the parliament of the United Kingdom of Great Britain and Ireland.

147. In case of the admission of Newfoundland and Prince Edward Island, or either of them, each shall be entitled to a representation in the senate of Canada of four members, and (notwithstanding anything in this act) in case of the admission of Newfoundland the normal number of senators shall be seventy-six; and their maximum number shall be eighty-two; but Prince Edward Island when admitted shall be deemed to be comprised in the third of the three divisions into which Canada is, in relation to the constitution of the senate, divided by this act, and accordingly, after the admission of Prince Edward Island, whether Newfoundland is admitted or not, the representation of Nova Scotia and New Brunswick in the senate shall, as vacancies occur, be reduced from twelve to ten members respectively, and the representation of each of those provinces shall not be increased at any time beyond ten, except under the provisions of this act for the appointment of three or six additional senators under the direction of the queen.

CANADIAN TABLES OF REFERENCE,

Relating to Population, Game Laws, Nativity of Inhabitants, Denominational Strength and Tariff Duties.

Population of Principal Cities of Canadian Dominion by Census of 1881.

Name of City.	Province Located In.	Population. 1871.	1881.	Increase.
Montreal	Quebec	107,225	140,747	33,522
Toronto	Ontario	56,092	86,415	30,323
Quebec	Quebec	59,699	62,446	2,747
Halifax	Nova Scotia	29,582	36,100	6,518
Hamilton	Ontario	26,716	35,961	9,245
Ottawa	Ontario	21,545	27,412	5,867
St. John	New Brunswick	28,805	26,127	*
London	Ontario	15,826	19,746	3,920
Portland	New Brunswick	12,520	15,226	2,706
Kingston	Ontario	12,407	14,091	1,684
Charlottetown	Prince Edward Island	8,807	11,485	2,678
Guelph	Ontario	6,878	9,890	3,012
St. Catharines	Ontario	7,864	9,631	1,767
Brantford	Ontario	8,107	9,616	1,509
Belleville	Ontario	7,305	9,516	2,211
Trois-Rivieres	Quebec	7,570	8,670	1,100
St. Thomas	Ontario	2,197	8,367	6,170
Stratford	Ontario	4,313	8,239	3,926
Winnipeg	Manitoba	241	7,985	7,744
Chatham	Ontario	5,873	7,873	2,000
Brockville	Ontario	5,102	7,609	2,507
Levis	Quebec	6,691	7,597	906
Sherbrooke	Quebec	4,432	7,227	2,795
Hull	Quebec		6,890	
Peterborough	Ontario	4,611	6,812	2,201
Windsor	Ontario	4,253	6,561	2,308
St. Henri	Quebec		6,415	
Fredericton	New Brunswick	6,006	6,218	212
Victoria	British Columbia	3,270	5,925	2,655

* The decrease of the population of the city of St. John is attributed to the great fire which occurred in the year 1877.

Fishery and Game Laws in Ontario and Quebec.

Seasons in which Fish must not be caught.

	Ontario.	Quebec.
Pickerel (Dore)	From Apr. 15 to May 15	From Apr. 15 to May 15
Maskinonge	From Apr. 15 to May 15	From Apr. 15 to May 15
Bass	From May 15 to June 15	From Apr. 15 to May 15
Salmon (with nets)		From Aug. 1 to May 1
Salmon (with the fly)		From Sept. 1 to May 1
Speckled Trout, Brook or River Trout	From Sept. 15 to May 1	From Oct. 1 to Dec. 31
Salmon Trout and Lake Trout	From Nov. 1 to 16	From Oct. 15 to Dec. 1
Whitefish	From Nov. 1 to 16	From Nov. 10 to Dec. 1

Seasons in which Game must not be killed.

	Ontario.	Quebec.
Deer and Cariboo	From Dec. 15 to Oct. 1.	From Feb. 1 to Sept. 1
Moose and Elk	From Dec. 15 to Oct. 1.	From Feb. 1 to Sept. 1
Partridge, Pheasant, Grouse	From Jan. 1 to Sept. 1.	From Mar. 1 to Sept. 1
Wild Turkey and Quail	From Jan. 1 to Oct. 1.	
Woodcock	From Jan. 1 to Aug. 1.	From Mar. 1 to Sept. 1
Snipe	From Jan. 1 to Aug. 15.	From Mar. 1 to Sept. 1
Duck	From Jan. 1 to Aug. 15.	From May 1 to Sept. 1
Swans and Geese	From May 1 to Aug. 15.	From May 1 to Sept. 1
Hares	From May 1 to Sept. 1.	From May 1 to Nov. 1
Wild Cat, Marten and Fisher	From May 1 to Nov. 1.	From Apr. 15 to Nov 1
Mink	From Apr. 1 to Nov. 1.	From Apr. 15 to Oct. 15
Otter	From May 1 to Nov. 1.	From May 1 to Oct. 1
Beaver	From May 1 to Nov. 1.	From Apr. 30 to Sept. 1
Muskrat	From May 1 to Nov. 1.	From May 1 to Apr. 1

Net or seine fishing without license is prohibited.

Nets must be raised from Saturday night until Monday morning of each week.

Nets cannot be set or seines used so as to bar channels or bays. Indians are forbidden to fish illegally the same as white men.

Each person guilty of violating these regulations is liable to fine and costs, or in default of payment is subject to imprisonment.

No person shall, during such prohibited times, fish for, catch, kill, buy, sell or have in possession any of the kinds of fish or game mentioned above.

Area, Population and Capitals of Canadian Provinces in 1881.

Provinces.	Area in Acres.	Population.	Males.	Females.	Capital of Province.	Population of Capital
Ontario	65,111,463	1,923,228	976,470	946,758	Toronto	86,415
Quebec	120,764,651	1,359,027	678,175	680,452	Quebec	62,446
Nova Scotia	13,382,063	440,572	220,534	220,034	Halifax	36,100
New Brunswick	17,393,410	321,233	164,119	157,114	Fredericton	6,218
British Columbia	218,435,200	4,945	29,503	19,966	Victoria	5,925
Prince Ed'd Island	1,365,400	108,891	54,729	54,162	Charlottetown	11,485
Manitoba	79,846,040	65,954	37,307	28,747	Winnipeg	7,985
N. W. Territories	1,705,761,280	56,446	28,113	28,333	Regina	
Total	2,221,061,447	4,324,810	2,188,954	2,135,856		

Birthplace of Inhabitants of Canadian Dominion by Census of 1881.

Canadian Dominion	3,715,492
British Isles	470,092
United States	77,753
Germany	25,328
Other British Provinces	8,143
Other Countries	7,455
Russia and Poland	6,376
Not Given	6,234
France	4,380
Norway and Sweden	2,076
Italy	777
At Sea	380
Spain and Portugal	215

Denominational Strength in Canadian Dominion, 1881.

Roman Catholics	1,791,982
Methodists	742,981
Presbyterians	676,165
Church of England	574,818
Baptists	296,525
Lutherans	46,350
Congregationalists	28,900
Disciples	20,193
Brethren	9,031
Jews	2,393

Of the above 1,170,718 Roman Catholics are in the Province of Quebec, and 320,839 are in Ontario.

TARIFF DUTIES UPON GOODS,

Collected by the Canadian and American Governments on Various Articles in Common Use, According to the Tariff Rates in Canada, and Adopted by the United States Congress, March 8, 1888.

Various articles upon which duty is paid are here omitted, for want of room, but those are given which, by general use, most directly concern the people.

Goods Subject to Duty.	Canadian Duty.	American Duty.	Goods Subject to Duty.	Canadian Duty.	American Duty.
Agricultural Implements, not otherwise herein provided for, twenty-five per cent. ad valorem..	25 per cent	35 per cent	Fruits in air-tight cans, including cans, three cents per pound if sweetened and two cents per pound, if not sweetened	3 c. pr ℔ and 2 c. per ℔	35 per c. and 25 per cent
Animals, living, of all kinds, except for breeding purposes, twenty per cent. ad valorem...	20 per cent	20 per cent	Fruits, preserved in brandy or other spirits, one dollar and ninety cents per imperial gallon......	$1.90 pr l. g.	35 per cent
Artificial Flowers and Feathers, twenty-five per cent ad valorem...............	25 per cent	50 per cent	FURS, VIZ.:		
Bird Cages of all kinds, thirty per cent ad valorem	30 per cent		Fur-skins, dressed, fifteen per cent. ad valorem	15 per cent	20 per cent
Blacking, shoe, and shoemakers' ink, twenty-five per cent ad valorem....................	25 per cent	25 per cent	Caps, hats, muffs, tippets, capes, coats, cloaks and other manufactures of fur, twenty-five per cent. ad valorem	25 per cent	30 per cent
BOOKS—			Furniture, house, cabinet or office, finished or in parts, including hair, spring and other mattresses, show-cases, caskets and coffins of any material, thirty-five per cent. ad valorem......	35 per cent	35 per cent
Books, printed, periodical and pamphlets, not elsewhere specified, not being foreign reprints of British copyright works, nor blank account-books, nor copy-books, nor books to be written or drawn upon, nor Bibles, prayer-books, psalm and hymn-books, fifteen per cent ad valorem................	15 per cent	25 per cent	Hair, curled, twenty per cent. ad valorem........	20 per cent	25 per cent
British copyright works, reprints of, fifteen per cent ad valorem, and in addition thereto twelve and a half per cent. ad valorem........	15 p. ct. and 12½ pr ct.	25 per cent	Hats, caps and bonnets, not elsewhere specified, twenty-five per cent ad valorem.......	25 per cent	30 per cent
Bibles, prayer-books, psalm and hymn-books, five per cent. ad valorem............	5 per cent	25 per cent	Honey, beer, in the comb or otherwise, three cents per pound...........	3 c. per ℔ 6 c. per ℔	20 c. pr gal. 8 c. per ℔
Blank-books, viz.: Account-books, copy-books, or books to be drawn or written upon, thirty per cent. ad valorem............	30 per cent	30 per cent	Hops, six cents per pound...........		
Printed, lithographed, or copper, or steel-plate bill-heads, checks, receipts, drafts, posters, cards, other commercial blank forms, labels of every description, advertising pictures or pictorial show-cards or bills, thirty per cent. ad valorem........	30 per cent	35 per cent	IRON AND MANUFACTURES OF, VIZ.		
			Pig, two dollars per ton........	$2 per ton	$6 per ton
Maps and charts, twenty per cent. ad valorem....	20 per cent	25 per cent	Old and scrap, two dollars per ton........	$2 per ton	$8 per ton
Playing-cards, thirty per cent. ad valorem.......	30 per cent	100 pr ct p pk	Iron and Manufactures of, whole, or heads, or parts of heads of sewing-machines, two dollars each, and in addition thereto twenty per cent. ad valorem..........	$2 & 20 pr ct	45 per cent
Printed music, bound or in sheets, six cents per pound........	6 c. per ℔	25 per cent	Ink, for writing, twenty-five per cent. ad valorem	25 per cent	30 per cent
BREADSTUFFS, VIZ.:			Jewelry and manufactures of gold and silver, twenty per cent. ad valorem.........	20 per cent	25 per cent
Barley, fifteen cents per bushel........	15 c. per bsh	10 c. per bsh	Lard, tried or rendered, two cents per pound......	2 c. per ℔	2 c. per ℔
Buckwheat, ten cents per bushel........	10 c. per bsh	10 per cent	Lard, untried, one and a half cents per pound.....	1½ c. per ℔	2 c. per ℔
Indian corn, seven-and-a-half cents per bushel..	7½ c. per bsh	10 c. per bsh	Lead, old and scrap, and in pigs, bars, blocks and sheets, ten per cent ad valorem............	10 per cent	2⅔ c pr ℔
Oats, ten cents per bushel........	10 c. per bsh	10 c. per bsh	Leather, sole, tanned but rough or undressed, ten per cent. ad valorem........	10 per cent	15 per cent
Rice, one cent per pound........	1 c. per ℔	1¼ per cent	Sole leather and belting leather, tanned but not waxed, and all upper leather, and French kid, fifteen per cent. ad valorem........	15 per cent	15 to 20 p c.
Rye, ten cents per bushel........	10 c. per bsh	10 c. per bsh			
Wheat, fifteen cents per bushel........	15 c. per bsh	20 c. per bsh	Boots and shoes and other manufactures of leather, including gloves and mitts and leather belting, twenty-five per cent. ad valorem........	25 per cent	30 per cent
Peas, ten cents per bushel........	10 c. per bsh	10 per cent	Malt, fifteen cents per bushel, upon entry for warehouse, subject to excise regulations......	15 c. per bsh	20 c. pr bsh
Beans, fifteen cents per bushel........	15 c. per bsh	10 per cent	Marble, in blocks from the quarry, in the rough, or sawn on two sides only and not specially shapen, containing fifteen cubic feet or over, ten per cent. ad valorem........	10 per cent	65 c. to $1.10 pr cubic ft.
Buckwheat meal or flour, one-fourth of one cent, per pound........	¼ c. per ℔	20 per cent			
Cornmeal, forty cents per barrel........	40 c. per brl	10 c. per bu.	Meats, fresh or salted, on actual weight as received in Canada, except shoulders, sides, bacon and hams, one cent per pound..........	1 c. per ℔	1 c. per ℔
Oatmeal, one-half cent. per pound........	½ c. per ℔	½ c. per ℔			
Rye flour, fifty cents per barrel........	50 c. per brl.	1¼ c. per ℔	Nuts of all kinds, except cocoa-nuts, twenty per cent. ad valorem........	20 per cent	2 c. per ℔
Wheat flour, fifty cents per barrel........	50 c. per brl.	21 per cent			
Rice and sago flour two cents per pound........	2 c. per ℔	20 per cent	Oil-cloth for floors, stamped, painted or printed: table covers similarly prepared, and oiled and painted window blinds, thirty per cent. ad valorem........	30 per cent	40 per cent
Brick, for building, twenty per cent. ad valorem..	20 per cent	20 per cent			
Butter, four cents per pound........	4 c. per ℔	4 c. per ℔			
Buttons of all kinds, twenty-five per cent. ad valorem........	25 per cent		Organs, cabinet, viz. All parlor organs having not more than two sets of reeds, a specific duty of ten dollars each, having over two and not over four sets of reeds, fifteen dollars each, having over four and not over six sets of reeds, thirty dollars; having over six sets of reeds, thirty dollars each; and in addition thereto, fifteen per centum ad valorem on the fair market value thereof........	$10 $15 $20 $30 and 15 pr ct.	25 per cent
Carriages, carts, railway-cars and carriages, wheelbarrows, and other like articles, thirty per cent. ad valorem........	30 per cent	35 per cent			
Cement, hydraulic, or water lime, ground, including barrels, forty cents per barrel........	40 c. per brl.	20 per cent			
China and porcelain ware, twenty-five per cent. ad valorem........	25 per cent	55 per cent	Paintings, drawings, engravings and prints, twenty per cent ad valorem........	20 per cent	30 per cent
Clocks, and parts thereof, thirty-five per cent. ad valorem........	35 per cent	30 per cent	Paper-hangings or wall paper, thirty per cent. ad valorem........	30 per cent	25 per cent
Coal, anthracite, fifty cents per ton of two thousand pounds........	50 c. per ton	75 c. per ton	Envelopes and all manufactures of paper not otherwise specified, twenty-five per cent ad valorem........	25 per cent	25 per cent 35 c p grme,
Coal, bituminous, sixty cents per ton of two thousand pounds........	60 c. per ton	75 c. per ton	Pencils, lead, in wood or otherwise, twenty-five per cent ad valorem........	25 per cent	30 per cent
Cocoa-nuts, one dollar per hundred........	$1 per 100	2 c. per ℔	Pianofortes, viz.: All square pianofortes, whether round cornered or not, not over seven octaves, twenty-five dollars each, on all other square pianofortes, thirty dollars each; on upright pianofortes, thirty dollars each on concert, semi-concert or parlor grand pianofortes, fifty dollars each; and in addition thereto fifteen per cent. ad valorem........	$25 $30 $30 $50 and 15 pr ct.	30 per cent
Coffee, green, two cents per pound........	2 c. per ℔	Free.			
Corks, and other manufactures of cork wood or cork bark, twenty per cent. ad valorem........	20 per cent	25 per cent			
Cotton, manufactures........	20 to 30 p ct	35 to 40 pr c.			
Earthenware and stoneware, brown or colored, and Rockinghamware, twenty-five per cent. ad valorem........	25 per cent	25 per cent	Plants, viz. Fruit, shade, lawn and ornamental trees, shrubs and plants, twenty per cent. ad valorem........	20 per cent	20 per cent
Essences, viz.; of apple, pear, pineapple, raspberry, strawberry, and other fruits, and vanilla, one dollar and ninety cents per imperial gallon and twenty per cent. ad valorem........	$1.90 pr imp gal. and 20 per cent	Some 50 pr c; some $2.50 per ℔	Plate engraved on wood, and on steel or other metal, twenty per cent. ad valorem........	20 per cent	25 per cent
Feathers, ostrich and vulture, undressed, fifteen and dressed, twenty-five per cent. ad valorem..	15 & 25 p ct	25 to 50 pr c.	Printing presses of all kinds, fifteen per cent. ad valorem........	15 per cent	45 per cent
Flax-seed, ten cents per bushel........	10 c. per bsh	20 c. per bsh.	Putty, twenty five per cent ad valorem........	25 per cent	$1 (?) p 100 ℔
Fruit, dried, viz. Apples, two cents per pound....	2 c. per ℔	2 c. per ℔	Sails for boats and ships, also tents and awnings, twenty-five per cent ad valorem........	25 per cent	Free
FRUIT, GREEN, VIZ.:					
Apples, forty cents per barrel........	40 c. per brl	10 per cent	Salt (except salt imported from the United Kingdom, or any British possession, or imported for		30 per cent
Blackberries, gooseberries, raspberries and strawberries, two cents per quart........	2 c. per qt.	10 per cent			
Cherries and currants, one cent per quart........	1 c. per qt.	10 per cent			
Cranberries, plums and quinces, thirty cents per bushel........	30 c. per bsh.	10 per cent			
Grapes, two cents per pound........	2 c. per ℔	20 per cent			
Oranges and Lemons twenty per cent. ad valorem	20 per cent	20 per cent			
Peaches, forty cents per bushel........	40 c. per bsh	10 per cent			

Goods Subject to Duty.	Canadian Duty.	American Duty.	Goods Subject to Duty.	Canadian Duty.	American Duty
the use of the sea or gulf fisheries, which shall be free of duty), in bulk, eight cents per one hundred pounds	8 c. pr 100 lbs	8 c. pr 100 lbs	hewn or sawn only, fifteen per cent. ad valorem	20 per cent	20 per cent
Seeds, viz.: Flower garden, field and other seeds, for agricultural purposes, when in bulk or in large parcels, fifteen per cent. ad valorem; when put up in small papers or parcels, twenty-five per cent. ad valorem	15 per cent 25 per cent	} 20 per cent	Lumber and timber, not elsewhere specified, twenty per cent. ad valorem	20 per cent	$2 p. m. ft., 1 c. p. cub ft.
Shingles, twenty-five per cent. ad valorem	20 per cent	35 c. per M.	WOOLS AND WOOLENS, VIZ.:		
Sewing silk and silk twist, twenty-five per cent ad valorem	25 per cent	30 per cent	Manufactures composed wholly or in part of wool, worsted, the hair of the alpaca goat, or other like animal, viz.: Shawls, blankets, and flannels of every description; cloths, doeskins, cassimeres, tweeds, coatings, overcoatings, felt cloth of every description, not elsewhere specified; horse-collar cloth; yarn, knitting yarn, fingering yarn, worsted yarn under number thirty; knitted goods, viz.: Shirts, drawers and hosiery of every description; seven and a half cents per pound, and in addition thereto twenty per cent. ad valorem		
Silk velvets and all manufactures of silk, or of which silk is the component part of chief value, not elsewhere specified, except church vestments thirty per cent. ad valorem	30 per cent	50 per cent		7½ c p ℔ and 20 per cent	
Soap, common brown and yellow, not perfumed, one cent and a half per pound	1½ c. per ℔	80 per cent			
Steel, and manufactures of, viz.: On and after the first day of January, 1883, steel in ingots, bars, sheets and coils, railway bars or rails and fish plates, ten per cent. ad valorem	10 per cent	$17 per ton			
Shovels, spades, hoes; hay, manure and potato-forks, rakes and rake teeth; carpenters', coopers', cabinetmakers' and all other mechanics' tools, including files, edge tools of every description, axes, scythes, and saws of all kinds, thirty per cent. ad valorem	30 per cent	2½ c. per ℔ to $2.50 p. doz.	Clothing, ready-made and wearing apparel of every description, including cloth caps, composed wholly or in part of wool, worsted, the hair of the alpaca goat, or other like animals, made up or manufactured wholly or in part by the tailor, seamstress or manufacturer; except knit goods, ten cents per pound, and in addition thereto twenty-five per cent ad valorem	10 c p ℔ and 25 per cent	
Stereotypes and electrotypes of standard books, ten per cent. ad valorem	10 per cent	25 per cent	All manufactures composed wholly or in part of wool, worsted, the hair of the alpaca goat, or other like animals, not herein otherwise provided for, twenty per cent. ad valorem	20 per cent	
Grindstones, two dollars per ton	$2.00 per ton	$1.75 per ton	Treble ingrain, three-ply and two-ply carpets, composed wholly of wool, ten cents per square yard; and in addition thereto twenty per cent. ad valorem	10 c. p. sq. yd and 20 per cent	
Tea, viz.: Black two cents per pound and ten per cent. ad valorem	2 c. pr ℔ and 10 per cent	Free.			
Green and Japan tea three cents per pound and ten per cent. ad valorem	3 c. pr ℔ and 10 per cent	Free.	Two-ply and three-ply ingrain carpets, of which the warp is composed wholly of cotton, or other material than wool, worsted, the hair of the alpaca goat, or other like animals, five cents per square yard, and in addition thereto twenty per cent. ad valorem	5 c. p. sq. yd. and 20 per cent	
Trunks, satchels, valises and carpet-bags, thirty per cent. ad valorem	30 per cent	30 per cent			
Twines of all kinds, not otherwise specified, twenty-five per cent ad valorem	25 per cent	40 per cent	Felt for boots and shoes and skirts, when imported by the manufacturers for use in their factories, fifteen per cent. ad valorem	15 per cent	
Type for printing, twenty per cent. ad valorem	20 per cent	25 per cent			
Vegetables, viz.: Potatoes, ten cents per bushel	10 c. per bsh.	15 c. per bsh.	Felt for glove linings, and endless felt for paper makers, when imported by the manufacturers for use in their factories, ten per cent. ad valorem	10 per cent	
Tomatoes, thirty cents per bushel	30 c. per bsh.	10 per cent			
Tomatoes, in cans, two cents per pound	2 c. per ℔	30 per cent			
And all other vegetables, including sweet potatoes, twenty per cent ad valorem	20 per cent	10 per cent 30 per cent	Wool, class one, viz.: Leicester, Cotswold, Lincolnshire, Southdown combing wools, or wools known as lustre-wools, and other like combing wools such as are grown in Canada, three cents per pound	3 c. per ℔	
Vinegar, twelve cents per imperial gallon	12 c. per I. g.	7½ c. p. w. g.			
Watches and watch cases, twenty-five per cent. ad valorem	25 per cent	35 per cent	Whips twenty-five per cent. ad valorem	25 per cent	35 per cent
Wood and manufactures of, and woodenware, viz.: Pails, tubs, churns, brooms, brushes and other manufactures of wood not elsewhere specified, twenty-five per cent ad valorem	25 per cent	25 per cent			
Hubs, spokes, felloes, and parts of wheels, rough					

VARIOUS ARTICLES WHICH MAY BE IMPORTED FREE OF TARIFF DUTY INTO THE UNITED STATES,

Not the entire free list, but including those which most generally interest the people.

Acids, boracic.
Acids, carbolic, for chemical or manufactur'g purposes.
Acids, muriatic.
Acids, nitric, not chemically pure.
Acids, sulphuric.
Adhesive-felt, for sheathing vessels.
African Fibre, unmanufactured, for beds.
Agates, unmanufactured.
Albumen.
Almond-oil.
Almond-shells.
Aloes.
Amber in the gum.
American artists, works of.
Ammonia, crude.
Angelica-root.
Angora Goats, alive.
Angora Skins, without wool.
Aniline-oil, crude.
Animal-carbon.
Animal Manures.
Animals, specially imported for breeding purposes, must be of superior breed for improvement of stock
Anise-seed.
Anise-oil.
Annotta or Annotto, and all extracts of, and seed.
Antiquities, for cabinets.
Aquafortis.
Arsenic.
Ashes, beet-root.

Baggage of immigrants or returning tourists, in actual use.
Bagging Waste, fit only for making paper.
Bags, gunny, old or refuse, fit only to be remanufactured.
Balm of Gilead.
Balsams, copaiva or copaiba.
Balsams, fir, or Canada.
Balsams, Peruvian.
Bamboo sticks, canes, or for umbrella sticks.
Basswood-bark.
Beads, amber.
Bed-feathers, or downs.
Beds, curled hogs-hair, for.
Bees, of superior stock for breeding.
Beet-root Ashes.
Belladonna, root and leaf.
Bell-metal.
Bergamot-oil.
Berries, for dyeing.
Berries, juniper and laurel.
Birds, living or stuffed.
Bleaching Powders.
Bologna Sausages.
Bone-ash and bone-dust, for manufacture of phosphates and fertilisers.
Bones, crude, burned, not manufactured, ground, calcined or steamed.
Books which have been printed over twenty years.
Books specially imported in

good faith for the use or by the order of any college, school or seminary of learning, and not more than two copies of any one book on one invoice.
Books, professional, of persons arriving in the United States.
Books, as household effects of immigrants, when they have been used abroad for more than one year and are not intended for sale.
Box-wood.
Brazil or cream-nuts.
Brazil-wood.
Bronze, statuary, the'original creative work of American artists
Buchu-leaves.
Bullion, gold and silver.
Burgundy Pitch.
Cabinet-woods.
Calf-skins, raw.
Caraway, oil of caraway-seeds.
Cardamom-seed.
Cars, Canadian, used only in through business between Canada and U. S.
Cattle, specially imported for breeding purposes, must be of superior breed for improvement of stock.
Chalk, unmanufactured.
Chamomile-flowers.
Charcoal.
Charts for library of Congress, United States.

Cinnamon, oil of.
Clothing, in actual use of persons arriving in the United States.
Coal, anthracite.
Coal stores of American vessels not unladen.
Cocoons, silk.
Coffee, in the natural berry.
Coins, cabinets of.
Coriander seed.
Cork, bark or wood manufactured.
Cotton, raw.
Cotton Waste, for making paper.
Cream-nuts.
Croton-bark.
Cubebs.
Cummin-seed.
Cuttlefish-bone.
Deer-skins, raw.
Diamond-dust.
Diamonds, rough or uncut.
Dried Flowers.
Dried Skins, not otherwise specified.
Drugs, crude, used in dyeing or tanning.
Eggs.
Elephants' teeth.
Elecampane-root.
Fence-posts, cedar, round and unmanufactured.
Fennel-seed.
Fertilisers.
Fire-wood.
Fish, all kinds, the produce

of the fisheries of the Dominion of Canada, Prince Edward's Island, Newfoundland, or Labrador (but not British Columbia), except fish of the inland lakes, or of the rivers falling into them, and except fish preserved in oil.
Fish, simply packed in ice for preservation while in transit to market and intended for immediate consumption.
Fish oil, the product of the sea -fisheries of Canada, Prince Edward Island, Newfoundland and Labrador (but not British Columbia)
Flax Waste for paper stock.
Flint, flints and ground flint-stones.
Flowers, natural, dried and prepared.
Fossils.
Fowls, land or water, living.
Fruit-plants, tropical and semi-tropical for propagation or cultivation.
Fur-skins, not dressed in any manner.
Gentian-root.
Ginger-root, green, fresh or dried.
Glass, fit only to be remanufactured.
Glaziers' Diamonds.
Glue, fish.
Gold-beaters' moulds and skins.
Gold Bullion.

Gold Coin.
Gold Medals.
Gold, old and unfit for use without remanufacture
Gold fine.
Gold Sweepings.
Grasses and Pulp of, for making paper.
Grease, for use as soap-stock only, not otherwise specified.
Guitar Strings, gut.
Gums, all not otherwise specified.
Gut, cat or whip, unmanufactured.
Gut and Worm-gut, for whip and other cord, manufactured or not.
Gut-cord or cat-gut strings.
Gut-rope or whip-gut strings.
Guts, salted.
Gutta - percha, unmanufactured or crude.
Gypsum, unground.

Hair, hogs', curled, for beds and mattresses, not fit for bristles.
Hair, horse and cattle, cleaned or uncleaned, drawn or undrawn, but unmanufactured.
Hair, sheep-skins, sheared.
Harp-strings, gut.
Hemp, Indian.
Hide-rope.
Hides, raw, hair removed by liming.
Hoofs.
Hoop-timber, round, in its natural condition, with the bark on.
Hop-roots, for cultivation.
Horn, in strips.
Horn, tips.
Horses, of superior breed for the improvement of stock.
Ice.
Iceland Moss.
Indian-hemp, crude.
India-rubber, crude.
India-rubber, crude, in rough sheets.
Isinglass.
Ivory, and vegetable ivory, unmanufactured.
Ivory Nuts, unmanufactured.
Japan-wax.

Juniper Berries.
Junk, old.
Jute, rags for making paper.
Jute, thread waste, fit only for making paper.
Lamb-skins, not dressed in any manner.
Laurel-berries.
Lava, unmanufactured.
Lavender, essence or oil of.
Leather, old scrap leather.
Leaves, all not otherwise specified.
Leaves, palm-leaves, unmanufactured.
Leeches.
Lemon-peel, not preserved, candied or otherwise prepared.
Leopard-skins, raw.
Licorice-root.
Life-boats, for the saving of human life.
Lime, phosphate of, crude, for fertilizing purposes.
Linen Rags, for making paper.
Linseed-cake.
Lithographic Stones, not engraved.
Loadstones.
Logs, unmanufactured, not otherwise specified.
Machinery, models of.
Madder, ground or prepared.
Madder, extracts of,
Madder-root.
Magnets.
Mahogany.
Medals, cabinets of
Mercury.
Metal, bell.
Mineral or Medicinal Waters, natural waters.
Mineral Waters, natural, artificially charged with gas.
Models of Inventions and other Improvements in the Arts.
Models, for instruction or illustration in schools.
Mother of Pearl.
Musk, crude, in natural pod.
Mustard-seed.
Myrrh-gum.
Necklaces, amber beads strung on threads.

Newspapers, imported by the mails, not exceeding 1,000 grammes (2 lbs. 3 ozs).
Newspapers, to be reconverted into paper.
Nutgalls.
Oak-bark.
Oakum.
Oilcake, of linseed. .
Oil-stone.
Oils, almonds.
Oils, bergamot.
Oils, lavender.
Oils, ottar or otto, of roses.
Oils, poppies.
Oils, rosemary.
Oils, valerian.
Oils, vitriol or sulphuric acid.
Oils, whale, American fisheries.
Orange-flowers or buds.
Orange-peel, not preserved.
Ores, gold and silver.
Paintings by American artists.
Paintings for municipal corporations.
Palm-leaf, unmanufactured.
Paper-stock, crude, of every description.
Pearl, mother of.
Pebbles, for spectacles, Brazil or other, rough.
Pelts, raw, not otherwise specified.
Pewter, old, fit only to be remanufactured.
Photographs, specially imported for exhibition, not for sale.
Piling, rough logs with bark on.
Pitch, Burgundy.
Plants, crude, used exclusively for dyeing or making dyes.
Plants, for use of United States.
Plants, medicinal, crude.
Plants, tropical and semi-tropical for propagation or cultivation.
Plaster of Paris, unground.
Plates, plain.
Polishing-stones, natural.
Poppy-heads, crude drug.
Posts, round, unmanufactured wool

Poppy-seed Oil.
Pulp, grass, for making paper.
Quassia-wood.
Quinine, salts and sulphates of.
Rags, for making paper.
Railroad-cars, for business between Canada and United States.
Railroad-ties, wood.
Rattans, unmanufactured.
Regalia, specially imported for the use of any society incorporated or established for philosophical, literary, or religious purposes, or for the encouragement of the fine arts.
Rennets, raw or prepared.
Rhubarb.
Rope, of raw hides, cut into strips.
Rose-leaves.
Saffron, and safflower, and extract of.
Samples, small strips of silk, cotton or other fabrics, small quantities of raw material, and articles of any description having little or no intrinsic value as merchandise.
Sandal-wood.
Sarsaparilla.
Sassafras Bark and Root.
Scrap-leather, old.
Seal-skins, raw or undressed.
Seeds, for use of United States.
Seeds, garden, not otherwise specified.
Seeds, hemlock.
Seeds, medicinal, crude, not otherwise specified.
Shrimps.
Silk, all raw, or as reeled from the cocoon, not being doubled, twisted, or advanced in manufacture any way.
Silk, waste.
Silk Bolting-cloth.
Silkworm Eggs.
Silver, bullion.
Silver, coins.
Silver, medals.
Silver, old, fit only for remanufacture.

Silver, sweepings
Singing-birds.
Size, gold.
Skeletons, and other preparations of anatomy.
Skins, fur, all not otherwise specified.
Skins, wool of no commercial value.
Skins, mats and robes.
Skins, shark.
Spanish-flies.
Stones, lithographic, not engraved.
Straw, unmanufactured.
Tanning, articles in a crude state, used in tanning, not otherwise specified.
Tapioca.
Tea.
Tea-plants.
Teasels. ·
Telegraph-poles, wood.
Theatrical Wardrobes, intended in good faith for the personal use of the actor or actress bringing them, and of a reasonable amount.
Timber, all round unmanufactured.
Tin, bars, blocks or pigs.
Tortoise - shell, unmanufactured.
Trees, for use in the United States.
Types, old, fit only to be remanufactured.
Vaccine-virus.
Vanilla Beans and Plants.
Vegetable substances for beds.
Veneers of cabinet-woods, unmanufactured.
Violin-strings, gut.
Walking-sticks, cut into suitable lengths.
Whetstones.
White Chalk.
Wood.
Wood. All logs and round, unmanufactured timber, not otherwise specified.
Wood. All ship timber.
Wood. All cabinet - woods, unmanufactured.
Wood. All dye - woods in sticks.
Yeast-cakes.

VARIOUS ARTICLES WHICH MAY BE IMPORTED FREE OF TARIFF DUTY INTO CANADA, ·

Including those in Most General Use Among the People.

Articles for the use of the governor-general.
Articles for the use of foreign consuls-general.
Articles imported by and for the use of the Dominion government, or any of the departments thereof, or for the senate or house of commons.
Army and navy and Canadian militia, for the use of, viz Arms, clothing, musical instruments for bands, military stores and munitions of war.
Bells for churches.
Berries for dyeing or used for composing dyes.
Bones, crude and not manufactured, burned, calcined, ground or steamed.
Bone-dust and bone-ash for

manufacture of phosphates and fertilisers.
Botany, specimens of.
Bristles.
Brimstone, crude or in roll or flour.
Broom-corn.
Buchu leaves.
Bullion, gold and silver.
Burgundy pitch.
Burr-stones in blocks, rough or unmanufactured, and not bound up into millstones.
Carriages of travelers and carriages laden with merchandise, and not to include circus troupes nor hawkers, under regulations to be prescribed by the minister of customs.
Cabinets of coins, medals and other collections of antiquities.

Casts, as models for schools of design.
Canvas for manufacture of floor oil-cloth, not less than forty-five inches wide and not pressed or calendered.
Cat-gut strings or gut cord for musical instruments
Chalk and cliff stone, unmanufactured.
Chamomile flowers.
Citron and rinds of, in brine for candying.
Clothing, donations of for charitable purposes.
Cochineal.
Cocoa, bean, shell or nibs.
Coins, gold and silver, except United States silver coin.
Communion plate and plated ware for use in churches.
Diamonds, unset, including black diamonds for borers.

Dyeing or tanning articles in a crude state, used in dyeing or tanning, not elsewhere specified.
Eggs.
Embossed books for the blind.
Entomology, specimens of.
Extract of logwood.
Fish-bait.
Fish-oil, and fish of all kinds, the produce of the fisheries of the United States (except fish of the inland lakes and of the rivers falling into them, and fish preserved in oil).
Fish-hooks, nets and seines, and lines and twines, for the use of the fisheries, but not to include sporting fishing-tackle or hooks with flies or trawling-spoons.

Fur-skins of all kinds, not dressed in any manner.
Flint, flints and ground flint-stones.
Fossils.
Grease and grease scrap, for manufacture of soap.
Guano, and other animal and vegetable manure.
Hair, angola, buffalo and bison, camel, goat, hog, horse and human, cleaned or uncleaned, but not curled or otherwise manufactured.
Hemlock bark.
Hemp, undressed.
Hides, whether dry, salted or pickled.
Horses, cattle, sheep or swine, for the improvement of stock, under regulations to be made by the treasury board and approved by the

governor-general in council.
Hoofs, horn and horn tips.
Ice.
India rubber, manufactured.
Licorice root.
Lemons, and rinds of, in brine, for candying.
Logs, and round unmanufactured timber, not elsewhere provided for.
Lumber and timber, plank and boards, sawn, of boxwood, cherry, walnut, chestnut, mahogany, pitch-pine, rosewood, sandalwood, Spanish cedar, oak, hickory and whitewood, not shaped or otherwise manufactured.
Locomotives and railway passenger, baggage and freight cars, being the property of railway companies in the United States, running upon any line of road crossing the frontier, so long as Canadian locomotives and cars are admitted free under similar

circumstances in the United States, under regulations to be prescribed by the minister of customs.
Medals of gold, silver or copper.
Mineralogy, specimens of.
Models of inventions and other improvements in the arts; but no article or articles shall be deemed a model or improvement which can be fitted for use.
Menageries — horses, cattle, carriages, and harness of, under regulations prescribed by the mininster of customs.
Newspapers and quarterly, monthly and semi-monthly magazines, unbound.
Oak-bark.
Oil-cake, cotton-seed cake, palm nut cake and meal.
Oils, cocoanut and palm, in their natural state.
Oranges and rinds of, in brine, for candying.

Ores of metals of all kinds.
Paintings, in oil or water colors, by artists of well-known merit, or copies of the old masters by such artists.
Palm-leaf, unmanufactured.
Pearl, mother of, not manufactured.
Philosophical instruments and apparatus, including globes and pictorial illustrations of insects, etc., when imported by and for the use of colleges and schools, scientific and literary societies.
Pelts.
Pitch (pine).
Pumice and pumice stone.
Rattans and reeds, unmanufactured.
Rhubarb root.
Salt, imported from the United Kingdom or any British possession or imported for the use of the sea or gulf fisheries.
Sand.

Silk, raw or as reeled from the cocoon, not being doubled, twisted or advanced in manufacture in any way, silk cocoons and silk waste.
Skins, undressed, dried, salted or pickled.
Settlers' effects, viz.: Wearing apparel, household furniture, professional books, implements and tools of trade, occupation or employment which the settler has had in actual use for at least six months before removal to Canada, not to include machinery, or live stock, or articles imported for use in any manufacturing establishment, or for sale; provided that any dutiable article entered as settlers' effects shall not be sold or otherwise disposed of without payment of duty, until after two years' actual use in Canada: provided also

that under regulations to be made by the minister of customs, live stock, when imported into Manitoba or the Northwest Territory by intending settlers, shall be free, until otherwise ordered by the governor in council.
Tanners' bark.
Tassels.
Tortoise and other shells, unmanufactured.
Turpentine, raw or crude.
Turtles.
Varnish, black and bright for ships' use.
Veneers of wood and ivory, sawn only.
Whalebone, unmanufactured.
Whale-oil, in casks from on shipboard, and in the condition in which it was first landed.
Willow for basket-makers.
Wool, unmanufactured, hair of the alpaca goat and other like animals.

THE CUSTOMS TARIFF OF GREAT BRITAIN.

No protective duties are now levied on goods imported—customs duties being charged solely for the sake of revenue. Formerly the articles subject to duty numbered nearly a thousand; now they are only twenty-two—the chief being tobacco, spirits, tea and wine. The following is a complete list:

Articles.	Duty. £ s. d.	Articles.	Duty. £ s. d.
Ale or beer, specific gravity not exceeding 1085°, per bbl	0 8 0	Naptha purified, per gallon	0 10 5
Ale or beer, specific gravity not exceeding 1090°, per bbl	0 11 0	Pickles, in vinegar	0 0 1
Ale or beer, specific gravity exceeding 1090°, per bbl	0 16 0	Plate, gold, per ounce	0 17 0
Beer, mum, per bbl	1 1 0	Plate, silver, per ounce	0 1 6
Beer, spruce, specific gravity not exceeding 1190°, per bbl	1 1 0	Spirits, brandy, Geneva rum, etc., per gallon	0 10 5
Beer, spruce, specific gravity exceeding 1190°, per bbl	1 4 0	Spirits, rum, from British colonies, per gallon	0 10 2
Cards, playing, per dozen packs	3 3 9	Spirits, Cologne water	0 16 6
Chicory (raw or kiln dried), per cwt	0 13 3	Tea, per lb	0 0 6
Chicory (roasted or ground), per lb	0 0 2	Tobacco, unmanufactured, per lb	0 3 1½
Chloral hydrate, per lb	0 1 3	Tobacco, containing less than 10 per cent. of moisture, per lb	0 3 6
Chloroform, per lb	0 3 0	Tobacco, cavendish or negro-head, per lb	0 4 6
Cocoa, per lb	0 0 1	Tobacco, other manufactured, per lb	0 4 0
Cocoa husks and shells, per cwt	0 2 0	Snuff containing more than 13 per cent. of moisture, per lb	0 3 9
Cocoa paste and chocolate, per lb	0 0 2	Snuff containing less than 13 per cent. of moisture, per lb	0 4 8
Coffee, raw, per cwt	0 14 0	Tobacco, cigars, per lb	0 5 0
Coffee, kiln dried, roasted or ground, per lb	0 0 2	Varnish containing alcohol, per gallon	0 12 0
Collodion, per gallon	0 1 4	Vinegar, per gallon	0 0 3
Essence of spruce, 10 per cent. ad valorem		Wine containing less than 26 degrees proof spirit, per gallon	0 1 0
Ethyl, iodide of, per gallon	0 13 0	Wine containing more than 26 degrees and less than 42 degrees	
Ether, iodide of, per gallon	0 1 5	spirit, per gallon	0 2 6
Fruit, dried, per cwt	0 7 0	Wine, for each additional degree of strength beyond 42 degrees, per	
Malt, per quarter	1 4 0	gallon	0 0 3

THE POST-OFFICE SAVINGS-BANK, CANADA.

Post-office savings-banks in Ontario and Quebec are open daily for the receipt and repayment of deposits, during the ordinary hours of post-office business.

The direct security of the Dominion is given by the statute for all deposits made.

Any person may have a deposit account, and may deposit yearly any number of dollars, from $1 up to $300, or more with the permission of the postmaster-general.

Deposits may be made by married women, and deposits so made, or made by women who shall afterward marry, will be repaid to any such woman.

Deposits for children under ten years of age may be made:

Firstly. By a parent or friend as trustee for the child, in which case the deposits can be withdrawn by the trustee until the child shall attain the age of ten years, after which time repayment will be made only on the joint receipts of both trustee and child.

Secondly. In the child's own name—and, if so deposited, repayment will not be made until the child shall attain the age of ten years.

A depositor in any of the savings-bank post-offices may continue his deposits at any other of such offices, without notice or change of pass book, and can withdraw money at that savings-bank office which is most convenient to him.

Each depositor is supplied with a pass-book, which is to be produced to the

postmaster every time the depositor pays in or withdraws money, and the sums paid in or withdrawn are entered therein by the postmaster receiving or paying the same.

Each depositor's account is kept in the postmaster-general's office, in Ottawa, and in addition to the postmaster's receipt in the pass-book, a direct acknowledgment from the postmaster-general for each sum paid in is sent to the depositor. If this acknowledgment does not reach the depositor within ten days from the date of his deposit, he must apply immediately to the postmaster-general, by letter, being careful to give his address, and, if necessary, write again, because the postmaster's receipt or entry in the pass-book is not sufficient without the further receipt for the money from Ottawa.

Every depositor must send his book once a year, viz., on the anniversary of his first deposit, for comparison with the books of the department, and for insertion of interest. The book will be returned to him by first mail   At no other time should a depositor suffer his book to be out of his own possession.

When a depositor wishes to withdraw money, he can do so by applying to the postmaster-general, who will send him by return mail a check for the amount, payable at whatever savings-bank post-office the depositor may have named in his application.

Interest at the rate of four per cent. per annum is allowed on deposits, and the interest is added to the principal on the 30th of June in each year.

CANADIAN LEGAL FORMS.

In General Use in the Transaction of Various Kinds of Business.

AS WILL be seen by examination, the forms for the writing of legal documents in Canada are essentially the same, with slight alterations, as are used in the United States. Several of the forms, in most frequent use in the Dominion, for which credit is due "O'Sullivan's Practical Conveyancer," are herewith given. These, with others elsewhere presented, give the reader a very extended list of legal forms for reference and use.

AGREEMENT.—Formal Parts of an Agreement.

Memorandum of agreement made this ....day of ...., A. D. 188 , between .... of the first part, and .... of the second part:

Witnesseth, that the said parties hereto do hereby agree, each with the other, in manner following:

1. That, etc. (*Here add the terms of the particular agreement.*)

In witness whereof, the parties have hereunto set their hands and seals the day and year first above written.

Signed, sealed and delivered }
   in the presence of   ...., L.S.
          Witness   ...., L.S.

ASSIGNMENTS.--Assignment by Endorsement.

KNOW ALL MEN BY THESE PRESENTS, that I, the within-named A. B., in consideration of $.... to me paid by C. D., have assigned to the said C. D., and his assigns, all my interest in the within-written instrument, and every clause, article, or thing therein contained; and I do hereby constitute the said C. D. my attorney, in my name, but to his own use, to take all legal measures which may be proper for the complete recovery and enjoyment of the assigned premises, with power of substitution.

In witness, etc.

Assignment of an Entire Interest in a Patent.

In consideration of $.... to me paid by ......, of ......, I do hereby sell and assign to the said ...... all my right, title and interest in and to the patent of Canada, No...., for an improvement in.......... granted to me ...., the same to be held by and enjoyed by the said .... to the full end of the term for which said patent is granted, as fully and entirely as the same could be held and enjoyed by me if this assignment and sale had not been made.

Witness my hand and seal this .... day of ...., one thousand eight hundred and ...., at ....

          ...., L.S.

BILL OF SALE.---Bill of Sale of Chattels.

THIS INDENTURE, etc., between ......, bargainor, and ......, bargainee:

WHEREAS the said ...... is possessed of the .... hereinafter set forth, described and enumerated, and hath contracted and agreed with ......, for the absolute sale to .... of the same, for the sum of $..... Now this indenture witnesseth, that in pursuance of the said agreement, and in consideration of the sum of $...., of lawful money of Canada, paid by the .... to the said ...., at or before the sealing and delivery of these presents (the receipt whereof is hereby acknowledged) ...... the said ...... ha.. bargained, sold, assigned, transferred and set over, and by these presents do.. bargain, sell, assign, transfer and set over unto the said ...., executors, administrators and assigns, ... all those, the said .... and all the right, title, interest, property, claim and demand whatsoever, both at law and at equity, or otherwise howsoever, of ...... the said ...... of, in, to, and out of the same, and every part thereof; to have and to hold the said hereinbefore assigned ...... and every of them and every part thereof, with the appurtenances, and all the right, title and interest of the said .... thereto and therein, as aforesaid, unto and to the use of the said ...., executors, administrators and assigns, to and for .... sole and only use forever; and the said .... do.. hereby, for .... heirs, executors and administrators, covenant, promise and agree with the said ...., executors and administrators, in manner following, that is to say: That .... the said .... now rightfully and absolutely possessed of and entitled to the said hereby assigned .... and every of them, and every part thereof; and that the said .... now ha.. in.. good right to assign the same unto the said ...., executors, administrators and assigns, in manner aforesaid, and according to the true intent and meaning of these presents; and that the said ......, executors, administrators and assigns shall and may, from time to time, and at all times hereafter peaceably and quietly have, hold, possess and enjoy the said hereby assigned ...... and every of them, and every part thereof, to and for .... own use and benefit, without any manner of hindrance, interruption, molestation, claim or demand whatsoever, of, from or by ...., the said ...., or any person or persons whomsoever: And that free and clear, and freely and absolutely released and discharged, or otherwise, at the cost of the said ...., effectually indemnified from and against all former and other bargains, sales, gifts, grants, titles, charges and encumbrances whatsoever: And moreover, that ......, the said ......, and all persons rightfully claiming or to claim any estate, right, title or interest of, in or to the said hereby assigned .... and every of them, and every part thereof, shall and will from time to time, and at all times hereafter upon every reasonable request of the said ......, executors, administrators or assigns, but at the cost and charges of the said ......, make, do and execute or cause or procure to be made, done and executed, all such further acts, deeds and assurances for the more effectually assigning and assuring the said hereby assigned ...... unto the said .... executors, administrators and assigns, in manner aforesaid, and according to the true intent and meaning of these presents, as by the said ......, executors, administrators or assigns, or his .... counsel shall be reasonably advised or required.

In witness, etc.

Signed, sealed, etc.

COUNTY OF ......, }
    To wit: }   I, ..., (the bargainee) in the foregoing bill of sale named, make oath and say: That the sale therein made is real, and for good consideration, namely: ...... and not for the purpose of holding or enabling me, this deponent, to hold the goods mentioned therein against the creditors of the said bargainor.

Sworn before at ......, in the county of ......, this .... day of ...... A. D., 18...   ...., a Commissioner.

Gift of Personal Property.

THIS INDENTURE, made ...... between A., of ...., of the one part, and B., of ......, of the other part.

WHEREAS, (setting out the reason and reality of the gift).

Now, this indenture witnesseth, that in pursuance of his said desire, and in consideration of his natural love and affection for the said B., he, the said A., doth hereby give and assign unto the said B.,

All and every the goods, chattels and effects in the schedule hereunto annexed, marked A.,

Together with full power and authority for the said B., and his assigns to enter into and upon any dwelling-house, lands and hereditaments, for the time being, belonging to or occupied by the said A., in or upon which any property comprised in or assigned by this indenture shall be, or be supposed to be, and stay therein or upon, and return therefrom to inspect and take an inventory or inventories of the properties and effects hereby assigned, and to remove the same at his or their pleasure.

And the said A., doth hereby, for himself and his heirs, covenant with the said B , that he, the said A., hath full power to assign and give the said goods and chattels hereby assigned in manner aforesaid,

And that it shall be lawful for the said B., and his assigns to take, hold and enjoy the same, free from any disturbance or hindrance whatever, and that free from any encumbrance.

In witness, etc.

INCORPORATION.---Declaration of Incorporation.

We (setting out the names of at least five of the intended corporators) do solemnly declare that it is our intention to become incorporated under the Act Respecting Benevolent, Provident and other Societies, Revised Statutes of Ontario, chaptered 167.

1. That the intended corporate name of our society (or institution, etc., as the case may be) is ....

2. That the objects of the said society are as follows:

3. That the manner in which our first trustees or managing officers are to be appointed is as follows:

In witness whereof we have hereunto set our hands at ...., in the county of ......, this .... day of ...... 168...

Declared before me.   A. B.

.............., Witness.   C. D.
                                           E. F.
                                           G. H.
                                           I. J.

CERTIFICATE ON THE FOREGOING FOR THE JUDGE TO SIGN.

The within declaration having been presented to me after execution by the parties thereto, as appears by the affidavit of ...., thereunto attached, I certify that the said declaration appears to me to be in conformity with the provisions of the Act Respecting Benevolent, Provident and other Societies, R. S. O. chap. 167.

Justice of the High Court of Justice, ... Division;
or
Judge of the County Court of the County of ......

LEASE.---General Form of Lease.

THIS INDENTURE, made the .... day of ...., in the year of our Lord one thousand eight hundred and ...., in pursuance of the act respecting short forms of leases, between ...., of the first part, and ...., of the second part:

WITNESSETH, that in consideration of the rents, covenants and agreements hereinafter reserved and contained on the part of the said party of the second part, his executors, administrators and assigns to be paid—observed and performed—the said party of the first part ha.. demised and leased, and by these presents do.. demise and lease unto the said party of the second part ...., executors, administrators and assigns, all that messuage or tenement situate .... To have and to hold the said demised premises for and during the term of ...., to be computed from the ..... day of ......, one thousand eight hundred and ....., and from thenceforth next ensuing and fully to be complete and ended.

Yielding and paying therefor, yearly, and every year during the said term hereby granted unto the the said party of the first part, ... heirs, executors, administrators or assigns, the sum of ......, to be payable on the following days and times, that is to say, on, etc. ; the first of such payments to become due and to be made on the ...... day of ...... next.

And the said party of the second part covenants with the said party of the first part to pay rent; and to pay taxes; and to repair; and to keep up fences, and not to cut down timber; and that the said party of the first part may enter and view state of repair; and that the said party of the second part will repair according to notice; and will not assign or sub-let without leave; and that .... will leave the premises in good repair.

Clause as to renewal may be as follows:

And also, that immediately after the expiration of the said term of .... years, he, the said party of the first part, his heirs and assigns, shall and will grant another lease of the said hereby demised premises, with the appurtenances, containing the like covenants, conditions, provisos and agreements as are in this lease contained and expressed, and at and under a yearly rent, payable in quarterly payments, the amount to be ascertained in manner following, that is to say: To be fixed on, and determined upon, and declared by two appraisers, to be named and appointed, one of them by the said party of the first part, his heirs and assigns, the other by the said party of the second part, ... executors, administrators and assigns, with power to them, the said appraisers, to name and call in a third if they cannot agree; such appraisement to be made within fourteen days after the end of the term hereby granted; such rent to be payable in quarterly payments as aforesaid, and to commence from and immediately after the termination of the first term.

Notice to Quit by Landlord.

To A. B., or whom else it may concern:

I hereby give you notice to quit and deliver up to me, on or before the ...... day of ...., 18.., the peaceable and quiet possession of the premises you now hold of me, with the appurtenances, situate at ...., in the ...... of ....

Dated this ...... day of ...., A. D. 18..

.............., Witness.   Yours, etc.,
                         ...., Lessor.

Notice to Quit by Tenant.

To A. B., Esq. :

I hereby give you notice that it is my intention to determine the said lease, and to quit and deliver up, on or before the .... day of ...., 18.., the possession of the premises now held by me, with the appurtenances, situate at ...., in the township of ...., in the county of ....

Dated this ...... day of ...., A. D. 18..

.............., Witness.   Yours, etc.,
                         ...., Lessee

Notice to Claim Double Rent.

To A. B. :

I give you notice that if you do not deliver up possession of the house and premises situate No. .... in .... street, in the .....

.... of ...., on the ...... day of ...., according to my notice to quit, dated the ...... day of ...., I shall claim from you double the yearly value of the premises for so long as you shall keep possession of them after the expiration of the said notice, according to the statute in such case made and provided.

Distress Warrant Upon Goods When Tenant Does Not Pay Rent.

To A. B., my bailiff, ... greeting:

Distrain the goods and chattels of ...., the tenant in the house he now dwells in or upon the premises in his possession, situated ...., for the sum of ...., being the amount of .... rent due to me on the same, on the ...... day of ...., 18.., and for your so doing, this shall be your sufficient warrant and authority.

Dated the .... day of ...., A. D. 18..

Oath of Appraisers of Goods Attached.

You, and each of you, shall well and truly appraise the goods and chattels mentioned in this inventory, according to the best of your judgment. So help you God.

Inventory of Goods Attached.

An inventory of the several goods and chattels distrained by me ...., the ...... day of ......, in the year 18.., in the house, out-houses and lands of ...., situate ...., by authority and on behalf of .... your landlord, for the sum of .... being .. .. rent due to the said .... on the ...... day of ...., 18...

In the dwelling-house:

On the premises:

Mr. ....: Take notice, that as the bailiff to .... your landlord, I have this day distrained on the premises above-mentioned, the several goods and chattels specified in the above inventory for the sum of ...., being .... rent due to the said .... the ...... day of ...., 18.., for the said premises; and that unless you pay the said rent, with the charges of distraining for the same, or replevy within five days from the date hereof, the said goods and chattels will be appraised and sold according to law.

Given under my hand, the ...... day of ...., A. D. 18.. ...., Witness.

Appraisement of Goods Attached.

Memorandum: That on the ...... day of ...., in the year of our Lord 18.., ..., of ...., sworn appraisers, were sworn upon the Holy Evangelists by me, ..., of ...., well and truly to appraise the goods and chattels mentioned in the inventory, according to the best of their judgment.

Present at the swearing of }
the said .... and } ...., Constable.
witness thereto. }

Memorandum to be Endorsed on the Inventory.

Memorandum: That on the ...... day of ...., in the year of our Lord 18.., ..., of ...., and ...., of ...., were sworn on the Holy Evangelists by me, ... of ...., constable, truly to appraise the goods and chattels mentioned in this inventory, according to the best of their judgment. As witness my hand.

[Signatures, etc., as above.]

Bailiff's Sale of Goods Attached.

Notice is hereby given, that the cattle, goods and chattels, distrained for rent on the ...... day of ...., 18.., by me, ..., as bailiff to ...., the landlord of the premises of .... the tenant, will be sold by public auction, on the ...... day of ......,

18.., at .... o'clock, which cattle, goods and chattels are as follows, that is to say:

[Describe the property.]
.... day of ...., 18..

Surrender of Lease.

Where a surrender of lease is required to be in writing, it must be by deed, and may be conveniently written on the back of the lease intended to be surrendered. No particular form of words is necessary, if the intention can be gathered that the lessee intends to surrender and yield up to the lessor the lease in question for the unexpired portion of the term. A covenant may be added that the lessee has, in himself, good right, full power, and lawful and absolute authority to surrender and yield up the premises to the lessor.

MORTGAGE.—Mortgage of Land.

THIS INDENTURE, made (in duplicate) the ...... day of ...., A. D. 18.., in pursuance of the Act Respecting Short Forms of Mortgages, between ....

WITNESSETH, that in consideration of .... of lawful money of Canada, now paid by the said mortgagee.. to the said mortgagor.. (the receipt whereof is hereby acknowledged), the said mortgagor.. do*. grant and mortgage unto the said mortgagee.., ... heirs and assigns forever:

All and singular, th.. certain parcel or tract of land and premises ....

Provided this mortgage to be void on payment of .... of lawful money of Canada, with interest ...... at .... per cent. per annum, as follows: .... and taxes and performance of statute labor.

The said mortga v.. covenant.. with the said mortgagee.. that the mortgagor will pay the mortgage-money and interest, and observe the above proviso;

That the mortgagor.. ha.. a good title in fee simple to the said lands; and that ..he.. ha., the right to convey the said lands to the said mortgagee.., and that on default the mortgagee.. shall have quiet possession of the said lands, free from all encumbrances. And that the said mortgagor.. will execute such further assurance of the said lands as may be requisite.

And also, that the said mortgagor.. will produce the title-deeds enumerated hereunder, and allow copies to be made at the expense of the mortgagee.

And that the said mortgagor.. ha.. done no act to encumber the said lands; and that the said mortgagor.. will insure the building on the said lands to the amount of not less than .... currency; and the said mortgagor.. do.. release to the said mortgagee.. all .... claims upon the said lands, subject to the said proviso:

Provided that the said mortgagee.., on default of payment for .... month, may .... enter on, and lease or sell the said lands:

Provided that the mortgagee.. may distrain for arrears of interest: provided that in default of the payment of the interest hereby secured, the principal hereby secured shall become payable; provided that until default of payment the mortgagor.. shall have quiet possession of the said lands.

And the said A. B., wife of the said mortgagor, hereby bars her dower in the said lands.

IN WITNESS WHEREOF, the said parties hereto have hereunto set their hands and seals.

Mortgage on Chattels.

THIS INDENTURE, made the ...... day of ...., 18.., between A. B , of, etc., and C. D., of, etc. :

WITNESSETH, that the said ...., for and in consideration of the sum of $......, of lawful money of Canada, to him in hand well and truly paid by the said ...., at or before the sealing and delivery of these presents, the receipt whereof is hereby acknowledged, doth bargain, sell and assign unto the said ...., his executors, administrators and assigns, all and every the goods, chattels, furniture and effects in and about the dwelling-house (or store) of the said A. B., situate at, etc., and hereinafter particularly mentioned, that is to say: (*Here specify the chattels; or you may refer to a schedule, saying after the word etc. "which are particularly specified in the schedule hereunder written.*")

To have, receive and take the said goods and chattels hereby assigned, or intended so to be, unto the said ...., his executors, administrators or assigns, as his and their own proper goods and effects.

Provided always, that if the said ...., his executors, or administrators, shall pay unto the said ...., his executors, administrators or assigns, the full sum of $...... with interest thereon at the rate of .... per cent., on the ...... day of .... next, then these presents shall be void.

And the said .... doth hereby, for himself, his executors and administrators, covenant, promise and agree to and with the said ...., his executors, administrators and assigns, that he the said ...., his executors or administrators, or some or one of them, shall and will, well and truly pay, or cause to be paid, unto the said ...., his executors, administrators and assigns, the said sum of money in the above proviso mentioned, with interest for the same as aforesaid, on the days and time, and in the manner above limited for the payment thereof.

And, also, that in case default shall be made in the payment of the said sum of money in the said proviso mentioned, or the interest thereon, or any part thereof, or in case the said .... shall attempt to sell or dispose of, or in any way part with the possession of the said goods and chattels, or any of them, or to remove the same or any part thereof out of the .... without the consent of the said ...., his executors, administrators and assigns, to such sale, removal or disposal therefrom, first had and obtained in writing; then and in such case, it shall and may be lawful for the said ...., his executors, administrators and assigns, peaceably and quietly to receive and take unto his or their absolute possession, and thenceforward to hold and enjoy all and every or any of the goods, chattels and premises hereby assigned or intended so to be, and with his or their servant or servants, and with such other assistant or assistants as he may require, at any time during the day to enter into and upon any lands, tenements, houses and premises belonging to and in the occupation of the ...., where the said goods and chattels, or any part thereof, may be, and to break and force open any door, lock, bolt, fastening, hinge, gate, fence, house, building, enclosure and place, for the purpose of taking possession of and removing the said goods and chattels; and to sell the said goods and chattels, or any of them, or any part thereof, at public auction or private sale, as to them, or any of them, may seem meet; and from and out of the proceeds of such sale, in the first place, to pay and reimburse himself or themselves all such sums of money as may then be due, by virtue of these presents, and all such expenses as may have been incurred by the said ...., his executors, administrators and assigns, in consequence of the default, neglect or failure of ...., his executors, administrators and assigns, in payment of the said sum of money, with interest thereon, as above mentioned, or in consequence of such sale or removal as above mentioned; and, in the next place, to pay unto the said ...., his executors, administrators and assigns, all such surplus as may remain after such sale and after payment of all such sum or sums of money, and interest thereon, as may be due by virtue of these presents at the time of such seizure, and after payment of the costs, charges and expenses incurred by such seizure and sale as aforesaid.

And the said .... doth hereby further covenant, promise and agree to and with the said ...., his executors, administrators and assigns, that in case the sum of money realized under such sale, as above mentioned, shall not be sufficient to pay the whole amount due at the time of such sale, then he, the said ...., his executors or administrators, will forthwith pay any deficiency to

the said ...., his executors, administrator and assigns.

In witness whereof, the parties to these presents have hereunto set their hands and seals the day and year first above written,

Signed, sealed and deliv- }
ered in presence of   }   .... [L.S.]
.... }

Affidavit of Mortgagee.

ONTARIO,   } to wit:
County of ...... }   I, C. D., of the .... of ...., in the county of ...., the mortgagee in the within bill of sale, by way of mortgage named, make oath and say, that A. B., the mortgagor in the within bill of sale, by way of mortgage named, is justly and truly indebted to me, this deponent C. D., the mortgagee therein named, in the sum of $......, mentioned therein. That the said bill of sale, by way of mortgage, was executed in good faith, and for the express purpose of securing the payment of the money so justly due, as aforesaid, and not for the purpose of protecting the goods and chattels mentioned in the said bill of sale, by way of mortgage, against the creditors of the said A. B., the mortgagor therein named, or preventing the creditors of such mortgagor from obtaining payment of any claim against him.

                               C. D.

Sworn before me, at the .... of .... in the county of ...., this ...... day of ...., 18...

               E. F., a Commissioner.

Notice of Sale Where Mortgagee Does Not Pay

To.........:

In the matter of the sale of .... lot .... under "An Act to Give to Mortgagees Certain Powers, now Commonly Inserted in Mortgages;"

I, ..., hereby require you, on or before the .... day of ...., 18.., to pay off the principal money and interest secured by a certain indenture of mortgage, dated the .... day of ......, 18.., and expressed to be made between .... on all th...., which said mortgage was registered in the registry office for the .... on the ...... day of ...., 18.., under the number ...., and has since become the property of the undersigned.

And I hereby give you notice that the amount due on the said mortgage for principal, interest and costs respectively, is as follows:

And unless the said principal money and interest and costs are paid on or before the said ...... day of ......, 18.., I shall sell the said property, comprised in the said indenture (and above described), under the authority of the act entitled "An Act to Give to Mortgagees Certain Powers, now Commonly Inserted in Mortgages," at ....

Dated at .... the .... day of ...., 18..

.............., Witness.

Discharge of Chattel Mortgage.

DOMINION OF CANADA, }
   Province of Ontario. }   To the clerk of the count.... of ...., I, ... do certify, that .... ha.. satisfied all money due on or to grow due on a certain chattel mortgage made by .... to .... which mortgage bears date the ...... day of ......, A. D. 18.., and ...... registered .... in the office of the clerk of the county court of the ...... count... of .... on the ...... day of ...., A. D. 18...... as No. ..., that such chattel mortgage has ... been assigned ...., and that I am the person entitled by law to receive the money, and that such mortgage is therefore discharged.

Witness my hand this ...... day of .... A. D. 18..

.............., Witness, Residence,.........., Occupation..........

[*Usual affidavit of execution to be added.*]

TIMBER MARKS.

An application for the registration of a timber mark or marks shall be made in duplicate after the following form:

To the Minister of Agriculture, (Trade-Mark and Copyright Branch,) Ottawa:

I (*name of person or firm*), of (*residence*), engaged in the business of lumbering (*or getting out timber and floating or rafting the same*), within the provinces of Ontario and Quebec, hereby request the registration of the accompanying timber mark (*or marks*) which I (*name of person or firm*), declare was not in use, to my knowledge, by any other person than myself at the time of my adoption thereof, and of which the following are a description and drawing (*or impression*) in duplicate.

I herewith forward the fee of $2 required by the " Act Respecting the Marking of Timber. "

In testimony thereof I have signed this application in the presence of the two undersigned witnesses, at the place and date hereunder mentioned.

(*Place and date.*)   (*Signature of the proprietor.*)
(*Signature of two witnesses.*)

WILL.—Form of Will.

This is the last will and testament of me, A. B., of, etc., made this ...... day of ... ., in the year of our Lord one thousand eight hundred and ....

I, A. B., of ...., in the county of ...., gentleman, being of sound and disposing mind and memory, do make and publish this my last will and testament, hereby revoking all former wills by me at any time heretofore made.

First. I hereby constitute and appoint my wife, E. B., to be sole executrix of this my last will, directing my said executrix to pay all my just debts and funeral expenses, and the legacies hereinafter given, out of my estate.

Second. After the payment of my said debts and funeral expenses, I give to each of my children the sum of .... Dollars, to be paid to each of them as soon after my decease (but within one year), as conveniently may be done.

Third. And for the payment of the legacies aforesaid, I give and devise to my said executrix, all the personal estate owned by me at

my decease (except my household furniture and wearing-apparel), and so much of my real estate as will be sufficient, in addition to the said personal estate herein given, to pay the said legacies.

Fourth. I give to my said executrix all my household furniture and wearing apparel for her sole use

Fifth. I devise to my said executrix all the rest and residue of my real estate, as long as she shall remain unmarried and my widow, with remainder thereof, on her decease or marriage, to my said children and their heirs respectively, share and share alike.

In witness whereof, I have hereunto set my hand to this my last will and testament.

Signed by the testator, as and for his last will and testament, in the presence of us, who, in his presence and at his request, and in the presence of each other, have hereunto subscribed our names as witnesses.

      C. D., Merchant.
      E. F., Clerk.

A. B,
Testator.

Codicil to a Will.

This is a codicil to the last will and testament of me, A. B., of, etc., bearing date the .... day of ...., A. D. 18.., (*the date of the will*).

I do hereby revoke the bequest to my son John, and do give and bequeath the same to my daughter Jane, to and for her own absolute use and benefit forever.

In all other respects I do confirm my said will.

In witness whereof, I have hereunto set my hand this .... day of ...., A. D. 18..

Signed, published and declared by the said A. B., the testator, as and for the codicil to his last will and testament, in the presence of us who, at his request, and in the presence of each other, have hereunto subscribed our names as witnesses to the due execution hereof.

      R. S., Merchant.
      X. Z., Clerk.

A. B.

COPYRIGHT IN CANADA.

Who May Copyright.—Copyrights may be secured by any person domiciled in Canada, or any part of the British possessions, or being a citizen of any country having an international copyright treaty with the United Kingdom, who is the author of any book, map, chart, musical composition, or of any original painting, drawing, design, etc., upon the following conditions: The books, maps, etc., must be published in Canada; and in the case of a work of art, it must be produced in Canada, either prior to or simultaneously with its production elsewhere. Two copies of

books, maps, etc., must be sent to the minister of agriculture; and in the case of paintings, statuary, etc., a written description of the same must be furnished.

Fee for Copyright.—The fee for registering a copyright is one dollar, and it runs for twenty-eight years. It may also be renewed for a further term of fourteen years upon the same conditions.

Period of Copyright.—An interim copyright may be obtained, pending the publication of any literary, scientific or artistic work, by depositing in the office of the minister of agricul-

ture a copy of the title, or a description of such work. The interim copyright runs for one month, and the fee is fifty cents. The work, however, must be published inside the time specified, or the author incurs a penalty not exceeding one hundred dollars.

Penalty for Infringement.—The penalty for infringing a copyright is the forfeiture of every copy of the work to the owner of the copyright, and the payment of a fine of not less than ten cents, nor more than one dollar, for every copy found in possession.

THE QUEEN AND THE ROYAL FAMILY, Jan. 1, 1883.

THE QUEEN—VICTORIA, of the United Kingdom of Great Britain and Ireland, Queen, Empress of India, Defender of the Faith. Her majesty was born at Kensington Palace, May 24, 1819· succeeded to the throne June 20, 1837, on the death of her uncle, King William IV.; was crowned June 28, 1838, and married February 10, 1840, to his Royal Highness Prince Albert. Her majesty is the only child of his late Royal Highness Edward, Duke of Kent, son of King George III. The children of her majesty are:

Her Royal Highness VICTORIA ADELAIDE MARY LOUISA, PRINCESS ROYAL OF ENGLAND AND PRUSSIA, born November 21, 1840, and married to his Royal Highness William, the Crown Prince of Germany, January 25, 1858, and has had issue four sons and four daughters.

His Royal Highness ALBERT EDWARD, PRINCE OF WALES, born November 9, 1841, married March 10, 1863, Alexandra of Denmark (Princess of Wales), born December 1, 1844, and has had issue, Prince Albert Victor, born January 8, 1864, George Frederick Ernest Albert, born June 3, 1865, Louise Victoria Alexandra Dagmar, born February 20, 1867; Victoria Alexandra Olga Mary, born July 6, 1868; and Maude Charlotte Mary Victoria, born November 26, 1869.

Her Royal Highness ALICE MAUD MARY, born April 25, 1843; married to His Royal Highness Prince Frederick Louis of Hesse, July 1, 1862, and has issue five daughters and one son: second son killed by accident May, 1873. Died December 14, 1878.

His Royal Highness ALFRED ERNEST ALBERT, Duke of Edinburgh, born Aug. 6, 1844; married Her Imperial Highness the Grand Duchess Marie of Russia, January 23, 1874, and has issue one son

Her Royal Highness HELENA AUGUSTA VICTORIA, born May 25, 1846; married to His Royal Highness Prince Frederick Christian Charles Augustus of Schleswig-Holstein-Sonderburg-Augustenburg, July 5, 1866, and has issue two sons and two daughters.

Her Royal Highness LOUISA CAROLINA ALBERTA, born March 18, 1848; married to the Marquis of Lorne, eldest son of the Duke of Argyle, March, 1871

His Royal Highness ARTHUR WILLIAM PATRICK ALBERT, born May 1, 1850.

His Royal Highness LEOPOLD GEORGE DUNCAN ALBERT, born April 7, 1853, married April 27, 1882, to Princess Helen of Waldeck

Her Royal Highness BEATRICE MARY VICTORIA FEODORE, born April 14, 1857.

Exemptions from Forced Sale.

ABSTRACT OF STATE LAWS.
Showing Property Exempt from Attachment, or Levy and Sale on Execution.

ALABAMA.—*Home worth $2,000, and Personal Property $1,000.* The exempted home may consist of a house and lot in an incorporated town, village or city, or of 160 acres of land, with buildings, in the country, either not exceeding $2,000 in value. The exempted personal property comprises wages for labor or service, $25 per month, burial-places, pews in churches, household furniture, all necessary and proper wearing-apparel for the whole family, family portraits, books used in the family, etc., worth not more than $1,000.

ARIZONA.—*Home worth $5,000, and Personal Property $600.*—The homestead may include a quantity of land and a dwelling-house and its appurtenances, with water-right sufficient to irrigate the land; also, stoves in use in dwellings, church pews, burial places of families, all arms and accoutrements kept for use, all wearing-apparel of families, all library and school-books to the value of $150, family pictures; ten sheep or goats owned by a householder, with their fleeces, and the yarn or cloth made from them; two cows, five swine, and enough provisions for the household to last six months; all household goods, furniture and utensils not exceeding $150 in value; the tools, implements, materials, animals, etc., necessary to carry on any trade profession or business, not exceeding in value $300; one sewing-machine and one musical instrument, with hay, grain and other food for exempted animals sufficient for three months.

ARKANSAS.—*Home $2,500, and Personal Property $500.*—The homestead in towns and cities may comprise one acre of land, in the country, 160 acres; but if the homestead be no more than eighty acres in the country, or one-quarter of an acre in a town or city, its value is unlimited. The personal property of an unmarried man exempted from execution, besides his necessary wearing apparel, must not exceed in value $200, nor, if married, $500, to be selected by the owners.

CALIFORNIA.—*Home $5,000, and Personal Property.*—An unmarried person's homestead, consisting of an indefinite quantity of land and a dwelling-house thereon, is limited to $1,000; a married person's to $5,000 in value. The other exemptions are chairs, tables, desks and books, to the value of $200; necessary household, table and kitchen furniture, including one sewing-machine, stoves, stove-pipe and stove furniture; wearing apparel, beds, bedding and bedsteads, hanging pictures, oil paintings and drawings, drawn or painted by a member of the family; family portraits, in their frames; provisions sufficient for three months; farming utensils or implements of husbandry; also two oxen, or two horses, or two mules, and their harness, one cart or wagon, and food for such animals, etc., for one month, all seed, grain or vegetables, actually provided for planting or sowing within the ensuing six months, not exceeding $300 in value; seventy-five bee-

hives; one horse and vehicle of a maimed and crippled person when necessary in his business; tools of a mechanic or artisan necessary to his trade; notarial seal, records and office furniture of a notary; instruments and chest of a surgeon, physician, surveyor, dentist, necessary to their profession, with their scientific or professional libraries and office furniture; the law professional libraries and office furniture of attorneys and judges, and libraries of ministers of the gospel; the cabin or dwelling of a miner not exceeding $500 in value; also his sluices, pipes, hose, windlass, derricks, cars, pumps, tools, implements, and appliances necessary for mining operations, not exceeding $500 in value; a miner's claim worked by him, not exceeding $1,000 in value, and two horses, oxen or mules, and harness, and food of horses, etc., for one month, when necessary to be used in any windlass, derrick, car, pump or hoisting gear, two oxen, horses, or mules, with harness, and hack, carriage, cart, etc., by which a cartman, drayman, peddler, teamster, etc., earns his living; and the horse, vehicle, and harness of a physician or minister of the gospel, with food for one month; three cows with their sucking calves, and four hogs with their sucking pigs; poultry, not exceeding $25 in value; earnings of debtor for services rendered within thirty days before levy, necessary for the use of his family residing in the State, supported by his labor; shares in a homestead corporation not exceeding $1,000 in value, when the holder does not own a homestead; all benefits of life insurance whose annual premiums do not exceed $500; firearms, etc., of fire companies; arms and accoutrements required to be kept by law; court-houses, jails, and buildings, and lots, cemeteries, and certain other public property.

COLORADO.—*Home worth $2,000, and Personal Property.*—There is exempted a homestead worth not to exceed $2,000, and to the head of a family owning and occupying the same, there are exempted various articles of personal property, as follows: Household furniture $100; provisions for the family six months; tools, implements or stock in trade $200; library and implements of any professional $300; working animals worth $200; one cow and calf, ten sheep, cattle-feed for six months; farm wagon, cart or dray, plow, harrow, and $50 worth of other farming implements.

CONNECTICUT.—*No Home exempted. Personal Property of the following value:* Necessary apparel and bedding, and household furniture necessary for supporting life; militia arms, uniforms, equipments and musical instruments, implements of the debtor's trade; library worth $500; one cow and ten sheep (the latter not exceeding in value $150); a liberal portion of specified amounts of household provisions, fuel, etc.; the horse, saddle, bridle, buggy and harness, of value not more than $200, belonging to any practicing surgeon or physician; one sewing-machine in use; one church pew in use, and one boat used in fishing, with its necessary tackle, sails and implements, worth not more, in all, than $200, and the family burial-place.

DAKOTA.—*Home of 160 acres, with buildings, or, in a village or city, a house and one acre of land, with Personal Property.*—The homeholder's homestead, as above described, is without limit in value. Besides the following family possessions, the householder may select $1,500 worth of other personal property, which is also exempt: The family pictures, a church pew, a burial lot, a family Bible, school-books and other books worth $100, all necessary wearing apparel of the family, and a year's supply of provisions and fuel.

DELAWARE.—*No Home exempted. Personal Property worth $200.*—There is no homestead exemption in this State. Local laws regulate exemptions of personal property in various portions of the State, covering the family Bible, library, school-books, pictures, church pew, burial-ground, clothing, and implements of trade (ranging in value from $50 to $75), and from $150 to $200 worth of other property. Sussex county does not give the additional personal property exemption.

DISTRICT OF COLUMBIA.—*No Home exempted. Personal Property of the following value:* The following property of a householder is exempt from distraint, attachment, or sale on execution, except for use rents' or laborers' wages due: Wearing apparel, household furniture to the amount of $300; provisions and fuel for three months; mechanics' tools or implements of any trade, to the value of $200, with stock to the same amount; the library and implements of a professional man or artist, to the value of $300, a farmer's team and other utensils, to the value of $100; family pictures and library, in value $400; earnings not exceeding $100 per month, and one cow, one swine and six sheep.

FLORIDA.—*Farm, or House and Lot, and Personal Property.*—Homestead of 160 acres of land and improvements, if in the country; a residence and one-half acre of ground, if in a village or city; together with $1,000 worth of personal property. An additional sum of $1,000 worth of property is exempt from all debts incurred prior to May 10, 1865.

GEORGIA.—*Real or Personal Property, or both, worth $1,600.*—The constitution of 1877 and statutes of 1878 absolutely exempt from levy, except for purchase-money, taxes, or liens for labor or materials, etc., real or personal property, or both, to the value of $1,600, the debtor choosing whatever he desires shall be exempted.

IDAHO.—*Home worth $500, and Personal Property.*—The head of a family, being a householder, either husband or wife, may select a homestead not exceeding in value $5,000. Exemption extends to chairs, tables, books and desks, worth $200; necessary household, table and kitchen furniture, a sewing-machine, stoves, stove-pipe and stove furniture, clothing, beds and bedding, family paintings and pictures and their frames, provisions for the family for three months, two cows and calves, and two sows and pigs; farming implements, teams, seed-grain and vegetables, etc., worth $200; mechanics' tools, etc., worth $500; instruments of medical practitioners; libraries of professional men, and office furniture of lawyers and judges; miners' cabins to the value of $500, and their mining tools and implements $200; earnings of laborers, etc.

ILLINOIS.—*Home worth $1,000, and Personal Property.*—Lot of ground and buildings thereon, occupied as a residence by the debtor, being a householder and having a family, to the value of $1,000. Exemption continues after the death of the householder for the benefit of widow and family, some one of them occupying the homestead until the youngest child shall become twenty-one years of age, and until death of widow. Insurance money received or due upon burned buildings of the homestead is also exempt. There is no exemption from sale for taxes, assessments, debt or liability incurred for the purchase or improvement of such homestead. No release or waiver of exemption is valid, unless in writing, and subscribed by such householder and wife, if he have one, and acknowledged as conveyances of real estate are required to be acknowledged. The following articles of personal property owned by the debtor are exempt from execution, writ of attachment, and distress for rent: *First*—Necessary wearing-apparel, Bibles, school-books, and family pictures of every person. *Second*—Other property worth $100 to be selected by the debtor. When the debtor is the head of a family, and resides with the same, in addition, other property worth $300 may be selected; though such exemption shall not be allowed from any money due such debtor. A debtor taking the benefit of this act shall make a schedule, subscribed and sworn to, of all his or her personal property, including all moneys on hand and due the debtor; and any property owned by the debtor and not included in said schedule, shall not be exempt as aforesaid. And thereupon the officer having an execution against the same, shall summon three householders who, upon oath, will appraise and fix a fair value upon each article in said schedule, and the debtor shall then select from such schedule such articles as he or she may desire to retain, the aggregate value of which shall not exceed the amount exempted, to which he or she may be entitled, and deliver the remainder to the officer having the writ. The officer having the writ is authorized to administer the oath to the debtor and appraisers. To head of family the sum of $50 is exempt from garnishment for wages.

INDIANA.—*Personal property to the value of $600.*—There is no specific homestead exemption in this State. On contracts made since May 31, 1879, a householder may claim, as exempt, real estate or personal property to the value of $600. Exempt goods may be removed from one part of the State to another without molestation. In case of debts founded upon contracts made previous to May 31, 1879, the exemption is only $300. A debtor's property must be scheduled and sworn to by the debtor, appraised under direction of the law officer. Exemptions do not affect liens for labor, purchase-money or taxes.

IOWA.—*Farm of 40 acres, or House and Lot in City, and Personal Property.*—The homestead must embrace the house used as a home by the owner thereof, and if he has two or more houses thus used by him, at different times and places, he may select which he will retain as a homestead. If within a town plat, it must not exceed one-half acre in extent, and if not in a town plat it must not embrace in the aggregate more than forty acres; in each case comprising all the buildings and improvements thereon, without limitation of value. All wearing apparel kept for actual use, and suitable to the condition of the party, and trunks to contain the same, one shot-gun, or rifle, the proper tools, instruments or books of any farmer, mechanic, surveyor, clergyman, lawyer, physician, teacher or professor; the horse or team, consisting of not more than two horses or mules, or two yoke of cattle and wagon with harness, by use of which any physician, public officer, farmer, teamster, or other laborer, habitually earns his living. All private libraries, family Bibles, portraits, pictures, musical instruments and paintings not kept for sale. If the debtor is the head of a family there are further exempt, two cows, one calf, one horse, fifty sheep, their wool and goods manufactured therefrom, six stands of bees, five hogs and all pigs under six months; the necessary food for all animals exempt for six months; all flax raised by the defendant on not exceeding one acre; one bedstead and necessary bedding for every two in the family; all cloth manufactured by the defendant, not exceeding 100 yards in quantity; household and kitchen furniture not exceeding $200 in value; all spinning-wheels, one sewing-machine, looms, and other instruments of domestic labor kept for actual use; the necessary provisions and fuel for the use of the family for six months; a pew in church, and a lot in burying-ground not exceeding one acre. The printer has exempted the necessary type, presses, etc., for his office to the value of $1,200. The earnings of a debtor for personal services, or those of his family, at any time within ninety days next preceding the levy are also exempt from attachment and execution. None of the foregoing exemptions are for the benefit of a single man not the head of a family, nor of non-residents, nor of those who have started to leave the State, but their property is liable to execution, with the exception of ordinary wearing-apparel and trunks to contain the same; and, in the latter case, of such wearing-apparel and such property as the defendant may select, not to exceed $75, to be selected by the debtor and appraised. But no exemptions shall extend to property against an execution issued for the purchase-money thereof.

KANSAS.—*Home of 160 acres of Farm, or House and One Acre in a Village or City, and Personal Property.*—A homestead to the extent of 160 acres of farming land, or of one acre within the limits of an incorporated town or city, occupied as a residence by the family of the owner, together with all the improvements on the same, shall be exempt from forced sale under any process of law, and shall not be alienated except by joint consent of husband and wife, when that relation exists. No money value is limited in the homestead. Exemptions do not affect indebtedness for taxes, purchase-money or improvement in homesteads. The law exempts, to heads of families, family books and musical instruments, a church pew, a burial lot, clothing, bedsteads, bedding, stoves and cooking utensils used by the household, one sewing-machine, all working tools, $500 worth of other household furniture, two cows, ten hogs, one yoke of oxen, and one horse or mule, or in lieu of one yoke of oxen and one horse or mule, a span of horses or mules, and twenty sheep and their wool; necessary food for the support of the stock for one year; one wagon, two plows, drag, and other farming utensils not exceeding $300; fuel and provisions for the family one year; the tools and implements of any mechanic, miner, or other person, kept for the purpose of carrying on his business, and in addition thereto stock in trade not exceeding $400 in value; library, implements, and office furniture of any professional man. Single persons may hold, exempt, their clothing, church pew, burial lot, necessary tools and implements used in business, and stock in trade to the value of $400; if professional, their libraries, office furniture, etc., are exempt.

KENTUCKY.—*Home worth $1,000, and Personal Property.*—On all debts or liabilities created after the first day of June, 1866, so much land, including the dwelling-house and appurtenances, as shall not exceed in value $1,000; one work-beast or one yoke of oxen, two cows and calves, five sheep; wearing apparel, and the usual household and kitchen furniture, of about the value of $100; also one sewing-machine, and the instruments and libraries of professional men to the amount of $500.

LOUISIANA.—*The Home and $2,000 in Personal Property.*—The homestead lands and tenements of a debtor, whether in city or country, and without specified money valuation, are exempt, if properly declared as such and recorded in the book of mortgages of the parish where the land is located. Heads of families also hold, exempt from execution, one work-horse and one wagon, or cart, one yoke of oxen, two cows and calves, twenty-five hogs (or 1,000 lbs of bacon or pork instead), and on a farm sufficient feed for the year and farming implements worth $2,000, together with clothing and necessary household furniture, bedding, etc.

MAINE.—*Home worth $500, and Personal Property.*—There is exempted a lot of land, dwelling-house, etc., not exceeding $500 in value; necessary apparel; a bed, bedstead and bedding for every two members of a family; one cooking-stove, all stoves used for warming buildings, and other necessary furniture to the value of $50, one sewing-machine for use, not exceeding $100 in value; all tools necessary for the debtor's occupation; all Bibles and school-books for the use of the family, one copy of the statutes of the State, and a library not exceeding $150 in value; one heifer, two swine, ten sheep, and the wool and lambs from them; one yoke of working cattle, or instead thereof, one pair of mules, or two horses, not exceeding $300 in value; all produce of farms until harvested; corn and grain for use of debtor and family, not exceeding thirty bushels; all potatoes raised or purchased for use in family; one barrel of flour; a sufficient quantity of hay to winter all exempted stock; all flax raised for use, on one-half acre of land; lumber to the amount of $10, twelve cords of fire-wood, five tons of anthracite coal, fifty bushels of bituminous coal, and all charcoal for use in the family; one pew in church; domestic fowls to value of $50, one horse-sled or ox-sled, $20 in value; one harness worth $20 for each horse or mule; one cart or truck-wagon, one harrow, one plow, one yoke, two chains, and one mowing-machine; for fishermen, one boat not exceeding two tons burthen.

MARYLAND.—*No Homestead exemption, but Personal Property.*—No home is secure from execution; but the law exempts to householders wearing apparel, books, and mechanics' tools (except books and tools kept for sale, or unless execution issues upon judgment for seduction or breach of promise of marriage), together with $100 worth of other property, to be selected by the debtor; or, in case no such division of the property can be agreed upon, then the debtor receives the equivalent of his exemption in money, after his goods have been sold. Equitable interests in personal property cannot be levied upon.

MASSACHUSETTS.—*Home worth $800, and Personal Property.*—Every householder, having a family, is entitled to a homestead, valued at $800, in farm, or lot of land, and buildings thereon, if he records his design to hold it as such. Necessary clothing, one bedstead, bed, and necessary bedding for every two of the family; one stove used for the dwelling, and fuel not exceeding the value of $20, for the use of the family; one sewing-machine, of a value not exceeding $100, in actual use by such debtor, or family; other household furniture necessary for him and his family, not exceeding $300 in value; Bibles, school-books, and library used by him or his family, not exceeding $50 in value; one cow, six sheep, one swine, and two tons of hay; the tools, implements and fixtures necessary for carrying on his trade or business, not exceeding $100 in value; materials and stock necessary for carrying on his trade or business, and intended to be used therein, not exceeding $100 in value; provisions necessary for the family not exceeding $50 in value; the boat, fishing tackle, and nets of fishermen, actually used by them in the prosecution of their business, to the value of $100; the uniform of an officer or soldier in the militia, and the arms and accoutrements required by law to be kept by him; one pew in church, unless required to be sold because of some tax legally laid thereon, and shares in co-operative associations, not exceeding $20 in the aggregate; also rights of burial, and tombs while in use as repositories for the dead.

MICHIGAN.—*Home worth $1,500, and Personal Property.*—Any quantity of land, not exceeding forty acres, and the dwelling-house thereon, with its appurtenances, and not included in any recorded town plat, city or village, or, instead thereof, at the option of the owner, a quantity of land not exceeding in amount one lot, being within a recorded town plat, or city, or village, and the dwelling-house thereon, and its appurtenances, owned and occupied by any resident of the State, not exceeding in value $1,500. Household furniture to amount of $250; stock-in-trade, a team or other things which may be necessary to carry on the pursuit of particular business, up to $250; library and school-books not exceeding $150; to a householder, ten sheep, two cows, five swine, and their food for six months.

MINNESOTA.—*Home of Eighty Acres in Farm Lands, or House and Lot in Village or City, and Personal Property.*—Eighty acres of land selected as a homestead, or a lot and dwelling-house thereon in any incorporated town plat, city, or village, being a homestead; the family Bible, family pictures, school-books, or library, and musical instruments; all wearing apparel of the debtor and his family, all beds, bedsteads, and bedding kept and used by the debtor and his family; all stoves and appendages put up or kept for the use of the debtor and his family; all cooking utensils, and all other household furniture not herein enumerated, not exceeding $500 in value; three cows, ten swine, one yoke of oxen and a horse, or in lieu of one yoke of oxen and a horse, a span of horses or mules, twenty sheep and the wool from the same, either in the raw material or manufactured into cloth or yarn; the necessary food for all the stock mentioned in this section, for one year's support, either provided or growing, or both, as the debtor may choose; also, one wagon, cart, or dray, one sleigh, two plows, one drag, and other farming utensils, including tackle for teams, not exceeding $300 in value; seed-grain and vegetables; the provisions for the debtor and his family necessary for one year's support, either provided or growing, or both, and fuel necessary for one year; the tools and instruments of any mechanic, miner or other person, used and kept for the purpose of carrying on his trade, and, in addition thereto, stock-in-trade not exceeding $400 in value; also the library and implements of any professional man; one sewing-machine; the earnings of minor children and laboring men and women, not exceeding $20. None of these articles of personal property are exempt from execution or attachment for the purchase-money thereof.

MISSISSIPPI.—*Home worth $2,000, and Personal Property.*—A homestead is allowed to every householder, with a family, not exceeding

160 acres of land, nor worth more than $2,000. Of personal property: The tools of a mechanic, agricultural implements of a farmer, implements of a laborer; wearing apparel; books of a student, libraries, books and maps owned by teachers; life-insurance policy, not exceeding $10,000; two cows and calves, five hogs, five sheep, 150 bushels of corn, 300 bundles of cattle-feed, ten bushels of wheat or rice, 200 pounds of meat, one cart or wagon, one sewing-machine, household furniture worth $100, and growing crops. In towns, villages and cities, instead of the foregoing, personal property is allowed to householders of the value of $250.

MISSOURI.—*Home worth $1,500 to $3,000, and Personal Property.*—Married men are allowed a homestead of 160 acres of land to the value of $1,500. In cities of 40,000 inhabitants or over, homesteads shall not include more than eighteen square rods of ground, nor exceed in value $3,000. In cities of less size, homestead shall not include over thirty square rods, nor exceed $1,500 in value. Personal property to the value of *not less* than $300 to the heads of families, besides spinning-wheels, cards, a loom, yarn, thread, and cloth woven for family use, 25 pounds each of hemp, wool and flax; all wearing apparel of the family, four beds and bedding, and other household furniture, worth not more than $100.

MONTANA.—*Home worth $2,500, and Personal Property.*—A homestead not exceeding in value $2,500; in a city or village not to exceed one-quarter of an acre, or farm land not exceeding 160 acres, the debtor taking his choice and selecting either, with all improvements thereon included in the valuation. The lien of a mechanic, laborer, or mortgage lawfully obtained upon the same, is not affected by such exemption. In addition to the homestead, personal property to the value of about $1,400, according to value of articles enumerated by statute, is allowed to the householder occupying the same.

NEBRASKA. — *Home worth $2,000, and Personal Property $500.*—A homestead not exceeding in value $2,000, consisting of the dwelling-house in which the claimant resides and its appurtenances, and the land on which the same is situated, not exceeding 160 acres, to be selected by the owner thereof, not in any city or incorporated village; or, instead thereof, at the option of the claimant, contiguous land, not exceeding two lots in any such city or village, owned and occupied by the head of a family. All heads of families who have no lands, town lots or houses, have exempt from forced sale the sum of $500 in personal property. Other personal property is exempted, which is enumerated by statute.

NEVADA.—*Home worth $5,000, and Personal Property.*—The husband, wife, or other head of the family, is entitled to a homestead not exceeding in value $5,000, and a debtor has exempted from attachment personal property not exceeding in value $1,500, enumerated in the statute.

NEW HAMPSHIRE.—*Home worth $500, and Personal Property.*—Homestead to the value of $500; necessary apparel and bedding and household furniture to the value of $100; Bibles and school-books in use in the family; library to the value of $200; one cow, one hog and one pig, and pork of same when slaughtered; tools of occupation to the value of $100; six sheep and their fleeces; one cooking stove and its furniture; provisions and fuel to the value of $50, and one sewing-machine; beasts of the plow, not exceeding one yoke of oxen, or a horse; military arms and equipments.

NEW JERSEY.—*Home worth $1,000, and Personal Property $200.*—A householder with a family may own, exempt, a house and lot worth $1,000, with all wearing apparel, and other personal property of the value of $200.

NEW MEXICO.—*Home worth $1,000; Provisions, $25; Furniture, $10; Tools, $20.* — Real estate to the value of $1,000 is exempt in farms if the heads of families reside on the same; also the clothing, beds and bed-clothing necessary for the use of the family, and fire-wood sufficient for thirty days, when actually provided and intended therefor; all Bibles, hymn-books, Testaments, and school-books, used by the family, and family and religious pictures; provisions actually provided to the amount of $25, and kitchen furniture to the amount of $10, both to be selected by the debtor; also tools and instruments belonging to the debtor that may be necessary to enable him to carry on his trade or business, whether agricultural or mechanical, to be selected by him, and not to exceed $20 in value. Real estate, when sold, must be first appraised by two freeholders of the vicinity, and must bring two-thirds of the appraised value.

NEW YORK. — *Home worth $1,000, and Personal Property.*—The homestead, consisting of a house and lot, is exempt to the value of $1,000, if properly recorded as such. This exemption extends to married women, widows and minor children of deceased householders. The necessary furniture of the household, working tools and teams, professional instruments, furniture and library worth not more than $250, ninety days' food for team, and debtor's earnings for sixty days, if necessary to support the family.

NORTH CAROLINA. — *Home worth $1,000, Personal Property $500.*—Every homestead, and dwellings and building used therewith, not exceeding in value $1,000, to be selected by the owner thereof; or, in lieu thereof, at the option of the owner, any lot in a city, town or village, with the dwellings used thereon, owned and occupied by any resident of the State, and not exceeding the value of $1,000. Personal property to the value of $500, selected by the debtor.

OHIO. — *Home worth $1,000, and Personal Property.*—There is exempted by law the family homestead, not exceeding in value $1,000; the wearing apparel of such family; beds, bedsteads, bedding necessary for the use of the family; two stoves and fuel necessary for sixty days; domestic animals and their food for sixty days, to the value of $65, or, instead, household furniture of equal value; other necessary household furniture worth $50; family provisons to the value of $50, mechanical or agricultural tools worth $100, if in use in business. In case the debtor is not the owner of a homestead, he is entitled to hold, exempt from levy and sale, personal property not exceeding $500, in addition to the chattel property as aforesaid.

ONTARIO, CANADA.—*Grants that are Free, and Homesteads that are in the possession of actual settlers*, in the Algoma and Nippissing Districts, and certain lands between the river Ottawa and Georgian Bay, are exempt from seizure, while in personal property, beds, bedding, and wearing apparel of the debtor and his family, household furniture, provisions, farm stock, tools and implements, to the value of $60, are exempt from seizure.

OREGON.—*Personal Property.*—Books, pictures, and musical instruments to the value of $75; wearing apparel to the value of $100, and, if a householder, to the value of $50 for each member of the family; tools, implements, apparatus, team, vehicle, harness, or library, when necessary in the occupation or profession of a judgment-debtor, to the amount of $400; if the judgment-debtor be a householder, ten sheep with one year's fleece, two cows, five swine, household goods, furniture, and utensils, to the value of $300. No article of property is exempt from execution issued upon a judgment for the purchase-price.

PENNSYLVANIA. — *Real or Personal, $300.*—Property, either real or personal, to the value of $300, besides wearing apparel, Bibles and school-books. Homesteads are not exempt.

QUEBEC, CANADA.—*Personal Property enumerated as follows* is exempt from forced sale, being used and owned by the debtor: Bed, bedding, and bedstead; necessary apparel for himself and family; set of table and stove furniture; all spinning-wheels and weavers' looms in use in the family, one ax, one gun, one saw, six traps, fish-nets in common use, and ten volumes of books; fuel and food for thirty days, worth $20; one cow, four sheep, two hogs, with necessary food for thirty days; tools and instruments used in his trade to the value of $30; fifteen hives of bees, and wages and salaries not yet due; besides certain other properties granted by the courts.

RHODE ISLAND.—*No Home exempted, but Personal Property.*—The law exempts from sale on execution the household furniture, and family stores of a housekeeper, provided the same do not exceed in value $300, all the necessary wearing apparel of a debtor and his family; one cow, one hog, and the tools or implements of a debtor's profession to the value of $200. There is no homestead exemption.

SOUTH CAROLINA. — *Home worth $1,000, Personal Property $500.*—There is exempt from sale and execution in the State a homestead not exceeding in value $1,000, and personal property, in the household of a family, worth $500. The products of the homestead are, however, not exempt. The homestead cannot be sold, except for the purchase of another, nor can the homestead right be alienated or waived.

TENNESSEE.—*Home worth $1,000, and Personal Property.*—The homestead, consisting of the dwelling house outbuildings, and land appurtenant, to the value of $1,000, also a generous allowance of household goods and utensils, with working tools and agricultural implements, amounting to several hundred dollars.

TEXAS.—*Home worth $5,000, and Personal Property.*—To every citizen, householder, or head of a family, two hundred acres of real estate, including homestead, in the country, or any lot or lots in a town or city, used as a homestead, not to exceed $5,000 in value at the time of their designation as a homestead (subsequent increase in value by improvements or otherwise does not subject it to forced sale); household and kitchen furniture, $500. To every citizen not the head of a family, one horse, saddle and bridle, all wearing apparel, and tools, books, and apparatus of his trade or profession. To the family, all household and kitchen furniture, cemetery lots, books, family portraits and pictures, five milch-cows, twenty hogs, working animals, twenty sheep and family provisions.

UTAH. — *Home worth $1,000, and Personal Property. To each member of the family $250.*—To the head of a family is allowed a homestead not exceeding in value $1,000, to be selected by the debtor, and personal property to the value of $700 or more, according to the value of articles exempt by statute; aside from the homestead, each member of the family is allowed $250. No property shall be exempt from sale on a judgment received for its price, on a mechanic's lien, or a mortgage thereon.

VERMONT.—*Home worth $500, and Personal Property.*—Homestead to the value of $500, and products; suitable apparel, bedding, tools, and articles of furniture as may be necessary for upholding life, one sewing-machine kept for use; one cow, the best swine, or the meat of one swine, ten sheep, one year's product of said sheep in wool, yarn or cloth; forage sufficient for keeping ten sheep and one cow through one winter; ten cords of firewood, or five tons of coal; twenty bushels of potatoes; such military arms and accoutrements as the debtor is by law required to furnish; all growing crops, ten bushels of grain, one barrel of flour, three swarms of bees and hives, together with their produce in honey; 200 pounds of sugar, and all lettered gravestones, the Bibles and all other books used in a family; one pew in church; live poultry not exceeding in value $10; the professional books and instruments of physicians; professional books of clergymen and attorneys, to the value of $200; one yoke of oxen or steers, or two horses, used for work, as the debtor may select, in lieu of oxen or steers, but not exceeding in value the sum of $200, with sufficient forage for the keeping of the same through the winter; also one two-horse wagon with whiffletrees and neckyoke, or one ox-cart, as the debtor may choose; one sled, or one set of traverse sleds, either for oxen or horses, as the debtor may select; two harnesses, two halters, two chains, one plow and one ox-yoke, which, with the oxen, or steers, or horses which the debtor may select for team-work shall not exceed in value $250.

VIRGINIA.—*Home and Personal Property $2,000.*—Every householder or head of a family shall be entitled to hold exempt from levy his real and personal property, or either, including money or debts due him, to a value not exceeding $2,000, to be selected by him. The personal property exempted is defined by the statute of the State.

WASHINGTON TERRITORY. — *Home worth $1,000, and Personal Property.*—To each householder, being the head of a family, a homestead worth $1,000, while occupied by such family. All wearing apparel, private libraries, family pictures and keepsakes; to each householder, one bed and bedding, and one additional bed and bedding for every two additional members of the family, and other household goods of the coin value of $150; two cows and their calves, five swine, two stands of bees, twenty-five domestic fowls, and provisions and fuel for six months. To a farmer, one span of horses and harness, or two yoke of oxen, and one wagon, with farming utensils not exceeding $200, coin value. To attorneys, physicians and clergymen, their libraries valued at not to exceed $500, with office furniture and fuel. Small boats and firearms kept for use, not exceeding $50 in coin value, parties engaged in lightering, two lighters and a small boat, valued at $250; the team of a drayman. To a mechanic, the tools and implements of his trade and materials not exceeding in value $500. To a person engaged in logging, three yoke of cattle and yokes, chains, and tools to the value of $300.

WEST VIRGINIA.—*Home worth $1,000, and Personal Property.*—The head of a family, or the infant children of deceased parents, may possess, exempt from execution, a homestead valued at $1,000, if it is properly recorded in the public land records, before debt is contracted, and may also select personal property, which shall be exempt, worth $200. Working tools to the value of $50, belonging to mechanics, artisans or laborers, are also exempt.

WISCONSIN. — *Farm of Forty Acres, or House and Lot in Village or City, and Personal Property.*—A homestead, of land not exceeding forty acres, used for agricultural purposes, and the dwelling-house thereon and its appurtenances, and not included in any town, city or village, or instead thereof, land not exceeding in amount one-fourth of an acre within an organized town, city or village, and the dwelling-house thereon, and its appurtenances, owned and occupied by any resident of the State, is not subject to forced sale on execution or any other final process from a court. Persons married, or supporting families, who do not own a homestead, except for debts contracted before June 1, 1882, may retain money or property, secure from attachment or execution, worth $500 instead of a home. Family pictures, Bibles, school-books, library books, and other household furniture valued at $200; two cows, ten swine one yoke of oxen and one horse, or a span

of horses or mules; ten sheep and the wool from same, either raw or manufactured; the necessary food for above stock for a year's support; one wagon, cart or dray, one sleigh, one plow, one drag and other farming utensils, including tackle for teams, not exceeding $50 in value; provisions and fuel for one year; tools and implements or stock in trade of a mechanic or miner, or other person, not exceeding $200 in value; library or implements of any professional man, not exceeding $200 in value; all moneys from insurance of exempt property; earnings of all persons for sixty days next preceding the issue of any process, all sewing-machines kept for use; any swords, plate, books, or other articles, presented by Congress or the members thereof

WYOMING.—Home worth $1,500, and Per- sonal Property—A homestead consisting of a house and lot in a village or city or land not exceeding one hundred and sixty acres, the value not to exceed [illegible] [illegible] is allowed to a householder comprising the same. Also the following property of a householder being the head of a family is exempt. Wearing apparel, family Bibles, pictures, school books, cemetery lots and dug furniture, provisions and household articles not to exceed in value [illegible] All earnings and [illegible] [illegible] Library, instruments and implements of any professional man worth not to exceed [illegible] The person claiming exemptions must be a resident of the territory.

Suggestions Relating to Collection of Debt.

Facts Concerning Judgments and Circumstances Under Which Debtors May be Imprisoned.

Imprisonment for debt has been abolished in every State and Territory. It was considered of so much importance that in some States it is prohibited in their constitutions. At the same time there are some fraudulent acts committed when incurring the debt, or in refusing to pay it, for which there is imprisonment to a certain extent.

The first limitation is, that the creditor must advance the board-bill to the jailor. Another is, the writ of arrest cannot be issued unless indorsed (by some judicial officer) with the amount for which the debtor is required to enter into bonds not to leave the jail limits, which usually embraces the county. On giving bond in such sum the debtor may live anywhere within the limits. Another is, that the writ cannot issue until proof by affidavits of the requisite facts is furnished to the judicial officer who is authorized to allow the writ. Finally, the debtor may make, under the insolvent law, a genuine assignment of all his property exempt from execution, and then he is discharged. He may have a trial of the truth of the charges, and if they are found untrue he will be discharged.

Imprisonment after judgment is usually a satisfaction of it. An action of trespass lies against the plaintiff if the writ issues without authority, and an action on the case when the charges are false and the arrest malicious. For the above reasons creditors rarely imprison fraudulent debtors.

The cases in which there can be an arrest may be classified. Thus: The debtor may be arrested at the commencement of the suit or after the judgment. There are few States in which he may be arrested before judgment, in cases resting on contract. On the other hand, the defendant may be arrested at the commencement of the suit in all States for wrong-doing. In addition to the affidavit stating the grounds for the arrest, and the allowance of the writ by the officer, the plaintiff is generally required to give a bond to the defendant, conditioned to pay all damages.

There are few cases connected with a debt where it is safe to arrest; many where it is dangerous, and very many where it is useless.

METRIC SYSTEM OF WEIGHTS AND MEASURES.

The following system of Measures and Weights, owing to its complete decimal character, and the consequent freedom from labor it affords in calculation, by converting one denomination into another, has been adopted by most European nations.

Its use has also been legalized in the United States, and its ultimate adoption, as a uniform system of measurement and weight, by all the civilized countries, it is believed, will be only a matter of time.

MEASURES OF CAPACITY.

		Dry Meas're	Liquid Measure				
		Peck	Bus.	Gills.	Pints	Qrts.	Gals.
Centilitre.	¹⁄₁₀₀ of a litre			.05			
Decilitre.	¹⁄₁₀ of a litre			.84	.211		
Litre.	Unit of capacity.				2.11	1.05	0.26
Dekalitre.	10 litres	1.13					2.64
Hectolitre.	100 litres		2.83				26.41

WEIGHTS.

		Weight or quantity of water at maximum density.	Equiv. in English Weigh		
			Troy Grains	Avoird. Ounces.	Pound
Milligramme..	¹⁄₁₀₀₀ of a gramme.	1 millimetre..	.0154		
Centigramme..	¹⁄₁₀₀ of a gramme.	10 millimetre..	.1543		
Decigramme..	¹⁄₁₀ of a gramme.	1 cubic centimetre.	1.543		
Gramme..	Unit of weight.	1 cubic decimetre.	15.43		
Dekagramme..	10 grammes.	10 cubic decimetre.		.3527	
Hectogramme..	100 grammes.	100 decimetre..		3.527	
Kilogramme..	1,000 grammes.	1 litre..			2.2046
Myriagramme..	10,000 grammes.	10 litre..			22.046
Quintal	100,000 grammes.	1 hectolitre.			220.46
Millier or Tonneau.	1,000,000 grammes.	1 cubic metre.			2204.6

MEASURES OF LENGTH.

		Equivalents in English Standard Measures.				
		Inches	Feet.	Yards.	Rods.	Furlongs.	Miles
Millimetre	¹⁄₁₀₀₀ of a metre	0.0397					
Centimetre	¹⁄₁₀₀ of a metre	0.3937					
Decimetre.	¹⁄₁₀ of a metre	3.937					
Metre.	Unit of measure	39.37	3.28	1.09			
Dekametre.	10 metres	393.7	32.80	10.94	1.99		
Hectometre	100 metres		328.	109.36	19.9	.497	
Kilometre.	1,000 metres		3280.	1093.33	199.		.62
Myriametre	10,000 metres						6.21

MEASURES OF SURFACE.

		Equivalent in English Standard Measures.					
		Inches	Square Feet.	Square Yards.	Square Poles.	Roods.	Acres.
Square Centimetre		.155					
Square Decimetre		15.50	.107				
Square Metre		1,550.06	10.76	1.20			
Sqr. Dekametre, or Are.				119.60	3.95	.099	0.247
Hectare.				11,960.33	395.33	9.88	2.47

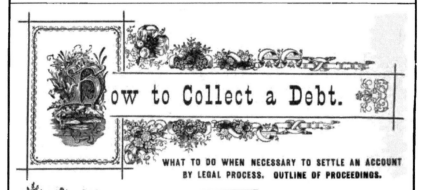

How to Collect a Debt.

WHAT TO DO WHEN NECESSARY TO SETTLE AN ACCOUNT BY LEGAL PROCESS. OUTLINE OF PROCEEDINGS.

ALTHOUGH an earnest effort be made to do business upon a strictly cash basis, debts will be incurred which dishonest, careless, improvident and unfortunate people will neglect to pay. To understand the necessary steps to be taken in the collection of such debts is a matter which, while it concerns all, is nevertheless understood only by the few; and, thus lacking acquaintance with the course which should be pursued, vast numbers of people are defrauded of their hard earnings and honest dues, and themselves frequently thrown into bankruptcy, when prompt and decisive measures pursued in the collection of debts would have saved to them fortune and independence.

Indebtedness having occurred, and the party owing the same neglecting to pay, what shall be the first step taken in its collection? Naturally that will very materially depend upon the nature of the indebtedness and the circumstances under which the debt was made. To illustrate, the following are among the various means by which debts are incurred:

How Debts are Made.

By buying goods to be paid for when convenient.

By buying goods on credit, settlement being made at certain times.

By employing service, to be paid for at certain stated periods.

By obtaining the use of lands, houses and other property, and contracting to pay for the same as per agreement.

By purchasing houses, lands and other property, giving a mortgage on the same as security for balance unpaid.

By borrowing money; usually secured by note and mortgage, or responsible indorsement, as the case may be.

General Suggestions.

To avoid any of these various classes of indebtedness, the following safeguards can be used:

First, do a strictly cash business. Mark goods in the beginning as low as you intend they shall be sold, and then part with them only for cash in hand, unless in cases of emergency. This is the best way to obviate all necessity of collecting, and is by far the best course to pursue alike for the buyer and the seller.

By adopting the cash system as the method of dealing, the price would rule much lower, and yet the merchant would suffer no loss, while the customer would thus be enabled to buy much cheaper, and paying for everything at time of purchase, would buy more sparingly, more economically, and hence would save and lay up money.

Precautionary Measures.

Send goods abroad only to be paid for when taken.

If goods are bought on account, to be paid for at stated periods, let such period be as short as possible, and collect promptly at the time specified.

If engaged in the service of others, secure payment if possible once a week, unless engaged in working for a strictly responsible firm who make it a rule to pay monthly.

If furnishing boarding-house or hotel accommodations, make it a positive rule to collect all bills at periods not exceeding a week apart. To do otherwise is almost certainly to meet with loss, though there are exceptional cases with strictly responsible parties who may arrange to pay monthly.

If renting houses, lands or other property, always have leases made in duplicate, one of which should be kept by the landlord, and the other by the tenant; the wording of the lease being specific as to the conditions of payment, and forfeiture, (*see "Landlord and Tenant," elsewhere*) if payment be not made promptly. In cities it is customary to have rent paid weekly or monthly, in advance. The payments should always be made at the landlord's residence or place of business. Acknowledgment of the payment should be made on the back of the lease when rent is paid.

Loaning Money.

If loaning money, always require a promissory note of the borrower. (*See "Promissory Notes," elsewhere*). Some exceptions may be made, of course, where the amount is quite small, among very intimate friends. Ordinarily, however, always take a note; and if the amount is considerable, or the responsibility of the borrower in the least doubtful, have the payment of the note secured by a mortgage on property worth several times the amount loaned. (*See "Mortgages," elsewhere*). When difficulty is experienced in collecting an account, get the same, if possible, converted into a note, as it is much easier to handle and collect.

Be very certain, when loaning money on real estate, that the amount of security is not only sufficient to pay the note, but that it is free from encumbrance. If a loan is made taking personal property as security, covered by chattel mortgage, see that no other mortgage has been placed on the same property before.

If the loan is secured by mortgage on real estate, which is much the safest, an Abstract of Title should be required of the borrower, signed by the county clerk or other responsible person, showing that the property mortgaged is entirely free from encumbrance. Or, if there be encumbrance already upon the same, ascertain what its amount may be. See also that your mortgage, taken as security, is recorded immediately.

We have thus enumerated some of the means with which loss by credit may be avoided; but should credits be given, and the parties owing neglect or refuse to pay, the following suggestions, it is hoped, may aid in the collection of the debt.

Preliminary Proceedings.

Of course the first steps to be taken in the collection of a debt will depend upon circumstances. The party owing may have met with a sudden reverse of fortune—may be willing, but unable, without great sacrifice, to pay at present; and thus a variety of circumstances will tend to determine the action to be pursued in the commencement—whether it be sharp, positive and energetic, or mild and lenient.

We will suppose, however, that the debtor neglects or refuses to pay a just debt. It becomes necessary, therefore, to proceed to its collection by the various discreet and legal steps at command. These are:

First, To write a letter calling attention to the account unpaid, stating the time when the obligation was due, and accompanying the same with a bill of goods bought, when, etc.

Second, Another letter, a little more pointed than the first, urging the necessity of immediate settlement.

Third, To sue for the same before a competent legal officer.

First Efforts at Collection.

The necessary forms will be very similar to the following:

DUNNING LETTER NO. 1.

MR. A. B. CUSHMAN,   ELYRIA, O., Feb. 10, 1877.
    Oberlin, O.
    Dear Sir: Please find enclosed a statement of your account to January first, at which time we had hoped to have settled with all our customers. Early attention to this will greatly oblige,
                                        Yours Respectfully,
                                            BROWN, MEYER & CO.

DUNNING LETTER NO. 2.

MR. A. B. CUSHMAN,   ELYRIA, O., Feb. 20, 1877.
    Oberlin, O.
    Dear Sir: We are compelled to place some of our accounts in the hands of collectors for settlement; but our relations with you have always been so pleasant, we wish to avoid doing so in your case. As all uncollected bills go into the hands of the collector next Monday, you will please call upon us before then, and oblige,
                                        Yours Respectfully,
                                            BROWN, MEYER & CO.

Borrowed Money.

In case the indebtedness is for borrowed money, possibly a small amount, for which no promissory note was given, the easiest method, probably, of disposing of the matter, when it is discovered that the individual does not intend to pay, is to erase the transaction from the memorandum and forget the affair entirely, if possible; considering yourself fortunate in discovering, before loaning a larger amount, that the borrower was a dead beat. It may be best that you continue on friendly terms, and you cannot afford to break pleasant relations for a small amount of money, though by this neglect the borrower has forever forfeited your confidence, unless the matter is satisfactorily explained. Should you propose, however, to press collection, a letter similar to the following may be written:

REMINDER NO. 1.

                                        GALESBURG, ILL., Aug 15, 1877.
MR. WEBSTER:
    The ten dollars borrowed by you on the Fourth of July was to have been paid, according to agreement, on last Monday. Thinking that, possibly, the matter had escaped your recollection, I take this means of reminding you of the fact.
                                        Respectfully Yours,
                                            CHAS. B. WEEKS.

No attention being paid to this letter, it may be well enough to write one letter more, as follows:

REMINDER NO. 2.

                                        GALESBURG, ILL., Aug. 24, 1877.
MR. WEBSTER:
    I mailed a note to your address some days since, in relation to money borrowed of me on the Fourth. I fear you must have failed to receive it, otherwise you surely would have given it your attention. As I put all unsettled accounts into the hands of a justice for collection next week on Wednesday, I should like to see you before that time.
                                        Respectfully Yours,
                                            CHAS. B. WEEKS.

Legal Proceedings.

You have exhausted the usual moral means of collecting your due, and the debt is not yet paid. It is proposed now to collect it, if possible, by legal process.

In the first place, can it be collected? Is the debtor worth enough to be compelled to pay it, aside from the property which the law exempts? What does the law exempt? (*See* "*Exemptions from Forced Sale,*" *elsewhere*), which applies to heads of families; also, ("*Limitations,*" *elsewhere.*

Being satisfied that the debt is collectible, you now place the account in the hands of a Justice of the Peace, unless the amount to be collected is so large as to be out of the justice's jurisdiction. The amount which can be collected through a justice varies in different States.

Limit of Jurisdiction with Justice of the Peace.

The following shows the largest amount in the different States and Territories which the justice of the peace, through his official position, can have jurisdiction over:

Alabama $100	Louisiana $100	Ohio..........$300
Arkansas 300	Maine.......... 20	Oregon 250
California...... 300	Maryland...... 100	Pennsylvania ... 300
Colorado 300	Massachusetts .. 300	Rhode Island.... 100
Connecticut 100	Michigan 300	South Carolina.. 100
Dakota Ter. 100	Minnesota 100	Tennessee 500
Delaware 100	Mississippi 150	Texas.......... 200
Florida 100	Missouri 300	Utah Ter....... 300
Georgia........ 100	Nebraska...... 200	Vermont........ 200
Idaho Ter. 100	Nevada 300	Virginia........ 50
Illinois......... 200	New Hampshire 100	Washington Ter. 100
Indiana 200	New Jersey ... 100	West Virginia... 100
Iowa 100*	New Mexico Ter 100	Wisconsin 300
Kansas 300	New York 200	Wyoming Ter... 100
Kentucky 100	North Carolina.. 200	

* By consent of parties, $300.

First Legal Steps.

The amount to be collected being within the jurisdiction of the justice, he will issue a *Summons,* which will be taken by a constable to the debtor, if he can be found, and read to him, which is termed "serving a summons" upon the person owing the debt.

Form of Summons.

The wording of this summons will be somewhat as follows:

STATE OF —— } ss.
  ——COUNTY, }
  The People of the State of —— *to any Constable of said County—*
      GREETING:
  You are hereby commanded to summon A. B. to appear before me at —— on the —— day of ——, at —— o'clock ——M., to answer the complaint of C. D. for a failure to pay him a certain demand not exceeding ——; and hereof make due return as the law directs. Given under my hand this —— day of —— 18—.
                                        JOHN DOE, *J. P.*

It may be remarked that the law varies in different States as to where a debtor may be sued. In some States he cannot be sued out of the town where he resides. In others more latitude is given, the facts concerning which the justice will explain, upon application, as to his own State.

Upon the issuance of a summons, the constable will proceed to serve the same immediately. But if the defendant cannot be found, or shall evade the service of process by refusing to listen, or by secreting himself, the constable may leave a copy of the summons with some member of his family of the age of ten years or upward;

and afterward report to the justice when and how his summons was served, and the circumstances attending the same.

In the summons the justice will specify a certain place, day and hour for the trial, not less, usually, than five, nor more than fifteen days from the date of such summons, at which place and time defendant is notified to appear. A summons is usually served at least three days before the trial is to take place.

The justice indorses on the summons the amount demanded by the plaintiff, with the costs due on the same, and upon the serving of the summons the debtor may pay to the constable the demand and sts, taking his receipt for the same, which will satisfy the debt and prevent all further costs.

The Costs.

The average costs accruing up to this point are: justice for issuing summons, 25 cents; constable for serving, 35 cents; the entire cost depending, somewhat, upon how far the constable has to travel, he being entitled, ordinarily, to five cents per mile each way for mileage.

In many cases, when served with a summons, the debtor will immediately settle the claim rather than allow a greater accumulation of costs; but should he refuse to make settlement, the constable will return the summons indorsed somewhat as follows:

"Served by reading the within to the defendant on the 5th day of July, 1876.   JOHN SMITH, *Constable.*"

In suing an incorporated company, a copy of the summons must be left with the president. If he is absent, then with the secretary, general agent, cashier, or principal clerk, if either can be found in the county in which suit is brought. If neither can be found in the county, then by leaving a copy of the summons with any clerk, engineer, director, station agent, conductor, or any such agent found in the county.

At the time appointed for the trial, both the plaintiff and defendant, or their representatives, are required to be promptly in attendance, the plaintiff being present for the purpose of proving his claim, and the defendant for the purpose of stating his defense, or the reasons why the claim should not be paid. Should either party fail to appear, he must suffer the penalty hereafter explained.

Trial by Justice and Jury.

When the parties appear, the justice will proceed to try the case, and after hearing the allegations and proofs, will, if the claim is proved, give judgment against the defendant, including costs and such interest as the law allows. If no claim is proved, the judgment will be against the plaintiff, who will be held responsible for costs.

Should either party demand a jury, he can have the same in all cases of trial before a justice of the peace, upon making a deposit with the justice of the jury fees. The jury shall comprise any number from six to twelve, as the parties may agree, though the number usually provided by law is six or twelve.

Upon determining to have the case tried by jury, the justice will put into the hands of the constable, or other authorized officer, the following

FORM OF WRIT FOR SUMMONING JURORS.

STATE OF ——
—— COUNTY, } ss.

The People of the State of —— to any Constable of said County— GREETING:

We command you to summon —— lawful men of your county to appear before me at —— o'clock —— M., who are not related to —— plaintiff, or to —— defendant, to make a jury between said parties in a certain cause pending before me; and have then and there the names of this jury and this writ.

Witness my hand this —— day of ——, 18—.
        JOHN DOE, *J. P.*

In the case of jury trial, the justice will enter judgment according to the verdict of the jury.

Who are Competent as Jurors.

In most States the following requisites are necessary to make the individual competent to serve on a jury

1. He should be a resident of the county, and not exempt from serving on jury.

2. Twenty-one years old and under sixty.

3. Of fair character, in the possession of natural faculties, free from legal exceptions, of sound judgment, well informed, and who under stands the English language.

Who are Exempt from Serving on Juries.

In general, the following persons, according to the statutes of many States, are exempt from serving on juries, namely: the governor, lieutenant governor, secretary of state, auditor of public accounts, treasurer, superintendent of public instruction, attorney general, members of the general assembly during their term of office, judges of courts, clerks of courts, sheriffs, coroners, postmasters, mail carriers, practicing attorneys, all officers of the United States, officiating ministers of the gospel, school teachers during their terms of school, practicing physicians, constant ferrymen, mayors of cities, policemen, and active members of the fire department.

The Result of Failing to Appear.

Should the plaintiff fail to appear within the hour appointed, the jury, or the justice, alone, being in readiness to hear the trial, and no good reason being given for his non-attendance, the suit is dismissed, unless the defendant should desire to have the case tried then or at another time.

Should the defendant fail to appear, the justice will hear the case, and if the claim is proved, he will enter *Judgment* against the defendant for the amount which is due the plaintiff, and will issue an *Execution* for its collection.

A "Judgment" is simply the decision of the court that a certain demand or claim shall be paid, and no particular form is required in rendering it.

The Execution.

An execution is a writ which authorizes an officer, to whom it is directed, to carry into effect the decision of the court. In some States the law permits the imprisonment of a debtor if he refuses to pay the claim against him, and an execution can be issued directing the proper officer to imprison the delinquent until the claim is satisfied. It is more common, however, to issue an execution authorizing an officer to levy upon personal property of the debtor, and a judgment being rendered by the justice against a party, the next step usually taken is to issue an execution for the collection of the amount due.

If the plaintiff is satisfied that the debt will be lost unless execution issue immediately, he may take oath to that effect, and the justice will issue an execution authorizing an officer to make levy upon goods at once, but sale of the same usually will not take place under twenty days.

If no fear of losing the debt is expressed, execution will issue, generally, in about twenty days from the time judgment was rendered, and the officer usually has about seventy days to make a levy and sell the property to satisfy said execution.

FORM OF EXECUTION AGAINST GOODS AND CHATTELS.

STATE OF ——
—— COUNTY, } ss.

The People of the State of —— to any Constable of said County— GREETING:

We command you, that of the goods and chattels of A. B. in your county, you make the sum of —— dollars and —— cents, judgment, and —— dollars and —— cents, costs, which C. D. lately recovered before me in a certain plea against the said A. B., and hereof make return to me within seventy days from this date.

Given under my hand this —— day of ——, 18—.
        JOHN DOE, *J. P.*

When the Writ of Execution against personal property is placed in his hands, it is the duty of the constable to make a levy upon and sell such personal property as he can find sufficient to satisfy the debt, which is not exempted from sale by law, giving ten days' previous notice of such sale by advertisement in writing to be posted up at three of the most public places in the vicinity where the sale is to be made, and on the day appointed for the sale, the constable sells to the highest bidder the property levied upon, or as much of the same as may be necessary to pay the judgment, interest and costs.

Of course discretion must be used by the constable in selecting property not exempted from sale, and not already attached or covered by chattel mortgage; and when covered by the latter, whether it will sell for enough to pay both claims.

Attachment of Goods.

If a creditor, his agent or attorney, has good reason to believe that there is danger of losing his claim, because the debtor is a non resident of the State, or conceals himself, in defiance of an officer, so that process cannot be served upon him, or has departed from the State with the intention of removing his goods from the State, or has fraudulently conveyed or assigned his effects so as to hinder or delay his creditors, or is about to do so, he can go before a justice of the peace and make affidavit setting forth the nature and amount of the indebtedness, after allowing all just credits and set-offs, for any one or more of the causes mentioned. He will also state the place of residence of defendant, if known, and file a bond with said justice in double the amount sworn to be due, with sufficient security, payable to defendant, against whom the writ is issued, conditioned for satisfying all costs and damages awarded to such defendant, for wrongfully suing out said attachment.

That being done, the justice will issue a Writ of Attachment, which authorizes the constable in whose hands it is placed to proceed at once to the residence or place of business of the debtor, or elsewhere where he may have goods and effects within the jurisdiction of the court, and immediately take possession of a sufficient amount of personal property with which to pay the claim and all costs; provided, however, if at the residence of the debtor he is allowed to enter. Should the debtor be present when the constable has got possession, he will read the writ to him, the time being specified in the same when his trial will take place. In the meantime the constable or officer will take possession of the goods by removing them or putting them in charge of some person until the day of the trial. If the goods are being removed to another county, in most States, follow and take them there.

The Trial.

At the trial, if it is proven that the debtor had no intention of leaving or refusing to pay his just due, and any damage has been done by the seizure of the property, the creditor will be held responsible for such damage. If the defendant or his representative does not put in an appearance, after having been notified, the justice, at the day appointed, which is usually within a month from the time the attachment was issued, will hear the case, and if the claim be proved, will render judgment accordingly, and order a sale of the necessary amount of goods to pay the debt and all costs.

Attaching the Body.

Where an attachment has been issued against a defendant and the constable returns no property found, and yet the plaintiff is satisfied that the defendant has property concealed, removed or assigned with intent to defraud his creditors, and that there is danger of losing his claim unless the debtor is held to bail, it is common in several States for the justice to issue a Capias for the arrest of the debtor, the form of which is as follows:

FORM OF CAPIAS.

STATE OF ——— } ss.
——— COUNTY,

The People of the State of ——— to any Constable of said County— GREETING:

You are hereby commanded to take the body of ——— and bring him forthwith before me, unless special bail be entered; and if such bail be entered, you will then command him to appear before me at ———, on the ——— day of ———, at ——— o'clock —M., to answer to the complaint of A. B. for failure to pay him a certain demand not exceeding ——— dollars; and hereof make due return as the law directs.

Given under my hand, this ——— day of ———, 18—.

JOHN DOE, *J. P.*

Before issuing a capias, the justice will take from the plaintiff, or his representative, a bond with approved surety, which is substantially in the following form:

FORM OF BOND FOR CAPIAS.

A— B—, }
vs. } Before ———, Justice of the Peace.
C— D—, }

STATE OF ——— } ss.
——— COUNTY,

We hereby bind ourselves to pay all damages and costs, if any, which may be wrongfully occasioned by a *capias* in this case.

Dated this ——— day of ———, 18—. ——— ——— [SEAL.]
——— ——— [SEAL.]

Ordinarily the capias is issued only as a last resort, and when it is evident that the claim can only be collected by arresting the defendant and depriving him of his liberty, unless he give satisfactory bail.

Being provided with a warrant for the apprehension of the debtor, the defendant is arrested, if found, and brought forthwith before the justice, unless some friend or other person will guarantee that the debtor will promptly appear at the hour and place appointed for trial. This guarantee, termed "giving bail," is in the following form, written on the back of the capias:

FORM OF SPECIAL BAIL.

I, A. B., acknowledge myself special bail for the within named C. D. Witness my hand, this ——— day of ———, 18—.

A. B.

This indorsement must be signed by one or more responsible persons whom the constable is willing to take as security, the condition being that the defendant, if judgment is rendered against him, at the time of trial will pay the same, with costs, or surrender himself, according to the terms of the capias. And in case he fails to pay, or surrender, the persons who signed the bail are held for the payment of the claim.

Who Cannot be Arrested.

By constitutional right, the following persons are privileged from arrest: Members of congress, except for treason, felony, and breach of the peace, are not liable to arrest during their attendance upon the session of their respective houses, nor while going to or returning from the same. Electors are also privileged from arrest, except for treason, felony or breach of the peace, while in attendance upon elections, or while going to or returning from the same. In many States, also, the militia, except in the above cases, are exempt during their attendance at musters, or while going or returning. Attorneys and counselors at law, judges, clerks, sheriffs, and all other officers of the several courts are likewise free from arrest while attending court, and while going to and returning from the same, as are also witnesses and other persons necessarily attending any courts of record on business.

Suing the Garnishee.

Another means left open for the collection of a claim in various States of the Union, is that of securing the debt by suing a third person who may be owing the defendant. In such case the plaintiff can proceed against this third person, who is called the garnishee, in the same manner as against the debtor, though a certain amount of the money owing is, in some States, exempt, and cannot be garnisheed.

Levying upon Real Estate.

When no personal property can be found with which to pay the debt, and the debtor is known to possess real estate in sufficient amount to pay the claim, then it is allowable, in certain States, for the justice to certify to the clerk of the circuit court, in the county where judgment was rendered, a transcript of the judgment, which shall be filed by the clerk; and thereupon the same will become a lien upon the real estate of the debtor, and execution may issue from that court, and proceedings be had for the sale of the land and payment of the debt and costs from the proceeds of the sale.

Appealing to Higher Courts.

Where an action has been brought before a justice to secure a claim, a summons has been issued, the day has been set for a hearing, and judgment has been rendered by a justice or a jury, and the decision is that the debtor must pay the claim with costs, the debtor can then appeal to the next higher legal tribunal, being the circuit, district court, court of common pleas, or other courts, which are known by different names in different States.

Before the defendant can appeal, however, he is required to give a bond, which must be signed by one or more responsible persons, by which he guarantees, in a sum twice the amount of the claim, to pay the debt and all costs if he is beaten in the higher court.

The case is then entered upon the docket of the clerk of the higher court for trial, and if time permits will be tried at the next term of that court.

Upon trial in this court, if the defendant is beaten again, he can, by giving bond as before, in double the amount of the debt and costs then accrued, carry the case for trial up to the Supreme Court of the State, where the matter generally ends.

How Soon the Debt may be Collected.

Thus it will be seen where, in each trial, the defendant promptly defends his case and appeals to the higher courts when he finds himself beaten, he can escape the payment of the original debt for one, two or more years. As each appeal is attended with heavy costs, however, few men care to punish themselves so much for the sake of wreaking revenge upon anybody else. In most cases the debtor will pay the debt in the earlier part of the prosecution, unless he thinks he has good reason for not doing so.

What does Law Cost?

What will it cost to collect the debt? That question naturally arises, and is, very properly, one that should be considered. Of course it is impossible to determine, definitely, what the costs will be. If a lawyer be employed for an ordinary justice suit, occupying the time but an hour or so, his fee will be five dollars. Should the claim be of considerable amount, and the time of the attorney be employed a day or two, the lawyer's charge will be from ten to twenty dollars. Should the plaintiff come off victorious, and obtain judgment against the debtor, the other costs will be mainly borne by the debtor. Should it be shown that the plaintiff has no just claim, the justice, or jury, if there be a jury, will decide that there was no cause of action, and will assess the costs of suit to the plaintiff.

The costs of an ordinary justice suit in most States, will average about as follows:

Docketing the suit, 25 cents; issuing summons, 25 cents; constable for serving summons, 35 cents; each mile traveled in serving summons by constable, 5 cents; justice fee for entering up judgment, 25 cents; for discharge of docket, 25 cents; fee of justice for hearing statement of each party and giving decision, $2.

The above are the inevitable costs which will be incurred if the plaintiff and defendant have a trial without witnesses, lawyers or jury, and then settle according to the decision of the justice.

If witnesses are called, the expense is 50 cents per day for each witness, to be claimed at time of trial. Fee of justice for issuing each subpœna for witness, 25 cents; constable for serving each subpœna, 25

cents; for mileage each way in serving a subpœna, 5 cents; for administering oath to each witness, 5 cents.

Should the suit be tried by a jury, each juryman is entitled, before a justice, to 50 cents for hearing the case, should the jury agree ; for entering verdict of the jury, 15 cents; fee of constable for waiting on jury, 50 cents; for entering satisfaction of judgment, 10 cents.

Should judgment be obtained against the debtor, and he refuse to settle, the justice will issue an execution to levy upon and sell a sufficient quantity of debtor's goods to pay the debt and all costs. Fee for execution, 50 cents; fee of constable for serving and returning execution, 50 cents; for advertising property for sale, 50 cents; commissions on sales, not exceeding ten dollars, 10 per cent.; for all in excess of that amount, 5 per cent.; except, when through settlement or other cause the property is not sold, in that case the commissions will be one half the above amount.

The defendant, thinking that equity may not be had before a certain justice, may have the case tried before the nearest justice; this procedure is termed a "Change of Venue." Fee of justice for transcript in change of venue, 50 cents.

Should either party desire to appeal to a higher court, the expenses of appeal before the justice will be: For bond, 35 cents; for entering appeal, 25 cents; for transcript of judgment and proceedings in case of appeal, 50 cents.

In the higher court the cost of trial will usually average from twenty to fifty dollars.

Collecting Large Amounts.

When the amount to be collected exceeds the jurisdiction of the justice, the plaintiff will apply to the clerk of such higher court as has jurisdiction in the case. This is the circuit court, district court, court of common pleas, or other court of similar character. The clerk of this court, upon application, will issue a summons, which is placed in the hands of a sheriff or his deputy, is served upon the debtor as before, and the case is tried usually before a jury of twelve persons at the next term of that court.

The proceedings in this court are usually so intricate as to make it advisable for the person unaccustomed to legal technicalities to employ an attorney to conduct the case, as is also generally most convenient even in the lower courts.

The Law of Different States.

We have given thus, in outline, the principal methods resorted to in the different States for the collection of debt. The forms here shown, while not conforming fully to the exact methods pursued in different States, are yet sufficiently accurate to enable the reader to possess a general understanding of the methods of procedure.

The special law of the State where the creditor may reside, as it relates to the collection of debt, can be learned by application to the justice of the peace in that State, who, upon the plaintiff stating the circumstances, will usually give the necessary information with which legal proceedings may be commenced.

GENERAL FORMS OF POWER OF ATTORNEY.

BUSINESS firms and individuals having a large trade, where indebtedness is unavoidably incurred, for a long or short time, frequently find it necessary to employ collectors whose special and entire duty it is to promptly collect such indebtedness or see that the same is paid when due. Oftentimes their work of collection will be in portions of the country hundreds or thousands of miles from the place of business or residence of the creditor. It is usual under these circumstances to invest such an agent, thus doing business, with what is termed "Power of Attorney," which is done by a written instrument usually under seal. The person or persons so authorized are called attorneys, and the person or persons so appointing are termed constituents.

If a power of attorney is to be recorded, it should be acknowledged. Where any act of the attorney is to be by deed, the authority to execute it must also be by deed. A document authorizing the attorney to execute a sealed instrument, must of itself be under seal, and a power to convey lands requires the same regulations in its acknowledgment by both husband and wife, in many States, as a deed by them would require. The following illustrates the general form and wording of such a document, together with other papers related thereto:

GENERAL FORM OF POWER OF ATTORNEY.

KNOW ALL MEN BY THESE PRESENTS, that I, Henry G. Holden, of Londonderry, in the County of Windham, and State of Vermont, have made, constituted and appointed, and by these presents do make, constitute and appoint James H. Hill, of Downer's Grove, County of Dupage, and State of Illinois, a true and lawful attorney for me, and in my name, place and stead, and in my behalf, to [here insert the things which the attorney is to do], hereby giving and granting unto my said attorney full power and authority in the premises to use all lawful means in my name and for my sole benefit, for the purposes aforesaid. And generally to do and perform all such acts, matters and things as my said attorney shall deem necessary and expedient for the completion of the authority hereby given, as fully as I might and could do were I personally present.

In witness whereof, I, the said Henry G. Holden, have hereunto set my hand and seal, this first day of December, in the year of our Lord one thousand eight hundred and seventy-six.

Signed and sealed in presence of { HENRY G. HOLDEN. [SEAL]
....

Letter of Substitution Appended to Power of Attorney.

It is customary to authorize the attorney to employ another to assist him when necessary, which person so appointed is termed a substitute. The power to appoint such sub-agent generally accompanies the document giving power of attorney, and is worded as follows:

KNOW ALL MEN BY THESE PRESENTS, that I, Jas. H. Hill, of Downer's Grove, in the County of Dupage and State of Illinois, named in the letter of attorney above mentioned, have made, appointed and substituted, and by these presents do make, appoint and substitute John Holland, of said Downer's Grove, to be the true and lawful attorney of the said Henry G. Holden in the above letter of attorney named, to do and perform all such acts, matters and things as he may deem necessary or expedient for the complete execution of the authority therein given, as fully in all respects, and to all intents and purposes, as I myself might and could do by virtue of the power and authority therein delegated, if I were personally present.

In witness whereof, I, the said Jas. H. Hill, have hereunto set my hand and seal, the fifth day of December, in the year of our Lord one thousand eight hundred and seventy-six.

Signed and sealed in presence of { JAS. H. HILL. [SEAL]
....

GENERAL POWER OF ATTORNEY TO COLLECT DEBTS.

KNOW ALL MEN BY THESE PRESENTS, that I, Henry G. Holden, in the town of Londonderry, County of Windham, and State of Vermont, have made, constituted and appointed, and by these presents do make, constitute and appoint Jas. H. Hill my true and lawful attorney, for me and in my name, to ask, demand, sue for, recover and receive of John Holland, and of all and every person and persons whomsoever indebted to me by note, account, or otherwise, all such sums of money, debt, and demands whatsoever, as now are or may be due and owing to me from them or either of them. And in default of payment of the same by them or either of them, to take all lawful means, in my name or otherwise, for the recovery thereof, by attachment, arrest or otherwise, and to arrange and agree for the same; and on receipt thereof to discharge the same, and seal and deliver in a lawful manner, and do all lawful acts concerning the premises as I would do myself were I personally present; and make and revoke such attorneys under him as may be necessary for the purposes aforesaid.

Hereby confirming all my said attorney shall in my name lawfully do, or cause to be done, in or about the premises.

In witness whereof, I, the said Henry G. Holden, have hereto set my hand and seal, this ninth day of December, one thousand eight hundred and seventy-six.

Signed and sealed in presence of { HENRY G. HOLDEN. [SEAL]
....

LETTER OF REVOCATION.

Whereas I, Henry G. Holden, of Londonderry, County of Windham, and State of Vermont, did on the first day of December, in eighteen hundred and seventy-six, by a certain instrument in writing or letter of attorney, make and appoint Jas. H. Hill, of Downer's Grove, County of Dupage, State of Illinois, to be my lawful attorney in my name and for my use, to [*here set forth what the attorney was authorized to do, precisely in the language of the original power*], as by the same writing, reference thereto being had, will fully appear: Now know all men by these presents, that I, the said Henry G. Holden, for a just cause, have revoked, recalled and made void the said letter of attorney, and all powers or authorities therein granted, and all acts which shall or may be done by virtue thereof.

[*If another attorney is to be appointed continue thus:*] And further know ye, that I, the said Henry G. Holden, do by these presents name, constitute and appoint John N. Hurd, of Aurora, County of Kane, and State of Illinois, to be my lawful attorney.

Signed and sealed in presence of | HENRY G. HOLDEN. [SEAL.]
...............................|

DUTIES OF CORONERS.

The office of coroner is one which the people of every community must provide for. Sudden deaths, which take place through violence, poison, suicide, and accident, demand investigation by persons competent to determine the cause of such death; hence in every State there are statutes regulating the manner of holding the coroner's inquest.

The duty of the coroner, upon being notified of a person being found dead, supposed to have come to his or her death through violence or unnatural means, is to summon a jury of six men, usually. Upon their assembling he will appoint one of the number a foreman, who, upon their being sworn to do their duty, will carefully proceed to investigate the cause of the death, witnesses being sworn by the coroner, and all other measures taken calculated to arrive at the true facts of the case.

As soon as the inquest is held and the verdict of the jury is rendered, if the deceased is unknown and is unclaimed by friends, immediate measures are taken to bury the body, which is done at the expense of the deceased person's estate if such there be. If not, then at the expense, generally, of the county. All goods found, after ten days' notice, according to the law of various States, are sold, and the proceeds, along with the moneys, papers or other valuable thing or things, deposited with the county treasurer, the coroner taking a receipt therefor. In the hands of the county treasurer they are to remain five years, subject to the order of the legal representatives of the deceased. If in that time they are not called for, then the property vests in the county.

It is made the duty of the coroner to keep a book of record in which is fully detailed all the circumstances attending every inquest, the testimony of witnesses, etc., and where any person or persons are implicated in the death, to arrange to have such witness or witnesses knowing the fact appear at the next term of court.

It is made the duty of the foreman to bring in the verdict, which will vary according to circumstances, as follows:

VERDICT IN CASE OF MURDER.

STATE OF ——— } ss.
COUNTY, ——— }

At an inquest held at the house of A. B. in the town of ———, county of ———, on the —— day of ———, 18—, before C. D., a coroner or justice of the peace in said county, upon the body of E. F. [*or*, a person unknown], there lying dead, the following jurymen being sworn to inquire into all the circumstances attending the death of the said E. F. [*or*, a person unknown], decide that one G. H., of [*or*, late of] the town of ———, in the county of ———, aforesaid, [*or as the case may be*] on the —— day of ———, in the year 18—, at —— o'clock in the afternoon of that day, made an assault upon the body of the deceased with a rod of iron [*or as the case may be*], from which assault wounds were inflicted on his left breast, causing the death of the deceased on the —— day of ———, 18—.

[*If others were implicated in the murder, state the fact, and who.*]

In witness whereof, the jurors have to this verdict set their hands on the day of the inquest.

[*To be signed by the jurors.*]

The justice or coroner should indorse on the verdict of the jury his acceptance thereof, which may be as follows:

The within verdict was made, signed and delivered to me this —— day of ———, 18—.   A. B., *Coroner or Justice of the Peace.*

VERDICT IN CASE OF SUICIDE.

At an inquest held [*proceed as in case of verdict for murder*], decide that the said O. P. [*or*, person unknown] did on the —— day of ———, 18—, at the town of ——— in said county of ———, voluntarily and with his own hand [*here state the nature of his death*], from which act he instantly died [*or as the case may be*].

In witness whereof, etc. [*as in case of verdict for murder*].

VERDICT WHERE DROWNED BY ACCIDENT.

STATE OF ——— } ss.
COUNTY, ——— }

At an inquest held [*proceed as in case of verdict for murder*], decide that the said R. H., on the —— day of ———, at —— o'clock —. M., at ———, in the county aforesaid, went into —— river in the town of ———, to bathe, and was accidentally drowned.

In witness, etc. [*as in case of verdict for murder*].

VERDICT IN CASE OF NATURAL DEATH.

STATE OF ——— } ss.
COUNTY, ——— }

At an inquest held [*proceed as in case of verdict for murder*], decide that the said E. H. on the —— day of ———, at —— in the town of ———, in the county aforesaid, being found lying on the highway in the town of [*or as the case may be*], with no marks of violence upon his body, came to his death from natural causes.

In witness whereof, etc. [*as in case of verdict for murder.*]

REPORTS OF COMMITTEES.

It is common with societies and assemblies of various kinds to entrust the special work of such society or assembly, requiring considerable investigation, to a committee usually consisting of three, five or more, who are expected to examine the subject which they are appointed to investigate, and at a certain specified time, or at their earliest convenience, bring in a written report of their conclusions.

It is customary to have such committee of an odd number, as three, five, etc., so that in case of the committee failing to agree there can be a majority vote, and a majority as well as a minority report.

The following may serve as specimens of various kinds of reports:

MAJORITY REPORT.

To the Mayor and Aldermen of the City of Aurora, in Common Council assembled:

Your committee, to whom was referred the proposition of John Jones to sell to the city a gravel bed, comprising a piece of land of four rods by ten in size, being lot four in block ten in the original plat of the city of Aurora, having had the same under advisement, ask leave to report as follows, to wit:

The gravel in this bed, though not of the uniform quality that may be desired, is yet sufficiently good to answer the purpose of grading the streets. The quantity in this lot, according to estimate, will be sufficient for the city's use in the east division of the city for the next five years, and, considering its accessibility, the city is recommended to buy the lot at the price offered, namely, five hundred dollars.

L. O. HILL,
H. H. EVANS.

MINORITY REPORT.

To the Mayor and Aldermen of the City of Aurora, in Common Council assembled:

The undersigned, the minority of a committee to whom was referred the proposition of John Jones to sell to the city a gravel bed, comprising a piece of land four rods by ten in size, being lot four in block ten in the original plat of the city of Aurora, having had the same under advisement, asks leave to report as follows, to wit:

The gravel in this bed is not such as the city should purchase as a covering for the streets, being in certain veins too fine, and in other places altogether too coarse. As there are other points in the city where lots can be purchased containing gravel which is much better adapted to the purpose of graveling streets, just as accessible and quite as cheap, the undersigned therefore recommends that the city do not purchase the lot at the price offered, namely, five hundred dollars.

S. B. HAWLEY.

REPORT OF THE TREASURER OF AN ASSOCIATION.

The undersigned, treasurer of the New York Mutual Benefit Association, herewith submits his annual report:

The balance in the treasurer's hands at the commencement of the present year, was forty-four (44) dollars. During the year, as shown by the accompanying exhibit A, which is hereto appended, there have been received into the treasury, from all sources, five hundred and ninety one (591) dollars and eighty-four (84) cents. During the same time the expenditures have been two hundred and fifty-seven (257) dollars and ten (10) cents, leaving a balance in the treasury, and subject to the order of the society, the sum of three hundred and thirty-four (334) dollars and seventy-four (74) cents.

All of which is respectfully submitted.

A. VAN OSDEL, *Treasurer, N. Y. M. B. A.*

A.

Dr. NEW YORK MUTUAL BENEFIT ASSOCIATION,
To A. VAN OSDEL, Treas., *Cr.*

1877.			1877.		
Dec. 31.	To cash paid to assist various members........	$110.00	Jan. 1.	By balance on hand from last year's account..........	$44.00
	To rent paid S. B.,..	70.00	Dec. 31.	By dues..........	452.00
	" carpet........	41.00		" initiation fees ..	64.00
	" stationery	5.10		" fines	1.84
	" advertising	31.00			
		$257.10			
	Balance on hand..	334.74			
		$591.84			$591.84

The undersigned, a committee appointed for the purpose, have compared the foregoing account with the vouchers, and find it to be correct.
ARTHUR H. KING,
L. A. BRADLEY.

REPORT OF A SPECIAL COMMITTEE ON CITY HALL.

The Committee on City Hall beg leave to submit the following report:

The present state of the building requires the early attention of the city, both in reference to needed changes in the arrangement of some of the rooms and in general repairs.

The roof is in need of immediate repair, the paint being so worn away as to leave much of the tin exposed to the weather, which is, consequently, badly rusted. The ceiling, walls and seats of the upper hall also require calcimining and painting, and many lights of glass need resetting. They recommend that this room be generally repainted, which, by the painter's estimate, annexed and marked A, can be done for ninety-one (91) dollars.

In connection with this improvement, they recommend the remodeling of the office of city clerk, by constructing a platform eight inches in height and seven feet in width on the south and west sides of the room,

with a low railing on the outer side of the same. This change can be cheaply made from the present high railing in the room, which should be taken down. The outer doors should also be changed to swing out, instead of in as they now do. The cost of these changes will be but eighty-nine (89) dollars. The entire sum required for the above purposes will amount to one hundred and eighty (180) dollars.

All of which is respectfully submitted.
A. B. CUMMINGS,
N. E. CUSHMAN, } *Committee on City Hall.*
A. W. HARTMAN.

A.

ESTIMATE FOR PAINTING ROOF AND INTERIOR OF UPPER HALL.

For painting roof two coats, mineral paint........................	$26.00
For calcimining ceiling of upper hall........................	14.00
For setting seventeen panes of large glass........................	9.00
For painting walls two coats........................	24.00
For painting and graining seats........................	18.00
	$91.00

BARNARD & STONE, *Painters.*

REPORT OF COMMITTEE AT AN AGRICULTURAL FAIR.

To the President and Superintendent of the Washington County Fair:

GENTLEMEN — Your committee to whom was assigned the duty of deciding concerning the relative merit of swine on exhibition at this show, make the following report:

The exhibit of different breeds is good, there being nine distinct classes in the exhibition. Of these, for size, cleanliness and generally superior condition, the first premium is awarded to four animals of the Poland China breed, in pen C, division four. The second premium is given to pen D, division three, containing three animals, Suffolks, which are to be commended for their great weight, considering their age.

Very Respectfully
ARTHUR MONROE,
WILBUR HANCHETT,
DEXTER D. BROWN.

DIRECTIONS FOR SECURING COPYRIGHTS.

PRINTED TITLE FOR ENTRY BEFORE PUBLICATION.

1. A printed copy of the title of the book, map, chart, dramatic or musical composition, engraving, cut, print, photograph, or a description of the painting, drawing, chromo, statue, statuary, or model or design for a work of the fine arts, for which copyright is desired, must be sent by mail, prepaid, addressed

LIBRARIAN OF CONGRESS,
WASHINGTON, D. C.

This must be done before publication of the book or other article.

COPYRIGHT FEES.

2. A fee of 50 cents, for recording the title of each book or other article, must be enclosed with the title as above, and 50 cents in addition (or $1 in all) for each certificate of copyright under seal of the Librarian of Congress, which will be transmitted by return mail.

WHAT IS REQUIRED TO PERFECT COPYRIGHT.

3. Within ten days after publication of each book or other article, two complete copies of the best edition issued must be sent, to perfect the copyright, with the address

LIBRARIAN OF CONGRESS,
WASHINGTON, D. C.

It is optional with those sending books and other articles to perfect copyright to send them by mail or express; but, in either case, the charges are to be prepaid by the senders. Without the deposit of copies above required, the copyright is void, and a penalty of $25 is incurred. No copy is required to be deposited elsewhere.

NOTICE OF COPYRIGHT TO BE GIVEN BY IMPRINT.

4. No copyright hereafter issued is valid unless notice is given by inserting in every copy published, on the title page, or the page following, if it be a book; or, if a map, chart, musical composition, print, cut, engraving, photograph, painting, drawing, chromo, statue, statuary, or model or design intended to be perfected as a work of the fine arts, by inscribing upon some portion of the face or front thereof, or on the face of the substance on which the same is mounted, the following words, viz.: *Entered according to act of Congress, in the year* ——, *by* ——, *in the office of the Librarian of Congress, at Washington.* Or thus: *Copyright,* 18——, *by A. B.*

The law imposes a penalty of $100 upon any person who has not obtained copyright who shall insert the notice "*entered according to act of Congress,*" etc., or words of the same import, in or upon any book or other article.

TRANSLATIONS, ETC.

5. Any author may reserve the right to translate or to dramatize his own work. In this case, notice should be given by printing the words, *Right of translation reserved,* or *All rights reserved,* below the notice

of copyright entry, and notifying the Librarian of Congress of such reservation, to be entered upon the record.

DURATION OF COPYRIGHT.

6. Each copyright secures the exclusive right of publishing the book or article copyrighted for the term of twenty-eight years. At the end of that time, the author or designer, or his widow or children, may secure a renewal for the further term of fourteen years, making forty-two years in all. Applications for renewal must be accompanied by explicit statement of ownership, in the case of the author, or of relationship, in the case of his heirs, and must state definitely the date and place of entry of the original copyright.

TIME OF PUBLICATION.

7. The time within which any work copyrighted may be issued from the press is not limited by any law or regulation, but depends upon the discretion of the proprietor. A copyright may be secured for a projected work as well as for a completed one.

ASSIGNMENTS.

8. Any copyright is assignable in law by any instrument of writing, but such assignment must be recorded in the office of the Librarian of Congress within sixty days from its date. The fee for this record is fifteen cents for every 100 words, and ten cents for every 100 words for a copy of the record of assignment.

COPIES, OR DUPLICATE CERTIFICATES.

9. A copy of the record (or duplicate certificate) of any copyright entry will be furnished under seal, at the rate of fifty cents each.

SERIALS OR SEPARATE PUBLICATIONS TO BE COPYRIGHTED SEPARATELY.

10. In the case of books published in more than one volume, if issued or sold separately, or of periodicals published in numbers, or of engravings, photographs, or other articles published with variations, a copyright is to be taken out for each volume of a book, or number of a periodical, or variety, as to size or inscription, of any other article.

COPYRIGHTS FOR WORKS OF ART.

11. To secure a copyright for a painting, statue, model or design intended to be perfected as a work of the fine arts, so as to prevent infringement by copying, engraving, or vending such design, a definite description must accompany the application for copyright, and a photograph of the same, at least as large as "cabinet size," must be mailed to the Librarian of Congress within ten days from the completion of the work.

FULL NAME OF PROPRIETOR REQUIRED.

12. Every applicant for a copyright must state distinctly the name and residence of the claimant, and whether the right is claimed as author, designer, or proprietor. No affidavit or formal application is required

Important Facts and Tables for Reference

Tabulated and Arranged for Writers and Speakers.

VALUE OF FOREIGN COINS IN U. S. MONEY.

Proclaimed by the Secretary of the Treasury, Jan. 1, 1881.

Country.	Monetary Unit.	Standard.	Value in U.S. Money.	Standard Coin.
Austria	Florin	Silver	.40.7.	
Belgium	Franc	Gold and silver	.19.3.	5, 10 and 20 francs
Bolivia	Boliviano	Silver	.88.3.	Boliviano
Brazil	Milreis of 1000 reis	Gold	.54.6.	
British Poss. in N. A.	Dollar	Gold	.$1.00	
Chili	Peso	Gold	.91.8.	Condor, doubloon and escudo.
Denmark	Crown	Gold	.26.8	10 and 20 crowns
Ecuador	Peso	Silver	.88.3.	Peso
Egypt	Piaster	Silver	.04.9	5, 10, 25, and 50 piasters.
France	Franc	Gold and silver	.19.3.	5, 10 and 20 francs
Great Britain	Pound Sterling	Gold	.4.86.6½	½ sovereign and sovereign.
Greece	Drachma	Gold and silver	.19.3.	5, 10, 25, 50 and 100 drachmas
German Empire	Mark	Gold	.23.8.	10 and 20 marks.
India	Rupee of 16 annas	Silver	.39.	
Italy	Lira	Gold and silver	.19.3.	5, 10, 25, 50 and 100 lire.
Japan	Yen (gold)	Gold and silver	.99.8.	5, 2, 5, 10 and 20 yen.
Liberia	Dollar	Gold	.1.00.	
Mexico	Dollar	Silver	.89.4.	Peso or dollar, 5, 10, 25 and 50
Netherlands	Florin	Gold and silver	.40.2.	[centavo
Norway	Crown	Gold	.26.8.	10 and 20 crowns
Peru	Sol	Silver	.88.3.	Sol
Portugal	Milreis of 1000 reis	Gold	.1.08.	2, 5 and 10 milreis
Russia	Rouble of 100 copecks	Silver	.66.3.	¼, ½ and 1 rouble.
Sandwich Islands	Dollar	Gold	.1.00.	
Spain	Peseta of 100 centimes	Gold and silver	.19.3.	5, 10, 20, 50 and 100 pesetas.
Sweden	Crown	Gold	.26.8.	10 and 20 crowns
Switzerland	Franc	Gold and silver	.19.3.	5, 10 and 20 francs
Tripoli	Mahbub of 20 piasters	Silver	.74.9.	
Turkey	Piaster	Gold	.04.4.	25, 50, 100, 250 and 500 piasters
U. S. of Columbia	Peso	Silver	.88.3.	Peso
Venezuela	Bolivar	Gold and silver	.19.3.	5, 10, 20, 50 and 100 Bolivar

GOVERNORS, STATE SENATORS AND REPRESENTATIVES.

Salaries and Terms of Office.*

States and Territories.	Salary of Governor.	Term of office of Governor.	Pay of Members of the Legislature.	Term of office of Senators.	Term of Representatives.	When the Legislature meets.	Limit of Session.
Alabama	$3,000.	2 years.	$4 per day	4 years	2 years	Biennially.	50 days
Arizona	2,600.					Biennially.	60.
Arkansas	3,500.					Biennially.	60.
California	6,000.					Biennially.	60.
Colorado	3,000.					Biennially.	40.
Connecticut	2,000.		300 per session			Annually.	None
Dakota	2,400.		4 per day			Biennially.	40 days
Delaware	2,000.					Biennially.	None
Florida	3,500.					Biennially.	60 days
Georgia	3,000.					Biennially.	40.
Idaho	2,000.					Biennially.	40.
Illinois	6,000.					Biennially.	None
Indiana	3,000.					Biennially.	60 days
Iowa	3,000.		550 per session			Biennially.	None
Kansas	3,000.		3 per day			Biennially.	50 days
Kentucky	5,000.					Biennially.	60 days
Louisiana	4,000.					Biennially.	60.
Maine	2,500.		150 per session			Biennially.	None
Maryland	4,500.		.5 per day			Biennially.	90 days
Massachusetts	5,000.		650 per session			Annually.	None
Michigan	1,000.		3 per day			Biennially.	60 days
Minnesota	3,000.					Biennially.	None
Mississippi	4,000.		500 per session			Biennially.	70 days
Missouri	5,000.		5 per day			Biennially.	70 days
Montana	2,600.					Biennially.	40.
Nebraska	2,500.					Biennially.	40.
Nevada	5,000.					Biennially.	60.
New Hampshire	1,000.		500 per session			Biennially.	40 days
New Mexico	2,600.					Annually.	None
New Jersey	5,000.		500 per session			Annually.	None
New York	10,000.		1500			Annually.	None
North Carolina	3,000.		4 per day			Biennially.	60 days
Ohio	4,000.					Biennially.	None
Oregon	1,500.					Biennially.	40 days
Pennsylvania	10,000.		1000 per session			Biennially.	None
Rhode Island	4,000.		1 per day			Annually.	None
South Carolina	3,500.					Annually.	None
Tennessee	4,000.					Biennially.	75 days
Texas	4,000.					Biennially.	60 days
Utah	2,000.					Biennially.	60 days
Vermont	1,000.		540 per session			Biennially.	None
Virginia	5,000.					Biennially.	40.
Washington	2,700.					Biennially.	40.
West Virginia	2,700.		4 per day			Biennially.	45.
Wisconsin	5,000.		350 per session			Annually.	None
Wyoming	2,600.		4 per day			Biennially.	40 days

*From 5 cents to 40 cents per mile is allowed representative, in some States, in going to and from the seat of government.

Annual Salaries of Principal United States Civil, Military and Naval Officers.

Legislative.

President	$50,000
Vice President	8,000
Secretary of State	8,000
Secretary of Treasury	8,000
Secretary of Interior	8,000
Secretary of Navy	8,000
Secretary of War	8,000
Postmaster General	8,000
Attorney General	8,000
Speaker House of Representatives	8,000
United States Senators	5,000
Representatives in Congress	5,000

U. S. Minister to

England	$17,500
Germany	17,500
France	17,500
Russia	17,500
China	12,000
Brazil	12,000
Spain	12,000
Japan	12,000
Mexico	12,000
Central America	10,000
Chili	10,000
Peru	10,000
Venezuela	7,500
Turkey	7,500
Sweden and Norway	7,500
Netherlands	7,500
Denmark	5,000
Greece	5,000
Uruguay	5,000
Portugal	5,000
Switzerland	5,000
Liberia	4,000

Judges.

Chief Justice U. S. Supreme Court	$10,500
Associate Judges	10,000
United States Circuit Judges	6,000
U. S. District Judges	from 3,500 to 5,000
Judge of U. S. Court of Claims	4,500

Heads of Departments.

Director of Geological Survey	$6,000
Auditor of Railroad Accounts	5,000
Superintendent of Census	5,000
Superintendent Naval Observatory	5,000
Commissioner of Patents	4,500
Director of the Mint	4,500
Commissioner of General Land Office	4,000
Superintendent Signal Service	4,000
Commissioner of Pensions	3,600
Superintendent Nautical Almanac	3,500
Commander of Marine Corps	3,500
Commissioner of Agriculture	3,000
Commissioner of Indian Affairs	3,000
Commissioner of Education	3,000

Army and Navy.

MILITARY OFFICERS.

General of the Army	$13,500
Lieutenant General	11,000
Major Generals	7,500
Brigadier Generals	5,500
Colonels	3,500
Lieutenant Colonels	3,000
Majors	2,500
Captains, Mounted	2,000
Captains, not Mounted	1,800
First Lieutenants, Mounted	1,600
First Lieutenant, not Mounted	1,500
Second Lieutenants, Mounted	1,500
Second Lieutenants, not Mounted	1,400
Chaplains	1,500

NAVAL OFFICERS.

Admirals	$13,000
Vice Admirals	9,000
Rear Admirals	6,000
Commodores	5,000
Captains	4,500
Commanders	3,500
Lieutenant Commanders	2,800
Lieutenants	2,400
Masters	1,800
Ensigns	1,200
Midshipmen	1,000

TABLES OF WEIGHTS, MEASURES, AND VARIATION OF TIME.

WEIGHTS.

Troy.

24 grains (gr.) 1 pennyw'ht,—dwt.
20 dwts .... 1 ounce,—oz.

3.2 grains, 1 carat, diamond wt.

By this weight gold, silver, and jewels only are weighed. The ounce and pound in this, are the same as in apothecaries' weight.

Apothecaries'.

20 grains .... 1 scruple.
3 scruples .... 1 drachm.
8 drs. .... 1 ounce.
12 ozs. .... 1 pound.

Avoirdupois.

16 drams (drs.) 1 ounce,—oz.
16 ozs. .... 1 pound,—lb.
25 lbs. .... 1 quarter,—qr.*
4 quarters ..... 100 weight,—cwt.
20 cwts. .... 1 ton.

* Formerly 28 lbs. were allowed to the quarter, but the practice is now nearly out of use excepting in the coal mines in Pennsylvania, the Eastern fish markets, and the U. S. Custom House.

Grains are the same in each of the above weights.

5,760 grains, apothecaries' or troy weight .... 1 lb.
7,000 grains, avoirdupois weight .... 1 lb.

Therefore, 144 lbs. avoir. equal 175 lbs. apoth. or troy.

Of Liquids.

1 gallon oil weighs 9.32 lbs. avoir.
1 gallon distilled water, 8.35 lbs.
1 gallon sea water, 10.32 lbs.
1 gallon proof spirits, 9.08 lbs.

Miscellaneous.

IRON, LEAD, ETC.

14 lbs. .... 1 stone.
21½ stones .... 1 pig.
8 pigs .... 1 fother.

BEEF, PORK, ETC.

200 lbs. .... 1 barrel.
196 lbs. (flour) .... 1 barrel.
100 lbs. (fish) .... 1 quintal.

MEASURES.

Dry.

2 pints .... 1 quart,—qt.
8 quarts .... 1 peck,—pk.
4 pecks .... 1 bushel,—bu.
36 bushels .... 1 chaldron.

1 United States standard (Winchester) bushel—18½ inches in diameter, and 8 inches deep—contains 2150.42 cubic inches.

Liquid or Wine.

4 gills .... 1 pint—pt.
2 pints .... 1 quart—qt.
4 quarts .... 1 gallon—gal.
31½ gallons ..... 1 barrel—bbl.
2 barrels .... 1 hogshead—hhd.
U. S. standard gallon .... 231 cubic inches.
Beer gallon ... 281 " "
31 " " .... 1 bbl.

Time.

60 seconds .... 1 minute.
60 minutes .... 1 hour.
24 hours .... 1 day.
7 days .... 1 week.
4 weeks .... 1 lunar month.
28, 29, 30, or 31 days } 1 calendar month.
30 days .... 1 month, (in computing interest).
52 weeks and 1 day ....
12 calendar months ... } 1 year.
365 days, 5 hours, 48 minutes, and 49 seconds ...... 1 solar year.

Circular.

60 seconds .... 1 minute.
60 minutes .... 1 degree.
30 degrees .... 1 sign.
90 degrees .... 1 quadrant.
4 quadrants ....
360 degrees .... } 1 circle.

A convenient method of finding the difference in time between two places, is to notice their distance apart in degrees of longitude, and allow 4 minutes to each degree, based on the following

CALCULATION:

1440 minutes .... 1 day, or revolution of the earth.
1 revolution of the earth is 360 degrees; therefore,
1 degree .... 4 minutes.

MEASURES.

Long.

DISTANCE.

3 barleycorns .. 1 inch,—in.
12 ins. .... 1 foot,—ft.
3 ft. .... 1 yard,—yd.
5½ yds. .... 1 rod,—rd.
40 rds .... 1 furlong,—fur.
8 fur .... 1 mile.

CLOTH.

2¼ inches .... 1 nail.
4 nails .... 1 quarter.
4 quarters .... 1 yard.

MISCELLANEOUS.

3 inches .... 1 palm.
4 inches .... 1 hand.
9 inches .... 1 span.
18 inches .... 1 cubit.
21.8 inches .... 1 Bible cubit.
2½ feet .... 1 military pace.
3 feet .... 1 common pace.

Square.

144 sq. ins. .... 1 sq. foot.
9 sq. ft. .... 1 sq. yard.
30¼ sq. yds. .... 1 sq. rod.
40 sq. rods .... 1 rood.
4 roods .... 1 acre.

Surveyors'.

7.92 inches .... 1 link.
25 links .... 1 rod.
4 rods .... 1 chain.
10 square chains.
160 square rods ... } 1 acre.
640 acres .... 1 square mile

Cubic.

1728 cubic inches. .. 1 cubic foot.
27 cubic feet .... 1 " yard.
128 cubic feet ..... 1 cord (wood.)
40 cubic feet ... 1 ton (shipping.)
2150.42 cubic in ... 1 standard bu.
268.8 " " ... 1 " gal.
1 cubic ft., four-fifths of a bushel.

To find the number of bushels in a bin of any dimensions, find the number of cubic feet by multiplying the three dimensions of the bin in feet; deduct one-fifth, and the result is the number of bushels.

PAPER.

The Sizes in Inches.

Flat Writing-Papers.

Flat Letter	10 x 16
Flat Cap	14 x 17
Double Flat Letter	16 x 20
Flat Foolscap	13 x 16
Crown	15 x 19
Folio Post	17 x 22
Demy	16 x 21
Medium	18 x 23
Check Folio	17 x 24
Back Folio	19 x 24
Double Cap	17 x 28
Royal	19 x 24
Super Royal	20 x 28
Imperial	23 x 31

Of the different sizes there are also several different weights of each size, as Demy 20, 22, 24, 26, and 28 lbs. per ream.

Stationers usually rule, cut and fold the sizes required to make the various styles of letter and note papers—a flat sheet making one, two or four sheets of letter or note paper.

Ledger Papers.

Flat Cap	14 x 17
Crown	15 x 19
Folio	17 x 22
Demy	16 x 21
Medium	18 x 23
Royal	19 x 24
Super Royal	20 x 28
Imperial	23 x 31
Elephant	23 x 28

Book Papers.

The usual sizes of these, from the different American and English manufacturers, differ but little from the above, except to fill special orders.

Paper Counts.

24 sheets .... 1 quire.
10½ quires .... 1 token.
20 quires .... 1 ream.
2 reams .... 1 bundle.
5 bundles .... 1 bale.

Units of Anything.

12 pieces .... 1 dozen.
12 dozen .... 1 gross.
12 gross .... 1 great gross.
20 units .... 1 score.

Railway Signals.

One pull of bell-cord signifies "stop."

Two pulls mean "go ahead."

Three pulls signify "back up."

One whistle signifies "down brakes."

Two whistles mean "off brakes."

Three whistles signify "back up."

Continued whistles indicate "danger."

Rapid short whistles, "a cattle alarm."

A sweeping parting of the hands, on a level with the eyes, signifies "go ahead."

A slowly sweeping meeting of the hands, over the head, means "back slowly."

Downward motion of the hands, with extended arms, signifies "stop."

Beckoning motion of one hand, indicates "back."

A red flag waved up the track, signifies "danger."

A red flag standing by the roadside, means "danger ahead."

A red flag carried on a locomotive, signifies "an engine following."

A red flag raised at a station, is a signal to "stop."

A lantern at night raised and lowered vertically, is a signal to "start."

A lantern swung at right angles across the track, means "stop."

A lantern swung in a circle, signifies "back the train."

Difference of Time between Washington and other Cities of the World.

12.00 o'clock (noon) at .... WASHINGTON.
12.12 .. " ..... P.M. .... New York.
12.24 .. " ..... " .... Boston.
12.27 .. " ..... " .... Portland.
1.37 .. " ..... " .... St. John (N. F).
3.19 .. " ..... " .... Angra (Azores).
4.31 .. " ..... " .... Lisbon.
4.43 .. " ..... " .... Dublin.
4.55 .. " ..... " .... Edinburgh.
5.07 .. " ..... " .... London.
5.17 .. " ..... " .... Paris.
5.58 .. " ..... " .... Rome.
6.02 .. " ..... " .... Berlin.
6.14 .. " ..... " .... Vienna.
6.22 .. " ..... " .... Cape Town.
7.04 .. " ..... " .... Constantinople.
11.01 .. " ..... " .... Calcutta.
12.54 .. " ..... A.M. .... Pekin.
2.48 .. " ..... " .... Melbourne.
4.51 .. " ..... " .... Auckland.
8.58 .. " ..... " .... San Francisco.
9.40 .. " ..... " .... Salt Lake.
11.08 .. " ..... " .... New Orleans.
11.18 .. " ..... " .... Chicago.
11.52 .. " ..... " .... Buffalo.
12.00 .. " .... (noon) .... Lima (Peru).

United States Land Measure.†

TOWNSHIP.

6	5	4	3	2	1
7	8	9	10	11	12
18	17	16	15	14	13
19	20	21	22	23	24
30	29	28	27	26	25
31	32	33	34	35	36

SECTION.

N. W.	N. E.
S. W.	S. E.

Each section has four quarter-sections, designated as above, each containing 160 acres.

† In Several States.

The township is six miles square, divided into 36 square miles or sections, numbered as above, each containing 640 acres.

SMALLER LAND DIVISIONS.

The following table will assist in making an estimate of the amount of land in fields and lots.

§ 10 rods x 16 rods .... 1 acre.
† 5 yards x 968 yards .... 1 "
‡ 220 feet x 198 feet .... 1 "
25 feet x 125 feet .... .0717 "
4356 sq. ft., .10 acre. 10890 sq. ft., .25 "
21780 " .50 " 32670 " .75 "

§ Or any two numbers whose product is 160.
† Or any two numbers whose product is 4,840.
‡ Or any two numbers whose product is 43,560.

Weights of a Cubic Foot.

Metals.

WEIGHT OF A CUBIC FOOT.

Substance.	Lbs.	Oz.
Platina	1,218	12
Pure Gold*	1,203	10
Mercury	848	12
Lead	709	8
Pure Silver*	655	13
Steel	487	13
Tin	455	1
Cast Iron	450	1
Copper	547	4
Brass	545	
Zinc	428	12

*The value of a ton of pure gold is $602,799.21.
†The value of a ton of silver is $37,704.84.
*$1,000,000 gold coin weigh 3,685.8 lbs. avordupois.
*$1,000,000 silver coin weigh 55,929.9 lbs. avordupois.

Earth, Stone, &c.

Substance.	Lbs.	Oz.
Italian Marble	169	4
Vermont Marble	165	9
Window Glass	165	8
Common Stone	157	3
Moist Sand	128	8
Clay	120	10
Brick	125	12
Mortar	109	6
Mud	101	14
Loose Earth	95	12
Lehigh Coal, loose	50	4
Lackawanna, loose	48	10

Liquids.

Substance.	Lbs.	Oz.
Honey	90	10
Vinegar	67	8
Blood	65	14
Beer	62	10
Milk	64	
Cider	58	3
Tar	62	7
Rain Water	62	
Linseed Oil	57	12
Brandy	57	12
Ice	57	8
Alcohol	49	10

Groceries.

WEIGHT OF A CUBIC FOOT.

Substance.	Lbs.	Oz.
Sugar	100	5
Beeswax	60	8
Lard	59	3
Butter	56	14
Tallow	56	12
Castile Soap	56	15

Miscellaneous.

Substance.	Lbs.	Oz.
India Rubber	58	7
Pressed Hay	25	
Pressed Cotton	25	

Woods.

Substance.	Lbs.	Oz.
Lignum Vitæ	83	5
Ebony	83	5
Boxwood	65	2
Mahogany	66	13
White Oak	54	13
Ash	53	13
Red Hickory	53	9
Apple	49	6
Maple	49	11
Cherry	44	8
Shellbark Hickory	43	2
Pitch Pine	41	4
Chestnut	41	8
Birch	40	7
Cedar	35	1
White Poplar	33	1
Spruce	31	4
Yellow Pine	29	8
Butternut	43	3
Cork	15	4

Difference in Weight of Wood, Green and Dry.

GREEN.

Substance.	Lbs.	Oz.
English Oak	71	10
Beech	60	
Ash	58	3
American Pine	44	12

DRY.

Substance.	Lbs.	Oz.
English Oak	48	8
Beech	53	4
Ash	35	4
American Pine	30	11

Woods for Fuel.

Taking shellbark hickory as the highest standard of our forest trees, and calling that one hundred, other trees will compare with it in real value, for fuel, as follows:

Shellbark Hickory	100
Pignut Hickory	96
White Oak	84
White Ash	77
Dogwood	75
Scrub Oak	73
White Hazel	72
Apple Tree	70
White Beech	69
Black Birch	65
Hard Maple	65
Black Walnut	62
Yellow Oak	60
White Elm	58
Red Oak	56
Red Cedar	55
Wild Cherry	55
Yellow Pine	54
Chestnut	52
Yellow Poplar	51
Butternut	43
White Birch	43
White Pine	30

Quantity Per Acre.

The following shows the average yield of different grasses and vegetables per acre.

Article.	Amount.
Barley	30 bushels
Buckwheat	25 bushels
Beans, bush.	20 bushels
Beets	10 tons
Cabbages, without stalks	20 tons
Carrots	10 tons
Corn	70 bushels
Clover hay	4 tons
Millet seed	30 bushels
Meadow hay	1¾ tons
Oats	40 bushels
Peas	20 bushels
Parsnips	10 tons
Potatoes	200 bushels
Rice	75 bushels
Rye	20 bushels
Rutabagas	10 tons
Turnips	10 tons
Wheat	30 bushels

Heat and Cold.

Degrees of heat above zero at which substances melt.

Substance.	Deg.
Wrought Iron	3,980
Cast Iron	3,479
Platinum	3,080
Gold	2,590
Copper	2,548
Steel	2,500
Glass	2,377
Brass	1,900
Silver	1,250
Antimony	951
Zinc	740
Lead	594
Tin	421
Arsenic	365
Sulphur	226
Beeswax	151
Gutta Percha	145
Tallow	97
Lard	95
Pitch	91
Ice	32

Degrees of cold above zero at which substances freeze.

Olive Oil	36
Water	32
Milk	30
Sea Water	28
Vinegar	28
Wines	20
Spirits of Turpentine	14

Degrees below zero at which the following freeze:

Brandy	7
Proof Spirit	7
Mercury	40

Cold experienced by Arctic Navigators.....70
Greatest Artific'l Cold. 220

Degrees of heat above zero at which substances boil.

Ether	98
Alcohol	173
Water	212
Petroleum	306
Linseed Oil	640
Blood Heat	98
Eggs Hatch	104

Ages of Animals.

Animal.	Yrs.
Whale, estima'd	400
Elephant	400
Swan	300
Tortoise	100
Eagle	100
Raven	100
Camel	100
Lion	70
Porpoise	30
Horse	30
Bear	20
Cow	20
Deer	20
Rhinoceros	20
Swine	20
Wolf	20
Ox	15
Fox	15
Dog	10
Sheep	10
Rabbit	8
Squirrel	7

Rates of Speed.

At which Birds Fly.

	PER HOUR.
Birds.	Miles.
Hawks	150
Sparrows	92
Ducks	90
Falcon	75
Crows	25

Fair winds make their flight much more rapid.

Interest.

Money Doubles at Compound Interest as follows:

At 3 per cent.	in 23 years.
" 4 "	17 "
" 5 "	14 "
" 6 "	12 "
" 7 "	10 "
" 8 "	9 "
" 9 "	8 "
" 10 "	7 "

TABLE OF WAGES;
COMPUTED ON A BASIS OF TEN HOURS LABOR PER DAY.

Hours.	$1.00	$1.50	$2.00	$2.50	$3.00	$3.50	$4.00	$4.50	$5.00	$5.50	$6.00	$6.50	$7.00	$7.50	$8.00	$9.00	$10	$11	$12
¼	.1	.1¼	.1¾	.2	.2¼	.3	.3⅜	.4¼	.4½	.5	.6	.6¼	.6⅞	.7½	.8	.9			
1	.3¼	.3¾	.2¼	.4½	.3	.6	.6⅜	.7¼	.8¼	.9	.10	.11	.11⅝	.12½	.13½	.15			
2	.5¼	.5	.6⅝	.8¾	.10	.11⅜	.13¼	.15	.16¼	.18½	.21⅜	.23¾	.25	.27⅝	.30	.35			
3	.5	.7¼	.10	.12½	.15	.17¼	.20	.22½	.25	.27⅛	.30	.32¼	.35	.37⅝	.40	.45			
4	.6¾	.10	.13¼	.16⅜	.20	.23⅜	.26⅜	.30	.33¼	.36½	.40	.43¼	.46½	.50	.53¼	.60			
5	.8¼	.12¾	.16⅜	.21	.25	.29¼	.33⅜	.37¼	.41⅜	.45	.50	.54¼	.58⅜	.62½	.66⅝	.75			
6	.10	.15	.20	.25	.30	.35	.40	.45	.50	.55	.60	.65	.70	.75	.80	.90			
7	.11¾	.17½	.23⅜	.29¼	.35	.41	.46⅝	.52¼	.58⅜	.64¼	.70	.76	.81⅜	.87½	.93⅜	1.05			
8	.13⅜	.20	.26⅜	.33¼	.40	.46⅝	.53¼	.60	.66⅝	.73¼	.80	.86¾	.93¼	1.00	1.06⅝	1.20			
9	.15	.22¼	.30	.37½	.45	.52¼	.60	.67¾	.75	.82½	.90	.97¼	1.05	1.12½	1.20	1.35			

Days.																			
1	.16⅝	.25	.33⅜	.41¼	.50	.58⅜	.66⅝	.75	.83⅜	.91⅜	1.00	1.08⅜	1.16⅝	1.25	1.33⅜	1.50	1.66	1.83⅜	2.00
2	.33¼	.50	.66⅝	.83¼	1.00	1.16⅝	1.33⅜	1.50	1.66⅝	1.83⅜	2.00	2.16⅝	2.33⅜	2.50	2.66⅝	3.00	3.33⅜	3.66⅝	4.00
3	.50	.75	1.00	1.25	1.50	1.75	2.00	2.25	2.50	2.75	3.00	3.25	3.50	3.75	4.00	4.50	5.00	5.50	6.00
4	.66⅝	1.00	1.33⅜	1.66⅝	2.00	2.33⅜	2.66⅝	3.00	3.33⅜	3.66⅝	4.00	4.33⅜	4.66⅝	5.00	5.33⅜	6.00	6.66⅝	7.33⅜	8.00
5	.83⅜	1.25	1.66⅝	2.08⅜	2.50	2.91⅜	3.33⅜	3.75	4.16⅝	4.58⅜	5.00	5.41⅜	5.83⅜	6.25	6.66⅝	7.50	8.33⅜	9.16⅝	10.00
6	1.00	1.50	2.00	2.50	3.00	3.50	4.00	4.50	5.00	5.50	6.00	6.50	7.00	7.50	8.00	9.00	10.00	11.00	12.00

EXPLANATION.

The large figures at the top of the columns show the rate per week, while the smaller figures indicate the amount per hour or per day. Thus if it is desired to find the amount per hour when working for $3.00 per week, we commence with the figure 1, in the left hand column under the head of "hours," and trace towards the right till we reach the column headed by $3.00, where we find 13¼ cents, the equivalent of one hour's labor at $3.00 per week. In like manner we find the price of several hours, one day, or several days.

To find wages at $13, $14, $15, $16, or more, per week, find the amount at $6.50, $7, $7.50, $8, etc., and multiply by 2.

POPULATION AND GROWTH OF THE UNITED STATES.

States and Territories.	Area in Square Miles.	No. of Inhabitants. 1870	No. of Inhabitants. 1880	No. Inhab. to Sq. Mile in 1880.*	M's R.R. in each State Jan 1, 1882
Alabama	52,250	996,992	1,262,505	24	2,495¾
Arkansas	53,850	484,471	802,525	44	709¾
California	158,360	560,247	864,694	5	3,260½
Colorado	103,925	39,864	194,327	1	2,188½
Connecticut	4,990	537,454	622,700	124	1,233¾
Delaware	2,050	125,015	146,608	71	247¾
Florida	58,680	187,748	269,493	4	813½
Georgia	59,475	1,184,109	1,542,180	25	2,888½
Illinois	56,650	2,539,891	3,077,871	54	13,575½
Indiana	36,350	1,680,637	1,978,301	54	7,578
Iowa	56,025	1,191,792	1,624,615	28	2,494½
Kansas	82,080	364,399	996,096	12	3,784½
Kentucky	40,400	1,321,011	1,648,690	40	3,270¾
Louisiana	48,720	726,915	939,946	19	1,762
Maine	33,040	626,915	648,936	19	1,301½
Maryland	12,210	780,894	934,943	76	1,746½
Massachusetts	8,315	1,457,351	1,783,085	214	3,667¾
Michigan	58,915	1,184,059	1,636,937	27	5,278¾
Minnesota	83,365	439,706	780,773	9	4,253½
Mississippi	46,810	827,922	1,131,507	24	488½
Missouri	69,415	1,721,295	2,168,380	31	5,062¾
Nebraska	76,855	123,993	452,402	5	2,859¾
Nevada	110,700	42,491	62,266		507
N. Hampshire	9,305	318,300	346,991	37	1,056¾
New Jersey	7,815	906,096	1,131,116	144	2,996¾
New York	49,170	4,382,759	5,082,871	103	10,410¾
North Carolina	52,250	1,071,361	1,399,750	26	1,710¾
Ohio	41,060	2,665,260	3,198,062	77	10,219
Oregon	96,030	90,923	174,768	1	812¾
Pennsylvania	45,215	3,521,791	4,282,891	94	11,110¾
Rhode Island	1,250	217,353	276,531	221	223¾
South Carolina	30,570	705,606	995,577	32	1,446
Tennessee	42,050	1,258,520	1,542,359	36	1,823¾
Texas	265,780	818,579	1,591,749	5	8,842
Vermont	9,565	330,551	332,286	34	965¾
Virginia	42,450	1,225,163	1,512,565	35	2,890
West Virginia	24,780	442,014	618,457	24	271¾
Wisconsin	56,040	1,054,670	1,315,497	23	5,861
TERRITORIES.					
Alaska	577,390		30,178		
Arizona	113,020	9,658	40,440		401¾
Dakota	149,100	14,181	135,177	1	55
Dist of Columb	70	131,700	177,624	2537	* *
Idaho	84,800	14,999	32,610		
Indian Territ'y	64,690		75,000	1	
Montana	146,080	20,595	39,159		
New Mexico	122,580	91,874	119,565		527¾
Utah	84,970	86,786	143,963	1	1,007¾
Washington	69,180	23,955	75,116	1	
Wyoming	97,890	9,118	20,789		472
Other lands	5,740				
	3,602,270	38,555,983	50,155,783		130,556

*In several states there is nearly one person more to the square mile than is here mentioned.

* * Included in the railroad mileage of Maryland.

Principal Countries of the World; Population, Area, Religion and Government.

Country.	Population.	Date of Census.	Area of Square Miles.	Inhabitants to Sq. Mile.	Capital.	Population.	Prevailing Religion.	Form of Government.
China (Est.), including Corea	388,631,975	1882	4,508,788	86.3	Peking	1,648,800	Buddhic	Empire
British India	254,899,516	1881	1,425,723	178.7	Calcutta	684,658	Hindoo	Empire
Russia	98,297,407	1879	8,387,816	11.7	St. Petersburg	876,575	Greek Church	Empire
United States, with Alaska	50,442,066	1880	3,602,290	14	Washington	147,307	Protestant	Republic
German Empire	45,234,061	1880	212,091	213	Berlin	1,122,360	Protestant	Monarchy
Austria-Hungary	37,786,246	1880	240,942	157	Vienna	726,105	Catholic	Monarchy
France	37,672,048	1881	204,092	184.6	Paris	2,269,023	Catholic	Republic
Japan	35,925,313	1880	148,700	241.6	Tokio	811,510	Buddhic	Empire
Great Britain and Ireland	35,262,762	1881	120,879	291	London	4,764,312	Protestant	Monarchy
Italy	28,452,639	1881	114,296	248	Rome	300,467	Catholic	Monarchy
Turkish Empire	42,213,400	1882	2,396,692	17.6	Constantinople	1,075,000	Mohammedan	Monarchy
Spain	16,625,860	1877	182,752	90	Madrid	397,690	Catholic	Monarchy
British America	4,324,810	1881	3,470,392	1.2	Ottawa	27,412	Protestant	Monarchy
Brazil	9,883,622	1872	3,287,963	3	Rio Janeiro	274,972	Catholic	Monarchy
Mexico (Estimated)	10,025,649	1881	743,948	12.1	Mexico City	238,300	Catholic	Republic
Belgium	5,519,844	1880	11,373	485	Brussels	394,940	Catholic	Monarchy
Bavaria	5,284,778	1880	29,292	180	Munich	230,023	Catholic	Monarchy
Sweden (Estimated)	4,572,245	1881	170,979	27	Stockholm	168,775	Protestant	Monarchy
Persia (Estimated)	7,653,600	1881	610,000	12.5	Teheran	200,000	Mohammedan	Monarchy
Portugal	4,160,315	1878	36,510	113.9	Lisbon	246,343	Catholic	Monarchy
Holland-Netherlands	4,114,077	1881	12,648	325.1	The Hague	123,409	Protestant	Monarchy
Colombia	3,001,323	1870	504,773	5.9	Bogota	46,000	Catholic	Republic
Switzerland	2,846,102	1880	15,992	178	Berne	44,087	Protestant	Confederation
Peru	3,049,945	1876	503,718	6	Lima	101,488	Catholic	Republic
Australasia	2,862,103	1881	3,156,841	.0	*		Protestant	Monarchy
Chili (Estimated)	2,223,434	1882	207,350	10.7	Santiago	387,081	Catholic	Republic
Bolivia	2,300,000	1880	Unknown		La Paz	78,372	Catholic	Republic
Denmark	1,969,039	1880	13,784	143	Copenhagen	273,323	Protestant	Monarchy
Wurtemberg	1,971,118	1880	7,675	256.8	Stuttgart	117,303	Protestant	Monarchy
Norway	1,925,000	1881	122,869	15	Christiania	122,036	Protestant	Monarchy
Venezuela	2,075,245	1881	439,120	4.7	Caracas	55,638	Catholic	Republic
Argentine Republic	2,540,000	1882	1,500,000	1.7	Buenos Ayres	289,925	Catholic	Republic
Greece	1,979,305	1881	25,041	79	Athens	140,000	Greek Church	Monarchy
Baden	1,570,254	1880	5,851	271.8	Karlsruhe	49,008	Catholic	Grand Duchy
Guatemala	1,252,497	1881	41,830	29	New Guatemala	55,728	Catholic	Republic
Ecuador (Estimated)	1,066,137	1875	251,322	4.3	Quito	80,000	Catholic	Republic
Hesse	936,340	1880	2,866	326.9	Darmstadt	48,153	Protestant	Grand Duchy
Liberia	1,068,000	1880	14,300	74.7	Monrovia	13,000	Protestant	Republic
Hayti (Estimated)	800,000	1880	10,204	78.2	Port au Prince	22,000	Catholic	Republic
Uruguay	438,245	1880	73,538	5.9	Montevideo	73,353	Catholic	Republic
San Salvador	554,785	1878	7,225	77	San Salvador	14,000	Catholic	Republic
Nicaragua	350,000		49,500	6.9	Managua	8,000	Catholic	Republic
Honduras	350,000		39,600	9	Tegucigalpa	12,000	Catholic	Republic
San Domingo	300,000	1880	18,045	16	San Domingo	10,000	Catholic	Republic
Paraguay	293,844	1876	91,970	3.2	Asuncion	48,000	Catholic	Republic
Costa Rica	180,000	1879	26,040	7	San Jose	2,000	Catholic	Republic
Hawaii	64,131		6,400	10	Honolulu	14,852	Protestant	Monarchy

* Australasia has seven organized colonies—New South Wales, Victoria, Queensland, South Australia, Western Australia, New Zealand and Tasmania, whose respective capitals, with the population of each city in 1881, are as follow: Sydney, 220,427; Melbourne 282,981, Brisbane, 31,109, Adelaide 38,479; Perth, 5,007, Auckland, 39,966, Hobart-Town, 19,449. There is no general seat of government in Australasia, the whole being controlled by the home government in England.

GEOGRAPHICAL, HISTORICAL, AND STATISTICAL TABLES.

Area and Population of the Earth.

The Longest Rivers of the World.

Oceans, Seas, Bays and Lakes.

Historical Facts Relating to the United States.

Highest Mountains and Cities in the World.

Principal Exports of Various Countries.

Presidents of the United States.

NAME.	Residence.	Born.	Inaug'd	Age at Inaug.	Term of Office.	Died.	Age at Death.
George Washington	Va.	1732	1789	57	8 yrs.	Dec. 14, 1799	68
John Adams	Mass.	1735	1797	62	4 "	July 4, 1826	91
Thomas Jefferson	Va.	1743	1801	58	8 "	July 4, 1826	83
James Madison	Va.	1751	1809	58	8 "	June 28, 1836	85
James Monroe	Va.	1759	1817	58	8 "	July 4, 1831	72
John Quincy Adams	Mass.	1767	1825	58	4 "	Feb. 23, 1848	80
Andrew Jackson	Tenn.	1767	1829	62	8 "	June 8, 1845	78
Martin Van Buren	N. Y.	1782	1837	55	4 "	July 24, 1862	80
William H. Harrison	Ohio	1773	1841	68	1 month	April 4, 1841	68
John Tyler	Va.	1790	1841	51	3 yrs. 11 mos.	Jan. 17, 1872	72
James K. Polk	Tenn.	1795	1845	49	4 "	June 15, 1849	54
Zachary Taylor	La.	1784	1849	65	1 y. 4 m. 5 d.	July 9, 1850	66
Millard Fillmore	N. Y.	1800	1850	50	2 y. 7 m. 26 d.	March 8, 1874	74
Franklin Pierce	N. H.	1804	1853	49	4 yrs.	Oct. 8, 1869	65
James Buchanan	Penn.	1791	1857	66	4 "	June 1, 1868	77
Abraham Lincoln	Ill.	1809	1861	52	4 y. 1 m. 10 d.	April 15, 1865	56
Andrew Johnson	Tenn.	1808	1865	57	3 y. 10 m. 20 d.	July 31, 1875	67
Ulysses S. Grant	Ill.	1822	1869	47	8 yrs.		
Rutherford B. Hayes	Ohio	1822	1877	55	4 "		
James A. Garfield	Ohio	1831	1881	50	6 mo. 15 dys.	Sept. 19, 1881	50
Chester A. Arthur	N. Y.	1830	1881	51			

* Abraham Lincoln died from the effects of a pistol shot, fired by John Wilkes Booth, at Ford's theater, Washington, on the evening of April 14, 1865. He lived ten hours, and died the next morning.
† President Garfield was shot by Charles J. Guiteau, at Washington, July 2, 1881, and died at Long Branch, N. J., Sept. 19, 1881. For this crime, Guiteau was hung at Washington, D. C., June 30, 1882.

Height of Monuments, Towers, Etc.

NAME.	PLACE.	FEET.
Cathedral of Cologne	Germany	500
Pyramid of Cheops	Egypt	543
Cathedral of St. Stephen	Vienna, Austria	470
Cathedral at Strasburg	Germany	468
Pyramid of Cephrenes	Egypt	456
Nicolai Church	Hamburg	455
St. Peter's Church at Rome	Italy	448
St. Michael's Church	Hamburg, Germany	426
St. Martin's Church	Landshut, Germany	411
Cathedral at Antwerp	Belgium	404
Cathedral at Cremona	Lombardy	396
Cathedral at Florence	Italy	387
Church at Fribourg	Germany	385
St. Paul's Church	London, Eng.	365
Cathedral of Seville	Spain	360
Cathedral of Utrecht	Holland	356
Cathedral of Milan	Lombardy	355
Cathedral of Notre Dame	Munich, Bavaria	348
Church of St. Mark	Venice, Italy	323
Asinelli Tower	Bologna, Italy	314
Trinity Church	New York, N. Y.	284
Town Hall at Berlin	Germany	274
Column at Delhi	India	262
Porcelain Tower at Nankin	China	260
Church of Notre Dame	Paris, France	224
Bunker Hill Monument	Boston, Mass.	221
Leaning Tower of Pisa	Italy	179
Washington Monument	Baltimore, Md.	175

Capacity of Large Rooms.

Estimating a person to occupy an area of 19.9 inches square.

CHURCHES:	Will Contain No. Persons.
St. Peter's, Rome	54,000
Cathedral, Milan	37,000
St. Paul's, Rome	32,000
St. Paul's, London	25,600
St. Petronio, Bologna	24,400
Cathedral, Florence	24,300
Cathedral, Antwerp	24,000
St. Sophia, Constantinople	23,000
St. John's, Lateran	22,900
Notre Dame, Paris	21,000
Cathedral, Pisa	13,000
St. Stephen's, Vienna	12,400
St. Dominic's, Bologna	12,000
St. Peter's, Bologna	11,400
Cathedral, Vienna	11,000
St. Mark's, Venice	7,000

Opera-Houses and Theaters.	
Barnum's Hippodrome, New York	8,488
Stadt Theater, New York	3,000
Academy of Music, Philadelphia	2,865
Carlo Felice, Genoa	2,560
Acad. of Music, Brooklyn	
Opera-House, Munich	2,307
Alexander, St. Petersburg	2,332
San Carlos, Naples	2,240
Adelphi Theater, Chicago	2,258
Imperial, St. Petersburg	2,160
La Scala, Milan	2,113
Academy of Paris, Paris	2,092
Covent Garden, London	2,684
Academy of Music, N. Y.	2,526
Boston Theater, Boston	2,972
Music Hall, Boston	2,585
Grand Opera-Hall, New Orleans	2,052
St. Charles Theater, New Orleans	2,178

Grand Opera-House, N. Y.	1,883
Booth's Theater, N. York	1,807
Opera-House, Detroit	1,790
McVicker's Theater, Chicago	1,786
Grand Opera-House, Chicago	1,786
Ford's Opera-House, Baltimore	2,001
National Theater, Washington	1,500
De Bar's Opera-House, St. Louis	1,696
California Theater, San Francisco	1,651
Euclid Ave. Opera-House, Cleveland	1,650
Opera-House, Berlin	1,636
Opera-House, Albany	1,404
Hooley's Theater, Chicago	1,374
Conter Opera-House, Aurora, Ill.	1,004
Opera-House, Montreal	928

Periods of Digestion.

Substance.	Hrs. Min.
Rice, boiled	1
Eggs, whipped, raw	1 30
Trout, fresh, fried	1 30
Soup, barley, boiled	1 30
Apples, sweet, mellow, raw	1 30
Venison steak, broiled	1 35
Sago, boiled	1 45
Tapioca, boiled	2
Barley, boiled	2
Milk, boiled	2
Liver, beef, fresh, broiled	2
Eggs, fresh, raw	2
Apples, sour, mellow, raw	2
Cabbage, with vinegar, raw	2
Milk, raw	2 15
Eggs, fresh, roasted	2 15
Turkey, domestic, roasted	2 30
Goose, wild, roasted	2 30

Periods of Digestion (cont.)

Substance.	Hrs. Min.
Cake, sponge, baked	2 30
Hash, warmed	2 30
Beans, pod, boiled	2 30
Parsnips, boiled	2 30
Potatoes, Irish, baked	2 30
Cabbage, head, raw	2 30
Custard, baked	2 45
Apples, sour, hard, raw	2 50
Oysters, fresh, raw	2 55
Eggs, fresh, soft boiled	3
Beefsteak, broiled	3
Mutton, fresh, broiled	3
Soup, bean, boiled	3
Chicken soup, boiled	3
Dumpling, apple, boiled	3
Oysters, fresh, roasted	3 15
Pork, salted, broiled	3 15
Parsnips, broiled	3 15
Mutton, fresh, roasted	3 15
Bread, corn, baked	3 15
Carrot, orange, boiled	3 15
Sausage, fresh, broiled	3 20
Oysters, fresh, stewed	3 30
Butter, melted	3 30
Cheese, old, raw	3 30
Oyster soup, boiled	3 30
Bread, wheat, fresh, baked	3 30
Turnips, flat, boiled	3 30
Potatoes, Irish, boiled	3 30
Eggs, fresh, hard boiled	3 30
Eggs, fresh, fried	3 30
Green corn & beans, boiled	3 45
Beets, boiled	3 45
Salmon, salted, boiled	4
Beef, fried	4
Veal, fresh, broiled	4
Fowls, domestic, boiled	4
Beef, old, salted, boiled	4 15
Pork, salted, fried	4 15
Veal, fresh, fried	4 30
Cabbage, boiled	4 30
Pork, roasted	5 15
Suet, beef, boiled	5 30

Capacity of a Freight Car.

A load, nominally, is 20,000 pounds. The following number can be carried:

Whisky	60 barrels.
Salt	70 "
Lime	70 "
Flour	90 "
Eggs	180 to 160 sacks.
Flour	200 sacks.
Wood	6 cords.
Cattle	18 to 20 head.
Hogs	50 to 80 "
Sheep	80 to 100 "
Lumber	6,000 feet.
Barley	300 bushels.
Wheat	340 "
Flax Seed	360 "
Apples	370 "
Corn	400 "
Potatoes	430 "
Oats	680 "
Bran	1,000 "
Butter	20,000 pounds.

Capacity here based on estimates made of two hundred empty cars. Freight cars of this size vary.

Quantity of Seed to Plant.

Asparagus Roots.—1,000 plants to the 4 x 10 feet.

Beans—1 qt. plants 150 ft. of row.
Beets—1 oz. plants 150 ft. of row.
Cabbage—1 oz. gives 3,000 plants.
Celery—1 oz. gives 7,000 plants.
Cucumber—1 oz. for 50 hills.
Lettuce—1 oz. gives 7,000 plants.
Melon—1 oz. for 120 hills.
Onion—Four pounds to the acre.
Radish—1 oz. to 150 ft. of ground.
Spinage—1 oz. to 250 ft. of row.
Squash—1 oz. to 75 hills.
Tomato—1 oz. gives 3,500 plants.
Turnip—1½ pound to the acre.

CHRONOLOGY OF IMPORTANT EVENTS.

Before Christ.

The Deluge	2348
Babylon Built	2247
Birth of Abraham	1996
Death of Joseph	1635
Moses born	1571
Athens founded	1556
The Pyramids built	1250
Solomon's Temple finished	1004
Rome founded	753
Jerusalem destroyed	587
Babylon taken by Jews	538
Death of Socrates	400
Rome taken by the Gauls	385
Paper invented in China	170
Carthage destroyed	148
Cæsar landed in Britain	55
Cæsar killed	44
Birth of Christ	0

After Christ.

Death of Augustus	14
Pilate, governor of Judea	27
Jesus Christ crucified	33
Claudius visited Britain	43
St. Paul put to death	67

Death of Josephus	93
Jerusalem rebuilt	131
The Romans destroyed 580,000 Jews and banished the rest from Judea	135
The Bible in Gothic	373
Horseshoes made of iron	481
Latin tongue ceased to be spoken	580
Pens made of quills	635
Organs used	660
Glass in England	664
Bank of Venice established	1157
Glass windows first used for lights	1180
Mariner's compass used	1200
Coal dug for fuel	1234
Chimneys first put to houses	1236
Spectacles invented by an Italian	1240
The first English House of Commons	1258
Tallow candles for lights	1290
Paper made from linen	1302
Gunpowder invented	1340
Woolen cloth made in England	1341
Printing invented	1436
The first almanac	1470
America discovered	1492
First book printed in England	1507

After Christ.

Luther began to preach	1517
Interest fixed at ten per cent. in England	1547
Telescopes invented	1549
First coach made in England	1564
Clocks first made in England	1568
Bank of England incorporated	1594
Shakespeare died	1616
Circulation of the blood discovered	1619
Barometer invented	1626
First newspaper	1630
Death of Galileo	1642
Steam engine invented	1649
Great fire in London	1666
Cotton planted in the United States	1759
Commencement of the American war	1775
Declaration of American independence	1776
Recognition of American independence	1783
Bank of England suspended cash paym'ts	1797
Napoleon I. crowned emperor	1804
Death of Napoleon	1821
Telegraph invented by Morse	1832
First daguerreotype in France	1839
Beginning of the American civil war	1861
End of the American civil war	1865
Great fire in Chicago	1871

POPULATION OF CITIES OF THE UNITED STATES,

Having 10,000 inhabitants and over, by the census of 1880, accompanied by a statement of the public debt of each city, to which is added a table showing the debt per person of each man, woman and child of each city.

Name of City.	Population 1880.	Debt 1880.	Debt per each Person.	Name of City.	Population 1880.	Debt 1880.	Debt per each Person.	Name of City.	Population 1880.	Debt 1880.	Debt per each Person.
Akron, Ohio	16,512	$17,619	$1.06	Grand Rapids, Mich	32,015	$471,000	$14.71	Newport, R. I	15,693	$116,693	$7.44
Albany, N. Y	90,903	3,158,500	34.36	Galveston, Tex	22,253	1,025,949	45.97	New Britain, Conn	13,978	456,063	38.49
Alleghany, Pa	78,681	1,506,429	20.29	Gloucester, Mass	19,329	193,270	10.90	Norwalk, Conn	15,956	572,695	37.62
Allentown, Pa	18,063	450,643	23.53	Galesburg, Ill	11,446	55,356	4.65	New Lots, N. Y	13,681	.....	.....
Alexandria, Va	13,658	1,037,088	75.92	Hempstead, N. Y	18,160	.....	.....	Nashua, N. H	13,397	656,961	36.23
Altoona, Pa	19,714	368,896	18.70	Hartford, Conn	62,553	3,689,555	58.71	Norristown, Pa	13,064	81,900	6.22
Amsterdam, N. Y	11,711	.....	.....	Hoboken, N. J	30,999	1,009,250	35.46	Northampton, Mass	12,176	827,500	64.15
Atchison, Kan	15,106	449,687	29.76	Harrisburg, Pa	30,762	1,065,300	34.62	New London, Conn	10,529	499,511	47.14
Atlanta, Ga	34,398	2,150,000	63.58	Holyoke, Mass	21,951	878,454	40.02	North Adams, Mass	10,192	287,594	28.20
Attleborough, Mass	11,111	16,600	1.49	Houston, Tex	18,646	1,501,561	80.53	Nashville, Tenn	43,461	1,008,500	26.95
Auburn, N. Y	21,924	530,000	23.12	Haverhill, Mass	18,475	365,488	21.97				
Augusta, Ga	22,025	1,961,319	85.18	Hyde Park, Ill	15,716	.....	.....	Oakland, Cal	34,556	609,195	13.55
Aurora, Ill	11,855	25,506	2.16	Hamilton, Ohio	12,122	48,047	3.96	Omaha, Neb	30,518	227,575	7.45
Austin, Tex	10,960	106,744	9.74	Hannibal, Mo	11,074	144,087	13.00	Oswego, N. Y	21,117	1,864,295	86.96
								Oshkosh, Wis	15,749	199,500	5.55
Baltimore, Md	332,190	27,008,600	81.56	Indianapolis, Ind	75,076	1,916,500	25.50	Orange, N. J	13,906	265,852	19.59
Bangor, Maine	16,887	2,561,000	158.13					Oyster Bay, N. Y	11,923	.....	.....
Bay City, Mich	20,695	655,100	20.93	Jersey City, N. J	120,722	15,598,435	129.16	Ogdensburg, N. Y	10,346	135,000	13.00
Belleville, Ill	10,683	217,719	20.38	Johnstown, N. Y	16,268	.....	.....				
Biddeford Maine	12,652	183,874	14.53	Joliet, Ill	16,165	54,000	3.34	Pittsburgh, Pa	156,381	14,136,896	90.37
Binghamton, N. Y	17,315	299,500	17.29	Jackson, Mich	16,105	183,500	11.50	Providence, R. I	104,850	.....	.....
Bloomington, Ill	17,184	521,463	30.35	Jacksonville, Ill	10,927	273,356	25.10	Paterson, N. J	50,887	1,250,909	24.71
Boston, Mass	362,535	28,244,017	77.90	Jeffersonville, Ind	10,492	240,350	23.06	Portland, Maine	33,810	4,338,154	128.13
Bridgeport, Conn	29,148	831,000	28.51	Jamaica, N. Y	10,089	.....	.....	Peoria, Ill	29,315	718,500	24.46
Brockton, Mass	13,606	71,300	5.25					Petersburg, Va	21,656	1,126,100	34.46
Brooklyn, N. Y	566,663	38,060,000	67.15	Kansas City, Mo	55,813	1,359,394	23.99	Poughkeepsie, N. Y	20,207	1,359,196	35.46
Buffalo, N. Y	155,137	3,211,994	56.92	Kingston, N. Y	18,342	644,880	35.15	Pawtucket, R. I	19,030	925,009	49.13
Burlington, Vt	11,364	383,487	33.74	Keokuk, Iowa	12,117	378,375	30.73	Pittsfield, Mass	13,367	325,341	24.32
Burlington, Iowa	19,450	132,092	6.56	Kalamazoo, Mich	11,937	25,900	2.09	Pottsville, Pa	13,253	.....	.....
Brookhaven, N. Y	11,544	.....	.....					Portsmouth, Va	11,388	252,814	24.35
				Louisville, Ky	123,645	8,548,355	39.10	Portsmouth, Ohio	11,314	317,000	28.00
Cambridge, Mass	52,740	3,403,723	64.55	Lowell, Mass	59,485	1,554,275	26.12	Philadelphia, Pa	846,984	16,353,896	19.16
Camden, N. J	41,656	1,164,300	27.96	Lawrence, Mass	39,197	1,712,000	43.68				
Canton, Ohio	12,956	180,657	14.72	Lynn, Mass	38,284	2,079,815	54.14	Quincy, Ill	27,275	1,917,888	70.31
Castleton, N. Y	12,679	.....	.....	Lancaster, Pa	25,769	464,148	18.01	Quincy, Mass	10,592	105,200	9.93
Cedar Rapids, Iowa	10,104	40,878	4.04	Lewiston, Maine	19,083	1,058,102	54.30				
Charleston, S. C	49,990	4,129,105	82.58	Long Island City, N. Y	17,117	900,000	55.50	Rochester, N. Y	89,363	3,701,896	42.30
Chattanooga, Tenn	12,892	71,546	5.55	Lexington, Ky	16,656	84,315	5.06	Richmond, Va	63,503	4,000,031	65.92
Chelsea, Mass	21,785	1,584,446	71.20	Leavenworth, Kan	16,550	366,913	22.56	Reading, Pa	43,290	959,300	22.16
Chester, Pa	14,996	357,064	23.81	Lynchburg, Va	15,959	794,827	49.80	Racine, Wis	16,031	213,532	13.42
Chicago, Ill	503,304	12,794,871	25.42	Lafayette, Ind	14,860	None	.....	Rockford, Ill	13,136	175,000	13.35
Cincinnati, Ohio	255,708	21,992,500	86.00	Leadville, Col	14,820	.....	.....	Richmond, Ind	12,763	167,000	13.30
Cleveland, Ohio	160,142	4,076,946	25.45	La Crosse, Wis	14,505	135,000	9.26	Rutland, Vt	12,149	182,400	15.06
Columbia, S. C	10,566	.....	.....	Lincoln, N. J	13,765	50,000	3.63	Rome, N. Y	12,045	160,000	13.29
Columbus, Ohio	51,566	1,969,182	84.37	Lockport, N. Y	13,529	106,867	8.03	Rock Island, Ill	11,609	329,609	28.73
Covington, Ky	29,720	1,050,000	34.66	Little Rock, Ark	13,185	335,943	25.48				
Cohoes, N. Y	19,417	141,214	7.27	Lincoln, Neb	13,004	199,615	15.35	St. Louis, Mo	350,522	22,561,761	65.13
Council Bluffs, Iowa	18,050	138,600	7.64	Los Angeles, Cal	11,311	310,177	27.42	San Francisco, Cal	229,956	3,059,285	13.12
Concord, N. H	13,832	615,500	44.46	Logansport, Ind	11,196	656,376	40.77	Syracuse, N. Y	51,791	1,551,500	26.00
Cortland, N. Y	12,664	.....	.....	Lennox, N. Y	10,969	.....	.....	Scranton, Pa	45,850	325,896	7.09
Chickopee, Mass	11,325	109,000	8.83					St. Paul, Minn	41,090	3,055,715	36.76
Chillicothe, Ohio	10,928	None	.....	Milwaukee, Wis	115,578	2,160,529	18.69	Springfield, Mass	33,340	1,929,600	57.32
				Minneapolis, Minn	46,887	1,137,667	24.95	St. Joseph, Mo	32,484	2,445,520	75.74
Detroit, Mich	116,342	1,288,778	11.02	Memphis, Tenn	33,569	None	.....	Savannah, Ga	30,681	3,625,000	111.63
Dayton, Ohio	38,677	1,101,580	29.45	Manchester, N. H	32,630	929,600	29.19	Salem, Mass	27,566	1,162,487	42.66
Denver, Col	35,630	20,000	.56	Mobile, Ala	31,205	8,671,100	85.91	Somerville, Mass	24,955	1,806,574	52.56
Des Moines, Iowa	22,408	578,000	25.79	Meriden, Conn	18,340	788,317	42.98	Sacramento, Cal	21,489	901,600	40.19
Dubuque, Iowa	22,254	804,611	36.15	Montgomery, Ala	16,714	847,900	33.91	Salt Lake City, Utah	20,765	47,000	2.32
Dover, N H	11,687	456,830	39.95	Macon, Ga	12,748	743,000	58.25	Springfield, Ohio	20,799	55,607	1.66
Danbury, Conn	11,669	255,415	21.88	Malden, Mass	12,017	483,562	40.53	San Antonio, Tex	20,561	120,209	7.15
Derby, Conn	11,649	80,943	6.86	Middletown, Conn	11,731	.....	.....	Springfield, Ill	19,749	778,720	39.40
Dallas, Tex	10,358	304,356	29.36	Muskegon, Mich	11,868	180,000	15.96	Sandusky, Ohio	15,838	321,215	21.41
Davenport, Iowa	21,834	290,675	13.31	Madison, Wis	10,325	136,768	13.54	Schenectady, N. Y	13,675	116,690	8.53
				Marlborough, Mass	10,186	151,961	15.00	South Bend, Ind	13,279	337,889	25.30
Evansville, Ind	29,280	None	.....					San Jose, Cal	12,567	None	.....
Elizabeth, N. J	28,229	5,512,638	195.55	Newburyport, Mass	13,537	422,706	31.66	Steubenville, Ohio	12,093	30,190	2.61
Erie, Pa	27,730	1,201,329	43.71	New York, N. Y	1,206,540	109,495,516	90.99	Stamford, Conn	11,298	160,000	14.30
Elmira, N Y	20,541	470,400	13.17	New Orleans, La	216,140	.....	.....	Shreveport, La	11,917	.....	.....
East Saginaw, Mich	19,016	611,055	32.13	Newark, N. J	136,400	9,070,022	56.41	Saratoga Springs, N. Y	10,822	997,000	27.30
Easton, Pa	11,924	219,949	18.45	New Haven, Conn	62,882	1,310,619	21.02	Saugerties, N. Y	10,275	.....	.....
Eau Claire, Wis	10,118	101,000	9.98	New Bedford, Mass	26,875	1,046,000	40.57	Saginaw, Mich	10,525	202,205	19.50
				Norfolk, Va	21,966	2,187,571	99.57	Stockton, Cal	10,267	365,615	37.00
Fall River, Mass	48,906	3,169,765	64.68	Norwich, Conn	21,141	1,191,956	56.34	Shenandoah, Pa	10,166	.....	.....
Fort Wayne, Ind	26,880	856,900	31.87	Newport, Ky	20,433	966,618	46.61				
Flushing, N. Y	15,919	.....	.....	Newburgh, N. Y	18,050	313,400	17.36	Troy, N. Y	56,747	984,048	16.33
Fond du Lac, Wis	13,091	165,000	12.60	New Brunswick, N J	17,167	1,616,945	94.30	Toledo, Ohio	50,143	2,232,000	44.46
Fitchburg, Mass	12,606	770,788	62.11	Newton, Mass	16,995	993,591	58.46	Trenton, N. J	29,910	1,664,501	54.70
Fishkill, N. Y	10,732	.....	.....	New Albany, Ind	16,423	355,462	21.62	Terre Haute, Ind	26,840	367,724	14.45
								Taunton, Mass	21,213	409,770	21.19
Georgetown, D. C	12,578	.....	.....					Topeka, Kan	15,451	333,349	21.30

Presidents of the United States.

Name.	Residence.	Born.	Installed into Office.	Age at that time.	Term of Office.	Died.	Age at Death.
George Washington	Va.	1732	1789	57	8 yrs.	Dec. 14, 1799	68
John Adams	Mass.	1735	1797	62	"	July 4, 1826	91
Thomas Jefferson	Va.	1743	1801	58	"	July 4, 1826	83
James Madison	Va.	1751	1809	58	"	June 28, 1836	85
James Monroe	Va.	1758	1817	58	"	July 4, 1831	73
John Quincy Adams	Mass.	1767	1825	58	"	Feb. 23, 1848	80
Andrew Jackson	Tenn.	1767	1829	62	"	June 8, 1845	78
Martin Van Buren	N. Y.	1782	1837	55	"	July 24, 1862	80
William H. Harrison	Ohio	1773	1841	68	1 month	April 4, 1841	68
John Tyler	Va.	1790	1841	51	3 yrs. 11 mos.	Jan. 17, 1871	71
James K. Polk	Tenn.	1795	1845	49	4 "	June 15, 1849	54
Zachary Taylor	La.	1784	1849	65	1 y. 4 m. 5 d.	July 9, 1850	66
Millard Fillmore	N. Y.	1800	1850	50	2 y. 7 m. 26 d.	March 8, 1874	74
Franklin Pierce	N. H.	1804	1853	49	4 yrs.	Oct. 8, 1869	65
James Buchanan	Penn.	1791	1857	65	"	June 1, 1868	77
Abraham Lincoln	Ill.	1809	1861	52	1 y. 1 m. 10 d.	April 15, 1865	56
Andrew Johnson	Tenn.	1808	1865	57	3 y. 10 m. 20 d.	July 31, 1875	67
Ulysses S. Grant	Ill.	1822	1869	47	8 yrs.		
Rutherford B. Hayes	Ohio	1822	1877	55	"		
James A. Garfield	Ohio	1831	1881	50	6 ms. 15 dys.	Sept. 19, 1881	50
Chester A. Arthur	N. Y.	1830	1881	51			

* Abraham Lincoln died from the effects of a pistol shot, fired by John Wilkes Booth, at Ford's theater, Washington, on the evening of April 14, 1865. He lived ten hours, and died the next morning.

† President Garfield was shot by Charles J. Guiteau, at Washington, July 2, 1881, and died at Long Branch, N. J., Sept. 19, 1881. For this crime, Guiteau was hung at Washington, D. C., June 30, 1882.

Height of Monuments, Towers, Etc.

Name.	Place.	Feet.
Cathedral of Cologne	Germany	533
Pyramid of Cheops	Egypt	543
Cathedral of St. Stephen	Vienna, Austria	470
Cathedral at Strasburg	Germany	468
Pyramid of Cephrenes	Egypt	456
Nicolai Church	Hamburg	450
St. Peter's Church at Rome	Italy	448
St. Michael's Church	Hamburg, Germany	426
St. Martin's Church	Landshut, Germany	411
Cathedral at Antwerp	Belgium	401
Cathedral at Cremona	Lombardy	396
Cathedral at Florence	Italy	387
Church at Friburg	Germany	386
St. Paul's Church	London, Eng.	365
Cathedral of Seville	Spain	360
Cathedral of Utrecht	Holland	356
Cathedral of Milan	Lombardy	355
Cathedral of Notre Dame	Munich, Bavaria	333
Church of St. Mark	Venice, Italy	323
Asinelli Tower	Bologna, Italy	314
Trinity Church	New York, N. Y.	284
Town Hall at Berlin	Germany	274
Column at Delhi	India	262
Porcelain Tower at Nankin	China	200
Church of Notre Dame	Paris, France	204
Bunker Hill Monument	Boston, Mass.	221
Leaning Tower of Pisa	Italy	179
Washington Monument	Baltimore, Md.	176

Capacity of Large Rooms.

Estimating a person to occupy an area of 19.9 inches square.

CHURCHES.	Will Contain No. Persons.
St. Peter's, Rome	54,000
Cathedral, Milan	37,000
St. Paul's, Rome	32,000
St. Paul's, London	25,600
St. Petronio, Bologna	24,400
Cathedral, Florence	24,300
Cathedral, Antwerp	24,000
St. Sophia's, Constantinople	23,000
St. John's, Lateran	22,900
Notre Dame, Paris	21,000
Cathedral, Pisa	13,000
St. Stephen's, Vienna	12,400
St. Dominic's, Bologna	12,000
St. Peter's, Bologna	11,400
Cathedral, Vienna	11,000
St. Mark's, Venice	7,000

Opera-Houses and Theaters.	
Barnum's Hippodrome, New York	9,453
Stadt Theater, New York	5,000
Academy of Music, Philadelphia	3,865
Carlo Felice, Genoa	2,560
Acad. of Music, Brooklyn	
Opera-House, Munich	2,307
Alexander St. Petersburg	2,332
San Carlos, Naples	2,240
Adelphi Theater, Chicago	2,235
Imperial, St. Petersburg	2,160
La Scala, Milan	2,113
Academy of Paris, Paris	2,092
Covent Garden, London	2,684
Academy of Music, N. Y.	2,526
Boston Theater, Boston	2,972
Music Hall, Boston	2,565
Grand Opera-Hall, New Orleans	2,052
St. Charles Theater, New Orleans	2,178

Grand Opera-House, N. Y.	1,883
Booth's Theater, N. York	1,807
Opera-House, Detroit	1,790
McVicker's Theater, Chicago	1,786
Grand Opera-House, Chicago	1,786
Ford's Opera-House, Baltimore	2,001
National Theater, Washington	1,500
De Bar's Opera-House, St. Louis	1,896
California Theater, San Francisco	1,651
Euclid Ave. Opera-House, Cleveland	1,650
Opera-House, Berlin	1,636
Opera-House, Albany	1,404
Hooley's Theater, Chicago	1,378
Comillet Opera-House, Aurora, Ill.	1,004
Opera-House, Montreal	928

Periods of Digestion.

Substance.	Hrs. Min.
Rice, boiled	1 00
Eggs, whipped, raw	1 30
Trout, fresh, fried	1 30
Soup, Barley, boiled	1 30
Apples, sweet, mellow, raw	1 30
Venison steak, broiled	1 35
Sago, boiled	1 45
Tapioca, boiled	2 00
Barley, boiled	2 00
Milk, boiled	2 00
Liver, beef, fresh, broiled	2 00
Eggs, fresh, raw	2 00
Apples, sour, mellow, raw	2 00
Cabbage, with vinegar, raw	2 00
Milk, raw	2 15
Eggs, fresh, roasted	2 15
Turkey, domestic, roasted	2 30
Goose, wild, roasted	2 30

Substance.	Hrs. Min.
Cake, sponge, baked	2 30
Hash, warmed	2 30
Beans, pod, boiled	2 30
Parsnips, boiled	2 30
Potatoes, Irish, baked	2 30
Cabbage, head, raw	2 30
Custard, baked	2 45
Apples, sour, hard, raw	2 50
Oysters, fresh, raw	2 55
Eggs, fresh, soft boiled	3 00
Beefsteak, broiled	3 00
Mutton, fresh, broiled	3 00
Mutton, fresh, boiled	3 00
Soup, bean, boiled	3 00
Chicken soup, boiled	3 00
Dumpling, apple, boiled	3 00
Oysters, fresh, roasted	3 15
Pork, salted, broiled	3 15
Porksteak, broiled	3 15
Mutton, fresh, roasted	3 15
Bread, corn, baked	3 15
Carrot, orange, boiled	3 15
Sausage, fresh, broiled	3 20
Oysters, fresh, stewed	3 30
Butter, melted	3 30
Cheese, old, raw	3 30
Oyster soup, boiled	3 30
Bread, wheat, fresh, baked	3 30
Turnips, flat, boiled	3 30
Potatoes, Irish, boiled	3 30
Eggs, fresh, hard boiled	3 30
Beans, fresh, boiled	3 30
Green corn & beans, boiled	3 45
Beets, boiled	3 45
Salmon, salted, boiled	4 00
Beef, fried	4 00
Bread, brown	4 00
Fowls, domestic, boiled	4 00
Beef, old, salted, boiled	4 15
Veal, fresh, broiled	4 00
Pork, salted, boiled	4 30
Veal, fresh, fried	4 30
Cabbage, boiled	4 30
Pork, roasted	5 15
Suet, beef, boiled	5 30

Capacity of a Freight Car.*

A load, nominally, is 20,000 pounds. The following number can be carried.

Whisky	60 barrels.
Salt	70 "
Lime	70 "
Flour	90 "
Eggs	180 to 160 "
Flour	200 sacks.
Wood	6 cords.
Cattle	18 to 20 head.
Hogs	50 to 60 "
Sheep	80 to 100 "
Lumber	6,000 feet.
Barley	300 bushels.
Wheat	340 "
Flax Seed	360 "
Apples	370 "
Corn	400 "
Potatoes	430 "
Oats	680 "
Bran	1,000 "
Butter	20,000 pounds.

*The table is for 18-ton cars. Freight cars of larger capacity have been made of late.

Quantity of Seed to Plant.

Asparagus Roots	1,000 plants to bed 4 x 225 feet.
Beans	1 qt. plants 150 ft. of row.
Beets	1 oz. plants 150 ft. of row.
Cabbage	1 oz. gives 2,000 plants.
Celery	1 oz. gives 7,000 plants.
Cucumber	1 oz. for 150 hills.
Lettuce	1 oz. gives 7,000 plants.
Melon	1 oz. for 120 hills.
Onion	Four pounds to the acre.
Radish	1 oz. to 100 ft. of ground.
Spinage	1 oz. to 250 ft. of row.
Squash	1 oz. to 75 hills.
Tomato	1 oz. gives 2,500 plants.
Turnip	1½ pound to the acre.

CHRONOLOGY OF IMPORTANT EVENTS.

Before Christ.

The Deluge	2848
Babylon built	2247
Birth of Abraham	1996
Death of Joseph	1635
Moses born	1571
Athens founded	1556
The Pyramids built	1250
Solomon's Temple finished	1004
Rome founded	753
Jerusalem destroyed	587
Babylon taken by Jews	538
Death of Socrates	400
Rome taken by the Gauls	385
Paper invented in China	170
Carthage destroyed	146
Caesar landed in Britain	55
Caesar killed	44
Birth of Christ	0

After Christ.

Death of Augustus	14
Pilate, governor of Judea	27
Jesus Christ crucified	33
Claudius visited Britain	43
St. Paul put to death	67

After Christ.

Death of Josephus	96
Jerusalem rebuilt	131
The Romans destroyed 580,000 Jews and banished the rest from Judea	135
The Bible in Gothic	373
Horseshoes made of iron	481
Latin tongue ceased to be spoken	580
Pens made of quills	635
Organs used	660
Glass in England	687
Bank of Venice established	1157
Glass windows first used for lights	1180
Mariner's compass used	1200
Coal dug for fuel	1234
Chimneys first put to houses	1236
Spectacles invented by an Italian	1240
The first English House of Commons	1258
Tallow candles for lights	1290
Paper made from linen	1302
Gunpowder invented	1340
Woolen cloth made in England	1341
Printing invented	1436
The first almanac	1470
America discovered	1492
First book printed in England	1507

After Christ.

Luther began to preach	1517
Interest fixed at ten per cent. in England	1547
Telescopes invented	1549
First coach made in England	1564
Clocks first made in England	1568
Bank of England incorporated	1594
Shakespeare died	1616
Circulation of the blood discovered	1619
Barometer invented	1626
First newspaper	1629
Death of Galileo	1642
Steam engine invented	1649
Great fire in London	1666
Cotton planted in the United States	1759
Commencement of the American war	1775
Declaration of American Independence	1776
Recognition of American Independence	1783
Bank of England suspended cash paym't	1797
Napoleon I. crowned emperor	1804
Death of Napoleon	1821
Telegraph invented by Morse	1832
First daguerreotype in France	1839
Beginning of the American civil war	1861
End of the American civil war	1865
Great fire in Chicago	1871

19

GOLD AND SILVER PRODUCTION AND AMOUNT OF MONEY IN CIRCULATION.

From reports by the Director of the United States mint. Condensed from Financial Tables in the "American Almanac."

Precious Metals in the United States.

Statistics showing where our gold and silver come from.

Where Gold Comes From.

Deposits of domestic productions of gold at the U. S. Mints from 1792 to June 30, 1881.

State.	Amount.
California	$709,234,400 24
Montana	50,141,207.90
Colorado	36,233,128.18
Idaho	34,663,354.70
Oregon	18,194,017.72
Nevada	15,139,000.96
North Carolina	10,671,306.23
Dakota	10,644,852.72
Georgia	7,313,347.58
Arizona	5,623,300.50
Virginia	1,653,436.70
New Mexico	1,804,613.02
South Carolina	1,419,732.91
Wyoming	722,561.61
Utah	467,345.56
Washington Ter	208,364.38
Alabama	220./1.97
Tennessee	4,756 57
Alaska	21,295.53
New Hampshire	11,00.55
Vermont	10,981.27
Maryland	562.06
Michigan (L. Superior)	123.99
Indiana	60 13

Where Silver Comes From.

Deposits of domestic productions of silver at the U. S. Mints from 1792 to June 30, 1881.

State.	Amount.
Nevada	$77,435,742 67
Colorado	23,158,448.27
Utah	10,288,337.96
Arizona	5,761,551.49
Montana	3,387,397.19
Michigan (L. Sup'r)	2,477,519.00
New Mexico	2,452,697.29
California	2,314,745.72
Idaho	904,781.96
North Carolina	46,016.71
Oregon	23,584.91
Dakota	21,276.28
Wyoming	11,796.00
Massachusetts	917.56
Georgia	537.98
Washington Ter	116.96
South Carolina	74.37
Vermont	63.50
Virginia	39.45
Alaska	5.08
Tennessee	1.99

Amount of Specie

In the United States Nov. 1, 1881, according to the report of the Director of the Mint, was

Gold	$459,000,000
Silver	191,000,000
Total	$650,000,000

Amount of Paper Money

In circulation in the United States Nov. 1, 1881, was as follows:

Paper money ... $705,622,504

Amount of paper in excess of specie in U. S. ... $55,622,504

The Total Production

Of precious metals from surface and mines of the earth, from the earliest period to the close of 1879, is estimated to be as follows:

Gold	$14,062,275,000
Silver	11,215,000,000
Total	$25,283,275,000

Estimate of the Total Production of Gold and Silver.

Gold From All Countries.

Estimated total yield of gold in all countries, from 1493 to 1875.

United States	$995,236,615
Austria	559,963,800
New Granada	506,561,675
Brazil	509,547,197
Russia	507,749,853
Africa	550,322,360
Austria-Hungary	226,245,267
Bolivia	144,396,100
Mexico	130,174,300
Chili	129,467,140
Various countries	74,458,346
Peru	60,227,542
Total	6,043,607,905

Silver From All Countries.

Estimated total yield of silver, in all countries, from 1493 to 1875.

Mexico	92,000,250,656
Bolivia	1,206,999,947
Peru	1,063,357,085
Austria-Hungary	354,961,603
Other European countries	251,888,684

Gold From All Countries.	
United States	179,074,330
Chili	90,668,358
Russia	80,668,851
Various countries	93,344,500
Germany	985,731,330
Total	6,130,581,962

Total Gold and Silver from 1493 to 1875.

Mexico	2,730,454,656
Bolivia	1,432,386,047
United States	1,175,699,132
Peru	1,143,684,808
Austria	909,962,300
New Granada	506,341,675
Russia	508,669,344
Brazil	509,547,197
Austria-Hungary	601,299,860
Africa	550,322,360
Germany	985,731,330
Other European countries	251,888,684
Chili	219,491,438
Various countries	148,782,340
Total	$16,902,929,343

AMOUNT OF MONEY IN CIRCULATION FOR EACH PERSON IN DIFFERENT COUNTRIES.

Estimated amount of gold and silver and paper money in circulation in twenty-four countries, from the report of the Director of the Mint, Dec. 1879.

Countries.	Year.	Paper.	Specie.	Money per each person.	Countries.	Year.	Paper.	Specie.	Money per each person.	Countries.	Year.	Paper.	Specie.	Money per each person.
Austria	1869	$9.00	$21 96	$30.96	Germany	1875	$5.38	$12.71	$18.06	Peru	1876	$4.86	$6.97	$11 86
Australia	1879	8.31	19.23	27.54	Great Britain	1871	6.41	23.30	30.11	Portugal	1875	4.62	16.60	24 22
Belgium	1876	10.96	38.60	43.56	Greece	1879	8.35	4.80	13.55	Russia	1876	6.76	1 87	8 63
Brazil	1872	9.00			Italy	1871	5.66	1.38	6.49	Spain	1876	2.96	13.33	14 41
Canada	1871	2.06	9.86	10.92	Japan	1874	4.65	1.18	5.45	Sweden	1876	2.64	4.09	6.73
Colombia	1870	.45	1.50	1.96	Mexico	1871	.16	5.39	5.55	Switzerland	1879	7 72	34.31	42 06
Denmark	1879	9.56	13.00	22.55	Netherlands	1866	30.46	21.78	52.24	Turkey		3.16		
France	1876	22.55	31.41	54.06	Norway	1875	8.70	3.20	11.90	United States	1879	18.55	5 00	23.44

LUMBER MEASURE.

To find the number of feet in a board 1 inch thick from 3 to 30 inches wide, and from 4 to 24 feet long, see the following table. Explanation —The figures at the top of the columns indicate the number of feet in length; those at the extreme left the width of the board in inches. To ascertain the number of feet multiply the number of feet in length by the number of inches in width and divide the product by 12. the result will be the number in feet and inches. Thus, multiply 9 inches wide by 13 feet long, and the result will be 117. Divide this by 12 and we have the product 9 feet and 9 inches. See the table.

LENGTH IN FEET.

	4 feet	5 feet	6 feet	7 feet	8 feet	9 feet	10 feet	11 feet	12 feet	13 feet	14 feet	15 feet	16 feet	17 feet	18 feet	19 feet	20 feet	21 feet	22 feet	23 feet	24 feet
	ft in	ft in	ft in	ft in	ft in	ft in	ft in	ft in	ft in	ft in	ft in	ft in	ft in	ft in	ft in	ft in	ft in	ft in	ft in	ft in	ft in
3 inches wide	1 00	1 03	1 06	1 09	2 00	2 03	2 06	2 09	3 00	3 03	3 06	3 09	4 00	4 03	4 06	4 09	5 00	5 03	5 06	5 09	6 00
4 inches wide	1 04	1 08	2 00	2 04	2 08	3 00	3 04	3 08	4 00	4 04	4 08	5 00	5 04	5 08	6 00	6 04	6 08	7 00	7 04	7 08	8 00
5 inches wide	1 08	2 01	2 06	2 11	3 04	3 09	4 02	4 07	5 00	5 05	5 10	6 03	6 08	7 01	7 06	7 11	8 04	8 09	9 02	9 07	10 00
6 inches wide	2 00	2 06	3 00	3 06	4 00	4 06	5 00	5 06	6 00	6 06	7 00	7 06	8 00	8 06	9 00	9 06	10 00	10 06	11 00	11 06	12 00
7 inches wide	2 04	2 11	3 06	4 01	4 08	5 03	5 10	6 05	7 00	7 07	8 02	8 09	9 04	9 11	10 06	11 01	11 08	12 03	12 10	13 05	14 00
8 inches wide	2 08	3 04	4 00	4 08	5 04	6 00	6 08	7 04	8 00	8 08	9 04	10 00	10 08	11 04	12 00	12 08	13 04	14 00	14 08	15 04	16 00
9 inches wide	3 00	3 09	4 06	5 03	6 00	6 09	7 06	8 03	9 00	9 09	10 06	11 03	12 00	12 09	13 06	14 03	15 00	15 09	16 06	17 03	18 00
10 inches wide	3 04	4 02	5 00	5 10	6 08	7 06	8 04	9 02	10 00	10 10	11 08	12 06	13 04	14 02	15 00	15 10	16 08	17 06	18 04	19 02	20 00
11 inches wide	3 08	4 07	5 06	6 05	7 04	8 03	9 02	10 01	11 00	11 11	12 10	13 09	14 08	15 07	16 06	17 05	18 04	19 03	20 02	21 01	22 00
12 inches wide	4 00	5 00	6 00	7 00	8 00	9 00	10 00	11 00	12 00	13 00	14 00	15 00	16 00	17 00	18 00	19 00	20 00	21 00	22 00	23 00	24 00
13 inches wide	4 04	5 05	6 06	7 07	8 08	9 09	10 10	11 11	13 00	14 01	15 02	16 03	17 04	18 05	19 06	20 07	21 08	22 09	23 10	24 11	26 00
14 inches wide	4 08	5 10	7 00	8 02	9 04	10 06	11 08	12 10	14 00	15 02	16 04	17 06	18 08	19 10	21 00	22 02	23 04	24 06	25 08	26 10	28 00
15 inches wide	5 00	6 03	7 06	8 09	10 00	11 03	12 06	13 09	15 00	16 03	17 06	18 09	20 00	21 03	22 06	23 09	25 00	26 03	27 06	28 09	30 00
16 inches wide	5 04	6 08	8 00	9 04	10 08	12 00	13 04	14 08	16 00	17 04	18 08	20 00	21 04	22 08	24 00	25 04	26 08	28 00	29 04	30 08	32 00
17 inches wide	5 08	7 01	8 06	9 11	11 04	12 09	14 02	15 07	17 00	18 05	19 10	21 03	22 08	24 01	25 06	26 11	28 04	29 09	31 02	32 07	34 00
18 inches wide	6 00	7 06	9 00	10 06	12 00	13 06	15 00	16 06	18 00	19 06	21 00	22 06	24 00	25 06	27 00	28 06	30 00	31 06	33 00	34 06	36 00
19 inches wide	6 04	7 11	9 06	11 01	12 08	14 03	15 10	17 05	19 00	20 07	22 02	23 09	25 04	26 11	28 06	30 01	31 08	33 03	34 10	36 05	38 00
20 inches wide	6 08	8 04	10 00	11 08	13 04	15 00	16 08	18 04	20 00	21 08	23 04	25 00	26 08	28 04	30 00	31 08	33 04	35 00	36 08	38 04	40 00
21 inches wide	7 00	8 09	10 06	12 03	14 00	15 09	17 06	19 03	21 00	22 09	24 06	26 03	28 00	29 09	31 06	33 03	35 00	36 09	38 06	40 03	42 00
22 inches wide	7 04	9 02	11 00	12 10	14 08	16 06	18 04	20 02	22 00	23 10	25 08	27 06	29 04	31 02	33 00	34 10	36 08	38 06	40 04	42 02	44 00
23 inches wide	7 08	9 07	11 06	13 05	15 04	17 03	19 02	21 01	23 00	24 11	26 10	28 09	30 08	32 07	34 06	36 05	38 04	40 03	42 02	44 01	46 00
24 inches wide	8 00	10 00	12 00	14 00	16 00	18 00	20 00	22 00	24 00	26 00	28 00	30 00	32 00	34 00	36 00	38 00	40 00	42 00	44 00	46 00	48 00
25 inches wide	8 04	10 05	12 06	14 07	16 08	18 09	20 10	22 11	25 00	27 01	29 02	31 03	33 04	35 05	37 06	39 07	41 08	43 09	45 10	47 11	50 00
26 inches wide	8 08	10 10	13 00	15 02	17 04	19 06	21 08	23 10	26 00	28 02	30 04	32 06	34 08	36 10	39 00	41 02	43 04	45 06	47 08	49 10	52 00
27 inches wide	9 00	11 03	13 06	15 09	18 00	20 03	22 06	24 09	27 00	29 03	31 06	33 09	36 00	38 03	40 06	42 09	45 00	47 03	49 06	51 09	54 00
28 inches wide	9 04	11 08	14 00	16 04	18 08	21 00	23 04	25 08	28 00	30 04	32 08	35 00	37 04	39 08	42 00	44 04	46 08	49 00	51 04	53 08	56 00
29 inches wide	9 08	12 01	14 06	16 11	19 04	21 09	24 02	26 07	29 00	31 05	33 10	36 03	38 08	41 01	43 06	45 11	48 04	50 09	53 02	55 07	58 00
30 inches wide	10 00	12 06	15 00	17 06	20 00	22 06	25 00	27 06	30 00	32 06	35 00	37 06	40 00	42 06	45 00	47 06	50 00	52 06	55 00	57 06	60 00

Name of City.	Population 1880.	Debt 1880.	Debt per cent 1 person.	Name of City.	Population 1880.	Debt 1880.	Debt per cent 1 Person.	Name of City.	Population 1880.	Debt 1880.	Debt per cash Persons.
Utica, N. Y.	33,913	$764,000	$22.55	Wheeling, W. V.	31,266	$531,888	$17.00	Watertown, N. Y.	10,697	$407,500	$38.00
				Wilkesbarre, Pa.	23,336	95,096	4.07	Weymouth, Mass.	10,571	64,302	6.09
Virginia City, Nev.	13,705	112,000	5.17	Watervliet, N. Y.	22,202			Winona, Minn.	10,208	183,000	17.92
Vicksburg, Miss.	11,814	375,215	31.50	Waterbury, Conn.	20,200	361,508	17.80	Waltham, Mass.	11,711	677,000	60.76
				Williamsport, Pa.	18,934	651,873	34.40				
Washington, D. C.	147,307	23,310,146	158.25	Wilmington, N C.	17,361	539,845	31.09	Yonkers, N. Y.	18,892	1,388,000	73.47
Warwick, R. I.	12,163	57,500	4 72	Woonsocket, R. I.	16,053	230,000	14.50	Youngstown, Ohio	15,431	193,406	12 50
Worcester, Mass.	58,395	2,467,543	41.98	Wallkill, N. Y.	11,483			York, Pa.	13,940	35,000	2 38
Wilmington, Del.	42,499	1,372,450	32.06	Woburn, Mass.	10,938	988,602	57 26	Zanesville, Ohio	18,120	529,097	29.91

Great Cities of the World, Outside of the United States, Having 100,000 Inhabitants. *

Cities.	Countries.	Census.	Population.	Cities	Countries.	Census	Population.	Cities	Countries.	Census	Population.
Alexandria	Egypt	1882	212,054	Genoa	Italy	1861	179,515	Oldham	England	1881	152,511
Agra	India	1881	160,207					Osaka	Japan	1877	284,105
Ahmenabad	India	1881	127,621	Hangtscheu-fu	China	Est	400,000				
Allahabad	India	1881	148,547	Hangjang	China	Est	100,000	Patna	India	1881	170,654
Amsterdam	Holland	1881	328,047	Hankkow	China	Est	600,000	Puna	India	1881	129,751
Antwerp	Belgium	1881	577,282	Hutscheu	China	Est	300,000	Pernambuco	South America	1872	116,671
Aberdeen	Scotland	1881	105,189	Hutscheu-fu	China	Est	100,000	Prague	Austria-Hun'y	1880	162,323
Amritsar	India	1881	151,896	Hwangjuer	China	Est	130,000	Paris	France	1861	2,269,023
Aboukqta	Africa	Est	130,000	Hyderabad	India	Est	120,000	Portsmouth	England	1881	127,953
				Hakhdate	Japan	1877	113,494	Palermo	Italy	1881	244,991
Berlin	Germany	1881	1,122,360	Hamburg	Germany	1880	290,054	Porto	Portugal	1878	108,346
Bahia	Brazil	1872	129,109	Hanover	Germany	1880	122,843	Porto Novo	Africa	Est	100,000
Buenos Ayres	South America	1881	289,925	Hague	Holland	1881	123,409	Peking	China	Est	1,648,800
Bombay	India	1881	773,196								
Bareilly	India	1881	109,844	Jangtschau	China	Est	360,000	Rio de Janeiro	South America	1872	274,972
Benares	India	1881	199,700	Jongpin	China	Est	200,000	Rangoon	India	1881	134,176
Brussels	Belgium	1881	394,940	Jondpore	India	Est	150,000	Rouen	France	1881	105,906
Bangalore	India	1871	142,513					Rome	Italy	1880	300,467
Bangkok	India	Est	600,000	Kesho	India	Est	150,000	Rotterdam	Holland	1881	157,270
Baroda	India	1871	112,053	Kagoshima	Japan	1877	200,000	Riga	Russia	1881	168,944
Bordeaux	France	1881	221,305	Kanagawa	Japan	1877	108,283				
Barmen	Germany	1880	95,941	Kiota	Japan	1877	229,810	Santiago	South America	1875	129,807
Bremen	Germany	1880	112 158	Konigsberg	Germany	1881	140,909	Shaohing	China	Est	500,000
Breslau	Germany	1880	272,390	Kingston	England	1881	154,350	Shanghai	China	Est	300,000
Belfast	Ireland	1881	207,671	Kijew	Russia	1874	127,250	Siangtan	China	Est	1,000,000
Birmingham	England	1881	400,757	Kischenew	Russia		102,427	Singan-fu	China	Est	1,000,000
Blackburn	England	1881	104,012					Sutschau	China	Est	500,000
Bolton	England	1881	105,422	Lima	South America	1876	101,488	Saoul	Corea	Est	500,000
Bradford	England	1881	180,459	Leinkong	China	Est	250,000	Sainagar	India	1873	132,681
Brighton	England	1881	128,407	Lahore	India	1881	149,349	Surat	India	1871	107,149
Bristol	England	1881	206,503	Lucknow	India	1881	261,303	Smyrna	Turkey in Asia	Est	150,000
Bucharest	Roumania	1876	221,805	Lille	France	1881	178,144	Sydney	Australia	1881	220,427
Bologna	Italy	1881	123,274	Lyons	France	1881	376,613	St. Etienne	France	1881	123,813
Barcelona	Spain	1877	249,106	Leipzig	Germany	1880	148,780	Strasburg	Germany	1880	104,471
Buda-Pesth	Austria-Hun'y	1880	300,551	Leeds	England	1881	309,126	Stuttgart	Germany	1880	117,303
				Leicester	England	1881	122,351	Salford	England	1881	176,233
Constantinople	Turkey	1879	1,075,000	Liverpool	England	1881	552,425	Sheffield	England	1881	284,410
Cairo	Egypt	1878	349,883	London	England	1881	4,764,312	Sunderland	England	1881	124,980
Canton	China	1881	1,600,000	Lisbon	Portugal	1878	246,343	St. Petersburg	Russia	1881	876,575
Calcutta	India	1881	684,058	Lemberg	Austria-Hun'y	1880	109,726	Seville	Spain	1877	133,938
Cawnpore	India	1881	151,444	Liege	Belgium	1880	663,607	Stockholm	Sweden	1880	168,775
Columbo	Ceylon	1881	111,942								
Copenhagen	Denmark	1880	273,323	Marseilles	France	1881	360,099	Tunis	Africa	Est	120,000
Cologne	Germany	1880	144,772	Manchester	England	1881	393,676	Taiwan-fu	China	Est	235,000
Charkow	Russia	1879	101,175	Messina	Italy	1881	126,497	Tengtschau-fu	China	Est	230,000
Christiania	Sweden	1880	119,407	Munich	Bavaria	1880	230,023	Tientsin	China	Est	950,000
				Milan	Italy	1861	321,836	Tschantschau-fu	China	Est	1,000,000
Delhi	India	1881	173,393	Madrid	Spain	1877	397,690	Tschanjang	China	Est	200,000
Dhar	India	Est	100,000	Malaga	Spain	1877	115,882	Tschingtn-fu	China	Est	800,000
Damascus	Turkey-in-Asia	Est	150,000	Moscow	Russia	1882	748,000	Tschungking-fu	China	Est	600,000
Danzig	Germany	1880	108,551	Madras	India	1881	405,848	Tokio	Japan	1877	811,510
Dresden	Germany	1880	220,818	Mandalah	India	Est	100,000	Tabris	Persia	Est	165,000
Dublin	Ireland	1881	249,486	Manilla	Indian Arch'go	Est	160,000	Teheran	Persia	Est	200,000
Dundee	Scotland	1881	140,239	Melbourne	Australia	1881	252,000	Tiflis	Russia-in-Asia	1876	104,024
				Montreal	Canada	1881	140,747	Trieste	Austria-Hun'y	1880	144,844
Edinburgh	Scotland	1881	236,002	Mexico	Mexico	1879	236,500	Toulouse	France	1881	140,289
				Mukden	China	Est	170,000	Turin	Italy	1881	252,832
Fez	Africa	Est	100,000								
Frankfort-on-Main	Germany	1880	136,819	Nangkin	China	Est	450,000	Valencia	Spain	1877	143,856
Florence	Italy	1881	169,001	Nantes	France	1881	124,319	Victoria	China	Est	102,000
Fatschau	China	Est	400,000	Newcastle	England	1881	145,228	Vienna	Austria-Hun'y	1880	726,105
Foochow	China	Est	630,000	Nottingham	England	1881	111,631	Venice	Italy	1881	132,826
				Naples	Italy	1881	494,314				
Glasgow	Scotland	1881	674,095	Nagoya	Japan	1877	135,715	Warsaw	Russia	1881	383,973
Gwalior	India	Est	200,000					Welhein	China	Est	250,000
Ghent	Belgium	1881	131,431	Odessa	Russia	1877	193,513	West Ham	England	1881	128,692

*For population of great cities not here given, see "Principal Countries of the World," mentioned elsewhere in this volume.

United States Soldiers in the Late Civil War.

Number of men furnished from April 10, 1861, to June 30, 1865.

States and Territories.	Men Furnished	States and Territories.	Men Furnished	States and Territories.	Men Furnished
New York	467,047	Maryland	50,316	Colorado Ter.	4,903
Pennsylvania	366,107	New Hampshire	34,629	Indian Nations.	3,530
Ohio	319,650	Vermont	35,262	Nebraska Ter.	3,157
Illinois	259,147	West Virginia	32,068	North Carolina	3,156
Indiana	197,147	Tennessee	31,092	Alabama	2,576
Massachusetts	152,048	Minnesota	25,052	Texas	1,965
Missouri	109,111	Rhode Island	23,699	Oregon	1,810
Wisconsin	96,424	Kansas	20,151	Florida	1,290
Michigan	89,372	Dist. of Columbia	16,872	Nevada	1,080
Iowa	76,309	California	15,725	Washington Ter.	964
New Jersey	81,010	Delaware	13,670	Mississippi	545
Kentucky	79,025	Arkansas	8,289	Dakota Ter.	206
Maine	72,114	New Mexico Ter.	6,561	Colored Troops	186,017
Connecticut	57,379	Louisiana	5,224	Total	2,861,708

Religious Denominations in the United States.

Denominations.	No. of Members	No. of Churches.	No. of Ministers.
Roman Catholics—adherents and church members, claimed	6,370,856	5,975	6,366
Baptist	2,133,044	34,794	15,401
Methodist Episcopal	1,990,779	16,721	9,261
Methodist Episcopal (South)	826,913		3,563
Lutheran	984,370	5,556	3,162
Presbyterian	573,377	5,536	4,820
Christian (Disciples of Christ)	567,448	4,081	3,658
Congregational	383,685	3,980	3,586
Protestant Episcopal	342,500	3,049	3,498
United Brethren in Christ	155,437	3,207	3,200
Reformed Church in the United States	154,742	1,384	752
United Evangelical	144,000	596	963
Presbyterian Church (South)	119,970	1,928	1,081
Protestant Methodist	118,170	1,501	2,130
Cumberland Presbyterians	111,855	2,474	1,380
Mormons	110,377	654	3,906
Evangelical Association	130,607	1,332	1,340
Dunkards—The Brethren	60,000	710	1,065
United Presbyterians	80,236	795	656
Reformed Church in America	78,017	480	519
Free-Will Baptists	76,708	1,445	1,296
Methodist Episcopal (colored)	74,193	1,659	648
Friends	67,643	921	876
Second Adventists	63,500	583	501
Anti-Mission Baptist	40,000	1,946	888
Universalists	39,236	710	713
Winnebrennerians (Church of God)	30,224	449	498
Unitarian Congregational	17,960	342	384
Wesleyan Methodist	17,847	289	472
Moravian	10,112	74	96
Seventh-Day Adventists	14,703	638	138
Jews	13,126	261	202
Free Methodists	12,100	397	601
Adventists	11,100	91	107
Reformed Episcopal	10,656	55	103
Seventh-Day Baptist	8,606	97	103
Reformed Presbyterian	6,020	41	31
New Jerusalem—Swedenborgian	4,774	91	80
Primitive Methodist	3,370	121	50
New Mennonite	2,180	31	44
American Communities	2,608	14	8
Shakers	2,400	17	58
Independent Methodists	2,100	15	14
Six-Principle Baptist	2,075	20	17
Total	15,345,326	92,167	77,280

Foreigners in the United States.

ACCORDING TO CENSUS OF 1880.

Where Born.	Number.	Where Born.	Number.
German Empire	1,966,742	West Indies	9,404
Ireland	1,854,571	Portugal	8,138
British America	717,094	Atlantic Islands	7,512
England	662,670	Cuba	6,917
Sweden	194,337	Spain	5,121
Norway	181,729	Australia	4,100
Scotland	170,136	South America	4,508
France	106,971	At Sea, under foreign flags	4,109
China	104,541	Europe, not specified	3,314
Switzerland	88,621	Africa, not specified	2,204
Bohemia	85,361	India	1,707
Wales	83,302	Great Britain, not specified	1,484
Mexico	68,391	Turkey	1,205
Denmark	64,196	Sandwich Island	1,147
Holland	58,090	Asia, not specified	1,056
Poland	48,557	Pacific Islands	849
Italy	44,230	Greece	776
Austria	38,663	Central America	707
Russia	35,722	Japan	401
Belgium	15,545	Malta	300
Luxemburg	12,836	Gibraltar	167
Hungary	11,526	Greenland	129

Strength of Ice.

Thickness.	Strength.
Two inches—Will support a man.	
Four inches—Will support a man on horseback.	
Five inches—Will support an eighty-pounder cannon.	
Eight inches—Will support a battery of artillery with carriages and horses attached.	
Ten inches—Will support an army, an innumerable multitude.	

Education of Presidents.

Washington.. Fair English education.
Adams......... Harvard.
Jefferson ...... William and Mary
Madison ...... Princeton.
Adams, J. Q... Harvard.
Jackson....... Limited education
Van Buren..... Academic course.
Harrison....... Hampden College.
Tyler......... William and Mary.
Polk......... University of N. C.
Taylor....... Slight rudiments.
Fillmore ...... Limited education.
Pierce........ Bowdoin.
Buchanan .... Dickinson
Lincoln....... Education limited.
Johnson....... Self-educated.
Grant........ West Point.
Hayes....... Kenyon College.
Garfield....... Williams College.
Arthur....... Union College.

Monroe and Harrison did not graduate. Monroe left college to join the revolutionary army. Financial embarrassment prevented Harrison from pursuing a full course. Polk graduated at 23, Tyler at 17. The majority graduated at 20.

Political Representation.

Number of Presidential Electors, United States Senators and Representatives in Congress that each State is entitled to by Congressional apportionment between 1883 and 1893.

States.	Electors.	Senators.	Representatives.
Alabama	10	2	8
Arkansas	7	2	5
California	8	2	6
Colorado	3	2	1
Connecticut	6	2	4
Delaware	3	2	1
Florida	4	2	2
Georgia	12	2	10
Illinois	22	2	20
Indiana	15	2	13
Iowa	13	2	11
Kansas	9	2	7
Kentucky	13	2	11
Louisiana	8	2	6
Maine	6	2	4
Maryland	8	2	6
Massachusetts	14	2	12
Michigan	13	2	11
Minnesota	7	2	5
Mississippi	9	2	7
Missouri	16	2	14
Nebraska	5	2	3
Nevada	3	2	1
N. Hampshire	4	2	2
New Jersey	9	2	7
New York	36	2	34
North Carolina	11	2	9
Ohio	23	2	21
Oregon	3	2	1
Pennsylvania	30	2	28
Rhode Island	4	2	2
South Carolina	9	2	7
Tennessee	12	2	10
Texas	13	2	11
Vermont	4	2	2
Virginia	12	2	10
West Virginia	6	2	4
Wisconsin	11	2	9
Totals	401	76	325

The Territories of Arizona, Dakota, Idaho, Montana, New Mexico, Utah, Washington and Wyoming, have each one delegate.

The Time of Fast Trotters.

Horses that have trotted a mile in 2 minutes and 19¾ seconds and less, up to and including the season of 1882.

Name.	Time.	Year.
Maud S.	2.10¾	1881
St. Julien	2.11¼	1880
Rarus	2.13¼	1878
Clingstone	2.14	1882
Trinket	2.14	1882
Goldsmith Maid	2.14	1874
Hopeful	2.14¾	1878
Lula	2.15	1875
Smuggler	2.15¼	1876
Hattie Woodward	2.15¼	1881
Lucille Golddust	2.16¼	1877
American Girl	2.16½	1874
Darby	2.16½	1879
Edwin Thorne	2.16½	1882
Jerome Eddy	2.16½	1882
Charlie Ford	2.16½	1875
Occident	2.16¾	1873
Gloster	2.17	1874
Black Cloud	2.17¼	1882
Dexter	2.17¼	1867
Piedmont	2.17¼	1881
So-So	2.17¼	1881
Santa Claus	2.17¼	1882
Hannis	2.17¼	1882
Red Cloud	2.18	1874
Nettie	2.18	1874
Judge Fullerton	2.18	1874
Great Eastern	2.18	1877
Edwin Forrest	2.18	1878
Protine	2.18	1879
Dick Swiveller	2.18	1881
Josephus	2.18	1880
Kate Sprague	2.18	1881
Robert McGregor	2.18	1881
Fanny Witherspoon	2.18¼	1881
Lady Thorn	2.18¼	1869
Lucy	2.18¼	1872
Lady Maud	2.18¼	1875
Midnight	2.18¼	1879
Monroe Chief	2.18¼	1881
Ross Wilkes	2.18¼	1882
Slow-Go	2.18¼	1881
Col. Lewis	2.18½	1875
Nutwood	2.18½	1880
J. B. Thomas	2.18½	1882
William H	2.18½	1881
Patchen	2.18½	1882
Cleora	2.18½	1879
Cozette	2.18	1878
Albemarle	2.18	1876
Edward	2.18	1881
Alley	2.18	1880
Bonesetter	2.18	1881
Alexander	2.18	1873
Daisydale	2.18	1882
Adele Gould	2.18	1882
Graves	2.18	1880
Jay Eye See	2.18	1882
Kitty Bates	2.18	1882
Minnie R.	2.18	1882
Wedgewood	2.18	1878
George Palmer	2.18	1875
Bodine	2.18½	1874
Cosure	2.18½	1882
Crosie	2.18	1882
P. ana	2.18¾	1882
Keene Jim	2.18¾	1882
Aldine	2.18¾	1875
T. L. Young	2.19	1879
Mouse	2.19	1882
Will Cody	2.19	1880
Driver	2.19	1880
Romero	2.19¼	1882
Troublesome	2.19¼	1882
Von Arnim	2.19½	1882

Seven Wonders of the World.

Pyramids of Egypt.

Tower, Walls and Terrace Hanging Gardens of Babylon.

Statue of Jupiter Olympus, on the Capitoline Hill, at Rome.

Temple of Diana, at Ephesus.

Pharos, or watch-tower, at Alexandria, Egypt.

Colossus of Rhodes, a statue 105 feet high, overthrown by an earthquake 224 B. C.

Mausoleum at Halicarnassus, a Grecian Persian city in Asia Minor.

EXPENSE OF BOARD PER DAY.

The following table will be found convenient for the proprietors of hotels and boarding-houses in giving the price per day where the board is a certain specified price per week. Thus, if it is desired to find the price of five days' board at $5.00 per week, it will be found by reference to be $3.57. (See table). When the board exceeds $10.00 per week, double the numbers.

Days.	50c.	75c.	$1.00	$1.25	$1.50	$1.75	$2	$2.25	$2.50	$3	$3.50	$4	$4.50	$5	$6	$7	$8	$9	$10
1	.7	.11	.14	.18	.21	.25	.29	.32	.36	.43	.50	.57	.64	.71	.86	1 00	1 14	1.29	1 43
2	.14	.21	.29	.36	.43	.50	.57	.64	.71	.86	1.00	1.14	1.29	1.43	1.71	2.00	2.29	2 57	2.86
3	.21	.32	.43	.54	.64	.75	.86	96	1.07	1 29	1.50	1.71	1 93	2 14	2 57	3 00	3 43	3 86	4.29
4	.29	43	.57	.71	.86	1 00	1.14	1.29	1.43	1.71	2 00	2 29	2.57	2.86	3 43	4 00	4.57	5 14	5 71
5	36	.54	.71	.89	1 07	1.25	1.43	1.61	1.79	2.14	2.50	2.86	3.21	3.57	4.29	5 00	5.71	6.43	7.14
6	.43	.64	.82	1.07	1.29	1.50	1.71	1.93	2.14	2.57	3.00	3.43	3 86	4.29	5.14	6.00	6.86	7.71	8.57
7	.50	.75	1.00	1.25	1.50	1.75	2.00	2.25	2.50	3.00	3 50	4.00	4.50	5 00	6 00	7.00	8.00	9.00	10.00

LEGAL WEIGHT OF A BUSHEL IN DIFFERENT STATES.*

States and Territories.	Wheat.	Rye.	Oats.	Barley.	Buck wheat.	Shelled Corn.	Corn on Cob	Corn Meal	Pota toes	Sweet Pota toes	Onions	Dried Apples	Beans	Peas	Dried peach	Flax seed	Timothy seed	Blue grass seed	Clover seed.	Coal, anthracite.
	lbs.	lbs.	lbs.	lbs.	lbs.	lbs.	lbs.	lbs.	lbs.	lbs.	lbs.	lbs.	lbs.	lbs.	lbs.	lbs.	lbs.	lbs.	lbs.	lbs.
Arkansas	60	56	32	48	52		70	50	60	50	57		60	46	24	33	50	45	14	60	80
Arizona	60	56	32	45		54						60									
California	60	54	32	50	40	52															
Colorado	60	56	32	48	52	56	70	50	60		57		60				45	14	60		
Connecticut	60	56	32	48	48	56		50	60		60	60									
Dakota	60	56	32	48	42	56	70		60	46	52	60	60	60			56	42		60	80
Delaware	60					56		48													
District Columbia	60	56	32			56		48	60												
Georgia	60	56	32	47	52	56	70	48	60	55	57	55	60	60	24	33	56	45	14	60	80
Illinois	60	56	32	48	52	56	70	48	60	55	57	55	60		24	33	56	45	14	60	80
Indiana	60	56	32	48	48	56	68	50	60		48		60		24	33	56	45	14	60	80
Iowa	60	56	32	48	52	56	70		60	46	57		60		24	33	56	45	14	60	80
Kansas	60	56	32	48	50	56	70	50	60	50	57	55	60	60	24	33	56	45	14	60	80
Kentucky	60	56	32	47	55	56	70	50	60	55	57	60	60	60	24	39	56	45	14	60	76
Louisiana	60	32	32	32		50															
Maine	60	56	30	48	48	56		50	60		32	50	64	60							
Maryland	60	56	32	47	48	56	70	48		56	56		60				45	14	64		
Massachusetts	60	56	32	48	48	56		50	60	56	52										
Michigan	60	56	32	48	48	56	70	50	60	56	58	60	60	60	22	28	56	45	14	60	
Minnesota	60	56	32	48	42	56			60					28	28		56	45	14	60	
Missouri	60	56	32	48	52	56			60		57		60		24	33	56	45	14	60	
Montana	60	56	35	48		56		50	60		57	50	60				45	14	60		
Nebraska	60	56	34	48	52	56	70	50	60		57	55	60		24	33	56	45	14	60	
Nevada	60	56	32	50	40	52	70		60		57	55	60		24	33	56	45	14	60	80
New Hampshire	60	56	32			56		50	60			60									
New Jersey	60	56	30	48	50	56			60	54	57		60	60	25	33	55			64	
New York	60	56	32	48	48	56			60		62		60		25		55	44		60	
North Carolina	60	56	30	48	50	54		46					60							60	
Ohio	60	56	32	48	50	56	70		60	50			60		22	33	56	45		60	
Oregon	60	56	36	46	42	56			60					28	28					60	
Pennsylvania	60	56	32	47	48	56			60		57		60							62	
Rhode Island		56	32	48		56		50	60												
South Carolina	60	56	33	48	56	56	70	50	60	50	57		60	60	26	33	44		14	60	
Tennessee		56	32	48	50	56	72	50	60	50	60	60	60	60	26	56	45	14			
Vermont	60	56	32	46	46	56			60		52	50	60	60			45			60	
Virginia	60	56	32	48	52	56	70	50	60	57	57	53	60	60	26	52	56	45	14	60	80
Washington Ter.	60	56	36	48	45	42	56		60		50	50	60		26		58	40		60	
West Virginia	60	56	32	48	52	56			60				60		25	33	56	45		60	
Wisconsin	60	56	32	48	50	56	70		60		60		60		22	33	56	45		60	

* Some States, not here mentioned, only legalize and recognize the Standard United States bushel, without reference to weight.

SHORT INSURANCE RATES.

By the following table may be seen the customary short rates of insurance for periods less than a year or month.

EXPLANATION.—When the rate is one per cent., or $1 on $100 for a year, the rate for one month is 4-90 of the annual rate, or 20 cents. (See table.) For six months it would be 14-90, or 70 cents. (See following table, which, by a little study, will be readily understood.)

For Periods of Several Years.

1 YEAR.	2 YEARS.	3 YEARS.	4 YEARS.	5 YEARS.	Charge this Proportion of whole Premium.
1 mo.	2 mo.	3 mo.	4 mo.	5 mo.	1/20 or 20 per cent.
2 "	4 "	6 "	8 "	10 "	30 " "
3 "	6 "	9 "	12 "	15 "	40 " "
4 "	8 "	12 "	16 "	20 "	50 " "
5 "	10 "	15 "	20 "	25 "	60 " "
6 "	12 "	18 "	24 "	30 "	70 " "
7 "	14 "	21 "	28 "	35 "	75 " "
8 "	16 "	24 "	32 "	40 "	80 " "
9 "	18 "	27 "	36 "	45 "	85 " "
10 "	20 "	30 "	40 "	50 "	90 " "
11 "	22 "	33 "	44 "	55 "	95 " "

For Periods Less than One Year.

1 month, 4/90 of annual rate.		7 mo's, 48/90 of annual rate.	
2 "	8/90 " "	8 "	58/90 " "
3 "	17/90 " "	9 "	68/90 " "
4 "	25/90 " "	10 "	78/90 " "
5 "	33/90 " "	11 "	88/90 " "
6 "	41/90 " "		

For Periods Less than One Month.

5 days, 1/6 of monthly rate | 15 days, 3/6 of monthly rate
10 " 2/6 " " | 20 " 4/6 " "

United States Soldiers in the Late Civil War.

Number of men furnished from April 10, 1861, to June 30, 1865.

States and Territories	Men Furnished	States and Territories	Men Furnished	States and Territories	Men Furnished
New York	467,047	Maryland	50,316	Colorado Ter.	4,903
Pennsylvania	366,107	New Hampshire	34,924	Indian Nations	3,530
Ohio	310,654	Vermont	35,262	Nebraska Ter.	3,157
Illinois	259,147	West Virginia	32,068	North Carolina	3,156
Indiana	197,147	Tennessee	31,092	Alabama	2,576
Massachusetts	152,048	Minnesota	25,052	Texas	1,965
Missouri	109,111	Rhode Island	23,248	Oregon	1,810
Wisconsin	91,424	Kansas	20,151	Florida	1,290
Michigan	89,372	Dist. of Columbia	16,872	Nevada	1,080
Iowa	76,309	California	15,725	Washington Ter.	964
New Jersey	81,010	Delaware	13,670	Mississippi	545
Kentucky	75,625	Arkansas	8,289	Dakota Ter.	206
Maine	72,114	New Mexico Ter.	6,561	Colored Troops	186,017
Connecticut	57,379	Louisiana	5,224	Total	2,759,798

Religious Denominations in the United States.

Denominations.	No. of Members.	No. of Churches.	No. of Ministers.
Roman Catholic—adherents and church members, claimed	6,370,858	5,975	6,998
Baptist	2,123,044	24,794	15,401
Methodist Episcopal	1,980,779	16,721	9,283
Methodist Episcopal (South)	828,013	......	3,593
Lutheran	684,570	5,556	3,102
Presbyterian	573,377	5,598	4,920
Christian (Disciples of Christ)	567,448	4,081	3,656
Congregational	382,985	3,680	3,589
Protestant Episcopal	342,530	3,045	3,490
United Brethren in Christ	155,437	2,207	2,200
Reformed Church in the United States	134,742	1,394	752
United Evangelical	144,000	806	363
Presbyterian Church (South)	119,970	1,928	1,081
Protestant Methodist	118,170	1,501	2,115
Cumberland Presbyterians	111,855	2,474	1,386
Mormons	110,377	454	3,906
Evangelical Association	99,697	382	1,240
Dunkards—The Brethren	90,000	716	1,985
United Presbyterians	80,236	785	658
Reformed Church in America	78,917	498	519
Free-Will Baptists	76,708	1,485	1,286
Methodist Episcopal (colored)	74,185	1,759	648
Friends	67,843	621	876
Second Adventists	63,500	585	501
Anti-Mission Baptists	40,000	1,030	888
Universalists	36,238	719	713
Winnebremerians (Church of God)	20,224	568	466
Unitarian Congregational	17,980	342	384
Wesleyan Methodist	17,847	290	472
Moravians	16,112	74	98
Seventh-Day Adventists	14,723	606	198
Jews	13,683	265	202
Free Methodists	12,130	287	601
Adventists	11,300	......	107
Reformed Episcopal	10,450	55	98
Seventh-Day Baptist	8,906	87	108
Reformed Presbyterian	6,920	41	31
New Jerusalem—Swedenborgian	4,734	91	81
Primitive Methodist	3,370	121	50
New Mennonite	2,980	31	44
American Communities	2,888	14	8
Shakers	2,400	17	68
Independent Methodists	2,100	18	14
Six-Principle Baptist	2,075	20	17
Total	**15,345,828**	**92,167**	**77,290**

Foreigners in the United States.

ACCORDING TO CENSUS OF 1880.

Where Born.	Number	Where Born.	Number
German Empire	1,947,749	West Indies	9,484
Ireland	1,854,571	Portugal	8,138
British America	717,086	Atlantic Islands	7,512
England	662,676	Cuba	6,917
Sweden	194,337	Spain	5,121
Norway	181,729	Australia	4,906
Scotland	170,136	South America	4,566
France	106,971	At sea, under foreign flags	4,068
China	104,541	Europe not specified	3,314
Switzerland	88,621	Af. &c. not specified	2,204
Bohemia	85,361	India	1,707
Wales	83,302	Great Britain, not specified	1,464
Mexico	68,399	Turkey	1,205
Denmark	64,196	Sandwich Islands	1,147
Holland	58,090	Asia, not specified	1,064
Poland	48,557	Pacific Islands	808
Italy	44,230	Greece	776
Austria	38,663	Central America	707
Russia	35,722	Japan	401
Belgium	15,535	Malta	305
Luxemburg	12,836	Gibraltar	167
Hungary	11,526	Greenland	129

Strength of Ice.

Thickness.	Strength.	Thickness.	Strength.
Two inches—Will support a man.		**Eight inches**—Will support a battery of artillery, with carriages and horses attached.	
Four Inches—Will support a man on horseback.			
Five Inches — Will support an eighty-pounder cannon.		**Ten inches**—Will support an army; an innumerable multitude.	

Education of Presidents.

Washington .. Fair English education.
Adams .... Harvard.
Jefferson .... William and Mary
Madison ..... Princeton.
Adams, J. Q.. Harvard.
Jackson ...... Limited education
Van Buren ... Academic course.
Harrison ..... Hampden College.
Tyler .... William and Mary.
Polk .... University of N. C.
Taylor .... Slight rudiments.
Fillmore ..... Limited education.
Pierce .... Bowdoin.
Buchanan ... Dickinson
Lincoln ...... Education limited.
Johnson ..... Self-educated.
Grant .... West Point.
Hayes .... Kenyon College.
Garfield...... Williams College.
Arthur........ Union College.

Monroe and Harrison did not graduate. Monroe left college to join the revolutionary army. Financial embarrassment prevented Harrison from pursuing a full course. Polk graduated at 21, Tyler at 17. The majority graduated at 20.

Political Representation.

Number of Presidential Electors, United States Senators and Representatives in Congress that each State is entitled to by Congressional apportionment between 1883 and 1893.

States.	Electors.	Senators.	Representatives.
Alabama	10	2	8
Arkansas	7	2	5
California	8	2	6
Colorado	3	2	1
Connecticut	6	2	4
Delaware	3	2	1
Florida	4	2	2
Georgia	12	2	10
Illinois	22	2	20
Indiana	15	2	13
Iowa	13	2	11
Kansas	9	2	7
Kentucky	13	2	11
Louisiana	8	2	6
Maine	6	2	4
Maryland	8	2	6
Massachusetts	14	2	12
Michigan	13	2	11
Minnesota	7	2	5
Mississippi	9	2	7
Missouri	16	2	14
Nebraska	5	2	3
Nevada	3	2	1
N. Hampshire	4	2	2
New Jersey	9	2	7
New York	36	2	34
North Carolina	11	2	9
Ohio	23	2	21
Oregon	3	2	1
Pennsylvania	30	2	28
Rhode Island	4	2	2
South Carolina	9	2	7
Tennessee	12	2	10
Texas	13	2	11
Vermont	4	2	2
Virginia	12	2	10
West Virginia	6	2	4
Wisconsin	11	2	9
Totals	**401**	**76**	**325**

The Territories of Arizona, Dakota, Idaho, Montana, New Mexico, Utah, Washington and Wyoming, have each one delegate.

The Time of Fast Trotters.

Horses that have trotted a mile in 2 minutes and 19¾ seconds and in less time, during the following years, up to and including the season of 1882.

Name.	Time.	Year.
Maud S.	2.10¾	1881
St. Julien	2.11¼	1880
Rarus	2.13¼	1878
Clingstone	2.14	1882
Trinket	2.14	1881
Goldsmith Maid	2.14	1874
Hopeful	2.14¾	1878
Lula	2.15	1875
Smuggler	2.15¼	1876
Hattie Woodward	2.15¼	1880
Lucille Golddust	2.16¼	1877
American Girl	2.16½	1874
Darby	2.16½	1879
Edwin Thorne	2.16½	1882
Gloster	2.17	1874
Jerome Eddy	2.16½	1882
Charlie Ford	2.16½	1881
Occident	2.16¾	1873
Gloster	2.17	1874
Black Cloud	2.17¼	1882
Dexter	2.17¼	1867
Piedmont	2.17¼	1881
So-So	2.17¼	1881
Santa Claus	2.17¼	1881
Hannis	2.17¼	1880
Red Cloud	2.18	1874
Nettle	2.18	1875
Judge Fullerton	2.18	1874
Great Eastern	2.18	1876
Edwin Forrest	2.18	1870
Protine	2.18	1874
Dick Swiveller	2.18	1879
Josephus	2.18¼	1881
Kate Sprague	2.18¼	1882
Robert McGregor	2.18	1881
Fanny Witherspoon	2.18¼	1882
Lady Thorn	2.18¼	1869
Lucy	2.18¼	1872
Lady Maud	2.18¼	1875
Midnight	2.18¼	1874
Monroe Chief	2.18¼	1882
Rosa Wilkes	2.18¼	1882
Slow-Go	2.18¼	1877
Col. Lewis	2.18¼	1881
Nutwood	2.18¾	1879
J. B. Thomas	2.18¾	1882
William H	2.18¾	1882
Patchen	2.18¾	1881
Cleora	2.18¾	1881
Cozette	2.19	1876
Albemarle	2.19	1879
Edward	2.19	1874
Alley	2.19	1879
Bonsetter	2.19	1879
Alexander	2.19	1881
Daisydale	2.19	1882
Adele Gould	2.19	1882
Graves	2.19	1882
Jay Ey-See	2.19	1882
Kitty Bates	2.19	1882
Minnie R.	2.19	1882
Wedgewood	2.19	1882
George Palmer	2.19¾	1882
Bodine	2.19¼	1877
Comee	2.19¼	1879
Crozie	2.19¼	1879
J. B.	2.19¼	1881
Keene Jim	2.19¼	1881
Alcina	2.19¾	1882
Y. L. Young	2.19¾	1875
Moore	2.19¾	1880
Will Cody	2.19¾	1882
Driver	2.19¾	1881
Romero	2.19¾	1882
Troubadour	2.19¾	1882
Von Arnim	2.19¾	1882

Seven Wonders of the World.

Pyramids of Egypt.

Tower, Walls and Terrace Hanging Gardens of Babylon.

Statue of Jupiter Olympus, on the Capitoline Hill, at Rome.

Temple of Diana, at Ephesus.

Pharos, or watch-tower, at Alexandria, Egypt.

Colossus of Rhodes, a statue 105 feet high, overthrown by an earthquake 224 B. C.

Mausoleum at Halicarnassus, a Grecian Persian city in Asia Minor.

Facts Concerning Production of Soil, Amount of Rainfall, Condition of Temperature, Weights, Foods, Etc.

297

Foreigners in the U. S.

By the census of 1890 there was in the States and Territories a population as follows:

Males	32,518,890
Females	31,636,963
Native born	53,473,540
Foreign born	6,679,943

Summary of the Bible.

The following table is published as containing accurate particulars of the English version of the Bible:

In the Old Testament.

Letters	2,728,100
Words	592,493
Verses	23,214
Chapters	929
Books	39

In the New Testament.

Letters	838,380
Words	181,253
Verses	7,959
Chapters	260
Books	27

Total.

Letters	3,566,480
Words	773,746
Verses	31,173
Chapters	1,189
Books	66

Average Annual Rainfall

—At different parts of the United States and Territories.

Places.	Inches.
Noah Bay, Wash. Ter.	123
Sitka, Alaska	83
Ft. Haskins, Or.	66
Mt. Vernon, Ala.	66
Baton Rouge, La.	60
Meadow Valley, Cal.	57
Ft. Tunson, Ind. Ter.	57
Ft. Myers, Fla.	56
Washington, Ark.	54
Huntsville, Ala.	54
Natches, Miss.	51
New Orleans, La.	51
Savannah, Ga.	48
Springdale, Ky.	48
Fortress Monroe, Va.	47
Memphis, Tenn.	45
Newark, N. J.	44
Boston, Mass.	44
Brunswick, Me.	44
Cincinnati, O.	44
New Haven, Conn.	44
Philadelphia, Pa.	44
Charleston, S. C.	43
New York City	43
Gaston, N. C.	43
Richmond, Ind.	43
Marietta, O.	43

Place.	Inches.
St. Louis, Mo.	42
Muscatine, Ia.	42
Baltimore, Md.	41
New Bedford, Mass.	41
Providence, R. I.	41
Fort Smith, Ark.	40
Hanover, N. H.	40
Ft. Vancouver.	38
Cleveland, O.	37
Pittsburgh, Pa.	37
Washington, D. C.	37
White Sulphur Springs, Va.	37
Ft. Gibson, Ind. Ter.	36
Key West, Fla.	36
Peoria, Ill.	35
Burlington, Vt.	34
Buffalo, N. Y.	33
Ft. Brown, Tex.	33
Ft. Leavenworth, Kan.	31
Detroit, Mich.	30
Milwaukee, Wis.	30
Penn Yan, N. Y.	28
Ft. Kearney.	25
Ft. Snelling, Minn.	25
Salt Lake City. U. T.	23
Mackinac, Mich.	23
San Francisco, Cal.	21
Dallas, Or.	21
Sacramento, Cal.	21
Ft. Massachusetts, Col.	17
Ft. Marcy, N. M.	16
Ft. Randall, D. T.	16

Place.	Inches.
Ft. Laramie, Wy. T.	15
Ft. Defiance, Ariz.	14
Ft. Craig, N. M.	11
San Diego, Cal.	9
Ft. Colville, Wash. Ter.	9
Ft. Bliss, Tex.	9
Ft. Bridger, Utah	8
Ft. Garland, Col.	6

Average Temperature

—In different States and Territories.

Place of Observation	State or Territory	Average Temperature.
Tucson	Ariz.	68
Jacksonville	Fla.	68
New Orleans	La.	66
Austin	Tex.	67
Mobile	Ala.	66
Jackson	Miss.	64
Little Rock	Ark.	62
Columbia	S. C.	62
Ft. Gibson Ind. Ter.		60
Raleigh	N. C.	59
Atlanta	Ga.	58
Nashville	Tenn.	58
Richmond	Va.	57
Louisville	Ky.	56
San Francisco	Cal.	55
Washington	D. C.	55

City.	State.	Degree.
St. Louis	Mo.	55
Baltimore	Md.	54
Harrisburg	Pa.	54
Wilmington	Del.	53
Trenton	N. J.	53
Columbus	O.	52
Portland	Or.	52
Ft. Boise	Idaho	52
Salt Lake City	Utah	52
Romney	W. Va.	52
Indianapolis	Ind.	51
Leavenworth	Kan.	51
Santa Fe	N. M.	51
Steilacoom	W. Ter.	51
Hartford	Conn.	50
Springfield	Ill.	50
Camp Scott	Nev.	50
Des Moines	Iowa.	49
Omaha	Neb.	49
Denver	Col.	48
Boston	Mass.	48
Albany	N. Y.	48
Providence	R. I.	48
Detroit	Mich.	47
Ft. Randall	Dak.	47
Sitka	Alaska.	46
Concord	N. H.	46
Augusta	Maine.	45
Madison	Wis.	45
Helena	Mont.	43
Montpelier	Vt.	43
St. Paul	Minn.	42

Weights by Railroad.

When not able to ascertain the weight definitely, railway companies make the following standard of weights in bulk.

Articles.	Pounds.	Articles.	Pounds.
Salt	Per bushel..70	Beef, pork, bacon	Per hhd...1,000
Eggs	Barrel...200	Salt fish and meat	Per firkin...100
Bark	Cord...2,000	Ashes, pot or pearl	Barrel...446
Barley	Bushel...45	Butter, tallow, lard	Per bbl...232
Apples	Bushel...50	Coke, and oake meal	Bushel...40
Liquors	Per gallon...10	Resin, tar, turpentine	Barrel...300
Charcoal	Bushel...22	Onions, wheat, potatoes	Bushel...60
Buckwheat	Bushel...48	Bran, feed, shipstuffs, oats	Bushel...35
Wood—oak	Cord...3,500	Liquors, malt and distilled	Barrel...350
Clover seed	Bushel...56	Apples, and barrelled fruits	Barrel...200
Hides (green)	Each...25	Grain and seeds, not stated	Bushel...60
Ice, coal, lime	Bushel...80	Timothy and light grass seed	Bushel...46
Stone, dressed	Cubic feet...160	Hides (dry), salted or Spanish	Each...23
Plastering lath	Per 1,000...600	Shingles	Per M., short, 900 lbs., Long...1,500
Wood—hickory	Cord...4,500	Lumber—pine, poplar, hemlock..Ft. b. m.	3
Bricks, common	Each...5	Lumber—oak, walnut, cherry, ash, Ft. b. m.	5
Nails and spikes	Keg...106	Oysters	Per bushel, 100 lbs., per 1,000...250
Sand, gravel, etc.	Per cubic feet...150	Flour and meal	Per bushel, 54 lbs., Barrel...216
Stone, undressed	Perch...4,600		

Landholders of Great Britain.

The English law of entailment, which provides that the eldest son shall inherit his parents' lands and tenements, has brought about the following results:

Amount of Land.	Number Owners.	Acres Land.
Less than 1 acre	816,894	179,342
From 1 to 10 acres	131,454	509,006
From 10 to 50 acres	72,166	1,827,695
From 50 to 100 acres	37,653	1,675,680
From 100 to 500 acres	34,454	7,343,718
From 500 to 1,000 acres	5,685	3,900,419
From 1,000 to 2,000 acres	3,316	4,634,640
From 3,000 to 5,000 acres	2,482	7,272,342
From 5,000 to 10,000 acres	921	5,791,392
From 10,000 to 20,000 acres	388	5,466,725
From 20,000 to 50,000 acres	146	4,925,364
From 50,000 to 100,000 acres	47	3,296,554
100,000 acres and over	15	5,113,509
No acres stated	6,945	
No rentals stated	134	3,570

Facts Concerning Poultry.

—Different breeds, their live weight, when full grown, the annual number of eggs they will lay, etc.

Breeds.	Live weight of Males.	Live weight of Hens.	No. of Eggs laid per year.	No. of Eggs laid to the pound.
Brahmas, light	11½	8	150	7
Brahmas, dark	11½	7	150	8
Cochins, black	10	7	170	9½
Cochins, buff	10	7½	150	8
Cochins, white	9	5	140	6
Cochins, partridge	11	8	150	8
Common	3½	3	140	11
Dorkings	8½	6	120	9
Dominiques, American	5	4	170	10
Games, black-breast'd, red	7½	5	170	10
Hamburg	5	3	130	17
Houdans	7½	6	170	9
Leghorns, black	6½	5½	200	10
Leghorns, brown	4½	3½	200	10
Leghorns, dominique	4½	3½	200	10
Leghorns, white	6½	5½	200	10
Plymouth Rocks	8½	6½	175	8½
Polish	6½	3½	170	9
Spanish, black	7	5	170	9½
Ducks, common	5	5	80	9
Ducks, Aylesbury	7	6	80	8
Ducks, Cayuga	6	5½	100	8
Ducks, Pekin	6	5½	75	8
Ducks, Rouen	7½	6½	80	6
Geese, common	6	7	90	4
Geese, African	20	15	20	4
Geese, Egyptian	7	6	40	6
Geese, Embden	18	15	20	2½
Geese, Toulouse	22	20	60	2½
Turkeys, common	18	10	50	7
Turkeys, black	15	12	50	6
Turkeys, bronze	24	15	50	6
Turkeys, buff	15	12	50	6
Turkeys, Narragansett	22	14	50	6

Foods for Sheep.

In the course of several experiments by De Raumer, a French scientist, it was found that 1,000 pounds of different kinds of foods produced the following results. It will be seen by examination that wheat proved the most valuable food, barley came next, while mangolds stood lowest in the scale.

Substances	Increase of weight in living animals	Wool produced	Tallow produced
Potatoes with salt	46½ lbs.	8½ lbs.	13½ lbs.
Potatoes without salt	44 lbs.	8½ lbs.	11½ lbs.
Mangold-Wurzels	38½ lbs.	5½ lbs.	6½ lbs.
Wheat	156 lbs.	14 lbs.	60½ lbs.
Oats	146 lbs.	16 lbs.	49½ lbs.
Barley	136 lbs.	11½ lbs.	60 lbs.
Peas	136 lbs.	14½ lbs.	41 lbs.
Rye, with salt	123 lbs.	16 lbs.	26 lbs.
Rye, without salt	90 lbs.	12 lbs.	43 lbs.
Corn-meal, wet	150 lbs.	13½ lbs.	17½ lbs.
Buckwheat	130 lbs.	10 lbs.	22 lbs.

AGRICULTURAL TABLES FOR FARMERS, GARDENERS AND OTHERS.

For many facts and figures in these various reference tables, credit is due the "American Almanac," edited by A. R. Spofford, "Moore's Universal Assistant," by R. Moore, the "American Farm and Home Cyclopædia," by H. R. Allen, "Farmers' and Mechanics' Manual," by Geo. E. Warring, "Statesman's Year Book," by Frederick Martin, "The Circle of Useful Knowledge" and other valuable works.

Vitality of Seeds.

Length of time that the seeds of various herbs and vegetables retain their powers of germination.

Vegetables.	*Years.*	*Vegetables.*	*Years.*
Cucumber	8 to 10	Leek	2 to 3
Melon	8 to 10	Onion	2 to 3
Pumpkin	8 to 10	Parsley	2 to 3
Squash	8 to 10	Parsnip	2 to 3
Broccoli	5 to 6	Pepper	2 to 3
Cauliflower	5 to 6	Salsify	2 to 3
Artichoke	5 to 6	Tomato	2 to 3
Endive	5 to 6	Egg-plant	1 to 2
Pea	5 to 6		
Radish	4 to 5	*Herbs.*	
Beets	3 to 4	Anise	3 to 4
Cress	3 to 4	Hyssop	3 to 4
Lettuce	3 to 4	Balm	2 to 3
Mustard	3 to 4	Caraway	2 ....
Okra	3 to 4	Coriander	1 ....
Rhubarb	3 to 4	Dill	2 to 3
Spinach	3 to 4	Fennel	2 to 3
Turnip	3 to 4	Lavender	2 to 3
Asparagus	2 to 3	Sweet Marjoram	2 to 3
Beans	2 to 3	Summer Savory	1 to 2
Carrots	2 to 3	Sage	2 to 3
Celery	2 to 3	Thyme	2 to 3
Corn (on cob)	2 to 3	Wormwood	2 to 3

Number to an Acre

Of plants or trees set at regular distances apart.

Distances apart.	No. of plants.	*Distances apart.*	No. of Plants.
3 inches by 3 inches	696,960	6 feet by 6 feet	1,210
4 inches by 4 inches	392,040	6½ feet by 6½ feet	1,031
6 inches by 6 inches	174,240	7 feet by 7 feet	881
9 inches by 9 inches	77,440	8 feet by 8 feet	680
1 foot by 1 foot	43,560	9 feet by 9 feet	537
1½ feet by 1½ feet	19,360	10 feet by 10 feet	435
2 feet by 1 foot	21,780	11 feet by 11 feet	360
2 feet by 2 feet	10,890	12 feet by 12 feet	302
2½ feet by 2½ feet	6,960	13 feet by 13 feet	257
3 feet by 1 foot	14,520	14 feet by 14 feet	222
3 feet by 2 feet	7,260	15 feet by 15 feet	193
3 feet by 3 feet	4,840	16 feet by 16 feet	170
3½ feet by 3½ feet	3,555	16½ feet by 16½ feet	160
4 feet by 1 foot	10,890	17 feet by 17 feet	150
4 feet by 2 feet	5,445	18 feet by 18 feet	134
4 feet by 3 feet	3,630	19 feet by 19 feet	120
4 feet by 4 feet	2,722	20 feet by 20 feet	108
4½ feet by 4½ feet	2,151	25 feet by 25 feet	69
5 feet by 1 foot	8,712	30 feet by 30 feet	48
5 feet by 2 feet	4,356	33 feet by 33 feet	40
5 feet by 3 feet	2,904	40 feet by 40 feet	27
5 feet by 4 feet	2,178	50 feet by 50 feet	17
5 feet by 5 feet	1,742	60 feet by 60 feet	12
5½ feet by 5½ feet	1,417	66 feet by 66 feet	10

Cost of Producing Pork.

The cost of producing a pound of pork depends upon the cost of corn per bushel, as follows:

Corn per Bushel in Cents.	Will make the cost of pork per hundred.
12½ cts	$1 50
15	1 75
17	2.00
20	2 38
22	2.62
25	2 96
30	3.57
33	3.96
35	4.00
38	4 52
40	4 76
42	5.00
45	5.35
50	5.95
55	6.54
60	7 14
65	7.74
70	8.57

Cost of Small Quantities of Hay.

Price per Ton.	50 lbs. worth.	100 lbs worth	200 lbs worth.	300 lbs. worth	400 lbs. worth.
Four dollars	10 cts.	20 cts.	40 cts.	60.	$ .80
Five dollars	12	25	50	75	1.00
Six dollars	15	30	60	90	1.20
Seven dollars	17	35	70	1.05	1.40
Eight dollars	20	40	80	1.20	1.60
Nine dollars	22	45	90	1.35	1.80
Ten dollars	25	50	1.00	1.50	2.00
Eleven dollars	27	55	1.10	1 65	2.20
Twelve dollars	30	60	1.20	1,80	2.40
Thirteen dollars	32	65	1.30	1.95	2.60
Fourteen dollars	35	70	1.40	2.10	2.80
Fifteen dollars	37	.75	1.50	2.25	3.00

Facts About Sheep.

The weight of any animal at a certain age, will, of course, depend upon the manner in which it is fed and cared for. Supposing sheep to be well fed and sheltered, the following presents an average yield of flesh and wool at a certain age.

Breeds.	Bucks weigh.	Ewes weigh	Age at maturity Years.	Annual yield of w. lbs.
Cotswold	300	200	2	14
Lincoln	300	200	2	11
Leicester	250	150	2½	8
Merino, American	150	120	2	9
Merino, Spanish	125	110	3	10
Southdown	200	140	2	6
Shropshire	200	140	2	6
Common "Scrub"	120	90	3	4

Weight of Horses.

Breeds.	Stallions.	Geldings and Mares.	Age when Matured.
Cleveland Bay	1,400	1,300	6
Clydesdale	1,900	1,700	4½
English draft	1,800	1,650	4
Hambletonian	1,150	1,100	5
Mambrino	1,200	1,150	5
Morgan	950	900	5
Percheron—Norman	1,700	1,550	4
Pony—Canadian	950	900	4
Pony—Mustang	800	650	3
Pony—Shetland	300	250	3
"Scrub," or Native	1,000	850	4½
Thoroughbred	1,150	1,000	3
Ass	700	600	5
Mule		1,000	5

Quantity of Seed Required to Sow or Plant an Acre.

Kind of Seed.	*Quantity.*
Asparagus in 12-inch drills	16 qts
Asparagus plants, 4 by 1½ feet	8,000
Barley	2½ bu
Beans, bush, in drills 2½ feet	1½ bu
Beans, pole, Lima, 4 by 4 feet	20 qts
Beans, Carolina, prolific, etc., 4 by 3	10 qts
Beets and mangold, drills, 2½ feet	6 lbs
Broom corn in drills	12 lbs
Cabbage, outside, for transplanting	12 oz
Cabbage, sown in frames	4 oz
Carrot in drills, 2½ feet	4 lbs
Celery, seed	8 oz
Celery, plant, 4 by ½ feet	25,000
Clover, white Dutch	12 lbs
Clover, Lucerne	10 lbs
Clover, Alsike	6 lbs
Clover, large red with timothy	12 lbs
Clover, large red without timothy	16 lbs
Corn, sugar	10 qts
Corn, field	8 qts
Corn, salad, drill 10 inches	25 lbs
Cucumber, in hills	3 qts
Cucumber, in drills	4 qts
Egg plant, plants 3 by 2 feet	4 oz
Endive, in drills 2½ feet	3 lbs
Flax, broadcast	20 qts
Grass, timothy with clover	6 qts
Grass, timothy without clover	10 qts
Grass, orchard	25 qts
Grass, red top or herds	20 qts
Grass, blue	28 qts
Grass, rye	30 qts
Grass, millet	32 qts
Hemp, broadcast	½ bu
Kale, German greens	3 lbs
Lettuce, in rows 2½ feet	3 lbs
Leek	4 lbs
Lawn grass	35 lbs
Melons, water, in hills 8 by 8 feet	3 lbs
Melons, citrons, in hills 4 by 4 feet	2 lbs
Oats	2 bu
Okra, in drills 2½ by ½ feet	20 lbs
Onion, in beds for sets	50 lbs
Onion, in rows for large bulbs	7 lbs
Parsnip, in drills 2½ feet	5 lbs
Pepper, plants, 2½ by 1 foot	17,500
Pumpkin, in hills 8 by 8 feet	2 qts
Parsley, in drills 2 feet	4 lbs
Peas, in drills, short varieties	2 bu
Peas, in drills, tall varieties	1 to 1½ bu
Peas, broadcast	3 bu
Potatoes	8 bu
Radish, in drills 2 feet	10 lbs
Rye, broadcast	1½ bu
Rye, drilled	1¼ bu
Salsify, in drills 2½ feet	10 lbs
Spinach, broadcast	30 lbs
Squash, bush, in hills 4 by 4 feet	3 lbs
Squash, running, 8 by 8 feet	2 lbs
Sorghum	6 qts
Turnips, in drills 2 feet	3 lbs
Turnips, broadcast	3 lbs
Tomatoes, in frames	3 oz
Tomatoes, seed in hills 3 by 3 feet	8 oz
Tomatoes, plants	3,800
Wheat, in drills	1½ bu
Wheat, broadcast	2 bu

Facts Concerning Production of Soil, Amount of Rainfall, Condition of Temperature, Weights, Foods, Etc.

297

Foreigners in the U. S.

By the census of 1880 there was in the States and Territories a population as follows:

Males.....................25,518,820
Females....................24,636,963
Native born...............43,475,840
Foreign born...............6,679,943

Summary of the Bible.

The following table is published as containing accurate particulars of the English version of the Bible:

In the Old Testament.

Letters.................2,728,100
Words....................592,493
Verses....................23,214
Chapters.....................929
Books.........................39

In the New Testament.

Letters..................838,380
Words....................181,253
Verses.....................7,959
Chapters.....................260
Books.........................27

Total.

Letters................3,566,480
Words....................773,746
Verses....................31,173
Chapters...................1,189
Books.........................66

Average Annual Rainfall

—At different parts of the United States and Territories.

Place.	Inches.
Neah Bay, Wash. Ter.	123
Sitka, Alaska	83
Ft. Haskins, Or.	66
Mt. Vernon, Ala	66
Baton Rouge, La.	60
Meadow Valley, Cal.	57
Ft. Tomson, Ind. Ter.	57
Ft. Myers, Fla.	56
Washington, Ark.	54
Huntsville, Ala.	54
Natchez, Miss.	53
New Orleans, La.	51
Savannah, Ga.	48
Springdale, Ky.	48
Fortress Monroe, Va.	47
Memphis, Tenn.	46
Newark, N. J.	46
Boston, Mass.	44
Brunswick, Me.	44
Cincinnati, O.	44
New Haven, Conn.	44
Philadelphia, Pa.	44
Charleston, S. C.	43
New York City	43
Gaston, N. C.	43
Richmond, Ind.	43
Marietta, O.	43

Place.	Inches.
St. Louis, Mo.	43
Muscatine, Ia.	42
Baltimore, Md.	41
New Bedford, Mass.	41
Providence, R. I.	41
Fort Smith, Ark.	40
Hanover, N. H.	40
Ft. Vancouver	39
Cleveland, O.	37
Pittsburgh, Pa.	37
Washington, D. C.	37
White Sulphur Springs, Va.	37
Ft. Gibson, Ind. Ter.	36
Key West, Fla.	36
Peoria, Ill.	35
Burlington, Vt.	34
Buffalo, N. Y.	33
Ft. Brown, Tex.	33
Ft. Leavenworth, Kan.	31
Detroit, Mich.	30
Milwaukee, Wis.	30
Penn Yan, N. Y.	28
Ft. Kearney.	26
Ft. Snelling, Minn.	26
Salt Lake City, U. T.	23
Mackinac, Mich.	22
San Francisco, Cal.	21
Dallas, Or.	21
Sacramento, Cal.	21
Ft. Massachusetts, Col.	17
Ft. Marcy, N. M.	16
Ft. Randall, D. T.	16

Place.	Inches.
Ft. Laramie, Wy. T.	15
Ft. Defiance, Ariz.	14
Ft. Craig, N. M.	11
San Diego, Cal.	9
Ft. Colville, Wash. Ter.	9
Ft. Bliss, Tex.	9
Ft. Bridger, Utah	6
Ft. Garland, Col.	6

Average Temperature

—In different States and Territories.

Place of Observation.	State or Territory.	Average Temperature.
Tucson	Ariz.	69
Jacksonville	Fla.	69
New Orleans	La.	69
Austin	Tex.	67
Mobile	Ala.	66
Jackson	Miss.	64
Little Rock	Ark.	63
Columbia	S. C.	62
Ft. Gibson Ind. Ter.		60
Raleigh	N. C.	59
Atlanta	Ga.	58
Nashville	Tenn.	58
Richmond	Va.	57
Louisville	Ky.	56
San Francisco	Cal.	55
Washington	D. C.	55

City.	State.	Degree.
St. Louis	Mo.	55
Baltimore	Md.	56
Harrisburg	Pa.	54
Wilmington	Del.	53
Trenton	N. J.	53
Columbus	O.	53
Portland	Or.	52
Ft. Boise	Idaho.	52
Salt Lake City	Utah.	52
Romney	W. Va.	52
Indianapolis	Ind.	51
Leavenworth	Kan.	51
Santa Fe	N. M.	51
Steilacoom	W. Ter.	51
Hartford	Conn.	50
Springfield	Ill.	50
Camp Scott	Nev.	50
Des Moines	Iowa.	49
Omaha	Neb.	49
Denver	Col.	49
Boston	Mass.	48
Albany	N. Y.	48
Providence	R. I.	48
Detroit	Mich.	47
Ft. Randall	Dak.	47
Sitka	Alaska.	46
Concord	N. H.	46
Augusta	Maine.	46
Madison	Wis.	45
Helena	Mont.	43
Montpelier	Vt.	42
St. Paul	Minn.	42

Weights by Railroad.

When not able to ascertain the weight definitely, railway companies make the following standard of weights in bulk.

Articles.		Pounds.
Salt	Per bushel	70
Eggs	Barrel	800
Bark	Cord	2,000
Barley	Bushel	48
Apples	Bushel	50
Liquors	Per gallon	10
Charcoal	Bushel	22
Buckwheat	Bushel	48
Wood—oak	Cord	3,500
Clover seed	Bushel	62
Hides (green)	Each	85
Ice, coal, lime	Bushel	80
Stone, dressed	Cubic feet	150
Plastering lath	Per 1,000	600
Wood—hickory	Cord	4,600
Bricks, common	Each	5
Nails and spikes	Keg	106
Sand, gravel, etc.	Per cubic feet	150
Stone, undressed	Perch	4,000

Articles.		Pounds.
Beef, pork, bacon	Per hhd.	1,000
Salt fish and meat	Per firkin	100
Ashes, pot or pearl	Barrel	450
Butter, tallow, lard	Per bbl.	333
Coke, and cake meal	Bushel	40
Resin, tar, turpentine	Barrel	300
Onions, wheat, potatoes	Bushel	60
Bran, feed, shipstuffs, oats	Bushel	32
Liquors, malt and distilled	Barrel	350
Apples, and barrelled fruits	Barrel	200
Grain and seeds, not stated	Bushel	60
Timothy and light grass seed	Bushel	45
Hides (dry), salted or Spanish	Each	25
Shingles	Per M., short, 900 lbs. Long	1,400
Lumber—pine, poplar, hemlock	Ft. b. m.	3
Lumber—oak, walnut, cherry, ash	Ft. b. m.	5
Oysters	Per bushel. 100 lbs., per 1,000	350
Flour and meal	Per bushel, 56 lbs., Barrel	216

Landholders of Great Britain.

The English law of entailment, which provides that the eldest son shall inherit his parents' lands and tenements, has brought about the following results:

Amount of Land.	Number Owners.	Acres Land.
Less than 1 acre	816,294	179,345
From 1 to 10 acres	121,434	566,096
From 10 to 50 acres	76,109	1,827,496
From 50 to 100 acres	27,952	1,878,963
From 100 to 500 acres	34,654	7,352,718
From 500 to 1,000 acres	5,425	3,900,419
From 1,000 to 2,000 acres	3,210	4,434,549
From 2,000 to 5,000 acres	2,406	7,373,568
From 5,000 to 10,000 acres	931	5,701,565
From 10,000 to 20,000 acres	393	5,865,795
From 20,000 to 50,000 acres	166	4,955,864
From 50,000 to 100,000 acres	47	3,220,554
100,000 acres and over	35	5,113,500
No acres stated	6,945	
No rentals stated	194	3,370

Facts Concerning Poultry,

—Different breeds, their live weight, when full grown, the annual number of eggs they will lay, etc.

Breeds.	Live weight of Males.	Live weight of Hens.	No. of Eggs laid per year.	No. of Eggs to the pound.
Brahmas, light	11½	8	130	7
Brahmas, dark	10½	7	150	8
Cochins, black	10	7	170	8½
Cochins, buff	10	7½	130	8
Cochins, white	11	8	140	8
Cochins, partridge	11	8	150	8
Common	5½	3	160	11
Dorkings	6½	5	190	9
Dominiques, American	5	4	170	10
Games, black-breast'd, red	7½	5	170	10
Hamburgs	5	3	180	12
Houdans	7½	5	180	9
Leghorns, black	4½	3½	200	10
Leghorns, brown	4½	3½	200	10
Leghorns, dominique	4½	3½	200	10
Leghorns, white	4½	3½	200	10
Plymouth Rocks	8½	6½	175	8½

Breeds.	Live weight of Males.	Live weight of Hens.	No. of Eggs laid per year.	No. of Eggs to the pound.
Polish	5½	3½	170	9
Spanish, black	7	5	170	9½
Ducks, common	8	5	50	9
Ducks, Aylesbury	7	6	50	8
Ducks, Cayuga	6	5½	130	8
Ducks, Pekin	6	5½	75	8
Ducks, Rouen	7½	6½	50	8
Geese, common	8	7	30	4
Geese, African	20	16	30	4
Geese, Egyptian	7	6	60	4
Geese, Embden	15	13	30	3½
Geese, Toulouse	18	15	80	3½
Turkeys, common	18	10	60	6
Turkeys, black	18	12	50	6
Turkeys, bronze	24	15	50	5
Turkeys, buff	18	12	50	7
Turkeys, Narragansett	22	14	50	5

Foods for Sheep.

In the course of several experiments by De Raumer, a French scientist, it was found that 1,000 pounds of different kinds of foods produced the following results. It will be seen by examination that wheat proved the most valuable food, barley came next, while mangolds stood lowest in the scale.

Substances.	Increase of weight in living animals	Wool produced	Tallow produced
Potatoes with salt	46½ lbs.	6¼ lbs.	12½ lbs.
Potatoes without salt	44 lbs.	6½ lbs.	11½ lbs.
Mangold-Wurzels	38½ lbs.	3½ lbs.	6½ lbs.
Wheat	155 lbs.	16 lbs.	50½ lbs.
Oats	148 lbs.	10 lbs.	42½ lbs.
Barley	158 lbs.	11½ lbs.	60 lbs.
Peas	136 lbs.	14½ lbs.	61 lbs.
Rye, with salt	133 lbs.	14 lbs.	35 lbs.
Rye, without salt	90 lbs.	12 lbs.	43 lbs.
Corn-meal, wet	139 lbs.	13½ lbs.	17½ lbs.
Buckwheat	139 lbs.	10 lbs.	33 lbs.

Healthiest Regions, Value of Foods, Educational Advancement, Etc.

Healthiest Regions for Consumptives.

The following table, in a scale of 100, shows the per cent. of deaths from consumption. From this it will be seen that the Atlantic States have a much higher death rate from this disease than most of the Western States and Territories.

State.	No. of Deaths in each 100
Vermont	36
Maine	25
Massachusetts	25
New Hampshire	25
Rhode Island	25
Connecticut	20
Delaware	20
District of Columbia	20
New Jersey	20
New York	20
Maryland	16
Michigan	16
Ohio	16
Pennsylvania	16
Washington Territory	16
West Virginia	16
California	14
Indiana	14
Kentucky	14
Minnesota	14
Wisconsin	14
Dakota	12
Iowa	12
Oregon	12
Tennessee	12
Virginia	12
Illinois	11

State.	No. of Deaths in each 100
Nebraska	9
Missouri	9
Montana	8
Colorado	8
Kansas	8
Louisiana	7
North Carolina	6
Alabama	6
Florida	6
Mississippi	6
Utah	6
Arkansas	5
Georgia	5
South Carolina	5
Texas	5
New Mexico	4

Relative Value of Foods.

One hundred pounds of good hay for stock are equal to—

Articles.	Pounds.
Beets, white silesia	660
Turnips	600
Rye of Genoa	629
Clover, red, green	372
Carrots	371
Mangolds	366½
Potatoes, kept in pit	350
Oat-straw	317
Potatoes	280
Carrot leaves (tops)	135
Hay, English	100
Lucerne	99
Clover, red, dry	88

Articles.	Pounds.
Buckwheat	78½
Corn	62½
Oats	56
Barley	55
Rye	53½
Wheat	64½
Oil-cake, linseed	43
Peas, dry	37½
Beans	35

Amount of Oil in Seeds.

The amount of oil in a certain seed will vary according to conditions of growth. In a scale of 100 this is considered about an average per cent.

Kind of Seeds.	Per Cent. of Oil
Rapeseed	55
Sweet almond	47
Turnip seed	45
White mustard	37
Bitter almond	37
Hempseed	19
Linseed	17
Indian corn	7
Oats	6½
Clover hay	5
Wheat bran	3½
Oat-straw	3
Meadow hay	3½
Wheat-straw	2
Wheat flour	2
Barley	2½
Potatoes, turnips, cabbages	1½

Canning Fruit.

A general rule for the canning of fruit is to add one pound of sugar to four pounds of fruit, and water sufficient to keep it from burning. If the fruit be very tart, more sweet may be added if desired. Whether glass or tin, the cans must, of course, be air-tight. The following gives the requisite time for boiling and the amount of sugar it is well to add at the time of canning.

Fruit.	Time for boiling. Min.	Quantity of sugar per qt.
Small pears, whole	30	5
Siberian apples	25	5
Bartlet pears	20	6
Tomatoes	20	None
Quinces, sliced	15	10
Pine apples, sliced	15	6
Peaches, whole	15	4
Pie-plant, sliced	10	10
Plums	10	8
Wild grapes	10	8
Sour apples	10	5
Blackberries	6	6
Strawberries	8	8
Gooseberries	8	8
Peaches, halved	8	4
Ripe currants	6	8
Raspberries	6	4
Cherries	5	6
Whortleberries	5	4

Cannot Read or Write.

The per cent. of illiteracy in the scale of 100 among the people of different countries is shown in the following table, as taken from Kiddle & Schem's Cyclopedia of Education, New York, 1877.

Country.	Year	Per Ct of Illiteracy
India	1871	95
Mexico	Recent	93
Poland	Recent	91
Russia	Recent	91
Argentine Rep.	Recent	83
Greece	Recent	82
Spain	1860	75
Italy	1861	73
Hungary	Recent	50
China	Recent	50
Austria	Recent	40
Ireland	Recent	40
England	Recent	32
Belgium	Recent	30
France	1876	30
United States	1870	20
Netherlands	Recent	16
Scotland	Recent	14
Japan	Recent	10

Illiteracy in the U. S.

By the census of 1880, persons over ten years old that could not write:

Whites	3,261,311
Colored	2,796,688
Natives	4,080,771
Foreigners	777,971
Could not read, total	6,325,628

Salaries of Kings, Queens, Presidents and other Rulers.

The following table, condensed from the "Statesman's Year Book," shows the yearly salary paid to kings, queens and members of royal households and presidents of various republics, according to the most reliable authorities in 1880. Out of these salaries some rulers have much to pay, in order to maintain the character of their position, so that their actual clear savings, annually, cannot be easily shown.

Country.	Ruler.	Salary.
Turkey	Sultan and royal household	$10,800,000.00
Russia	Emperor and royal household	9,000,000.00
Italy	King	3,166,000.00
	Prince Amadeo	58,000.00
	Duke of Genoa	38,780.00
Germany Prussia	Emperor and King and royal family	3,867,077.84
Morocco	Sultan	2,450,000.00
Austria-Hungary	As Emperor	2,250,000.00
	As King	2,250,000.00
Spain	King	1,350,000.00
	Queen	87,250.00
	Parents of King	202,250.00
	King's Sisters	154,500.00
Bavaria	King and royal family	1,393,940.13
Japan	Mikado and royal family	845,548.00
Egypt	Khedive	786,000.00
	His father	243,000.00
	Royal family	336,800.00
Saxony	King	711,480.00
	Royal family	125,855.00
Belgium	King	603,860.00
Wurtemberg	King	417,965.55
	Royal family	80,719.40
Portugal	King	396,880.00
	Queen	64,372.00
	Royal family	182,468.00
Baden	Grand Duke and royal family	362,666.04
Hesse	Grand Duke and royal family	318,191.28

Country.	Ruler.	Salary.
Great Britain and Ireland, including queen and members of the royal household, making a total annual salary for the government to pay of $1,939,310	Queen (Privy Purse)	$290,400.00
	Prince of Wales	400,000.00
	Princess of Wales	48,400.00
	Duke of Edinburgh	121,000.00
	Duke of Connaught	121,000.00
	Prince Leopold	58,780.00
	Princess Fredrich Wilhelm of Prussia	38,720.00
	Princess Christian of Schleswig-Holstein	29,040.00
	Princess Louise, Marchioness of Lorne	29,040.00
	Duchess of Cambridge	29,040.00
	Grand Duchess of Mecklenb'g Strelitz	14,520.00
	Princess Teck	24,250.00
	Duke George of Cambridge	58,000.00
Denmark	King	266,556.00
	Heir apparent	39,363.14
Greece	King	252,541.38
Netherlands	King	942,000.00
	Royal family	60,560.00
Brunswick	Duke	242,000.00
Saxe Weimar	Grand Duke	303,290.00
Roumania	Prince	174,240.00
Anhalt	Duke and royal family	140,360.00
India	Governor-General	121,000.00
Schaumburg-Lippe	Prince	121,000.00
France	President	116,160.00
	State household	58,080.00
Schwarzburg Sonderhausen	Prince	108,680.00
Saxe-Altenburg	Duke and royal family	103,818.00

Country.	Ruler.	Salary.
Saxe Meiningen	Duke	991,300.00
Sweden and Norway	King	89,363.44
	Royal family	615,936.30
Saxe-Coburg-Gotha	Duke	72,000.00 to 87,342.00
Oldenburg	Grand Duke	99,300.00
	Royal family. Private income	
Schwarzburg-Rudolstadt	Prince	76,296.00
United States	President	50,000.00
Victoria	Governor	42,489.40
Lippe	Prince	43,585.80 and Private income
Canada	Governor-General	48,480.00
Ceylon	Governor	38,793.00
New Zealand	Governor	38,302.00
New South Wales	Governor	35,380.00
Hong Kong	Governor	30,040.00
Mauritius	Governor	38,865.00
Cape Colony, Africa	Governor	34,328.04
Queensland	Governor	36,330.00
South Australia	Governor	34,380.00
Chili	President	21,780.00
Argentine Republic	President	19,380.00
Tasmania	Governor	16,305.00
Natal, Africa	Governor	12,105.00
Western Australia	Governor	22,308.00
Switzerland	Federal Council— President	5,304.00
	Members	1,929.00

Astronomical Tables, Giving Facts Relative to the Heavenly Bodies,

Condensed from chapter on Astronomy in "HILL'S ALBUM OF BIOGRAPHY AND ART."

Distant From the Sun.

Distances of the different planets from the sun.

Name of Planet.	Miles distant from the sun.
Neptune	2,745,998,000
Uranus	1,822,360,000
Saturn	872,132,000
Jupiter	480,000,000
Mars	145,000,000
Earth	92,000,000
Venus	68,000,000
Mercury	37,000,000
Earth's Moon distant from Earth	140,000

The enormous distances from us of the fixed stars, which are supposed to be suns, are beyond conception. One of these, Sirius (the Dog Star), is supposed to be twenty trillion miles away.

Size of Planets.

The following gives the diameter of the sun and the known principal planets that revolve around it, together with the number of moons belonging to the several planets.

Heavenly Body.	Diameter Miles.	No. of Moons.
Sun	882,000	
Jupiter	91,000	4 moons
Saturn	71,903	8 moons
Neptune	35,000	1 moon
Uranus	34,331	6 moons
Venus	7,661	
Mars	4,222	2 moons
Mercury	2,984	
Earth	8,000	1 moon

Diameter of Earth's Moon, 2,162 miles.

Time of Revolution.

The following is the time of revolution of the various planets around the sun

Planet.	Time in going around the sun.
Neptune	164½ years
Uranus	84 years
Saturn	29½ years
Jupiter	12 years
Mars	1 yr. 10½ months
Earth	1 year
Venus	224 2-3 days
Mercury	88 days

Our moon makes its revolution around the earth in 29 days, 12 hours, 44 minutes and 3 seconds, and is supposed to revolve once upon its own axis in that time.

Velocity of Motion.

The velocity of speed with which the various planets move through space as they go around the sun, is shown in the following.

Planet.	Miles per hour
Mercury	110,725
Venus	80,000
Earth	68,000
Jupiter	30,000
Saturn	22,300
Uranus	15,000
Neptune	12,000

Light moves at the rate of 192,000 miles a second, and yet passing with that velocity it would take three years and nine months to reach Alpha, the nearest star, which is nineteen trillions of miles away.

Revolution on its Axis.

The length of the day on each planet is indicated by the following table, which shows the length of time required for revolution on its axis.

Planet.	Daily revolution in hours, minutes and seconds.
Mars	24 h. 39 m. 21½ s.
Mercury	24 h. 5 m. 28 s.
Venus	23 h. 21 m. 7 s.
Earth	24 h.
Saturn	10½ h.
Jupiter	9 h. 56 m.
Uranus	7 h. 5 m.

The sun revolves upon its own axis at the rate of 4,564 miles per hour, and yet requires 25½ days to complete one entire revolution.

Solidity of Foods, Strength of Liquors, Weights, Measures, Etc.

Solidity of Different Foods.

Showing the proportion of solid matter and water in 100 parts each of the following articles of diet.

Articles	Solid Matter	Water	Articles	Solid Matter	Water
Wheat	87	13	Pork	24	76
Peas	87	13	Codfish	21	79
Rice	86	14	Blood	20	80
Beans	86	14	Trout	19	81
Rye	86	14	Apples	18	82
Corn	86	14	Pears	16	84
Oatmeal	74	26	Carrots	13	87
Wheat Bread	51	49	Beets	13	87
Mutton	29	71	Milk	13	87
Chicken	27	73	Oysters	13	87
Lean Beef	26	74	Cabbage	8	92
Eggs	26	74	Turnips	7	93
Veal	25	75	Watermelons	5	95
Potatoes	25	75	Cucumbers	3	97

Bricks Required.

Number of bricks required in a wall of different thickness per square foot of surface wall. The dimensions of common bricks are from 7¾ to 8 inches long by 4¼ wide, and 2¼ inches thick.

Thickness of wall	Bricks
4 inches	7½
8 inches	15
12 inches	22½
16 inches	30
20 inches	37½
24 inches	45
28 inches	52½
32 inches	60
36 inches	67½
42 inches	75

Per Cent. of Alcohol in Liquors.

In a scale of 100, the following shows the per cent. of alcohol in various kinds of liquors. The reader will understand that the per cent. here given is founded upon the fact that each liquor is tested under the most favorable conditions. Various conditions would change the rate per cent.

Kind of Liquor.	Per cent.	Kind of Liquor.	Per cent.
Scotch Whisky	54½	Malaga	17¾
Rum	53¾	Claret	15
Brandy	53½	Burgundy	14
Irish Whisky	53	Champagne (still)	13¾
Gin	51	Champagne (sparkling)	12½
Madeira	22½	Rhenish	12
Port	22	Gooseberry Wine	11½
Currant Wine	20½	Elder	8¾
Teneriffe	19¾	Ale	6¾
Constantia	19¾	Cider	5 to 9
Sherry	19¾	Porter	4
Cape Muscat	18¾	Small Beer	1

Weights and Measures for Cooks.

1 lb. of Wheat Flour is equal to	1 quart
1 lb. 2 oz. of Indian Meal make	1 quart
1 lb. of Soft Butter is equal to	1 quart
1 lb. of Broken Loaf Sugar is equal to	1 quart
1 lb. 2 oz. of Best Brown Sugar make	1 quart
1 lb. 1 oz. of Powdered White Sugar make	1 quart
10 Eggs make	1 pound
4 Large Tablespoonfuls make	½ gill
1 Common-sized Tumbler holds	½ pint
1 Common-sized Wine-glass is equal to	½ gill
1 Tea-cup holds	1 gill.
1 Large Wine-glass holds	2 ounces
1 Tablespoonful is equal to	½ ounce

Cost of Street Pavement.

The cost of paving will vary slightly in different sections, according to the supply of materials near by. The following is the average cost in Chicago, Ill.

Kind of Pavement.	Per Square Yard.
Stone block, about	$2.50 to $3.25
Asphaltum block	2.25 to 2.50
Cedar block	1.25 to 1.50
Macadam	1.40 to 1.60
Curbstone, per lineal foot	.70 to .75

On a street eighty feet wide there will be two and two-thirds yards, and on a sixty-six foot street two and one-ninth yards of pavement for each foot of frontage on each side of the street, excepting on streets occupied by railway tracks.

Interest Table.

The following will be found convenient in the absence of extended interest tables.

To find the interest on a given sum, for any number of days, at any rate of interest.

At five per cent., multiply the principal by the number of days, and divide by	72
At 6 per cent., as above, and divide by	60
At 7 per cent., as above, and divide by	52
At 8 per cent., as above, and divide by	45
At 9 per cent., as above and divide by	40
At 10 per cent., as above, and divide by	36
At 12 per cent., as above, and divide by	30
At 15 per cent., as above, and divide by	24
At 20 per cent., as above and divide by	18

Distances Around the World.

The following includes the principal stopping places, and distances between them, in a direct line around the world.

	Miles.
New York to San Francisco	3,450
San Francisco to Yokohama	4,764
Yokohama to Hong Kong	1,620
Hong Kong to Singapore	1,150
Singapore to Calcutta	1,200
Calcutta to Bombay	1,400
Bombay to Aden	1,664
Aden to Suez	1,308
Suez to Alexandria	250
Alexandria to Marseilles	1,300
Marseilles to Paris	536
Paris to London	316
London to Liverpool	205
Liverpool to New York	3,000

Average Velocity.

Object	Per hour	Per sec
Electricity moves		288,000 miles
Light moves		192,000 miles
A rifle ball moves	1,000 miles, or	1,466 feet
Sound moves	743 miles, or	1,142 feet
A hurricane moves	80 miles, or	117 feet
A storm moves	36 miles, or	52 feet
A horse runs	20 miles, or	29 feet
Steamboat runs	18 miles, or	26 feet
Sailing vessel runs	10 miles, or	14 feet
Slow rivers flow	3 miles, or	4 feet
Rapid rivers flow	7 miles, or	10 feet
A moderate wind blows	7 miles, or	10 feet
A horse trots	7 miles, or	10 feet
A man walks	3 miles, or	4 feet

Boxes of Different Measure.

A box 24 inches long by 16 inches wide, and 28 inches deep, will contain a barrel (3 bushels).

A box 24 inches long by 16 inches wide, and 14 inches deep, will contain half a barrel.

A box 16 inches square and 8 2-5 inches deep, will contain one bushel.

A box 16 inches by 8 2-5 inches wide, and 8 inches deep, will contain half a bushel.

A box 8 inches by 8 2-5 inches square, and 8 inches deep, will contain one peck

A box 8 inches by 8 inches square, and 4 1-5 inches deep, will contain one gallon.

A box 7 inches by 4 inches square, and 4 4-5 inches deep, will contain half a gallon.

A box 4 inches by 4 inches square, and 4 1-5 inches deep, will contain one quart.

In purchasing anthracite coal, 28 bushels are generally allowed for a ton.

Debt of Different Countries, How Various Colors are Made, Length and Cost of American Canals, Center of Gravity of Population, Etc.

Average Height and Weight
Of Human Beings, at Different Ages.

Males.			Females.		
Age.	Feet.	Lbs.	Age.	Feet.	Lbs.
Birth.......	1¾	7	Birth.......	1¾	6½
2 years....	2¾	25	2 years....	2¼	23½
4 years....	3	31½	4 years....	3	28¾
6 years....	3½	45	6 years....	4	35½
9 years....	4	50	9 years....	4	47
11 years...	4½	60½	11 years...	4½	56½
12 years...	4¾	75 4-5	13 years...	4 3-5	72 2-3
15 years...	5	96½	15 years...	5	99
17 years...	5½	116½	17 years...	5	104½
18 years...	5½	127½	18 years...	5½	113½
20 years...	5½	132½	20 years...	5 1-6	115½
30 years...	5½	140½	30 years...	5 1-6	119 4-5
40 years...	5½	140½	40 years...	5 1-6	121 4-5
50 years...	5½	140	50 years...	5	122 4-5
60 years...	5½	136	60 years...	5	119½
70 years...	5½	131½	70 years...	5	115½
80 years...	5½	127½	80 years...	5	108 6-6
90 years...	5½	127½	90 years...	5	108 6-5

Bait for Different Game.

Animal.	Bait Required.
Squirrel............	Grain, nuts, or ear of corn.
Muskrat...........	Carrots, potatoes, apples, etc.
Woodchuck.......	Roots, fruit, corn or bread.
Mink...............	Fowl, flesh or roasted fish.
Skunk.............	Mice, meat, piece of a fowl.
Fox.................	Fowl, flesh, fish, toasted cheese.
Opossum.........	Nuts, corn, mice, piece of fowl.
Raccoon..........	Chicken, fish or frog.
Badger...........	Mice, or flesh of any kind.
Otter..............	Fish, piece of a bird, or otter musk.
Marten..........	Head of a fish, piece of meat, or fowl.
Beaver...........	Fresh roots.
Wolf..............	Waste parts of tame or wild fowl.

The Pulse in Health.

New-born infants..............	From 140 down to 130
During 1st year................	From 130 down to 115
During 2d year................	From 115 down to 100
During 3d year................	From 105 down to 95
From 7th to 14th year.......	From 90 down to 80
From 14th to 21st year......	From 85 down to 75
From 21st to 60th year......	From 75 down to 70
In old age.....................	From 75 up to 80

Center of Gravity of Population.

The change of center of population each ten years, in the United States, is shown in the following table. In ninety years the center of gravity has moved westward 467 miles, on almost a straight line from east to west. The very rapid settlement of the northwest of late would indicate that the line will move considerably northward in the next ten years.

Date.	Location.	Westward move. Miles.
1790, 23 miles east of Baltimore................		
1800, 18 miles west of Baltimore...............		41
1810, 40 miles northwest by west of Washington		36
1820, 16 miles north of Woodstock, Va..........		50
1830, 19 miles southwest of Moorefield, W. Va.		39
1840, 16 miles south of Clarksburg, W. Va......		55
1850, 23 miles southeast of Parkersburg, W. Va.		55
1860, 20 miles south of Chillicothe, O..........		81
1870, 48 miles east by north of Cincinnati, O.		42
1880, 8 miles west by south of Cincinnati, O.		58
Total....		467

Capacity of Cisterns.

In calculating the capacity of cisterns, 31½ gallons are estimated to one barrel and 63 gallons to one hogshead.

Circular Cistern one foot in depth.

5 feet in diam. holds....	4½ barrels.
6 feet in diam. holds....	6½ barrels.
7 feet in diam. holds....	9 barrels.
8 feet in diam. holds....	12 barrels.
9 feet in diam. holds....	15 barrels.
10 feet in diam. holds....	18½ barrels.

Square Cisters one foot in depth.

5 feet by 5 feet holds....	6 barrels.
6 feet by 6 feet holds....	8½ barrels.
7 feet by 7 feet holds....	11½ barrels.
8 feet by 8 feet holds....	15½ barrels.
9 feet by 9 feet holds....	19½ barrels.
10 feet by 10 feet holds....	23½ barrels.

Audible Sounds.

The distance at which sounds can be distinguished depends much on favoring winds.

Description of Sound.	Feet.	Miles
A powerful human voice in the open air and no wind.................	460	
Beating a drum..........	10,560	2
Music of a heavy brass band...............	15,840	3
A strong human voice with a breeze barely felt...................	15,840	3
Report of a musket........	16,000	3
Cannonading, very strong................	475,000	90

National Debt of Principal Countries.

The following table, from Porter's Census Book, shows the increase and decrease of the public debt of these different countries in the past twenty years:

Countries.	1860.	1870.	1880.
France...........	$1,554,126,500...	$2,777,563,000...	$3,369,932,350
Great Britain....	3,893,220,000...	3,825,467,000...	3,766,571,400
Russia...........	1,134,161,500...	1,079,620,000...	2,312,845,000
Spain............	525,562,000...	1,386,962,500...	2,570,968,000
Italy.............	430,965,500...	1,909,606,000...	2,160,312,000
United States....	64,842,288...	2,480,672,400...	2,120,415,371
Austria-Hungary.	1,163,093,500...	1,654,419,500...	1,881,115,250
Turkey...........	100,564,500...	602,446,000...	1,376,666,250
Portugal.........	136,962,000...	301,900,000...	457,451,000
Australia.........		138,065,000...	462,858,200
Holland..........	652,250,500...	569,664,000...	560,399,000
Canada..........		62,736,000...	175,191,000
Roumania........		53,000,000...	118,742,600
Sweden-Norway..		29,199,000...	97,530,000
Greece..........	35,832,000...	60,000,000...	95,351,425
German Empire*.	694,456,400...	730,562,000...	48,217,365
Denmark.........	50,964,500...	63,364,500...	45,083,000

* The debt given for the German Empire in 1880 does not include the debts of any of the States composing it, but only the Empire Proper.

American Canals---Their Length and Cost.

The following table comprises the canals of the United States and Canada, of which the cost has exceeded $1,000,000.

Name.	State.	Miles.	Cost.
Chesapeake and Ohio..............	Maryland.	181	$16,000,000
Delaware and Hudson............	New York and Pa.	108	9,000,000
Illinois and Michigan.............	Illinois.	102	6,054,337
Erie............................	New York.	363	7,143,789
Welland........................	Canada.	26	7,000,000
Central Division.................	Pennsylvania.	173	5,907,853
James River and Kanawha........	Virginia.	147	5,029,050
Ohio and Erie...................	Ohio.	307	4,695,224
Lehigh.........................	Pennsylvania.	85	4,455,000
Miami..........................	Ohio.	178	3,750,000
North Branch Extension..........	Pennsylvania.	90	3,588,300
Morris and Essex................	New Jersey.	101	3,100,000
West Division...................	Pennsylvania.	104	3,008,523
Wabash and Erie................	Indiana.	469	3,057,120
Chesapeake and Delaware.......	Delaware and Md.	13½	2,750,000
Delaware and Raritan...........	New Jersey.	43	2,844,105
Schuylkill Division..............	Pennsylvania.	108	2,500,176
Chenango.......................	New York.	97	2,419,960
Cornwall........................	Canada.	12	2,000,000
Lachine........................	Canada.	8½	2,000,000
Beauharnois....................	Canada.	21	1,500,000
Sandy and Beaver...............	Ohio.	76	1,500,000
Delaware Division...............	Pennsylvania.	60	1,275,715
Champlain......................	New York.	63	1,257,604
North Branch...................	Pennsylvania.	73	1,006,173
Susquehannah..................	Pennsylvania.	39	1,039,354
St. Lawrence...................	Canada.	10	1,000,000

Combinations of Shades that Make Different Colors.

Mixing Red and Black...............	makes........	Brown
Mixing Lake with White..............	makes........	Rose
Mixing Umber and White............	makes........	Drab
Mixing White and Brown............	makes........	Chestnut
Mixing Yellow and Brown...........	makes........	Chocolate
Mixing Red with Light Blue	makes........	Purple
Mixing Carmine with Straw.........	makes........	Flesh Color
Mixing Blue with Lead Color........	makes........	Pearl
Mixing Carmine with White........	makes........	Pink
Mixing Lamp-Black with Indigo.....	makes........	Silver Gray
Mixing Lamp-Black with White.....	makes........	Lead Color
Mixing Paris Green with White.....	makes........	Bright Green
Mixing Yellow Ochre and White....	makes........	Buff
Mixing White tinted with Purple....	makes........	French White
Mixing Black with Chrome Green...	makes........	Dark Green
Mixing Chrome Green with White...	makes........	Pea Green
Mixing Emerald Green with White..	makes........	Brilliant Green
Mixing Vermilion with Chrome Yellow	makes........	Orange
Mixing Chrome Yellow with White Lead	makes........	Straw Color
Mixing White tinted with Red and Yellow	makes........	Cream
Mixing White with tints of Black and Purple	makes	Ashes of Rose
Mixing White, tinted with Black and Purple	makes	French Gray
Mixing Chrome Yellow, Blue, Black and Red	makes	Olive

Size of Animals.

Man—4 to 5 feet in Lapland and Labrador; 5½ to 5¾ feet in Europe and Asia; 5 to 5¾ in Africa and America; and 6 to 8 feet in Patagonia.

Name of Animal.	*Size.*
Fox	1½ to 2 feet
Mole	6 inches
Stag	4 to 5 feet
Wolf	2½ to 3 feet
Lion	6 to 8 and 9 feet
Otter	3½ feet
Lynx	4 feet
Civet	2 feet
Sable	11 inches
Lama	6 feet
Tapir	6 feet
Hyena	3 feet
Jackal	2½ feet
Ferret	14 inches
Ermine	10 inches
Polecat	17 inches
Weasel	7½ inches
Badger	2½ feet
Giraffe	15 or 16 feet high
Marmot	10 inches
Roebuck	3¾ feet
Raccoon	2 feet
Vampire	6 to 12 inches
Wild Cat	2 to 5 feet
Antelope	3½ feet
Chamois	3 feet
Opossum	15 to 18 inches
Dormouse	6 inches
Kangaroo	3 to 4 feet
Hedgehog	10 inches
Porcupine	2½ feet
Musk-Deer	3½ feet
Ichneumon	15 inches
Maned Seal	10 to 14 feet
Pigmy Apes	2 feet
Barbary Ape	3½ feet
Common Bat	4 or 5 inches
Spectrum Bat	7 inches
Common Seal	4 to 6 feet
Hippopotamus	12 to 20 feet
Flying Squirrel	6 inches
Ourang Outang	4½ to 5½ feet
Great Ant-eater	4 feet
Pigmy Antelope	10 inches
Walrus or Morse	15 to 18 feet
Vaulting Monkey	13 inches
Bottle-nosed Seal	11 to 18 feet
Ordinary Squirrel	8 inches
Dog-faced Baboon	5 feet
Armadillo and tail	5 feet
Elephant	10 or 11 feet 8 to 11 feet high
Lioness	5 to 6 and 7 feet Tail 3 feet, height 3 to 5
Tiger	8 to 9 feet Tail 3 feet, height 4 feet
Ant-eater	1 foot Spines 4 feet
Dromedary	6 or 7 feet 9 feet high to top of head
Rhinoceros	12 feet 6 or 7 feet high

Legal Holidays in the U. S.

Fourth of July—in all the States and Territories.

Christmas Day—*Dec. 25*—in all the States and Territories.

Thanksgiving Day—*usually the last Thursday in November*—whenever appointed by the President of the United States or the Governors of States—in all the States and Territories.

Fast Days—whenever appointed by the Presidents of the United States or by the Governors—in all the States.

New Year's Day—*Jan. 1*—in all States except Arkansas, Delaware, Georgia, Kentucky, Maine, Massachusetts, New Hampshire, North Carolina, Rhode Island and South Carolina.

Washington's Birthday—*Feb. 22*—in all States except Alabama, Arkansas, Florida, Indiana, Iowa, Kansas, Maine, Missouri, North Carolina, Ohio, Oregon, Tennessee and Texas.

General Election Day—*usually on Tuesday after the first Monday in November*—in California, Illinois, Maine, Missouri, New Jersey, New York, Oregon, South Carolina and Wisconsin.

Decoration Day — *May 30* — in Colorado, Connecticut, Maine, Michigan, New Hampshire, New Jersey, New York, Pennsylvania, Rhode Island and Vermont.

Good Friday — *Friday before Easter Sunday*—in Florida, Louisiana, Minnesota and Pennsylvania. Easter Sunday is the first Sunday after the full moon which happens on or after March 21st. If full moon happens on Sunday, Easter Sunday is the Sunday thereafter.

Shrove Tuesday — *the Tuesday preceding the first day of Lent*—in Louisiana, and the cities of Selma, Mobile, and Montgomery, Ala.

Memorial Day — *April 26* — in Georgia.

March 2 — Anniversary of the Independence of Texas, in Texas.

April 21 — Anniversary of the Battle of San Jacinto, in Texas.

January 8—Anniversary of the Battle of New Orleans, fought 1815, in Louisiana.

February 12 — Lincoln's Birthday, in Louisiana.

March 4—Firemen's Anniversary, in Louisiana.

Different Nations, the Name of their People and the Language they Speak.

Country.	Name of People.	Language they Speak
Austria	Austrians	German, Hungarian and Slavonic.
Arabia	Arabs, Arabians	Arabic.
Afghanistan	Afghans	Persian and Hindoostanee.
Algeria	Algerines	Chiefly Arabic.
Abyssinia	Abyssinians	Abyssinian.
Australasia	Australasians	Dutch and English. Various native languages are spoken.
Brazil	Brazilians	Portuguese.
Bolivia	Bolivians	Spanish.
Belgium	Belgians	Flemish and French.
Beloochistan	Beloochees	Beloochee and Hindoostanee.
Canada	Canadians	English and French.
Chili	Chilians	Spanish.
China	Chinese	Chinese.
Denmark	Danes	Danish.
Egypt	Egyptians	Chiefly Arabic and Italian.
England	English	English.
East Indies	East Indians	Hindoostanee, Bengalee, Siamese, Malay, etc.
France	French	French.
Greenland	Greenlanders	Danish and Esquimaux.
Germany	Germans	German.
Greece	Greeks	Greek.
Holland	Dutch	Dutch.
Hindoostan	Hindoos	Hindoostanee and others.

Country.	Name of People.	Language they Speak.
Iceland	Icelanders	Icelandic.
Ireland	Irish	English and Irish.
Italy	Italians	Italian.
Japan	Japanese	Japanese.
Mexico	Mexicans	Spanish.
Norway	Norwegians	Danish.
Poland	Poles	Polish.
Peru	Peruvians	Spanish.
Paraguay	Paraguayans	Spanish.
Prussia	Prussians	German.
Portugal	Portuguese	Portuguese.
Persia	Persians	Persian.
Russia	Russians	Russian
Sweden	Swedes	Swedish.
Switzerland	Swiss	German, French, and Italian.
Spain	Spaniards	Spanish.
Siberia	Siberians	Russian (mostly).
Siam	Siamese	Siamese.
Scotland	Scotch	English and Gaelic.
Turkey	Turks	Turkish.
United States	Americans	English.
Venezuela	Venezuelans	Spanish.
West Indies	West Indians	Spanish.
Wales	Welsh	English and Welsh.

MULTIPLICATION TABLE.

For the convenience of those who, though once familiar with the Multiplication Table, may have forgotten portions of it, or may not at the moment be able to recall the amount which results from one number being multiplied by another, this table is given. The × signifies *multiplied by*, and — signifies *equal to.*

1 × 0 — 0	2 × 0 — 0	3 × 0 — 0	4 × 0 — 0	5 × 0 — 0	6 × 0 — 0	7 × 0 — 0	8 × 0 — 0	9 × 0 — 0	10 × 0 — 0	11 × 0 — 0	12 × 0 — 0
1 × 1 — 1	2 × 1 — 2	3 × 1 — 3	4 × 1 — 4	5 × 1 — 5	6 × 1 — 6	7 × 1 — 7	8 × 1 — 8	9 × 1 — 9	10 × 1 — 10	11 × 1 — 11	12 × 1 — 12
1 × 2 — 2	2 × 2 — 4	3 × 2 — 6	4 × 2 — 8	5 × 2 — 10	6 × 2 — 12	7 × 2 — 14	8 × 2 — 16	9 × 2 — 18	10 × 2 — 20	11 × 2 — 22	12 × 2 — 24
1 × 3 — 3	2 × 3 — 6	3 × 3 — 9	4 × 3 — 12	5 × 3 — 15	6 × 3 — 18	7 × 3 — 21	8 × 3 — 24	9 × 3 — 27	10 × 3 — 30	11 × 3 — 33	12 × 3 — 36
1 × 4 — 4	2 × 4 — 8	3 × 4 — 12	4 × 4 — 16	5 × 4 — 20	6 × 4 — 24	7 × 4 — 28	8 × 4 — 32	9 × 4 — 36	10 × 4 — 40	11 × 4 — 44	12 × 4 — 48
1 × 5 — 5	2 × 5 — 10	3 × 5 — 15	4 × 5 — 20	5 × 5 — 25	6 × — 30	7 × 5 — 35	8 × 5 — 40	9 × 5 — 45	10 × 5 — 50	11 × 5 — 55	12 × 5 — 60
1 × 6 — 6	2 × 6 — 12	3 × 6 — 18	4 × 6 — 24	5 × 6 — 30	6 × 6 — 36	7 × 6 — 42	8 × 6 — 48	9 × 6 — 54	10 × 6 — 60	11 × 6 — 66	12 × 6 — 72
1 × 7 — 7	2 × 7 — 14	3 × 7 — 21	4 × 7 — 28	× 7 — 35	6 × 7 — 42	7 × 7 — 49	8 × 7 — 56	9 × 7 — 63	10 × 7 — 70	11 × 7 — 77	12 × 7 — 84
1 × 8 — 8	2 × 8 — 16	3 × 8 — 24	4 × 8 — 32	5 × 8 — 40	6 × 8 — 48	7 × 8 — 56	8 × 8 — 64	9 × 8 — 72	10 × 8 — 80	11 × 8 — 88	12 × 8 — 96
1 × 9 — 9	2 × 9 — 18	3 × 9 — 27	4 × — 36	5 × 9 — 45	6 × 9 — 54	7 × 9 — 63	8 × 9 — 72	9 × 9 — 81	10 × 9 — 90	11 × 9 — 99	12 × 9 — 108
1 × 10 — 10	2 × 10 — 20	3 × 10 — 30	4 × 10 — 40	5 × 10 — 50	6 × 10 — 60	7 × 10 — 70	8 × 10 — 80	9 × 10 — 90	10 × 10 — 100	11 × 10 — 110	12 × 10 — 120
1 × 11 — 11	2 × 11 — 22	3 × 11 — 33	4 × 11 — 44	5 × 11 — 55	6 × 11 — 66	7 × 11 — 77	8 × 11 — 88	9 × 11 — 99	10 × 11 — 110	11 × 11 — 121	12 × 11 — 132
1 × 12 — 12	2 × 12 — 24	3 × 12 — 36	4 × 12 — 48	5 × 12 — 60	6 × 12 — 72	7 × 12 — 84	8 × 12 — 96	9 × 12 — 108	10 × 12 — 120	11 × 12 — 132	12 × 12 — 144

Expectation of Life and Present Value of Widow's Dower.

Age.	Expectation in years.	Age.	Expectation in years.	Age.	Expectation in years.	Age.	Expectation in years.	Age.	Expectation in years.
0	28.15	20	34.22	40	26.04	60	15.45	80	5.85
1	36.78	21	33.84	41	25.61	61	14.86	81	5.50
2	38.74	22	33.46	42	25.19	62	14.26	82	5.16
3	40.01	23	33.08	43	24.77	63	13.66	83	4.87
4	40.73	24	32.70	44	24.35	64	13.05	84	4.66
5	40.88	25	32.33	45	23.92	65	12.43	85	4.57
6	40.69	26	31.93	46	23.37	66	11.96	86	4.21
7	40.47	27	31.50	47	22.83	67	11.48	87	3.90
8	40.14	28	31.08	48	22.27	68	11.01	88	3.67
9	39.72	29	30.66	49	21.72	69	10.50	89	3.56
10	39.23	30	30.25	50	21.17	70	10.06	90	3.73
11	38.64	31	29.83	51	20.61	71	9.60	91	3.33
12	38.02	32	29.43	52	20.05	72	9.14	92	3.12
13	37.41	33	29.02	53	19.49	73	8.69	93	2.40
14	36.79	34	28.62	54	18.92	74	8.25	94	1.98
15	36.17	35	28.22	55	18.35	75	7.83	95	1.62
16	35.76	36	27.78	56	17.78	76	7.40		
17	35.37	37	27.34	57	17.20	77	6.99		
18	34.98	38	26.91	58	16.63	78	6.59		
19	34.59	39	26.47	59	16.04	79	6.21		

In the settlement of estates where the widow is entitled to a third interest in the real estate, or a "dower" interest, as it is termed, as long as she may live, it becomes necessary that some definite calculation be made as to how long the widow will probably live to receive this interest. This matter being determined, a calculation can readily be made as to how much she is entitled to at present, which being ascertained, the estate can be satisfactorily settled. To illustrate, by the above table, which is generally adopted in the settlement of estates, it will be seen that, if the widow be 60 years of age, she will probably live 15 and 45×100 years longer, or until her age is 75 and 45×100 years.

By the following table is given the value of an annuity of one dollar from 1 to 35 years at 5 per cent. per annum. Thus for 15 years the value of one dollar will be $10.3796. Suppose the widow's dower interest in the estate to be $100 per year. To find the present value of the widow's interest, therefore, multiply the $100 by 10.3796, and the result is $1,037.96, which is the amount that the widow is entitled to in the settlement.

Years	Dollars, Cents and 100ths.	Years	Dollars, Cents and 100ths.	Years	Dollars, Cents and 100ths.	Years	Dollars, Cents and 100ths.
1	.9523	10	7.7217	19	12.0853	28	14.8981
2	1.8594	11	8.3064	20	12.4622	29	15.1401
3	2.7232	12	8.8632	21	12.8211	30	15.3724
4	3.5459	13	9.3935	22	13.1630	31	15.5928
5	4.3204	14	9.8986	23	13.4886	32	15.8026
6	5.0756	15	10.3796	24	13.7986	33	16.0025
7	5.7863	16	10.8377	25	14.0939	34	16.1929
8	6.4632	17	11.2740	26	14.3751	35	16.3741
9	7.1078	18	11.6895				

Distances From New York City to

	Miles.		Miles.		Miles.		Miles.
Adrian, Mich.	775	Chattanooga, Tenn.	980	Lafayette, Ind.	903	Quincy, Ill.	1,176
Akron, Ohio	610	Chicago, Ill	911	Lansing, Mich.	755	Racine, Wis	976
Albany, N. Y.	143	Chillicothe, Ohio	645	Lawrence, Mass	262	Raleigh, N. C.	669
Alexandria, Va	238	Cincinnati, Ohio	744	Leavenworth, Kan.	1,385	Reading, Pa	128
Algiers, La.	1,551	Circleville, Ohio	640	Lexington, Ky.	840	Richmond, Va.	350
Allegheny, Pa.	434	Cleveland, Ohio	581	Lexington, Mo.	1,354	Rochester, N. Y.	386
Allentown, Pa.	92	Columbia, S. C.	744	Little Rock, Ark.	1,430	Rock Island, Ill.	1,093
Alton, Ill.	1,060	Columbus, Ohio	624	Lockport, N. Y.	507	Rome, N. Y.	264
Annapolis, Md.	222	Concord, N. H.	308	Louisville, Ky.	900	Roxbury, Mass	237
Ann Arbor, Mich.	716	Covington, Ky.	745	Lowell, Mass.	261	Sacramento, Cal.	2,900
Atchison, Kansas	1,368	Cumberland, Md.	304	Lynchburg, Va.	404	St. Joseph, Mo.	1,334
Atlanta, Ga.	1,018	Davenport, Iowa	1,093	Macon, Ga.	1,131	St. Louis, Mo.	1,084
Auburn, N. Y.	325	Dayton, Ohio	804	Madison, Wis.	1,049	St. Paul, Minn	1,242
Augusta, Me.	407	Denver City, Col.	1,980	Memphis, Tenn.	1,289	Salem, Mass.	252
Augusta, Ga.	887	Des Moines, Iowa	1,251	Milledgeville, Ga.	1,100	Salt Lake City, Utah	2,410
Aurora, Ill.	951	Detroit, Mich.	670	Milwaukee, Wis.	996	San Francisco, Cal.	3,023
Baltimore, Md.	188	Dover, N. H.	304	Mobile, Ala.	1,370	Sandusky, Ohio	642
Bangor, Me.	482	Dubuque, Iowa	1,100	Montgomery, Ala.	1,193	Savannah, Ga.	974
Bath, Me.	382	Dunkirk, N. Y.	460	Montpelier, Vt.	454	Scranton, Pa.	144
Baton Rouge, La.	1,330	Elmira, N. Y.	274	Nashua, N. H.	275	Springfield, Ill	1,062
Belfast, Me.	424	Erie, Pa.	508	Nashville, Tenn.	1,085	Springfield, Mass.	138
Bellefontaine, Ohio	658	Evansville, Ind.	1,021	New Albany, Ind.	903	Springfield, Ohio.	558
Binghamton, N. Y.	215	Fall River, Mass.	180	New Bedford, Mass	181	Staunton, Va.	426
Blackstone, Mass.	272	Fitchburg, Mass.	218	New Brunswick, N.J	32	Stonington, Conn	143
Bloomington, Ill.	1,037	Fort Kearney, Neb.	1,598	Newburg, N. Y.	53	Syracuse, N. Y.	302
Boston, Mass.	236	Fort Wayne, Ind.	763	New Haven, Conn.	76	Taunton, Mass.	210
Bristol, R. I.	215	Fredericksburg, Va.	276	New Orleans, La.	1,550	Tallahassee, Fla.	1,100
Bucyrus, Ohio	632	Galena, Ill.	1,083	Newport, Ky.	744	Terre Haute, Ind.	912
Buffalo, N. Y.	433	Galesburg, Ill.	1,076	Newport, R. I.	168	Toledo, Ohio	712
Burlington, N. J.	74	Galveston, Texas	1,900	Norwalk, Conn	45	Tonawanda, N. Y.	463
Burlington, Iowa	1,122	Georgetown, D. C.	228	Omaha, Neb.	1,455	Trenton, N. J.	57
Burlington, Vt.	280	Hamilton, Ohio.	766	Oswego, N. Y.	337	Troy, N. Y.	148
Cambridge, Mass.	239	Harrisburg, Pa.	182	Paterson, N. J.	17	Utica, N. Y.	240
Camden, N. J.	91	Hartford, Conn	112	Peoria, Ill.	1,072	Vicksburg, Miss.	1,542
Canandaigua, N. Y.	377	Indianapolis, Ind.	838	Petersburg, Va.	378	Washington, D. C.	230
Carson City, Nevada	2,300	Jackson, Miss.	1,408	Philadelphia, Pa.	88	Wheeling, W. Va.	512
Chambersburg, Pa.	246	Jefferson City, Mo.	1,210	Pittsburgh, Pa.	431	Wilmington, Del.	116
Charleston, S. C.	874	Kalamazoo, Mich.	822	Portland, Me.	344	Wilmington, N. C.	604
Charlestown, Mass.	235	Kansas City, Mo.	1,361	Providence, R. I.	193	Worcester, Mass.	194

Distances by Water From New York City to

	Miles.		Miles.		Miles.		Miles.
Amsterdam	3,510	Chagres	2,308	Lisbon	3,175	Rio Janeiro	3,840
Barbadoes	1,905	Charleston	750	Liverpool	3,210	Sandwich Islands	15,300
Batavia	13,065	Columbia River	15,075	London	3,375	San Francisco	15,858
Bermudas	660	Constantinople	5,140	Madras	11,850	St. Petersburg	4,420
Bombay	11,574	Copenhagen	3,640	Melbourne	12,844	Singapore	13,710
Bordeaux	3,310	Dublin	3,225	Monrovia	3,825	Smyrna	5,000
Boston	310	Gibraltar	3,300	Naples	4,330	Stockholm	4,050
Botany Bay	13,205	Halifax	612	New Orleans	2,045	Tahiti	12,125
Buenos Ayres	7,110	Hamburg	3,775	Panama	2,358	Trieste	5,130
Calcutta	12,425	Havana	1,420	Pekin	15,125	Valparaiso	9,750
Canton	13,900	Havre	3,310	Pernambuco	4,760	Vera Cruz	2,250
Cape Horn	8,115	Kingston	1,740	Philadelphia	240	Washington	400
Cape of Good Hope	6,850	Lima	11,310	Quebec	1,400	Round the Globe	25,000

The Influence of the Moon on the Growth of Plants.

Does the light of the moon affect the growth of plants? Does it make any difference in the growth of a plant what time in the moon it is planted? Undoubtedly it does.

Light is a great promoter of growth, and, the more brilliant the light, the stronger and more vigorous the growth, all the other conditions being favorable. It is a fact, also, with certain plants, that when young they require, like young animals, considerable time for rest and sleep. To have this sleep is to give them ultimate strength and vigor, which is essential to their subsequent complete development.

To illustrate: The seeds of certain vines and other plants sown in the new of the moon will vegetate, and the plants are likely to appear above ground, near the old of the moon, at a time when the moon's radiance is so brilliant that they are compelled to grow under its strong light. Upon the rising of the sun, the growth is still forced forward, and the tender plant, thus in its infancy, gets no rest.

The seed sown in the old of the moon will bring forth the plant in the new of the moon, or during the dark nights; at which time it obtains the needed rest and sleep, in the darkness, which is essential to its future productiveness.

That the light of the moon has thus a very perceptible and important influence upon the growth of plants when very young and tender, is a fact which thousands have verified, though few understand the philosophy of the same.

FOREIGN WORDS AND PHRASES.

LATIN WORDS AND PHRASES.

Ad captandum, For the purpose of captivating.
Ad infinitum, To an unlimited extent.
Ad libitum, At pleasure.
Alias, Otherwise.
Alibi, Elsewhere.
Alma mater, Gentle mother; often applied to the institution where one is educated.
Amor patriæ, Love of country.
Anglicè, In English
Annus mirabilis, A year of wonders.
A priori, Beforehand; from previous knowledge.
Bona fide, In good faith; genuine.
Beatæ memoriæ, Of blessed memory.
Cacoethes scribendi, A ridiculous fondness for writing
Casus belli, A case for war.
Caveat, Let him beware.
Contra, On the other hand; against.
De facto, In fact.
De jure, By right.

Dramatis personæ, Characters of the play.
Ergo, Therefore.
Et id genus omne, And all of that sort.
Ex officio, By virtue of the office.
Exit, He (or she) goes out.
Exeunt omnes, They all go out.
Ex parte, On one side only.
Ex tempore, On the moment.
Fac simile, An exact copy.
Facetiæ, Witty sayings.
Fiat, Let it be done; a command.
Fiat justitia ruat cœlum, Let justice be done though the heavens crash.
Finis, The end.
Genius loci, The genius of the place.
In propria persona, In person.
In transitu, On the way.
Imprimis, In the first place.
Impromptu, Off-hand.
Interim, In the mean time.
Item, Also.
Lapsus linguæ, A slip of the tongue.
Magna charta, The great charter.

Maximum, The greatest quantity.
Mens sana in corpore sano, A sound mind in a healthy body.
Meum et tuum, Mine and thine.
Minimum, The least quantity.
Ne plus ultra, The greatest extent attainable.
Nil desperandum, Never despair.
Nolens volens, Willing or not.
Non compos mentis, Not of sound mind.
Non est inventus, Not to be found
Non sequitur, It does not follow.
Nota bene, Mark well.
Omnia vincit amor, Love conquers all things.
Onus probandi, Burden of proving
Orator fit, poeta nascitur, The orator is made, but the poet is born.
Otium cum dignitate, Ease with dignity.
Par nobile fratrum, A noble pair of brothers; two alike.

Passim, Everywhere.
Paterfamilias, Father of a family.
Per capita, By the head.
Per diem, By the day.
Per fas et nefas, Through right or wrong.
Per se, By itself.
Prima facie, On the first view.
Pro et con, For and against.
Pro forma, For form's sake.
Pro tempore, For the time being.
Quondam, Former.
Quid nunc? What now?
Rus in urbe, The country in town.
Semper idem, Always the same.
Sub rosa, Privately.
Sui generis, Of its own kind; unique.
Tempus fugit, Time flies.
Vale, Farewell.
Veni, vidi, vici, I came, I saw, I conquered.
Verbum sat, A word is enough.
Viva voce, By the living voice.
Vice versa, The case being reversed.

FRENCH WORDS AND PHRASES, With Pronunciation.

A bas (ah-bah), Down with.
A bon marché (ah-bong-mar-shaī), Cheap.
A cheval (ah-sheh-val), On horseback.
Affaire d'amour (ah-faire-dah-moor), A love affair.
Affaire d'honneur (af-faire-don-ot-ur), An affair of honor.
A la mode (ah-lah-mod), In the fashion.
A l'improviste (ah-lam-pro-rist), Unawares.
Amateur (ah-ma-tair), An admirer of and unprofessional practitioner in any art.
Amour (ah-moor), Love.
A l'outrance (ah-loo-trangse), To the utmost.
A propos (ah-pro-poo), By the way; to the purpose.
A tout prix (au-too-pree), At any cost.
A contraire (a-kong-trayre), On the contrary.
Au fait (o-fay), All right; instructed.
Au revoir (o-ruh-voo-ar), Till we meet again.
Avant coureur (ah-vang-koo-rayre), Fore-runner.
A votre santé (au-votr-sang-tai), To your health.
Bas bleu (bah-bluhe), Blue-stocking.
Beau monde (bo-mongde), The gay world.
Belles-lettres (bell-lay-tr), Polite literature.
Blasé (blah-sai), Time-worn, faded.
Bijou (be-joo), A jewel or gem.
Billet-doux (be-yay-doo), A love letter.
Bon gré malgré (bon-grai-mal-grai), Willing or not.
Bonhomie (bun-no-mee), Good nature.
Bon jour (bong-joor), Good-day.
Bon-mot (bong-mo), A witticism.
Bon soir (bong-soo-ar), Good night.
Bon ton (bong-tong), High fashion.
Bon vivant (bong-vi-vang), A high liver.
Bonne bouche (bun-boo-she), A tid-bit.
Bonne foi (bun-foo-ah), Good faith.
Canaille (kan-ayh), The rabble.
Carte blanche (kart-blansh), Full power.
Chacun a son goût (shah-koo-ah son-goo), Every one to his taste.
Château en Espagne (shah-to ong-es-pan-ye), Air-castles.
Chef d'œuvre (shay-duhvr), A masterpiece.

Cher ami (shair-ah-me), Dear friend (male.)
Chère amie (shayre-ah-mee), Dear friend, (female.)
Ci-devant (se-duh-vang), Formerly.
Comme il faut (kom-ill-foh), As it should be.
Compagnon de voyage (kong-pang-yong), Traveling companion.
Contretemps (kongtr-tang), Disappointment, accident.
Coup d'état (koo-daih-tah), A stroke of policy.
Coup de grâce (koo-de-grass), The finishing stroke.
Coup d'œil, A glance.
Coûte qu'il coûte (koot-key-koot), Cost what it may.
Début (dai-boo), First appearance.
Dénouement (dai-noo-mang), Solution; result.
Dieu et mon droit, God and my right.
Dot (doh), A dowry.
Double entendre (doo-bl-ang-tangdr), Double meaning.
Doux yeux (doox-yuke), Tender glances.
Éclat (ai-klah), Splendor; brilliancy.
Élite (ai-lit), Choice; select.
Embonpoint (ong-bong-poo-aing), Plumpness, fatness.
En ami (ang-ah-me), As a friend.
Encore (ong-kor), Again.
Enivre (ai-ne-vrai), Intoxicated.
En masse (ong-mass), In a body.
Ennui (ah-noo-e), Weariness.
En revanche (ung-ruh-vanghshe), In return.
Entente cordiale (ong-tangte-kor-dyol), Good understanding.
Entrée (ang-trale), Entrance.
Entre nous (angtr-noo), Between ourselves.
Esprit de corps (es-pree-duh-kor), Pride of association.
Faux pas (foe-paw), False step; misconduct.
Fête (fayte), A festival.
Feu de joie (fuh-dh-joo-au), Bonfire; illumination.
Gensdarmes (jang-darm), Soldier police.
Haut ton (ho-tong), Highest fashion.

Honi soit qui mal y pense, Shamed be he that evil thinks.
Jeu de mots, A play upon words
Jeu d'esprit (juh-des-pree), A witticism.
Le bon temps viendra There is a good time coming.
L'homme propose et Dieu dispose, Man proposes and God disposes.
Matinée (mah-te-nale), A daytime entertainment.
Mise en scène (meese-ang-seyne), Putting on the stage; getting up.
Nom de plume (nong-du-ploom), Literary nickname.
Nous verrons (noo-vai-rong), We shall see.
On dit (ong-de), It is said.
Outré (oo-tray), Extravagant; outlandish.
Papier maché (pah-pyai-ma-shai), Paper pulp prepared for use and ornament.
Par exemple, For example.
Parvenu, An upstart.
Petit (puh-te), Small, little; (feminine, *petite*.)
Protégé (pro-tai-kjai), One protected by another; (feminine, *protégée*.)
Qui vive (ke-rir), (On the), On the alert.
Recherché (ruh-sher-shai), Of rare attraction.
Résumé (rai-zoo-mai), A summary.
Rôle (role), Part in a drama or performance.
Sans façon (sang-fah-song), Without formality.
Sans peur et sans reproche, Without fear and without reproach.
Sans souci (sang-soo-se), Without care.
Savant (sah-rang), A man of science.
Savoir vivre, Good breeding.
Soi-disant (soo-ah-de-sang), Self-styled.
Soirée (soo-ah-raie), An evening entertainment.
Tête à tête (tayte-ah-tayte), Face to face.
Tout à vous (tool-ah-voo), Wholly yours.
Tout ensemble (too-ang-sangbl), The whole together.
Vis à vis (vee-sah-vee), Opposite.
Vive le roi (veve-luh-roo-ah), Long live the king.
Voilà tout (voo-ah-lah-too), That is all.

SPANISH WORDS AND PHRASES.

A Dios, Good-bye.
Adobe, A sun-baked brick.
Alma mia, My dear.
Cañon, A deep gulch or gorge.
Carrai! Zounds!

Chaparral, A thicket of shrub oak.
Corral, An inclosure for horses, etc.
Hacienda, A farm.
Hidalgo, An aristocrat.
Olla podrida, An incongruous mass.

Poco tempo, In a little while.
Poco dinero, Little money.
Pronunciamento, A declaration.
Quien sabe? Who knows?
Señor, Mr. or Master.

Señora, Mrs. or Mistress.
Señorita, Miss.
Sierra, Chain of mountains.
Vamos! Let us go.

ITALIAN WORDS AND PHRASES.

Cantatrice, A singer.
Conversazione, Social gathering.
Dilettante, A lover of the fine arts.

Dolce far niente, Pleasant idleness
Impresario, A theatrical proprietor or manager.

Prima donna, First lady, or "star," in an opera.
Signor, Mr. or Master.

Signora, Mrs or Mistress.
Signorina, Miss.
Virtù, Curious or fine.

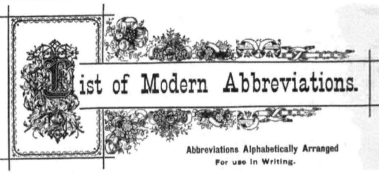

List of Modern Abbreviations.

Abbreviations Alphabetically Arranged
For use in Writing.

a.—In commerce, to.

@.—In commerce, at.

A. A. G. — Assistant Adjutant-General.

A. A. P. S.—American Association for the Promotion of Science.

A. A. S.—*Academiæ Americanæ Socius*, Fellow of the American Academy (of Arts and Sciences).

A. A. S. S.—*Americanæ Antiquarianæ Societatis Socius*, Member of the American Antiquarian Society.

A. B.—*Artium Baccalaureus*, Bachelor of Arts.

A. B. C. F. M. — American Board of Commissioners for Foreign Missions.

Abp.—Archbishop.

Abr.—Abridgment.

Abbr.—Abbreviation.

A. B. S.—American Bible Society.

A. C.—*Ante Christum*, before Christ; Arch-Chancellor.

Acad.—Academy.

Acct.—Account; Accent.

A. C. S.—American Colonization Society.

A. D.—*Anno Domini*, in the year of our Lord.

A. D. C.—Aid-de-camp.

Ad. — Advertisement.

Adj.—Adjective.

Adjt.—Adjutant.

Adjt.-Gen.—Adjutant-General.

Ad lib.—*Ad libitum*, at pleasure.

Adm.—Admiral; Admiralty.

Adm. Ct.—Admiralty Court.

Admr.—Administrator.

Admx.—Administratrix.

Ad v.—*Ad valorem*, at (or on) the value.

Adv.—Adverb; Advent; Advertisement.

Æt.—*Ætatis*, of age, Aged.

A. F. & A. M.— Ancient Free and Accepted Masons.

A. F. B. S.—American and Foreign Bible Society.

A. G.—Adjutant-General.

Alaska—Alaska Territory.

Agr.—Agriculture.

A. G. S. S.—American Geographical and Statistical Society.

Agt.—Agent.

A. H.—*Anno Hegiræ*, in the year of the Hegira.

A. H. M. S.—American Home Missionary Society.

Ala.—Alabama.

Ald.—Alderman.

A. L. of H. — American Legion of Honor.

Alex.—Alexander.

Alg.—Algebra.

Alt.—Altitude.

A. M.—*Anno Mundi*, in the year of the world. *Artium Magister*, Master of Arts. *Ante meridiem*, before noon; morning.

Amb.—Ambassador. (See Emb.)

Amer.—American.

AMM.—*Amalgama*, amalgamation.

Amt.—Amount.

An.—*Anno*, in the year.

An. A. C.—*Anno ante Christum*, in the year before Christ.

Anat.—Anatomy.

Anc.—Ancient; Anciently.

And.—Andrew.

Ang.-Sax.—Anglo-Saxon.

Anon.—Anonymous.

Ans.—Answer.

Ant.—Antiquity.

Anth.—Anthony.

Aor. or aor.—Aorist.

A. O. S. S.—*Americanæ Orientalis Societatis Socius*, Member of the American Oriental Society.

A. O. U. W.—Ancient Order of United Workmen.

Ap.—Apostle; Appius.

Ap.—*Apud*, in the writings of; as quoted by.

Apo.—Apogee.

Apoc.—Apocalypse.

App.—Appendix.

Apr.—April.

A. Q. M. G.—Assistant Quartermaster-General.

A. R.—*Anno Regina*, Queen Anne. *Anno regni*, year of the reign.

R. R. A. — Associate of the Royal Academy.

Arab.—Arabic, or Arabia.

Ariz. Ter.—Arizona Territory.

Arg.—*Argumento*, by an argument drawn from such a law.

Arith.—Arithmetic.

Ark.—Arkansas.

A. R. R.—*Anno regni regis*, in the year of the reign of the king.

Arr.—Arrived. Arrs., Arrivals.

A. R. S. S.—*Antiquariorum Regiæ Societatis Socius*, Fellow of the Royal Society of Antiquaries.

Art.—Article.

A. S. or Assist. Sec.—Assistant Secretary.

A. S. A.—American Statistical Association.

A. S. S. U.—American Sunday-School Union.

Astrol.—Astrology.

Astron.—Astronomy.

A. T. – Arch-Treasurer.

A. T. S.—American Tract Society.

Ats.—At suit of.

Atty.—Attorney.

Atty.-Gen.—Attorney-General.

A. U. A.—American Unitarian Association.

Aub. Theol. Sem. — Auburn Theological Seminary.

A. U. C.—*Anno urbis conditæ*, or *ab urbe condita*, in the year from the building of the city (Rome).

Aug.—August.

Aur.—*Aurum*, gold.

Auth. Ver.—Authorised Version (of the Bible.)

Av.—Average. Avenue.

Avoir.—Avoirdupois.

A. Y. M.—Ancient York Masons.

b.—Born.

B. A.—Bachelor of Arts.

Bal.—Balance.

Balt.—Baltimore.

Bar.—Baruch.

Bart. or Bt.—Baronet.

Bbl.—Barrel.

B. C.—Before Christ.

B. C. L.—Bachelor of Civil Law.

B. D. — *Baccalaureus Divinitatis*, Bachelor of Divinity.

Bds. or bds.—Boards (bound in).

Benj.—Benjamin.

Bk.—Book.

B. LL.—*Baccalaureus Legum*, Bachelor of Laws.

B. M.—*Baccalaureus Medicinæ*, Bachelor of Medicine.

B. R.—Bills Receivable.

B. P.—Bills Payable.

Boat.—Boston.

Bot.—Botany.

Bp.—Bishop.

B. R.—*Banco Regis* or *Reginæ*, the King's or Queen's Bench.

Brig.—Brigade; Brigadier.

Brig.-Gen.—Brigadier-General.

Brit. Mus.—British Museum.

Bro.—Brother.

Br. Univ.—Brown University.

B. S.—Bachelor in the Sciences.

B. V.—*Beata Virgo*, Blessed Virgin. *Bene vale*, farewell.

B. V. M.—Blessed Virgin Mary.

C., Ch. or Chap.—Chapter.

C. or Cent.—*Centum*, a hundred.

cæt. par.—*Cæteris paribus*, other things being equal.

Cal.—California; Calends.

Can.—Canon.

Cant.—Canticles.

Cap. or c. — *Caput*, *capitulum*, chapter.

Caps.—Capitals.

Capt.—Captain.

Capt.-Gen.—Captain-General.

Cash.—Cashier.

ca. resp.—*Capias ad respondendum*, a legal writ.

ca. sa.—*Capias ad satisfaciendum*, a legal writ.

Cath.—Catherine.

C. B.—Companion of the Bath. *Communis Bancus*, Common Bench.

C. C.—Caius College; Account Current; Chancellor Commander, County Commissioner.

C. C. C.—Corpus Christi College.

C. C. P.—Court of Common Pleas.

C. E.—Canada East; Civil Engineer.

Cel. or Celt.—Celtic.

Cf. or ef.—*Confer*, compare.

C. G.—Commissary-General; Consul-General.

C. H.—Court-house.

Ch.—Church; Chapter.

Chanc.—Chancellor.

Chap.—Chapter.

Chas.—Charles.

Chem.—Chemistry.
Chic.—Chicago.
Chr.—Christopher.
Chron.—Chronicles.
Cin.—Cincinnati.
C.J.—Chief-Justice.
Clk.—Clerk.
C.M.—Common Meter.
C.M.G.—Companion of the Order of St. Michael and St. George.
Co.—Company; County.
C.O.D.—Cash (or collect) on delivery.
Cochl.—A spoonful.
Col.—Colonel; Colossians.
Coll.—Collector; Colloquial; College; Collection.
Colo.—Colorado.
Com.—Commerce; Committee; Commentary; Commissioner; Commodore.
Com. Arr.—Committee of Arrangements.
Comdg.—Commanding.
Comm.—Commentary.
Comp.—Compare; Compound; Compositor.
Com. Ver.—Common version (of the Bible).
Con.—*Contra*, against; in opposition.
Con. Cr.—Contra, credit.
Conch.—Conchology.
Cong.—Congress.
Conj. or conj.—Conjunction.
Conn. or Ct.—Connecticut.
Const.—Constable; Constitution.
Cont.—Continent; Contract; Continued.
Cor.—Corinthians.
Corol.—Corollary.
Cor. Sec.—Corresponding Secretary.
C.P.—Common Pleas; Court of Probate.
C.P.S.—*Custos Privati Sigilli*, Keeper of the Privy Seal.
C.R.—King (*Rex*) Charles.
C.R.—*Custos Rotulorum*, Keeper of the Rolls.
Cr.—Creditor; Credit.
Crim. Con.—Criminal conversation; Adultery.
C.S.—Court of Sessions. *Custos Sigilli*, Keeper of the Seal.
Ct., cts.—Cent. Cents.
C. Theod.—*Codex Theodosiano*, in the Theodosian Code.
C.W.—Canada West.
Cwt.—Hundredweight.
Cyc.—Cyclopedia.

d.—*Denarius* or *Denarii*, penny or pence; Died.
D.—Five hundred.
Dak.—Dakota.
Dan.—Daniel; Daniah.
D.C.—*Da Capo*, again; District of Columbia.
D.C.L.—Doctor of Civil Law.
D D.—*Divinitatis Doctor*, Doctor of Divinity.
Dea.—Deacon.
Dec.—December; Declaration; Declination.
Deg.—Degree or degrees.
Del.—Delaware; Delegate.
Del. or del.—*Delineavit*, he (or she) drew it.
Dep.—Deputy.
Dept.—Department.
Deut.—Deuteronomy.

D.F.—Dean of the Faculty.
Dft. or Deft.—Defendant.
D.G.—*Dei gratia*, by the grace of God.
D.G.—*Deo gratias*, thanks to God.
Diam.—Diameter.
Dict.—Dictator; Dictionary.
Dim.—Diminutive.
Disc.—Discount.
Diss.—Dissertation.
Dist.—District.
Dist. Atty.—District-Attorney.
Div.—Division; Dividend.
D.M.—Doctor of Music.
Do.—*Ditto*, the same.
Dols.—Dollars.
D.O.M.—*Deo optimo maximo*, to God, the best, the greatest.
Doz.—Dozen.
D.P.—Doctor of Philosophy.
Dr.—Debtor; Doctor; Drachm.
D.S.—*Dal segno*, from the sign.
d.s.b.—*Debit sans breve*.
D.T.—*Doctor Theologiæ*, Doctor of Theology.
D.V.—*Deo volente*, God willing.
Dwt.—Pennyweight.

E.—East.
ea.—Each.
E. by S.—East by South.
Eben.—Ebenezer.
Eccl.—Ecclesiastes.
Ecclus.—Ecclesiasticus.
Ed.—Editor; Edition.
Edm.—Edmund.
Edw.—Edward.
E.E.—Errors excepted.
e.g.—*Exempli gratia*, for example. *Ex grege*, from the flock; Among the rest.
E.I.—East Indies, or East India.
E.I.C.—East India Company.
Elec.—Electric; Electricity.
Eliz.—Elizabeth.
E. lon.—East longitude.
Emb.—Embassador.
Encyc.—Encyclopedia.
E.N.E.—East-Northeast.
Eng.—England, English.
Ent.—Entomology.
Env. Ext.—Envoy Extraordinary.
Ep.—Epistle
Eph.—Ephesians; Ephraim.
Esd.—Esdras.
E S.E.—East-Southeast.
Esq.—Esquire.
Esth.—Esther.
et al.—*Et alii*, and others.
et seq.—*Et sequentia*, and what follows.
etc. or &c.—*Et cæteri, et cætera, et cætera*, and others; and so forth.
Ex.—Example, Exodus.
Exc.—Excellency; Exception.
Exch.—Exchequer.
Exec. Com.—Executive Committee.
Execx.—Executrix.
Exr. or Exec.—Executor.
Ez.—Ezra.
Ezek.—Ezekiel.
E.&O.E.—Errors and omissions excepted.
Fahr.—Fahrenheit.
F.A.M.—Free and Accepted Masons.
Far.—Farthing.
F A.S.—Fellow of the Antiquarian Society.
fcap. or fcp.—Foolscap.
F.D.—*Fidei Defensor* or *Defensa-

trix*, Defender of the Faith.
Fe.—*Ferrum*, iron.
Feb.—February.
Fec.—*Fecit*, he did it.
Fem.—Feminine.
F.E.S.—Fellow of the Entomological Society; of the Ethnological Society.
Ff.—The Pandects.
F.G.S.—Fellow of the Geological Society.
F.H.S.—Fellow of the Horticultural Society.
fi. fa.—*Fieri facias*, cause it to be done.
Fid. Def.—Defender of the Faith.
Fig.—Figure.
Fir.—Firkin.
Fla.—Florida.
F.L.S.—Fellow of the Linnæan Society.
F.O.B.—Free on Board.
Fol.—Folio.
For.—Foreign.
Fort.—Fortification.
F.P.S.—Fellow of the Philological Society.
Fr.—Franc, francs; French. *Pragmentum*, fragment. Francis.
F.R.A.S.—Fellow of the Royal Astronomical Society.
F.R.C.S.L.—Fellow of the Royal College of Surgeons, London.
Fred.—Frederick.
F.R.G.S.—Fellow of the Royal Geographical Society.
Fri.—Friday.
F.R.S.—Fellow of the Royal Society.
Frs.—Frisian.
F.R.S.E.—Fellow of the Royal Society, Edinburgh.
F.R.S.L.—Fellow of the Royal Society, London; Fellow of the Royal Society of Literature.
F.S.A.—Fellow of the Society of Arts.
F.S.A.E.—Fellow of the Society of Antiquaries, Edinburgh.
Ft.—Foot; feet; Fort.
Fur.—Furlong.
F.Z.S.—Fellow of the Zoological Society.

G. or g.—Guinea.
G.A.—General Assembly.
Ga.—Georgia.
Gal.—Galatians; Gallon.
G.B.—Great Britain.
G.C.—Grand Chancellor; Grand Chapter.
G.C.B.—Grand Cross of the Bath.
G.C.H.—Grand Cross of Hanover.
G.C.L.H.—Grand Cross of the Legion of Honor.
G.E.—Grand Encampment.
Gen.—Genesis, General.
Gent.—Gentleman.
Geo.—George, Georgia.
Geog.—Geography.
Geol.—Geology.
Geom.—Geometry.
Ger.—Germany; German.
G.L.—Grand Lodge.
Gl.—*Glossa*, a gloss.
G.M.—Grand Master.
G.O—General Order.
Goth.—Gothic.
Gov.—Governor.
Gov. Gen.—Governor-General.
G.R.—*Georgius Rex*, King George.
Gr.—Greek; Gross; Grains.

Gram.—Grammar.
Gro.—Gross.
Grot.—Grotius.
h.a.—*Hoc anno*, this year.
Hab.—Habakkuk.
Hab. corp.—*Habeas corpus*, you may have the body.
Hab fa. poss.—*Habere facias possessionem*.
Hab fa. seis.—*Habere facias seisinam*.
Hag.—Haggai.
Ham. Coll.—Hamilton College.
H.B.C.—Hudson's Bay Company.
H H.M.—His (or Her) Britannic Majesty.
H C.—House of Commons.
Hdkf.—Handkerchief.
h.e.—*Hoc est*, that is, or this is.
Heb.—Hebrews.
Her.—Heraldry.
Hf.-bd.—Half-bound.
Hg.—*Hydrargyrum*, mercury.
Hhd.—Hogshead.
H.H.S.—Fellow of the Historical Society.
Hist.—History.
H.J.S.—*Hic jacet sepultus*, Here lies buried.
H.L.—House of Lords.
H.M.—His (or Her) Majesty; Hill's Manual.
H.M.P.—*Hoc monumentum posuit*, Erected this monument.
H.M.S.—His (or Her) Majesty's Ship.
Hon.—Honorable.
Hon'd.—Honored.
Hort.—Horticulture.
Hos.—Hosea.
h.p.—half-pay.
H.R.—House of Representatives.
H.R.E.—Holy Roman Emperor.
H R.H.—His Royal Highness.
H.R.I.P.—*Hic requiescat in pace*, Here rests in peace.
H.S.—*Hic situs*, Here lies.
H S.B.Co—Hill Standard Book Company.
H.S.H.—His Serene Highness.
h.t.—*Hic titulus*, this title, Hoc titulo, in or under this title.
h.v.—*Hoc verbum*, this word; *his verbis*, in these words.
Hund.—Hundred.

I, II, III.—One, two, three, or first, first, second, third.
Ia.—Iowa.
Ib. or Ibid.—*Ibidem*, in the same place.
Ich.—Ichthyology.
Ictus.—*Jurisconsultus*, Counselor at Law.
Id.—*Idem*, the same.
Idaho.—Idaho Territory.
i.e.—*Id est*, That is.
I.H.S.—*Jesus hominum Salvator*, Jesus the Saviour of men.
ij.—Two (*medical*).
Ill.—Illinois, Illustrious; Illustrated.
Imp.—Imperial
In.—Inch, inches.
Incog.—*Incognito*, unknown.
Incor.—Incorporated.
Ind.—Indiana, Index
Ind. Ter.—Indian Territory.
Indef.—Indefinite
Inf.—*Infra*, beneath or below.
in f.—*In fine*, at the end of the title, law, or paragraph quoted.

In lim.—*In limine*, at the outset.

In loc.—*In loco*, in the place; on the passage.

In pr.—*In principio*, in the beginning and before the first paragraph of a law.

I.N.R.I.—*Jesus Nazarenus, Rex Judæorum*, Jesus of Nazareth, King of the Jews.

Inst.—Instant, of this month; Institutes.

In sum.—*In summa*, in the summary.

Int.—Interest.

Interj.—Interjection.

In trans.—*In transitu*, on the passage.

Introd.—Introduction.

I.O.G.T.—Independent Order of Good Templars.

I.O.F.—Independent Order of Foresters.

I.O.O.F.—Independent Order of Odd-Fellows.

I.O.U.—I owe you.

I.q.—*Idem quod*, the same as.

Isa.—Isaiah.

Isl.—Island.

I.S.M.—*Jesus Salvator mundi*, Jesus the Saviour of the world.

Ital.—Italic; Italian.

Itin.—Itinerant, or Itinerary.

IV.—Four or fourth.

IX.—Nine or ninth.

J.—Justice or Judge. JJ.—Justices.

ʒ.—One (*medical*).

J.A.—Judge-Advocate.

Jac.—Jacob.

Jam.—Jamaica.

Jan.—January.

Jas.—James.

J.C.D.—*Juris Civilis Doctor*, Doctor of Civil Law.

J.D.—*Jurum Doctor*, Doctor of Laws.

Jer.—Jeremiah.

Jno.—John.

Jonas.—Jonathan.

Jos.—Joseph.

Josh.—Joshua.

J.P.—Justice of the Peace.

J. Prob.—Judge of Probate.

J.R.—*Jacobus Rex*, King James.

Jr. or Jun.—Junior.

J.U.D. or J.V.D.—*Juris utriusque Doctor*, Doctor of both Laws (of the Canon and the Civil Law).

Jud.—Judith.

Judg.—Judges.

Judge-Adv.—Judge Advocate.

Jul.—July; Julius.

Jul Per.—Julian Period.

Jun.—June; Junius; Junior.

Jus. P.—Justice of the Peace.

Just.—Justinian.

J. W.—Junior Warden.

K.—King.

K.A.—Knight of St. Andrew, in Russia.

K.A.N.—Knight of St. Alexander Nevskoj, in Russia.

Kas.—Kansas.

K.B.—King's Bench; Knight of the Bath.

K.B.A.—Knight of St. Bento d'Avis, in Portugal.

K.B.E.—Knight of the Black Eagle, in Russia.

K.C.—King's Council; Knight of the Crescent, in Turkey.

K.C.B.—Knight Commander of the Bath.

K.C.H.—Knight Commander of Hanover.

K.C.S.—Knight of Charles III. of Spain.

K.E.—Knight of the Elephant, in Denmark.

K.F.—Knight of Ferdinand of Spain.

K.F.M.—Knight of St. Ferdinand and Merit, in Sicily.

K G.—Knight of the Garter.

K.G.C.—Knight of the Grand Cross.

K.G.C.B.—Knight of the Grand Cross of the Bath.

K.G.F.—Knight of the Golden Fleece, in Spain.

K.G.H.—Knight of the Guelphs of Hanover.

K.G.V.—Knight of Gustavus Vasa, in Sweden.

K.H.—Knight of Hanover; Knights of Honor.

Ki.—Kings.

Kil. or kil.—Kilderkin.

Kingd.—Kingdom.

K.J.—Knight of St. Joachim.

K.L. or K.L.A.—Knight of Leopold of Austria.

K.L.H.—Knight of the Legion of Honor; Knights and Ladies of Honor.

K.M.—Knight of Malta.

K Mess.—King's Messenger.

K.M.H.—Knight of Merit, in Holstein.

K.M.J.—Knight of Maximilian Joseph, in Bavaria.

K.M.T.—Knight of Maria Theresa, in Austria.

K.N.—Know-Nothing.

Knick.—Knickerbocker.

K.N.S.—Knight of the Royal North Star, in Sweden.

Knt.—Knight.

K.P.—Knight of St. Patrick; Knight of Pythias.

K.R.C.—Knight of the Red Cross.

K.R.E.—Knight of the Red Eagle, in Prussia.

K.S.—Knight of the Sword, in Sweden.

K.S.A.—Knight of St. Anne, in Russia.

K.S.E—Knight of St Esprit, in France.

K.S.F.—Knight of St. Fernando, in Spain.

K.S.G.—Knight of St. George, in Russia.

K.S.H.—Knight of St. Hubert, in Bavaria.

K.S.J.—Knight of St. Januarius of Naples.

K.S.L.—Knight of the Sun and Lion, in Persia.

K.S.M. & S.G.—Knight of St. Michael and St. George, in the Ionian Islands.

K.S.P.—Knight of St. Stanislaus, in Poland.

K.S.S—Knight of the Southern Star, in Brazil; Knight of the Sword, in Sweden.

K.S.W.—Knight of St. Wladimir, in Russia.

K.T.—Knight of the Thistle; Knight Templar.

Kt.—Knight.

K.T.S.—Knight of the Tower and Sword, in Portugal.

K.W.—Knight of William, in the Netherlands.

K.W.E.—Knight of the White Eagle, in Poland.

Ky.—Kentucky.

L.—Fifty or fiftieth. *Liber*, book. Latin.

L, £, or l.—*Libra* or *Libræ*, pound or pounds sterling.

L, or £, s. d.—*Libra, solidi, denarii*, Pounds, shillings, pence.

La.—Louisiana.

Lam.—Lamentations.

Lat.—Latitude; Latin.

Lb. or lb.—*Libra* or *Libræ*, Pound or pounds in weight.

L.C.—Lord Chancellor; Lord Chamberlain; Lower Canada.

l.c.—Lower-case.

L.C.B.—Lord Chief Baron.

L.C.J.—Lord Chief-Justice.

L.D.—Lady-Day.

Ld.—Lord.

Ldp.—Lordship.

Leg.—Legate.

Legis.—Legislature.

Lev.—Leviticus.

Lex—Lexicon.

L. I.—Long Island.

Lib.—*Liber*, book.

Lieut.—Lieutenant.

Lieut.-Col.—Lieutenant-Colonel.

Lieut.-Gen.—Lieutenant-General.

Lieut.-Gov.—Lieutenant-Governor.

Linn.—Linnæan.

Liq.—Liquidation.

Lit.—Literally; Literature.

Liv.—*Livre*, book.

LL B.—*Legum Baccalaureus*, Bachelor of Laws.

LL.D.—*Legum Doctor*, Doctor of Laws.

loc. cit.—*Loco citato*, in the place cited.

Lon.—Longitude.

Lond.—London.

L.S.—*Locus sigilli*, place of the seal.

Lt.—Lieutenant.

LX.—Sixty or sixtieth.

LXX.—Seventy or seventieth; The Septuagint (Version of the Old Testament).

LXXX.—Eighty or eightieth.

M.—*Meridies*, noon.

M.—*Mille*, a thousand.

M. or Mons.—*Monsieur*, Sir.

M.A.—Master of Arts.

Macc.—Maccabees.

Mad.—Madam.

Mad. Univ.—Madison University.

Maj.—Major.

Maj.-Gen.—Major-General.

Mal.—Malachi.

Man.—Manasses.

Mar.—March.

March.—Marchioness.

Marg.—Margin.

Marg. Tran.—Marginal Translation.

Marq.—Marquis.

Masc.—Masculine.

Mass.—Massachusetts.

Math.—Mathematics; Mathematician.

Matt.—Matthew.

Max.—Maxim.

M.B.—*Medicinæ Baccalaureus*, Bachelor of Medicine.

M.B.—*Musicæ Baccalaureus*, Bachelor of Music.

M.B.G. et H.—*Magna Britannia, Gallia et Hibernia*, Great Britain, France, and Ireland.

M.C.—Member of Congress.

Mch.—March.

M.D.—*Medicinæ Doctor*, Doctor of Medicine.

Md—Maryland.

Mdlle.—*Mademoiselle*.

Mdse.—Merchandise.

M.E.—Methodist Episcopal; Military or Mechanical Engineer.

Me.—Maine.

Mech.—Mechanics, or Mechanical.

Med.—Medicine.

Mem.—Memorandum. *Memento*, remember.

Merc.—Mercury.

Messrs. or MM.—*Messieurs*, Gentlemen.

Met.—Metaphysics.

Metal.—Metallurgy.

Meteor.—Meteorology.

Meth.—Methodist.

Mex.—Mexico, or Mexican.

M.-Goth.—Mœso-Gothic.

M. H. S.—Massachusetts Historical Society; Member of the Historical Society.

Mic.—Micah.

Mich.—Michigan.

Mil.—Military.

Mil. Acad.—Military Academy.

Min.—Mineralogy; Minute.

Minn.—Minnesota.

Min. Plen.—Minister Plenipotentiary.

Miss.—Mississippi.

M. L. A.—Mercantile-Library Association.

MM.—Their Majesties. *Messieurs*, Gentlemen, Two thousand.

M.M.S.—Moravian Missionary Society.

M.M.S.S.—*Massachusettensis Medicinæ Societatis Socius*, Fellow of the Massachusetts Medical Society.

Mo—Missouri; Month.

Mod.—Modern.

Mon.—Monday.

Mons.—*Monsieur*, Sir.

Mos.—Months.

Mont. Ter.—Montana Territory.

M.P.—Member of Parliament. Member of Police.

M.P.P.—Member of Provincial Parliament.

M. R.—Master of the Rolls.

Mr.—Mister.

M.R.A.S.—Member of the Royal Asiatic Society; Member of the Royal Academy of Science.

M.R.C.C.—Member of the Royal College of Chemistry.

M.R.C.S.—Member of the Royal College of Surgeons.

M.R.G.S.—Member of the Royal Geographical Society.

M.R.I.—Member of the Royal Institute.

M.R.I.A.—Member of the Royal Irish Academy.

Mrs.—Mistress.

M.R.S.L.—Member of the Royal Society of Literature.

M.S.—*Memoriæ sacrum*, Sacred to the Memory; Master of the Sciences.
MS.—*Manuscriptum*, manuscript.
MSS.—Manuscripts.
Mt.—Mount, or Mountain.
Mus. B.—Bachelor of Music.
Mus. D.—Doctor of Music.
M.W.—Most Worthy; Most Worshipful.
Myth.—Mythology.

N.—North; Number; Noun; Neuter.
n.—Note.
N.A.—North America.
Nah.—Nahum.
Nat.—Natural.
Nat. Hist.—Natural History.
Nath.—Nathanael, or Nathaniel.
N.B.—New Brunswick; North British. *Nota Bene*, mark well; take notice.
N.C.—North Carolina; New Church.
N.E.—New England; Northeast.
Neb.—Nebraska.
Neh.—Nehemiah.
n.e.i.—*Non est inventus*, He is not found.
nem. con. or nem. diss.—*Nemine contradicente*, No one opposing; unanimously.
Neut.—Neuter (gender).
Nev.—Nevada.
New Test. or N.T.—New Testament.
N.F.—Newfoundland.
N.G.—New Granada; Noble Grand.
N.H.—New Hampshire; New Haven.
N.H.H.S.—New Hampshire Historical Society.
Ni. pri.—*Nisi prius* (law).
N.J.—New Jersey.
n.l.—*Non liquet*, It does not appear.
N. lat.—North latitude.
N. Mex.—New Mexico.
N.N.E.—North-Northeast.
N.N.W.—North-Northwest.
N.O.—New Orleans.
No.—*Numero*, number.
Nol. pros.—*Nolens prosequi*, Unwilling to prosecute.
Nom. or nom.—Nominative.
Non con.—Not content; dissenting (House of Lords).
Non cul.—*Non culpabilis*, Not guilty.
Non obst.—*Non obstante*, notwithstanding.
Non pros.—*Non prosequitur*, He does not prosecute.
Non seq.—*Non sequitur*, It does not follow
Nos.—Numbers.
Nov.—November.
N.P.—Notary Public; New Providence
N.S.—New Style (after 1752), Nova Scotia.
N.T.—New Testament.
N.n.—Name, or names, unknown.
Num.—Numbers; Numeral.
N.V.M.—Nativity of the Virgin Mary.
N W.—Northwest.
N.W.T.—Northwestern Territory.
N Y.—New York.
N.Y.H.S.—New York Historical Society.

O.—Ohio.
Ob.—*Obiit*, He (or she) died.
Obad.—Obadiah.
Obj.—Objection; Objective.

O K.—A slang phrase for "All correct."
Obt. or obdt.—Obedient.
Oct.—October.
O.F.—Odd-Fellow, or Odd-Fellows.
O.F.P.—Order of Friar Preachers.
Old Test. or O.T.—Old Testament.
Olym.—Olympiad.
Ont.—Ontario.
Opt.—Optics; Optical; Optional.
Or.—Oregon.
Ord.—Ordinance; Order; Ordnance; Ordinary.
Orig.—Originally.
Ornith.—Ornithology.
O.S.—Old Style (before 1752).
O.S.F.—Order of St. Francis.
O.T.—Old Testament.
O U.A.—Order of United Americans.
Oxf.—Oxford.
Oxon.—*Oxoniensis Oxonii*, of Oxford, at Oxford.
Oz.—Ounce.

P.—*Ponders*, by weight.
P. or p.—Page; Part; Participle.
Pa.—Pennsylvania.
Pal.—Palæontology.
Par.—Paragraph.
Par. Pas.—Parallel passage.
Parl.—Parliament.
Pathol.—Pathology.
Payt.—Payment.
Pb —*Plumbum*, lead.
P. B.—*Philosophiæ Baccalaureus*, Bachelor of Philosophy.
P C.—*Patres Conscripti*, Conscript Fathers; Senators.
P.C.—Privy Council; Privy Councilor.
P.D—*Philosophiæ Doctor*, Doctor of Philosophy.
Pd.—Paid.
P.E.—Protestant Episcopal.
P.E I.—Prince Edward Island.
Penn.—Pennsylvania.
Pent.—Pentecost.
Per or pr.—By the.
Per an.—*Per annum*, by the year.
Per cent.—*Per centum*, by the hundred.
Peri.—Perigee.
Pet.—Peter.
P. G.—Past Grand.
Phar.—Pharmacy.
Ph. B.—*Philosophiæ Baccalaureus*, Bachelor of Philosophy.
Ph D.—*Philosophiæ Doctor*, Doctor of Philosophy.
Phil —Philip; Philippians; Philosophy; Philemon.
Phila. or Phil.—Philadelphia.
Philom. — *Philomathes*, Lover of Learning.
Philomath.—*Philomathematicus*, A lover of the mathematics.
Phil. Trans.—Philosophical Transactions.
Phren.—Phrenology.
P.H S — Pennsylvania Historical Society.
Pinx.—*Pinxit*, He (or she) painted it.
Pk.—Peck.
Pl. or plur —Plural.
Plff —Plaintiff.
P. M.— *Post Meridiem*, Afternoon, Evening; Postmaster; Passed Midshipman.
P M G — Postmaster-General; Professor of Music in Gresham College.

P.O.—Post-Office.
Poet.—Poetical.
Pop.—Population.
Port.—Portugal; Portuguese.
Pos.—Position; Positive; Possession.
P.P.—*Pater Patriæ*, Father of his Country; Parish Priest.
P.P.C.—*Pour prendre conge*, to take leave.
Pp. or pp.—Pages.
Pph.—Pamphlet.
Pr.—By.
P.R.—*Populus Romanus*, the Roman People; Porto Rico; Proof-reader; Prize Ring.
P.R.A.—President of the Royal Academy.
P.R.C.—*Post Romam conditam*, After the building of Rome.
Pref.—Preface.
Prep.—Preposition.
Pres.—President.
Prin.—Principally.
Pro.—For; in favor of.
Prob.—Problem.
Prof.—Professor.
Pron.—Pronoun; Pronunciation.
Prop.—Proposition.
Prot.—Protestant.
Pro tem.—*Pro tempore*, for the time being
Prov.—Proverbs; Provost.
Prox.—*Proximo*, next (month).
P.R.S.—President of the Royal Society.
P.S.—*Post scriptum*, Postscript.
P.S.—Privy Seal.
Ps.—Psalm or Psalms.
Pt.—Part; Pint; Payment; Point; Port; Post-town.
P.Th.G.—Professor of Theology in Gresham College.
Pub.—Publisher; Publication; Published; Public.
Pub. Doc.—Public Documents.
P. v.—Post-village.
Pwt.—Pennyweight; pennyweights.
Pxt.—*Pinxit*, He (or she) painted it.

Q.—Queen; Question.
q.—*Quasi*, as it were; almost.
Q. B.—Queen's Bench.
Q.C.—Queen's College; Queen's Counsel.
q.d.—*Quasi dicat*, as if he should say; *quasi dictum*, as if said; *quasi dixisset*, as if he had said.
q e.—*Quod est*, which is.
q.e.d.—*Quod erat demonstrandum*, which was to be proved.
q.e.f.—*Quod erat faciendum*, which was to be done.
q.e.i.— *Quod erat inveniendum*, which was to be found out.
q.l.—*Quantum libet*, as much as you please.
Q.M —Quartermaster.
qm.—*Quomodo*, how; by what means.
Q.M.G —Quartermaster-General.
q.p. or q pl.—*Quantum placet*, as much as you please.
Qr.—Quarter.
Q.S.—Quarter - sessions; Quarter-section.
q.s.—*Quantum sufficit*, a sufficient quantity.
Qt.—Quart.
qu. or qy.—*Quære*, inquire; query.
Quar.—Quarterly.

Ques.—Question.
q.v.—*Quod vide*, which see; *quantum vis*, as much as you will.
R.—*Recipe*, take. *Regina*, Queen; *Rex*, King. River; Rod; Rood; Rises.
R.A.—Royal Academy; Royal Academician; Royal Arch; Royal Arcanum; Royal Artillery.
RC.—*Rescriptum*, a Rescript, rewritten.
R.E.—Royal Engineers.
Rec.—Recipe, or Recorder.
Recd.—Received.
Rec. Sec.—Recording Secretary.
Rect.—Rector; Receipt.
Ref.—Reference; Reform.
Ref. Ch.—Reformed Church.
Reg.—Register; Regular.
Reg. Prof.—*Regius Professor*.
Regr.—Registrar.
Regt.—Regiment.
Rel.—Religion.
Rep. — Representative; Reporter. Republic.
Rev.—Reverend; Revelation (Book of); Review; Revenue; Revise.
Rhet.—Rhetoric.
R.I.—Rhode Island.
Richd.—Richard.
R.I.H.S. — Rhode Island Historical Society.
R.M.—Royal Marines; Royal Mail.
R M S —Royal Mail Steamer.
R.N.—Royal Navy.
R.N.O. — *Riddare af Nordstjerne Orden*, Knight of the Order of the Polar Star.
Ro.—*Recto*, Right-hand page.
Robt.—Robert.
Rom.—Romans (Book of).
Rom Cath.—Roman Catholic.
R.P.—*Regius Professor*, the King's Professor.
R.R.—Railroad.
R.S.—Recording Secretary.
Rs.—*Responsum*, answer; *respondere*, to answer.
R.S.A. — Royal Society of Antiquaries; Royal Scottish Academy.
R.S.D.—Royal Society of Dublin.
R.S.E. — Royal Society of Edinburgh.
R.S.L.—Royal Society of London.
R.S.V.P.—*Repondez s'il vous plait*, Answer, if you please.
Rt. Hon.—Right Honorable.
Rt. Rev.—Right Reverend.
Rt. Wpful —Right Worshipful.
R W.—Right Worthy.
R W O. — *Riddare af Wasa Orden*, Knight of the Order of Wasa.
S.—South; Saint, Scribe; Sulphur; Sunday; Sun; Series.
S —*Solidus*, a shilling.
S. A.—South America; South Africa, South Australia.
s.a.—*Secundum artem*, according to art.
Sam.—Samuel.
Sancs.—Sanscrit.
S.A.S. — *Societatis Antiquariorum Socius*, Fellow of the Society of Antiquaries.
Sat.—Saturday.
Sax.—Saxon.
Sax. Chron.—Saxon Chronicle.
S C —*Senatus Consultum*, A decree of the Senate; South Carolina.

[faded] ...., he (or she) engraved it.
.... —*Scilicet,* namely.
.... —*Scandalum magnatum,*
.... or *scandalum magnum,*
.... —scandal.
.... —Small capitals.
.... —*Scholium,* a note.
.... —Schnauer.
.... —*Scire facias,* make known
....
.... —*Sclavonic.*
.... or *sculp.* —*Sculpsit,* he (or
.... engraved it.
.... —Scotland; Scottish; Scotch.
Scr. —Scruple.
S. D. —*Salutem dicit,* sends health.
s. E. —Excellence.
Sec. —Secretary; Second, Section.
Sec. Leg. —Secretary of Legation.
Sec. reg. —*Secundum legem,* accord-
ing to law.
Sec. reg. —*Secundum regulam,* ac-
cording to rule.
Sect. —Section.
Seem. —*Semble* it seems.
Sen. —*Senate* Senator; Senior.
Sept. —*Septuaginta,* Septuagint.
Seq. —*Sequentia,* following; sequi-
tur, it follows.
Ser. —Series.
Serg. —Sergeant.
Serg. Maj. —Sergeant-Major.
Serv. —Service.
S. G. —Solicitor General.
S. H. S. —*Societatis Historiæ Socius,*
Fellow of the Historical Society.
Shak. —Shakspere.
S. I. —Sandwich Islands.
Society of all Jesus, Society of
....
S. J. C. —Supreme Judicial Court.
SL. —Scilicet.
S. L. —Solicitor at Law (Scots).
S. M. —Sacred ministre
S. M. —*Sanctæ Mariæ* Knight Mary;
...... Knight of Malta.
S. P. Q. R. —*Senatus
...... populusque Romanus, ...
.... Member
...... Society
S. P. —*secundum artem,* accord-
....
Secr. —*secundum l'usage*
Sem. —......
Sem. —......
S. P. G. —...... ....
S. P. D. —...... *Philosophiæ*
...... Member of the
...... Society
S. P. G. —...... for the Propagation
of the ......

Sp. gr. —Specific gravity.
S. P. Q. R. —*Senatus Populusque Ro-
manus,* the Roman Senate and
people.
Sq. ft. —Square foot or square feet.
Sq. in. —Square inch or inches.
Sq. m. —Square mile or miles.
Sq. r. —Square rood or roods.
Sq. yd. —Square yard.
Sr. —Sir or Senior.
S. R. I. —*Sacrum Romanum Im-
perium,* Holy Roman Empire.
S. R. S. —*Societatis Regiæ Socius,* Fel-
low of the Royal Society.
S. S. —Sunday-school.
SS. —Saints.
SS. or ss. —*Scilicet,* to wit.
ss. —*Semis,* half.
S. S. C. —Solicitor before the Supreme
Court (Scotland).
S. S. E. —South-Southeast.
S. S. W. —South-Southwest.
St. —Saint; Street; Strait; Stone.
Stat. —Statute.
S. T. D. —*Sacræ Theologiæ Doctor,*
Doctor of Sacred Theology.
Ster. or Stg. —Sterling.
S. T. P. —*Sacræ Theologiæ Professor,*
Professor of Sacred Theology.
Su. —Sunday.
Subj. —Subjunctive.
Subst. —Substantive.
Su.-Goth. —Suio-Gothic.
Sun. or Sund. —Sunday.
Sup. —Supplement; Superfine; Supe-
rior.
Supt. —Superintendent.
Surg. —Surgeon; Surgery.
Surg.-Gen. —Surgeon-General.
Surv. —Surveyor.
Surv.-Gen. —Surveyor-General.
Sus. —Susannah.
s. v. —*Sub verbo,* under the word or
title.
S. W. —Southwest.
Switz. —Switzerland.
Syn. —Synonym; Synonymous.

T. —Territory; Town; Township;
Tutti, all together.
T. or tom. —Tome, volume.
Ta. —*Tantalum* (Columbium).
T. E. —Topographical Engineers.
Tenn. —Tennessee.
Ter. —Territory.
Tex. —Texas.
Text. Rec. —*Textus Receptus,* the
Received Text.
Th. or Thurs. —Thursday.
Theo. —Theodore.
Theol. —Theology; Theological.
Theoph. —Theophilus.
Thess. —Thessalonians.
Tho'. —Though.
Thos. —Thomas.
Thro'. —Through.

Tim. —Timothy.
Tit. —Titus.
T. O. —Turn over.
T. R. —T-bar.
Topog. —Topography; Topograph-
ical.
Tr. —Transpose, Translator, Trans-
lation; Trustee. Trs. —Trustees.
tr. —*Tragic,* a shake.
Trans. —Translator; Translation;
Transactions.
Treas. —Treasurer.
Trin. —Trinity.
Tues. or Tu. —Tuesday.
Typ. —Typographer.

U. E. I. C. —United East India Com-
pany.
U. J. D. —*Utriusque Juris Doctor,*
Doctor of both Laws (Civil and
Canon).
U. K. —United Kingdom.
ult. —*Ultimo,* last, of the last month.
Unit. —Unitarian.
Univ. —University.
U. S. —United States.
u. s. —*Ut supra* or *uti supra,* as
above.
U. S. A. —United States Army; United
States of America.
U. S. M. —United States Mail; United
States Marine.
U. S. M. A. —United States Military
Academy.
U. S. N. —United States Navy.
U. S. N. A. —United States Naval
Academy.
U. S. S. —United States Senate.
Utah —Utah Territory.
V. —Five or fifth; Violin.
VV. —Violins.
v. or vid. —*Vide,* see.
v. or vs. —*Versus,* against; *Versi-
culo,* in such a verse.
Va. —Virginia.
Vat. —Vatican.
V. C. —Vice-Chancellor.
V. D. M. —*Verbi Dei Minister,* Min-
ister of God's Word.
Ven. —Venerable.
Ver. —Verse.
V. G. —Vicar-General.
v. g. —*Verbi gratia,* as for example.
VI. —Six or sixth.
VII. —Seven or seventh.
VIII. —Eight or eighth.
Vice-Pres. or V. P. —Vice-President.
Visc. —Viscount.
viz. or vi. —*Videlicet,* to wit;
namely; that is to say
Vo. —Verso, left-hand page.
Vol. —Volume.
V. R. —*Victoria Regina,* Queen
Victoria.
V. S. —Veterinary Surgeon.

Vt. —Vermont
Vul. —Vulgate (Latin version of the
Bible).
W. —West.
Wash. Ter. —Washington Territory
Wed. —Wednesday.
West. Res. Coll. —Western Reserve
College.
w. f. —Wrong font.
Whf. —Wharf
W. I. —West Indies.
Wis. —Wisconsin.
Wisd. —Wisdom (Book of).
Wk. —Week.
W. lon. —West longitude.
W. M. —Worshipful Master
Wm. —William.
W. M. S. —Wesleyan Missionary So-
ciety.
W. N. W. —West-Northwest.
W. P. —Worthy Patriarch
Wp. —Worship.
Wpful. —Worshipful.
W. S. —Writer to the Signet.
W. S. W. —West-Southwest
Wt. —Weight.
W. Va. —West Virginia.
Wyo. Ter. —Wyoming Territory.

X. —Ten or tenth.
XI. —Eleven.
XII. —Twelve.
XIII. —Thirteen.
XIV. —Fourteen.
XV. —Fifteen.
XVI. —Sixteen.
XVII. —Seventeen.
XVIII. —Eighteen.
XIX. —Nineteen.
XX. —Twenty.
XXX. —Thirty.
XL. —Forty.
XC. —Ninety.
X. or Xt. —Christ.
Xmas or Xm. —Christmas.
Xn. or Xtian. —Christian.
Xnty or Xty. —Christianity.
Xper or Xr. —Christopher.

Yd. —Yard.
y. or y⁻ —The
yᵐ —Them.
yⁿ —Then.
yʳ —Their; Your.
yˢ —This.
yᵗ —That.
Y. M. C. A. —Young Men's Christian
Association.
Yrs. —Years; Yours.

Zach. —Zachary.
Zech. —Zechariah.
Zeph. —Zephaniah.
Zool. —Zoology.
Zn. —Zinc.
&. —And.
&c. —*Et cetera,* and the rest; and so
forth.

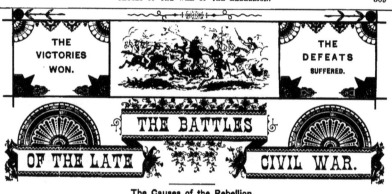

THE
VICTORIES
WON.

THE
DEFEATS
SUFFERED.

THE BATTLES

OF THE LATE

CIVIL WAR.

The Causes of the Rebellion.

EAVING DESOLATION in its track, throughout many parts of the South, was a four-years' war, waged between the people of the Northern and Southern portions of the United States, extending over a period of time from April 12, 1861, to the surrender of Lee, April 9, 1865.

Among the causes that produced the war, briefly stated, were these: The staple productions in the South, prior to the war, were cotton and sugar. To sell these productions in the markets of the world at the highest figures, and purchase the necessaries of life at the lowest price, was regarded by the Southern people as legitimate. To have unrestricted commercial intercourse, therefore, with the people of all nations, being free to export their productions without hindrance, and import goods from abroad free of duty, was considered for the best interests of the South.

There existed a decided difference of opinion between the people of the Northern and Southern States on this subject. A large body of people at the North believed that home industries could best be built up through the shutting out of foreign production by a high protective tariff. This party favored the placing of a high tax on all goods from abroad.

Protective tariff against free trade, which became a sectional issue, was one of the causes. Another was the black man. For generations the colored people had been regarded by most persons at the South as property that could be rightfully bought and sold.

In many parts of the North, in the early history of the country, slavery was common. Washington was a prominent owner of slaves,

as were many other great and good men; and the institution of slavery having for generations been protected by legislation, a vast body of people at the South regarded it as perfectly right to buy, sell, and own slaves.

Gradually a public sentiment grew up in the North antagonistic to the idea of one class owning another class. This feeling extended into the halls of national legislation, and in time developed very bitter sectional feeling.

The final result was that the Southerners, thinking of the triumph of the United States when they cut loose from England, and that the people of the South should have the right to make such laws as they deemed best for their own interests, inaugurated the work of separating the South from the North by the act of secession, passed by the legislature of South Carolina, in which that State seceded from the Union, December 20, 1860. This example was followed by others of the Southern States in the following order, eleven States passing ordinances of secession between the fifteenth day of December, 1860, and June 10, 1861: Mississippi, January 9, 1861; Florida, January 10, 1861; Alabama, January 11, 1861; Georgia, Janua., 19, 1861; Louisiana, January 26, 1861; Texas, February 1, 1861; Virginia, April 17, 1861; Arkansas, May 6, 1861; North Carolina, May 21, 1861; Tennessee, by a vote of the people, June 8, 1861. The Western portion of Virginia refused to secede, and in 1863 was admitted into the Union as the loyal State of West Virginia.

The people of the South were then desirous of having the authorities of the United States withdrawn from the seceded States, and in order to hasten and compel this, an attack was made on Fort Sumter, April 12, 1861. This precipitated the war of the Rebellion—a four-years' struggle—that caused a loss of near 500,000 lives, and fastened upon the United States a debt, at the close of the war, of near $3,000,000,000.

An outline of each prominent battle, the numbers killed, wounded and taken prisoners, are given in the succeeding pages:

THE BATTLES OF THE FIRST YEAR OF THE WAR.

Battle of Fort Sumter — Fort Sumter, in Charleston harbor, S. C., occupied by Major Robert Anderson and a force of 47 effective United States soldiers and 68 other persons, and mounting 58 cannon, was by General Beauregard, commanding ———, in Charleston, April 12 and ——— was set on fire by the Confederates, after a fair defense, by

Major Anderson. His loss was only one man, who was killed by the bursting of a gun inside the fort; the Confederate losses are not generally known.

Skirmish at Fairfax Court House, Va. — Fought May 31, 1861, between 47 Unionist cavalry, under Lieutenant Tompkins, and a force of 1,500 Confederates.

Battle at Phillippi—Fought June 3, 1861, at Phillippi, W. Va., between 2,000 Confederates and

several regiments of Unionists, under Colonel Kelly and Colonel Lander, resulting in the retreat of the Confederates, with a loss of 15 killed, a number wounded and taken prisoners, and $35,000 worth of arms surrendered. Colonel Kelly was severely wounded.

Battle of Big Bethel — Fought June 10, 1861, at Big Bethel, Va., between 3,500 Unionists, under General Pierce, and 1,800 Confederates.

Debt of Different Countries, How Various Colors are Made, Length and Cost of American Canals, Center of Gravity of Population, Etc.

Average Height and Weight
Of Human Beings, at Different Ages.

Males.			Females.		
Age.	Feet.	Lbs.	Age.	Feet.	Lbs.
Birth..	1¾	7	Birth..	1¾	6¼
2 years..2¾..		25........	2 years..2¾ ..		23¾
4 years..3..31¾..		4 years...3....22¾			
6 years..3¾..36 4-5..		6 years..3....35¼			
8 years..4......50..		8 years....4....47			
11 years..4½...60¾...		11 years....4¼ ..56¾			
13 years..4¾..75 4-5....13 years...4 3-5..78 2-3					
15 years...5..96¼...		15 years.....5....89			
17 years..5¼..116½....17 years...5....104¼					
18 years..5¼..127½....18 years...5¼..112¾					
20 years..5¼..135¾...20 years....5 1-6.115½					
30 years..5½..140¾...30 years...5 1-6.118 4-5					
40 years..5½..140¾...40 years...5 1-6.121 4-5					
50 years..5½..140.....50 years...5....123 4-5					
60 years..5½..139.....60 years...5....119¾					
70 years..5½..131½...70 years...5....113¾					
80 years..5½..127½...80 years...5....106 4-5					
90 years..5½..127½...90 years...5....106 4-5					

Bait for Different Game.

Animal.	Bait Required.
Squirrel...............Grain, nuts, or ear of corn.	
Muskrat.......Carrots, potatoes, apples, etc.	
Woodchuck........Roots, fruit, corn or bread.	
Mink................Fowl, flesh or roasted fish.	
Skunk............Mice, meat, piece of a fowl.	
Fox........Fowl, flesh, fish, toasted cheese.	
Opossum......Nuts, corn, mice, piece of fowl.	
Raccoon...................Chicken, fish or frog.	
Badger...........Mice, or flesh of any kind.	
Otter ......Fish, piece of a bird, or otter musk.	
Marten..Head of a fish, piece of meat, or fowl.	
Beaver ....Fresh roots.	
Wolf............Waste parts of tame or wild fowl.	

The Pulse in Health.

New-born infants..........From 140 down to 130	
During 1st year............From 130 down to 115	
During 2d year.............From 115 down to 100	
During 3d year.............From 106 down to 95	
From 7th to 14th year......From 90 down to 80	
From 14th to 21st year.....From 85 down to 75	
From 21st to 60th year.....From 75 down to 70	
In old age..................From 75 up to 80	

Center of Gravity of Population.

The change of center of population each ten years, in the United States, is shown in the following table. In ninety years the center of gravity has moved westward 467 miles, on almost a straight line from east to west. The very rapid settlement of the northwest of late would indicate that the line will move considerably northward in the next ten years.

Date.	Location.	Westward move. Miles.
1790.	23 miles east of Baltimore...............	
1800.	18 miles west of Baltimore...............	41
1810.	40 miles northwest by west of Washington.	36
1820.	16 miles north of Woodstock, Va.........	50
1830.	19 miles southwest of Moorefield, W. Va..	39
1840.	16 miles south of Clarksburg, W. Va.....	55
1850.	23 miles southeast of Parkersburg, W. Va.	55
1860.	20 miles south of Chillicothe, O........	81
1870.	48 miles east by north of Cincinnati, O..	42
1880.	8 miles west by south of Cincinnati, O...	58
	Total....	**467**

Capacity of Cisterns.

In calculating the capacity of cisterns, 31½ gallons are estimated to one barrel, and 63 gallons to one hogshead.

Circular Cistern one foot in depth.

5 feet in diam. holds....4½ barrels.	
6 feet in diam. holds....6¾ barrels.	
7 feet in diam. holds....9 barrels.	
8 feet in diam. holds....12 barrels.	
9 feet in diam. holds....15 barrels.	
10 feet in diam holds...18½ barrels.	

Square Cistern one foot in depth.

5 feet by 5 feet holds....6 barrels.	
6 feet by 6 feet holds....8¼ barrels.	
7 feet by 7 feet holds...11½ barrels.	
8 feet by 8 feet holds...15¼ barrels.	
9 feet by 9 feet holds...19½ barrels.	
10 feet by 10 feet holds...23½ barrels.	

Audible Sounds.

The distance at which sounds can be distinguished depends much on favoring winds.

Description of Sound.	Feet.	Miles
A powerful human voice in the open air and no wind............	460	
Beating a drum..........	10,560	2
Music of a heavy brass band...........	15,840	3
A strong human voice with a brass barely felt..........	15,840	3
Report of a musket.......	16,000	3
Cannonading, very strong............	575,000	90

National Debt of Principal Countries.

The following table, from Porter's Census Book, shows the increase and decrease of the public debt of these different countries in the past twenty years:

Countries.	1850.	1870.	1888.
France..............	$1,254,136,500...	$2,777,363,000...	$3,929,932,360
Great Britain........	3,893,330,000...	3,835,497,000...	3,706,671,088
Russia..............	1,154,161,500...	1,070,430,000...	2,312,363,668
Spain...............	529,588,000...	1,396,406,500...	2,579,465,026
Italy...............	436,063,500...	1,900,006,000...	2,349,213,085
United States.......	64,843,260...	2,480,672,488...	2,196,415,371
Austria-Hungary.....	1,163,083,500...	1,654,410,000...	1,881,115,339
Turkey..............	160,564,500...	669,446,665...	1,376,488,559
Portugal............	136,966,000...	291,900,000...	457,431,486
Australia...........		136,668,000...	442,531,500
Holland.............	645,666,500...	369,164,500...	362,329,000
Canada..............		66,720,560...	173,191,088
Roumania...........		63,600,000...	118,762,088
Sweden-Norway.......		29,196,000...	97,229,088
Greece..............	32,962,000...	60,400,000...	94,351,428
German Empire*......	494,455,400...	729,363,000...	48,217,388
Denmark.............		62,364,500...	62,688,000

* The debt given for the German Empire in 1888 does not include the debts of any of the States composing it, but only the Empire Proper.

American Canals---Their Length and Cost.

The following table comprises the canals of the United States and Canada, of which the cost has exceeded $1,000,000.

Name.	State.	Miles.	Cost.
Chesapeake and Ohio..........Maryland.......191.......$10,000,000			
Delaware and Hudson......New York and Pa...108........9,000,000			
Illinois and Michigan........Illinois.......108.......8,654,337			
Erie........................New York.......363.......7,143,789			
Welland....................Canada.........36........7,000,000			
Central Division..........Pennsylvania...173........2,307,852			
James River and Kanawha......Virginia.....147........5,080,050			
Ohio and Erie...............Ohio...........307........4,695,854			
Lehigh....................Pennsylvania....55........4,455,000			
Miami......................Ohio...........178........3,750,900			
North Branch Extension......Pennsylvania...98........3,100,000			
Morris and Essex..........New Jersey.....101........3,004,532			
West Division............Pennsylvania....84........3,007,120			
Wabash and Erie...........Indiana........409........2,750,000			
Chesapeake and Delaware...Delaware and Md..13½.......2,844,168			
Delaware and Raritan......New Jersey.....43........2,830,000			
Schuylkill Division........Pennsylvania...108........2,500,178			
Chenango..................New York........97........2,419,000			
Cornwall..................Canada.........18........2,000,000			
Lachine...................Canada.........8½........2,000,000			
Beauharnois...............Canada.........21........1,500,000			
Sandy and Beaver..........Ohio...........74........1,500,000			
Delaware Division.........Pennsylvania...90........1,275,715			
Champlain.................New York........82........1,257,604			
North Branch.............Pennsylvania...73........1,006,172			
Susquehannah.............Pennsylvania...39........1,030,354			
St. Lawrence..............Canada.........10........1,000,000			

Combinations of Shades that Make Different Colors.

Mixing Red and Black............makes........Brown	
Mixing Lake with White...........makes........Rose	
Mixing Umber and White...........makes........Drab	
Mixing White and Brown...........makes........Chestnut	
Mixing Yellow and Brown..........makes........Chocolate	
Mixing Red with Light Blue.......makes........Purple	
Mixing Carmine with Straw........makes........Flesh Color	
Mixing White with Lead Color.....makes........Pearl	
Mixing Carmine with White........makes........Pink	
Mixing Lamp-Black with Indigo....makes........Silver Gray	
Mixing Lamp-Black with White.....makes........Lead Color	
Mixing Paris Green with White....makes........Bright Green	
Mixing Yellow Ochre and White....makes........Buff	
Mixing White tinted with Purple..makes........French White	
Mixing Black with Chrome Green...makes........Dark Green	
Mixing Chrome Green with White...makes........Pea Green	
Mixing Emerald Green with White..makes........Brilliant Green	
Mixing Vermilion with Chrome Yellow.makes.... Orange	
Mixing Chrome Yellow with White Lead.makes....Straw Color	
Mixing White tinted with Red and Yellow..makes....Cream	
Mixing White with tints of Black and Purple, makes....Ashes of Rose	
Mixing White, tinted with Black and Purple, makes....French Gray	
Mixing Chrome Yellow, Blue, Black and Red, makes....Olive	

BATTLES OF THE SECOND YEAR OF THE WAR.

Fight in South Carolina — In a cannon-fight at Fort Pickens, January 1, 1862, General Stevens, commanding a Union land force, advanced from Beaufort, and, with the assistance of the gunboats, captured the (Confederate) Coosaw batteries, held by General Bragg, losing 8 killed and 8 wounded.

Fight at Huntersville, W. Va.—January 4, 1862, the Union troops, under General Milroy, defeated a Confederate force at Huntersville, and captured $80,000 worth of stores.

Battle of Prestonburg, Ky. — Fought January 10, 1862, between about 3,000 Unionists, under General Garfield, and about 2,500 Confederates, with three guns, under General Humphrey Marshall. Garfield, after fighting for several hours, and then being reinforced, finally routed the Confederates, whose loss was about 60 killed, besides prisoners, horses and stores.

A River Combat—Fought January 11, 1862, between two Union steamers and four Confederate boats, about 20 miles south of Cairo, Ill. The latter were compelled to seek refuge under the Confederate batteries at Columbus, Ky.

Battle of Mill Springs, Ky.—Fought January 19, 1862, between about 8,000 Confederates, under Generals Crittenden and Zollicoffer, and 3,000 Union troops, under Generals Thomas and Schoepf. The Confederates were defeated, with the loss of Generals Zollicoffer and Peyton, and 192 killed and 62 wounded, 8 cannon, 1,000 stand of arms, 1,700 horses and mules, a drove of cattle, 100 wagons, quartermaster's stores, etc. The Union loss was 39 killed and 203 wounded.

Capture of Fort Henry, Tenn.—General Grant, with a force of Unionists, and Commodore Foote, with 7 Union gunboats, formed an expedition which left Cairo, Ill., to reduce Fort Henry, on the Tennessee river, then in possession of the Confederates, under General Tighlman. On the 6th of February, 1862, without waiting for General Grant, who was detained by bad roads, Commodore Foote attacked the fort with his squadron. Within two hours General Tighlman unconditionally surrendered the fort, mounting 20 cannon, with barracks and tents, and about 130 prisoners. The Union loss was 2 killed and 37 wounded; the Confederates had 6 killed and 10 wounded.

Battle of Roanoke Island, N. C.—Fought February 8, 1862, between a Union expedition by land and sea, and the Confederate fortifications on the islands held by 2,000 men. The Union force consisted of more than 100 vessels and 11,500 troops, commanded by Commodore Goldsborough and General Burnside. The result was the capture of 6 Confederate forts, 40 guns, 2,000 Confederate prisoners, 3,000 small arms, ammunition, etc. The Union loss was 50 killed and 212 wounded, the Confederates had 5 killed and 18 wounded.

Battle of Fort Donelson, Tenn.—Fought February 15 and 16, 1862, between 20,000 Confederates, under Generals Pillow, Floyd and Buckner, within the fort and its outworks, and about 30,000 Unionists under General Grant, assisted by Commodore Foote, with his fleet of gunboats. On the second day General Buckner unconditionally surrendered the fort, with between 12,000 and 15,000 prisoners, 40 cannon, and a large amount of stores. The Union losses included 321 in killed, 1,046 wounded, and 150 missing. Floyd escaped with part of the Confederate force.

Battle of Fort Craig, N. M. — Fought February 21, 1862, between Union troops under General Canby and a Texan force. The Unionists were defeated with a loss of 62 killed and 162 wounded.

Captures on the Sea-coast—Commodore Dupont, commanding the Union fleet on the Southern coast, on the 4th of March, 1862, captured Brunswick, Ga., and Forts Clinch, Fernandina, and St. Mary's, Fla.

Battle of Pea Ridge, Ark. — Fought March 6, 7 and 8, 1862, between about 12,000 Unionists, under General Curtis, and 20,000 Confederates, under Van Dorn, Price and McCulloch, resulting in the defeat of the latter. The Unionists lost 203 killed, 972 wounded, and 176 missing. The loss of the Confederates was much greater.

The Fight at Hampton Roads — On the 8th of March, 1862, the Confederate steam war-vessels Merrimack, Jamestown and Yorktown, attacked the Union fleet at Hampton roads, Va., destroying the Cumberland and Congress, and damaging several other Government vessels. Next day occurred the battle between the iron-clad Monitor (Union), commanded by Lieutenant Worden, and the Merrimack (Confederate), in which the latter was disabled. The Federal loss of men, killed and drowned, besides the vessels, was 234, and 62 wounded and prisoners. The Confederate loss was 6 killed and a number wounded.

Surrender of New Madrid, Mo. — The Confederates had fortified Island No Ten, in the Mississippi river, a few miles above New Madrid, which was also fortified and defended by a Confederate force. Commodore Foote, with his river fleet of armed boats, and General Pope, with a land force, having threatened their works, the Confederates, March 13, 1862, evacuated New Madrid, leaving 25 cannon, and military stores valued at $1,000,000 in the hands of the Unionists.

Capture of Newbern, N. C. — Newbern was occupied by a Confederate force. On the 14th of March, 1862, General Burnside attacked the city with a fleet of gunboats and three brigades of Unionists. A four-hours' fight ensued, when the Confederates retreated, and the Unionists took possession of the city, with 69 heavy cannon and field-pieces, large quantities of ammunition, naval and military stores, steamers, vessels, etc., valued at $2,000,000. The Union loss was 91 killed and 466 wounded, many mortally. The Confederate loss was not so heavy, they being under cover.

Battle of Winchester, Va. — Fought March 23, 1862, between Union troops, numbering 8,000 men and 24 cannon, under Generals Banks and Shields, and 13,200 Confederate infantry and cavalry, with 28 cannon, under Jackson and Garnett. After five hours' fighting, the Confederates were defeated, and retreated to Strasburg, followed by their victors. The Union loss was 103 killed, 441 wounded, and 46 missing. The loss of the Confederates was very large, 270 being buried on the field.

Battle of Pigeon Ranch, N. M.—Fought March 28, 1862, between 3,000 Unionists, under Colonel Hough, and 1,100 Texan Confederates; a drawn battle.

Battles of Pittsburg Landing and Shiloh General Grant was encamped at Pittsburg Landing on the Tennessee river, with 45,000 Unionists awaiting reinforcements under General Buell. April 6, 1862, they were attacked by 40,000 Confederates, under Generals Johnston and Beauregard and driven back to the river, with the loss of a number of prisoners. Next day, General Buell, with more Unionists, having arrived the battle was renewed, lasting throughout the day. The Confederates, however, were finally defeated and driven to their fortifications at Corinth, Miss. The Confederates lost General A. S. Johnston. The Union loss is set down at 1,700 killed, 7,495 wounded, and 3,022 prisoners. The Confederate losses, as reported by Beauregard, were 1,728 killed, 8,012 wounded, and 959 missing.

Capture of Island No. Ten — The Confederates having fortified Island No. Ten, in the Mississippi river, 10 miles above New Madrid, and so commanding a strong position, General Pope, with a force of Unionists, also secured another commanding position, just below the island. After several ineffectual attempts to dislodge him by the Confederate gunboats, on the 16th of March, 1862, Commodore Foote and his flotilla arrived to assist General Pope. The island was well fortified with earthworks and heavy cannon, and manned by 20,000 Confederates. The bombardment was so hot and heavy, however, as to seriously incommode the Confederates, and on April 8, 1862, the Unionists attacked them with such vigor that the works were carried. The result was the capture of 5,000 prisoners, 124 cannon, 5,000 stand of small arms, 2,000 hogsheads of sugar and a large quantity of clothing, tents, ammunition, etc.

Bombardment of Fort Pulaski, Ga.—Fort Pulaski, twelve miles from Savannah, occupied by the Confederates and defended by 128 cannon and mortars, was invested by 11 Union batteries, under command of General Gilmore. On the 10th of April, 1862, the bombardment of the fort began, and on the 11th the fort was unconditionally surrendered to the Unionists, who had lost 1 killed and 3 wounded. The Confederates had 5 wounded, and 380 prisoners were taken with the fort.

Capture of Huntsville, Ala. — On the 11th of April, 1862, General Mitchel, Unionist, occupied Huntsville, capturing 200 Confederate prisoners, 15 locomotives and a number of cars.

Skirmish at Monterey, Va., and Capture at Chattanooga. — April 12, 1862, Confederates attacked General Milroy's Union force at Monterey, but were repulsed. On the same day, the Union general, Mitchel, captured 2,000 Confederates at Chattanooga.

Second Siege of Yorktown, Va.—Yorktown was strongly fortified by the Confederates, under General J. E. Johnston, who occupied it on April 17, 1862, with 53,000 men, exclusive of cavalry. The siege of this stronghold, which began April 5, 1862, was conducted by General McClellan, who had a force of 118,000 Unionists. It continued for a month. On the 4th of May, Johnston and his men evacuated the place, with whatever he could take, and started toward Richmond. Union cavalry, under Hancock, and Hooker's division, engaged 30,000 of them near Williamsburg, and a severe fight ensued. The Confederates at length retired, but most of their trains had by that time escaped beyond the lines. The Unionists lost 1,856 killed and wounded and 372 missing. The Confederate loss is believed to have been at least 2,600 killed and wounded.

Bombardment of Forts Jackson and Saint Philip, La.—Commodore Farragut and the Union fleet designed to capture New Orleans from the Confederates, and sailed early in February, 1862. On the 18th of April, 1862, he began the bombardment of the two Confederate forts, Saint Philip and Jackson, in the Mississippi, below New Orleans, with such success that the obstructions were removed, and the fleet passed the forts on its way to New Orleans, April 24.

Fights in North Carolina—April 19, 1862, the Unionists, under General Burnside, defeated a body of Confederates near Elizabeth City, N. C. The Union loss was 11 killed. On the same day, General Reno, with 2,000 Unionists, defeated some Confederate troops at Camden, N. C., in which the former lost 99 wounded and 14 killed.

Capture of New Orleans Part of Commodore Farragut's fleet of Union vessels [illegible] flotilla, and a land force of Unionists, under General Butler, appeared before New Orleans then held by the Confederates April 25, 1862. Forts Saint Philip and Jackson, the Confederate strongholds, capitulated April 28. General Lovell with his Confederate troops retreated into the interior of the State and General Butler took possession of the city May 1, 1862. The Confederates lost, besides the forts, including 11 gunboats, the ram Manassas, and the iron-clad Louisiana. The Confederates destroyed immense quantities of cotton, steamboats, ships, sugar, and other property in the city to prevent its falling into the hands of the Unionists. The loss of the Unionists in passing the Confederate forts was 30 killed and 110 wounded.

Fight at Lebanon, Tenn.—Fought May 5, 1862, between the Union troops under General Dumont and Morgan's Confederate cavalry. The latter had 66 killed and 133 taken prisoners; the Unionists lost 10 killed and 86 wounded and missing.

Battle of West Point, Va.—Fought May 7, 1862, between a formidable force of Confederates—a part of Lee's army—and Generals Franklin and Sedgwick's divisions of about 30,000 Unionists. The battle lasted six hours, when the Confederates were repulsed. The Union loss was 194 killed and wounded.

Battle at McDowell's, Va.—On the 8th of May, General Milroy's force of Unionists attacked a body of Confederates, but after a fight of five hours he was obliged to withdraw, having sustained a loss of 29 killed and about 200 wounded.

Evacuation of Pensacola, Fla. — The 3,000 Confederates, under General Bragg, who had occupied Pensacola since January 12, 1861, fearing a visit from Commodore Porter's Union mortar-fleet, evacuated the city May 9, 1862. When leaving, they fired the navy-yard, destroying the extensive workshops, warehouses, forts McRae and Barrancas, the lighthouse and the magnificent naval hospital. The Unionists at Fort Pickens, by a heavy cannonade, succeeded in driving the Confederates from the forts and buildings, thus arresting the work of destruction.

Capture of Norfolk, Va.—May 10, 1862, the Confederate authorities of Norfolk surrendered the city to General Wool and his 5,000 Unionists, without a fight. The navy-yard was in ruins, the iron-clad Merrimack had been blown up, and many guns spiked. The Confederates left behind them some 200 cannon and considerable ammunition.

A Naval Fight—May 10, 1862, a fight occurred between 8 Confederate and 4 Union gunboats on the Mississippi river, near Fort Wright, in which the former were defeated, losing 2 of their vessels.

Surrender of Natchez, Miss. — May 12, 1862, Commodore Farragut's fleet captured Natchez, which was then occupied by a small Confederate force, and was soon after abandoned by the Unionists.

Naval Fight in Virginia — A squadron of 4 Union war vessels, under Commodore Rodgers, encountered a Confederate force at Fort Darling, on the James river, eight miles from Richmond, May 14, 1862, and after a sharp fight the fleet withdrew, having lost 13 killed and 14 wounded.

On the Chickahominy—May 17, 1862, McClellan's left wing, drove a body of Confederates across the Chickahominy, at Bottom bridge, 13 miles from Richmond.

Battle at Lewisburgh, Va. — May 23, 1862, a force of Confederates, under Colonel Heath, attacked a body of Unionists, and, after an hour's contest, were defeated. The Unionists lost 14 killed and wounded.

Battle of Front Royal, Va. — Fought May 23, 1862, between Colonel Kenley, commanding a Union regiment, three companies and part of a battery, and a large force of Confederates, near Manassas gap, Va. After a desperate defense, Kenley retired across the Shenandoah, and rallied again; but was finally compelled to retreat, with a very heavy loss.

A Union Defeat — May 25, 1862. General Banks, with about 4,000 Unionists, encountered more than 25,000 Confederates, under Jackson and Ewell, at Strasburg, Va. Against such odds, after the first attack, and having held Winchester for two hours, Banks retreated to Williamsburgh to await reinforcements.

Battle of Hanover Court House, Va. —Fought May 27, 1862, between Fitz John Porter's division of Unionists and 13,000 Confederates. The latter were dislodged with the loss of about 200 killed, 730 prisoners, 2 railroad trains, arms, and ammunition. The Union loss was 53 killed and 344 wounded and missing.

Movements at Corinth, Miss.—May 28, 29 and 30, 1862, Corinth was invested by the Unionists under Generals Halleck, Pope and W. T. Sherman. On the 29th the Confederates, under Beauregard, evacuated their position, and on the 31st the Unionists, under General Halleck, occupied the town. General Pope, with 40,000 Unionists, pursued the fugitives (whose retreat had been obstructed by another Union force), and took many prisoners. Beauregard, however, again rallied his forces at Okolono, Miss.

Battle of Seven Pines, Va.—Fought May 31, 1862, between a large force of Confederates, under Longstreet, D. H. Hill, and Smith, and the Union troops in Casey's division of McClellan's army. Casey sustained his position for three hours against superior numbers, but finally fell back to the Seven Pines. They were dislodged from that position by the Confederates, and driven to a belt of woods, where the 1,800 Unionists, under Heintzelman, made so strong a resistance as to check the assault. Both armies then separated and encamped for the night.

Battle of Fair Oaks, Va. — While the battle of the Seven Pines was in progress, May 31, 1862, another battle was fought at Fair Oaks, hardly a mile away, between the Unionists in Sumner's division of McClellan's army and about 18,000 Confederates under Johnston and Smith. The contest continued from four o'clock in the afternoon until twilight when the Unionists charged upon the foe, driving them back in confusion at about the time that the struggle at the Seven Pines closed. Johnston was severely wounded in the last attack. Both armies bivouacked on the field, but a short distance from each other. Next morning hostilities were renewed at Fair Oaks, but not at the Seven Pines. Sumner being reinforced by Hooker, after an hour's hard fighting the Confederates were driven from the shelter of the woods and retreated in confusion to Richmond.

Losses at the Seven Pines and Fair Oaks—The losses of the Unionists in both battles were 890 killed, 3,627 wounded, 1,222 missing. The total loss of the Confederates is estimated at 6,733.

Fort Pillow Besieged—Fort Pillow, about 40 miles north of Memphis, Tenn., was erected by the Confederates. After a siege of 54 days by Union gunboats, under Commodore Foote, the fort, occupied by 6,000 Confederates, under General Villipigue, was abandoned, it having been dismantled and destroyed, June 5, 1862.

Battle Near Memphis, Tenn. — Fought June 6, 1862, between 8 Confederate war-vessels, under Commodore Montgomery, and a Union fleet of 5 gunboats and 9 rams, commanded by Colonel Ellet. Four of the Confederate vessels were sunk and 3 were run ashore. After the battle, the city of Memphis was surrendered to the Unionists, and was always afterwards retained by them.

Skirmish Near Harrisonburg, Va. — Fought June 6, 1862, between Unionists and Confederates, under General Ashby, who was killed.

Battle of Cross-Keys, Va.—Fought June 8, 1862, between a Union force under General Fremont, and 5,000 Confederates under General Ewell, a contest that retarded Fremont's advance. The Union loss was 664, that of the Confederates is unknown.

Battle of James Island, S. C. — Fought near Charleston, June 16, 1862, between Unionists, under General Stevens, and Confederates, the former being defeated with a loss of 85 killed, 472 wounded, and 128 missing.

Battle at Saint Charles, Ark.—Fought June 17, 1862, between Unionists, under Colonel Fitch, and a Confederate battery, which was destroyed. An explosion in a Union gunboat killed 125.

Battles Before Richmond—June 26, 1862, McClellan's Union army of 105,000 was gathered on the Chickahominy confronted by about 100,000 Confederates, under Robert E. Lee. Richmond, the Confederate capital, was in no condition to withstand a siege. Lee, therefore, decided to attack McClellan and raise the siege. He, therefore, divided his army and posted it at several points. The contest opened at Mechanicsville, where the Confederates attacked McClellan's right wing. In this action 6,000 Unionists contended with 12,000 Confederates. The latter were repelled, and fell back, having lost 1,500 men, while the Union loss was barely 300, owing to their sheltered position. On the 27th the battle of Cold Harbor was fought with great severity, between about 56,000 Confederates and 33,000 Unionists. During this day's fight the Confederates lost 9,500 in killed and wounded, and the Unionists 4,000 killed and wounded, 2,000 prisoners, and 22 cannon. During one skirmish the Confederates lost 800 out of 850 men. The victory at the close of the day was apparently with Lee, although he had suffered double the losses that he had inflicted, and his position was perilous. June 29, a series of engagements occurred at Savage's Station, McClellan having fallen back from his advantageous position. At Peach Orchard the Confederates attacked the Unionists, but were repulsed. Later in the day they renewed the attack at Savage's Station, which lasted until nine o'clock in the evening. The Union loss was about 600; that of the Confederates about 400. The Union wounded and sick (2,500) fell into the hands of the Confederates. June 30, McClellan continued his retreat to the James river. On this day was fought the battle of Frazier's Farm, between the Union divisions of McCall, Hooker, and Kearney, and the Confederates under A. P. Hill and Longstreet. The attempt to break the Union line failed. The Unionists lost about 300 killed, and 1,500 wounded, the Confederates, 325 killed and 1,700 wounded. The battle of Malvern Hill was fought July 1, 1862. McClellan had about 80,000 men; Lee only about 60,000 with which to attack McClellan's position. McClellan's artillery and musketry, well-placed, served to repel the Confederates' repeated charges upon his lines. The attacking party was not more than 28,000 strong. At dark the contest ceased, the Confederates having been repulsed at every point. The Union loss, that day, was about 375 killed and 1,800 wounded; the Confederate loss, 900 killed and 3,500 wounded. During the engagements from June 26 to July 1, it is estimated that the Unionists lost 1,582 killed, 7,709 wounded, and 5,958 missing; while the Confederates lost 3,150 killed, 15,255 wounded, and about 1,000 prisoners.

Skirmish at Bayou Cache, Ark. — Fought July 7, 1862, between a portion of General Curtis' Union army and the Confederates under General Rust, the latter being defeated, with 110 killed. Curtis lost but 8 killed and 45 wounded.

Skirmish at Jasper, Ala. — Fought July 7, 1862, between Unionists and Confederates, the former being worsted.

Capture of Hamilton, N. C. — July 9, 1862, Hamilton was captured by the Unionists.

Battle of Murfreesboro, Tenn.—Fought July 13, 1862, between a small force of Unionists, by whom it had been previously occupied, and a body of Confederates, under Forrest, a Michigan regiment being taken prisoners, and $30,000 worth of commissary stores were captured.

Capture of Kentucky Towns — July 11, 1862, the Confederate, General Morgan, raided Lebanon, Ky., burned part of the town and despoiled the bank. July 17, he captured Cynthiana, Ky., and burned several railroad bridges.

A Raid in Indiana — July 18, 1862, a band of Confederates raided Newburgh, Ind., destroyed some hospital stores, captured 250 stand of arms, and retreated across the Ohio.

Skirmish at Memphis, Tenn. — Fought July 19, 1862, between Unionists and Confederates, the former losing 6 killed and 32 wounded.

Bombardment of Vicksburg, Miss. — In June, 1862, the Union fleets of gunboats, respectively commanded by Commodore Farragut, from below, and Commanders Davis and Ellet, from above, met at Vicksburg, which was then strongly fortified and occupied by a Confederate force estimated at 10,000, and from time to time bombarded the city without any definite results. July 14, 1862, the commanders made a general attack upon the fortifications and heavily bombarded them for two hours. The upper batteries were silenced, and the city was set on fire in several places. Farragut's fleet passed the batteries and steamed down the river. The Confederates were not dislodged. On the 22d of July, the siege was abandoned.

Battle at Moore's Hill, Mo. — Fought between Confederates and Unionists, July 28, 1862, the former being defeated. The Unionists lost 10 killed and 30 wounded.

Capture of Orange Court House, Va. —August 1, 1862, Union cavalry, under General Crawford, after a short skirmish, drove out 2 regiments of Confederates, killing 11, and taking over 50 prisoners.

Skirmish Near Memphis, Tenn. — Fought August 3, 1862, between a Confederate force, under General Jeff. Thompson, and Union troops, in which Thompson was defeated.

A Naval Fight — Fought August 4, 1862, between 3 Union gunboats, under Commodore Porter, and the monster ram Arkansas, belonging to the Confederates. They met above Baton Rouge, on the Mississippi river, and on being attacked with incendiary shells the Arkansas was set on fire and destroyed.

Battle at Baton Rouge, La. — Fought August 5, 1862, between Confederates, under General Breckinridge, and a small force of Unionists, under General Williams. Confederate and Union gunboats were also engaged. Under a sharp shelling by the Union boats the Confederates were repulsed. The Unionists lost 56 killed, including General Williams, and 175 wounded and missing.

Battle of Cedar Mountain, Va.—Fought August 9, 1862, between the Confederate army, numbering about 21,000, under Generals Jackson, Ewell and Longstreet, and about 7,000 Unionists, under General Banks. The latter was forced to retire about 1½ miles from his first position. Banks being reinforced, the Confederates next day fell back two miles, and on the 11th retired across Robertson river. The Union loss was 450 killed, 660 wounded, and 290 prisoners, besides cannon and a large quantity of ammunition. The Confederate loss was nearly as heavy in killed, wounded and missing, including Generals Winder and Trimble.

Fight at Fort Donelson, Tenn.—August 25, 1862, the Confederates made an unsuccessful attack on the Unionists at Fort Donelson.

Fights at Manassas and Haymarket, Va.—August 26, 1862, the Confederates, under General Ewell, attacked a portion of the Union army, under Pope, at Manassas, and drove them out. Next day Pope fell back toward Warrenton, and was reinforced by Hooker's command. Overtaking the Confederates at Haymarket, a severe fight ensued between Hooker and Ewell, in which the Confederates were vanquished, Ewell losing his camp with 300 killed and wounded.

Reduction of City Point, Va. — On the 27th of August, 1862, the Union gunboats destroyed the Confederate fortifications at City Point.

Skirmish Near Centerville, Va. — Fought August 28, 1862, between Gibbon's brigade of McDowell's Union corps, and a force of Confederates under Stonewall Jackson. The fight was severe, but ended with the coming on of darkness.

Battle of Gainesville, Va.—Fought August 29, 1862, between Sigel and Reynolds' divisions of McDowell's Union corps, reinforced by Reno and Heintzelman's divisions, and the Confederate army under Stonewall Jackson, with reinforcements arriving. The battle raged furiously for several hours, in which the enemy was driven back, leaving his dead and wounded on the field. Darkness put an end to the contest, and General Pope claimed a victory. His losses were estimated at between 5,000 and 8,000 men, and those of the Confederates much greater.

The Second Battle of Bull Run — Fought August 30, 1862, between Stonewall Jackson's entire army of Confederates, reinforced by Longstreet and the advance of Lee's army (about 46,000 in all), and 35,000 Unionists under Pope. The contest was severe, lasting all day, at dark, exhausted, the Unionists retired to Centerville in good order, leaving the Confederates in possession of the field. The Unionists lost at least 11,000 in killed and wounded, and, perhaps, 9,000 prisoners, the Confederates about 8,500 killed and wounded.

Battle at Richmond, Ky. — Fought August 30, 1862, between the Confederates, under Kirby Smith, and the Unionists, under Generals Manson and Nelson. The latter were defeated with a loss of about 200 killed, 700 wounded, and 2,000 prisoners.

Skirmish at Bolivar, Tenn. — Fought August 30, 1862, between Unionists and Confederates, the latter being defeated.

Destruction of Bayou Sara, La. — August 31, 1862, Bayou Sara, a prosperous shipping port of Louisiana, on the Mississippi river 155 miles from New Orleans, was almost entirely destroyed by the Union fleet of Admiral Porter, in consequence of his being fired upon by Confederate guerrillas.

Battle at Britton's Lane, Tenn. — Fought September 1, 1862, between Unionists and Confederates, the latter retiring and leaving their dead on the field. The Unionists lost 5 killed, 78 wounded and 92 missing.

Battle at Chantilly, Va.—Fought September 1, 1862, between the Unionists under Generals Hooker, Reno, and Kearney, and the Confederate army under Ewell and Hill. General Pope endeavored to transfer his forces from Centerville to Germantown, and while doing so was attacked. The fight lasted for several hours, ending with the darkness. The Union generals,

Kearney and Stevens, were killed. Under an impetuous bayonet charge the Confederates were driven from the field; but the losses of the Unionists were heavy.

Battle at Washington, N. C.—September 6, 1862, the Confederates attacked the Union garrison, but were repulsed. The Unionists lost 8 killed and 36 wounded.

Battle at Middletown, Md. — Fought September 12, 1862, between Unionists and Confederates, the former losing 80 killed and wounded.

Battle of South Mountain, Md. — Fought September 14, 1862, between the Union army under Generals Hooker, Reno, Franklin, Cox and others, and the Confederate forces under Longstreet and Hill. The engagement was general and severe, and resulted in the retreat of the Confederates. The Union general, Reno, was killed. The Union losses were 312 killed, 1,234 wounded, and 22 missing. The Confederate loss was quite as large, including 1,500 prisoners.

Surrender of Harper's Ferry—A force of 12,000 Unionists, under General Miles, who held Harper's Ferry, W. Va., was attacked September 13, 1862, by a strong Confederate army, under Stonewall Jackson, and after a two-days' contest, the place was surrendered on the 15th to the Confederates. General Miles was killed, and the Unionists sustained a loss of about 11,000 prisoners, 73 cannon, 13,000 small arms, and a considerable amount of stores. Union cavalry, 2,000 strong, cut their way through the rebel lines, and escaped.

Battle of Munfordsville, Ky.—Fought between about 5,000 Unionists, under Colonel Dunham, who held the place, and a strong force of Confederates under Price. After three days' fighting, September 14, 15 and 16, 1862, Dunham surrendered about 4,500 men and their artillery, and turned the town over to the Confederates. September 21, General McCook and a force of Unionists recaptured the place.

Battle of Antietam, Md.—Fought September 17, 1862, near Sharpsburg, Md., between 85,000 Confederates, under Lee and Jackson, and 85,000 Unionists, under McClellan, Hooker, Burnside, Sumner, and Mansfield. The contest was severe, and lasted from early morning until evening. During the succeeding night the Confederates retreated, leaving in the hands of their foes 3,500 prisoners, 39 stand of colors, and 13 cannon. Their total loss was about 9,000 men. The Unionists lost 2,010 killed, 9,416 wounded, and 1,043 missing. The Union General Mansfield lost his life while endeavoring to regain the ground lost by Hooker. It is classed as a drawn battle.

The Evacuation of Maryland and Harper's Ferry—On the 18th of September, 1862, the Confederate army of Lee and Jackson withdrew from Maryland to Virginia, after having invaded the first-named State for a fortnight. Harper's Ferry, W. Va., was also evacuated by the Confederates on the same day.

Battle of Iuka, Miss. — General Price, with about 15,000 Confederates, occupied Iuka early in September, 1862. On the 19th of September, Generals Rosecrans and Ord advanced with a force of Unionists to capture this point, and for two hours the contest was severe and bloody. During the following night the Confederates evacuated the town. Their losses included more than 300 buried on the field, and 500 severely wounded, 200 of whom died within a few days. The Union losses were 300 killed and 500 wounded.

Battle of Augusta, Ky.—Fought September 27, 1862, between an attacking force of Confederates and the Union garrison of 120. The latter surrendered with a loss of 9 killed, 15 wounded, and the rest taken prisoners.

Battle of Corinth, Miss.—Fought October 3 and 4, 1862, between 25,000 Unionists, under General Rosecrans, who held the town and its outposts, and more than 35,000 Confederates, under Generals Van Dorn, Price, and Lovell. On the first day, the Unionists outside were driven into the town. The battle was renewed with terrible severity next morning, the Unionists having been reinforced by McPherson, and the Confederates were obliged to retreat, leaving in the hands of their foes 2,248 prisoners, 14 stand of colors, 2 cannon, 2,300 stand of small arms, a large amount of ammunition etc. The Confederates had 1,423 men and officers killed, and more than 5,000 wounded. The Unionists lost 315 killed, 1,812 wounded, and 232 prisoners and missing.

Battle at Lavergne, Tenn. — Fought October 6, 1862, between a Confederate force and a brigade of Unionists, under General Palmer; the former were repulsed, with a loss to the latter of 5 killed and 13 wounded and missing. The Confederate loss was about 80 killed and wounded, 175 prisoners, 2 cannon, provisions, camp equipage, etc.

Battle of Perryville, Ky. — Fought October 8, 1862, between 15,000 Unionists, under Colonel Daniel McCook, of Buell's army, and four divisions of the Confederate army, under Generals Bragg, Polk, and Hardee. The battle lasted from three o'clock in the morning until after dark that evening and resulted in a victory for the Unionists. The loss of the latter, besides the killing of Generals Jackson and Terrell, was 466 killed, 1,463 wounded and 160 missing. The Confederate loss is estimated at about the same figures.

Raid on Chambersburg, Pa. — On the 10th of October, 1862, the Confederate general, Stuart, with 2,000 cavalry, made a dash on Chambersburg, seized a considerable amount of clothing designed for McClellan's Union army, destroyed property belonging to the government, burned the railroad depot, captured fresh horses, passed clear around McClellan's army, and escaped without loss.

Battle Near Gallatin, Tenn. — October 19, 1862, the Confederates, under General Forrest, were defeated by a force of Unionists.

Operations in Florida—During the latter part of October, 1862, an expedition of Unionists, under Colonel Beard, of New York, destroyed 9 large salt works on Florida rivers, and brought back 150 good colored recruits for the Northern army.

Battle of Pocotaligo, S. C. — Fought October 22, 1862, between about 5,000 Union soldiers, with three batteries and an engineer corps, under General Brannon, and a force of Confederates. In the struggle of nearly six hours to gain possession of the Charleston and Savannah railroad, the Unionists were repulsed, with the loss of 30 killed and 180 wounded.

Battle of Maysville, Ark. — Fought October 22, 1862, between 10,000 Unionists, under General Blunt, and 7,000 Confederates. After a severe action of an hour's duration, the latter were totally routed, with the loss of all their artillery, a large number of horses, and a part of their garrison equipments.

Battle of Labadie, La.—Fought October 27, 1862, between a party of Confederates and a Union force. The latter won the field, with a loss of 17 killed and 74 wounded.

Fight at Garrettsburg, Ky. — Fought November 11, 1862, between Unionists under General Ransom, and Confederates under General Woodward. The latter were defeated.

Battle of Kinston, N. C.—Fought November 17, 1862, between 6,000 Confederates, under General Evans, and a Union force under General Foster. After a fight of five hours the Confederates were defeated, with the loss of 11 cannon and about 400 prisoners. The Union loss was about 200 killed and wounded. This fight and several other encounters of more or less importance occurred during a ten days' expedition of General Foster from Newbern to Goldsboro, for the purpose of cutting off railroad communication between Richmond, Va., and Charleston, S. C. He appears to have been successful.

Battle of Cane Hill, Ark. — Fought November 28, 1862, between 2,000 Unionists (cavalry and artillery), under Generals Blunt and Heron, and 2 regiments of Confederate cavalry. After a sharp skirmish the latter retreated to Van Buren, leaving their killed and some of their wounded on the field. The Unionists followed them to Van Buren, and completely routed them there, capturing 100 prisoners, 4 steamers, a large quantity of corn, camp equipage, mules and horses. The Confederates retreated, leaving behind 600 wounded and sick soldiers.

Skirmish near Charleston, Va.—Fought December 2, 1862, between Unionists and Confederates. The latter were defeated, with a loss of 70 killed and wounded and 145 prisoners.

Battle of Prairie Grove, Ark.—Fought December 7, 1862, between about 7,000 Unionists (infantry and artillery), under General Heron, reinforced by about 5,000 more and 24 cannon, under General Blunt and 28,000 men of Hindman's Confederate army, with 18 cannon, under Marmaduke, Parsons, Frost, and Rains. The Confederates were defeated with a loss of more than 2,000 killed and wounded, and during the succeeding night retreated from the field. The Union army lost 495 killed and 500 wounded, including upward of 40 field and line officers.

Fight at Hartsville, Tenn. — Fought December 7, 1862, between Morgan's Confederate cavalry and a brigade of Unionists of Dumont's command, under Colonel Moore. After an hour's fight, the brigade consisting of the 104th Illinois, the 106th and 108th Ohio, part of the 2d Indiana cavalry and a battery, surrendered to the Confederates and were paroled. The Unionists also lost 55 killed.

Battle of Fredericksburg, Va. — December 11, 1862, the Union army under Burnside, began the bombardment of Fredericksburg, then occupied by the Confederates under Lee. During this bombardment Burnside transferred [illegible] of his men across the Rappahannock in front of Fredericksburg. December 13, the battle was fought, Burnside bringing about 32,000 men into action under Sumner, Hooker and Franklin. Lee had of his [illegible] troops only about [illegible] in the fight, under Jackson and Longstreet. The Unionists, after a severe contest, were repulsed. Their losses were [illegible] killed, [illegible] wounded, [illegible] missing. The Confederates lost only 595 killed, 4,061 wounded, and 653 missing.

Skirmish at Zurich, Va.—Fought on the 13th December, 1862, between Unionists and Confederates, the latter being defeated, with the capture of a portion of their force.

Capture of Baton Rouge, La. — On December 14, 1862, a part of General Banks' command, under General Grover, took peaceable possession of Baton Rouge, the capital of the State, the Confederates having evacuated the town.

Capture of Holly Springs, Miss. — December 19, 1862, the Confederate general, Van Dorn, with several thousand cavalry, invested Holly Springs, which was then occupied by the Unionists. Once in, after a feeble resistance by the Unionists, they destroyed and carried off public and private property valued at nearly $6,000,000. They then evacuated the town.

A Raid into East Tennessee—A notable cavalry raid was made into East Tennessee, beginning December 21, 1862, by the Unionist General Carter, with about 1,000 men. They were gone from Winchester, Ky., 20 days, during which, without tents, they marched 470 miles (170 in the enemy's country); burned 2 important railroad bridges across the Holston and Wautaga rivers; damaged 10 miles of track; had 2 skirmishes with the Confederates; captured 400 prisoners, 700 stand of arms, and a train of cars with a locomotive, besides a considerable quantity of stores, and returned with the loss of 2 men killed and 8 others wounded, captured or missing.

Skirmish at Dumfries, Va. — Fought December 23, between the Unionists, under General Sigel, and a party of Confederates. The latter were repulsed.

Battle of Davis' Mills, Miss. — Fought between the Confederates, under Van Dorn, and a small force of Unionists, under Colonel Morgan, of the 25th Indiana regiment, December 21, 1862. After a severe conflict the Confederates retreated, leaving their dead and wounded on the field.

Second Siege of Vicksburg, Miss. — December 27, 1862, General Sherman attacked the advanced works of the Confederate defenses, about six miles from Vicksburg, on the Yazoo river. At the same time the gunboats attacked the Confederate batteries on Haines' Bluff. December 28, the Unionists drove the Confederates from the first and second lines of defense, and advanced to within 2½ miles of Vicksburg. December 29, the Confederates attacked General Sherman with their whole force, and drove him back to the first line of defense. December 30, after burying their dead and transferring their wounded to transports, the Unionists abandoned the siege, General Sherman returning to camp at Milliken's Bend. The Union loss was about 600 killed, 1,500 wounded, and 1,000 missing.

Battles of Stone River, Tenn.—Fought December 31, 1862, and January 1, 2, 3, 1863, between 43,400 Unionists under General Rosecrans, and 62,490 Confederates under Hardee, Polk, and Kirby Smith. The main attack of the Confederates was made December 31 on General Rosecrans' right, commanded by General McCook. This Union division was driven back four miles, and lost 28 cannon, but being reinforced from the left and center, the Confederates were in turn repulsed and the lost ground regained. Confederate attacks were made on the Federal lines January 1 and 2, but were repulsed. On the night of January 3 the Confederates retreated. The Union losses were 1,553 killed, 7,000 wounded, and 3,000 prisoners. The Confederate loss is estimated at 10,000 in all.

Battle of Parker's Cross Roads, Tenn.—Fought December 31, 1862, between 7,000 Confederate cavalry, under Forrest, with 10 cannon, and a body of Unionists under Generals Dunham and Sullivan. After a sharp fight, the Confederates retreated, losing their cannon, 500 horses, caissons, ammunition, small arms, wagons, camp equipage and more than 1,000 men killed, wounded, or taken prisoners.

BATTLES OF THE THIRD YEAR OF THE WAR.

Battle of Galveston, Tex. — Fought January 1, 1863, between a Confederate force of 5,000 men, under General Magruder, and the 300 Unionists who occupied the town. At the same time the Confederate batteries and 2 steamers attacked the Union blockading fleet in the harbor. After a contest of several hours, the small Union force on shore and the Union steamer Harriet Lane were captured by the Confederates. The Union vessel Westfield was blown up to prevent her falling into the hands of the enemy, and Commodore Renshaw perished with her. The Confederates captured, also, a large quantity of arms, ammunition, etc. The Unionists lost 26 killed.

Fight at Springfield, Mo. — Fought January 7, 1863, between a force of Confederates, and a force of Unionists under General Brown, who held the place and defeated the Confederates. The place contained a large quantity of stores owned by the Unionists, whose loss in the defense was 17 killed.

Battle of Arkansas Post, Ark. — Fought January 10 and 11, 1863, by the Union river fleet under Admiral Porter, and the Union land forces under General McClernand, against the Confederate force who held the post. On the second day the fortifications were carried by the Unionists. The Confederate loss was about 200 killed, 4,500 prisoners, about 4,500 stand of arms, and 20 cannon. The Unionists lost about 100 killed and 500 wounded.

A Naval Battle—January 10, 1863, two Confederate iron-clads undertook to break up the Union blockade at Charleston, S. C. Two Union vessels were seriously injured, and the inner line of the fleet disturbed. Otherwise the attack was a failure.

Capture of Transports—January 12, 1863, three Union transports and a gunboat surrendered to the Confederates on the Cumberland river, Tenn.

Battle at Bayou Teche, La. — Fought January 15, 1863, between a party of Unionists and the Confederate force which held the place. The latter were captured, and the Confederate gunboat Cotton was destroyed.

Battle at Sabine City, Tex. — Fought January 20, 1863, between Confederates and 2 vessels of the blockading squadron. The latter were captured, and 1 was destroyed.

Third Siege of Vicksburg—January 22, 1863, General McClernand resumed the Union siege of Vicksburg, Miss., and work was renewed on the Union cut-off canal at that point. The Union ram, Queen of the West, ran the blockade at Vicksburg, February 2, but was afterwards captured by the Confederates. February 13, the iron-clad Indianola also ran the blockade, and was captured by the Confederates. February 18, 1863, the Union gunboats began to shell Vicksburg, but without accomplishing anything.

Fight at Fort McAllister, Ga.—Fought between the Union iron-clad Montauk, sailed by Commander Worden, and 3 wooden gunboats and a force of Confederates in the fort. Two unsuccessful efforts were made, January 27 and February 1, 1863, to capture the fort. February 27, the Confederate steamer Nashville, while attempting to run the Union blockade, got aground and was destroyed by the fleet.

Battle of Blackwater, Va. — Fought January 30, 1863, between a force of Confederates, under General Pryor, and the Union army, under Generals Peck and Corcoran. After 3 severe engagements, the Confederates were repulsed, with a Union loss of 24 killed and 80 wounded.

Skirmish at Rover, Tenn. — Fought January 31, 1863, between a party of Unionists and another of Confederates, the latter being defeated with a loss of 12 killed and 300 wounded.

Battle Near Middletown, Tenn. — Fought February 2, 1863, between Stokes' Union Tennessee cavalry and a Kentucky Union regiment and a Confederate camp. The camp was captured, the occupants dispersing.

Fight at Bradyville, Tenn. — Fought March 1, 1863, between 2,300 infantry and cavalry, under General Stanley, and a force of about 800 Confederate cavalry. After a sharp skirmish the latter were routed and driven more than three miles, some of them being cut down as they ran.

Skirmish at Eagleville, Tenn.—Fought March 2, 1863, between a brigade from the regular Union army and a force of Confederates, in which the latter were routed.

Skirmish Near Thompson's Station, Tenn. — Fought March 5, 1863, between 7 regiments of Union soldiers, with a battery, under Colonel Coburn, and a force of Confederates, numbering 30,000 men, under Van Dorn. Overcome by superior numbers, after an unequal struggle, Coburn surrendered, part of his command escaping safely The Unionists lost 100 killed, 300 wounded, and about 1,200 prisoners. The Confederates admitted a loss of 150 killed and 450 wounded.

Battle at Unionville, Tenn. — Fought March 7, 1863, by a force of Unionists under General Minty and a body of Confederate cavalry, the latter being defeated, with the loss of their wagons, horses and tents and about 60 prisoners.

Battle of Fairfax, Va.—Fought March 9, 1863, between General Stoughton, with a Union force, and a band of rebel cavalry. The latter passed through the Union lines, and captured the General and some of his men.

Fight at Newbern, N. C. — Fought March 13, 1863, between an attacking force of Confederates and the Unionists who held the place. The attempt resulted in a failure to recapture the place.

Battle at Port Hudson, La.—March 13, 1863, Commodore Farragut's Union fleet attempted to pass the Confederate batteries, but only a part of the vessels succeeded. One—the Mississippi—ran aground and was destroyed.

Battle Near Kelly's Ford, Va.—March 17, 1863, a force of 300 Union cavalry, under General Averill crossed the Rappahannock river, where only one horseman could pass the ford at once, and, notwithstanding a galling fire from the Confederate rifle-pits and sharpshooters, charged upon the Confederate intrenchments, killing or capturing nearly the entire force of their enemies. They then encountered a body of Confederate cavalry, under Stuart, with whom they had a hand-to-hand encounter for five hours. The Confederates were routed with great slaughter, and the Unionists took 80 of them prisoners.

Battle at Milton, Tenn. — Fought March 20, 1863, between 4,000 Confederates under Wheeler and Morgan, and 1,323 mounted Unionists, under Colonel Hall. The Confederates were totally defeated, with a loss of 400.

Capture of Jacksonville, Fla. — March 20, 1863, the Confederates were driven from the city by a Union brigade of colored soldiers.

Battle of Steele's Bayou, Miss. — Fought March 22, 1863, between about 4,000 Confederates and General Sherman's division of the Union army, assisted by Union gunboats. The brief contest resulted in the retreat of the Confederates, with heavy loss, while the Unionists lost but one man, who was killed.

Capture of Mount Sterling, Ky. — March 22, 1863, a force of Confederates, under Clark, captured Mount Sterling.

The Brentwood, Tenn., Affair — March 25, 1863, Brentwood was occupied by about 500 Unionists. That day the place was captured and sacked by about 3,000 Confederates under Wheeler, Forrest, Armstrong and Stearns. Green Clay Smith, with a body of Union cavalry pursued them as they departed with their spoils and prisoners, in the direction of Columbia. About nine miles from Brentwood he overtook them, charged upon them, killing many and driving them six miles further. The Confederates having been reinforced by Wheeler's cavalry, 2,500 strong, Clay slowly withdrew from the advancing foe, retreating two miles, when the Confederates gave up the pursuit. The Confederate loss was estimated at fully 400 men, many horses, ambulances, etc. Smith did not lose a man as prisoner, but brought away 47 of the enemy.

Battle of Somerset, Ky. — Fought March 29, 1863, between a force of Unionists, under Carter and Gilmore, and a body of Confederate cavalry, under Pegram. The battle resulted in the total defeat of the Confederates, and their evacuation of Kentucky.

Battle near Woodbury, Tenn.—Fought April 1, 1863, between a Union force under General Hazen, and 800 Confederates, under Colonel Smith The latter were defeated, with a loss of 30 killed and wounded, 20 prisoners, 50 horses, besides mules and wagons.

Battle near Nashville, Tenn. — Fought between General Mitchell, with 300 Union cavalry, and an encampment of Confederates, April 6, 1863. Mitchell made a sabre charge, killing 15 Confederates, taking 5 prisoners and capturing all their arms, tents, horses and equipments.

Attack on Charleston, S. C.—April 7, 1863, Commodore Dupont, with nine Union iron-clad war vessels, attacked Charleston. The fight continued for two hours, under a sharp fire from Forts Sumter and Moultrie, when the Union fleet retired, five of the vessels being disabled, and one—the Keokuk—subsequently sank at her anchorage. The Union loss was 16 wounded—1 fatally.

Fight at Franklin, Tenn.—Fought April 10, 1863, between a large Confederate force under Van Dorn, and the Union troops occupying the town, under General Granger. After a protracted fight the Confederates were driven off and pursued until nightfall.

Three Battles in Louisiana — April 11, 1863, General Banks, with the Union troops under Emory and Weitzel, started from Berwick, at the mouth of the Atchafalaya river. In three sharp engagements with the Confederate forces in the Bayou Teche region, on April 15, 16 and 17, he took nearly 2,000 prisoners, caused the destruction of their 3 gunboats and several transport vessels, with a large amount of other Confederate property, dispersing their army in that section. The Union loss was 700.

Porter's Fleet Runs Past Vicksburg —April 17, 1863, Commodore Porter succeeded in running six vessels of his Union fleet safely past the Confederate batteries at Vicksburg.

Battle of Fayetteville, Ark. — Fought April 18, 1863, between 2,000 Union troops occupying the town and an attacking party of Confederates, numbering 3,000, with four cannon. The Confederates were repulsed, the Unionists losing 5 killed and 17 wounded.

Capture of a Union Steam-Ram — April 22, 1863, the Union ram, Queen of the West, was captured by the Confederates, in Grand Lake, La., with her commander, Captain Fuller, and all her officers and crew, numbering 90 The same day General Banks occupied Washington and Opelousas, Miss.

Battle at Fairmont, W. Va. — Fought April 30, 1863, between the Union forces, under Colonel Mulligan, and Confederate troops. The former were repulsed, and the Baltimore & Ohio railroad bridges, at Fairmont and Cheat river were blown up.

Battle at Monticello, Ky.—Fought May 1, 1863, between 5,000 Union troops, under General Carter, and the Confederate forces under Pegram. The latter were driven from the field, with a loss of 86 men. On the same day the Confederate troops, under Marmaduke, were driven out of Missouri by the Union General Vandever.

Battle of Port Gibson, Miss.—Fought May 1, 1863, between the united Union armies of Generals Grant and McClernand and the Confederate force under General Bowen. The latter, after a severe fight, were defeated with the loss of 1,550 men and 5 cannon.

Grierson's Raid in Mississippi—Colonel Grierson, of the 6th Illinois regiment, with his own and the 7th Illinois cavalry, 900 strong, and 6 cannon, started from La Grange, Tenn., April 17, 1863, to march southerly through the center of Mississippi. May 2, 1863, they reached Baton Rouge, La., having traveled nearly 800 miles in 16 days, and having passed through 17 counties. As they went they destroyed Confederate railroads, bridges, cars, locomotives and stores of all kinds, fought successfully against several attempts to capture them and brought into Baton Rouge more than 1,000 horses and a large number of cattle, besides 500 colored people who followed them.

Battle of Chancellorsville, Va. — The Army of the Potomac, under General Hooker, made its second attempt to capture the Confederate fortifications at Fredericksburg, Va., between April 27 and May 3 1863. The main body of the Union army crossed the Rappahannock river April 27, at Kelly's ford, about 20 miles northwest of Fredericksburg, taking a position 10 miles west of that stronghold, at Chancellorsville. The main battle, after two days' severe skirmishing, took place May 3, between the Confederate army, under Lee and Jackson, and Hooker's army. The Unionists, in this battle, were defeated. In the meantime the Union General Sedgwick had crossed the Rappahannock river and occupied Fredericksburg, but he, too, was defeated and compelled to retire. Hooker's army recrossed the river on the night of May 5. Hooker's whole effective force was about 95,000, Lee's, in all, 60,000 The Union losses were about 17,000—12,000 killed and wounded—5,000 missing, the Confederates, 13,000—10,300 killed and wounded.

Stoneman in Virginia.—During the battles of Chancellorsville, May 1-4, 1863, the Union General Stoneman, with a large body of cavalry raided Virginia destroying large quantities of Confederate provisions at different points and a portion of the railroad between Gordonsville and Charlottesville, and considerably damaging one or two other railroads.

Capture of Alexandria, La. — May 5, 1863, Admiral Porter and his Union gunboats captured this town.

Streight's Surrender—After effective service and hard fighting in the enemy's country May 3, 1863, Union Colonel Streight, with 1,300 men, was captured by the Confederate cavalry under Forrest, near Cedar Bluff, Ala.

Fight on the Cumberland River—Fought May 9, 1863, between Union Kentucky cavalry, under Colonel Jacobs, and a Confederate guerrilla force, near Horseshoe Bend, Tenn. The latter were defeated, with the loss of a number killed, 8 prisoners and the destruction of their camp.

Battle at Raymond, Miss.—Fought May 12, 1863, between a Union force, under General McPherson, of Grant's army, and two divisions of Confederates, under Gregg and Walker. After a fierce fight of two hours, the place was captured, the Confederates losing 103 killed, 720 wounded and prisoners. Union loss, 69 killed, 341 wounded, and 32 missing.

Battle Near Jackson, Miss.—Fought May 13, 1863, between Grant's Union army and Confederate troops under Joseph S. Johnson. The latter was defeated, losing the town, 7 cannon, 400 prisoners, and large quantities of military stores. The State House was burned.

Fight at Linden, Tenn.—Fought May 13, 1863, between 55 men of the 1st Tennessee cavalry, under Colonel Breckenridge, and twice that number of Confederates. The latter were defeated, with the loss of 43 officers and privates, 50 horses and a quantity of other property.

Battle at Suffolk, Va.—Fought May 15, 1863, between a Confederate detachment and a party of Unionists, in which the former were defeated.

Battle Near Holly Springs, Miss.—Fought May 15, 1863, between Faulkner's Confederate cavalry and a Union force, the former being defeated.

Battle of Baker's Creek, Miss.—Fought May 16, 1863, between the Confederates, under General Pemberton, and the Union army, under General Grant, about 25,000 men being engaged on each side. The fight ended in the defeat of the Confederates, who lost 2,600 killed and wounded, 2,000 prisoners and 29 cannon.

Battle of Big Black River, Miss.—Fought May 17, 1863, between the Confederates under Pemberton and Grant's Union army, the former being again defeated, with a loss of 2,600 men and 17 cannon.

Destruction at Austin, Miss.—May 24, 1863, Colonel Ellet's Union marine brigade burned the town, which had been occupied by the Confederates.

A Navy-Yard Destroyed—May 25, 1863, the Unionists destroyed the Confederate navy-yard at Yazoo city, Miss.

Loss of a Union Gunboat—May 28, 1863, in an encounter between the Union gunboat Cincinnati, on the Mississippi river, and the Confederate batteries at Vicksburg, Miss., the former was sunk, going down with flying colors. The Union loss was 25 killed and wounded and 15 drowned.

A Raid in South Carolina—June 3, 1863, the second South Carolina Union regiment (colored), under Colonel Montgomery, numbering 800 men, passed up the Coosa river, landing in full view of two Confederate regiments, who retreated. Penetrating 25 miles into the country, Montgomery brought away 725 negroes, a lot of blooded horses, and other property belonging to the Confederates, valued at $600,000.

Battle at Triune, Tenn.—Fought June 11, 1863, between 5,000 Confederate cavalry and two batteries, under Forrest, and a force of Union cavalry, under Colonel R. B. Mitchell. The Confederates were defeated, with a loss of 21 killed and 70 others wounded and taken prisoners. Mitchell's loss was 6 killed.

Sinking of a Blockade-Runner—Off Charleston, June 11, 1863, the Confederate and notorious blockade-runner, the Herald, was sunk by a broadside from the Union blockading fleet.

Battle of Winchester, Va.—Fought June 14, 1863, between about 7,000 Unionists, under Milroy, and the advance of Lee's army on its way to Pennsylvania. Besides a small number killed and wounded, Milroy lost 4,000 prisoners, about 30 guns, many small arms, and 300 wagons.

A Naval Fight—Fought June 17, 1863, in Wilmington waters, off the coast of North Carolina, between the Confederate ram Atlanta and the Union war vessel Weehawken, commanded by Captain John Rodgers. The Atlanta was decoyed and captured.

Battle Near Aldie, Va.—Fought June 17, 1863, between Union troops, under Colonel Kilpatrick, and 5 regiments of Confederate cavalry, under Fitzhugh Lee, with artillery. After a desperate hand-to-hand encounter, the Confederates retreated, leaving 100 prisoners in the hands of the Unionists.

Second Battle of Big Black River, Miss.—Fought June 23, 1863, between a Confederate force, under Johnston, and a division of the Union army, under Osterhaus. The latter was defeated.

Fights in Tennessee—June 24, 1863, the Union general, Rosecrans, began his advance from Murfreesboro, Tenn. On the same day, Willich's brigade, of McCook's division of the Union army, wrested Liberty Gap from the Confederates, sustaining a loss of 75 killed and wounded. Next day, Willich, Wilder and Carter's brigades of Rosecrans' army defeated a division of Confederates, under Claiborne. The Unionists lost 40 killed and 100 wounded; the Confederates, who retreated in disorder, suffered a much greater loss. June 24, 1863, Wilder's mounted Union brigade captured Hoover's Gap from the Confederates. His loss was 53 killed and wounded. June 26, 1863, Wilder's Union brigade destroyed the Decherd bridge in the rear of the Confederate general, Bragg, between Tullahoma and Chattanooga. Other fights and skirmishes were features in this nine days' campaign by the Unionists under Rosecrans, whose total loss was 85 killed, 462 wounded and 13 missing. The Confederates lost 1,364 prisoners and 11 cannon, and were expelled from Middle Tennessee.

Morgan's Raids—June 27, 1863, John Morgan, with 2,500 Confederate guerrillas and 4 cannon, began a raid in Kentucky. On the 3d of July, a sharp fight occurred between them and a reconnoitering party of Unionists under Captain Carter. The captain was killed, his men retreated, and Morgan occupied Columbia. On the 4th of July, Morgan fought 200 Unionists, under Colonel Moore, at Tebb's Bend, on Green river, Ky. For four hours the battle raged, when Morgan was repulsed and retreated, leaving his dead on the field. At Lebanon, Morgan captured 300 Union militia, robbed and paroled them. Morgan then raided Southern Ohio and Indiana. At Corydon, Ind., in a fight, Morgan had 2 men killed and 7 wounded, while the opposing Unionists lost 15 killed and wounded. There and at other places large amounts of merchandise and horses were seized by the raiders, money was extorted as a ransom for property, and their operations created general excitement. In the meantime, a pursuit by armed men to capture Morgan was vigorously prosecuted. At Buffington's island, in the Ohio river, July 19, Morgan encountered a force of Unionists under General Judah, Lieutenant O'Neil of the 5th Indiana cavalry, and two gunboats, and a bloody battle ensued, which resulted in the utter rout and dispersion of Morgan's band. They left behind them about 1,000 prisoners, all their artillery and large quantities of stolen plunder. John Morgan and 500 of his men escaped, but were hotly pursued by General Shackleford, of the Union army, and on July 26 at West Point, Ohio, Morgan, finding himself surrounded by a superior force, unconditionally surrendered, his band having been slain, dispersed or captured.

Battle of Grey's Gap, Tenn.—Fought June 30, 1863, between Union cavalry and infantry under Stanley and Granger and a force of Confederate cavalry and infantry. The latter were driven from point to point, hotly pursued, and many of them were killed, drowned and wounded in their flight. The capture of Shelbyville, Tenn., by the Unionists, with a large number of prisoners and a quantity of arms and commissary stores, were the results of this day's work.

Capture of Tullahoma, Tenn.—July 1, 1863, the Unionists under Brannon, Negley and Sheridan occupied Tullahoma, which the Confederates had evacuated on the previous night. This was one step in the campaign which drove the Confederates from Middle Tennessee.

Battle of Gettysburg, Pa.—Fought July 1-3, 1863, between the invading Confederate army under General R. E. Lee, and the Union army of the Potomac under General Meade. The forces engaged or near at hand, July 2, were about equal, each numbering between 70,000 to 80,000 infantry and artillery. The battle, one of the most terrible of the war, resulted in the defeat of the Confederates, their compulsory evacuation of Pennsylvania and Maryland, their withdrawal from the valley of the Shenandoah, and heavy losses, as follows: 5,000 killed, 23,000 wounded left on the field, 8,000 prisoners, 3 cannon and 41 battle flags; 24,978 small arms were collected on the battle field. The Union loss was 2,834 killed, 13,713 wounded, and 6,643 missing.

Battle at Helena, Ark.—Fought July 4, 1863, between about 4,000 Unionists, under General Prentiss, and 7,600 Confederates under General Holmes, the latter being defeated with the loss of of 173 killed, 687 wounded, and 776 missing. The Union loss did not exceed 250 in killed and wounded.

Surrender of Vicksburg, Miss.—General Grant began his siege of Vicksburg, May 18, prosecuting it with great vigor until July 4, 1863, when Pemberton, the Confederate General occupying the place, surrendered to the Union army 27,000 prisoners, 132 cannon and 50,000 stand of arms. Thus the Mississippi river was opened to the Gulf of Mexico.

Battle of Port Hudson, La.—General Banks' Union army invested Port Hudson in May, 1863, the place being strongly fortified and defended by a force of Confederates under General Gardner. Three important assaults were made upon this stronghold by land and water, May 27, June 11 and 14, in which some of the Confederate works were captured, but the Unionists were on both days repulsed, with the loss of about 3,000 men. The siege was continued until July 7, when Gardner capitulated (owing to the surrender of Vicksburg), and on the 9th of July, 1863, General Banks entered the town, taking 6,408 prisoners, 2 steamers, 51 cannon, and a quantity of small arms.

Draft Riots at the North.—From July 13 to 16, 1863, New York, Boston and other Northern cities, were the scene of riots in opposition to the drafting of soldiers for the Union army. In New York mobs held possession of the city for three days; the drafting offices were demolished and the buildings burned. A colored orphan asylum was pillaged and burned down. Collisions were frequent between the authorities and the mob, and many persons were killed. These riots cost the city more than $1,500,000 for losses by them.

Battle at Jackson, Miss.—Fought July 17, 1863, between the Union army under Sherman and the Confederates under Johnston. The result was the occupation of the city by Sherman, the capture of a large quantity of stores, 40 locomotives and the rolling stock of three railroads.

Capture of Natchez, Miss.—July 17, 1863, General Ransom and a party of Unionists captured this city from the Confederates, taking a large quantity of ammunition, 13 cannon, 2,000 cattle and 4,000 hogsheads of sugar.

Battle of Elk Creek, Ark.—Fought July 17, 1863, between 2,400 Unionists under General Blunt, and 5,000 Confederates under General Cooper. The latter were defeated, with the loss of 184 men. The Unionists lost 40 men.

Union Cavalry in North Carolina—July 20, 1863, the cavalry expedition sent out by the Union General Foster, attacked the Wilmington & Weldon railroad at Rocky Mount, burned the long bridge over Tar river, tore up two miles of track, destroyed the depot, a large cotton factory, a supply train and 5,000 bales of cotton belonging to the Confederates.

Battle at Wytheville, Va.—Fought July 20, 1863, between Union cavalry under Colonel Tolland, of the 34th Ohio mounted infantry, and a Confederate force; it resulted, after a severe conflict, in the defeat of the Confederates, the burning of the town, the seizure of 3 cannon, 700 stand of arms and 120 prisoners. The Confederates also lost 75 men killed and many wounded. The Unionists lost 65 killed and wounded, including among the former Colonel Tolland.

Bombardment of Chattanooga, Tenn.—July 22, 1863, Colonel Wilder, of Rosecrans' army, shelled Chattanooga, creating considerable agitation among its Confederate occupants, but without definite results.

Recapture in Louisiana—July 22, 1863, the Union gunboat Sachem recaptured Brashear city from the Confederates

Battle Near Manassas Gap, Va.—Fought July 23, 1863, between 800 Unionists, under General Spinola, and about twice as many Confederate troops from Georgia and North Carolina. The latter were utterly routed.

Battle in the Southwest—Fought July 22, 1863, between Kit Carson's Union 1st New Mexico regiment and a party of Navajos, near Fort Canby. The Indians were defeated.

Kentucky Invaded—The Confederates re-invaded Kentucky, July 23, 1863. July 31, 1863, the Unionists in that State, commanded by Colonel Sanders, completely routed the Confederate forces under Scott and Pegram, and martial law was declared.

Battle at Culpeper, Va.—Fought August 2, 1863, between Union cavalry under Buford, and Confederate cavalry under Stuart. The battle was indecisive, but 100 prisoners were taken by the Unionists.

Battle of Grenada, Miss.—Fought 17th of August, 1863, between a Union expedition sent out by General Hurlbut, under Lieutenant-Colonel Phillips, of the 9th Illinois mounted infantry, and a Confederate force of 2,000 men under General Slimmer, who occupied Grenada. The Confederates were so hardly pressed by the attacking party that they fled in confusion, leaving behind an immense quantity of ordnance and stores. These, with the depot, the machine-shop, the railroad track, 57 locomotives, and more than 400 cars, were destroyed by the Unionists.

The War in Arkansas—August 22, 1863, the Union force under General Blunt, numbering 4,500, attacked 11,000 Confederates under General Cooper, in the Indian Territory, and compelled the latter to retreat to Red river. On the same day, Union cavalry under Colonel Woodson, successfully attacked numerous Confederate guerrilla bands in Arkansas, capturing the Confederate general, Jeff. Thompson, with his entire staff. On the 29th of July, 1863, the Confederate army under General Price, then in Arkansas, was severely pressed by the Union forces under General Steele. The same day, Steele's advance, under General Davidson, drove 3,000 Confederates, under Marmaduke, out of Brownsville and across the Arkansas river. September 1, 1863, General Blunt defeated the Confederates under Cooper and Cabell, and captured Fort Smith, Ark. The same day the Confederates evacuated Little Rock, and General Steele occupied it September 10, 1863.

Quantrell's Raid—A force of Confederate guerrillas, numbering 350, collected in Cass county, Mo., under the leadership of Quantrell. In the dead of night, August 20, 1863, they unexpectedly attacked the town of Lawrence, in Kansas, set it on fire, burned 182 buildings to the ground, destroying $2,000,000 of property; killed 145 persons, including helpless women and children, and wounded 581 citizens, many of them mortally. Soon afterwards, the guerrillas having departed, the citizens organized a force, commanded by General James H. Lane, and pursued the marauders to Grand River, Mo. There, when attacked, the murderers dispersed in various directions, but about 80 of them were slain.

Occupation of Knoxville, Tenn.—The Confederate General Buckner, evacuated Knoxville, leaving behind a considerable quantity of quartermaster's stores, with other valuable property, and General Burnside, with his Union force, occupied the place September 3, 1863, to the delight of the inhabitants.

Battle at Sabine City, Texas—Fought September 8, 1863, between the Confederate force occupying the fortifications of the town and the 19th Union army corps under General Franklin, with 4 Union gunboats. The fight was quite severe, but resulted in the repulse of the Unionists and the loss of 2 of their gunboats.

Affairs at Chattanooga, Tenn.—After the battle of Stone river, at the beginning of 1863, the Confederate army under Bragg occupied Chattanooga. September 8, 1863, when Rosecrans and his Union army approached, the Confederates abandoned the place, and, on the 9th, Crittenden's division of the Union army occupied it. Bragg's army having been reinforced by Longstreet, managed to drive the Unionists out of Chattanooga, while Rosecrans attempted to force the Confederates from their threatening position in that vicinity. The result was the battle of Chickamauga.

Affairs at Cumberland Gap, Tenn.—This narrow pass, which separates Kentucky from Tennessee, and became an important point during the civil war, was occupied early in the contest by the Confederates, then by the Unionists, and again by the Confederates. September 9, 1863, General Burnside's Union army recaptured it, with 2,000 prisoners and 14 cannon, from General Fraser.

Battle of Chickamauga, Tenn.—Fought September 19 and 20, 1863, between about 50,000 Confederates, under Bragg, who began the contest, and about 55,000 Union soldiers, besides cavalry, under Rosecrans. The cavalry and about 10,000 of Bragg's infantry were not, however, long in the action. At the close of the first day both armies occupied nearly the same position that they did in the morning. The battle occupied the whole of both days, and resulted in defeat and the retreat of the Unionists to Chattanooga. The Union loss was 1,644 killed, 9,262 wounded, and 4,945 prisoners. The Confederate loss is estimated at not far from 18,000 men.

A Cavalry Defeat—Confederate cavalry, under Wheeler, which had come north of the Tennessee river for the purpose of operating against Rosecrans' Union army, encountered Union forces October 9, 1863, at Farmington, Tenn., and near Shelbyville, Ky., and was defeated, with considerable loss, at both points.

Battle of Missionary Ridge, Tenn.—General Thomas, who succeeded Rosecrans in command of the Union army, was practically besieged by the Confederates at Chattanooga. A battle was fought November 24, 25 and 26, 1863, at this point, between about 80,000 Unionists, under Grant, who had partially raised the siege and reinforced the garrison, and about 50,000 Confederates under Bragg. The latter's army occupied strong positions above Chattanooga, on Lookout mountain at the south and Missionary ridge on the east. Hooker, with 10,000 Unionists, went to Lookout mountain to assail the Confederate left. Sherman, Sheridan, and other Union commanders, with their several divisions, stormed and carried the Confederate redoubts, as did Hooker those on Lookout mountain. The Confederates fled from a galling fire from their own cannon, and were vigorously pursued. The Union losses were 757 killed, 4,529 wounded, and 330 missing. The Confederate loss in killed and wounded did not, probably, exceed 4,000; but they lost 6,142 prisoners, 40 cannon, and 7,000 stand of small arms. This battle ended the war in Tennessee for a year.

The Storming of Knoxville, Tenn.—Under instructions from superior officers, General Burnside prepared for a vigorous defense of Knoxville. The second division of the 23rd army corps under General Julius White, and other troops, was to co-operate with Burnside. November 14, 1863, a fight occurred in the vicinity between General White's command and Confederates on Huff's hill, in which the Confederates were dislodged with considerable loss on both sides. November 16, another severe fight occurred near Knoxville, between the 23rd and 9th Army corps, with artillery, and a Confederate force at Campbell's station, but the Unionists were obliged to retreat, which they did in good order, although hotly pursued. On the 17th a close siege of Knoxville began, which terminated, November 29, in an attempt of the Confederates to carry the fortifications by storm, commanded by General Longstreet. The assault, however, was repulsed with so much vigor, that, in connection with the defeat of Bragg at Missionary Ridge, the Confederates deemed it advisable to raise the siege. Longstreet, therefore, retreated, followed by Burnside's forces, while another army, under Foster, started from Cumberland Gap to cut off their retreat. The number of Unionists engaged in this siege was about 12,000, their loss was less than 50, the loss of the attacking party was about 500.

BATTLES OF THE FOURTH YEAR OF THE WAR.

Battles Near Newbern, N. C.—February 1, 1864, a Confederate force, estimated at 15,000, attacked a small number of Union troops, under General Palmer, at Bachelor's creek, an outpost of the Unionists at Newbern. The latter, finding themselves outnumbered, fell back in good order, with only a slight loss, although the fight was severe, and they were pursued by the Confederates. Next morning a Confederate force in boats boarded the Union gunboat Underwriter, which had run aground and, after a sharp struggle, captured her with about one-third of her crew. Engineer Allen and part of the crew of the gunboat, rose up against the crew of the Confederate barge that was carrying them off, overcame them and rescued the commander and crew, bringing them safely into port.

Battle at Stevensburg, Va.—Fought all day, February 6, 1864, between the second and third corps of the Union army, under General Sedgwick, and a Confederate force. The Unionists withdrew, having lost 200 men in killed and wounded.

Sherman's Raid in Mississippi—February 3, 1864, General Sherman, with a Union force of 25,000 men, marched from Big Black river on a grand raid through the Confederate State of Mississippi, returning to Vicksburg, March 4, 1864. At Messenger's station there was a sharp skirmish with a Confederate force, resulting in a Union loss of 12 killed and 35 wounded, and a much larger one on the part of the Confederates. At Canton Sherman's troops captured artillery, ammunition and prisoners. Jackson, Brandon, Morton, and Meridian were visited, with some opposition, but with loss to the Confederates. At Meridian the Unionists remained seven days, destroying Confederate stores, ammunition and public buildings, the arsenal, hotels, etc. Other places visited by the Unionists were Enterprise, Marion, Quitman, Hillsboro, Lake station, Decatur, Bolton and Lauderdale springs. At these places railroad property, machine shops, lumber and flour mills were destroyed. Near Decatur a skirmish occurred, in which the Confederates were repulsed with the loss of 5 killed and three prisoners. The expedition marched more than 400 miles in 24 days, liberated 10,000 slaves, and brought away an immense amount of booty. The estimated losses of the Unionists during this raid were 50 men killed and wounded and about 100 prisoners. The Confederate losses in killed and wounded were considered much larger, and in deserters and prisoners were estimated at more than 600.

Escape of Union Prisoners—February 9, 1864, a large number of Union prisoners escaped from the Confederate Libby prison, at Richmond, Virginia.

Battle of Plymouth, N. C.—Fought February 17, 1864, between about 10,000 Confederates, under General R. F. Hoke, and about 1,500 Unionists, under General Wessel, who occupied Fort Williams, one of the defenses of Plymouth. Six times the Confederates assaulted this stronghold without capturing it, but on the fourth day, after fighting six times his own force, Wessel gave up the unequal contest and surrendered.

Battle of Olustee, Fla.—Fought February 20, 1864, between a Union force of about 4,500 infantry and 400 cavalry, with 20 cannon, under General Seymour, and an estimated Confederate force, under General Finnegin, of 3,000. The fight lasted three and a half hours, and resulted in the retreat of the Unionists before a superior force to Barber's station. Union loss 2,000 men, besides artillery, ammunition and wagon trains. Confederate loss about 1,000 men.

A Raid on Richmond, Va.—February 28, 1864, a Union cavalry expedition, under General Kilpatrick, started from the army of the Potomac to liberate Union prisoners at Richmond. After several skirmishes, March 4, 1864, Kilpatrick withdrew from the raid, having destroyed a large amount of Confederate property in the vicinity. Colonel Ulric Dahlgren had command of a branch expedition of Union cavalry in another direction, which also destroyed a large amount of property; but on the third of March his command fell into a Confederate ambush, and he lost his life, and a large number of his men were taken prisoners.

Capture of Fort de Russey, La.—March 15, 1864, a large Union force under General Mower, of Smith's Red river expedition, stormed this formidable fortress of the Confederates. The veterans, however, after a short but sturdy fight, carried the fort, capturing 12 cannon, 2,000 barrels of powder a large supply of army stores and ammunition, with 325 prisoners.

Surrender of Union City, Tenn.—March 24, 1864, between the Confederate force under Forrest and 500 Unionists under Hawkins, who occupied the place. The latter repulsed the attacking party several times, but at length surrendered.

Battle at Paducah, Ky.—Fought March 25, 1864, between 6,000 Confederates under Forrest, Buford, Harris and Thompson, and the 40th Illinois regiment under Colonel S. G. Hicks, numbering 655 Unionists, assisted by some Union gunboats. Hicks made a stand at Fort Anderson, and repelled several attacks and refused to surrender. Three more attacks were then made on the fort, but were repulsed with heavy losses each time, Thompson being killed. The Confederates retired next day, having suffered an estimated loss of 300 killed and from 1,000 to 1,200 wounded. The Union loss was 14 killed and 46 wounded.

Battles in Arkansas—March 26, 1864, a small Union force, from Rosecrans' army, marched from Pine Bluff, Ark., to Mount Elba and Longview, on the Washita river, destroying at the latter place several pontoon bridges, 35 wagons loaded with camp and garrison equipage, ammunition, stores, etc., and capturing 320 prisoners. March 30, 1864, this Union force encountered 1,200 Confederates at Monticello, routing them, capturing a large quantity of arms, wagons, and 300 horses and mules, and losing but 15 men during the expedition.

Battle of Natchitoches, La.—Fought March 31, 1864, between a cavalry division, under Lee, of General Banks' Union army, and a Confederate force under Taylor, estimated at 1,000. After a brisk but brief skirmish the Confederates were completely routed, with a loss of 6 or 8 killed and wounded and 25 prisoners. The Unionists lost none.

Battle of Crump's Hill, La.—Fought April 2, 1864, between 3 brigades of Union troops under Lee, and a body of Confederates. The former made a charge which caused the Confederates to retreat and the Unionists pursued them seven miles, killing and wounding a number. The Confederates made a stand, however, and a severe fight of an hour's duration ensued. Then the Confederates again retreated. A number of prisoners fell into the hands of the Unionists.

Fight Near Pleasant Hill, La.—Fought April 7, 1864, between the cavalry of Banks' and Smith's Union armies and about 3,000 Confederate cavalry under Green. At first it was a running fight, but the Confederates being reinforced, Colonel Haral Robinson, of Lee's Union cavalry brigade, dashed upon them with so much vigor that Green's force was whipped and driven from the field. This engagement lasted two and a half hours, and the losses on each side were estimated at 40 killed and wounded. Robinson pursued the retreating enemy until the latter reached a superior reinforcement. He then retired.

Battle Near Sabine Cross Roads, La.—Fought April 8, 1864, between the advance of General Banks' Union army, under General Stone and from 18,000 to 22,000 Confederates under Kirby Smith, Dick Taylor, Green, Price and Mouton. The Unionists were repulsed on that day, but on the next, after a severe conflict, the Confederates were defeated, 2,000 of them throwing away their arms during their flight. The losses in killed and wounded were very heavy, being estimated at 2,000 on each side. The Confederate General Mouton was slain, and 700 Confederate prisoners were captured.

Battle of Fort Pillow, Tenn.—The Unionists occupied the garrison with 19 officers, 276 white infantry and 262 colored infantry, a section of light artillery (colored), and 1 battalion of white cavalry, the whole being commanded by Major Booth. On April 12, 1864, the Confederates under Forrest attacked the fort, but by the aid of a gunboat they were kept at bay by the garrison. Major Booth was killed, and Major Bradford took command of the beleaguered fort. A demand to surrender from Forrest was refused by Bradford. New and commanding positions having been gained by the Confederates, their attack was resumed, and they soon carried the fort. No quarter was shown to its inmates, either black or white, male or female, and even children were slain by the invaders. Thus the Unionists were destroyed.

Gunboat Battles in North Carolina—April 17 and 18, 1864, at Plymouth, N. C., the Confederate iron-clad ram Albemarle, with the aid of a battery, destroyed 2 Union gunboats. On May 5, 1864, an effort was made by Union gunboats to destroy the Albemarle, but the attempt failed. October 27, 1864, Lieutenant Cushing, of the Union navy, succeeded with a torpedo in blowing this formidable craft to pieces, narrowly escaping his own destruction.

Battles of the Wilderness, Va.—May 4, 1864, General Grant, commanding the Union army of the Potomac, about 130,000 strong, crossed the Rapidan river into the "wilderness" of Virginia, to dislodge the Confederate General Lee and his 80,000 troops from their position between the Unionists and the Confederate capital. As Grant advanced, Lee prepared for a stubborn contest. From May 5 to May 31 there was fought a terrible series of battles, unprecedented in American annals for their sanguinary results. During those 27 bloody days various fortunes of war were experienced by both armies, and closed, leaving Lee on the south side of the North Anna river, and the Union force on the shores of the Pamunky river. The Union losses during these battles were 5,586 killed, 28,364 wounded, and 7,450 missing—a total of 41,398—which does not include the losses in Burnside's corps. No trustworthy statement of the Confederate losses was made, but they are estimated at about 30,000.

Butler's Operations on the James River, Va.—On May 5, 1864, General Butler and a Union force started from fortress Monroe, for a cruise up the James river in transports toward Richmond, destroying railroads, bridges, etc. Occasional skirmishes were had with Confederates, and on the 16th of May occurred

The Battle of Fort Darling, Va.—Fought between Butler's Union army and a force of Confederates under Beauregard. Butler's troops were forced to retire, with the loss of about 5,000 men, mostly prisoners, and several cannon. The fight was resumed on the 19th, and after a short conflict the Confederates were repulsed. Next day the Confederates drove the Unionists out of their intrenchments. Another fight ensued, and the Unionists recovered their rifle-pits.

Second Battle of Fort Darling—Fought May 21, 1864, between the Unionists under Gilmore, of Butler's army, occupying the intrenchments, and a large force of Confederates of Beauregard's army, who advanced upon the fort. Gilmore's batteries opened upon them at short range, and the several fierce charges of the Confederates were repulsed, with heavy loss. The Union gunboats also assisted in shelling the Confederates during this battle.

Battle of the Kulp House, Va.—Fought May 22, 1864, between a force of Confederates, under Hood and Hooker, and Schofield's divisions of Sherman's Union army. Hood made the attack, but was repulsed and driven off, leaving his dead and wounded on the field, and losing many prisoners.

Battle of Wilson's Wharf, Va.—Fought May 24, 1864, between a brigade of Confederate cavalry, under Fitzhugh Lee, and two regiments of negro Union troops, under General Wild, who occupied a strong position on the north bank of the James river. Lee demanded the surrender of the post, which was refused. A severe conflict followed for several hours, but the Confederate attempts to capture the position proved fruitless, and they finally abandoned the assault.

Battle of New Hope Church, Ga.—Sherman's Union army, in pursuit of Johnston's Confederate forces in Georgia, after several unimportant skirmishes, found themselves confronted with the Confederates about three miles from Dallas, Ga., May 25, 1864. After a general action the Confederates were driven three miles and into their inner intrenchments.

Battle of Powder Springs, Ga.—Fought in May, 1864, between McPherson's division of Sherman's Union army and a considerable force of Confederates of Johnston's army. After a sharp engagement the latter were driven toward Marietta, with a loss of 2,500 killed and wounded (left on the field), and about 300 prisoners. The Union losses did not, it is officially stated, exceed 300.

Sherman's Expedition from Chattanooga, Tenn., to Atlanta, Ga.—In the spring of 1864, General Sherman, with a force of 100,000 Unionists and 254 cannon, aided by Generals Thomas, McPherson and Schofield, commanding divisions, started to march from Chattanooga, through the Confederates' country, to Atlanta. Opposing this expedition was the Confederate General J. E. Johnston, aided by Hardee, Hood, and Polk, with Wheeler's cavalry, their entire force numbering about 60,000 men, including 10,000 cavalry and artillery. The Union expedition began its operations May 7, 1864, and closed them successfully at Atlanta, Ga., September 2, of the same year, occupying Dalton, May 8.

Sheridan's Raid in Virginia—May 13, 1864, General Sheridan, with his Union cavalry force, reached the rear of Lee's army, near Hanover junction, breaking 2 railroads, capturing several locomotives, and destroying Lee's depot for supplies at Beaver Dam, containing more than 1,000,000 rations.

Battle of Resaca, Ga.—Fought May 15, 1864, between General Sherman's Union troops and Johnston's Confederate army. The battle lasted two days, and resulted in the evacuation of Resaca by the Confederates and their pursuit by the Unionists. The losses were estimated at 3,500 killed and wounded, including among the latter Generals Hooker, Willich, Kilpatrick, and Manson. The Confederates lost, it is estimated, 2,000 killed and wounded, including 3 general officers reported among the former, several hundred prisoners, and 7 cannon.

Second Battle of Cold Harbor, Va.—Fought June 3, 1864, between the Union army, under Grant and Meade, and the Confederate forces, under Lee and Longstreet. Grant had about 150,000, and Lee about 56,000 men. The fight was brief but desperate, lasting less than half an hour, and resulted in the repulse of the Union army at every point. Grant's loss in killed, wounded and missing, including 3 brigadier-generals killed, was about 7,500 men; Lee's loss, including one general officer, was less than half that number.

Battle of Pine Mountain, Ga.—Fought June 14, 1864, between a body of Confederates, who held the place, and a force of Union artillery under Sherman. During this fight the Confederate General Leonidas Polk was killed, and on the next day the stronghold was found to have been abandoned, the Confederates having intrenched themselves along the lines of hills connecting Kenesaw and Lost mountains; this line was abandoned, however, on the 17th. Being pressed by the Unionists under McPherson, the Confederates took to Kenesaw mountain and there were strongly intrenched.

Sheridan's Raid in Virginia—June 7, 1864, General Sheridan and a Union cavalry force set out to destroy the Confederate railroads leading from Gordonsville. On the 11th, at Buck Childs', he encountered a force of Confederate cavalry, which was driven back and outflanked. The result was a complete rout of the Confederates, who left their dead and nearly all their wounded on the field, besides the capture of 20 officers, 500 men and 300 horses by the Unionists. About five miles from Gordonsville the Confederates had constructed rifle-pits, and on the 12th there was a cavalry engagement of considerable importance. The Confederates lost heavily, including several general officers. Sheridan lost about 85 killed and 490 wounded. The raid was successful.

Morgan's Second Guerrilla Raid—The Confederate guerrilla General Morgan again invaded Kentucky, June 7, 1864. After plundering Lexington and taking Cynthiana, he was attacked and had nearly all his force captured or dispersed by the Union General Burbridge. By the 17th of June, Morgan was discomfited and his raid ended. Morgan's operations were finally ended September 5, 1864, at Greenville, Tenn., where he was killed.

Averill's Raid in the Shenandoah Valley, Va.—June 16, 1864, General Averill, with a body of Unionists proceeded to destroy the Virginia and East Tennessee railroad, in order to cut off Lee's communications with Richmond. He succeeded in destroying 15 miles of the track, and burned five bridges, depots, cars, large quantities of Confederate stores, and captured 200 prisoners and 150 horses. His loss was 6 men drowned, 5 wounded, and 14 missing, during his rugged expedition of 355 miles.

First Battle at Petersburg, Va.—Fought June 15 and 18, 1864, between the Confederate army under Lee (about 70,000 strong), which occupied the town, and Grant's army, about 150,000. A series of engagements resulted first in the repulse of the Unionists under W. F. Smith, and subsequently other repulses, which cost the Union army a loss of 1,198 killed, 6,853 wounded, and 2,217 missing. June 21, 1864, an attempt was made by the Unionists to seize the Weldon railroad, which cost them 3,000 men. Afterwards this and other roads were seized by them, which prevented supplies reaching Lee's army at Petersburg. July 30, 1864, a mine containing 8,000 pounds of powder was exploded under a Confederate fort at Petersburg by the Unionists. The effect was not so beneficial as was expected by the Unionists, the earth being blown into an inaccessible position, so that entrance to the city was extremely difficult by that route. The Confederates poured in shell upon the attacking party, and after four hours' ineffectual assault the Union forces withdrew, having lost 4,003 men killed, wounded and missing, while the Confederate loss is set down at less than 1,000. August 5, the Confederates exploded a mine in front of a Union corps, without inflicting serious injury, and considerable fighting ensued, without important results or serious losses on either side.

Battle of Rood's Hill, Va.—Fought in June, 1864, between 5 regiments of Unionists under General Sigel and about 7,000 Confederate infantry, with cavalry and artillery, of Breckenridge's army. Sigel was defeated with the loss of about 600 killed, wounded and missing, and 5 cannon.

A Naval Victory—June 19, 1864, in the French port of Cherbourg, the famous Confederate ocean-cruiser Alabama, commanded by Raphael Semmes, was defeated and sunk by the United States war-ship Kearsarge, commanded by Commodore Winslow. Semmes escaped.

Battles of Kenesaw Mountain, Ga.—Finding the Confederates strongly intrenched upon Kenesaw mountain, June 27, 1864, General Sherman ordered his Union troops to attempt to dislodge them. This assault was participated in by McPherson, Thomas, Blair, Dodge, Logan and other division commanders of the Union army. The assault was well made, but the Confederate intrenchments could not be carried. A flank movement was at once made, with such effect that early on the morning of July 3, 1864, the Union skirmishers appeared on the mountain above the Confederate intrenchments, which had been abandoned on the previous night. In the attack of June 27, the Unionists lost from 2,000 to 3,000 men.

Battle of Monocacy River, Md.—On the 9th July, 1864, an action occurred between 15,000 Confederates, under Early, and Rickett's division of the sixth Union army corps, under General Wallace. The latter were outflanked and forced to fall back, with the loss of about 1,200, including about 600 prisoners.

Battle Near Washington, D. C.—Fought July 11, 1864, about 5 miles from the city between Union troops, under General Augur—a brigade of veteran infantry—and Confederate skirmishers. The former were the attacking party. The Confederates were completely routed, leaving about 100 of their dead and wounded on the field. The Union loss was about 200.

Battle of Peach-Tree Creek, Ga.—Fought July 20, 1864, between Sherman's Union army and the Confederate forces under Johnston. Hooker's Union corps suffered in the severe conflict, but the Confederates were driven to their intrenchments, leaving more than 500 of their number killed and over 1,000 wounded on the field, 7 stand of colors and many prisoners. Their entire loss was estimated at 5,000. Sherman lost 1,500 killed, wounded and missing.

Battle of the Howard House, Ga.—Fought July 22, 1864, between the Confederate army under Hood (who had superseded Johnston) and Sherman's Union army, the former attacking the latter. The conflict was general and stubborn until the Confederates gave way, repulsed. Sherman's loss, including the death of General McPherson, was 3,722 killed, wounded and prisoners. The Confederates, it is estimated, lost 2,000 killed, or 8,000 in all.

Another Fight in Front of Atlanta, Ga.—Fought July 28, 1864, between the Confederate army, under Hood, and a portion of Sherman's Union army, under Howard and Logan, the former coming out of their Atlanta intrenchments to attack the latter. This bloody conflict resulted in the complete repulse of the attacking party, with a loss of about 650 killed, and probably not less than 4,300 wounded. Sherman lost less than 600 in killed, wounded and missing.

Battle Near Winchester, Va.—General Crook, with a small Union force, was defeated on the 24th of July, 1864, by the Confederates under General Early.

Union Raids in Georgia—In the latter part of July, 1864, General Sherman organized two cavalry expeditions to destroy the Macon railroad, which was a source of Confederate supplies. They consisted of General Stoneman, with 5,000 Union cavalry, and General McCook with 4,000 cavalry. Another object was to release the Union prisoners at Andersonville. In making a premature descent upon Andersonville, Stoneman encountered a superior force of Confederates, who defeated him and took him and 700 of his men prisoners. McCook proceeded to the Macon railroad, but Stoneman failing to meet him there, he withdrew to Newman, Ga., where he fell in with a considerable force of Confederate infantry. Surrounding McCook's command they forced him into a battle, compelling him to fight his way out, which he did with the loss of 500 of his men. He then returned to the main army at Marietta. Substantially the raid was a serious failure.

Chambersburg, Pa., Plundered and Burned—July 30, 1864, a cavalry force under the Confederate General McCausland, entered Chambersburg, plundered the citizens, and burned about 250 buildings, at an estimated loss of $1,000,000.

Battle of Moorefield, W. Va.—Fought August 7, 1864, between Union cavalry under Averill and a body of Confederate cavalry, the latter being defeated with the loss of all their artillery, 50 prisoners, many wagons and small arms. The remainder were driven to the mountains.

Farragut's Fleet at Mobile, Ala.—August 5, 1864, the Union fleet commanded by Rear Admiral Farragut, commenced the attack on Mobile bay by blowing up and causing the evacuation of the Confederate Fort Powell, permitting the passage of 17 Union vessels into the bay. One had been sunk by the fort batteries; the Confederate war vessel Tennessee surrendered after a sharp engagement and her commander, Buchanan, was killed; another Confederate vessel was captured and another was beached. On August 7, Farragut opened fire on the Confederate Fort Gaines, which contained [illegible] men. On the 8th this fort was surrendered by its commander. A co-operating Federal force, under General Granger, assisted in the reduction of another Confederate fort on August 23, leaving Farragut in control of the entrance of the bay.

Sheridan in the Shenandoah Valley, Va.—From August 9 to the 15th, 1864, General Sheridan's Union cavalry had several encounters of more or less severity with the Confederates under Early. Skirmishes occurred within ten miles of Winchester; Sulphur Springs bridge, when Custer's Union cavalry were repulsed; near White Post, the Confederates retiring after a 3 hours' contest; at Newtown, which Early succeeded in holding; near Strasburg, Early retiring, and the Unionists occupying the town; at Berryville, where Mosby's force captured Sheridan's supply train, destroying a large number of wagons and driving off several hundred horses, mules and beef cattle. Sheridan's force, August 15, 1864, retired to Charlestown.

Battle at Deep Bottom, Va.—Fought August 16, 1864, between the Federal forces and a superior number of Confederates, the former being obliged to retire, though without heavy losses.

Fights on the Weldon Railroad, Va., —August 18, 1864, the Unionists made an advance upon this road, in order to cut off the enemy's supplies, but were driven back by the Confederates. A sharp fight followed, and the lost ground retaken and fortified. Next day the fight was renewed and the Union lines were broken. This battle cost the Unionists about 3,000 men, a great proportion being taken prisoners. On the 21st the Confederates made another vigorous attempt to dislodge the Unionists from the road, but were repulsed with a severe loss; the Unionists suffered but slightly in comparison.

Battle of Ream's Station, Va.—Fought August 25, 1864, between the Union corps under Hancock and a heavy force of Early's Confederate army, the latter being the attacking party. Both sides fought desperately, and Hancock withdrew from Ream's station, having lost 9 cannon and 2,000 men killed, wounded and taken prisoners. The Confederates lost 1,500 killed and wounded. This battle gave the Confederates repossession of the Weldon railroad southward, although the track had previously been destroyed by the Unionists.

Kilpatrick's Raid in Georgia—General Kilpatrick, of Sherman's Union army, with 5,000 cavalry, August 18, 1864, broke the track of the West Point railroad, near Fairburn, and then struck the Macon road, near Jonesboro. Here he encountered a heavy force of Confederates, under Ross, but maintained possession of the road for several hours. Finding himself likely to be overwhelmed by numbers, he retreated, made a circuit and again struck the road at Lovejoy's station. Here he was once more menaced by the Confederates. Making a charge upon them, capturing 4 cannon and a number of prisoners, he retired to Decatur, without having very seriously broken up the Macon railroad.

Battle of Jonesboro, Ga.—Fought August 31, 1864, between a force under Howard, of Sherman's Union army, and a heavy force of Confederates from Hood's army, under Hardee, and Lee's command. The conflict in front of Jonesboro lasted two hours, when the Confederates withdrew to their fortifications. Their loss, as officially reported by Hood, was 1,400 killed and wounded. Union losses were comparatively light. On the first of September General Davis, with a body of Union cavalry, attacked the Confederate lines at Jonesboro, carrying their fortifications, and the Confederates effected their escape southward. In the meantime the Unionists were busily engaged in destroying the Macon railroad.

Raiders in Georgia, Tennessee and Kentucky—The Confederate cavalry under Wheeler, after breaking the Union railroad and destroying property at Adairsville and Calhoun, Ga., August 14, 1864, demanded the surrender of Dalton, then occupied by less than 500 Unionists under Colonel Laibold. This was refused, and Wheeler sharply attacked Laibold's position, but the latter having been reinforced next morning, Wheeler was driven off. Wheeler then passed into Tennessee, and formed a Union with Forrest and other raiders; but the whole were driven from the State by the Union forces under Generals Rousseau, Steadman and Granger. September 4, 1864, the famous Confederate guerrilla, John Morgan, was surprised and killed near Greenville, Tenn., by a Union force under General Gillem, his band being dispersed or captured. September 8, 1864, the Confederate raider, Jessie, and 100 of his men were captured at Ghent, in Kentucky.

Surrender of Atlanta, Ga.—The grand object of Sherman's Union expedition to Atlanta was achieved on the night of September 1, 1864, by the Confederate General Hood and his forces evacuating the city and its fortifications. Before leaving, he blew up seven trains of cars and destroyed other property. General Slocum, of the 20th Union Army corps, occupied the city September 2, and it then became the headquarters of the Federal army in Georgia. Hood withdrew to Macon.

Battle of Winchester, Va.—Fought September 19, 1864, between a heavy force of Confederates under Early, in position near Winchester, and Union troops under Averill and Sheridan. The fight lasted from noon until five o'clock in the evening, when the Confederates retreated, pursued by Sheridan's troops. Union loss 653 killed, 3,719 wounded, and 618 captured. Confederate loss, about 6,000—2,000 wounded were found in the hospitals at Winchester, and about 3,000 were taken prisoners.

Battle of Fisher's Hill, Va.—Fought September 22, 1864, between Sheridan's Union army and Early's Confederate troops, who were intrenched at that point. A flanking movement and a general charge along the Confederate lines compelled the latter to evacuate their fortifications, the Unionists pursuing them through the night. Early's loss was about 300 killed and wounded, and also 1,100 prisoners, 16 cannon, with his camp equipage, wagons, horses, small arms, and ammunition. Sheridan's loss was about 300 men. By the 29th of September, the Confederates had been driven from the Shenandoah valley.

Battle of Pilot Knob, Mo.—The Confederate General Price, with a force estimated at 10,000 men invaded Missouri, from Arkansas, September 23, 1864, raiding the country with apparently but little opposition. On the 26th Price attacked the little town of Pilot Knob, then occupied by a Union brigade under General Ewing, but was repulsed in all his attempts with severe losses. Price then occupying Shepherd's mountain, in that vicinity, Ewing blew up his magazine and retired to Harrison's station, where he intrenched. Price closely pursued him, breaking up the railroad, but Ewing finally escaped to Rolla, with little loss, from the dangers that surrounded him.

Price Defeated—During the month of October, 1864, the Confederate General Price committed various depredations in Missouri, although harassed and watched by Union forces under several commanders. October 25, when on the Fort Scott (Kas.) railroad, Price was beaten with serious loss. On the 26th, at Mine Creek, his Generals Marmaduke and Cabell, with a large number of their men, were captured; and he was defeated also at Des Cygnes, Kas., on the 27th, and on the 28th at Newtonia. This ended the invasion of Missouri. Price lost 10 cannon, a large number of small arms, 1,958 prisoners (besides his killed, wounded and deserters), and nearly all his trains and plunder. His defeat was caused by the exertions of 7,000 Union cavalry, whose total losses in killed, wounded and missing, were less than 350.

Battle of Allatoona, Ga.—On the 5th October, 1864, a strong force of Confederates under General French, unsuccessfully attacked the small Union garrison under General Corse, with a loss of 2,000 men, killed and captured. Union loss 700 men, over one-third of the entire command. General Corse was wounded in the face.

Battle of Thoms' Brook, Va.—Fought October 8, 1864, between Union cavalry, under Generals Merritt and Custer, and the Confederate cavalry divisions of Generals Rosser and Lomax. The latter were defeated and driven twenty miles, with the loss of about 330 prisoners and several cannon. The Union loss was less than 100.

Battle of Cedar Creek, Va.—Fought October 19, 1864, between Sheridan's Union army (he being temporarily absent, but returning before the fight was over), and Early's Confederate forces in the valley of the Shenandoah. The latter were the attacking party, but their assault was steadily met, after the first panic, by the Unionists, who subsequently repulsed and routed their foes. During the first part of the battle it is estimated that the Unionists lost 1,300 prisoners, 20 cannon, considerable camp equipage, ambulances, wagons and medical supplies. Before the close of the contest the Unionists, it is estimated, captured and recaptured the following: 1,300 prisoners, 48 cannon, 300 horses and mules, 65 ambulances, 50 wagons, 15,000 rounds of artillery ammunition, 1,500 small arms, 10 battle-flags, harness, medical stores, etc. The Confederates lost about 3,000 men in killed, wounded and prisoners. The Unionists lost 5,990, including 2,000 temporarily missing, and a large number of officers. But the victory, though gained at heavy loss, was considered decisive for the Unionists.

Bombardment and Capture of Plymouth, N. C.—Commodore Macomb, with 7 Union gunboats, began bombarding the Confederate stronghold of Plymouth, N. C., October 29, 1864. The attack lasted until the 31st, when a Union shell exploded the Confederate magazine, and soon afterwards the Union commander took possession of the place without further resistance.

Sherman's March from Atlanta to Savannah, Ga.—On the 1st of November, 1864, the Confederate force under Hood in Georgia was estimated at 35,000 infantry and 10,000 cavalry. About this time Sherman arranged the details for his expedition from Atlanta to the sea-coast through the Confederate State of Georgia. The Union army for this enterprise comprised 60,000 infantry, 5,500 cavalry, and between 60 and 70 pieces of artillery. On the 14th of November the storehouses, depot buildings and machine shops, covering 200 acres in the city of Atlanta, were burned by the Unionists, and but little more than the dwellings and churches of the place survived the flames. On the 15th of November the advance guard of the expedition left Atlanta, followed on the next day by the main army.

Battle Near Morristown, Tenn.—Fought November 13-14, 1864, between General Breckenridge, with a Confederate force estimated at 3,000 strong, and General Gillem, with 1,500 Unionists and 6 cannon. The latter were routed losing several hundred prisoners and artillery. Gillem then escaped, with the remainder of his force, to Knoxville.

Battle of Hollow-Tree Gap, Tenn.—Four miles from Franklin, Thomas' Union cavalry overtook Hood's retreating Confederate army, November 17, 1864, and attacked it in front and rear, capturing 413 prisoners and three battle-flags.

Another Battle at Franklin, Tenn.—Hood's Confederate army then fell back to Franklin, but Johnson's division of Thomas' Union army repulsed them on the Harpeth river bank, and Union cavalry took possession of the town, capturing the Confederate hospitals, containing more than 2,000 wounded men, 200 of whom were Unionists. Hood was still pursued after leaving Franklin, but escaped into the interior of Georgia, with but little additional loss.

Battle of Griswoldville, Ga.—Fought November 22, 1864, between a detachment of Kilpatrick's Union cavalry (from Sherman's army) with a brigade of Union infantry, and about 5,000 Confederates, mostly militia, with some of Hardee's corps. The latter were the attacking party. The fight was brief but sanguinary, and resulted in the retreat of the Confederates, who left more than 300 of their dead on the field, and lost more than 1,000 in wounded and prisoners. The Union loss was about 40 killed and wounded.

Occupation of Milledgeville, the Capital of Georgia—Sherman's Union army occupied Milledgeville, November 23, 1864. The Confederate legislature in session there hastily adjourned, and the citizens were panic stricken. The Unionists burned the magazines, arsenals, depot buildings, various factories, store-houses, containing large amounts of Confederate public property, and about 1,700 bales of cotton. Private property was everywhere respected. Railroads were generally torn up and destroyed.

Capture of Fort McAllister, near Savannah, Ga.—The fort was manned by about 200 men, Confederate infantry and artillery, and lay in Sherman's way to the objective point of his expedition, the city of Savannah. December 13, 1864, the fort was carried, in a single assault, by nine regiments of Unionists. On the same day Sherman was enabled to communicate with the Union naval squadron at the mouth of the Ogeechee river, under Admiral Dahlgren and General Foster.

Capture of Savannah, Ga.—A demand from the Union General Sherman upon the Confederate General Hardee, who then occupied Savannah, for the surrender of the city, November 17, 1864, was refused. Sherman, therefore, prepared to carry the place by a military and naval assault. Hardee, recognizing the exigencies of the times, evacuated the city on the night of November 28, first destroying the Confederate war vessels in the harbor; and thus Sherman's expedition successfully terminated. Hardee's command moved toward Charleston, S. C.

Results of Sherman's Expedition from Atlanta to Savannah—Sherman's Union army brought with them to Savannah 15,000 slaves, more than 1,000 prisoners, 150 cannon, 13 locomotives in good order, 190 railroad cars, a very large supply of ammunition and other war material, three steamers and 32,000 bales of cotton, besides achieving national benefits growing out of the success of his expedition.

Hood in Tennessee and Alabama—The Confederate General Hood, who had retired before Sherman's Union army to Gaylesville, in Northeastern Alabama, visited Jacksonville, and thence proceeded northwesterly toward the Tennessee river, watched by the Union forces under General Thomas. The Confederate troops began their northward march about November 20, 1864, approaching Pulaski, Tenn. At this point, General Schofield and General A. J. Smith concentrated their Union forces, on learning of Hood's approach. The latter moved directly upon Gaynesboro, thus flanking Schofield, who fell back to Columbia, and being pursued by Hood, retreated to Franklin.

Battle of Spring Hill, Tenn.—Hood, with his Confederate army, attacked Schofield's Union cavalry November 29, 1864. A fight ensued, in which Schofield lost less than 300 men, and then he retreated to Franklin, 18 miles from Nashville. Here he formed his lines in a strong position and prepared for a battle with Hood.

Battle of Franklin, Tenn.—Fought November 30, 1864, between Schofield's Union force, consisting of two army divisions, commanded by Generals Stanley and Cox, and two corps of Hood's Confederate army, under Generals Lee and Cheatham. The fight was extremely hot, the Confederates making repeated charges upon the Union batteries; but the Confederates were finally repulsed, and Schofield was reinforced by General Smith's corps. The Union loss was 189 killed, 1,033 wounded, and 1,104 missing. Hood's loss was 1,750 killed, 3,800 wounded, and 702 taken prisoners.

Skirmish at Overall's Creek, Tenn.—Fought December 4, 1864, at the blockhouse, occupied by a Union force and Bates division of Cheatham's Confederate corps, the latter attacking the former, and using artillery. The Union General Milroy coming up with infantry, cavalry and artillery, attacked the Confederates and drove them off.

Battle Near Murfreesboro, Tenn.—Fought December 5, 6, and 7, 1864. General Rousseau and about 8,000 Unionists were occupying Fortress Rosecrans, and were approached by two divisions of Lee and Cheatham's Confederate corps, with 2,500 of Forrest's Confederate cavalry. The Confederates hesitating to attack the fort General Milroy, with seven regiments of Union infantry, was sent out to engage them. He found them a short distance off, posted behind rail breastworks. A fight ensued, in which the Confederates were routed, with the loss of 30 killed, 175 wounded, 207 prisoners, and two cannon. On the same day Buford's Confederate cavalry entered Murfreesboro and shelled it, but were speedily driven out by a regiment of Union infantry and a section of artillery.

A Union Raid in Virginia—By orders from General Grant, December 6, 1864, a Union force of 20,000 men, with 22 cannon, proceedec down the line of the Weldon railroad, with instructions to destroy the road and penetrate the enemy's country, capturing such points and supplies as should come in their way. The weather was bad, but the expedition, which was absent a week, was mainly successful. Some opposition was encountered, but the entire loss of the Unionists did not exceed 100 men. They destroyed 3 railroad bridges, 15 miles of track, burned Sussex Court-house, and brought in a few prisoners.

Battle of Nashville, Tenn.—Fought December 15 and 16, 1864, between General Thomas, with four corps of Union infantry and Wilson's cavalry, dismounted, aided by a division of Rear-Admiral Lee's Mississippi naval squadron, and Hood's concentrated army of Confederates. The first day's fight resulted in driving the Confederates from their intrenchments with a loss of ab ut 600 killed and wounded, 1,000 prisoners and 18 great guns. The Union loss that day was about 500 killed and wounded. The attack was renewed by the Unionists next morning on Hood's new position, and resulted, soon after noon in the complete rout of the Confederates, sufferig severe losses. All their dead and wounded were left on the field of battle. The Confederate losses in the two days' contests footed up about 2,300 killed and wounded, 4,462 prisoners captured, including 287 officers, 53 cannon and thousands of small arms. The Confederates were pursued.

Stoneman's Raid in Virginia—December 15, 1864, Generals Stoneman and Burbridge of the Union army in Tennessee, sallied out to Glade's Spring, W. Va., destroying a railroad track east of Abingdon, and mining the principal salt works in that region. This movement severed the Confederate communication between Richmond and East Tennessee, and deprived the Confederates of important public property.

The Finish at Fort Fisher, N. C.—In December, 1864, an expedition was fitted out under the Union Generals Butler and Weitzel and the North Atlantic naval squadron, under Admiral Porter, to break up the Confederate blockade-runner's depot at Wilmington, N. C. A preliminary explosion, December 23, 1864, having failed to reduce the fort to splinters, the fleet attacked it next day. Five hours' cannonading, resisted by the Confederate garrison, resulted in blowing up two magazines within the inclosure and setting it on fire in several places. Decembe 25 the assault was renewed on sea and shore by the Union forces, but General Weitzel reporting, after a reconnoissance, that it would be inexpedient to carry the fort by assault, the attempt was abandoned, leaving the fort substantially uninjured, and the expedition retired.

BATTLES OF THE FIFTH YEAR OF THE WAR.

Battle at Beverly, W. Va.—Fought January 11, 1865, between a Union force occupying the town and Confederate troops under General Rosser. The former were defeated, the latter capturing the town and a large portion of the force defending it.

Capture of Fort Fisher, N. C.—The Union assault upon Fort Fisher, the formidable Confederate stronghold at Wilmington, N. C., mounting 72 great guns, was resumed January 13, 1865, by about 8,000 Union troops under General Terry, with Admiral Porter's fleet and 1,000 or more marines—a Confederate force of 2,300 men occupying the fort. The fleet began the bombardment of the fort on that day, and in the afternoon of the 15th the Union soldiers, with the sailors and marines, attacked the fort by land and sea. At 4 o'clock one-half of the fort had been captured. That evening reinforcements of Union soldiers arrived, and the Confederate defense surrendered. The fighting had been very severe. Of the garrison, 217 were killed or wounded, besides the force surrendered. The Union loss was about 1,000, besides which were 200 men killed or wounded on the next day by the accidental blowing up of a magazine.

Fight at Fort Anderson, N. C.—Fort Anderson, one of the defenses of the mouth of Cape Fear river, near Wilmington, defended by about 6,000 Confederates, under General Hoke, strongly intrenched, was attacked, January 18, 1865, by 8,000 Union soldiers of Cox's division, under General Schofield, and Admiral Porter, with 16 gunboats and a monitor. A heavy fire from the fleet and the operations of the land force continued during the day, and before daylight on the 19th the Confederates evacuated the fort. The Confederate loss was 12 cannon, a quantity of ammunition, and about 50 prisoners. The Unionists lost 3 killed and 5 wounded in the fleet, and less than 50 killed and wounded in the skirmishes of the land forces.

Skirmishes on Town Creek, N. C.—Fought January 20, 1865, between a Confederate force in rifle-pits and Union troops under Terry. The latter lost 10 killed and 47 wounded, but drove the Confederates inside their works. A similar Union force soon afterwards charged upon some Confederates in the same vicinity. They were met with grape and canister. Another charge was then made by the Union soldiers, and the Confederates were routed, with the loss of 2 cannon and 373 prisoners, the rest escaping. The Union loss was about 30.

Evacuation of Wilmington, N. C.—January 21, 1865, finding themselves beleaguered with a heavy Union force, the Confederates prepared to evacuate Wilmington. That night they burned their war material and stores, about 1,000 bales of cotton, 15,000 barrels of resin, extensive cotton-sheds and presses, an unfinished iron-clad, three steam-mills, three large turpentine factories, with wharves, railroad bridges and other property, and moved out. At daylight on the 22d, the Union troops under Generals Terry and Cox occupied the city, taking about 700 prisoners, and capturing a large amount of Confederate property.

Sherman's March to Wilmington, N. C., from Savannah, Ga.—January 13, 1865, Sherman's Union advance corps left Beaufort, N. C. On the 15th a skirmish occurred with a Confederate force on the Charleston railroad for the possession of a Confederate pontoon and trestle bridge. The Unionists succeeded in saving the bridge from being burned and drove off the Confederates. The Union loss was about 50 killed and wounded. January 19, the march of the main Union army from Savannah, under Sherman, began. By a system of feints the Unionists misled the Confederates as to their intentions. At the Salkehatchie river, Mower and Smith's divisions captured a bridge from the Confederate force which held it, losing 18 killed and 70 wounded in the struggle. February 16, the Confederates surrendered the city of Columbia, S. C., to Colonel Stone, of the 25th Iowa infantry. The Confederate soldiers set fires in the city, and that night the city was burned, and within two or three days afterwards the arsenal, railroad depots, and tracks, machine shops, foundries, etc., were destroyed by the Unionists. March 9, Wade Hampton's Confederate troops surprised Kilpatrick's and Spencer's Union forces, rescuing their jeopardised camp equipage, artillery and horses, and driving off the Unionists. March 12-14 the Unionists spent in destroying all the buildings and much valuable military and public property. March 8, the Confederates under Hoke captured two Union regiments, commanded by Colonel Upham, securing over 1,000 prisoners. March 10, Hoke's Confederate force fought Cox's Union brigade, but the latter were the victors, driving off Hoke, who left his killed and wounded on the field, besides losing about 300 prisoners.

Battles at Fort Steadman and Hatcher's Run, Va.—Fought February 6 and 7, 1865, between the 2d, 6th and 9th corps and Griffin's division of the 5th corps of Grant's army in Virginia and Lee's Confederate army. Steadman's fort, occupied by the 14th New York Union heavy artillery, was carried by the Confederates at the outset, and its guns were turned against the Unionists. The Confederates also captured two Union batteries between Fort Steadman and Fort Haskell, and with them fought the Union troops. They failed, however, to carry the Union Fort Haskell. A tremendous cannonade followed, the Union batteries being massed against Fort Steadman with so much vigor that some of the Confederates retreated, first into the fortress and then out of it, leaving all the guns that they had captured. A large portion of the escaping Confederates, 1,758 in all, were captured. The Confederate loss at this point was estimated at 2,500. The Union forces on the left then moved out against the Confederate intrenched lines of pickets, which were swept right and left, resulting in the capture of about 300 prisoners. Another attack by the Unionists, reconnoitering across Hatcher's Run, resulted in driving in another Confederate picket line, with the capture of 70 more prisoners. Subsequently the Confederates rallied their forces and attacked the 6th and 2d corps of Grant's army. The fight was severe and continued until dark and even into the night, but the Unionists were the victors. The Confederate total losses in both battles were set down at 5,000 men—1,883 prisoners. The Unionists lost 171 killed, 1,236 wounded, and 983 missing.

Evacuation of Charleston, S. C.—February 18, 1865, the city of Charleston was evacuated by the Confederates, and occupied by the Union General Gilmore. A large amount of valuable property was destroyed, including 5,000 bales of cotton. Ammunition stored in the railroad depot exploded, and many lives were lost. General Gilmore displayed the American flag over the ruins of Fort Sumter.

Sheridan's March Through the Shenandoah Valley, Va.—General Sheridan, with a strong Union force, left Winchester, Va., February 26, 1865. This expedition was principally distinguished by

Sheridan's Capture of Early's Army.—March 2, 1865, near Waynesboro, Va., Sheridan's Union force encountered the Confederates under Early. The latter fired one volley, when General Custer's division advanced upon them. The Confederate line suddenly broke, and Custer's force surrounded them, capturing 17 Confederate officers, 1,166 enlisted men, 13 flags, 2 cannon, more than 100 horses and mules and about 100 wagons and ambulances. Custer's brigades immediately pursued the fleeing Confederates, destroying the depot at Greenwood station, with their artillery and other captured war material. Next day the prisoners were sent to Winchester. An attempt to rescue them by the Confederate General Rosser only succeeded in his being beaten off, with the loss of 27 more prisoners. March 26, 1864, Sheridan arrived at City Point, Va., having made a most successful raid. His total losses were 2 officers and about 50 men in killed, wounded and prisoners.

Battle of Averysboro, N. C.—Fought March 16, 1865, between four divisions of Sherman's Union army, under General Slocum, and about 20,000 Confederates under Hardee. After a severe action the latter retreated, leaving 108 of his dead on the field. The Union loss was 77 killed, 477 wounded and no prisoners.

Battle near Bentonville, N. C.—Fought March 19-21, 1865, between General Sherman's Union army and Johnston's Confederate army.

The latter were defeated, with heavy losses, including 267 killed and 1,625 prisoners. The Union loss in killed, wounded and missing, was 1,643. Sherman now had possession of Goldsboro, N. C., and concentrated his army there.

Skirmish on the Quaker Road, Va.—Fought March 29, 1865, between one division of Meade's Union 5th corps, with 3 batteries, and a detachment of Lee's Confederate army. After a short and sharp conflict, the Confederates withdrew to their original position, they having made the attack. The Union loss was 450 killed, wounded and missing. That night, under a heavy Confederate cannonade, the Union 9th corps lost 51 men.

Skirmish on the Boydton Road, Va.—Fought March 30, 1865, between Merritt's corps of Meade's Union army and Confederate infantry and cavalry. Another smart skirmish occurred between detachments of the same armies on the same day, and the total Union losses were something less than 300 men.

A Federal Repulse.—Proceeding along the Boydton (Va.) road toward Five Forks, March 31, 1865, Meade's Union advance and Sheridan's Union cavalry encountered a strong force of Confederates, who stubbornly resisted the Federal advance and brought on a conflict, which resulted in the repulse of the Unionists, with a loss of from 2,500 to 3,000 men. Between 300 and 400 Confederate prisoners were captured. Subsequently, under the fire of the Union batteries, the Confederates withdrew.

Battle of Five Forks, Va.—Fought April 1, 1865, between a part of Lee's Confederate army and three divisions of Union infantry and four of Union cavalry, commanded by Sheridan, while Meade's army threatened the Confederate line from Dinwiddie to Petersburg. After a preliminary contest, Sheridan broke through the Confederate lines, inclosing the Five Forks fortification and its Confederate garrison and capturing it. The battle for two hours was one of the most terrific of the war, and resulted in the utter defeat of the Confederates. They lost nearly 3,000 killed and wounded and

prisoners. The Union loss was about 1,000 men, including General Winthrop, who was killed.

Evacuation of Petersburg, Va.—Saturday night and Sunday morning, April 1 and 2, 1865, Grant's Union army, under Meade and Sheridan, invested Petersburg with such vigor that on the afternoon of the second day Lee evacuated the place, his communications with Richmond being severed. The losses were very heavy on both sides.

Evacuation of Richmond, Va.—Petersburg having been lost, President Davis, of the Southern Confederacy, retired from its capital, on Sunday, April 2, 1865, and on the following morning General Weitzel with his force entered Richmond, capturing about 500 cannon, 5,000 stand of arms, and 5,000 prisoners. Thirty locomotives and 300 cars were abandoned by the Confederates. The Confederate fleet was destroyed, and as the rear-guard of Lee's army moved out of the city they fired it, burning considerable property and stores.

Surrender of General Lee.—Lee's army was followed by Grant's Union forces after the evacuation of Richmond, and on the 9th of April, 1865, Lee surrendered to General Grant, at Appomattox Court House, Virginia, and his officers and men were paroled as prisoners of war. They numbered over 27,000. Lee's losses in killed and wounded, from March 31 to April 9, 1865, were something more than 10,000. There were released 250 wagons, 10,000 small arms, and 36 cannon.

Capture of Southern Cities.—April 12, 1865, Mobile was captured by the Union army under General Canby, who captured 1,000 Confederate prisoners, 150 cannon, and 3,000 bales of cotton. On the same day the Unionists captured Salisbury, N. C., and Columbus, Ga. On the following day they captured Raleigh, N. C., taking Governor Vance prisoner.

The End of the War.—General Johnston, of the Confederate army, surrendered to the Unionists, April 26, 1865, at Durham's station, near Greensboro, N. C. This closed the war of the Rebellion.

Distinguished Officers in the Union Service During the Civil War.†

Robert Anderson. Maj.-Gen.; b. near Louisville, Ky.; died in France in 1871.

Edward D. Baker. Colonel; U. S. Sen. from Or.; b. in London, Eng., in 1811; killed at Ball's Bluff, Va., in 1861.

Don Carlos Buell. Maj.-Gen.; b. at Marietta, O., in 1818.

Ambrose E. Burnside. Maj.-Gen.; b. at Liberty, Ind., 1824; Gov. R.I., and M. C.; d. in 1880.

Benjamin F. Butler. Maj.-Gen.; b. at Deerfield, N. H., 1818, has been M.C. from Mass.

Edward R. S. Canby. Brig.-Gen.; b. in Ky. in 1819; shot by Modoc Indian chief, in Cal. in 1873.

John C. Fremont. Maj.-Gen.; b. at Savannah, Ga., in 1813; Repub. can for Pres. in 1856; has been U. S. Sen. from Cal., and later Gov. of Ariz.

Ulysses S. Grant. Gen.-in-Chief of the U. S. during the latter part of the war; was b. at Pt. Pleasant, O., in 1822. Eight years Pres. of the U. S.

Henry W. Halleck. Gen.-in-Chief of the U. S. Army for a time; b. at Waterville, N. Y., in 1815; d. at Louisville, Ky., in 1872.

Winfield S. Hancock. Maj.-Gen.; b. in Montg. Co., Pa., in 1824; Dem. can. for Pres., 1880.

Joseph Hooker. Brevet Maj.-Gen.; b. at Hadley, Mass., in 1815; d. in 1879.

Oliver O. Howard. Brevet Maj.-Gen.; b. at Leeds, Me.

Philip Kearney. Maj.-Gen.; b. in N. Y. City, in 1815, wounded at Second Bull Run, where he d., in 1862.

John A. Logan. Maj.-Gen.; b. in Jefferson Co., Ill., in 1826; U. S. Sen. from Ill.

Nathaniel Lyon. Brig.-Gen.; b. at Ashford, Conn., in 1819; slain at Wilson's Creek, Mo., in 1861.

Geo. B. McClellan. Gen.-in-Chief of the U. S. Army, for a time; b. at Phila., Pa., in 1826; was Dem. can. for Pres. in 1864; elected Gov. of N.J. in 1878.

Irvin McDowell. Maj.-Gen.; b. at Franklinton, O., in 1818.

James B. McPherson. Maj.-Gen. of vols. b. at Clyde, O., in 1828; k. at Atlanta, in 1864.

Geo. G. Meade. Maj.-Gen.; b. at Cadiz, Spain, in 1815; d. at Phila. in 1872.

T. F. Meagher. Brig.-Gen.; b. at Waterford, Ireland, in 1823; accidentally drowned by falling from a steamer near Ft. Benton, Montana, in 1867.

John A. McClernand. Maj.-Gen.; b. in Breckenridge Co., Ky.; has been M. C.

Ormsby M. Mitchel. Maj.-Gen.; b. in Union Co., Ky., in 1810; d. of yellow fever at Beaufort, S. C., in 1862.

Richard J. Oglesby. Maj.-Gen.; b. in Oldham Co., Ky., in 1824; has been Gov. of Ill., and U. S. Sen. from that State.

Alfred Pleasanton. Maj.-Gen.; b. at Washington, D. C., in 1824; author of treatise on healing effect of sunlight passing through blue glass.

John Pope. Maj.-Gen.; b. at Kaskaskia, Ill., in 1823.

Fitz John Porter. Maj.-Gen.; b. at Portsmouth, N. H., in 1822.

Thomas E. G. Ransom. Brig.-Gen.; b. in 1834; d. in Chicago in 1864.

Wm. S. Rosecrans. Maj.-Gen.; b. at Kingston, O., in 1819.

Franz Sigel. Maj.-Gen.; b. at Zinsheim, Baden, Germany.

John M. Schofield. Maj.-Gen.; b. at Chautauqua Co., N. Y., in 1831; U. S. Secretary of War in 1868.

John Sedgwick. Maj.-Gen.; b. at Cornwall, Conn., in 1813; k. at Spottsylvania, Va., in 1864.

Philip H. Sheridan. Maj.-Gen.; b. at Somerset, O., in 1831; present Lieut.-Gen. U. S. A.

Wm. T. Sherman. Major-Gen. in the war; present Gen. U. S. A.; b. at Lancaster, O., in 1820.

Alfred H. Terry. Maj.-Gen.; b. at Hartford, Conn., in 1827.

Geo. H. Thomas. Maj.-Gen.; b. in Southham Co., Va., in 1816; d. at San Fran., Cal., in 1870.

Leading Officers in the Confederate Service.*

Peter G. T. Beauregard.* Gen.; b. at New Orleans, La., in 1818.

Braxton Bragg.* Maj.-Gen.; born in N.C. about 1815; d. at Galveston, Tex., in 1876.

Jefferson Davis. Col.; b. in Christian Co., Ky., in 1808; was President of the Southern Confederacy; formerly U.S. Senator from Miss., and was Sec. of War under Pres. Pierce.

J. A. Early.* Maj.-Gen.; b. in Va. about 1815.

Richard S. Ewell. Lieut.-Gen.; born in D. C., in 1820; d. at Springhill, Tenn., in 1872.

Wade Hampton, Jr. Lieut.-Gen.; b. at Columbia, S. C., in 1818; has been Gov. of S. C. and member of U. S. Senate.

Wm. J. Hardee.* Brig.-Gen.; b. at Savannah, Ga., in 1818; d. at Wytheville, Va., in 1873.

Ambrose P. Hill.* Maj.-Gen.; b. in Culpeper Co., Va., about 1825; k. at Petersburg, Va., in 1865.

Dan'l H. Hill.* Gen.; b. in S. C. about 1822.

John B. Hood.* Lieut.-Gen.; b. in Bath Co., Ky., about 1830.

Benj. Huger.* Maj.-Gen.; b. at Charleston, S. C., in 1806.

Thos. J. Jackson (Stonewall).* Lieut.-Gen.; b. at Clarksburg, Va., in 1824; d. from wounds received at battle of Chancellorsville.

Albert S. Johnston.* Gen.; b. in Mason Co., Ky., in 1803; k. at Shiloh, in 1862.

Joseph E. Johnston.* Maj.-Gen.; b. in Pr. Edward Co., Va., in 1807.

George W. C. Lee.* Gen.; b. in Va. about 1833.

Robert E. Lee.* Gen.-in-Chief of the Confederate army. b. at Stafford, Va., in 1807; d. at Lexington, Va., in 1870.

Fitz Hugh Lee.* Gen.; b. in Va. about 1835.

James Longstreet.* Lieut.-Gen.; b. in S. C. about 1820.

Benj. McCulloch. Maj.-Gen.; b. in Rutherford Co., Tenn., in 1814; k. at Pea Ridge, Ark., Mar. 7, 1862.

Leonidas Polk.* Maj.-Gen.; b. at Raleigh, N. C., in 1806; k. at Pine Mountain, near Marietta, Ga., in 1864.

Sterling Price. Maj.-Gen.; b. in Pr. Edward Co., Va., in 1809; M. C. from Mo., and was Gov. of that State; d. at St. Louis in 1867.

Kirby E. Smith.* Maj.-Gen.; b. at St. Augustine, Fla., about 1825.

Jas. E. B. Stuart. Maj.-Gen.; b. in Patrick Co., Va., in 1833; k. in battle near Richmond in 1864.

Earl Van Dorn. Maj.-Gen.; b. in Miss. in 1821; d. in 1863.

EXPLANATORY.—* Graduated at West Point; b., born; d., died; k., killed. † Many other distinguished names should be here mentioned, but lack of space prevents.

1. Alabama.
2. Arkansas.
3. California.
4. Colorado.
5. Connecticut.
6. Delaware.
7. Florida.
8. Georgia.
9. Illinois.
10. Indiana.
11. Iowa.
12. Kansas.
13. Kentucky.
14. Louisiana.
15. Maine.
16. Maryland.
17. Massachusetts.
18. Michigan.
19. Minnesota.

20. Mississippi.
21. Missouri.
22. Nebraska.
23. Nevada.
24. N. Hampshire.
25. New Jersey.
26. New York.
27. N. Carolina.
28. Ohio.
29. Oregon.
30. Pennsylvania.
31. Rhode Island.
32. S. Carolina.
33. Tennessee.
34. Texas.
35. Vermont.
36. Virginia.
37. West Virginia.
38. Wisconsin.

OW THE UNITED STATES ARE GOVERNED.

Duties and Privileges of
PERSONS IN OFFICIAL POSITIONS.

Early Discovery, Settlement and Government of the Country.

THE RECORD of North American discovery and settlement may be thus briefly told: Greenland, by Icelanders, in A. D. 980; Bahama Islands, by Christopher Columbus, in 1492; Isthmus of Darien, by Columbus, in 1494; Florida, by Sebastian Cabot, in 1497; Newfoundland and Canada, by John and Sebastian Cabot, in 1497; North and South Carolina, by Sebastian Cabot, in 1498; Hudson bay, by Sebastian Cabot, in 1512; the Mississippi river, by De Soto, about 1541; Davis' strait, by John Davis, in 1585; the Hudson river, by Henry Hudson, in 1608; and Baffin bay, by William Baffin, in 1616. In 1500, Americus Vespucci explored Brazil, S. A., and gave his name to both of the American continents.

The Spaniards early settled the West India Islands and New Mexico. The French occupied Canada in 1534, with the valley of the Mississippi, and other regions south and west. The English made their first permanent settlement at Jamestown, Va., in 1607, and a few years later several districts (including the present city of New York) were populated by Hollanders and Swedes. In 1620, the Puritan Pilgrims landed on the bleak coast of Massachusetts. By 1770, England, after a series of conflicts, had captured the country, occupied by the French, Dutch, and Swedish settlers, and was in possession of nearly the whole of North America, except Mexico, which was held by Spain. Soon afterwards, Russia acquired territory on the northwestern coast. Such was the ownership of the continent when the war of the Revolution began, in 1775.

At that time there were thirteen American colonies. These afterwards became the thirteen original States.

The colonists, who were subjects of Great Britain, became restive under various restrictions placed upon them by the mother country. Among these were a species of search warrant, which permitted government officials to enter stores and private houses to search for goods upon which prescribed taxes had not been paid.

Another was a stamp tax, which required every document used in the trade or legal business of the colonies to bear a stamp costing not less than an English shilling each, and a larger sum in proportion to the value of the document used.

This tax was afterwards repealed, but in 1767 another act of parliament provided for taxing paper, glass, tea and other goods imported into the colonies.

This enactment being resisted upon the part of the people, the English government sent troops to Boston to enforce the law, when a collision ensued between the troops and the citizens, in which several of the latter were killed and wounded.

Owing to the bitter opposition these taxes were soon repealed, excepting that of threepence on each pound of tea imported. But even this tax the colonists refused to pay, and when the first shipload of tea arrived in Boston harbor, the citizens went upon the vessel and threw the tea overboard.

In order to subdue and punish her American subjects, the English government thereupon devised other oppressive measures and annoyances, which, in the spring of 1775, resulted in the conflicts between the British soldiers and citizens at Concord and Lexington, and commenced the seven years war, known as the War of the Revolution for American Independence. The war had been in progress for about a year, when the Continental Congress in session at Independence Hall, in Philadelphia, July 2, 1776, adopted a resolution, introduced by Richard Henry Lee, declaring:

That these united colonies are, and of right ought to be, free and independent States; that they are absolved from all allegiance to the British crown, and that all political connection between them and the State of Great Britain is, and ought to be, totally dissolved.

Two days later the Declaration of Independence, prepared by Thomas Jefferson, was brought into Congress, and, amid intense excitement on the part of the citizens, was adopted. The announcement that it had been signed was made by the ringing of a bell in the cupola of the building. Such was the birth of American freedom.

INDEPENDENCE HALL, PHILADELPHIA.

Signers of the Declaration of Independence.

John Hancock	Quincy,	Mass.
Samuel Adams	Boston,	Mass.
Robert Treat Paine	Boston,	Mass.
William Whipple	Kittery,	Mass.
Matthew Thornton		Ireland.
William Ellery	Newport,	R. I.
John Hart	Hopewell,	N. J.
Benjamin Franklin	Boston,	Mass.
John Morton	Ridley,	Penn.
George Clymer	Philadelphia,	Penn.
James Smith		Ireland.
George Taylor		Ireland.
James Wilson	St. Andrew's, Scotland
George Ross	Newcastle,	Del.
Cæsar Rodney	Dover,	Del.
George Read	Cecil County,	Md.
Thomas Stone	Charles County,	Md.
Charles Carroll	Annapolis,	Md.
Richard Henry Lee	Stratford,	Va.
Francis Lightfoot Lee	Stratford,	Va.
Carter Braxton	Newington,	Va.
William Hooper	Boston,	Mass.
Joseph Hewes	Kingston,	N. J.
John Penn	Carolina County,	Va.
Button Gwinnett		England.
Lyman Hall		Connecticut.
George Walton	Frederick County,	Va.

Signers of the Declaration of Independence.

Elbridge Gerry	Marblehead,	Mass.
Stephen Hopkins	Scituate,	R. I.
Josiah Bartlett	Amesbury,	Mass.
Roger Sherman	Newton,	Mass.
Francis Lewis	Llandaff,	Wales
Philip Livingston	Albany,	N. Y.
William Floyd	Suffolk Co.,	N. Y.
Oliver Wolcott	Windsor,	Conn.
William Williams	Lebanon,	Conn.
Samuel Huntington	Windham,	Conn.
Lewis Morris	Morrisania,	N. Y.
Richard Stockton	Princeton,	N. J.
John Witherspoon	Yester,	Scotland
F. Hopkinson	Philadelphia,	Pa.
A. Clark	Elizabethtown,	N. J.
Robert Morris	Liverpool,	England
Benjamin Rush	Proprietine Co's,	Pa.
Thomas McKean	Chester Co.,	Pa.
Samuel Chase	Somerset Co.,	Md.
William Paca	Hartford Co.,	Md.
George Wythe	Elizabeth City,	Va.
Thomas Jefferson	Monticello,	Va.
Benjamin Harrison	City Point,	Va.
Thomas Nelson, Jr.	York Co.,	Va.
Edward Rutledge	Charleston,	S. C.
Thomas Heyward, Jr.	St. Luke's Par.,	S. C.
Thomas Lynch, Jr.	Pr. George Par.,	S. C.
Arthur Middleton	Ashley River,	S. C.

The Declaration of Independence.

DECLARATION by the representatives of the United States of America, in Congress assembled. Passed, Thursday, July 4, 1776.

When, in the course of human events, it becomes necessary for one people to dissolve the political bands which have connected them with another, and to assume among the powers of the earth the separate and equal station to which the laws of nature, and of nature's God, *entitle them*, a decent respect to the opinions of mankind requires that they should declare the causes which impel them to the separation.

We hold these truths to be self-evident; that all men are created equal; that they are endowed, by their Creator, with certain inalienable rights; that among these are life, liberty, and the pursuit of happiness. That, to secure these rights, governments are instituted among men, deriving their just powers from the consent of the governed; that, whenever any form of government becomes *destructive of* these ends, it is the right of the people to alter or to abolish it, and to institute a new government, laying its foundation on such principles, and organizing its powers in such form, as to them shall seem most likely to effect their safety and happiness. Prudence, indeed, will dictate that governments, long established, should not be changed for light and transient causes; and accordingly, all experience hath shown, that mankind are more disposed to suffer, while evils are sufferable, than to right themselves, by abolishing the forms to which they are accustomed. But when a long train of abuses and usurpations, pursuing invariably the same object, evinces a design to reduce them under absolute despotism, it is their right, it is their duty, to throw off such government, and to provide new

guards for their future security. Such has been the patient sufferance of these colonies; and such is now the necessity which constrains them to alter their former systems of government. The history of the present king of Great Britain is a history of repeated injuries and usurpations, all having, in direct object, the establishment of an absolute tyranny over these states. To prove this, let facts be submitted to a candid world.

He has refused his assent to laws the most wholesome and necessary for the public good.

He has forbidden his governors to pass laws of immediate and pressing importance, unless suspended in their operation till his assent should be obtained; and, when so suspended, he has utterly neglected to attend to them.

He has refused to pass other laws for the accommodation of large districts of people, unless those people would relinquish the right of representation in the legislature, a right inestimable to them, and formidable to tyrants only.

He has called together legislative bodies at places unusual, uncomfortable, and distant from the depository of their public records, for the sole purpose of fatiguing them into compliance with his measures.

He has dissolved representative houses, repeatedly, for opposing, with manly firmness, his invasions on the rights of the people.

He has refused, for a long time, after such dissolutions, to cause others to be elected; whereby the legislative powers, incapable of annihilation, have returned to the people at large for their exercise; the state remaining, in the meantime, exposed to all the dangers of invasion from without, and convulsions within.

He has endeavored to prevent the population of these states; for that purpose, obstructing the laws for naturalization of foreigners; refusing to

pass others to encourage their migration hither, and raising the conditions of new appropriations of lands.

He has obstructed the administration of justice, by refusing his assent to laws for establishing judiciary powers.

He has made judges *dependent* on his will alone, for the tenure of their offices, and the amount and payment of their salaries.

He has erected a multitude of new offices, and sent hither swarms of officers to harrass our people, and eat out their substance.

He has kept among us, in time of peace, standing armies, without the consent of our legislatures.

He has affected to render the military independent of, and superior to, the civil power.

He has combined with others, to subject us to a jurisdiction foreign to our constitution, and unacknowledged by our laws; giving his assent to their acts of pretended legislation:

For quartering large bodies of armed troops among us:

For protecting them, by a mock-trial, from punishment for any murders which they should commit on the inhabitants of these states:

For *cutting off* our trade with all parts of the world:

For imposing taxes on us, without our consent:

For depriving us, in many cases, of the benefit of trial by jury:

For transporting us beyond seas, to be tried for pretended offences.

For abolishing the free system of English laws in a neighboring province, establishing therein an *arbitrary* government, and enlarging its boundaries, so as to render it, at once, an example and a fit instrument for introducing the same absolute rule into these colonies:

For taking away our charters, abolishing our most valuable laws, and altering fundamentally, the forms of our government; for suspending our own legislatures, and declaring themselves invested with power to legislate for us, in all cases whatsoever.

He has abdicated government here, by declaring us out of his protection, and waging war against us.

He has plundered our seas, ravaged our coasts, burnt our towns, and destroyed the lives of our people.

He is at this time, transporting large armies of foreign mercenaries, to complete the works of death, desolation, and tyranny, already begun with circumstances of cruelty and perfidy, scarcely paralleled in the most barbarous ages, and totally unworthy the head of a civilized nation.

He has constrained our fellow-citizens, taken captive on the high seas, to bear arms against their country, to become the executioners of their friends and brethren, or to fall themselves by their hands.

He has excited domestic insurrections amongst us, and has endeavored to bring on the inhabitants of our frontiers, the merciless Indian savages, whose known rule of warfare is an undistinguished destruction of all ages, sexes, and conditions. In every stage of these oppressions, we have petitioned for redress, in the most humble terms; our repeated petitions have been answered only by repeated injury. A prince, whose character is thus marked by every act which may define a tyrant, is unfit to be the ruler of a free people. Nor have we been wanting in attentions to our British brethren. We have warned them, from time to time, of attempts, by their legislature, to extend an unwarrantable jurisdiction over us. We have reminded them of the circumstances of our emigration and settlement here. We have appealed to their native justice and magnanimity, and we have conjured them, by the ties of our common kindred, to disavow these usurpations, which would inevitably interrupt our connections and correspondence. They too, have been deaf to the voice of justice and of consanguinity. We must, therefore, acquiesce in the necessity which

denounces our separation, and hold them, as we hold the rest of mankind, enemies in war, in peace friends.

We, therefore, the representatives of the UNITED STATES OF AMERICA IN GENERAL CONGRESS assembled, appealing to the Supreme Judge of the world, for the rectitude of our intentions, do, in the name, and by the authority, of the good people of these colonies, solemnly publish and declare, That these united colonies are, and of right ought to be, FREE AND INDEPENDENT STATES; and that they are absolved from all allegiance to the British crown, and that all political connection between them and the State of Great Britain is, and ought to be, totally dissolved; and that, as FREE AND INDEPENDENT STATES, they have full power to levy war, conclude peace, contract alliances, establish commerce, and to do all other acts and things, which independent states may of right do. And, for the support of this declaration, with a firm reliance on the protection of Divine Providence, we mutually pledge to each other, our lives, our fortunes, and our sacred honor.

The End of The Revolution. Adoption of The Constitution.

The Ratification of the Constitution by the Thirteen Original States.

AFTER the signing of the Declaration of Independence, the thirteen British colonies were known as the "Thirteen United States of America." Beyond the efforts of Congress to sustain the conflict between the States and the "mother country," and to encourage Washington in his design to free the soil from British domination, the political changes were unimportant, until England dispatched a messenger to New York with offers of peace, about the beginning of the year 1782. November 30, 1782, the preliminaries of peace were signed at Paris, France, and, on September 3, 1783, the treaty was concluded, the independence of each of the

several States was acknowledged, and boundary lines established.

The government of the States was then principally vested in Congress and their own legislation; but, May 14, 1787, a national convention met at Philadelphia. After four months' deliberation, the present Constitution of the United States was adopted, and submitted to the people of each State for ratification or rejection. Their action was tardy in the extreme, for although Delaware, the first State to accept it, voted for it December 7, 1787, Rhode Island, the last, did not ratify it until May 27, 1790; but every State voted in its favor. Congress ratified it March 4, 1789, at which time it became the law of the land.

THE CONSTITUTION OF THE UNITED STATES.

WE, THE PEOPLE of the United States, in order to form a more perfect union, establish justice, insure domestic tranquility, provide for the common defense, promote the general welfare, and secure the blessings of liberty to ourselves and our posterity, do ordain and establish this Constitution for the United States of America.

ARTICLE I.—Section 1. All legislative powers herein granted shall be vested in a Congress of the United States, which shall consist of a Senate and House of Representatives.

House of Representatives.

Sect. II—1. The House of Representatives shall be composed of members chosen every second year by the people of the several States, and the electors in each State shall have the qualifications requisite for electors of the most numerous branch of the State Legislature.

2. No person shall be a Representative who shall not have attained to the age of twenty-five years, and been seven years a citizen of the United States, and who shall not, when elected, be an inhabitant of that State in which he shall be chosen.

3. Representatives and direct taxes shall be apportioned among the several States which may be included within this Union, according to their respective numbers, which shall be determined by adding to the whole number of free persons, including those bound to service for a term of years, and excluding Indians not taxed, three-fifths of all other persons. The actual enumeration shall be made within three years after the first meeting of the Congress of the United States, and within every subsequent term of ten years, in such manner as they shall by law direct.

The number of Representatives shall not exceed one for every thirty thousand, but each State shall have at least one Representative; and until such enumeration shall be made, the State of New Hampshire shall be entitled to choose three, Massachusetts eight, Rhode Island and Providence Plantations one, Connecticut five, New York six, New Jersey four, Pennsylvania eight, Delaware one, Maryland six, Virginia ten, North Carolina five, South Carolina five and Georgia three.

4. When vacancies happen in the representation from any State, the executive authority thereof shall issue writs of election to fill such vacancies.

5. The House of Representatives shall choose their Speaker and other officers, and shall have the sole power of impeachment.

The Senate.

Sect. III. The Senate of the United States shall be composed of two senators from each State, chosen by the Legislature thereof for six years, and each senator shall have one vote.

1. Immediately after they shall be assembled in consequence of the first election, they shall be divided as equally as may be into three classes. The seats of the senators of the first class shall be vacated at the expiration of the second year, of the second class at the expiration of the fourth year, and of the third class at the expiration of the sixth year, so that one-third may be chosen every second year; and if vacancies happen by resignation or otherwise during the recess of the Legislature of any State the Executive thereof may make temporary appointments until the next meeting of the Legislature, which shall then fill such vacancies. No person shall be a Senator who shall not have attained to the age of thirty years, and been nine years a citizen of the United States, and who shall not, when elected, be an inhabitant of that State for which he shall be chosen.

2. The Vice-President of the United States shall be President of the Senate but shall have no vote, unless they be equally divided.

3. The Senate shall choose their other officers, and also a President *pro tempore*, in the absence of the Vice-President or when he shall exercise the office of President of the United States.

4. The Senate shall have the sole power to try all impeachments. When sitting for that purpose, they shall be on oath or affirmation. When the President of the United States is tried, the Chief Justice shall preside: and no person shall be convicted without the concurrence of two-thirds of the members present.

5. Judgment in cases of impeachment shall not extend further than to removal from office and disqualification to hold and enjoy any office of honor, trust or profit under the United States; but the party convicted shall nevertheless be liable and subject to indictment, trial, judgment and punishment according to law.

Election of Congressmen.

Sect. IV. Times, places and manner of holding elections for Senators and Representatives shall be prescribed in each State by the Legislature thereof; but the Congress may at any time by law make or alter such regulations, except as to the places of choosing Senators. The Congress shall assemble at least once in every year, and such meeting shall be on the first Monday in December, unless they shall by law appoint a different day.

Sect. V.—1. Each House shall be the judge of the elections, returns, and qualifications of its own members, and a majority of each shall constitute a quorum to do business; but a smaller number may adjourn from day to day, and may be authorised to compel the attendance of absent members, in such manner and under such penalties as each House may provide.

General Rules.

2. Each House may determine the rules of its proceedings, punish its members for disorderly behavior, and, with the concurrence of two-thirds, expel a member.

3. Each House shall keep a journal of its proceedings, and from time to time publish the same, excepting such parts as may in their judgment require secrecy; and the yeas and nays of the members of either House on any question shall, at the desire of one-fifth of those present, be entered on the journal.

4. Neither House, during the session of Congress, shall, without the consent of the other, adjourn for more than three days, nor to any other place than that in which the two Houses shall be sitting.

Sect. VI—1. The Senators and Representatives shall receive a compensation for their services, to be ascertained by law, and paid out of the Treasury of the United States. They shall in all cases, except treason, felony, and breach of the peace, be privileged from arrest during their attendance at the session of their respective Houses, and in going to or returning from the same; and for any speech or debate in either House, they shall not be questioned in any other place.

2. No Senator or Representative shall, during the time for which he was elected, be appointed to any civil office under the authority of the United States, which shall have been created, or the emoluments whereof shall have been increased during such time; and no person holding any office under the United States shall be a member of either House during his continuance in office.

Sect. VII—1. All bills for raising revenue shall originate in the House of Representatives, but the Senate may propose or concur with amendments as on other bills.

How Law is Made.

2. Every bill which shall have passed the House of Representatives and the Senate, shall, before it becomes a law, be presented to the President of the United States. If he approve, he shall sign it; but if not, he shall return it, with his objections, to that House in which it shall have originated, who shall enter the objections at large on their journal, and proceed to reconsider it. If, after such reconsideration, two-thirds of that House shall agree to pass the bill, it shall be sent, together with the objections, to the other House, by which it shall likewise be reconsidered, and if approved by two-thirds of that House, it shall become a law. But in all such cases the votes of both Houses shall be determined by yeas and nays, and the names of the persons voting for and against the bill shall be entered on the journal of each House respectively. If any bill shall not be returned by the President within ten days (Sundays excepted) after it shall have been presented to him, the same shall be a law, in like manner as if he had signed it, unless the Congress, by their adjournment, prevent its return, in which case it shall not be a law.

3. Every order, resolution, or vote to which the concurrence of the Senate and House of Representatives may be necessary (except on a question of adjournment) shall be presented to the President of the United States; and before the same shall take effect, shall be approved by him, or, being disapproved by him, shall be repassed by two-thirds of the Senate and House of Representatives, according to the rules and limitations prescribed in the case of a bill.

The Powers of Congress.

Sect. VIII. The Congress shall have power—

1. To lay and collect taxes, duties, imposts and excises, to pay the debts and provide for the common defense and general welfare of the United States; but all duties, imposts, and excises, shall be uniform throughout the United States;

2. To borrow money on the credit of the United States;

3. To regulate commerce with foreign nations and among the several States, and with the Indian tribes;

4. To establish a uniform rule of naturalisation, and uniform laws on the subject of bankruptcy throughout the United States.

5. To coin money, regulate the value thereof, and of foreign coin, and fix the standard of weights and measures;

6. To provide for the punishment of counterfeiting the securities and current coin of the United States;

7. To establish post offices and post roads;

8. To promote the progress of science and useful arts, by securing for limited times to authors and inventors the exclusive right to their respective writings and discoveries.

9. To constitute tribunals inferior to the Supreme Court;

10. To define and punish piracies and felonies committed on the high seas, and offenses against the law of nations;

11. To declare war, grant letters of marque and reprisal, and make rules concerning captures on land and water,

12. To raise and support armies, but no appropriations of money to that use shall be for a longer term than two years;

13. To provide and maintain a navy;

14. To make rules for the government and regulation of the land and naval forces,

15. To provide for calling forth the militia to execute the laws of the Union, suppress insurrections, and repel invasions;

16. To provide for organizing, arming, and disciplining the militia, and for governing such parts of them as may be employed in the service of the United States, reserving to the States respectively, the appointment of the officers, and the authority of training the militia according to the discipline prescribed by Congress.

17. To exercise exclusive legislation in all cases whatsoever, over such district (not exceeding ten miles square) as may, by cession of particular States and the acceptance of Congress, become the seat of government of the United States, and to exercise like authority over all places purchased by the consent of the Legislature of the State in which the same shall be, for the erection of forts, magazines, arsenals, dock-yards, and other needful buildings; and,

18. To make all laws which shall be necessary and proper for carrying into execution the foregoing powers and all other powers vested by this Constitution in the Government of the United States, or in any department or officers thereof.

Emigration and Taxes.

Sect. IX.—1. The migration or importation of such persons as any of the States now existing shall think proper to admit, shall not be prohibited by the Congress prior to the year one thousand eight hundred and eight, but a tax or duty may be imposed on such importation, not exceeding ten dollars for each person.

2. The privilege of the writ of habeas corpus shall not be suspended, unless when in cases of rebellion or invasion the public safety may require it.

3. No bill of attainder or ex post facto law shall be passed.

4. No capitation, or other direct tax shall be laid, unless in proportion to the census or enumeration hereinbefore directed to be taken.

5. No tax or duty shall be laid on articles exported from any State. No preference shall be given by any regulation of commerce or revenue to the ports of one State over those of another: nor shall vessels bound to or from one State, be obliged to enter, clear, or pay duties in another.

6. No money shall be drawn from the Treasury, but in consequence of appropriations made by laws; and a regular statement and account of the receipts and expenditures of all public money shall be published from time to time.

Titles Forbidden.

7. No title of nobility shall be granted by the United States, and no person holding any office of profit or trust under them shall, without the consent of the Congress, accept of any present, emolument, office, or title, of any kind whatever, from any king, prince or foreign state.

Sect. X.—1. No State shall enter into any treaty, alliance, or confederation; grant letters of marque and reprisal; coin money; emit bills of credit; make anything but gold and silver coin a tender in payment of debts; pass any bill of attainder, ex post facto law, or law impairing the obligation of contracts, or grant any title of nobility.

2. No State shall, without the consent of the Congress, lay any impost or duties on imports or exports, except what may be absolutely necessary for executing its inspection laws; and the net produce of all duties and imposts, laid by any State on imports or exports, shall be for the use of the Treasury of the United States, and all such laws shall be subject to the revision and control of the Congress.

3. No State shall, without the consent of Congress, lay any duty of tonnage, keep troops or ships of war, in time of peace, enter into any agreement or compact with another State, or with a foreign power, or engage in war, unless actually invaded, or in such imminent danger as will not admit of delay.

Election of President.

ARTICLE II.—Sect. I.—1. The executive power shall be vested in a President of the United States of America. He shall hold his office during the term of four years, and together with the Vice-President, chosen for the same term, be elected, as follows:

2. Each State shall appoint, in such manner as the Legislature thereof may direct, a number of electors, equal to the whole number of Senators and Representatives to which the State may be entitled in the Congress; but no Senator or Representative, or person holding an office of trust or profit under the United States shall be appointed an elector.

3. (Annulled, see amendments, Article XII.)

4. The Congress may determine the time of choosing the electors, and the day on which they shall give their votes: which day shall be the same throughout the United States.

5. No person except a natural-born citizen, or a citizen of the United States at the time of the adoption of this Constitution, shall be eligible to the office of President; neither shall any person be eligible to that office who shall not have attained to the age of thirty-five years, and been fourteen years a resident within the United States.

6. In case of the removal of the President from office, or of his death, resignation, or inability to discharge the powers and duties of the said office, the same shall devolve on the Vice-President, and the Congress may by law provide for the case of removal, death, resignation, or inability, both of the President and Vice-President, declaring what officer shall then act as President, and such officer shall act accordingly, until the disability be removed, or a President shall be elected.

7. The President shall, at stated times, receive for his services, a compensation, which shall neither be increased or diminished during the period for which he shall have been elected, and he shall not receive within that period, any other emolument from the United States, or any of them.

8. Before he enters on the execution of his office, he shall take the following oath or affirmation:

"I DO SOLEMNLY SWEAR (OR AFFIRM) THAT I WILL FAITHFULLY EXECUTE THE OFFICE OF THE PRESIDENT OF THE UNITED STATES; AND WILL, TO THE BEST OF MY ABILITY, PRESERVE, PROTECT, AND DEFEND THE CONSTITUTION OF THE UNITED STATES."

Powers of the President.

Sect. II.—1. The President shall be commander-in-chief of the army and navy of the United States, and of the militia of the several States when called into the actual service of the United States; he may require the opinion, in writing, of the principal officer in each of the executive departments, upon any subject relating to the duties of their respective offices, and he shall have power to grant reprieves and pardons for offenses against the United States, except in cases of impeachment.

2. He shall have power, by and with the advice and consent of the Senate, to make treaties, provided two-thirds of the Senators present concur; and he shall nominate, and by and with the advice and consent of the Senate, shall appoint embassadors and other public ministers and consuls, judges of the Supreme Court, and all other officers of the United States, whose appointments are not herein otherwise provided for, and which shall be established by law; but the Congress may, by law, vest the appointment of such inferior officers as they think proper, in the President alone, in the courts of law, or in the heads of departments.

3. The President shall have power to fill up all vacancies that may happen during the recess of the Senate, by granting commissions which shall expire at the end of their next session.

Sect. III. He shall from time to time give to the Congress information of the state of the Union, and recommend to their consideration, such measures as he shall judge necessary and expedient; he may, on extraordinary occasions, convene both Houses, or either of them, and in case of disagreement between them, with respect to the time of adjournment, he may adjourn them to such time as he shall think proper; he shall receive embassadors and other public ministers; he shall take care that the laws be faithfully executed and shall commission all officers of the United States.

Sect. IV. The President, Vice-President, and all civil officers of the United States, shall be removed from office on impeachment for, and conviction of, treason, bribery, or other high crimes and misdemeanors.

Administration of Justice.

ARTICLE III.—Sect. I. The Judicial power of the United States, shall be vested in one Supreme Court, and in such inferior courts as the Congress may from time to time ordain and establish. The Judges, both of the Supreme and Inferior Courts, shall hold their offices during good behavior, and shall, at stated times, receive for their services a compensation, which shall not be diminished during their continuance in office.

Sect. II.—1. The Judicial power shall extend to all cases in law and equity, arising under this Constitution, the laws of the United States, and treaties made, or which shall be made, under their authority; to all cases affecting embassadors, other public ministers and consuls; to all cases of admiralty and maritime jurisdiction; to controversies to which the United States shall be a party; to controversies between two or more States; between a State and citizens of another State; between citizens of different States; between citizens of the same State claiming lands under grants of different States, and between a State or the citizens thereof and foreign States, citizens, or subjects.

2. In all cases affecting embassadors, other public ministers and consuls, and those in which a State shall be a party, the Supreme Court shall have original jurisdiction. In all the other cases before mentioned, the Supreme Court shall have appellate jurisdiction, both as to law and fact, with such exceptions, and under such regulations as the Congress shall make.

3. The trial of all crimes, except in cases of impeachment, shall be by jury; and such trial shall be held in the State where the said crimes shall have been committed; but when not committed within any State, the trial shall be at such place or places as the Congress may by law have directed.

Sect. III.—1. Treason against the United States shall consist only in levying war against them, or in adhering to their enemies, giving them aid and comfort. No person shall be convicted of treason unless on the testimony of two witnesses to the same overt act, or on confession in open court.

2. The Congress shall have power to declare the punishment of treason, but no attainder of treason shall work corruption of blood or forfeiture, except during the life of the person attainted.

Rights of the Several States.

ARTICLE IV.—Sect. I. Full faith and credit shall be given in each State to the public acts, records and judicial proceedings of every other State. And the Congress may by general laws, prescribe the manner in which such acts, records and proceedings shall be proved, and the effect thereof.

Sect. II.—1. The citizens of each State shall be entitled to all privileges and immunities of citizens in the several States.

2. A person charged in any State with treason, felony, or other crime, who shall flee from justice and be found in another State, shall, on demand of the executive authority of the State from which he fled, be delivered up, to be removed to the State having jurisdiction of the crime.

3. No person held to service or labor in one State under the laws thereof, escaping into another, shall, in consequence of any law or regulation therein, be discharged from such service or labor, but shall be delivered up on claim of the party to whom such service or labor may be due.

Sect. III.—1. New States may be admitted by the Congress of this Union; but no new States shall be formed or erected within the jurisdiction of any other State; nor any State be formed by the junction of two or more States, or parts of States, without the consent of the Legislatures of the States concerned as well as of the Congress.

2. The Congress shall have power to dispose of and make all needful rules and regulations respecting the territory or other property belonging to the United States; and nothing in this Constitution shall be so construed as to prejudice any claims of the United States, or of any particular State.

Sect. IV. The United States shall guarantee to every State in this Union a Republican form of government, and shall protect each of them against invasion; and on application of the Legislature or of the executive (when the Legislature cannot be convened), against domestic violence.

How Amendments May be Made.

ARTICLE V. The Congress, whenever two-thirds of both Houses shall deem it necessary, shall propose amendments to this Constitution, or, on the application of the Legislatures of two-thirds of the several States, shall call a convention for proposing amendments, which, in either case, shall be valid to all intents and purposes, as part of this Constitution, when ratified by the Legislatures of three-fourths of the several States, or by conventions in three-fourths thereof, as the one or the other mode of ratification may be proposed by the Congress; provided that no amendment which may be made prior to the year one thousand eight hundred and eight, shall in any manner affect the first and fourth clauses in the ninth section of the first article; and that no State, without its consent shall be deprived of its equal suffrage in the Senate.

ARTICLE VI.—1. All debts contracted, and engagements entered into, before the adoption of this Constitution, shall be as valid against the United States under this Constitution, as under the confederation.

2. This Constitution, and the laws of the United States which shall be made in pursuance thereof; and all treaties made or which shall be made, under authority of the United States, shall be the supreme law of the land; and the judges in every State shall be bound thereby, anything in the constitution or laws of any State to the contrary notwithstanding.

3. The Senators and Representatives before mentioned, and the members of the several State Legislatures, and all executive and judicial officers both of the United States and of the several States, shall be bound by oath or affirmation to support this Constitution; but no religious test shall ever be required as a qualification to any office or public trust under the United States.

ARTICLE VII. The ratification of the conventions of nine States, shall be sufficient for the establishment of this Constitution between the States so ratifying the same.

AMENDMENTS TO THE CONSTITUTION.

ARTICLE I. Congress shall make no law respecting an establishment of religion, or prohibiting the free exercise thereof; or abridging the freedom of speech or of the press; or the right of the people peaceably to assemble and to petition the government for a redress of grievances.

ARTICLE II. A well regulated militia being necessary to the security of a free State, the right of the people to keep and bear arms shall not be infringed.

ARTICLE III. No soldier shall, in time of peace, be quartered in any house without the consent of the owner, nor in time of war, but in a manner to be prescribed by law.

ARTICLE IV. The right of the people to be secure in their persons, houses, papers, and effects, against unreasonable searches and seizures, shall not be violated; and no warrants shall issue, but upon probable cause, supported by oath or affirmation, and particularly describing the place to be searched, and the persons or things to be seized.

ARTICLE V. No person shall be held to answer for a capital or otherwise infamous crime, unless on a presentment or indictment of a Grand Jury, except in cases arising in the land or naval forces, or in the militia, when in actual service in time of war or public danger; nor shall any person be subject for the same offense to be twice put in jeopardy of life or limb; nor shall be compelled in any criminal case to be a witness against himself, nor be deprived of life, liberty, or property, without due process of law; nor shall private property be taken for public use, without just compensation.

Trial by Jury.

ARTICLE VI. In all criminal prosecutions, the accused shall enjoy the right to a speedy and public trial, by an impartial jury of the State and district wherein the crime shall have been committed, which district shall have been previously ascertained by law, and to be informed of the nature and cause of the accusation; to be confronted with the witnesses against him; to have compulsory process for obtaining witnesses in his favor; and to have the assistance of counsel for his defense.

ARTICLE VII. In suits at common law, where the value in controversy shall exceed twenty dollars, the right of trial by jury shall be preserved, and no fact tried by a jury shall be otherwise re-examined in any court of the United States, than according to the rules of the common law.

ARTICLE VIII. Excessive bail shall not be required, nor excessive fines imposed, nor cruel and unusual punishments inflicted.

ARTICLE IX. The enumeration, in the Constitution, of certain rights, shall not be construed to deny or disparage others retained by the people.

ARTICLE X. The powers not delegated to the United States by the Constitution, nor prohibited by it to the States, are reserved to the States respectively, or to the people.

ARTICLE XI. The judicial power of the United States shall not be construed to extend to any suit in law or equity, commenced or prosecuted against one of the United States by citizens of another State, or by citizens or subjects of any foreign State.

The Electoral Vote.

ARTICLE XII.—1. The electors shall meet in their respective States, and vote by ballot for President and Vice-President, one of whom at least shall not be an inhabitant of the same State with themselves. They shall name in their ballots the person voted for as President, and in distinct ballots the person voted for as Vice-President; and they shall make distinct lists of all persons voted for as President, and of all persons voted for as Vice President, and of the number of votes for each, which lists they shall sign and certify, and transmit sealed to the seat of the Government of the United States, directed to the President of the Senate. The President of the Senate shall, in the presence of the Senate and House of Representatives, open all the certificates, and the votes shall then be counted. The person having the greatest number of votes for President shall be the President, if such number be a majority of the whole number of electors appointed; and if no persons have such majority, then from the persons having the highest numbers, not exceeding three on the list of those voted for as President, the House of Representatives shall choose immediately, by ballot, the President. But in choosing the President, the votes shall be taken by States, the representation from each State having one vote. A quorum for this purpose shall consist of a member or members from two-thirds of the States, and a majority of all the States shall be necessary to a choice. And if the House of Representatives shall not choose a President whenever the right of choice shall devolve upon them, before the fourth day of March next following, then the Vice President shall act as President, as in the case of the death or other constitutional disability of the President.

2. The person having the greatest number of votes as Vice-President shall be the Vice President, if such number be a majority of the whole number of electors appointed, and if no person have a majority, then from the two highest numbers on the list, the Senate shall choose a Vice-President. A quorum for the purpose shall consist of two-thirds of the whole number of Senators, and a majority of the whole number shall be necessary to a choice.

3. But no person constitutionally ineligible to the office of President, shall be eligible to that of Vice-President of the United States.

ARTICLE XIII.—1. Neither slavery nor involuntary servitude, except as a punishment for crime, whereof the party shall have been duly convicted, shall exist within the United States or any place subject to their jurisdiction.

2. Congress shall have power to enforce this article by appropriate legislation.

Who are Citizens.

ARTICLE XIV.—Sect. 1. All persons born or naturalized in the United States, and subject to the jurisdiction thereof, are citizens of the United States and of the State in which they reside. No State shall make or enforce any law which shall abridge the privileges or immunities of citizens of the United States. Nor shall any State deprive any person of life, liberty, or property, without due process of law, nor deny to any person within its jurisdiction the equal protection of the laws.

Sect. II. Representatives shall be apportioned among the several States according to their respective numbers, counting the whole number of persons in each State, excluding Indians not taxed. But when the right to vote at any election for the choice of electors for President and Vice-President of the United States, Representatives in Congress, the executive and judicial officers of a State, or the members of the Legislatures thereof, is denied to any of the male inhabitants of such a State, being twenty-one years of age and citizens of the United States, or in any way abridged, except for participation in rebellion or other crime, the basis of representation therein shall be reduced in the proportion which the number of such male citizens shall bear to the whole number of male citizens twenty-one years of age in such State.

Sect. III. No person shall be a Senator or Representative in Congress, or elector of President and Vice-President, or hold any office, civil or military, under the United States or under any State, who, having previously taken an oath as a member of Congress, or as an officer of any State Legislature, or as an executive or judicial officer of any State, to support the Constitution of the United States, shall have engaged in insurrection or rebellion against the same, or given aid or comfort to the enemies thereof, but Congress may, by a vote of two-thirds of each House, remove such disability.

What Debts Shall be Paid.

Sect. IV. The validity of the public debt of the United States, authorized by law, including debts incurred for payment of pensions and bounties for services in suppressing insurrection or rebellion, shall not be questioned; but neither the United States nor any State shall assume or pay any debt or obligation incurred in aid of insurrection or rebellion against the United States, or any claim for the loss or emancipation of any slave; but all such debts, obligations, and claims, shall be held illegal and void.

Sect. V. The Congress shall have power to enforce, by appropriate legislation, the provisions of this article.

ARTICLE XV.—Sect. I. The right of citizens of the United States to vote shall not be denied or abridged by the United States or any State on account of race, color, or previous condition of servitude.

Sect. II. The Congress shall have power to enforce this article by appropriate legislation.

The First Congresses.

THE first Continental Congress, formed while the thirteen colonies were yet under British dominion, exerted no political influence, and had no part in the government of the United States, for it dissolved before the signing of the Declaration of Independence. It met in Carpenters' Hall, Philadelphia, Pa., September 5, 1774, and adjourned October 26, the same year.

The second Congress assembled at the Pennsylvania State House, Philadelphia, May 10, 1775, and on July 4, 1776, adopted the Declaration of Independence.

The third Congress was held at Baltimore, Md., beginning December 20, 1776.

The fourth Congress opened at Philadelphia, March 4, 1777.

The fifth Congress began its session at Lancaster, Pa., September 27, 1777.

The sixth Congress met at York, Pa., September 30, 1777.

The seventh Congress gathered at Philadelphia, July 2, 1778.

The eighth Congress was held at Princeton, N. J., June 30, 1783.

The ninth Congress opened at Annapolis, Md., November 26, 1783, and here, December 23, 1783, Washington resigned his office of commander-in-chief of the army.

The tenth Congress began at Trenton, N. J., November 1, 1784.

The eleventh Congress assembled at the City Hall, in New York, January 11, 1785, where the new government was organized, and Washington, the first president, was inaugurated in 1789. The Federal capital remained at New York until 1790.

Congress met again at Philadelphia, December 6, 1790, and the seat of government remained here until 1800, at which time the Federal capital was permanently established at Washington, D. C., Congress first assembling in that city November 17, 1800.

The First Presidential Election.

EACH of the thirteen original States having duly accepted the Federal Constitution, it was ratified by Congress, and went into operation in 1789. At this time public opinion pointed unmistakably to General Washington as the first President of the new republic. The first Wednesday of January, 1789, was set apart for the choice of presidential electors in each of the States by the voters thereof; the first Wednesday of February, 1789, was fixed upon for the selection of a President by the chosen electors, and the first Wednesday of March, 1789, as the date when the new administration of governmental affairs should commence operations.

The first Congress of the Federal Union met without a quorum in the House of Representatives, and did not organize until March 30, 1789, nor did the Senate convene until April 6, following, at which time presidential ballots were counted. All the States, except New York (which neglected, through indifference, to hold an election), had chosen presidential electors, and Washington was their unanimous choice for President, receiving sixty-nine votes, while John Adams, having received thirty-four votes, was declared Vice-President.

April 30, 1789, the new executive officers were publicly inaugurated at the City Hall, in New York; and thus the Republic began its long career of prosperity, with a government as complete as that of either Great Britain or France.

Duties of Principal Federal Officers.

IN ORDER to become acquainted with the general government of the country, the reader should first carefully study the Constitution of the United States, which is herewith given, with headings, displayed in a manner such as to make it easily understood.

To become familiar with the State, county, town and municipal government, and the duties of persons in the several State, county, town and city offices, the student should acquaint himself or herself with the Constitution of the State in which he or she may be a resident, and follow with a reading of the statutes of that particular State.

The object of this chapter is to give the reader an understanding of the duties of some of the leading federal officers, together with a view of the manner in which Congressional law is made and the country governed.

The article on the duties of Congressmen very fully reveals the method of procedure in the passage of bills that make up the laws of the land, some of which may be only for personal benefit, while others are necessary and are framed for the general good.

Through laws thus passed by Congress, have the general federal offices been created. The succeeding pages quite fully outline the frame-work of the general government.

President's Mansion, Washington, D. C.

The President of the United States.

1st President. 2d President.

3d President. 4th President.

5th President. 6th President.

7th President. 8th President.

9th President. 10th President.

POLK 11th President. TAYLOR 12th President.

FILLMORE 13th President. PIERCE 14th President.

BUCHANAN 15th President. LINCOLN 16th President.

17th President. GRANT 18th President.

HAYES 19th President. GARFIELD 20th President.

THE PRESIDENT must be thirty-five years old, a native of the United States, and a resident of the United States fourteen years.

He holds office for four years, and swears to preserve, protect and defend the Constitution of the United States, to the best of his ability.

He is commander-in-chief of the army and navy of the United States, and of the militia of the several States, when it is called into actual service of the nation; and may require the opinion, in writing, of the principal officer in each of the executive departments upon any subject relating to the duties of their respective offices.

He has power to grant pardons for offenses against the United States, except in cases of impeachment; has power, by and with the advice and consent of the United States Senate, to make treaties (provided that two-thirds of the Senators present concur); and shall nominate and, by and with the advice and consent of the Senate, appoint ambassadors, ministers, and consuls to foreign countries, judges of the Supreme Court of the United States, and all other officers of the United States, whose appointments are not otherwise provided for in other ways or established by law. If vacancies occur during the recess of the Senate, the President may grant commissions to new appointees which shall expire at the end of the next session of the Senate.

From time to time he is to give Congress information of the state of the Union, and recommend such legislation as shall to him seem necessary and expedient; on extraordinary occasions, or in a national emergency, he may call either house of Congress, or both, as he pleases, to convene, and if they disagree as to the time when they shall adjourn, he may adjourn them, as he may deem best.

He shall sign all bills passed by Congress before they can become law; but he may return to the house where it originated, any bill, order, or resolution, with his objections, which he cannot approve. If he fails to sign it, or return it to Congress within ten days after its passage, it becomes a law without his approval.

His term of office begins on the 4th day of March next succeeding his election; his salary shall be $50,000 a year, to be paid monthly, and he has the use of the furniture and other effects, belonging to the United States, that are usually kept in the President's mansion, known as the "White House," at Washington, where he resides.

The President's official house-

hold, at annual salaries, such persons being selected by himself, consists of the following officers:

ARTHUR.

1 Secretary	$3,250
1 Assistant	2,250
2 Clerks	2,000
1 Stenographer	1,800
1 Steward	1,800
1 Clerk	1,800
1 Clerk	1,600
1 Clerk	1,200
1 Usher	1,400
2 Doorkeepers, etc.	1,200
1 Watchman	900
1 Fireman	864

Duties of the Vice-President and Cabinet Officers.

Their Eligibility, Requirements and Privileges.

THE Vice-President is elected at the same time and by the same process as the President of the United States. No man who is ineligible for the office of President can be elected Vice-President. He goes into office with the President, and their terms of office expire on the same day.

In case the President resigns or dies, or becomes unable to exercise the functions of his office, or is removed from it, the duties of his position shall be performed by the Vice-President during the remainder of the term for which both were elected. In case both die or resign or become unable to perform the duties required of them, or are removed from office, Congress has the power to declare by law what other officer shall then act as President.

The Vice-President is, by virtue of his office, the President of the United States Senate, and in case of his death, removal, resignation, or inability, the Senate may elect a presiding officer of the Senate, who shall also be President of the United States should any cause create a vacancy in that office. The Vice-President may be removed from his office on impeachment for, and conviction of, treason, bribery, or other high crimes or misdemeanors.

As presiding officer of the Senate, he cannot vote except when there is an equal division of the Senate on any question, and his vote is decisive.

It is his duty, also, as presiding officer of the Senate, to open, in the presence of the assembled Senate and House of Representatives, all the certificates of the election of the President and Vice-President of the United States, and superintend the counting of the votes accompanying the certificates.

Officers of the Cabinet.

Duties of the Several Members of the President's Cabinet.

THE EXECUTIVE departments of the United States government are seven in number: the Department of State, the Department of War, the Department of the Treasury, the Department of Justice, the Department of the Navy, the Department of the Interior, the Post-office Department. The Department of Justice is governed by the Attorney-General, the Post-office Department by the Postmaster-General, and the others by secretaries, respectively. Each head of a department is entitled to a salary of $8,000 a year, payable monthly.

The head of each department is authorized to prescribe regulations, not inconsistent with law, for its government, the conduct of its officers and clerks, the distribution and performance of its business, and the custody, use and preservation of the records, papers and property pertaining to it.

From the first day of October until the first day of April, in each year, all the bureaus and offices in the State, War, Treasury, Navy and Post-office Departments, and in the General Land Office (at Washington) are required to be open for the transaction of the public business at least eight hours in each day; and from the first day of April until the first day of October, in each year, at least ten hours in each day, except Sundays and days designated by law as public holidays.

The clerks in the departments are arranged in four classes, distinguished as the first, second, third and fourth classes. No clerk can be appointed in either of these classes, in any department, until he has been examined and found qualified by a board of three examiners, consisting of the chief of the bureau or office into which such clerk is to be appointed, and two other clerks to be selected by the head of the department. Women may, at the discretion of the head of any department, be appointed to any of the clerkships therein authorized by law, upon the same qualifications, requisites and conditions, and with the same compensations as are prescribed for men. Each head of a department may, from time to time, alter the distribution among the various bureaus and offices of his department of the clerks prescribed by law, as he may find it proper and necessary so to do.

Clerks and employes in the departments, whose compensation is not otherwise prescribed, receive the following salaries per year:

First Class Clerks, $1,200 | Fourth Class Clks.. $1,800 | Asst. Messengers... $720
Second do .. 1,400 | Women Clerks..... 900 | Laborers 720
Third do .. 1,600 | Messengers .... 840 | Watchmen 720

Temporary clerks, performing duties similar to those in either class, are entitled to a salary of the same rate as permanent clerks.

Each head of a department is authorized to employ as many clerks of all classes, and such other employes, at such rates of compensation, respectively, as Congress may, from year to year, appropriate money for paying them. No money can be paid to any clerk employed in either department at an annual salary, as compensation for extra services, unless expressly authorized by law. Further restrictions are also placed upon the employment of extra and temporary clerks and subordinate assistants in the departments, and the law prescribes the rates of their compensation, in case their employment becomes necessary.

The chief clerks in the several departments and bureaus and other offices connected therewith have supervision, under their immediate superior, over the duties of the other clerks therein, and see that they are faithfully performed. And it is also the business of the chief clerks to take care, from time to time, that the duties of the other clerks are distributed among them with equality and uniformity, according to the nature of the case. The chief clerks also report monthly to their superior officers any existing defects that they may know of in the arrangement or dispatch of the public business; and each head of a department, chief of a bureau, or other superior officer must examine the facts as stated, and take proper measures to amend such existing defects.

The disbursing clerks authorized by law in any department are appointed by the heads of the departments from clerks of the fourth class. Each of these clerks is required to give a bond to the United States for the faithful discharge of the duties of his office, according to law, in such amount as may be directed by the Secretary of the Treasury, and with sureties approved by the Solicitor of the Treasury, and renew, strengthen and increase the amount of such bond, from time to time, as the Secretary of the Treasury may direct.

Each disbursing clerk, except the one employed in the Treasury Department, may, when so directed by the head of his department, superintend the building which it occupies.

Each disbursing clerk, in addition to his salary as a clerk of the fourth class, is entitled to receive $200 more a year, or $2,000 in all.

In case of the death, resignation, absence or sickness of the head of any department, the first or sole assistant thereof, unless the President directs otherwise, performs the duties of such head until a successor is appointed or the sickness or absence ceases.

In case of the death, resignation, absence or sickness of the chief of any bureau, or any officer thereof whose appointment is not vested in the head of the department, the assistant or deputy of such chief or officer, or his chief clerk, may perform the duties of his superior, unless the President orders otherwise.

The President, in case of the vacancies created as above mentioned, may authorize and direct the head of any other department, or any other officer in either department (whose appointment is vested in the President) to perform the duties of the vacant office until a successor is appointed, or the sickness or absence of the incumbent ceases. But no vacancy of this kind, occasioned by death or resignation, may be temporarily filled for a longer time than ten days. And any officer performing the duties of another office, during such vacancy, is not entitled to any compensation beyond his own proper salary.

Officers or clerks of any department, when lawfully detailed to investigate frauds or attempts to defraud the government, or any official misconduct or irregularity, are authorized to administer oaths to witnesses; and any head of a department or bureau may, when any investigation in his department requires it, subpœna witnesses before the proper officer, to testify in the case, and resort to compulsion by the court to enforce the attendance of such witnesses. Heads of departments or bureaus are furnished the necessary legal assistance by the Attorney-General; and evidence is to be furnished by the departments in suits pending in the court of claims.

Each department is allowed to expend $100 a year for newspapers, to be filed in that department. The head of each department makes an annual report to Congress, giving a detailed statement of the manner in which the contingent fund for his department has been expended, the names of every person to whom any of it has been

President Lincoln and His Cabinet.

THE above pictorial illustration is from F. B. Carpenter's painting, made at the White House, in Washington, in 1864, representing the memorable meeting of Lincoln and his cabinet assembled to listen to the first reading of the Emancipation Proclamation.

Some of the sketches will be readily recognized. In the picture William H. Seward, Secretary of State, who sits in front of the table, is evidently considering certain features of the document. Edwin M. Stanton, head of the War Department, sitting at the extreme left, listens intently; so, also does Salmon P. Chase, Secretary of the Treasury, who stands with arms folded. Lincoln, as he sits with paper in hand, is all attention; so is Gideon Welles, head of the Navy, who, in long, white beard, sits opposite Seward. Caleb Smith, Secretary of the Interior, stands next to Welles; Montgomery Blair, Postmaster-General, stands beside Smith, and Edward Bates, Attorney-General sits at the extreme right.

Altogether the faces and the scene represented will go down into the future as one of the memorable events connected with the efforts made for the preservation of the American Union in the dark and troublous days of the rebellion.

paid, the nature of the service rendered, the kind of property furnished, and its price, etc. ; he also reports to Congress, annually, the names of the clerks and other persons who have been employed in his department and its offices, the time and manner of their employment, the sums paid to each, whether they have been useful, need to be removed, etc.

The Secretaries of State, the Treasury, the Interior, War and Navy, the Postmaster-General, the Attorney-General and the Commissioner of Agriculture, are required to keep a complete inventory of all the property belonging to the United States in the buildings, rooms, offices and grounds occupied by them, respectively, and under their charge, as well as an account of the sale or other disposition of

any of such property, except supplies of stationery and fuel in the public offices, and books, pamphlets and papers in the library of Congress.

The head of each department is required, as soon as practicable after the last day of September, in the year whenever a new Congress assembles, to cause to be filed in the office of the Secretary of the Interior, a full and complete list of all officers, agents, clerks and employes in his department, or in any of the offices or bureaus connected with it. Such list must include, also, all the statistics peculiar to his department required to enable the Secretary of the Interior to prepare the Biennial Register.

THE SECRETARY OF STATE.

A Summary of His Duties.

HE duties of the Secretary of State are from time to time prescribed by the President of the United States, and relate principally to carrying on correspondence, issuing commissions or instructions to or with public ministers or consuls from the United States or to negotiations with public ministers from foreign states or princes, or to memorials or other applications from foreigners, or to such other matters respecting foreign affairs as the President of the United States assigns to the department; and he conducts the business of the department in such manner as the President shall direct. He has custody of the seal of the United States, and of the seal of the Department of State, and of all the books, records, papers, furniture, fixtures and other property in or belonging to the department.

When the President has approved and signed any bill, order, resolution or vote passed by Congress, or which becomes a law in any other prescribed manner, the Secretary of State shall receive it from the President or the Speaker of the House of Representatives, and give it due publication in print in the manner ordered by law. Also, when any new amendment to the national Constitution has been legally adopted, the Secretary of State shall give it due publication as prescribed in the statutes.

Annual Reports.

He shall report annually to Congress the following particulars:

An abstract of all the returns made to him pursuant to law by customs collectors at the various ports of the country, of seamen registered by them, and impressments of seamen and detention of vessels by foreign authorities.

A statement of all such changes and modifications in the commercial systems of other nations, in any manner made, as shall have been communicated to his department.

Important information communicated by diplomatic and consular officers if he deems it valuable for publication to the people.

A full list of all consular officers.

A report of any rates or tariff of fees to be received by diplomatic or consular officers, prescribed by the President during the preceding year.

A statement of such fees as have been collected and accounted for by such officers during the preceding year.

A statement of lists of passengers arriving in the United States from foreign places, returned to him every three months by collectors of customs.

Names of any consular officers of foreign citizenship who may have been employed under salaries, and the circumstances of their appointment.

A statement of expenditures from the contingent fund required to be made by him, which must include all the contingent expenses of foreign intercourse and of all foreign ministers and their offices, except such expenditures as are settled upon the certificate of the President.

Every act of Congress that becomes a law of the land by regular process, together with every foreign treaty, postal convention, or congressional joint resolution adopted, must be sent to the public printer for legal publication by the Secretary of State, who is also to publish in one or more newspapers (not exceeding three) such commercial information that he may receive from diplomatic and consular officers as he may consider important to the public interests.

Passports.

It is from this department, also, that passports are furnished, free of charge, to all persons who desire to travel in foreign countries where passports are necessary. Copies of records in this department are copied by clerks for all persons at a cost to the applicant of ten cents for each 100 words in the desired statement.

Annual Salaries of Assistant Officers.

The subordinate officers of this department, with their salaries, are as follows:

3 Asst. Secretaries $3,500	11 Clerks $1,800	3 Clerks $1,600
1 Chief Clerk..... 3,500	4 do 1,600	10 do 900
1 Translator..... 2,100	9 do 1,400	1 Engineer 1,000
4 Bureau Chiefs.. 2,100	10 do 1,000	1 Assistant 1,000
Messengers, Watchmen, Firemen, Laborers, etc., ranging from $600 to $840.

Each chief clerk has the supervision of the clerks in his bureau or division of the department, and regulates the amount and character of the duties of each, reporting particulars concerning such clerks, their short-comings, etc., to his superior officer monthly. In case of the death, removal, resignation, sickness, or incapacity of the head of any bureau, the next officer below him performs his duties until a successor is appointed.

SECRETARY OF WAR.

An Outline Sketch of His Official Work, the Number of His Assistants and their Salaries.

HE EXECUTIVE of War is appointed by the President to assist in carrying on the government of the country, and performs such duties as shall from time to time be enjoined on or intrusted to him by the President relative to military commissions, the military forces, the warlike stores of the United States, or to other matters respecting military affairs.

He must prepare and communicate to Congress estimates of necessary expenditures and needed appropriations for his department, including estimates for such sums as will be required to print and bind documents relating to his department, and for the compensation of his subordinate officers and clerks, and estimates for the construction of public works. All estimates for the public service in this and all other Cabinet departments are transmitted to Congress by the Secretary of the Treasury.

The Secretary of War has the custody and charge of all the books, records, papers, furniture, fixtures, and other property belonging to his department; controls the collection at the seat of government of all flags, standards, and military colors captured by the army from the enemies of the country; defines and prescribes the kinds and amounts of supplies to be purchased by the subsistence and quartermasters' departments of the army; regulates the transportation of supplies from the places of purchase to the several military posts or stations at which they are required, and the safe-keeping and storage of such supplies, provisions, etc., and the transportation of troops, munitions of war, equipments and stores; provides for the taking of weather observations at military stations in the interior of the continent, and other points in the States and Territories; for giving notice on the Northern lakes and sea-coast, by magnetic telegraph, of the approach and force of storms, and for the establishment and reports of signal offices in various parts of the country concerning the weather, for the benefit of agricultural and commercial interests, with telegraph lines to connect weather-reporting stations, etc. ; furnishes non-commissioned officers and soldiers who have in any manner lost their certificates of discharge from the army with duplicate certificates; details employes of the department to administer proper oaths in the settlement of officers' accounts for clothing, camp and garrison equipage, quartermasters' stores, cannon, etc.

The Secretary of War must report to Congress annually a statement of the appropriations of the preceding fiscal year (beginning always July 1) for his department, showing how much was appropriated under each specific bureau or branch of the department, and the balance that remained on hand unexpended, together with his estimates of the amounts of appropriations, specifically stated, that will probably be needed for the ensuing year, aside from what may remain of the balances in his hand; also a statement of all his official contracts for supplies or services during the preceding year, military expenses, etc.

Another important duty of the Secretary is to submit to Congress reports of river and harbor examinations and surveys made by order of Congress, with statements showing the extent to which the commerce of the country will be promoted by the contemplated improvement of these rivers and harbors, with a view to the wisest appropriation and expenditure of the public money in this direction.

Once a year, he reports to Congress an abstract of the returns of the Adjutants-General relative to the militia of the several States.

The annual reports of the Secretary to Congress are made at the beginning of each regular session, and embrace the transactions of his department during the preceding year.

The War Department is divided into branches, governed by the following army officers: The Adjutant-General, Quartermaster-General, Paymaster-General, Commissary-General, Surgeon-General, Chief of Engineers, Chief of Ordnance, and the Court of Military Justice.

Annual Salaries of Assistant Officers.

1 Chief Clerk....	$2,750	1 Printer.........	$1,600	6 Compositors ...	$1,600
1 Disbursing Clk.	2,000	95 Clerks.........	1,400	22 Clerks.........	900
7 Bureau Chiefs.	2,500	1 Engineer.......	1,600	1 Messenger	840
55 Clerks.........	1,800	290 Clerks.......	1,200	64 Messengers, etc.	780
1 Draughtsman..	1,800	2 Engineers......	1,260	50 Laborers.......	660
58 Clerks.........	1,600	1 Pressman......	1,200	8 Charwomen....	150
1 Anatomist.....	1,600	191 Clerks.......	1,000		

There are also 125 private physicians, at Washington and various military posts, who receive $100 a month, with quarters and fuel; 185 hospital stewards, at $30 to $35 a month, with rations, quarters, fuel, and clothing; about fifty paymaster's clerks, at $1,200 a year; ninety national cemetery keepers, at from $720 to $900 a year, with residence; 450 weather observers in the Signal service, at from $25 to $100 a month, with allowances; about 500 employes at armories and arsenals, and 450 clerks, superintendents, janitors of the several buildings of the department, at rates ranging from $40 to $800 a month.

Equipment, Salaries and Duties of Army Officers.

HE PRESIDENT of the United States is the commander-in-chief of the army.

The army of the United States, on a peace footing, consists of five regiments of artillery, ten regiments of cavalry, twenty-five regiments of infantry, an Adjutant-General's department, an Inspector-General's department, a Quartermaster's department, a Subsistence department, a corps of engineers, a battalion of engineer soldiers, an Ordnance department, the enlisted men of the Ordnance department, a Medical department, with its corps of hospital stewards, a Pay department, a Bureau of Military Justice, a force of Indian scouts, not exceeding 1,000; officers on the army retired list, and the Professors and corps of Cadets, and a military band at the West Point Military academy.

What Constitutes a Regiment.

A regiment of artillery consists of twelve batteries of artillery (or cannoniers), and each battery has not exceeding 122 private soldiers attached to it. One battery in each regiment is equipped as light or flying artillery, so called from the rapidity with which it can be moved: seats being contrived for the men who work it, with sufficient horses to enable them to proceed at a gallop.

A regiment of cavalry consists of twelve troops of mounted soldiers, each troop containing not more than seventy-eight enlisted privates. Two regiments of the cavalry are made up of enlisted colored privates. Any of the cavalry force may be dismounted and armed and drilled as infantry, at the discretion of the President.

A regiment of infantry consists of ten companies, each company containing from fifty to 100 privates, as the exigencies of the service may require. The enlisted men of two regiments of infantry are colored men.

There can not be in the army, at one time, more than 30,000 enlisted men.

Duty of Quartermasters.

The Quartermaster's department has charge of purchasing and distributing to the army (and marines in land service) all military stores and supplies requisite for their use, which other corps are not directed by law to provide; to furnish means of transportation for the army, its military stores and supplies, and to pay for, and to provide for and pay all incidental expenses of the military service, which other corps are not directed to provide for and pay.

The Subsistence department is in charge of picked subordinate officers, whose duty it is to receive, at each military post or place of deposit and preserve, the subsistence supplies of the army, under regulations prescribed by the Secretary of War, and to purchase and issue to the army such supplies as enter into the composition of the army ration.

Duty of Military Engineers.

The Corps of Engineers regulates and determines, with the approval of the Secretary of War, the number, quality, form, and dimensions of the necessary vehicles, pontoons, tools, implements, arms and other supplies for the use of the battalion of engineer soldiers. This battalion consists of five companies of enlisted privates of the first and second class, each company containing not more than sixty-four privates of each class. This battalion is recruited and organized, with the same limitations, provisions, allowances, and benefits, in every respect like other troops on a peace footing.

The enlisted men are instructed in, and perform the duties of, sappers, miners, and pontoonlers; aid in giving practical instruction in those branches at the West Point military academy, and may be detailed to oversee and aid laborers upon fortifications and other works in charge of the engineer corps of the government, and, as fort-keepers, to protect and repair finished fortifications; but engineers cannot assume nor be ordered on any duty beyond the line of their immediate profession, except by a special order of the President, who may also transfer engineers from one corps to another, regard being paid to rank.

Ordnance Department.

The Ordnance department has in charge the enlistment, under the direction of the Secretary of War, of master-armorers, master-carriage makers, and master-blacksmiths, who are mustered in as sergeants; subordinate armorers, carriage-makers and blacksmiths are mustered as corporals; artificers, as privates of the first-class, and laborers, as privates of the second-class. The Chief of Ordnance, subject to the approval of the Secretary of War, organises and details to other military organisations or garrisons such numbers of ordnance enlisted men, furnished with proper tools, carriages and apparatus as may be necessary, and makes regulations for their government; he also furnishes estimates, and, under the direction of the Secretary of War, makes contracts and purchases, for procuring the necessary supplies of ordnance and ordnance stores for the use of the United States army; directs the inspection and proving of the same, and the construction of all cannon and carriages, and ammunition wagons, traveling forges, arti-

ficers' wagons, and of every implement and apparatus for ordnance, and the preparation of all kinds of prescribed ammunition and ordnance stores; establishes depots of ordnance and ordnance stores, in such parts of the United States, and in such numbers as may be deemed necessary; executes, or causes to be executed, all orders of the Secretary of War, and (in time of war) the orders of any general or field officer commanding an army or detachment, for the required supply of all ordnance and ordnance stores for active service; and, half-yearly, or oftener, he makes a report to the Secretary of War of all the officers and enlisted men in his department, and of all ordnance and ordnance stores under his control.

The Army Medical Department.

The Medical department furnishes surgical or medical aid to members of the army; has supervision of the purchase and distribution of the hospital and medical supplies; unites with the line officers of the army, under the rules and regulations of the Secretary of War, in superintending the cooking done by the enlisted men; attends, under the direction of the Surgeon-General, to the proper preparation of the rations for the enlisted men; provides such quantities of fresh or preserved fruits, milk, butter and eggs, as may be necessary for the proper diet of the sick in hospitals, and trusses for ruptured soldiers or pensioners.

The Pay department is charged with the punctual payment of the troops, and is presided over by the Paymaster-General, and as many assistant paymasters as are required to perform that duty.

The Bureau of Military Justice has control of the proceedings of courts-martial, courts of military inquiry, military commissions, etc.

Salaries of Leading Army Officers.

The General of the army ranks next in command to the President in the control of the national troops. He has a salary of $13,500 a year, and selects from the army such a number of aids, not exceeding six, as he may deem necessary, who, while serving on his staff, bear the rank of colonels of cavalry.

The Lieutenant-General of the army ranks next below the General; has a salary of $11,000 a year, and is allowed to select from the army two aids and a military secretary, who rank as lieutenant-colonels of cavalry while serving on his staff.

Three Major-Generals have command under the Lieutenant-General. Each is entitled to $7,500 a year, forage for five horses, and three aids, whom he may select from captains or lieutenants in the army, whose pay over and above the pay of their rank is $200 a year.

Six Brigadier-Generals, each drawing $5,500 a year, and each having two aids, who may be selected by him from lieutenants in the army. Each draws forage for four horses.

Officers of a Regiment of Artillery.

Each regiment of artillery is commanded by one Colonel, one Lieutenant-Colonel, one Major for every four batteries, one Adjutant, one Quartermaster and Commissary, one Sergeant-Major, one Quartermaster-Sergeant, one chief musician (who is an instructor of music), and two principal musicians; the Adjutant and Quartermaster and Commissary are extra Lieutenants, selected from the first or second lieutenants of the regiment. Each battery of artillery is officered by one Captain, one First Lieutenant, one Second Lieutenant, one First Sergeant, one Quartermaster-Sergeant, four Sergeants, four Corporals, two musicians, two artificers and one wagoner; but one First Lieutenant, one Second Lieutenant, two Sergeants and four Corporals may be added to each battery, at the discretion of the President.

Officers of a Regiment of Cavalry.

Each regiment of cavalry has for its officers one Colonel, one Lieutenant-Colonel, three Majors, one Surgeon, one Assistant-Surgeon, one Adjutant, one Quartermaster, one Veterinary Surgeon (with the rank of regimental Sergeant-Major), one Sergeant-Major, one Quartermaster-Sergeant, one Saddler-Sergeant, one chief musician (who is an instructor of music), and one chief trumpeter. Two Assistant-Surgeons may be allowed to each regiment, and four regiments have an additional Veterinary Surgeon. The Adjutant and the Quartermaster of each regiment are extra Lieutenants, selected from the first or second lieutenants of the regiment. Each troop of cavalry is officered by one Captain, one First Lieutenant, one Second Lieutenant, one First Sergeant, one Quartermaster-Sergeant, five Sergeants, four Corporals, two trumpeters, two farriers, one saddler and one wagoner.

Officers of a Regiment of Infantry.

The officers of each infantry regiment consist of one Colonel, one Lieutenant-Colonel, one Major, one Adjutant, one Quartermaster, one Sergeant-Major, one Quartermaster-Sergeant, one chief musician, two principal musicians. The Adjutant and the Quartermaster are extra lieutenants, selected from the first or second lieutenants of the regiment. Each company of infantry is officered by one Captain, one First Lieutenant, one Second Lieutenant, one First Sergeant, one Quartermaster-Sergeant, four Sergeants, four Corporals, two artificers, two musicians, and one wagoner.

Salaries of Regimental Officers.

Colonels receive as compensation $3,500 a year, and forage for two horses; Lieutenant-Colonels, $3,000 a year, and forage for two horses; Majors, $2,500 a year, and forage for two horses; Captains, mounted, $2,000 a year, and forage for two horses; Captains, not mounted, $1,800 a year; Adjutants, $1,800 a year, and forage for two horses; Regimental Quartermasters, $1,800 a year, and forage for two horses; First Lieutenants, mounted, $1,600 a year, and forage for two horses; First Lieutenants, not mounted, $1,500 a year; Second Lieutenants, mounted, $1,500 a year, and forage for two horses; Second Lieutenants, not mounted, $1,400 a year; Chaplains, $1,500 a year, and forage for two horses; Acting Assistant Commissaries, $100 a year in addition to the pay of their rank. Ordnance Store-keeper and Paymaster at the Springfield (Mass.) Armory, $2,500, and forage for

two horses; all other Store-keepers, $2,000 a year, and forage for two horses. Each non-commissioned officer below the rank of a Brigadier-General, including Chaplains and others whose rank or pay assimilates, are allowed 10 per cent. of their current yearly pay for each term of five years of service.

The Pay of Enlisted Men.

The following enlisted men are paid these sums monthly during their first terms of enlistment, with some modifications prescribed by law: Sergeant-Majors of cavalry, artillery and infantry, $23 each; Quartermaster-Sergeants of cavalry, artillery and infantry, $23 each; chief trumpeters of cavalry, $22; principal musicians of artillery and infantry, $22; chief musicians of regiments, $60, and the allowances of a Quartermaster-Sergeant; Saddler Sergeants of cavalry, $22; First Sergeants of cavalry, artillery and infantry, $22; Sergeants of cavalry, artillery and infantry, $17; Corporals of cavalry and light artillery, $15; Corporals of artillery and infantry, $15; saddlers of cavalry, $15; blacksmiths and farriers of cavalry, $15; trumpeters of cavalry, $13; musicians of artillery and infantry, $13; privates of cavalry, artillery and infantry, $13; Sergeant-Majors of engineers, $36; Quartermaster-Sergeants of engineers, $36; Sergeants of engineers and ordnance, $34; Corporals of engineers and ordnance, $20; musicians of engineers, $13; privates (first class) of engineers and ordnance, $17; privates (second class) of engineers and ordnance, $13. To these rates of pay $1 a month is added for the third year of enlistment, $1 for the fourth year, and one more for the fifth year, making $3 a month increase for the last year of enlistment; but this increase is "retained pay," and is not given to the soldier until his term is ended, and it is forfeited if he misbehaves himself before he receives his discharge. Occasional extra services by soldiers and non-commissioned officers also entitle them to additional pay.

Hospital Stewards.

Hospital stewards are either enlisted for that position, or appointed from the enlisted men in the army, and are permanently attached to the medical corps, under the regulations of the Secretary of War. There is one hospital steward for each military post; and they are graded as of the first, second and third classes. The first class receive $30 a month, the second $22, and the third $20. Hospital matrons in post or regimental hospitals receive $10 a month, and female nurses in general hospitals, 40 cents a day; but one military ration, or its equivalent, is allowed to each. Women are employed as matrons and nurses in post or regimental hospitals in such numbers as may be necessary, and as nurses in general or permanent hospitals at such times and in such numbers as the Surgeon-General or the medical officer in charge of any such hospital deems proper.

Pay Department in the Army.

The pay department of the army consists of one Paymaster General, with the rank of colonel, two Assistant Paymasters-General, with the rank of colonel of cavalry, two Deputy Paymasters-General, with the rank of lieutenant of cavalry, and sixty Paymasters, with the rank of major of cavalry. Officers of the pay department are not entitled, by virtue of their rank, to command in the line or in other staff corps. When volunteers or militia are called into the service of the United States, and the officers in the pay department are not deemed by the President sufficient for the punctual payment of the troops, he may appoint and add to such corps as many paymasters, called

additional paymasters, ranking as majors (not exceeding one for every two regiments of volunteers or militia) as he may deem necessary; but these additional paymasters may only be retained in service so long as they are required to perform the special duty for which they are appointed. Paymasters and additional paymasters are allowed a capable non-commissioned officer or private as a clerk. If suitable persons for this office cannot be found in the army, they are authorized, with the approval of the Secretary of War, to employ citizens as clerks, at a salary of $1,200 a year.

The Paymaster-General performs his duties under the direction of the President. The army is paid in such a manner that the arrears shall at no time exceed two months, unless circumstances render further arrears unavoidable. The Deputy Paymasters-General, in addition to paying troops, superintend the payment of armies in the field. The paymasters and additional paymasters pay the regular troops and all other troops in the service of the United States, when required to do so by order of the President.

The Signal Service.

The chief signal officer is of high rank in the army, with a corps of seven or more first lieutenants as acting signal officers, one scientific professor, and assistants, besides six inspectors ranking as first and second lieutenants. The work is divided into several divisions, each in charge of a proper officer, as follows: General correspondence—in charge of letters and records; property and disbursing—in charge of supplies and accounts; station—for instructing observers; telegraph—in charge of army telegraph lines; indications—issues weather warning, etc.; weather review and international bulletin; scientific and study; instruction; printing; instrument and observatory.

Judge Advocates.

The Bureau of Military Justice consists of one Judge Advocate-General, with the rank of Brigadier-General, and one Assistant Judge Advocate-General, with the rank of colonel of cavalry. It is the duty of the Judge Advocate-General to receive, revise and cause to be recorded the proceedings of all courts-martial, courts of inquiry and military commissions, and perform such other duties as have been prescribed for that office, from time to time, by the laws of the country.

There are eight Judge Advocates of the army, holding the rank of major of cavalry. They perform their duties under the direction of the Judge Advocate-General, and preside over courts-martial, courts of inquiry, etc.; have power to issue a like process to compel witnesses to appear and testify which courts of criminal jurisdiction within the State, Territory or district where such military courts are held may lawfully issue, and have power to appoint a reporter, who records the proceedings of such court and the testimony taken before it, and sets down the same, in the first instance, in short-hand writing. The reporter, before entering upon this duty is sworn, or makes affirmation, faithfully to perform the same.

Brevet Officers.

In the army, promotions of officers to higher grades in the service are regulated by law. In time of war, the President may confer commissions by brevet (giving a higher rank and title, without increase of pay) upon commissioned officers of the army for distinguished conduct and public service in presence of the enemy. Such commissions bear date from the particular action or service for which the brevet rank was conferred. Such officers may be assigned to duty or command according to their brevet rank by a special assignment of the President; but brevet rank does not entitle an officer to precedence or command, except when so assigned, nor is he entitled to wear, while on duty, any uniform other than that of his actual rank, nor to be addressed in orders or official communications by any title other than that of his actual rank.

Military Cadets.

When any cadet (student) of the United States Military Academy at West Point has gone through its classes and received a regular degree from the academical staff, he is considered a candidate for a commission in any portion of the army for whose duties he may be deemed competent. But should there be no vacancy then existing in such corps, he may be brevetted as a supernumerary officer, with the rank of second lieutenant, until a vacancy occurs.

Non-commissioned Officers.

Under regulations established by the Secretary of War, non-commissioned officers may be examined by a board of four officers as to their qualifications for the duties of commissioned officers in the line of the army, and are eligible for appointment as second lieutenants in any corps for which they are qualified.

Meritorious Privates.

Whenever a private soldier distinguishes himself in the army, the President may, on the recommendation of the commanding officers of the regiment to which such private soldier belongs, grant him a certificate of merit.

Educational.

Schools are established at all posts, garrisons, and permanent camps, at which troops are stationed, in which the enlisted men are instructed in the common English branches of education, and especially in the history of the United States. It is the duty of the post or garrison commander to set apart a suitable room or building for school and religious purposes, and the Secretary of War details such officers and enlisted men as may be necessary to carry out this measure.

Retiring Boards---Veteran Officers.

From time to time the Secretary of War, under the direction of the President, assembles an Army Retiring Board, consisting of not more than nine, nor less than five, officers, two-fifths of whom are selected from the Medical corps, and besides these the board is composed, as far as may be, of seniors in rank to the officer whose disability is the subject of inquiry. The members of the board are sworn to discharge their duties honestly and impartially. The board inquires into and determines the facts touching the nature and occasion of the disability of any officer who appears to be incapable of performing the duties of his office, and shall have such powers of a court-martial and of a court of inquiry as may be necessary for that purpose. The proceedings and decision of the board are transmitted to the Secretary of War, and are by him laid before the President for his approval or disapproval and orders in the case.

When an officer has served forty consecutive years as a commissioned officer, he may, upon making application to the President, be retired from active service and placed upon the retired list, at the discretion of the President. When any officer has served forty five years as a commissioned officer, or is sixty-two years old, he may, at the discretion of the President, be retired from active service.

When any officer has become incapable of performing the duties of his office, he shall either be retired from active service, or wholly retired from the service by the President, in the manner

provided by law. Officers are retired from active service upon the actual rank held by them at the date of their retirement; are withdrawn from command and the line of promotion; are entitled to wear the uniform of their rank; continue to be borne on the army register; are subject to the rules and articles of war, and to trial by court-martial for any breach thereof. The whole number of officers on the retired list cannot at any time exceed 360.

Retired officers may be assigned to duty at the Soldiers' Home (Dayton, Ohio) when selected by the commissioners of the home, approved by the Secretary of War; and a retired officer cannot be assigned to any other duty, but may, on his own application, be detailed to serve as professor in any college. No retired officer, in these positions, however, will be allowed any additional compensation—only his regular pay as a retired officer.

Rights of Enlisted Men.

No enlisted man can, during his term of service, be arrested on mesne process, or taken or charged in execution for any debt unless it was contracted before his enlistment and amounted to $20 when first contracted.

Cooks.

Cooks for the army are detailed, in turn, from the privates of each company of troops in the service of the United States, at the rate of one cook for each company numbering less than thirty men, and two cooks for each company numbering more than thirty men, and they serve on each detail ten days.

Officers as Teachers.

The President may, upon the application of any established college or university within the United States, having capacity to educate at the same time not less than 150 male students, detail an officer of the army to act as president, superintendent or professor thereof; but the number of such officers may not exceed thirty at any time; are to be apportioned throughout the United States, as nearly as practicable, according to population, and are governed by general rules prescribed, from time to time, by the President.

Officers' Reports.

Every officer commanding a regiment, corps, garrison or detachment, is required, once in two months, or oftener, to make a report to the chief of ordnance, stating all damages to arms, implements or equipments belonging to his command, noting those occasioned by negligence or abuse, and naming the officer or soldier by whose negligence or abuse such damages were occasioned.

Every officer who receives clothing or camp equipage for the use of his command, or for issue to troops, must render to the Quartermaster-General, quarter-yearly, returns of such supplies, according to prescribed forms, with the requisite vouchers.

Army Officers as Civil Officers.

No army officer in active service can hold any civil office, either by election or appointment, and if he accepts or exercises the functions of a civil office he ceases to be an officer of the army and his commission is vacated. Should he accept a diplomatic or consular appointment under the government, he is considered as having resigned his place in the army, and it is filled as a vacancy.

Musicians and Their Pay.

The leader of the band at the military academy receives $75 a month, and the chief musicians of regiments $40 and the allowances of a quarter-master sergeant.

Army Clothing.

The uniform of the army, and the quantity and kind of clothing issued annually to the troops, are prescribed by the President.

West Point Military Academy.

The officers of the West Point Academy consist of a superintendent, a commandant of cadets, a senior instructor of artillery tactics, a senior instructor of cavalry tactics, a senior instructor of infantry tactics, a professor and an assistant professor of civil and military engineering, a professor and an assistant professor of natural and experimental philosophy, a professor and an assistant professor of mathematics; one chaplain, who is also professor of history, geography and ethics, aided by an assistant professor; a professor and an assistant professor of chemistry, mineralogy and geology, a professor and an assistant professor of drawing, a professor and an assistant professor of the French language, a professor and an assistant professor of the Spanish language, one adjutant, one master of the sword, and one teacher of music.

The superintendent, the commandant of cadets and the professors are appointed by the President, and the assistant professors, acting assistant professors and the adjutant are officers of the army, detailed to such duties by the Secretary of War, or cadets (students) assigned by the superintendent, under the direction of the Secretary of War.

The superintendent and commandant of cadets may be selected, and all other officers on duty at the Military academy may be detailed from cavalry, infantry or artillery; but the academic staff (as such) is not entitled to any command in the army, outside of the academy. The superintendent and the commandant of cadets, while serving as such, have, respectively, the local rank of colonel and lieutenant-colonel of engineers.

The superintendent and, in his absence, the next in rank, has the immediate government and military command of the academy, and is commandant of the military post at West Point.

The commandant of cadets has the immediate command of the battalion of cadets, and is the instructor in the tactics of artillery, cavalry and infantry.

Supervision of the Military Academy.

The supervision and charge of the academy is vested in the War Department, under such officers, or officer, as the Secretary of War may assign to that duty.

Leaves of absence are granted by the superintendent, under regulations prescribed by the Secretary of War, to the professors, assistant professors and other officers of the academy for the entire period of the suspension of the ordinary academic studies, without deductions from their respective pay or allowances.

The professors are placed on the same footing, as to retirement—from active service, as officers of the army.

Salaries of Military Teachers.

Pay of the Academic staff: Superintendent, same as a colonel. Commandant of cadets, same as a lieutenant-colonel. Adjutant, same as an adjutant of the cavalry service. Professors, who have served more than ten years at the academy, the pay and allowances of a colonel, and all other professors those of a lieutenant-colonel; the instructors of ordnance and science of gunnery and of practical engineering have the pay of a major, besides ten per centum of their current yearly pay for each and every term of five years' service in the army and at the academy, and such professors are placed upon the same footing, as regards restrictions upon pay and retirement from active service, as officers of the army; each assistant professor and each senior instructor of cavalry, artillery and infantry tactics, and the instructor of practical military engineering, receives the pay of a captain; the master of the sword receives at the rate of $1,500 a year, with fuel and quarters; the librarian and assistant librarian of the academy each receive $120 additional pay; the non-commissioned officer in charge of mechanics and other labor at the academy, the soldier who acts as clerk in the adjutant's office, and the four enlisted men in the philosophical and chemical departments and the lithographic office, receive each $36 additional pay.

Requirements of Military Cadets.

The corps of cadets consists of one from each congressional district in the United States, one from each Territory, one from the District of Columbia and ten from the United States at large, and are appointed by the President.

Appointees to cadetships are required to be between seventeen and twenty-two years old; but if they had served faithfully in the Southern rebellion as Union volunteers, the law allowed them to be two years older, and no person who served in the rebellion against the Union could receive a cadet's appointment. Cadets are appointed one year in advance of the time of their admission to the academy; they draw no pay or allowances until they are admitted; they are examined under regulations prescribed by the Secretary of War before their admission, and they are required to be well-versed in reading, writing and arithmetic, and to have a knowledge of the elements of English grammar, descriptive geography (particularly of our country), and of the history of the United States. Previous to admission, also, each cadet is required to take an oath of fidelity to his country and his duties, and to sign articles binding himself to serve the Government eight years, unless sooner discharged.

How Cadets are Drilled.

The cadets are arranged into companies, under the direction of the superintendent, each of which is commanded by an officer of the army for the purpose of military instruction. Each company is allowed four musicians. The corps is taught and trained in all the duties of a private soldier, non-commissioned officer and officer, goes into encampment at least once a year for three months, and is instructed and drilled in all the duties incident to a regular camp. Cadets are also subject to do duty in such places and on such service as the President may direct.

No cadet who is reported as deficient in either conduct or studies, and recommended to be discharged from the academy, can, except upon the recommendation of the academic board, be returned or reappointed, or appointed to any position in the army before his class have left the academy and received their commissions.

The superintendent of the academy has power to convene general courts-martial for the trial of cadets, and to execute the sentences of such courts (except sentences of suspension or dismission), subject to the limitations and conditions existing as to other general courts-martial.

The Board of Visitors.

A Board of Visitors is appointed once a year to attend the annual examination of cadets at the Military academy. Seven persons are appointed by the President of the United States, and two United States Senators and three Representatives in Congress are designated by the presiding officers in the Senate and House of Representatives, respectively, at the session of Congress next preceding the examination.

It is the duty of this Board of Visitors to inquire into the actual state of the discipline, instruction, police administration, financial affairs, and other concerns of the academy. The visitors appointed by the President report the results of their examination to the Secretary of War, for the information of Congress at the beginning of the next session; the Congressional visitors report directly to Congress, within twenty days after its meeting, their action as visitors, with their views and recommendations concerning the academy.

These visitors receive no compensation for their services, except the payment of their expenses for board and lodging while visiting West Point, and an allowance of not more than eight cents per mile for traveling expenses, going and returning by the shortest mail routes.

Articles of War.

The statutes of the United States contain a code of laws for the government of the army, known as the "Articles of War," and to these every officer and soldier is required to yield implicit obedience or suffer the penalties therein provided. These articles number 128. They include all ranks and conditions of the army, the formation, jurisdiction and conduct of general courts-martial, field-officers' courts, regimental courts, and garrison courts. Officers can only be tried by general courts-martial. (See "Judge Advocates-General.") The other courts are composed of officers chosen by commandants in the field, in the regiment, and in the garrison for the trial of minor offenses committed by soldiers and non-commissioned officers.

Military Prison.

A military prison has been established at Rock Island, Ill., by the government, for the confinement and reformation of offenders against the rules, regulations and laws for the government of the army of the United States, in which are confined and employed at labor, and governed according to law, all such offenders as have been convicted before any court-martial or military commission of the United States and sentenced to imprisonment therein.

The Secretary of War appoints a board of five members, consisting of three officers of the army and two civilians, who each hold their office for three years (unless sooner removed), and are each paid $5 a day while on duty, besides their necessary traveling expenses. With the Secretary of War, twice a year, and oftener if deemed expedient, they visit the prison for the purpose of examination, inspection and correction, and to inquire into all abuses and neglect of duty on the part of the officers or other persons in charge of the prison, and make such changes in the general discipline of the institution as they deem essential.

The officers of the prison consist of a commandant and such subordinate officers as may be necessary, a chaplain, a surgeon and a clerk, all of whom are detailed by the Secretary of War from the commissioned officers of the army, and he also details a sufficient number of enlisted men to act as turnkeys, guards and assistants in the prison.

The commandant controls the prison, has charge of the prisoners and their employments, and custody of all the property of the government connected with the prison, receives and pays out all money used for the prison, causes accounts to be kept of all the property, expenses, income, business and concerns of the prison, and transmits full and regular reports thereof to the Secretary of War. Under the direction of the Secretary of War, he employs (for the benefit of the United States) the convicts at such labor and in such trades as may be deemed best for their health and reformation, has power to sell and dispose of the articles manufactured by the convicts, regularly accounting for the proceeds thereof, takes note and makes record of the good conduct of the convicts, and shortens the daily time of hard labor for those who earn such consideration by their obedience, honesty, industry or general good conduct.

One of the inspectors of the army, at least once in three months, visits the prison for the purpose of examining into the books and all the affairs thereof, and to ascertain whether the laws, rules and regulations relating to it are complied with, whether the officers are competent and faithful, and whether the convicts are properly governed and employed and humanely and kindly treated. Of the results of his inspection he makes full and regular reports to the Secretary of War.

National Service.

Should the United States be invaded or be in imminent danger of invasion from any foreign nation or Indian tribe, or of rebellion against the government of the United States, the President may call forth such number of the militia of the State or States most convenient to the place of danger or scene of action as he may deem necessary to repel such invasion, or to suppress such rebellion, and issue his orders for that purpose to such officers of the militia as he may think proper. If the militia of more than one State is called into the active service of the United States by the President, he apportions them among such States according to representative population. In a time of rebellion the militia is subject to the same rules and articles of war as the regular troops of the United States.

When called into actual service, however, the militia is reorganized in a manner similar to regular troops. Each regiment of infantry then has one colonel, one lieutenant-colonel, one major, one adjutant (a lieutenant), one quartermaster (a lieutenant), one surgeon, two assistant surgeons, one sergeant-major, one regimental quartermaster-sergeant, one regimental commissary-sergeant, one hospital steward and two principal musicians; the regiment composed of ten companies, each company consisting of one captain, one first lieutenant, one second lieutenant, one first sergeant, four sergeants, eight corporals, two musicians, one wagoner, and from sixty-four to eighty-two privates. The militia is then also further organized into divisions of three or more brigade each, and each division has a major-general, three aids-de-camp, and one assistant adjutant-general (with the rank of major). Each brigade is made up of four or more regiments, and has one brigadier-general, two aids-de-camp, one assistant adjutant-general (with the rank of captain), one surgeon, one assistant quartermaster, one commissary of subsistence, and sixteen musicians as a band.

When thus called into actual service, the President may specify the period for which such service will be required of the militia, not exceeding nine months. During the time of service they will be entitled to the same pay, rations, clothing, and camp equipage provided by law for the regular army of the United States. They are also allowed mileage for the distance between their places of residence and the place of rendezvous from which they start for the field of military operations, with forage for the animals of mounted regiments, loss of horses, etc.

Courts-martial for the trial of militia are composed of militia officers only.

National Armories.

At each United States arsenal (or place where military arms and munitions of war are stored) is established a national armory, where muskets and carbines for the military service are manufactured. These armories are each in charge of one superintendent, who must be an officer of the ordnance corps of the army.

His Duties as Manager of the United States Moneys.

AMONG THE requirements it is stipulated that the Secretary of the Treasury shall not be interested, directly or indirectly, in carrying on any business of trade or commerce, or own any interest in a sea-vessel; that he shall not purchase or own any public lands or public property, or be concerned in buying or selling government securities, whether of the United States or any State thereof, or profit by any negotiation or transaction relating to the business of his department, other than his legal allowances, under penalty of fine and removal from his office, and he shall further be incapable of holding any other office under the United States Government. Every clerk in the department is also under similar restrictions and subject to similar penalties in a lighter degree.

The general duties of the Secretary require him, from time to time, to consider and prepare plans for the improvement and management of the national revenue and the support of the public credit; to superintend collection of the revenue; to prescribe the forms of keeping and rendering all public accounts and making proper returns; granting, under certain restrictions, all warrants for moneys to be issued from the Treasury in accordance with the laws of Congress; report to, or inform, either house of Congress, in person or in writing, respecting all matters referred to him by the Senate or House of Representatives, or which pertain to his office, and to perform such general duties relative to the national finances as he shall be directed, with considerable discretionary power: such as the collection of duties on imports and tonnage, under his superintendence. Whenever it is possible, he shall cause all accounts of the expenditure of public money to be settled within the fiscal year.

It is the duty of the Secretary of the Treasury to make and issue, from time to time, such instructions and regulations to the several collectors, receivers, depositaries, officers and others who may receive Treasury notes, United States notes, or other securities of the United States, and to those employed to prepare and issue such notes and securities, as he shall deem best to promote the convenience and security of the public, and protect the government or individuals against loss or fraud.

He prescribes forms of entries, oaths, bonds and other papers, with rules and regulations, in accordance with law, to be used in carrying out the various provisions of the internal revenue law, or the law relating to raising revenue from imported goods by duties or warehouse charges.

He prescribes such directions, rules, and forms to revenue collectors as are necessary for the proper observation of the law.

He prescribes the forms of the annual statements to Congress, which show the actual condition of commerce and navigation between the United States and foreign countries, or along the coasts between the collection districts of the government, in each year.

He, under the direction of the President, from time to time, establishes regulations to secure a just, faithful, and impartial appraisal of all goods, wares and merchandise imported into the United States, with proper entries of their true values and amounts.

When the revenue received at any port of the United States by collections does not amount to $10,000 a year, the Secretary may discontinue it as a port of delivery.

The Secretary of the Treasury is authorized to receive deposits of gold coin or bullion, by the Treasurer or Assistant-Treasurers of the United States, in sums of not less than $20, and issue certificates of deposit therefor of not less than $20 each; and these certificates shall be received in payment of public dues, as duties on imported goods, etc., the same as gold or bullion.

The Secretary may designate any recognized officer of the government as a disbursing agent, for the payment of all moneys appropriated for the construction of government buildings in the district to which such officer belongs.

When any person or corporation unjustly withholds from the government any moneys belonging to it, the Secretary may employ individuals (not exceeding three) to recover such moneys upon terms and conditions prescribed by himself; and the persons so employed receive no compensation except out of the moneys so recovered, and if they accept money or emolument for themselves from the persons from whom they attempt to recover said moneys, they become liable to fine and imprisonment by the government.

Plans for Raising Money.

In his annual report to Congress the Secretary shall present: Estimates of the public revenue and public expenditures for the current fiscal year, with plans for improving and increasing the revenues from time to time; a statement of all contracts for supplies or services which have been made by him, or under his direction, during the preceding year; a statement of the expenditure of moneys appropriated for the payment of miscellaneous claims against the government not otherwise provided for; a statement of the rules and regulations made by him, with his reasons for making them, to secure a just and faithful appraisal of all goods, wares, and merchandise imported into the United States, and their amounts and values; a full and complete statement of the sums collected from seamen, and expended for sick and disabled seamen, as a hospital tax for that purpose.

The secretary shall make other reports to Congress, at prescribed times: A statement of the amount of money expended at each custom-house during the preceding fiscal year, with the detailed number, occupation and salaries of all persons employed at each custom-house during the same period.

A statement showing the results of the information collected during the preceding year by the Bureau of Statistics concerning the condition of the agriculture, manufactures, domestic trade, currency, and banks in the States and Territories.

The reports made to him by the auditors relating to the accounts of the war and navy departments respectively, showing the application of the money appropriated by Congress for those departments for the preceding year.

An abstract, in tabular form, of the separate accounts of moneys received from internal duties or taxes in each of the States, Territories and collection districts, required to be kept at the Treasury.

A copy of each of the accounts kept by the superintendent of the Treasury buildings of all contingent expenses of the several bureaus of the department, and of all amounts paid for furniture, repairs of furniture, or of the sale of old furniture.

Also the number, names, and salaries of persons employed in surveying the lake and sea-coasts, their respective duties, and the amounts expended by the superintendent of this branch of the government service.

Statistics of Commerce.

The secretary is also charged with the duty, under prescribed regulations, of printing and presenting to Congress the annual report of the statistics of commerce and navigation, prepared by the Bureau of Statistics; of printing annually a condensed statement of the whole amount of the exports and imports to and from foreign countries during the preceding fiscal year; of publishing in some newspaper at Washington, every three months, a statement of the whole receipts, during the previous quarter-year, showing the amounts received from customs, public lands, and miscellaneous sources, and also the payments made during said quarter to civil officers and employes, the army or the navy, for Indian affairs, fortifications or pensions; of publishing in some newspaper at Washington, on the first day of each month, the last preceding weekly statement of the Treasurer of the United States, showing the amount to his credit in the different banks, in the mints or other depositories, the amounts for which drafts have been given and those unpaid, the amount remaining subject to his draft, and any recent changes in the depositories of the Treasury.

Bureau of Statistics.

The Bureau of Statistics is superintended by a division clerk, who is appointed for that purpose by the Secretary of the Treasury.

The purpose of the bureau is the collection, arrangement and classification of such statistical information as may be procured, tending to show, each year, the condition of the agriculture, manufactures, domestic trade, currency and banks of the several States and Territories. Under the direction of the Secretary of the Treasury, the chief of the Bureau of Statistics prepares annually a report, containing in detail statements substantially showing: Statistics concerning the commerce and navigation of the United States with foreign countries, to the close of the fiscal year; comprehending all goods, wares and merchandise exported from the United States to foreign countries, and all goods, wares and merchandise imported into

Treasury Building, Washington, D. C.

the United States from foreign countries, and all navigation employed in the foreign trade of the United States. These statistics exhibit the kinds, qualities and values of the articles exported or imported, minutely stated; also what articles are of foreign or native production. The statistics of navigation show the amount of tonnage of all vessels arriving from foreign countries in the United States, and all vessels departing from the United States to foreign ports; the amount of tonnage of vessels belonging to the United States, and the amount of tonnage of vessels owned in foreign countries, arriving in and departing from the United States, with other particulars.

Bureau of the Mint.

The Bureau of the Mint is under the general direction of the Secretary of the Treasury. Its chief officer is the Director of the Mint, who is appointed by the President; serves five years, unless he dies, resigns or is removed for cause, and has a salary of $4,500, besides his necessary traveling expenses. The Bureau of the Mint has under its control all the government mints for the manufacture of gold, silver and other coins, and all the assay offices for the stamping of bullion in order to establish its fineness and coin value. In his annual report to the Secretary of the Treasury, the Director of the Mint sets forth what and how valuable have been the operations of the mints during the preceding fiscal year, and the estimates for their operation during the next succeeding year.

The Secretary of the Treasury appoints the number of classified clerks necessary to carry on the duties of this bureau.

Suggestions
And Facts Relating
TO THE
PUBLIC DOMAIN.

First Home in the Wilderness.

Inspectors,
Revenue Officers,
Sub-Treasurers and
Superinten't of Mint.

How to Secure a Home on Government Land. *

THE Government of the United States owns and controls the public lands, not previously disposed of, where the Indian title has been extinguished by purchase or otherwise.

The public lands are open to pre-emption by citizens of the United States, except in the following cases: Lands reserved by any treaty, law or Presidential proclamation, for any purpose; lands lying within the limits of any incorporated city or town; lands actually settled or used for business purposes, and not for farming, and lands on which salt-springs or mines are situated.

Who May Pre-empt Land.

Every head of a family, or widow, or single person, more than twenty-one years old, being a citizen of the United States, or having filed his written intention to become such, or who may, himself or herself, actually settle on land subject to pre-emption, inhabiting, building a residence thereon, and improving the land, may enter at the proper land-office any quantity of such land, not exceeding 160 acres, upon which he or she may reside, by paying to the government the sum of $1.25 per acre.

Who May Not Pre-empt Land.

No person who owns 320 acres of land in any State or Territory, or who abandons his or her own land to settle on public lands in the same State or Territory, has a right to pre-emption.

No person is entitled to more than one pre-emption, and cannot secure a second tract of public land by this means.

Where the Land-Offices are Located.

Most of the public lands subject to pre-emption lie west of the Mississippi river. Land-offices, where all necessary information relative to the settlement and entry of these lands may be obtained, are located in the several States and Territories, as follows:

Alabama—Huntsville and Montgomery.

Arkansas—Little Rock, Camden, Harrison and Dardanelle.

Arizona Ter.—Prescott and Tucson.

California—San Francisco, Marysville, Humboldt, Stockton, Visalia, Sacramento, Los Angeles, Shasta, Susanville and Lodie.

Colorado—Denver City, Leadville, Central City, Pueblo, Del Norte, Lake City, Gunnison and Durango.

Dakota Ter.—Mitchell, Watertown, Fargo, Yankton, Bismarck, Deadwood, Aberdeen, Grand Forks, Huron and Creelsburg.

Florida—Gainesville.

Idaho Ter.—Boise City, Lewiston, Oxford and Hailey.

Iowa—Des Moines.

Kansas—Topeka, Salina, Independence, Larned, Wichita, Kirwin, Concordia, Wa-Keeny, Oberlin and Garden City.

Louisiana—New Orleans and Natchitoches.

Michigan—Detroit, East Saginaw, Reed City and Marquette.

Minnesota—Taylor's Falls, Saint Cloud, Duluth, Fergus Falls, Worthington, Tracy, Benson, Crookston and Redwood Falls.

Mississippi—Jackson.

Missouri—Boonville, Ironton and Springfield.

Montana Ter.—Miles City, Bozeman and Helena.

Nebraska—Neligh, Beatrice, Lincoln, Niobrara, Grand Island, North Platte, Bloomington, McCook and Valentine.

Nevada—Eureka.

New Mexico Ter.—Santa Fe and Las Cruces.

Oregon—Oregon City, Roseburg, Le Grand, Lakeview and The Dalles.

Utah Ter.—Salt Lake City.

Washington Ter.—Olympia, Vancouver, Walla Walla, Colfax and Yakima.

Wisconsin—Menasha, Falls of St. Croix, Eau Claire, Wausau, La Crosse and Bayfield.

Wyoming Ter.—Cheyenne and Evanston.

The Pre-emptor's Oath.

Previous to making a pre-emption, every citizen must make oath before the land register or receiver in the district where the desired tract is located, that he has never availed himself, on a former occasion, of his privilege to pre-empt public land; that he does not own 320 acres of land in any State or Territory; that he has not settled upon and improved such land to sell it on speculation, but for his own exclusive use; that he has not, in any way, contracted or agreed with any other person that the title of the said land, in whole or part, shall be for the benefit of any one except himself.

The certificate of this oath is filed in the land office of each district, and a copy of it is also sent to the General-Land Office for preservation.

Penalty for False Swearing.

Any person taking this oath and swearing falsely forfeits the money he has paid for the specified land and all his right and title to the land itself, and if he has previously bargained to transfer his pre-emptive title to any other person, that conveyance is null and void.

Preliminary Steps.

Before any person can enter land as above described, he must give satisfactory proof to the register and receiver of the land-office that he has properly settled upon and improved the land that he desires to pre-empt.

Within thirty days after first settling upon said land, the pre-emptor must file with the register of the proper land-office a written declaration of his intention to enter such tract of land under the pre-emption laws. Failing to make this statement within the prescribed time, or in furnishing the necessary proof of settlement and improvement of such land, or make the required payment, within one year after settling upon it, any other person may enter the same tract.

When two or more persons settle on the same tract of land, the right of pre-emption is in the one who made the first settlement.

The head of any family, or single person, twenty-one years old, being a citizen of the United States, is entitled to enter one quarter-section (160 acres), or less, but no more, of public lands not otherwise disposed of, after having filed a pre-emption claim, (if such land is subject to pre-emption), at $1.25 per acre, or eighty acres or less, in one tract, at $2.50 per acre.

Those possessing land may enter adjoining public land, if the tracts do not exceed 160 acres.

Upon applying to the register of the proper land office, he must swear that he is the head of a family, or twenty-one years old, or has served in the army or navy of the United States, as the case may be, and that he is securing the desired tract for his own use, for actual settlement and cultivation; taking this oath, and paying to the register of the land-office the sum of five dollars, where the land does not exceed eighty acres, and ten dollars for a larger amount.

When Ownership is Actually Acquired.

The certificate of the register of the land office, however, does not issue to the applicant for five years, at the end of which time, or two years later, he, or his widow, or his heirs, must prove by competent witnesses that he, she, or they

* Though belonging to the Department of the Interior this subject is treated here, as the revenues from land sales belong to the Treasury Department.

resided upon or cultivated the tract for five successive years after the the above affidavit was made, and that they still retain the land, and then take an oath of allegiance to the United States Government. He, she, or they will then be entitled to receive a patent for the land. Any false swearing concerning these particulars is punished, as in other cases of perjury.

The register of the land-office keeps a record of all the proceedings touching each tract of land claimed as a homestead.

No such homestead can be levied upon and sold for any debt contracted before the government patent is issued.

When the Payment Must be Made.

The payment for the homestead, besides the five or ten dollars prepaid when the land is entered, must be all paid before the expiration of the five years previous to the issue of the patent. Further information on this and other points can be obtained by applying to the land-office.

Tree Culture on Homesteads.

Any person having a homestead, who, at the end of the third year of his residence thereon, shall have had for two years, one acre of timber, the trees thereon not being more than twelve feet apart, and in a good, thrifty condition, for each and every sixteen acres of such homestead, upon due proof of the fact by two credible witnesses, receives his patent for such homestead.

Land Officers.

The President appoints a Register of the Land-Office and a Receiver of public moneys for each of the land districts of the United States, and each is required to reside at the place where the land-office to which he is appointed is directed to be kept. Each receives a salary of $500 a year, with liberal fees and commissions for locating land-warrants, issuing land-certificates, etc; but the salary, fees and commissions cannot in any case exceed an aggregate of $3,000. All balances received and remaining in the hands of registers and receivers above this amount, must be paid into the United States Treasury, as other public moneys.

The receivers make to the Secretary of the Treasury monthly returns of the moneys received in their several offices, and pay them over pursuant to his instructions.

Applicants for Land.

Should any person apply to any register to enter any land whatever, and the Register knowingly and falsely informs the person so applying that the same has been already entered, and refuses to permit the person so applying to enter such land, the Register is liable therefor to the applicant for five dollars for each acre of land which the latter offered to enter, to be recovered in an action for debt in any proper court.

Custom-House Officers.

The laws of the United States provide for the collection of duties on imported goods and merchandise in 110 collection districts of the Union, with one Collector of Customs, appointed by the President, for each district.

Collectors of Customs.

Collectors of customs at the various ports of entry of the United States are appointed by the President, for the term of four years.

The oath of office, taken and subscribed by each collector before some magistrate authorized to administer oaths within the collector's own district, affirms his past and present fidelity to the Government of the United States, and that he will use his best endeavors to detect and prevent frauds against the laws of the United States imposing duties upon imports.

Duty of the Collector.

At each of the ports to which there are appointed (by the President) a collector, naval officer and customs surveyor, it is the duty of the collector to receive all reports, manifests and documents to be made or exhibited on the entry of any ship or vessel, according to the customs laws of the United States; to record all manifests; to receive the entries of all ships or vessels, and of the goods, wares and merchandise imported in them; to estimate, with the naval officer, when there is one, or alone, when there is none, the amount of the dues payable thereon, indorsing such amount upon the respective entries; to receive all moneys paid for duties, and take all bonds for securing the payment thereof; to grant all permits for the unlading and delivery of goods; to employ, with the approval of the Secretary of the Treasury, proper persons as weighers, gaugers, measurers, and inspectors at the several ports within his district, to provide, with the like approval, at the public expense, storehouses for the safe keeping of goods, and such scales, weights and measures as may be necessary.

It is his business to furnish statistics of commerce and navigation for the use of the Bureau of Statistics, at Washington, relating to the kinds and quantities of all imported articles free from duty, subject to specific and ad valorem duties; the value of articles exported from his district to foreign countries; an accurate account of the characters and tonnage of all vessels sailing from his district to foreign countries; a similar record of all vessels arriving within his district from foreign countries, and an account of the kinds, quantities and value of merchandise entered and cleared coastwise at ports within his collection district.

It is his duty to cause the seizure of any vessel fitted out for piratical or aggressive purposes in violation of the law of nations.

Duties of Naval Officers.

The Naval Officer of any port is appointed by the President, and holds his office four years, unless sooner removed. His duties are as follows: To examine quarter-yearly, or oftener, if directed so to do by the Secretary of the Treasury, the books, accounts, returns and money on hand of the collector, and make a full, accurate and faithful report of their condition to the Secretary of the Treasury; to receive copies of all manifests and entries; to estimate, together with the collector, the duties on all merchandise subject to duty, and no duties can be received without such estimates; to keep a separate record of such estimates, to countersign all permits, clearances, certificates, debentures and other documents to be granted by the collector; to examine the collector's abstract of duties (taxation) and other accounts of receipts, bonds and expenditures, and certify to their correctness if found right.

Every naval officer is entitled to a maximum compensation of $5,000 a year out of any and all fees and emoluments received by him. Deputy naval officers may be appointed by the respective naval officers, when necessary, and in several of the largest commercial cities of the United States they each receive a salary of $2,500 a year. The naval officers are responsible for the acts of their respective deputies.

Duty of Surveyors of Customs.

The Surveyor of Customs at any port is appointed by the President, and holds his office four years, unless sooner removed.

At ports where a collector, naval officer and surveyor are appointed, it is the duty of the latter, subject to the direction of the collector, to superintend and direct all inspectors, weighers, measurers, gaugers at his port, to report weekly to the collector the name or names of all the above-named subordinates who are absent from or neglect their business; to visit or inspect the vessels which arrive in his port from foreign ports each day, and to report the same, with all necessary particulars concerning them, to the collector every morning; to put on board of each of such vessels, immediately after their arrival in port, one or more inspectors of cargoes; to ascertain the proof, quantities and kinds of distilled spirits imported, rating such spirits according to their respective degrees of proof as defined by the laws imposing duties on this class of merchandise; to examine whether the goods imported in any vessel, and the deliveries thereof, agreeably to the inspector's returns, correspond with the permits for landing the same, and to report any disagreement or error in the same to the collector, and to the naval officer, if there is one; to superintend the lading for exportation of all goods entered for the benefit of any drawback, bounty or allowance, and examine and report whether the kind, quantity and quality of the goods so laden on any vessel for shipment to a foreign port correspond with the entries and permits granted therefor; to examine, and from time to time, especially twice a year, try the weights, measures, and other instruments used in ascertaining the duties on imports, with standards provided by each collector for that purpose, to report errors and disagreements in the same to the collector, and to obey and execute such directions as he may receive for correcting the same agreeably to the standards.

Authority to Employ Assistance.

Every collector of customs has authority, with the approval of the Secretary of the Treasury, to employ within his district as many proper persons as deputy-collectors as he deems necessary, and they are declared to be officers of the customs. During the absence or sickness of collectors, such deputy may exercise the powers of a collector, the collector being responsible for the acts of his deputies.

The Secretary of the Treasury has power, except in cases otherwise provided, to limit and fix the number and compensation of the clerks employed by collector, surveyor or naval officer, and may fix and limit the salaries of their respective deputies.

Rules Must be Posted Up.

Every collector, naval officer and surveyor is required to keep posted up in his office a fair table of the rates of fees and duties demandable by law, and to give receipts for fees received by him whenever they may be requested, under a penalty of $100 for non-compliance, recoverable to the use of the informer. And every officer of the customs who demands or receives any other or greater fee or compensation than the law allows for any duty of his office, is liable to the aggrieved party in the sum of $200 for each offense.

Restrictions upon Collectors.

No person employed in the collection of duties on imports or tonnage may own, either in whole or in part, any vessel, or act as agent, attorney or consignee for the owner of any vessel, or of any cargo or lading on any vessel, nor import, or be concerned in the importation of any merchandise for sale, under a penalty of $500

Collectors, naval officers and surveyors must attend in person at the ports to which they are respectively appointed, keeping fair and true accounts and records of all their transactions as officers of the customs, subject to the inspection of the Secretary of the Treasury, who prescribes the form and manner of keeping such accounts and records, or to the inspection of such persons as he may appoint for that purpose; the neglect of this duty involves a penalty of $1,800.

Appraisers of Merchandise.

Four appraisers of merchandise are appointed by the President, who are employed in visiting such ports of entry, under the direction of the Secretary of the Treasury as may be deemed useful by him for the security of the revenue, and who at such ports afford such aid and assistance in the appraisement of merchandise as may be deemed necessary by the secretary to protect and insure uniformity in the collection of customs duties.

Whenever an appraisement of imported merchandise is to be made at any port for which no appraiser is provided by law, the collector of that district may appoint two respectable resident merchants, who shall be the appraisers of such merchandise. Any such merchant who refuses to assist at such appraisement, is liable to a fine not exceeding $50 and the costs of prosecution.

Assistant Treasurers.

Assistant Treasurers are appointed by the President, to serve for four years, at Boston, New York, Philadelphia, Baltimore, New Orleans, St. Louis, San Francisco, Chicago and Cincinnati.

The Assistant Treasurers have the charge and care of the rooms, vaults and safes assigned to them respectively, and there perform the duties required of them relating to the receipt, safekeeping, transfer and disbursement of the public moneys.

All collectors and receivers of public money of every description in the cities where there are sub-treasuries are required to deposit with the sub-treasurers all the public moneys collected by them or in their hands, there to be safely kept until otherwise disposed of according to law.

If any assistant treasurer fails safely to keep all public moneys deposited by any person, he is deemed guilty of embezzlement and punished by fine and imprisonment.

Officers of Internal Revenue.

The United States are divided into 131 internal revenue collection districts.

The President appoints for each of these districts one Collector of Internal Revenue, who must be a resident of the district for which he is appointed.

Appointment of Deputy Collectors.

Each collector is authorized to appoint, in writing, as many deputy-collectors as he may think proper, to be by him compensated for their services; to revoke any such appointments, giving notice thereof to the Commissioner of Internal Revenue, and to require and accept bonds or other security from such deputies.

Duty of Internal Revenue Collectors.

It is the duty of the collector and his deputies (each of whom has equal authority with the collector) to collect all internal revenue taxes levied or assessed against individuals or corporations within the portion of the district assigned to him; but each collector is in every respect responsible both to the United States and to individuals, as the case may be, for all moneys collected, and for every act done or neglected to be done by any one of his deputies while acting in that position.

Superintendent of Exports.

In any port of the United States where there is more than one Collector of Internal Revenue, the Secretary of the Treasury may designate one of them to have charge of all matters relating to the exportation of articles subject to tax under the internal revenue laws, and there may be appointed under such collector an officer to superintend all matters of exportation and drawback. This officer is known as Superintendent of Exports.

Inspectors of Tobacco and Cigars.

In every collection district where it is necessary the Secretary of the Treasury appoints one or more inspectors of tobacco and cigars. This officer is entitled by authority of the Treasury to receive such fees as the latter may prescribe to be paid by the owner or manufacturer of the inspected articles.

Internal Revenue Gaugers.

In every collection district where it may be necessary, the Secretary of the Treasury appoints one or more internal revenue gaugers, whose duty it is to determine the amount of articles which he is called to examine.

Requirements and Penalties.

Collectors of internal revenue are required to report violations of the revenue laws to the district attorney of his district for prosecution.

Every collector, deputy collector and inspector is authorized to administer oaths and take evidence in reference to matters in his department of the public service.

Any officer of internal revenue may be specially authorized by the commissioner to make seizures of property which may become forfeited or jeopardized by a violation of the revenue laws.

Any revenue officer who discloses to any other person the operations, style of work or apparatus of any manufacturer whose establishment comes under his inspection, is liable to be fined heavily and imprisoned. Neither can any internal revenue officer be or become interested in the manufacture of tobacco, snuff, cigars or spirits, under penalty of being dismissed from office, besides a heavy fine; and the law also provides severe penalties for extortion, receiving unlawful fees, etc., by revenue officers.

Superintendents of the Manufacture of Money.

The United States Government has mints at Philadelphia, San Francisco, New Orleans, Carson, (Nev.), and Denver, and assay offices at New York, Boise City (Idaho), and Charlotte, N. C. The officers of a mint are a superintendent, an assayer, a melter and refiner, a coiner, and, at Philadelphia, an engraver. Besides these are various assistants. and clerks, and numerous workmen.

Restrictions upon Employes.

Every officer, assistant and clerk of a mint must take the oath of fidelity, which oath is deposited with the Secretary of the Treasury, and the superintendent may require any employe of the mint to take such an oath.

The assayer, the melter and refiner, and the coiner of every mint, before entering upon the duties of his office, is required to execute a bond to the United States, with one or more securities.

In the temporary absence of the superintendent, the chief clerk acts in his place, and in that of the Director of the Mint, the Secretary of the Treasury designates some one to act for him.

Duties of the Superintendent of the Mint.

The Superintendent of each mint has the control of it, the superintendence of the officers and other persons employed in it, and the supervision of its business, subject to the direction of the Director of the Mint, to whom he makes reports at such times and in such form as the director prescribes. These reports exhibit in detail, and classified, the deposits of bullion, the amount of gold, silver and minor coinage, and the amount of unparted, standard and refined bars issued, and such other statistics and information as may be required.

He receives and safely keeps, until legally withdrawn, all moneys or bullion designed for the use or expenses of the mint. He receives all bullion brought to the mint for assay or coinage, is the keeper of all bullion or coin in the mint, except when it is in the hands of other officers, and delivers all coins struck at the mint to the persons to whom they are lawfully payable.

From the report of the assayer and the weight of the bullion, he computes the value of each deposit and the amount of the charges or deductions, if any, of all which he gives a detailed memorandum to the depositor; and he also gives, at the same time, a certificate of the net amount of the deposit, to be paid in coins or bars of the same species of bullion as that deposited, the assayer verifying the correctness of such certificate by countersigning it.

Duties of the Assayer.

The Assayer assays all metals and bullion whenever assays are required in the operations of the mint. From every parcel of bullion deposited for coinage or bars, the superintendent delivers to the assayer a sufficient portion for the purpose of being assayed, and the assayer reports to the superintendent the quality or fineness of the bullion assayed by him, with such information as will enable the superintendent to compute the amount of charges to be made against the depositor.

Duty of the Melter and Refiner.

The Melter and Refiner executes all the operations necessary to form ingots of standard silver or gold and alloys for minor coinage, suitable for the coiner, from the metals legally delivered to him for that purpose, or to form bars conformably with the law from gold and bullion delivered to him for that purpose. He keeps a careful record of all transactions with the superintendent, noting the weight and character of the bullion, and is responsible for all bullion placed in his care until he returns it to the superintendent, receiving proper vouchers therefor.

Duty of the Coiner.

The Coiner executes all the operations necessary in order to form coins, conformable in all respects to the law, from the standard gold and silver ingots and alloys for minor coinage legally delivered to him for that purpose, and is responsible for it until it is returned to the superintendent. As coins are prepared from time to time, the coiner delivers them to the superintendent, who receipts for them and keeps a careful record of their kind, number and actual weight. The coiner, also, from time to time, delivers to the superintendent the clippings and other portions of bullion remaining, after the process of coining, the superintendent receipting for the same and keeping a careful record of their weight and character.

At the end of every calendar year the coiner, in the presence of the superintendent and assayer, defaces and destroys the obverse (or date) working-dies, so that no more coins of that date can be issued.

Duty of the Engraver.

The Engraver prepares all the working-dies (or moulds) required for use in the coinage of the mint, and when new coins or devices are required, under the supervision of the Director of the Mint, he engraves the models, moulds and matrices, or original dies for the same; but the director has power to engage, temporarily, the services of other artists for such work.

The Light-House Board.

The President appoints two officers of the navy, of high rank; two officers of the corps of engineers of the army, and two citizens in civil life, of high scientific attainments, whose services are at the disposal of the President, together with an officer of the navy and an officer of engineers of the army as secretaries; and these gentlemen constitute the lighthouse board.

This board is attached to the office of the Secretary of the Treasury, and under his superintendence discharges all administrative duties relating to the construction, illumination, inspection and government of light-houses, light-vessels, beacons, sea-marks, and whatever belongs to them, embracing the foundations of works already in existence, procuring illuminating and other apparatus, supplies, and materials of all kinds for building and for rebuilding, when necessary, and keeping in good repair the light-houses, light-vessels, beacons and buoys of the United States; has charge and custody of all the archives, books, documents, drawings, models, returns, apparatus and other things pertaining to the light-house service. Upon the requisition of the Secretary of the Treasury, the board furnishes all the estimates of expense which the several branches of the light-house system may require, and such other information as it may be necessary to lay before Congress at each session.

The board is authorized, whenever an appropriation may be made by Congress for a new light-house on land not belonging to the United States, to purchase the necessary site for such light-house with money appropriated for that purpose.

Who Build Light-Houses.

The President causes, from time to time, such officers to be detailed from the engineer corps of the army as are necessary to superintend the construction and renovation of light-houses. The plans, drawings, specifications and estimates of cost of all illuminating and other apparatus, and of construction and repair of towers, buildings, etc., connected with the light-house service, are prepared by the engineer-secretary of the board.

Who May be Light-House Inspectors.

The Atlantic, Gulf of Mexico, Pacific and lake coasts of the United States are divided into fifteen light-house districts, each of which is under the supervision of either a commodore, captain or commander of the navy, who is called the inspector. The engineer in charge of each district is either a colonel, lieutenant-colonel, major or captain of the Engineer Corps of the United States.

The laws provide that there be detailed from the engineer corps of the army such officers as may be necessary to superintend the construction and renovation of light-houses; also, that an officer of the army or the navy be assigned to each district as a light-house inspector, subject to the orders of the light-house board, who receives no pay or emolument beyond his own lawful compensation in the regular line of his profession, with mileage while traveling under orders connected with his duties.

Working Force in Light-House Offices.

Each inspector and engineer has an office in every district to which they are assigned, and are allowed (according to their various locations and duties) the assistance of certain employes, paid by the Government, as follows. In the inspector's offices—one or two clerks, one messenger, one keeper of the buoy depot, one superintendent of construction, one or more assistant superin-

tendents of construction, a store-keeper, a foreman of depot, a copyist, and a watchman of the buoy depot.

Engineers in Light-House Department.

In the engineer's department are employed, but not in every office: One assistant engineer, a superintendent of construction, and one or more assistant superintendents of construction, a foreman of the lamp-shop, one lampist, a foreman of laborers, a draughtsman, and a messenger.

In both the inspectors' and engineers' departments are employed steam-tugs, or vessels, for the conveyance of supplies, implements, etc., generally officered as follows: One master, one mate, one engineer, assistant engineer, and a pilot occasionally.

The Light-House Keeper.

At light-houses are employed One keeper, at from $375 to $1,000 a year, according to location, with assistant keepers, with salaries ranging from $160 to $450 a year; keepers of light-ships receive $600 or $1,000 a year.

The Life-Saving Service.

By law the Secretary of the Treasury is authorized to establish stations at certain points on the Atlantic coast and the shores of the Northern lakes, for affording aid to the shipwrecked vessels and rescuing their crews and passengers.

Articles Used for Saving Life.

This life-saving service is divided into seven ocean districts and three lake districts. The various stations are supplied with the requisite apparatus as may, in the judgment of the Secretary of the Treasury, be best adapted to the purposes of each station, such as life-boats, ropes, mortars for sending ropes on board wrecked vessels, contrivances for getting passengers safely on shore, etc. Each district is in charge of a superintendent, who possesses the powers and performs the duties of an inspector of the customs for each of the coasts on which stations are established. These districts number seven on the Atlantic coast, and three on the great lakes, and each superintendent receives from the Secretary of the Treasury the proper instructions relative to the duties required of them.

Each station is in charge of a keeper, who is instructed in his duties by the Secretary of the Treasury. At some stations experienced surfmen are engaged to assist in aiding wrecked vessels.

Quarantines.

The law provides for the restraint, stoppage and government of all vessels arriving at seaports and inland ports from places where infectious diseases prevail, or vessels on which cases of such infectious diseases exist.

This law, the health-laws of the several States, and the regulations of the Secretary of the Treasury, are required to be duly observed by the officers of the customs-revenue of the United States, by the masters and crews of the several revenue-cutters belonging to the Government, and by the military officers commanding in any fort or station upon the coast, and all such officers of the United States must faithfully aid in the execution of such quarantines and health-laws, according to their respective powers and within their respective precincts, as directed, from time to time, by the Secretary of the Treasury.

The Revenue Marine Service.

The President, for the better security of the collection of import or tonnage duties on commercial vessels and cargoes, causes the maintenance of as many revenue-cutters as may be necessary for the protection of the Government revenues,

the expense of which is paid out of the sum annually appropriated by Congress for this service.

Duties of Officers in this Service.

The officers of the revenue-cutters are respectively deemed officers of the customs, and are subject to the direction of such collectors of the revenue, or other customs officers, as, from time to time, may be designated for that purpose. They are required to board all vessels arriving within the United States or within twelve miles of the United States coasts, if bound for United States ports, and search and examine every part of such vessels, and demand and receive and certify the manifests required to be on board of certain vessels; to affix and put proper fastenings on the hatches and other communications with the hold of such vessels, and remain on board such vessels until they arrive at the port or place of their destination.

How Revenue-Cutters are Known.

The revenue-cutters on the Northern and Northwestern lakes are specially charged with the duty of aiding vessels in distress on the lakes.

Revenue-cutters are distinguished by a peculiar flag or ensign; and the officers are empowered to stop any vessel liable to seizure or examination by firing upon her after hoisting the revenue flag, if the merchant-vessel's officers refuse to let the revenue officers board her.

The Coast Survey.

Surveys of the sea-coasts and lake-coasts of the United States are authorized by Congress for the purpose of aiding navigation by the production of correct charts of courses, distances, depth of water, etc., along such coasts. The public vessels in actual service and officers of the navy and army are employed, as far as practicable, in this survey.

What is Done With the Surveys.

The Secretary of the Treasury is authorized to dispose of the maps and charts of the survey of the coast, from time to time, and under such regulations as he may prescribe, besides those distributed gratuitously among foreign governments, the departments of our own Government, and literary and scientific associations.

Steamboat Inspectors.

The laws of the United States provide for the inspection of the hulls and steamboilers of merchant, passenger, and excursion vessels propelled by steam in United States waters, owned in the United States, except on canals.

From time to time the President appoints a Supervising Inspector-General, who is selected with reference to his fitness and ability to reduce to a system and carry into effect all the provisions of the law relating to steamboat inspection.

Under the direction of the Secretary of the Treasury, it is his business to superintend the administration of the steamboat inspection laws and regulations; preside at the meetings of the board of supervising inspectors; receive all reports of inspectors; receive and examine all accounts of inspectors, and report fully, at stated periods, to the Secretary of the Treasury, upon all matters pertaining to his official duties.

Inspection Districts.

The United States are divided into ten inspection districts, each of which is in charge of a supervising inspector, appointed by the President, each of whom is chosen for his knowledge, skill and practical experience in the uses of steam for navigation, and who must be a competent judge of the character and qualities of steam vessels and all parts of the machinery used in steaming.

Annual Meetings.

The supervising inspectors and Supervising Inspector-General assemble as a board at Washington once a year (in January), and at such other times as the Secretary of the Treasury may require, for joint consultation, and assign to each supervising inspector the limits of territory in which he is to perform his duties. The board also establishes all essential regulations necessary to carry out in the most effective manner the provisions of the laws. These regulations, when approved by the Secretary of the Treasury, have the force of law.

Each supervising inspector watches over all parts of the territory assigned to him; visits and confers with, and examines into the doings of the local boards of inspectors within his district, and instructs them in the proper performance of their duties; and, whenever he deems it expedient, he visits any licensed vessels at his discretion, and examines their condition with reference to the inspection laws and regulations having been observed and complied with, both by the owners or masters, or the board of inspectors.

Restrictions Upon Inspectors.

No person who is directly or indirectly interested in any patent required to be used on any steamer by the steamboat inspection laws, or who is a member of any association of owners, masters, engineers or pilots of steamboats, or who is directly or indirectly interested in any steam-vessel, or who is intemperate in his habits, or who does not possess the required skill or experience, may not hold the office of either supervising or local inspector, and if any such person attempts to perform the functions of an inspector, he is punishable by a fine of $500 and dismissal from office.

Must Not Employ Unlicensed Officers.

The boards of local inspectors license and classify the masters, chief mates, engineers and pilots of all steam-vessels, and it is a punishable offense for any steamboat owner to employ an unlicensed officer of these grades.

Whenever a supervising inspector ascertains that any of the above-named steamboat officers fails to perform his duty according to law, he is required to report him to the board of local inspectors in the district where the vessel was inspected or belongs, and if necessary or expedi-ent, to have the offending party prosecuted; and if the local board is in fault for licensing him the facts must be investigated, and the delinquent inspectors are liable to removal from office.

It is the duty of the inspecting supervisors to see that the local boards faithfully perform their duties of inspection; to inspect boats and grant licenses in districts where there are no local boards, or where it is difficult to apply to them; to furnish to local inspectors all needful information concerning licensed persons, individuals from whom licenses have been withheld, or whose licenses have been revoked or suspended; boats whose owners have refused or neglected to have them properly repaired, and persons who have been refused certificates.

United States Fish Commissioner.

The laws provide that the President shall appoint from among the civil officers or employes of the government a Commissioner of Fish and Fisheries, who must be a person of proved scientific and practical acquaintance with the fishes of the sea-coast, and who receives no salary additional to that which he drew before his appointment. It is his business to prosecute investigations and inquiries on the subject, with the view of ascertaining whether any, and what, diminution in the number of the food fishes of the coast and lakes of the United States has taken place, and, if so, to what causes this diminution is due, and, also, whether any, and what, protective, prohibitory, or precautionary measures should be adopted in the premises, and report the same to Congress. He may take, or cause to be taken, at all times, in the waters of the sea-coast of the United States, where the tide ebbs and flows, and also in the waters of the lakes, such fish or specimens thereof as may, in his judgment, from time to time, be needful or proper for the conduct of his duties, any law, custom, or usage of any State to the contrary notwithstanding.

Pension Agents.

The President is authorized to appoint all pension-agents, who hold their respective offices for four years, unless sooner removed or suspended. Each pension-agent, whether man or woman, is required to execute an official bond, with sufficient security, for such an amount and in such form as the Secretary of the Interior may approve. The President may establish pension-agencies, not exceeding three in any State or Territory, whenever in his judgment the public interest and the convenience of pensioners require.

Agents for paying pensions receive a commission of two per centum on all disbursements made by them to pensioners. They are also allowed, where an agent disburses $50,000 annually to pensioners, not exceeding $500 for clerk-hire, office-rent, and office expenses; where an agent disburses $100,000 annually, not exceeding $750 a year for such office expenses; and for every $50,000 additional disbursed by an agent, he or she is allowed not more than $250 a year additional income; but no agent can receive from fees and commissions more than $4,000 a year. Each agent is, however, entitled to thirty cents in full for each voucher prepared and paid by him or her, including necessary postage, which sum is paid to the United States. Pension-agents and their clerks are authorized to take and certify the affidavits of all pensioners and their witnesses who come before them for that purpose, but they receive no fee for this service. In paying a pension the pension-agent is authorized to deduct from the amount of it the attorney's fee for aiding the pensioner, as agreed upon or as prescribed by the Commissioner of Pensions, where no sum was agreed upon. For this service the pension-agent may retain thirty cents.

Pension Surgeons.

The Commissioner of Pensions is authorized to organize, at his discretion, boards of examining surgeons, not to exceed three members, to examine the physical condition of pensioners or applicants for pensions in the interest of the government. In ordinary examinations each surgeon receives a fee of one dollar, and for special ones three dollars each. The Secretary of the Interior also appoints a surgeon as medical referee, who, under the control and direction of the Commissioner of Pensions, has charge of the examination and revision of the reports of examining surgeons, and performs other duties touching medical and surgical questions in the Pension-Office as the interests of the service may demand. His salary is $2,500 a year.

The Secretary of the Interior may also appoint qualified surgeons, not exceeding four in number to perform the duties of examining surgeons when so required, and they are borne on the rolls of his office as clerks of the fourth class, with salaries of $1,800 a year each.

A Sketch of the Work in the Department of the Interior.

THE DEPARTMENT of the Interior, at Washington, is governed by the Secretary of the Interior. There is also an Assistant Secretary of the Interior, appointed by the President, whose duties are prescribed by the Secretary, or by law.

There are in the Department of the Interior the following bureaus, controlled by their respective commissioners: The General Land Office, Bureau of Indian Affairs, Pension Office, Patent Office, and Office of Education.

Duties of the Secretary of the Interior.

The Secretary of the Interior has supervision of the census, when directed by law; the public lands, including mines; the Indians; pensions and bounty lands; patents for inventions; the custody and distribution of government publications; the educational interests; the Government Hospital for the Insane, and the Columbia Asylum for the Deaf and Dumb.

He exercises all the powers and performs all the duties in relation to the Territories of the United States that were by law or custom performed, previous to March 1, 1873, by the Secretary of State. He has, also, supervisory and appellate powers in relation to all acts of United States marshals, and others, in taking and returning the census of the country. He has also supervision of all the expenditures of his department. He also reports annually to Congress the nature, character, and amounts of all claims presented to him during the preceding year, under laws or treaty stipulations for compensation for depredations committed by Indians, whether allowed by him or not, and the evidence on which he based his action; also, the quantity and kind of the copies of public journals, books and documents received from the government for distribution, and the manner of their distribution in detail.

DUTIES OF OFFICERS IN THE INTERIOR DEPARTMENT.

General Land Office.

The Commissioner of the General Land-Office performs, under the directions of the Secretary of the Interior, all executive duties pertaining to the survey and sale of the public lands of the United States, or in anywise respecting such public lands, such as relate, also, to private claims of land, and the issue of patents for all grants of land under the authority of the government. He makes plats of lands surveyed under the authority of the United States, and gives such information respecting the public lands and concerning the business of his office as may be directed.

All patents issued from the Land-office bear the authority of the United States, are signed by the President, countersigned by the Commissioner of the General Land-Office, and are recorded in that office.

Duty of the Recorder.

It is the duty of the Recorder of the General Land-Office, under instructions from the commissioner, to certify and affix the seal of the office to all patents for public lands, and to attend to their correct engrossing, recording and transmission; to prepare alphabetical indexes of the names of persons entitled to patents and those who receive them, and to prepare copies and exemplifications of matters on file or records in the General Land-Office as the commissioner may direct.

Duties of the Commissioner of Indian Affairs.

The Commissioner of Indian Affairs has the management of all Indian affairs and all matters arising out of Indian relations. To him are transmitted, for examination, all accounts and vouchers for claims and disbursements connected with Indian affairs, and by him they are passed to the proper accounting officer of the department of the Treasury for settlement.

The President may prescribe such regulations as he deems proper for carrying into effect the various legal provisions relating to the control of Indian affairs; and the Secretary of the Interior also prepares and publishes regulations, at his discretion, establishing the method of presenting claims, arising under treaty stipulations or Congressional laws, for compensation for depredations committed by Indians, and the character of the evidence brought to support such claims.

It is the duty of the Secretary of the Interior, also, to make and maintain such rules as are necessary to prohibit the sale of arms or ammunition within any district or country occupied by uncivilized or hostile Indians.

It is the duty of the Commissioner of Indian Affairs to report annually to Congress a tabular statement showing distinctly the separate objects of expenditure under his supervision, during the fiscal year next preceding each report. In his annual report he embodies the statements of all agents or commissioners issuing food, clothing or supplies of any kind to Indians, with the number of Indians present and actually receiving such supplies.

Commissioner of Pensions.

The Commissioner of Pensions performs such duties in the execution of the various pension and bounty-land laws of the United States as the President directs.

The commissioner is authorized, with the approval of the Secretary of the Interior, to appoint a person to sign the name of the commissioner to certificates or warrants for bounty lands to soldiers, sailors, etc.

The commissioner is authorized to detail, from time to time, any of the clerks in his office to investigate any suspected attempts to defraud the United States in or affecting the administration of any law relative to pensions, and to aid in the prosecution of any person implicated, with such additional compensation as is customary in cases of special service; and such person is empowered to administer oaths in the course of such investigation.

Officers of Indian Affairs.

The Board of Indian Commissioners consists of not more than ten persons, appointed by the President; men eminent for intelligence and philanthropy, who receive no compensation for performing their duties under such appointment. The board has power to appoint one of, its members as its secretary, who is entitled to such reasonable salary as may be agreed upon by the board, to be paid from any moneys appropriated by the government for the expenses of the commission. The board supervises all expenditures of money appropriated for the benefit of Indians within the limits of the United States, and inspects all goods purchased for Indians, in connection with the Indian service, and has access to all books and papers relating thereto in any government office; but the examination of vouchers and accounts by the executive committee of the board is not necessary to secure their payment.

Duty of Indian Inspectors.

The President is authorized to appoint several Indian inspectors, not exceeding five in number, each of whom holds his office for four years, unless sooner removed.

As often as twice a year one or more of the inspectors is required to visit each Indian superintendency and agency and fully investigate all matters pertaining to the business of each, including an examination of its accounts, the manner of expending money, the number of Indians provided for, contracts of all kinds connected with the business, the condition of the Indians, their advancement in civilization, the extent of the reservations, and what use is made of the lands set apart for that purpose, and, generally, all matters belonging to the Indian service.

Each inspector has power to examine on oath all officers and other persons in and about the superintendencies and agencies, and to suspend from office any superintendent, agent, or employe, and appoint another person temporarily to fill the vacancy created by the suspension, reporting his action to the President. The inspectors are, also, each empowered to enforce the laws and prevent the violation of the laws in the several agencies and superintendencies. It is so arranged that the same inspector may not investigate the affairs of any superintendency or agency twice in succession.

Indian Superintendents.

The President is authorized, from time to time, to appoint four or more superintendents of Indian affairs, and each holds his office four years.

Each superintendent, within his district, exercises a general supervision and control over the official conduct and accounts of all officers and persons employed by the government in Indian affairs, under such regulations as are established by the President, and may suspend such officers and persons from their offices or employments for reasons forthwith to be communicated to the Secretary of the Interior; and, also, to perform within his district such duties as may be properly assigned to him. The Secretary of the Interior may, at his discretion, authorize the temporary employment of clerks by superintendents of Indian affairs whenever the public interests seem to require it.

Whenever a superintendency is discontinued by the President, or abolished by law, the agents in that district report directly to the Commissioner of Indian Affairs.

Indian Agents.

From time to time the President is authorized to appoint numerous Indian agents, locating them among the Indian tribes west of the Mississippi river, and from Texas to Oregon. The President has power to discontinue any agent at his discretion, or to require one agent to perform duty at two agencies for one salary. Each agent holds his office four years, and before entering upon his duties is required to give a bond with such security as the President or Secretary of the Interior may require. Within his agency he manages and superintends the intercourse with the Indians according to law, and executes and performs such regulations and duties as may be prescribed by the President, the Secretary of the Interior, the Commissioner of Indian Affairs, or the Superintendent of Indian Affairs.

Where Indian Agents Must Live.

Every agent is required to reside and keep his agency within or near the tribe of Indians to which he is assigned, and at such place as the President may designate, and may not leave the limits of his agency without permission.

The President may require any military officer of the United States to execute the duties of an Indian agent, and such officer receives no other compensation than his army pay and actual traveling expenses.

Legal Powers of Agents.

Indian agents are authorized to take acknowledgments of deeds and other instruments of writing, and to administer oaths in investigations committed to them in the Indian country, under rules and regulations prescribed by the Secretary of the Interior.

The President also appoints a competent number of sub-Indian agents, to be employed and to reside wherever the President may direct.

Location of Each Agency.

The limits of each superintendency, agency and sub-agency are established by the Secretary of the Interior, either by tribes or geographical boundaries. All special agents and commissioners not appointed by the President are appointed by the Secretary of the Interior.

Indian Interpreters.

An interpreter is allowed to each agency. Where there are several tribes in the same agency speaking different languages, one interpreter may be allowed by the Secretary of the Interior for each of such tribes. Interpreters may be nominated by the proper agents to the Department of the Interior for approval, and may be suspended by the agent, for cause, from pay and duty, and the circumstances reported to the Department of the Interior for final action.

Indian Interpreters Preferred.

Whenever persons of Indian descent can be found who are properly qualified for the performance of the necessary duties, preference is given to them in all cases of appointments of interpreters and other persons employed for the benefit of the Indians.

The Secretary of the Interior must, under the direction of the President, cause the discontinuance of the services of such agents, sub-agents, interpreters, etc., as may from time to time become unnecessary in consequence of the emigration of the Indians, or other causes.

No person employed in Indian affairs may have

any interest or concern in any trade with the Indians, except for and on account of the United States, under a penalty of $5,000 and removal from office.

Teachers Among the Indians.

In every case where the President may judge improvement in the habits and condition of Indians practicable, and ascertains that the means of instruction can be introduced among them with their own consent, he may employ capable persons of good moral character to instruct them in the mode of agriculture suited to their situation, and to teach their children in reading, writing and arithmetic, under such regulations as the President may prescribe. And when any of the Indian tribes are, in the opinion of the Secretary of the Interior, competent to direct the employment of their blacksmiths, mechanics, teachers, farmers or other persons engaged for them, the direction of such persons may be given to the proper authority of the tribe.

Indian Traders.

Any loyal citizen of the United States, of good moral character, may be permitted to trade with any Indian tribe upon giving a bond to the United States of not less than $5,000, with good security, approved by the proper authorities, conditioned that he will faithfully observe all laws and regulations made for the government of trade and intercourse with the Indian tribes, and in no respect violate the same.

United States Surveyors.

The President appoints one Surveyor-General in the States and Territories named below, each embracing one surveying district: Louisiana, Florida, Minnesota, Kansas, Nebraska, Iowa, Dakota Territory, Oregon, Washington, Colorado, New Mexico, California, Idaho, Nevada, Montana, Utah, Wyoming and Arizona. Each Surveyor-General has but one office in his district, located from time to time, as the President shall direct, and must reside in the district to which he is appointed. The term of office of Surveyor-General is four years.

The Records of Surveys.

The Secretary of the Interior takes the necessary measures for the completion of the surveys in the general surveying districts for which Surveyors-General have been appointed, as the earliest practicable period, and when the surveys are finished, the field notes, maps, records and other papers pertaining to land-titles within the same are turned over to the Secretary of State of the respective States, and the office of Surveyor-General in every such district ceases and is discontinued.

Every Surveyor-General is authorized to employ a sufficient number of skilful surveyors as his deputies, who are sworn to a faithful performance of their duties. He frames regulations for their direction, and has power to remove them for negligence or misconduct in office.

What Shall be Surveyed.

Each Surveyor-General is required to cause to be surveyed, measured, and marked all base and meridian lines through such potato, and perpetuated by such monuments and such other correction parallels and meridians as are prescribed by law and instructions from the General Land-Office, in respect to the public lands within his surveying district to which the Indian title has been or may be extinguished. He causes to be surveyed all private land-claims within his district after they have been confirmed by authority of Congress, so far as may be necessary to complete the survey of the public lands. He transmits to the register of the respective land-offices within his district general and particular plats of all lands surveyed by him for each land district, forwarding copies of such plats to the Commissioner of the General Land-Office.

As far as is compatible with his other duties, he is required occasionally to inspect the surveying operations in his district, sufficiently to satisfy himself that the field-work is being faithfully executed according to contract. In case he cannot give his personal attention to such inspection, he is authorized to appoint a confidential deputy to make the required examination.

There is allowed for the several offices of the Surveyors-General, for clerk-hire, office-rent, fuel, books, stationery, and other incidental expenses, such sums as Congress may appropriate from year to year.

Whenever he thinks that the public interest requires it, the President is authorized to transfer the duties of Land Register and Receiver in any district to the Surveyor-General of the district in which such land district is located.

The Patent-Office.

The Patent-Office is a bureau of the Interior Department, wherein are kept and preserved all the records, books, models, drawings, specifications and other papers and things pertaining to patents for inventions.

In the Patent-Office are the following officers, appointed by the President: A Commissioner of Patents, an Assistant Commissioner of patents, and three Examiners-in-chief.

All the other officers, clerks and employés, named below, are appointed by the Secretary of the Interior, on the nomination of the Commissioner of Patents, their salaries varying from $900 to $3,500 per year: A chief clerk, an examiner in charge of interferences, one examiner in charge of trade-marks, twenty-four principal examiners, twenty-four first assistant examiners, twenty-four second assistant examiners (two of whom may be females), twenty-four third assistant examiners, a librarian, one machinist, three skilled draughtsmen, thirty-five copyists of drawings, one messenger and purchasing clerk, one skilled laborer, eight attendants in the model room, and eight others in the same room.

The Patent-Office has a seal, with which letters-patent and papers issued from it are authenticated.

The Commissioner of Patents and the chief clerk are severally required to give a bond for the faithful discharge of their duties, and a true accounting of public moneys coming into their hands.

Must Not be Pecuniarily Interested.

No officer or employé of the Patent-Office is allowed to acquire or take, during his or her term of service, any right or interest, directly or indirectly, except by inheritance or bequest, in any patent issued by the office.

Under the direction of the Secretary of the Interior, the Commissioner of Patents superintends or performs all duties respecting the granting and issuing of patents directed by the laws, and has charge of all books, records, papers, models, machines and other things belonging to the Patent-Office.

He, subject to the approval of the Secretary of the Interior, from time to time, establishes regulations, consistent with law, for the conduct of proceedings in his office. He also causes to be classified and arranged in suitable cases, in rooms and galleries of the Patent-Office, set apart for that purpose, the models, specimens of composition, fabrics, manufactures, works of art and designs which are deposited in the Patent-Office;

and these rooms and galleries are kept open during suitable hours for inspection by visitors.

He may restore to the respective applicants such models accompanying rejected applications for patents as he deems it unnecessary to preserve, or he may sell or otherwise dispose of them after the application has been finally rejected for a year, paying the purchase-money into the Treasury, as other patent-moneys are directed to be paid.

Description of Patents.

He may cause to be printed copies of the patent-claims of current issue, and copies of such laws, decisions, regulations and circulars as may be necessary for the information of the public.

He is authorized to have printed, from time to time, for free distribution a limited number of the complete specifications and drawings of each patent, together with suitable indexes, one copy being placed for free public inspection in each State-house of every State and Territory, copies for the like purpose in the clerks' offices of the Federal district courts, and one in the library of Congress—all being certified under the hand of the Commissioner and seal of the Patent-Office, and not to be taken from their places of deposit for any other purpose than as evidence in suits at law.

He is also authorized to have printed such additional copies of these specifications and drawings, duly certified, for sale at a price as low as may be warranted by the actual cost and demand for them, and to furnish a complete set of them to any public library that will pay for binding and transporting them and will provide suitable places of deposit, open to the public.

The lithographing and engraving are done by contract after competitive bidding, and the printing is done at the Government Printing-office.

Report of Commissioner of Patents.

Annually, the Commissioner of Patents lays before Congress a report, setting forth the amount of moneys received for patents, for copies of records or drawings, and all other sources; details of all the moneys paid out for contingent and miscellaneous expenses; a list of all the patents granted during the preceding year, generally classified; an alphabetical list of all the patentees and their places of residence; a list of all the patents that have been extended during the year, with such other information of the condition of the Patent-Office as may be useful to Congress or the public.

Superintendent of Public Documents.

The Superintendent of Public Documents, appointed by the Secretary of the Interior, collects, arranges, preserves, packs and distributes the publications received at the Department of the Interior for distribution, and performs other duties belonging to his office, including the compiling and supervising of the "Biennial Register," for the use of Congress and the several States.

The Returns Office.

The Secretary of the Interior is directed to provide, from time to time, a proper apartment in his department, to be called the Returns office, in which he causes to be filed the returns of contracts made by the Secretary of War, the Secretary of the Navy and the Secretary of the Interior, and appoints a clerk to attend to its business. His duty is to file all returns made to the office, so that they may be easy of access, keeping all returns made by the same officer in the same place, and numbering them in the order in which they are made. He also keeps an index-book, with the names of the contracting parties and the number of each contract opposite to the names, and this book is to be open for public

inspection. He also furnishes copies of these returns to any person who is willing to pay five cents for copying every 100 words; he has also to certify to the correctness of each copy made.

The Office of Education.

The Office of Education is a bureau of the Department of the Interior, the duties of which include the collection of facts and figures showing the condition and progress of education in the several States and Territories, and to diffuse such information respecting the organization and management of schools and methods of teaching as shall aid the people of the United States in the establishment and maintenance of efficient school systems, and otherwise promote the cause of education throughout the country.

The office of education is managed by a commissioner of education, who is appointed by the President.

The persons employed in the office of education include a chief clerk, one statistician, and one translator.

Hospitals.

Besides the foregoing bureaus and offices of the Department of the Interior, the Secretary of the Interior is charged with the supervision of the Government Hospital for the Insane, in the District of Columbia, which has for its objects the most humane care and enlightened curative treatment of the insane of the army and navy of the United States and the District of Columbia; and the Columbia Institution for the Deaf and Dumb, in the District of Columbia, which was established for the education of deaf mutes from the several States and Territories.

Department of Agriculture.

Congress, some years since, made provision for a Department of Agriculture at Washington.

The general design and duties of the Government Department of Agriculture are to acquire and distribute among the people of the United States useful information on subjects connected with agriculture in the most general and comprehensive sense of that word, and to procure, propagate, and distribute among the people new and valuable plants and seeds. The chief officer of this department is the Commissioner of Agriculture, who is appointed by the President. Besides a chief clerk, the commissioner appoints the following assistants: One chemist, one assistant chemist, one entomologist, one microscopist, one botanist, one statistician, one superintendent of experimental gardens and grounds, one assistant superintendent of the same, one disbursing clerk, one superintendent of the seed-room, one assistant superintendent of the seed-room, one librarian, one engineer, one superintendent of the folding-room, two attendants in the museum, and one carpenter.

Duties of the Commissioner of Agriculture.

The Commissioner of Agriculture has charge of the building and premises appropriated to the use of that department at Washington, and of the library, furniture, fixtures, records, and other property belonging to it.

It is his duty to procure and preserve all information concerning agriculture which he can obtain by means of books and correspondence, and by practical and scientific experiments (official records, accurately kept, are made in his office), by the collection of statistics, and by any appropriate means within his power.

He is also required to collect new and valuable seeds and plants, and to test, by cultivation, the value of such of them as ought to be thus tested; propagate such as may be worthy of propagation, and distribute them among agriculturists.

The Bureaus of the Naval Department.

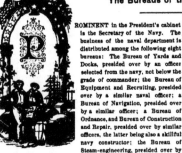

ROMINENT in the President's cabinet is the Secretary of the Navy. The business of the naval department is distributed among the following eight bureaus: The Bureau of Yards and Docks, presided over by an officer selected from the navy, not below the grade of commander; the Bureau of Equipment and Recruiting, presided over by a similar naval officer; a Bureau of Navigation, presided over by a similar officer; a Bureau of Ordnance, and Bureau of Construction and Repair, presided over by similar officers, the latter being also a skillful navy constructor; the Bureau of Steam-engineering, presided over by one of the chief engineers of the navy, who is also a skillful engineer; the Bureau of Provisions and Clothing, presided over by a paymaster of the navy, of not less than ten years' standing; the Bureau of Medicine and Surgery, presided over by one of the surgeons of the navy. The chiefs of these bureaus are appointed by the President, hold their offices for four years, and receive only the salary pertaining to each of their official grades in the navy.

Duties of the Secretary of the Navy.

The duties of the Secretary of the Navy are as follows: To execute such orders as he shall receive from the President relative to procuring naval stores and materials, and the construction, armament, equipment and employment of vessels of war, and other matters connected with the naval establishment; to have custody and charge of all the books, records and property in and belonging to the Navy Department; to cause the collection of all flags, standards and colors taken by the navy from the enemies of the United States.

The annual reports of the secretary to Congress shall present: A statement of the appropriations of the preceding fiscal year, how much money was expended, and in what manner, and the probable demand of the balances of appropriations remaining unused in each department of the navy; a statement of all offers for contracts for supplies and services made during the year, and accepted, by classes; a statement showing how much money was expended during the preceding fiscal year for wages of mechanics and laborers employed in building, repairing or equipping vessels, or in handling stores, and how much money was spent in purchasing stores and materials, with the cost and value of articles received, used, and remaining on hand, at the navy-yards; a statement of all sales of vessels and materials of the navy, by whom bought, the amounts realized from such sales, etc. The respective bureaus of the department furnish to the secretary all estimates for the specific, general and contingent expenses of the department and bureaus.

The Hydrographic Office.

Attached to the Bureau of Navigation in the Navy Department is a hydrographic office, for improving the means for navigating safely the vessels of the navy and merchant marine by providing, under the authority of the Secretary of the Navy, accurate and cheap nautical charts, sailing directions, navigators and manuals of instruction for the use of all such vessels. The Secretary of the Navy is authorized to provide such charts, maps, etc., to be prepared and printed and distributed to navigators at the cost of printing and paper. The moneys thus received from the sale of maps, charts, etc., is to be applied to the purchase and preparation of more of the same articles.

Nautical Observations.

The Naval Observatory at Washington is in charge of a naval officer, who receives only the pay of an officer of his grade for shore duty. The "Nautical Almanac," containing the result of naval and astronomical observations, is supervised annually by a naval officer or professor of mathematics in the navy, appointed by the secretary for that purpose.

The meridian of the Naval Observatory, at Washington, is established as the American meridian for all astronomical purposes, and the meridian of Greenwich, England, for all nautical purposes.

Facts Concerning the Various Branches of the United States Navy.

THE ACTIVE officers of the United States Navy are graded as follows: Admiral, Vice-Admiral, rear-admirals, commodores, captains, commanders, lieutenant-commanders, lieutenants, masters, ensigns, and midshipmen.

When the present Admiral and Vice-Admiral die, resign, or are removed, the grade will cease to exist, as no vacancy in it can be filled by promotion from the next lower rank.

The relative rank between officers of the navy and officers of the army is as follows:

The Vice-Admiral ranks with the lieutenant-general, Rear-admirals with major-generals, Commodores with brigadier-generals, Captains with colonels, Commanders with lieutenant-colonels, Lieutenant-Commanders with majors, Lieutenants with captains, Masters with first lieutenants, and Ensigns with second lieutenants.

How Many Naval Officers are Allowed.

There are allowed on the active list of naval officers of the line, one Admiral, one Vice-Admiral, ten rear-admirals, twenty-five commodores, fifty captains, ninety commanders, eighty lieutenant-commanders, 280 lieutenants, 100 masters and 100 ensigns. During war, rear-admirals are selected from those officers on the active list, not below the grade of commanders, who eminently distinguish themselves by their courage, skill and genius in their profession, and not then unless they have, upon the recommendation of the President, received the thanks of Congress for distinguished service. During peace, vacancies in the grade of rear-admiral are filled by regular promotion from the list of commodores.

Requisites in the Medical Service.

The active list of the Medical corps of the navy consists of fifteen medical directors, fifteen medical inspectors, fifty surgeons, and 100 assistant surgeons. All appointments in the Medical corps are made by the President. No person can be appointed assistant surgeon until he has been examined and approved by a board of naval surgeons, nor be less than twenty-one years old, nor more than twenty-six. No person can be appointed surgeon until he has served as an assistant surgeon at least two years in the navy, at sea, nor until he has been approved for such appointment by a board of naval surgeons.

The President selects the surgeons, and appoints to every fleet or squadron one who is denominated "surgeon of the fleet," and is surgeon of the flag-ship.

The Pay Department of the Navy.

The active list of the Pay corps of the Navy consists of thirteen pay directors, thirteen pay inspectors, fifty paymasters, thirty passed assistant paymasters and twenty assistant paymasters. All appointments in the pay corps are made by the President.

No person can be appointed assistant paymaster who is less than twenty-one years old or more than twenty-six years, nor until his physical, mental and moral qualifications have been approved by a board of paymasters appointed by the Secretary of the Navy.

The President may designate among the paymasters in the service, and appoint one to every fleet or squadron, who is denominated "paymaster of the fleet."

The Engineer Corps of the Navy.

The active list of the Engineer corps of the Navy consists of seventy chief engineers, divided into three grades, ten having the relative rank of captain, fifteen of commander, and forty-five of lieutenant-commander, or lieutenant. One engineer in-chief is selected by the President to serve in each fleet or squadron of the navy, and is denominated "engineer of the fleet." There are also in the navy 100 first assistant engineers, who have the relative rank of lieutenant or master in the navy, and 100 second assistant engineers, with the relative rank of master, or ensign.

Religious Service in the Navy.

The laws provide for the appointment by the President, for service in the public armed vessels of the United States, a number of chaplains (or ministers of the gospel), not exceeding twenty-four. A chaplain must not be less than twenty-one, nor more than thirty-five years old at the time of his appointment. Every chaplain is permitted to conduct public worship according to the manner and forms of the church of which he may be a member, and each chaplain must report annually to the Secretary of the Navy the official services performed by him during the previous year.

Mathematicians in the Naval Service.

The number of professors of mathematics

employed in the navy cannot exceed twelve, and they are appointed and commissioned by the President. They perform such duties as may be assigned to them by order of the Secretary of the Navy, at the Naval Academy, at the Naval Observatory, and in ships of war, instructing midshipmen of the navy, or otherwise. Three have the relative ranks of captains, four of commanders, and five of lieutenant-commanders, or lieutenants.

Naval Constructors.

The President may appoint naval constructors, who have rank and pay as naval officers, and are required to perform duty at any navy-yard or other station. Cadet engineers, who graduate with credit in the scientific and mechanical class of the Naval Academy, may, upon the recommendation of the academic board, be immediately appointed as assistant naval constructors.

Store-Keepers.

The President may appoint a civil engineer and a naval store-keeper at each of the navy-yards where such officers are necessary. The Secretary of the Navy may appoint citizens who are not officers of the navy to be store-keepers at foreign stations, when suitable officers of the navy cannot be ordered on such service, or when, in his opinion, the public interest will be thereby promoted.

Number Who May Enlist, and their Age.

The number of persons who may at one time be enlisted in the navy, including seamen, ordinary seamen, landsmen, mechanics, firemen, coal-heavers, apprentices, and boys, may not exceed 7,500.

Boys between the ages of sixteen and eighteen years may be enlisted to serve in the navy until they arrive at the age of twenty-one years, and other persons may be enlisted to serve for a period not exceeding five years unless sooner discharged by the direction of the President. No minor between sixteen and eighteen years old can be enlisted without the consent of his parents or guardian No boy less than sixteen years old, no insane or intoxicated person, and no deserter from the navy or army can be enlisted in the naval service. Any person enlisted in the military service may, on application to the Navy Department, approved by the President, be transferred to the navy or marine corps, to serve therein the remainder of his term of enlistment, subject to the laws and regulations of the naval service. But such tranfer does not release the soldier from any indebtedness to the government. Provision is also made in the laws for sending men from distant stations to the places of their enlistment at the expiration of their terms of service Honorable discharges may be granted to seamen, ordinary seamen, landsmen, firemen, coal-heavers and boys who have enlisted for three years; and it is the duty of every commanding officer, on returning from a cruise, to report to the Secretary of the Navy a list of his crew who enlisted for three years as being entitled to an honorable discharge as a testimonial of obedience and fidelity. And every commanding officer of a vessel is required to discourage his crew from selling any part of their prize-money, bounty-money, or wages.

Flag-Officers.

The President may select any officer not below the grade of a commander on the active list, and assign him to the command of a squadron, with the rank and title of "flag-officer;" and any officer so assigned has the same authority and receives the same obedience from the commanders of ships in his squadron, even though they hold commissions of an older date than his, that he would be entitled to receive if his commission were the oldest.

The laws prescribe with great minuteness the naval system of promotion from a lower rank to a higher one.

The Naval Academy.

The Naval Academy of the United States is established at Annapolis, Md. The students are styled "cadet midshipmen," and of these one is allowed to be appointed for every member or delegate of the House of Representatives in Congress, one for the District of Columbia, and ten are appointed annually from the United States at large.

How Cadets Are Appointed.

In March, every year, the Secretary of the Navy notifies (in writing) every member and delegate in Congress of any cadet vacancy that may exist in his district. The nomination of a candidate to fill such vacancy is made upon the recommendation of the member or delegate, if made before the first day of July of that year; but if it is not made by that time, the Secretary of the Navy must fill the vacancy. The candidates for the District of Columbia and the United States at large are selected by the President. All candidates from Congressional or Territorial districts and the District of Columbia must be actual residents, respectively, of the localities from which they are nominated.

Age of Candidates.

All candidates must be between the ages of fourteen and eighteen years, and physically sound, well formed and robust, and each is examined, how and where the Secretary of the Navy may prescribe. Any candidate rejected at such examination does not have the privilege of another examination for admission to the same class, unless recommended by the board of examiners. Should any candidate be found to be mentally or morally disqualified for admission, the member of Congress or Territorial delegate is notified to appoint another, who will be also duly examined and admitted or rejected.

Length of Time in School.

The academic course of cadet midshipmen continues for six years. Cadet midshipmen who are found to be deficient at any examination shall not be continued at the academy or in the service, unless the academic board of examiners so recommend.

When cadet midshipmen have successfully passed the graduating examination at the academy, they receive appointments as midshipmen in the navy, and take rank according to their proficiency in academic studies.

Who Determines the Course of Study.

The Secretary of the Navy has authority to issue regulations for the education, at the naval academy, as naval constructors and steam engineers, of midshipmen and other persons who exhibit a peculiar aptitude for such professions. For this purpose such persons are formed into a separate class at the academy, to be styled cadet engineers, or are otherwise supplied with all proper facilities for such a scientific mechanical education as will fit them for their proposed professions. These students may not at any time exceed fifty in number, and are selected by the Secretary of the Navy. No person other than a midshipman can be eligible for appointment to this class unless he first produces satisfactory evidence of mechanical skill and proficiency, and passes an examination as to his mental and physical qualifications.

The course of study for cadet engineers is four years, including two years' service on naval steamers. They are examined from time to time, and if found deficient, or if dismissed for misconduct, they cannot remain at the academy or in the service, except upon the recommendation of the academic board.

How Vessels are Ranked and Classified.

The classification of vessels in the navy includes four grades, commanded as follows: First rate vessels by commodores, second rate by captains, third rate by commanders, and fourth rate by lieutenant-commanders. Steamships, carrying forty or more guns, are classed as first rates, those of twenty guns and under forty as second rates, and all those of less than twenty guns as third rates.

How Vessels are Named.

The vessels of the navy are named by the Secretary of the Navy, under the direction of the President, according to the following rule: Sailing vessels of the first class, after the States of the Union, those of the second class after the rivers and principal cities and towns of the United States, and those of the third class as the President may direct. Steamships of the several classes are named in the same manner precisely, care being taken that not more than one vessel in the navy shall have the same name.

The Secretary of the Navy may change the names of any vessels purchased for the naval service.

Punishment for Offenses.

Congress has prepared sixty articles for the government of the officers and men in the navy. They have special reference to offenses committed against discipline, good order and morality, and the penalties attached to these and infractions of duty; the composition and powers of courts-martial and courts of inquiry, the sale or misuse of government property, the treatment of prize vessels and prisoners of war, the general conduct of all persons in the navy, etc.

Punishment with Death.

The following offenses are punishable with death, and the code applies to all persons in the navy. Mutiny, disobedience of orders, striking a superior officer, murder, acting as a spy, intercourse with an enemy without leave, receiving secret messages from an enemy, desertion in time of war, deserting a trust, sleeping on watch, leaving a station without orders, willful stranding or injuring of a vessel, unlawful destruction of public property, striking his flag or treacherously yielding to an enemy, cowardice in battle, deserting duty in battle, neglecting orders to prepare for battle, neglecting to clear ship for action, or to join in attack when signal is made to give battle, failing to encourage the men to fight, failing to seek an encounter with an enemy when duty requires it, or failing to relieve and assist other vessels of the fleet or squadron when in battle.

Other Punishment.

Courts-martial may adjudge the penalties of imprisonment for life, or for a stated term, at hard labor, and have jurisdiction in this respect over the offense of profanity, falsehood, drunkenness, gambling, fraud, theft or other conduct tending to the destruction of good morals, cruelty, oppression, quarreling and fomenting quarrels; challenging or fighting duels, or acting as a second in a duel; contempt of superior officers; seeking to form combinations against a commanding officer to weaken his authority; using mutinous words; neglect of orders; not endeavoring to prevent the destruction of public property; negligent stranding of any vessel of the navy, misconduct in convoying merchant or other vessels; receiving goods or merchandise for freight on board of a naval vessel without high authority; aiding or abetting in making false muster-roll; wasting public property; plundering or abusing citizens on shore; refusing to apprehend offenders or to receive prisoners; absence from duty without leave; violating general orders or regulations; desertion in time of peace; harboring deserters, etc.

Duties of commanders in active service are designated respecting accurate accounts of men transferred to and from their respective ships, showing their exact positions in the navy at the date of transfer; complete lists of the officers, men and passengers, sent quarterly to headquarters; noting deaths and desertions on board ship; care of the property of deceased persons, inspection of provisions, the health of their crews; presence at the final payment of crews; promulgation of the articles for the government of the navy, etc., and liability to be court-martialed for neglect of these rules and restrictions.

What Constitutes a Court-Martial.

Rules prescribe that no officer shall be dismissed from the service except by an order of the President, or by the sentence of a general court-martial. A general court-martial may be convened by the President, the Secretary of the Navy, or the commander-in-chief of a fleet or squadron. It consists of not more than thirteen nor less than five commissioned officers, not more than one-half of lower rank than the officer to be tried.

The Duty of a Court-Martial.

It is the duty of a court-martial, in all cases of conviction, to adjudge a punishment adequate to the nature of the offense. In a sentence to suffer death, two-thirds of the members must vote in favor of such sentence, or it cannot be inflicted. In all other cases, sentences are decided by a majority of the votes of the members. No sentence of a court-martial extending to the taking of life or to the dismissal of a commissioned or warrant-officer can be carried into execution until confirmed by the President. All other sentences may be carried into execution on confirmation of the commander of the fleet or officer ordering the court.

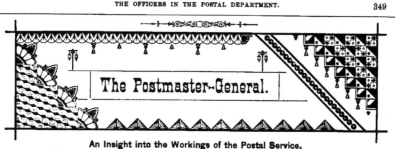

The Postmaster-General.

An Insight into the Workings of the Postal Service.

THIS EXECUTIVE department of the Government is superintended by the Postmaster-General. His term continues through that of the President, by whom he is appointed, and one month more, unless he sooner dies or resigns, or is removed for cause.

In this department are also three Assistant Postmasters-General, appointed by the President. There is also in this department an Assistant Attorney-General, appointed by the Postmaster-General.

Oath of Persons in the Postal Service.

Before entering upon his or her duties, or drawing any salary, every person employed in the postal service, from the Postmaster-General down, has to go before some civil or military officer and take the following oath of office:

I, A. B., do solemnly swear, (or affirm) that I will faithfully perform all the duties required of me, and abstain from everything forbidden by the laws in relation to the establishment of post-offices and post-roads within the United States; and that I will honestly and truly account for, and pay over, any money belonging to the said United States which may come into my possession or control· So help me God.

Duties of the Postmaster-General.

The duties of the Postmaster-General are as follows: To establish and discontinue post-offices; to instruct all persons in the postal service with reference to their duties; to decide on the forms of all official papers; prescribe the manner of keeping and stating postal accounts; to inforce the prompt rendering of postal returns relative to said accounts; to control, subject to the settlement of the Sixth Auditor of the Treasury Department, all expenses incident to the service of his department; to superintend disposal of the moneys of his department; to direct the manner in which balances shall be paid over; issue warrants to deposit money into the treasury, and to pay it out; to superintend generally the business of the department, and execute all laws relative to the postal service; to keep an account of all property in charge of the department, and report the same to Congress annually; to negotiate and conclude postal arrangements with foreign countries, and may reduce or increase the rates of postage between this and foreign countries; to publish the results of postal conventions with foreign countries; to deliver to the Sixth Auditor of the Treasury a copy of mail-carrying contracts; to issue warrants (on the quarterly statements of the Sixth Auditor) of payments of postmasters on account of the postal service, for carrying such amounts to the credit of the postal revenues on the books of the Auditor; to discharge from custody any person confined in jail on a judgment in a civil case in favor of the department if the defendant can show that he has no property of any kind; to prepare estimates and transmit them to Congress annually through the Secretary of the Treasury, for the necessary appropriations of money for his department, specifying in detail the purposes for which it is needed, such as printing, binding, salaries of employes, and other items.

Postmaster-General's Reports.

The Postmaster-General shall report to Congress annually: All contracts for carrying the mails made within the preceding year, with all particulars concerning them, and no person employed in the Post-Office Department shall become interested in any such contract, or act as agent, with or without compensation, for any mail-contractor, under pain of instant dismissal from office and other penalties; a statement of all land and water mail routes established or ordered within the preceding year, besides those contracted for at the annual mail-lettings, with the particulars attending them, and of all allowances made to mail contractors within the preceding year above the original contract prices, and the reasons therefor, etc. ; a statement in detail of all expenses curtailed within the preceding year; a detailed statement of the finances of the department for the preceding year, showing its resources, engagements, and liabilities; a report of the fines assessed against mail contractors and deductions from their pay, with the particulars; a copy of each contract for carrying mails between the United States and foreign countries, and a statement showing its benefits to the department; a report of all contracts, except for carrying mails, with the details thereof. a report on the postal business and agencies in foreign countries; a statement of the money expended in the department for the preceding fiscal year, with details. All of these reports and statements are to be printed at the public printing office, together or separately.

THE UNITED STATES POSTAL SERVICE.

Division of Labor in Large Post-Offices.

The postmaster, with a private secretary, has an office, where he maintains a general supervision over the entire post-office and its business, answering correspondence relating to postal business, and giving the public such information concerning the postal service as may be necessary for the general good. In his office, also, is an "inquiry clerk," whose business it is to receive all complaints concerning missing letters and other mail-matter, to institute searches therefor in his own or other interested post-offices, etc.

In the larger post-offices, like that at Chicago, the work is divided into sections. The general laws provide for clerks, at various salaries, and the postmasters, with the consent of the Post-master-General, assign to each a distinctive branch of labor. In the Chicago Post-Office, for instance, there are five divisions, embracing all' the operations of the office, as follows:

THE EXECUTIVE DEPARTMENT—Composed of the assistant postmaster, the auditor of post-office accounts, the book-keeper, the cashier, the watchmen, etc.

THE MAILING DEPARTMENT — Devoted to the reception and sending-off of mail-matter passing into and through the office, and out of it, in the regular course of business.

THE LETTER DELIVERY—Including the superintendent of free delivery and the letter-carriers, with the general delivery, the box-delivery, etc.

THE REGISTERED-LETTER DEPARTMENT — For the registry and mailing of valuable letters and the delivery of registered letters to the proper parties.

THE MONEY-ORDER DEPARTMENT — In which money-orders upon other post-offices in the United States and several foreign countries are issued, and similar orders from other post-offices are paid to the proper persons.

Special Postal Agents.

Connected with the principal post-offices are also two or more special agents of the Post-Office Department, whose business it is to superintend the railway postal service, and special agents employed in the free delivery and money-order service, in the interest of the Department.

Assistant Postmaster.

This officer is appointed by the postmaster, who is responsible for his acts. He is, as his title indicates, the active assistant of the postmaster in supervising the work of the post-office. He cannot be a contractor for carrying any mail, nor be interested in any mail-carrying contract, and his salary varies according to the location and circumstances of his appointment.

Post-Office Auditor.

The auditor is charged with the examination and correction of the accounts of the postmaster with the Government, his subordinate officers, clerks and employes of the post-office.

The Post-Office Book-keeper.

The book-keeper is charged with the duty of correctly opening, keeping and closing, from time to time, the accounts of the postmaster with the Government and with every individual doing business with or for his post-office, subject to the orders of the postmaster and assistant postmaster, by whom his salary is fixed.

The Post-Office Cashier.

This officer has supervision of all the money paid into or out of the post-office, subject to the orders of the postmaster and assistant postmaster, and provides for its safe keeping and proper deposit with the United States Sub-Treasurer, or in some other designated place.

The Post-Office Watchmen.

The duties of the watchmen are principally confined to the custody of the post-office building and its contents at night and other designated periods during the absence of officers and employes.

Interior Work of Large Post-Offices.

The duties of mailing clerks are varied according to the departments in which they are employed, as for instance: To open all packages of letters addressed to that office, to count and compare them with the post-bill accompanying the package and to check any error in the bill; to file the bill, and send the letters to the letter-carriers' department, the general delivery, the box-delivery, the registry office or the money-order office, as may be necessary for their proper care and safe delivery.

If the office is a "distributing post-office," letters for various other places within the distributing limits of the office are sorted, billed, repacked and forwarded to their proper destination by mail.

Some of the clerks sort out newspapers and periodicals, and send them to the proper delivery, or mail them for other points. Newspapers and periodicals for other newspapers and periodicals within the delivery of that office are sent to the "exchange clerks," to be sorted and properly distributed, so, also, transient newspapers and periodicals are sorted and sent to the proper deliveries in the post-office.

Other clerks receive, sort, stamp, bill and mail letters designed for other places. Others receive, examine and mail transient packages of newspapers and periodicals directed to other post-offices. Others receive regular daily, weekly and other newspapers and periodicals sent from publishing houses direct to subscribers, exchanges, etc., weigh them, to ascertain the amount of postage to be prepaid by the publishers, and send the accounts to the proper officer, after which such papers and periodicals can be forwarded by mail to any part of the country without further charge to the publishers or subscribers.

Delivery clerks receive domestic and foreign letters, newspapers, periodicals not directed to any special box, street or number. These go into the general delivery, to be there called for by their owners. Other letters and papers, directed to a specified box, are placed in that box to remain until called for.

Post-Office Stamp Department.

In large offices there is a wholesale stamp department and a retail stamp department. In the first, stamps are sold to merchants and others by the sheet, or in greater quantities; stamped envelopes by the package or larger quantity, and postal cards by packages or hundreds.

In the retail department sales extend from a single one-cent stamp to a dozen or more of any required sorts. In this department, also, the clerk weighs transient packages to be sent by mail, to ascertain the required amount of postage to be prepaid, if requested so to do.

Letter Delivery.

The superintendent of free delivery is placed in charge of the letter-carriers and their work. He sees that letters are promptly and properly sorted by the clerks for the branch offices or the various letter-carriers.

One or more clerks are stationed in the general delivery to promptly and carefully assort and deliver the letters and papers, domestic and foreign, sent to their department. In some offices there is a foreign-letter delivery, conducted like the ordinary general delivery. When letters remain a designated time in the general delivery uncalled for, they are advertised in some public newspaper, kept a certain time longer, and are then forwarded to the dead-letter office of the Post-Office Department at Washington.

All letters not properly directed for mailing, or on which the postage is not prepaid, are also sent to the dead-letter office at stated periods. In the box-delivery, clerks are stationed to wait upon those who call for the contents of their boxes, and properly distribute whatever mail-matter is sent to their department. Those persons who rent lock-boxes and drawers wait upon themselves, having the proper keys to their respective compartments of this delivery.

Registered-Letter Division.

For the greater security of valuable mail-matter, the Postmaster-General established a uniform system for the registration of letters. Mail-matter can only be registered on the application of the party who posts the same, and the fee for registration, in addition to the regular postage, is ten cents, to be in all cases prepaid. The registry clerk in the post-office gives the person registering the letter a receipt for it, properly describing it. The letter is classified on the books of the office sending it as a registered letter; it is then carefully mailed to the postmaster at the post-office to which it is directed; is classified there as a registered letter, and delivered to the person to whom it is addressed only upon his giving a receipt therefor as a registered letter. The proper number of clerks is detailed to the registered-letter department of a large office by the postmaster thereof. In smaller offices the postmaster and his ordinary clerks attend to the registration of letters, as they are presented, and the delivery thereof whenever they arrive.

The Money-Order Division.

In order to promote public convenience, and to insure greater security in the transfer of money through the mails, the Postmaster-General has established and maintains, under rules and regulations which he deems expedient, a uniform money-order system at all suitable post-offices, known as "money-order offices." The postmaster of every city where branch post-offices are in operation subject to his supervision, is authorized, under the direction of the Postmaster-General, to issue, or cause to be issued, by his clerks and assistants in charge of such branch offices or stations, postal money-orders, payable at his own or at any other money-order office, or at any branch post-office or station of his own or any other money-order office, as the remitters thereof may direct; and the postmaster and his sureties are, in every case, held accountable upon his official bond for all moneys received by him or his designated assistants or clerks in charge of stations, from the issue of money-orders, and for all moneys which may come into his or their hands, or be placed in his or their custody by reason of the transaction by them of money-order business.

Any postmaster who issues a money-order without having previously received the money therefor, is deemed guilty of a misdemeanor, and may be fined not less than $50 nor more than $500.

Prices of Postal Money-Orders.

Money-orders not exceeding $15, ten cents.
"   "   30, fifteen cents.
"   "   40, twenty cents.
"   "   50, twenty-five cents.

None are sold exceeding $50, nor can one individual or firm send more than three orders amounting to $50 to one and the same party on the same day.

Money-orders are payable only to the persons in whose names they are drawn, but the right to collect the amount may be transferred in writing on the money-order to one other (and no other) individual by the person in whose favor the order is originally drawn.

Blank applications for money-orders are kept at money-order offices, which each applicant can fill up with his name, the name and address of the party to whom the order is to be paid, the amount and date of the application, and all such applications are preserved in the money-order office for a stated time after the money-order is issued.

The postmaster who issues a money-order sends a notice thereof by mail, without delay, to the postmaster on whom it is drawn.

After a money-order has been issued, if the purchaser desires to have it modified or changed, the postmaster who issued it can take it back and give a new one instead, for which a new fee has to be paid.

The postmaster who issues a money-order shall repay the amount of it upon the application of the person who obtained it and the return of the order, but the fee paid for it is not returned.

The Postmaster-General transfers money-order funds from one postmaster to another, and from the postal revenue to the money-order fund; and also to the postmaster at any money-order office, by a warrant on the United States Treasury, and payable out of the postal revenue, such sums as may be required over and above the current revenues at his office to pay the money-orders drawn upon him. He also requires each postmaster at a money-order office to render to the Post-Office Department weekly, semi-weekly, or daily accounts of all money-orders issued and paid, of all fees received for issuing them, of all transfers and payments made from money-order funds, and of all money received to be used for the payment of money-orders or on account of money-order business.

Commissions to Postmasters.

Postmasters at money-order offices are allowed, as compensation for issuing and paying money-orders, not exceeding one-third of the whole amount of fees collected on orders issued, and one-fourth of one per cent. on the gross amount of orders paid at their respective offices, provided that such compensation, together with the postmaster's salary, does not exceed $4,000 a year, except in the case of the postmaster at New York city.

There is at Washington an officer of the Government known as the superintendent of the money-order system, whose salary is $3,000 a year.

Officers in the Money-Order Department.

The officers in charge of the postal money-order division of the Chicago Post-Office, aside from the postmaster and assistant postmaster, are a superintendent, an examiner and a cashier. The superintendent supervises and controls the direct operations of his office under the instructions of the Postmaster-General and the postmaster. The examiner examines the correctness of each money-order presented from another post-office before passing it to the cashier for payment, reserving a minute of it, which must compare with the order in name, place of issue, number and amount. The cashier, upon receiving the order from the examiner, pays it to the proper person waiting to receive the money.

The cost of the stationery and incidental expenses of the money-order division of each post-office are, if possible, paid out of the fees received from the sale of money-orders.

The Dead-Letter Office.

The dead-letter office is a branch of the Post-Office Department at Washington, for the purposes herein named.

The Postmaster-General regulates the period during which undelivered letters may remain in any post-office, and when they shall be returned to the dead-letter office, and he makes regulations for their return from the dead-letter office to the

writers when they cannot be delivered to the persons to whom they are addressed.

When Letters are Advertised.

As often as the Postmaster-General may prescribe, but not oftener than once a week, postmasters are required to advertise the list of letters remaining uncalled-for and unclaimed in their respective offices. This is done by inserting the list in a newspaper of the vicinity having the largest circulation within that post-office delivery, or by a written list posted in some public place. After the list has been published, the postmaster is required to post up in a conspicuous place in his office a copy of such list.

Sent to the Dead-Letter Office.

At the end of the time prescribed by the Postmaster-General for keeping undelivered letters in his office after advertising them, the postmaster sends them to the dead-letter office, together with the following other letters: Letters deposited in that office to be mailed to other offices, on which the name of the post-office was accidentally omitted, or on which the address was too imperfect to be properly understood; letters on which prepayment of postage was neglected, and letters addressed to a known fraudulent institution or firm.

What is Done With Dead Letters.

At the dead-letter office, all letters sent to it are opened and examined. If they contain valuable inclosures they are registered, and when they cannot be delivered to the party addressed nor to the writer, the contents are disposed of, and a careful account is kept of the amount realized in each case, and may be reclaimed within four years by the sender or the party addressed. All other letters of value or importance to the party addressed or the writer, and which cannot be returned to either, are disposed of as the Postmaster-General directs.

Letters with Writer's Address on Envelope.

Prepaid letters, bearing upon the outside the name and address of the writer, are not advertised, but if not called for within a time set by the writers, are returned to the persons sending them, without charge.

Mail Contractors.

Before making any contract for carrying the United States mails, except on railways, and, under certain circumstances, upon steamboats or other vessels, the Postmaster-General must give public notice by advertising once a week for six weeks, in one or more newspapers published in the State or Territory where the mail service is to be performed (one of which papers must be published at the State or Territorial capital), and such notice must describe the route, the time at which the mail is to be made up, the time at which it is to be delivered, and the frequency of the service.

Proposals for Carrying the Mail.

Every proposal for carrying the mail over any specified route must be accompanied by the oath of the bidder, that he has the pecuniary ability to fulfill his obligations and that his bid is made in good faith and with the intention to enter into contract and perform the service in case his bid is accepted, that the signatures of his guarantors are genuine, and that he believes them pecuniarily responsible for and able to pay all damages to the United States arising from his failure to fulfill his contract. The guarantors must be one or more responsible persons. Proposals for carrying mails are delivered sealed, and are kept sealed until the bidding is closed, and are then opened and marked in the presence of the Postmaster-

General and one or two of the Assistant Postmasters-General, or any other two officers of the Post-Office Department, to be designated by the Postmaster-General. Any bidder may withdraw his bid, in writing, twenty-four hours before the time for opening it.

Bids are Recorded.

All bids are recorded and preserved by the Postmaster-General. Postmasters are forbidden to give any bidder a certificate of the sufficiency of his guarantor or surety before the guarantee or contract is signed by such guarantor or surety, and if he "knowingly makes any false or illusory certificate," may be forthwith dismissed from office and fined or imprisoned, or both.

Contracts Run for Only Four Years.

No contract for carrying mails on land can be made for a longer term than four years, nor on the sea for more than two years. No mail contractor can receive any pay until he has executed his contract according to law and the regulations of the department. The laws prescribe the manner of carrying mails in detail, prohibit sending letters by private expresses, provide for carrying letters on vessels, steamboats, etc., and punishment for obstructing or delaying the mail.

The Railway Postal Service.

Railway routes on which mails are carried, including those in which the service is partly by railway and partly by steamboat, are divided into three classes, according to the size of the mails, the speed at which they are carried and the frequency and importance of the service, so that each railway company receives, as far as practicable, a proportionate and just rate of compensation, according to the service performed. The pay for carrying mails on any railway of the first class does not exceed $300 per mile a year, on railways of the second class not more than $100 per mile a year, and on those of the third class not more than $56 per mile a year, unless one-half the service on any railway is required to be performed in the night, when twenty-five per cent. additional may be paid by the Postmaster-General.

Postal Clerks Carried Free.

On all railways carrying mails, the person in charge of them is transported free, and mail-matter and the route agent are to be carried on any train. The pay for carrying mails on railways which receive government aid is fixed by Congress.

Postal Car Accommodations.

Among the conditions of the railway postal service are the following: That the railway shall furnish mail trains with postal cars sufficiently large, properly fitted up, furnished, warmed and lighted for the accommodation of route-agents and the necessary clerks to accompany and distribute the mails.

The clerks sort the mails for each station on the route and the post-roads connecting therewith, while traveling, and deliver the mail bag thus made up at mail stations, by kicking or throwing it from the car at places where the train does not stop, or by handing it to the authorized mail-messengers at depots where the train halts.

Different Classes of Postmasters.

The Postmaster-General establishes post-offices at all such places on post-roads defined by law as he may deem expedient.

Postmasters are divided into five classes. Those of the fourth and fifth classes, who do the least business, are appointed and may be removed by the Postmaster-General, and the others are appointed by the President, holding their offices for four years, unless sooner removed.

Where Postmasters Must Live.

Every postmaster must reside within the delivery of the office to which he is appointed, and before entering upon its privileges, emoluments and responsibilities, must execute a bond to the Government with good and approved security; and if it is designated as a money-order office, his bond contains an additional condition for the performance of his duties and obligations in connection with the money-order business.

The bond of any married woman who may be appointed postmaster is as binding upon her and her sureties, and she is as liable for misconduct in office, as if she were a man.

What the Post-Office Department Requires.

Every person employed in the postal service must take and subscribe to an oath that he (or she) will faithfully perform all the duties required of him (or her), and abstain from everything forbidden by the laws in relation to the establishment of post-offices and post-roads within the United States; and that he (or she) will honestly and truly account for and pay over any money belonging to the United States which may come into his (or her) possession or control. Every person employed in the postal service is subject, however, to all penalties and forfeitures for violations of the laws relating to such service, whether he has taken the oath of office or not.

Requirements of Postmasters.

Every postmaster keeps an office in which one or more persons must be on duty during such hours of the day as the Postmaster-General directs, for the purpose of receiving, delivering, making up and forwarding all mail-matter received thereat. He must also keep a record, in prescribed form, of all postage-stamps, envelopes, postal books, blanks, and property received from his predecessor, or from the Post-Office Department or its agents; of all receipts of money for postage and box-rents, and of all other receipts on account of the postal service, and of any other transactions which are required by the Postmaster-General. These records are preserved and delivered to his successor, and shall at all times be subject to examination by any special agent of the department.

He renders to the Postmaster-General, under oath, once in three months, in such form as the latter prescribes, an account of all moneys received or charged by him, or at his office, for postage, rent of boxes or other receptacles for mail-matter, or by reason of keeping a branch post-office, or for the delivery of mail-matter in any manner whatever.

The Postmaster-General may also require him to send with his quarterly accounts a sworn statement of the truth of such accounts, showing, besides, that he has not knowingly delivered, or permitted to be delivered, any mail-matter on which the postage was not at the time paid.

Penalty for Neglect.

If he neglects for a month to make his quarterly returns to the department, he and his sureties forfeit and pay double the amount of the gross receipts at such office during any previous or subsequent equal period of time; and if at the time of trial no account has been rendered, they are liable to a penalty in such sum as the court and jury estimate to be equivalent thereto.

Where Postmasters Must Keep Money.

He is required to safely keep, without loaning, using, depositing in an unauthorized bank, or exchanging for other funds, all public money collected by him, or which comes into his possession, until it is ordered by the Postmaster-General to be transferred or paid out. Postmasters in cities where there is an Assistant Treasurer of the United States, must deposit the postal revenues and all money accruing at their offices with such assistant treasurer as often as once a week, and oftener if the Postmaster-General requires it. Every postmaster must promptly report to the Postmaster-General every delinquency, neglect or malpractice of mail-contractors, their agents or mail-carriers, that comes to his knowledge.

When More Post-Office Clerks are Allowed.

Whenever unusual business accrues at any post-office, the Postmaster-General may make a special order allowing reasonable compensation for clerks, and a proportionate increase of salary to the postmaster during the time of such extraordinary business.

The Postmaster-General may designate offices at the intersection of mail-routes as distributing or separating offices, and if any such office is of the third, fourth, or fifth class, he may make a reasonable allowance to the postmaster for the necessary cost of clerk-hire arising from such duties. The Postmaster-General may discontinue any post-office where the safety and security of the postal service and revenues are endangered from any cause, or where the efficiency of the service requires it.

What Persons in the Postal Service May Not Do.

No postmaster, assistant postmaster or clerk employed in any post-office, may be a mail-contractor or concerned in any contract for carrying the mail. No postmaster can act as an agent for any lottery office, or, under any pretense of purchase, or otherwise, sell lottery-tickets; nor can he receive or send any lottery-scheme, circular or ticket free of postage, under penalty of $50 for each violation of this regulation.

Salaries of Postmasters.

The salaries of postmasters must be readjusted by the Postmaster-General once in two years, and in special cases as much oftener as he may deem expedient. The salary of a postmaster, and such other expenses of the postal service authorized by law as may be incurred by him, and for which appropriations have been made by Congress, may be deducted out of the receipts of his office, under the direction of the Postmaster-General.

Whenever, by reason of the extension of the free delivery of letters, the box-rents of any post-office are decreased, the Postmaster-General may allow, out of the receipts of that office, a sum sufficient to maintain the salary at the amount fixed upon before the decrease in box-rents. No postmaster can, under any pretense whatever have, receive, or retain for himself, in the aggregate, more than the amount of his salary and his commission on the money-order business of his office.

When a Town May Have Letter-Carriers.

As frequently as the public convenience may require, at every city or town containing a population of 20,000 within the delivery of its post-office, letter-carriers may be employed for the free delivery of mail-matter.

Letter-Boxes.

The Postmaster-General may establish, in places where letter-carriers are employed, and in other places where, in his judgment, the public convenience requires it, receiving-boxes for the deposit of mail-matter, and cause the matter deposited therein to be collected as often as may be for general accommodation.

The compensation of letter-carriers is established by a law of Congress, and graded according to service or location.

The uniform dress worn by letter-carriers is prescribed by the Postmaster-General, and it is a penal offense for any person not connected with the letter-carriers' department of the postal service to wear such uniform.

Every letter-carrier must execute a bond, with sureties, to be approved by the Postmaster-General, for the safe custody and delivery of all mail-matter and the faithful account and payment of all money received by him.

If any person wilfully or maliciously injures, tears down or destroys any public letter-box, or assaults a letter-carrier while performing his duty, he is liable to prosecution, a fine of not less than $100 nor more than $1,000, or to imprisonment from one to three years. The Postmaster-General may establish branch offices for the receipt and delivery of mail-matter and the sale of postage-stamps and envelopes, within any post-office delivery, and prescribe the rules and regulations for their government.

No Gifts to Letter-Carriers.

No extra postage or carriers' fees may be charged or collected upon any mail-matter collected or delivered by carriers, nor can any person employed in the postal service receive any fees or perquisites on account of duties performed by him in his official position.

All expenses of letter-carriers, branch offices and receiving boxes, or incident thereto, are kept and reported in a separate account by the postmaster, and the Postmaster-General is guided in the expenditures for this branch of the service by the income derived from it.

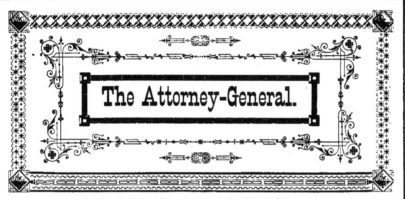

The Judiciary Department of the United States.

THIS EXECUTIVE department of the Government is in charge of the Attorney-General of the United States. He is assisted by another officer, learned in the law, called the Solicitor-General; also three officers, learned in the law, called Assistant Attorneys-General; a Solicitor of the Treasury, an Assistant Solicitor of the Treasury, a Solicitor of Internal Revenue, a Naval Solicitor, and an Examiner of Claims for the Department of State. All of the officers above designated are appointed by the President, each and all of whom hold their positions for four years, unless for sufficient cause they are sooner removed.

Duties of the Attorney-General.

It is the duty of the Attorney-General to give his advice and opinion upon questions of law whenever required by the President. No public money can be expended upon any building, site or land purchased by the Government on which to erect any armory, arsenal, fort, fortification, navy-yard, custom-house, lighthouse or other public building until the Attorney-General, in writing, decides upon the validity of the land-title and the Legislature of the State in which the land is located has given its consent to such purchase; and other government officers are named as assistants in procuring sound title to such lands.

The head of any executive department may require the Attorney General to give his opinion concerning any question of law arising in his department, including the Secretary of War and the Secretary of the Navy, who may call upon him for legal advice.

Most of the questions of law referred to the Attorney-General, he may submit to his subordinate officers for examination and opinion, but not any questions involving a construction of the Constitution of the United States, and his approval of their opinions is required to make them valid.

He has a general superintendence over district attorneys and marshals of the United States in any State or district, and when the public interest requires it, he may employ other counsel to aid district attorneys in their duties. Should the head of any department require the attendance of counsel in examining witnesses in any claim case, the Attorney-General must furnish a subordinate lawyer for that purpose, and regulations exist for the appointment and preparation of such counsel. He may also send the Solicitor-General, or any officer of the Department of Justice, to any State or district of the United States to attend to the interests of the Government in any Federal or State court. He has also a general supervision of the accounts of district attorneys, marshals, clerks or other officers of United States courts. He shall also sign all requisitions for the advance or payment of all moneys in the Treasury, appropriated for the use of the Department of Justice. He is also authorized to publish in book form, from time to time, such opinions of the officers of the Department of Justice as he shall deem valuable for preservation, with indexes and foot-notes, the work to be done at the Government Printing-office.

At the beginning of each regular session of Congress, he has to make a report of the business of the Department of Justice for the last preceding fiscal year, including the expense accounts of the Federal courts, statistics of crime in the United States, the number of pending suits, etc.; also a report of the additional counsel and attorneys employed to assist in United States law cases.

The officers of the Department of Justice, under the direction of the Attorney-General, shall assist in performing all legal services required for other departments, in prosecuting or defending government claims, suits, etc., and the Attorney-General may require any solicitor or officer of his department to perform any duty required of the department or any of its officers.

Unless the Attorney-General otherwise directs, he and the Solicitor-General shall conduct and argue suits and writs of error and appeals in the Supreme Court, and suits in the courts of claims, in which the Government is interested.

The traveling expenses of the officers of this department, while visiting courts, etc., in remote States and districts, are paid in addition to their salaries.

Administration of Justice.

The United States Supreme Court.

THE CONSTITUTION declares that the judicial power of the United States is vested in one Supreme Court and in such inferior courts as Congress may, from time to time, ordain and establish. The judges, both of the Supreme and inferior courts, hold their offices during good behavior, and receive for their services compensation that may not be diminished during their continuance in office. This judicial power extends to all cases in law and equity arising under the Constitution, the laws of the United States, and all treaties with foreign countries made under their authority.

The Supreme Court of the United States consists of a Chief Justice and eight associate justices, appointed by the President, any six of whom constitute a quorum. The associate justices have precedence according to the dates of their commissions, or, when the commissions of two or more of them bear the same date, according to their ages. Should a vacancy occur in the office of Chief Justice, or he become unable to perform the labors and exercise the powers of his office, his duties devolve upon the associate justice who is first in precedence, until such disability is removed or another associate justice is appointed and qualified. This provision applies to every associate justice who succeeds to the office of Chief Justice.

The Supreme Court has power to appoint a clerk, a marshal, and a reporter of its decisions.

The clerk is under the same obligations, the same restrictions, the same oath or affirmation of office, and the same bond, as is the clerk of a United States district court.

One or more deputy clerks may be appointed by the court on the application of the clerk, and may be removed at the pleasure of the court; and their duties and responsibilities are similar to those of deputy clerks in a United States district court.

The marshal of the Supreme Court is required to attend the court at its sessions; to serve and execute all processes and orders issuing from it, or made by the Chief or associate justices, in pursuance of law, and to take charge of all property of the United States used by the court or its members; and with the approval of the Chief Justice he may appoint assistants and

messengers to attend the court, with the same compensation allowed to similar officers in the lower house of Congress.

The reporter of the Supreme Court is required to see that its decisions, made during his term of office, are printed and published within eight months after they are made, and in any subsequent year he must print and publish another volume of the same sort. He also delivers a specified number of copies of such printed decisions to the Secretary of the Interior. At the completion of his first volume of reports he is entitled to receive $7,500, and for every subsequent volume prepared and published by him, $1,500; but all his work must be done within the legally-prescribed time and manner. The law also provides for the proper distribution of these decisions to officers of the United States Government, and the price at which other persons may buy them. Thus are preserved, from year to year, most valuable additions to our national legal lore, which, substantially bound in volumes, are gradually enlarging the law libraries of the land.

The Supreme Court holds one session annually, beginning on the second Monday in October, and such adjourned or special terms as it may deem necessary for the dispatch of its business.

The Supreme Court has exclusive jurisdiction of all controversies of a civil nature where a State is a party, except between a State and its citizens, or between a State and citizens of other States, or

The Judges of the United States Supreme Court.

Jos. P. Bradley, Stephen J. Field, Sam. F. Miller, Nathan Clifford, M. R. Waite, N. A. Swayne, David Davis, W. Strong, Ward Hunt.

THE above illustration, from a photograph by S. M. Fassett, of Washington, represents the Judges of the Supreme bench, as they appeared in 1876. The picture is valuable as showing the dress worn and the position assumed by the judges when together in session, the Chief Justice being in the center, and the eight Associate Justices sitting four upon each side.

aliens, in which last-named cases it has original, but not exclusive, jurisdiction. And it has, exclusively, all such jurisdiction of suits or proceedings against embassadors, or other public ministers, or their domestics, or domestic servants, as a court of law can have consistently with the law of nations; and original, but not exclusive, jurisdiction of all suits brought by public ministers or embassadors, or in which a consul or vice-consul is a party.

It has power, also, to issue writs of prohibition in the district courts when proceeding as courts of admiralty and maritime jurisdiction: and writs of mandamus in cases warranted by the principles and usages of law to any courts appointed under the authority of the United States, or to persons holding office under the authority of the Government, where a State, or an embassador, or other public minister, or a consul or vice-consul is a party. The trial of issues of fact in the Supreme Court, in all actions at law against citizens of the the United States, are by jury. The laws provide largely for the character of the practice in this Supreme tribunal, which is final in its action and decrees.

What is Required of Judges.

The Justices of the Supreme Court and the United States district and circuit courts, before entering upon their public duties, are solemnly sworn, or made to affirm, that they will administer justice without respect to persons, and do equal right to the poor and to the rich, and that they will faithfully and impartially discharge and perform all the duties incumbent on them, according to the best of their abilities and understanding, agreeably to the Constitution and laws of the United States.

Continuance of Salary in Old Age.

None of these judges may exercise the profession or employment of counsel or attorney, or be engaged in the practice of the law, and disobedience in this direction is deemed a high misdemeanor and treated accordingly.

When any one of these judges resigns his office after having held it at least ten years, and has attained the the age of seventy years, he receives, during the remainder of his life, the same salary that was by law payable to him at the time of his resignation.

Division into Districts.

The United States are divided into fifty-five federal judicial districts. A district judge is appointed for each district by the President of the United States, unless otherwise provided for by the statutes. Each judge must reside in the district for which he is appointed. The records of the district court are kept at the place where it is held.

The jurisdiction of the district courts in suits, and the places and times of holding such courts, are regulated by law. The law also provides for the government of the judges in holding, changing or postponing courts, according to circumstances.

Restrictions upon Clerks.

No clerk, assistant, or deputy clerk of any United States court is allowed to act as solicitor, proctor, attorney or counsel in any cause pending in either of said courts, or in any district for which he is acting as said officer, and, if he does, he may be stricken from the roll of attorneys upon complaint.

Within thirty days after the adjournment of each term of court, the clerk is required to forward to the Solicitor of the Treasury a list of all judgments and decrees, to which the United States are parties, that have been entered in said court during such term, showing the amount

adjudged or decreed in each case, for or against the United States, and the term to which execution thereon will be returnable.

Duties of Clerks.

At each regular session of any court of the United States, the clerk presents to the court an account of all moneys remaining therein or subject to its order, stating in detail in what causes they are deposited, and in what causes payments have been made.

In the absence or disability of the judges the clerks administer oaths to all persons who identify papers in admiralty causes.

The Attorney-General exercises general supervisory powers over the accounts of clerks and other officers of United States courts.

Judges of district courts, in cases of absence or sickness, hold terms of court for each other, with the same powers and effects as if held in their own district.

United States Circuit Courts.

The judicial districts of the United States are divided into nine circuits. The Chief Justice and associate justices of the Supreme Court of the United States are allotted among these circuits by an order of that court. For each circuit there is also appointed a circuit judge, who has the same power and jurisdiction as the justice of the Supreme Court allotted to the circuit.

Circuit courts are usually held in each judicial district of the United States, (see District Courts), and are presided over by the circuit justice of the United States Supreme Court, or by the circuit judge, or by the district judge of the district sitting alone, or by any two of said judges sitting together.

It is the duty of the Chief Justice of the Supreme Court, and of each justice of that court, to attend at least one term of the circuit court in each district of the circuit to which he is allotted during every period of two years. Cases may be ,heard and tried by each of the judges holding a circuit court sitting apart, by direction of the presiding justice or judge, who designates the business to be done by each.

Circuit courts may be held at the same time in the different districts of the same circuit. Special terms are arranged in certain circuits of the United States. The law also regulates the circumstances under which district judges may sit in circuits, in cases of error or appeal from their own decisions; when suits may be transferred from one circuit to another; when causes may be certified back to the courts from which they came, and under what circumstances circuit justices may hold courts of other circuits at the request of another circuit justice, or when no justice has been allotted to a circuit, after a vacancy occurs.

The circuit judges of each circuit, except in cases otherwise provided for by law, appoints a clerk for each circuit court. The court also, at the request of the circuit clerks, appoints deputy clerks, and both clerks and deputies are governed by the regulations concerning district clerks and their deputies.

District Attorneys.

In nearly every district where United States circuit and district courts are established throughout the nation, the President appoints a person learned in the law to act as attorney for the United States in such district, who holds his position for four years, and is sworn to the faithful execution of his office.

It is the duty of each district attorney to prosecute, in his district, all delinquents for crimes and offenses cognizable under the authority of the United States, and all civil actions in which the United States are concerned,

and, unless otherwise instructed by the Secretary of the Treasury, to appear in behalf of the defendants, in all suits or proceedings pending in his district against collectors or other officers of the revenue, for any act done by them or for the recovery of money exacted by or paid to such officers, and by them paid into the Treasury. On instituting any suit for the recovery of any fine, penalty or forfeiture, he is required to immediately transmit a statement of the case to the Solicitor of the Treasury. Also, immediately after the close of every term of the circuits and district courts for his district, he forwards to the Solicitor of the Treasury (except in certain cases, as provided by law) a full and particular statement, accompanied by the certificates of the clerks of the respective courts, of all causes pending in said courts, and of all causes decided therein during the term in which the United States are party.

Marshals and their Duties.

A marshal is appointed in nearly every district, by the President, and holds his office for four years.

It is the duty of the marshal of each district to attend the district and circuit courts when in session, and to execute throughout the district all lawful precepts directed to him and issued under the authority of the United States; and he has power to command all necessary assistance in the execution of his duty.

The marshals and their deputies have, in each State, the same powers as sheriffs and their deputies, in executing the laws of the United States.

If a marshal dies, his deputies continue to perform their official duties, and are held responsible for their acts under the bond of the deceased marshal, the same as if he were still alive.

Marshals and their deputies whose term of office expires, or who are removed, have legal power to execute all processes remaining in their hands.

Within a month before the commencement of each term of the circuit and district courts in his district, every marshal is required to make returns to the Solicitor of the Treasury of the proceedings had upon all writs of execution or other processes in his hands for the collection of moneys adjudged and decreed to the United States, respectively, by such courts. And every marshal to whom any execution upon a judgment in any suit for moneys due on account of the Post-Office Department has been directed, is required to make returns to the sixth auditor, whenever he directs, of the proceedings which have taken place upon such process of execution.

When Vacancies Occur.

Should a vacancy occur in the office of the district attorney or marshal within any circuit, the circuit justice of such circuit may fill it, and the person so appointed serves until an appointment is made by the President; and the marshal thus appointed must give a bond, as if he had been appointed by the President, and the bond shall be approved by the circuit justice, and filed in the office of the clerk of the court.

Juries.

Jurors chosen to serve in the courts of the United States, in each State respectively, must possess the same qualifications (subject to modifications), and be entitled to the same exemptions, as the jurors in the highest court of law in such State may have and be entitled to at the time when such jurors for service in the United States courts are summoned, and they are selected by ballot, lot, or otherwise, in accordance with the custom in such State court, so far as that mode may be found practicable in a United States court or by its officers. And for this purpose the United States courts may, by rule or order, conform the selection and impaneling of juries, in substance, to the laws and usages relating to jurors in the State courts in such State.

Number of the Grand Jury.

Every grand jury impaneled before any district or circuit court must consist of not less than sixteen, nor more than twenty-three persons. If less than sixteen attend they are placed on the grand jury, and the marshal is ordered, at a date fixed by the court, to summon from the body of the district, and not from bystanders, a sufficient number of persons to complete the grand jury. Vacancies in the jury arising from the challenging of jurors are also filled in a similar manner. From the persons summoned and accepted as grand jurors, the court appoints a foreman, who has power to administer oaths and affirmations to witnesses appearing before any jury.

Grand juries are not summoned to attend the United States courts, except at the discretion and upon the orders of the presiding judge. The circuit and district courts of the States and Territories and the supreme court of the District of Columbia, discharge their juries whenever they consider their attendance unnecessary.

No person can be summoned as a juror in any circuit or district court oftener than once in two years, and any juror summoned to serve oftener than once in two years is ineligible, if challenged.

The grand jury impaneled and sworn in any district court may take cognizance of all crimes and offenses within the jurisdiction of the circuit court for such district as well as of the district court. Laws in relation to grand jurors, however, differ in certain localities.

Who May Not Serve on Juries.

Every person summoned to serve as a grand or petit juror in United States courts, are disqualified and subject to challenge who have willfully or voluntarily taken up arms or joined in any rebellion or insurrection against the United States, giving it aid and comfort, or any assistance, directly or indirectly, in money, arms, horses, clothes, or anything whatever for the benefit of any person engaged in such insurrection, or about to join it; or who has resisted, or is about to resist, with force and arms, the execution of the laws of the United States.

At every term of any United States court, the district attorney, or other person acting in behalf of the United States in such court, may move, and the court may require the clerk to administer to every person summoned to serve as a grand or petit jury in that court, an oath embodying the substance of the above-named cause for disqualification as a juror, and liable to be challenged; and unless such persons can truly take such oath, they cannot be allowed to serve on juries in that court.

Nor can any person serve as a juror in a United States court in any proceeding or prosecution based upon or arising under the provisions of laws enforcing the fourteenth amendment of the Federal Constitution (relative to the equality of civil rights of all citizens, regardless of their color), unless such person can take and subscribe an oath, in open court, that he has never counseled, advised or voluntarily aided in any combination or conspiracy against said amendment and the laws enforcing it.

the court must report to Congress the cases of such removal.

The chief clerk has authority to disburse, under the direction of the court, the contingent fund which may from time to time be appropriated to its use by Congress; and his accounts are settled by the proper accounting officers of the Treasury in the same way as the accounts of other disbursing agents of the Government are adjusted.

Statement of Judgments Rendered.

At the beginning of the annual session of Congress, the clerk transmits to it a full and complete statement of all the judgments rendered by the court during the previous year, stating the amounts thereof and the parties in whose favor they were rendered, together with a brief synopsis of the nature of the claims; and at the end of every term of the court he transmits copies of the decisions to the heads of the various departments of the Government, to specified government officials, and to other officers charged with the adjustment of claims against the United States.

No member of either branch of Congress can practice as an attorney or counselor in the court of claims.

The court of claims has jurisdiction over all claims founded on statutes or contracts, or which are referred to it by either house of Congress; all set-off and counter-claims of the Government against persons presenting claims upon it; the claims of disbursing officers for relief from responsibility on account of the captures, while in the line of his duty, of Government funds, vouchers, records  or papers in his charge, and claims for captured or abandoned property, arising from the exigencies of insurrection or other cause. The methods of procedure and practice in such court of claims are particularly described in the United States statutes. It has also power to appoint commissioners to take testimony to be used in the investigation of claims that come before it, to prescribe the fees which they receive for their services, etc.

Any final judgment against a claimant on any claim prosecuted in the court of claims according to the provisions of the law forever bars any further claim or demand against the United States arising out of the matters involved in the controversy.

These brief sketches of the various United States tribunals will serve to give the reader a fair idea of the power and dignity that distinguish our national judicial system.

The Court Room.

THE illustration shown above represents the usual attendants upon a lawsuit during its trial in court.

Behind the desk is seated the judge; in front is the clerk of the court and beside him sits the court crier. Seated in a chair by the judge's desk is the witness being questioned by the lawyer who sits with his client at the end of the table. At the adjoining table several reporters are writing; at the extreme right are the twelve jurymen; on the opposite side of the room are four lawyers, one of whom is standing and is objecting to the course pursued by the lawyer who is examining the witness. Inside the railing and near the entrance sits the deputy sheriff, who has general charge of the court-room; at the extreme left and outside the railing sit spectators and individuals who may be called as witnesses.

The United States court of claims, is located at Washington, in apartments provided at the expense of the Government. It consists of one chief justice and four judges, who are appointed by the President, and hold their offices during good behavior. Each of them is required to take an oath to support the Constitution and faithfully discharge his duties.

When Court is in Session.

The court of claims holds one annual session, beginning early in December and continuing as long as the prompt transaction of its business may require. Any two of the judges constitute a quorum and can hold a court.

The court appoints a chief clerk, an assistant clerk (if necessary), a bailiff and a messenger. The clerks are required to take the constitutional oath of fidelity, and perform their duties under the direction of the court. For misconduct or incapacity they may be removed by the court, but

A Sketch of the Capitol at Washington.

BOUT one and one-half miles easterly from the President's Mansion is the United States Capitol, a structure distinguished as much by its size and elegance of finish as by being the place in which the two houses of Congress assemble to enact the national laws.

The corner-stone was laid by Washington in September, 1793, and it was first occupied by Congress in November, 1800. In 1814 it was partially burned by the British soldiery; the reconstruction of the burned wings was begun in 1815; the corner-stone of the main building was laid in March, 1818, and it was finished in 1827. In 1850 it was decided to extend the structure, and the corner-stone of the new work was laid July 4, 1851, with an address by Daniel Webster. The structure was completed in 1867.

The whole edifice has an eastern front, and its entire length is 751 feet four inches, and its greatest depth, including steps and porticoes, is 348 feet. The building covers about three and a half acres of ground. The main or old portion is built of sandstone, painted white, and the extensions are of white marble, slightly variegated with blue. The outside of the building is adorned with architectural ornaments and several groups of sculpture. An iron dome rises from the center to a height of 287½ feet above the basement floor, having a diameter of 135½ feet. The top of this dome is surmounted by Crawford's bronze statue of Liberty, nineteen and a half feet high. The inside of the Capitol is liberally decorated with frescoes, sculptures and paintings. The rotunda, inside of the dome, is a circular apartment, ninety-six feet in diameter and 180 feet high.

The chamber occupied by the United States Senate is situated in the center of the northern extension of the Capitol; is of rectangular form, being over 113 feet in length, more than eighty feet in width, and thirty-six feet in height. The galleries surrounding it will seat 1,200 persons.

The House of Representatives occupies the center of the southern extension of the Capitol, and is 139 feet long, ninety-three feet wide and thirty-six feet high. The galleries will seat 1,000 people.

The Supreme Court of the United States holds its sessions in the old Senate chamber, on the east side of the north wing of the central building. It is a semicircular apartment, seventy-five feet long and forty-five feet high. The former Hall of Representatives, also of a semi-circular form, ninety-six feet long, and fifty-seven feet high, is in the south wing of the central building, and is used as a depository for the historical statues contributed by the several States, in accordance with the invitation of Congress, in 1864, with other statuary and paintings. It is considered the most stately and beautiful apartment in the Capitol.

The Library of Congress is another attractive room, ninety-one and a half feet long, thirty-four feet wide and thirty-eight feet high, on the west side of the rotunda, together with two wings, each ninety and a half feet long, twenty-nine and a half feet wide.

The Capitol grounds cover an area of fifty-one and a half acres, handsomely laid out, and containing a great variety of trees.

THE PRESIDENT'S MANSION.*

T THE western end of the city of Washington stands the staid and venerable home of the Presidents of the United States, during their terms of office. Close by it, and surrounding it, are the Government buildings occupied by the State Department, the Treasury Department, the War Department and the Navy Department, representing, in one group, the executive, diplomatic, pecuniary, and defensive sinews of the nation. Having an attractive location, with handsomely ornamented grounds in front, and a fine park in its rear reaching to the Potomac river, the President's house occupies a prominent position in the national capital.

The corner-stone of the mansion was laid October 13, 1792, and the structure was first occupied in 1800 by President John Adams. It is properly called the "White House," owing to its freestone walls having been painted white. Its designer was Mr. James Hoban, who embodied in it a resemblance to the palace of the Duke of Leinster, in Great Britain. It contains two stories and a basement, is 170 feet long and eighty-six feet wide. The portico on the north front is supported by eight columns of the Ionic order of architecture; on the south front is a semicircular colonnade of six other Ionic columns, and the roof is surrounded with a handsome balustrade.

During the war of 1812, when the British army invaded Washington, President Madison was forced to flee, and the English troops destroyed the mansion. This was in 1814. In the following year Congress authorized its reconstruction, and in 1818 the new edifice was first occupied by President Monroe.

The main entrance to the mansion is in the north front, where a massive door-way opens into the main hall, divided midway by a row

* For view of President's mansion see page devoted to President's Duties.

of pillars resembling marble, and along its walls are ranged the portraits of the chief magistrates who formerly occupied it. On the left of the hall the visitor is ushered into the celebrated "East room," which occupies the entire lower eastern portion of the mansion. It is in this apartment, which is handsomely furnished, that the Presidents hold their levees and state assemblages. It is eighty-six feet long, forty feet wide and twenty-eight feet high, and is warmed with four fire-places.

Three other apartments of some celebrity,—the "Green," the "Blue," and the "Red,"—adjoin the East room, each deriving its name from the color which distinguishes it from the adjacent ones,

and all are handsomely furnished. The Red room is sometimes used as a general reception parlor. The north front of the mansion has six rooms, which are chambers used by the President and his family, and on the south front are seven rooms, described as the ante-chamber, audience room, cabinet-room, ladies' parlor, the President's private office, and two others used for various purposes. The main or state dining-room is west of the Red room, and joining it is the ordinary dining-room used by the President's family. The ladies' parlor is for the private use of the President's family, and is considered the handsomest apartment in the building. The basement contains eleven rooms, including kitchens, pantries, etc.

The Duties of a Congressman.

How Bills are Passed and Laws Made.

 ALTHOUGH the Constitution of the United States quite fully details the work to be done by Congress, the following outline of the form of procedure will doubtless be interesting, it being much the same as that observed in the State legislatures in the passage of State laws:

The day having arrived for the regular meeting of a new Congress, the members of the House of Representatives gather in their hall in the Capitol at Washington, at three o'clock in the afternoon, and come to order.

The Clerk of the last previous Congress rises and says: "The hour fixed by law for the meeting and organization of the House of Representatives of the Forty-—— Congress having arrived, the Clerk of the House of Representatives of the Forty-—— Congress will proceed to read the list of members-elect to the House of Representatives for the Forty-—— Congress, prepared by him in accordance with law."

He then reads the list by States, comprising about 260 names. During the reading, some member, whenever a certain name is called (each member answering to his name), says "I reserve a point of order on that name," intimating that he has objections to the called member's right to a seat in Congress.

The list being called through, the Clerk says: "One hundred and ninety-three persons have answered to the call. Being a quorum of the body, the Clerk is now ready to receive motions."

Sometimes, at this point, members rise and state their objections to seating certain new members, making motions to refer the credentials of such members to the Committee on Elections, etc. This business consumes considerable time in discussion, with more or less bitterness of feeling and speech.

At length the Clerk says, "The Clerk appeals to members of the House to preserve order."

Sometimes the confusion continues after this. At length the Clerk is heard to say: "The gentleman from Tennessee is out of order. The tellers will please take their places"—to aid in the organization of the House.

Selection of a Speaker.

Nominations for Speaker are then made by several members. A vote is taken by voice, counted by the tellers, and announced: "Whole number of votes cast, ——; necessary to a choice. ——; Mr. A. has ——; Mr. B., ——."

The Clerk announces: "Mr. A., of New York, having received a majority of all the votes given, is duly elected Speaker of the House of Representatives for the Forty-—— Congress. The gentleman from Wisconsin (Mr. Brown) and the gentleman from Connecticut (Mr. Jones) will please conduct the Speaker-elect to the chair, and the gentleman from Pennsylvania (Mr. Robinson), the senior member of the body, will please administer to him the oath required by the Constitution and laws of the United States."

Mr. Brown and Mr. Jones then conduct Mr. A. to the chair, where he stands and expresses, in a brief speech, his thanks for the honor conferred upon him, and pays a handsome compliment to the intelligence and political strength of the new Congress. The oath of fidelity to the Constitution, the laws and his duties, is then administered to him by Mr. Robinson.

Admitting the Members.

The Speaker then says: "The first business in order is the swearing-in of members. The various delegations (by States) will present themselves in a convenient number as they are called."

As the various members present themselves, the other members listen in silence, or occasionally interpose an objection to a certain member being qualified. These objections properly take a written form, and are referred to the Committee on Elections for examination, with the necessary affidavits to show why the members objected to should not have a seat in Congress. Long discussions sometimes intervene, and if the objec-

tions are not withdrawn, the oath is not administered to the member in dispute until the Committee on Elections report favorably in his case.

The Delegates elect from the several Territories are also sworn in.

Ready for Business.

A member offers a resolution, which meets with no opposition, but is immediately read, considered and agreed to, as follows "That the Senate be informed that a quorum of the House of Representatives has assembled, and that Mr. A., one of the Representatives from New York, has been chosen Speaker, and that the House is now ready to proceed to business."

Mr. C, of Illinois, rises and presents a resolution, which is read, considered and adopted, appointing the Speaker and four members a committee to revise the rules of the House for its better government, to report at an early day.

Mr. G., the Secretary of the Senate, now appears on the floor of the House to announce. "Mr Speaker—I am directed to inform the House that a quorum of the Senate has assembled, and that the Senate is ready to proceed to business."

Presently, a member rises and asks unanimous consent to take up and concur in a resolution just received from the Senate. No objection being made, the resolution is read, announcing the appointment of two members of the Senate to join certain members of the House (to be selected by the House) to wait upon the President of the United States, and inform him that a quorum of each House has assembled, and that Congress is ready to receive any communication that he may be pleased to make.

Waiting Upon the President.

Mr. E. moves that the House appoint three members to join the committee on the part of the Senate. The motion being agreed to, the Speaker appoints Mr. L., of Georgia; Mr M., of Tennessee, and Mr. N., of New Jersey, as the committee on the part of the House.

During the absence of this committee but little business is done, beyond discussions upon the eligibility of certain members, or the election of the following officers of the House of Representatives: A Clerk, a Sergeant-at-Arms, a Doorkeeper, Postmaster and Chaplain, in the order named. Members nominate candidates for each office as their own names are called, if they choose; the Speaker appoints tellers, and the voting is done by voice.

The vote having been announced, the successful candidate is declared elected by the Speaker. He then comes forward and qualifies for his new position by taking the Constitutional oath of fidelity. Sometimes the election of Chaplain is postponed, in order to find a candidate who is entirely satisfactory to the majority.

Somebody then proposes a regular hour for the daily meeting of the House, and the hour of twelve, noon, is usually adopted.

The drawing of seats for the members of the House is usually next in order, either by themselves or their colleagues.

This is also considered a good time to lay before the House the papers in the various contested election cases of members of the House, to be referred to the Committee on Elections when that committee has been appointed by the Speaker, within a few days after the organization.

The Joint Committee of the two Houses of Congress, appointed to announce to the President the readiness of Congress to receive any communication from him, having fulfilled their duty, return to their respective houses and report what they have done, and are then discharged from further duty in the case.

The President's annual or inaugural message is, about this time, delivered to both houses, in joint session in the House of Representatives, being usually read by the Clerk of the House and his assistants. After it has been read, the Senate retires to its own chamber and both houses proceed to refer certain portions of the message to appropriate committees for consideration and future action.

A resolution is usually adopted in the House of Representatives, authorizing the printing of several thousand copies of the message for the use of members and others.

By this time the first day's session has drawn to a close. A motion to adjourn is therefore made, seconded and adopted, and the House dissolves until the next hour of meeting.

In the Senate Chamber.

In the Senate, on the first day of the new session, the proceedings are usually marked by less feeling and confusion, but the organization is similarly effected. The Vice-President of the United States is inducted into the chair of the Senate; the new Senators are sworn in, or have their credentials referred to the Committee on Elections, and but little other business is, generally, transacted.

The New Member.

Among the members of the House of Representatives whose credentials were found to be all right, and whose eligibility and claim to a seat in Congress are therefore undisputed, is Mr. Sempronius Smith, from the Tenth District of Wisconsin. Mr. Smith has been a prosperous merchant, and mill-owner, a wide-awake and useful citizen, and his popularity resulted in his being sent to Congress to represent the interests of a large and thrifty constituency. For a few days after the organization, he wisely refrains from making himself conspicuous in the councils

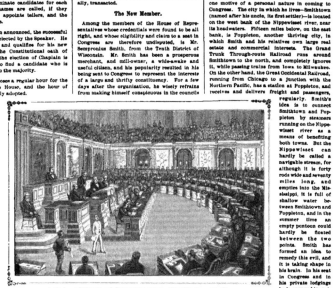

Interior of House of Representatives, Washington, D. C.

THIS ILLUSTRATION represents the members of the House of Representatives in session during the meeting of Congress. The full number entitled to vote, from 1883 to 1893 is 325. The speaker of the house occupies the upper seat, at one end of his desk sits the door-keeper, at the other end the sergeant-at-arms; at the desk in front are the clerks, and at the lower desk, are the official reporters. In the gallery above the speaker, newspaper correspondents have their seats; the remainder of the gallery, which will hold about 1,000 persons, being allotted to spectators. The members occupy the seats in the body of the house, the individuals standing on the floor being pages, who serve the members when they desire to communicate with the clerks or with each other.

of the nation. He is "learning the ropes." He confers with his colleagues and a few new acquaintances in the House upon national topics. Naturally he is shrewd and honest, and he comes to Congress fully decided to do his duty.

A Local Bill for Personal Gain.

That more or less of personal selfishness should sometimes reveal itself in Congressional legislation is a natural consequence. In order to show the routine work of introducing a bill, the nature of the lobby, the means which may influence the passage of a law in Congress, where personal benefits are conferred, the following illustration is given. This class of bill is presented as illustrative of the work of the lobby and the means sometimes used to influence legislation in securing appropriations for personal profit.

Mr. Smith does not believe that any man ever

goes to Congress without at least one selfish motive—one "axe to grind." Pott, his predecessor, had half a dozen axes to grind, and came very near ruining a good portion of his constituency by advocating his selfish measures. Smith confesses (to himself only, however,) that he has one motive of a personal nature in coming to Congress. The city in which he lives—Smithtown (named after his uncle, its first settler)—is located on the west bank of the Nippewisset river, near its headwaters. Fifteen miles below, on the east bank, is Poppleton, another thriving city, in which Smith and his relatives own large real estate and commercial interests. The Grand Trunk Through-route Railroad runs around Smithtown to the north, and completely ignores it, while passing trains from Iowa to Milwaukee. On the other hand, the Great Occidental Railroad, running from Chicago to a junction with the Northern Pacific, has a station at Poppleton, and receives and delivers freight and passengers, regularly. Smith's idea is to connect Smithtown and Poppleton by steamers running on the Nippewisset river as a means of benefiting both towns. But the Nippewisset can hardly be called a navigable stream, for although it is forty rods wide and seventy miles long, and empties into the Mississippi, it is full of shallow water between Smithtown and Poppleton, and in the summer time an empty pontoon could hardly be floated between the two points. Smith has formed an idea to remedy this evil, and it is taking shape in his brain. In his seat in Congress and in his private lodgings he is engaged in putting it upon paper.

INTRODUCTION OF THE BILL.

One day, when the introduction of bills is in order, he rises in his seat in the House, and, catching the Speaker's eye, he says:

"Mr. Speaker—I hold in my hand a bill entitled: 'An Act to build a dam across the Nippewisset river at a point three miles below the town of Poppleton, Lomax county, Wisconsin, and appropriating $15,000 for that purpose.' This bill, sir, is in the interest of a large and populous section of my district, and is offered for the purpose of facilitating trade and commerce between the great Northwest and the metropolitan city of Chicago and the Atlantic sea-board. I desire, sir, to have it read and referred to the Committee on Appropriations." Smith "fairly ached" to make a speech on his bill, but he wisely refrained until it should regularly come before the House. He sent it to the Speaker by a page. Smith's colleague (Benson) requested that it be read before being referred, as it was short. He thought that an internal improvement bill of this sort had sufficient public interest to demand this consideration.

The fact is that Benson only preferred his request to satisfy his own curiosity. He had no special interests in Smith's district, and if the bill did no injury to the State, it might pass and welcome.

The Speaker said: "If there are no objections, the bill will be read by the Clerk."

TEXT OF THE BILL.

The Clerk read as follows:

"Be it enacted by the Senate and House of Representatives of the United States of America in Congress assembled, That permission is hereby granted to Robert Sweet, Thomas P. Glade and John Q. A. Sweet to construct and maintain a substantial dam across the Nippewisset river, three miles below the city of Poppleton, in the county of Lomax and State of Wisconsin.

"SECTION 2. The said dam shall be constructed of natural stone and timber, and earth, put together as crib-work, and extend from the present east shore of the Nippewisset river, at a point known as Winkle's ford, to the west shore of said river to a point known as the northeast corner of Tripp's farm

"SECTION 3. The lands likely to be overflowed by reason of the construction of the said dam are swamp-lands, owned by the State of Wisconsin; and the said Robert Sweet, Thomas P. Glade and John Q. A. Sweet, their heirs and successors, are hereby authorized and required to build and maintain strong and substantial dykes, or levees along the line of the banks of said river, between the river and said swamp-lands, to prevent the overflow of the river into said swamps.

"SECTION 4. There is also appropriated to the said Robert Sweet, Thomas P. Glade and John Q. A. Sweet, to aid in the construction of said dam and dykes, or levees, the sum of $15,000, to be paid from moneys in the Treasury of the United States not otherwise appropriated."

One word of explanation which was not granted to the House by Smith. The parties named in this bill were brothers-in-law to Smith.

REFERRED TO A COMMITTEE.

The Speaker: "If there is no objection, the bill will be sent to Committee on Appropriations."

A Member: "I move that it be ordered printed and sent to the Committee on Commerce."

Another Member. "I second that motion."

The yeas and nays being called for, the motion prevailed, Smith himself voting in the affirmative.

That afternoon Smith's bill was sent to the room of the Committee on Commerce by a messenger, with other bills that had been referred to them during the day.

THE WORK OF THE LOBBY.

Smith had a lobby force at the capital, a number of personal friends from Smithtown and Poppleton, who knew the value of Smith's project to the interests of their respective towns and their own pockets. Ostensibly the surrounding country was to be greatly benefited by the passage of the bill. Now the lobby went to work in good earnest. They advocated the measure to every member of the House who would listen to them. They were liberal in dinners, wines and cigars. They had an argument to meet every objection. It was not a trumpery affair. A whole district would be benefited; towns would flourish, farmers be encouraged, commerce be increased, and labor enlisted. They all understood the merits of the bill. Smith was modest; he only pleaded the best interests of his constituents. Glade, one of the parties named in the bill, was there. He got in some good arguments also. Smith knew two or three of the Committee on Commerce, and by his manly bearing and quiet demeanor gave them a favorable unpression of himself.

THE BILL BEFORE THE COMMITTEE.

When the full bill came up in the committee for consideration, Smith was requested to be present with one or two of his friends to explain anything that might be deemed questionable. Smith and his friends did their best to convince the committee of the fairness and utility of the measure They described the geographical position with neat diagrams, and the commercial interests with nicely-arranged statistics. They represented the value of the Nippewisset river below the proposed dam as already worthless for commercial purposes—a thing of swamps and shoals and bars. They pointed with much enthusiasm to the increased value of lots and lands made available by making the river navigable above the dam The committee courteously dismissed Smith and his friends, and then discussed the question of reporting the bill favorably to the House. One or two opposition members argued against the measure on political grounds, and one or two more objected otherwise, but the value of the levees or dykes to the commerce of that section of country was a strong argument. The chairman thought the improvement was richly worth the sum it would cost for its promotion of commerce in the Northwest. He had known railroads that promised less to receive large grants of land and great subsidies of money without a murmur of opposition. Now 15,000 people and 500 farms were to be benefited by the appropriation of an insignificant sum of money. He believed in encouraging steamboats, canal-boats, sail vessels or railroads impartially, in proportion to their relative business. A railroad company needed more help than a steamboat company, and always got it. He should vote for the measure as one of the committee, or as its chairman with his casting vote. Then the vote was taken. It stood five to three before the chairman voted; then it stood six to three.

REPORT OF THE COMMITTEE.

Next day the chairman of the Committee on Commerce stood up in the House and favorably reported Smith's bill without amendment.

The House went into Committee of the Whole that afternoon to consider some appropriations for special objects. Smith's bill was among them. Smith was a little nervous. It is true he had won an important victory. The Committee on Commerce was made up of men of good common sense and ability, and their recommendation was on the side of the dominant political party in the House. But now the bill had to run the gauntlet of the entire House—friends and foes. Smith made an able plea in behalf of it, and his colleague (Benson) made another. One or two Eastern members, with pardonable sectional indifference, briefly objected to the West swallowing up so much of the public money; but an old stalwart veteran from Massachusetts said that the East had no reason to be ashamed of the West and its energetic commercial prosperity. The two sections were no longer divided in their interests. Massachusetts was the older and the better cultivated State in the matter of intellect and commercial affairs, but Wisconsin was fast overtaking any of the New England States in both of these advantages. Then he wound up with an oratorical slap at New York's overgrown steamship and railroad monopolies, and said be should vote for Smith's bill. Two or three other gentleman spoke of Wisconsin in the most favorable terms. Her war record was briefly reviewed and compared favorably with her agricultural, manufacturing and political position in the Union. Many members listened to the discussion with perfect indifference. One man suggested an amendment by striking out the appropriation. This bit of waggery caused a general smile and hastened the vote on the bill. The yeas and nays were called for and taken: the bill received a handsome majority on the question of reporting it favorably to the House, and then the committee rose.

One secret of the success of Smith's bill, thus far, is found in the real benefit that it proposed to bring to everybody living above the dam; the population below the dam had not yet found out enough about it to oppose it intelligently.

On the following day, the action of the Committee of the Whole was duly reported to the assembled House, and the bills favorably passed upon by the committee were called up in rotation for action by the House. That is, the members moved the second reading of each one as it came up, and it was so ordered.

Debate followed the second reading. Some of the bills were discussed at length, some were laid on the table, some were postponed; others were ordered to be engrossed for a third reading and put upon their passage. One or two were passed by good majorities. One or two more were recommitted to their respective committees for further consideration and amendment.

A SPEECH IN FAVOR OF THE BILL.

Smith's bill was read a second time. Benson good naturedly spoke in favor of its passage. He had been in Congress one or two terms, and always spoke to the point and pleasantly. In consideration of its having favorably passed the Committee on Commerce and the Committee of the Whole, he felt it due to his colleague (Smith) and the State which they both represented, to move its third reading and passage by the House.

An opposition member, from a district in another portion of the Union, wished to know if the lobby had come well-primed to urge this bill through the House.

Benson indignantly repelled the insinuation of corrupting influences. The parties named in the bill were business men in good standing—not millionaires, and men who had no money to throw away in buying votes for a paltry sum of $15 000 Suppose they had a prospective money interest in the bill So had every business man in the county. The lobby were a unit in advocating the measure, and not a word of genuine opposition had been heard except from the opponents of the dominant party in this House "I," said Benson, in conclusion, "I move, sir, that the bill go to a third reading and be put upon its passage"

Smith seconded the motion. The crisis had come in the House, but he felt rather sure of success. The men from below the dam had not been heard from. The other eight members from Wisconsin knew of no good reason why the bill should not pass, and they said little or nothing in regard to it. Besides, they might need the votes of Smith and Benson in some little measures of their own during the session; so they were a unit on this question.

The yeas and nays on the passage of the bill were called. The vote showed political bias and considerable indifference as to the result It stood: Yeas, 94; nays, 65; not voting, 27 So the bill was passed.

THE BILL GOES TO THE SENATE.

A day later, Smith's bill, with others, is taken to the Senate Chamber by the Clerk of the House of Representatives and handed to the Secretary of the Senate. The latter officer, at the proper time, announces to the Senate the receipt of these bills which have been sent to that branch of Congress for its concurrence. As the title of each is read, some Senator moves its reference to a committee or to be laid on the table, or to be read in full a first or a first and second time.

A Senator, hearing the title of Smith's bill read, requested that it be read in full. Having heard it read, the Senator moved that the bill be sent to the Committee on Commerce.

Another Senator moved that it go to the Committee on Appropriations This last motion being seconded, the first Senator withdrew his motion.

The President: "Unless objection is made, the bill will be sent to the Committee on Appropriations."

No one objected; and the bill was referred to the Committee on Appropriations.

PERSONAL INTERVIEWS WITH A CONGRESSMAN.

One of the Senators from Wisconsin was on this committee. When Smith learned the reference of his bill in the Senate, he sought the Senator from Wisconsin, with whom he had considerable acquaintance; had a conference with him in regard to its merits, and reported the action of the House Committees and the House in detail. Some of Smith's lobby friends also interviewed the Senator from Wisconsin, and favorably impressed him with the merits of the enterprise

In the afternoon of the following day, Smith's bill was brought up in the committee. Smith was not present, nor was it necessary. He had fully explained matters to the Senator from his State. When the bill had been read by the clerk of the committee, the members of the committee naturally turned to the Senator from Wisconsin, with gentlemanly deference, and he briefly and comprehensively expressed a favorable opinion of it. Smith could not have done better The State would really derive benefit from the passage of the bill. He would not deprecate the value of any other public work authorized by Congress, but this comparatively insignificant appropriation would have an effect upon the interests of inter-State commerce far outside of Wisconsin The whole Union was more or less benefited, frequently, by these little aids to commerce

One of the committee objected to the largeness of the amount of the appropriation. In his opinion the dam and dykes ought not to cost more than the amount named in the bill, but the parties to be benefited directly by this appropriation and improvement ought to pay at least one-third of the expense out of their own pockets. He proposed to amend the bill by striking out "$15,000," and substituting therefor "$10,000" The Senator from Wisconsin was on his feet in a moment Only the week before he had assisted the objecting Senator to increase the appropriation in a bill of a similar character, but of no more merit than this. He made a little speech in which he denounced the niggardly spirit in public enterprises, under a senseless cry of "retrenchment and reform." He begged permission to introduce a witness to show that $15,000 was the smallest possible sum that could be beneficially expended in making the Nippewisset river navigable for boats. The parties who requested the passage of the bill had asked nothing for the erection of the necessary wharves and piers at Poppleton or Smithtown. They were willing to bear the burden of this expense themselves. He sent a messenger for one of Smith's lobby, a gentleman familiar with the entire county mentioned in the bill. The committee questioned him in reference to the amount of work that $15,000 would accomplish. He said it might possibly build the dam, and, perhaps, most of the dykes, yet he thought that $20,000 would be none too much to finish the work proposed but the county would willingly make up any deficiency remaining after the expenditure of the appropriation.

FAVORABLE CONSIDERATION BY THE COMMITTEE.

The committee was favorably impressed by this testimony, and the Senator cheerfully withdrew his proposed amendment. No other objection was made to the bill as it came from the House. One member of the committee thought the matter should have been put into the general appropriation for rivers and harbors, but that was all. A vote was taken on the concurrence of the committee on the merits of the measure. There are always members of committees who talk and vote against the dominant party in Congress. There was one in this committee, and he voted against Smith's bill. Otherwise the committee agreed unanimously to report the bill favorably to the Senate.

Next day the chairman of the committee so reported it to the Senate, without amendment.

The Tenure-of-Office law being then under consideration, a Senator moved that Smith's bill be read a second time, ordered printed, and laid on the table for future consideration. To this the Senate agreed.

Several days passed, for the discussion of the Tenure-of-Office law was vigorously and extensively pressed.

As soon as he saw his way clearly to gain the attention of the Senate, the Senator from Wisconsin, who had considered Smith's bill in the Committee on Appropriations, having in the meantime conferred with Smith, called up the Nippewisset river-dam bill for a third reading. This motion brought the bill squarely before the Senate. The Senator from Wisconsin recited the action of the committee in favorably recommending it for passage without amendment, and also the favor with which it had passed the House. He briefly dwelt upon the benefit which the bill endeavored to confer upon a large class of intelligent and industrious citizens in Lomax county and upon the interests of inter-State commerce.

It was in the days when the civil service and tenure-of-office questions deeply agitated both branches of Congress. The debates had been exciting and tedious, and the minds of the Senators were filled with conflicting views upon these subjects. They gave little attention to minor matters; hence the explanations of the Senator from Wisconsin easily served to settle any doubts of the constitutionality or practical benefit of Smith's bill.

So the bill was read a third time and put upon its final passage without a dissenting voice. The vote on its passage stood: Yeas, 37, nays, 15, absent or not voting, 13.

Then the Secretary of the Senate announced that the bill had passed.

An hour afterwards, in the House of Representatives, the Secretary of the Senate announced that the Senate had passed, and the Vice-President had signed, the House bill to construct a dam across the Nippewisset river, in Lomax county, Wisconsin.

SIGNED THE BILL.

The Speaker of the House thereupon signed Smith's bill also, and it was dispatched to the President of the United States for his approval or veto. (See "Duties of the President.")

A day or two subsequent to this, the President's Private Secretary appeared in the House of Representatives and announced that the President had approved and signed the bill to build a dam across the Nippewisset river, in Lomax county, Wisconsin.

Smith was happy, and received the congratulations of his friends for so successfully getting his first bill safely through Congress, within ten days.

Smith now owns two steamboat lines on the Nippewisset river

A Bill of General Interest.

IN THE HOUSE.

On the last day of the last session of the Fortieth Congress, the President of the United States signed and thus approved, a bill, which had been regularly passed by both Houses of Congress, entitled "An Act making appropriations for sundry civil expenses of the Government for the year ending June 30, 1870, and for other purposes."

On the 9th of April, 1869, at the first session of the Forty-first Congress, in the House of Representatives, Mr. Dawes, from Massachusetts, addressed the speaker as follows: "I ask unanimous consent to report from the Committee on Appropriations a bill making available an appropriation heretofore made for furniture for the Presidential Mansion. The appropriation made

at the last session of Congress cannot be made available until next July, unless this bill is passed."

The bill introduced by Mr. Dawes, who was at that time chairman of the Standing Committee of the House on Appropriations, was a perfectly legitimate piece of legislation. He also presented to the House, at the same time a letter from the Secretary of the Treasury, Mr. Boutwell, who stated that the appropriation bill of the previous session, mentioned above, had been referred to the Comptroller of the Currency for his views, and that the comptroller had expressed the opinion that the money appropriated to purchase furniture for the President's House could not be drawn before July 1, 1869. The Secretary also requested that a bill similar to that now introduced by Mr. Dawes might be passed by Congress.

The House received the bill presented by Mr. Dawes, which was read a first and second time, without opposition. It was in substance as follows:

"Be it enacted by the Senate and House of Representatives of the United States of America, in Congress assembled, That the sum of $25,000 appropriated by the act approved March 3, 1869, entitled 'An act making appropriations for sundry civil expenses of the government for the year ending June 30, 1870,' for the purpose of refurnishing the President's House, may be made available for that purpose without increasing the amount."

Mr. Brooks, of New York, asked: "Can the gentleman name what is the amount appropriated for the White House this year?"

Mr. Dawes replied: "There has been none made by this Congress. The last Congress appropriated $25,000—the usual amount at the coming in of a new administration. It has never been less than that. On one occasion it was more."

No further remarks being made, the bill was ordered to be engrossed and read a third time, and being engrossed, it was accordingly read a third time, and passed by the House as it was introduced by Mr. Dawes.

For some unexplained cause, Mr. Dawes then moved to reconsider the vote by which the House had passed the bill, and also moved that the motion to reconsider such vote be laid on the table.

The bill was now ready to go to the Senate for concurrence, amendment or defeat.

IN THE SENATE.

On the following day, in the Senate, a message was received from the House of Representatives, by its Clerk, Mr. McPherson, announcing that the House had passed the bill making available an appropriation heretofore made for furniture for the Presidential Mansion, and requesting the concurrence therein of the Senate

Mr. Fessenden, of Maine, said: "That is a very short bill, and I move that it be taken up at once and acted upon. It is absolutely necessary to pass it, because the money which has been appropriated for that purpose cannot be used in the present fiscal year as the law stands. This bill is merely to allow the money to be used at once."

He then called attention to the letter from the Secretary of the Treasury, expressing the opinion of the Comptroller of the Currency as to the unavailability of the appropriation in its present condition.

Mr. Stewart, referring to the bill, said "It had better be read"

By unanimous consent, the bill was read twice by its title, and was then considered as in Committee of the Whole

Mr. Conkling said: "Let us hear the letter read of which the chairman told us."

The Chief Clerk then read Secretary Boutwell's letter in reference to the appropriation

Mr Fessenden said: "I notice that the bill reads that 'the sum of $25 000, etc , is hereby made available for such purpose.' It is available now, but not until the close of the fiscal year I think, therefore, that it will be necessary to amend it. I move to amend it by inserting after the word 'available' the words, 'during the present fiscal year '"

The amendment was agreed to as in Committee of the Whole.

The bill was next reported to the Senate as amended, and the Senate concurred in the amendment.

It was ordered that the amendment be engrossed, and the bill read a third time.

So the bill was read a third time and passed.

IN THE HOUSE.

A message from the Senate, by its Secretary, Mr Gorham, announced to the House that the Senate had passed the bill, with an amendment, in which he was directed to ask the concurrence of the House.

Mr. Dawes said: "I ask unanimous consent that the bill just returned from the Senate may be taken up, and the amendment of the Senate concurred in.

Messrs. Kerr, Brooks, and others objected.

IN THE SENATE.

Mr Fessenden, in the Senate, on the same day, said: "In regard to the bill authorizing the $25,000 appropriate [for] furnishing the President's House to be used, finding it essential that where it would lead, I therefore [move] that word used [unless] and that it come to beg up in the House, owing to the objections of Messrs. Kerr, Brooks and others, and if it was not back to the indiscipline with the request that it be passed as it is. I move therefore regarding the bill as it lies by unanimous consent that an amendment that suits be struck out and another vote down the amendment, and pass it, the bill as it came from the House at first, without amendment

Mr Edmunds of Vermont said It has not been returned formally

Mr Edmunds said No, but informally

The President of the Senate said The vote will be reconsidered as [doubtless] if there is no objection

Mr Edmunds and others said Let it be done by unanimous consent

The President of the Senate said This being a motion to take the vote on the passage of the bill making available an appropriation heretofore made for furniture for the Presidential Mansion which is not dependent on reconsideration, the amendment will be regarded as struck out and the bill passed with an amendment of [there] to be objection."

IN THE HOUSE.

In the House a message from the Senate, by its Clerk, Mr. Gorham, announced that the Senate had passed, without amendment, an act making available the appropriation heretofore made for furniture for the Presidential Mansion.

IN THE SENATE.

A message from the House, by its Clerk, Mr. McPherson, announced that the Speaker of the House had signed the bill making available the appropriation for furniture for the White House, and the President of the Senate then signed it. It was then ready to be sent to the President of the United States for approval and signature, in the same form as that in which Mr. Dawes introduced it in the House of Representatives on the previous day

REMARKS.

The history of this bill is something unusual, and the action upon it irregular, but the legality of the measure is unquestioned. After the Senate had passed the bill with the amendment, it was the duty of the House to either accept or reject the amendment by ballot This it failed to do It was irregular, also, for the Senate to reject its own amendment without having the bill before it, as it should have had, but it could not have it. The bill having, therefore, finally passed both houses without amendment, and the presiding officers having both signed it it became a law, for it is not likely that the President would veto a bill of so much importance to the house in which he lived. It was something unusual, too, for the Senate to first consider the bill "as in Committee of the Whole," there agree to it, report it to the Senate as a body, and then put it on its passage.

Congressional Committees.

Territorial Laws.

The Duties of United States Officers in the Territories.

THE executive power of the Territories of the United States is vested in a governor, who is appointed by the President, and who holds his office for four years, unless sooner removed. He resides in the Territory to which he is assigned, although appointed from some other portion of the United States.

Powers of the Governor.

In his office he is commander-in-chief of the militia of his Territory, grants pardons and reprieves, remits fines and forfeitures for offenses against the laws of the Territory; issues respites for offenses against the laws of the United States, till the decision of the President can be made known thereon; commissions all officers appointed under the laws of such Territory, and takes care that the statutes are faithfully executed. The governor has also the same powers to either approve or veto any bill passed by the Territorial legislature, and the process in either case is similar to that indicated in the description of the government of the several States of the Union.

Duties of the Territorial Secretary.

The President also appoints a secretary for each Territory, who resides in the Territory to which he is appointed, and who holds his office for four years, unless sooner removed. In case of the death, removal, resignation or absence of the governor from the Territory, the secretary executes all the powers and performs all the duties of the governor during such vacancy or absence. It is the duty of the secretary, also, to record and preserve all the laws and proceedings of the legislative assembly, and all the acts and proceedings of the governor in the executive department; transmit copies of the laws and journals of the legislature, after each session thereof, to the President and Congress, and copies of the executive proceedings and official correspondence of the Territory to the President twice a year; prepare the laws passed by the legislature for publication, and furnish the copy to the public printer of the Territory.

Territorial Legislature.

The legislature consists of two branches—the council and house of representatives, members of both branches being duly qualified voters, are elected by the people in the various districts in the Territory. They remain in office two years, and hold their regular sessions once in two years, each legislature appointing its own day of meeting. Members must reside in the county or district from which they are respectively elected. The apportionment of districts and the election of legislators are established by the laws of the United States.

Territorial Laws Submitted to Congress.

Laws passed in certain Territories have to be submitted to Congress, and if they are not there approved, they become null and void. The Territorial legislatures are not allowed to pass laws interfering with the primary disposal of the soil, imposing taxes upon property of the United States, or taxing the land or property of non-resident owners higher than that of persons residing in the Territory.

Length of Time Legislature is in Session.

The sessions of each Territorial legislature are limited to forty days. The president of the council and the speaker of the house are both elected by their respective branches of the legislature. The qualifications of members and their rights to hold other offices while they are members, etc., are regulated by United States law. The legislature cannot pass any law altering the salary of the governor, or the secretary, or the officers or members of the legislature as fixed by the laws of the United States.

The subordinate officers of each branch of every Territorial legislature consist of one chief clerk, one assistant clerk, one enrolling clerk, one engrossing clerk, one sergeant-at-arms, one door-keeper, one messenger and one watchman.

Territorial Representation in Congress.

Every Territory has a right to send a Delegate to the House of Representatives of the Congress of the United States, to serve during each term of Congress, and this Delegate is elected by a majority of the qualified voters of the Territory. Such Delegate has a seat in Congress with the right of debating, but not of voting.

How Minor Offices are Filled.

Justices of the peace, and all general officers of the militia of the Territory, are appointed or elected by the people in such manner as may be prescribed by the governor and legislature; all other officers not otherwise provided for by the laws of the United States are appointed by the governor, with the advice of the Territorial council, vacancies being filled temporarily by the governor's appointment during a recess of the legislature until it meets again.

When a Resident May Vote.

Voters must be twenty-one years old, and citizens of the United States, or persons who have legally declared their intentions of becoming such, and without regard to "race, color or previous condition of servitude." No officer, soldier, seamen, mariner or other person in the service of the United States can vote in any Territory until he has been permanently domiciled there for six months, and no person belonging to the army or navy can be elected to, or hold, any civil office or appointment in any Territory. All township, district and county officers, except justices and general officers of the militia, are appointed or elected in such manner as the governor and legislature provide.

Territorial Supreme Courts.

The supreme court of every Territory consists of a chief justice and two associate justices, any two of whom constitute a quorum for business. They are appointed by the President, hold their offices for four years, unless sooner removed, and open a term of their court annually at the seat of Territorial government.

Each Territory is divided into three judicial districts, in each of which a Territorial district court is held by one of the justices of the supreme court, at such time and place as the law prescribes; and each judge, after his assignment, resides in the district to which he is assigned.

The supreme court and the district courts, respectively, of the Territories, possess chancery as well as common law jurisdiction.

Territorial Prisoners.

A penitentiary established in some of the Territories when ready for the reception of convicts, is placed in charge of the attorney-general of the Territory, who makes all needful rules and regulations for its government, and the marshal having charge over such penitentiary must cause them to be duly executed and obeyed; and the reasonable compensation of the marshal and his deputies for their services under such regulations are fixed by the attorney-general.

Diplomatic Officers of the United States.

THE diplomatic officers of the United States include the following:

EMBASSADORS. — Persons sent by one sovereign power to another sovereign power to transact public business of importance and interest to one or both of them.

ENVOYS—Extraordinary—Public ministers, or officers, sent from one sovereignty to another on special business of importance.

MINISTERS — Plenipotentiary—Embassadors, or negotiators, or envoys, sent to a foreign seat of government with full diplomatic powers.

MINISTERS—Resident—Embassadors with diplomatic powers who reside continually at a foreign seat of government.

COMMISSIONERS—Persons appointed by a sovereign power to confer with similar persons from another sovereign power, and decide any special and disputed question of international interest or importance.

CHARGES D'AFFAIRES—Ministers of the third or lowest class, sent to a foreign seat of government.

AGENTS—Officers sent to a foreign country, with limited powers, to treat upon specified international matters.

SECRETARIES OF LEGATION — Officers appointed by the President to accompany ministers to foreign governments to assist them in their official duties.

Appointed by the President.

The foregoing diplomatic officers are appointed by the President, and confirmed by the United States Senate.

But one minister resident is accredited to Guatemala, Costa Rica, Honduras, Salvador, and Nicaragua, living in either of these States that he may select.

Ministers resident and consuls-general, combined in the same person, are accredited to the Republics of Hayti and Liberia.

The consul-general at Constantinople is the secretary of legation to Turkey, but receives compensation only as a consul-general.

Any regularly-appointed diplomatic officer upon whom devolves another similar office while holding the first, is allowed 50 per cent. additional pay as long as he holds the second office.

All fees collected at the legations are accounted for to the Secretary of the Treasury.

Consular Officers.

"Consul general," "consul," and "commercial agent," denote full, principal and permanent consular officers, as distinguished from subordinates and substitutes.

Either of these terms designate an officer of greater or less degree, appointed to reside at a certain place in a foreign country, to protect the commerce and commercial interests of the United States.

"Deputy-consul" and "consular agent" denote consular officers who are subordinate to such principals, exercising the powers and performing the duties within the limits of their consulates or commercial agencies, respectively, the former at the same ports or places, and the latter at ports or places different from those at which such principals are respectively located.

"Vice-consuls" and "vice-commercial agents" denote consular officers who are temporarily substituted to fill the places of consuls-general, consuls or commercial agents when they are temporarily absent, or relieved from duty.

The term "consular officer" includes the foregoing persons and none others.

No consul-general or consul may hold those offices at any other place than that to which each is appointed.

Restrictions Upon Consuls.

All consular officers whose salaries exceed $1,000 a year, cannot, while holding office, be interested in or transact any business as merchants, factors, brokers or other traders, or as clerks or agents for any such persons.

Consular Clerks.

The President has authority to appoint consular clerks, not exceeding thirteen in number, who must be citizens of the United States and over eighteen years old when appointed, and assign them from time to time to such consulates and with such duties as he shall direct. Such clerks must be duly examined as to their qualifications by an examining board, who report to the Secretary of State, before their appointment.

Duties of Consular Officers.

Consuls and vice-consuls have the right, in the ports or places to which they are severally appointed, of receiving the protests or declarations which captains, masters, crews, passengers or merchants, who are citizens of the United States, may choose to make there, and also such as any foreigner may make before them relative to the personal interest of any citizen of the United States. Every consular officer is also required to keep a list of all seamen and mariners shipped and discharged by him, giving the particulars of each transaction, the payments made on account of each man, if any; also, of the number of vessels arrived and departed, the amounts of their tonnage, the number of their seamen and mariners, and of those who are protected, and whether citizens of the United States or not, and as nearly as possible the nature and value of their cargoes and where produced, making returns of the same to the Secretary of the Treasury; also to take possession of the personal estate left by any citizen of the United States (other than seamen belonging to any vessel), who dies within the jurisdiction of that consulate, leaving no representative or relative by him to take care of his effects.

The consul inventories the effects, collects debts due to the deceased, pays those due from him, sells such of the property of the deceased as is perishable in its nature, and after one year the remainder, unless, in the meantime, some relative or representative of the deceased comes to claim his effects, paying the accrued fees. In case no relative or representative appears, the consul forwards the remainder of the effects, the accounts, etc., to the Secretary of the Treasury in trust for the legal claimants.

Persons dying abroad may appoint consular officers their agents for the disposal of their effects, etc., or any other person instead, and the consular officer may be called upon to assist in caring for the property and interests of the deceased.

Consular officers are required to procure and transmit to the Department of State authentic information concerning the commerce of such countries, of such character, in such manner and form, and at such times as the Department of State may prescribe; also, the prices-current of all articles of merchandise usually exported to the United States from the port or place at which the consular officer is stationed. Other duties of a commercial character are fully prescribed by the laws, with restrictions and penalties for violations of the rules and regulations governing consulates.

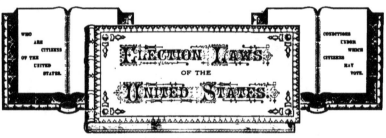

WHO ARE CITIZENS OF THE UNITED STATES.

ELECTION LAWS
OF THE
UNITED STATES.

CONDITIONS UNDER WHICH CITIZENS MAY VOTE.

Who May and Who May Not Vote.

ALL PERSONS born in the United States, and not subject to any foreign power, excluding Indians not taxed; all children born out of the limits and jurisdiction of the United States, whose fathers were or may be at the time of their birth citizens thereof, and any woman who is now or may hereafter be married to a citizen of the United States, and who might herself be lawfully naturalized, are deemed citizens of the United States; but the rights of citizenship do not descend to children whose fathers never resided in the United States.

Rights of Citizens in Foreign Countries.

All naturalized citizens of the United States, while in foreign countries, are entitled to and receive from this Government the same protection of persons and property which is accorded to native-born citizens; and it is the duty of the President, whenever an American citizen is unjustly deprived of his liberty by any foreign government, to demand the reason for his imprisonment, and, if his imprisonment is unjust or in violation of the rights of American citizens, to demand his release; should this demand be refused or unreasonably delayed, the President may take measures (not amounting to acts of war) to have him released, communicating all facts and proceedings relative to the case to Congress, as soon as practicable. After that, any invasion of the rights of any such American citizen by a foreign government is a reasonable ground for diplomatic adjustment or a declaration of war by the United States.

Military Force Not Allowed at Elections.

The laws of the United States forbid any naval or military officer to bring any armed troops to places of election, general or special, unless it be to repel armed enemies of the United States, or to keep peace at the polls; and no military or naval officer is permitted to prescribe or fix, or attempt to prescribe or fix, by proclamation, order, or otherwise, the qualifications of voters in any State, or in any manner interfere with the freedom of any election in any State, or with the exercise of the free right of suffrage therein. The laws also provide that neither "race, color,

or previous condition of servitude" can affect the rights of citizens to vote, and prescribe penalties for refusing to let citizens vote lawfully, for wrongfully refusing to receive a lawful vote at an election, and for unlawfully hindering a person from voting.

Supervisors of Election.

In order to correct any abuses of this sort, it is decreed that on the application of any two citizens in any city or town of more than 20,000 inhabitants, or whenever in any county or parish, in any Congressional district, ten citizens of good standing, previous to any registration of voters for an election for Representatives or Delegate in Congress, or previous to any election at which such Representative or Delegate is to be voted for, may make known in writing to the judge of the United States circuit court, in that circuit, their desires to have such registration or election, or both, guarded and scrutinized, the judge, within not less than ten days prior to the registration or election, as the case may be, is required to open the circuit court at the most convenient point in his circuit. He then proceeds to appoint and commission, from day to day and from time to time, under his hand and the seal of his court, two citizens, residents of the city, town, election district or voting precinct of the town, city, county and parish, who shall be of different political parties, and able to read and write the English language; and these citizens shall be known and designated as "supervisors of election." Any circuit judge may appoint a United States district judge to perform this duty for him, in case he is unable to perform it himself.

What Supervisors of Election Shall Do.

The supervisors of election, so appointed, are authorized and required to attend, at all times and places fixed for the registration of legal voters, and challenge any person offering to register; to attend at all times and places when the names of registered voters may be marked for challenge, and to cause such names registered to be, as they deem proper, so marked; to make, when required, the lists of persons whose right to register and vote is claimed and verify the same; and upon any occasion, and at any time when in attendance upon the duty here noted, to personally inspect and scrutinize such registry, and for purposes of identification, to sign their names to each page of the original list and of each copy of any such list of registered voters, at such time when any name may be received or registered, and in such a manner as will, in their judgment, detect

and expose improper removal or addition of any name therefrom or thereto.

The Duty to Challenge Votes.

The supervisors of election are authorized at all times and places for holding elections of Representatives or Delegates in Congress, and for counting the votes cast at such elections to challenge any such vote offered by any person whose legal qualifications the supervisors, or either of them, may doubt; to be and remain where the ballot-boxes are kept at all times after the polls are open until every vote cast at such time and place has been counted, the canvass of all votes polled wholly completed, and the proper and requisite returns or certificates made, as required by any State, Territorial, municipal or Federal law; and to personally inspect and scrutinize, from time to time, and at all times, on the day of election, the manner in which the voting is done, and the way and method in which the poll-books, registry lists, and tallies or check-books are kept.

In order that each candidate for Delegate or Representative in Congress may obtain the benefit of every vote cast for him, the supervisors of election are, and each of them is, required to personally scrutinize, count and canvass each ballot cast in their election district or voting precinct, whatever the indorsement on the ballot, or in whatever box it may have been placed or is found, to make and forward to the officer known as chief supervisor such certificates and returns of all such ballots as such officer may direct and require, and to certify on all registry lists any statement as to the truth or accuracy of the lists or to the truth or fairness of the election and canvass, that they deem honest and proper to be made, in order that the facts may become known.

Must Stand Where Each Voter Can be Seen.

The better to enable the supervisors of election to discharge their duties, they are authorized and required, in their respective election districts or voting precincts, on the day of registration, on the day when registered voters may be marked to be challenged, or on the day of election, to take such a position, from time to time, as will, in their judgment, best enable them to see each person who offers himself for registration or to vote, and permit them to scrutinize the manner in which the registration or voting is being done; and at the closing of the polls for the reception of votes, they are required to sit or stand in such a position near the ballot-boxes as will best enable them to canvass the ballots and see that the election has been fairly conducted.

HOW FOREIGNERS ARE NATURALIZED AND BECOME CITIZENS.

PERSONS born in foreign nations and coming to the United States to reside, are required to submit to certain forms of law before they can become citizens of any State or Territory, as follows:

Going before either a district or circuit court of the United States, or a district or supreme court of any Territory, or any court of record having jurisdiction in such cases, he must declare on oath that he intends to become a citizen of the United States, and to renounce forever his allegiance to any foreign sovereign or State, especially naming the kingdom or empire of which he was formerly a subject.

Two years, or more, after thus declaring his intention to become a citizen, he applies to the court for admission to all the rights and privileges of a citizen of the United States. At this time he must clearly state, under oath, that he will support the Constitution of the United States and again renounce all allegiance to any foreign sovereign or government, especially the one under whom he formerly lived. He must also show, to the satisfaction of the court, that he has resided within the United States five years, and within the State or Territory in which the court is then held for a certain period; that he has during that time behaved as a man of good moral character, attached to the principles of the Federal Constitution; that he is well disposed to the good order and happiness of the United States, and that he expressly renounces and abandons any hereditary title of nobility or association with any of the orders of nobility which he possessed in his native or adopted foreign country, and this renunciation is recorded in the court. Witnesses are necessary to prove the fact of his having resided in the country the requisite time before applying for citizenship, his own oath not being sufficient.

Any person who immigrates into the United States from a foreign country three years before coming of age, and maintains his residence here until twenty-one years old and two years longer, may, at the expiration of the whole five years, be admitted to all the rights and privileges of a citizen without making the preliminary declaration of his intention to become such; but he must then make oath that for two years past such has been his intention, and fully comply with all the other requirements of the naturalization laws.

The provisions of this law apply equally to white persons of foreign birth, of African nativity or African descent.

When Native-Born Citizens and Foreigners May Vote.

THE CONDITIONS under which a person born in the United States or Territories may vote at general State elections are: That the person shall be a male, twenty-one years of age, and have resided in the State where he votes a definite period of time. Certain States require educational and property qualifications.

After arriving in the United States, a foreigner may go before a competent court and make oath that he desires to become a citizen of the United States. The paper given him by the court is a certificate that he has "declared his intention" to become a citizen.

Five years afterwards he may go again before a proper court and take out papers of naturalization. The foreigner is then naturalized, and is a citizen of the United States, entitled to vote the same as a native-born citizen.

Each State has its own law as to the time a foreigner shall have lived in the United States before he can vote in that State. Thus in Illinois the law requires that the voter must be a citizen. This makes it necessary that the foreigner must have taken out his naturalization papers, and have been a resident in the United States for five years preceding the time when he can vote. This is the law in several States.

Other States require only that the foreigner, in order to be allowed to vote, shall have declared his intention to become a citizen. He then has the same privileges as the native-born, concerning the length of time he shall remain in the State where voting. Different States, it will be seen, have different laws as to the time the voter shall be a resident of the State.

In most of the States voters are required to be registered before election.

The length of time that those persons entitled to vote must remain in the State, county, or election precinct before voting, is shown in the following list of States.

Time of Residence Required in State, County and Precinct.

Alabama—State, one year, county, three months; ward or precinct, thirty days.

Arizona—Territory, one year; county, ten days.

Arkansas—State, one year; county, six months, precinct or ward, thirty days.

California—State, one year; county, ninety days, precinct, thirty days. Foreigners must be naturalized. Chinamen not allowed to become citizens.

Colorado—State, six months; women vote at school elections.

Connecticut—State, one year, town, six months. Must be able to read State laws. Foreigners required to be naturalized. Must have good moral character and a freehold yielding $7 annually, or pay State tax, or have done military duty.

Dakota[a]—Territory, ninety days. Women allowed to vote.

Delaware[a]—State, one year; county, one month. Must pay a county tax. Foreigners must be naturalized. Paupers not allowed to vote.

District of Columbia—No elections are held here The various local officers are appointed by Congress and the President.

Florida—State, one year; county, six months.

Georgia—State, one year; county, six months. Voters must have paid their taxes.

Idaho[a]—Territory, four months, county, thirty days. Foreigners must be naturalized.

Illinois—State, one year; county, ninety days; election district, thirty days. Foreigners must be naturalized.

Indiana[a]—State, six months; town, sixty days; ward or precinct, thirty days. Foreigners must be residents of the United States one year.

Iowa—State, six months; county, sixty days; town or ward, ten days. Foreigners required to be residents of the State two years.

Kansas—State, six months; township or ward, thirty days.

Kentucky[a]—State, two years; county, town, or city, one year; precinct, sixty days. Foreigners must be naturalized.

Louisiana—State, one year; parish, ten days.

Maryland—State, one year; city or county, six months. Foreigners must be naturalized.

Maine—State, three months. Paupers and Indians not allowed to vote. Foreigners must be naturalized.

Massachusetts—State, one year; Congressional district, town or city, six months. Must have paid a State or county tax. Must be able to read and write. Paupers not allowed to vote. Foreigners must be naturalized.

Michigan[a]—State, three months; township or ward, ten days. Foreigners must be residents of the State two years and six months.

Minnesota—State, four months; election district, ten days. Foreigners must have lived in the United States one year.

Mississippi—State, six months, county, one month. Foreigners must be naturalized.

Missouri—State, one year; county, city or town, sixty days.

Nebraska—State, six months; county, forty days; ward or precinct, ten days.

Nevada—State, six months county or district, thirty days. Foreigners must be naturalized.

New Hampshire—Town, six months. Must be tax-payers. Foreigners must be naturalized.

New Jersey—State, one year; county, five months. Foreigners must be naturalized.

New Mexico—Territory, six months; county three months; precinct, thirty days. Foreigners must be naturalized.

New York—State, one year; county, four months, district, town, or ward, thirty days. Foreigners must be naturalized.

North Carolina—State, one year; county, thirty days. Voter must own fifty acres of land or have paid taxes.

Ohio—State, one year; county, thirty days, town, village or ward, twenty days. Foreigners must be naturalized.

Oregon—State, six months; county or district, ninety days.

Pennsylvania—State, one year; election district, two months. Must have paid State or county taxes within two years Formny citizens returned from abroad may vote after six months' residence. Foreigners must be naturalized.

Rhode Island—State, one year; town or city, six months. Must own property in his town and pay taxes on it. Foreigners must be naturalized.

South Carolina—State, one year; county, sixty days. Foreigners must be naturalized.

Texas[a]—State, one year; county or election district, six months. Paupers not allowed to vote.

Tennessee[a]—State, one year; county, six months, and must pay poll-tax. Foreigners must be naturalized.

Utah—Territory, six months. Wives, widows and daughters of citizens can vote.

Vermont[a]—State, one year; town, three months. Foreigners must be naturalized.

Virginia—State, one year; county, city, or town, six months. Foreigners must be naturalized. Paupers not allowed to vote.

West Virginia—State, one year; county, thirty days. Foreigners must be naturalized. Paupers not allowed to vote.

Wisconsin—State, one year. Paupers not allowed to vote.

Wyoming—Territory, ninety days. Women allowed to vote.

* No registration required.

Forms of Constitutions.

ARTICLES AND SECTIONS.

General Directions Relating to Constitutions and By-Laws.

Constitutions.

A S A BASIS of action in the government of an association of people, who propose to hold regular and frequent meetings, it becomes necessary to make a specific agreement by such association of the course of action they will pursue, and the rules by which they shall be governed in their deliberations. This agreement is termed a "CONSTITUTION."

In its preparation, care should be taken, while making it sufficiently explicit, to have the document as concise, clear and distinct as possible.

In the adoption of a constitution by an assembly, it is usually customary to consider it section by section. After it has been accepted, the secretary should make record of the constitution in a blank-book suitable for the purpose. This should be signed by the members of the society, who consent to accept of the same as their fundamental rule of action.

Amendments to the constitution should be made in the same book with convenient marks for reference showing where they may be found.

By-Laws.

When it is desired to add matter more clearly defining certain articles of the Constitution, such explanatory notes are termed 'BY-LAWS.' When the Constitution is quite explicit, for most associations by-laws are unnecessary. If it is desirable, however, to be very minute in explanation, that members of an association may fully understand their rights and duties, by-laws are sometimes quite essential. When added, they should follow immediately after the Constitution.

Explanatory words giving the character of each article in the Constitution, may be placed above, or at the left side of the article, as shown in the following forms.

Prevention of Cruelty to Animals.

PREAMBLE.

CRUELTY to Animals being a prevailing fault, calculated to cultivate the baser passions of man's nature, it becomes necessary, in order to counteract the same, to take individual and united action in opposition thereto. The better to accomplish a reform in this direction, the undersigned agree to form an association, and be governed in their fundamental action by the following

CONSTITUTION

TITLE.

ARTICLE I. The title and name of this Society shall be "THE SACRAMENTO SOCIETY FOR THE PREVENTION OF CRUELTY TO ANIMALS."

OBJECTS.

ARTICLE II. The objects of this Society are to provide effective means for the prevention of cruelty to animals within the limits of the City of Sacramento; to enforce all laws which are now or may hereafter be enacted for the protection of dumb animals, and to secure by lawful means the arrest, conviction and punishment of all persons violating such laws.

OFFICERS.

ARTICLE III. The officers of this Society shall be a President, six Vice-Presidents, a Counsel, a Secretary, a Treasurer, and an Executive Committee of nine persons, who shall constitute the Board of Directors. The President, Counsel, Secretary, and Treasurer shall be ex-officio members of the Executive Committee. The officers shall be elected annually by ballot, and shall hold their offices until others are elected to fill their places.

MEMBERS.

ARTICLE IV. Any person, male or female, may become a member of this Society upon election by the Society, or Executive Committee, and the payment of the sum of two dollars; and the annual membership fee shall not exceed that amount.

Sec. 2.—Any person may become a life-member of this Society, upon the payment to the Treasurer of the sum of twenty-five dollars.

ANNUAL MEETING.

ARTICLE V. The annual meeting of this Society shall be held on the first Thursday in April of each year, when the annual election of officers shall take place.

Sec. 2.—Every member of the Society who has been such for ten days or more, and who is not in arrears for dues, shall be entitled to vote at the said election.

Sec. 3.—At the annual meeting the Executive Committee shall present a general report of its proceedings during the past year, and the Secretary and Treasurer shall also present their annual reports.

Sec. 4.—Special meetings of the Society may be called by the President, (or in case of his absence or inability, by one of the Vice-Presidents,) and shall be so called upon the written request of fifteen members. Notice of such meeting shall be inserted in at least two daily papers of the city of Sacramento.

COUNSEL.

ARTICLE VI. The Counsel shall be the legal adviser of the Society, its Officers and Executive Committee, and shall have general charge and conduct of all suits and proceedings instituted by or against it, or them, or either of them, or in which the Society may be interested. He shall receive for his services such pecuniary compensation, or fees, as shall be determined by the Executive Committee.

SECRETARY.

ARTICLE VII. It shall be the duty of the Secretary to keep minutes of all the proceedings of the Society and of the Executive Committee, and to record the same in the Society's books provided for that purpose ; to conduct the correspondence and keep copies thereof, and to perform such other duties as are customary for such an officer, under the direction of the Executive Committee.

TREASURER.

ARTICLE VIII. The Treasurer shall have charge of all the funds belonging to the Society, and shall disburse the same under the direction of the Executive Committee. He shall, previous to the annual meeting of the Society, prepare and submit to the Executive Committee for audit, a detailed account of his receipts and disbursements during the past year, which annual account, duly audited, he shall present to the Society at its annual meeting.

AGENTS.

ARTICLE IX. The Executive Committee may appoint from time to time such special agents as it may deem advisable, and shall have the power to remove the same at its pleasure.

Sec. 2.—The appointment of every agent of the Society shall be in writing, and he shall receive such pecuniary compensation for his services as may be determined by the Executive Committee.

EXECUTIVE COMMITTEE.

ARTICLE X. The Executive Committee shall have the management, control and disposition of the affairs, property and funds of the Society, and shall have the power to fill for the unexpired term any vacancy that may occur in any of the offices of the Society or in its own body.

Sec. 2.—No member of the Executive Committee, except the Counsel and the Secretary, shall receive or derive any salary or pecuniary compensation for his services.

Sec. 3.—The Executive Committee shall hold meetings for the transaction of business at least once in every month, and at all such meetings five members shall constitute a quorum.

ALTERATIONS OR AMENDMENTS.

ARTICLE XI. This constitution may be altered or amended by a two-thirds vote of all the members present, at any regular or special meeting of the Society, provided such alteration or amendment has been proposed and entered on the minutes, together with the name of the member proposing it, at a previous meeting of the Society.

By - Laws.

HOURS OF MEETING.

ARTICLE I. The hours of assembling for the stated meetings of the Society shall be as follows: From the 1st of April until the 1st of October, at eight o'clock P. M., and from the 1st of October until the 1st of April, at half-past seven o'clock, P. M.

ADMISSION OF MEMBERS.

ARTICLE II. The names of all persons desiring admission to this Society shall be presented to the Secretary, who shall bring the same before the members of the Society for election at any regular meeting.

DUTIES OF AGENTS.

ARTICLE III. It shall be the duty of agents appointed to use their utmost efforts to secure kind and gentle treatment to all dumb animals, by rigid prosecution of violation of law relating to the same.

Sec. 2. The agent shall be empowered, and is expected to use his best efforts to distribute all tracts, papers and literature placed in his hands which may be calculated to accomplish the work for which the Society is organized.

Sec. 3. The agent is authorized, if in a locality where no Society exists, to organize an association to be governed by such officers, and such action as will most effectually abolish cruelty to animals.

At each regular meeting of the Society, the following shall be, after calling the meeting to order, and the opening exercises, the

Order of Business.

1. Reading of the minutes.
2. Report of the Board of Directors.
3. Reports of Standing and Special Committees.
4. Reports of officers.
5. Receiving communications and bills.
6. Admission of new members, and election of officers at the annual meeting.
7. New business.
8. Reports of the Secretary and Treasurer
9. Adjournment.

CONSTITUTION OF A VILLAGE LYCEUM

PREAMBLE.

GROWTH and development of mind, together with readiness and fluency of speech, being the result of investigation and free discussion of religious, educational, political, and other topics, the undersigned agree to form an association, and for its government, do hereby adopt the following

CONSTITUTION.

Name and Object.

ARTICLE I. The name and title of this organization shall be

"The Cambridge Literary Association,"

and its object shall be the free discussion of any subject coming before the meeting for the purpose of diffusing knowledge among its members.

Officers of the Society.

ARTICLE II. The officers of the Association shall consist of a President, two Vice-Presidents, a Corresponding Secretary, a Recording Secretary, a Treasurer and a Librarian, who shall be elected annually by ballot, on the first Monday in January of each year, said officers to hold their position until their successors are elected.

Duties of the Officers.

ARTICLE III. It shall be the duty of the President to preside at all public meetings of the Society. The first Vice-President shall preside in the absence of the President, and in case of the absence of both President and Vice-President, it shall be the duty of the second Vice-President to preside.

The duty of the Secretary shall be to conduct the correspondence, keep the records of the Society, and read at each meeting a report of the work done at the preceding meeting.

The Treasurer shall keep the funds of the Society, making an annual report of all moneys received, disbursed, and amount on hand.

It shall be the duty of the Librarian to keep, in a careful manner, all books, records and manuscripts in the possession of the Society.

Appointment of Committees.

ARTICLE IV. There shall be appointed by the President, at the first meeting after his election, the following standing committees, to consist of three members each, namely: On lectures, library, finance, and printing, whose duties shall be designated by the President.

The question for debate at the succeeding meeting shall be determined by a majority vote of the members present.

Conditions of Membership.

ARTICLE V. Any lady or gentleman may become a member of this Society by the consent of the majority of the members present, the signing of the constitution and the payment of two dollars as membership fee. It shall be the privilege of the Society to elect any person whose presence may be advantageous to the Society, an honorary member, who shall not be required to pay membership fees or dues.

Times of Meeting.

ARTICLE VI. This association shall meet weekly, and at such other times as a majority, consisting of at least five members of the association, shall determine. The President shall be authorized to call special meetings upon the written request of any five members of the Society, which number shall be sufficient to constitute a quorum for the transaction of business.

Collection of Dues.

ARTICLE VII. It shall be the duty of the finance committee to determine the amount of dues necessary to be collected from each member, and to inform the Treasurer of the amount, who shall promptly proceed to collect the same at such time as the committee may designate.

Parliamentary Authority.

ARTICLE VIII. The parliamentary rules and general form of conducting public meetings, as shown in HILL'S MANUAL, shall be the standard authority in governing the deliberations of this association.

Penalty for Violating Rules.

ARTICLE IX. Any member neglecting to pay dues, or who shall be guilty of improper conduct, calculated to bring this association into disrepute, shall be expelled from the membership of the Society by a two-thirds vote of the members present at any regular meeting. No member shall be expelled, however, until he shall have had notice of such intention on the part of the association, and has been given an opportunity of being heard in his own defense.

Alterations and Amendments.

ARTICLE X. By giving written notice of change at any regular meeting, this constitution may be altered or amended at the next stated meeting by a vote of two-thirds of the members present.

Calls for Public Meetings.

Forms of Wording in Calling Public Meetings.

AMONG the duties of the projector of a public meeting will be the writing of the "Call," which should be clear, distinct, and brief, yet sufficiently explicit to enable people to know when, where, and for what object they meet.

The following, which may be varied according to circumstances, will sufficiently illustrate the general form :

Democratic Rally!

AT THE COURT ROOM, Monday Evening, Nov. 7, at 8 o'clock. The DEMOCRATS OF PAXTON, WORKING MEN, BUSINESS MEN, AND CITIZENS GENERALLY, are *cordially invited* to be present. The meeting will be addressed by the HON. JOSIAH ADAMS, HON. T. M. BAXTER, AND OTHER ABLE SPEAKERS.

School Meeting.

The Friends of Education are requested to meet at the house of Solomon Biggs, in Walnut Grove, Saturday evening, Sep. 1st, at 7 o'clock, to take action relative to opening a public school in this vicinity. The meeting will consider the selection of directors, the location of the school building, and the propriety of opening a school this fall, before the building is complete.

Old Settlers' Reunion.

All persons in Adams and adjoining counties, who settled here prior to 1850, are requested to meet at the Court House, in Clinton, Saturday afternoon, June 10, at two o'clock, to make arrangements for an Old Settlers' Reunion, to be held at such place and time as the meeting shall determine.

Firemen's Review.

The entire Fire Department of this city is hereby notified to appear on dress parade, Saturday afternoon, at 1.30, on Broadway, between Green and Spruce streets, provided the weather is pleasant, and the streets dry. If the weather does not permit, due notice of postponement will be given.

GEO. H. BAKER,
Fire Marshal.

Woman Suffrage Convention.

The Friends of Woman Suffrage are invited to meet in mass convention, at Dixon's Hall, in Chester, June 14, at ten o'clock, A. M., at which time the session will commence, and continue two days, closing on Friday evening. Hon. Asa Cushing, Rev. H. W. Cooper, Mrs. Gardner, Mrs. Chas. Fuller, and other distinguished speakers will be present, and participate in the proceedings of the convention.

Hot for Horse Thieves!

All Citizens of Jonesville and surrounding country, favorable to protecting their stock from the depredations of thieves, are expected to be present at the Eagle School House, in District No. 10, on Saturday evening, July 13, at 8 o'clock, sharp, to aid in forming an association that will give horse and cattle thieves their just dues.

Railroad Meeting.

The Midland and Great Western Railroad Company are about locating their railway through this county, having surveyed three routes, one through Hastings, one by way of Brownsville, and the other through this village, passing up the river just east of Fuller's mill. The Company propose to take this route on one condition, namely: that we furnish depot grounds and right of way through this village.

Citizens of Pikeville! what action shall we take in this matter? Shall we have a railroad at our own doors, or be compelled henceforth to go ten miles to the nearest depot? Every citizen interested in the growth of our beautiful village is requested to be present at the Town Hall, next Tuesday evening, May 7, at half past seven o'clock, to consider this subject. Let there be a full expression from all the people at this meeting.

Fourth of July!

The liberty-loving citizens of Eagleville, who desire to participate this year at home in a genuine, old-fashioned Fourth of July celebration, such as will make-the American Eagle proud of the village that bears his name, will meet at Allen's Hall next Saturday evening, at 8 o'clock, to consider the advisability of holding such celebration.

Shall We have an Agricultural Fair?

Agriculturists, Horticulturists, Mechanics, Artists and others, favorable to the establishment of an Agricultural and Mechanics' Fair, are desired to meet at the Town Hall, next Monday evening, June 20, at 8 o'clock, to take the necessary steps towards perfecting such organization.

Eight Hour Meeting.

All mechanics, artisans, laborers, and others, who favor making eight hours a legal day's work, that they may occasionally see their wives and children during the winter months, in the day time, are requested to meet in Boyd's Hall, Monday evening, June 14, at 8 o'clock, on which occasion the meeting will be addressed by that distinguished advocate of the rights of the working man, Hon. Archibald P. Green.

Temperance Convention.

The Friends of Temperance, independent of party or sect, are invited to meet in convention at Fullerton Hall in Fairbury, Wednesday, Oct. 9, at 10 A.M., to consider and discuss the means by which we may arrest the present increasing tide of intemperance in this vicinity, by which our youth are corrupted, our Sabbaths desecrated, and our homes impoverished and desolated.

Come up and help us, sons, husbands, fathers! Come up and aid us, daughters, wives, mothers! We want the influence of your presence. Dr. Carr, the eloquent champion of temperance, will be with us. Mrs. Arnold, Mrs. John Berryman, Rev. Dr. Williams, and others will participate in the discussions of the convention, and Prof. Carter, the world-renowned musician, will add interest to the occasion by leading in the singing.

The convention will continue in session two days, being addressed Wednesday evening by Rev. H. D. Williams, and on Thursday evening, in the closing address, by Mrs. John Berryman.

Vermonters Attention!

All Vermonters, resident in this city and vicinity, who are favorable to holding a Vermonters' pic nic sometime during July or August, are requested to meet next Wednesday afternoon, June 15, at Judge Miller's office in Canton, to arrange time, place, and programme of exercises for that occasion.

RESOLUTIONS.

Appropriate for Many Occasions.

RESOLUTIONS are a brief, terse method of expressing the opinions and sentiments of a company of people relative to any subject which it is desirable to discuss or place on record.

They are applicable to nearly any subject, and should be characterized by the utmost brevity consistent with a clear expression of the idea sought to be conveyed.

Resolutions Complimenting a Teacher.

"At the close of Mr. Hall's writing school, lately in session at Springfield, which was very fully attended, numbering over one hundred pupils, Prof. Hamilton, Principal of Springfield Academy, offered the following preamble and resolutions, which were unanimously adopted:

"WHEREAS, Prof. Geo. B. Hall, in giving instruction in penmanship to a very large and interesting class in this place, has given most unbounded satisfaction as a teacher of writing, therefore:

"*Resolved*, That, as a teacher and penman he is pre-eminently superior, changing as he does the poorest scribblers almost invariably into beautiful penmen, during his course of lessons.

"*Resolved*, That his lectures on epistolary correspondence, punctuation, use of capital letters, and the writing of business forms, of themselves are worth infinitely more than the cost of tuition in his schools.

"*Resolved*, That we recommend him to the people of the entire country, as a teacher whose schools will be found a great intellectual good in any community so fortunate as to secure his services.

"*Resolved*, That, while we thank him for the very efficient instruction given this class here, we tender him a cordial invitation to visit our city again, professionally, at his earliest convenience."

Resolutions of Respect and Condolence.

On the Death of a Freemason.

"At a regular communication of Carleton Lodge, No. 156, A. F. and A. M., held Feb. 10, 18—, the following preamble and resolutions were unanimously adopted:

"WHEREAS, It has pleased the Great Architect of the Universe to remove from our midst our late brother Benjamin W. Rust: and

"WHEREAS, It is but just that a fitting recognition of his many virtues should be had: therefore be it

"*Resolved*, By Carleton Lodge, No 156, on the registry of the Grand Lodge of ——, of Ancient Free and Accepted Masons, that, while we bow with humble submission to the will of the Most High, we do not the less mourn for our brother who has been taken from us.

"*Resolved*, That, in the death of Benjamin W. Rust, this Lodge laments the loss of a brother who was ever ready to proffer the hand of aid and the voice of sympathy to the needy and distressed of the fraternity; an active member of this society, whose utmost endeavors were exerted for its welfare and prosperity; a friend and companion who was dear to us all; a citizen whose upright and noble life was a standard of emulation to his fellows.

"*Resolved*, That the heartfelt sympathy of this Lodge be extended to his family in their affliction.

"*Resolved*, That these resolutions be spread upon the records of the Lodge, and a copy thereof be transmitted to the family of our deceased brother, and to each of the newspapers of Carleton."

On the Death of a Member of any Society, Club, or Other Association.

"WHEREAS, in view of the loss we have sustained by the decease of our friend and associate, —— ——, and of the still heavier loss sustained by those who were nearest and dearest to him; therefore, be it

"*Resolved*, That it is but a just tribute to the memory of the departed to say that in regretting his removal from our midst we mourn for one who was, in every way, worthy of our respect and regard.

"*Resolved*, That we sincerely condole with the family of the deceased on the dispensation with which it has pleased Divine Providence to afflict them, and commend them for consolation to Him who orders all things for the best, and whose chastisements are meant in mercy.

"*Resolved*, That this heartfelt testimonial of our sympathy and sorrow be forwarded to the —— of our departed friend by the secretary of this meeting."

On the Death of a Clergyman.

"WHEREAS, the hand of Divine Providence has removed our beloved pastor from the scene of his temporal labors and the congregation who sat under his ministry, and profited by his example, are desirous of testifying their respect for his memory, and expressing their earnest and affectionate sympathy with the household deprived by this dispensation of its earthly head; therefore, be it

"*Resolved*, That we tenderly condole with the family of our deceased minister in their hour of trial and affliction, and devoutly commend them to the keeping of Him who looks with pitying eye upon the widowed and the fatherless.

"*Resolved*, That in our natural sorrow for the loss of a faithful and beloved shepherd, we find consolation in the belief that it is well with him for whom we mourn.

"*Resolved*, That while we deeply sympathize with those who were bound to our departed pastor by the nearest and dearest ties, we share with them the hope of a reunion in that better world where there are no partings, and bliss ineffable forbids a tear.

"*Resolved*, That these resolutions be transmitted to the family of the deceased, as a token of our respect and veneration for the Christian character of a good man gone to his rest, and of the interest felt by his late congregation in those he loved and cherished.

Resolutions Complimenting a Public Officer upon Retirement.

"WHEREAS, the retirement of our esteemed fellow citizen, —— ——, from the office of ——, presents a suitable opportunity for expressing the esteem in which we hold him as a faithful and courteous public servant; therefore, be it

"*Resolved*, That the thanks of this meeting and the community are due to ——, for the able and impartial manner in which he has uniformly performed his public duties, and that we sincerely regret his determination to retire from public life.

"*Resolved*, That he carries with him, on leaving the position which he has so satisfactorily filled, the regard and good wishes of all who had occasion to transact official business with him.

"*Resolved*, That his late associates in office regard his return to private life as a loss to them, while they sincerely hope that it will prove a gain to him, and trust that his future will be as bright and prosperous as he can anticipate or desire.

"*Resolved*, That the secretary of the meeting be requested to transmit to him the preamble and resolutions adopted on this occasion.

Resolutions Complimenting a Captain of a Steamer on a Successful Voyage.

"At a meeting of the cabin passengers of the steamship ——, Captain ——, arrived at this port from ——, on the —— inst., the following preamble and resolution were unanimously adopted:

"In token of our grateful remembrance of the watchful seamanship and agreeable social qualities displayed by Captain —— and his officers during our late voyage from —— to this port; be it

"*Resolved*, That if skill in navigation, urbane and gentlemanly attention to the wants and wishes of the passengers, and a sound, swift, and comfortable vessel, are among the essentials of a pleasant voyage, then we have reason to congratulate ourselves on having crossed the sea in the good ship ——, Captain ——; that we tender to him, and to all the officers of the vessel, our thanks for the kindness with which they administered to our comfort; that we commend the ship, her appointments, her commander, and his subordinates, to the favor of the voyaging public, because we are of opinion that they deserve it; and, that we hereby request the gentleman acting as secretary of this meeting to see that a copy of this testimonial be placed in the hands of Captain ——."

(Signed by ——, etc.)

Resolutions Thanking a Conductor, and Commending a Railway.

"At a meeting of the passengers on the Palace Sleeping and Dining Car ——, nearing their journey's end, June 2, 1872, at ——, the following preamble and complimentary resolutions were unanimously adopted:

"WHEREAS, It has been the good fortune of the persons comprising this meeting to make a safe, quick, and most delightful passage from —— to ——, over the —— railroad; therefore be it

"*Resolved*, That our thanks are due, and are hereby tendered, to the Conductor of the Palace Car ——, for the numerous favors received at his hand throughout the journey; and we commend him for the many gentlemanly and agreeable qualities which characterize him as a man, and eminently fit him for the position he now holds.

"*Resolved*, That commendation is especially due the railroad company for the excellent accommodations furnished travelers in their comfortable and luxurious coaches, and the superior condition of the track and road-bed, which is so smooth that the traveler rides over the same resting with almost as much ease and pleasure as when seated in his own parlor.

AT A MEETING OF THE

Citizens of East Saginaw

MICHIGAN,

HELD AT THE

Common Council Rooms, August 14, 1882.

the following preamble and resolutions were unanimously adopted, viz:

WHEREAS,

Almighty God in the exercise of His divine will, has removed from this world, and the busy cares of life,

JESSE HOYT

OF NEW YORK CITY,

Therefore, we the Citizens of the City of East Saginaw, Michigan,

have assembled here to-night to pay our last sad tribute to the

MEMORY

of the departed, and to express our deep appreciation of the many and lasting obligations that we, as citizens, owe to him, and by words and actions, to him, to express our sincere sorrow for the irreparable loss our city has sustained by his death.

Thirty-two years ago the tract of land which is now occupied by our prosperous city was a wilderness and Mr. Hoyt's keen perception and observing mind foresaw the growth and development of the Saginaw Valley, and here, in the wilderness, he laid the foundation of a great and prosperous community; and during all the various phases of its development, from its infancy to the present time, his faith and confidence in our city never faltered. Look whatever way we find the evidences of his acute business judgment, sagacity, and intelligence, in the many enterprises that he has fostered, which have materially advanced the substantial growth and development of our city; hundreds of happy families owe their happiness to him; no manner did or could doubt his integrity, and we sincerely deplore his loss and

express our heartfelt sympathy with his sorrowing family.

Resolved,

That the Secretary be instructed to cause a copy of this preamble and resolutions to be published in the daily papers of this city, and that he transmit a copy thereof to the Common Council, with the request that they may be spread at large upon its records, and that a copy thereof be sent to the family of the departed.

Resolved,

That the Mayor be requested to issue a proclamation, requesting our citizens

to close their respective places of business

between the hours of ten and twelve o'clock A.M., on August 17th inst. (as his funeral occurs at that time)

AS

A token of respect for the deceased.

Copied Expressly
For Ell's Manual from Specimen of Pen-Work
Executed by D. T. Ames.

Secretary.

President of Citizens Meeting.

RESOLUTIONS.

Suitable for Forming Associations, Remonstrance, On the Departure of Friends, Expression of Wishes, etc.

Resolutions at a Temperance Meeting.

" Mr. Chairman: Your committee on resolutions respectfully submit the following : —

" WHEREAS, The saloons of this city are being kept open at all hours of the day and night, in violation of the ordinances governing the same ; and

" WHEREAS, Drunkenness is evidently on the increase, in consequence of the total lack of necessary legal restraint, which should close their doors at proper hours of night, and Sundays ; therefore, be it

" *Resolved,* That a committee of five be appointed by this meeting to investigate the extent of this violation, and report the same to the city council at their next meeting.

" *Resolved,* That we call upon the mayor, aldermen, and city marshal of this city to enforce the law relating to the sale of liquors, and we hereby remind them that the people will hold them to strict accountability for allowing the ordinances governing and restraining saloon keepers to be violated."

Resolutions on the Departure of a Clergyman.

" At a meeting of the Presbyterian society, held in the lecture room of their church, on Tuesday evening, the 10th instant, the following preamble and resolutions were adopted :

" WHEREAS, Our pastor, the Rev. Hiram G. Morgan, has received a call from the First Presbyterian church of ——, and, for the purpose of accepting the same, has tendered his resignation as pastor of the Presbyterian church in this city ; and

" WHEREAS, We all realize that none but a selfish interest can prompt us to retain him, when a broader field with nobler opportunities is open to him ; therefore, be it

" *Resolved,* That we accept the resignation which severs our relation as pastor and people with feelings of heartfelt sadness.

" *Resolved,* That the ten years of faithful service rendered by him to this society have been greatly blessed in upbuilding our church, increasing its membership, and creating feelings of Christian fellowship and good will among other denominations.

" *Resolved,* That for his ministering to the temporal wants of the poor, and the spiritual needs of all; for the tender solicitude and earnest sympathy which have always brought him to the bedside of the sick and dying; for his efforts in behalf of the education of the masses; and for his exertions to ameliorate the condition of suffering humanity at all times and under all circumstances, the members of this parish, and the people of this city, owe him a debt of gratitude which they can never repay.

" *Resolved,* That, in parting, our kindest wishes will ever attend him, and that we recommend him to the parish to which he is to minister as one worthy their full confidence and highest esteem.

———————————— }
———————————— } *Committee.*

Resolutions on the Departure of a Sunday School Teacher.

" WHEREAS, Mr. Grant Watkins is about to remove from our midst and sever his connection with this school, in which he has so long and faithfully labored as teacher ; therefore, be it

" *Resolved,* That we deeply regret the necessity of losing him in the Sunday School work, and most fervently wish for him a future of active usefulness in his chosen field of new associations and interests, ever praying that by a well ordered life and a Christian consecration he may at last unite, with all the truly faithful, in sweeter songs of redemption in the bright hereafter."

Resolutions Favorable to Forming an Association.

" Mr. Chairman : Your committee, to whom was referred the duty of preparing resolutions expressive of the sense of this meeting, beg leave to report the following :

" WHEREAS, Our county is being infected by a band of organized horse thieves and highwaymen, making property and human life insecure ; and

" WHEREAS, The safety of the people demands that some immediate action be taken looking to the protection of life and property ; therefore, be it

" *Resolved,* That an association of citizens favorable to such protection be formed, to be known and styled ' The Grant County Protective Association.'

" *Resolved,* That this association be governed by five directors, chosen by this meeting. Such directors to choose their president, secretary, and treasurer from their number, any one of whom, upon hearing of the loss of property belonging to any member of this association, shall have authority, upon consulting with two other directors, to take the necessary steps to recover the same, and punish the thief, the expense of recovery not to exceed the value of said property.

" *Resolved,* That each member of this association shall pay to the treasurer two dollars, as membership fee, upon signing the constitution, and shall bear his share of the necessary expense incurred in recovering stolen property, and convicting thieves.

" *Resolved,* That a committee of three be appointed by this meeting to draft articles of association for the government of the society, regulating dues, times of meeting, etc., for each member to sign, essentially embodying the ideas expressed in these resolutions."

Resolutions Remonstrating against a Nuisance.

" *Resolved,* That the continuance of the bone boiling establishment and glue factory of Messrs. Smith & Jones in the midst of a densely populated neighborhood, is an intolerable nuisance, which is incompatible with the health and comfort of those who reside in the vicinity.

" *Resolved,* That a committee of three be appointed by the chair, whose duty it shall be to apprise the authorities of the existence and nature of the nuisance; and, in case such action shall not produce its abatement, then, to employ counsel, and take such other legal steps as the case may require."

Resolutions at a Stockholders' Meeting, in Favor of a Certain Route.

" *Resolved,* That the proposed railroad bridge of this company, at Jackson, be located north, rather than south, of the village, for these reasons:

" 1. To build a bridge south of the town will necessitate placing a depot so far from the center of the village as to prevent the people of Jackson from patronizing the road, inasmuch as the South Western railway already has a depot near the center of the town.

"2. The south line will require more than double the amount of trestle work for the bridge.

"3. The right of way by the southern route is much the most expensive. Even with the purchase of the Jackson foundry grounds (which will remove the abrupt curve in the upper route), the right of way will cost less than by the south survey, to say nothing of bringing the depot nearer the center of the village, and lessening the expense of trestle work; therefore

"*Resolved*, That, for the foregoing and other reasons, the directors are recommended to take the northern instead of the southern route, for the proposed railway through the town of Jackson."

Resolution Instructing Members of the Legislature.

"*Resolved*, That we are opposed to the present oppressive law on our statute books relative to stock running at large, and we hereby pledge ourselves to vote for no candidate for either house of the legislature who is not pledged to its speedy repeal.

"*Resolved*, That the secretary is instructed to furnish a report of this meeting, together with this resolution, to such papers as will bring the subject most generally before the people."

Resolution of Thanks to the Officers of a Convention.

The following resolution, presented just before the close of a convention, is put by the member who makes the motion — it being personal to the presiding officer.

"*Resolved*, That the thanks of this convention are hereby given to the president, for the able, dignified, and impartial manner in which he has presided over its deliberations, and to the other officers for the satisfactory manner in which they have fulfilled the duties assigned to them."

PETITIONS.

A PETITION is a formal request or supplication, from the persons who present or sign the paper containing it, to the body or individual to whom it is presented, for the grant of some favor.

It is a general rule, in the case of petitions presented to courts that an affidavit accompany them, setting forth that the statements therein made, so far as known to the petitioner, are true, and that these facts, by him stated as within his knowledge and that of others, he believes to be true.

PETITIONS TO A CITY COUNCIL.

The people of a town or city very frequently have occasion to petition their town authorities or city government for the granting of favors or the enactment of laws.

The following are among the forms of petition to a city council:

For Opening a Street.

To THE MAYOR AND ALDERMEN OF THE CITY OF ————, IN COMMON COUNCIL ASSEMBLED

Gentlemen —The undersigned respectfully solicit your honorable body to open and extend Walnut street, which now terminates at Adams street, through blocks Nos. 10 and 12 in Hall's addition to ————, to Benton street, thereby making Walnut a nearly straight and continuous street for two miles, and greatly accommodating the people in that portion of the city.

[*Signed by two hundred tax-payers, more or less.*]

Remonstrating Against a Nuisance.

To THE MAYOR AND ALDERMEN OF THE CITY OF ————, IN COMMON COUNCIL ASSEMBLED

Gentlemen —Your petitioners respectfully represent that during the past summer John Jones has converted the barn located at No. 134 Monroe street, between Van Buren and Jackson into a slaughter house, which, with the decaying offal about the premises, produces a stench that is unbearable to the citizens living in that vicinity. In all respects the affair is a nuisance to the neighborhood, and we ask your honorable body to have the same removed.

[*Signed by one hundred persons, more or less, residing in the neighborhood.*]

Asking for a Policeman.

To THE MAYOR AND ALDERMEN OF THE CITY OF ————, IN COMMON COUNCIL ASSEMBLED

Gentlemen —The undersigned citizens and tax-payers of ————, feeling that life and property are very insecure after dark in portions of this town, respectfully ask your honorable body to appoint a night policeman to have supervision of the streets and alleys from Harrison to Walnut streets, on Broadway.

[*Signed by one hundred tax-payers, more or less.*]

PETITIONS TO THE STATE LEGISLATURE.

Petition from Farmers Asking for the Extermination of the Canada Thistle.

To THE HONORABLE THE SENATE AND HOUSE OF REPRESENTATIVES OF THE STATE OF ————, IN LEGISLATURE CONVENED

The undersigned citizens of ———— county, respectfully represent that this, and neighboring counties, are becoming infested with that pest, the Canada thistle. As yet they are not in sufficient quantity to be beyond control, but it is feared if they are allowed to go without restraint two years longer, they will be so spread as to make their extermination next to impossible. We, therefore, respectfully request your honorable body to take some action looking to their immediate subjection, thus saving the farming community from an evil which cannot be removed if allowed to exist much longer.

[*Signed by one thousand farmers, more or less.*]

Petition from Farmers, Relative to Stock Running at Large.

To THE HONORABLE THE SENATE AND HOUSE OF REPRESENTATIVES OF THE STATE OF ————, IN LEGISLATURE CONVENED

Your petitioners, residents and tax payers of ———— county, respectfully represent to your honorable body that the farmers of this State are at present subjected to an immense drain on their resources, by being compelled to build thousands of miles of fence, not for their own use, but for the purpose of preventing the encroachment of others. At a low estimate, it is costing millions of dollars every year for this needless fencing. The man who wishes to keep stock may fence the necessary pasturage for the same, but to compel the farmer who does not have stock in any considerable quantity to keep up miles of fence, continually to rot down and be rebuilt, is an oppression which is causing many farmers to remain in poverty, who otherwise might be in comparatively independent circumstances.

We, therefore, petition you to enact a law to prevent stock of every description from running at large.

[*Signed by five hundred farmers, more or less.*]

Petition to the Governor Asking for Pardon.

To JOHN M. PALMER, GOVERNOR OF THE STATE OF ILLINOIS

The Petition of the undersigned citizens respectfully represents·

That on the ninth day of July, 1871, John Jones, of the city of Chicago, was convicted before the criminal court, in the said city, of the crime of manslaughter, and sentenced therefor to the State prison at Joliet, where he now remains, for the term of twelve years; that the evidence upon which he was convicted, as will be seen by the summary appended, was not altogether conclusive, that previous to that time the said Jones had maintained the reputation of being a peaceable and upright man and that his conduct since imprisonment, according to the letter of the warden, filed herewith, has been most exemplary. The said Jones has a family who need his support, and under the impression that the well-being of society will not be injured by his enlargement, and that the ends of justice, under the circumstances of the case, have been sufficiently answered, they respectfully implore executive clemency in his behalf.

[*Signed by etc., etc.*]

Celebrations and Festivals.

SUGGESTIONS
CONCERNING FOURTH OF JULY
CELEBRATIONS, Etc.

HINTS RELATING TO
PUBLIC DINNERS, PICNICS
FESTIVALS, Etc.

The Committees Necessary and the Plan of Organization.

PLEASING variety in the routine of life is an occasional celebration. These are given often by certain societies, and comprise festivals, public dinners, picnics, excursions, reunions, etc.

FOURTH OF JULY.

A very appropriate day for a general celebration, in the United States, is the Fourth of July.

In preparing for such a celebration it is first necessary to appoint suitable committees to carry out the details of the work incident to such an occasion. This is done by calling a meeting of the citizens at some public place, "*for the purpose of making arrangements for celebrating the forthcoming anniversary of American Independence!*" which meeting should organize in the usual form, by the appointment of a president and secretary.

The meeting should consider the feasibility of such celebration, and, if it is deemed advisable to celebrate this anniversary, should appoint an executive committee of three, to have general supervision of the whole affair, to be assisted by:

1. A finance committee, who will solicit the necessary funds.
2. A committee on grounds, to select a suitable place for holding the celebration, furnishing speakers' stand, seats for people, etc.
3. Committee on orator, who will provide speakers, reader of Declaration of Independence, etc.
4. Committee on music, to provide band, singing by the glee club, etc.
5. Committee on procession, who will induce the various societies, and a representation from the different trades, to appear in street procession, along with the representation of the different States in the Union.
6. Committee on military display, who will organize any military exhibition that may be thought advisable, take charge of firing guns, etc.
7. Committee on fireworks, who will attend to the arrangements for such exhibition in the evening.
8. Committee on amusements, whose especial duty it shall be to organize such street display of burlesque, etc., as will entertain and amuse the people.

The executive committee may appoint the president of the day, the necessary marshals, and arrange for additional attractions and novelties calculated to secure the success of the celebration.

Let these arrangements be made three or four weeks before the "Fourth." Now, let the executive committee thoroughly advertise the list of committees, and what it is proposed to accomplish. In the meantime, the finance committee should report to the executive what amount of money may be relied upon, and the committee on orator should report the names of their speakers, while the various other committees will report what the attractions are to be in their several departments.

Then the executive committee should prepare their posters and programmes, descriptive of what may be seen by strangers from abroad who attend the celebration, and crowds of people will come from near and far.

It is not necessary for many people to be interested at first in the celebration, to make the same a success. The resolve by *one* person to have a grand celebration, who will call a public meeting, associate with himself two others, as an executive committee, and follow by the appointment of the necessary committees, publishing the whole to the world, and *going ahead*, will generally make a very successful celebration.

In the smaller towns so many committees may not be necessary, but having a good executive committee, the work is made much lighter by being distributed among a good many persons, though it will always devolve upon two or three individuals to carry the affair through to a successful conclusion.

PUBLIC DINNERS.

The same regulations, to a certain extent, as in the Fourth of July celebration, may be observed in other public entertainments, though it may not be necessary to have as many committees.

Where it is resolved to give a public dinner to a distinguished man, the first move is to extend to the person an invitation, as numerously signed as possible. If he accepts, he either fixes the day himself, or leaves that to the option of the party inviting him. In the latter case, they designate a time that will best suit his convenience.

Arrangements having been made thus far, committees may be appointed on table, invitations, toasts, etc., the affair being conducted according to the etiquette of such occasions.

PICNICS AND FESTIVALS.

These social entertainments, which are usually conducted in the interest of certain societies, are mostly pleasant affairs in proportion as they are agreeably conducted by the managers.

They should be especially noticeable in the absence of all formality, jollity and mirth reigning supreme. If another committee is appointed, outside of the executive, let it be a committee on *fun*

AMONG the delightful titbits that afford variety and merriment on certain festal occasions, may be toasts and sentiments, thus:

For a Christmas Dinner.

" Christmas hospitality: And the ladies who make it delightful by their *mincing* ways."

" The sports of the holidays: Sleighing the *Dears*, and taking comfort among the *Buffaloes*."

For the Thanksgiving Festival.

" Our opinion on the Eastern Question: We agree with Russia, that *Turkey* ought to be *gobbled*."

" The health of our venerable host: Although an American citizen, he is one of the best *Grand Seniors* that ever presided over *Turkey*."

" Thanksgiving: The magnetic festival that brings back erratic wanderers to the Old Folks at Home."

" The thanksgiving board: While it *groans* with plenty within, who cares for the whistling of the wind without."

" Thanksgiving: The religious and social festival that converts every family mansion into a Family Meeting House."

For the Fourth of July.

" The American Eagle: The older he grows the louder he screams, and the higher he flies."

" The Union of the States, and the Union of the Sexes: The one was the beginning of man's independence, the other is the end of it."

" Our Standard Sheet: It has often been badly mangled, and terribly scorched, but is, nevertheless, the noblest sheet that ever covered a hero on the bed of glory."

For a Wooden Wedding.

" Our Host and Hostess: The fire of affection they mutually kindled five years ago has not gone out; on the contrary, we are glad to see them *wooding up*."

" The Wooden Wedding of our Friends: And may all the children be *chips of the old block*."

" The Hero and Heroine of this Wooden Festival: May they flourish like green bay trees in their youth, and retain all their *pith* when they become elders."

For the Tin Wedding.

" The Golden Rule of Matrimony: Marry the first time for love — the second time for *Tin*."

" The Fair Bride: She blushed at her first marriage, but she shows more *metal* to-day."

" Tin Weddings: And the bright reflections to which they give rise."

For the Crystal Wedding.

" Crystal Weddings: The medium through which the bliss of enduring affection is *magnified*, *reflected*, and made *transparent* to everybody."

" The fifteenth year of Wedlock: A matrimonial *Stage*, chiefly remarkable for its *Tumblers*."

" Our Hospitable Hostess: And may it never be her fate to look on life 'as through a glass darkly.'"

" The New Married Couple: They will not find the friendship of their friends as brittle as their gifts."

For a Silver Wedding.

" A quarter of a century of Married Happiness: The best five-twenty bond in the world."

" The Bridal Pair: Their admirable performances in double harness well entitle them to the plate."

" Our Kind Entertainers: Know all men, by these presents, how sincerely we love them."

For the Golden Wedding.

" Matrimony's Pleasant Autumn: May it always bear golden fruit."

" The Bridegroom's Prize: Not toys of gold, but the more attractive metal by his side."

* Selected from Barber's Ready-made Speeches, published by Dick & Fitzgerald, New York.

HOW TO CALL, ORGANIZE AND CONDUCT PUBLIC ASSEMBLAGES.

Duties of Officers, Order of Business, Introduction of Resolutions, and Parliamentary Usages in the Government of Public Gatherings.

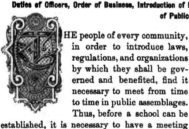

HE people of every community, in order to introduce laws, regulations, and organizations by which they shall be governed and benefited, find it necessary to meet from time to time in public assemblages. Thus, before a school can be established, it is necessary to have a meeting of the citizens, to take the preliminary steps towards obtaining the school. Before a church organization can be had, a meeting of persons favorable to such proceeding must first take place, to secure sufficient concert of action to accomplish the object. To obtain unity of sentiment, and harmony of action, in the carrying forward of any important enterprise, the people must be called together, and the minds of a sufficient number directed into the desired channel to effect the contemplated purpose.

In educating public sentiment, calling the people together, and introducing the resolutions that shall embody the sense of the meeting, much written business is required that may properly be considered here.

To show the manner in which a meeting is convened, called to order, organized, and conducted, we will take a political gathering as an example.

To illustrate: William Jones, who lives in the town of Monroe, being a zealous politician, is desirous of having a republican meeting in his town, just before election. He, therefore, consults with John Belden, Arthur Bennett, George Moody, and others, who have a certain influence, as to time and place. Arrangements are also made with two or three persons, accustomed to public speaking, to address the meeting.

Notice is then given, by written placards or printed posters, as follows :

"Republican Meeting.

ALL CITIZENS of Monroe, who favor the principles of the REPUBLI-CAN PARTY, are requested to meet on THURSDAY EVENING, OCT. 1st, at the TOWN HALL, at SEVEN O'CLOCK, to take such action as may be deemed best to promote the *Success of the Party* in the COMING ELECTION. The Meeting will be addressed by the HON. WILLIAM SPENCER, THOMAS HOPKINS, Esq., and OTHERS."

The projectors assemble at the Hall early, and decide, from an examination of the audience, who will make a suitable presiding officer, and secretary, or these persons may be selected previous to the meeting, with the understanding that they will be present.

Selection of Chairman.

Half or three-quarters of an hour is usually given from the time when the meeting is appointed, for general conversation, while the audience is assembling. At half-past seven, Wm. Jones steps forward, and says:

"The meeting will please come to order."

As soon as the audience becomes still, Mr. Jones continues:

"I move that Samuel Lockwood act as President of this meeting."

Mr. Arthur Belden says:

"I second the motion."

Then, Mr. Jones puts the question thus:

"It has been moved and seconded, that Mr. Samuel Lockwood act as President of this meeting. All in favor of the motion will manifest the same by saying, 'Aye.'"

As soon as the affirmative vote has been expressed, he will say:

"Those who are opposed will say, 'No.'"

If the "Ayes" predominate, he will say:

"The 'Ayes' have it. Mr. Lockwood will take the chair."

If, however, the 'Noes' are in the majority, he will say:

"The 'Noes' have it; the motion is lost."

Thereupon, he will nominate another person, or put the question upon the nomination of some one else. *

As soon as the chairman is chosen, he will take his place.

Appointment of Secretary.

Mr. Arthur Bennett then says:

"I move that Mr. Hiram Cooper act as Secretary of this meeting."

This motion being seconded, the Chairman puts the question, and declares the result.

The meeting is now organized. The Chairman will direct the Secretary to read the call, or, if a copy of the call is not to be obtained, he will ask one of the projectors to state the object of the meeting.

Order of Business.

That speech being concluded, the President will say:

"You have heard the call, and understand its object; what is the further pleasure of the meeting?"

Mr. Jones, thereupon, says:

"I move that a Committee of three be appointed by the chair to draft resolutions expressive of the sense of this meeting."

This is seconded.

The Chairman then says:

"Gentlemen, you have heard the motion; are you ready for the question?"

If any one desires to speak against the motion, or has any remark to make, he arises, and says:

"Mr. Chairman."

The Chairman turns towards the speaker, and listens to him, and each in succession. When they are all done, or in case no one responds to the call, he puts the question in the previous form, and declares the result.

Committee on Resolutions.

The resolution being adopted, the Chairman says:

"I will appoint as such Committee—William Jones, Albert Hawkins, and Henry Peabody."

Where a motion is made moving the appointment of a committee, it is parliamentary usage to appoint, as the first person selected on such committee, the mover of the resolution.

The Committee withdraws to prepare the resolutions, or to examine those previously prepared for the purpose.

Upon the retirement of the Committee, the audience will call for the leading speakers of the evening to address the meeting. When the speeches are concluded, the Chairman of the Committee comes forward, and says:

* If considerable political excitement exists in the community, the opposite party will sometimes gather in large force, which is termed "packing" the meeting; will vote their own officers into place, and conduct the meeting according to their own wishes. When, however, a meeting is called in the interest of a certain political party, it is considered disreputable for another party to seek, through overwhelming force, to control the meeting in their own interest.

"Mr. Chairman, the Committee report the following resolutions."

He then reads the resolutions, and gives them to the Secretary.

The Chairman now says:

"You have heard the resolutions. What shall be done with them?"

Arthur Bennett says:

"I move they be adopted."

The motion is seconded.

The Chairman then says:

"The question on the passage of the resolutions is now before the house. Are there any remarks to be made on the subject?"*

If no objections are made, the President will put the question, and declare the result. The formality of appointing a Committee on Resolutions may be avoided by the resolutions being introduced and read by one of the projectors of the meeting.

The resolutions adopted, and the speeches concluded, the Chairman will ask:

"What is the further pleasure of the meeting?"

Adjournment.

If there be no further business, some one moves an adjournment. As the question is not debatable the Chairman puts it direct. If carried, he says:

"The meeting is adjourned."

If thought best to convene another meeting, the Chairman will declare:

"The meeting is adjourned to the time fixed upon."

The foregoing, it will be seen, by varying the call, and changing the business to suit, will answer for most political gatherings, or any public meeting.

If it is desirable to make the proceedings public, it is the duty of the Secretary to fully write up the business of the meeting, and transmit the same to the nearest newspaper favorable to the cause. If the meeting be of sufficient

* If there is a good deal of business before the meeting, the chairman may dispatch such business much more rapidly by immediately putting a question, when moved and seconded, without inviting remarks.

importance, it may be well for him, immediately after being chosen to fill the position, to move the appointment of two Assistant Secretaries, who will aid him in writing up the proceedings for two or three newspapers.

The Secretary's Report.

The Secretary's report of a meeting, will, of course, vary according to circumstances. In the record of the foregoing meeting, it would read as follows:

Pursuant to call, a meeting of the Republican citizens of Monroe was held in the Town Hall on Thursday evening, Oct. 10th. Samuel Lockwood being chosen president of the meeting, and Hiram Cooper appointed secretary.

On motion of Mr. William Jones, the chairman appointed as a committee on resolutions, Messrs Wm. Jones, Albert Hawkins, and Henry Peabody.

During the absence of the committee, the meeting was very ably addressed by Hon. W. Spencer, of Belmont, who reviewed the work that had been done by this party, in a speech of some forty minutes.

Mr. Spencer was followed by Thomas Hopkins, Esq., of Cambridge, in a half hour's speech, in which he particularly urged upon all Republicans the necessity of vigilant effort from this time forward till the election.

The committee on resolutions reported the following, which were unanimously adopted.

(*Here the Secretary inserts the Resolutions.*)

On motion, the meeting was adjourned.

Government of Conventions.

While the foregoing form is applicable, with suitable variations, to the management of ordinary public meetings, it is generally necessary in political conventions, which contain frequently a large number of delegates with a great diversity of interests to subserve, several candidates being often before the convention seeking position, to make first a temporary, and afterwards a permanent organization.

Comprised, as the convention is, of delegates, who are representatives from constituencies of different parts of the county, or state, the assemblage is a legislature of the party, and is governed by nearly the same rules. The strictest application of these rules is often necessary, in order to preserve decorum in its discussions, and dignity in its action.

A convention may be called, either by some committee appointed by previous conventions to make the call, or it may be convened by invitation of the leading friends of a particular cause, or measure. The call should contain some general directions as to the mode of electing delegates.

The night before the convention a caucus is generally held in the several towns of the county, for the purpose of selecting delegates to attend the same. These delegates are sometimes instructed by the meeting to vote for certain men or measures, in the convention.

Two sets of officers are chosen in the convention — temporary, and permanent. The first is for the purpose of conducting the business preparatory to organization.

The temporary chairman is chosen in the manner heretofore designated. In selecting the permanent officers, it is usual to allow the delegation from each county, district or township, the right to name one member of the committee on permanent organization. In order to save time, it is common to appoint a committee, at the same time, on credentials, whose duty it is to ascertain if each delegate is entitled to vote in the convention.

During the interval that follows, it is customary, while the committees are engaged in their labors, to call upon various prominent men to address the gathering.

The officers recommended by the committee chosen for the purpose, are generally elected; the real business of the convention can now be performed.

It is customary to give the thanks of the convention to its officers just previous to adjournment. In that case, the member who makes the motion puts the question upon its adoption, and declares the result.

PARLIAMENTARY RULES.*

THE foregoing illustration of the method of conducting public meetings and conventions will give the reader a general idea of the mode of procedure in the organization and management of any public gathering; as many questions arise, however, concerning parliamentary usage on disputed questions, the following rules of order will be of interest to all persons who may have occasion to participate in the work of public meetings:

Duties of the President of a Meeting.

The presiding officer of a meeting should possess acuteness of hearing, a clear, distinct voice, positiveness of manner, self-possession, and a clear understanding of his duties, which are as follows:

First, if the meeting be temporary in its character, the president, having been appointed by the members of the congregation present, will, after taking the chair, proceed to state the object of the meeting, or call upon some member in the audience, who is supposed to know the object of the gathering, to do so.

SELECTION OF A SECRETARY.

Should no one move the appointment of a secretary, the president will suggest the necessity of a recording officer, and will call upon the meeting to nominate a suitable person for the position. Upon his nomination the chairman will put the same to vote and announce the result, as he will all motions and propositions properly presented, that may necessarily arise in the course of the proceedings.

In making a statement to the assembly, or putting a question, it is customary for the chairman to arise and stand while doing so, though he may retain his seat if much more convenient, while reading any communication or message to the meeting.

ORDER.

He should strictly maintain order, or call upon some one or more persons in authority to do so; should see that members of the meeting, while engaged in the presenting of motions or in debate, observe the order and decorum enjoined by parliamentary rules; should decide all questions of order; should appoint members of committees when required by motion to do so, and should not leave his chair unless the same be filled by a vice president (if there be one) or by the appointment of a *pro tempore* chairman.

QUORUM.

When presiding over a deliberative assembly, such as a council or legislature, his actions will be largely governed

* Parliamentary rules are called *parliamentary* from the fact that the rules and regulations that now govern public bodies, throughout this country, are substantially those that have been long in use by the British Parliament in England.

by the rules and regulations of the body itself. In such cases it is customary for the chairman to ascertain whether or not a quorum of members be present. Should such not prove to be the case within thirty minutes from the time appointed for the opening of the meeting, it will be in order to adjourn from lack of a quorum, though it will be proper to send an officer in authority to secure the attendance of a sufficient number of members to make a quorum, whereby business may be transacted.

At any time during the session, should it be ascertained that less than a quorum of members is in attendance, the chairman must announce the fact, and suspend the transaction of business, as the proceedings of the meeting are illegal when less than a quorum is present.

Should the meeting open with a quorum of members, some of whom should afterwards leave, and the fact be discovered when calling the yeas and nays upon any question, that a quorum is not present, the meeting should adjourn. It will be in order to take up the uncompleted business at the next meeting exactly at the same point it was when the absence of a quorum was ascertained at the preceding meeting.

SIGNING PUBLIC DOCUMENTS.

It is the duty of the presiding officer to place his signature to all documents and proceedings of the assembly, when necessary, in order to authenticate the same.

In general, the chairman being created by the meeting, as a representative of the members present, his duty is to obey their commands, and declare the will of the assemblage in a just and impartial manner.

Duties of the Secretary.

The secretary, upon taking the chair at a temporary meeting, will provide himself with the necessary stationery with which to note the proceedings on the occasion.

READING CALL, ETC.

He will, upon request of the president, read the call for the meeting, all communications, messages, and resolutions that may be offered; will furnish a copy of the proceedings for publication, if desirable, or for any person interested who may wish to examine the same; and will preserve the record of proceedings for presentation and examination at a subsequent meeting, if held.

WHAT TO MAKE RECORD OF.

The secretary of a deliberative assembly will, after reading the minutes of preceding meeting, make note of and enter upon his journal the substance of all proceedings and enactments passed by the assemblage. All discussions, motions proposed, and other matter not voted upon, are not entered. Such is the rule in legislative assembles. In other meetings it is frequently customary to present a report, not only of what is actually done, but also an outline of the discussions and proceedings in the meeting.

PRESERVATION OF IMPORTANT PAPERS.

The secretary should file all papers of importance, after having read the same, and being the custodian of all such, should never allow any member or other person to remove them without permission from or direction of the assembly.

CALLING ROLL AND SIGNING PAPERS.

He should call the roll when ordered, for the purpose of either noting the absentees or taking a vote of the yeas and nays. He will inform committees of their appointment, the nature of the business they are chosen to consider, will authenticate all proceedings, acts, and orders of the meeting by his signature, and will issue calls for special sittings.

It is customary for the secretary to stand while reading any extended document or calling the roll of members in large assemblages, and to retain his place throughout the session of the meeting unless some one be appointed *pro tempore* to act as secretary during his absence. Where one or several assistant secretaries are chosen, less inconvenience is occasioned by the temporary absence of the secretary.

The Treasurer.

The office of treasurer, while often distinct, is frequently coupled with that of secretary. This portion of his duty consists in entering in a book provided for the purpose, an account of all moneys received and disbursed in behalf of the body which he serves.

ORDERS TO PAY MONEY.

The rule is, to pay out no moneys without an order bearing the signatures of the president and secretary, or the chairman of a finance committee, who is empowered to audit bills, which orders the treasurer should carefully preserve as vouchers.

BONDS.

It is further customary to require bonds of such officer for the faithful performance of his duty, where any considerable amount of money is handled, he being also required to yield possession of his books to his successor, in good order.

The Committees.

All public bodies find it necessary, in order to systematize their work and expedite business, to appoint certain individuals of their number to have charge and control of certain departments of the work, relating to their deliberations.

SELECT AND STANDING COMMITTEES.

Where appointed for a particular occasion, the committee is known as and called a select committee; where appointed at the beginning of a session, to consider all matters of a certain nature, it is termed a standing committee.

COMMITTEE OF THE WHOLE.

A "committee of the whole" consists of all the members. As it is the duty of the *standing* and *select* committees to prepare measures to be acted upon by the full assembly, so it is the duty of the "committee of the whole" to consider and arrange the preliminaries of the business that the assembly is to consider. This committee can act with much less formality than is consistent with the customary forms of parliamentary usage in full assemblage.

Appointment of Committees.

The constitution and by-laws of an association usually provide for the appointment of standing committees, who sit permanently during the session. The members of such committees in deliberative assemblies, unless otherwise ordered, are appointed by the presiding officer.

The necessity of a select committee is usually suggested by some member of the assembly, who frequently moves that a certain number be appointed, either by the chairman or the meeting. Should this committee be appointed by the meeting, it is customary to select by majority vote one at a time, thus giving the assembly ample time to consider the fitness of each candidate for the proposed committee ; though the entire number may be voted upon at once, if thought desirable, to save time.

CHAIRMAN OF A COMMITTEE.

While the members of the committee possess the right to select their chairman, it is a recognized courtesy to select the first person appointed on the committee as chairman of such committee.

The necessity of appointing a new committee is sometimes obviated, if there be already a committee appointed, by assigning the matter to be considered to such committee.

VARIOUS COMMITTEES.

In most legislative bodies the committees appointed by the presiding officer at the opening of the session, are sufficient in number to appropriately consider any subject that may be brought before the meeting. Thus, in the City Council, there is usually provision made for the appointment of a committee on "police," on "fire and water," on "abatement of taxes," on "streets and alleys," on "license," public grounds," etc. Committees are also appointed by legislative assemblies, whose duty it is to consider everything of a judicial character, matters relating to taxation, public institutions, etc. Any matter arising during the session, decidedly distinct in its character, and requiring considerable deliberation, is usually referred, by motion of one of the members of the assembly, to the committee having jurisdiction over that kind of business.

CALLING THE COMMITTEE TOGETHER.

When a committee is appointed, it is usual for the first named member to call such committee together as soon as possible, though it is not allowable for a committee to hold its meeting during the session of the main body, unless ordered to do so.

Committee Reports.

No order is necessary to require a committee to report. Whenever a conclusion is arrived at by the majority, a report should be made by the chairman of the committee to the main body. The minority of a committee can also present a report, by obtaining leave to do so. If a majority cannot be obtained, or an agreement made, the committee should report the fact and ask to be discharged. Upon being discharged, a new committee may be appointed as before, or the matter may be disposed of by the main body.

RECEIVING THE REPORT.

When a report is made, the chairman, or person appointed to present the report of the committee, rises in the assembly, and states to the presiding officer that the committee which he represents is ready to make their report concerning the matter which they have had under consideration. The person making this announcement may himself move that the report be received and (if a select committee) the committee discharged, though it is more usual for some other member of the assembly to make such motion. The question is then put by the presiding officer to the meeting, as to whether the report will be received then ; or, if not then, a time is fixed upon when it will be received.

REPORT IN WRITING.

The person making the report usually presents the same in writing, reading the document in his place, after which he presents the report, and all papers relating to the subject, to the secretary ; or the report may be given to the secretary to read, after which the meeting will consider the matter of its acceptance. As a rule, upon some one member of the meeting moving the acceptance of the report, the same being seconded, the presiding officer will announce the report accepted, without taking a vote thereon. If, however, decided objection is made, a vote by the meeting will be taken.

A report by a select committee being accepted, the committee is dissolved, though anything further arising on the question, the matter may be recommitted to the same committee. When accepting a report, it is common to move that the report be accepted and the committee discharged.

Reports may be made by the simple expression of opinion by the committee, or by resolution or resolutions.

Committee of the Whole.

When it becomes necessary for the assembly to form itself into a committee of the whole, such action is taken on motion of some member of the meeting. The motion being carried, the presiding officer appoints a chairman of the committee, and himself takes a seat with the other members of the assembly, the chairman of the committee taking his seat with the clerk at the secretary's desk.

CHAIRMAN OF THE COMMITTEE OF THE WHOLE.

The chairman appointed by the presiding officer is usually accepted by the meeting, though the meeting possesses the power to select another chairman, should the members see fit to enforce the privilege, some one member of the meeting putting the question on the selection of another candidate.

QUORUM.

The same number is necessary in the committee of the whole to form a quorum as in the main body, and should the number be less than a quorum, the committee is compelled to rise, when the chairman informs the presiding officer that the committee is unable to transact business for want of a quorum.

DISSOLVING THE COMMITTEE.

While the committee of the whole is in session the president usually remains in the room, so that, should any disturbance arise in the committee, he may take the chair, dissolve the committee, and restore the body to order. Should such action be taken, the motion must be put as before, that the committee may sit again.

The secretary makes no record in his journal of the proceedings of the committee, but only the report of such committee to the main body.

COMMITTEE OF THE WHOLE CANNOT ADJOURN.

A committee of the whole cannot adjourn; it must rise. Neither does it take the ayes and noes, nor take up the previous question.

If unable to finish the business before time for adjournment, the committee may rise; the presiding officer will resume the chair; the chairman of the committee will report progress and ask leave to sit again, which leave is usually granted upon motion.

REPORT TO THE MAIN BODY.

Should the subject be concluded, on motion the committee will rise, the president will resume his seat, and the committee will report its proceedings and conclusions to the main body, upon the motion of some member, as with other reports.

With the exception that members may speak as often as they can obtain the floor in committee of the whole, the same rules apply to the committee of the whole as govern the main body.

THE SECRETARY.

The assistant clerk usually acts as secretary of the committee of the whole, and the presiding officer of the main body may participate in the proceedings of the committee of the whole, along with the other members of the assembly.

EXAMINATION OF MATTER BEFORE THE COMMITTEE.

In the case of any communication referred to a committee, it is usual to proceed to have it read by the clerk, section by section, or paragraph by paragraph, he noting such suggestions as the members may see fit to make, and adding such amendments as may be thought best.

Should the paper originate in the committee, erasures and interlineations may be made on such paper, in such number as may be thought best, though a clean copy of the same should be made when completed. Should the paper originate outside of the committee, amendments and changes should be made on a separate sheet of paper. When the amendments are complete, the committee should rise, and report to the general assembly.

Duties of Members of a Meeting.

Having defined the duties of the officers and committees, it is equally important that members of the assembly also understand their duties and privileges.

EQUALITY OF MEMBERS.

An assemblage of citizens, meeting in deliberative assembly is, in the highest sense of the term, a representation of a free and independent people, standing, for the time, upon a plane of exact equality. Every member of the meeting will assume the position he is fitted to fill, and will win the esteem and respect of his associates there, in proportion to his worth, perhaps more nearly than anywhere else.

APPRECIATION OF EACH MEMBER'S ABILITY.

If well informed in parliamentary usage, the fact is very clearly seen. If possessed of a high degree of intellectual culture — if gifted with fluency of speech and readiness in debate — the fact is clearly shown on such an occasion as this. Wealth and poverty stand side by side. Eminence in position and lowliness of condition are lost sight of for the time, and the real worth of the speaker, and active participator in the public meeting, is revealed in the proceedings of the assembly.

The same rights being accorded to all, it therefore becomes each member to exhibit such deportment as will, in the highest degree, promote the harmony and efficiency of the meeting.

ORDER AND DEPORTMENT OF MEMBERS.

Upon calling the meeting to order, every member should, if possible, become seated, with head uncovered. The member wishing to speak will arise and address the presiding officer, when the president, upon hearing such address, will call the member by name, or indicate him by position, that the body may give attention to his remarks.

It is customary for a member to stand while speaking, if able to do so, and the rules of decorum forbid any unseemly conduct upon the part of other members, calculated to disturb the speaker, such as general conversation, laughing, hissing, or passing about the room between the speaker and the presiding officer.

Right to the Floor.

Two or more persons arising to speak at nearly the same time, the chairman will decide who was first up, by calling the name or otherwise indicating such person, whereupon he proceeds, unless he voluntarily withdraws in favor of another. In case the president is unable to decide the matter, it should be left for the meeting to determine who is entitled to the floor. Readiness of discernment, and promptness of decision, however, upon the part of the chairman, usually render this appeal unnecessary.

TREATMENT OF A DISORDERLY PERSON.

In cases of persistency in any improper course of action, or breaches of decorum, it is in order for any member of the assembly to make complaint of such offending member to the chairman, who names the offender, states in presence of the meeting the offence complained of, and offers the offender an opportunity for explanation of his conduct.

WITHDRAWAL FROM THE ASSEMBLY.

If the offence is of such grave character as to require the action of the meeting upon the same, the member so offending should withdraw, though the privilege may be given him of remaining. It is optional with the meeting whether the member be allowed to remain or not, while his conduct is being considered by the assembly. In no case, however, should he vote upon matters relating to himself. If he does so, the vote should not be received, as no person has a right to act as judge upon his own conduct.

KINDS OF PUNISHMENT INFLICTED.

After a due consideration of the offense, the assembly may reprimand the offender; may deprive him of the privilege of voting, or speaking, for a certain length of time; may compel him to apologize, or suffer expulsion; or, if deemed for the best interests of the assembly, may expel him from the association.

Speaking to the Question.

No one can speak more than once to the same question, without permission from the assembly, even though he may change his mind on the subject; when he obtains the floor, he may speak as long as he chooses, unless a regulation exists to the contrary. The person introducing the subject, however, after every one else wishing to speak on the matter has spoken, may close the debate.

MAKING EXPLANATION.

A member may, however, be permitted to make an explanation relating to any material part of his speech, though he is not allowed to review the same at length for the purpose of introducing additional arguments.

RESPECT DUE THE CHAIRMAN.

Upon the chairman rising to make any explanation or statement, the member occupying the floor at the time should resume his seat, giving the president an opportunity of being heard.

DESIGNATING MEMBERS OF THE ASSEMBLY.

The rule of a well conducted meeting, in order to prevent personalities, is to avoid calling any person by name during a debate in assembly; it being customary to designate the person referred to by number, or as the member from such a state, such a county or district, or "my opponent," "my colleague," or the member who spoke last, etc.

Impropriety of Personalities.

To secure continued harmony among members of a public assembly, everything of a personal nature should be studiously avoided. Any allusion to the personal appearance of another member, reference to his peculiarities, ridicule of his private opinions on political or religious matters, is all very ungentlemanly, and will, in the end, react to the injury of the person making the remarks. Such a course of action will sometimes make a lifelong enemy of the person alluded to. It is desirable for each member of the assembly to secure all the friends in the meeting it is possible to obtain; to do this, he should treat every member of the meeting as he would wish to be treated, under like circumstances. The speaker should confine himself closely to principles involved in the subject he is treating, though he may criticise the position taken by his adversary. Any personal allusions, however, should be of a courteous and complimentary character.

NECESSITY OF THE CHAIRMAN PRESERVING ORDER.

When a member fails to observe the rules of decency and decorum, becomes personal and offensive, it is the duty of the chairman to call the speaker immediately to order, and check such language. The neglect of a presiding officer to do this will frequently cause a body that meets in continuous session to become greatly demoralized, and cause it to lose its power and efficiency for good.

CALLING TO ORDER.

When a member is called to order by the president he should take his seat, unless allowed to explain. In case the meeting be appealed to, the question is decided without debate. If the body is not appealed to, the question shall be decided by the chair. If the decision be favorable, the speaker is allowed to proceed; if unfavorable, the speaker is not allowed to proceed without permission of the assembly.

Introducing the Business of a Meeting.

The officers and members of an assembly understanding their duties, they are then in readiness for the transaction of such business as may come before the meeting, or any work they may have met to consider.

In legislative assemblies, generally, the order of business is provided for in the by-laws of the association, and generally comes in the following order:

1. The secretary reads his record of the preceding meeting. 2. Reports of standing committees. 3. Reports of special committees. 4. Special orders. 5. Unfinished business. 6. New business.

Official Form of Conducting a Meeting.

The rapidity with which business may be transacted in a deliberative assembly will greatly depend upon the readiness of action, and executive ability of the presiding officer. If such officer be thoroughly informed in parliamentary usage, quick and positive in decision, the council or association that otherwise would be detained in discussions and business half the day or night, may have the same business dispatched in an hour.

PROMPTITUDE OF THE PRESIDING OFFICER.

The president should be promptly in his seat at the minute appointed, and should strictly enjoin upon members the necessity of punctuality. Thus, much time is gained in the early part of a meeting.

Upon taking the chair, the president will give the signal, and will say, "The meeting (or council, society, club, association, as the case may be) will please come to order."

READING OF THE MINUTES.

If a previous meeting has been held, and the record of the same has been kept by the secretary, the president will say ·

"The secretary will please read the minutes."

The minutes of the preceding meeting should be as brief as possible, and plainly state the work transacted at the last meeting. At the close of their reading, the president will say:

"You have heard the minutes read; what action will you take on them?"

If the minutes are correct, some member will say · "I move the minutes stand approved." This motion is seconded, when the president says:

"It is moved and seconded that the minutes stand approved All in favor of the motion manifest the same by saying 'Aye!'"

"Those of the contrary opinion, 'No!'"

The formality of a vote on the minutes is dispensed with in many associations, as follows:

At the close of the reading of the minutes, the president says:

"You have heard the reading of the minutes; what action will you take thereon?"

A member says, "I move that the minutes, as read, stand approved."

The president says, "If no objection is offered, the minutes will stand approved."

The president will then promptly call for reports of "standing committees," if there be a standing rule to that effect, "special committees," etc., reports, petitions, etc., from the members, passing in under each head.

New Business.

New business usually comes in under the head of communications or petitions, and is presented by some member rising to his feet and saying:

"Mr. president (or Mr. chairman)."

The attention of the president having been arrested, he will call the member by name, or designate his number, and announce his willingness for the member to proceed.

TWO PERSONS RISING AT THE SAME TIME.

If two members should rise at nearly the same time, the president will determine who was first up. If his opinion is appealed from, the matter will be decided by a majority vote of the meeting. Should there be a tie, the president will vote and determine the matter.

A member making a statement relating to some matter, or presenting a communication or petition in writing from some person or persons, such communication or petition should be signed by the petitioner or petitioners.

Presenting Petitions.

The member who presents a petition should be so informed of the character of his petition, as to be able to make a plain statement of the nature of its contents, and whether it is worthy of consideration or not.

The person presenting the petition, or some other member, may move that the communication be received, and referred to the committee having charge of that class of business. At the same time, he should give the paper to the secretary.

His motion being seconded, the president will say:

"If no objection is offered, the communication (or petition, as the case may be) is so referred."

The secretary makes note of the fact, and holds the paper in his custody, until given to the proper committee.

IMMEDIATE ACTION ON THE PETITION.

If it is desirable to have the petition acted upon at once, the person presenting it offers a motion to that effect, and upon its being seconded it is put to vote by the president, as follows ·

"It has been moved and seconded that (here the president should so distinctly state the question that all may understand the proposition before the meeting). All in favor of the motion will manifest the same by saying 'Aye!'"

When the ayes have voted, he will say:

"All opposed to the motion, 'No!'"

Or the motion having just been made, the president may say:

"It has been moved and seconded that (here he states the question) be passed. All in favor of the same, etc."

Calling the Ayes and Noes.

Frequently the member who makes a motion, for the purpose of placing the ayes and noes of each member on record, will say:

"I move the adoption of the resolution, and that the clerk call the ayes and noes thereon."

The president will then state the question, and say:

"The clerk will please call the ayes and noes."

As a rule, unless a motion receives a second, the question is not put to vote; the idea being that if a motion does not possess sufficient popularity to secure a second, it is not worth the while to take up the time of the assembly in putting the same to vote.

Stating the Question.

A motion that has been made and seconded, has next to be stated by the president. Until it is so stated, no action can be taken thereon, as it is not yet before the meeting for discussion. Having been stated, and being before the meeting, it can only be withdrawn by motion and second, the same as it was introduced.

EXPLANATION OF THE QUESTION.

Whenever any member fails to understand the question, the president should state the same for the information of the member, if desired.

The assembly can consider but one question at a time, which should be disposed of before another question can be introduced.

INTRODUCTION OF MOTIONS.

As a rule, to insure the passage of a resolution, it is safest for the person introducing the same to have the proposition plainly reduced to writing (see chapter on resolutions). Thus the clerk or president having occasion to announce the motion, is much more likely to bring the matter clearly before the meeting.

Whether the proposition readily receive the sanction of the assembly or not will depend upon the following conditions:

1. The assembly should completely understand the objects, tendency, and character of the resolution, or

2. If the resolution relate to a matter of public interest, and is obviously a subject that requires immediate attention, and its passage will be of very decided benefit, an assembly will be apt to consider it favorably at once, and will be likely to take immediate action relating to its passage.

TEMPORARY SUPPRESSION OF THE QUESTION.

If, however, the body deem the proposition of no especial consequence, or wish more time for the investigation of the subject, or an opportunity to make amendments and changes rendering it more acceptable, then they may cause its suppression, at least for a time, by some member moving that the question lie on the table. If this is seconded, this question takes precedence of any other before the assembly.

If this motion is decided in the affirmative, the main question, and all matters relating to it, is removed from before the meeting, until such time as it suits the convenience of the assembly to take the matter up.

If decided in the negative, the business relating to the principal motion before the house will proceed, as though the motion to "lie on the table" had not been made.

Previous Question.

A question may be postponed by moving the previous question, which is done as follows:

Upon a motion being made to adopt a resolution, it is allowable for a member to move that "the question be now put." This last motion, which is termed moving the previous question, becomes the immediate question before the house, and at once shuts off debate on the main question. When the friends of a measure are afraid to have the same discussed, it is common for them to move that "the question be now put;" hoping to have strength enough, if the resolution is not discussed, to carry their point. If their motion is carried, then the original question is put, and immediately disposed of.

It is common, also, for the party anxious to defeat a measure, being fearful that its discussion will make a favorable impression on the members, to move "that the question be now put;" their hope being that the members, being unacquainted with the resolution, will not consent to its adoption, until it has been more thoroughly discussed.

POSTPONEMENT OF THE QUESTION.

When it is decided that the question should not then be put, all further discussion of the original question is usually postponed for that day. This depends upon the standing rule of assembly, however. With some state legislatures it is the rule, if the question is decided in the negative, to resume the debate and proceed with the discussion.

Formerly, in the English parliament, when it was decided that the question be not put, the question could not be brought up again during the session. At the present time, however, the decision that the motion shall not be put, effects a postponement only until the next day.[*]

[*] "The operation of a negative decision is different in different assemblies; in some, as for example, in the house of representatives of congress, it operates to dispose of the principal or main question, by suppressing or removing it from before the house for the day; but in others, as in the house of representatives of Massachusetts, and in the house of assembly of New York (in the former by usage only, and in the latter by rule), the effect of a negative decision of the previous question is to leave the main question under debate for the residue of the sitting, unless sooner disposed of by taking the question, or in some other manner.

In England, the previous question is used only for suppressing a main question; the object of the mover is to obtain a decision of it in the negative; and the effect of such a decision, though in strictness only to suppress the question for the day, is, practically and by parliamentary usage, to dispose of the subject altogether. In this country, the previous question is used chiefly for suppressing debate on a main question; the object of the mover is to obtain a decision of it in the affirmative; and the effect of a decision the other way, though in some

Suppression of Questions.

When it is desirable to suppress a question, or prevent its passage, there are several plans resorted to by parliamentarians. Among these are:

1st. Moving an adjournment, which is immediately in order; and if the hour be late, will oftentimes be passed.

2d. Moving that the question be laid on the table for the present; the argument being that, on a subsequent occasion the meeting will have more time and better opportunity to consider the merits of the question, and hence will be better informed concerning its merits.

3d. To secure, if possible, an indefinite postponement of the question, which virtually defeats it. If the maker of the motion for postponement is fearful that the question is so popular with the assembly that the members will not submit to an *indefinite* postponement, he will

4th. Aim to secure at least a postponement to a certain time in the future, hoping that it will be subsequently forgotten, or the pressure of business will be such that it cannot be taken up at the time appointed.

Or, the member, trusting to the unpopularity of the question, or the unwillingness of the meeting to pass a measure without due consideration, may move the "previous question," by

5th. Moving that the question be now put.

The member may suggest indefinite changes in the question, sufficient to show the importance of some amendment, and thereupon

6th. Move its reference to a committee having jurisdiction over that class of questions, or a select committee, as the case may be. If the question has been once considered in committee, it may be recommitted. Or the member may

7th. Move an amendment to the question, which will greatly change, modify, or weaken the force of the question.

Should all these means fail, and the question be put and carried, subsequent light on the subject may cause the members to change their opinions, in which case

8th. The question may be taken up at the next sitting or any subsequent meeting, and be reconsidered.

To Secure the Passage of a Question.

1st. The member introducing a question should have given the matter very careful and considerate attention; being thus thoroughly informed concerning its merits, and consequently able to fully illustrate and represent the claims of the measure he advocates.

2d. Personal acquaintance, conversation, and explanation with various members of the assembly relative to the question to be brought forward, will aid much in securing favorable consideration of the subject.

3d. The introduction of the motion when adjournment is

assemblies operating technically to suppress the main question for the day only, is, in general, merely to suspend the taking of the question for that day; either leaving the debate to go on during the residue of the day, or the subject to be renewed on the next or some other day. The operation of an affirmative decision is the same. In both countries, namely, the putting of the main question immediately, and without further debate, delay, or consideration." — *Cushing's Manual.*

not probable, and, if possible at a time when there is not a sufficient amount of business before the meeting to make an excuse for laying the question on the table, will aid in having it passed.

4th. The motion being seconded, the member introducing the same should then obtain the floor, and properly present the claims of the question to the members of the assembly.

5th. If the meeting is adjourned, the question laid on the table, or the consideration of the motion postponed to a certain time, the motion should be promptly brought up at the first opportunity.

6th. Should the matter be referred to a committee, the privilege may be obtained of fully acquainting the committee with the claims of the question.

7th. Should the question be so amended as to entirely change the character of the original question, and thus passed, the member may subsequently, under another name, introduce a question embracing essentially the same principles, indirectly, as the original question, and perhaps secure for the proposition favorable consideration.

8th. Another trial. Subsequent events may so change the opinions of members of an assembly as to induce them to vote favorably upon a question that they have before rejected.

The Disposal of Questions.

Motions and *questions* while nearly synonymous in parliamentary usage, are somewhat different in meaning. To *move* that an act be passed, is termed a *motion*. The subject, however, to be acted upon, is called a *question*. The action of the assembly is termed a *resolution* or *vote*. The *motion* being put, and the *question* adopted by a vote of the assembly, the decision is then known as an ordinance, order, law, statute, resolution, etc., according to the character of the meeting.

To move the previous question by moving that the question be now put, if carried in the affirmative, causes the question to be put immediately, and is thus at once disposed of without further debate. If decided in the negative, the question was formerly disposed of for the session. At the present time, it disposes of the question for the day only. In some parliamentary bodies, according to the standing rules, the debate goes on.

The effect of securing a postponement of a question without date, is to suppress the motion entirely. If postponed to a certain day, it can be taken up on that day, or as soon as the business of that day is completed.

PUTTING THE QUESTION.

In putting a question to the assembly, after it has been carefully considered, altered, amended, etc., as the case may be, the presiding officer should ask if the assembly is ready for the question? If no further suggestions are offered by the members, the chairman will then state the question, and call for a vote of the members, in the first place on the affirmative, the form of which has been heretofore considered.

TAKING UP THE QUESTION.

A question having been postponed to a certain time, the member interested in the question has a right to insist, at the appointed time, that the question be taken up. No delay or debate is allowed on the matter of taking it up. The presiding officer will then put the motion whether the meeting proceed to take up the order of the day. If the decision be favorable, the members will proceed to consider the business appointed for the day.

Referring to a Committee.

If it be thought best to refer a question to a committee, it is done on motion. Such reference to a committee is termed a "commitment" of the question. If to a special committee, the chair may name such committee, or they may, upon request of the presiding officer, be appointed by the meeting. Frequently, the person moving that the question be referred, not desiring to be on the committee himself, will, with the motion, suggest the name of some one as chairman of the committee. If no objection is made, such person may be selected.

APPOINTMENT OF THE COMMITTEE.

It is more common, however, for the person interested in a measure, to move its reference to a committee, the presiding officer to appoint the same. If it be a select committee, it is in accordance with parliamentary rule for the presiding officer to appoint as chairman on the committee, the mover of the resolution.[*]

When a question is referred, the committee may be instructed by the assembly to take such course of action in the examination of the subject as is desired, and report upon the whole, or portions of the subject, as may seem advisable. A portion may be referred to one committee, and the remainder of the proposition, involving a different principle, may be given to another committee.

The clerk may give the bill to any member, but it is usual to hand it to the one first named on the committee.

PLACE OF MEETING.

The committee may meet where they please, unless ordered to meet in a certain place by the assembly; and can meet at such time as they desire, when the main body is not in session.

Any member of the main body may be present at the meeting of the committee, but cannot vote.

Amendments to the Question.

The committee having given their report to the meeting, or the question having been considered by the assembly itself, may lack yet a few essential points necessary to make the same what it should be when passed. To add these is what is termed amending the question.

DIVIDING THE QUESTION.

Mr. Cushing recommends where a question contains two or more parts that are so distinct from each other as to form separate propositions, some of which the assembly may favor, and the others not, that the motion be divided, and submitted in

---

[*] "Though the majority on a committee should be favorable to a measure, the minority may be of those who are opposed to it in some particulars. But those totally opposed to it should never be appointed: and if any one of that view be named, he should rise and state the fact, when the main body will excuse him from serving." — (*Chairman's Assistant.*)

parts to the assembly, for their approval or rejection. This is thought a more expeditious manner of disposing of the same than to add several amendments to the question, the result in the end being the same.

This division may be made by motion ; the mover designating in his motion the manner in which he would have the division made.

JUDGMENT OF THE ASSEMBLY.

It is, of course, for the presiding officer and the assembly to consider whether the question is of such a complicated nature as to require such division. As a rule, no division should be made, unless the parts are so separate and distinct that either alone would form a separate and distinct proposition.

BLANKS.

The member of an assembly who introduces a long and complicated question, containing several points, yet one so dependent on the other as not to be separable, may prepare his questions with blanks for the assembly to fill up.

The proposition before the meeting, in such case, may contain an outline of all that is required, while the members of the assembly will very readily fill the blanks with the time, amount, cost, or whatever they may wish to particularize.

Amendments.

Much time may frequently be saved in a deliberative assembly by the member who introduces a motion, carefully considering the question himself before presenting it, as well as learning the wishes of the members by private consultation. As this is not always practicable, however, many questions must first be made ready for being voted upon by being amended in the public assembly itself.

For the purpose of effecting such changes in a question as the members may desire, the question may be altered:

1st. By an amendment.
2d. By an amendment to an amendment.

As there must be a line drawn somewhere, parliamentary law prevents there being any more amendments to amendments than the foregoing ; but still more changes may be made in the proposition before the meeting, by alterations in the amendments.

AN AMENDMENT TO AN AMENDMENT.

To illustrate : John Smith, member of the assembly, says.

" I move that a committee of five be appointed by this meeting to collect funds for the poor of this town."

The motion being seconded, and the question stated by the chairman, William Jones says:

" I move an amendment ; that this committee to collect funds consist of seven persons, to be appointed by the chair.

The amendment being seconded, and stated as before, James Brown says:

" I move an amendment to the amendment ; that the chairman of this meeting appoint seven persons a committee to collect funds, to be used wholly in the interests of the poor of the west division of this city."

The question being again before the house as in the former case, Walter Harper says:

" I move another amendment ; that one half of the funds collected go to the children's aid society, the other half to the general poor fund of the entire city."

The chairman here remarks that the last amendment is out of order, as there can be but one amendment to an amendment.

He further says:

" The amendment to the amendment is first in order. It is moved " *(here he states the amendment to the amendment, or calls upon the mover to do so, puts the question and declares the result).*

If the motion is lost, he says :

" The next question in order is the amendment to the question, *(here he states the amendment, and puts the same as before).* Should this be lost, he says :

" The question is now on the original motion." *(He here states the question, puts the motion as before, and announces the result.)*

Nature of Amendments.

Amendments cannot be made to privileged questions ; such as a motion to adjourn, the previous question, or to lay on the table.

An amendment to an amendment, even though greatly at variance with the amendment, will still be in order, it being left to the discretion of the assembly to determine whether they will change from their previous action.

SPEAKING TO AN AMENDMENT.

A member who may have spoken to the main question, may speak to the amendment, after the same is moved.

If it is desired to add to a sentence a new paragraph, it is important that the paragraph be very carefully considered, being made as perfect as possible, as it cannot be changed after being adopted in that form. Or, should it be resolved to strike out a paragraph, the same care should be taken to have the sentence as complete as may be, after the words are stricken out.*

COMMITMENT TO A COMMITTEE.

When a long and complicated question is before the house, if there be a standing committee, the easiest method of disposing of the question is to refer the same to such committee. If, however, the time of the convention will admit, and there be no other business appointed or occupying the present attention of the assembly, it will be in order for the members to immediately proceed to the disposal of the question, by the following process :

1st. By amendments striking out all unnecessary matter.
2d. By the addition of all essential matter.
3d. By combining two or three propositions, where it can be done, in one.

* When it is moved to amend by striking out certain words, and inserting others, the manner of stating the question is, first to read the whole passage to be amended, as it stands at present, then the words proposed to be struck out ; next, those to be inserted ; and lastly, the whole passage, as it will be when amended. And the question, if desired, is then to be divided, and put, first, on striking out. If carried, it is next on inserting the words proposed. If that be lost, it may be moved to insert others. —*Hatsall.*

4th. By voting separately on each distinct proposition, until all are disposed of.

WHAT AMENDMENTS ARE IN ORDER.

An amendment may be made to the question; and an amendment to that amendment is in order; but no amendment to the amendment of the amendment can be made.

If it is desired to introduce a change, it is best to state the objection to the amendment of the amendment, and, if possible, defeat such amendment, when another amendment may be introduced and possibly carried, in the place of the one defeated.

If an amendment has been accepted by the assembly, it cannot afterwards be altered or rejected, but the amendment may be so amended as to present the question in the desired shape.

Thus, if the amendment consist of *one, two, three,* and it is moved to insert *four,* and the motion prevails, *four* cannot afterwards be rejected, for it has been adopted in that form. Should it be moved to strike out *two, three,* and the motion be lost, *two, three,* cannot afterwards be stricken out, as the meeting resolved to allow them to remain.

The only alternative now left the meeting, should it seem very desirable to strike out *two, three,* is to make the proposition to strike out *one, two, three,* or the amendment may be to strike out *two, three, four.*

The rule in parliamentary practice is, that while certain words, which have been accepted or rejected, cannot afterwards be changed, such words may afterwards be adopted or rejected, if accompanied by other words.*

Inserting Clauses and Striking Out.

When it is proposed to amend by adding a certain paragraph, and such paragraph or words are rejected, such paragraph or words can only be subsequently added by the adding of other words with the same, thereby changing the sense of the words intended to be added.

When it is proposed to reject certain words or a paragraph, and the meeting vote to allow such words to remain, those words cannot afterwards be stricken out, unless other words be added with these words, thereby changing the sense of what it was before designed to strike out.

Amendments Changing the Question, by Striking Out Certain Words and Adding Others.

The following changes may be made in a proposition:

1. To strike out certain words and insert nothing in their place.

---

* When a motion for striking out words is put to the question, the parliamentary form always is, whether the words *shall stand as part* of a principal motion, and not whether they *shall be struck out.* The reason for this form of stating the question probably is, that the question may be taken in the same manner on a part as on the whole of the principal mo ion; which would not be the case if the question was stated on striking out; inasmuch as the question on the principal motion, when it comes to be stated, will be on agreeing to it, and not on striking out or rejecting it. Besides, as an equal division of the assembly would produce a different decision of the question, according to the manner of stating it, it might happen, if the question on the amendment was stated on striking out, that the same question would be decided both affirmatively and negatively by the same vote. The common, if not the only mode of stating the question, in the legislative assemblies of this country, is on *striking out. — Cushing's Manual.*

2. To insert other words in the place of those stricken out.

Amendments may then be made, striking out a part of the words added, with others, or adding words stricken out with others.

Fixing Time, Amount, Etc., by Amendments.

In determining the time at which the assembly shall convene in the future, or the number of anything desired, the rule is not in the amendment to fix the time and amount at so short a period or small an amount as to be certain to unite the members upon the proposition at first; as to adopt a *less* would preclude the adoption of a *greater;* but the vote is to be taken on the greater, and recede until a sufficient number of votes can be secured to carry the amendment.*

Privileged Questions.

Parliamentary usage has determined that when a question is being debated, no motion shall be received except the following, which are termed " privileged questions," and come in the following order:

1st. A question having been moved, seconded, and put by the chair, must be decided by a vote of the assembly before anything else is in order.

2d. A motion to adjourn takes precedence over all others, for the reason that, otherwise, the assembly might be compelled to continue in session, without such motion, an indefinite time against its will. This question, however, cannot be entertained after a question has been actually put, and while the members of the meeting are voting upon the same.

3d. An order of the day stands next in precedence. That is, a question that has been postponed to a certain hour; should the person interested in the question move that it be taken up and disposed of then, such motion is in order. Thus, if a question has been postponed to 9 o'clock, and at that time it is moved to take up that question, even though there be another question before the house, that motion must be received by the chair.

4th. The previous question stands next in order, and when moved and seconded, must be put. This question admits of no lesser motion, such as amendment or postponement to a certain time.

---

* In Senate, January 25, 1798, a motion to postpone until the second Tuesday in February, some amendments proposed to the constitution. The words "until the second Tuesday in February" were struck out by way of amendment. Then it was moved to add "until the first day of June." Objected, that it was not in order, as the question should first be put on the longest time; therefore, a shorter time decided against, a longer cannot be put to question. It was answered, that this rule takes place only in filling blanks for a time. But when a specific time stands part of a motion, that may be struck out as well as any other part of the motion; and when struck out, a motion may be received to insert any other. In fact, it is not till they are struck out, and a blank for the time thereby produced, that the rule can begin to operate, by receiving all the propositions for different times, and putting the questions successively on the longest. Otherwise, it would be in the power of the mover, by inserting originally a short time, to preclude the possibility of a longer. For till the short time is struck out, you cannot insert a longer; and if, after it is struck out, you cannot do it, then it cannot be done at all. Suppose the first motion had been to amend, by striking out " the second Tuesday in February," and inserting, instead thereof, " the first of June." It would have been regular then to divide the question, by proposing first the question to strike out, and then to insert. Now this is precisely the effect of the present proceeding; only, instead of one motion and two questions, there are two motions and two questions to effect it; the motion being divided as well as the question. — *Jefferson's Manual.*

AMENDMENT AND POSTPONEMENT.

If an amendment and postponement are proposed, the latter is put first, because, in case of postponement, the amendment, at the time appointed, may be then brought up, when the main question is again considered.

A motion for postponement being followed by one referring the question to a committee, the latter must be put first.

Reading Papers.

A motion being made relative to reading papers which relate to the principal question, must be put before the main question.

In referring to a committee, the order of the commitment is as follows:

1st. Committee of the whole.
2d. Standing committee.
3d. Special committee.

A motion being made and seconded cannot be withdrawn, though, if no one object, the chairman need not put the question.

A motion having been made and it being subsequently moved to commit the question, or to postpone, to amend, or to lay on the table, the motion to lay on the table comes first. That being lost, the next question is on the amendment. Next comes the postponement; then the commitment, and lastly, the putting of the question.

POSTPONEMENT.

If it is moved that a question be postponed to a certain time, the time appointed can be amended, and the amendment can be amended. The amendment to the amendment comes first, and the amendment before the main question.

It being moved to insert or strike out anything, and the matter to be inserted or stricken out being amended, the amendment must be put first.

DATES AND NUMBERS.

Blanks being filled with different sums or dates, the question is to be put first on the longest time and largest sum.

A disagreement between members should be disposed of before the putting of the main question.

An appeal from the decision of the chair, or a motion to withdraw a question, must be acted upon before the putting of the main question.

Orders of the Day.

When several questions have been postponed to a certain day, such questions are termed the orders of the day. Upon a motion being made on the day appointed, that the orders of the day be taken up, such motion takes precedence of any other question that may be introduced at the time, and being decided in the affirmative, must be first put. The questions are then considered in the order of their priority, in their appointment for that particular day.

A question which has been postponed to a certain hour, or which lies on the table, it is regarded discourteous to call up in the absence of the mover or against his wishes, provided the matter has reference to private and local concerns in his particular charge; especially if the delay of the question does

not particularly interfere with the order of business before the general assembly.

Decisions as to Order.

Whenever, as is frequently the case, disagreements and questions of order arise among members of an assembly, and the chairman is appealed to as the arbitrator in such case, he will himself decide the matter, and the expression of his decision is in order before the transaction of other business. If, however, any member of the assembly objects to the ruling of the chair, he can appeal from the decision of the presiding officer, and have the matter decided by a vote of the meeting.

In such cases the presiding officer will put the question on the appeal as follows:

"*It is desired that an appeal be taken from the chair. Do the members of this meeting sustain the decision of the chairman?*"

The question is then before the assembly for consideration and debate, in which the chairman will take part if he desires to do so.

Vote of the Chairman.

As a rule in most assemblies, on ordinary questions, the chairman is not expected to participate in the debate, but simply to make statement of facts, maintain order, and facilitate the business of the meeting by affording information relative to questions in order, put questions, determine the vote, etc. While the chairman does not usually vote, he nevertheless retains the great advantage of being able to determine, if he chooses, in case of a tie vote, what the majority vote shall be.

A TIE VOTE.

In legislative assemblies, such as councils, legislatures, etc., the regulations of the code under which the assembly works sometimes give the presiding officer the privilege of voting only in case of a tie vote, and in that case he is compelled to vote. In all other meetings, the chairman may cast his vote when a ballot is taken. This privilege he does not usually exercise, however, unless he is desirous of making a tie, for the purpose of preventing the passage of a question.

AN EXAMPLE.

Thus, if there be eleven persons to vote besides the chairman, and the vote stands six for the adoption of the resolution and five against, the chairman may vote with the minority, and thus defeat the resolution by making the vote a tie.

HE MAY VOTE OR NOT.

Or, in case the vote is a tie, he may vote with the opponents of the measure, and thus defeat the proposition, or, if unwilling to have his vote go on record, he may decline to vote, as the question is defeated in either case.

Reading All Papers.

When papers are brought before the meeting, it is the conceded right of every member of the assembly to have them read at least once, before he can be compelled to vote on them, though no member should insist on the privilege of all papers, accounts, etc., being read, without the consent of the other members. To do so would so trespass on the time of the assembly as to seriously prevent the transaction of business. If, however, it is evident that when a member calls for the reading of any document pertaining to the question, that his object is information, and not delay, the chairman may instruct the clerk to read the paper without a vote of the members, unless the same be objected to, in which case the question must be put.

READING SPEECHES.

Neither has a member a right to insist on the clerk reading any book pertaining to the subject, nor can the member himself claim the privilege of reading a document, even his own speech, without leave of the house, if the same be objected to. If the speaker, however, is earnestly desirous of affording more light on the subject, without consuming time unnecessarily, he is usually allowed to proceed, without objection.

If the time of the assembly be taken up with a large amount of business, it is customary to read the title of a petition or communication to be considered, and refer the same to the appropriate standing committee. If, however, any member of the assembly insists that the paper shall be read, his right is admitted to exist.

Proper Time for Speaking on a Question.

The usual plan of procedure in speaking to a question is as follows:
1st. A motion is made by a member.
2d. The motion is seconded by another member.
3d. The question is then stated to the meeting by the chairman, with the further remark, as follows:
" *The question is now before the meeting, what is your pleasure in reference to it.*"
The question is now in condition for debate. Every member has a right to the expression of his opinion once upon the subject, either for or against. He has also the privilege of talking as long as he chooses, even adjourning to the next day, and the next, in legislative assemblies, unless by common consent a regulation has been imposed, restricting the time of speaking to a certain period.

HINTS TO CEASE SPEAKING.

If, however, the person speaking fails to secure the attention of the house, it should be a sufficient evidence that his remarks are without influence and effect, and good judgment will dictate that he should resume his seat. If disorder is caused by his continuance in speaking, it is the duty of the chairman to preserve decorum in the meeting, by calling the speaker to order, and requesting him to take his seat.

The Member Entitled to Speak First.

As between several speakers who may wish to speak upon a question which has been introduced, the person making the motion is, by courtesy, entitled to speak first. The person moving an adjournment is entitled to speak first upon the reassembling of the meeting, after the adjournment; and of two members rising at the same time, the person opposing the

question has a right to the floor before the member favoring the proposition.

LOSING THE RIGHT TO THE FLOOR.

A speaker having resigned his right to the floor, thereby forfeits his privilege of speaking any more to the question then under discussion, except by express permission of the assembly, unless for the purpose of offering some brief explanation in reference to his former remarks on the question.

The question having been put in the affirmative, and a vote taken on the same, any member who has not yet spoken may speak to the question before the negative is put. The coming of other members into the room after the affirmative of the question has been put, when the negative is under discussion, makes it necessary to put the affirmative again.

Times of Speaking.

As a rule, no member can speak more than once to the main question. Should the question be referred to a committee, however, he may speak on the report of the committee, though the question is the same as before.

Should there be an amendment, he may speak upon that, though it may involve essentially the same principles as the main question; and he may also speak upon an amendment to an amendment. Thus, a member desirous of speaking to a question again, may, by moving its reference to a committee, and the addition of amendments, obtain the floor several times, essentially upon the same question.

Suspension of Rules.

When it is discovered that a standing rule of the assembly is in conflict with a question of very considerable importance, which it is desirable should be acted upon, it has become the custom to suspend such rule, for the purpose of passing the question; such suspension taking place by motion, being seconded and passed by a majority vote.*

Taking a Vote.

There are several methods of putting a question to vote; these being by ballot, *viva voce*, by calling the yeas and nays, by raising of hands, by standing, and by dividing the house, one party going to one side of the room, the other to the opposite side.

The question is in all cases put first in the affirmative, and if the chairman cannot himself determine by either of the above methods, in consequence of there being a large number of persons present, he may appoint certain members to act as tellers, to take the vote in different divisions of the house, taking the affirmative vote first.

The method adopted will depend upon the number and character of the audience, and the size and convenience of the room in which the meeting convenes.

---

* It is usual, in the code of rules adopted in deliberative assemblies, and especially legislative bodies, to provide that a certain number exceeding a majority, as two thirds or three fourths, shall be competent to the suspension of a rule in a particular case; when this is not provided, there seems to be no other mode of disposing with a rule than by general consent. — *Cushing's Manual.*

Concluding Remarks.

The harmony and success of a public meeting will depend very largely upon the order preserved by the presiding officer.

If the assemblage be of a character where any trouble is to be apprehended, it is well for the projectors of the meeting to notify officers, having authority to preserve order, to be in attendance. The chairman, however, will greatly aid in the preservation of stillness, by requesting all persons in to room to come forward and be seated in his near presence. Let him see that every seat, if possible, is filled in front. A magnetic connection and sympathy exists between the presiding officer and the audience, when the congregation is placed closely around the chairman's desk, that is favorable for the president of a meeting. Seated near the chairman, the audience can more distinctly hear all that is said, they will take a greater interest in the meeting, and hence will observe better order.

HONORARY MEMBERS.

Veteran members of the meeting, and persons who have won honorable distinction in the cause that the meeting assembles to consider, distinguished past presiding officers, and other notabilities whose presence will lend dignit to the rostrum, the chairman may appropriately call to the stand, to occupy a seat beside him, all of which, well managed by the presiding officer, tends to give dignity, respectability, and influence to the proceedings of the assemblage.

The Ladies.

In the preparation of this work on parliamentary usages, the author has, for convenience sake, made reference to, and spoken only of, the masculine gender. Realizing, however, that the time is now at hand when the women of the country will take a much more active part in public affairs than they have done hitherto, this chapter is also prepared with special reference to the wants of conventions, and other assemblages, composed wholly, or in part, of ladies; the only change required in the wording being the personal pronouns, which make reference to the male sex.

Titles of Women who act as Officers.

When a woman acts as presiding officer of a meeting, the person addressing her should say, "Mrs. President," or "Miss President," as the case may be.

The presiding officer will designate the speaker, if a lady, by name, by number; or as the lady, the number, the delegate, the representative, etc., as may be most convenient.

The titles of clerk, secretary, recording officer, treasurer, etc., are the same, whether applied to ladies or gentlemen.

Adjournment.

If the meeting be a regular session of a legislature, or council, and it is moved and voted to adjourn, such adjournment is understood to be until the next regular meeting. If it is desired to meet before that, the meeting will adjourn to reassemble at the time specified.

If the meeting be not in regular session, it is necessary, if the business be unfinished at the time of adjournment, to adjourn to a certain time. If, however, the business for which the assembly was called is completed, and no subsequent assemblage is necessary, it is moved and seconded to adjourn, which being put by the president, and carried, the meeting is dissolved.

Writing for the Press.

IN writing for the Press, while being explicit, the writer should make the statement as brief as possible.

Though in ordinary conversation talk may be cheap, in the newspaper, words cost money. If sent by telegraph, they cost for transmission; time is consumed in their examination by the editor and proofreader; money is expended in putting them in type; ink and paper must be furnished on which they make their impress; and time is to be occupied by the reader in their perusal; therefore, each word should convey as much significance as possible.

General Directions.

1. If, unavoidably, a long article is written relating to a variety of subjects, it is well to break the sameness of the appearance by *sub-heads*, scattered through the article, relating to different subjects considered in the composition.

2. Write very plainly, on white paper with black ink, taking care to write names of persons, dates and places, with the utmost distinctness.

3. Use sheets of paper about six by nine inches in size, numbered in their order if more than one sheet be used. Very large sheets, on the compositor's case, make it inconvenient for the type setter.

4. Write on but one side of the sheet. Thus the paper containing your communication may be, if necessary, cut into parts, and distributed among several compositors who will place your composition in type.

5. As a rule, in short news articles, never use the pronouns *I* or *you*. A plain, succinct record of the news is all that is required. If necessary for the writer to refer to himself, it is better to say "Our reporter" or "The writer."

6. Never waste time in complimenting the editor or his paper, when writing a letter for publication. Commence at once with the subject in hand, and close when you have done.

Local Reporting.

That kind of journalistic writing most easily taken up, and yet quite difficult to do well, is that of presenting in attractive form a judicious report of home news.

Much demand exists for more reportorial talent, especially on the country newspaper. Thousands of exciting incidents and events transpire, the details of which, written up for the press, would greatly edify the readers of the country journal, the editor of which, knowing nothing of the affair, is compelled to fill his paper with foreign news of less interest to his subscribers.

As a general rule, there is not sufficient local matter to be obtained, nor space to be filled, in the weekly country journal, to make it an object for the publisher to employ, at a weekly salary, a person whose exclusive business shall be collecting local news; and yet the editor is desirous of obtaining all the important home intelligence there is, and will willingly pay for such as he may publish, at the rate of from $1 to $5 per column, when an arrangement may be made for the correspondent to write regularly.

Of course no writer should expect compensation until it is clearly shown that his or her writings are of decided service to the paper in which they are published. When they become so, editors and publishers readily concede the fact, and are willing to pay what the articles are worth.

Important Reportorial Qualifications.

The reporter should be truthful. In writing of any event, great care should be taken to state the actual facts. To do this, the reporter should possess the energy to go to the scene of action, if possible, himself, and learn the exact condition of affairs. It is often unsafe to depend upon hearsay.

The reporter should carefully guard against allowing his own opinions to warp or bias his report of the sayings or doings of others, thus giving, almost without his being conscious of the fact, an untruthful representation. A plain, unvarnished report should be made, and nothing else.

Much discretion should be exercised in the personal mention of individuals. A dozen words, thoughtlessly written, may do irreparable injury to the reputation of an innocent person : a paragraph in praise may add to the life-long happiness and prosperity of the individual upon whom it is bestowed. As a general rule, while praise may be personally given, if wrongs exist, it is better to speak of them in general terms, rather than couple them with names of the individuals at fault ; though, if the person be notoriously persistent in a course of wrong doing, justice demands newspaper exposure.

Subjects of Local and General Interest.

ITEMS FOR THE NEWSPAPER.

For the advantage of the inexperienced writer, making record of home news, the following partial list is given, containing subjects of general interest to the public.

Accidents.—When, where, to whom.

Amusements, Excursions, Etc.—When, where; character of amusement, etc.

Births.—When, where, name of parents and sex of child.

Burglary.—When, where, by whom. amount stolen, etc.

Change of Business Firms.—When, and names of the parties.

Crops.—Present condition and future prospects.

Crime of any kind.—Names of offenders ; nature of the crime.

Churches.—Change of pastors, revivals, election of church officers, etc.

Dissolutions of Partnership.—Names of parties, where going, what to do.

Deaths.—Who, when, where, cause.

Discoveries.—Of curiosities, or anything new or valuable.

Distinguished Arrivals.—At the hotels or elsewhere.

Divorces.—Who, when, where, cause. When and where married.

Elopements.—Names of parties and circumstances.

Election Intelligence.—Election takes place when, candidates to be, or are elected, etc.

Fires.—Whose property, when, where, cause, amount of insurance, names of companies insured in.

Facts and Figures.—Concerning any products raised in the vicinity, amount sold, profits, etc.

Festivals.—Held by whom, for what object, amount realised, etc.

Improvements.—By whom, where, and costs.

Inventions.—Patents granted to whom, what for, nature of the improvement.

Lectures.—Past, or to come ; when, where, by whom, substance of what was said.

Marriages.—Who, when, where, by whom married, where gone on bridal tour.

Murders.—When, where, who, by whom, object of the murder, circumstances.

New Comers.—Their business, where located, where from, etc.

New Manufactures.—In prospect, when, where, by whom established, kind, etc.

New Buildings.—To be or built, erected by whom, for what purpose, cost, etc.

Price of Staple Commodities.—In the market, prospect for the future, etc.

Parties Leaving Town.—Who, when, where going, business going into.

Presentations.—By whom, to whom, where given, what presented, why.

Railroads.—New roads in prospect, profits of present roads, etc.

Sales of Real Estate.—By whom, to whom, who will occupy, amount paid, etc.

Shows, Exhibitions, Fairs.—Where, when, who gives them, character of entertainment.

Schools.—Facts and figures concerning them, change of teachers, improvements needed, etc.

Secret Societies.—Election of officers, prosperity and condition of the society.

Strange Phenomena.—In the heavens, in the elements, on or in the earth, where, when.

Suggestions of Improvements Needed.—Where, when, by whom, cost, etc.

Surgical Operations.—By whom performed, of what character, condition of patient.

Sickness. — Who sick, cause, by what physician attended, health of the community.

Telegraphs. — What new lines are to be established, present cost of telegraphing, etc.

Violation of Law. — Whereby parties are arrested and fined, what offense, when, where, etc.

Writing for the Metropolitan Press.

In every locality something will occasionally transpire the details of which will be of general interest to the public at large, in which case the publishers of papers in the large cities will esteem it a favor for some person to give them the facts.

Should the town in which the correspondent is stationed be sufficiently large, and the news frequently occurring important, the publisher will pay an accepted regular correspondent for news that he prints, from $1 to $10 per article, as may be agreed between publisher and correspondent.

Only such matter is desired for the metropolitan journal as will interest the people throughout the entire country. Of such news are facts concerning : — *Enactments of Law. Severe accidents. Fires. Crops. Murders. Elopements. Burglary. Schools. Churches. New manufactures. Railroads. Elections. Weather. Discoveries. Inventions. Strange phenomena. Important Statistics. Personal mention of distinguished persons, etc.*

RESULTS OF BAD PENMANSHIP.

Especial pains should be taken, when writing for the press, to write legibly. The error is very common with some authors and prominent men, of writing in a manner such as to seriously trespass upon the time and patience of printers and correspondents upon whom they inflict their penmanship.

This fault is a very serious one, and causes much waste of time and pecuniary loss to printers. Lawyers frequently prepare their briefs, clergymen their sermons, and others their copy, in a penmanship so entirely illegible as to compel several re-settings of much of the same, in type, before it is correct. Of course this loss of time must be borne by the compositor, and frequently, with those printers employed in setting type by the thousand, bad manuscript entails a loss in their earnings of several dollars per week.

While to filch from the pocket of the printer, in this manner may not be deemed so dishonorable as to steal his purse, the result is, however, all the same.

Again, business men who would regard it a great intrusion for another to trespass on their time for even a half hour, will show the discourtesy to write a letter to a correspondent which may consume hours and even days of his time in deciphering the same.

This evil would be less if it stopped here. Unfortunately, however, it goes beyond and afflicts the coming penmanship of our youth. The boy that will pick up the half consumed cigar and smoke out the balance of the stump, thinking that thereby he makes a man of himself, will look upon bad penmanship, when executed by distinguished men, as an evidence of genius, and is not unlikely to imagine himself a great man, because he imitates their pot-hooks and scrawls.

Eminent men are liable to have faults. If the error is an illegible penmanship, this defect is none the less a fault, because the man may have distinguished reputation and redeeming qualities in other directions.

Young writers should not therefore ape bad penmanship as an evidence of genius. Of two articles written for the newspaper, all things else being equal, that one stands much the best chance for publication which is most plain in penmanship. Let the young author see that the composition is not only correctly written, when prepared for the press, but that it is so perfectly legible that its merit may be readily seen upon examination.

BOOKS.

THE accompanying illustrations, upon this page, represent the principal sizes of books, namely: *Folio*, a long book; *Quarto* (*4to*), nearly square, (shape of Hill's Manual); *Octavo* (*8vo*), the general size; and *Duodecimo* (*12mo*), a small book, as seen below.

FOLIO.

The standard size of book paper is 25 x 38 inches; one half of the sheet being 19 x 25 inches, which folded in two leaves, having four pages, makes a book of the size called a *folio*.

QUARTO.

When the half sheet is folded in four leaves, making eight pages, it forms a *quarto* in size.

OCTAVO.

The half sheet folded again, eight leaves, sixteen pages, forms an *octavo*, or folded into sixteen leaves forms a *sixteenmo*.

DUODECIMO.

By folding the same into twelve leaves, making twenty-four pages, we have a *duodecimo*. Folded into eighteen leaves, or thirty-six pages, we form an *18mo*; into 24 leaves, and we have a *24mo*, &c.

The words Post, Crown, Demy, Royal, etc., used in connection, as Royal Octavo, designate the sizes of paper of which books are made.

Modern facilities for the manufacture of paper enable publishers to have any desired size made to order, as has been done in the case of this book.

The marks a, b, c; 1, 2, 3; 1*, 2*, 3*, 1A, &c., occasionally found at the bottom of a page, are what printers term *signature* marks, being printed for the direction of the binders in folding the sheets.

FOLIO.

QUARTO, "4to."

OCTAVO, "8vo."

Duodecimo, "12mo."

The art of covering books in a superior manner, was in use long before the art of printing was discovered, some of the most beautiful and elaborate binding being executed as early as the 11th century. Books, which were in manuscript, in those days, were few, and so very valuable that great care was taken in their preservation, jewelers and other artisans engaging in the manufacture and ornamentation of their covers.

With the advanced civilization of the 19th century, however, the superior machinery for book binding has not only cheapened the cost, but the facilities in some large establishments, are such as to enable manufacturers to elegantly bind, in muslin, one hundred and fifty copies per hour.

NAMES OF THE DIFFERENT SIZES OF BOOK AND NEWSPAPER TYPE.

The poetry and other matter occupying the lower portion of the following oblong space, it will be seen, are printed in a style much more open than the matter occupying the upper part of the space. This results from placing a thin piece of metal, called a *lead*, between the lines. Reading matter having these leads between the lines is called *leaded*: thus, the reading matter in the following spaces is what is termed *solid* and *leaded*; the upper portion being *solid*, and the lower part *leaded*.

This page contains a specimen of fourteen kinds of n
This page contains a specimen of fourteen kinds of newsp
This page contains a specimen of fourteen kinds of newspaper and book type, fr
This page contains a specimen of fourteen kinds of newspaper and book type, from Bri
This page contains a specimen of fourteen kinds of newspaper and book type, from Brilliant to Tw
This page contains a specimen of fourteen kinds of newspaper and book type, from Brilliant to Two-line
This page contains a specimen of fourteen kinds of newspaper and book type, from Brilliant to Two-line Small Pica.
This page contains a specimen of fourteen kinds of newspaper and book type, from Brilliant to Two-line Small Pica. A
This page contains a specimen of fourteen kinds of newspaper and book type, from Brilliant to Two-line Small Pica. A B C D E
This page contains a specimen of fourteen kinds of newspaper and book type, from Brilliant to Two-line Small Pica. A B C D E 1234
This page contains a specimen of fourteen kinds of newspaper and book type, from Brilliant to Two-line Small Pica. A B C D E F G 123456789 10
This page contains a specimen of fourteen kinds of newspaper and book type, from Brilliant to Two-line Small Pica. A B C D E F G H I J K L M N O P 123456789 10 11 12
This page contains a specimen of fourteen kinds of newspaper and book type, from Brilliant to Two-line Small Pica. A B C D E F G H I J K L M N O P Q R S T U V W X Y Z & 123456789 10
This page contains a specimen of fourteen kinds of newspaper and book type, from Brilliant to Two-line Small Pica. A B C D E F G H I J K L M N O P Q R S T U V W X Y Z & 12345678 9 10 11 12 13 14 15 16

BRILLIANT.

Experience proves that the apprentice foreshadows the workman, just as surely as the bend of a twig foretells the inclination of the tree. The upright, obedient, industrious lad will graduate a steady, skillful, and capable man, as unmistakably as the perverse, idling, careless boy will ripen into the lazy, dissolute fellow. The fact is, a boy is measurably the maker of his own destiny; and if he fail to acquire a master-knowledge of the trade to which he is put, it will mainly be because he did not at the outset determine to be a master-workman. Good morals and steady industry are indispensable. Among the business habits that are highly valued in the apprentice are punctuality, order, neatness and dispatch. The boy who is promptly at his work in the morning soon wins the esteem of his employer. The lad who keeps the shop and store in a neat and orderly manner are long becomes a valuable assistant, and the youth who, in addition to these qualifications, is active in the dispatch of business, is certain to make himself useful to those with whom he may engage. The boy who is prompt at his work in the morning.

THE FUTURE LIFE.
By Wm. C. Bryant.

How shall I know thee in the sphere which keeps
The disembodied spirits of the dead,
When all of thee that time could wither, sleeps
And perishes among the dust we tread?

For I shall feel the sting of ceaseless pain,
If there I meet thy gentle spirit not;
Nor hear the voice I love, nor read again
In thy serenest eyes, the tender thought.

DIAMOND.

Experience proves that the apprentice foreshadows the workman, just as surely as the bend of a twig foretells the inclination of the tree. The upright, obedient, industrious lad will graduate a steady, skillful, and capable man, as unmistakably as the perverse, idling, careless boy will ripen into the lazy, dissolute fellow. The fact is, a boy is measurably the maker of his own destiny; and if he fail to acquire a master-knowledge of the trade to which he is put, it will mainly be because he did not at the outset determine to be a master-workman. Good morals and steady industry are indispensable. Among the business habits that are highly valued in the apprentice are punctuality, order, neatness and dispatch. The boy who is promptly at his work in the morning soon wins the esteem of his employer. The lad who keeps the shop and store in a neat and orderly manner are long becomes a valuable assistant, and the youth who, in addition to these qualifications, is active in the dispatch of business, is certain to make himself useful to those with whom he may engage. The boy who is prompt at his work in the morning soon wins the esteem of his employer. The boy should one resolution that are long becomes a valuable assistant, and the youth who, in addition to these qualifications, is active in the dispatch of business, is certain to make himself useful to those with whom he may engage. To attain the highest success in a tradesman and thereby obtain, he should not only form those serious habits of business, but he should carefully cultivate and maintain a pure, untarnished morality; upon which rests all permanent happiness and success.

PEARL.

Experience proves that the apprentice foreshadows the workman, just as surely as the bend of a twig foretells the inclination of the tree. The upright, obedient, industrious lad will graduate a steady, skillful, and capable man, as unmistakably as the perverse, idling, careless boy will ripen into the lazy, dissolute fellow. The fact is, a boy is measurably the maker of his own destiny; and if he fail to acquire a master-knowledge of the trade to which he is put, it will mainly be because he did not at the outset determine to be a master-workman. Good morals and steady industry are indispensable. Among the business habits that are highly valued in the apprentice are punctuality, order, neatness and dispatch. The lad who keeps the shop and store in a neat and orderly manner are long becomes a valuable assistant, and the youth who, in addition to these qualifications, is active in the dispatch of business, is certain to make himself useful to those with whom he may engage. The boy

Will not thy own meek heart demand me there?
That heart whose fondest throb to me was given?
My name on earth was ever in thy prayer,
And wilt thou never utter it in heaven?

AGATE.

EXPERIENCE proves that the apprentice foreshadows the workman, just as surely as the bend of a twig foretells the inclination of the tree. The upright, obedient, industrious lad will graduate a steady, skillful and capable man, as unmistakably as the perverse, idling, careless boy will ripen into the lazy, dissolute fellow. The fact is, a boy is measurably the maker of his own destiny, and if he fail to acquire a master-knowledge of the trade to which he is put, it will mainly be because he did not at the outset determine to be a master-workman. Good morals and steady industry are indispensable. Among the business habits that are highly valued in the apprentice are punctuality, order, neatness and dispatch. The boy who is promptly at his work in the morning soon wins the esteem of his employer. The lad who keeps the shop and store in a neat and orderly manner are long becomes a

In meadows fanned by heaven's life-breathing wind,
In the resplendence of that glorious sphere,
And larger movements of the unfettered mind,
Wilt thou forget the love that joined us here?

NONPAREIL.

EXPERIENCE proves that the apprentice foreshadows the workman, just as surely as the bend of a twig foretells the inclination of the tree. The upright, obedient, industrious lad will graduate a steady, skillful, and capable man, as unmistakably as the perverse, idling, careless boy will ripen into the lazy, dissolute fellow. The fact is, a boy is measurably the maker of his own destiny; and if he fail to acquire a master-knowledge of the trade to which he is put, it will mainly be because he did not at the outset determine to be a master-workman. Good morals and steady industry are indispensable. Among the business habits that are highly valued in the apprentice are punctuality, order, neatness and dispatch. The boy who is

The love that lived through all the stormy past,
And meekly with my harsher nature bore,
And deeper grew, and tenderer to the last,
Shall it expire with life, and be no more?

MINION.

EXPERIENCE proves that the apprentice foreshadows the workman, just as surely as the bend of a twig foretells the inclination of the tree. The upright, obedient, industrious lad will graduate a steady, skillful, and capable man, as unmistakably as the perverse, idling, careless boy will ripen into the lazy dissolute fellow. The fact is, a boy is measurably the maker of his own destiny; and if he fail to acquire a master-knowledge of the trade to which he is put, it will mainly be because he did not at the outset determine to be a master-workman.

A happier lot than mine, and larger light,
Await thee there; for thou hast bowed thy will
In cheerful homage to the rule of right,
And lovest all, and renderest good for ill.

BREVIER.

EXPERIENCE proves that the apprentice foreshadows the workman, just as surely as the bend of a twig foretells the inclination of the tree. The upright, obedient, industrious lad will graduate a steady, skillful, and capable man, as unmistakably as the perverse, idling, careless boy will ripen into the lazy, dissolute fellow. The fact is, a boy is measurably the maker of his own destiny; and if he fail to acquire a master-knowledge of the trade to which he is

For me, the sordid cares in which I dwell,
Shrink and consume my heart as heat the scroll,
And wrath has left its scar — that fire of hell
Has left its frightful scar upon my soul.

BOURGEOIS.

EXPERIENCE proves that the apprentice foreshadows the workman, just as surely as the bend of a twig foretells the inclination of the tree. The upright, obedient, industrious lad will graduate a steady, skillful, and capable man, as unmistakably as the perverse, idling, careless boy will ripen into the lazy, dissolute fellow. The fact is, a boy is measurably the maker of his own destiny; and if he fail to acquire a master-knowledge of the trade

Yet, though thou wearest the glory of the sky,
Wilt thou not keep the same beloved name,
The same fair, thoughtful brow, and gentle eye,
Lovelier in heaven's sweet climate, yet the same?

LONG PRIMER.

EXPERIENCE proves that the apprentice foreshadows the workman, just as surely as the bend of a twig foretells the inclination of the tree. The upright, obedient, industrious lad will graduate a steady, skillful, and capable man, as unmistakably as the perverse, idling, careless boy will ripen into the lazy, dissolute fellow. The fact is, a boy is

Shalt thou not teach me in that calmer home
The wisdom that I learned so ill in this —
The wisdom which is love — till I become
Thy fit companion in that land of bliss?

SMALL PICA.

EXPERIENCE proves that the apprentice foreshadows the workman, just as surely as the bend of a twig foretells the inclination of the tree. The upright, obedient, industrious lad will graduate a steady, skillful, and capable man, as unmistakably as the perverse, idling, careless boy will ripen into the lazy, dissolute fellow. The fact is, a boy is measurably the maker of his own destiny ; and if he fail to acquire a master-knowledge of the trade to which he is put, it

PICA.

EXPERIENCE proves that the apprentice foreshadows the workman, just as surely as the bend of a twig foretells the inclination of the tree. The upright, obedient, industrious lad will graduate a steady, skillful, and capable man, as unmistakably as the perverse, idling, careless boy will ripen into the lazy, dissolute fellow. The fact is, a boy is measurably the maker of

ENGLISH.

Experience proves that the apprentice foreshadows the workman, just as surely as the bend of a twig foretells the inclination of the tree. The upright, obedient, industrious lad will graduate a steady, skillful, and capable man, as unmistakably as the perverse, idling, careless boy will ripen into the

GREAT PRIMER.

Experience proves that the apprentice foreshadows the workman, just as surely as the bend of a twig foretells the inclination of the tree. The upright, obedient,

TWO LINE SMALL PICA.

Experience proves that the apprentice foreshadows the workman, just as surely as the bend of a twig foretells the inclina-

DIRECTIONS FOR READING PROOF.

TYPOGRAPHICAL MARKS   EXEMPLIFIED.

Though several differing opinions exist as to the individual by whom the art of printing was first discovered, yet all authorities concur in admitting Peter Schoeffer to be the person who invented *cast metal types*, having learned the art of cutting the letters from the Gutenbergs: he is also supposed to have been the first who engraved on copper plates. The following testimony is preserved in the family, by Jo. Fred. Faustus, of Ascheffenburg:

Peter Schoeffer, of Gernsheim, perceiving his master Faust's design, and being himself desirous ardently to improve the art, found out (by the good providence of God) the method of cutting (*incidendi*) the characters in a *matrix*, that the letters might easily be singly *cast* instead of bieng *cut*. He privately cut *matrices* for the whole alphabet: Faust was so pleased with the contrivance, that he promised Peter to give him his only daughter Christina in marriage, a promise which he soon after performed. But there were many difficulties at first with these *letters*, as there had been before with wooden ones, the metal being too soft to support the force of the impression: but this defect was soon remedied, by mixing a substance with the metal which sufficiently hardened it.

and when he showed his master the letters cast from these matrices.

Though several differing opinions exist as to the individual by whom the art of printing was first discovered, yet all authorities concur in admitting PETER SCHOEFFER to be the person who invented *cast metal types*, having learned the art of *cutting* the letters from the Gutenbergs: he is also supposed to have been the first who engraved on copper-plates. The following testimony is preserved in the family, by Jo. Fred. Faustus, of Ascheffenburg:

'PETER SCHOEFFER, of Gernsheim, perceiving his master Faust's design, and being himself ardently desirous to improve the art, found out (by the good providence of God) the method of cutting (*incidendi*) the characters in a *matrix*, that the letters might easily be singly *cast*, instead of being *cut*. He privately *cut matrices* for the whole alphabet: and when he showed his master the letters cast from these matrices, Faust was so pleased with the contrivance, that he promised Peter to give him his only daughter *Christina* in marriage, a promise which he soon after performed. But there were as many difficulties at first with these letters, as there had been before with *wooden ones*, the metal being too soft to support the force of the impression: but this defect was soon remedied, by mixing the metal with a substance which sufficiently hardened it.'

EXPLANATION OF THE CORRECTIONS.

ACKELLAR'S American Printer gives the following rules for correcting proof which will be found of convenience to all who write for the press :

A wrong letter in a word is noted by drawing a short perpendicular line through it, and making another short line in the margin, behind which the right letter is placed. (See No. 1.) In this manner whole words are corrected, by drawing a line across the wrong word and making the right one in the margin opposite.

A turned letter is noted by drawing a line through it, and writing the mark No. 2 in the margin.

If letters or words require to be altered from one character to another, a parallel line or lines must be made underneath the word or letter,—viz. for capitals, three lines ; small capitals, two lines ; and Italics, one line ; and, in the margin opposite the line where the alteration occurs, *Caps, Small Caps*, or *Ital.* must be written. (See No. 3.)

When letters or words are set double, or are required to be taken out, a line is drawn through the superfluous word or letter, and the mark No. 4 placed opposite in the margin.

Where the punctuation requires to be altered, the correct point, marked in the margin, should be encircled.

When a space is omitted between two words or letters which should be separated, a caret must be made where the separation ought to be, and the sign No. 6 placed opposite in the margin.

No. 7 describes the manner in which the hyphen and ellipsis line are marked.

When a letter has been omitted, a caret is put at the place of omission, and the letter marked as No. 8.

Where letters that should be joined are separated, or where a line is too widely spaced, the mark No. 9 must be placed under them, and the correction denoted by the marks in the margin.

Where a new paragraph is required, a quadrangle is drawn in the margin, and a caret placed at the beginning of the sentence. (See No. 10.)

No. 11 shows the way in which the apostrophe, inverted commas, the star and other references, and superior letters and figures, are marked.

Where two words are transposed, a line is drawn over one word and below the other, and the mark No. 12 placed in the margin ; but where several words require to be transposed, their right order is signified by a figure placed over each word, and the mark No. 12 in the margin.

Where words have been struck out, that have afterward been approved of, dots should be marked under them, and *Stet.* written in the margin. (See No. 13.)

Where a space sticks up between two words, a horizontal line is drawn under it, and the mark No. 14 placed opposite, in the margin.

Where several words have been left out, they are transcribed at the bottom of the page, and a line drawn from the place of omission to the written words (see No 15) ; but if the omitted matter is too extensive to be copied at the foot of the page, *Out, see copy,* is written in the margin, and the missing lines are enclosed between brackets, and the word *Out,* is inserted in the margin of the copy.

Where letters stand crooked, they are noted by a line (see No. 16) ; but, where a page hangs, lines are drawn across the entire part affected.

When a smaller or larger letter, of a different font, is improperly introduced into the page, it is noted by the mark No. 17, which signifies wrong font.

If a paragraph is improperly made, a line is drawn from the broken-off matter to the next paragraph, and *No* ¶ written in the margin. (See No. 18.)

Where a word has been left out or is to be added, a caret must be made in the place where it should come in, and the word written in the margin. (See No. 19.)

Where a faulty letter appears, it is marked by making a cross under it, and placing a similar one in the margin (see No. 20); though some prefer to draw a perpendicular line through it, as in the case of a wrong letter.

MARKS USED IN CORRECTING PROOF.

℘	Turn letter.
☐	Indent line one em quadrat.
℘	Take out ; expunge.
∧	The caret shows where the letter or word is omitted.
#	Insert space.
⌢	Less space.
◯	Close up entirely.
℘ #	Remove type, and insert a space, in place of what is removed.
℘ ◯	Take out type, and close up.
✕	Bad type.
⟊	Push down space.
⏟	Plane down a letter.
⌇	No paragraph.
------	Placed under erased words, restores them.
Stet.	Written in the margin, restores a cancelled word or words that have dots under them.
¶	Begin a paragraph.
/	Letters stand crooked.
/-/	Should be a compound word.
⊏ or ∟	Remove to the left.
⊐ or ⌐	Remove to the right.
⌐	Carry higher up on page.
⌣	Carry down.
≡	Three lines, beneath writing, denote capitals.
=	Two lines, beneath writing, denote small capitals.
—	One line, beneath writing, denotes italics.
w. /.	Wrong font type.
tr.	Transpose letters, words or sentences.
l. c.	Lower case, or small letters.
s. c.	Small capitals.
⊙	Period.
⊙	Colon.
?	Calls attention to some doubtful word or sentence.

Pen & Pencil Flourishing.

Carrie Belden.

Florence Gertrude.

"The path of sorrow and that path alone
Leads to the land where sorrow is unknown."

"For Time will teach thee soon the truth,
There are no birds in last year's nests."

Adelaide.

BRUSH LETTERS FOR MARKING PURPOSES—MODERN STYLE.

ABCDEFGHIJKLM NOPQRSTUVWX
YZ&.._ abcdefghijklmnopqrstuvwxyz.z
1234567890.

Enquire,Huntington,Chicago,Rochester,
Buffalo,Cleveland,Milwaukee,Ohio.

Hill Standard Book Co.,
No. 103 State St.,
Chicago, Ill's.

PLAIN ROMAN LETTERS.

A B C D E F G H I J K L
M N O P Q R S T U V W
X Y Z . & Æ Œ
a b c d e f g h i j k l m n o p q
r s t u v w x y z . æ œ 1 2 3 4 5
6 7 8 9 0 . $ £

ANTIQUE POINTED EXTENDED.

A B C D E F G H I J K L M N O P Q R S T U V W X Y Z &.

1 2 3 4 5 6 7 8 9 0 .

ONE-HAND DEAF AND DUMB ALPHABET.

DORIC.

A B C D E F G H I J K L M N O P Q R S T U V W X Y Z ?

a b c d e f g h i j k l m n o p q r s t u v w x y z & $ 1 2 3 4 5 6 7 8 9 0 .

POINTED CONDENSED.

A B C D E F G H I J K L M N O P Q R S T U V W X Y Z & $ 1 2 3 4 5 6 7 8 9 0 ? .

OLD ENGLISH TITLE TEXT.

$$A\ B\ C\ D\ E\ F\ G\ H\ I\ J\ K\ L\ M$$

$$N\ O\ P\ Q\ R\ S\ T\ U\ V\ W\ X\ Y\ Z$$

abcdefghijklmnopqrsturwxyz

OLD ENGLISH FANCY TEXT.

$$A\ B\ C\ D\ E\ F\ G\ H\ I\ J\ K\ L\ M\ N\ O\ P\ Q$$

$$R\ S\ U\ W\ X\ Y\ Z\ \&.$$

a b c d e f g h i j k l m n o p q r s t u v w x y z .

MEDIEVAL.

$$A\ B\ C\ D\ E\ F\ G\ H\ I\ J\ K\ L\ M\ N$$

$$O\ P\ Q\ R\ S\ T\ U\ V\ W\ X\ Y\ Z\ \&$$

a b c d e f g h i j k l m n o p q r s t u

v w x y z . 1 2 3 4 5 6 7 8 9 0 .

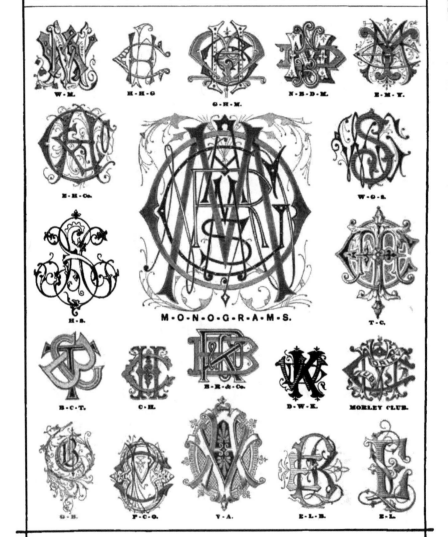

W·M.   H·H·G   G·H·M.   N·B·D·M.   E·M·Y.

E·H·Co.   W·G·S.

H·S.   M·O·N·O·G·R·A·M·S.   T·C.

B·C·T.   C·H.   B·R·&·Co.   D·W·K.   MORLEY CLUB.

G·B.   F·C·O.   V·A.   E·L·B.   E·L.

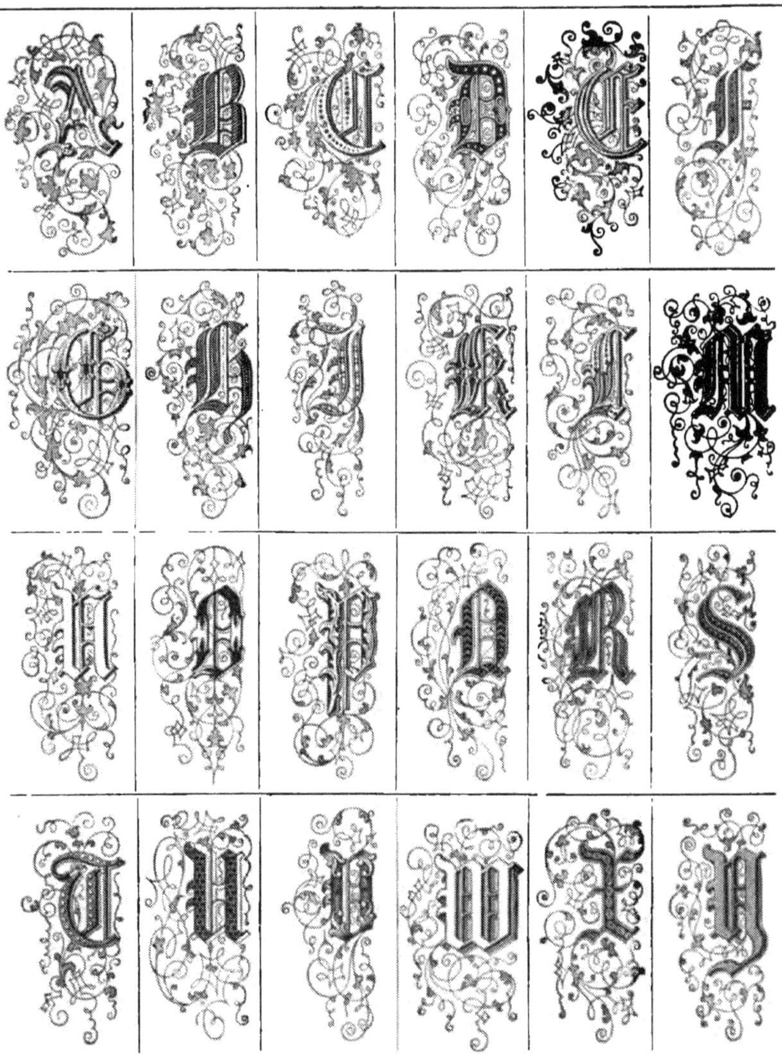

Sign Punctuation.

Illustrations of the Proper Wording and Punctuation of Sign Writing.

Unusually Large Marks are used to Distinctly Illustrate Punctuation.

The following samples of Signs will be found convenient by Sign Writers as showing correct punctuation.

BANK.

POST-OFFICE.

JOHN SMITH.

JOHN HENRY SMITH.

J. H. SMITH.

JOHN H. SMITH.

CHARLES SMITH. HENRY JONES.

C. SMITH & H. JONES.

SMITH & JONES.

The period (.) is used at the end of every sentence, even if it be but one word; as, *Bank. Merchant Tailor. John Smith. William Jones, Dealer in Hats, Caps and Furs.* The period is also used to show the omission of letters, at the last of a name or word, called abbreviation; as *Co.* for *Company; H. J. Smith* for *Henry James Smith.* In the abbreviation of *Chas., Wm., Thos., Jas., Robt., Bros.,* and *Saml.,* while the rule is to use the apostrophe, it is customary to use the period.

The comma (,) is used, in sign painting, to show the omission of words. This is shown in the following sentences:

Brown and West and Co. are Dealers in Paints and Oils and Glass, and so forth.

To avoid repeating the *and* we use the comma, thus:

Brown, West & Co., Dealers in Paints, Oils, Glass, &c.

The apostrophe (') is used to show the omission of letters, in the beginning or middle of a word, thus: *'t is* for *it is;* *'t were* for *it were;*

'78 for 1873; *comp'y* for *company*; *pack'g* for *packing*; *d's* for *days*; *m's* for *months*; *y's* for *years*; *gen'l ag't* for *general agent*, etc.

The apostrophe is also used to show the possessive, thus: *Brown's Bank*. If the owner's name terminates with an *s*, the apostrophe follows the *s*; as, *Wells' Bank, Briggs' Store*. If two or more persons are spoken of, in the possessive, the apostrophe follows the *s*; as, *Ladies' Entrance; Gents' Parlor; Tomlinson Brothers' Bank*. If, however, the person's name takes the character of an adjective, describing the article, no apostrophe is required; as, *Briggs House; Merchants Bank*.

This character (&) stands for *and*, and came originally from *Et.*, Etc. in script, the Latin abbreviation for *et cetera*—"and the rest." The first is used in connecting firm names, and the other at the end to avoid details. Thus, *Smith & Brown*; or *Smith, Brown & Co., Dealers in Groceries, Provisions, &c.*

Where the placing of a period or other mark, after a letter or figure, would decidedly injure the appearance of the same, good taste may suggest that such mark be omitted. See Nos. 44 and 42, next page.

For other marks in punctuation, see page 52.

A light faced letter is used in the following advertisements, to illustrate the punctuation conspicuously.

NORTH AMERICA
FIRE & MARINE INSURANCE COMPANY,
ST. LOUIS, MISSOURI.
CAPITAL, - - - - $200,000.
OFFICERS:
J. HARTLEY WELLS, *Pres't.*   DAVID BRIGGS, *Sec'y.*

S. & J.

EDITOR.

EDITOR'S ROOM.

SUPT'S OFFICE.

LADIES' PARLOR.

TREASURER'S OFFICE.

DRY GOODS.

MERCHANT TAILOR.

JONES SCHOOL.

BRIGGS HOUSE.

METROPOLITAN HOTEL.

JONES' STORE.

FRESH AND SALT MEATS.

FIRST NATIONAL BANK.

PROF. A. B. COOK.

DR. HENRY WING.

SAML. H. SMITH, M.D.

FIRE INS. COMP'Y.

A. M. EXPRESS CO.

AMERICAN PACK'G CO.

JONES BROS., WEST & HOYT.

PAGE BROS.' BLOCK.

WELLS, WADE BROS. & COOK.

Mc MICKEN & St. CLAIR.

St. CLAIR BROS.' EXCHANGE.

MEN'S AND BOYS' CLOTHING.
CHILDREN'S UNDERGARMENTS.

BENNETT & PETERS.
STOVES AND HARDWARE.

SMITH, JONES & BLACK.
HARDWARE, CUTLERY, ETC.

MRS. WM. HENRY WEST.
MILLINERY AND FANCY GOODS.

C. CLINTON BROWN,
ATTORNEY AND COUNSELOR.

De LAND & Mc GANN.

44   BROWN BROTHERS.   44

42   BRAINARD'S SONS.   42

C. S. BELDON, CLARK & CO.
DRUGGISTS' SUNDRIES.

F. BURT, SHAW & SONS,
REAL ESTATE AND LOAN AG'TS.

St. CLAIR BROS. & SONS,
GEN'L AGENTS.

D. O. WELLS, BRIGGS & SONS,
AG'TS N. W. MANUF'G CO.

HIRAM BROWN,
DEALER IN
BOOTS AND SHOES.

H. O. SMITH,
DEALER IN
LUMBER.

HOYT & WEBSTER,
DEALERS IN
PAINTS, OILS, GLASS, ETC.

WILLIAMS & CO.,
DEALERS IN
HATS, CAPS, FURS, ETC.

OLD ENGLISH TITLE TEXT.

𝔄𝔅ℭ𝔇𝔈𝔉𝔊ℌℑ𝔍𝔎𝔏𝔐

𝔑𝔒𝔓𝔔ℜ𝔖𝔗𝔘𝔙𝔚𝔛𝔜ℨ

abcdefghijklmnopqrstuvwxyz

OLD ENGLISH FANCY TEXT.

𝔄𝔅ℭ𝔇𝔈𝔉𝔊ℌℑ𝔍𝔎𝔏𝔐𝔑𝔒𝔓𝔔

ℜ𝔖𝔙𝔚𝔛𝔜ℨ&.

abcdefghijklmnopqrstuvwxyz.

MEDIEVAL.

𝔄𝔅ℭ𝔇𝔈𝔉𝔊ℌℑ𝔍𝔎𝔏𝔐𝔑

𝔒𝔓𝔔ℜ𝔖𝔗𝔘𝔙𝔚𝔛𝔜ℨ&

abcdefghijklmnopqrstu

vwxyz.1234567890.

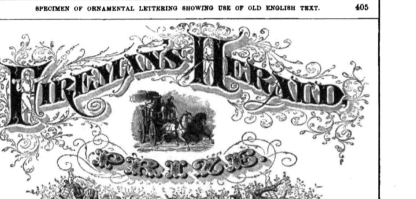

FIREMAN'S HERALD.

PRIZE.

WHEREAS

THE·PUBLISHERS·OF·THE

Fireman's Herald,

OF

New York City

UPON THE 19TH DAY IN JANUARY, 1882, OFFERED

a prize of an engrossed pen and ink premium for the best set of

COMPANY BY LAWS, BLANKS AND ROLL.

THIS IS TO CERTIFY THAT

THE *Passaic Steam Fire*

OF

PATERSON, N.J.

Engine Co. No. 1.

HAS BEEN AWARDED THE

SAID PRIZE.

In Testimony Whereof we the undersigned Judges have hereunto affixed our signatures on this the twelfth day of October A.D. 1882.

(The signatures of the committee of award are here omitted for want of room.)

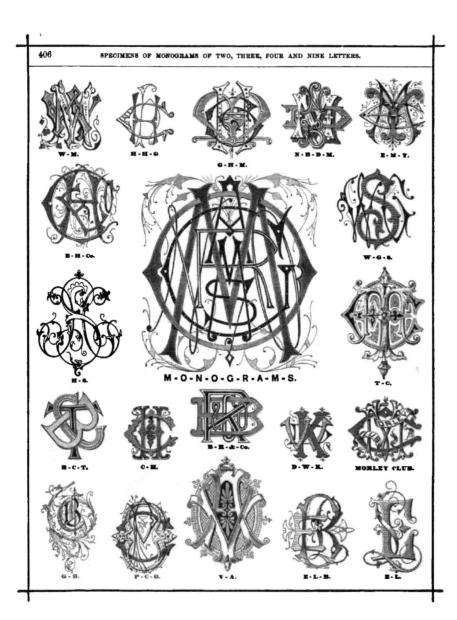

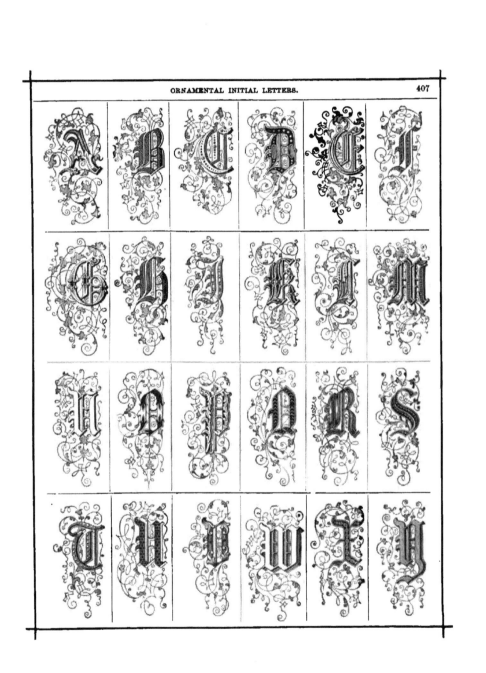

"Shed not for her the bitter tear,
  Nor give the heart to vain regret;
'T is but the casket that lies here,
  The gem that filled it sparkles yet."

———

"Sheltered and safe from sorrow."

———

" Ere sin could harm, or sorrow fade,
  Death came with friendly care;
The opening bud to heaven conveyed,
  And bade it blossom there."

———

" Happy infant, early blest!
  Rest, in peaceful slumbers, rest."

———

" This lovely bud, so young, so fair,
  Called hence by early doom,
Just came to show how sweet a flower
  In Paradise would bloom."

———

" Suffer little children to come unto me."

———

" There, in the Shepherd's bosom,
  White as the drifted snow,
Is the little lamb we missed one morn,
  From the household flock below."

———

" Sweet flower, transplanted to a clime
  Where never comes the blight of time."

———

" So the bird of my bosom fluttered up to the dawn,
A window was opened — my darling was gone !
A truant from time, from tears, and from sin,
For the angel on watch took the wanderer in."

———

" O Death! where is thy sting? O Grave! where
  is thy victory?"

———

" From meadows fanned by heaven's life-breathing
    wind,
In the resplendence of that glorious sphere,
And larger movements of the unfettered mind,
Come darling, oft, and meet me here."

" A happier lot than ours, and larger light, sur-
    rounds thee there."

———

" Gone to a land of pure delight,
  Where saints immortal reign;
Infinite day excludes the night,
  And pleasures banish pain."

———

" Though I walk through the valley of the shadow
  of death, I will fear no evil, for Thou
      art with me."

———

" Triumphant smiles the victor's brow,
  Fanned by some angel's purple wing.
Where is, O grave, thy victory now?
  And where, insidious death, thy sting?"

———

" Thy rod and Thy staff, they comfort me."

———

" Sweet is the scene when virtue dies!
  When sinks a righteous soul to rest,
How mildly beam the closing eyes,
  How gently heaves the expanding breast!"

———

" Here I lay my burden down,
  Change the cross into the crown."

———

" I shall know the loved who have gone before,
And joyfully sweet will the meeting be,
When over the river, the peaceful river,
The angel of death shall carry me."

———

" Because I lived, ye shall live also."

———

" Life is real, life is earnest,
  And the grave is not its goal;
' Dust thou art, to dust returnest,'
  Was not spoken of the soul."

———

" Of such is the kingdom of Heaven "

"Dear is the spot where Christians sleep,
   And sweet the strains that angels pour.
O! why should we in anguish weep?
   They are not lost, but gone before."

———

"I am the resurrection and the life."

———

"From darkness and from woe,
   A power like lightning darts;
A glory cometh down to throw
   Its shadow o'er our hearts."

———

"Heaven's eternal year is thine."

———

"Known and unknown, human, divine,
   Sweet darling hand and lips and eye;
Dear heavenly one, thou canst not die,
   Mine, mine forever, ever mine."

———

"Death loves a shining mark."

———

"Life's duty done, as sinks the day,
   Light from its load the spirit flies;
While heaven and earth combine to say,
   How blest the righteous when he dies. "

———

"He giveth his beloved sleep."

———

"Gone before us, O our brother,
   To the spirit land!
Vainly look we for another,
   In thy place to stand."

———

"Her children rise up and call her blessed."

"She was but as a smile,
   Which glistens in a tear,
Seen but a little while,
   But, oh! how loved, how dear!"

———

"We loved her."

———

"We only know that thou hast gone,
   And that the same returnless tide.
Which bore thee from us, still glides on,
   And we, who mourn thee, with it glide."

———

"There shall be no night there."

———

"Green be the turf above thee,
   Friend of my better days;
None knew thee but to love thee,
   Nor named thee but to praise."

———

"I know his face is hid
   Under the coffin lid;
Closed are his eyes; cold is his forehead fair.
   My hand that marble felt,
   O'er it in prayer I knelt;
Yet my heart whispers that — he is not here."

———

"Far off thou art, but ever nigh;
   I have thee still, and I rejoice."

———

"To us for sixteen anxious months,
   His infant smile was given,
And then he bade farewell to earth
   And went to live in heaven."

———

"Where immortal spirits reign,
   There we shall meet again."

"Poetry is the blossom and fragrance of all human knowledge, human thoughts, human passions, emotions, language."—COLERIDGE.

The GENTLE stillness of a spring-time evening, when, with heart attuned to the glories of the twilight scene, we listen enraptured to the closing song of busy nature, hushing to repose — *this is poetry!*

The coming storm, preceded by the rushing wind; the dark, angry, approaching clouds, capped with the flashing, darting lightning, with the low muttering, and anon the deep-toned thunder, coming nearer and nearer in its awful grandeur! To the lover of the grand and sublime — *this is poetry!*

The silvery quiet of the moonlight night, when we wander amid the jessamines and roses, with our darling, whispering words of love, and dreaming of the future — *this is poetry!*

The midnight hour in the attic, when, through the crevices of the roof and windows, we catch glimpses of the flashing lightning, and listen, slumber, and dream to the music of the pattering rain-drops on the roof — *this is poetry!*

The roaring cataract, the silvery rivulet, the towering mountain, the dark ravine, the open-ing rosebud, the cherub child, the waving grain, the modest violet, — *all breathe the music of poetry!*

The beautiful face, the gentle, thrilling pressure of the hand, the kettle singing for tea, the joyous meeting of the husband and wife on the return from labor at the twilight hour, the smile, the kiss — *all this is poetry!*

It flashes in the sky, it blossoms on the earth, it breathes music in the air, delighting the eye, charming the ear, and filling the soul with ineffable happiness — *all this is poetry!*

To appreciate, to comprehend, and to interpret this golden, sunny halo of beauty, is the gift of the poet.

Poetry is not necessarily told in rhyme. It is oftentimes revealed as beautifully in prose. B. F. Taylor illustrates this very strikingly in the following description of

The Old Church.

"Last evening we were walking leisurely along. The music of choirs in three churches came floating out into the darkness around us, and they were all new and strange tunes but one; and that one, it was not sung as we had heard it, but it awakened a train of long buried memories, that rose to us even as they were before the cemetery of the soul had a tomb in it. It was sweet old 'Corinth' they were singing — strains that we have seldom heard since the rose-color of life was blanched — and we were in a moment back again to the old church; and it was a summer afternoon, and yellow sunbeams were streaming through the west windows, and the silver hair of the old deacon who sat in the pulpit was turned to gold in its light, and the minister, who, we used to think, could never die, so good was he, had concluded 'application' and 'exhortation,' and the village choir were singing the last hymn, and the tune was 'Corinth.'

"It is years — we dare not think how many — since then, and the prayers of 'David the son of Jesse' are ended, and the choir scattered and gone — the girl with blue eyes that sang alto, and the girl with black eyes that sang air ; the eyes of one were like a June heaven at noon, and the other like the same heaven at night. They both became wives, and both mothers, and both died. Who shall say they are not singing 'Corinth' still, where Sabbaths never wane, and congregations never break up? There they sat, Sabbath after Sabbath, by the square column at the right of the 'leader,' and to our young ears their tunes were 'the very soul of music.' That column bears still their penciled names, as they wrote them in those days in life's June, 183—, before dreams of change had overcome their spirits like a summer's cloud.

"Alas! that with the old singers most of the sweeter tunes have died upon the air! But they linger in memory, and they shall yet be sung in the sweet reunion of song that shall take place by and by, in a hall whose columns are beams of morning light, whose ceiling is pearl, whose doors are gold, and where hearts never grow old. Then she that sang alto, and she that sang air, will be in their places once more."

More frequently, however, the poet gives expression to his emotions in rhyme, such form of expression having the advantage of musical sound, accompanied by sentiment. Unfortunately, however, much of that which passes for poetry is but rhyme, being devoid of sense or moral.

For the assistance and guidance of those who would correctly write poetry, we give herewith the rules of versification, accompanied by a vocabulary of rhymes, followed by a number of standard poems from the best authors, that are models in their respective kinds of verse.

Versification.

ERSIFICATION is the art of making verse. Verse is rhythmical language, keeping time like music; having syllables arranged according to accent, quantity, and generally rhyme; being so divided into lines as to promote harmony.

Two kinds of verse are in use by poets, namely, *blank verse* and *rhyme*. Rhyme is characterized by a similarity of sound at the end of one line with another; as

"Perhaps in this neglected spot is . . . . laid
  Some heart once pregnant with celestial . . . fire;
Hands, that the rod of empire might have . . swayed,
  Or waked to ecstasy the living . . . . lyre."

"The Assyrian came down like a wolf on the . . fold,
And his cohorts were gleaming with purple and gold."

Blank Verse.

Blank verse is the name given to a kind of poetry without rhyme, which was the form that the earlier poets almost entirely made use of. The poetry of the Greeks and Romans was generally without rhyme, and not until the Middle Ages, when introduced by the Goths from the North, did rhyme come into the Latin and the vernacular tongues of modern Europe.

Blank verse is particularly suited to the drama, and was very popular in the sixteenth century, during which time, and the beginning of the seventeenth century, Shakespeare wrote his plays. The following from Milton's " Paradise Lost " representing Eve's lament and farewell to Eden, written in 1667, illustrates the power of expression in blank verse:

"O unexpected stroke, worse than of death!
Must I thus leave thee, Paradise? thus leave
Thee, native soil! these happy walks and shades,
Fit haunt of gods? where I had hoped to spend,
Quiet though sad, the respite of that day
That must be mortal to us both. O, flowers
That never will in other climate grow,
My early visitation and my last
At even, which I bred up with tender hand
From the first spring bud, and gave ye names!
Who now shall rear thee to the sun, or rank
Your tribes, and water from the ambrosial fount?
Thee lastly, nuptial bower? by me adorn'd
By what to sight or smell was sweet! from thee
How shall I part, and whither wander down
Into a lower world, to this obscure
And wild? How shall we breathe in other air
Less pure, accustom'd to immortal fruits?"

Accent and Feet.

Upon careful observation, it will be seen that we involuntarily divide a line of rhythmical verse into meter, by a sort of keeping time with hands and *feet:* accenting at regular intervals certain syllables, thus giving the peculiar musical accompaniment which makes poetry attractive.

There are four kinds of feet in English verse called *Iambus, Trochee, Anapest* and *Dactyl.* The distinguishing characteristic of *Iambic* verse is, that we always accent the second syllable in reading the same; as " Behóld, how gréat."

The *Trochee,* like the Iambus, consists of two syllables, with the accent on the first syllable; as " Sée the dístant fórest dárk and wáving."

The *Anapest* has the first two syllables unaccented, and the last accented; as " O'er the lánd of the frée and the hóme of the bráve."

The *Dactyl* contains three syllables, with the accent on the first; as *dúrable, brávery.*

Meters.

Verse is also named according to the *number* of feet in each line; a foot in Iambic being two syllables. *Monometer* is a line of one foot; *dimeter,* of two feet; *trimeter,* of three feet; *tetrameter,* of four feet; *pentameter,* of five feet; *hexameter,* of six feet; *heptameter,* of seven feet; *octometer,* of eight feet.

Examples.

The following examples represent the *Iambic, Trochaic, Anapestic,* and *Dactylic,* in the different kinds of *meter.* A straight line (ˉ) over a syllable, shows that such syllable is accented. A curved line (˘) indicates the unaccented.

IAMBIC.—*One foot.*

" Thĕy gò
To sow."

IAMBIC.—*Two feet.*

" Tò mĕ | thĕ rōse
No longer glows,"
" Thĕir lŏve | ănd ăwe
Supply | the law."

IAMBIC.—*Three feet.*

" Blŭe light | nīngs sĭnge | thĕ wăves,
And thunder rends the rock."

IAMBIC.—*Four feet.*

" Ănd còld | ĕr stĭll | thĕ wĭnds | dĭd blŏw,
And darker hours of night came on."

IAMBIC.—*Five feet.*

" Fŏr prăise | tŏo dĕar | lў lŏv'd | ŏr wărm | lў sŏught,
Enfeebles all internal strength of thought."

IAMBIC.—*Six feet.*

" Hĭs heărt | ĭs săd, | hĭs hŏpe | ĭs gŏne, | hĭs lĭght | ĭs păssed;
He sits and mourns in silent grief the lingering day."

IAMBIC.—*Seven feet.*

" Thĕ lŏf | tў hĭll, | thĕ hŭm | blĕ lăwn, | wĭth cŏunt | lĕss beaŭ | tĭes shĭne ;
The silent grove, the solemn shade, proclaim thy power divine."

Note.—It has become common in writing modern poetry to divide this kind of verse into four lines; alternate lines having four and three feet; thus,—

" The lofty hill, the humble lawn,
With countless beauties shine;
The silent grove, the solemn shade,
Proclaim thy power divine."

IAMBIC.—*Eight feet.*

O ăll | yĕ pĕo | plĕ, clăp | yŏur hănds, | ănd wĭth | trŭm | phănt vŏic | ĕs sĭng ;
No force the mighty pow'r withstands of God the universal King.

Note.—It is common at present to reduce this verse into lines of eight syllables, as follows,—

" O all ye people, clap your hands,
And with triumphant voices sing,
No force the mighty pow'r withstands
Of God the universal King."

Stanza—Long, Short, and Common Meter.

A *stanza* is a combination of several lines in poetry, forming a distinct division of the poem ; thus,—

" The curfew tolls the knell of parting day,
The lowing herd winds slowly o'er the lea,
The ploughman homeward plods his weary way,
And leaves the world to darkness and to me."

A Verse.

Verse is but a single line of a stanza, thus ,—

" The curfew tolls the knell of parting day."

Long Meter.

The long, short, and common meters are known by the number of feet or syllables found in them. Long meter stanzas contain in each line four Iambic feet, thus —

> "Through every age, eternal God
> Thou art our rest, our safe abode ;
> High was thy throne ere heaven was made,
> Or earth, thy humble footstool, laid."

Short Meter.

Short meter stanzas contain three lines of six syllables, and one of eight syllables — the third line being the longest, and containing four Iambic feet, thus —

> " Sweet is the time of Spring,
> When nature's charms appear ;
> The birds with ceaseless pleasure sing,
> And hail the opening year."

Common Meter.

Iambic verse of seven feet, divided into two lines, the first containing four, and the latter three feet, makes what is known as common meter ; thus —

> " When all thy mercies, O, my God !
> My rising soul surveys,
> Transported with the view, I 'm lost
> In wonder, love, and praise."

Each species of Iambic verse will admit of an additional short syllable ; as

> Ŭpŏn ă moŭnt | ăin,
> Bĕsĭde ă foŭnt | ăin.

Trochaic Verse.

The accent in *Trochaic* verse occurs on the first syllable. The foot consists of two syllables.

TROCHAIC.— *One foot.*

> Chăngĭng.
> Ranging.

TROCHAIC.— *Two feet.*

> Fancў | viewĭng.
> Joys ensuing.

TROCHAIC.— *Three feet.*

> " Whĕn thў | heărt ĭs | moŭrnĭng."
> " Go where comfort waits thee."

TROCHAIC.— *Four feet.*

> " Roŭnd ă | hōlў | cālm dĭf | fūsĭng,
> Love of peace and lonely musing."

TROCHAIC.— *Five feet.*

> Āll thăt | wālk ŏn | fōot ŏr | rĭde ĭn | chărĭŏts,
> All that dwell in palaces or garrets.

TROCHAIC.— *Six feet.*

> Ōn ă | moŭntain | strētch'd bĕ | nĕath ă | hōarў | wĭllŏw,
> Lay a shepherd swain and viewed the roaring billow.

TROCHAIC.— *Seven feet.*

> Hăstĕn | Lŏrd tŏ | rĕscŭe | mĕ, ănd | sĕt mĕ | săfe frŏm | troŭblĕ,
> Shame thou those who seek my soul, reward their mischief double.

TROCHAIC.— *Eight feet.*

> Note.— Trochaic and Iambic are frequently found combined in one stanza.

> Ōnce ŭp | ŏn ă | mĭdnĭght | drĕary | whĭle I | pŏndered | wĕak and | wĕary
> Over many a quaint and curious volume of forgotten lore.

Anapestic Verse.

Anapestic verse contains three syllables to the foot, with the accent on the last syllable.

ANAPESTIC.— *One foot.*

> " Ŏn thĕ lănd,
> Lĕt mĕ stănd."

ANAPESTIC.— *Two feet.*

> " Bŭt hĭs coŭr | age 'găn făil,
> Fŏr nŏ ărts coŭld avăil."

This form admits of an additional short syllable ; as

> " Bŭt hĭs coŭr | age găn făil | hĭm,
> For no arts could avail him."

ANAPESTIC.— *Three feet.*

> Ŏ yĕ woŏds | sprĕad yōur brănch | ĕs spăce,
> Tŏ yŏur deĕpĕst rĕcĕssĕs I hie ;
> I woŭld hĭde wĭth thĕ bĕasts ŏf thĕ chăse,
> I woŭld vănĭsh frŏm ĕvĕrў ĕye.

ANAPESTIC.—*Four feet.*

Măy Ĭ gŏv | ĕrn mў păss | iŏns with ăb | sŏlūte swáy,
Ănd grŏw wisĕr ănd bĕttĕr ăs lĭfe wĕars ăwáy.

This measure admits of a short syllable at the end ; as

Ŏn thĕ wărm | cheĕk ŏf youth | smĭles ănd rŏ | sĕs ăre blĕnd
| ing.

Dactylic Verse.

In *Dactylic* verse the accent occurs on the first syllable of each successive three, being on the first, fourth, seventh, and tenth syllables.

DACTYLIC.—*One foot.*

Chĕerfullў,
Fearfully.

DACTYLIC.—*Two feet.*

Făthĕr ăll | glŏriŏŭs
O'er all victorious.

DACTYLIC.—*Three feet.*

Weăring ă | wăy ĭn hĭs | youthfulnĕss,
Loveliness, beauty, and truthfulness.

DACTYLIC.—*Four feet.*

" Bŏys wĭll ăn | tĭcĭpăte, | lăvĭsh ănd | dĭssĭpăte,
Ăll that yoŭr bŭsў păte hŏardĕd wĭth căre ;
And, in their foolishness, passion, and mulishness,
Charge you with churlishness, spurning your pray'r."

DACTYLIC.—*Five feet.*

" Nŏw thŏu dŏst | wĕlcŏme mĕ, | wĕlcŏme mĕ, | frŏm thĕ dark
| sĕa,
Land of the beautiful, beautiful land of the free."

DACTYLIC.— *Six feet.*

" Tĭme, thŏu ărt | ĕvĕr ĭn | mŏtiŏn, ŏn | wheĕls ŏf thĕ | dăys,
yĕars, ănd | āges,
Restless as waves of the ocean, when Eurus or Boreas rages."

DACTYLIC.— *Seven feet.*

" Oŭt ŏf thĕ | kĭngdŏm ŏf | Chrĭst shăll bĕ | găthĕrĕd, by |
ăngĕls ŏ'er Sătăn vĭctŏriŏus,
All that offendeth, that lieth, that faileth to honor his name
ever glorious."

DACTYLIC.— *Eight feet.*

Nĭmrŏd thĕ | hŭntĕr wăs | mĭghty ĭn | hŭntĭng, ănd | fămed ăs
thĕ | rŭlĕr ŏf | cĭties ŏf | yŏre ;
Babel, and Erech, and Accad, and Calneh, from Shinar's far
region his name afar bore.

Other Kinds of Poetical Feet.

Besides the foregoing there are other kinds of feet that sometimes occur. These are named the *pyrrhic*, the *spondee*, the *amphibrach*, and the *tribrach*. The *pyrrhic* consists of two short and the *spondee* of two long syllables. The *amphibrach* contains three syllables, of which the first and third are short and the second long. The *tribrach* consists of three short syllables.

Examples.

PYRRHIC.—" Ŏn thĕ tall tree."
SPONDEE.—" The păle mŏŏn."
AMPHIBRACH. — " Dĕlĭghtfŭl, Dŏmĕstĭc."
TRIBRACH.—" Nŭmĕrăblĕ, cŏnqŭĕrăblĕ."

Poetical Pauses.

The full effect in reading poetry is most completely given when a slight pause is made at the close of every line, even though the sense may not require a pause. Frequently a pause for sense is found in or near the middle of the line, particularly of long lines, in which it improves the rhythm, and brings out the meaning of the poem with much better effect. This pause is called the *cæsural* pause, and is shown in the following examples.

Cæsural Pause.

On her white breast | a sparkling cross she wore—
Which Jews might kiss | and infidels adore.
Her lively looks | a sprightly mind disclose,
Quick as her eyes | and as unfixed as those ;
Favors to none, | to all she smiles extends,
Oft she rejects, | but never once offends.
" Then her cheek | was pale, and thinner | | than should be '
for one so young ;
And her eyes, | on all my motions, | | with a mute observance
hung."

The *final pause* occurs at the end of each line whether the sense requires it or not, though it should not be too distinctly marked, as it consists merely in a brief suspension of the voice without any change in tone or accent. The following example shows its effect.

Final Pause.

Ye who have anxiously and fondly *watched*
Beside a fading friend, unconscious *that*
The cheek's bright crimson, lovely to the view,
Like nightshade, with unwholesome beauty bloomed.

Varieties of Poetry.

EVERAL leading kinds of poetry are named as follows: *Epic, Dramatic, Lyric, Elegiac, Pastoral, and Didactic.*

Epic Poetry.

Epic poetry pertains to the narrative, descriptive, and heroic in character, and is the highest and most difficult of poetry to write well. Among the best of the Epic poems may be mentioned, Homer's "*Iliad*" in Greek, Virgil's "*Æneid*" in Latin, and Milton's "Paradise Lost" in English.

Dramatic Poetry.

Dramatic poetry is also an elevated species of poetry, and takes nearly equal rank with the Epic. This kind of poetry includes the dramas, tragedies, comedies, melodramas, and operas.

Lyric Poetry.

Lyric poetry, as its name indicates, was the kind of verse originally written to be sung as an accompaniment to the lyre. This class of poetry is the oldest in the language of all nations, comprising, as it does, the songs of the people. In the Lyric are included the Songs, Hymns, Odes, and Sonnets.

Elegiac Poetry.

Elegiac poetry includes the elegies, such as Milton's "Lycidias," Tennyson's "In Memoriam," and poems of grave, solemn, and mournful character. Gray's "Elegy, Written in a Country Churchyard " is undoubtedly the most complete specimen of this class of poetry to be found in any language

Pastoral Poetry.

In the early history of the world, throughout certain portions of Europe, a distinct occupation was that of the shepherd, whose duty was to care for the flocks, as they roamed in the valleys and among the hills. Leading thus a life of dreamy ease among the charms of nature, the shepherds of better culture took readily to the writing of verse, which poetry, usually descriptive of rustic life, became known as Pastoral poetry.*

This class of poetry includes the poems that relate to country scenes, and the quiet, the simplicity, and the happiness found in rural life.

Of these may be included, in modern poems, "The Old Oaken Bucket," "The Sower," "Twenty Years Ago," "Maud Muller," and others of like character.

Didactic Poetry.

Didactic poetry pertains chiefly to the meditative and instructive, and includes such poems as Bryant's "Thanatopsis," Campbell's "Pleasures of Hope," Thomson's "Seasons," Pope's "E say on Man," and kindred poems.

Kinds of Poems.

ARIOUS kinds of poems are known by certain names, which are defined as follows:

Odes.—Sacred hymns, such as are sung in church.

Pæans.—Songs of praise and triumph.

Ballads.—An easy form of descriptive verse, written in such style as to be easily sung by the people, who may have little acquaintance with music.

---

* From the Latin word *pastor*, a shepherd.

Epigrams.—A short poem, witty and concise, treating of a single subject, usually ending with an unexpected, ingeniously expressed natural thought.

Sonnets.—The Sonnet is a poetical composition, consisting of fourteen lines, so constructed that the first eight lines shall contain but two rhymes, and the last six but two more; and so arranged that, in the first part, the first line is made to rhyme with the fourth, fifth, and eighth —the second rhyming with the third, sixth, and seventh, while in the second part, the first, third, and fifth; and the second, fourth, and sixth also rhyme with each other, as shown in the following:

Autumn.
" The blithe birds of the summer tide are flown ;
  Cold, motionless, and mute, stands all the wood,
  Save as the restless wind, in mournful mood,
Strays through the tossing limbs with saddest moan.
The leaves it wooed with kisses, overblown
  By gusts capricious, pitiless and rude,
  Lie dank and dead amid the solitude;
Where-through it waileth, desolate and lone.
But with a clearer splendor sunlight streams
Athwart the bare, slim branches ; and on high
Each star, in Night's rich coronal that beams,
  Pours down intenser brilliance on the eye ;
Till dazzled Fancy finds her gorgeous dreams
Outshone in beauty by the autumn sky."

Cantatas.—The Cantata is a musical composition, partaking of the nature of an anthem, being intermixed with airs and recitatives; and may be adapted to a single voice, or many.

Charades. The Charade may be in either prose or poetry, and contains as a subject a word of two syllables, each forming a distinct word ; these to be concealed in an enigmatical description, first separately and then together.

Canzonets.—A short song consisting of one, two, or three parts is termed a Canzonet. The following, of two parts, is an illustration.

BLACK EYES AND BLUE.
Black eyes most dazzle in the hall ;
Blue eyes most please at evening fall.
The black a conquest soonest gain ;
The blue a conquest most retain ;
The black bespeak a lively heart
Whose soft emotions soon depart ;

The blue a steadier flame betray,
That burns and lives beyond a day ;
The black may features best disclose ;
In blue may feelings all repose :
Then let each reign without control,
The black all MIND — the blue all SOUL.

Epitaphs.—An Epitaph is usually a stanza in poetry, which follows the inscription on a tombstone.*

Satires.—The Satire is a poem used in exposing folly and wickedness, in keen, cutting words; holding the same up to ridicule and contempt.

Parodies.—A ludicrous imitation of a serious subject, usually in rhyme, is termed a Parody, as follows —

" Hands that the rod of empire might have swayed —
  Close at my elbow stir their lemonade."

Prologues.—The Prologue is a short poem, introductory to a play or discourse, usually recited before the performance begins.

Epilogues.—The Epilogue is a short poem, which frequently reviews the principal incidents of the play, delivered by one of the actors at the close of a dramatic performance.

Impromptus.—An Impromptu is a poetical composition, made at the moment, without previous study.

Acrostics.—An Acrostic is a stanza of several lines, the first letters of which, taken in their order from top to bottom, make a word or sentence.

Friendship, thou 'rt false ! I hate thy flattering smile !
Return to me those years I spent in vain,
In early youth, the victim of thy guile,
Each joy took wing, ne'er to return again —
Ne'er to return ; for, chilled by hopes deceived,
Dully the slow-paced hours now move along :
So changed the time, when, thoughtless, I believed
Her honeyed words, and heard her syren song.
If e'er, as me, she lure some youth to stray,
Perhaps, before too late, he 'll listen to my lay.

---

* See chapter on Epitaphs.

Vocabulary of Rhymes.

The Poet's Assistant in Finding Words that Rhyme.

MONG the gems of literature that will live longest in the history of the world, will be various beautiful poems. Poetry is not always in rhyme, but generally it is.

As a rule, a prominent feature of beauty in the poem is the pleasant sensation produced by words coming near each other of similar sound.

In the stanza,

"Maud Muller, on a summer's day,
Raked the meadow, sweet with hay,"

it is seen that the pleasant jingling of "DAY" and "HAY" has much to do in making the verse attractive.

To express the same idea without rhyme thus:

Maud Muller raked one day in summer,
In a meadow where the hay was sweet,

is to deprive the sentiment of much of its charm.

Rhyme is, in fact, one of the prominent essentials of sweet verse, though to make the complete poem, common sense and truth must be expressed with rhyme.

It is sometimes the case that rhyme can be so ingeniously arranged, however, as to make a poem a success from the simple arrangement of rhyming words. Thus:

"Hi diddle diddle, the cat and the fiddle,
The cow jumped over the moon;
The little dog laughed to see such a craft,
And the dish ran away with the spoon."

Though nonsensical and ridiculous, this, with many others of the Mother Goose Melodies, is more attractive to the child than any of the choicest stanzas in Gray's Elegy.

A pleasant and intellectual pastime may be had by a company of young people, in the construction of impromptu rhymes. To conduct the exercise, one of the number is seated at the table, provided with paper and pencil. When all are in readiness, the hostess of the occasion announces a subject upon which they are to write a poem. Suppose the subject to be "SPRING." The person sitting next to the secretary will give the first line, the poetic feet decided upon, perhaps, being eight syllables to the line. The first line presented to the secretary may read,

In spring-time when the grass is green.

It is now in order for the second person in the group to give the next line ending with a word that rhymes with "green." Half a minute only will be allowed for the line to be produced. The individual, whose turn it is, gathers thought and says:

A thousand blossoms dot the scene.

This may not be very good poetry, but the

rhyme is complete and the poetry is as good as may be expected with so short a time in which to produce it. The next continues by presenting the third line as follows:

A perfume sweet loads down the air.

The fourth says,

The birds now sing, and mate, and pair.

The fifth continues,

O! charming season of the year.

The sixth may be at a loss for the suitable word to rhyme with "year," but must produce something in the half-minute, and here it is:

I wish that you was always here

Whether the word "you" is a suitable word in this place, the rhymsters have not time to de-termine, as the composition must progress rapidly so that a twenty-line metrical composition may be produced in ten minutes.

As poetry this extemporaneous effusion, when finally read by the secretary, will not be very good—it may be only doggerel rhyme—but it will be amusing to see it produced, and its production will be a decidedly intellectual exercise.

For the advantage of the student who may aim to write the best of verse, as well as the impromptu poet in the social circle, who may wish to test the ability to rapidly make rhyme, the following vocabulary, from Walker's Rhyming Dictionary, is given:

Classification of Words that Rhyme.

AB.—Bab, cab, dab, mab, nab, blab, crab, drab, scab, stab. *Allowable rhymes*, babe, astrolabe, etc.

ACE.—Ace, face, pace, face, lace, mace, race, brace, chace, grace, place, space, trace, apace, deface, efface, disgrace, displace, misplace, embrace, grimace, interlace, retrace, populace, etc. *Perfect rhymes*, bass, case, abase, debase, etc. *Allowable rhymes*, grass, glass, etc., peace, cease, etc., dress, less, etc.

ACH.—Attach, detach, etc. *Perfect rhymes*, batch, match, etc. *Allowable rhymes*, fetch, wretch, etc.

ACK.—Back, rack, hack, jack, lack, pack, quack, tack, sack, rack, black, clack, crack, knack, slack, smack, stack, track, wrack, attack, zodiac, demoniac, symposiac, almanac. *Allowable rhymes*, bake, take, etc., neck, speck, etc.

ACT.—Act, fact, pact, tract, attract, abstract, extract, compact, contract, detract, distract, exact, protract, enact, infract, subtract, transact, cataract, with the preterits and participles of verbs in ack as backed, hacked, etc. *Allowable rhymes, the preterits and participles of verbs in ake, as* baked, caked, etc.

AD.—Add, bad, dad, gad, had, lad, mad, pad, sad, brad, clad, glad, plad, shad, etc. *Allowable rhymes*, cade, fade, etc., glede, bead, read, etc.

ADE.—Cade, fade, made, jade, lade, wade, blade, glade, shade, spade, trade, degrade, evade, dissuade, invade, persuade, blockade, brigade, serenade, cavalcade, masquerade, renegade, retrograde, serenade, ambuscade, cannonade, palisade, etc. *Perfect rhymes*, aid, maid, braid, afraid, upbraid, etc., *and the preterits and participles of verbs in ay, ey, and eigh, as* played, obeyed, weighed, etc. *Allowable rhymes*, ad, bad, etc., bed, dead, etc., head, mead, etc., heed, need, etc.

AFE.—Safe, chafe, vouchsafe, etc. *Allowable rhymes*, leaf, sheaf, etc., deaf, etc., laugh, staff, etc.

AFF.—Gaff, chaff, draff, quaff, staff, engraff, epitaph, cenotaph, paragraph, etc. *Perfect rhyme*, laugh. *Allowable rhymes*, safe, chafe, etc.

AFT.—Aft, haft, raft, waft, craft, shaft, abaft, graft, draft, ingraft, handicraft. *Perfect rhymes, draught, the preterits and participles of verbs in aff and augh as* quaffed, laughed, etc. *Allowable rhymes, the preterits and participles of verbs in afe, as* chafed, vouchsafed, etc.

AG.—Bag, cag, fag, gag, nag, rag, tag, wag, brag, crag, drag, flag, knag, shag, snag, stag, wrag, scrag, Brobdignag.

AGE.—Age, cage, gage, page, rage, sage, stage, swage, assuage, enrage, disengage, enrage, presage, appendage, concubinage, heritage, hermitage, parentage, parsonage, personage, pasturage, patronage, pilgrimage, villanage, equipage. *Allowable rhymes*, edge, wedge, etc., liege, siege, oblige, etc.

AID, see ADE. AIGHT, see ATE. AIGN, see ANE.

AIL.—All, bail, fail, hail, jail, mail, nail, pail, quail, rail, sail, tail, wail, flail, frail, snail, trail, assail, avail, detail, bewail, entail, prevail, retail, countervail, etc. *Perfect rhymes*, ale, bale, dale, gale, hale, male, pale, sale, tale, vale, wale, scale, stale, swale, whale, impale, exhale, regale, veil, nightingale, etc. *Allowable rhymes*, peal, steal, etc., bell, cell, etc.

AIM, see AME.

AIN.—Cain, blain, brain, chain, fain, gain, grain, main, pain, rain, vain, wain, drain, plain, slain, Spain, stain, swain, train, twain, sprain, strain, abstain, amain, attain, complain, contain, constrain, detain, disdain, distrain, enchain, entertain, explain, maintain, ordain, pertain, obtain, refrain, regain, remain, restrain, retain, sustain, appertain. *Perfect rhymes*, bane, cane, dane, crane, fane, Jane, mane, pane, vane, wane, profane, hurricane, etc., deign, arraign, campaign, etc., feign, reign, etc., vein, rein, etc. *Allowable rhymes*, lean, mean, etc., queen, seen, etc., ban, can, etc., den, pen, etc.

AINT.—Faint, paint, plaint, quaint, saint, taint, acquaint, attaint, complaint, constraint, restraint, etc. *Perfect rhyme*, feint. *Allowable rhymes*, cant, pant, etc., lent, rent, etc.

AIR, see ARE. AISE, see AZE. AIT, see ATE. AITH, see ATH. AIZE, see AZE.

AKE.—Ake, bake, cake, lake, make, quake, rake, sake, take, wake, brake, drake, flake, shake, snake, stake, strake, spake, awake, betake, etc., sake, mistake, partake, overtake, undertake, bespake. *Perfect rhymes*, break, steak, etc. *Allowable rhymes*, back, rack, etc., beck, deck, etc., speak, weak, etc.

AL.—Cabal, canal, animal, admiral, cannibal, capital, cardinal, comical, conjugal, corporal, criminal, critical, festival, funeral, general, hospital, interval, liberal, madrigal, literal, magical, mystical, mineral, musical, natural, original, pastoral, pedestal, personal, physical, poetical, puritan, principal, prodigal, prophetical, rational, satirical, reciprocal, rhetorical, several, temporal, tragical, tyrannical, whimsical, arsenal, etc. *Allowable rhymes*, all, ball, etc., all, mall, etc., ale, pale, etc.

ALD.—Bald, scald, emerald, etc. *Perfect rhymes, the preterits and participles of verbs in all, aul and awl, as* called, mauled, crawled, etc.

ALE, see AIL.

ALF.—Calf, half, behalf, etc. *Allowable rhymes*, staff, laugh, etc.

ALK.—Balk, chalk, stalk, talk, walk, calk, etc. *Perfect rhyme*, hawk. *Allowable rhymes*, sock, clock, etc.

ALL.—All, ball, call, etc. *Perfect rhymes*, awl, bawl, brawl, crawl, scrawl, sprawl, squall. *Allowable rhymes*, cabal, equivocal, etc. *See* **AL.** *plurals and third persons singular rhyme with alms, as* calms, becalms, etc.

ALT.—Halt, malt, exalt, salt, vault, assault, default and fault, the last of which is, by Pope, rhymed with thought, bought, etc.

ALVE.—Calve, halve, salve, valve.

AM.—Am, dam, ham, jam, ram, cram, dram, flam, sham, swam, epigram, anagram, etc. *Perfect rhyme*, lamb. *Allowable rhymes*, dame, tame, etc.

AME.—Blame, came, dame, fame, flame, frame, game, lame, name, tame, shame, inflame, became, defame, nickname, misbecame came, etc. *Perfect rhymes*, aim, claim, maim, acclaim, declaim, exclaim, proclaim, reclaim. *Allowable rhymes*, dam, ham, etc., beam, theme, scheme, etc., dream, gleam, etc.

AMP.—Camp, champ, cramp, damp, stamp, vamp, lamp, clamp, decamp, encamp, etc.

AN.—Ban, can, Dan, man, Nan, pan, ran, tan, van, bran, plan, span, than, unman, fore-ran, began, trepan, courtesan, partisan, artisan, pelican, caravan, etc. *Allowable rhymes*, bane, cane, plain, mane, etc. bean, lean, wan, swan, etc., gone, upon, etc.

ANCE.—Chance, dance, glance, lance, trance, prance entrance, romance, advance, mischance, complaisance, circumstance, countenance, deliverance, consonance, dissonance, extravagance, ignorance, inheritance, maintenance, temperance, intemperance, exorbitance, ordinances, consonance, sufferance, sustenance, utterance, arrogance, vigilance, vengeance, enhance.

ANCH.—Branch, stanch, blanch, ranch, hanch. *Perfect rhymes*, haunch, paunch.

AND.—And, band, hand, land, rand, sand, brand, bland, grand, gland, stand, strand, command, demand, countermand, disband, expand, withstand, understand, reprimand, contraband, etc. *Allowable rhymes*, wand, fond, bond, etc., *and the preterits and participles of verbs in ain and an* as remained, leaned, etc.

ANE, see AIN.

ANG.—Bang, fang, gang, hang, pang, tang, twang, sang, rang, har angue, clang. *Allowable rhymes*, song, long, etc.

ANGE.—Change, grange, range, strange, estrange, arrange, exchange, interchange. *Allowable rhymes*, revenge, avenge, etc.

ANK.—Bank, blank, shank, clank, dank, drank, slank, frank, spank, stank, lank, plank, prank, rank, thank, disrank, mountebank, etc.

ANSE, see ANCE.

ANT.—Ant, cant, chant, grant, pant, plant, rant, slant, askant, enchant.

plaisant, displant, enchant, gallant, implant, recant, supplant, transplant, absonant, adamant, arrogant, combatant, consonant, cormorant, protestant, significant, visitant, covenant, dissonant, disputant, elegant, elephant, exorbitant, conversant, extravagant, ignorant, insignificant, inhabitant, militant, predominant, sycophant, vigilant, petulant, etc. *Allowable rhymes*, faint, paint, etc. *See* **AINT** *and* **ENT**.

AP.—Cap, gap, hap, lap, map, nap, pap, rap, sap, tap, chap, clap, trap, flap, knap, slap, snap, wrap, scrap, strap, enwrap, entrap, mishap, etc. *Allowable rhymes*, cape, tape, etc., cheap, heap *and* swap.

APE.—Ape, cape, chape, grape, rape, scrape, shape, escape, mape, crape, tape, etc. *Allowable rhymes*, heap, keep, etc.

APH, *see* **AFF**.

APSE.—Lapse, elapse, relapse, perhaps, *and the plurals of nouns and third persons singular of the present tense in* ap, *as* caps, maps, etc., he raps, he laps, etc. *Allowable rhymes, the plurals of nouns and third persons singular of verbs in* ape *and* eap, *as* apes, he apes, heaps, he heaps, etc.

APT.—Apt, adapt, etc. *Rhymes, the preterits and participles of the verbs in* ap, *as* tapped, slapped, etc. *Allowable rhymes, the preterits and participles of the verbs in* ape, *as* aped, escaped, etc.

AR.—Bar, car, far, jar, mar, par, tar, spar, scar, star, chair, afar, debar, unbar, catarrh, particular, perpendicular, secular, angular, regular, popular, singular, titular, vinegar, scimitar, calendar, collender. *Perfect rhyme, the plural verb* are. *Allowable rhymes*, bare, prepare, etc., pair, repair, wear, tear, war, etc, *and words ending in* er *or* or, *having the accent on the last syllable, or last but two.*

ARB.—Barb, garb, etc.

ARCE.—Farce, parse, Mars, etc. *Allowable rhyme*, scarce.

ARCH.—Arch, march, parch, starch, countermarch, etc.

ARD.—Bard, card, guard, hard, lard, nard, shard, yard, bombard, discard, regard, interlard, retard, disregard, etc., *and the preterits and participles of verbs in* ar, *as* barred, scarred, etc. *Allowable rhymes*, cord, reward, etc.

ARD.—Ward, award, reward, etc. *Allowable rhymes*, hard, card, *see the last article*, board, lord, bird, curd, *and the preterits and participles of the verbs in* ar, or, *and* ur, *as* barred, abhorred, incurred, etc.

ARE.—Bare, care, dare, fare, hare, mare, pare, tare, rare, ware, flare, glare, scare, share, snare, spare, square, stare, sware, prepare, aware, beware, compare, declare, ensnare. *Perfect rhymes*, air, hair, fair, lair, pair, chair, stair, affair, debonnair, despair, impair, repair, etc., bear, pear, swear, tear, wear, forbear, forswear, etc., there, were, where, ere, e'er, ne'er, elsewhere, whate'er, howe'er, howsoe'er, whene'er, where'er, etc., heir, co-heir, their. *Allowable rhymes*, bar, car, etc., err, prefer, *and* hear, here, etc., regular, singular, war, etc.

ARES.—Unawares. *Rhymes*, their's, *and the plurals of nouns and third persons singular of verbs in* are, air, eir, ear, *as* care, he cares, pair, he pairs, heirs, bear, he bears, etc. *The allowable rhymes are the plurals of nouns and the third persons singular of verbs which are allowed to rhyme with the termination* ars, *as* bars, cars, errs, prefers, etc.

ARF.—Scarf. *Allowable rhymes*, dwarf, wharf.

ARGE.—Barge, charge, large, targe, discharge, o'ercharge, surcharge, enlarge. *Allowable rhymes*, verge, emerge, gorge, forge, urge, etc.

ARK.—Bark, cark, Clark, dark, lark, mark, park, shark, spark, stark, embark, remark, etc. *Allowable rhymes*, cork, fork, etc.

ARL.—Snarl, marl, parl. *Allowable rhymes*, curl, furl, etc.

ARM.—Arm, barm, charm, farm, harm, alarm, disarm. *Allowable rhymes*, warm, swarm, storm, etc.

ARN.—Barn, yarn, etc. *Allowable rhymes*, warn, forewarn, etc., horn, morn, etc.

ARN.—Warn, forewarn. *Perfect rhymes*, horn, morn, etc. *Allowable rhymes*, barn, yarn, etc.

ARP.—Carp, harp, sharp, counterscarp. *Allowable rhyme*, warp.

ARSH.—Harsh, marsh, etc.

ART.—Art, cart, dart, hart, mart, part, smart, tart, start, apart, depart, impart, dispart, counterpart. *Perfect rhymes*, heart, etc. *Allowable rhymes*, wart, thwart, etc., hurt, etc., dirt, flirt, etc., pert, etc.

ART (*sounded* **ORT**).—Wart, thwart, etc. *Perfect rhymes*, short, retort, etc. *Allowable rhymes*, art, sport, court, etc.

ARTH, *see* **EARTH**.

ARVE.—Carve, starve, etc. *Allowable rhymes*, nerve, deserve, etc.

AS.—Was. *Allowable rhymes*, has, as.

ASS.—Ass, brass, class, grass, lass, mass, pass, alas, amass, cuirass, repass, surpass, morass, etc. *Allowable rhymes*, base, face, deface, etc., loss, toss, etc.

ASE, *see* **ACE**.

ASH.—Ash, cash, dash, clash, crash, flash, gash, gnash, hash, lash, plash, rash, thrash, slash, trash, abash, etc. *Allowable rhymes*, wash, quash, etc., leash, etc.

ASH.—Wash, quash, etc. *Allowable rhymes*, cash, dash, etc.

ASK.—Ask, task, bask, cask, flask, mask.

ASP.—Asp, clasp, gasp, grasp, hasp. *Allowable rhymes*, wasp, etc.

AST.—Cast, last, blast, mast, past, vast, fast, aghast, avast, forecast, overcast, outcast, repast. *Perfect rhymes, the preterits and participles of verbs in* ass, *as* classed, amassed, etc. *Allowable rhymes, the preterits and participles of verbs in* ace, *as* placed, etc. *Nouns and verbs in* aste, *as* taste, waste, etc.

ASTE.—Baste, chaste, haste, paste, taste, waste, distaste. *Perfect rhymes*, waist, *and the preterits and participles of verbs in* ace, *as* faced, placed, etc. *Allowable rhymes*, cast, fast, etc., best, nest, etc., *and the preterits and participles of verbs in* ess, *as* messed, dressed, etc.

AT.—At, bat, cat, hat, fat, mat, pat, sat, rat, tat, vat, brat, chat, flat, plat, sprat, that, gnat. *Allowable rhymes*, bate, hate, etc.

ATCH.—Catch, match, hatch, latch, patch, scratch, smatch, snatch, despatch.

ATE.—Bate, date, fate, gate, grate, hate, tate, mate, pate, plate, prate, rate, sate, state, skate, slate, abate, belate, collate, create, debate, elate, dilate, estate, ingrate, innate, rebate, relate, sedate, translate, abdicate, abominate, abrogate, accelerate, accommodate, accumulate, accurate, adequate, affectionate, advocate, adulterate, aggravate, agitate, alienate, animate, annihilate, antedate, anticipate, antiquate, arbitrate, arrogate, articulate, assassinate, calculate, capitulate, captivate, celebrate, circulate, coagulate, commemorate, commiserate, communicate, compassionate, confederate, congratulate, congregate, consecrate, contaminate, corroborate, cultivate, candidate, co-operate, considerate, consulate, capacitate, debilitate, dedicate, degenerate, delegate, deliberate, denominate, depopulate, dislocate, deprecate, discriminate, derogate, dissipate, delicate, disconsolate, desperate, educate, effeminate, elevate, emulate, estimate, elaborate, equivocate, eradicate, evaporate, exaggerate, exasperate, expostulate, exterminate, extricate, facilitate, fortunate, generate, gratulate, hesitate, illiterate, illuminate, irritate, imitate, immoderate, impenetrate, importunate, imprecate, inanimate, innovate, instigate, intemperate, intimate, intimidate, intoxicate, intricate, invalidate, inveterate, inviolate, legitimate, magistrate, meditate, mitigate, moderate, necessitate, nominate, obstinate, participate, passionate, penetrate, perpetrate, personate, potentate, precipitate, predestinate, predominate, premeditate, prevaricate, procrastinate, profligate, prognosticate, propagate, recriminate, regenerate, regulate, reiterate, reprobate, reverberate, ruminate, separate, sophisticate, stipulate, subjugate, subordinate, suffocate, terminate, tolerate, temperate, vindicate, violate, unfortunate. *Perfect rhymes*, bait, plait, strait, wait, await, great. *Nearly perfect rhymes*, eight, weight, height, straight. *Allowable rhymes*, beat, heat, etc., bat, cat, etc., bet, wet, etc.

ATH.—Bath, path, etc. *Allowable rhymes*, hath, faith, etc.

ATHE.—Bathe, swathe, lathe, rathe.

AUB, *see* **OB**. **AUCE**, *see* **AUSE**. **AUCH**, *see* **OACH**.

AUD.—Fraud, laud, applaud, defraud. *Perfect rhymes*, broad, abroad, bawd, *and the preterits and participles of verbs in* aw, *as* gnawed, sawed, etc. *Allowable rhymes*, odd, nod, etc., ode, bode, etc., *also the word* load.

AVE.—Cave, brave, gave, grave, crave, lave, nave, knave, pave, rave, save, shave, slave, stave, wave, behave, deprave, engrave, outbrave, forgave, misgave, architrave. *Allowable rhyme, the auxiliary verb* have.

AUGH, *see* **AFF**. **AUGHT**, *see* **OUGHT**. **AULT**, *see* **ALT**.

AUNCH.—Launch, paunch, haunch, staunch, etc.

AUNCE, *see* **ONSE**.

AUNT.—Aunt, daunt, gaunt, haunt, jaunt, taunt, vaunt, avaunt. *Perfect rhymes*, slant, aslant. *Allowable rhymes*, want, etc., pant, cant, etc.

AUSE.—Cause, pause, clause, applause, because. *Perfect rhymes, the plurals of nouns, and third persons singular of verbs in* aw, *as* laws, he draws, etc. *Allowable rhyme*, was.

AUST, *see* **OST**.

AW.—Craw, daw, law, chaw, claw, draw, flaw, gnaw, jaw, law, maw, paw, raw, straw, thaw, withdraw, foresaw.

AWD, *see* **AUD**. **AWK**, *see* **ALK**.

AWL.—Bawl, brawl, drawl, crawl, scrawl, sprawl, squall. *Perfect rhymes*, ball, call, fall, gall, small, hall, pall, tall, wall, stall, install, forestall, thrall, inthrall.

AWN.—Dawn, brawn, fawn, pawn, spawn, drawn, yawn, lawn, withdrawn.

AX.—Ax, tax, wax, relax, flax. *Perfect rhymes, the plurals of nouns and third persons singular of verbs in* ack, *as* backs, sacks, etc., he lacks, he packs, etc. *Allowable rhymes, the plurals of nouns and third persons singular of verbs in* ake, *as* cakes, lakes, etc., he makes, he takes, etc.

AY.—Bray, clay, day, dray, tray, flay, fray, gay, hay, jay, lay, may, nay, pay, play, ray, say, way, pray, spray, slay, spay, stay, stray, sway, affray, allay, array, astray, away, belay, bewray, betray, decay, defray, delay, disarray, display, dismay, essay, forelay, gainsay, inlay, relay, repay, roundelay, virelay. *Perfect rhymes*, neigh, weigh, inveigh, etc., prey, they, convey, obey, purvey, survey, disobey, grey. *Allowable rhymes*, tea, sea, fee, see, glee, etc.

AZE.—Craze, daze, blaze, gaze, glaze, maze, raze, amaze, graze. *Perfect rhymes*, raise, praise, dispraise, etc., paraphrase, etc., *and the nouns plural, and third persons singular of the present tense of verbs in* ay, eigh, *and* ey, *as* days, he inveighs, he obeys, etc. *Allowable rhymes*, ease, tease, seize, etc., *and* keys, *the plural of* key, *also the auxiliaries* has *and* was.

E

E *and* **EA**, *see* **EE**. **EACE**, *see* **EASE**.

EACH.—Beach, breach, bleach, each, peach, preach, teach, impeach. *Nearly perfect rhymes*, beech, leech, speech, beseech. *Allowable rhymes*, fetch, wretch, etc.

EAD, *see* **EDE** *and* **EED**. **EAF**, *see* **IEF**.

EAGUE.—League, Teague, etc. *Perfect rhymes*, intrigue, fatigue, etc. *Allowable rhymes*, Hague, vague, etc., leg, beg, etc., bag, rag, etc.

EAK, *see* **AKE**.—Beak, speak, bleak, creak, freak, leak, peak, sneak, squeak, streak, weak, tweak, wreak, bespeak. *Nearly perfect rhymes*, cheek, leek, creek, meek, reek, seek, sleek, pique, week, shriek. *Allowable rhymes*, beck, speck, etc., lake, take, thick, lick, etc.

EAL.—Deal, heal, reveal, meal, peal, seal, steal, teal, veal, weal, seal, squeal, repeal, conceal, congeal, anneal, appeal. *Nearly perfect rhymes*, eel, heel, feel, keel, kneel, peel, reel, steel, wheel. *Allowable rhymes*, bell, tell, etc., bale, tale, etc., bill, fill, etc., ail, fail, etc.

EALM, *see* **ALM**.

EALTH.—Health, wealth, stealth, commonwealth, etc.

EAM.—Bream, cream, gleam, seam, scream, steam, stream, team, beam, dream. *Perfect rhymes*, fleame, scheme, theme, blaspheme, extreme, supreme. *Nearly perfect rhymes*, deem, teem, beseem, misdeem, esteem, disesteem, redeem, seem, etc. *Allowable rhymes*, dame, lame, etc., limb, him, etc., them, hem, etc., lamb, dam, etc. *See* **AME**.

EAN.—Bean, clean, dean, glean, lean, mean, wean, yean, demean, unclean. *Perfect rhymes*, convene, demesne, intervene, mien. *Nearly perfect rhymes*, machine, keen, screen, seen, green, spleen, between, careen, foreseen, serene, obscene, terrene, etc., queen, etc. *Allowable rhymes*, bane, mane, etc., ban, man, etc., bin, thin, begin etc

EANS, *see* **ENSE**. **EANT**, *see* **ENT**. **EAP**, *see* **EEP** *and* **EP**. **EAR**, *see* **EER**.

EARD—Heard, hard, sherd, etc. *Perfect rhymes, the preterits and participles of verbs in ar, as erred, preferred, etc. Allowable rhymes, beard, the preterits and participles of verbs in ere, ear, and ar, as revered, feared, barred.*

EARCH.—Search, perch, research. *Allowable rhymes, church, smirch, lurch, perch, march, etc.*

EARN, see **ERN. EARSE,** see **ERSE. EART,** see **ART.**

EARTH.—Earth, dearth. *Perfect rhymes, birth, mirth, etc. Allowable rhymes, hearth, etc.*

EASE, sounded **EACE.**—Cease, lease, release, grease, decease, decrease, increase, surcease. *Perfect rhyme, peace. Nearly perfect rhymes, piece, niece, fleece, geese, frontispiece, apiece, etc. Allowable rhymes, less, mess, etc., lace, mace, etc., miss, hiss, etc., nice, vice, etc.*

EASH, see **ESH.**

EAST.—East, feast, least, beast. *Perfect rhymes, the preterits and participles of verbs in ease, as cease, increased, etc. Nearly perfect rhyme, priest. Allowable rhymes, haste, taste, etc., best, chest, etc., fist, list, etc., and the preterits and participles of verbs in ess and iss, as dressed, hissed.*

EAT.—Bleat, eat, feat, heat, meat, neat, seat, treat, wheat, beat, cheat, defeat, entreat, escheat, entreat, retreat. *Perfect rhymes, obsolete, replete, concrete, complete. Nearly perfect rhyme, feet, fleet, gleet, greet, meet, sheet, sleet, street, sweet, discreet. Allowable rhymes, bate, grate, hate, etc., get, met, etc., bit, hit, etc. See ATE.*

EATH.—Breath, death, etc. *Allowable rhymes, heath, sheath, teeth.*

EATHE.—Breathe, sheathe, etc. *Perfect rhymes, wreath, inwreath, bequeath, beneath, underneath, etc. Nearly perfect rhymes, seethe, etc.*

EAVE.—Cleave, heave, interweave, leave, weave, bereave, heave. *Perfect rhymes, receive, conceive, deceive, perceive. Nearly perfect rhymes, eve, grieve, thieve, aggrieve, achieve, believe, disbelieve, relieve, reprieve, retrieve. Allowable rhymes, live, give, etc., lave, cave, etc., and have.*

EBB—Ebb, web, etc. *Allowable rhymes, babe, astrolabe, etc., glebe, etc.*

ECK—Beck, check, deck, neck, speck, wreck. *Allowable rhymes, break, take, etc., beak, sneak, etc.*

ECT.—Sect, abject, affect, correct, incorrect, collect, deject, detect, direct, disrespect, disaffect, dissect, effect, elect, eject, erect, expect, indirect, infect, inspect, neglect, object, project, protect, recollect, reflect, reject, respect, select, subject, suspect, architect, circumspect, dialect, intellect. *Perfect rhymes, the preterits and participles of verbs in eck, as decked, checked, etc. Allowable rhymes, the preterits and participles of verbs in ake and oak, as baked, leaked.*

ED.—Red, bled, fed, fled, bred, led, shred, shed, sped, wed, abed, inbred, misled. *Perfect rhymes, said, bread, dread, dead, head, lead, spread, thread, tread, behead, o'erspread. Allowable rhymes, bead, mead, etc., blade, fade, etc., maid, paid, etc., and the preterits and participles of verbs in ay, ey, and eigh, as bayed, obeyed, weighed, etc.*

EDE, see **EED.**

EDGE.—Edge, wedge, fledge, hedge, ledge, pledge, sedge, allege. *Allowable rhymes, age, page, etc., siege, oblige, etc., privilege, sacrilege, sortilege.*

EE.—Bee, free, glee, knee, see, three, thee, tree, agree, decree, degree, disagree, o'ersee, pedigree, he, me, we, she, be, jubilee, Lee. *Nearly perfect rhymes, sea, plea, flea, tea, key. Allowable rhymes, all words of one syllable ending in y, ye, or ie, or polysyllables of these terminations having the accent on the ultimate or antepenultimate syllable.*

EECE, see **EASE. EECH,** see **EACH.**

EED.—Creed, deed, indeed, bleed, breed, feed, need, meed, heed, reed, speed, seed, steed, weed, proceed, succeed, exceed. *Perfect rhymes, knead, read, intercede, precede, recede, concede, impede, supersede, etc., bead, lead, mead, plead, etc. Allowable rhymes, bed, dead, etc., bid, hid, etc., made, blade, etc.*

EEF, see **IEF. EEK,** see **EAK. EEL,** see **EAL. EEM,** see **EAM. EEN,** see **EAN.**

EEP.—Creep, deep, sleep, keep, peep, sheep, steep, sweep, weep, asleep. *Nearly perfect rhymes, cheap, heap, reap, etc. Allowable rhymes, ape, rape, etc., step, nep, etc., hip, lip, etc.*

EER.—Beer, deer, fleer, gear, jeer, peer, meer, leer, sheer, steer, sneer, cheer, veer, pioneer, domineer, cannoneer, compeer, engineer, mutineer, pioneer, privateer, charioteer, chanticleer, career, mountaineer. *Perfect rhymes, here, adhere, cohere, interfere, persevere, revere, austere, severe, sincere, hemisphere, etc., car, clear, dear, fear, hear, near, sear, smear, spear, tear, year, appear, besmear, disappear, endear, auctioneer. Allowable rhymes, hare, dare, etc., preter, deter, character, etc.*

EESE, see **EEZE. EET,** see **EAT. EETH,** see **EATH.**

EEZE.—Breeze, freeze, sneeze, wheeze, squeeze *and the plurals of nouns and third persons singular, present tense, of verbs in ee, as bees, he sees. Perfect rhymes, cheese, these, etc. Nearly perfect rhymes, ease, appease, disease, displease, tease, seize, etc., and the plurals of nouns in ea, as teas, pleas, etc., and the polysyllables ending in ea, having the accent on the antepenultimate, as images, monarchies, etc.*

EFT.—Cleft, left, theft, weft, bereft, etc. *Allowable rhymes, lift, sift, etc., and the third person singular, present tense, of verbs in afe, aff, augh, and iff, as chafed, quaffed, laughed, whiffed, etc.*

EG.—Egg, leg, beg, peg. *Allowable rhymes, vague, plague, etc., league, Teague, etc.*

EIGN, see **AY. EIGHT,** see **ATE. EIGN,** see **AIN. EIL,** see **AIL. EIN,** see **AIN. EINT,** see **AINT. EIR,** see **ARE. EIT,** see **EAT. EIVE,** see **EAVE. EIZE,** see **EEZE.**

ELL.—Ell, dwell, fell, hell, knell, quell, sell, bell, cell, dispel, foretell, excel, compel, befell, yell, well, tell, swell, spell, smell, shell, parallel, sentinel, infidel, citadel, retel, repel, rebel, impel, expel. *Allowable rhymes, bale, sail, etc., beal, peal, etc., eel, steel, etc.*

ELD.—Held, geld, withheld, upheld, beheld, etc. *Perfect rhyme, the preterits and participles of verbs in ell, as swelled felled, etc. Allowable rhymes, the preterits and participles of verbs in ale, ail, etc., heal, seal, etc., as impaled, waled, etc., healed, sealed, etc.*

ELF.—Elf, pelf, self, shelf, himself, etc.

ELK.—Elk, whelk, etc.

ELM.—Elm, helm, realm, whelm, overwhelm, etc. *Allowable rhymes palm, film, etc.*

ELP.—Help, whelp, yelp, etc.

ELT.—Belt, gelt, melt, felt, welt, smelt, pelt, dwelt. *Perfect rhymes, dealt.*

ELVE.—Delve, helve, twelve, etc.

ELVES.—Elves, themselves, etc. *Perfect rhymes, the plurals of nouns and third persons singular of verbs in elf and elve, as twelves, delves, shelves, etc.*

EM.—Gem, hem, stem, them, diadem, stratagem, etc. *Perfect rhymes, condemn, contemn, etc. Allowable rhymes, lame, tame, etc., team, seam, theme, etc.*

EME, see **EAM.**

EMN,—Condemn, contemn, etc. *Perfect rhymes, gem, hem, etc. Allowable rhymes, lame, tame, etc., team, seam, etc.*

EMPT.—Tempt, exempt, attempt, contempt.

EN.—Den, hen, fen, ken, men, pen, ten, then, when, wren, denizen. *Allowable rhymes, bane, fane, etc., mean, bean, etc.*

ENCE.—Fence, hence, dense, pence, thence, whence, defence, expense, offense, pretense, commence, abstinence, circumference, conference, confidence, consequence, continence, benevolence, concupiscence, difference, diffidence, diligence, eloquence, eminence, evidence, excellence, impenitence, imperitinence, impotence, impudence, improvidence, inconstinence, indifference, indigence, indolence, inference, intelligence, innocence, magnificence, munificence, negligence, omnipotence, penitence, preference, providence, recompense, reference, residence, reverence, vehemence, violence. *Perfect rhymes, sense, dense, cense, condense, immense, intense, prepense, dispense, suspense, prepense, incense, frankincense.*

ENCH.—Bench, drench, retrench, quench, clench, stench, flench, trench, wench, wrench, intrench.

END.—Bend, mend, blend, end, fend, lend, rend, send, spend, tend, vend, amend, attend, ascend, commend, contend, defend, depend, descend, distend, expend, extend, forefend, intend, misspend, offend, offend, portend, pretend, protend, suspend, transcend, unbend, apprehend, comprehend, condescend, discommend, recommend, reprehend, dividend, reverend. *Perfect rhymes, friend, befriend, and the preterits and participles of verbs in en, as penned, kenned, etc. Allowable rhymes, the preterits and participles of verbs in ean, as gleaned, yeaned, etc.*

ENDS.—Amends. *Perfect rhymes, the plurals of nouns and third persons singular, present tense, of verbs in end, as friends, he mends, etc.*

ENE, see **EAN.**

ENGE.—Avenge, revenge, etc.

ENGTH.—Length, strength, etc.

ENSE (sounded **ENZE).**—Cleanse. *Perfect rhymes, the plurals of nouns and third persons singular, present tense, of verbs in en, as hens, hen he pens, he kens, etc.*

ENT.—Bent, lent, rent, pent, scent, sent, shent, spent, tent, vent, went, absent, assent, ascent, assent, attent, augment, consent, content, convent, descent, dissent, event, extent, foment, frequent, indent, intent, invent, lament, misspent, o'erspent, present, prevent, relent, repent, resent, orient, ferment, outvent, underwent, discontent, unbent, circumvent, represent, abstinent, accident, accomplishment, admonishment, acknowledgment, ailment, arbitrament, argument, banishment, battlement, blandishment, astonishment, armipotent, belipotent, benevolent, chastisement, competent, compliment, complement, confident, continent, corpulent, detriment, different, diffident, diligent, disparagement, document, element, eloquent, eminent, equivalent, establishment, evident, excellent, excrement, exigent, experiment, firmament, fraudulent, government, embellishment, imminent, impenitent, impertinent, implement, impotent, imprisonment, improvement, impudent, incident, incompetent, incontinent, indifferent, indigent, innocent, insolent, instrument, irreverent, languishment, ligament, lineament, magnificent, management, medicament, malcontent, monument, negligent, nourishment, nutriment, occident, omnipotent, opulent, ornament, parliament, penitent, permanent, pertinent, president, precedent, prevalent, provident, punishment, ravishment, regiment, rudiment, reticent, sacrament, sediment, sentiment, settlement, subsequent, supplement, succulent, tenement, temperament, testament, tourmament, turbulent, vehement, violent, virulent, reverent. Allowable rhymes, paint, saint, etc.*

ENTS.—Accoutrements. *Perfect rhymes, the plurals of nouns and third persons singular, present tense, of verbs in ent, as scents, he accents, etc.*

EP.—Step, nep, etc. *Allowable rhymes, leap, reap, etc., rape, tape, etc.*

EPT.—Accept, adept, except, intercept, etc. *Perfect rhymes, crept, slept, wept, kept. Allowable rhymes, the preterits and participles of verbs in ape, eep and cap, as peeped, reaped, shaped, etc.*

ERR.—Err, aver, defer, infer, deter, inter, refer, transfer, confer, prefer, parterre, administer, wagoner, islander, arbiter, character. *Village cottager, dowager, forager, pillager, voyager, manager, gardener, slanderer, flatterer, idolater, provender, theater, amphitheater, forager, lavender, messenger, passenger, scrivener, interpreter, officer, mariner, barrister, minister, register, canister, chorister, sophister, presbyter, astrologer, astrologer, loiterer, prisoner, grasshopper, astronomer, sepulcher, thunderer, traveler, murderer, usurer. Allowable rhymes, bare, care, etc., ear, fear, etc., bar, car, etc., air, fir, her, etc.*

ERCH, see **EARCH. ERCE,** see **ERSE. ERD,** see **EARD. ERE,** see **EER.**

ERGE.—Verge, emerge, absterge, immerge. *Perfect rhymes, dirge, Nearly perfect rhymes, urge, purge, surge. Allowable rhymes, barge, large, etc.*

ERN.—Fern, stern, discern, concern. *Perfect rhymes, learn, earn, yearn, etc. Allowable rhymes, barn, yarn, etc., burn, turn, etc.*

ERSE.—Verse, hearse, absterse, adverse, averse, converse, disperse, intersperse, perverse, reverse, traverse, asperse, intereperse, universe. *Perfect rhymes, amerce, coerce, etc., fierce, tierce, pierce, etc. Allowable rhymes, farce, parse, Mars, etc., purse, curse etc.*

ERT.—Wert, advert, assert, avert, concert, convert, controvert, divert, exert, expert, insert, invert, pervert, subvert. *Allowable rhymes, heart, part, etc., shirt, dirt, etc., hurt, spurt, etc.*

ERVE.—Serve, nerve, swerve, preserve, deserve, conserve, observe, reserve, disserve, subserve. *Allowable rhymes*, starve, carve, etc., curve, etc.

ESS.—Bless, dress, cess, chess, guess, less, mess, press, stress, acquiesce, access, address, assess, compress, confess, caress, depress, digress, dispossess, distress, excess, express, impress, oppress, possess, profess, recess, repress, redress, success, transgress, adulteress, bashfulness, bitterness, cheerfulness, comfortless, comeliness, dizziness, diocese, drowsiness, eagerness, easiness, embassadress, emptiness, evenness, fatherless, filthiness, foolishness, forgetfulness, forwardness, frowardness, fruitfulness, fulsomeness, giddiness, greediness, gentleness, governess, happiness, haughtiness, heaviness, idleness, heinousness, hoaryness, hollowness, holiness, lasciviousness, lawfulness, laziness, littleness, liveliness, loftiness, lioness, lowliness, manliness, masterless, mightiness, motherless, motionless, nakedness, neediness, noisomeness, numberless, patroness, peevishness, perfidiousness, pitiless, poetess, prophetess, ransomness, readiness, righteousness, shepherdess, sorceress, sordidness, spiritless, sprightliness, stubbornness, sturdiness, surliness, steadiness, tenderness, thoughtfulness, ugliness, uneasiness, unhappiness, votaress, usefulness, wakefulness, wantonness, weaponless, wariness, willingness, willfulness, weariness, wickedness, wilderness, wretchedness, drunkenness, childishness. *Allowable rhymes*, mass, pass, etc., mace, place, etc.

ESE, *see* **EEZE.**

ESH.—Flesh, fresh, refresh, thresh, afresh, mesh. *Allowable rhymes*, mash, flash, etc.

ESK.—Desk. *Perfect rhymes*, grotesque, burlesque, etc. *Allowable rhymes*, mask, ask, etc.

EST.—Best, chest, crest, guest, jest, nest, pest, quest, rest, test, vest, west, arrest, attest, bequest, contest, detest, digest, divest, invest, infest, molest, obtest, protest, retest, suggest, unrest, interest, manifest, etc. *Perfect rhymes*, breast, abreast, etc., *and the preterits and participles of verbs in ess, as* dressed, expressed, etc. *Allowable rhymes*, cast, fast, etc., haste, waste, etc., beast, least, etc. *See* **EAST.**

ET.—Bet, jet, fret, get, let, met, net, set, wet, whet, yet, debt, abet, beget, beset, forget, regret, alphabet, amulet, anchoret, cabinet, epithet, parapet, rivulet, violet, counterfeit, coronet, etc. *Perfect rhymes*, sweat, threat, etc. *Allowable rhymes*, bate, hate, etc., beat, heat, etc.

ETCH.—Fetch, stretch, wretch, sketch, etc. *Allowable rhymes*, match, latch, etc., peach, bleach, etc.

ETE, *see* **EAT. EVE**, *see* **EAVE. EUM**, *see* **UME.**

EW.—Blew, chew, dew, brew, drew, flew, few, grew, new, knew, hew, Jew, mew, view, threw, yew, crew, slew, anew, askew, bedew, eschew, renew, review, withdrew, screw, interview, etc. *Perfect rhymes*, blue, clue, cue, glue, hue, rue, sue, strue, accrue, ensue, endue, imbue, imbrue, pursue, subdue, adieu, purlieu, perdue, residue, avenue, revenue, retinue.

EWD, *see* **EUD. EWN**, *see* **UNE.**

EX.—Sex, vex, annex, convex, complex, perplex, circumflex, *and the plurals of nouns and third persons singular of verbs in eck, as* checks, he checks, etc. *Allowable rhymes*, ax, wax, etc., *and the plurals of nouns and third persons singular of verbs in* ake, ack, eak, eke, ique, ike, etc., breaks, rakes, etc., he takes, he breaks, racks, he ekes, pikes, he likes, he pipes, etc.

EXT.—Next, pretext, *and the preterits and participles of verbs in* ex, *as* vexed, perplexed, etc. *Allowable rhymes, the preterits and participles of verbs in* ax, *as* waxed, etc.

EY, *see* **AY.**

I

IB.—Bib, crib, squib, drib, glib, nib, rib. *Allowable rhymes*, bribe, tribe, etc.

IBE.—Bribe, tribe, scribe, ascribe, describe, superscribe, prescribe, proscribe, subscribe, transcribe, inscribe. *Allowable rhymes*, bib, crib, etc.

ICE.—Ice, dice, mice, nice, price, rice, spice, slice, thrice, trice, advice, entice, vice, device. *Perfect rhymes*, rise, concise, precise, paradise, etc. *Allowable rhymes*, miss, kiss, hiss, artifice, avarice, cockatrice, benefice, cicatrice, edifice, orifice, prejudice, precipice, sacrifice, etc., piece, fleece, etc.

ICH, *see* **ITCH.**

ICK.—Brick, sick, chick, kick, lick, nick, pick, quick, stick, thick, trick, arithmetic, asthmatic, choleric, catholic, phlegmatic, heretic, rhetoric, schismatic, splenetic, lunatic, politic, empiric. *Allowable rhymes*, like, pike, etc., weak, speak, etc.

ICT.—Strict, addict, afflict, convict, inflict, contradict, etc. *Perfect rhymes, the preterits and participles of verbs in* ick, *as* licked, kicked, etc. *Allowable rhymes, the preterits and participles of verbs in* ike, eak, *as* liked, leaked, etc.

ID.—Bid, chid, hid, kid, lid, slid, rid, bestrid, pyramid, forbid. *Allowable rhymes*, hide, chide, parricide, etc., *and the preterits and participles of verbs in y or ie, as* died, replied, etc., lead, bead, mead, deed, need, etc., *and the preterits and participles of verbs in* ee, *as* freed, agreed, etc.

IDE.—Bide, chide, hide, glide, pride, ride, slide, side, stride, tide, wide, bride, abide, guide, aside, astride, beside, bestride, betide, confide, decide, deride, divide, preside, provide, subside, misguide, subdivide, etc. *Perfect rhymes, the preterits and participles of verbs in* ie *and* y, *as* dyed, replied, etc., *and the participle* sighed. *Allowable rhymes*, bead, mead, etc., bid, hid, etc.

IDES.—Ides, besides. *Perfect rhymes, the plurals of nouns and third persons singular of verbs in* ide, *as* tide, he rides, etc. *Allowable rhymes, the plurals of nouns and third persons singular of verbs in* ead, id, *as* beads, he leads, etc., kids, he bids, etc.

IDGE.—Bridge, ridge, abridge, etc.

IDST.—Midst, amidst, etc. *Perfect rhymes, the second person singular, of the present tense of verbs in* id, *as* thou biddest, thou hiddest, etc. *Allowable rhymes, the second persons singular of the present tense of verbs in* ide, *as* thou hidest, thou readest, etc.

IE, or Y.—By, buy, cry, die, dry, eye, fly, fry, fie, hie, lie, pie, ply, pry, rye, shy, sly, spry, sky, sty, tie, try, vie, why, ally, apply, awry, belie, comply, decry, defy, descry, deny, imply, espy, outvie, outfly, rely, reply, supply, untie, amplify, beautify, certify, crucify, deify, dignify, edify, falsify, fortify, gratify, glorify, indemnify, justify, magnify, modify, mollify, mortify, pacify, petrify, purify, putrefy, qualify, ratify, rectify, sanctify, satisfy, scarify, signify, specify, stupefy, terrify, testify, verify, vilify, vitrify, vivify, prophesy. *Perfect rhymes*, high, nigh, sigh, thigh. *Allowable rhymes*, bee, she, tea, sea, etc., pleurisy, chemistry, academy, apostasy, conspiracy, confederacy, ecstasy, democracy, embassy, fallacy, legacy, supremacy, lunacy, privacy, piracy, malady, remedy, tragedy, comedy, cosmography, geography, geometry, etc., elegy, certainty, sovereignty, loyalty, disloyalty, penalty, casualty, ribaldry, chivalry, infamy, constancy, fealty, cavalry, bigamy, polygamy, vacancy, inconstancy, infancy, company, accompany, dittany, tyranny, villainy, anarchy, monarchy, lethargy, incendiary, infirmary, library, salary, sanctuary, votary, auxiliary, contrary, diary, granary, rosemary, urgency, infantry, knavery, livery, recovery, robbery, novelty, antipathy, apathy, sympathy, idolatry, galaxy, husbandry, cruelty, enemy, blasphemy, prophecy, clemency, decency, inclemency, emergency, regency, progeny, energy, poverty, liberty, property, adultery, artery, artillery, battery, beggary, bribery, bravery, delivery, drudgery, flattery, gallery, imagery, lottery, misery, mystery, nursery, raillery, slavery, sorcery, treachery, discovery, tapestry, majesty, modesty, immodesty, honesty, dishonesty, courtesy, heresy, poesy, poetry, secrecy, leprosy, perfidy, subsidy, drapery, symmetry, drollery, prodigy, policy, mutiny, destiny, scrutiny, hypocrisy, family, ability, activity, avidity, assiduity, civility, community, concavity, consanguinity, conformity, congruity, diuturnity, facility, falsity, familiarity, formality, generosity, gratuity, humidity, absurdity, adversity, affability, affinity, agility, alacrity, ambiguity, animosity, antiquity, austerity, authority, brevity, calamity, capacity, captivity, charity, chastity, civility, credulity, curiosity, finery, declivity, deformity, duty, dexterity, dignity, disparity, diversity, divinity, enmity, enormity, equality, equanimity, equity, eternity, extremity, fatality, felicity, fertility, fidelity, frugality, futurity, gravity, hostility, humanity, humility, immanity, immaturity, immensity, immorality, immortality, immunity, immutability, impartiality, impossibility, impetuosity, improbity, inanity, incapacity, incivility, incongruity, inequality, indemnity, infinity, inflexibility, instability, invalidity, jollity, lenity, lubricity, magnanimity, majority, mediocrity, minority, mutability, nicety, perversity, perplexity, perspicuity, prosperity, privity, probability, probity, propensity, rarity, rapidity, sagacity, sanctity, sensibility, sensuality, solidity, temerity, timidity, tranquillity, virginity, visibility, university, trumpery, apology, genealogy, etymology, simony, symphony, soliloquy, allegory, armory, factory, pillory, faculty, treasury, usury, augury, importunity, impunity, impurity, inaccuracy, inability, incredulity, indignity, infidelity, infirmity, iniquity, integrity, laity, liberality, malignity, maturity, morality, mortality, nativity, necessity, neutrality, nobility, obscurity, opportunity, partiality, perpetuity, prosperity, priority, prodigality, purity, quality, quantity, scarcity, security, severity, simplicity, sincerity, solemnity, sterility, stupidity, trinity, vacuity, validity, vanity, vivacity, unanimity, uniformity, unity, anxiety, gaiety, impiety, piety, satiety, sobriety, society, variety, customary, melody, philosophy, astronomy, anatomy, colony, gluttony, harmony, agony, gallantry, canopy, history, memory, victory, calumny, injury, luxury, penury, perjury, usury, industry.

IECE, *see* **EASE.**

IEF.—Grief, chief, fief, thief, brief, belief, relief, etc. *Perfect rhymes*, reef, beef, etc. *Nearly perfect rhymes*, leaf, sheaf, etc.

IEGE.—Liege, siege, oblige, disoblige, assiege, besiege.

IELD.—Field, yield, shield, wield, afield. *Nearly perfect rhymes, the preterits and participles of verbs in* eal, *as* healed, repealed, etc.

IEN, *see* **EEN. IEND**, *see* **END. IERCE**, *see* **ERSE. IEST**, *see* **EAST. IEVE**, *see* **EAVE.**

IFE.—Rife, fife, knife, wife, strife, life. *Allowable rhymes*, cliff, skiff, stiff, whiff, etc.

IFF, *see* **IFE.**

IFT.—Gift, drift, shift, lift, rift, sift, thrift, adrift, etc., *and the preterits and participles of verbs in* iff, *as* whiffed, etc.

IG.—Big, dig, gig, fig, pig, rig, sprig, twig, swig. *Allowable rhymes*, league, Teague, fatigue, etc.

IGE, *see* **IEGE. IGH**, *see* **IE. IGHT**, *see* **ITE. IGN**, *see* **INE. IGUE**, *see* **EAGUE.**

IKE.—Dike, like, pike, spike, strike, alike, dislike, oblique. *Allowable rhymes*, leak, speak, antique, etc., lick, pick, etc.

ILL.—Bill, chill, fill, drill, gill, hill, ill, kill, mill, quill, rill, shrill, skill, spill, still, swill, thrill, till, trill, will, distill, fulfill, instill, codicil, daffodil, utensil. *Perfect rhymes, all words ending in* ile, *with the accent on the antepenultimate syllable, as* volatile, etc. *Allowable rhymes*, byle, chyle, file, feel, reel, etc., meal, peal, seal, etc., *and words in* ble, *having the accent on the antepenultimate, as* suitable, etc.

ILD.—Child, mild, wild, etc. *Perfect rhymes, the preterits and participles of verbs of one syllable in* ile, *or of more syllables, provided the accent be on the last, as* piled, reviled, etc. *Allowable rhymes, the preterits and participles of verbs in* ill, *as* filled, willed, etc., *in* oil, *as* oiled, boiled, foiled, etc.

ILD. Gild, build, rebuild, etc. *Perfect rhymes, the preterits and participles of verbs in* illed, *as* filled, willed, etc. *Allowable rhymes*, child, mild, *and their allowable rhymes, which see.*

ILE.—Bile, chyle, file, guile, isle, mile, pile, smile, stile, style, tile, vile, while, awhile, compile, revile, defile, exile, erewhile, reconcile, beguile. *Allowable rhymes*, oil, boil, etc., bill, fill, etc.

ILK.—Milk, silk, bilk, etc.

ILT.—Gilt, jilt, built, quilt, guilt, hilt, spilt, stilt, tilt.

ILTH.—Filth, tilth, etc.

IM.—Brim, dim, grim, him, rim, skim, slim, trim, whim, prim. *Perfect rhymes*, limb, hymn, limn. *Allowable rhymes*, lime, time, climb, etc., team, gleam, etc.

IMB, *see* **IM.**

IME.—Chime, time, grime, climb, clime, crime, prime, mime, rhyme, slime, thyme, lime, sublime. *Allowable rhymes*, brim, dim, maritime, etc.

IMES.—Betimes, sometimes, etc. *Perfect rhymes, the plurals of nouns and third persons singular, present tense, of verbs in* ime, *as* chimes, he rhymes, etc. *Allowable rhymes, the plurals of nouns and third persons singular, present tense, of verbs in* eam *and* im, *as* dreams, brims, he swims, etc.

IMN, *see* **IM.**

IMP.—Imp, pimp, limp, gimp.

IMPSE.—Glimpse. *Rhymes, the plurals of nouns, third person present, of verbs in imp, as imps, he limps, etc.*

IN.—Chin, din, fin, gin, grin, in, inn, kin, pin, shin, sin, spin, skin, thin, tin, win, within, assassin, javelin, begin. *Allowable rhymes,* chine, dine, etc., lean, bean, etc., machine, magazine, etc.

INCE.—Mince, prince, since, quince, rinse, wince, convince, c¬ince.

INCH.—Clinch, flinch, winch, pinch, inch.

INCT.—Instinct, distinct, extinct, precinct, succinct, etc., *and the preterits and participles of verbs in* ink, *as* linked, pinked, etc.

IND.—Bind, find, mind, blind, hind, kind, grind, rind, wind, behind, unkind, remind, etc., *and the preterits and participles of verbs in* ine, *as* refined. *Allowable rhymes,* rescind, prescind, *and the noun* wind, *as it is frequently pronounced, also the participles of verbs in* oin, *as* joined.

INE.—Dine, brine, mine, chine, fine, line, nine, pine, shine, shrine, kine, trine, trine, twine, vine, wine, whine, combine, confine, decline, define, incline, inshrine, intwine, opine, calcine, recline, refine, repine, superfine, interline, countermine, undermine, supine, concubine, porcupine, divine. *Perfect rhymes,* sign, assign, consign, design, etc. *Allowable rhymes,* bin, thin, tin, origin, join, loin, etc., *polysyllables ending in* ine, *pronounced* in, *as* masculine, feminine, discipline, libertine, heroine, etc.

ING.—Bring, sing, ring, cling, ring, sling, spring, sting, swing, wing, wring, thing, etc., *and the participles of the present tense in* ing, *with the accent on the antepenultimate, as* recovering, altering, etc.

INGE.—Cringe, fringe, hinge, singe, springe, swinge, tinge, twinge, infringe.

INK.—Ink, think, wink, drink, blink, brink, chink, clink, link, pink, shrink, sink, stink, bethink, forethink.

INT.—Dint, mint, hint, flint, lint, print, squint, asquint, imprint.

IP.—Chip, lip, hip, clip, dip, drip, nip, sip, rip, scrip, ship, skip, slip, snip, strip, tip, trip, whip, equip, eldership, fellowship, workmanship, rivalship, *and all words in* ship, *with the accent on the antepenultimate. Allowable rhymes,* wipe, gripe, etc., leap, heap, etc.

IPE.—Gripe, pipe, ripe, snipe, type, stripe, wipe, archetype, prototype. *Allowable rhymes,* chip, lip, workmanship, etc.

IPSE.—Eclipse. *Rhymes, the plurals of nouns and third persons singular, present tense, of verbs in* ip, *as* gripe, strips, etc. *Allowable rhymes, the plurals of nouns and third persons singular, present tense, of verbs in* ipe, *as* gripes, wipes, etc.

IR, *see* **UR. IRCH,** *see* **URCH. IRD,** *see* **URD.**

IRE.—Fire, dire, hire, ire, lyre, mire, quire, sire, spire, squire, wire, tire, attire, acquire, admire, aspire, conspire, desire, inquire, entire, expire, inspire, require, retire, transpire. Tyre. *Perfect rhymes,* friar, liar, brier, *and nouns formed from verbs ending in* ie *or* y, *as* crier, dyer, *as also the comparative of adjectives of the same sounding terminations, as* nigher, shyer, etc.

IRGE, *see* **ERGE.**

IRL.—Girl, whirl, twirl. *Nearly perfect rhymes,* curl, furl, churl, etc.

IRM.—Firm, affirm, confirm, infirm. *Nearly perfect rhymes,* worm, term, etc.

IRST, *see* **URST. IRT,** *see* **URT.**

IRTH.—Birth, mirth. *Perfect rhymes,* earth, dearth, *which see.*

ISS.—Bliss, miss, hiss, kiss, this, abyss, amiss, submiss, dismiss, remiss. *Allowable rhymes,* mice, spice, etc., peace, lease, etc.

IS, *pronounced like* **IZ.**—Is, his, whiz.

ISE, *see* **ICE** *and* **IZE.**

ISH.—Dish, wish, fish, cuish, pish.

ISK.—Brisk, frisk, disk, risk, whisk, basilisk, tamarisk.

ISP.—Crisp, wisp, lisp.

IST.—Fist, list, mist, twist, wrist, assist, consist, desist, exist, insist, persist, resist, subsist, alchemist, amethyst, anatomist, antagonist, annalist, evangelist, eucharist, exorcist, herbalist, humorist, oculist, organist, satirist, etc., *and the preterits and participles of verbs in* iss, *as* missed, hissed, etc. *Allowable rhymes, the preterits and participles of verbs in* ice, *as* spiced, sliced, etc.

IT.—Bit, cit, hit, fit, grit, flit, knit, nit, pit, quit, sit, split, twit, wit, whit, writ, admit, acquit, commit, emit, omit, outwit, permit, remit, submit, transmit, refit, benefit, perquisite. *Allowable rhymes,* beat, heat, etc., bite, mite, light, etc.

ITCH *and* **HITCH.**—Ditch, pitch, rich, which, Fitch, bitch, flitch, hitch, itch, stitch, switch, twitch, witch, bewitch, niche, enrich.

ITE *and* **IGHT.**—Bite, cite, kite, mite, quite, rite, smite, spite, trite, white, write, contrite, dismite, despite, indite, invite, excite, incite, polite, requite, recite, unite, reunite, aconite, appetite, parasite, proselyte, expedite, *Perfect rhymes,* blight, benight, bright, fight, flight, fright, height, light, knight, night, might, plight, right, sight, slight, sprite, wight, affright, alight, aright, foreknight, delight, despite, unsight, upright, bedight, oversight. *Allowable rhymes,* eight, weight, etc., bit, hit, etc., favorite, hypocrite, infinite, requisite, opposite, apposite, exquisite, etc.

ITH.—Pith, smith, frith.

ITHE.—Hithe, blithe, tithe, scythe, writhe, lithe. *Allowable rhyme,* with.

IVE.—Five, dive, alive, gyve, hive, drive, rive, shrive, strive, thrive, arrive, connive, contrive, deprive, derive, revive, survive. *Allowable rhymes,* give, live, sieve, forgive, outlive, fugitive, laxative, narrative, prerogative, primitive, sensitive, vegetive affirmative, alternative, contemplative, demonstrative, diminutive, distributive, donative, inquisitive, lenitive, massive, negative, perspective, positive, preparative, provocative, purgative, restorative.

IX.—Fix, six, fix, mix, affix, infix, prefix, transmix, intermix, crucifix, etc., *and the plurals of nouns and third persons of verbs in* ick, *as* wicks, licks, etc. *Allowable rhymes, the plurals of nouns and third persons singular of verbs in* ike, *as* pikes, likes, etc.

IXT.—Betwixt. *Rhymes, the preterits and participles of verbs in* ix, *as* fixed, mixed, etc.

O

O, *see* **OO** *and* **OW.**

OACH.—Broach, croach, proach, abroach, approach, encroach, reproach. *Perfect rhyme,* loach. *Allowable rhymes,* botch, notch, etc., mutch, hutch, etc.

OAD, *see* **AUD** *and* **ODE. OAF,** *see* **OFF. OAK,** *see* **OKE. OAL,** *see* **OLE. OAM,** *see* **OME. OAN,** *see* **ONE. OAP,** *see* **OPE. OAR,** *see* **ORE. OARD,** *see* **ORD. OAST,** *see* **OST. OAT,** *see* **OTE. OATH,** *see* **OTH.**

OB.—Fob, bob, mob, knob, sob, rob, throb. *Perfect rhymes,* swab, squab. *Allowable rhymes,* daub, globe, robe, dub, etc.

OBE.—Globe, lobe, probe, robe, conglobe. *Allowable rhymes,* fob, mob, etc., rub, dub, etc., daub, etc.

OCE, *see* **OSE.**

OCK.—Block, cock, dock, clock, crock, dock, frock, flock, knock, mock, rock, shock, stock, sock. *Allowable rhymes,* oak, poke, cloak, etc., look, took, etc., buck, suck, etc.

OCT.—Concoct. *Rhymes, the preterits and participles of verbs in* ock *as* blocked, locked, etc. *Allowable rhymes, the preterits and participles of verbs in* oak *and* oke, *as* croaked, soaked, yoked, etc.

OD.—Clod, God, rod, sod, trod, nod, plod, odd, shod. *Allowable rhymes,* ode, code, mode, etc., *and the preterits and participles of verbs in* ow, *as* sowed, did sow, etc.

ODE *and* **OAD.**—Bode, ode, code, mode, rode, abode, corrode, explode, forbode, commode, incommode, episode, etc. *Perfect rhymes,* road, goad, load, etc., *and the preterits and participles of verbs in* ow *as* owed, showed, etc. *Allowable rhymes,* blood, flood, clod, bod, nod, broad, fraud, etc. *See* **OOD.**

OE, *see* **OW.**

OFF *and* **OUGH.**—Off, scoff, etc. *Perfect rhyme,* cough, trough, etc. *Allowable rhymes,* oaf, loaf, etc., proof, roof, etc. *See* **OOF.**

OFT.—Oft, croft, soft, aloft, etc., *and the preterits and participles of verbs in* off *and* uff, *as* ruffed, scoffed, etc.

OG.—Hog, bog, cog, dog, clog, fog, frog, log, jog, etc. *Perfect rhymes,* dialogue, epilogue, agog, synagogue, catalogue, pedagogue. *Allowable rhymes,* rogue, vogue, etc.

OGUE.—Rogue, vogue, prorogue, collogue, disembogue. *Allowable rhymes,* bog, log, dialogue, etc.

OICE.—Choice, voice, rejoice. *Allowable rhymes,* nice, vice, rice, etc.

OID.—Void, avoid, devoid, etc., *and the preterits and participles of verbs in* oy, *as* buoyed, cloyed, etc. *Allowable rhymes,* bide, tide, ride, etc.

OIL.—Oil, boil, coil, moil, soil, spoil, toil, despoil, embroil, recoil, turmoil, disembroil. *Allowable rhymes,* isle, while, tile, etc.

OIN.—Coin, join, subjoin, groin, loin, adjoin, conjoin, disjoin, rejoin, purloin, rejoin. *Allowable rhymes,* whine, wine, fine, etc. *See* **INE.**

OINT.—Oint, joint, point, disjoint, anoint, appoint, disappoint, counterpoint. *Allowable rhymes,* pint.

OISE.—Poise, noise, counterpoise, equipoise, etc., *and the plurals of nouns and third persons singular, present tense, of verbs in* oy, *as* buoys, cloys, etc. *Allowable rhymes,* wise, size, prize, *and the plurals of nouns and third persons singular, present tense, of verbs in* ie *or* y, *as* pies, tries, etc.

OIST.—Hoist, moist, foist. *Perfect rhymes, the preterits and participles of verbs in* oice, *as* rejoiced. *Allowable rhymes, the preterits and participles of verbs in* ice, *as* spiced.

OIT.—Coit, exploit, adroit, etc. *Allowable rhymes,* white light, might, sight, rite, etc.

OKE.—Broke, coke, smoke, spoke, stroke, yoke, bespoke invoke, provoke, revoke, etc. *Perfect rhymes,* choke, cloak, oak, soak. *Allowable rhymes,* stock, mock, etc., buck, luck, etc., talk, walk, etc., look, hook, etc. *See* **OCK** *and* **OOK.**

OL.—Loll, doll, droll, extol, capitol, etc. *Allowable rhymes,* ol, toll, etc., bawl, etc., bowl, roll, soul, dull, mull, etc.

OLD.—Old, bold, cold, gold, hold, mold, scold, sold, told, behold, unfold, unfold, uphold, withhold, foretold, manifold, marigold. *Perfect rhymes, preterits and participles of verbs in* oll, *owl, ole and oal, as* rolled, cajoled, foaled, bowled, etc.

OLE.—Bole, dole, jole, hole, mole, pole, sole, stole, whole shole, etc., condole, parole, patrol, pistole, etc. *Perfect rhymes,* coal, foal, goal, etc., bowl, droll, prowl, roll, scroll, toll, troll, control, carroll, etc. *Allowable rhymes,* gull, dull, etc., bull, full, etc., loll, etc.

OLEN.—Stolen, swollen.

OLT.—Bolt, colt, jolt, holt, dolt, molt, revolt, thunderbolt. *Allowable rhymes,* vault, fault, salt, etc.

OLVE.—Solve, absolve, resolve, convolve, involve, devolve, dissolve revolve.

OM, *see* **UM.**

OME.—Loam, dome, home, tome. *Perfect rhymes,* foam, roam, comb. *Allowable rhymes,* dum, hum, come, bomb, etc., troublesome, etc. *See* **OOM.**

OMB, *see* **OOM. OMPT,** *see* **OUNT. ON,** *see* **UN.**

ON.—Don, on, con, upon, anon, etc. *Perfect rhymes,* gone underwent, etc. *Allowable rhymes,* dun, run, won, etc., own, moan, etc. *See* **OAN.** Amazon, cinnamon, comparison, caparison, garrison, skeleton, etc., upon.

OND.—Pond, bond, fond, beyond, abscond, correspond, despond, diamond, vagabond, etc., *and the preterits and participles of verbs in* on, *as* donned, conned, etc. *Allowable rhymes, the preterits and participles of verbs in* one, oan *and* un, *as* stoned, moaned, stunned, etc.

ONCE, *see* **UNCE.**

ONE.—Prone, bone, drone, throne, alone, stone, tone, lone, zone, atone, enthrone, dethrone, postpone, etc. *Perfect rhymes,* grown, flown, disown, thrown, sown, own, loan, shown, overthrown, groan, blown, moan, known. *Allowable rhymes,* dawn, lawn, etc., on, con, etc., none, bun, dun, etc., moon, boon, etc.

ONG.—Long, prong, song, thong, strong, throng, wrong, along, belong, prolong. *Allowable rhymes,* bung, among, hung, etc.

ONGUE, *see* **UNG. ONK,** *see* **UNK.**

ONSE.—Sconse, ensconce, etc. *Allowable rhymes,* once, nonce, askance, etc.

ONT.—Font. *Perfect rhyme,* want. *Allowable rhymes,* front, affront, etc., confront, punt, runt, etc., *the abbreviated negatives,* won't, don't, etc.

OO.—Coo, woo. *Nearly perfect rhymes,* shoe, two, too, who, etc., do, ado, undo, through, you, true, blue, flew, strew, etc. *Allowable rhymes,* know, blow, go, toe, etc.

OOD.—Brood, mood, food, rood, etc. *Nearly perfect rhymes, the preterits and participles of verbs in* oo, *as* cooed, wooed, etc. *Allowable rhymes,* wood, good, hood, stood, withstood, understood, brotherhood, livelihood, likelihood, neighborhood, widowhood, etc., blood, flood, etc., feud, allude, habitude, etc., *the preterits and participles of verbs in* ue *and* ew, *as* brewed, strewed, etc., imbued, subdued, etc., bud, mud, etc., *and the three apostrophized auxiliaries,* would, could, should, *pronounced* wou'd, cou'd, shou'd, etc., ode, code, *and the preterits and participles of verbs in* ow, *as* crowed, rowed, etc., *also* nod, hod, etc.

OOF.—Roof, proof, roof, woof, aloof, disproof, reproof, behoof. *Allowable rhymes,* huff, ruff, rough, enough, etc., off, scoff, etc.

OOK.—Book, brook, cook, crook, hook, look, rook, shook, took, mistook, undertook, forsook, betook. *Allowable rhymes,* puke, flake, etc., duck, luck, etc., broke, spoke, etc.

OOL.—Cool, fool, pool, school, stool, tool, befool. *Allowable rhymes,* pule, rule, etc., dull, gull, etc., bull, pull, etc., pole, hole, etc.

OOM.—Gloom, groom, loom, room, spoom, bloom, doom, etc. *Perfect rhymes,* tomb, entomb, *and the city* Rome. *Nearly perfect rhymes,* whom, womb, etc. *Allowable rhymes,* come, drum, etc., bomb, thumb, clomb, etc., plume, spume, etc., *and* from, home, comb, etc.

OON.—Boon, soon, moon, noon, spoon, swoon, buffoon, lampoon, poltroon. *Allowable rhymes,* tune, prune, etc., bun, dun, etc., gone, done, etc., bone, alone, etc., moan, roan, etc. *See* **ONE.**

OOP.—Loop, poop, scoop, stoop, troop, droop, whoop, coop, hoop, etc. *Perfect rhymes,* soup, group, etc. *Allowable rhymes,* dupe, up, sup, tup, etc., cop, top, etc., cope, hope, etc.

OOR.—Boor, poor, moor, etc. *Perfect rhymes,* tour, amour, paramour, contour. *Allowable rhymes,* bore, pore, etc., pure, sure, etc., your, pour, etc., door, floor, etc., bur, cur, etc., sir, stir, etc.

OOSE.—Goose, loose, etc. *Nearly perfect rhymes, the nouns* deuce, use, etc., profuse, seduce. *Allowable rhymes,* dose, jocose, globose, etc., moss, toss, etc., us, pus, thus, etc.

OOT.—Root, boot, coot, hoot, shoot. *Nearly perfect rhymes,* suit, fruit, etc., lute, impute, etc. *Allowable rhymes,* rote, vote, etc., goat, coat, etc., but, hut, soot, etc., foot, put, etc., hot, got, etc.

OOTH.—Booth, sooth, smooth. *Allowable rhymes,* tooth, youth, uncouth, forsooth, etc. *Though these are frequent, they are very improper rhymes, the* th *in one class being flat, and in the other sharp.*

OOZE.—Ooze, noose. *Perfect rhymes,* whose, choose, lose. *Nearly perfect rhymes, the verbs* to use, abuse, etc. *Allowable rhymes,* dose, hose, etc., buzz *and* does, *the third persons singular of* do, *with the plurals of nouns and third persons singular, present tense, of verbs in* ow, o, oo, ew, ue, *as* foes, goes, throws, views, imbues, flues, etc.

OP.—Chop, hop, drop, crop, fop, top, prop, flop, shop, slop, sop, stop, swap, underprop. *Allowable rhymes,* cope, trope, hope, etc., tup, sup, etc., coop, etc.

OPE.—Sope, hope, cope, mope, grope, pope, rope, scope, slope, tope, trope, aslope, elope, interlope, telescope, heliotrope, horoscope, antelope, etc., *and* ope, *contracted in poetry for* open. *Allowable rhymes,* hoop, coop, etc., lop, top, etc., tup, sup, etc.

OPT.—Adopt *rhymes perfectly with the preterits and participles of verbs in* op, *as* hopped, lopped, etc. *Allowable rhymes, the preterits and participles of verbs in* ope, upe, oop, *and* up, *as* coped, duped, hooped, cupped, etc.

OR.—Or, for, creditor, counselor, confessor, competitor, emperor, ancestor, ambassador, progenitor, conspirator, successor, conqueror, governor, abhor, metaphor, bachelor, senator, etc., *and every word in* or, *having the accent on the last, or last syllable but two, as* abhor, orator, etc. *Allowable rhymes,* bore, tore, etc., boar, hoar, etc., pure, endure, etc., pur, demur, etc., stir, sir, etc.

ORCH.—Scorch, torch, etc. *Allowable rhymes,* birch, smirch, church, etc., porch, etc.

ORCE.—Force, divorce, enforce, perforce, etc. *Perfect rhymes,* corse, coarse, hoarse, course, discourse, recourse, intercourse, source, resource, etc. *Allowable rhymes,* worse, purse, etc., horse, endorse, etc.

ORD.—Cord, lord, record, accord, abhorred. *Allowable rhymes,* hoard, board, aboard, ford, afford, sword, etc., word, curd, bird, etc., *and the preterits and participles of verbs in* ore, ur *and* ir, *as* bored, incurred, stirred, etc.

ORE.—Bore, core, gore, lore, more, ore, pore, score, shore, snore, sore, store, swore, tore, wore, adore, afore, ashore, deplore, explore, implore, restore, forbore, forswore, heretofore, hellebore, sycamore. *Perfect rhymes,* boar, oar, roar, soar, four, door, floor, *and* o'er *for* over. *Allowable rhymes,* hour, sour, etc., pow'r *for* power, show'r *for* shower, etc., bur, cur, etc., poor, your, etc., abhor, orator, senator, etc. *See* **OOR** *and* **OR.**

ORGE.—Gorge, disgorge, regorge, etc. *Allowable rhymes,* forge, urge, dirge, etc.

ORK.—Ork, cork, fork, stork, etc. *Allowable rhymes,* pork, work.

ORLD.—World *rhymes perfectly with the preterits and participles of verbs in* url, *as* hurled, curled, etc.

ORM and ARM.—Form, storm, conform, deform, inform, perform, reform, misinform, uniform, multiform, transform. *Allowable rhymes,* form (*a seat*) *and* worm.

ORN, *rhyming with* **HORN.**—Born, corn, morn, horn, scorn, thorn, adorn, suborn, unicorn, Capricorn. *Allowable rhymes, the participles* borne, (*suffered*) shorn, etc., *the verb* mourn, *the nouns* urn, turn, etc.

ORN, *rhyming with* **MORN.**—Born, shorn, torn, worn, lorn, love-lorn, sworn, forsworn, overborn, forlorn. *Perfect rhyme,* mourn. *Allowable rhymes,* born, corn, etc., urn, burn, etc.

ORSE, *see* **ORCE.**—Horse, endorse, unhorse. *Allowable rhymes,* worse, curse, etc., remorse, coarse, course, corse, etc.

ORST, *see* **URST. ORT,** *see* **ART.**

ORT, *rhyming with* **WART.**—Short, sort, exhort, consort, distort, extort, resort, retort, snort. *Allowable rhymes,* fort, court, port, report, etc., dirt, shirt, etc., wort, hurt, etc.

ORT, *rhyming with* **COURT.**—Fort, port, sport, comport, disport, export, import, support, transport, report. *Allowable rhymes,* short, sort, etc., dirt, hurt, etc.

ORTH.—Forth, fourth. *Allowable rhymes,* north, worth, birth, earth, etc.

OSE, (*sounded*) **OCE.**—Close, dose, jocose. *Perfect rhymes,* morose, gross, engross, verbose. *Allowable rhymes,* moss, cross, etc., us, thus, etc.

OSE (*sounded*) **OZE.**—Close, dose, hose, pose, chose, gloze, froze, nose, prose, those, rose, compose, depose, disclose, dispose, discompose, expose, impose, inclose, interpose, oppose, propose, recompose, repose, suppose, transpose, arose, presuppose, foreclose, etc., *and the plurals of nouns and apostrophized preterits and participles of verbs in* ow, oe, o, etc., *as* rows, glows, foes, goes, etc. *Allowable rhymes, the verbs* choose, lose, etc., *and the plurals of nouns and third persons singular of verbs in* ow, *rhyming with* now, *as* cows, *and the word* buzz.

OSS.—Boss, loss, cross, dross, moss, toss, across, emboss. *Allowable rhymes, the nouns* close, dose, jocose, etc., *and* us, thus, etc.

OST.—Cost, frost, lost, accost, etc., *and the preterits and participles of words in* oss, *as* mossed, embossed, etc., *the verb* exhaust, *and the noun* holocaust. *Allowable rhymes,* ghost, host, post, compost, most, etc., coast, boast, toast, etc., bust, must, etc., roost, *and the preterits and participles of verbs in* oose, *as* loosed, etc.

OT, *see* **AT.**—Clot, cot, blot, got, hot, jot, lot, knot, not, plot, pot, scot, shot, sot, spot, apricot, trot, rot, grot, begot, forgot, allot, besot, complot, counterplot. *Allowable rhymes,* note, vote, etc., boat, coat, etc., but, cut, etc.

OTCH.—Botch, notch, etc. *Perfect rhyme,* watch. *Allowable rhymes,* much, such, etc.

OTE.—Note, vote, mote, quote, rote, wrote, smote, denote, promote, remote, devote, anecdote, antidote, etc. *Perfect rhymes,* boat, coat, bloat, doat, gloat, float, goat, oat, overfloat, afloat, throat, moat. *Allowable rhymes,* bout, flout, etc., bot, cot, etc., but, cut, etc., boot, hoot, etc.

OTH.—Broth, cloth, froth, moth, troth, betroth. *Perfect rhyme,* wrath. *Allowable rhymes,* both, loth, sloth, oath, growth, etc., forsooth, *the noun* mouth, *and the solemn auxiliary* doth, *to which some poets add* loathe, clothe, *but I think improperly. See* **OOTH.**

OU, *see* **OO** *and* **OW. OUBT,** *see* **OUT.**

OUCH.—Couch, pouch, vouch, slouch, avouch, crouch. *Allowable rhymes,* much, such, etc., coach, roach, etc.

OUD.—Shroud, cloud, proud, loud, aloud, crowd, overshroud, etc., *and the preterits and participles of verbs in* ow, *as* be bowed, vowed, etc. *Allowable rhymes, the preterits and participles of verbs in* ow, *as* owed, flowed, etc., blood, flood, etc., bud, mud, etc.

OVE.—Wove, inwove, interwove, alcove, clove, grove, rove, stove, strove, throve, drove. *Allowable rhymes,* dove, love, shove, glove, above, etc., move, behoove, approve, disprove, disapprove, improve, groove, prove, reprove, etc.

OUGH, *see* **OFF, OW** *and* **UFF.**

OUGHT.—Bought, thought, ought, brought, forethought, fought, nought, sought, wrought, besought, bethought, methought, etc. *Perfect rhymes,* aught, naught, caught, taught, etc., *sometimes* draught. *Allowable rhymes,* not, yacht, etc., note, vote, etc., butt, hut, etc., hoot, root, etc.

OUL, *see* **OLE** *and* **OWL.**

OULD.—Mould. *Perfect rhymes,* fold, old, cold, etc., *and the preterits and participles of verbs in* owl, ol *and* ole, *as* bowled, tolled, cajoled, etc. *Allowable rhymes, the preterits and participles of verbs in* ull, *as* gulled, pulled, etc.

OUNCE.—Bounce, flounce, renounce, pounce, ounce, denounce, pronounce.

OUND.—Bound, found, mound, ground, hound, pound, round, sound, wound, abound, aground, around, confound, compound, expound, profound, rebound, redound, resound, propound, surround, etc., *and the preterits and participles of verbs in* own, *as* frowned, renowned, etc. *Allowable rhymes, the preterits and participles of verbs in* one, oan *and* un, *as* toned, moaned, sunned, etc., *consequently* fund, refund, etc., *and* wound (*a hurt*), *pronounced* woond.

OUNG, *see* **UNG.**

OUNT.—Count, mount, fount, amount, dismount, remount, surmount, account, discount, miscount. *Allowable rhymes,* want, font, don't, won't, etc.

OUP, *see* **OOP.**

OUR.—Hour, lour, sour, our, scour, deflour, devour, etc., *rhymes perfectly with* bower, cower, flower, power, shower, tower, etc., *pronounced* bow'r, tow'r, etc. *Allowable rhymes,* bore, more, roar, pour, four, moor, poor, etc., pure, sure, etc., sir, stir, bur, cur, etc.

OURGE, *see* **URGE. OURNE,** *see* **ORN** *and* **URN.**

OURS.—Ours *rhymes perfectly with the plurals of nouns and third persons present of verbs in* our *and* ower, *as* hours, scours, deflours, bowers, showers, etc. *Allowable rhymes, the plurals of nouns and third persons present of verbs in oor and ure, as boors, moors, etc., cures, endures, etc.*

OURS.—Yours *rhymes perfectly with the plurals of nouns and third persons present of verbs in ure, as cures, endures, etc. Allowable rhymes, ours, and its perfect rhymes and the plurals of nouns and third persons present of verbs in oor, ore and ur, as boors, moors, etc., shores, pores, etc., burs, slurs, stirs, etc.*

OURSE, see ORCE. OURT, see ORT. OURTH, see ORTH. OUS, see US.

OUS, pronounced OUCE.—House, mouse, chouse, etc. *Allowable rhymes, the nouns close, dose, joccee, etc., deuce, use, produce, etc., us, thus, etc., mooce, and the noun nooce.*

OUSE, pronounced OUZE, *see* OWZE.

OUT.—Bout, stout, out, clout, pout, gout, grout, route, scout, shout, snout, spout, stout, sprout, trout, about, devout, without, throughout, etc., *rhymes perfectly with doubt, redoubt, misdoubt, drought, etc. Allowable rhymes, note, vote, etc., boat, coat, etc., lute, suit, etc., got, not, etc., hut, shut, hoot, boot, etc.*

OUTH.—Mouth, south, *when nouns have the th sharp. The verbs to mouth, to south, may allowably rhyme with booth, smooth, etc., which see.*

OW, *sounded* OU.—Now, how, how, mow, cow, brow, plow, sow, vow, prow, avow, allow, disallow, endow, etc. *Perfect rhymes, bough, plough, slough, (mire), etc., thou. Allowable rhymes, go, no, blow, so, etc.*

OW, *sounded* OWE.—Blow, stow, crow, bow, flow, glow, grow, know, low, mow, row, show, sow, strow, stow, slow, snow, throw, trow, below, bestow, foreknow, outgrow, overgrow, overthrow, reflow, foreshow, etc. *Perfect rhymes, go, ho, toe, foe, owe, wo, oh, lo, lo, though, hoe, ho, ago, forego, undergo, dough, roe, sloe, and the verb to sew (with the needle). Allowable rhymes, now, cow, vow, do, etc. See the last article.*

OWL, see OLE.—Cowl, growl, owl, fowl, howl, prowl, etc. *Perfect rhymes, scowl, foul, etc. Allowable rhymes, bowl, soul, shoal, goal, etc., dull, gull, etc.*

OWN, see ONE.—Brown, town, clown, crown, down, drown, frown, gown, adown, renown, embrown, etc. *Perfect rhyme, noun. Allowable rhymes, tone, bone, moan, own, and the participles thrown, shown, blown.*

OWSE, see OUSE.—Blouse. *Perfect rhymes, brouse, trouse, rouse, spouse, carouse, souse, espouse, the verbs to house, mouse, etc., and the plurals of nouns and third persons, present tense, of verbs in ow, as brows, allows, etc. Allowable rhymes, hose, those, to dose, etc.*

OX.—Ox, box, fox, equinox, orthodox, heterodox, etc. *Perfect rhymes, the preterits of nouns and third persons present of verbs in ock, as locks, stocks, etc. Allowable rhymes, the plurals of nouns and third persons present of verbs in oke, oak, and uck, as strokes, oaks, cloaks, sucks, etc.*

OY.—Boy, buoy, coy, employ, deploy, joy, toy, alloy, annoy, convoy, decoy, destroy, enjoy, employ.

OZE, see OSE.

U

UB.—Cub, club, dub, drub, grub, rub, snub, shrub, tub. *Allowable rhymes, cube, tube, etc., oob, rob, etc.*

UBE.—Cube, tube. *Allowable rhymes, club, cub, etc.*

UCE.—Truce, sluice, spruce, deuce, conduce, deduce, induce, introduce, produce, seduce, traduce, juice, reduce, etc., *rhyme perfectly with the nouns use, abuse, profuse, abstruse, disuse, excuse, misuse, obtuse, recluse.*

UCH, see UTCH.

UCK.—Buck, luck, pluck, suck, struck, tuck, truck, duck. *Allowable rhymes, puke, duke, etc., lock, took, etc.*

UCT.—Conduct, deduct, instruct, obstruct, aqueduct. *Perfect rhymes, the preterits and participles of verbs in uck, as ducked, sucked, etc. Allowable rhymes, the preterits and participles of verbs in uke and ook, as puked, hooked, etc.*

UD.—Bud, scud, stud, mud, cud, *rhyme perfectly with blood and flood. Allowable rhymes, good, hood, etc., rood, food, etc., beatitude, latitude.*

UDE.—Rude, crude, prude, allude, conclude, delude, elude, exclude, exude, include, intrude, obtrude, seclude, altitude, fortitude, gratitude, interlude, latitude, longitude, magnitude, multitude, solicitude, solitude, victimitude, aptitude, habitude, ingratitude, inaptitude, lassitude, plenitude, promptitude, servitude, similitude, etc. *Perfect rhymes, lewd, feud, etc., and the preterits and participles of verbs in ew, as stewed, viewed, etc. Allowable rhymes, bud, cud, etc., good, hood, etc., blood, flood, etc.*

UDGE.—Judge, drudge, grudge, trudge, adjudge, prejudge.

UE, see EW.

UFF.—Buff, cuff, bluff, huff, gruff, luff, puff, snuff, stuff, ruff, rebuff, counterbuff, etc. *Allowable rhymes, rough, tough, enough, slough (cast skin), chough, etc. Allowable rhymes, loaf, oaf, etc.*

UFT.—Tuft. *Perfect rhymes, the preterits and participles of verbs in uff, as cuffed, stuffed.*

UG.—Lug, bug, dug, drug, hug, rug, slug, snug, mug, shrug, pug. *Allowable rhymes, vogue, rogue, etc.*

UICE, see USE. UISE, see ISE and USE, see IE.

UKE.—Duke, puke, rebuke, etc. *Nearly perfect rhymes, cook, look, book, etc. Allowable rhymes, duck, buck, etc.*

UL and ULL.—Cull, dull, gull, hull, lull, mull, null, trull, skull, annul, disannul. *Allowable rhymes, fool, tool, etc., wool, bull, pull, full, bountiful, fanciful, sorrowful, dutiful, merciful, wonderful, worshipful, and every word ending in ful, having the accent on the antepenultimate syllable.*

ULE.—Mule, pule, yule, rule, overrule, ridicule, misrule. *Allowable rhymes, cull, dull, wool, full, bountiful. See the last article.*

ULGE.—Bulge, indulge, divulge, etc.

ULK.—Bulk, hulk, skulk.

ULSE.—Pulse, repulse, impulse, expulse, convulse.

ULT.—Result, adult, exult, consult, insult, occult, insult, difficult. *Allowable rhymes, colt, bolt, etc.*

UM.—Crum, drum, grum, gum, hum, mum, scum, plum, stum, sum, swum, thrum. *Perfect rhymes, thumb, dumb, succumb, come, become, overcome burthensome, cumbersome, frolicsome, humorsome, quarrelsome,*

troublesome, martyrdom, christendom. *Allowable rhymes, fume, plume, rheum, and room, doom, tomb, hecatomb*

UME.—Fume, plume, assume, consume, perfume, resume, presume, plume.

UMP.—Bump, pump, jump, lump, plump, trump, stump, rump, thump, p

UN.—Dun, sun, nun, pun, run, sun, shun, tun, stun, spun, begun. *Perfect rhymes, son, won, ton, done, one, none, undone. Allowable rhymes on, gone, etc., tune, prune, etc. See ON.*

UNCE.—Dunce, once, etc. *Allowable rhyme, sconce.*

UNCH.—Bunch, punch, hunch, lunch, munch.

UND.—Fund, refund. *Perfect rhymes, the preterits and participles of verbs in un, as shunned, etc.*

UNE.—June, rune, untune, jejune, prune, importune, etc. *Nearly perfect rhymes, moon, soon, etc. Allowable rhymes, bun, dun, etc.*

UNG.—Clung, dung, flung, hung, rung, strung, sung, sprung, slung, stung, swung, unsung. *Perfect rhymes, young, tongue, among. Allowable rhymes, song, long, etc.*

UNGE.—Plunge, spunge, expunge, etc.

UNK.—Drunk, sunk, shrunk, stunk, spunk, punk, trunk, stunk. *Perfect rhymes, monk.*

UNT.—Brunt, blunt, hunt, runt, grunt. *Perfect rhymes, wont (to be accustomed).*

UP.—Cup, sup, up. *Allowable rhymes, rope, scope, and dupe group.*

UPT.—Abrupt, corrupt, interrupt. *Perfect rhymes, the participles of verbs in up, as supped, etc.*

UR.—Blur, cur, bur, fur, slur, spur, concur, demur, incur. *Perfect rhymes, sir, stir. Nearly perfect rhymes, fir, etc. Allowable rhymes, pure oar, etc.*

URB.—Curb, disturb. *Nearly perfect rhymes, verb, herb, etc. Allowable rhyme, orb.*

URCH.—Church, lurch, birch. *Nearly perfect rhymes, perch, search. Allowable rhymes, perch.*

URD.—Curd, absurd. *Perfect rhymes, bird, word, and the preterits and participles of verbs in ur, as spurred. Allowable rhymes, board, ford — lord, etc., and the preterits and participles of verbs in ore, oar and ur as geared, oared, abhorred, etc., also the preterits and participles of verbs in ire, as aired, insnared, etc. See OED.*

URE.—Cure, pure, dure, lure, sure, adjure, allure, assure, demure m-a jure, endure, manure, enure, insure, immature, immure, mature, obscure, procure, secure, calenture, coverture, epicure, investiture, forfeiture, furniture, miniature, overture, portraiture, primogeniture, temperature *Allowable rhymes, poor, moor, power, sour, etc., cur, bur, etc.*

URF.—Turf, scurf, etc.

URGE.—Purge, urge, surge, scourge. *Perfect rhymes, verge, diverge, etc. Allowable rhymes, gorge, George, etc., forge, etc*

URK.—Lurk, Turk. *Perfect rhyme, work. Nearly perfect rhymes irk, jerk, perk.*

URL, see IRL.—Churl, curl, furl, hurl, purl, uncurl, unfurl. *Nearly perfect rhymes, girl, twirl, etc., pearl, etc.*

URN.—Burn, churn, spurn, turn, urn, return, overturn. *Perfect rhymes, sojourn, adjourn, rejourn.*

URSE.—Nurse, curse, purse, accurse, disburse, imburse, reimburse. *Perfect rhyme, worse Allowable rhymes, coarse, corse, force, verse, disperse, horse, etc.*

URST.—Burst, curst, accurst, etc. *Perfect rhymes, thirst, worst, first.*

URT.—Blurt, hurt, spurt. *Perfect rhymes, dirt, shirt, flirt, squirt, etc Allowable rhymes, port, court, short, sport, etc.*

US.—Us, thus, buss, truss, discuss, incubus, overplus, amorous, boisterous, clamorous, credulous, dangerous, degenerous, generous, garrulous, fabulous, frivolous, hazardous, idolatrous, infamous, miraculous, marvellous, mountainous, mutinous, necessitous, numerous, ominous, perilous, poisonous, populous, prosperous, ridiculous, riotous, ruinous, scandalous, scrupulous, sedulous, traitorous, treacherous, tyrannous, venemous, villainous, vigorous, adventurous, adulterous, ambiguous, blasphemous, dolorous, tumultuous, sonorous, gluttonous, gratuitous, lascivious, lecherous, libidinous, magnanimous, obstreperous, odoriferous, ponderous, ravenous, rumpidus, slanderous, solicitous, timorous, valorous, unanimous, calamitous Allowable rhymes, the nouns use, abuse, diffuse, excuse the verb to loose, and the nouns goose, deuce, juice, truce, etc. close, dose, hoses, moose, etc.*

USE, *with the* S *pure.*—The nouns use, disuse, abuse, deuce, truce. *Perfect rhymes, the verb to loose, the nouns goose, noose, moose. Allowable rhymes, us, thus, buss, etc.*

USE *(sounded)* UZE.—Muse, *the verbs to use, abuse, accuse, diffuse, excuse, infuse, misuse, peruse, refuse, suffuse, transfuse, accuse Perfect rhymes, bruise, the plurals of nouns and third persons singular of verbs in ew and ue, as dews, imbues, etc. Allowable rhymes, buzz, does etc*

USH.—Blush, brush, crush, gush, flush, rush, hush. *Allowable rhymes, bush, push.*

USK.—Dusk, tusk, dusk, husk, musk.

UST.—Bust, crust, dust, just, must, lust, rust, thrust, trust, adjust, adust, disgust, distrust, intrust, mistrust, unjust, robust. *Perfect rhymes, the preterits and participles of verbs in use, as trussed, discussed, etc.*

UT.—But, butt, cut, hut, gut, glut, jut, nut, shut, strut, engrut, rut, scut, slut, smut, abut. *Perfect rhyme, soot. Allowable rhymes, but doe dispute, etc., boot, etc.*

UTCH.—Hutch, crutch, Dutch. *Perfect rhymes, much, such, touch.*

UTE.—Brute, lute, flute, mute, acute, compute, confute, dispute, dilute depute, impute, minute, pollute, refute, repute, salute, absolute, attribute, constitute, destitute, dissolute, execute, institute, irresolute, persecute, prosecute, prostitute, resolute, substitute. *Perfect rhymes, fruit, recruit, etc. Allowable rhymes, boot, etc., boat, etc., note, etc., but, etc*

UX.—Flux, redux, crux. *Perfect rhymes, the plurals of nouns and third persons of verbs in uck, as ducks, trucks, etc. Allowable rhymes, the plurals of nouns and third persons of verbs in ook, uke, oak, etc., as cooks, pukes, oaks, etc.*

Y, see IE.

CHOICE
Selections
FROM
THE POETS.

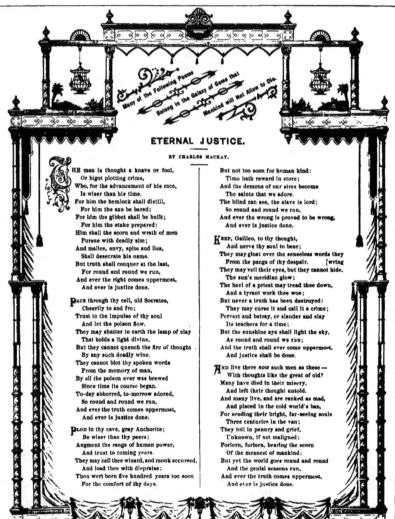

Many of the Following Poems Belong in the Galaxy of Gems that Mankind will Not Allow to Die.

ETERNAL JUSTICE.

BY CHARLES MACKAY.

THE man is thought a knave or fool,
  Or bigot plotting crime,
Who, for the advancement of his race,
  Is wiser than his time.
For him the hemlock shall distill,
  For him the axe be bared;
For him the gibbet shall be built;
  For him the stake prepared:
Him shall the scorn and wrath of men
  Pursue with deadly aim;
And malice, envy, spite and lies,
  Shall desecrate his name.
But truth shall conquer at the last,
  For round and round we run,
And ever the right comes uppermost,
  And ever is justice done.

PACE through thy cell, old Socrates,
  Cheerily to and fro;
Trust to the impulse of thy soul
  And let the poison flow.
They may shatter to earth the lamp of clay
  That holds a light divine,
But they cannot quench the fire of thought
  By any such deadly wine.
They cannot blot thy spoken words
  From the memory of man,
By all the poison ever was brewed
  Since time its course began.
To-day abhorred, to-morrow adored,
  So round and round we run,
And ever the truth comes uppermost,
  And ever is justice done.

PLOD in thy cave, gray Anchorite;
  Be wiser than thy peers;
Augment the range of human power,
  And trust to coming years.
They may call thee wizard, and monk accursed,
  And load thee with dispraise;
Thou wert born five hundred years too soon
  For the comfort of thy days.

But not too soon for human kind:
  Time hath reward in store;
And the demons of our sires become
  The saints that we adore.
The blind can see, the slave is lord;
  So round and round we run,
And ever the wrong is proved to be wrong,
  And ever is justice done.

KEEP, Galileo, to thy thought,
  And nerve thy soul to bear;
They may gloat over the senseless words they
  From the pangs of thy despair.   [wring
They may veil their eyes, but they cannot hide,
  The sun's meridian glow;
The heel of a priest may tread thee down,
  And a tyrant work thee woe;
But never a truth has been destroyed:
  They may curse it and call it a crime;
Pervert and betray, or slander and slay
  Its teachers for a time;
But the sunshine aye shall light the sky,
  As round and round we run;
And the truth shall ever come uppermost,
  And justice shall be done.

AND live there *now* such men as these —
  With thoughts like the great of old?
Many have died in their misery,
  And left their thought untold.
And many live, and are ranked as mad,
  And placed in the cold world's ban,
For sending their bright, far-seeing souls
  Three centuries in the van;
They toil in penury and grief,
  Unknown, if not maligned;
Forlorn, forlorn, bearing the scorn
  Of the meanest of mankind;
But yet the world goes round and round
  And the genial seasons run,
And ever the truth comes uppermost,
  And ever is justice done.

HEREAFTER.

LAND beyond the setting sun!
 O realm more fair than poet's
    dream!
How clear thy silvery streamlets run,
How bright thy golden glories
    gleam!

Earth holds no counterpart of thine;
 The dark-browed Orient, jewel-
    crowned,
Pales, as she bows before thy shrine,
 Shrouded in mystery so profound.

The dazzling North, the stately West,
 Whose rivers flow from mount to sea;
The South, flower-wreathed in languid rest,
 What are they all compared with thee?

All lands, all realms beneath yon dome,
 Where God's own hand hath hung the stars,
To thee with humblest homage come,
 O world beyond the crystal bars!

Thou blest hereafter! Mortal tongue
 Hath striven in vain thy speech to learn,
And fancy wanders, lost among
 The flowery paths for which we yearn.

But well we know, that fair and bright,
 Far beyond human ken or dream,
Too glorious for our feeble sight,
 Thy skies of cloudless azure beam.

We know thy happy valleys lie
 In green repose, supremely blest;
We know against thy sapphire sky
 Thy mountain peaks sublimely rest.

And sometimes even now we catch
 Faint gleamings from the far-off shore,
And still with eager eyes we watch
 For one sweet sign or token more.

For oh, the deeply loved are there!
 The brave, the fair, the good, the wise,
Who pined for thy serener air,
 Nor shunned thy solemn mysteries.

There are the hopes that, one by one,
 Died even as we gave them birth;
The dreams that passed ere well begun,
 Too dear, too beautiful for earth.

The aspirations, strong of wing,
 Aiming at heights we could not reach;
The songs we tried in vain to sing;
 Thoughts too vast for human speech;

Thou hast them all, Hereafter! Thou
 Shalt keep them safely till that hour
When, with God's seal on heart and brow,
 We claim them in immortal power!

NEVER AGAIN.

NEVER again will the roses blow
 For us as the roses we used to know.

Oh! never again will the wide sky hold
Such wealth of glory and sunset gold;

And never again will I whisper, dear,
The pleasant fancies you smiled to hear;

And never again, at the day's decline,
Shall I sit with your little hand in mine,

And look at the beauty of sunset skies,
And the sweeter beauty of your sweet eyes.

Never again! for the dream is done
That a word, and a look, and a touch begun.

Love, if we *always* could dream, ah, then!
The words are as sad as "it might have been!"

For us, there is nothing but memory,
In the coming days, *of what could not be!*

Love, you are near me, and yet as far
As the round earth is from the fartherest star.

Kiss me and smile in my eyes once more,
Tho' your lips should quiver, and tears run o'er.

Put your hand in mine for one moment, one,
And then, good-bye, for the dream is done!

HANNAH JANE.

BY PETROLEUM V. NASBY.

HE isn't half so handsome as when, twenty
years agone,
At her old home in Piketon, Parson Avery
made us one;
The great house crowded full of guests of
every degree,
The girls all envying Hannah Jane, the
boys all envying me.

Her fingers then were taper, and her skin as white as milk,
Her brown hair—what a mess it was! and soft and fine as silk;
No wind-moved willow by a brook had ever such a grace,
The form of Aphrodite, with a pure Madonna face.

She had but meagre schooling; her little notes, to me,
Were full of crooked pot-hooks, and the worst orthography;
Her "dear" she spelled with double e, and "kiss" with but one s;
But when one's crazed with passion, what's a letter more or less?

She blundered in her writing, and she blundered when she spoke,
And every rule of syntax, that old Murray made, she broke;
But she was beautiful and fresh, and I—well, I was young;
Her form and face o'erbalanced all the blunders of her tongue.

I was but little better. True, I'd longer been at school;
My tongue and pen were run, perhaps, a little more by rule;
But that was all. The neighbors round, who both of us well knew,
Said—which I believed—she was the better of the two.

All's changed: the light of seventeen 's no longer in her eyes;
Her wavy hair is gone—that loss the coiffeur's art supplies;
Her form is thin and angular; she slightly forward bends;
Her fingers, once so shapely, now are stumpy at the ends.

She knows but very little, and in little are we one;
The beauty rare, that more than hid that great defect, is gone.
My parvenu relations now deride my homely wife,
And pity me that I am tied, to such a clod, for life.

I know there is a difference; at reception and levee,
The brightest, wittiest, and most famed of women smile on me;
And everywhere I hold my place among the greatest men;
And sometimes sigh, with Whittier's judge, "Alas! it might have
been."

When they all crowd around me, stately dames and brilliant belles,
And yield to me the homage that all great success compels,
Discussing art and state-craft, and literature as well,
From Homer down to Thackeray, and Swedenborg on "Hell,"

I can't forget that from these streams my wife has never quaffed,
Has never with Ophelia wept, nor with Jack Falstaff laughed;
Of authors, actors, artists—why, she hardly knows the names;
She slept while I was speaking on the *Alabama* claims.

I can't forget—just at this point another form appears—
The wife I wedded as she was before my prosperous years;
I travel o'er the dreary road we traveled side by side,
And wonder what my share would be, if Justice should divide.

She had four hundred dollars left her from the old estate;
On that we married, and, thus poorly armored, faced our fate.
I wrestled with my books; her task was harder far than mine—
'Twas how to make two hundred dollars do the work of nine.

At last I was admitted; then I had my legal lore,
An office with a stove and desk, of books perhaps a score;
She had her beauty and her youth, and some housewifely skill,
And love for me and faith in me, and back of that a will.

I had no friends behind me—no influence to aid;
I worked and fought for every little inch of ground I made.
And how she fought beside me! never woman lived on less;
In two long years she never spent a single cent for dress.

Ah! how she cried for joy when my first legal fight was won,
When our eclipse passed partly by, and we stood in the sun:
The fee was fifty dollars—'t was the work of half a year—
First captive, lean and scraggy, of my legal bow and spear.

I well remember when my coat (the only one I had)
Was seedy grown and threadbare, and, in fact, most shocking bad,
The tailor's stern remark when I a modest order made:
"Cash is the basis, sir, on which we tailors do our trade."

Her winter cloak was in his shop by noon that very day;
She wrought on hickory shirts at night that tailor's skill to pay;
I got a coat, and wore it; but alas! poor Hannah Jane
Ne'er went to church or lecture till warm weather came again.

Our second season she refused a cloak of any sort,
That I might have a decent suit in which t' appear in court.
She made her last year's bonnet do, that I might have a hat:
Talk of the old-time, flame-enveloped martyrs after that!

No negro ever worked so hard: a servant's pay to save,
She made herself most willingly a household drudge and slave.
What wonder that she never read a magazine or book,
Combining as she did in one, nurse, house maid, seamstress, cook.

What wonder that the beauty fled, that I once so adored!
Her beautiful complexion my fierce kitchen fire devoured;
Her plump, soft, rounded arm was once too fair to be concealed;
Hard work for me that softness into sinewy strength congealed.

I was her altar, and her love the sacrificial flame:
Ah! with what pure devotion she to that altar came,
And, tearful, flung thereon—alas! I did not know it then—
All that she was, and more than that, all that she might have been!

At last I won success. Ah! then our lives were wider parted:
I was far up the rising road; she, poor girl! where we started.
I had tried my speed and mettle, and gained strength in every race;
I was far up the heights of life—she drudging at the base.

She made me take each fall the stump; she said 't was my career;
The wild applause of list'ning crowds was music to my ear.
What stimulus had she to cheer her dreary solitude?
For me she lived on gladly, in unnatural widowhood.

She couldn't read my speech, but when the papers all agreed
'T was the best one of the session, those comments she could read;
And with a gush of pride thereat, which I had never felt,
She sent them to me in a note, with half the words misspelt.

I to the legislature went, and said that she should go
To see the world with me, and, what the world was doing, know
With tearful smile she answered, "No! four dollars is the pay;
The Bates House rates for board *for one* is just that sum per day."

At twenty-eight the State-house; on the bench at thirty-three;
At forty every gate in life was opened wide to me.

I nursed my powers, and grew, and made my point in life; but she—
Bearing such pack-horse weary loads, what could a woman be?

What could she be? Oh, shame! I blush to think what she has been,
The most unselfish of all wives to the selfishest of men.
Yes, plain and homely now she is; she's ignorant, 't is true;
For me she rubbed herself quite out; I represent the two.

Well, I suppose that I might do as other men have done—
First break her heart with cold neglect, then shove her out alone.
The world would say 't was well, and more, would give great
      praise to me,
For having borne with "such a wife" so uncomplainingly.

And shall I? No! The contract 'twixt Hannah, God and me,
Was not for one or twenty years, but for eternity.
No matter what the world may think; I know, down in my heart,
That, if either, I'm delinquent; she has bravely done her part.

There's another world beyond this; and, on the final day,
Will intellect and learning 'gainst such devotion weigh?
When the great one, made of us two, is torn apart again,
I'll fare the worst, for God is just, and He knows Hannah Jane.

THE MOTHERLESS TURKEYS.

BY MARIAN DOUGLASS.

THE white turkey was dead! The white turkey
      was dead!
      How the news through the barn-yard went
      flying!
Of a mother bereft, four small turkeys were
      left,
      And their case for assistance was crying.
E'en the peacock respectfully folded his tail,
As a suitable symbol of sorrow,
And his plainer wife said, "now the old bird is dead,
Who will tend her poor chicks on the morrow?
And when evening around them comes dreary and chill,
Who above them will watchfully hover?"
"Two each night I will tuck 'neath my wings," said the Duck,
"Though I have eight of my own I must cover!"
"I have so much to do! For the bugs and the worms,
In the garden, 't is tiresome pickin';
I've nothing to spare—for my own I must care,"
Said then the Hen with one chicken.

"How I wish," said the Goose, "I could be of some use,
For my heart is with love over-brimming:

The next morning that's fine, they shall go with my nine
      Little yellow-backed goslings, out swimming' "
"I will do what I can," the old Dorking put in,
      "And for help they may call upon me too,
Though I've ten of my own that are only half grown,
      And a great deal of trouble to see to;
But these poor little things, they are all head and wings,
      And their bones through their feathers are stickin'! "
"Very hard it may be, but, Oh, don't come to me!"
      Said the Hen with one chicken.

Half my care, I suppose, there is nobody knows,
      I'm the most over-burdened of mothers!
They must learn, little elves! how to scratch for themselves,
      And not seek to depend upon others."
She went by with a cluck, and the Goose to the Duck
      Exclaimed with surprise, "Well, I never! "
Said the Duck, "I declare, those who have the least care,
      You will find are complaining forever!
And when all things appear to look threatening and drear,
      And when troubles your pathway are thick in,
For some aid in your woe, Oh, beware how you go
      To a Hen with one chicken."

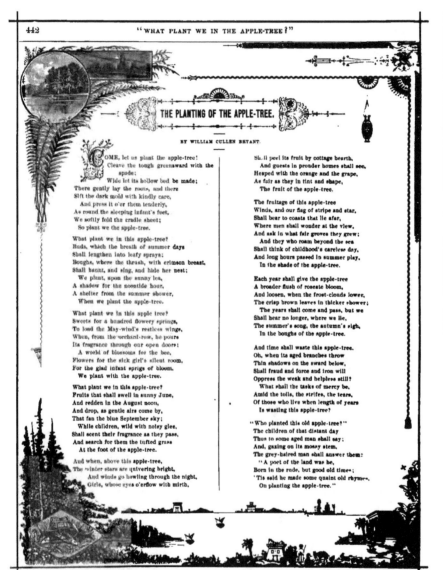

THE PLANTING OF THE APPLE-TREE.

BY WILLIAM CULLEN BRYANT.

COME, let us plant the apple-tree!
Cleave the tough greensward with the
spade;
    Wide let its hollow bed be made;
There gently lay the roots, and there
Sift the dark mold with kindly care,
And press it o'er them tenderly,
As round the sleeping infant's feet,
We softly fold the cradle sheet;
    So plant we the apple-tree.

What plant we in this apple-tree?
Buds, which the breath of summer days
Shall lengthen into leafy sprays;
Boughs, where the thrush, with crimson breast,
Shall haunt, and sing, and hide her nest;
    We plant, upon the sunny lea,
A shadow for the noontide hour,
A shelter from the summer shower,
    When we plant the apple-tree.

What plant we in this apple tree?
Sweets for a hundred flowery springs,
To load the May-wind's restless wings,
When, from the orchard-row, he pours
Its fragrance through our open doors;
    A world of blossoms for the bee,
Flowers for the sick girl's silent room,
For the glad infant sprigs of bloom,
    We plant with the apple-tree.

What plant we in this apple-tree?
Fruits that shall swell in sunny June,
And redden in the August noon,
And drop, as gentle airs come by,
That fan the blue September sky;
    While children, wild with noisy glee,
Shall scent their fragrance as they pass,
And search for them the tufted grass
    At the foot of the apple-tree.

And when, above this apple-tree,
The winter stars are quivering bright,
    And winds go howling through the night,
Girls, whose eyes o'erflow with mirth,

Shall peel its fruit by cottage hearth,
    And guests in prouder homes shall see,
Heaped with the orange and the grape,
As fair as they in tint and shape,
    The fruit of the apple-tree.

The fruitage of this apple-tree
Winds, and our flag of stripe and star,
Shall bear to coasts that lie afar,
Where men shall wonder at the view,
And ask in what fair groves they grew;
    And they who roam beyond the sea
Shall think of childhood's careless day,
And long hours passed in summer play,
    In the shade of the apple-tree.

Each year shall give the apple-tree
A broader flush of roseate bloom,
And loosen, when the frost-clouds lower,
The crisp brown leaves in thicker shower;
    The years shall come and pass, but we
Shall hear no longer, where we lie,
The summer's song, the autumn's sigh,
    In the boughs of the apple-tree.

And time shall waste this apple-tree.
Oh, when its aged branches throw
Thin shadows on the sward below,
Shall fraud and force and iron will
Oppress the weak and helpless still?
    What shall the tasks of mercy be,
Amid the toils, the strifes, the tears,
Of those who live when length of years
    Is wasting this apple-tree?

"Who planted this old apple-tree?"
The children of that distant day
Thus to some aged man shall say;
And, gazing on its mossy stem,
The grey-haired man shall answer them:
    "A poet of the land was he,
Born in the rude, but good old times;
'Tis said he made some quaint old rhymes,
    On planting the apple-tree."

The Old Oaken Bucket.

BY SAMUEL WOODWORTH.

HOW dear to this heart are the scenes of my childhood,
When fond recollection presents them to view!
The orchard, the meadow, the deep-tangled wildwood,
And every loved spot which my infancy knew!
The wide-spreading pond, and the mill that stood by it;
The bridge, and the rock where the cataract fell;
The cot of my father, the dairy-house nigh it,
And e'en the rude bucket that hung in the well:
The old oaken bucket, the iron-bound bucket,
The moss-covered bucket which hung in the well.

That moss-covered vessel I hailed as a treasure;
For often at noon, when returned from the field,
I found it the source of an exquisite pleasure,
The purest and sweetest that nature can yield.
How ardent I seized it, with hands that were glowing,

" The old oaken bucket, the iron-bound bucket,
The moss-covered bucket which hung in the well."

And quick to the white-pebbled bottom it fell!
Then soon, with the emblem of truth overflowing,
And dripping with coolness, it rose from the well:
The old oaken bucket, the iron-bound bucket,
The moss-covered bucket, arose from the well.

How sweet from the green, mossy brim to receive it,
As, poised on the curb, it inclined to my lips!
Not a full, blushing goblet could tempt me to leave it,
The brightest that beauty or revelry sips.
And now far removed from the loved habitation,
The tear of regret will intrusively swell,
As fancy reverts to my father's plantation,
And sighs for the bucket that hangs in the well:
The old oaken bucket, the iron-bound bucket,
The moss-covered bucket that hangs in the well.

BETSEY AND I ARE OUT.

BY WILL M. CARLETON.

DRAW up the papers, lawyer, and make 'em good and stout;
For things at home are cross-ways, and Betsey and I are out.
We who have worked together so long as man and wife,
Must pull in single harness the rest of our nat'ral life.

"What is the matter?" say you.   I vow! it's hard to tell:
Most of the years behind us we've passed by very well;
I have no other woman—she has no other man,
Only we've lived together as long as ever we can.

So I've talked with Betsey, and Betsey has talked with me;
And we've agreed together that we can't never agree;
Not that we've catched each other in any terrible crime;
We've been a gatherin' this for years, a little at a time.

There was a stock of temper we both had for a start;
Although we ne'er suspected 'twould take us two apart'
I had my various failings, bred in the flesh and bone,
And Betsey, like all good women, had a temper of her own.

The first thing I remember whereon we disagreed,
Was somethin' concerning heaven—a difference in our creed.
We arg'ed the thing at breakfast—we arg'ed the thing at tea—
And the more we arg'ed the question, the more we didn't agree.

And the next that I remember was when we lost a cow;
She kicked the bucket, certain—the question was only—How?
I held my own opinion, and Betsey another had;
And when we were done a talkin', we both of us was mad.

And the next that I remember, it started in a joke;
But full for a week it lasted, and neither of us spoke.
And the next was when I scolded because she broke a bowl;
And she said I was mean and stingy, and hadn't any soul.

And so that bowl kept pouring dissensions in our cup;
And so that blamed cow-critter was always a comin' up;
And so that heaven we arg'ed no nearer to us got;
But it gave us a taste of somethin' a thousand times as hot.

And so the thing kept workin', and all the self-same way;
Always somethin' to arg'e, and somethin' sharp to say.
And down on us come the neighbors, a couple dozen strong,
And lent their kindest service for to help the thing along.

And there has been days together—and many a weary week,
We was both of us cross and spunky, and both too proud to speak,
And I have been thinkin' and thinkin' the whole of the winter and fall,
If I can't live kind with a woman, why, then I won't at all.

And so I have talked with Betsey, and Betsey has talked with me,
And we've agreed together that we can't never agree;

And what is hers shall be hers, and what is mine shall be mine;
And I'll put it in the agreement, and take it to her to sign.

Write on the paper, lawyer—the very first paragraph—
Of all the farm and live stock, that she shall have her half;
For she has helped to earn it, through many a dreary day.
And it's nothing more than justice that Betsey has her pay.

Give her the house and homestead; a man can thrive and roam,
But women are skeery critters, unless they have a home.
And I have always determined, and never failed to say,
That Betsey never should want a home, if I was taken away.

There's a little hard money that's drawin' tol'rable pay;
A couple of hundred dollars laid by for a rainy day;
Safe in the hands of good men, and easy to get at;
Put in another clause, there, and give her half of that;

Yes, I see you smile, sir, at my givin' her so much;
Yes, divorce is cheap, sir, but I take no stock in such.
True and fair I married her, when she was blithe and young;
And Betsey was al'ays good to me, except with her tongue.

Once, when I was young as you, and not so smart, perhaps,
For me she mittened a lawyer, and several other chaps;
And all of 'em was flustered and fairly taken down,
And I for a time was counted the luckiest man in town.

Once, when I had a fever—I won't forget it soon—
I was hot as a basted turkey and crazy as a loon—
Never an hour went by when she was out of sight;
She nursed me true and tender, and stuck to me day and night.

And if ever a house was tidy, and ever a kitchen clean,
Her house and kitchen was as tidy as any I ever seen;
And I don't complain of Betsey or any of her acts,
Exceptin' when we've quarrelled and told each other facts.

So draw up the paper, lawyer; and I'll go home to-night,
And read the agreement to her and see if it's all right.
And then in the mornin' I'll sell to a tradin' man I know—
And kiss the child that was left to us, and out in the world I'll go.

And one thing put in the paper, that first to me didn't occur—
That when I'm dead at last, she shall bring me back to her.
And lay me under the maples I planted years ago,
When she and I was happy, before we quarrelled so.

And when she dies, I wish that she would be laid by me;
And lyin' together in silence, perhaps we will agree;
And if ever we meet in heaven, I wouldn't think it queer
If we loved each other the better because we quarrelled here.

HOW BETSEY AND I MADE UP.

BY WILL M. CARLETON.

IVE us your hand, Mr. Lawyer: how do you do to-day?
You drew up that paper—I s'pose you want your pay.
Don't cut down your figures; make it an X or a V;
For that 'ere written agreement was just the makin' of me.

Goin' home that evenin' I tell you I was blue,
Thinkin' of all my troubles, and what I was goin' to do;
And if my hosses hadn't been the steadiest team alive,
They'd 've tipped me over, certain, for I couldn't see where to
    drive.

No—for I was laborin' under a heavy load;
No—for I was travelin' an entirely different road;
For I was a-tracin' over the path of our lives ag'in,
And seein' where we missed the way, and where we might have
    been.

And many a corner we'd turned that just to quarrel led,
When I ought to've held my temper, and driven straight ahead;
And the more I thought it over the more these memories came,
And the more I struck the opinion that I was the most to blame.

And things I had long forgotten kept risin' in my mind,
Of little matters betwixt us, where Betsey was good and kind;
And these things flashed all through me, as you know things
    sometimes will
When a feller's alone in the darkness, and everything is still.

"But," says I, "we're too far along to take another track,
And when I put my hand to the plow I do not oft turn back;
And tain't an uncommon thing now for couples to smash in two;"
And so I set my teeth together, and vowed I'd see it through.

When I come in sight o' the house 'twas some'at in the night,
And just as I turned a hill-top I see the kitchen light;
Which often a han'some pictur' to a hungry person makes,
But it don't interest a feller much that's goin' to pull up stakes.

And when I went in the house, the table was set for me—
As good a supper 's I ever saw, or ever want to see;
And I crammed the agreement down my pocket as well as I could,
And fell to eatin' my victuals, which somehow didn't taste good.

And Betsey, she pretended to look about the house,
But she watched my side coat-pocket like a cat would watch a
    mouse;
And then she went to foolin' a little with a cup,
And intently readin' a newspaper, a-holdin' it wrong side up.

And when I'd done my supper, I drawed the agreement out,
And give it to her without a word, for she knowed what 'twas
    about;
And then I hummed a little tune, but now and then a note
Was bu'sted by some animal that hopped up in my throat.

Then Betsey, she got her specs from off the mantel-shelf,
And read the article over quite softly to herself;
Read it by little and little, for her eyes is gettin' old,
And lawyers' writin' ain't no print, especially when its cold.

And after she'd read a little, she gave my arm a touch,
And kindly said she was afraid I was 'lowin' her too much;
But when she was through she went for me, her face a-streamin'
    with tears,
And kissed me for the first time in over twenty years!

I don't know what you'll think, Sir—I didn't come to inquire—
But I picked up that agreement and stuffed it in the fire;
And I told her we'd bury the hatchet alongside of the cow;
And we struck an agreement never to have another row.

And I told her in the future I wouldn't speak cross or rash
If half the crockery in the house was broken all to smash;
And she said, in regards to heaven, we'd try to learn its worth
By startin' a branch establishment and runnin' it here on earth.

And so we sat a-talkin' three-quarters of the night,
And opened our hearts to each other until they both grew light;
And the days when I was winnin' her away from so many men
Was nothin' to that evenin' I courted her over again.

Next mornin' an ancient virgin took pains to call on us,
Her lamp all trimmed and a-burnin' to kindle another fuss;
But when she went to pryin' and openin' of old sores,
My Betsey rose politely, and showed her out-of-doors.

Since then I don't deny but there's been a word or two;
But we've got our eyes wide open, and know just what to do;
When one speaks cross the other just meets it with a laugh,
And the first one's ready to give up considerable more than half.

Maybe you'll think me soft, Sir, a-talkin' in this style,
But somehow it does me lots of good to tell it once in a while;
And I do it for a compliment—'tis so that you can see
That that there written agreement of yours was just the makin'
    of me.

So make out your bill, Mr. Lawyer: don't stop short of an X;
Make it more if you want to, for I have got the checks.
I'm richer than a National Bank, with all its treasures told,
For I've got a wife at home now that's worth her weight in gold.

Maud Muller.

BY JOHN G. WHITTIER.

MAUD MULLER, on a summer's day,
Raked the meadow, sweet with hay.

Beneath her torn hat glowed the wealth
Of simple beauty and rustic health.

The sweet song died, and a vague unrest
And a nameless longing filled her breast—

A wish, that she hardly dared to own,
For something better than she had known.

"Maud Muller, on a summer's day,
Raked the meadow, sweet with hay."

Singing, she wrought, and her merry glee
The mock-bird echoed from his tree.

But, when she glanced to the far-off town,
White from its hill-slope looking down,

The Judge rode slowly down the lane,
Smoothing his horse's chestnut mane.

He drew his bridle in the shade
Of the apple-trees to greet the maid,

She stooped where the cool spring bubbles up
And filled for him her small tin cup.

And blushed as she gave it, looking down
On her feet so bare, and her tattered gown.

"Thanks!" said the Judge, "a sweeter draught
From a fairer hand was never quaffed."

He spoke of the grass and flowers and trees,
Of the singing birds and the humming bees;

Then talked of the haying, and wondered whether
The cloud in the west would bring foul weather.

And Maud forgot her brier-torn gown,
And her graceful ankles bare and brown,

And listened, while a pleased surprise
Looked from her long-lashed, hazel eyes.

At last, like one who for delay
Seeks a vain excuse, he rode away.

Maud Muller looked and sighed: "Ah me!
That I the Judge's bride might be!

"He would dress me up in silks so fine,
And praise and toast me at his wine.

"My father would wear a broadcloth coat;
My brother should sail a painted boat.

"I'd dress my mother so grand and gay;
And the baby should have a new toy each day.

"And I'd feed the hungry and clothe the poor,
And all should bless me who left our door."

The Judge looked back as he climbed the hill,
And saw Maud Muller standing still:

"A form more fair, a face more sweet,
Ne'er hath it been my lot to meet.

"And her modest answer and graceful air
Show her wise and good as she is fair.

"Would she were mine, and I to-day,
Like her, a harvester of hay.

"No doubtful balance of rights and wrongs,
No weary lawyers with endless tongues,

"But low of cattle, and song of birds,
And health, and quiet, and loving words."

But he thought of his sister, proud and cold,
And his mother, vain of her rank and gold.

So, closing his heart, the Judge rode on,
And Maud was left in the field alone.

But the lawyers smiled that afternoon,
When he hummed in court an old love-tune.

And the young girl mused beside the well,
Till the rain on the unraked clover fell.

He wedded a wife of richest dower,
Who lived for fashion, as he for power.

Yet oft, in his marble hearth's white glow,
He watched a picture come and go;

And sweet Maud Muller's hazel eyes
Looked out in their innocent surprise.

Oft, when the wine in his glass was red,
He longed for the wayside well instead,

And closed his eyes on his garnished rooms,
To dream of meadows and clover-blooms;

And the proud man sighed with a secret pain,
"Ah, that I were free again!

"Free as when I rode that day
Where the barefoot maiden raked the hay."

*" But low of cattle, and song of birds,
And health, and quiet, and loving words."*

She wedded a man unlearned and poor,
And many children played round her door.

But care and sorrow, and child birth pain,
Left their traces on heart and brain.

And oft, when the summer sun shone hot
On the new-mown hay in the meadow lot,

And she heard the little spring brook fall
Over the roadside, through the wall,

In the shade of the apple-tree again
She saw a rider draw his rein,

And, gazing down with timid
    grace,
She felt his pleased eyes read her
    face.

Sometimes her narrow kitchen
    walls
Stretched away into stately halls;

The weary wheel to a spinnet
    turned,
The tallow candle an astral burned;

And for him who sat by the chim
    ney lug,
Dozing and grumbling o'er pipe
    and mug,

A manly form at her side she saw,
    And joy was duty and love was law.

"*And she heard the little spring-brook fall
Over the roadside, through the wall.*"

Then she took up her burden of life again,
    Saying only, "It might have been"

Alas for maiden, alas for Judge,
For rich repiner and household
    drudge!

God pity them both! and pity us
    all,
Who vainly the dreams of youth
    recall;

For of all sad words of tongue or
    pen,
The saddest are these: "It might
    have been!"

Ah, well! for us all some sweet
    hope lies
Deeply buried from human eyes;

And, in the hereafter, angels
    may
Roll the stone from its grave away!

ABSENCE.

BY FRANCES ANNE KEMBLE.

WHAT shall I do with all the days and hours
    That must be counted, ere I see thy face?
How shall I charm the interval that lowers
    Between this time and that sweet time of grace?

Shall I in slumber steep each weary sense—
    Weary with longing? Shall I flee away
Into past days, and with some fond pretense
    Cheat myself to forget the present day?

Shall love for thee lay on my soul the sin
    Of casting from me God's great gift of time?
Shall I, these mists of memory locked within,
    Leave and forget life's purposes sublime?

Oh, how, or by what means, may I contrive
    To bring the hour that brings thee back more near?
How may I teach my drooping hope to live
    Until that blessed time, and thou art here?

I'll tell thee; for thy sake, I will lay hold
    Of all good aims, and consecrate to thee,
In worthy deeds, each moment that is told,
    While thou, beloved one! art far from me.

For thee, I will arouse my thoughts to try
    All heavenward flights, all high and holy strains;
For thy dear sake, I will walk patiently
    Through these long hours, nor call their minutes pains.

I will this dreary blank of absence make
    A noble task-time; and will therein strive
To follow excellence, and to o'ertake
    More good than I have won since yet I live.

So may this doomed time build up in me
    A thousand graces, which shall thus be thine;
So may my love and longing hallowed be,
    And thy dear thought an influence divine.

THE LOST STEAMSHIP.

BY FITZ-JAMES O'BRIEN.

HO, THERE! fisherman, hold your hand!
    Tell me what is that far away—
        There, where over the Isle of Sand
        Hangs the mist-cloud sullen and gray?
Ses! it rocks with a ghastly life,
    Raising and rolling through clouds of spray,
    Right in the midst of the breakers' strife—
    Tell me, what is it, fisherman, pray?

"That, good sir, was a steamer, stout
    As ever paddled around Cape Race,
And many's the wild and stormy bout
    She had with the wind in that self-same place;
But her time had come; and at ten o'clock
    Last night she struck on that lonesome shore,
And her sides were gnawed by the hidden rock,
    And at dawn this morning she was no more."

"Come, as you seem to know, good man,
    The terrible fate of this gallant ship,
Tell me all about her that you can,—
    And here's my flask to moisten your lip.
Tell me how many she had on board—
    Wives and husbands, and lovers true—
How did it fare with her human hoard,
    Lost she many, or lost she few?"

"Master, I may not drink of your flask,
    Already too moist I feel my lip;
But I'm ready to do what else you ask,
    And spin you my yarn about the ship:
'Twas ten o'clock, as I said, last night,
    When she struck the breakers and went ashore,
And scarce had broken the morning's light,
    Than she sank in twelve feet of water, or more.

"But long ere this they knew their doom,
    And the captain called all hands to prayer;
And solemnly over the ocean's boom
    The orisons rose on the troubled air:
And round about the vessel there rose
    Tall plumes of spray as white as snow,
Like angels in their ascension clothes,
    Waiting for those who prayed below.

"So those three hundred people clung,
    As well as they could, to spar and rope;
With a word of prayer upon every tongue,
    Nor on any face a glimmer of hope.

But there was no blubbering weak and wild
    Of tearful faces I saw but one,
A rough old salt, who cried like a child,
    And not for himself, but the Captain's son.

"The Captain stood on the quarter-deck,
    Firm but pale, with trumpet in hand.
Sometimes he looked on the breaking wreck,
    Sometimes he sadly looked on land.
And often he smiled to cheer the crew—
    But, Lord! the smile was terrible grim—
Till over the quarter a huge sea flew,
    And that was the last they saw of him.

"I saw one young fellow, with his bride,
    Standing amidships upon the wreck;
His face was white as the boiling tide,
    And she was clinging about his neck.
And I saw them try to say good-bye,
    But neither could hear the other speak;
So they floated away through the sea to die—
    Shoulder to shoulder, and cheek to cheek.

"And there was a child, but eight at best,
    Who went his way in a sea we shipped,
All the while holding upon his breast
    A little pet parrot, whose wings were clipped.
And as the boy and the bird went by,
    Swinging away on a tall wave's crest,
They were grappled by a man with a drowning cry,
    And together the three went down to rest.

"And so the crew went one by one,
    Some with gladness, and few with fear;
Cold and hardship such work had done,
    That few seemed frightened when death was near.
Thus every soul on board went down—
    Sailor and passenger, little and great;
The last that sunk was a man of my town,
    A capital swimmer—the second mate."

"Now, lonely fisherman, who are you,
    That say you saw this terrible wreck?
How do I know what you say is true,
    When every mortal was swept from the deck?
Where were you in that hour of death?
    How do you know what you relate?"
His answer came in an underbreath—
    "Master, I was the second mate!"

A WISH FOR THEE

BY JOHN G. C. BRAINARD.

I SAW two clouds at morning,
Tinged by the
rising sun,
And in the
dawn they
floated
on,
And mingled
into one:
I thought that morning
cloud was blest,
It moved so sweetly to
the west.

I saw two summer cur-
rents
Flow smoothly to their
meeting,
And join their course
with silent force,

In peace each other greeting;
Calm was their course
through banks of
green,
While dimpling eddies
played between.

Such be your gentle
motion,
Till life's last pulse
shall beat;
Like summer's beam,
and summer's stream,
Float on in joy, to meet
A calmer sea, where
storms shall cease,
A purer sky, where all
is peace.

"I saw two clouds at morning, tinged by the rising sun."

THE SCULPTOR BOY.

CHISEL in hand stood a sculptor boy,
  With his marble block before him: —
And his face lit up with a smile of joy
  As an angel dream passed o'er him.
He carved that dream on the yielding stone
  With many a sharp incision;
In heaven's own light the sculptor shone,
  He had caught that angel vision.

Sculptors of life are we, as we stand,
  With our lives uncarved before us;
Waiting the hour when, at God's command,
  Our life dream passes o'er us.
Let us carve it then on the yielding stone,
  With many a sharp incision:—
Its heavenly beauty shall be our own—
  Our lives, that angel vision.

LITTLE AND GREAT.

BY CHARLES MACKAY.

A TRAVELER, through a dusty road,
  Strewed acorns on the lea;
And one took root and sprouted up,
  And grew into a tree.
Love sought its shade at evening time,
  To breathe his early vows;
And Age was pleased, in heats of noon,
  To bask beneath its boughs.
The dormouse loved its dangling twigs,
  The birds sweet music bore;
It stood a glory in its place,
  A blessing evermore.

A little spring had lost its way
  Amid the grass and fern;
A passing stranger scooped a well,
  Where weary men might turn.
He walled it in, and hung with care
  A ladle at the brink:
He thought not of the deed he did,
  But judged that Toil might drink.
He passed again—and lo! the well,
  By summers never dried,
Had cooled ten thousand parching tongues,
  And saved a life beside.

"And Age was pleased, in heats of noon, to bask beneath its boughs."

A dreamer dropped a random thought;
  'Twas old—and yet 'twas new;
A simple fancy of the brain,
  But strong in being true.
It shone upon a genial mind,
  And lo! its light became
A lamp of life, a beacon ray,
  A monitory flame.
The thought was small—its issue great;
  A watch-fire on the hill,
It sheds its radiance far adown,
  And cheers the valley still.

A nameless man, amid a crowd
  That thronged the daily mart,
Let fall a word of hope and love,
  Unstudied, from the heart.
A whisper on the tumult thrown,
  A transitory breath,
It raised a brother from the dust,
  It saved a soul from death.
O germ! O fount! O word of love!
  O thought at random cast!
Ye were but little at the first,
  But mighty at the last!

THERE IS NO SUCH THING AS DEATH.

THERE is no such thing as death—
  In nature nothing dies;
From each sad remnant of decay
  Some forms of life arise.

The little leaf that falls
  All brown and sere to earth,
Ere long will mingle with the buds
  That give the flower its birth.

THE VAGABONDS.

BY J. T. TROWBRIDGE.

WE ARE two travelers, Roger and I.
  Roger's my dog—Come here, you scamp!
Jump for the gentleman,—mind your eye!
  Over the table,—look out for the lamp!—
The rogue is growing a little old;
Five years we've tramped through wind and weather,
And slept out-doors when nights were cold,
  And ate and drank—and starved—together.

We've learned what comfort is, I tell you!
  A bed on the floor, a bit of rosin,
A bit of fire to thaw our thumbs (poor fellow!
  The paw he holds up there's been frozen,)
Plenty of catgut for my fiddle,
  (This out-door business is bad for strings,)
Then a few nice buckwheats, hot from the griddle,
  And Roger and I set up for kings!

No, thank ye, sir,—I never drink;
  Roger and I are exceedingly moral—
Aren't we Roger?—See him wink!
  Well, something hot, then, we won't quarrel,
He's thirsty, too, see him nod his head!
  What a pity, sir, that dogs can't talk!
He understands every word that's said,—
  And he knows good milk from water-and-chalk.

The truth is, sir, now I reflect,
  I've been so sadly given to grog,
I wonder I've not lost the respect
  (Here's to you, sir!) even of my dog;
But he sticks by, through thick and thin;
  And this old coat, with its empty pockets
And rags that smell of tobacco and gin,
  He'll follow while he has eyes in his sockets.

There isn't another creature living
  Would do it, and prove through every disaster,
So fond, so faithful, and so forgiving,
  To such a miserable, thankless master!
No, sir!—see him wag his tail and grin!
  By George! it makes my old eyes water—
That is, there's something in this gin
  That chokes a fellow. But no matter!

We'll have some music, if you're willing,
  And Roger (hem! what a plague a cough is, sir!)
Shall march a little.—Start, you villain!
  Stand straight! 'Bout face! Salute your officer!
Put up that paw! Dress! Take your rifle!
  (Some dogs have arms, you see!) Now hold your
Cap while the gentleman gives a trifle,
  To aid a poor, old, patriot soldier!

March! Halt! Now show how the rebel shakes
  When he stands up to hear his sentence.
Now tell us how many drams it takes
  To honor a jolly new acquaintance.
Five yelps,—that's five; he's mighty knowing!
  The night's before us, fill the glasses!—
Quick, sir! I'm ill,—my brain is going!—
  Some brandy,—thank you,—there, it passes.

Why not reform? That's easily said;
  But I've gone through such wretched treatment,
Sometimes forgetting the taste of bread,
  And scarce remembering what meat meant,
That my poor stomach's past reform;
  And there are times when, mad with thinking,
I'd sell out heaven for something warm,
  To prop a horrible inward sinking.

Is there a way to forget to think?
  At your age, sir, home, fortune, friends,
A dear girl's love,—but I took to drink;—
  The same old story; you know how it ends.
If you could have seen these classic features,
  You needn't laugh, sir; they were not then
Such a burning libel on God's creatures;
  I was one of your handsome men!

If you had seen HER, so fair and young,
  Whose head was happy on this breast!
If you could have heard the song I sung
  When the wine went round, you wouldn't have guessed
That ever I, sir, should be straying,
  From door to door, with fiddle and dog,
Ragged and penniless, and playing
  To you to-night for a glass of grog!

She's married since,—a parson's wife:
  'Twas better for her that we should part,
Better the soberest, prosiest life
  Than a blasted home and a broken heart.
Have I seen her? Once: I was weak and spent
  On a dusty road: a carriage stopped:
But little she dreamed as on she went,
  Who kissed the coin that her fingers dropped!

You've set me talking, sir, I'm sorry;
  It makes me wild to think of the change!
What do you care for a beggar's story?
  Is it amusing? You find it strange?
I had a mother so proud of me!
  'Twas well she died before—Do you know
If the happy spirits in heaven can see
  The ruin and wretchedness here below?

Another glass, and strong, to deaden
  This pain; then Roger and I will start.
I wonder, has he such a lumpish, leaden,
  Aching thing, in place of a heart?
He is sad sometimes, and would weep if he could,
  No doubt remembering things that were,—
A virtuous kennel, with plenty of food,
  And himself a respectable cur.

I'm better now; that glass was warming.
  You rascal! limber your lazy feet!
We must be fiddling and performing
  For supper and bed, or starve in the street.
Not a very gay life to lead, you think?
  But soon we shall go where lodgings are free,
And the sleepers need neither victuals nor drink;
  The sooner the better for Roger and me!

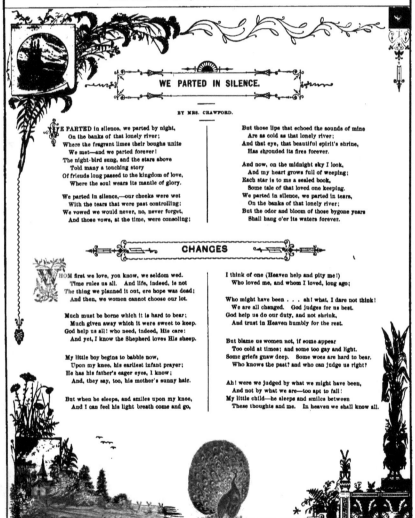

WE PARTED IN SILENCE.

BY MRS. CRAWFORD.

WE PARTED in silence, we parted by night,
  On the banks of that lonely river;
Where the fragrant limes their boughs unite
  We met—and we parted forever!
The night-bird sung, and the stars above
  Told many a touching story
Of friends long passed to the kingdom of love,
  Where the soul wears its mantle of glory.

We parted in silence,—our cheeks were wet
  With the tears that were past controlling:
We vowed we would never, no, never forget,
  And those vows, at the time, were consoling;

But those lips that echoed the sounds of mine
  Are as cold as that lonely river;
And that eye, that beautiful spirit's shrine,
  Has shrouded its fires forever.

And now, on the midnight sky I look,
  And my heart grows full of weeping;
Each star is to me a sealed book,
  Some tale of that loved one keeping.
We parted in silence, we parted in tears,
  On the banks of that lonely river;
But the odor and bloom of those bygone years
  Shall hang o'er its waters forever.

CHANGES

WHOM first we love, you know, we seldom wed.
  Time rules us all.   And life, indeed, is not
The thing we planned it out, ere hope was dead;
  And then, we women cannot choose our lot.

Much must be borne which it is hard to bear;
  Much given away which it were sweet to keep.
God help us all! who need, indeed, His care:
  And yet, I know the Shepherd loves His sheep.

My little boy begins to babble now,
  Upon my knee, his earliest infant prayer;
He has his father's eager eyes, I know;
  And, they say, too, his mother's sunny hair.

But when he sleeps, and smiles upon my knee,
  And I can feel his light breath come and go,

I think of one (Heaven help and pity me!)
  Who loved me, and whom I loved, long ago;

Who might have been . . . ah! what, I dare not think!
  We are all changed.   God judges for us best.
God help us do our duty, and not shrink,
  And trust in Heaven humbly for the rest.

But blame us women not, if some appear
  Too cold at times; and some too gay and light.
Some griefs gnaw deep.   Some woes are hard to bear.
  Who knows the past? and who can judge us right?

Ah! were we judged by what we might have been,
  And not by what we are—too apt to fall!
My little child—he sleeps and smiles between
  These thoughts and me.   In heaven we shall know all.

HANNAH BINDING SHOES.

BY LUCY LARCOM.

POOR lone Hannah,
  Sitting at the window, binding shoes!
    Faded, wrinkled,
  Sitting, stitching, in a mournful muse!
    Bright-eyed beauty once was she,
    When the bloom was on the tree.
      Spring and winter
  Hannah's at the window, binding shoes.

    Not a neighbor
  Passing nod or answer will refuse
    To her whisper:
  "Is there from the fishers any news?"
    O, her heart's adrift with one
    On an endless voyage gone!
      Night and morning
  Hannah's at the window, binding shoes.

    Fair young Hannah,
  Ben, the sun-burnt fisher, gayly woos;
    Hale and clever,
  For a willing heart and hand he sues.
    May-day skies are all a-glow,
    And the waves are laughing so!
      For her wedding
  Hannah leaves her window and her shoes.

    May is passing:
  'Mid the apple-boughs a pigeon coos.
    Hannah shudders;
  For the mild southwester mischief brews.
    Round the rocks of Marblehead,
    Outward bound, a schooner sped.
      Silent, lonesome,
  Hannah's at the window, binding shoes.

    'Tis November;
  Now no tear her wasted cheek bedews.
    From Newfoundland
  Not a sail returning will she lose.
    Whispering, hoarsely, "Fishermen,
    Have you, have you heard of Ben?"
      Old with watching,
  Hannah's at the window, binding shoes.

    Twenty winters
  Bleach and tear the ragged shore she views:
    Twenty seasons;
  Never one has brought her any news.
    Still her dim eyes silently
    Chase the white sails o'er the sea.
      Hopeless, faithful,
  Hannah's at the window, binding shoes.

LULLABY.

BY ALFRED TENNYSON.

WEET and low, sweet and low,
　　Wind of the western sea!
Low, low, breathe and blow,
　　Wind of the western sea!
Over the rolling waters go;
Come from the dying moon, and blow,
　　Blow him again to me;
While my little one, while my pretty one sleeps.

Sleep and rest, sleep and rest!
　　Father will come to thee soon.
Rest, rest on mother's breast;
　　Father will come to thee soon!
Father will come to his babe in the nest;
Silver sails all out of the west,
　　Under the silver moon.
Sleep, my little one! sleep, my pretty one, sleep!

ROCK ME TO SLEEP, MOTHER.

BY FLORENCE PERCY.

BACKWARD, turn backward, O Time, in your flight,
Make me a child again, just for to-night!
Mother, come back from the echoless shore,
Take me again to your heart as of yore;
Kiss from my forehead the furrows of care,
Smooth the few silver threads out of my hair;
Over my slumbers your loving watch keep—
Rock me to sleep, mother—rock me to sleep!

Backward, flow backward, O tide of the years!
I am so weary of toil and of tears—
Toil without recompense—tears all in vain—
Take them, and give me childhood again!
I have grown weary of dust and decay—
Weary of flinging my soul-wealth away;
Weary of sowing for others to reap—
Rock me to sleep, mother—rock me to sleep!

Tired of the hollow, the base, the untrue,
Mother, O Mother, my heart calls for you:
Many a summer the grass has grown green,
Blossomed and faded, our faces between;
Yet with strong yearning, and passionate pain,
Long I to-night for your presence again.
Come from the silence so long and so deep—
Rock me to sleep, mother—rock me to sleep!

Over my heart, in the days that are flown,
No love like a mother's love ever has shone
No other worship abides and endures—
Faithful, unselfish, and patient like yours;
None like a mother can charm away pain
From the sick soul and the world-weary brain.
Slumber's soft calm o'er my heavy lids creep—
Rock me to sleep, mother—rock me to sleep!

Come, let your brown hair just lighted with gold,
Fall on your shoulders again as of old;
Let it drop over my forehead to-night,
Shading my faint eyes away from the light;
For with its sunny-edged shadows once more
Happy will throng the sweet visions of yore—
Lovingly, softly, its bright billows sweep—
Rock me to sleep, mother—rock me to sleep!

Mother, dear mother, the years have been long
Since I last listened to your lullaby song;
Sing, then, and unto my heart it shall seem
Womanhood's years have been only a dream.
Clasped to your heart in a loving embrace,
With your light lashes just sweeping my face,
Never hereafter to wake or to weep—
Rock me to sleep, mother—rock me to sleep!

THE EVENING BELLS.

BY THOMAS MOORE.

WHOSE evening bells, those evening
    bells!
  How many a tale their music tells
Of youth, and home, and native clime,
When I last heard their soothing chime!

Those pleasant hours have passed away,
And many a heart that then was gay,

Within the tomb now darkly dwells,
And hears no more those evening bells.

And so it will be when I am gone:
That tuneful peal will still ring on,
When other bards shall walk these dells
And sing your praise, sweet evening bells.

A MESSAGE.

BY EBEN E. REXFORD.

YOU ARE dying, my friend!
  Your bark will go drifting, ere breaking of day,
Toward the shores lying over the shadowy bay;
And at morn you will see, rising fair through the
    mist,
    The hills which the sunshine eternal has kissed.

You are going away!
You will meet on the shores, which your vessel will find,
Dear friends who sailed outward, and left us behind;
You will know them, and clasp them, and kiss them once
    more,
Grown young again there, on the beautiful shore.

Dear friend, when you meet
The woman I loved, on the shore far away,
Will you give her the message I give you to-day?
You will know her, I know, by her face, that was fair
    As the face of an angel, and beautiful hair.

And her eyes, like a star,
In a clear summer night, shining out through the
    dew,

Falling down, like a kiss, from the furthermost blue.
And her voice, when she greets you, you'll know as of old,
Her voice, and her face in its tresses of gold.

O, tell her, my friend,
That I miss her so much since she left me that night,
When the mists of the sea drifted over my sight,
And hid her in shadows, so dense and so deep,
That, remembering the time, even now I must weep.

And tell her for me,
That I wait for the morn, which for her has begun,
When our ways, which were severed on earth, shall be one:
I shall come to her, over the wide solemn sea,
And clasp her, and claim her—that tell her for me.

Friend, you will not forget?
Already your bark is afloat on the tide,
That shall bear you out over the waters so wide;
At morn you will see her, and tell her for me,
That I love her, I miss her, this side of the sea.

THERE'S BUT ONE PAIR OF STOCKINGS
TO MEND TO-NIGHT.

AN OLD wife sat by her bright fireside,
  Swaying thoughtfully to and fro,
In an ancient chair whose creaky frame
  Told a tale of long ago;
While down by her side, on the kitchen floor,
Stood a basket of worsted balls—a score.

The good man dozed o'er the latest news,
  Till the light of his pipe went out,
And, unheeded, the kitten, with cunning paws,
  Rolled and tangled the balls about;
Yet still sat the wife in the ancient chair,
Swaying to and fro in the fire-light glare.

But anon a misty tear-drop came
  In her eye of faded blue,
Then trickled down in a furrow deep,
  Like a single drop of dew;
So deep was the channel—so silent the stream,
The good man saw naught but the dimmed eye-beam.

Yet he marvelled much that the cheerful light
  Of her eye had weary grown,
And marvelled he more at the tangled balls;
  So he said in a gentle tone:
"I have shared thy joys since our marriage vow,
Conceal not from me thy sorrows now."

Then she spoke of the time when the basket there
  Was filled to the very brim,
And how there remained of the goodly pile
  But a single pair—for him.
"Then wonder not at the dimmed eye-light,
There's but one pair of stockings to mend to-night.

"I cannot but think of the busy feet,
  Whose wrappings were wont to lie
In the basket, awaiting the needle's time,

Now wandered so far away;
How the sprightly steps, to a mother dear,
Unheeded fell on the careless ear.

"For each empty nook in the basket old,
  By the hearth there's a vacant seat!
And I miss the shadows from off the wall,
  And the patter of many feet;
'Tis for this that a tear gathered over my sight
At the one pair of stockings to mend to-night.

"'Twas said that far through the forest wild,
  And over the mountains bold,
Was a land whose rivers and dark'ning caves
  Were gemmed with the rarest gold;
Then my first-born turned from the oaken door,
And I knew the shadows were only four.

"Another went forth on the foaming waves
  And diminished the basket's store—
But his feet grew cold—so weary and cold—
  They'll never be warm any more—
And this nook, in its emptiness, seemeth to me
To give forth no voice but the moan of the sea.

"Two others have gone toward the setting sun,
  And made them a home in its light,
And fairy fingers have taken their share
  To mend by the fireside bright;
Some other baskets their garments fill—
But mine! Oh, mine is emptier still.

"Another—the dearest—the fairest—the best—
  Was ta'en by the angels away,
And clad in a garment that waxeth not old,
  In a land of continual day.
Oh! wonder no more at the dimmed eye-light,
While I mend the one pair of stockings to-night."

YOU AND I.

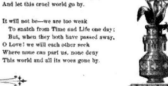

IF we could leave this world behind—
  Its gains and loss, its praise and blame,
  Nor seeking place, nor fearing shame,
Some fair land quite forgotten find,
We might be happy, you and I,
And let this foolish world go by.

No paradise of love and bliss,
  No dreams of youth in Eden bowers,
  But some dear home of quiet hours,

Where all of life we would not miss,
But find some day sweet ere we die,
And let this cruel world go by.

It will not be—we are too weak
  To snatch from Time and Life one day;
  But, when they both have passed away,
O Love! we will each other seek
Where none can part us, none deny
This world and all its woes gone by.

A SNOW-STORM.

BY CHARLES G. EASTMAN.

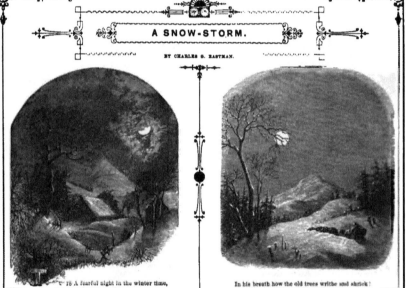

'T IS A fearful night in the winter time,
  As cold as it ever can be;
The roar of the blast is heard, like the chime
  Of the waves on an angry sea;
The moon is full, but her silver light
The storm dashes out with its wings to-night;
And over the sky from south to north
Not a star is seen, as the wind comes forth
  In the strength of a mighty glee.

All day had the snow come down—all day,
  As it never came down before;
And over the hills, at sunset, lay
  Some two or three feet or more;
The fence was lost, and the wall of stone,
The windows blocked, and the well-curbs gone;
The haystack had grown to a mountain lift,
And the woodpile looked like a monster drift,
  As it lay by the farmer's door.

The night sets in on a world of snow,
  While the air grows sharp and chill,
And the warning roar of a fearful blow
  Is heard on the distant hill;
And the Norther! See—on the mountain peak,

In his breath how the old trees writhe and shriek!
He shouts on the plain, Ho, ho, Ho, ho!
He drives from his nostrils the blinding snow,
  And growls with a savage will.

Such a night as this to be found abroad,
  In the drifts and the freezing air,
Sits a shivering dog in the field by the road,
  With the snow in his shaggy hair!
He shuts his eyes to the wind, and growls;
He lifts his head and moans and howls;
Then crouching low from the cutting sleet,
His nose is pressed on his quivering feet:
  Pray, what does the dog do there?

A farmer came from the village plain,
  But he lost the traveled way;
And for hours he trod, with might and main,
  A path for his horse and sleigh;
But colder still the cold wind blew,
And deeper still the deep drifts grew,
And his mare, a beautiful Morgan brown,
At last in her struggles floundered down,
  Where a log in a hollow lay.

In vain, with a neigh and a frenzied snort,
  She plunged in the drifting snow,
While her master urged, till his breath grew short,
  With a word and a gentle blow;
But the snow was deep, and the tugs were tight,
His hands were numb, and had lost their might;
So he wallowed back to his half-filled sleigh,
And strove to shelter himself till day,
   With his coat and the buffalo.

He has given the last faint jerk of the rein
  To rouse up his dying steed,
And the poor dog howls to the blast in vain,
  For help in his master's need;
For a while he strives, with a wistful cry,
To catch a glance from his drowsy eye,
And wags his tail if the rude winds flap
The skirt of the buffalo over his lap,
   And whines when he takes no heed.

The wind goes down, and the storm is o'er:
  'Tis the hour of midnight past;
The old trees writhe and bend no more
  In the whirl of the rushing blast;
The silent moon, with her peaceful light,
Looks down on the hills, with snow all white;
And the giant shadow of Camel's Hump,
The blasted pine and the ghostly stump,
   Afar on the plain are cast.

But cold and dead, by the hidden log,
  Are they who came from the town:
The man in his sleigh, and his faithful dog,
  And his beautiful Morgan brown—
In the wide snow-desert, far and grand,
With his cap on his head, and the reins in his hand,
The dog with his nose on his master's feet,
And the mare half seen through the crusted sleet,
   Where she lay when she floundered down.

LITTLE FEET.

BY FLORENCE PERCY.

TWO little feet so small that both may nestle
  In one caressing hand—
Two tender feet upon the untried border
  Of life's mysterious land;

Dimpled and soft, and pink as peach-tree blossoms
  In April's fragrant days—
How can they walk among the briery tangles
  Edging the world's rough ways?

These white-rose feet, along the doubtful future,
  Must bear a woman's load;
Alas! since woman has the heaviest burden,
  And walks the hardest road.

Love, for a while, will make the path before them
  All dainty, smooth and fair—
Will cull away the brambles, letting only
  The roses blossom there.

But when the mother's watchful eyes are shrouded
  Away from sight of men,
And these dear feet are left without her guiding,
  Who shall direct them then?

How will they be allured, betrayed, deluded,
  Poor little untaught feet—
Into what dreary mazes will they wander,
  What dangers will they meet?

Will they go stumbling blindly in the darkness
  Of Sorrow's tearful shades?
Or find the upland slopes of Peace and Beauty
  Whose sunlight never fades?

Will they go toiling up Ambition's summit,
  The common world above?
Or in some nameless vale, securely sheltered,
  Walk side by side in Love?

Some feet there be, which walk Life's track unwounded,
  Which find but pleasant ways;
Some hearts there be, to which this life is only
  A round of happy days.

But they are few. Far more there are who wander
  Without a hope or friend,
Who find the journey full of pains and losses,
  And long to reach the end!

How shall it be with her, the tender stranger,
  Fair-faced and gentle-eyed,
Before whose unstained feet the world's rude highway
  Stretches so strange and wide?

Ah! who may read the future? For our darling
  We crave all blessings sweet—
And pray that He who feeds the crying ravens
  Will guide the baby's feet.

BINGEN ON THE RHINE.

BY CAROLINE E. NORTON.

SOLDIER of the Legion lay dying in Algiers:
There was lack of woman's nursing, there was dearth
of woman's tears;
But a comrade stood beside him, while his life-blood
ebbed away,
And bent with pitying glances, to hear what he might say.
The dying soldier faltered, as he took that comrade's hand,
And he said, "I never more shall see my own, my native land.
Take a message and a token to some distant friends of mine;
For I was born at Bingen—at Bingen on the Rhine!

"Tell my brothers and companions, when they meet and crowd around,
To hear my mournful story, in the pleasant vineyard ground,
That we fought the battle bravely; and when the day was done,
Full many a corse lay ghastly pale beneath the setting sun.
And midst the dead and dying were some grown old in war,
The death-wounds on their gallant breasts the last of many scars;
But some were young, and suddenly beheld life's morn decline; .
And one had come from Bingen—fair Bingen on the Rhine!

"Tell my mother that her other sons shall comfort her old age,
For I was still a truant bird that thought his home a cage;
For my father was a soldier, and even as a child
My heart leaped forth to hear him tell of struggles fierce and wild;
And when he died, and left us to divide his scanty hoard,
I let them take whate'er they would—but kept my father's sword;
And with boyish love I hung it, where the bright light used to shine
On the cottage wall at Bingen—calm Bingen on the Rhine!

"Tell my sister not to weep for me, and sob with drooping head,
When the troops come marching home again, with glad and gallant
tread;
But to look upon them proudly, with a calm and steadfast eye,
For her brother was a soldier too, and not afraid to die;
And if a comrade seek her love, I ask her in my name
To listen to him kindly, without regret or shame;
And to hang the old sword in its place, my father's sword and
mine,
For the honor of old Bingen—dear Bingen on the Rhine!

"There's another, not a sister: in the happy days gone by
You'd have known her by the merriment that sparkled in her eye;
Too innocent for coquetry, too fond for idle scorning;
O friend! I fear the lightest heart makes sometimes heaviest mourning.
Tell her the last night of my life (for ere this moon be risen,
My body will be out of pain, my soul be out of prison),
I dreamed I stood with her, and saw the yellow sunlight shine

"A soldier of the Legion lay dying in Algiers."

On the vine-clad hills of Bingen—fair Bingen on the Rhine!

"I saw the blue Rhine sweep along; I heard, or seemed to hear,
The German songs we used to sing, in chorus sweet and clear;
And down the pleasant river, and up the slanting hill,
The echoing chorus sounded, through the evening calm and still:
And her glad blue eyes were on me, as we passed, with friendly talk;
Down many a path beloved of yore, and well-remembered walk;
And her little hand lay lightly, confidingly in mine:
But we'll meet no more at Bingen—loved Bingen on the Rhine!"

His voice grew faint and hoarse—his grasp was childish weak;
His eyes put on a dying look—he sighed, and ceased to speak;
His comrade bent to lift him, but the spark of life had fled:
The soldier of the Legion in a foreign land was dead!

And the soft moon rose up slowly, and calmly she looked down
On the red sand of the battle-field, with bloody corpses strown.
Yes, calmly on that dreadful scene her pale light seemed to shine,
As it shone on distant Bingen—fair Bingen on the Rhine!

THE CLOSING SCENE.

BY T. BUCHANAN READ.

WITHIN the sober realm of leafless trees,
  The russet year inhaled the dreamy air;
Like some tanned reaper, in his hour of ease,
  When all the fields are lying brown and bare.

The gray barns looking from their hazy hills,
  O'er the dun waters widening in the vales,
Sent down the air a greeting to the mills,
  On the dull thunder of alternate flails.

All sights were mellowed, and all sounds subdued,
  The hills seemed further, and the stream sang low,
As in a dream the distant woodman hewed
  His winter log with many a muffled blow.

The embattled forest, erewhile armed with gold,
  Their banners bright with every martial hue,
Now stood like some sad, beaten host of old,
  Withdrawn afar in time's remotest blue.

On sombre wings the vulture tried his flight;
  The dove scarce heard his sighing mate's complaint;
And, like a star slow drowning in the light,
  The village church vane seemed to pale and faint.

The sentinel cock upon the hill-side crew—
  Crew thrice—and all was stiller than before;
Silent till some replying warden blew
  His alien horn, and then was heard no more.

Where erst the jay, within the elm's tall crest,
  Made garrulous trouble round her unfledged young;
And where the oriole hung her swaying nest,
  By every light wind, like a censer, swung.

Where sang the noisy martins of the eaves,
  The busy swallows circling ever near—
Foreboding, as the rustic mind believes,
  An early harvest and a plenteous year;

Where every bird, that waked the vernal feast,
  Shook the sweet slumber from its wings at morn,
To warn the reaper of the rosy east;
  All now was sunless, empty, and forlorn.

Alone, from out the stubble, piped the quail;
  And croaked the crow through all the dreary gloom;
Alone the pheasant, drumming in the vale,
  Made echo in the distance to the cottage loom.

There was no bud, no bloom upon the bowers;
  The spiders wove their thin shrouds night by night,
The thistle-down, the only ghost of flowers,
  Sailed slowly by—passed noiseless out of sight.

Amid all this—in this most dreary air,
  And where the woodbine shed upon the porch
Its crimson leaves, as if the year stood there,
  Firing the floor with its inverted torch;

Amid all this, the center of the scene,
  The white-haired matron, with monotonous tread,
Plied the swift wheel, and, with her joyless mien,
  Sate like a fate, and watched the flying thread.

She had known sorrow. He had walked with her,
  Oft supped, and broke with her the ashen crust,
And in the dead leaves still, she heard the stir
  Of his thick mantle trailing in the dust.

While yet her cheek was bright with summer bloom,
  Her country summoned and she gave her all;
And twice war bowed to her his sable plume—
  Re-gave the sword to rust upon the wall.

Re-gave the sword but not the hand that drew,
  And struck for liberty the dying blow;
Nor him who, to his sire and country true,
  Fell 'mid the ranks of the invading foe.

Long, but not loud, the droning wheel went on,
  Like the low murmur of a hive at noon;
Long, but not loud, the memory of the gone
  Breathed through her lips a sad and tremulous tune.

At last the thread was snapped—her head was bowed;
  Life dropped the distaff through her hands serene.
And loving neighbors smoothed her careful shroud,
  While death and winter closed the autumn scene.

MIGNONETTE.

BY MARY BRADLEY.

PASSED before her garden gate:
　She stood among her roses,
And stooped a little from the state
　In which her pride reposes,
To make her flowers a graceful plea
For luring and delaying me.

"When summer blossoms fade so
　soon,"
　She said with winning sweetness,
"Who does not wear the badge of June
　Lacks something of completeness.
My garden welcomes you to-day,
Come in and gather, while you may."

I entered in: she led me through
　A maze of leafy arches,
Where velvet-purple pansies grew
　Beneath the sighing larches,—
A shadowy, still, and cool retreat
That gave excuse for lingering feet.

She paused; pulled down a trailing vine;
　And twisted round her finger
Its starry sprays of jessamine,
　As one who seeks to linger.
But I smiled lightly in her face,
And passed on to the open space.

Passed many a flower-bed fitly set
　In trim and blooming order,
And plucked at last some mignonette
　That strayed along the border;
A simple thing that had no bloom,
And but a faint and far perfume.

She wondered why I would not choose
　That dreamy amaryllis,—
"And could I really, then, refuse
　Those heavenly white lilies!
And leave ungathered on the slope
This passion-breathing heliotrope?"

She did not know—what need to tell
　So fair and fine a creature?—
That there was one who loved me well
　Of widely different nature;
A little maid whose tender youth,
And innocence, and simple truth,

Had won my heart with qualities
　That far surpassed her beauty,
And held me with unconscious ease
　Enthralled of love and duty;
Whose modest graces all were met
And symboled in my mignonette.

I passed outside her garden gate,
　And left her proudly smiling:
Her roses bloomed too late, too late
　She saw, for my beguiling.
I wore instead—and wear it yet—
The single spray of mignonette.

Its fragrance greets me unaware,
　A vision clear recalling
Of shy, sweet eyes, and drooping hair
　In girlish tresses falling,
And little hands so white and fine
That timidly creep into mine;

As she—all ignorant of the arts
　That wiser maids are plying—
Has crept into my heart of hearts
　Past doubting or denying;
Therein, while suns shall rise and set,
To bloom unchanged, my Mignonette!

A MUSICAL BOX

BY W. W. STORY

THOU knowest her, the thing of
laces, and silk,
And ribbons, and gauzes, and
ermine,
With her neck and shoulders as
white as milk,
And her doll-like face and
conscious mien?

A lay-figure fashioned to fit a
dress,
All stuffed within with screw
and bran—
Is that a woman to love, to
caress?
Is that a creature to charm a man?

Only listen! how charmingly she talks
Of conquests—and beaus—of the Paris mode—
Of the coming ball—of the opera box—
Of pajama, and flounces, and fashion abroad!

Not a bonnet in church but she knows it well,
And Fashion she worships with downcast eyes;
A matchmaker de modes is her oracle,
And Paris her earthly paradise.

She's perfect to whirl with in a waltz;
And her shoulders—how well on a soft divan,
As she lounges at night and spreads her silks,
And plays with her bracelets and flirts her fan,—

With a little laugh at whatever you say,
And rounding her "No!" with a look of surprise,

And lisping her "Yes," with an air distrait,
And a pair of aimless, wandering eyes.

Her duty this Christian never omits!
She makes her calls, and she leaves her cards,
And enchants a circle of half-fledged wits,
And slim attachés and six-foot Guards.

Her talk is of people who're nasty or nice,
And she likes little bon-bon compliments,
While she seasons their sweetness by way of spice,
By some witless scandal she often invents.

Is this the thing for a mother or wife?
Could love ever grow on such barren ways?
Is this the companion to take for a wife?
One might as well marry a musical box.

You exhaust in a day her full extent;
'Tis the same little tinkle of tunes always;
You must wind her up with a compliment,
To be bored with the only airs she plays.

ELEGY WRITTEN IN A COUNTRY CHURCHYARD.

BY THOMAS GRAY.

THE curfew tolls the knell of parting day;
  The lowing herd winds slowly o'er
    the lea,
The plowman homeward plods his weary
    way,
  And leaves the world to darkness and
    to me.

Now fades the glimmering landscape on
    the sight,
  And all the air a solemn stillness holds,
Save where the beetle wheels his droning
    flight,
  And drowsy tinklings lull the distant
    folds;

Save that, from yonder ivy-mantled tower,
  The moping owl does to the moon complain
Of such as, wandering near her secret bower,
  Molest her ancient, solitary reign.

Beneath those rugged elms, that yew-tree's shade,
  Where heaves the turf in many a mouldering heap,
Each in his narrow cell forever laid,
  The rude forefathers of the hamlet sleep.

The breezy call of incense-breathing morn,
  The swallow twittering from the straw-built shed,
The cock's shrill clarion, or the echoing horn,
  No more shall rouse them from their lowly bed.

For them no more the blazing hearth shall burn,
  Or busy housewife ply her evening care;
No children run to lisp their sire's return,
  Or climb his knees the envied kiss to share.

Oft did the harvest to their sickle yield,
  Their furrow oft the stubborn glebe has broke:
How jocund did they drive their team afield!
  How bowed the woods beneath their sturdy stroke!

Let not Ambition mock their useful toil,
  Their homely joys, and destiny obscure;
Nor Grandeur hear, with a disdainful smile,
  The short and simple annals of the poor.

The boast of heraldry, the pomp of power,
  And all that beauty, all that wealth e'er gave,
Await, alike, the inevitable hour—
  The paths of glory lead but to the grave.

Nor you, ye proud, impute to these the fault,
  If memory o'er their tomb no trophies raise,
Where, through the long-drawn aisle and fretted vault
  The pealing anthem swells the note of praise.

Can storied urn, or animated bust,
  Back to its mansion call the fleeting breath?
Can Honor's voice provoke the silent dust,
  Or Flattery soothe the dull, cold ear of death?

Perhaps, in this neglected spot, is laid
  Some heart once pregnant with celestial fire—
Hand, that the rod of empire might have swayed,
  Or waked to ecstacy the living lyre:

But Knowledge to their eyes her ample page,
  Rich with the spoils of time, did ne'er unroll;
Chill Penury repressed their noble rage,
  And froze the genial current of the soul.

Full many a gem, of purest ray serene,
  The dark unfathomed caves of ocean bear;
Full many a flower is born to blush unseen,
  And waste its sweetness on the desert air.

Some village Hampden, that, with dauntless breast,
  The little tyrant of his fields withstood—
Some mute, inglorious Milton here may rest,
  Some Cromwell, guiltless of his country's blood.

The applause of listening senates to command,
  The threats of pain and ruin to despise,
To scatter plenty o'er a smiling land,
  And read their history in a nation's eyes,

Their lot forbade; nor circumscribed alone
  Their growing virtues, but their crimes confined:—
Forbade to wade through slaughter to a throne,
  And shut the gates of mercy on mankind;

The struggling pangs of conscious Truth to hide,
  To quench the blushes of ingenuous Shame,
Or heap the shrine of Luxury and Pride
  With incense kindled at the Muse's flame.

Far from the maddening crowd's ignoble strife,
  Their sober wishes never learnt to stray;
Along the cool, sequestered vale of life
  They kept the noiseless tenor of their way.

Yet even these bones from insult to protect,
  Some frail memorial still erected nigh,
With uncouth rhymes and shapeless sculpture decked,
  Implores the passing tribute of a sigh.

Their names, their years, spelled by th' unlettered Muse,
  The place of fame and elegy supply;
And many a holy text around she strews,
  That teach the rustic moralist to die.

For who, to dumb forgetfulness a prey,
  This pleasing, anxious being e'er resigned,—
Left the warm precincts of the cheerful day,
  Nor cast one longing, lingering look behind?

On some fond breast the parting soul relies,
　Some pious drops the closing eye requires;
Even from the tomb the voice of Nature cries,
　Even in our ashes live their wonted fires.

For thee, who, mindful of th' unhonored dead,
　Dost in these lines their artless tale relate;
If chance, by lonely contemplation led,
　Some kindred spirit shall enquire thy fate—

Haply, some hoary headed swain may say,
　"Oft have we seen him, at the peep of dawn,
Brushing, with hasty steps, the dews away,
　To meet the sun upon the upland lawn.

"There, at the foot of yonder nodding beech,
　That wreathes its old, fantastic roots so high,
His listless length at noontide would he stretch,
　And pore upon the brook that babbles by.

"Hard by yon wood, now smiling, as in scorn,
　Muttering his wayward fancies, he would rove;
Now drooping, woful-wan, like one forlorn,
　Or crazed with care, or crossed with hopeless love.

"One morn I missed him on th' accustomed hill,
　Along the heath and near his favorite tree;
Another came,—nor yet beside the rill,
　Nor up the lawn, nor at the wood was he.

"The next, with dirges due, in sad array,
　Slow through the church-way path we saw him borne;
Approach and read (for thou canst read) the lay,
　Graved on the stone beneath yon aged thorn."

EPITAPH.

Here rests his head upon the lap of earth,
　A youth to fortune and to fame unknown;
Fair Science frowned not on his humble birth,
　And Melancholy marked him for her own.

Large was his bounty, and his soul sincere;
　Heaven did a recompense as largely send:
He gave to misery all he had,—a tear;
　He gained from heaven—'twas all he wished—a friend.

No farther seek his merits to disclose,
　Nor draw his frailties from their dread abode,—
(There they, alike, in trembling hope repose,)
　The bosom of his Father and his God.

TWO LITTLE PAIRS.

BY MRS. SUSAN TRALL PERRY.

TWO little pairs of boots, to-night,
　Before the fire are drying;
Two little pairs of tired feet
　In a trundle bed are lying;
The tracks they left upon the floor
　Make me feel like sighing.

Those little boots with copper toes!
　They run the livelong day;
And oftentimes I almost wish
　They were miles away;
So tired am I to hear so oft
　Their heavy tramp at play.

They walk about the new-ploughed ground
　Where mud in plenty lies;
They roll it up in marbles round,
　They bake it into pies,
And then, at night upon the floor,
　In every shape it dries!

To-day I was disposed to scold,
　But when I look to-night
At those little boots before the fire,

With copper toes so bright,
　I think how sad my heart would be
　To put them out of sight.

For in a trunk up stairs I've laid
　Two socks of white and blue;
If called to put those boots away,
　Oh God, what should I do?
I mourn that there are not to-night
　Three pairs instead of two.

I mourn because I thought how nice
　My neighbor 'cross the way,
Could keep her carpets all the year
　From getting worn or gray;
Yet well I know she'd smile to own
　Some little boots to day.

We mothers weary get, and worn,
　Over our load of care;
But how we speak to these little ones
　Let each of us beware:
For what would our fireside be to night,
　If no little boots were there?

THE FIRST SNOW-FALL.

BY JAMES RUSSELL LOWELL.

THE snow had begun in
  the gloaming,
   And busily, all the
    night,
Had been heaping field and
  highway
With a silence deep and
  white.

Every pine and fir and
  hemlock
Wore ermine too dear for
  an earl,
And the poorest twig on
  the elm-tree
Was ridged inch-deep with
  pearl.

From sheds new-roofed
  with carrara
Came chanticleer's muffled
  crow;
The stiff rails were softened
  to swan's-down;
And still wavered down
  the snow.

I stood and watched from
  my window
The noiseless work of the
  sky,
And the sudden flurries of
  snow-birds,
Like brown leaves whirl-
  ing by.

I thought of a mound in
  sweet Auburn
Where a little headstone
  stood;
How the flakes were fold-
  ing it gently,
As did robins the Babes in the Wood.

"Every pine and fir and hemlock wore ermine too dear for an earl."

Up spoke our own
  Mabel,
Saying, "Father, who
  makes it snow?"
And I told of the good
  Father
Who cares for us all
  below.

Again I looked at the snow-
  fall,
And thought of the leaden
  sky
That arched o'er our first
  great sorrow
When that mound was
  heaped so high.

I remember the gradual
  patience
That fell from that cloud
  like snow,
Flake by flake, healing and
  hiding
The scar of our deep-
  woe.

And again to the child I
  whispered
"The snow that husheth
  all,
Darling, the merciful
  Father
Alone can bid it fall."

Then with eyes that saw
  not I kissed her,
And she, kissing back,
  could not know
That my kiss was given
  her sister,
Folded close under deepening snow.

A DEATH-BED.

BY JAMES ALDRICH.

HER suffering ended with the day;
  Yet lived she at its close,
And breathed the long, long night away,
  In statue-like repose.

But when the sun, in all his state,
  Illumed the eastern skies,
She passed through glory's morning-gate,
  And walked in Paradise.

THE CROOKED FOOTPATH.

BY OLIVER WENDELL HOLMES.

Ah, here it is! the sliding rail
That marks the old remembered spot,
The gap that struck our schoolboy trail,
The crooked path across the lot.

It left the road by school and church:
A pencilled shadow, nothing more,
That parted from the silver birch
And ended at the farm-house door.

No line or compass traced its plan;
With frequent bends to left or right,
In aimless, wayward curves it ran,
But always kept the door in sight.

The gabled porch, with woodbine green,
The broken millstone at the sill,
Though many a rood might stretch between,
The truant child could see them still.

No rocks across the pathway lie,
No fallen trunk is o'er it thrown;

"*And yet it winds, we know not why, and turns as if for tree or stone.*"

And yet it winds, we know not why,
And turns as if for tree or stone.

Perhaps some lover trod the way,
With shaking knees and leaping heart:
And so it often runs astray,
With sinuous sweep or sudden start.

Or one, perchance, with clouded brain,
From some unholy banquet reeled:
And since, our devious steps maintain
His track across the trodden field.

Nay, deem not thus:—
no earth-born will
Could ever trace a faultless line;
Our truest steps are human still,—
To walk unswerving were divine.

Truants from love, we dream of wrath:
O, rather let us trust the more!
Through all the wanderings of the path
We still can see our Father's door!

THE OLD LOVE.

I MET her, she was thin and old,
She stooped and trod with tottering feet;
Her locks were gray that once were gold,
Her voice was harsh that once was sweet;
Her cheeks were sunken, and her eyes,
Robbed of their girlish light of joy,
Were dim: I felt a strange surprise
That I had loved her when a boy.

And yet a something in her air
Restored to me my youthful prime;
My heart grew young and seemed to wear
The impress of that long-lost time:
I took her wilted hand in mine,
Its touch awoke a world of joy;
I kissed her with a reverent sigh,
For I had loved her when a boy!

OVER THE HILL TO THE POOR-HOUSE.*

BY WILL M. CARLETON.

OVER the hill to the poor-house I'm trudgin' my weary
way—
  I, a woman of seventy, and only a trifle gray—
  I, who am smart an' chipper, for all the years I've
told,
  As many another woman, that's only half as old.

  Over the hill to the poor-house—I can't make it
quite clear!
  Over the hill to the poor-house—it seems so horrid
queer!
Many a step I've taken a-toilin' to and fro,
But this is a sort of journey I never thought to go.

What is the use of heapin' on me a pauper's shame?
Am I lazy or crazy? am I blind or lame?
True, I am not so supple, nor yet so awful stout,
But charity ain't no favor, if one can live without.

I am willin' and anxious an' ready any day,
To work for a decent livin', an' pay my honest way;
For I can earn my victuals, an' more too, I'll be bound,
If anybody only is willin' to have me round.

Once I was young and han'some—I was, upon my soul—
Once my cheeks was roses, my eyes as black as coal;
And I can't remember, in them days, of hearin' people say,
For any kind of reason, that I was in their way.

'Taint no use of boastin', or talkin' over free,
But many a house an' home was open then to me;
Many a han'some offer I had from likely men,
And nobody ever hinted that I was a burden then.

And when to John I was married, sure he was good and smart,
But he and all the neighbors would own I done my part;
For life was all before me, an' I was young an' strong,
And I worked the best that I could in tryin' to get along.

And so we worked together; and life was hard but gay,
With now and then a baby, for to cheer us on our way;
Till we had half a dozen, an' all growed clean an' neat,
An' went to school like others, an' had enough to eat.

So we worked for the childr'n, and raised 'em every one;
Worked for 'em summer and winter, just as we ought to 've done;
Only perhaps we humored 'em, which some good folks condemn,
But every couple's childr'n's a heap the best to them.

Strange how much we think of our blessed little ones!—
I'd have died for my daughters, I'd have died for my sons;
And God he made that rule of love; but when we're old and gray,
I've noticed it sometimes somehow fails to work the other way.

Strange, another thing: when our boys an' girls was grown,
And when, exceptin' Charley, they'd left us there alone;
When John he nearer an' nearer come, an' dearer seemed to be,
The Lord of Hosts he come one day an' took him away from me.

Still I was bound to struggle, an' never to cringe or fall—
Still I worked for Charley, for Charley was now my all;
And Charley was pretty good to me, with scarce a word or frown,
Till at last he went a-courtin', and brought a wife from town.

She was somewhat dressy, an' hadn't a pleasant smile—
She was quite conceity, and carried a heap o' style;
But if ever I tried to be friends, I did with her, I know;
But she was hard and proud, an' I couldn't make it go.

She had an edication, an' that was good for her;
But when she twitted me on mine 'twas carryin' things too fur;
An' I told her once 'fore company (an' it almost made her sick),
That I never swallowed a grammar, or et a 'rithmetic.

So 'twas only a few days before the thing was done—
They was a family of themselves, and I another one;
And a very little cottage for one family will do,
But I have never seen a house that was big enough for two.

An' I never could speak to suit her, never could please her eye,
An' it made me independent, an' then I didn't try;
But I was terribly staggered, an' felt it like a blow,
When Charley turned ag'in me, an' told me I could go.

I went to live with Susan, but Susan's house was small,
And she was always a-hintin' how snug it was for us all;
And what with her husband's sisters, and what with childr'n three,
'Twas easy to discover that there wasn't room for me.

An' then I went to Thomas, the oldest son I've got,
For Thomas' buildings 'd cover the half of an acre lot;
But all the childr'n was on me—I couldn't stand their sauce—
And Thomas said I needn't think I was comin' there to boss.

An' then I wrote to Rebecca,—my girl who lives out West,
And to Isaac, not far from her—some twenty miles at best;
And one of 'em said 'twas too warm there, for any one so old,
And t'other had an opinion the climate was too cold.

So they have shirked and slighted me, an' shifted me about—
So they have well-nigh soured me, an' wore my old heart out;
But still I've borne up pretty well, an' wasn't much put down,
Till Charley went to the poor-master, an' put me on the town.

Over the hill to the poor-house—my childr'n dear, good-bye!
Many a night I've watched you when only God was nigh;
And God 'll judge between us; but I will al'ays pray
That you shall never suffer the half I do to-day.

* From "Farm Ballads."   Published by Harper & Brothers.

OVER THE HILL FROM THE POOR-HOUSE.

BY WILL M. CARLETON.

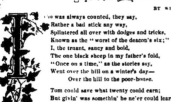

I was always counted, they say,
Rather a bad stick any way,
Splintered all over with dodges and tricks,
Known as the "worst of the deacon's six;"
I, the truant, saucy and bold,
The one black sheep in my father's fold,
"Once on a time," as the stories say,
Went over the hill on a winter's day—
　　Over the hill to the poor-house.

Tom could save what twenty could earn;
But givin' was somethin' he ne'er could learn;
Isaac could half o' the Scriptures speak,
Committed a hundred verses a week;
Never forgot, an' never slipped;
But "Honor thy father and mother" he skipped.
　　So over the hill to the poor-house.

As for Susan, her heart was kind
An' good—what there was of it, mind;
Nothin' too big an' nothin' too nice,
Nothin' she wouldn't sacrifice
For one she loved; an' that 'ere one
Was herself, when all was said an' done
An' Charley an' 'Becca meant well, no doubt,
But anyone could pull 'em about.

An' all our folks ranked well, you see,
Save one poor fellow, and that was me.
An' when, one dark an' rainy night,
A neighbor's horse went out of sight,
They hitched on me as the guilty chap
That carried one end of the halter-strap
An' I think, myself, that view of the case
Wasn't altogether out o' place;
My mother denied it, as mothers do,
But I'm inclined to believe 'twas true.

Though for me one thing might be said—
That I, as well as the horse, was led;
And the worst of whisky spurred me on,
Or else the deed would have never been done.
But the keenest grief I ever felt,
Was when my mother beside me knelt,
An' cried an' prayed till I melted down,
As I wouldn't for half the horses in town.
I kissed her fondly, then and there,
An' swore henceforth to be honest and square.

I served my sentence—a bitter pill
Some fellows should take, who never will;
And then I decided to "go out West,"
Concludin' 'twould suit my health the best;
Where, how I prospered, I never could tell,
But Fortune seemed to like me well.
An' somehow, every vein I struck
Was always bubblin' over with luck;
An' better than that, I was steady an' true,
An' put my good resolutions through.
But I wrote to a trusty old neighbor, an' said.
"You tell 'em, old fellow, that I am dead,
An' died a Christian; 'twill please 'em more
Than if I had lived the same as before."

But when this neighbor he wrote to me,
"Your mother is in the poor-house," says he;
I had a resurrection straightway,
An' started for her that very day;
And when I arrived where I was grown.
I took good care that I shouldn't be known;
But I bought the old cottage, through and through,
Of some one Charley had sold it to;
And held back neither work nor gold,
To fix it up as it was of old;
The same big fire-place, wide and high,
Flung up its cinders toward the sky;
The old clock ticked on the corner-shelf—
I wound it an' set it a-goin' myself;
An', if everything wasn't quite the same,
Neither I nor Manly was to blame;
　　Then—over the hill to the poor-house!

One bloomin', blusterin' winter's day,
With a team an' cutter I started away,
My fiery nags was as black as coal;
(They some'at resembled the horse I stole;)
I hitched an' entered the poor-house door—
A poor old woman was scrubbin' the floor;
She rose to her feet in great surprise
And looked, quite startled, into my eyes;
I saw the whole of her trouble's trace
In the lines that marred her dear old face;
"Mother!" I shouted, "your sorrows are done!
You're adopted along o' your horse-thief son
　　Come over the hill from the poor-house!"

She didn't faint; she knelt by my side,
An' thanked the Lord till I fairly cried.
An' maybe our ride wasn't pleasant and gay,
An' maybe she wasn't wrapped up that day.
An' maybe our cottage wasn't warm and bright;
An' maybe it wasn't a pleasant sight,
To see her a-gettin' the evenin's tea,
An' frequently stoppin' and kissin' me;
An' maybe we didn't live happy for years,
In spite of my brothers' and sisters' sneers,
Who often said, as I have heard,
That they wouldn't own a prison bird
(Though they're gettin' over that, I guess,
For all of them owe me more or less.)

But I've learned one thing, and it cheers a man
In always a-doin' the best he can;
That whether, on the big book, a blot
Gets over a fellow's name or not,
Whenever he does a deed that's white
It's credited to him fair and right.
An' when you hear the great bugle's notes,
An' the Lord divides his sheep and goats;
However they may settle my case,
Wherever they may fix my place,
My good old Christian mother, you'll see,
Will be sure to stand right up for me
　　So over the hill from the poor-house!

WEIGHING THE BABY.

BY ETHEL LYNN.

HOW MANY pounds does the baby weigh,—
    Baby, who came but a month ago;
How many pounds from the crowning curl
    To the rosy point of the restless toe?

Grandfather ties the handkerchief's knot,
    Tenderly guides the swinging weight,
And carefully over his glasses peers
    To read the record, "Only eight!"

Softly the echo goes around,
    The father laughs at the tiny girl;
The fair young mother sings the words,
    While grandmother smooths the golden curl.

And stooping above the precious thing,
    Nestles a kiss within a prayer;
Murmuring softly, "Little one,
    Grandfather did not weigh you fair."

Nobody weighed the baby's smile,
    Or the love that came with the helpless one;

Nobody weighed the threads of care
    From which a woman's life is spun.

No index tells the mighty worth
    Of a little baby's quiet breath!
A soft, unceasing metronome,
    Patient and faithful unto death.

Nobody weighed the baby's soul,
    For here, on earth, no weights there be
That could avail. God only knows
    Its value in eternity.

Only eight pounds to hold a soul
    That seeks no angel's silver wing,
But shrines it in this human guise—
    Within so fair and small a thing.

Oh, mother, laugh your merry note,
    Be gay and glad, but don't forget
From baby's eyes looks out a soul
    That claims a home in Eden yet.

JUDGE NOT.

JUDGE not! The workings of his brain
    And of his heart thou canst not see;
What looks to thy dim eyes a stain,
    In God's pure light may only be
A scar, brought from some well-won field,
    Where thou wouldst only faint and yield.

The look, the air, that frets thy sight,
    May be a token, that below
The soul has closed in deadly fight

With some infernal, fiery foe,
Whose glance would scorch thy smiling grace,
And cast thee shuddering on thy face.

The fall thou darest to despise—
    Perchance the slackened angel's hand
Has suffered it, that he may rise
    And take a firmer, surer stand;
Or, trusting less to earthly things,
May henceforth learn to use his wings.

THE LITTLE BOY THAT DIED.

BY JOSHUA D. ROBINSON.

I AM all alone in my chamber now,
And the midnight hour is near,
And the faggot's crack, and the clock's dull tick,
Are all the sounds I hear;
And over my soul in its solitude
Sweet feelings of sadness glide;
And my heart and my eyes are full when I think
Of the little boy that died.

I went home once night to my father's house—
Went home to the dear ones all,
And softly I oped the garden gate,
And softly the door of the hall;
My mother came out to meet her son,
She kissed me, and then she sighed,
At her head fell on my neck, and she wept
For the little boy that died.

And when I gazed on his innocent face,
As still and cold he lay,
And thought what a lovely child he had been,
And how soon he must decay;
"O Death, thou lovest the beautiful!"
In the woe of my spirit I cried,
For sparkled the eyes, and the forehead was fair,
Of the little boy that died.

Again I will go to my father's house—
Go home to the dear ones all,
And softly I'll open the garden gate,
And softly the door of the hall;
I shall meet my mother, but, nevermore,
With her darling by her side;
And she'll kiss me and sigh, and weep again
For the little boy that died.

I shall miss him when the flowers come,
In the garden where he played;
I shall miss him more by the fire-side,
When the flowers have all decayed;
I shall see his toys and his empty chair,
And the horse he used to ride:
And they will speak, with silent speech,
Of the little boy that died.

I shall see his little sister again,
With her playmates about the door,
And I'll watch the children at their sports,
As I never did before;
And if, in the group I see a child
That's dimpled and laughing-eyed,
I'll look to see if it may not be
The little boy that died.

We shall go home to our Father's house—
To our Father's house in the skies,
Where the hope of our souls shall have no blight,
And our love no broken ties:
We shall roam on the banks of the River of Peace,
And bathe in its blissful tide;
And one of the joys of our Heaven will be
The little boy that died.

And therefore, when I'm sitting alone,
And the midnight hour is near,
And the faggot's crack and the clock's dull tick
Are the only sounds I hear;
O sweet o'er my soul in its solitude
Are the feelings of sadness that glide,
Though my heart and my eyes are full when I think
Of the little boy that died.

CLEON AND I.

BY CHARLES MACKAY.

CLEON hath a million acres,
 Ne'er a one have I;
Cleon dwelleth in a palace,
 In a cottage, I;
Cleon hath a dozen fortunes,
 Not a penny, I;
Yet the poorer of the twain is
 Cleon, and not I.

Cleon, true, possesseth acres,
 But the landscape, I;
Half the charms to me it yieldeth,
 Money cannot buy;
Cleon harbors sloth and dullness,
 Freshening vigor, I;
He in velvet, I in fustian,
 Richer man am I

Cleon is a slave to grandeur,
 Free as thought am I;
Cleon fees a score of doctors,
 Need of none have I;
Wealth-surrounded, care-environed,
 Cleon fears to die;
Death may come, he'll find me ready,
 Happier man am I.

Cleon sees no charm in nature,
 In a daisy, I;
Cleon hears no anthems ringing
 In the sea and sky;
Nature sings to me forever,
 Earnest listener, I;
State for state, with all attendants,
 Who would change!—Not I.

IF I SHOULD DIE TO-NIGHT.

BY BELLE E. SMITH.

If I should die to-night,
My friends would look upon my quiet face
 Before they laid it in its resting-place,
 And deem that death had left it almost fair;
 And, laying snow-white flowers against my hair,
Would smooth it down with tearful tenderness,
And fold my hands with lingering caress;
Poor hands, so empty and so cold to-night!

 If I should die to-night,
My friends would call to mind, with loving thought,
 Some kindly deed the icy hand had wrought;
 Some gentle word the frozen lips had said;
Errands on which the willing feet had sped,
The memory of my selfishness and pride,
My hasty words, would all be put aside,
And so I should be loved and mourned to-night.

 If I should die to night,
Even hearts estranged would turn once more to me,
 Recalling other days remorsefully.
 The eyes that chill me with averted glance
Would look upon me as of yore, perchance,
And soften, in the old, familiar way,
For who could war with dumb, unconscious clay?
So I might rest, forgiven of all, to-night.

 Oh, friends, I pray to night,
Keep not your kisses for my dead, cold brow.
 The way is lonely, let me feel them now.
 Think gently of me; I am travel-worn;
My faltering feet are pierced with many a thorn.
Forgive, oh, hearts estranged, forgive, I plead!
When dreamless rest is mine I shall not need
The tenderness for which I long to-night.

WORDS FOR PARTING.

BY MARY CLEMMER.

WHAT shall I do, my dear,
In the coming years, I wonder,
When our paths, which lie so sweetly near,
Shall lie so far asunder?
O, what shall I do, my dear,
Through all the sad to-morrows,
When the sunny smile has ceased to cheer,
That smiles away all sorrows?

What shall I do, my friend,
When you are gone forever?
My heart its eager need will send,
Through the years to find you, never.
And how will it be with you,
In the weary world, I wonder!
Will you love me with a love as true,
When our paths lie far asunder?

A sweeter, sadder thing,
My life for having known you:
Forever, with my sacred kin,
My soul's soul, I must own you;
Forever mine, my friend,
From June till life's December;
Not mine to have and hold,
Mine to pray for, and remember.

The way is short, my friend,
That reaches out before us:
God's tender heavens above us bend,
His love is smiling o'er us.
A little while is ours,
For sorrow or for laughter;
I'll lay the hand you love in yours,
On the shore of the hereafter.

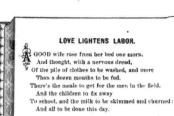

LOVE LIGHTENS LABOR.

GOOD wife rose from her bed one morn,
And thought, with a nervous dread,
Of the pile of clothes to be washed, and more
Than a dozen mouths to be fed.
There's the meals to get for the men in the field,
And the children to fix away
To school, and the milk to be skimmed and churned;
And all to be done this day.

It had rained in the night, and all the wood
Was wet as it could be;
There were puddings and pies to bake, besides
A loaf of cake for tea;
And the day was hot, and her aching head
Throbbed wearily as she said:
" If maidens but knew what good wives know,
They would be in no haste to wed."

"Jennie, what do you think I told Ben Brown?"
Called the farmer from the well;
And a flush crept up to his bronzed brow,
And his eyes half bashfully fell,

" It was this," he said—and coming near,
He kiss'd from her brow the frown;—
" 'Twas this," he said, " that you were the best,
And the dearest wife in town."

The farmer went back to the field, and the wife,
In a smiling and absent way,
Sang snatches of tender little songs
She'd not sung for many a day.
And the pain in her head was gone, and the clothes
Were white as the foam of the sea;
Her bread was light and her butter was sweet,
And as golden as it could be.

"Just think," the children all called in a breath,
" Tom Wood has run off to sea!
He wouldn't, I know, if he only had
As happy a home as we."
The night came down, and the good wife smiled
To herself as she softly said:
" 'Tis so sweet to labor for those we love,
It's not strange that maids will wed!"

JENNY KISSED ME.

BY LEIGH HUNT.

JENNY kissed me when we met,
   Jumping from the chair she sat in;
Time, you thief, who love to get
   Sweets into your list, put that in!
Say I'm weary, say I'm sad;
   Say that health and wealth have missed me;
Say I'm growing dull, but add,
      Jenny kissed me!

ROLL CALL.

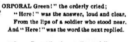

CORPORAL Green!" the orderly cried;
  "Here!" was the answer, loud and clear,
  From the lips of a soldier who stood near.
And "Here!" was the word the next replied.

"Cyrus Drew!"—then a silence fell—
  This time no answer followed the call;
  Only his rear man had seen him fall,
Killed or wounded he could not tell.

There they stood in the falling light,
  These men of battle, with grave, dark looks,
  As plain to be read as open books,
While slowly gathered the shades of night.

The fern on the hill-side was splashed with blood,
  And down in the corn, where the poppies grew,
  Were redder stains than the poppies knew;
And crimson-dyed was the river's flood.

For the foe had crossed from the other side,
  That day in the face of a murderous fire,
  That swept them down in its terrible ire;
And their life-blood went to color the tide.

"Herbert Kline!" At the call, there came
  Two stalwart soldiers into the line,
  Bearing between them this Herbert Kline,
Wounded and bleeding, to answer his name.

"Ezra Kerr!"—and a voice answered, "Here!"
  "Hiram Kerr!"—but no man replied.
  They were brothers, these two, the sad winds sighed,
And a shudder crept through the cornfield near.

"Ephraim Deane!"—then a soldier spoke:
  "Deane carried our Regiment's colors," he said;
  "Where our Ensign was shot, I left him dead,
Just after the enemy wavered and broke.

"Close to the roadside his body lies.
  I paused a moment and gave him to drink,
  He murmured his mother's name, I think,
And death came with it and closed his eyes."

'Twas a victory; yes, but it cost us dear.—
  For that company's roll, when called at night,
  Of a *hundred* men who went into the fight,
Numbered but *twenty* that answered "Here!"

UP-HILL.

BY CHRISTINA G. ROSSETTI.

DOES the road wind up-hill all the way?
　Yes, to the very end.
Will the day's journey take the whole long day?
　From morn to night, my friend.

But is there for the night a resting place?
　A roof for when the slow, dark hours begin?
May not the darkness hide it from my face?
　You cannot miss that inn.

Shall I meet other wayfarers at night?
　Those who have gone before.
Then must I knock, or call when just in sight?
　They will not keep you standing at the door.

Shall I find comfort, travel-sore and weak?
　Of labor you shall find the sum.
Will there be beds for me and all who seek?
　Yes, beds for all who come.

"Yes, beds for all who come."

OH, WHY SHOULD THE SPIRIT OF MORTAL BE PROUD?

BY WILLIAM KNOX.

OH, why should the spirit of mortal be proud?
Like a swift-fleeting meteor, a fast-flying cloud,
A flash of the lightning, a break of the wave,
Man passes from life to his rest in the grave.

The leaves of the oak and the willow shall fade,
Be scattered around and together be laid;
And the young and the old, and the low and the high,
Shall moulder to dust and together shall lie.

The infant a mother attended and loved,
The mother that infant's affection who proved;
The husband that mother and infant who blessed,
Each, all, are away to their dwellings of rest.

The maid on whose cheek, on whose brow, in whose eye,
Shone beauty and pleasure—her triumphs are by;
And the memory of those who loved her and praised,
Are alike from the minds of the living erased.

The hand of the king that the sceptre hath borne,
The brow of the priest that the mitre hath worn,
The eye of the sage and the heart of the brave,
Are hidden and lost in the depth of the grave.

The peasant, whose lot was to sow and to reap;
The herdsman, who climbed with his goats up the steep;
The beggar, who wandered in search of his bread,
Have faded away like the grass that we tread.

The saint who enjoyed the communion of heaven,
The sinner who dared to remain unforgiven,
The wise and the foolish, the guilty and just,
Have quietly mingled their bones in the dust.

So the multitude goes, like the flowers or the weed
That withers away to let others succeed;
So the multitude comes, even those we behold,
To repeat every tale that has often been told.

For we are the same our fathers have been.
We see the same sights our fathers have seen,—
We drink the same stream and view the same sun,
And run the same course our fathers have run.

The thoughts we are thinking our fathers would think,
From the death we are shrinking our fathers would shrink,
To the life we are clinging they also would cling;
But it speeds for us all, like a bird on the wing.

They loved, but the story we cannot unfold;
They scorned, but the heart of the haughty is cold;
They grieved, but no wail from their slumbers will come;
They joyed, but the tongue of their gladness is dumb.

They died, aye! they died; and we things that are now,
Who walk on the turf that lies over their brow,
Who make in their dwellings a transient abode,
Meet the things that they met on their pilgrimage road.

Yea! hope and despondency, pleasure and pain,
We mingle together in sunshine and rain;
And the smiles and the tears, the song and the dirge,
Still follow each other, like surge upon surge.

'Tis the wink of an eye, 'tis the draught of a breath;
From the blossom of health to the paleness of death,
From the gilded saloon to the bier and the shroud,—
Oh, why should the spirit of mortal be proud?

UNTIL DEATH.

AKE me no vows of constancy, dear friend,
  To love me, though I die, thy whole life long,
And love no other till thy days shall end,—
  Nay, it were rash and wrong.

If thou canst love another, be it so;
  I would not reach out of my quiet grave
To bind thy heart, if it should choose to go;—
  Love should not be a slave.

My placid ghost, I trust, will walk serene
  In clearer light than gilds these earthly morns,
Above the jealousies and envies keen,
  Which sow this life with thorns.

Thou wouldst not feel my shadowy caress,
  If, after death, my soul should linger here; ·
Men's hearts crave tangible, close tenderness,
  Love's presence, warm and near.

It would not make me sleep more peacefully
  That thou wert wasting all thy life in woe

For my poor sake; what love thou hast for me,
  Bestow it ere I go!

Carve not upon a stone when I am dead
  The praises which remorseful mourners give
To women's graves—a tardy recompense—
  But speak them while I live.

Heap not the heavy marble on my head
  To shut away the sunshine and the dew;
Let small blooms grow there, and let grasses wave,
  And rain-drops filter through.

Thou wilt meet many fairer and more gay
  Than I; but, trust me, thou canst never find
One who will love and serve thee night and day
  With a more single mind.

Forget me when I die! The violets
  Above my rest will blossom just as blue,
Nor miss thy tears; e'en nature's self forgets;
  But while I live, be true!

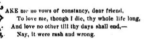

SOMETIME.

OMETIME, when all life's lessons
  have been learned,
And sun and stars for ever-
  more have set,
The things which our weak
  judgments here have spurned,
The things o'er which we
  grieved with lashes wet,
Will flash before us out of
  life's dark night,
As stars shine most in deeper tints of blue;
And we shall see how all God's plans were right,
And how what seemed reproof was love most true.

And we shall see how, while we frown and sigh,
  God's plans go on as best for you and me;
How, when we called, He heeded not our cry,
  Because His wisdom to the end could see.
And e'en as prudent parents disallow
  Too much of sweet to craving babyhood,
So God, perhaps, is keeping from us now
  Life's sweetest things because it seemeth good.

And if, sometimes, commingled with life's wine,
  We find the wormwood, and rebel and shrink,

Be sure a wiser hand than yours or mine
  Pours out this portion for our lips to drink.
And if some friend we love is lying low,
  Where human kisses cannot reach his face,
Oh, do not blame the loving Father so,
  But wear your sorrow with obedient grace!

And you shall shortly know that lengthened breath
  Is not the sweetest gift God sends His friend,
And that, sometimes, the sable pall of death
  Conceals the fairest boon His love can send.
If we could push ajar the gates of life,
  And stand within, and all God's workings see,
We could interpret all this doubt and strife,
  And for each mystery could find a key!

But not to-day. Then be content, poor heart!
  God's plans like lilies pure and white unfold;
We must not tear the close-shut leaves apart,
  Time will reveal the calyxes of gold.
And if, through patient toil, we reach the land
  Where tired feet, with sandals loose, may rest,
When we shall clearly know and understand,
  I think that we will say, "God knew the best!"

RAIN ON THE ROOF.

BY COATES KINNEY.

WHEN the humid shadows hover over
   all the starry spheres,
And the melancholy darkness gently
   weeps in rainy tears,
'Tis a joy to press the pillow of a cot
   tage chamber bed,
And listen to the patter of the soft
   rain overhead.

Every tinkle on the shingles has an
   echo in the heart,
And a thousand dreamy fancies into
   busy being start;
And a thousand recollections weave their bright hues into woof,
As I listen to the patter of the soft rain on the roof.

There, in fancy, comes my mother, as she used to years agone,
To survey the infant sleepers ere she left them till the dawn;

I can see her bending o'er me, as I listen to the strain
Which is played upon the shingles by the patter of the rain.

Then my little seraph sister, with her wings and waving hair,
And her bright-eyed cherub brother—a serene, angelic pair,—
Glide around my wakeful pillow, with their praise or mild reproof,
As I listen to the murmur of the soft rain on the roof.

And another comes to thrill me with her eyes' delicious blue.
I forget, as gazing on her, that her heart was all untrue;
I remember that I loved her as I ne'er may love again,
And my heart's quick pulses vibrate to the patter of the rain.

There is naught in art's bravuras that can work with such a spell,
In the spirit's pure, deep fountains, where the holy passions swell,
As that melody of nature,—that subdued, subduing strain,
Which is played upon the shingles by the patter of the rain.

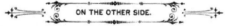

ON THE OTHER SIDE.

WE GO our ways in life too much alone;
   We hold ourselves too far from all our kind;
Too often we are dead to sigh and moan;
   Too often to the weak and helpless blind;
Too often, where distress and want abide,
We turn and pass upon the other side.

The other side is trodden smooth, and worn
   By footsteps passing idly all the day.
Where lie the bruised ones that faint and mourn,
   Is seldom more than an untrodden way;
Our selfish hearts are for our feet the guide,
They lead us by upon the other side.

It should be ours the oil and wine to pour
   Into the bleeding wounds of stricken ones;
To take the smitten, and the sick and sore,
   And bear them where a stream of blessing runs;
Instead, we look about—the way is wide,
And so we pass upon the other side.

Oh, friends and brothers, gliding down the years,
   Humanity is calling each and all
In tender accents, born of grief and tears!
   I pray you, listen to the thrilling call;
You cannot, in your cold and selfish pride,
Pass guiltlessly by on the other side.

AMBITION.

BY LORD BYRON.

He who ascends to mountain tops shall find
   The loftiest peaks most wrapt in clouds and snow;
He, who surpasses or subdues mankind,
   Must look down on the hate of those below.
Though high above the sun of glory glow,
   And far beneath the earth and ocean spread,
Round him are icy rocks, and loudly blow
   Contending tempests on his naked head;
And thus reward the toils which to those summits led.

BLESSED ARE THEY THAT MOURN.

BY WM. C. BRYANT.

There is a day of sunny rest
   For every dark and troubled night;
And grief may bide an evening guest,
   But joy shall come with early light.

For God hath marked each sorrowing day
   And numbered every secret tear,
And heaven's long age of bliss shall pay
   For all His children suffer here.

SONG OF THE BROOK.

BY ALFRED TENNYSON.

I COME from haunts of coot and hern;
   I make a sudden sally,
And sparkle out among the fern,
   To bicker down a valley.

By thirty hills I hurry down,
   Or slip between the ridges;
By twenty thorps, a little town,
   And half a hundred bridges.

Till last by Philip's farm I flow,
   To join the brimming river;
For men may come and men may go,
   But I go on forever.

I chatter over stony ways,
   In little sharps and trebles;
I bubble into eddying bays,
   I babble on the pebbles.

With many a curve my banks I fret,
   By many a field and fallow,
And many a fairy foreland set
   With willow-weed and mallow.

I chatter, chatter, as I flow
   To join the brimming river;
For men may come and men may go,
   But I go on forever.

I wind about, and in and out,
   With here a blossom sailing,
And here and there a lusty trout,
   And here and there a grayling.

And here and there a foamy flake
   Upon me, as I travel,
With many a silvery waterbreak
   Above the golden gravel;

And draw them all along, and flow
   To join the brimming river;
For men may come and men may go,
   But I go on forever.

I steal by lawns and grassy plots;
   I slide by hazel covers;
I move the sweet forget-me-nots
   That grow for happy lovers.

I slip, I slide, I gloom, I glance
   Among my skimming swallows;
I make the netted sunbeam dance
   Against my sandy shallows.

I murmur under moon and stars,
   In brambly wildernesses;
I linger by my shingly bars,
   I loiter round my cresses.

And out again I curve and flow
   To join the brimming river;
For men may come and men may go,
   But I go on forever.

THE DOORSTEP.

BY EDMUND CLARENCE STEDMAN.

THE conference meeting through at last,
  We boys around the vestry waited,
To see the girls come tripping past
  Like snow-birds willing to be mated.

Not braver he that leaps the wall
  By level musket-flashes litten,
Than I, who stepped before them all
  Who longed to see me get the mitten.

But no, she blushed and took my arm!
  We let the old folks have the highway,
And started toward the Maple Farm
  Along a kind of lovers' by-way.

I can't remember what we said,
  'Twas nothing worth a song or story,
Yet that rude path by which we sped
  Seemed all transformed and in a glory.

The snow was crisp beneath our feet,
  The moon was full, the fields were gleaming;
By hood and tippet sheltered sweet,
  Her face with youth and health was beaming.

The little hand outside her muff—
  O sculptor, if you could but mold it!
So lightly touched my jacket-cuff,
  To keep it warm I had to hold it.

To have her with me there alone—
  'Twas love and fear and triumph blended:
At last we reached the foot-worn stone
  Where that delicious journey ended.

She shook her ringlets from her hood,
  And with a " Thank you, Ned," dissembled,
But yet I knew she understood
  With what a daring wish I trembled.

A cloud passed kindly overhead,
  The moon was slyly peeping through it,
Yet hid its face, as if it said,
  "Come, now or never, do it, do it!"

My lips till then had only known
  The kiss of mother and of sister,
But somehow, full upon her own
  Sweet, rosy, darling mouth—I kissed her!

Perhaps 'twas boyish love, yet still,
  O listless woman! weary lover!
To feel once more that fresh wild thrill,
  I'd give—But who can live youth over.

LITTLE BOY BLUE.

BY ABBY SAGE RICHARDSON.

UNDER the haystack, little Boy Blue
Sleeps with his head on his arm,
While voices of men and voices of maids
Are calling him over the farm.

Sheep in the meadows are running wild,
Where a poisonous herbage grows,
Leaving white tufts of downy fleece
On the thorns of the sweet, wild rose.

Out in the fields where the silken corn
Its plumed head nods and bows,
Where the golden pumpkins, ripen below,
Trample the white-faced cows.

But no loud blast on the shining horn
Calls back the straying sheep,

And the cows may wander in hay or corn,
While their keeper lies asleep.

His roguish eyes are tightly shut,
His dimples are all at rest;
The chubby hand tucked under his head,
By one rosy cheek is pressed.

Waken him! No! Let down the bars
And gather the truant sheep,
Open the barn-yard and drive in the cows,
But let the little boy sleep.

For year after year we can shear the fleece,
And corn can always be sown;
But the sleep that visits little Boy Blue
Will not come when the years have flown.

EXTRACT FROM "THE BATTLE-FIELD."

BY W. C. BRYANT.

TRUTH crushed to earth shall rise again!
The eternal years of God are hers;
But Error, wounded, writhes with pain,
And dies among his worshipers.

KEEP PUSHING.

KEEP pushing! 'tis wiser than sitting aside,
And sighing and watching and waiting the tide;
In life's earnest battle they only prevail,
Who daily march onward and never say fail.

EXTRACT FROM "A PSALM OF LIFE."

BY H. W. LONGFELLOW.

LIVES of great men all remind us
We can make our lives sublime,
And, departing, leave behind us
Footprints on the sands of time.

SCATTER THE GERMS OF THE BEAUTIFUL.

SCATTER the germs of the beautiful,
By the wayside let them fall,
That the rose may spring by the cottage gate,
And the vine on the garden wall;
Cover the rough and the rude of earth
With a veil of leaves and flowers,
And mark with the opening bud and cup
The march of summer hours!

Scatter the germs of the beautiful
In the holy shrine of home;
Let the pure, and the fair, and graceful there
In the loveliest lustre come;
Leave not a trace of deformity
In the temple of the heart,
But gather about its hearth the gems
Of nature and of art.

Scatter the germs of the beautiful
In the temples of our God—
The God who starred the uplifted sky,
And flowered the trampled sod!
When he built a temple for himself,
And a home for his priestly race,
He reared each arm in symmetry,
And covered each line in grace.

Scatter the germs of the beautiful
In the depths of the human soul!
They shall bud, and blossom, and bear the fruit,
While the endless ages roll;
Plant with the flowers of charity
The portals of the tomb,
And the fair and the pure about thy path
In paradise shall bloom.

HEAVEN BY LITTLES.

BY J. G. HOLLAND.

Heaven is not reached by a single bound,
But we build the ladder by which we rise
From the lowly earth to the vaulted skies,
And we mount to its summit round by round.

I count these things to be grandly true:
That a noble deed is a step toward God—
Lifting the soul from the common sod,
To a purer air and a broader view.

We rise by the things that are under feet;
By what we have mastered of good and gain;
By the pride deposed and the passion slain,
And the vanquished ills that we hourly meet.

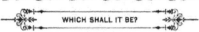

WHICH SHALL IT BE?

BY ETHEL LYNN BEERS.

WHICH shall it be? which shall it be?
I looked at John—John looked at me
(Dear patient John, who loves me yet
As well as though my locks were jet,)
And when I found that I must speak,
My voice seemed strangely low and weak.
"Tell me again what Robert said;"
And then I listening bent my head.
"This is his letter:"

  "I will give
A house and land while you shall live,
If, in return, from out your seven,
One child to me for aye is given."

I looked at John's old garments worn,
I thought of all that John had borne
Of poverty and work and care,
Which I, though willing, could not share;
I thought of seven months to feed,
Of seven little children's need,
And then of this.

  "Come, John," said I,
"We'll choose among them, as they lie
Asleep; so walking hand in hand,
Dear John and I surveyed our band.
First to the cradle lightly stepped
Where the new, nameless baby slept.
"Shall it be baby?" whispered John.
I took his hand, and hurried on
To Lily's crib. Her sleeping grasp
Held her old doll within its clasp;
Her dark curls lay like gold alight,
A glory 'gainst the pillow white.
Softly her father stooped to lay
His rough hand down in a loving way,
When dream or whisper made her stir,
And, huskily, John said, "Not her—not her."

We stooped beside the trundle-bed,
And one long ray of lamp-light shed

Across the boyish faces, three,
In sleep so pitiful and fair;
I saw, on Jamie's rough, red cheek,
A tear undried. Ere John could speak,
"He's but a baby too," said I,
And kissed him as we hurried by.
Pale, patient Robbie's angel face,
Still in sleep bore suffering's trace.
"No, for a thousand crowns, not him,"
We whispered while our eyes were dim.
Poor Dick! bad Dick! our wayward son,
Turbulent, reckless, idle one—
Could he be spared? "Nay, He, who gave,
Bids us befriend him to his grave;
Only a mother's heart can be
Patient enough for such as he;
And so," said John, "I would not dare
To send him from her bedside prayer."
Then stole we softly up above,
And knelt by Mary, child of love.
"Perhaps for her 'twould better be,"
I said to John. Quite silently
He lifted up a curl that lay
Across her cheek, in wilful way,
And he shook his head, "Nay, love, not thee,"
The while my heart beat audibly.
Only one more, our oldest lad,
Trusty and thoughtful, good and glad—
So like his father. "No, John, no—
I cannot, will not, let him go."

And so we wrote, in courteous way,
We could not give one child away;
And after that, toil lighter seemed,
Thinking of that of which we dreamed,
Happy, in truth, that not one face
Was missed from its accustomed place;
Thankful to work for all the seven,
Trusting the rest to One in Heaven.

WEEDS.

WE call them weeds, the while with slender fingers,
 Earth's wounds and scars they seek to cover o'er;
On sterile sands, where scarce the raindrop lingers,
 They grow and blossom by the briny shore.

We call them weeds; did we their form but study,
 We many a secret might unfolded find;
Each tiny plant fulfills its heaven-taught mission,
 And bears the impress of Immortal Mind.

We call them weeds; the while their uses hidden
 Might work a nation's weal, a nation's woe;

Send thro' each wasted frame the balm of healing,
 And cause the blood with youth's quick pulse to flow.

Weeds—yet they hold in bonds the mighty ocean!
 Their slender threads bind firm the sandy shore:
Navies may sink amid its wild commotion,
 These humble toilers ne'er their work give o'er.

And who shall say the feeblest thought avails not
 To bind the shifting sands upon life's beach?
Some heart may treasure what we've long forgot,
 The faintest word some soul with power may reach.

OVER THE RIVER.

BY NANCY AMELIA PRIEST.

OVER the river they beckon to me,
  Loved ones who've crossed to the farther side;
The gleam of their snowy robes I see,
  But their voices are lost in the dashing tide.
There's one with ringlets of sunny gold,
  And eyes, the reflection of heaven's own blue;
He crossed in the twilight gray and cold,
  And the pale mist hid him from mortal view.
We saw not the angels who met him there,
  The gates of the city we could not see;
Over the river, over the river,
  My brother stands waiting to welcome me.

Over the river the boatman pale
  Carried another, the household pet;
Her brown curls waved in the gentle gale,
  Darling Minnie! I see her yet.
She crossed on her bosom her dimpled hands,
  And fearlessly entered the phantom bark;
We felt it glide from the silver sands,
  And all our sunshine grew strange and dark.
We know that her fairy form had passed
  Where the tender reeds the banks bedight,
Over the river, the mystic river,
  My childhood's idol is waiting for me.

And I sit and think, when the sunset's gold
  Is flushing river and hill and shore,
I shall one day stand by the water cold,
  And list for the sound of the boatman's oar;
I shall watch for a gleam of the flapping sail,
  I shall hear the boat as it gains the strand,
I shall pass from sight with the boatman pale,
  To the better shore of the spirit land.
I shall know the loved who have gone before,
  And joyfully sweet will the meeting be,
When over the river, the peaceful river,
  The angel of death shall carry me.

OPINIONS OF THE PRESS.

The newspapers of the country have been of one voice in the praise of HILL's MANUAL. The following testimonials are a few of the hundreds of similar character.

IN NEW ENGLAND.

From the Boston Herald.

"A very valuable volume is 'Hill's Manual of Social and Business Forms.' It is a large quarto, handsomely produced as far as externals are concerned, but not less attractive and desirable on account of its contents, for, from its pages the self-instructing student can become familiar with all the forms in general use, and almost everything that a person should know in this practical age."

From the Nashua (N. H.) Telegraph.

"'Hill's Manual' is one of the most beautiful and useful books ever published. It is a book for everybody, man, woman and child. No one can fail to find much in it that is both entertaining and instructive, and that can be applied to practical use. It is an eminently useful book for public or private libraries, and a most valuable book for study and reference by every man in every possible business. No book on this continent was ever gotten up with such exquisite taste in its mechanical execution, and certainly none that will be of greater value to the masses of men and women—old and young. Whoever purchases the book will have in it alone a valuable library at very small cost."

From the Suffolk Co. (Mass.) Journal.

"Of its inestimable value one cannot judge fully without examining the work. Many of the most eminent men in our country have given it their unqualified praise, having bought and used it, and the general sentiment among them is, that having once possessed it and become acquainted with its worth, they could hardly be induced to part with it at any price. Among those in this section of country are Gov. Gaston, Gov. Rice, C. G. Atwood of the Boston Board of Trade, G. A. Somerby, Esq., and many others. The leading educational men of our country speak of it in the same terms of praise."

From the Fall River (Mass.) Border City Herald.

"'HILL'S MANUAL OF SOCIAL AND BUSINESS FORMS.'—This is a valuable new work of real excellence, and forms a manual comprehending instructions and examples to guide the scholar, the man of business, the teacher, and the general public in every branch of enterprise over the wide domain of human effort. The work is of the most varied character, and supplies alike the wants of the old and the demands of the young in every phase of human life. We assure all who purchase this work that a more elegant, useful, and comprehensive volume of instructions and examples, suiting all ages and conditions in life in both sexes, has never been laid upon our tables."

From the Cambridge (Mass.) Chronicle.

"'HILL'S MANUAL OF SOCIAL AND BUSINESS FORMS' is one of the most useful volumes ever placed upon the desk of a business or professional man, or upon the table of a drawing-room. It is a perfect treasure of valuable and practical information on social and business topics, which are of immense importance to every one. The items confined within the limits of the book embrace instructions and guides for the city officer, student, politician, clergyman, physician, clerk. In fact, every person who is in business or engaged in any calling whatever, will find information as to the proper manner in which to write any document entering into the various social and business relations of life."

IN THE MIDDLE STATES.

From the Phrenological (N. Y.) Journal.

"This work is exceedingly comprehensive. The author has evidently aimed to cover all the departments of practical life in which the pen is an essential instrumentality, and his endeavor has not failed of eminent success in producing a most useful book. We have been informed that upward of 50,000 copies have been sold in a short time; and no wonder, as it is such a work as an agent can talk about, if talk be at all necessary besides its examination."

From the Akron (Ohio) Beacon.

"Let it be placed where young people may have access to it; and in the hands of every family, where children can, as it were, GROW UP with it, so that its principles may become a kind of second nature to them, and many a stream will be bridged which would otherwise separate them from positions in both social and business life, which by nature they are fitted to fill. The work certainly belongs to the list of articles which should be considered a NECESSITY in every household, and a timely, helping hand to those of mature years."

From the Easton (Penn.) Free Press.

"'Hill's Manual' is a work of which no written description can give a properly adequate idea. It must be examined, that its merits may be appreciated. The author seems to have studied the wants of almost every person and family, and more perfectly met these wants than it would seem possible to do in volumes; and yet we find it in one compact book, which comes within the reach of all."

From the Syracuse (N. Y.) Daily Journal.

"It has often been remarked of individuals that 'they have forgotten more in a minute' than others have learned in a lifetime. Whether the remark is to be taken as a compliment to the former or a reflection upon the latter, matters not particularly, since it is a well-known fact, and one most frequently and sincerely regretted by everybody, that thousands of little things that contribute to daily pleasure, convenience or knowledge are absolutely forgotten and beyond recall at the very moment when most they are needed. What heart burning, what vexation of spirit would be averted, what incalculable material benefits, even, would often accrue were there at our elbow some monitor, visible or invisible, embodying in its inexhaustible resources the *multum in parvo* which forgetful mortals crave.

"Such a mentor, nearly if not altogether infallible, has been provided in 'Hill's Manual of Social and Business Forms and Guide to Correct Writing,' a copy of which lies before us, and the examination of which suggests the fitness of the above title. Its external appearance and internal composition fit it, in all respects, to be the guide of young and old, male and female, business man of whatever trade, calling or profession, and man of leisure, dunce and scholar. 'Hill's Manual' best speaks for itself, for its compactness, brevity and comprehensiveness brings within its covers thousands upon thousands of items of information in daily practical use, the topical enumeration of which, in the general index, occupies seven pages.

"The book is a marvel of patience and painstaking care. It is the work of years, and a triumph at last. No more useful book can be found in existence."

IN THE WEST AND SOUTH.

From the Chicago Evening Journal, March 8, 1876.

"The people of Aurora, Ill., yesterday elected Thomas E. Hill mayor of their city, without opposition. The press and the people unanimously declared him to be so eminently fitted for the place, by wealth, public spirit and enterprise, that all classes united in choosing him for the place, irrespective of party or politics 're ing. Though formerly, for several years, engaged in teaching, Mr. Hill has lately made journalism his profession. He is best known to the world, however, as the author of 'Hill's Manual of Social and Business Forms,' a book which, though a very large volume, has had the remarkable sale of over 50,000 copies in a very brief time."

From the Chicago Evening Post.

"One of the most useful volumes that was ever laid upon the counting-room desk or the drawing-room table, is 'Hill's Manual of Business Forms.' It is a perfect treasury of knowledge; a complete encyclopedia of practical information. Scanning the table of contents, it is puzzling to conceive how so much can have been crowded into the confines of a single book.—impossible to believe that the half what is there promised can be fulfilled. But turning over the pages, one by one, observing the freight they bear, the method of its arrangement, its variety and completeness, incredulity is succeeded by astonishment and admiration. The work is a marvel of ingenuity and industry, a prodigy of patient and skilful labor."

The Preston (Minn.) Republican says:

"Hill's Manual, as a whole, is the outgrowth of many years of preparation, the object of the author being to give in a concise form, and in one compendium, much that has been heretofore inaccessible, and also much that could be obtained elsewhere only at great cost, thus placing the important information in convenient form for ready reference, within the reach of all. The varied departments of practical, every day life, it will be found at once the faithful tutor, the reliable guide, and the safe adviser.

"For the business man or mechanic, the professional man or farmer, for every lady, the student, the young or old, and pre-eminently for the family, the work has never had its equal as regards real practical utility.

"Meeting an existing want among all classes of people, the sale of the work at the present time, in proportion to the population, has rarely, if ever, been equaled by any other work, even in the most prosperous years of the last decade."

From the Louisville Commercial.

"HILL'S MANUAL.—We learn that the useful book is meeting with the favor it so well deserves. It is a peculiar work, in the respect that no description will give a person a true idea of it, owing to the diversity of subjects treated; hence, only those who examine the work can really appreciate it. We are all, to some extent, specialists, having given more attention to some one line of business or study, leaving other matters of equal importance but partially covered, and just here this work will be found to meet a want which almost every one has felt. It certainly belongs to the list of articles which should be considered a necessity in every office and library, and is a helping hand to those of useless years."

COMMENDATIONS

FROM

DISTINGUISHED EDUCATORS AND EMINENT MEN.

N O work of an educational character, of late years, has met with such universal approval from teachers and learned men as this. While the book is most warmly welcomed by the illiterate, it is equally sought for by the educated. Hundreds of testimonials from distinguished individuals might be given similar to the following:

From Samuel Fellows, ex-State Supt. Pub. Schools, Wisconsin.

"I am highly delighted with the plan and execution of Hill's Manual."

From Prof. J. G. Cross, Principal of the Northwestern Business College, Naperville, Ill.

"It is a most valuable book, which ought to be multiplied as many times as there are families in the United States. I have adopted it as a book of daily reference for our business students."

From D. S. Burns, Supt. Pub. Schools, Harrisburg, Pa.

"I know of no work that contains so great a variety of valuable information on social and business topics as 'Hill's Manual of Social and Business Forms.' I think it a work of special value to those who have not had opportunities of an extended school course, or becoming familiar by contact with the conventionalities of society."

From Wm. Cornell, Supt. Pub. Schools in Fall River, Mass.

"I most cheerfully recommend "Hill's Manual of Social and Business Forms" as a very full work on the various 'Forms' which every person is likely to have occasion to use in his relations with persons in society. A thorough study of the 'book' by our young men and women would repay them by their acquiring a large fund of very valuable and practical knowledge from its pages. It should meet with a large circulation."

From M. M. Ballou, Distinguished Author, formerly Publisher of " Boston Globe," " Ballou's Monthly," etc.

"'Hill's Manual' is one of those indispensable books of reference which both business men and families should always have at hand. It is such a natural outgrowth of the spirit of the age to condense and put in available form important information upon every subject, that, while we are much gratified to possess this volume, we are also surprised that such a book has not before been produced. It is exactly what its title indicates, a book of 'Social and Business Forms'; but it would require too much space to give even a synopsis of this valuable compendium of instruction and important knowledge."

From D. P. Lindsley, Author of Lindsley's System of Tachygraphy, Andover, Mass.

"'Hill's Manual' is really the most comprehensive, thorough and elegant volume, treating on 'Social and Business Forms,' that has ever been issued in this country."

From Gov. Gaston, of Massachusetts.

"'Hill's Manual of Social and Business Forms' *contains much valuable and useful information.* I think *it well meets a public want,* and can therefore be safely and properly commended to public favor."

From President McCollister, of Buchtel College, Akron, Ohio.

"'HILL'S MANUAL' is a timely book, meeting a public want which has not been filled before. Every family should own this book. It contains information important and useful to all classes. I feel all who examine it will want it."

From Wm. M. Cubery, of Cubery & Co., Publishers of the " Pacific Churchman," San Francisco, Cal.

"'Hill's Manual of Social and Business Forms' is not only a luxury, but a necessity — eminently serviceable in the social circle, and indispensable to the man of business who would save time and money. I keep a copy in my counting-room for ready reference."

From Stephen Walkley, Treasurer of the Peck, Stow & Wilcox Co., Southington, Conn.

"Hill's Manual is remarkable as containing a great variety of forms for numberless little things which all people have to do at sometime in their lives, but which most people do so seldom that they entirely forget the methods in ordinary use, and do them awkwardly or not at all. I have known even well-educated persons travel one or two miles to have a subscription paper drawn, just for the lack of such a book as this. I am surprised at the great scope of the work, and have yet to discover any social or business form needed by people in the ordinary walks of life which is not there given."

From Newton Bateman, ex-State Supt. of Public Schools, Illinois.

"KNOX COLLEGE, GALESBURG, ILL. "'Hill's Manual of Social and Business Forms ' is the best and most complete work of the kind that has yet fallen under my notice. Indeed I do not see how it could well be more comprehensive and exhaustive in respect to the matters of which it treats. It contains, in comparatively small compass, an immense amount of useful information upon a great variety of practical matters, general and special, with which every person in every community ought to be acquainted."

From Geo. Soule, President of Soule's Commercial and Literary Institute, New Orleans.

"I am pleased to say that I regard 'Hill's Manual' as one of the most valuable works for all classes of society which the nineteenth century has produced."

From Prof. Worthy Putnam, Author of Putnam's Elocution and Oratory, Berrien Springs, Mich.

" have bought Hill's Manual—I like it—I admire it; and so says my household. It is a little encyclopædia of use, ornament, and knowledge for both men and women. It is a gem of authorship, artistic execution and usefulness."

From the venerable Jared P. Kirtland, M. D., LL.D.

"After a THOROUGH AND CRITICAL EXAMINATION of 'Hill's Manual,' I have subscribed for three copies: one to accompany Webster's Unabridged Dictionary on my writing desk for my own use, the others for my two eldest greatgrandsons. * * * It should be in the possession of every class of persons, from the young student to the most active business man or woman." JARED P. KIRTLAND.

President Grant Subscribes.

The agent of Hill's Manual at Long Branch writes: "By ten A. M. I was at the president's cottage, tipped and doffed my hat, announced my business, when the president promptly said he did not want to subscribe. I obtained permission to show it to him, and did so very hurriedly. At the conclusion, he took my specimen copy, paid me the cash, and added his name to my autograph book."

From Major Merwin, Editor "American Journal of Education," St. Louis.

"After having given 'Hill's Manual' a very careful and thorough examination, I do not hesitate to say that it will be found one of the most *useful* and *practical* works to put into the schools of the country that has ever been published. IT IS A FIT AND ALMOST INDISPENSABLE COMPANION TO WEBSTER'S UNABRIDGED DICTIONARY; containing in a compact form just those things every person who transacts *any* business needs to know. There is scarcely a subject which comes within the purview of any individual, either in public or private life, but what is explained in this elegant volume. If it could be consulted in the drawing side of contracts, nearly all the mistakes which occur might be avoided, and the ill feeling and litigation growing out of misunderstandings would be a thing of the past. I wish every person in the State could be supplied with a copy."

SOLD ONLY BY SUBSCRIPTION, and not at Bookstores. AGENTS WANTED. Address, for terms,

HILL STANDARD BOOK CO., Publishers,

No. 103 State Street, CHICAGO, ILL.

[OVER]

THE PURPOSE of Hill's Album has been to present in a condensed form the leading and essential facts concerning the lives of the most noted persons who have ever lived.

The Plan has been followed of arranging distinct classes together. Thus the great Religious Founders, including Moses, Buddha, Confucius, Zoroaster, Christ, Mohammed and others, accompanied by fine illustrations, biographies, History and Beliefs of Denominations, Dictionary of Religious Terms, etc., are included in one chapter. The Great Military Heroes at all times, including Wellington, Bonaparte, Washington, Grant and many others, together with a list of memorable battles fought, a Dictionary of Military Terms, etc., form another chapter, and so through the volume.

The Lessons drawn from these biographies as they are presented, are of themselves a peculiar feature of this work. In the histories of the Rothschilds, the Astors, Vanderbilt, Girard, Peabody, A. T. Stewart, Jay Gould, Longworth, Mackey, Flood and others, the secret of their success in money-getting is very clearly stated, so that the reader desirous of making money may greatly profit by the reading. And thus throughout the volume the causes that led to success, in whatever direction, is very clearly pointed out. Much light under this head is given in the chapter devoted to phrenology.

The Examples presented through the struggles of inventors, including Howe, Goodyear, Stephenson, Watt, and multitudes of others celebrated for triumphs in war, finance, exploration, science, literature and art, are worthy of careful study and imitation by the young who aspire to supremacy.

General Matter. The chapters relating to the History and Beliefs of the Great Denominations; the Illustrated Darwinian Philosophy, showing the world's progress at different epochs of time; the department devoted to Astronomy, presenting the subject in simple language, clearly illustrated; the chapter relating to Phrenology, accompanied by views and diagrams of heads; the portion concerning Household Decoration and that treating of Landscape Gardening, all profusely illustrated, are each intensely interesting and instructive.

The Scope of the work it is impossible to enumerate here; suffice it to say eleven pages are devoted to giving the table of contents. The range of the work includes the men who have formed the religious beliefs, that have been brilliant lights in the commercial world, that have wrought great improvements, that have discovered new continents, that have opened the book of science, that have made the people happy through laughter, that have written our sweetest songs, that have produced the most thrilling tales, that have presented the world the most truthful portraitures with the brush and chisel, and that have stirred the hearts of the people through powerful oratory.

The Typographic Display of the ALBUM is a distinguishing feature of the book. In elegant, artistic finish it is without a rival, the secret of its superior embellishment lying in the fact that the power to produce the book mechanically rests with the author, who, by his knowledge of the artistic, is able to produce the matter in such attractive form.

SOLD BY SUBSCRIPTION ONLY. AGENTS WANTED.

[OVER.]

What They Say of the "Album."

Brief Extracts From Hundreds of Similar Testimonials.

The following are from papers published at Aurora, Ill., where the author of the ALBUM resided twelve years, during the last of which he was Mayor of the city.

From the Aurora Beacon.

THE business career of Mr. Thos. E. Hill, who was at one time a resident of Aurora, and mayor of the city, has been very successful, and some have been inclined to think it the result of good luck. Every enterprise of which he took hold seemed to turn him money, and schemes which would have been abortive in the hands of ordinary men blossomed into rare success under his management. The same good fortune follows him and his enterprises to this day. There is no "luck" in it at all. It grows first from his intense industry, energy and application; second from his enthusiasm; and third from his keen appreciation of *what the public desires*, drawn from long contact with it and close study. In his youth he was eminently successful as a canvasser, as a teacher of writing and lecturer on penmanship. In Aurora, for a number of years he published and edited the *Herald* with great success. When he sold his newspaper, and established the system of city messenger, which has since become so popular between minor cities and Chicago, he exploited new ground which was for a time very profitable; and it was during the hours when he was passing between Aurora and Chicago, that he conceived and did the first work upon the "Manual," that splendid product of the brain, of the compiler, the printer and the book-binder, which has made Thos. E. Hill's name familiar from the Atlantic to the Pacific oceans, and from Minnesota to Florida.

"For two years or more past, Mr. Hill has been of opinion that there existed room for another work besides the "Manual," which should be equally popular and useful—and meet a demand as universal as that enjoyed by his first great work. He has devoted a large amount of labor and inventive genius to the accomplishment of his ideal, and we now have it before us in "HILL'S ALBUM OF BIOGRAPHY AND ART." It is a large quarto volume of 327 pages, printed upon heavy tinted paper, with hundreds of fine portraits, miscellaneous illustrations, unique, artistic and elegant designs. In its preparation he has called to his aid the most modern and refined skill of the type-maker, engraver and typographer, and he has thus, in the "ALBUM," surpassed, in artistic and typographical display, all his former efforts.

"The new work is divided into eighteen departments, as follows: 1st, Religion and its Founders; 2d, Military Chieftains and Famous Battles; 3d, Discoverers and Explorers; 4th, Sketches of Leading Inventors; 5th, History of Financiers; 6th, Sketches of the Scientists; 7th, the Theory of Progression; 8th, Astronomical Science; 9th, Phrenology and Science of Mind; 10th, Humorists and Caricaturists; 11th, Physicians, Lawyers and Sovereigns; 12th, Orators and Statesmen; 13, Actors and Play Writers; 14th, Historians, Novelists, Essayists, etc.; 15th, Poets and Song Writers; 16th, Painters and

Sculptors; 17th, Household Ornamentation; 18th, Beautiful Homes. Under these heads are given very many beautiful engravings of men, incidents and places, with sketches, biographical and pertinent, interspersed with very many things valuable to every person who would be reasonably well informed. We doubt if there is any one volume where so much useful information of the kind is gathered, and certainly there is none where it is put in more methodical form, or presented in a manner so pleasing to the eye and taste."

From the Aurora Blade.

"Every page of HILL'S ALBUM is *a model of typography* and originality, each differing from the other in mechanical construction, and each succeeding leaf a surprise from an artistic standpoint. The question one asks, instinctively, is, how can a man conceive so many elegant designs? The contents of the book, however, are what prove its most forcible recommendation. The name of the author of this valuable work, Hon. Thomas E. Hill, is in itself enough to recommend it to all. Our readers are advised to examine the book carefully when they have the opportunity.

From the Aurora Herald.

"'HILL'S ALBUM OF BIOGRAPHY AND ART,' is the name of a new book by Hon. Thos. E. Hill, author of "Hill's Manual of Social and Business Forms." It is gotten up very much after the style of the Manual, but more elaborate and expensive, as nearly every page has some engraving especially for it. The title of the book does not give any adequate idea of the immense amount of information it contains. We suppose it is called an ALBUM because of the many pictures it contains, but in addition thereto it contains short biographical sketches of distinguished men, from the time of Moses and Aaron down to the present. It gives a sketch of Moses, with his portrait, and an outline of his teachings; of Buddha, portrait and doctrines, also the same of Confucius, Jesus Christ, Mohammed, Swedenborg. Andrew Jackson Davis, and Joseph Smith, and an outline of the belief of the different Christian denominations. It also gives sketches and portraits of numerous warriors, inventors, financiers, scientists, actors, humorists, explorers, poets, lawyers, doctors, statesmen, orators, artists, etc., and gives as much about each as most people would care to remember. It is, in short, *a complete library in one volume*, and must have been the work of years to gather the information and put it in this condensed form. Of the typographical excellence it is unnecessary to speak, as all know that whatever Mr. Hill undertakes in that line, is done in the best style known to the art. We know of no other book which has so many new and original designs."

[OVER.]

From the People and the Press in General.

The Universal Testimony is that Hill's Album is one of the Most Unique, Elegant and Useful Books in the World. Read the Verdict.

"One of the Most Instructive and Entertaining Books."
[From Rev. H. W. Thomas, Chicago.]

I THINK 'Hill's Album' is *one of the most instructive and entertaining books* I ever saw."

"Most Fascinatingly Interesting."
[From the *Passaic* (N. J.) *Item.*]

" We know of no volume so comprehensive in its information as this, and arranged in such a manner as to be *most fascinatingly interesting.*"

"The Most Beautiful and Complete."
[From the *Chicago Inter-Ocean.*]

" One of the *most beautiful and complete* books of the year. Not only is it wholly creditable as a fine specimen of the printer's art, but the elegant, unique and artistic designs are worthy of special commendation. But the value of the book is in its reading contents, and the admirable system and method of its arrangement. The author is the Hon. Thomas E. Hill, author of 'Hill's Manual of Social and Business Forms,' another of the practical books. The book, under many headings, gleans the most interesting and valuable acts of history bearing upon the subject."

"We Have Examined It and Were Captured."
[From the *Sandwich* (Ill.) *Argus.*]

" ' 'Hill's Album' is a wonder of art and industry. *We have examined it and were captured.* Mr. Hill made a great success of his 'Manual,' and this work gives evidence of his old-time industry and thoroughness. It is full of information upon matters of science, art, architecture, mechanics, biography, religion, etc., and is embellished and illustrated in the highest perfection. The amount of persistent labor needed for Mr. Hill to accomplish this perfect 'Album,' is as wonderful as the skill shown in gathering in so small a compass the pith of the world's history."

Must be Largely Sought and Highly Prized."
[From the *Penman's Art Journal*, New York.]

" The subject-matter of the work, in its extent and skillful manner of presentation, bears unmistakable evidence of great labor and profound research, as well as a liberal expenditure of money on the part of the author. The embellishments are upon a scale most liberal and excellent in taste. The work, as a whole, is one that *must be largely sought and highly prized* by all classes, not alone as a handbook of valuable and interesting information, but as a beautiful and appropriate ornament for the parlor or drawing-room. It is a fitting companion of 'Hill's Manual,' which has proved the most popular and ready-selling work of its day, having already reached its thirtieth edition, and into the hundreds of thousands of copies sold. Like the 'Manual,' the new work is to be sold only on subscription, through agents."

"It is a Marvel."
[From the *Chicago Tribune.*]

" In the preparation of a work like this a vast amount of labor was required, and *it is a marvel* that the author was able to condense so much valuable information into so little space."

"Extreme Beauty, Wise Brevity and Charming Variety."
[From Rev. J. B. Lockwood, Mt. Joy, Pa.]

" *Extreme beauty, wise brevity, charming variety* and practical utility are some of the evident characteristics of this second venture in book-making by Mr. Hill. We predict an immense demand for the 'Album.' In the drawing-room it will be an elegant ornament, in the sitting-room an entertaining companion; in the study a handy volume of biographical reference. Like its predecessor — the 'Manual'—it will be a special educator in the family, and will largely aid in promoting intelligent citizenship in the community."

"One of the Most Valuable Works to Place in a Family."
[From the Chicago *Youths' Examiner.*]

" We supposed when we saw 'Hill's Manual of Social and Business Forms,' we saw as fine a work as was ever issued in this country, and were not satisfied until the work was numbered among our books. As we examine the new book, now before us, by Hon. Thos. E. Hill, we feel how unequal we are to the task of giving the work anything like the description it deserves, in a notice of this character. Nothing but a personal examination will give even a fair idea of its merits. We can honestly say that it is *one of the most valuable works to place in a family* that it has ever been our pleasure to examine."

"Far Ahead of Anything Ever Issued of Like Nature."
[From the *Joliet* (Ill.) *Signal.*]

" It is dedicated 'to those striving for excellence in the various departments of human action, and who would know how others have won success.' It comprises eighteen different departments, and it is a model, not only for the vast number of interesting subjects treated upon, and the conciseness and brevity of the articles and amount of useful and desirable information contained, but for the beauty of its typography and the charming manner in which the subjects are grouped and illustrated. It is *far ahead of anything ever issued of like nature*, and is an elegant and attractive volume for any parlor or library."

"I Consider This a Fair Test."

J. J. MOORE, *from St. Charles, Mo.*, *writes:*

" I have taken **twenty-seven** orders in this place for the 'Album,' in four days *I consider this a fair test* of what I can do."

CHARLES N. THOMAS, *Gen. Agt. in New England writes:*

" The agent I put at work in Maine took **seventeen** orders for 'Albums,' his first week, working half his time."

B. W. KRAYBILL, *reporting from Lancaster, Pa.*, *says:*

" My first day netted me **ten** sales for the 'Album.'"

[OVER]

One Opinion and One Voice Concerning the Album.

"Regardless of Time, Cost and Labor."
[From the Chicago *Humane Journal*.]

"The 'Album' exhibits an immense amount of work gotten up *regardless of time, cost and labor*, and is bound to please. It is a book which every student should possess, and which every person with limited time for reading can refer to and at once obtain almost any desired information. At the same time it is so attractively illustrated and elegantly bound that it would constitute an ornament to any parlor table. The book is doubly interesting because the author is so well known in Chicago and vicinity. Besides being a gentleman of exceedingly fine tastes and the highest culture, he is known as one of great kindness of heart and instinctively humane. The *Journal*, always deeply interested in this phase of a man's character, takes pleasure in recognizing this element in that of Mr. Hill, and brings to mind a bright instance of it at the time he held the office of Mayor of the city of Aurora, Ill. The subject of kindness to animals had long engaged his attention, and he then and there proceeded to put in practice the principles he had long upheld. He made it his business to go around the city daily, and if there was a horse standing unfed, exposed to bitter cold or undue heat, he caused it to be provided with food and shelter until the heartless owner had come to reason and was likely to take better care of his animal himself. The good that one man in such a position can accomplish is great, and if each official in high position would openly censure and aid in punishing the brutal acts which he can scarcely fail to witness upon our streets daily, it would do much toward preventing the abuse of the dumb and patient servants of mankind."

"A Condensed Popular Encyclopædia."
[From the Chicago *Evening Journal*.]

"'Hill's Album' is an illustrated compendium of biography, history, literature, art and science—in fact, a *condensed popular encyclopædia*. One is astonished, on glancing through its ample pages, that so much and so vast a variety of highly instructive and useful matter could have been crowded into one book, and at the same time presented in a form and style so tasteful and attractive. Almost every man or woman whose name has become conspicuous in modern times in connection with great works or great thoughts or great systems is included in the sketches, and many of them in the illustrations of this remarkable 'Album.' Religious systems and leaders, wars and war heroes, great inventions and inventive geniuses, systems of finance and great financiers, the sciences and the great men of science, celebrities in the various departments of literature, music and great musicians, the drama and its chief actors, the law and the great lawyers, medicine and the great physicians, statesmanship and politics and famous leaders in the affairs of State, and art and the great artists, are sketched in a manner which gives the reader a good degree of information regarding each and all; and in addition to all these, Mr. Hill has gathered a mass of facts and hints for the benefit of the housekeeper and the student which are invaluable and always in order.

"The people of America are aware of the great practical value of 'Hill's Manual,' which can be found in almost every counting-room and household in the land; and when we assure them that his 'Album,' which is published in form and style similar to that of the 'Manual,' is, in its peculiar line, equally valuable, and that it as surely fills a popular want as that did, they will need no further suggestion as to the desirability of possessing it."

"Goes to the Root of Everything."
[From the *Piano* (Ill.) *News*.]

"Hon. Thos. E. Hill, once editor of the Aurora *Herald*, and author of that almost indispensable volume, 'Hill's Manual of Social and Business Forms,' which has found its way into so many homes in Kendall county, has just presented a new volume to the world, entitled 'Hill's Album of Biography and Art.' It is altogether one of the finest volumes ever produced, besides being a regular encyclopædia of information that no person in this age should be without. "To those who have read 'Hill's Manual,' we need say but little in praise of the 'Album,' for they know that the author of both could not but make a success of such a work as is comprised in the latter.

"The book treats not alone of the biographies of men and women eminent in the world of art, literature, music and the drama, but of religion and its founders, military men, discoverers, lawyers, statesmen, physicians, and it also gives synopses of some of the different scientific theories that have at once startled the world. Without delving into Darwin's intricacies, for instance, one may yet obtain a clear idea of his theory of progression, by the synopsis in this work, which will impress itself deep enough on the mind to enable one to comprehend it thoroughly; and so with other subjects—astronomical science, science of mind, finance, household ornamentation, and all he touches on. The author is not superficial, but where such an array of subjects is treated in a work of this magnitude, the articles must necessarily be brief, yet he *goes to the root of everything*, discarding superfluities, and telling facts in an interesting style peculiarly his own."

"Gotten Up on the Same Elegant Scale."
[From the *Phrenological Journal*, New York.]

"It is in fine a cyclopædia of eminent persons and of the subjects in religion, science, art and literature which are deemed by the world of importance to civilization. Upward of six hundred and fifty historical men and women are sketched, and a large proportion of these have their portraits given. We are informed of the tenets of ancient religions, and, in contrast with them, a brief exposition of Christianity. Mormonism, Spiritualism and other later forms of belief receive their share of consideration also. It should be added that the prominent Christian sects are described as to their history and growth. Following the religious department, which is very properly put first, we have a summary of the great military heroes of history, and of important battles fought in Europe and America—the late war for the Union receiving a good share of the compiler's attention. Then follows a department of exploration and discovery; then a very interesting (because fresh in most of its details) section related to inventors and invention. The rich men of the world come in for a share of the printed space, and then science, politics and philanthropy fill fifty or more of the large pages. The author evidently places much confidence in the doctrine of Gall and Spurzheim, for a considerable section is devoted to a synopsis of phrenology, with several well selected illustrations. The humorists and the artists who please the public with their facetious talk and drawing, are well represented, and so are the writers, essayists, poets and orators who direct attention to the serious side of life. The practical has its place in the book, especially in the space given to penmanship, household decoration and architectural designs. Mr. Hill has prepared a very attractive book, and its success will probably match that of his 'Manual,' which was *gotten up on the same elegant scale*."